PETERSON'S®

MASTER THE™ CATHOLIC HIGH SCHOOL ENTRANCE EXAMS

About Peterson's®

Peterson's has been your trusted educational publisher for more than 50 years. It's a milestone we're quite proud of as we continue to offer the most accurate, dependable, high-quality educational content in the field, providing you with everything you need to succeed. No matter where you are on your academic or professional path, you can rely on Peterson's for its books, videos, online information, expert test-prep tools, the most up-to-date education exploration data, and the highest quality career success resources—everything you need to achieve your education goals. For our complete line of products, visit **www.petersons.com**.

For more information, contact Peterson's, 4380 S. Syracuse St., Suite 200, Denver, CO 80237; 800-338-3282 Ext. 54229; or visit us online at **www.petersons.com**.

ISBN-13: 978-0-7689-4586-7

Printed in the United States of America

10 9 8 7 6 5 4 3 2   24 23 22

Twenty-Sixth Edition

CONTENTS

Part I: Tackling the Exams

Part II: Diagnostic Tests

CONTENTS

Part III: Verbal Skills

CONTENTS

Part IV: Quantitative and Nonverbal Skills

Part V: Six Practice Tests

CONTENTS

Part VI: Appendixes

Credits

Excerpt from *A Christmas Carol* by Charles Dickens

Excerpt from *Rip Van Winkle* by Washington Irving

Excerpt from *The Nightingale* by Hans Christian Andersen

"The Rhodora" by Ralph Waldo Emerson

Anne of Green Gables by Lucy Maud Montgomery

"The Moon was but a Chin of Gold" by Emily Dickinson

Excerpt from *Around the World in Eighty Days* by Jules Verne

Excerpt from *The Adventures of Tom Sawyer* by Mark Twain

Excerpt from *1984* by George Orwell

Excerpt from "Emerging Space: The Evolving Landscape of 21st Century American Spaceflight" as produced by the Office of the Chief Technologist at NASA

Excerpt from *Mysterious Island* by Jules Verne

"April's Charms" by William H. Davies

Excerpt from *Pennsylvania Dutch Cooking* by Unknown

Excerpt from *The Outline of Science*, Vol. 1 by J. Arthur Thomson

Excerpt from *White Fang* by Jack London

Excerpt from *The Colors of Animals* by Sir John Lubbock

Excerpt from *American Leaders and Heroes:*
A preliminary text-book in United States History by Wilbur F. Gordy

Excerpt adapted from *The Book of Tea* by Kakuzo Okakura

Excerpt from *Mountaineering in the Sierra Nevada* by Clarence King

Excerpt from *The Story of Napoleon* by Harold F. B. Wheeler

BEFORE YOU BEGIN

OVERVIEW

Why You Should Use This Book

How This Book Is Organized

How to Use This Book

Special Study Features

Top 10 Ways to Raise Your Score

Peterson's® Publications

Give Us Your Feedback

You're Well on Your Way to Success

If you're graduating from junior high or middle school and exploring your options for high school, it's an exciting time in your life. This may be your first opportunity to make a big decision about your education— and if you're reading this book, you're taking that responsibility seriously.

You may have a few target schools in mind and, because you have this book in your hands, it's likely that you're considering continuing your education at a Catholic high school. If that's true, then you also know that an essential part of getting into the Catholic high school of your choice is taking and passing an entrance exam.

While some students have no fear of important, high-stakes exams like the TACHS (Test for Admission into Catholic High Schools) and the HSPT (High School Placement Test)—the two most commonly used Catholic high school entrance exams—other students feel they could use a confidence boost and a bit more help to make sure they are a step ahead of the competition on test day.

If this sounds like you, then fear not—you've come to the right place!

WHY YOU SHOULD USE THIS BOOK

Peterson's *Master the™ Catholic High School Entrance Exams* is designed by test experts and educators with real-life classroom experience to fully prepare you for test-day success, regardless of which entrance exam you're preparing to take. This helpful guide includes the following:

ESSENTIAL TEST INFORMATION

We take the stress out of planning for your entrance exam by providing all the information you'll need to know before the big day in one place—including how to decide which test is right for you, how to register, where to go, and even what to bring on the day of the exam. We've got you covered!

COMPREHENSIVE COVERAGE OF THE TACHS AND HSPT TEST FORMATS

After using this book, you'll know the structure and format of your exam from start to finish and have all the information you'll need for success on test day.

THOROUGH TEST TOPIC REVIEW

You'll get both a thorough review of *every topic* tested on the TACHS and HSPT and help creating an effective study plan for reaching your goal score. So not only will there be *no surprises* on test day, but you'll also have the confidence of knowing that you're thoroughly prepared for the exam.

PLENTY OF REALISTIC TEST QUESTION PRACTICE

Every topic chapter in this book contains tests and activities those you'll encounter during the actual exam. In addition, you can customize your preparation based on your target test. Take a full-length diagnostic exam for either the TACHS or the HSPT to help you determine your strengths and weaknesses and target your study time effectively. Build your confidence with 4 (3 in the book and 1 online) full-length practice exams for each test to help you strengthen your test skills and get comfortable with the timing and pace of the actual exams. There's no better way to practice for the big day!

EXPERT TIPS, ADVICE, AND STRATEGIES

We *know* what it takes to get a top score on the TACHS and HSPT—you'll get expert tools that have proven to be effective on exam day, putting you a step ahead of the test-taking competition. Consider this your *inside edge* as you prepare to conquer your entrance exam!

We *know* that doing well on your Catholic high school entrance exam is important, both to you and your family—and we're here to help you through *every step* of your journey. Consider this book your all-in-one test preparation package to get you through the exam and on your way to the Catholic high school of your choice.

HOW THIS BOOK IS ORGANIZED

This book is divided into six parts that can help you with your preparation. Use **Part I** to learn more about each exam type and how it's scored. Here and throughout the book, you'll find examples of typical questions from each exam. Take the diagnostic test for the TACHS or HSPT in **Part II** to determine your strengths and weaknesses so you can best plan your test preparation. Use **Part III** to review verbal skills, such as analogies, verbal logic, reading, and composition, which are tested on the TACHS, HSPT, and other exams. Use **Part IV** to review quantitative and nonverbal skills, such as mathematics and ability questions. **Part V** includes practice exams for the TACHS and the HSPT. The **Appendix** section includes a word list and a useful synonyms/antonyms list to help boost your test-prep confidence on the Language Arts sections of the admissions tests. It also includes a useful summary sheet of math formulas that you can tear out and review throughout your day.

HOW TO USE THIS BOOK
Diagnostic Test Method

One way to use this book is to start with a diagnostic test for the TACHS or HSPT. A diagnostic test is a test that helps you understand your strengths and weaknesses on the exam. It "diagnoses" the skills that need the most improvement.

In this method, you take a diagnostic test first, and then you use the results of your test to develop a study plan. Use one of the diagnostic tests in Part II, Chapter 4 or 5, depending on whether you are preparing for the TACHS or HSPT. This test will give you a sampling of the kinds of questions you are likely to see on your test, and it will show you where you might need to focus your test-prep efforts.

Once you've taken your diagnostic test, score yourself to see your strengths and weaknesses. How did you do? Make a list of your stronger and weaker areas. If you scored well on math but struggled with verbal skills, then you can count math as a strength. Your verbal skills, on the other hand, will need some work. Rank the different sections in terms of your strongest and weakest skills.

Use your ranking list to develop your study plan. Your plan should prioritize boosting those areas where you need the most improvement. You don't need to spend as much time brushing up on your strengths. However, you should still plan to spend *some* time on "strong skills" exercises—just to stay in shape.

Once you've got a study plan, put it to work. Read the introduction to your test in Part I. Then, focus on improving your weaker skills by studying those sections first in Parts III and IV. After you've reviewed the content sections, take a practice test in Part V. This test should show an improvement in your score!

Front-to-Back Method

Another way to use this book is the front-to-back method. In this method, you work through the book the way it is organized.

Start at Part I of the book and carefully read through the introductory section on your exam. This will help you understand the exam and how it's scored. Then, take a diagnostic test in Part II to figure out where you are starting from as you prepare for the exam. Next, study the content sections in Parts III and IV. Focus on the sections that relate to your exam. If you know your stronger and weaker areas, you might devote extra time to sections where you need the most improvement.

After you've reviewed the content, take a practice test or two in Part V. Even taking one test will help you be more prepared for exam day. Sometimes, the process of taking the test itself can help increase your score. This is because you become more familiar with the test, which increases your confidence.

After you complete each test, review your answers with the explanations provided. If you still don't understand how to answer a certain question, you might ask a teacher for help. A review session with a friend might prove helpful, too.

NOTE

You have the option to take the practice tests either in the book or online. For more information, go to **www.petersons.com/testprep/high-school-entrance-exams.**

The expert subject review and skill-specific exercises in Peterson's *Master the™ Catholic High School Entrance Exams* can help familiarize you with the unique content, structure, and format of the test. Test-taking tips and advice guide you smoothly from your first day of test preparation to test day.

In addition, taking online practice tests is desirable because you get immediate feedback and automated scoring. Peterson's *Master the™ Catholic High School Entrance Exams* gives you access to not only the tests in this book but also additional practice tests online, each with detailed feedback to help you understand the concepts presented. The content in these practice tests was created by the test-prep experts at Peterson's to help you boost your test-prep confidence. You can access the TACHS and HSPT practice tests at **www.petersons.com/testprep/product/master-the-catholic-high-school-entrance-exams-online-book-component**. Use coupon code **MTC2022** for complimentary access with the purchase of this book.

Important: Usage of the coupon code to access online content is intended for the original purchaser of the book and not for resellers or library patrons. Access will expire 18 months after the copyright date printed in this title.

TIP

Looking for Additional Practice? Check out Peterson's Test Prep Subscriptions
Our subscription plans allow you to study as quickly as you can, or as slowly as you'd like. How does it work? Subscribers get unlimited usage of our entire test prep catalog for over 150 exams, including high school entrance exams like the TACHS, HSPT, ISEE, SSAT, and SHSAT. For more information, go to
www.petersons.com/testprep/high-school-entrance-exams

SPECIAL STUDY FEATURES

You will find the following kinds of special study features scattered throughout the book:

Overview

Each chapter begins with a bulleted overview listing the topics to be covered in the chapter. This will allow you to quickly target the areas in which you are most interested.

Tools to Guide You through the Book

- Each chapter ends with **Summing It Up**, a point-by-point summary that captures the most important points contained in the chapter.

- **Tips** point out valuable information you need to know when taking the TACHS and HSPT exams. Tips provide quick and simple hints for selecting the correct answers for the most common question types.

- **Alerts** identify potential pitfalls in the testing format or question types that can cause common mistakes in selecting answers.

- **Notes** address information about the test structure itself.

- **Cautions** provide warnings, such as common grammatical errors or possible errors in computation or formulas that can result in choosing incorrect answers.

QR Codes

Throughout this book, you'll find QR codes that link to supplemental video content. These videos are designed to provide you with focused lessons on specific topics. If you find yourself struggling with a specific concept, look for a QR code in the section or chapter for additional instruction. To scan a QR code, first make sure that you are using a compatible mobile device. Then, open the camera app and focus the camera on the QR code. This should populate a link to the corresponding video.

Word List and List of Synonyms and Antonyms

Questions that require a robust knowledge of vocabulary appear throughout both of these exams. The broader, more varied, and more accurate your vocabulary knowledge, the better your chances of answering questions quickly and correctly. To help you with this task, we've put together a list of about 500 commonly used words that may appear on your exam, including hundreds of related words—words that are variants of the primary words or words that share a common root word. We've also included a list of synonyms and antonyms for many of the terms on the word list as well as additional terms. You'll find the word list and the list of synonyms and antonyms at the back of the book. We hope they will enhance your vocabulary study for any of the Catholic high school entrance exams.

TOP 10 WAYS TO RAISE YOUR SCORE

When it comes to taking your entrance exam, some test-taking skills will do you more good than others. There are concepts you can learn, techniques you can follow, and tricks you can use that will help you to do your very best. Here are our picks for the top 10 ways to raise your score:

01 Regardless of which plan you will follow, get started by reading Part I to familiarize yourself with the test formats.

02 Make sure you understand the information in Chapter 2 on effective learning and studying. Apply it as you work through this book.

03 Use the QR codes throughout the book to see things explained in video form.

04 Make sure to complete the exercises in each chapter you read.

05 When you are one third of the way through your preparation, take a practice test. Make sure you are applying new test-taking strategies.

06 Revisit challenging chapters and their summaries.

07 After you have completed all the study sections, take your second practice test. You should find the second practice test much easier now, and, after your study and practice, you should be able to answer more questions than you could on the first practice test.

08 If you have the time, you might find it instructive to take the practice tests for the other exams. For example, if you're required to take the TACHS, you might also test yourself with the HSPT exam.

09 During the last phase of your study, review the practice tests.

10 The night before your exam, RELAX. You'll be prepared.

PETERSON'S® PUBLICATIONS

Peterson's publishes a full line of books—career preparation, education exploration, test prep, and financial aid. Peterson's books are available for purchase online at **www.petersons.com**. Sign up for one of our online subscription plans and you'll have access to our entire test prep catalog of more than **150 exams** *plus* instructional videos, flashcards, interactive quizzes, and more! Our subscription plans allow you to study as quickly as you can or as slowly as you'd like. For more information, and access to practice for high school entrance exams like the TACHS, HSPT, ISEE, SSAT, and SHSAT, go to **www.petersons.com/testprep/high-school-entrance-exams**.

GIVE US YOUR FEEDBACK

Peterson's publications can be found at high school guidance offices, college libraries and career centers, and your local bookstore and library. Peterson's books are also available for purchase online at **petersons.com**.

We welcome any comments or suggestions you may have about this publication. Your feedback will help us make education dreams possible for you—and others like you.

YOU'RE WELL ON YOUR WAY TO SUCCESS

Remember that knowledge is power. By using this book, you will be studying the most comprehensive guide available.

The *first step* to acing your high school entrance exam is to know the structure and format of the exam you're going to take inside and out, including all the basics you need to know.

We *know* you're eager to get to the test practice and review, but having a thorough understanding of the exam from top to bottom will give you a real advantage—and put you ahead of the test-taking competition. We'll go carefully through each exam—the TACHS, HSPT, ISEE, SSAT, and SHSAT—and guide you through each step so you'll be confident and prepared for test day success. Let's get started!

Good luck!

PART I
PREPARING FOR THE EXAMS

CHAPTER

All About the Exams

ALL ABOUT THE EXAMS

OVERVIEW

All about the Test for Admission into Catholic High Schools (TACHS)

All about the High School Placement Test (HSPT®)

All about the Independent School Entrance Exam (ISEE)

All about the Secondary School Admission Test (SSAT)

All about the Specialized High School Admissions Test (SHSAT)

Test Day Checklist

Summing It Up

There are several types of Catholic high school entrance exams, so knowing which one you are going to take is important. This chapter covers five of the exams: We'll focus on the Test for Admission into Catholic High Schools (TACHS) and the High School Placement Test (HSPT), but we'll also cover the basics for the Independent School Entrance Exam (ISEE), the Secondary School Admission Test (SSAT), and the Specialized High School Admissions Test (SHSAT). That's a lot of different tests (and acronyms), but we'll help you figure out which one applies to you and how you can use this book to study for what's on your exam. Throughout this book, the first page of each chapter will include a legend that tells you which tests the chapter is relevant to; at a glance, you'll be able to see if the content covered in the chapter is on the exam you are going to take.

As a result of the COVID-19 pandemic, all the tests covered here now offer a remote testing option. The protocol for online remote testing varies depending on the exam. Make sure that you fully understand the system requirements, code of conduct, and testing protocol for the remote testing option for the exam you plan to take.

ALL ABOUT THE TEST FOR ADMISSION INTO CATHOLIC HIGH SCHOOLS (TACHS)

The Test for Admission into Catholic High Schools (TACHS) is the entrance test for eighth grade students who want to attend a Catholic high school in the Diocese of Brooklyn/Queens or Archdiocese of New York City. In 2021, the Catholic High Schools of Long Island (Diocese of Rockville Center) used an online TACHS exam in lieu of the Catholic High School Entrance Exam (CHSEE), and this will be the case for 2022 as well. The TACHS is a multiple-choice exam that lasts about 2 hours, including time to give directions. There are no breaks during the TACHS.

If you are currently in the eighth grade and plan to attend a Catholic high school in this area, you'll take the TACHS exam as part of your admissions application. If, however, you plan to enter a school in this area as a tenth, eleventh, or twelfth grader, you *don't need* to take the TACHS. Instead, you'll apply directly to the high school you wish to attend.

Along with your school records, your TACHS score is sent to the principals of up to three high schools that you're applying so that they can make an admissions decision. Unlike the ACT and SAT, the official TACHS Handbook says **you may take the TACHS only once**. This is an important test, but don't worry—we'll help you fully prepare for it!

Registering for the TACHS

There are two ways to register for the TACHS:

1 Online—Visit **https://www.tachsinfo.com/howtoregister.aspx** to register online. This process is open to students, parents, guardians, and principals. This is the preferred method of registration, as there is no waiting involved. After you're registered, you can have your confirmation instantly emailed to you. Be sure to bookmark your confirmation email for easy reference on test day.

2 By phone—Students, parents, and guardians can also register for the TACHS by calling 1-866-61TACHS and speaking with a representative who will guide you through the process. As of this writing, the hours for phone registration are Monday through Friday from 8:00 a.m. to 7:00 p.m. and Saturday and Sunday from 10 a.m. to 2 p.m., Eastern Standard Time. Options for those who speak languages other than English are available. Once you're registered, you'll get a verbal confirmation. You can also ask to have your confirmation emailed. Be sure to bookmark your confirmation email for easy reference on test day.

NOTE

THE OFFICIAL TACHS STUDENT HANDBOOK
Download or browse a copy of the TACHS Student Handbook for detailed information about exam contents and requirements, as well as information about scholarships and financial aid for Catholic high schools throughout New York City: https://tachsinfo.com/handbook.aspx

Once you've registered for the exam, make sure that you enter your three high school choices by the deadline to ensure that they receive a copy of your exam results. About a week after the registration deadline, you will receive an email with your test session date, time, and code. You will be randomly assigned either an 8:30 a.m. or 10:00 a.m. time slot on your test date. Due to the ongoing COVID-19 pandemic, the only option available in 2022 is online remote testing.

ALERT

2022 TACHS REGISTRATION
Mark your calendars—internet registration for the TACHS opens on **November 13, 2022**.

Complete registration information, including important dates, registration procedures, registration fees, and testing locations can be found online at **www.tachsinfo.com**.

TACHS Exam Fee

The current fee for taking the TACHS is $65. This is a *nonrefundable* fee and includes a copy of the student handbook, test materials, and up to three score reports for the Catholic high schools of your choice.

Special Exam Accommodations

There is an option for extended testing time (time and a half) for students who have a documented need. Those who will need extra time are required to submit an eligibility form. You can find the form on the TACHS website. Pay careful attention to the deadline and instructions for submitting the form.

Online Testing Protocol

This year, the TACHS exam is only offered online. As such, you will need to carefully read the system requirements, which can be found on the TACHS website, to ensure that your device is compatible with the online testing system. On the TACHS website, you will also need to read the Proctorio setup and installation guide. Proctorio is the automated proctoring service you will use to take the exam remotely. The setup and installation guide will walk you through the process of downloading and accessing the Proctorio extension. Be sure to do this well in advance of your test day to avoid any last-minute software issues. To use Proctorio, your operating system and internet connection must meet specific requirements, and you will also need a webcam and microphone (or headphones with audio capability) during the exam. Tablets and mobile devices are not supported, so you must have access to a desktop or laptop computer. Your parent or guardian must also sign a consent form, which outlines the code of conduct for remote testing.

In preparation for test day, be sure to test out the Proctorio system as well as your webcam and microphone or headphones on your computer. Check your internet connection to ensure that everything is running smoothly and quickly, and as an extra precaution, you can turn off other devices that are using the internet. On test day, keep your student ID (your 7-digit TACHS ID assigned to you at registration) and your session code handy because you will need both in order to take the exam. Also, make sure to have any troubleshooting information for Proctorio easily accessible in case you encounter technical difficulties during the test. Keep your laptop or computer plugged in to ensure that your computer is fully charged while you're taking the exam.

Before you can start the exam, you must complete a room scan to ensure that there are no unauthorized resources or supplemental materials in your exam space. Your webcam and microphone will monitor you to ensure that you are not violating the remote testing code of conduct. You must share your screen for the duration of the exam; do not click the Stop Sharing button at any time. Try not to get distracted by seeing yourself on camera; focus on the exam itself and follow instructions closely.

It's important that you take the test in a comfortable and quiet location with adequate lighting. Minimize any distractions by silencing notifications and alerts on both your computer and your phone. During the exam, you are permitted to have snacks and water. You can also use a pen/pencil and scratch paper only during approved subtests—Reading, Written Expression, and Mathematics. Once the Mathematics subtest is over, you must discard the scratch paper.

After each of the first three subtests, you will be offered a 5-minute break. You can choose to take the break or you can skip to the next subtest. If you opt to take a break, then you'll have five minutes to use the restroom, grab a snack, etc. However, the next subtest will automatically begin as soon as the five-minute break is over, so if you are not back at your device by the end of the break, you will lose testing time. There will only be one-minute pauses after subtests 4 and 5, so plan accordingly.

TACHS Format and Focus

The TACHS is a multiple-choice exam that tests your knowledge in the following key areas: **reading, written expression, mathematics, and general reasoning ability**. The questions you see will match the content a typical eighth-grade student should have mastered. It's not designed to trick you, give you impossible challenges, or test your patience. So, breathe easy!

Questions on the TACHS will have either four or five answer choices, with alternating letter options ('A, B, C, D, E' or 'J, K, L, M, N'). Your job is to pick the choice that best answers each question.

The following is a general overview of what you can expect on each subtest of the TACHS.

 NOTE

While the practice tests presented in the book and online reflect the content you will find on the TACHS, the question sequence, time allotment, and number of questions found within each subtest are subject to change.

The TACHS Reading Subtest (35 minutes long)

The Reading subtest of the TACHS features several passages of varying length. Your task is to read and answer questions that test your factual, interpretative, and evaluative understanding of the text. Some passages will be fiction; this might include fables, narrative stories, and excerpts from previously published works. Others will be nonfiction; these may include topics like science and social studies.

It's important to note that the exam will test your ability to comprehend what you read, *not* your general understanding of the topics, such as social studies or science.

For the most part, you'll be asked to infer or generalize about what you read. You may also be asked to identify the meaning of words or phrases in their literary context, to identify the main idea of a passage, and to determine what should come next in the passage. Reading the text closely is your greatest ally here.

Let's look at a sample reading question:

EXAMPLE:

> **Directions:** This is a test of how well you understand what you read. Read the following passage and then answer the questions. Four choices are given for the question. Choose the answer that you think is better than the others.

Paul Grisham, as a young boy, sold newspapers on the street corner to help his family. He went to work before sunrise, worked until it was time for school, and then returned home after school. Paul walked everywhere he went, regardless of the weather. The work ethic he developed as a youngster contributed to his eventual financial success as an adult.

Which of the following can be inferred about Paul's family when he was a child?

  A. Paul's family had very little money.
  B. Paul's family was very wealthy.
  C. Paul's family lived in the country.
  D. Paul's family was very large.

The correct answer is A. Paul worked before school and "walked everywhere he went." It can be inferred from the passage that he worked because he needed the money and walked because the family had no other means of transportation.

The TACHS Written Expression Subtest (30 minutes long)

The Written Expression subtest of the TACHS will test your skills in the proper use of Standard English. The questions cover sentence structure, organization, clarity, effectiveness or appropriateness of expressions, spelling, capitalization, punctuation, usage, and expression.

The first part of the test features pieces of writing followed by questions about how the writing should be changed. The second part features short pieces of writing with mistakes that you'll need to identify.

Let's look at a sample written expression question:

EXAMPLE:

> **Directions:** This is a test about writing in Standard English. Four answers are given for this question. Choose the answer that you think is better than the others.

- A. Clarisse, though a fast runner, a match for her cousin Arnold she was not.
- B. Though she was fast; Clarisse was a runner but was no match for her cousin Arnold.
- C. Though Clarisse was a fast runner, she was no match for her cousin Arnold.
- D. As a runner, though fast, a match for her cousin Arnold Clarisse was not.

The correct answer is C. In this sentence, the clause "though Clarisse was a fast runner" is followed by a comma, which is the correct punctuation.

The TACHS Mathematics Subtest (40 minutes long)

The Mathematics subtest of the TACHS tests your ability to solve math problems. For each math question, you'll be given a set of choices and will need to choose the correct answer.

Topics covered on the Mathematics subtest include geometry, measurement, algebraic patterns and connections, number sense and operations, data analysis, probability, and statistics. Questions can involve the use of formulas, equations, word problems, symbols, operations, estimation, data interpretation, and working with charts and graphs.

Let's look at a sample mathematics question:

EXAMPLE:

> **Directions:** This is a test of your knowledge and understanding of math. Four answers are given for this question. Choose the answer that you think is better than the others.

Gail has $\frac{2}{3}$ as many french fries as Mindy. Mindy has 12 french fries. How many french fries does Gail have?

- A. 8
- B. 9
- C. 10
- D. Not given

The correct answer is A. $\frac{2}{3} \times 12 = 8$

The TACHS Ability Subtest
(32 minutes long)

The Ability subtest of the TACHS exam will test your abstract reasoning abilities—skills you have honed both in the classroom and in everyday life. Question types in this section include Paper Folding, Figure Classification, and Figure Matrices. You'll be presented with visual tasks that require you to generalize from one item or series of items to another. Don't worry if this sounds different or new to you; we're testing general reasoning skills here, not academic knowledge. Identifying patterns within a series and looking ahead to logical outcomes are the skills required in this section.

Let's look at a sample figure classification question:

EXAMPLE:

Directions: In the following question, the first three figures are alike in certain ways. Choose the figure that corresponds to the first three figures.

The correct answer is L. Each of the figures is divided in half with the bottom half shaded.

ALL ABOUT THE HIGH SCHOOL PLACEMENT TEST (HSPT®)

Like the TACHS, the Scholastic Testing Service High School Placement Test—HSPT for short—is part of the admissions process for many Catholic high schools. The HSPT is a multiple-choice, 298-question exam designed to test your **reading**, **mathematics**, **verbal**, **quantitative**, and **language skills**.

There's also an optional forty-question test in either science, mechanical aptitude, or religion. Because many schools do not use any of the optional tests, and because these test results are *not* included as part of your composite score, this book doesn't cover the optional tests in depth. To give you some idea of what you can expect on an optional test, you'll find an outline of the Science test at the end of this section. The outline shows you the typical structure and scope of the optional tests. If you need to take one of the optional tests, be sure to get study advice from the schools you want to attend.

The exam takes about 2 hours and 30 minutes; along with your school records, your HSPT score will be sent to the high schools you're applying to, so they can make an admissions decision. Keep reading, and we'll help you prepare for success on this important exam!

The Pre-HSPT is an edition of the Closed HSPT designed to help seventh-grade students prepare for the HSPT. Families with seventh-grade students interested in taking the Pre-HSPT should contact the student's current school to see if the test is offered.

NOTE

CLOSED VS. OPEN HSPT

There are two different kinds of HSPT exams: the Closed HSPT and the Open HSPT. The Closed HSPT is administered by the school but scored by the Scholastic Testing Service (STS), the official HSPT creators and administrators. Closed HSPT scores are compared to national standard distribution norms, so nationwide percentiles can be computed. The Open HSPT is administered and scored by the school, so STS does not deal directly with student results. The Open HSPT uses old versions of the Closed HSPT.

Registering for the HSPT®

The HSPT is ordered and administered by individual schools or dioceses throughout the country. To schedule the HSPT, contact the school you want to attend and ask about their registration process. There are several options for taking the HSPT exam: in-person testing with proctoring and paper test booklets; in-person testing with proctoring, an online answer sheet, and a paper test booklet; and internet-based testing with or without a proctor.

Unlike other standardized admissions exams, the STS does not have set days for testing. Rather, individual schools and dioceses determine their own test days. For more information, contact the school where you'd like to take the HSPT.

The STS strongly recommends that each student take the HSPT only once. However, each school can allow a student to retest due to extenuating circumstances; this process is handled on a case-by-case basis.

Special Exam Accommodations

Each school administering the HSPT has its own policy regarding special exam accommodations. The STS suggests that if a student needs any accommodations, the parents or guardians should contact the schools directly for additional information.

Upon a school's request, the STS does provide large-print test booklets and answer sheets for visually impaired test takers. If your child requires large-print materials, please contact the school where you are taking the test, who will contact STS.

 TIP

You *don't* lose points for incorrect answers on the HSPT— this means you should try to answer *every* question you encounter on test day, even if you need to guess! Visit **https://www.ststesting.com/hsp/index.html** for more information.

Online Testing Protocol

Due to the COVID-19 pandemic, there is now an online testing option for the HSPT. To take the HSPT online, you will need to carefully read the HSPT Online Quick Start Guide, which can be found on the Scholastic Testing Service website, and complete the student tutorial in advance of your test date. Prior to test day, the test administrator must provide you with the required information for testing online, such as the scheduled test date and time, test code, list of materials allowed during testing, and any additional instructions required for video conferencing if you are being monitored virtually during testing. Test administrators may have their own individual requirements for testing, so familiarize yourself with any additional instructions in advance to avoid any last-minute issues. The quick start guide will walk you through the process of using your test code to claim your student ID for the test and logging in to HSPT Online. After you've logged in, you must sign the code of conduct for remote testing.

The only software requirements for the exam are internet access and an up-to-date web browser. Mobile devices are not recommended for testing. In preparation for test day, check your internet connection to ensure that everything is running smoothly and quickly. As an extra precaution, you can turn off other devices that are using the internet. Keep your laptop or computer plugged in to ensure that your computer is fully charged while you're taking the exam. On test day, keep your test code handy in order to claim your student ID and log in to the exam site. If you encounter any technical difficulties during the exam, contact your school or testing administrator.

It's important that you take the test in a comfortable and quiet location with adequate lighting. Minimize any distractions by silencing notifications and alerts on both your computer and your phone. Test administrators will likely have their own requirements for breaks and materials allowed during testing, such as snacks, water, scratch paper, etc.

How the HSPT® is Scored

High schools nationwide use score results on the HSPT to make admissions decisions, scholarship award selections, and curriculum placement determinations. That said, there are no set guidelines for how schools should use score results, empowering each school to set its own rules for evaluating your scores.

To determine your HSPT scores, the number of questions you answered correctly on each of the subtests are added up, which will give you a set of *raw scores.* Your raw scores are then converted into standardized scores and national percentile rankings for each subtest ranging from one to 99, clearly showing how you stack up against other test takers nationwide.

Your HSPT® Score Report

Each individual school, cooperative, or diocese decides on the type of score report it wishes to receive, its process for distributing scores, and what information will be shared and distributed to test takers.

If a test taker is taking the HSPT at a school that is part of a cooperative of several high schools, they may have the option of sending their scores to several schools by coding their answer sheets accordingly.

 TIP

While the practice tests presented in this book and online are much like the *content* you will find on the actual test, the sequence, time allotment, and number of questions found within each section will vary from one HSPT test session to the next.

HSPT® Format and Focus

As mentioned previously, the HSPT is a multiple-choice exam with five distinct sections:

1. Verbal Skills
2. Quantitative Skills
3. Reading
4. Mathematics
5. Language Skills

You'll have approximately 2 hours and 30 minutes to answer the 298 questions you'll encounter on test day. Let's take a closer look at each of the sections on the exam.

Verbal Skills Section
(16 minutes long)

The Verbal Skills Section of the HSPT is designed to measure your ability to perform reasoning tasks that involve the use of words. This is a core performance ability that spans a wide array of content areas, including language, reading, and various areas within social studies.

The following is a breakdown of the topics you will encounter in the HSPT Verbal Skills section:

- Analogies
- Logic
- Verbal Classifications
- Synonyms
- Antonyms

Let's look at a sample verbal skills question:

EXAMPLE:

Directions: Mark one answer—the answer you think is best—for the problem.

Throw is to ball as shoot is to

   A. policeman.
   B. kill.
   C. arrow.
   D. hunting.

The correct answer is C. This analogy describes an action-to-object relationship. You *throw* a *ball*, and you *shoot* an *arrow*.

Quantitative Skills Section
(30 minutes long)

The quantitative component measures your ability to answer reasoning problems involving numbers and quantities. This is a core performance ability that spans a wide array of content areas, including mathematics and science.

This section of the exam will test the cognitive skills you've acquired and built up this far, both in the classroom and in your everyday life.

The following is a breakdown of the topics you will encounter in the HSPT Quantitative Skills section:

- Sequence
- Reasoning
- Geometric Comparison
- Non-Geometric Comparison

The following geometric comparison is an example of a quantitative skills question:

EXAMPLE:

Directions: Mark one answer—the answer you think is best—for the problem.

A

B   C   D

A. $\overline{AD}$ is greater than $\overline{CD}$.

B. $\overline{BA}$ and $\overline{AD}$ are each less than $\overline{BC}$.

C. $\overline{AB}$ is equal to $\overline{BC}$.

D. $\overline{AB}$ is equal to $\overline{AC}$ plus $\overline{BC}$.

The correct answer is A. The line drawn from point *A* to the base of triangle *ABD* divides the triangle into two right angles, one of which is ∠*ACD*. $\overline{AD}$ is the hypotenuse of this right triangle, whose length must be greater than the length of $\overline{CD}$, the base of ∠*ACD*.

Reading Section (25 minutes long)

The Reading Section of the HSPT tests your effective reading comprehension, your recognition of key details and ideas, your ability to identify central thoughts and premises, how well you make logical inferences, and your understanding of vocabulary in context. This section tests the skills you've acquired in the classroom and in your everyday life.

Here is a breakdown of the topics you will encounter in the HSPT Reading Section:

Comprehension

- Vocabulary in Context
- Literal Comparison
- Inferential Comparison
- Main Idea
- Drawing Conclusions
- Reasoning
- Implied Characterization
- Critical Composition
- Primary Purpose
- Compare/Contrast
- Predictions
- Fact vs. Fiction

Vocabulary

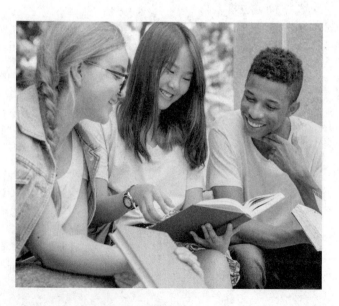

Let's look at a sample reading comprehension question:

EXAMPLE:

Directions: Read the passage below and then answer the question. Four answers are given for the question. Choose the answer that you think is better than the others.

Sample Passage

Most of us know that physical exercise is important for a healthy lifestyle. We know that people who exercise live longer lives and resist many fatal diseases. We know, in short, that exercise is a good thing. What we might not realize, however, is exactly how *many* benefits physical activity provides. Research conducted by the Harvard University School of Public Health has shed light on this issue by describing the effects of exercise in detail.

The Harvard® studies show that physical exercise helps prevent many diseases, including obesity, stroke, heart disease, and many types of cancers. Exercise increases our balance as well as the strength of our muscles and bones. Exercise helps us concentrate, enables us to burn more fat, keeps our joints healthy, and fortifies our immune systems. If all that weren't enough, exercise also has an important psychological benefit: it causes us to feel more positive and to maintain better moods.

Which of the following is true regarding the Harvard University School of Public Health?

A. It conducted research studies showing that physical activity prevents many diseases.

B. It ran many tests on exercise and published a book on the benefits of exercise.

C. It developed technology to measure what happens to the joints of people who exercise.

D. It ran scientific studies to examine how athletes can be harmed by too much exercise.

The correct answer is A. To answer a question like this one, it is helpful to re-read the part of the passage that contains the reference to the Harvard University School of Public Health. This reference occurs at the end of the first paragraph and the beginning of the second one. We learn that the Harvard University School of Public Health has conducted research about the benefits of exercise. According to paragraph two, the school's studies have shown that "physical exercise helps prevent many diseases," so choice A is correct.

Mathematics Section (45 minutes long)

The Mathematics Section of the HSPT is designed to measure your ability to perform arithmetic operations, apply key math concepts, and utilize sound mathematical reasoning to solve problems. The math skills you've acquired and built up thus far, both in the classroom and in your everyday life, will be tested during this section of the exam.

Here is a breakdown of the topics you will encounter in the HSPT Mathematics Section:

Numbers & Numeration

- Procedural Operations
- Roots/Exponents/Place Values
- Ratios/Proportions
- Properties/Factors/Multiples
- Word Problems

Measurements

- Weight/Length/Dry/Liquid
- Metric/Monetary Conversions

Geometry

- Points/Lines/Angles
- Plane/Cubic Figures
- Perimeter/Area/Volume
- Diameter/Radius/Circumference
- Congruency/Symmetry/Pythagorean Theorem

Algebra

- Equality/Inequality
- Functions/Coordinates

Statistics & Probability

- Mean/Median/Mode/Range
- Probability/Concepts
- Data Graphs/Tables

Let's look at a sample measurements question:

EXAMPLE:

Directions: Mark one answer—the answer you think is best—for the problem.

On a map, 1 inch represents 500 miles. How many miles apart are two cities that are $1\frac{1}{2}$ inches apart on the map?

    A. 750

    B. 1,000

    C. 1,250

    D. 1,500

The correct answer is A. If 1 inch = 500 miles, then $\frac{1}{2}$ inch = 250 miles. Therefore, $1\frac{1}{2}$ inches = 500 + 250 = 750 miles.

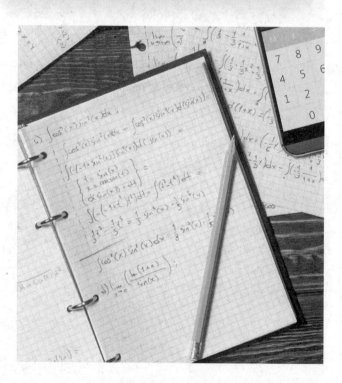

Language Skills Section
(25 minutes long)

The Language Skills Section of the HSPT is designed to measure your knowledge of proper English language capitalization, punctuation, grammar, spelling, usage, and composition. The language skills you've acquired and built up thus far, both in the classroom and in your everyday life, will be tested during this section of the exam.

The following is a breakdown of the topics you will encounter in the HSPT Language Skills section:

Punctuation

Capitalization

Incorrect/Correct Usage

- Noun/Pronoun
- Verb/Adverb/Adjective
- Other Parts of Speech

Spelling

Composition

Let's look at a sample incorrect usage question:

EXAMPLE:

> **Directions:** Find the sentence that has an error in usage. If you find no mistake, mark D as your answer.

> **A.** Many children adopt the beliefs of their parents.
> **B.** "Is he always so amusing?" she asked.
> **C.** All the officers declined except she.
> **D.** *(No mistakes)*

The correct answer is C. This sentence has an error in usage. The word *she* should be *her* since it acts as the object of the preposition *except.*

The Optional HSPT® Tests

Some schools might require that you take one of the three optional tests described at the beginning of this section: Mechanical Aptitude, Science, or Catholic Religion. If you must take an optional test, the test is chosen by the school, and, like the basic HSPT exam, the test will involve multiple-choice questions and answers.

Your score on the optional test will not be included with your score on the basic HSPT exam. Rather, the school will receive a report on your overall performance on the optional exam and a topic-by-topic evaluation of your performance. The school will use this information to place you in appropriate classes. It might also use the information to determine the background of the student body in preparing the curriculum for the following year.

The optional science test consists of forty questions covering a wide variety of topics. The questions are not neatly categorized. For example, a biology question might be followed by a physics question, then a laboratory methods question might be followed by a chemistry question. The following outline gives you an idea of how many topics are covered on the science test.

Distribution of Topics on HSPT® Optional Science Test

Biological Sciences

- Plants
- Animals
- Life Processes
- Health and Safety
- Ecology

Earth Sciences

- Astronomy
- Geology
- Weather
- Air
- Water

Physical Sciences

- Matter and Energy
- Machines and Work
- Magnetism and Electricity
- Sound
- Heat and Light
- Chemistry

Implications of Scientific Technology

- Societal Benefits
- Technical Applications

Principles of Scientific Research and Experimentation

- Laboratory Methods
- Research Practices

OTHER TESTS YOU CAN USE THIS BOOK TO STUDY FOR

While we focus on the TACHS and HSPT in this book, we'll also provide a quick overview of other common Catholic high school entrance exams: the ISEE, SSAT, and SHSAT.

All about the Independent School Entrance Exam (ISEE)

The Independent School Entrance Exam (ISEE) can be taken by students as part of their application to a private high school. The Upper Level of the ISEE exam is offered to students applying for grades 9 through 12. The ISEE lasts about 2 hours and 40 minutes, not including two 5- to 10-minute breaks. The ISEE is broken into five parts: Verbal Reasoning, Quantitative Reasoning, Reading Comprehension, Mathematics Achievement, and an unscored Essay component. On the ISEE, there are no penalties for incorrect answers, so you'll want to answer every question, even if you need to guess.

ISEE TEST STRUCTURE		
Section	Number of Questions	Duration
Verbal Reasoning	40	20 minutes
Quantitative Reasoning	37	35 minutes
Break		5–10 minutes
Reading Comprehension	36	35 minutes
Mathematics Achievement	47	40 minutes
Break		5–10 minutes
Essay	1	30 minutes

Along with your school records, your ISEE score is sent to the principals of the schools that you're applying to so that they can make an admissions decision. You can take the ISEE up to three times in a 12-month admission cycle. However, the test can only be taken once per season: fall (August to November), winter (December to March), and spring/summer (April to July).

How the Test is Scored

The Verbal Reasoning, Quantitative Reasoning, Reading Comprehension, and Mathematics Achievement sections consist of multiple-choice questions. Students will be scored based on the number of questions they answer correctly, with no penalties for incorrect answers. Scores are reported in percentile ranks, so your performance on the exam will be weighed against the performance of other students in the same grade as you who took the exam over the past three years. The Essay section is not scored. The schools you are applying to will receive a copy of your score report along with your essay.

Format and Focus

The ISEE is offered in both online and paper testing formats, and each format follows the same rules, guidelines, and timing requirements. If you opt for the paper format of the exam, you can take the test at school, at an office, or at a testing center. Depending on your needs and preferences, you may find it more convenient to test at your local school or at an office in a smaller group environment. If you go to a testing center, a parent or guardian is required to stay at the testing center for the duration of your exam. If you opt for the online testing format, you can take the ISEE from home.

The ISEE consists of five sections: Verbal Reasoning, Quantitative Reasoning, Reading Comprehension, Mathematics Achievement, and an Essay component. The exam only consists of multiple-choice questions, except the Essay component, which requires a written response. On the Verbal Reasoning portion of the exam, you will have 20 minutes to answer 40 questions. The Verbal Reasoning section will include vocabulary and sentence completion items. For vocabulary items, you will be given a word and asked to select a synonym for that word from four answer options. For sentence completion items, you will be asked to fill in two blanks within a sentence; you will be given four pairs of words and you must choose the pair that best completes the sentence.

On the Quantitative Reasoning section, which is one of two math sections on the exam, you will have 35 minutes to answer 37 questions. The emphasis of this section is on your ability to think and reason mathematically, so very few calculations will be required. Instead, you will likely be using logic and reason to solve problems, analyzing and interpreting data, comparing and contrasting quantities, and other tasks.

On the Reading Comprehension section of the exam, you will have 35 minutes to answer 36 questions. There will be six passages on topics such as history, science, literature, and contemporary life. Questions may ask you to identify the main and supporting ideas, make inferences, define words, identify the structure of the passage, and interpret literary elements within the passage.

The Mathematics Achievement section of the exam tests your mathematical abilities on a variety of topics, including numbers and operations, algebra, geometry, measurement, data analysis and probability, and problem solving. For this section of the exam, you will have 40 minutes to answer 47 questions. In contrast to the Quantitative Reasoning section, you will need to perform calculations in order to determine the correct answer to certain problems on this part of the exam. The good news is that you do not have to memorize any conversion factors; if required, they will be given to you in the question. You cannot use a calculator and you won't be given scratch paper for the paper format of the exam, but you can write in the test booklet.

For the Essay component of the exam, you will be given a prompt and asked to write a short essay in 30 minutes. The Essay section of the ISEE serves two purposes: First, you can showcase your personality to the schools to which you are applying. Second, you can demonstrate your writing skills, specifically your ability to organize and express your thoughts and ideas. The essay prompts focus on topics that allow you to talk more about yourself, including your interests, your strengths, and your goals. On the exam, you can use a piece of scratch paper to create a short outline for your response before you start drafting.

All about the Secondary School Admission Test (SSAT)

The Secondary School Admission Test (SSAT) is an entrance exam that can be taken by students as part of their application to a private high school. The Upper Level of the SSAT exam is offered to students applying for grades 9 through 12. The SSAT lasts about 3 hours and 10 minutes, including two 10-minute breaks. The SSAT is broken into the following sections: Quantitative (Math), Verbal, Reading, an unscored Writing Sample, and an unscored Experimental section, which includes a mix of verbal, reading, and math questions.

Along with your school records, your SSAT score is sent to the principals of the schools that you're applying to so that they can make an admissions decision. You are allowed to take the SSAT multiple times, depending on which format of the test you are taking. For computer-based SSAT exams, you can take the exam up to 3 times per testing year (August 1st through July 31st). For paper-based SSAT exams, you can take the Standard test up to six times, and you can take the Flex test twice, once per Flex period. See the SSAT website for details.

How the Test is Scored

The Quantitative, Verbal, Reading, and Experimental sections consist of multiple-choice questions with five possible answers. Students will be scored based on the number of questions they answer correctly. You receive one point for each correct answer, but you will lose one quarter of a point for each incorrect answer. As such, only guess if you are confident that you can eliminate at least one wrong answer. Scores are reported in percentile ranks, so your performance on the exam will be weighed against the performance of other students in the same grade as you who have taken the exam. The Writing Sample section is not scored. The schools you are applying to will receive a copy of your score report along with your essay.

Format and Focus

The SSAT is offered in both online and paper testing formats, and each format follows the same rules, guidelines, and timing requirements. If you opt for the paper format of the exam, you can take the test at school, at

SSAT TEST STRUCTURE		
Section	Number of Questions	Duration
Writing Sample (unscored)	1	25 minutes
Break		10 minutes
Quantitative (Part 1)	25	30 minutes
Reading	40	40 minutes
Break		10 minutes
Verbal	60	30 minutes
Quantitative (Part 2)	25	30 minutes
Experimental (unscored)	16	15 minutes

an office, or at a testing center. Depending on your needs and preferences, you may find it more convenient to test at your local school or at an office in a smaller group environment. If you go to a testing center, a parent or guardian is required to stay at the testing center for the duration of your exam. If you opt for the online testing format, you can take the SSAT from home.

The SSAT is broken into the following sections: Quantitative (Math), Verbal, Reading, an unscored Writing Sample, and an unscored Experimental section, which includes a mix of verbal, reading, and math questions. The exam only consists of multiple-choice questions, except the Writing Sample component, which requires a written response. For the Writing Sample component of the exam, you will be given two prompts to choose from, one personal and one general. You will be asked to choose one and write a short essay response in 25 minutes. The Writing Sample section of the SSAT serves two purposes: First, you can showcase your personality to the schools to which you are applying. Second, you can demonstrate your writing skills, specifically your ability to organize and express your thoughts and ideas.

The Quantitative (Math) section consists of 50 questions, given in two 30-minute sections on the exam.

1

These questions test your ability in arithmetic, algebra, and geometry, as well as other topics. You are not permitted to use a calculator on this section of the exam.

On the Reading Comprehension section of the exam, you will have 40 minutes to answer 40 questions. There will be both argumentative and narrative passages ranging from 250 to 350 words in length. Reading comprehension passages are taken from sources such as literary fiction; the humanities, including biography, art, and poetry; science, including anthropology, astronomy, and medicine; and social studies, including history, sociology, and economics. Questions may ask you to identify the main idea, find details, make inferences, define words, determine the author's purpose and tone, evaluate arguments, and make predictions based on information in the text.

On the Verbal Reasoning portion of the exam, you will have 30 minutes to answer 60 questions. The Verbal Reasoning section will include synonym and analogy items. For synonym items, you will be given a word and asked to select the word that means most nearly the same from among five answer choices. For analogy items, you will be given a comparison and asked to determine the logical relationship between the words by selecting the word that best completes the analogy.

The Experimental section on the exam is unscored and is designed to test future questions for the SSAT.

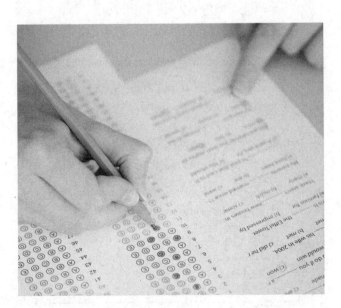

All about the Specialized High School Admissions Test (SHSAT)

Students in grades 8 and 9 who reside in New York City can take the Specialized High School Admissions Test (SHSAT) as part of their application to enroll in a local Catholic high school. The test consists of two sections: an English Language Arts section and a Math section. English language learners will also be given a glossary with word-to-word translations of mathematics terms, but these glossaries do not include definitions. You will have 180 minutes to complete the test, and you can divide your time between both the English Language Arts section and the Math section however you want.

How the Test is Scored

The English Language Arts section consists of 57 multiple-choice questions, 10 of which are field test questions and are unscored, though you won't know which are scored and which are unscored. The Math sections consists of 52 multiple-choice questions and five grid-in questions. Like the English Language Arts section, 10 of the questions are unscored and you will not know which questions are scored and which are unscored. Each question is worth one point, and there is no penalty for incorrect answers. The number of questions you answer correctly adds up to your raw score. Your raw score is converted to a scaled score in order to make comparisons between your score and other students who took different forms of the SHSAT in the same year as you. Your composite score is the sum of your scaled scores for both English Language Arts and Math. The more questions you get right in each section, the higher your scaled scores and composite score will be. The maximum score for each section is typically 350, and the maximum composite score is 700, though these numbers may vary depending on the year you take the exam. Your results are reported as scaled scores to the schools to which you are applying, and your personal score report will include your scaled scores and composite score.

Format and Focus

The English Language Arts section consists of two parts: Revising/Editing and Reading Comprehension. There are 9–19 questions in the Revising/Editing subsection, which tests your ability to recognize and correct language errors and to improve the overall quality of writing. Part A will ask you to answer questions based on an individual sentence or paragraph, while questions in Part B are based on a single, multi-paragraph text. There are 38–48 questions on the Reading Comprehension subsection, which tests your ability to understand, analyze, and interpret texts from a variety of genres. There will be 5-6 texts with 6-10 questions for each. The passages will include texts that middle school students should be familiar with: Nonfiction texts may include expository/explanatory texts, argumentative texts, and essays or opinion pieces on a variety of topics, and some accounts may be historical, scientific, or technical in nature but written for a general audience. Literary texts may include poetry, historical fiction, science fiction, allegories, satire, and more.

The Math section will include both word problems and computational problems in either multiple-choice or grid-in format, meaning you must record your number on the score sheet instead of selecting it from multiple-choice options. Definitions or explanations for terms, symbols, and formulas will not be provided on the exam. Questions on the exam may ask you to perform basic operations, set up equations based on word problems, set up and solve proportion problems, work with angles, lines, and figures, and more. You are not permitted to use a calculator.

TEST DAY CHECKLIST

No matter what test you're taking, you already know how important it is to study and prepare. But it's *equally* important to know what you must—and must not—bring with you to your testing location on the day of your exam; this will help you avoid any unpleasant delays or surprises.

What to bring on exam day (in-person testing):

 A form of identification (e.g., a student ID or library card)

 A few sharpened No. 2 pencils with good erasers

What NOT to bring on exam day (in-person testing):

 Preparation materials (notes, notebooks, study guides, flashcards, etc.)

 Battery-operated or electronic devices including calculators, watches, phones, tablets, and laptop computers

 Food or drinks

What to have with you during the exam (online, remote testing):

 Your registration code (test code, session code, student ID number, etc.)

 Your computer or laptop, fully charged, plugged in, and connected to the internet

 Webcam or microphone (or headphones with audio capability) if your test administrator is monitoring your testing environment virtually

 A stable and fast internet connection

 Water and healthy snacks (if permitted)

 A pencil or pen and blank paper to use as scratch paper (if permitted)

What NOT to have with you during the exam (online, remote testing):

 Preparation materials (notes, notebooks, study guides, flashcards, etc.)

 Battery-operated or electronic devices including calculators, watches, phones, and tablets

NOTES

SUMMING IT UP

- Make sure that you know which exam you're taking, how to register for it, the format and focus of the test, how to take the test online (if applicable), and how your exam is scored.

- The Test for Admission into Catholic High Schools (TACHS) is the entrance examination for eighth-grade students who want to attend a Catholic high school in the Diocese of Brooklyn/Queens or the Archdiocese of New York City.

  ○ This year, all testing will be online, so make sure that you are familiar with the system requirements and that you set up the automated proctoring system in advance.

  ○ The TACHS is a multiple-choice exam that lasts about 2 hours and tests your knowledge in the following key areas: reading, written expression, mathematics, and general reasoning ability.

- The High School Placement Test (HSPT) is an entrance examination for eighth-grade students who want to attend a Catholic high school.

  ○ The HSPT exam takes about 2 hours and 30 minutes to complete 298 questions designed to test your reading, mathematics, verbal, quantitative, and language skills.

  ○ There are three options for taking the HSPT: in person and on paper, in person with an electronic answer sheet and paper test booklet, and online.

  ○ Each individual school, cooperative, or diocese decides on how to conduct online testing as well as the type of score report it wishes to receive, its process for distributing scores, and what information will be distributed to test takers.

- The Independent School Entrance Exam (ISEE) is an entrance exam that can be taken by students as part of their application to a private high school.

  ○ The ISEE is offered in both online and paper testing formats, and each format follows the same rules, guidelines, and timing requirements.

  ○ The Upper Level of the ISEE exam is offered to students applying for grades 9 through 12. The ISEE lasts about 2 hours and 40 minutes, not including two 5- to 10-minute breaks.

  ○ The ISEE is broken into five parts: Verbal Reasoning, Quantitative Reasoning, Reading Comprehension, Mathematics Achievement, and an Essay component.

  ○ Scores are reported in percentile ranks, so your performance on the exam will be weighed against the performance of other students in the same grade as you who took the exam over the past three years.

- The Secondary School Admission Test (SSAT) is an entrance exam that can be taken by students as part of their application to a private high school.

  ○ The Upper Level of the SSAT exam is offered to students applying for grades 9 through 12.

- The SSAT lasts about 3 hours and 10 minutes, including two 10-minute breaks.
- The SSAT is broken into the following sections: Quantitative (Math), Verbal, Reading, an unscored Writing Sample, and an unscored Experimental section, which includes a mix of verbal, reading, and math questions. Students will be scored based on the number of questions they answer correctly. You receive one point for each correct answer, but you will lose one quarter of a point for each incorrect answer.
- Scores are reported in percentile ranks, so your performance on the exam will be weighed against the performance of other students in the same grade as you who have taken the exam.

- Students in grades 8 and 9 who reside in New York City can take the Specialized High School Admissions Test (SHSAT) as part of their application to enroll in a local Catholic high school.

  - The test consists of two sections: an English Language Arts section and a Math section, each with 57 questions.
  - You will have 3 hours to complete the test, and you can divide your time between both the English Language Arts section and the Math section however you want.
  - Each question is worth one point, and there is no penalty for incorrect answers.

- For in-person testing, be sure to bring these on exam day:
  - A form of identification (e.g., a student ID or library card)
  - A few sharpened No. 2 pencils with good erasers

- For in-person testing, be sure to **NOT** bring these on exam day:
  - Notes, books, or scratch paper
  - Food or beverages
  - Battery-operated or electronic devices, including calculators, watches, phones, tablets, or laptops

- For remote online testing, be sure to have the following:
  - Your registration code
  - Your computer or laptop
  - Webcam and microphone (if required)
  - A stable internet connection
  - Water and snacks
  - A pencil or pen and blank paper to use as scratch paper (if permitted)

- For remote online testing, do **NOT** use the following:
  - Preparation materials (notes, notebooks, study guides, flashcards, etc.)
  - Battery-operated or electronic devices including calculators, watches, phones, and tablets

CHAPTER

Learning How to Learn

LEARNING HOW TO LEARN

OVERVIEW

What Is Learning?

How Does Learning Work?

What Does Effective Learning Look Like?

Techniques and Strategies for Effective Studying

Study Time Surveys

Summing It Up

Whether someone is an expert in astrophysics, algebra, English grammar, social media, or dog grooming, they likely possess traits that are common to most if not all experts. Research says that experts are different than most people not because of their intellect but because they've built a set of skills that take full advantage of how humans learn.

Learning how to learn isn't something we are exposed to every day. That may vary from school to school, classroom to classroom, and even student to student, but in general, more classroom time is spent on what we're trying to learn rather than how to learn it well.

To help you get the most out of this book, we want to put you in an expert mindset. To do that, let's look at ideas related to what learning is and how it works so that you can make better choices to not only learn more but learn everything better.

NOTE

This chapter is all about learning and studying effectively. There's a lot to take in here, so set a reminder to revisit this information as you work through this book to make sure you're preparing for your test in the best way possible.

WHAT IS LEARNING?

What does it mean to learn something? What even is *learning*? In school, learning is the acquisition, formation, and application of knowledge. You do this through lectures, readings, and studying. But you're also learning any time your ideas, behaviors, beliefs, skills, and/or attitudes change. And the process of changing any of those things is often about practice.

Changing who you are and how you think isn't something you do lightly, though. More than likely, you want to have as much control over that process as possible so that you can become exactly who you need to be to accomplish what you want.

HOW DOES LEARNING WORK?

There are some things that you only have to experience once to learn well. The wisdom behind the label "HOT! DO NOT TOUCH!" becomes pretty clear after you lean on a glowing stove. Your first encounter with a spider (harmless or not) may have "taught" you that every trip to a dark and dusty closet could be a life-or-death ordeal. But then there are concepts that just don't seem to stick. Maybe you can't remember the differences between mean, median, and mode. Maybe you can't remember all the rules for comma usage. For whatever reason, those things may not be cemented into your thinking the same way as the painful or the unpleasant. Depending on your goals, though, you may need that slippery information to stick around too. So, since learning seems so inconsistent, how does it actually work?

According to recent findings from the fields of psychology and neurobiology, learning is about making changes to a physical system: your brain. When you're acquiring information, your brain cells (neurons) are "firing." And when neurons fire together, they "wire" together. This leads to the creation or modification of "pathways" throughout your brain. Creating those neural pathways is not a perfect process, though. You have all sorts of routines that already have well-developed pathways, and they may have to change (or resist change) to accommodate something new. Then there's everything your body is going through when learning—sleep deprivation, dehydration, distraction, and more. But the more you use a pathway, the more efficient that pathway becomes.

All of that is one way of saying that your brain is a complex organ and learning is not a path from A to B. It's a pathfinding process that requires time and energy. But we can try to think about learning as a sequence of basic processes and conditions. Let's start with memory.

NOTE

The description of memory used in this chapter is referred to as the Atkinson-Shiffrin multi-store model of memory. It suggests that human memory works, most of the time, like saving a file on a computer. You enter the information, choose to save it, and then can access it later.

The Memory Process

You are constantly bombarded with sensory information and you don't remember most of it. In fact, only a tiny fraction of what you experience every day is stored for later use. The details of why that is can get a little complicated, but let's look at memory as a series of steps taking place in different kinds of memory. You have several different forms of memory: sensory memory, short-term memory (STM), and long-term memory (LTM). Remembering something requires use of all three. The process itself starts with sensing and transforming information and ends with you retrieving it from the vast storage of your long-term memory.

Encoding

To start the process of memory, your brain takes in information through your senses. Anything you touch, taste, hear, see, or smell. That info flashes in your sensory memory. This is happening constantly at high volume, but you ignore most of what you experience. If you pay attention to something, though, you kick-start a sort of memory transfer process. What would have been a fleeting sensation has now moved into your short-term memory. Your STM is all about what your

mind is working with and really only information from within the past 60 seconds that you've selected.

You then hold the information in your short-term memory and encode the info—change it into some usable form in your mind. After handling the info, you might find that you can recall it later on. All of this constitutes a process called encoding.

Sometimes remembering things feels automatic. You may not have been paying perfect attention to something or manipulating it but somehow you still remember it (yesterday's breakfast, what someone was wearing last Tuesday, etc.). Most of the time, however, to keep things from being forgotten almost immediately, you need to focus on the information and change it into a new form.

Once upon a time, people had to memorize each other's phone numbers, a process that, for most, meant saying the numbers again and again under their breath. That's not a bad way of doing things because it can work, since it has the person see the numbers then work with those numbers in STM. By repeating them (acoustic encoding), the digits then might be stored for retrieval in long-term memory. The key word, though, is "might." There's never a guarantee that things will transfer—at least not perfectly.

TYPES OF MEMORY

SENSORY MEMORY

- High-capacity
- 2-3 seconds long
- Information must be brought in by senses

SHORT-TERM MEMORY

- 5-9 items
- Less than 60 seconds
- Information must be selected with attention

LONG-TERM MEMORY

- Nearly unlimited capacity
- A day to an entire lifetime
- Information must be encoded, stored, and maintained

TIP

Pause regularly throughout this chapter to check that you understand how learning works and the choices that can make your learning more effective.

Let's assume that you want to make the chance of that happening as great as possible; instead of trying to just hammer each number into memory with simple repetition, there are some better routes to take. Repetition (what's called "rehearsal") is necessary, but just hearing or picturing info is shallow processing. You can encode more effectively when you try to process information deeply—which requires thinking about the meaningful characteristics of that information (what's called semantic encoding).

For instance, instead of trying to memorize the individual numbers that make up the phone number, someone could think of the digits as forming a "chunk." Chunking is the process of looking at information as meaningful wholes rather than individual pieces. The average limit for short-term memory is seven items, so by grouping things into chunks, your STM can hold more at one time. Say someone gave you a phone number with the following starting digits: 718-555. Instead of trying to remember each digit individually, the information could be divided into meaningful chunks: 718 is a New York area code, 555 is a group of 5s. Instead of six individual items, you now have two chunks in memory. That gives you plenty of capacity to rehearse the last four digits of the number if you can't think of any way to chunk them.

But you can chunk in all sorts of ways. For another example, each sequence could be visualized as a series of strange images: imagine the 7 is a construction crane that builds a radio tower, 1, which then falls through a pair of pink sprinkled donuts, 8, and so on. That stream of images is distinct and will probably stick in your memory.

If the digits were like another number you already knew, connecting it to that prior knowledge would make recall easier later on. All of those moments of processing, or "recoding," make encoding more effective and thus create better conditions for the next stages of memory.

Before moving on, rehearse the process of encoding: after you're exposed to information, you have to select info with your attention and then encode it by changing or repeating its form in your short-term memory. There are multiple conditions that lead to better encoding—if information is:

- distinct (or odd) in the context of what you're experiencing
- connected with strong emotions or prior knowledge
- visualized in your mind's eye
- processed for its meaning and not just its superficial qualities (what it looks like, sounds like, etc.)
- received in multiple different forms (auditory, visual, haptic)
- chunked into more manageable and meaningful parts

Scan this QR code for a playlist of videos on learning strategies and study skills.

NOTE

Look up "memory palaces" to see how people with even average memories can remember incredible amounts of information. Clemens Mayer, a World Memory Champion, once used the memory palace technique to memorize and recall 1040 random digits in a half-hour.

Storage

As information is moving through your different forms of memory and encoding, it's going through the process of storage. Storage is all about getting the information to persist in your memory. To do that, it has to pass through each form of memory. You know that at the start of the memory process, the information went from your sensory memory (a few seconds long but high volume) to your short-term memory (less than a minute and very limited in its capacity). In your short-term memory, you did some encoding, and then, the hope is, that information started to travel into your long-term memory (something that may have a near infinite capacity). Some form of storage is happening in each of those different memory spaces and is aided by rehearsal (selection and repetition).

Essentially, storage is when your brain is doing some rewiring to accommodate what you've encoded. This often requires some maintenance (saying it to yourself, picturing it again, etc.) to send that signal. Storage is not a perfect process. Not everything survives the trip from your STM to your LTM. It all depends on memory traces, little biochemical changes to the brain's structure. Those traces, like anything that occurs in a physical system, may have flaws and can even be impacted by your current mood or mindset. But the greater the repetition of signals through the newly forming neural pathways, the greater the chance that the information will take hold in your LTM—which is the key to the next step in the process.

Retrieval

Once information has gone through the storage process and is saved to your long-term memory, it's ready for retrieval. Retrieval is the act of accessing your stored memories. Sometimes retrieval feels involuntary. You

NOTE

A survey in 2021 found data to suggest that every month, more than half of Americans have to reset at least five of their online passwords. How could that be? Often, people select a new password but maybe don't pay attention to it, so it's forgotten. Or it gets encoded poorly so that it's only stored as a weak memory. When it comes time to retrieve it, it's not all there (was there capitalization, numbers, an exclamation point?). But if a password is typed frequently, it can be maintained and stored more effectively for later recall.

MULTI-STORE MODEL OF MEMORY

might hear someone mutter a phrase and suddenly you're humming the chorus to a song you haven't heard in years. Retrieval is often considered the true purpose and power of memory. After all, what would be the point of encoding and storing information if we couldn't use it when we needed to?

As such, the goal is to gain control over what's accessible in long-term memory. You want to be able to retrieve the information you want when you need it. So how do you do that? Let's use a simple metaphor: your memory is a garden. Once you've got the seeds and planted them, you need to periodically walk through, pull some weeds, and water what you care about. Some things just won't survive when left on their own.

For strong retrieval, you have to periodically revisit the information that's important for your goals. To do that, you have to pull information from your long-term memory into your short-term memory and rehearse it. That retrieval should be done periodically (soon after learning, multiple times per week, and over longer intervals). This act of tending to memory is a step that a lot of learners skip in their learning process. Students just like you assume that because they were exposed to it (encoding) and maybe felt like they remember it (storage), that they can actually use it (retrieval). Often, they can't. The interval between memorization and retrieval is too great and leads to forgetting.

For the most part, the more often and thoroughly you retrieve, the more engrained information becomes. By repeatedly walking that pathway in your brain, you make it easier to traverse in the future. As you'll see later in this chapter, you need to take the time to actively quiz yourself on what you need to remember. But that's just one part of the process because learning doesn't end with memory.

Learning Is More Than Memory

To learn, you have to acquire knowledge. You now know a bit about how memory works; however, learning is also about using knowledge. To use knowledge, you have to understand it. But what "understanding" is or exactly how it works in the brain is less clear in the science of today. Nonetheless, we can say what some of the outcomes of understanding are. If someone understands something, then they might be able to execute a procedure. Or a person might be able to express the relationships between different topics or state why something works the way that it does.

In those outcomes, someone is using various facts, ideas, concepts, and processes and connecting them together. That network may be present because of how information was initially learned or because of what the learner has chosen to do with their knowledge since. Remember that neurons that fire together wire together. To improve your network of neural pathways, you can activate different pathways at the same time.

Activation of more parts of the brain depends on the use of higher-level cognitive processes. Those higher-level processes include the following and more:

- setting goals
- identifying what information is important and what's not
- organizing information
- using information in different situations
- adapting behavior to new situations
- evaluating understanding
- determining relationships between ideas

By thinking about what you know and what you're doing in those ways, you're working to create those new connections. Those connections lead not only to better recall but also even better understanding, what you can think of as expertise. It may all sound like a paradox: To reach understanding, you have to try to understand. But it seems to work. It's leads to a cycle of thinking that compounds what you know, how well you know it, and what you can do with your knowledge.

All of this is to help you understand that while you may be able to remember certain things sometimes, true mastery requires more than memory. You need to take steps that allow you to access and apply information when you need it. So, now that you know a little about your brain's inner workings, let's explore what you can do to hack the mechanics of learning to work better for you.

WHAT DOES EFFECTIVE LEARNING LOOK LIKE?

So, based on what learning is and how it works, what do you need to do to learn well? Learning is supported by all sorts of activities. But you can probably guess that not all learning strategies and study techniques are equal. Some methods are going to support how your brain works and others aren't.

Unfortunately, even the strategies that work may not work all the time or for everyone. This is where we can start thinking about experts again. In general, experts are experts because they approach learning differently. Experts are always trying to build upon their skills and expand their knowledge. That means that they're always trying to acquire new strategies and improve on their old ones.

In fact, research indicates that one of the key differences between experts and other learners is that experts frequently reflect on their learning to make changes to how they learn[*]. In many ways, experts play a different game than the one most people learn to play in school: Experts are both strategic and deep learners. That means they're persistent, creative, reflective, and highly active. As you might guess, you can get more from your learning by trying to be all those things too.

In the following sections, you'll see that effective learning and studying is supported by the following choices:

- Being active rather than passive while studying
- Practicing metacognition to make meaningful decisions about studying
- Using higher-level thinking to connect ideas
- Alternating between focused and diffused modes of thinking
- Adopting a growth mindset

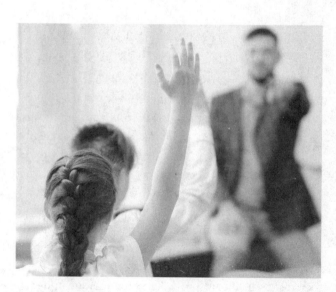

[*]National Research Council. 2000. *How People Learn: Brain, Mind, Experience, and School: Expanded Edition.* Washington, DC: The National Academies Press.

Active vs. Passive Learning

Research shows that when most learners are preparing for a test, they use a strategy called *rereading*. The word "strategy" is generous for what is essentially just looking over notes or a textbook. And students do this again and again, on repeat, until they're either too tired to continue or run out of time. Students do it because it's easy, then they believe that simply because they recognize the material on the page that they must also remember and understand it. Educators have taken to describing this situation as an illusion of competence. Students feel like they know it, but when it comes time to use it, that knowledge is nowhere to be found.

This is just one of many examples of what's called "passive studying." Passive studying occurs any time a student tries to absorb the information in front of them without injecting intention and energy. The problem stems from the idea that people will perfectly remember and understand a topic after watching a video or reading something for the first time. By default, there's no activity in that process. Nothing is created and no choices are being made; rereading a chapter or rewatching a video multiple times doesn't really change that. Rereading will serve neither the purpose nor the mechanics of learning. Yes, repetition is important for memory, but it needs to be made more efficient and effective through "active" processes.

You learned earlier that changing your knowledge, skills, and behaviors requires time and energy. After-all, learning is a top-down process, meaning that to remember information well and approach understanding, you must also make choices for your learning. You need to actively select what you're going to remember, organize that information, and build upon it. You must engage your memory and your thinking.

Just like watching someone play a game or dance doesn't necessarily make you better at either of those things, neither will you improve by staring at a page in a book. You need to be active.

While working through this book, active learning might look like the following:

1. Plan out your work time
2. Preview the chapter or section
3. Connect information to your prior knowledge
4. Read strategically
5. Take some form of notes
6. Create something to study from
7. Work for sustained, focused periods free of distractions
8. Test yourself regularly and intensely
9. Take periodic breaks during studying to reflect on and connect ideas
10. Review often (multiple times per week)
11. Assess whether your studying is working and what you can do differently

All that activity will come from multiple practices: planning, evaluating, and reviewing (metacognition), practicing higher-level thinking, alternating between different modes of thinking, maintaining an all-around practice of a growth mindset, and using a variety of effective study strategies. The combination of those behaviors is the best way to be active and support how you actually learn.

NOTE --

Did you know that there's an amount of stress that's good for you? Eustress is moderate stress that helps you perform better. Exactly how much stress that is varies from person to person. Finding that stressful sweet spot, though, will actually help you perform better in all sorts of circumstances. However, if your stress level goes too high or too low, your performance can suffer.

Metacognition

One major part of active learning is something called metacognition. It's a practice of thinking about your thinking. Research shows that metacognition is one of the top three traits among people we would call experts—people who know a lot in a particular field but continue to build on their knowledge all the time.

To start thinking about what metacognition is, let's think through a scenario. Imagine you're training for a marathon. Your ultimate goal is to go 26.2 miles. However, that doesn't mean you're going to put on your running gear, head out your front door, and take off at a dead sprint.

Most likely, you'll make a plan. You'll set up a training schedule. You'll train for different periods of time and in different conditions. You'll have some short routes and some longer ones. Eventually, you'll give that marathon-length route a try. Perhaps you'll find yourself wheezing and panting at only a quarter of the way, but perhaps not. Regardless, you'll take that trial as an opportunity to evaluate what's working in your training routine and what's not. Then you'll modify what you're doing to get the gains you're looking for.

That process of planning, monitoring, and evaluating is called metacognition. It's a cycle of thinking that helps people perform better, and it is a crucial part of effective learning.

There are three essential steps for metacognition:

1. Plan > 2. Evaluate > 3. Review

Each step is focused on asking yourself questions before, during, and after studying (like those shown in the graphic).

STEP 1 — **PLAN**
What do I know and what will I do to build on that knowledge?

STEP 2 — **EVALUATE**
How well am I doing while I'm learning and what can I do differently?

STEP 3 — **REVIEW**
What do I still need to work on and how can I guarantee that I'm prepared?

Let's see the cycle in action in an educational setting. Imagine Ivan. He's a typical student. He studies when he has tests, but sports, clubs, friends, and family routinely get in the way of studying as much as he might say he should. Sometimes he's also just not in the mood.

Ivan just learned that he failed his last math test. He's always been strong in the subject, but this semester has felt harder. On top of that, Ivan knows that if he fails another test, his grade point average could slip, which may even affect his eligibility for sports.

Instead of wallowing in his bad grade, though, Ivan pushes himself to think: "Why did I fail?"

Ivan starts thinking about how he got to this point. He evaluates his studying process and realizes: "Well, I only started studying the night before the test. I didn't give myself a lot of time. I know that the more time I have to review something, the better chance I have of remembering it."

Going deeper, Ivan might think: "I also wasn't remembering things while studying. I recognized things on the page, but I didn't test myself. All I really did was look over my notes."

Ivan now knows that how he studied just wasn't effective; he needs to do something different. He's thinking about his thinking and making some informed decisions about what he knows works for him. Ivan is practicing metacognition.

Ivan now thinks, "Next time, I need to start studying earlier. I also need to watch videos about the topics in the chapters instead of just reading. I know that I have an easier time remembering and understanding when I watch something. From the class syllabus, I also know that the next test is about something I don't understand at all. I'm going to need to study more and be active."

That's Ivan's starting point. Because he plans to start studying earlier, he can also take time to evaluate the progress of his studying as he goes. When he does that, he can evaluate his strategies and make changes to serve his current level of understanding.

At some point, he might think "The videos definitely help, but I'm still having trouble remembering all of this information. I need to make some flashcards, draw things out, and do some practice questions too." Ivan might have any number of those thoughts as he evaluates his strategies for individual problems, quizzes, videos, or even an entire textbook chapter.

At the same time, during Ivan's new and improved study sessions, he also needs to ask questions such as "Do I understand this?" and "Can I put this into my own words?" He might realize, "I actually don't get this. I know the terms and individual parts, but I couldn't explain it if someone asked me to. I need to go through it again, change my approach, or even try another resource."

Once Ivan's test comes around and he improves, he'll have created a working framework for how to approach not only his next unit test but also tests in his other courses. By self-directing his learning, Ivan will have empowered himself to achieve better results.

That's the process of metacognition, of thinking about thinking. It's not the WHAT of learning; it's the HOW Because learning is not just what you know but how you know what you know. Recognizing this makes you much more likely to achieve your learning goals.

Remember: Plan your studying, evaluate what's working and what's not as you go, and review what you know and what you need to do differently next time.

Keep in mind that to practice metacognition, you'll want to try to meet several conditions:

- See beyond the subject matter—not just the *what* of learning but the *how*
- Know different learning strategies and be curious enough to learn how to apply them
- Understand your personal strengths and weaknesses—how you learn and how your brain works
- Identify the limits of your knowledge—what you know, how well you know, and what you still need to learn

Higher-Level Thinking

The thoughts you have can be divided into different levels of thinking. There's higher-level and lower-level thinking. We can say that the lowest level of thinking is gathering information. Gathering can mean either remembering something or simply finding it online or on a page. Higher-level thinking still needs you to gather, but it also requires some degree of understanding.

For example, imagine you were asked to do the following tasks:

1. List the colors of a standard Rubik's cube.
2. Explain the relationship between the different colors on a Rubik's cube.
3. Demonstrate how to solve a Rubik's cube.
4. Design a new device that is similar to a Rubik's cube.

If you were to perform those tasks, what kinds of thinking would each of them require?

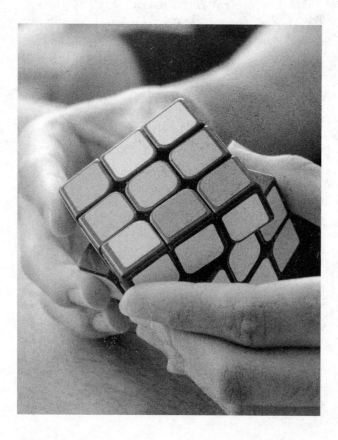

Task 1 asks for the colors of a standard Rubik's cube. You can accomplish that task either by recalling the colors or pointing to them on an actual cube. Task 2 requires a bit more thought, since you will need to not only know the colors but also understand how they're positioned. Task 3 then complicates the situation even further by asking you to solve a Rubik's cube; while there are methods for doing that, it requires significant knowledge and practice to do so. The complexity of your thinking is dramatically higher while demonstrating such knowledge. Predictably, task 4 requires an even higher degree of thinking, since you are asked to design a new device. To do so, you need to have complete knowledge of how the original puzzle works and must also be able to devise a method of solving whatever new contraption you come up with to verify that it functions. That's a powerful combination of memory, understanding, and creativity all used to achieve a specific result.

Each of those tasks demands more and more from the learner, who must not only acquire and retain knowledge but also use it in increasingly complex ways. Each of those tasks represents a different level of thinking. And it's those higher levels of thinking that people aspire to when beginning a new hobby or preparing for a test—recall, comprehend, create.

How does that help you, though? Well, if you can perform those different actions (remembering and understanding) with a topic, then you have some degree of mastery over said topic. If you can't perform higher-level thinking, then that tells you all you need to know about whether you're prepared for your test—most likely, you're not ready.

Additionally, just as you're making connections between ideas, so too are those connections forming in your brain. Furthermore, the greater the number of connections, the more ingrained that information is in your brain's structure. That all translates to greater expertise and recall ability.

Here, we've provided a table that offers a sample of some of the different actions that you might be expected to take with a topic when conducting different levels of thinking. The level of thinking increases from

LEVELS OF THINKING AND EXAMPLE VERBS*					
Remember	**Understand**	**Apply**	**Analyze**	**Evaluate**	**Create**
Define	Compare	Demonstrate	Combine	Assess	Compose
Gather	Discuss	Estimate	Debate	Judge	Design
List	Explain	Implement	Experiment	Monitor	Generate
Recognize	Paraphrase	Modify	Illustrate	Recommend	Produce
Select	Translate	Use	Predict	Test	Transform

*Adapted from Anderson, L.W., & Krathwohl, D.R. (Eds.) (2001). *A taxonomy for learning, teaching, and assessing: A revision of Bloom's taxonomy of educational objectives.* New York: Longman.

left to right. These actions are the type that teachers often use to create objectives for a class or unit. They know that if a student can perform the higher-level verbs by the end of the term, then the student has mastered the related topics. Think like a teacher: if you can't perform the higher-level actions, then it means that you may need to do more to remember or understand a topic—more studying, different study strategies, etc.

The levels of thinking that you'll need to apply on your exams tend to be more limited because of the nature of multiple-choice questions. But being able to practice higher levels of thinking and pushing yourself there in your studying—especially for entirely new topics—isn't going to hurt you on the test; in fact, it can only help.

For the tests in this book, you'll need to remember what a fraction is or the different rules for comma usage. You'll also need to apply rules for operations with fractions in word problems. Sometimes it won't be immediately clear what the operation or even the fraction is. You won't need to perform every level of thinking with every concept. But you should take the time when you're studying to check that you not only remember the information but can also use it in different ways.

Focused and Diffused Thinking

Just as your thoughts can be divided into different levels, they can be used in different modes too. We can think about two of those modes when it comes to learning things: focused and diffused.

When you're reading or trying to work through a problem, you're in your focused mode. That mode kicks on any time you're really concentrating to try to figure something out. In that mode, your thinking is traveling the pathways that exist in your brain, the ones that you've used in the past. Those pathways become more refined and more efficient with use.

 TIP

The next time you see a question on your homework or on a test, try assessing what level of thinking it requires. It's a good exercise to see the kinds of things your teachers are expecting of you and whether you're on track with your mastery.

NOTE

The name of the transition state from waking to sleep is called hypnagogia. The brain is incredibly active as it transitions; it's during this period that people may experience lucid dreaming, sleep paralysis, the Tetris effect, and other phenomena.

Alternatively, you've got your diffused mode. This mode is what was just active whenever you catch your mind wandering. The diffused mode of thinking turns on when you're doing things that don't require that much attention. You likely experience it when you go for a walk, take a shower, or play a song you've played many times before. In the diffused mode, your brain is great at making connections. You might have some epiphany about how two things are related or figure out a new way to do something.

Those modes represent two very different ways of thinking that serve very different purposes. One is for getting things done (focused). The other is for making surprising connections (diffused). When you're dealing with a new topic, you might get stuck in that laser-focused thinking mode because your thoughts are being forced to travel the pathways your brain already has built. If the situation is similar enough to something you've done before, you might figure it out. But if it's truly new information or a new way of thinking, then your existing chunks aren't going to be enough; instead, they'll keep you from seeing what's new. To fix that, you're going to need to let your mind wander off the beaten path to form some new connections.

There are plenty of stories of famous inventors and artists hacking their brains to come up with new ideas. People like Thomas Edison and Salvador Dali figured out that their brains were at their most creative right before they fell asleep. Supposedly, Thomas Edison used to sit in a chair while holding a piece of metal in his hand. Beneath his hand, he would position a plate. He would then close his eyes and as soon as he started to drift off, the metal piece would fall from his hand and clatter onto the plate. The sound would stir him

NOTE

Setting strict time limits for your work and breaks can improve not only your motivation and attention but also trigger a diffused state of mind when you step away. The Pomodoro technique is one such time management method. It has you work in short, concentrated bursts with short breaks in between. Give it a try: Choose your task. Set a 25-minute timer. Work on that task and nothing else until the timer expires. Take a 5-minute break. For every four 25-minute periods, take a 15-30 minute break. Keep that up until you're done for the day to see how it can improve your productivity and focus.

awake, and he would use his brain's creative state to ease him through a difficult problem or give him a glimpse of some potential invention.

Even just closing your eyes—taking a long blink—can help you step away from your current mode of thinking and allow your mind to, potentially, forge new connections. Sometimes, you're going to need to give your mind a larger incentive to switch modes than that. That's when it's time to take an actual break.

When you're trying to learn something new, if you feel like you're running into a wall, you should do something that allows your brain to not focus on anything in particular. To initiate that mode of thinking, you can try the following:

- Go for a walk
- Take a shower
- Exercise
- Draw
- Listen to instrumental music
- Take a nap

However, this doesn't mean taking breaks every few minutes. Your breaks need to come after intense active studying. This is because studying that doesn't require energy and won't do you any good. You need to alternate between your focused and diffused thinking to study most effectively. When you get back from your break, whether you had some grand epiphany or not, switch back to focused thinking and practice retrieval (see what you can remember without looking back at the material) and some higher-level thinking. Then review to make sure you're remembering correctly and

that you actually understand. Your diffused mode of thinking is a great asset, but spending too much time in that aimless state will often stall your learning.

Growth vs. Fixed Mindset

Learning new things is hard. You're trying to internalize a wealth of information, develop new skills, and change behaviors. In short, you're trying to grow. There are all sorts of barriers to your improvement, though. One that we have to contend with every day is our attitude or mindset. Our beliefs tend to impact what we do and how we do it, and if we're stuck in the mindset that we can't do something or are no good at it, we usually don't even try.

To be a successful and self-directed learner, then, demands that you believe you can be successful. This isn't to encourage blind optimism but to simply let you know that you need to want to change. Positivity isn't just a personality trait. It is a crucial tool for learning. To approach challenging situations with what's called a "growth mindset" improves learning outcomes. A growth mindset replaces the all-too-easy phrase "I can't . . ." with "How can I . . .?"

 NOTE -

Not everything will get you into a relaxed state for your diffused thinking to take over. Choose things that are easy for your brain and free of stress. While things like playing a video game or hopping on social media for a few minutes might be good rewards for hard work, they're not going to let your mind wander.

Because here's the reality: we don't grow when we avoid doing the hard things, and no one gets better by not practicing.

With practice, though, you can be a math person, a better writer, a better reader, or a better thinker. But, like everything, it requires work. Just like it takes you time to improve at a sport, build muscle at the gym, play a new song on an instrument, or make skillful drawings, your brain requires time and repetition to build expertise for academic topics.

While your brain is trying to grow, you need to frame what you're doing with growth in mind. Say to yourself, "I'm struggling now, but I'll keep getting better. I just need to keep working." From there, you get to make the critical decisions that can help you overcome frustration and continue to learn.

Take people who say, "I'm just not a math person." They think that because they've struggled with math in the past that it will always be a struggle. Despite what you may have heard, math ability is not limited by "talent" or "gifts." Persistence is the key to long-term math success. Sooner or later, even someone who may be naturally "good at math" has to work hard to succeed. For some people, that need starts earlier than for others. But if you're one of those people, that doesn't mean you should fall into the trap of a fixed mindset.

The real secret to learning is that perseverance is more important than intelligence. High intelligence may make things seem easier for a while, but sooner or later, everyone hits a wall. The difference between good learners and those who struggle is what happens when they reach what feels like a breaking point.

In recent years, a mountain of research has emerged showing that your intellectual abilities are not fixed. You can and will improve when you use the knowledge that you can grow to make better decisions. It sounds too simple, but students who know that their abilities can change recognize the importance of effort. That belief in effort and pursuit of hard work translates to better performance over time.

When you're aware of that, it's hard to make excuses for how you can't improve. If you know that your mindset matters, that it is your limiting factor, then you have to acknowledge the importance of practice and persistence. In doing so, you must decide whether you'll study the right way or the "easy way," which by now you know simply doesn't work.

Someone with a growth mindset may still sometimes say "I'm not good at math" or "I can't do this. . .", but they'll always end those sentences with the word "yet."

You can say it right now: "I can't do some things in math. . . yet." Then make it about what you *can* be: "I can be a better reader or a better writer or student or thinker." Understand that all of that comes "with practice." Because once you understand that it is only a matter of time and effort, you can make decisions that help you perform better. You don't need to resign yourself to the silly idea that you'll never improve, grow, or change because it's just not true. You may not be a "math person" or a "great learner" now, but know that you can be.

TECHNIQUES AND STRATEGIES FOR EFFECTIVE STUDYING

There are many different ways to study that check the boxes for effective and active learning. Here, we've suggested a few that can help you maximize your retention and encourage understanding. Some work for when you first read through a chapter or watch a video. Others are techniques that require intense retrieval and higher-level thinking. They all ask you to recall information and form relationships in different ways. Often, you'll spend more time up front creating something, but then you'll have a new resource on hand that you can use to test yourself.

You'll see that some of these strategies and techniques have you complete similar tasks. Try to experiment with different ones, even merging some together, to suit your preferences and also capitalize on what you know about how learning works. Each item is accompanied by an explanation of what it is, how it should be done, and why it can help you be a more effective and efficient learner.

SQ3R

What Is It?

SQ3R is a strategic reading technique. It stands for **S**urvey, **Q**uestion, **R**ead, **R**ecite, **R**eview. It is a five-step process that has you preview what you're going to read before you read it and review once you're done. To get the most out of a book chapter or section, you can prime yourself to identify what is most important or what you're less familiar with. You can then check your understanding at the end to make sure you took away the key points.

How Do You Do It?

Break down your reading of a chapter or section into five distinct steps:

1. **Survey:** Preview the entire chapter, reading section headings and examining graphics, captions, and the text's structure.

2. **Question:** Generate questions based on the information you surveyed.

3. **Read:** Read through the text.

4. **Recite:** Recite information from the text and try to answer your questions.

5. **Review:** Review the chapter or section to check your understanding and retention of what you read.

Why Does It Help?

SQ3R makes reading easier. By approaching reading as a multi-part process, you reduce the burden of having to try to learn everything in a single shot. By taking steps to find the purpose of a text (survey), identify points of confusion (questioning), read, retrieve key information (recite), and generate a cohesive summary of the text (review), you've done a lot to improve encoding and increase understanding of what you read.

Mind Maps

What Is It?

Mind maps are diagrams that illustrate the relationships between different ideas. They can be used to represent the topic of a book, a mathematical or scientific concept, an entire field of study, and more. A mind

TIP

Read through this information now but return here after you complete your diagnostic test and have identified what areas you'll need to work on. Mark strategies that you think you'll want to try when you start studying.

map makes use of text, images, and colors to depict and relate different characteristics or parts of a topic to one another. Imagine it like a tree: a major topic branches off into minor topics, all with their own detailed leaves.

How Do You Do It?

Draw and/or label the main topic of the map in the center of a document. From the central topic, place subtopics in the space around the main topic. For the subtopics, provide important details, categories, characteristics, views, etc. Use color, arrows, images, and other diagramming features to add greater detail.

Why Does It Help?

A mind map helps you identify the key features of a topic while developing spatial and logical relationships between said features. Mind maps capitalize on the brain's strong visual capacity while also asking you to retrieve, organize, and connect information—all higher-level processes that reinforce, once again, retention and understanding.

Feynman Technique

What Is It?

Richard Feynman was a Nobel prize-winning physicist. He made incredible discoveries in the field and was always looking to learn more. He was a true expert credited with developing a widely used study strategy called the Feynman technique. The Feynman technique is all about identifying, refining, and communicating what you know. Your goal is to create a short document that communicates a complex topic in a way that anyone reading it can understand.

An example of a mind map for the topic of ecology.

How Do You Do It?

List the topic in question at the top of a sheet of paper or blank document on your computer or phone. Describe the topic in terms that could be understood by almost anyone. Be sure to identify what it is, how it works, why it works that way, why it is important, or what topics it is connected to. Avoid using technical terms and jargon. After completing a paraphrase, reread what you wrote. Identify any gaps in your understanding and consult other resources as necessary. Continue to revise your paraphrase until the topic is absolutely clear—you both remember and understand the topic and could teach it to someone else. You can even share the document with others to see if they understand what you wrote. Use any feedback to revise.

Why Does It Help?

If you can teach someone how to do something, that usually means that you understand it completely. Not only does this technique force you to go through the process of retrieving and translating information (a form of higher-level thinking), but it also creates a resource that you can use to test yourself in the future.

Practice Testing

What Is It?

If your goal in studying is to do well on a test, then the best thing that you can do to support your preparation is to take practice tests that feel like the real thing. This strategy is likely why you're using this book. But as you might infer from the earlier sections of this chapter, just doing practice questions isn't quite enough. You can get more out of practice tests when you take time to make a plan for how you'll complete them, evaluate your performance as you're working, and review how well you did after finishing. This method of practice testing is all about injecting greater activity.

How Do You Do It?

Find practice questions, set a timer, review your test-taking strategies, and take the test. Once you finish, check your score and record it so you can track your performance over time. Then ask yourself the following questions:

- How well did I do?
- How well did I use my time?
- What kinds of questions were harder?
- What kinds of questions did I miss?
- Why did I miss those questions?
- Were there any topics with which I consistently struggled?
- What can I do differently to improve for my next test?

Take the time to answer those questions thoroughly and determine what's next for your study process before you take your next test.

Why Does It Help?

Time and time again, research has shown that taking practice tests has a significant impact on future test performance. That's largely the result of the "practice effect" wherein practicing for a test with similar material will lead to gains. It's intuitive, but many students either skip the step (not knowing where to find practice tests) or think they're done once they check their scores. But you need to assess your strengths and weaknesses and use that information to make choices for what you need to do differently next time (study more, read questions more slowly, etc.). If you don't take the time to think through those metacognitive questions, you might miss an opportunity to change something in your studying that just isn't working. Remember, you need to reflect. Your answers to those reflection questions are going to put you in a better position to make decisions that will help you do better next time.

Self-Questioning

What Is It?

Self-questioning asks you to create your own questions or problems based on the facts, concepts, and applications of the topics you're learning.

How Do You Do It?

You know that thinking has multiple different levels and that it is essential that you be able to remember information. Once you can remember information, you need to construct meaning—or develop relationships between different topics. After you understand something, you need to be able to apply it—or use information in different situations.

- First, pick topics with which you struggle.
- Then start asking questions that require defining, listing, or identifying different ideas (e.g., define mean, median, and mode).
- Next, ask questions that compare, summarize, or classify ideas (e.g., comparing usage of different punctuation).
- Finally, pursue higher-level thinking by responding to, using, judging, or generating applications for the ideas (e.g., developing practice word problems).

Why Does It Help?

Those three kinds of "thinking" encompass the cognitive processes required by most tests. As such, if you can develop and answer questions that demand those tasks, you know that you're prepared for your assessment. Know that this strategy is very similar to practice testing. When practice tests are unavailable or inaccessible, you can try to make some of your own.

Cornell Notes

What Is It?

Cornell notes is a multi-step note-making process. It asks you to take, review, and revise your notes while also turning them into a method for self-quizzing. While most students typically take notes and then stuff them away for later, the Cornell method asks that you practice retrieval as soon after note-taking as possible. Once you've reviewed, you go through the process of revising your notes, making questions, and writing a summary. You then have a study resource you can refer to rather than having to consult a book chapter or video again.

How Do You Do It?

There are lots of variations on the Cornell note-taking method, but the following outlines the basic process of the method's structure and usage:

1. Format a document into two columns (1/3 of the page for the left column, 2/3 of the page for the right) with space for a topic name at the top of the document and a gap of roughly two inches at the bottom of the document.

2. While reading, watching a video, or listening to a lecture, record short, complete sentences in the right-hand column that describe the topic of the reading/video/lecture. After finishing the source material, reread what you wrote—this should happen as soon after recording has finished as possible.

3. Mark places where more information may be needed or any places of confusion. Add details that you may recall.

4. Then, in the left-hand column, record questions (either from the materials or ones that you generate) that may be answered by the information in the right-hand column.

5. Cover the right-hand column in some way and answer the self-generated questions without looking at the noted information. Check your accuracy and mark questions that you're unable to answer effectively.

6. Once you've completed that initial quizzing, use the gap at the bottom of the page to write a summary that describes the topic of the notes.

7. Revisit this document to study: read the summary and then answer the questions in the left-column while covering up the notes column.

Why Does It Help?

Revisiting information soon after your first exposure is a critical step that many students neglect, and skipping that step contributes to poor memory storage. A good note-making process will encourage you to revisit notes soon after taking them and regularly revisit them to maintain retention. As described previously, the Cornell method has a built-in system of review in the form of questions and a format that allows you to easily quiz yourself on the content of the notes without a partner. At the same time, the summary creates a quick reference point so that you can get the gist of a topic without having to fully reread the entire set of notes.

ADEPT

What Is It?

ADEPT is actually a common teaching strategy for introducing a new concept. It stands for **A**nalogy, **D**iagram, **E**xample, **P**lain English Definition, **T**echnical Definition. By presenting information in that order, students tend to encode more easily. However, it can also be used in the reverse to work through different levels of thinking for a concept. If you work through ADEPT in reverse, you go from simple recalling to understanding and even applying.

How Do You Do It?

To make use of ADEPT as a studying technique, do the following:

1. Select your topic.
2. Recall and write out the technical definition.
3. Paraphrase it into plainer English.
4. Create an example of the topic in action.
5. Draw a diagram to make it visual.
6. Create an analogy to compare the topic to something else.

If any of those steps prove difficult, consult your resources again to clarify the definition and your understanding of the topic. Like the Feynman technique, you can then use this resource to test your memory and understanding later on.

Why Does It Help?

New topics often require complex thinking, but you can breach the complexity of a new topic by starting with the basics and changing the way you look at the information. By bridging knowledge you already have in the analogy stage, you can also forge new connections. That process can then break down the barriers between what you know and what you're trying to learn. By moving through different types of communication for a new or complex topic, your higher-level thinking skills must grapple with examining a new idea from multiple perspectives. That serves to expand understanding and reinforce your memory.

STUDY TIME SURVEYS

You now know a lot more than you probably did when you started this chapter about what learning is, how learning works, and what will make your studying more effective. But, as you know, there's a big difference between being exposed to information and actually making use of it.

As you work through this book, you'll need to use what you've started to learn here to make your learning more effective in the other chapters. To assist with that goal, the following are surveys you can use when you study to determine whether you're doing everything you can to make your learning as active and effective as possible.

Studying the Right Way

You know that your studying needs to meet certain criteria to serve how learning works. Ask yourself the following as you work through this book:

- Are you being active when you study? Are you retrieving information from your memory, creating study tools, and practicing higher-level thinking?

- Are you practicing metacognition? Are you planning, evaluating, and reviewing your performance regularly (before, during, and after studying)?

- Are you taking breaks to practice diffused thinking? Are you engaging your diffused thinking when learning new thing to help forge new connections between different parts of your brain?

- Are you practicing a growth mindset? Are you tracking your progress, maintaining effort, and developing a positive attitude about your ability to change?

Metacognition Questions

Throughout the various stages of studying, you need to think through the following questions to practice metacognition.

Before Studying

- Have you previewed what you're going to be learning?
- Have you reviewed your prior knowledge about the topic?
- Can you connect the topic to something else?
- Do you know what you need to focus on?
- What strategies will you use?
- How will you test yourself?

During Studying

- What can you remember?
- What do you understand?
- What still doesn't make sense?
- How are you performing with the exercises?
- Is there anything you can do differently right now?

After Studying

- What did you learn?
- What do you still need to work on?
- What will you do differently next time?
- How can you review between now and the next time you study?

SUMMING IT UP

- Learning is all about changing your brain. That requires time and energy.

- Neurons that fire together wire together. If you study in different ways, you're going to develop more connections between different memories and concepts, making them easier to access.

- Your memory has three stages: encoding (receiving the information), storage (keeping the information), and retrieval (recalling the information). Certain choices and situations make encoding more effective. But retrieval is the most important part of memory. Retrieve often and rigorously.

- Learning something well means that you can remember it and that you understand it.

- To learn effectively, you have to study actively rather than passively. If you're not testing yourself (retrieving information), creating something when studying, or reflecting on what you understand and what you don't, then you're not getting the most out of your study time.

- Use metacognition to plan what you'll study and how you'll do it (what strategies or techniques you'll use), evaluate how well you're doing as you're practicing or working on different topics, and, at the end of your session, review what you learned and what strategies seemed to work and which ones didn't. You can do this at different scales: for your study session, for the entire week, etc.. But do it regularly to assess what works for you and where you need to make changes.

- Thinking occurs at different levels, and expertise with a topic means that you remember it, understand it, and can apply that knowledge in different situations. The more you practice that higher-level thinking, the more readily accessible information will be in your mind.

- Intense study sessions will help you grow, but when dealing with new material, it's also important to take breaks to let your brain sort things out. Make use of your diffused thinking for new topics, especially in math. If you feel like you're hitting a wall, go for a walk, listen to some music, or take a timed nap to see what insights arise.

- Adopt a growth mindset. You're not fixed as any one type of person. Just because you can't do something now doesn't mean you won't be able to do it in the future. If ever you find yourself saying "I can't. . ." always finish that sentence with "yet." And then make a plan for how to improve and execute it.

- Effective study techniques will help you not only remember information but put it to use.

- Return to this chapter throughout your time with this book to reflect on whether you're learning as effectively as you can.

PART II
DIAGNOSTIC TESTS

CHAPTER

TACHS Diagnostic Test

TACHS DIAGNOSTIC TEST

DIAGNOSTIC TEST

This diagnostic test is designed to help you recognize your strengths and weaknesses. The questions cover information from all the different sections of the TACHS. Use the results to help guide and direct your study time.

ANSWER SHEETS: TACHS DIAGNOSTIC TEST

Reading

1. Ⓐ Ⓑ Ⓒ Ⓓ	11. Ⓐ Ⓑ Ⓒ Ⓓ	21. Ⓐ Ⓑ Ⓒ Ⓓ	31. Ⓐ Ⓑ Ⓒ Ⓓ	41. Ⓐ Ⓑ Ⓒ Ⓓ
2. Ⓙ Ⓚ Ⓛ Ⓜ	12. Ⓙ Ⓚ Ⓛ Ⓜ	22. Ⓙ Ⓚ Ⓛ Ⓜ	32. Ⓙ Ⓚ Ⓛ Ⓜ	42. Ⓙ Ⓚ Ⓛ Ⓜ
3. Ⓐ Ⓑ Ⓒ Ⓓ	13. Ⓐ Ⓑ Ⓒ Ⓓ	23. Ⓐ Ⓑ Ⓒ Ⓓ	33. Ⓐ Ⓑ Ⓒ Ⓓ	43. Ⓐ Ⓑ Ⓒ Ⓓ
4. Ⓙ Ⓚ Ⓛ Ⓜ	14. Ⓙ Ⓚ Ⓛ Ⓜ	24. Ⓙ Ⓚ Ⓛ Ⓜ	34. Ⓙ Ⓚ Ⓛ Ⓜ	44. Ⓙ Ⓚ Ⓛ Ⓜ
5. Ⓐ Ⓑ Ⓒ Ⓓ	15. Ⓐ Ⓑ Ⓒ Ⓓ	25. Ⓐ Ⓑ Ⓒ Ⓓ	35. Ⓐ Ⓑ Ⓒ Ⓓ	45. Ⓐ Ⓑ Ⓒ Ⓓ
6. Ⓙ Ⓚ Ⓛ Ⓜ	16. Ⓙ Ⓚ Ⓛ Ⓜ	26. Ⓙ Ⓚ Ⓛ Ⓜ	36. Ⓙ Ⓚ Ⓛ Ⓜ	46. Ⓙ Ⓚ Ⓛ Ⓜ
7. Ⓐ Ⓑ Ⓒ Ⓓ	17. Ⓐ Ⓑ Ⓒ Ⓓ	27. Ⓐ Ⓑ Ⓒ Ⓓ	37. Ⓐ Ⓑ Ⓒ Ⓓ	47. Ⓐ Ⓑ Ⓒ Ⓓ
8. Ⓙ Ⓚ Ⓛ Ⓜ	18. Ⓙ Ⓚ Ⓛ Ⓜ	28. Ⓙ Ⓚ Ⓛ Ⓜ	38. Ⓙ Ⓚ Ⓛ Ⓜ	48. Ⓙ Ⓚ Ⓛ Ⓜ
9. Ⓐ Ⓑ Ⓒ Ⓓ	19. Ⓐ Ⓑ Ⓒ Ⓓ	29. Ⓐ Ⓑ Ⓒ Ⓓ	39. Ⓐ Ⓑ Ⓒ Ⓓ	49. Ⓐ Ⓑ Ⓒ Ⓓ
10. Ⓙ Ⓚ Ⓛ Ⓜ	20. Ⓙ Ⓚ Ⓛ Ⓜ	30. Ⓙ Ⓚ Ⓛ Ⓜ	40. Ⓙ Ⓚ Ⓛ Ⓜ	50. Ⓙ Ⓚ Ⓛ Ⓜ

Written Expression

1. Ⓐ Ⓑ Ⓒ Ⓓ Ⓔ	11. Ⓐ Ⓑ Ⓒ Ⓓ	21. Ⓐ Ⓑ Ⓒ Ⓓ	31. Ⓐ Ⓑ Ⓒ Ⓓ	41. Ⓐ Ⓑ Ⓒ Ⓓ
2. Ⓙ Ⓚ Ⓛ Ⓜ Ⓝ	12. Ⓙ Ⓚ Ⓛ Ⓜ	22. Ⓙ Ⓚ Ⓛ Ⓜ	32. Ⓙ Ⓚ Ⓛ Ⓜ	42. Ⓙ Ⓚ Ⓛ Ⓜ
3. Ⓐ Ⓑ Ⓒ Ⓓ Ⓔ	13. Ⓐ Ⓑ Ⓒ Ⓓ	23. Ⓐ Ⓑ Ⓒ Ⓓ	33. Ⓐ Ⓑ Ⓒ Ⓓ	43. Ⓐ Ⓑ Ⓒ Ⓓ
4. Ⓙ Ⓚ Ⓛ Ⓜ Ⓝ	14. Ⓙ Ⓚ Ⓛ Ⓜ	24. Ⓙ Ⓚ Ⓛ Ⓜ	34. Ⓙ Ⓚ Ⓛ Ⓜ	44. Ⓙ Ⓚ Ⓛ Ⓜ
5. Ⓐ Ⓑ Ⓒ Ⓓ Ⓔ	15. Ⓐ Ⓑ Ⓒ Ⓓ	25. Ⓐ Ⓑ Ⓒ Ⓓ	35. Ⓐ Ⓑ Ⓒ Ⓓ	45. Ⓐ Ⓑ Ⓒ Ⓓ
6. Ⓙ Ⓚ Ⓛ Ⓜ Ⓝ	16. Ⓙ Ⓚ Ⓛ Ⓜ	26. Ⓙ Ⓚ Ⓛ Ⓜ	36. Ⓙ Ⓚ Ⓛ Ⓜ	46. Ⓙ Ⓚ Ⓛ Ⓜ
7. Ⓐ Ⓑ Ⓒ Ⓓ Ⓔ	17. Ⓐ Ⓑ Ⓒ Ⓓ	27. Ⓐ Ⓑ Ⓒ Ⓓ	37. Ⓐ Ⓑ Ⓒ Ⓓ	47. Ⓐ Ⓑ Ⓒ Ⓓ
8. Ⓙ Ⓚ Ⓛ Ⓜ Ⓝ	18. Ⓙ Ⓚ Ⓛ Ⓜ	28. Ⓙ Ⓚ Ⓛ Ⓜ	38. Ⓙ Ⓚ Ⓛ Ⓜ	48. Ⓙ Ⓚ Ⓛ Ⓜ
9. Ⓐ Ⓑ Ⓒ Ⓓ Ⓔ	19. Ⓐ Ⓑ Ⓒ Ⓓ	29. Ⓐ Ⓑ Ⓒ Ⓓ	39. Ⓐ Ⓑ Ⓒ Ⓓ	49. Ⓐ Ⓑ Ⓒ Ⓓ
10. Ⓙ Ⓚ Ⓛ Ⓜ Ⓝ	20. Ⓙ Ⓚ Ⓛ Ⓜ	30. Ⓙ Ⓚ Ⓛ Ⓜ	40. Ⓙ Ⓚ Ⓛ Ⓜ	50. Ⓙ Ⓚ Ⓛ Ⓜ

Mathematics

1. Ⓐ Ⓑ Ⓒ Ⓓ

2. Ⓙ Ⓚ Ⓛ Ⓜ

3. Ⓐ Ⓑ Ⓒ Ⓓ

4. Ⓙ Ⓚ Ⓛ Ⓜ

5. Ⓐ Ⓑ Ⓒ Ⓓ

6. Ⓙ Ⓚ Ⓛ Ⓜ

7. Ⓐ Ⓑ Ⓒ Ⓓ

8. Ⓙ Ⓚ Ⓛ Ⓜ

9. Ⓐ Ⓑ Ⓒ Ⓓ

10. Ⓙ Ⓚ Ⓛ Ⓜ

11. Ⓐ Ⓑ Ⓒ Ⓓ

12. Ⓙ Ⓚ Ⓛ Ⓜ

13. Ⓐ Ⓑ Ⓒ Ⓓ

14. Ⓙ Ⓚ Ⓛ Ⓜ

15. Ⓐ Ⓑ Ⓒ Ⓓ

16. Ⓙ Ⓚ Ⓛ Ⓜ

17. Ⓐ Ⓑ Ⓒ Ⓓ

18. Ⓙ Ⓚ Ⓛ Ⓜ

19. Ⓐ Ⓑ Ⓒ Ⓓ

20. Ⓙ Ⓚ Ⓛ Ⓜ

21. Ⓐ Ⓑ Ⓒ Ⓓ

22. Ⓙ Ⓚ Ⓛ Ⓜ

23. Ⓐ Ⓑ Ⓒ Ⓓ

24. Ⓙ Ⓚ Ⓛ Ⓜ

25. Ⓐ Ⓑ Ⓒ Ⓓ

26. Ⓙ Ⓚ Ⓛ Ⓜ

27. Ⓐ Ⓑ Ⓒ Ⓓ

28. Ⓙ Ⓚ Ⓛ Ⓜ

29. Ⓐ Ⓑ Ⓒ Ⓓ

30. Ⓙ Ⓚ Ⓛ Ⓜ

31. Ⓐ Ⓑ Ⓒ Ⓓ

32. Ⓙ Ⓚ Ⓛ Ⓜ

33. Ⓐ Ⓑ Ⓒ Ⓓ

34. Ⓙ Ⓚ Ⓛ Ⓜ

35. Ⓐ Ⓑ Ⓒ Ⓓ

36. Ⓙ Ⓚ Ⓛ Ⓜ

37. Ⓐ Ⓑ Ⓒ Ⓓ

38. Ⓙ Ⓚ Ⓛ Ⓜ

39. Ⓐ Ⓑ Ⓒ Ⓓ

40. Ⓙ Ⓚ Ⓛ Ⓜ

41. Ⓐ Ⓑ Ⓒ Ⓓ

42. Ⓙ Ⓚ Ⓛ Ⓜ

43. Ⓐ Ⓑ Ⓒ Ⓓ

44. Ⓙ Ⓚ Ⓛ Ⓜ

45. Ⓐ Ⓑ Ⓒ Ⓓ

46. Ⓙ Ⓚ Ⓛ Ⓜ

47. Ⓐ Ⓑ Ⓒ Ⓓ

48. Ⓙ Ⓚ Ⓛ Ⓜ

49. Ⓐ Ⓑ Ⓒ Ⓓ

50. Ⓙ Ⓚ Ⓛ Ⓜ

Ability

Figure Classification

1. Ⓐ Ⓑ Ⓒ Ⓓ Ⓔ   5. Ⓐ Ⓑ Ⓒ Ⓓ Ⓔ   9. Ⓐ Ⓑ Ⓒ Ⓓ Ⓔ   13. Ⓐ Ⓑ Ⓒ Ⓓ Ⓔ   17. Ⓐ Ⓑ Ⓒ Ⓓ Ⓔ

2. Ⓙ Ⓚ Ⓛ Ⓜ Ⓝ   6. Ⓙ Ⓚ Ⓛ Ⓜ Ⓝ   10. Ⓙ Ⓚ Ⓛ Ⓜ Ⓝ   14. Ⓙ Ⓚ Ⓛ Ⓜ Ⓝ   18. Ⓙ Ⓚ Ⓛ Ⓜ Ⓝ

3. Ⓐ Ⓑ Ⓒ Ⓓ Ⓔ   7. Ⓐ Ⓑ Ⓒ Ⓓ Ⓔ   11. Ⓐ Ⓑ Ⓒ Ⓓ Ⓔ   15. Ⓐ Ⓑ Ⓒ Ⓓ Ⓔ   19. Ⓐ Ⓑ Ⓒ Ⓓ Ⓔ

4. Ⓙ Ⓚ Ⓛ Ⓜ Ⓝ   8. Ⓙ Ⓚ Ⓛ Ⓜ Ⓝ   12. Ⓙ Ⓚ Ⓛ Ⓜ Ⓝ   16. Ⓙ Ⓚ Ⓛ Ⓜ Ⓝ   20. Ⓙ Ⓚ Ⓛ Ⓜ Ⓝ

Figure Matrices

1. Ⓐ Ⓑ Ⓒ Ⓓ Ⓔ   5. Ⓐ Ⓑ Ⓒ Ⓓ Ⓔ   9. Ⓐ Ⓑ Ⓒ Ⓓ Ⓔ   13. Ⓐ Ⓑ Ⓒ Ⓓ Ⓔ   17. Ⓐ Ⓑ Ⓒ Ⓓ Ⓔ

2. Ⓙ Ⓚ Ⓛ Ⓜ Ⓝ   6. Ⓙ Ⓚ Ⓛ Ⓜ Ⓝ   10. Ⓙ Ⓚ Ⓛ Ⓜ Ⓝ   14. Ⓙ Ⓚ Ⓛ Ⓜ Ⓝ   18. Ⓙ Ⓚ Ⓛ Ⓜ Ⓝ

3. Ⓐ Ⓑ Ⓒ Ⓓ Ⓔ   7. Ⓐ Ⓑ Ⓒ Ⓓ Ⓔ   11. Ⓐ Ⓑ Ⓒ Ⓓ Ⓔ   15. Ⓐ Ⓑ Ⓒ Ⓓ Ⓔ   19. Ⓐ Ⓑ Ⓒ Ⓓ Ⓔ

4. Ⓙ Ⓚ Ⓛ Ⓜ Ⓝ   8. Ⓙ Ⓚ Ⓛ Ⓜ Ⓝ   12. Ⓙ Ⓚ Ⓛ Ⓜ Ⓝ   16. Ⓙ Ⓚ Ⓛ Ⓜ Ⓝ   20. Ⓙ Ⓚ Ⓛ Ⓜ Ⓝ

Paper Folding

1. Ⓐ Ⓑ Ⓒ Ⓓ Ⓔ   3. Ⓐ Ⓑ Ⓒ Ⓓ Ⓔ   5. Ⓐ Ⓑ Ⓒ Ⓓ Ⓔ   7. Ⓐ Ⓑ Ⓒ Ⓓ Ⓔ   9. Ⓐ Ⓑ Ⓒ Ⓓ Ⓔ

2. Ⓙ Ⓚ Ⓛ Ⓜ Ⓝ   4. Ⓙ Ⓚ Ⓛ Ⓜ Ⓝ   6. Ⓙ Ⓚ Ⓛ Ⓜ Ⓝ   8. Ⓙ Ⓚ Ⓛ Ⓜ Ⓝ   10. Ⓙ Ⓚ Ⓛ Ⓜ Ⓝ

READING

50 Questions—35 Minutes

Turn to the Reading section of your answer sheet to answer the questions in this section.

Directions: This is a test of how well you understand what you read.

- Read each passage and then answer the questions.

- Four answers are given for each question. You are to choose the answer that you think is better than the others.

Questions 1–4 are based on the following passage.

PASSAGE 1

Everything was white, from the top of Mount Franklin to the coast—forests, prairie, lake, river, beach. The waters of the Mercy ran under a vault of ice, which cracked and broke with a loud noise at every change of tide. Thousands of birds—ducks and wood-peckers—flew over the surface of the lake. The rocks between
Line which the cascade plunged to the borders of the Plateau were blocked up with ice. One would have said that
5 the water leaped out of a huge gargoyle, cut by some fantastic artist of the Renaissance. To calculate the damage done to the forest by this hurricane would be impossible until the snow had entirely disappeared.

    Spilett, Pencroff, and Herbert took this opportunity to look after their traps and had hard work finding them under their bed of snow. There was danger of their falling in themselves; a humiliating thing to be caught in one's own trap! They were spared this annoyance, however, and found the traps had been
10 untouched; not an animal had been caught, although there were a great many footprints in the neighborhood, among others, very clearly impressed marks of claws.

    Herbert at once classified these carnivora among the cat tribe, a circumstance which justified the engineer's belief in the existence of dangerous beasts on Lincoln Island. Doubtless these beasts dwelt in the dense forests of the Far West; but driven by hunger, they had ventured as far as Prospect Plateau. Perhaps
15 they scented the inhabitants of Granite House.

—Excerpt from *Mysterious Island*, by Jules Verne

1. In the first paragraph of this passage, the word *fantastic* most likely means

   A. good.

   B. unrealistic.

   C. terrible.

   D. funny.

2. Where does the passage take place?

   J. Mount Franklin

   K. Lincoln Island

   L. The Far West

   M. Prospect Plateau

3. Which of these words best describes Spilett, Pencroff, and Herbert?

   A. Brave

   B. Cowardly

   C. Annoying

   D. Dangerous

4. From this passage, you can infer that the characters

   J. will soon leave the island.

   K. are experts at trapping animals.

   L. do not like animals.

   M. are in peril.

Questions 5–10 are based on the following passage.

PASSAGE 2

April's Charms

When April scatters coins of primrose gold
Among the copper leaves in thickets old,
And singing skylarks from the meadows rise,
To twinkle like black stars in sunny skies;

Line
5 When I can hear the small woodpecker ring
Time on a tree for all the birds that sing;
And hear the pleasant cuckoo, loud and long—
The simple bird that thinks two notes a song;

When I can hear the woodland brook, that could
10 Not drown a babe, with all his threatening mood:
Upon whose banks the violets make their home,
And let a few small strawberry blossoms come;

When I go forth on such a pleasant day,
One breath outdoors takes all my care away;
15 It goes like heavy smoke, when flames take hold
Of wood that's green and fill a grate with gold.

—William H. Davies

5. The poet believes that

   A. April is the only decent month.

   B. the cuckoo makes the prettiest sound.

   C. this particular day in April is extremely nice.

   D. skylarks ruin the view of the sky.

6. The second stanza describes

   J. the sounds of woodpeckers and cuckoos.

   K. the sound and appearance of skylarks.

   L. the appearance of the brook.

   M. the appearance of birds in a tree.

7. The poet likely

   A. enjoys seeing violets.

   B. prefers woodpeckers to cuckoos.

   C. has never eaten a strawberry.

   D. thinks the day is too cold.

8. When he writes, "April scatters coins of primrose gold / Among the copper leaves in thickets old," the poet means

   J. someone named April has dropped her coins.

   K. he sees golden rays of sunlight through the trees.

   L. he lives in a fantasy world where leaves are made of copper.

   M. the environment appears to be messy.

9. In this passage, *thickets* most likely means

   A. days.

   B. woods.

   C. copper.

   D. songs.

10. The tone of the poem is

    J. simple.

    K. threatening.

    L. heavy.

    M. pleasant.

Questions 11–16 are based on the following passage.

PASSAGE 3

Soups are a traditional part of Pennsylvania Dutch cooking and the Dutch housewife can apparently make soup out of anything. If she has only milk and flour she can still make rivel soup. However, most of their soups are sturdier dishes, hearty enough to serve as the major portion of the evening meal. One of the fa-
Line
vorite summer soups in the Pennsylvania Dutch country is Chicken Corn Soup. Few Sunday School picnic
5   suppers would be considered complete without gallons of this hearty soup.

   Many of the Pennsylvania Dutch foods are a part of their folklore. No Shrove Tuesday would be complete without raised doughnuts called "fastnachts." One of the many folk tales traces this custom back to the burnt offerings made by their old country ancestors to the goddess of spring. With the coming of Christianity, the custom became associated with the Easter season and "fastnachts" are eaten on Shrove
10 Tuesday to insure living to next Shrove Tuesday. Young dandelion greens are eaten on Maundy Thursday in order to remain well throughout the year...

   The apple is an important Pennsylvania Dutch food. Dried apples form the basis for many typical dishes. Each fall barrels of apples are converted into cider. Apple butter is one of the Pennsylvania Dutch foods which has found national acceptance. The making of apple butter is an all-day affair and has the
15 air of a holiday to it. Early in the morning the neighbors gather and begin to peel huge piles of apples that will be needed. Soon the great copper apple butter kettle is brought out and set up over a wood fire. Apple butter requires constant stirring to prevent burning. However, stirring can be light work for a boy and a girl when they're young and the day is bright and the world is full of promise. By dusk the apple butter is made, neighborhood news is brought up to date and hunger has been driven that much further away for
20 the coming winter.

—Excerpt from *Pennsylvania Dutch Cooking*, by Unknown

11. Which of these sayings is best illustrated by this passage?

   A. "Necessity is the mother of invention."

   B. "Out with the old, in with the new."

   C. "Old habits die hard."

   D. "Too many cooks spoil the broth."

12. The word *hearty* in the first paragraph most likely means

   J. energetic.

   K. enthusiastic.

   L. cheerful.

   M. substantial.

13. What are the Pennsylvania Dutch people most likely to eat on Shrove Tuesday?

   A. Rivel soup

   B. Chicken corn soup

   C. Fastnachts

   D. Dandelion greens

14. The purpose of burnt offerings is to

   J. appease the goddess of spring.

   K. eat at a Sunday school picnic.

   L. contact ancient ancestors.

   M. bake doughnuts called fastnachts.

15. This passage is intended to be

   A. informative.

   B. persuasive.

   C. humorous.

   D. personal.

16. The phrase "the air of a holiday to it" is another way of saying which of the following?

   J. It involves the giving of gifts.

   K. It only happens once a year.

   L. It is a fun event that communities enjoy together.

   M. It occurs on the same day as Christmas.

PASSAGE 4

Animals below the level of zoophytes and sponges are called Protozoa. The word obviously means "First Animals," but all that we can say is that the very simplest of them may give us some hint of the simplicity of the original first animals. For it is quite certain that the vast majority of the Protozoa today are far too complicated to be thought of as primitive. Though most of them are microscopic, each is an animal complete in itself, with the same fundamental bodily attributes as are manifested in ourselves. They differ from animals of higher degree in not being built up of the unit areas or corpuscles called cells. They have no cells, no tissues, no organs, in the ordinary acceptation of these words, but many of them show a great complexity of internal structure, far exceeding that of the ordinary cells that build up the tissues of higher animals. They are complete living creatures that have not gone in for body-making.

—Excerpt from *The Outline of Science, Vol. 1*, by J. Arthur Thomson

17. What alternate title best expresses the main idea of the passage?

 A. "The Only Complete Living Creature"
 B. "The Complex First Animal"
 C. "The Primitive Protozoa"
 D. "It Is Quite Certain"

18. In this passage, the word *fundamental* most likely means

 J. useless.
 K. complete.
 L. basic.
 M. unusual.

19. All the following characteristics of protozoa are mentioned in this passage *except* their

 A. complexity.
 B. appearance.
 C. size.
 D. internal structures.

20. Animals more complex than Protozoa are made up primarily of

 J. organs.
 K. flesh.
 L. cells.
 M. bones.

21. What does the author mean when he states, "Animals below the level of zoophytes and sponges are called Protozoa"?

 A. Zoophytes and sponges are smaller than Protozoa.
 B. Zoophytes and sponges are more intelligent than Protozoa.
 C. Zoophytes and sponges are more dangerous than Protozoa.
 D. Zoophytes and sponges are more complex than Protozoa.

22. In this passage, the word *exceeding* most likely means

 J. greater than.
 K. moving over.
 L. as much as.
 M. trying harder.

Questions 23–28 are based on the following passage.

PASSAGE 5

An hour went by, and a second hour. The pale light of the short sunless day was beginning to fade, when a faint far cry arose on the still air. It soared upward with a swift rush, till it reached its topmost note, where it persisted, palpitant and tense, and then slowly died away. It might have been a lost soul wailing, had it not
Line been invested with a certain sad fierceness and hungry eagerness. The front man turned his head until his
5 eyes met the eyes of the man behind. And then, across the narrow oblong box, each nodded to the other.

A second cry arose, piercing the silence with needle-like shrillness. Both men located the sound. It was to the rear, somewhere in the snow expanse they had just traversed. A third and answering cry arose, also to the rear and to the left of the second cry.

"They're after us, Bill," said the man at the front.
10 His voice sounded hoarse and unreal, and he had spoken with apparent effort.

"Meat is scarce," answered his comrade. "I ain't seen a rabbit sign for days."

Thereafter they spoke no more, though their ears were keen for the hunting-cries that continued to rise behind them.

—Excerpt from *White Fang,* by Jack London

23. In this scene, Bill appears to be

A. hungry.

B. bored.

C. angry.

D. frightened.

24. The phrase *hunting-cries* probably refers to

J. the sounds Bill and his friend are making.

K. the sounds the animals are making.

L. the sounds the rabbits are making.

M. the sound the wind is making.

25. The characters were probably

A. on a fun camping trip.

B. spending several days outdoors.

C. hunting for rabbits.

D. escaped prisoners.

26. The person observing all of this is

J. Bill.

K. Bill's friend.

L. a rabbit hunter.

M. an unknown narrator.

27. The passage takes place as

A. evening approaches.

B. the day begins.

C. the winter approaches.

D. the summer is ending.

28. Which statement best reflects the main idea of the passage?

J. "Never fear what you cannot see in the dark."

K. "There is nothing to fear but fear itself."

L. "Be respectful of nature, because nature has no respect for you."

M. "Always let nature take its course."

Questions 29–34 are based on the following passage.

PASSAGE 6

The color of animals is by no means a matter of chance; it depends on many considerations, but in the majority of cases tends to protect the animal from danger by rendering it less conspicuous. Perhaps it may be said that if coloring is mainly protective, there ought to be but few brightly colored animals. There are, however, not a few cases in which vivid colors are themselves protective. The kingfisher itself, though so brightly colored, is by no means easy to see. The blue harmonizes with the water, and the bird as it darts along the stream looks almost like a flash of sunlight; besides which, protection is not the only consideration. Let us now consider the prevalent colors of animals and see how far they support the rule.

Desert animals are generally the color of the desert. Thus, for instance, the lion, the antelope, and the wild ass are all sand-colored. "Indeed," says Canon Tristram, "in the desert, where neither trees, brushwood, nor even undulation of the surface afford the slightest protection to its foes, a modification of color which shall be assimilated to that of the surrounding country is absolutely necessary. Hence, without exception, the upper plumage of every bird, whether lark, chat, sylvain, or sand grouse, and also the fur of all the smaller mammals and the skin of all the snakes and lizards, is of one uniform sand color."

—Excerpt from *The Colors of Animals,* by Sir John Lubbock

29. Based on the passage, *plumage* most likely means which of the following?

    A. Camouflage

    B. Color

    C. Fur

    D. Feathers

30. How does a kingfisher protect itself?

    J. It has a sharp beak it uses to peck at other animals.

    K. It flies too quickly for any other animal to catch it.

    L. Its enormous size keeps other animals from trying to hunt it.

    M. Its coloring causes it to blend in with its surroundings.

31. In paragraph 1, *conspicuous* most likely means

    A. hidden.

    B. realistic.

    C. visible.

    D. friendly.

32. All the following animals are mentioned in this passage *except*

    J. sand grouses.

    K. cobras.

    L. antelopes.

    M. lizards.

33. The lion is adapted to blend in with

    A. the desert.

    B. grass.

    C. forests.

    D. countrysides.

34. Based on this passage, which animal is most likely adapted to survive in a grassy environment?

    J. Grasshoppers

    K. Elephants

    L. Raccoons

    M. Skunks

Questions 35–40 are based on the following passage.

PASSAGE 7

American independence, the beginnings of which we have just been considering, was accomplished after a long struggle. Many brave men fought on the battle-field, and many who never shouldered a musket or drew a sword exerted a powerful influence for the good of the patriot cause. One of these men was Ben-

Line jamin Franklin.

5   He was born in Boston in 1706, the fifteenth child in a family of seventeen children. His father was a candle-maker and soap-boiler. Intending to make a clergyman of Benjamin, he sent him, at eight years of age, to a grammar-school, with the purpose of fitting him for college. The boy made rapid progress, but before the end of his first school-year his father took him out on account of the expense, and put him into a school where he would learn more practical subjects, such as writing and arithmetic. The last study

10   proved very difficult for him.

Two years later, at the age of ten, he had to go into his father's shop. Here he spent his time in cutting wicks for the candles, filling the moulds with tallow, selling soap in the shop, and acting the part of errand-boy.

Many times he had watched the vessels sailing in and out of Boston Harbor, and often in imagination

15   had gone with them on their journeys. Now he longed to become a sailor, and, quitting the drudgery of the candle-shop, to roam out over the sea in search of more interesting life. But his father wisely refused to let him go. His fondness for the sea, however, took him frequently to the water, and he learned to swim like a fish and to row and sail boats with great skill. In these sports, as in others, he became a leader among his playmates.

20   With all his dislike for the business of candle-making and soap-boiling, and with all his fondness for play, he was still faithful in doing everything that his father's business required. His industry, together with his liking for good books and his keen desire for knowledge, went far toward supplying the lack of school training. He spent most of his leisure time reading and devoted his savings to collecting a small library.

His father, noting his bookish habits, decided to apprentice Benjamin to his older brother, James, a

25   printer in Boston. Benjamin was to serve until he was 21 and to receive no wages until the last year. In this position he was able to see more books and made good use of his opportunities. Often, he would read far into the night, a borrowed book that had to be returned in the morning. He also wrote some verses and peddled them about the streets, until his father discouraged him by ridiculing his efforts.

—Excerpt from *American Leaders and Heroes: A Preliminary Text-book in United States History,* by Wilbur F. Gordy

35. The author refers to Benjamin Franklin as "a leader among his playmates" because

A. he was captain of an athletic team.

B. he was stronger than the other children.

C. the other children probably admired him.

D. the other children feared him.

36. As used in sentence 2 of paragraph 1, what does the word *shouldered* most likely mean?

J. Built

K. Sold

L. Threw

M. Carried

37. Benjamin Franklin probably disliked making candles because

   A. the work was too difficult.

   B. he was not smart enough to make candles.

   C. he wanted to become a writer.

   D. it was not challenging work.

38. In the second sentence of paragraph 5, *keen* most likely means

   J. eager.

   K. intense.

   L. biting.

   M. blunt.

39. Why did Benjamin Franklin's father send him to apprentice for his brother, James?

   A. He wanted Benjamin to make more money than he did as a candle maker.

   B. He knew that Benjamin always wanted to become a printer.

   C. He could tell that Benjamin was interested in printed materials.

   D. He though Benjamin might learn to read if he worked as a printer.

40. What would be an appropriate alternate title for this passage?

   J. "Benjamin Franklin: The Early Years"

   K. "The Life of a Founding Father"

   L. "Benjamin Franklin: The Complete Biography"

   M. "The Art of Making Candles"

Questions 41–46 are based on the following passage.

PASSAGE 8

Like Art, Tea has its periods and its schools. Its evolution may be roughly divided into three main stages: the Boiled Tea, the Whipped Tea, and the Steeped Tea. We moderns belong to the last school. These several methods of appreciating the beverage are indicative of the spirit of the age in which they prevailed. For life
Line
5 is an expression, our unconscious actions the constant betrayal of our innermost thought. Confucius said that "man hideth not." Perhaps we reveal ourselves too much in small things because we have so little of the great to conceal. The tiny incidents of daily routine are as much a commentary of racial ideals as the highest flight of philosophy or poetry. Even as the difference in favorite vintage marks the separate idiosyncrasies of different periods and nationalities of Europe, so the Tea-ideals characterize the various moods of Asian culture. The Cake-tea which was boiled, the Powdered-tea which was whipped, the Leaf-tea which was
10 steeped, mark the distinct emotional impulses of the Tang, the Sung, and the Ming dynasties of China. If we were inclined to borrow the much-abused terminology of art-classification, we might designate them respectively, the Classic, the Romantic, and the Naturalistic schools of Tea.

    The tea-plant, a native of southern China, was known from very early times to Chinese botany and medicine. It is alluded to in the classics under the various names of Tou, Tseh, Chung, Kha, and Ming, and
15 was highly prized for possessing the virtues of relieving fatigue, delighting the soul, strengthening the will, and repairing the eyesight. It was not only administered as an internal dose, but often applied externally in paste form to alleviate rheumatic pains. The Taoists claimed it as an important ingredient of the elixir of immortality. The Buddhists used it extensively to prevent drowsiness during their long hours of meditation.

—Excerpt adapted from *The Book of Tea*, by Kakuzo Okakura

41. Who used tea to stay awake?

    A. Taoists

    B. Confucians

    C. Mohists

    D. Buddhists

42. In the fourth sentence of paragraph 1, the word *indicative* most likely means

    J. opposite.

    K. unrelated.

    L. representative.

    M. following.

43. How was tea administered to relieve rheumatic pains?

    A. As a paste

    B. Brewed in water

    C. As a pill

    D. As dry leaves

44. Which kind of tea was whipped?

    J. Powdered tea

    K. Cake tea

    L. Leaf tea

    M. Ming tea

45. In the last sentence of paragraph 1, the word *designate* most likely means

    A. solve.

    B. name.

    C. detail.

    D. move.

46. Based on this passage, which of the following is true?

    J. Tea is the most important influence on Chinese philosophy.

    K. The only correct Chinese name for tea is Chung.

    L. Tea was believed to have many uses in Chinese culture.

    M. Tea does not really repair weak eyesight.

Questions 47–50 are based on the following passage.

PASSAGE 9

The western margin of this continent is built of a succession of mountain chains folded in broad corrugations, like waves of stone upon whose seaward base beat the mild, small breakers of the Pacific.

By far the grandest of all these ranges is the Sierra Nevada, a long and massive uplift lying between
Line the arid deserts of the Great Basin and the Californian exuberance of grain-field and orchard; its eastern
5 slope, a defiant wall of rock plunging abruptly down to the plain; the western, a long, grand sweep, well watered and overgrown with cool, stately forests; its crest a line of sharp, snowy peaks springing into the sky and catching the *alpenglow* long after the sun has set for all the rest of America.

The Sierras have a structure and a physical character which are individual and unique. To Professor Whitney and his corps of the Geological Survey of California is due the honor of first gaining a scientific
10 knowledge of the form, plan, and physical conditions of the Sierras.

—Excerpt from *Mountaineering in the Sierra Nevada*, by Clarence King

47. Why does the author claim the Sierra Nevada is the grandest of the western mountain ranges?

    A. It is huge with several unique features.

    B. It is the biggest of the mountain ranges.

    C. It has several snowy peaks.

    D. It is part of a great desert.

48. In regards to the Sierra Nevada range, Professor Whitney was the first person to

    J. discover it.

    K. climb it.

    L. record its features.

    M. measure it.

49. What makes up the eastern side of the Sierra Nevada range?

    A. Forests

    B. Rock

    C. A grain field

    D. An orchard

50. In the first sentence of paragraph 2, the word *arid* most likely means

    J. rainy.

    K. small.

    L. pleasant.

    M. dry.

WRITTEN EXPRESSION
50 Questions—30 Minutes

Turn to the Written Expression section of your answer sheet to answer the questions in this section.

Directions: This is a test of how well you can find mistakes in writing. You will be given questions that deal with spelling, capitalization, punctuation, usage, and expression. Based on the instructions given for each section, you will either choose the answer you think is better than the others or determine how to correct a mistake in the way words or sentences are used. If no correction is needed, choose the last answer choice.

For questions 1–10, identify the misspelled word. If all the words are spelled correctly, choose the last option, (*No mistakes*).

1. A. cantaloupe
    B. porcupine
    C. acquire
    D. explaination
    E. (*No mistakes*)

2. J. definitly
    K. license
    L. noticeable
    M. publicly
    N. (*No mistakes*)

3. A. seperate
    B. until
    C. calendar
    D. leisure
    E. (*No mistakes*)

4. J. jewelry
    K. accommodate
    L. priviledge
    M. restaurant
    N. (*No mistakes*)

5. A. camouflage
    B. foreign
    C. defendant
    D. grammar
    E. (*No mistakes*)

6. J. apology
    K. precede
    L. disappoint
    M. existance
    N. (*No mistakes*)

7. A. development
    B. pronounciation
    C. recommend
    D. knowledge
    E. (*No mistakes*)

8. J. occasion
    K. pleasant
    L. necessery
    M. labeled
    N. (*No mistakes*)

9. A. obstacle
    B. pallor
    C. escalater
    D. width
    E. (*No mistakes*)

10. J. generation
    K. frivolous
    L. overbearing
    M. tawnt
    N. (*No mistakes*)

Directions: For questions 11–25, identify the line of text that contains an error in capitalization, punctuation, usage, or expression. If there are no errors, choose the last option, (*No mistakes*).

11. **A.** In the movie *King Kong*,
    B. a giant gorilla climbs up the
    C. side of the Empire State building.
    D. (*No mistakes*)

12. **J.** We just got a new kitten,
    K. and my little sister gave him an
    L. adorable name Pookie.
    M. (*No mistakes*)

13. **A.** I asked my cousin Tim if
    B. he has ever read the poem "The Raven"
    C. by Edgar Allan Poe.
    D. (*No mistakes*)

14. **J.** The first chapter of Herman Melville's
    K. novel *Moby Dick*
    L. is called *Loomings*.
    M. (*No mistakes*)

15. **A.** "Für Elise" is one of the most famous
    B. compositions by Ludwig van Beethoven,
    C. but no one really knows who elise is.
    D. (*No mistakes*)

16. **J.** Did you know that Khandi
    K. has an article in the latest addition
    L. of the school newspaper?
    M. (*No mistakes*)

17. **A.** Pluto was once considered to be a
    B. planet, but it has recently been
    C. demoted to a Planetoid.
    D. (*No mistakes*)

18. **J.** Mrs Shahi is going to
    K. be my art teacher
    L. next semester.
    M. (*No mistakes*)

19. **A.** My sister works in a glass factory
    B. on highway 61 called
    C. Super Glass Works, LTD.
    D. (*No mistakes*)

20. **J.** I haven't seen Jimmy,
    K. Maria said, despite just
    L. taking math class with him.
    M. (*No mistakes*)

21. **A.** This is not the same car
    B. we drove here, so our car must be
    C. parked someplace else?
    D. (*No mistakes*)

22. **J.** Willow is running for class
    K. president; Buffy is the captain of
    L. the cheerleading squad.
    M. (*No mistakes*)

23. **A.** When you pack for the trip,
    B. be sure to include, a warm sweater,
    C. a heavy jacket, and ski pants.
    D. (*No mistakes*)

24. **J.** Shara and Lashawn are going
    K. to that new movie on Saturday,
    L. and I really want to see it with her.
    M. (*No mistakes*)

25. **A.** Last year I attended JFK Junior
    B. High School, but next year I will be
    C. going to St. Mary's High School.
    D. (*No mistakes*)

Directions: For questions 26–30, choose the best way of expressing the idea.

26. **J.** They were anxious, the explorers were, because dangerous terrain they knew they were entering.

   K. The explorers, because they knew that they were entering dangerous terrain, were anxious.

   L. The explorers were anxious because they knew that they were entering dangerous terrain.

   M. The explorers, knowing that they were entering dangerous terrain, were anxious.

27. **A.** At the tournament, John, because he lost his confidence, fared poorly despite months of practice.

   B. Despite months of practice, John lost his confidence and fared poorly at the tournament.

   C. John, at the tournament, despite months of practice, lost his confidence and fared poorly.

   D. Losing his confidence, at the tournament despite months of practice, John fared poorly.

28. **J.** Putting aside their differences on the project allowed Marc and Jason to collaborate on it.

   K. Marc and Jason, once they put aside their differences on the project, collaborated.

   L. Collaborating on the project, Marc and Jason were able to once they put aside their differences.

   M. Marc and Jason were able to collaborate on the project once they put aside their differences.

29. **A.** The Louisiana Purchase and the Gold Rush sparked westward expansion in the nineteenth century.

   B. Sparking westward expansion were the Louisiana Purchase and the Gold Rush in the nineteenth century.

   C. The Louisiana Purchase in the nineteenth century and the Gold Rush sparked westward expansion.

   D. In the nineteenth century, westward expansion of the Louisiana Purchase and the Gold Rush sparked.

30. **J.** From Monday to Friday long hours my mother works, but she always makes plenty of time to spend with me on the weekend.

   K. My mother works long hours from Monday to Friday, but she always makes plenty of time to spend with me on the weekend.

   L. My mother, but she always makes plenty of time to spend with me on the weekend, from Monday to Friday works long hours.

   M. My mother long hours from Monday to Friday works, but she always makes plenty of time to spend with me on the weekend.

Directions: For questions 31–50, choose the best answer based on the following paragraphs. You may see additional errors beyond those in the underlined words and phrases of the paragraphs.

(1) Most photographers snap photos because they <u>wanted to capture</u> beautiful or interesting images. (2) However, Dorothea Lange had a higher purpose behind her work. (3) She took pictures of impoverished people during the Great Depression to expose the personal cost of the vast economic crisis. (4) She took pictures of unemployed people and migrant workers often with captions featuring quotations from the people in her pictures. (5) She performed her work as an investigative project for the U.S. Farm Security Administration, and it served as a powerful, unforgettable portrait of a difficult time in U.S. history.

31. What is the best way to write the underlined portion of sentence 1?

    A. want to capture

    B. wants to capture

    C. wanted to captured

    D. *(No change)*

32. Choose the best last sentence to add to this paragraph.

    J. Dorothea Lange was born on May 26, 1895, in Hoboken, New Jersey.

    K. The U.S. Farm Security Administration employed Dorothea Lange, and her pictures chronicled a tough time for America.

    L. For that reason, Dorothea Lange will always be remembered as a great artist and human being.

    M. Another great photographer is Ansel Adams, who is beloved for his landscape pictures and environmental work.

(1) However, collage is an art form that anyone can perform. (2) It simply involves taking existing pictures and reconfiguring them into interesting new images. (3) Some artists create collages by clipping pictures out of magazines and pasting them onto <u>oak tag; but collages</u> can also be made digitally using a computer. (4) A collage may follow a particular theme, or it may be a random assortment of pictures that capture the artist's fancy. (5) There are no rules to making a collage, which is another reason why it is such a fabulous and accessible art form.

33. Choose the best first sentence to add to this paragraph.

    A. Making collages is something anyone can do.

    B. Some people shy away from the arts because they do not know how to draw or sculpt.

    C. Art forms include painting, sculpting, drawing, making collages, dancing, making music, writing, and anything else that is creative.

    D. A collage artist must study for years to become good at their craft.

34. What is the best way to write the underlined portion of sentence 3?

    J. oak tag, but collages

    K. oak tag collages

    L. oak tag: but collages

    M. *(No change)*

(1) A rhinoceros may look like a huge, horned pig, or even a distant relative of horned <u>dinosaurs such as the triceratops</u>. (2) However, this animal is actually related to the horse. (3) It is a member of the odd-toed ungulates, which includes several other <u>animals horses, donkeys, and zebras</u>. (4) All of these creatures are characterized by their odd number of toes and the fact that they digest plant cellulose in their intestines instead of their stomachs. (5) A rhinoceros may be related to the horse, but it still might not be a smart idea to try to ride one!

35. What is the best way to write the underlined portion of sentence 1?

   A. dinosaurs such as the Triceratops

   B. Dinosaurs such as the triceratops

   C. Dinosaurs such as the Triceratops

   D. *(No change)*

36. What is the best way to write the underlined portion of sentence 3?

   J. animals: horses, donkeys, and zebras

   K. animals; horses, donkeys and zebras

   L. animals, horses, donkeys, and zebras

   M. *(No change)*

(1) *Dracula* is one of the most popular novels ever written. (2) It <u>tells the tail</u> of a mysterious Transylvanian count who is actually an ancient blood-drinking creature known as the vampire. (3) Yet as successful as *Dracula* was, its writer never managed to write another book that was as well-loved. (4) In fact, few people even read books such as *The Jewel of Seven Stars* and *Miss Betty*. (5) His final novel, <u>The lair of the white worm</u>, is considered almost laughably poor and borderline nonsensical. (6) So although Stoker had a major hit with his chilling tale of creeping vampires, he will forever be remembered as a one-hit wonder.

37. What is the best way to write the underlined portion of sentence 2?

   A. tells the tale

   B. tells the tails

   C. tell the tail

   D. *(No change)*

38. What is the best way to write the underlined portion of sentence 5?

   J. *The Lair Of The White Worm*

   K. *The lair of The white worm*

   L. *The Lair of the White Worm*

   M. *(No change)*

(1) Finding a fossil from a long-extinct dinosaur is always an amazing discovery for scientists. (2) Few places are <u>as rife in fossils</u> as the southeast side of the Uinta Mountains. (3) That is why it has earned the title of Dinosaur National Monument! (4) Exploration of the site began in 1909 when paleontologist Earl Douglass first discovered an abundance of plant and animal fossils there. (5) Yet discoveries continue into the present age. (6) In 2010, a team of paleontologists discovered a previously unknown <u>herbivore called: Abydosaurus mcintoshi</u>. (7) However, you do not need to be a professional scientist to explore Dinosaur National Monument—just ask the explorers of all ages who view the 1,500 bones pulled from the site displayed at the Dinosaur Quarry Exhibit Hall!

3

39. What is the best way to write the underlined portion of sentence 2?

   A. as rich of fossils

   B. as rich in fossils

   C. as rife of fossils

   D. *(No change)*

40. What is the best way to write the underlined portion of sentence 6?

   J. herbivore called; *Abydosaurus mcintoshi*

   K. herbivore called *Abydosaurus mcintoshi*

   L. herbivore called—*Abydosaurus mcintoshi*

   M. *(No change)*

(1) The Taj Mahal is one of the most spectacular buildings in the world. (2) Although its name translates to "Crown of the Palace," the Taj Mahal is not actually a palace; it is a mausoleum entombing Mumtaz Mahal. (3) She was the wife of emperor <u>Shah Jahan of the Mughal empire</u>. (4) He so adored his wife that when she died, he had a massive, architecturally spectacular construction made to serve as her final resting place. (5) Two thousand artisans were required to build it at a cost of $827 million in contemporary US currency.

41. Choose the best final sentence to add to this paragraph.

   A. The Taj Mahal remains one of the most recognizable buildings in the world and an essential destination for visitors to Pradesh, India.

   B. Shah Jahan, who reigned from 1628 to 1658, commissioned the building of the Taj Mahal in 1632.

   C. Mumtaz Mahal's birth name was Arjumand Banu Begum, and she was born in Agra, a city on the banks of the Yamuna River in Uttar Pradesh.

   D. The Taj Mahal is designated a UNESCO World Heritage Site, and so is Dinosaur Provincial Park in Alberta, Canada.

42. What is the best way to write the underlined portion of sentence 3?

   J. Shah Jahan of the mughal empire

   K. Shah Jahan of the Mughal Empire

   L. shah Jahan of the Mughal Empire

   M. *(No change)*

(1) Considered one of <u>the Seven Natural Wonders of the World</u>, Paracutin is a cinder volcano that varies between 9,101 and 10,397 feet above ground. (2) Although it has been dormant since 1952, Paracutin is still considered to be an active volcano. (3) However, these are not the reasons it is considered a natural wonder. (4) The amazing thing about <u>Paracutin is that its birth</u> was actually witnessed by people. (5) While most volcanoes originated during prehistoric times, Paracutin dates back less than 80 years ago. (6) In fact, it is the youngest volcano in the world, which makes it wholly unique.

43. What is the best way to write the underlined portion of sentence 1?

   A. the Seven Natural Wonders Of the World

   B. the Seven Natural Wonders Of The World

   C. the seven natural wonders of the world

   D. *(No change)*

44. What is the best way to write the underlined portion of sentence 4?

   J. Paracutin is that it's birth

   K. Paracutin is that it is birth

   L. Paracutin is that its' birth

   M. *(No change)*

(1) If you enters any souvenir shop in New York City, you are likely to find abundant merchandise depicting the Statue of Liberty. (2) The statue is regarded as one of the most recognizable symbols of the Big Apple. (3) However, most people do not realize that the Statue of Liberty is technically not located in New York City. (4) In fact, it is not even located in the state of New York. (5) The Statue of Liberty is actually positioned within New Jersey, even though the statue is officially within the territorial jurisdiction of New York. (6) The Statue of Liberty can even be reached from ferries out of Jersey City's Liberty State Park, named in honor of the major but rather misunderstood New Jersey landmark.

45. What is the best way to write the underlined portion of sentence 1?

   A. If you enter any

   B. If they enters any

   C. If we enters any

   D. *(No change)*

46. What is the best way to write the underlined portion of sentence 6?

   J. major. But rather misunderstood. New Jersey

   K. major—but rather misunderstood—New Jersey

   L. major; but rather misunderstood; New Jersey

   M. *(No change)*

(1) People often travel to Hawaii for its natural beauty. (2) However, there is a human-made attraction that is just as lush and green and gorgeous as any palm tree framed shore. (3) On Honolulu's Dole Plantation, you will find the Pineapple Garden Maze. (4) It is the largest hedge maze in the world, spanning almost three acres of land. (5) To walk through all its paths is to walk almost two and a half miles. (6) While it is a marvelous place to simply stroll at a leisurely pace, some visitors race through the Pineapple Garden Maze as quickly as possible because those with the fastest exit time are allowed to sign their names at the entrance of the maze. (7) Its considered quite an honor among maze enthusiasts.

47. What is the best way to write the underlined portion of sentence 2?

   A. as any palm tree-framed-shore

   B. as any palm-tree framed shore

   C. as any palm tree-framed shore

   D. *(No change)*

48. What is the best way to write the underlined portion of sentence 7?

   J. It's considered quite

   K. Its' considered quite

   L. It is' considered quite

   M. *(No change)*

(1) With the enacting of the Emergency Quota Act of 1921, the United States drastically restricted immigration, especially from non-Northern European countries. (2) Many saw the act as discriminatory and in need of revision. (3) This <u>revision finally is occurring in 1965</u> when New York Representative Emanuel Celler proposed the Immigration and Nationality Act. (4) The new act removed the racial and national specifics of the Emergency Quota Act, allowing more diverse immigration into the United States. (5) With support from Senators Phillip Hart and Ted Kennedy, the bill passed heralded the age of a more welcoming America.

49. What is the best way to write the underlined portion of sentence 3?

   A. revision finally will be occurring in 1965

   B. revision finally occurred in 1965

   C. revision finally occurs in 1965

   D. *(No change)*

50. What is the best way to write sentence 5?

   J. With support from Senators Phillip Hart and Ted Kennedy, the bill passed and heralded the age of a more welcoming America.

   K. With support from Senators Phillip Hart and Ted Kennedy, the bill passed, heralded the age of a more welcoming America.

   L. With support from Senators Phillip Hart and Ted Kennedy.

   M. *(No change)*

MATHEMATICS
50 Questions—40 Minutes

Turn to the Mathematics section of your answer sheet to answer the questions in this section.

Directions: Four answers are given for each problem. Choose the best answer.

---

1. Which of these is equivalent to $(5 \times 10^4) + (3 \times 10^2) + (1 \times 10^1) + (4 \times 10^{-2})$?

   A. 531.4

   B. 5,031.004

   C. 5,031.04

   D. 50,310.04

2. What is the sum of four squared and three cubed?

   J. 16

   K. 17

   L. 27

   M. 43

3. The ratio of bathrooms to bedrooms in a mansion is 2:3. If there are 18 bedrooms, how many bathrooms are there?

   A. 9

   B. 12

   C. 15

   D. 21

4. Which of these is equal to $5\frac{11}{25}$?

   J. 0.522

   K. 2.2

   L. 5.22

   M. 5.44

5. Compute: $1.111 - 0.919$

   A. 0.108

   B. 0.192

   C. 0.202

   D. 0.292

6. Which of these numbers is composite?

   J. 17

   K. 23

   L. 51

   M. 71

7. Which of these statements is true?

   A. $1 - (-4) < 4 - (-2)$

   B. $(-2)(3) > (-1)(-6)$

   C. $6 \div \left(-\frac{1}{2}\right) > \left(\frac{1}{4}\right) \div \left(-\frac{1}{4}\right)$

   D. $-(5 - 3) = -5 - 3$

8. The ratio of camp counselors to campers is 1:25. If there are 9 counselors, how many campers are there?

   J. 34

   K. 125

   L. 225

   M. 450

9. Compute: $2\left(\frac{5}{2} - 2\right) \div \frac{1}{2}$

   A. $\frac{1}{2}$

   B. 1

   C. 2

   D. 6

10. Solve for x: $x + \dfrac{5}{4} = \dfrac{17}{8}$

   J. $\dfrac{27}{8}$

   K. 3

   L. $\dfrac{7}{8}$

   M. $\dfrac{17}{20}$

Use the following diagram for Questions 11 and 12:

A family has several tasks to complete in preparation for Halloween each year. The pie chart below shows the time devoted to each of these tasks.

11. How much total time is spent preparing for Halloween each year?

   A. 5 hours

   B. 7.5 hours

   C. 11.5 hours

   D. 13.5 hours

12. What is the approximate percentage of the total time spent on trick-or-treating?

   J. 17%

   K. 22%

   L. 35%

   M. 43%

13. Which of these is NOT equal to $(3 + 4)^2$?

   A. $(3 + 4)(3 + 4)$

   B. $3^2 + 2 \times 3 \times 4 + 4$

   C. $(3 + 4)(4 + 3)$

   D. $3^2 + 4^2$

14. What is the perimeter of the rhombus $ABCD$?

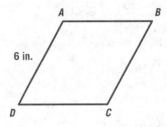

   J. 12 inches

   K. 18 inches

   L. 24 inches

   M. 36 inches

15. A batch of brownies takes $\dfrac{2}{3}$ hour to bake.

   If Cherie bakes 4 batches of brownies, one at a time, each day for 3 days, how many hours total are spent baking?

   A. 2 hours

   B. 4 hours

   C. 6 hours

   D. 8 hours

16. A credit card company charges a 4% balance transfer fee. If you want to transfer a balance of $2,100 to this credit card, what fee would you pay?

   J. $40

   K. $84

   L. $400

   M. $840

17. 4 hours minus 1 hour, 59 minutes, 58 seconds equals

    A. 2 hours, 2 seconds.

    B. 3 hours, 1 minute, 2 seconds.

    C. 2 hours, 1 minute, 1 second.

    D. 3 hours, 2 seconds.

18. If it is p miles from home to school, how many round trips can be made if your car gets q miles per gallon of gasoline and there are 5 gallons of gasoline in its tank?

    J. $\dfrac{5q}{2p}$

    K. $5q + 2p$

    L. $\dfrac{q}{p}$

    M. $\dfrac{5}{2} + pq$

19. Compute: $\left(-\dfrac{1}{2}\right) \cdot (-6) \div \left(-\dfrac{3}{2}\right)$

    A. $-\dfrac{9}{2}$

    B. -2

    C. 2

    D. $\dfrac{9}{4}$

20. Find x:

    J. 58°

    K. 70°

    L. 111°

    M. 121°

Use the following stacked bar chart for Questions 21–23:

21. How many boys selected "Watching TV" as their favorite activity?

    A. 20

    B. 40

    C. 60

    D. 80

22. For which activity is there the largest difference between the number of girls selecting it as their favorite and the number of boys doing so?

    J. Watching TV

    K. Playing video games

    L. Playing sports

    M. Reading

23. What is the ratio of the number of boys to the number of girls selecting "Playing Sports" as their favorite activity?

    A. 3:6

    B. 2:1

    C. 3:2

    D. 1:1

Use the following chart for Questions 24 and 25:

Three traffic officers record the number of speeding tickets they issue to drivers each week for six weeks. The results are as follows:

Week	Officer Ken	Officer Michelle	Officer Pat
1	8	6	1
2	5	10	2
3	0	3	1
4	7	4	10
5	11	3	9
6	2	8	6

24. How many more tickets did Officer Michelle issue than Officer Ken during this six-week period?

J. 1

K. 4

L. 5

M. 7

25. During which week were the least number of tickets issued?

A. Week 3

B. Week 1

C. Week 5

D. Week 6

26. 500% of 0.01 is _____.

J. 0.05

K. 0.5

L. 5

M. 50

27. The temperature is 96° on the beach at 1 p.m. on Monday. If the temperature decreases by 25% by 5 a.m. Tuesday morning and then increases by 10% by noon that same day, what is the approximate temperature at noon on Tuesday?

A. 72°

B. 76°

C. 79°

D. 82°

28. If $x = -1$ and $y = 2$, what is the value of $(y - x)^3$?

J. 1

K. 9

L. 27

M. 81

29. Which of these equals $2^5 \cdot 3^2$?

A. $(2 \cdot 3)^{5+2}$

B. $(2 \cdot 3)^{5 \cdot 2}$

C. $(2 \cdot 5)(2 \cdot 3)$

D. $2^3 \cdot 6^2$

Use the following graph for Questions 30 and 31:

The number of weighted lunges that Nancy and Laura completed during a workout session each day of a certain week is shown below.

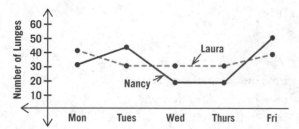

30. What is the difference between the number of lunges Nancy completed and the number Laura completed during this five-day period?

   J. 0

   K. 10

   L. 20

   M. 30

31. What fraction of the total number of lunges that Laura completed did she complete on Friday?

   A. $\frac{3}{17}$

   B. $\frac{4}{17}$

   C. $\frac{2}{11}$

   D. $\frac{4}{5}$

32. What is the area of the shaded region inside the square *ABCD*?

   J. 48 square feet

   K. 96 square feet

   L. 120 square feet

   M. 144 square feet

33. What is the complete set of factors common to 12, 18, and 48?

   A. {1, 3, 6, 12, 18}

   B. {1, 2, 3, 4, 6}

   C. {1, 2, 3, 6}

   D. {1, 2, 3, 12}

34. What is the area of the shaded region pictured below?

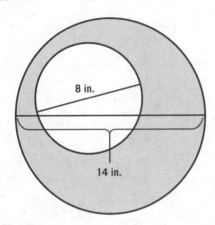

8 in.

14 in.

J. 6π square inches

K. 33π square inches

L. 49π square inches

M. 132π square inches

35. Which of the following does *not* result in an integer?

A. $9 \div \frac{1}{4}$

B. $2 - 16$

C. $\left(\frac{1}{2}\right)^2$

D. $\frac{5 + 11}{5 + 3}$

36. In what quadrant of the *xy*-plane does the point (−5, 6) lie?

J. Quadrant I

K. Quadrant II

L. Quadrant III

M. Quadrant IV

37. Find the value of *x*:

36°

x°

A. 54°

B. 72°

C. 90°

D. 144°

38. Stella leaves her home at 5 a.m. for a road trip to the beach. She arrives at the hotel at 1 p.m. If she drove 560 miles, what was her average speed?

J. 60 miles per hour

K. 65 miles per hour

L. 70 miles per hour

M. 80 miles per hour

39. Rick likes playing classic video games. He plays three rounds of a game and earns the following scores: 6,500; 13,000; and 16,500. What is his average score for these three games?

A. 9,000

B. 11,500

C. 12,000

D. 13,000

40. If *x* is an odd integer, which of these is also an odd integer?

J. $x + 2$

K. $2x$

L. $x + 1$

M. $\frac{x}{2}$

Directions: For the following questions, estimate the answer in your head. No scratch work is allowed. Do NOT try to compute exact answers.

41. What is the closest estimate for $(8.04)^2$?

    A. 62

    B. 65

    C. 68

    D. 70

42. What is the closest estimate for $4(1.7 + 8.1) + 3(12.1 + 7.6)$?

    J. 60

    K. 80

    L. 90

    M. 100

43. What is the closest estimate to $8,112 - 4,978$?

    A. 2,000

    B. 3,000

    C. 4,000

    D. 5,000

44. What is the closest estimate to $4\frac{7}{8} + 7\frac{1}{16} + 9\frac{8}{9}$?

    J. 20

    K. 22

    L. 25

    M. 30

45. A recipe calls for 9 ounces of canola oil. If the recipe were made 32 times, how many ounces of canola oil would be needed?

    A. 40

    B. 100

    C. 288

    D. 400

46. A survey of local teachers revealed that 5% were not in favor of the field trip to the city art museum. If 612 teachers responded to the survey, about how many were not in favor of the field trip?

    J. 30

    K. 45

    L. 60

    M. 75

47. What is the closest estimate to 286×193?

    A. 30,000

    B. 40,000

    C. 60,000

    D. 100,000

48. What is the closest estimate to 39.08 ÷ 2.13?

   J. 15
   K. 20
   L. 40
   M. 80

49. Tim bowled nine games and acquired a total of 1,819 points. What is the best estimate of the average number of points he scored per game?

   A. 190
   B. 192
   C. 195
   D. 200

50. It takes Cooper 8 minutes to complete an exercise circuit. If he completed 9 circuits, how long did it take him?

   J. 17 minutes
   K. 58 minutes
   L. 72 minutes
   M. 90 minutes

ABILITY
50 Questions—32 Minutes

Figure Classification

Turn to the Ability section of your answer sheet to answer the questions in this section.

Directions: In questions 1–20, the first three figures are alike in certain ways. Choose the answer choice that best corresponds to the first three figures.

14.

15.

16.

17.

18.

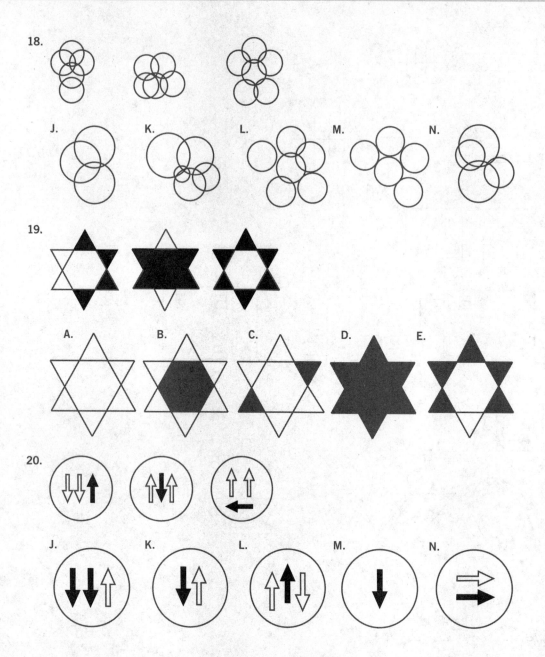

19.

20.

Figure Matrices

Directions: In questions 1–20, select the image that would continue the pattern or sequence.

1.

A.   B.   C.   D.   E.

2.

J.   K.   L.   M.   N.

3.

A.   B.   C.   D.   E.

4.

5.

6.

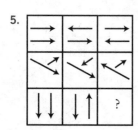

J. ☐ ☐   K.   L. ☐ ☐ ☐   M. ☐   N. ✕ ✕ ✕

   ✕   ✕ ✕   ✕   ✕ ✕   ☐   ☐

7.

8.

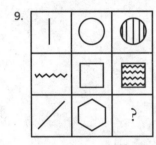

J.   K.   L.   M.   N.

9.

A.   B.   C.   D.   E.

10.

J.   K.   L.   M.   N.

11.

A.   B.   C.   D.   E.

12.

J.   K.   L.   M.   N.

13.

A.   B.   C.   D.   E.

14.

J.   K.   L.   M.   N.

15.

A.   B. C. D.   E.

16.

J. K. L.   M. N.

17.

A.   B. C.   D.   E.

18.

J.   K.   L.   M.   N.

19.

A.   B.   C.   D.   E.

20.

J.   K.   L.   M.   N.

Paper Folding

Directions: In questions 1–10, look at the top row to see how a square piece of paper is folded and where holes are punched into it. Then, look at the bottom row to decide which answer choice shows how the paper will look when it is completely unfolded.

9.

10.

ANSWER KEYS AND EXPLANATIONS
Reading

1. B	11. A	21. D	31. C	41. D
2. K	12. M	22. J	32. K	42. L
3. A	13. C	23. D	33. A	43. A
4. M	14. J	24. K	34. J	44. J
5. C	15. A	25. B	35. C	45. B
6. J	16. L	26. L	36. M	46. L
7. A	17. B	27. A	37. D	47. A
8. K	18. L	28. L	38. K	48. L
9. B	19. B	29. D	39. C	49. B
10. M	20. L	30. M	40. J	50. M

1. **The correct answer is B.** The word *fantastic* is used to refer to an artist who sculpts unrealistic creatures such as gargoyles. While *fantastic* can sometimes be used to mean "extremely good," choice A is too mild a word to ever be a synonym of *fantastic*. *Terrible* (choice C) is an antonym. *Funny* (choice D) is not a synonym of fantastic.

2. **The correct answer is K.** All the reader knows is that the passage takes place on Lincoln Island. While the narrator refers to Mount Franklin (choice J), the Far West (choice L), and Prospect Plateau (choice M), there is no evidence that the characters are actually in any of these locations in this particular passage.

3. **The correct answer is A.** According to the narrator, Spilett, Pencroff, and Herbert risked falling into the traps, but they decided to check them anyway, and since they faced such risks but still did what they had to do, they can be characterized as brave. Choice B can be eliminated since *cowardly* is the opposite of *brave*. The narrator refers to an annoyance that the three men might have faced, but he does not actually refer to the men as annoying, so choice C is incorrect. While the three men do something dangerous (choice D), they are not dangerous themselves.

4. **The correct answer is M.** Herbert believes that dangerous beasts with large claws are stalking the island, so it is likely that the characters are in peril. There is no evidence in the passage that supports choice J. Since the characters have not caught any animals in this passage, there is no reason to draw the conclusion in choice K. The characters are trying to trap animals because they are afraid that there are dangerous ones on the island, not because they do not like animals in general, so choice L is not the best answer.

5. **The correct answer is C.** The poem describes how a particular day in April makes the poet feel happy, so choice C is the best answer. Choices A and B reach extreme conclusions that the information in the poem does not support. While the poet refers to how skylarks change the view of the sky, he does not suggest that the skylarks ruin the view, so choice D lacks support.

6. **The correct answer is J.** In the second stanza, the poet describes the sounds of woodpeckers and cuckoos. Choice K refers only to the second couplet of the first stanza. Choice L describes the third stanza, not the first one. In the second stanza, the poet describes sounds, not appearances, so choice M is incorrect.

7. **The correct answer is A.** As a whole, the poem describes all of the pleasant things the poet sees during his walk. Since he mentions violets among those things, it is reasonable to conclude that the poet enjoys seeing violets. The other answer choices all reach conclusions that are unsupported by the information in the poem.

8. **The correct answer is K.** Choice K is the likeliest interpretation of the figurative language in the poem's opening couplet. Choice J is too literal a translation of that opening couplet, and April is a month, not a person, in this poem. Choice L is also too literal. Choice M misinterprets the author's use of the word *scattered*; he thinks the environment looks nice, not messy.

9. **The correct answer is B.** In the first stanza, the poet is talking about leaves. That should provide a clue that he is talking about the woods. Evidence in the poem does not support the other answer choices.

10. **The correct answer is M.** The poet spends the poem discussing all of the nice things he sees and hears and the pleasant way they make him feel. While the poet uses the words *simple* (choice J), *threatening* (choice K), and *heavy* (choice L) in the poem, none of them convey the niceness of the day in April he describes.

11. **The correct answer is A.** The first paragraph of the passage explains how a cook, who only has a few ingredients, can still create a soup out of it. Eating is a necessity, and the desire to eat causes these cooks to create—or invent—a meal out of them. Therefore, the saying "Necessity is the mother of invention" suits the passage well. The passage is about the importance of tradition and old ways, but choices B and C put a negative spin on tradition and old ways, so they are not the best answers. While the passage is about cooking, there is nothing in the passage that supports the saying in choice D.

12. **The correct answer is M.** Each of the answer choices can be used as a synonym for *hearty*, but only *substantial* makes sense in this context since *hearty* is used to describe soup. One would not

refer to a soup as energetic (choice J), enthusiastic (choice K), or cheerful (choice L).

13. **The correct answer is C.** According to the passage, "No Shrove Tuesday would be complete without raised doughnuts called 'fastnachts.'" The author does not provide a day on which rivel soup (choice A) is traditionally eaten. Chicken corn soup (choice B) is traditionally eaten in the summertime, and dandelion greens (choice D) are traditionally eaten on Maundy Thursday.

14. **The correct answer is J.** According to the passage, "No Shrove Tuesday would be complete without raised doughnuts called 'fastnachts.' One of the many folk tales traces this custom back to the burnt offerings made by their old country ancestors to the goddess of spring." Chicken corn soup, not burnt offerings, is eaten at Sunday school picnics, so choice K is incorrect. Burnt offerings were not used to contact ancestors (choice L), nor were they used as ingredients in fastnachts (choice M).

15. **The correct answer is A.** The sole purpose of the passage is to inform the reader about traditional Pennsylvania Dutch cooking. It is not written to persuade the reader (choice B) or be funny (choice C). It is also not written from a first-person point of view (choice D).

16. **The correct answer is L.** A holiday is a fun event a community can enjoy together, and this is how the author describes the making of apple butter in the third paragraph. Choice J describes certain holidays, but it does not describe the making of apple butter. The author never suggests that apple butter can be made on only one day of the year, so choice K is incorrect. The author does not suggest that it can only be made on Christmas, so choice M is also incorrect.

17. **The correct answer is B.** The passage is about how the protozoa (which means "first animal") may seem simple but is actually complex, and this title suits that theme well. This also eliminates choice C. While the passage identifies protozoa as "complete living creatures," it never suggests that there are no other such creatures, so choice A would make a misleading title. Choice D is a random

phrase from the passage that fails to capture its main idea in any meaningful way.

18. **The correct answer is L.** As it is used in the passage, *fundamental* means "basic." Almost no body parts are useless, so choice J is incorrect. Since *fundamental* is used to compare the body parts of a protozoa to those of a person, choice K has to be incorrect; human bodies are not identical to those of protozoa. There is no reason to believe the body attributes in question are unusual, so choice M is not the best answer.

19. **The correct answer is B.** The author never describes how protozoa look. However, their complexity (choice A), microscopic size (choice C), and internal structures (choice D) are all mentioned in the passage.

20. **The correct answer is L.** According to the passage, protozoa "differ from animals of higher degree in not being built up of the unit areas or corpuscles called cells." The passage offers no evidence that animals more complex than protozoa are primarily made up of organs (choice J), flesh (choice K), or bones (choice M).

21. **The correct answer is D.** When the author states that "Animals below the level of zoophytes and sponges are called Protozoa," he means that zoophytes and sponges are more complex than protozoa.

22. **The correct answer is J.** The phrase "great complexity" is a clue that the word *exceeding* means "greater than." The other answer choices do not make as much sense if used in place of *exceeding* in the passage.

23. **The correct answer is D.** Bill feels that animals are after him, and his voice is hoarse. These details are clues that he is frightened. The man with Bill suggests that the animals are hungry; he does not suggest that Bill is hungry, so choice A is not the best answer. Bill is too concerned to be bored, so choice B is not the best answer. He does not seem particularly angry, so choice C is not a strong answer either.

24. **The correct answer is K.** The phrase "hunting-cries" possibly refers to the sounds that animals are making. Bill and his friend hear the sounds; they are not making them, so choice J is incorrect. Bill's friend says there is no sign of rabbits, so choice L does not make sense. Wind is never mentioned in the passage, so choice M is not the likeliest answer.

25. **The correct answer is B.** Bill's friend says that he hadn't seen a rabbit in days, and the men seem to be in danger from animals with no way to escape them by going indoors. Therefore, the most logical conclusion is that the characters were probably spending several days outdoors. Choice A is too specific, and the situation in this passage is not very fun. Choice C is also too specific; although rabbits are mentioned in the passage, there is no evidence that the men are actually hunting rabbits. There is no evidence to support choice D either.

26. **The correct answer is L.** This passage is written from the third-person point of view, which is an unknown narrator. Neither Bill (choice J) nor Bill's friend (choice K) is telling his own story in this passage. There is no rabbit hunter in this passage, so choice M is incorrect.

27. **The correct answer is A.** The passage states, "The pale light of the short sunless day was beginning to fade," which supports the idea that it takes place as evening is approaching. This eliminates choice B. There are no clues regarding which season it is, so choices C and D can be eliminated too.

28. **The correct answer is L.** The men in this passage are out in nature, and they are in danger of being harmed by wild animals, so the phrase, "Be respectful of nature, because nature has no respect for you" captures the idea in the passage well. Choices J and K imply that the men have nothing to fear, when they are in very real danger. Choice M refers to nature, but it fails to reflect the main idea of the passage in any meaningful way.

29. **The correct answer is D.** The passage draws a parallel between the fur of mammals and the plumage of birds. Since fur covers mammals, plumage must cover birds, and feathers cover birds. Therefore,

feathers is correct and *fur* (choice C) can be eliminated. While plumage can be used as camouflage (choice A) or have color (choice B), neither of these words defines it as *feathers* does.

30. **The correct answer is M.** Choice M is confirmed by the discussion of the kingfisher in the first paragraph of the passage. Choices J and L are never mentioned in the passage. While the author does suggest that the kingfisher flies fast, he discusses a different way the bird protects itself.

31. **The correct answer is C.** The passage discusses how animals use their coloring to make them more difficult to see, so if its coloring makes an animal less conspicuous, then it makes that animal less visible. *Hidden* (choice A) is the opposite of *conspicuous*. The passage simply provides no evidence to support choice B or choice D.

32. **The correct answer is K.** All of these animals are mentioned in the second paragraph except for cobras. While snakes are mentioned, the specific snake called the cobra is not.

33. **The correct answer is A.** The passage mentions lions among the animals that have adapted to blend into a desert environment. The other environments are not mentioned in the passage.

34. **The correct answer is J.** The passage is all about how the coloring of animals helps them to survive by camouflaging them in their given environments. Since grasshoppers are green like grass, choice J is the best answer. The other answer choices do not describe green animals.

35. **The correct answer is C.** Based on information in the passage, Benjamin Franklin had many skills and, for these, the other children probably admired him. While he may have been athletic, choice A reaches a specific conclusion the passage does not support. Choice B reaches an extreme conclusion, since Franklin's abilities are never compared to those of the other children. While some people fear their leaders, there is no reason to believe the other children feared Benjamin Franklin.

36. **The correct answer is M.** *Shouldered* means "carried." The other answer choices would not make much sense if used in place of *shouldered* in paragraph 1.

37. **The correct answer is D.** The passage shows that Franklin was a very bright boy with many skills, but the process of making candles seems like dull work that required running errands for other people. Therefore, it is reasonable to conclude that the work was not challenging enough for him. This eliminates choices A and B. While Franklin did become a writer as an adult, there are no clues that this would happen in the passage, so choice C lacks supporting evidence.

38. **The correct answer is K.** As it is used in the context of paragraph 5, *keen* means "intense." *Eager* (choice J) and *biting* (choice L) can be used as synonyms for *keen*, but they do not fit this particular context. *Blunt* (choice M) is the opposite of *keen*.

39. **The correct answer is C.** Benjamin Franklin's father knew his son was "bookish," which means Benjamin liked reading printed materials such as newspapers and books. According to the passage, the apprenticeship was mostly unpaid, so choice A is unlikely and never given as a reason in the passage. There is no evidence for choice B either. Benjamin already knew how to read, so choice D is incorrect.

40. **The correct answer is J.** The passage as a whole is about Benjamin Franklin's youth, so choice J is the best answer. Choices K and L imply that the passage is about Franklin's entire life, which it is not. Although Benjamin Franklin helped make candles when he was a boy, choice M implies that the passage is more about making candles than it is about Benjamin Franklin, which is inaccurate.

41. **The correct answer is D.** According to the final sentence of the passage, Buddhists used tea "extensively to prevent drowsiness during their long hours of meditation." Taoists used tea as an elixir of immortality, so choice A is incorrect. While Confucius is mentioned in the passage, Confucians are not, so choice B is incorrect. Mohists are not mentioned either, which eliminates choice C.

42. **The correct answer is L.** The word *indicative* means "representative." *Opposite* (choice J) and *unrelated* (choice K) are almost antonyms of *indicative*. *Following* (choice M) suggests a sequence of events that the passage does not support.

43. **The correct answer is A.** According to the passage, tea was "often applied externally in paste form to alleviate rheumatic pains." While the passage does indicate that people drank tea by saying that it was taken as an "internal dose," the author never suggests that tea was brewed in water to relieve rheumatic pains, so choice B is incorrect. Administering tea in pill form (choice C) or as dry leaves (choice D) is never mentioned in the passage.

44. **The correct answer is J.** According to the passage, powdered tea was whipped. Cake tea (choice K) was boiled, and leaf tea (choice L) was steeped. *Ming* is the name of a dynasty, not a kind of tea, so choice M is incorrect.

45. **The correct answer is B.** After stating that teas can be designated, the author names a few different teas, which is a clue that *designate* means "to name." Choices A, C, and D would not make sense if used in place of *designate* in the sentence.

46. **The correct answer is L.** The passage details many uses of tea in Chinese culture. While the author references philosophy, the passage provides no strong evidence to support the extreme conclusion in choice J. The author provides a number of names for tea but does not suggest that any of the names are the "only correct" one for tea, so choice K is not the best answer. The passage states that tea was believed to be capable of repairing weak eyesight; it does not comment on whether or not this is true, so choice M lacks supporting evidence.

47. **The correct answer is A.** The author notes that the Sierra Nevada is grand because it is "long and massive," which means that it is huge, and then describes its many unique features. Choice B reaches a conclusion that the passage does not support. The author states only that the Sierra Nevada is huge; he does not say that it is the biggest. Choice C mentions only one of the details about the Sierra Nevada, and it is not a particularly unique one among mountain ranges. Choice D describes the features on one side of the Sierra Nevada; this is not a feature of the mountain range itself.

48. **The correct answer is L.** According to the passage, Professor Whitney was the first person to gain "a scientific knowledge of the form, plan, and physical conditions of the Sierras," which supports choice L. There is no support for choices J, K, or M.

49. **The correct answer is B.** According to the passage, the range's eastern slope is "a defiant wall of rock plunging abruptly down to the plain." Forests are found on the western range, so choice A is incorrect. Choices C and D describe the features on one side of the Sierra Nevada; these are not features of the mountain range itself.

50. **The correct answer is M.** The author describes a desert as "arid," and deserts are dry. Deserts are not rainy, so choice J can be eliminated. *Small* (choice K) and *pleasant* (choice L) are not words associated with deserts, so there are no context clues to suggest that either of these words is a synonym of *arid*.

Written Expression

1. D	11. C	21. C	31. A	41. A
2. J	12. L	22. M	32. L	42. K
3. A	13. D	23. B	33. B	43. D
4. L	14. L	24. L	34. J	44. M
5. E	15. C	25. D	35. D	45. A
6. M	16. K	26. L	36. J	46. K
7. B	17. C	27. B	37. A	47. C
8. L	18. J	28. M	38. L	48. J
9. C	19. B	29. A	39. B	49. B
10. M	20. J	30. K	40. K	50. J

1. **The correct answer is D.** The correct spelling is *explanation.*

2. **The correct answer is J.** The correct spelling is *definitely.*

3. **The correct answer is A.** The correct spelling is *separate.*

4. **The correct answer is L.** The correct spelling is *privilege.*

5. **The correct answer is E.** *No mistakes.*

6. **The correct answer is M.** The correct spelling is *existence.*

7. **The correct answer is B.** The correct spelling is *pronunciation.*

8. **The correct answer is L.** The correct spelling is *necessary.*

9. **The correct answer is C.** The correct spelling is *escalator.*

10. **The correct answer is M.** The correct spelling is *taunt.*

11. **The correct answer is C.** *Building* is part of the name of the structure, so it should be capitalized.

12. **The correct answer is L.** The clarifying information—the kitten's name—needs to be introduced with a colon in this sentence.

13. **The correct answer is D.** *No mistakes.*

14. **The correct answer is L.** While the title of a novel should be italicized, a chapter title should be placed within quotation marks.

15. **The correct answer is C.** *Elise* is someone's name, so it should be capitalized.

16. **The correct answer is K.** There is a homonym error in this sentence. *Addition* means "something added"; *edition* means "an issue of a periodical, such as a school newspaper."

17. **The correct answer is C.** *Planetoid* is not a proper noun, so it should not be capitalized.

18. **The correct answer is J.** An abbreviated title such as *Mrs.* needs to end with a period.

19. **The correct answer is B.** Since Highway 61 is the proper name of a specific road, it should be capitalized.

20. **The correct answer is J.** The line "I haven't seen Jimmy" is something Maria said, and quotes belong within quotation marks.

21. **The correct answer is C.** This sentence is a declarative statement, so it should end with a period, not a question mark.

22. **The correct answer is M.** *No mistakes.*

23. **The correct answer is B.** There should not be a comma at the beginning of the list. Therefore, the comma after *include* is misplaced.

24. **The correct answer is L.** There is a pronoun/antecedent error in this sentence. *Shara* and *Lashawn* are two people, yet *her* is a singular pronoun. It should be replaced with *them*.

25. **The correct answer is D.** *No mistakes.*

26. **The correct answer is L.** This sentence expresses the ideas clearly: "The explorers were anxious because they knew that they were entering dangerous terrain." Its independent and dependent clauses are separate, distinct, and straightforward.

27. **The correct answer is B.** This sentence expresses the ideas clearly: "Despite months of practice, John lost his confidence and fared poorly at the tournament." The subject immediately follows a brief introductory phrase, and it is not separated from the predicate by any clauses or phrases.

28. **The correct answer is M.** This sentence expresses the ideas directly and concisely: "Marc and Jason were able to collaborate on the project once they put aside their differences." The plural subject begins the sentence and is immediately followed by the verb, which helps to clearly convey the action taking place.

29. **The correct answer is A.** This sentence expresses the ideas directly and concisely: "The Louisiana Purchase and the Gold Rush sparked westward expansion in the nineteenth century." The compound subject begins the sentence and is immediately followed by the verb, which helps to clearly convey the action taking place.

30. **The correct answer is K.** This sentence expresses the ideas directly and concisely: "My mother works long hours from Monday to Friday, but she always makes plenty of time to spend with me on the weekend." The subject begins the sentence, and it is immediately followed by a verb, which helps to clearly convey the action taking place.

31. **The correct answer is A.** Use of the present-tense verb *snap* establishes this sentence in the present tense, but *wanted* is in the past tense. The best way to correct this problem is to write the verb in the present tense as *want*.

32. **The correct answer is L.** This sentence does the best job of wrapping up the passage by naming Lange again and summing up her significance. Choice J is information that would make much more sense earlier in the passage since it describes the beginning of a life. Choice K basically just rewords sentence 5 and introduces no new information. Choice M changes the topic from Dorothea Lange to another photographer.

33. **The correct answer is B.** Sentence 1 begins with the word *However*, which indicates that it introduces an exception to the sentence that would precede it, and choice B is something to which sentence 1 would be an exception. Choice A just rewords sentence 1, so it is unnecessary. Choice C simply lists art forms without providing information that would be followed by *However*. Choice D states the opposite of sentence 1.

34. **The correct answer is J.** Sentence 3 is a compound sentence with two independent clauses, and clauses should be connected with a semicolon only if there is no conjunction. However, these clauses are connected with the conjunction *but*, so the correct punctuation is a comma, not a semicolon. Choice K would turn sentence 3 into a run-on. A colon is used to introduce a list or a clarifying word; it is not used to connect independent clauses. Therefore, choice L is incorrect.

35. **The correct answer is D.** *No change.* Neither *dinosaurs* nor *triceratops* is a proper name, so neither word should be capitalized. Sentence 1 is correct as written.

36. **The correct answer is J.** Sentence 3 ends with a list, and a colon is used to introduce a list. A semicolon (choice K) separates complete clauses in a compound sentence; a comma (choice L) is used to separate items in a list.

37. **The correct answer is A.** There is a word choice error in sentence 2. A tail is the body part on the back of an animal. However, this sentence is referring to a story, and *tale* means "story." Neither making the word *tail* plural (choice B) nor changing the word *tells* to the plural form *tell* (choice C) corrects that error.

38. **The correct answer is L.** When capitalizing a title, all of the words are capitalized except for articles and prepositions in the center of the title. Only choice L is capitalized correctly. Choice J capitalizes the article and preposition in the center of the title. Choice K capitalizes the article in the center of the title and fails to capitalize the words *Lair, White,* and *Worm.*

39. **The correct answer is B.** There is a word choice error in the original sentence, because the correct phrase is "rife with," not "rife in." Therefore, the best way to correct this sentence is to replace *rife* with *rich,* which has a similar meaning but works with the preposition *in.*

40. **The correct answer is K.** A colon would be necessary to introduce the dinosaur's name only if the word *called* did not already serve that introductory function. The best fix is to delete the unnecessary punctuation altogether.

41. **The correct answer is A.** This sentence effectively confirms the idea that the Taj Mahal is a significant site. Choice B is a detail that should have appeared earlier in the passage, not at the passage's end. Choice C would also work better earlier in the passage, but since it focuses on details about Mumtaz Mahal when the passage is really about the Taj Mahal, it is somewhat unnecessary information. Choice D starts as a strong concluding sentence, but its second clause provides unnecessary information about another UNESCO World Heritage Site that has nothing to do with the passage's main idea.

42. **The correct answer is K.** The entire name of the empire, the *Mughal Empire,* is a proper noun, so both words should be capitalized. Choice J fails to capitalize either word. Choice L capitalizes both words but fails to capitalize *Shah,* which should be capitalized since it is a title.

43. **The correct answer is D.** *Seven Natural Wonders of the World* is the official title of a series of spectacular natural features of the earth, so it should be capitalized. However, prepositions, such as *of,* and articles, such as *the,* should not be capitalized in titles unless they are the first word of the title.

44. **The correct answer is M.** *No change. It's* is a contraction of *it is; its* is the possessive form of *it,* which is what is required in sentence 4.

45. **The correct answer is A.** As sentence 1 is originally written, there is a pronoun-verb error. Choice A corrects that error by changing the verb *enters* to *enter.* Choices B and C create different pronoun-verb errors.

46. **The correct answer is K.** The phrase "but rather misunderstood" is nonessential additional information, so it should be set off from the rest of the sentence. Choice K corrects the original sentence's lack of punctuation by offsetting the phrase with em dashes. Choice J converts the original sentence into three fragments. Choice L incorrectly uses semicolons to offset the nonessential information.

47. **The correct answer is C.** In sentence 2, *palm tree framed* is a compound adjective, so it needs a hyphen to connect *tree* and *framed.* However, there should not be a hyphen between a compound adjective and the noun it modifies, so choice A is incorrect. Choice B places the hyphen incorrectly.

48. **The correct answer is J.** *Its* is the possessive form of *it; it's* is a contraction of *it is,* which is what is required in sentence 7. Writing out *it is* completely would solve the problem if an unnecessary apostrophe were not added to it, as in choice L.

49. **The correct answer is B.** Sentence 3 describes something that happened in the past, so the verb needs to be written in the past tense as *occurred.* Choice A rewrites it in the future tense, and choice C writes it in the present tense.

50. **The correct answer is J.** As originally written, the independent clause in sentence 5 has a compound predicate (*passed* and *heralded*) that is not joined correctly. Choice J corrects this error by adding the conjunction *and* between the two verbs. A comma would not be used to join a two-verb compound predicate, so choice K is incorrect. Choice L reduces the run-on to a fragment and deletes relevant information.

Mathematics

1. D	11. C	21. B	31. B	41. B
2. M	12. K	22. K	32. L	42. M
3. B	13. D	23. D	33. C	43. B
4. M	14. L	24. J	34. K	44. K
5. B	15. D	25. A	35. C	45. C
6. L	16. K	26. J	36. K	46. J
7. A	17. A	27. C	37. B	47. C
8. L	18. J	28. L	38. L	48. K
9. C	19. B	29. D	39. C	49. D
10. L	20. L	30. K	40. J	50. L

1. **The correct answer is D.** The given expression equals $50{,}000 + 300 + 10 + 0.04 = 50{,}310.04$.

2. **The correct answer is M.**
$4^2 + 3^3 = 16 + 27 = 43$

3. **The correct answer is B.** Let x be the number of bathrooms. Set up and solve the proportion $\frac{2}{3} = \frac{x}{18}$. Cross-multiply to get $36 = 3x$. Finally, dividing by 3 yields $x = 12$.

4. **The correct answer is M.**
$5\frac{11}{25} = 5 + \frac{11}{25} = 5 + \frac{44}{100} = 5.44$

5. **The correct answer is B.**
$1.111 - 0.919 = 0.192$

6. **The correct answer is L.** Since $51 = 3(17)$, it is not prime. So, it must be composite, which means it has factors other than 1 and itself.

7. **The correct answer is A.** Observe that $1 - (-4) = 1 + 4 = 5$ and $4 - (-2) = = 4 + 2 = 6$. Since $5 < 6$, the inequality in A is true.

8. **The correct answer is L.** Multiply 9 times 25 to conclude that 225 is the number of campers.

9. **The correct answer is C.** Use the order of operations:

$$2\left(\frac{5}{2} - 2\right) \div \frac{1}{2} = 2\left(\frac{1}{2}\right) \div \frac{1}{2} = 1 \div \frac{1}{2} = 1 \cdot 2 = 2$$

10. **The correct answer is L.** Subtract $\frac{5}{4}$ from both sides to get the following:

$$x + \frac{5}{4} = \frac{17}{8}$$
$$x = \frac{17}{8} - \frac{5}{4}$$
$$x = \frac{17}{8} - \frac{10}{8}$$
$$x = \frac{7}{8}$$

11. **The correct answer is C.** Add the number of hours in each wedge to get $5 + 2 + 2 + 2.5 = 11.5$ hours.

12. **The correct answer is K.** 2.5 hours are spent trick-or-treating, and there are 11.5 hours total. So, the percentage of the time spent trick-or-treating is $\frac{2.5}{11.5} \times 100\% \approx 22\%$.

13. **The correct answer is D.** Note that $(3 + 4)^2 = 7^2 = 49$, while $3^2 + 4^2 = 9 + 16 = 25$. Therefore they are not equal.

14. **The correct answer is L.** All four sides of a rhombus have the same length. So, the perimeter is $4(6) = 24$ inches.

15. **The correct answer is D.** Multiply $\frac{2}{3}$ times 4 times 3 to get 8 hours.

3

16. **The correct answer is K.** 4% of $2,100 is $0.04(\$2,100) = \$84$.

17. **The correct answer is A.**

$\overset{3}{\cancel{4}}$ hours	$\overset{59}{\cancel{60}}\;\overset{60}{\cancel{0}}$ minutes	$\overset{60}{\cancel{0}}$ seconds
$-\quad$ 1 hour	59 minutes	58 seconds
2 hours	0 minutes	2 seconds

18. **The correct answer is J.** One round trip is $2p$ miles. The car can travel $5q$ miles on 5 gallons of gasoline. So, the number of round trips that can be made is $\dfrac{5q}{2p}$.

19. **The correct answer is B.** Use the order of operations:

$$\left(-\frac{1}{2}\right)\cdot(-6) \div \left(-\frac{3}{2}\right) =$$
$$3 \div \left(-\frac{3}{2}\right) =$$
$$3 \cdot \left(-\frac{2}{3}\right) = -2$$

20. **The correct answer is L.** The sum of the four interior angles of a trapezoid is 360°. So, $x° + 121° + 58° + 70° = 360°$. This is equivalent to $249° + x° = 360°$. So, $x = 111°$.

21. **The correct answer is B.** The length of the shaded portion of the bar above "Watching TV" is $80 - 40 = 40$.

22. **The correct answer is K.** The number of boys selecting "Playing Video Games" as their favorite activity is 50, while the number of girls selecting this as their favorite activity is 10. The difference is 40, which is larger than the other three differences.

23. **The correct answer is D.** The number of boys and the number of girls selecting "Playing Sports" as their favorite activity is both 30. So the ratio is 1:1.

24. **The correct answer is J.** Officer Michelle issued 34 tickets and Officer Ken issued 33 tickets during this six-week period. So the difference in the number of tickets issued is $34 - 33 = 1$.

25. **The correct answer is A.** Add the cells in each row. The smallest sum occurs in Week 3.

26. **The correct answer is J.** Since 500% of $1 = 5$, it follows that 500% of 0.01 is $5(0.01) = 0.05$.

27. **The correct answer is C.** The temperature at 5 a.m. Tuesday is $96° - 0.25(96°) = 96° - 24° = 72°$. So the temperature at noon that same day is $72° + 0.10(72°) = 72° + 7.2° \approx 79°$.

28. **The correct answer is L.** $(2 - (-1))^3 = 3^3 = 27$

29. **The correct answer is D.** Simplify as follows:

$$2^5 \cdot 3^2 = 2 \cdot 2 \cdot 2 \cdot 2 \cdot 2 \cdot 3 \cdot 3$$
$$= 2 \cdot 2 \cdot 2 \cdot (2 \cdot 3) \cdot (2 \cdot 3)$$
$$= 2 \cdot 2 \cdot 2 \cdot 6 \cdot 6$$
$$= 2^3 \cdot 6^2$$

30. **The correct answer is K.** Nancy completed $30 + 40 + 20 + 20 + 50 = 160$ lunges, and Laura completed $40 + 30 + 30 + 30 + 40 = 170$ lunges. So, the difference is $170 - 160 = 10$.

31. **The correct answer is B.** Laura completed 40 lunges on Friday and a total of 170 lunges for the week. So, the fraction completed on Friday is $\dfrac{40}{170} = \dfrac{4}{17}$.

32. **The correct answer is L.** The area of the entire square is $(12)(12) = 144$ square feet. The base of the unshaded triangle is 4 feet (since $\overline{AD}$ is divided into three congruent segments, and one of them is the base of the unshaded triangle). Since its height is 12 feet, the area of the unshaded triangle is $\dfrac{1}{2}(4)(12) = 24$ square feet. So the area of the shaded region is $144 - 24 = 120$ square feet.

33. **The correct answer is C.**

Factors of 12: 1, 2, 3, 4, 6, 12

Factors of 18: 1, 2, 3, 6, 9, 18

Factors of 48: 1, 2, 3, 4, 6, 8, 12, 16, 24, 48

The complete set of factors common to all three is {1, 2, 3, 6}.

34. The correct answer is K. The radius of the large circle is 7 inches, so its area is $\pi \cdot 7^2 = 49\pi$ square inches. The radius of the small inner circle is 4 inches, so its area is $\pi \cdot 4^2 = 16\pi$. So, the area of the shaded region is $49\pi - 16\pi = 33\pi$ square inches.

35. The correct answer is C. $\left(\dfrac{1}{2}\right)^2 = \dfrac{1}{2} \cdot \dfrac{1}{2} = \dfrac{1}{4}$, which is not an integer.

36. The correct answer is K. The point is plotted as follows:

37. The correct answer is B. The triangle is isosceles, so the base angles are congruent; call both of their measures $x°$. Since the sum of the three interior angles of a triangle is 180°, we have $36° + x° + x° = 180°$. Solve for x as follows:

$$36° + x° + x° = 180°$$
$$36° + 2\left(x°\right) = 180°$$
$$2\left(x°\right) = 144°$$
$$x° = 72°$$

38. The correct answer is L. The number of hours she travels is 8. So, the average speed is $560 \div 8 = 70$ miles per hour.

39. The correct answer is C. Add the three scores and divide the sum by 3:

$$\frac{6,500 + 13,000 + 16,500}{3} = \frac{36,000}{3} = 12,000$$

40. The correct answer is J. If you start with an odd integer and add 1 to it, you get an even integer. If you add 1 to this, you get another odd integer. So, adding 2 to an odd integer gives an odd integer.

41. The correct answer is B. $8^2 = 64$, and since 8.04 is slightly larger than 8, it follows that 8.04^2 is closer to 65 than it is to 62.

42. The correct answer is M. The expression is approximately $4(10) + 3(20) = 100$.

43. The correct answer is B. The expression is approximately $8,000 - 5,000 = 3,000$.

44. The correct answer is K. The expression is approximately $5 + 7 + 10 = 22$.

45. The correct answer is C. The number of ounces of canola oil needed to make 32 batches would be 9×32, or 288.

46. The correct answer is J. Approximate 612 as 600. Since 10% of 600 is 60, it follows that 5% of 600 is half of this, or 30.

47. The correct answer is C. The expression is approximately $300(200) = 60,000$.

48. The correct answer is K. The expression is approximately $40 \div 2 = 20$.

49. The correct answer is D. Approximate 1,819 as 1,800 and divide by 9. Doing so, the expression is approximately $1,800 \div 9 = 200$. Since 1,819 is greater than 1,800, the average would be a little higher than that, but 200 is the closest option.

50. The correct answer is L. Multiply 8 times 9 to get 72 minutes.

Ability

Figure Classification

1. E	5. B	9. B	13. D	17. D
2. K	6. J	10. K	14. N	18. J
3. A	7. E	11. D	15. A	19. D
4. J	8. M	12. L	16. M	20. L

1. **The correct answer is E.** All figures comprise line segments and no curves.

2. **The correct answer is K.** All figures are closed regions that comprise five line segments.

3. **The correct answer is A.** The interiors of the figures are cut in half and the shading is done using line segments perpendicular to the line used to cut the figure in half.

4. **The correct answer is J.** All the given figures are small. Since choice J is small and the other four are large, it is the logical choice.

5. **The correct answer is B.** The points on the circles of the given figures are equally spaced around the entire circle.

6. **The correct answer is J.** The figures are symmetric about the dotted line shown.

7. **The correct answer is E.** The pattern exhibited in the figures is one unshaded circle between two parallel horizontal lines, then two shaded circles between two parallel horizontal lines, then three unshaded circles between two parallel horizontal lines. Following this pattern, the next logical choice should be four shaded circles between two parallel horizontal lines.

8. **The correct answer is M.** The given figures are all triangles.

9. **The correct answer is B.** An odd number of congruent portions of each of the given figures are shaded.

10. **The correct answer is K.** The given figures are all rotations about the center point of the square.

The figure in choice K is obtained by rotating the second given figure 90 degrees counterclockwise.

11. **The correct answer is D.** All figures contain one shaded circle fewer than the number of sides that comprise the figure.

12. **The correct answer is L.** The pairs of triangles in each of the given figures are obtained by translating the leftmost triangle to the right and then reflecting it over the dotted line.

13. **The correct answer is D.** The inner and outer shapes in each figure are similar (that is, the inner one is a smaller version of the outer shape).

14. **The correct answer is N.** The figures comprise two sets of intersecting lines which, when added, equal an odd number of lines.

15. **The correct answer is A.** The ratio of X's to E's is 5:2.

16. **The correct answer is M.** The arrows inside each of the figures all point in a clockwise direction, and no two figures are similar.

17. **The correct answer is D.** The given figures all contain the same internal configuration, with circles included at vertices to form a triangle pattern that encompdonkeys a quarter of the figure's area.

18. **The correct answer is J.** All pattern options feature interlocking circles of equal size. In choices K and N, the circles are different sizes. In choice L, two of the circles are not interlocked with the rest. In choice M, all the circles are touching, but none of them interlock with one another.

19. **The correct answer is D.** This pattern features a hexagram with a decreasing number of unshaded parts. The first is missing three parts, the second two parts, and the third one part. Choice D would continue this pattern because it's a hexagram that's missing zero parts. Choice A is missing all parts, choice B is missing six parts, choice C is missing 5 parts, and choice E is missing 2 parts.

20. **The correct answer is L.** Each circle includes two white arrows and one black arrow in its interior.

NOTES

Figure Matrices

1. B	5. E	9. D	13. D	17. C
2. N	6. K	10. L	14. L	18. L
3. D	7. C	11. C	15. B	19. D
4. J	8. M	12. J	16. N	20. K

1. **The correct answer is B.** The pattern across the rows is to start with a figure (either empty or bisected), add something to it, and then put only what was added in the final column. Doing so here yields choice B.

2. **The correct answer is N.** The pattern across the rows is to insert a smaller version of the figure in the first square inside the figure in the second square to get the figure for the third square. Choice N is a better option than choices K or M, as it preserves the orientation of the original triangle.

3. **The correct answer is D.** The pattern across the rows has nothing to do with the first column. The third square is simply the interior figure from the second square.

4. **The correct answer is J.** The pattern across the rows is to start with the figure in the first square, insert intersecting lines to get the figure in the second square, and then replace those lines with circles that appear at the ends of each of the segments that appeared in the second square.

5. **The correct answer is E.** The pattern across the rows is to start with two arrows in the first square, change the direction of one of the arrows to get the second square, and then change the direction of both arrows from what they were in the second square to get the figure in the third square.

6. **The correct answer is K.** The pattern across the rows is to remove one square and add one X to go from the first to the second figure, and then do the same to go from the second to the third figure.

7. **The correct answer is C.** This time, the pattern occurs in the columns, not the rows. The pattern going down the columns is to start with a figure and remove the bottom portion labeled A to get

the second square. Then to get the figure in the third square, add the removed figure A portion back to a horizontally flipped figure B of the image found in the second square.

8. **The correct answer is M.** The pattern across the rows is to remove one circle from the interior to go from the first to the second square. Then, do the same to go from the second to the third square.

9. **The correct answer is D.** The pattern across the rows is to use the type of segment (and the direction of the segment, i.e., horizontal, diagonal, zig zag, vertical, etc.) in the first square to shade the interior of the figure in the second square to get the figure in the third square.

10. **The correct answer is L.** The pattern across the rows is to affix the next consecutive vertex of the figure moving in a clockwise fashion to go from the first to the second square. Then, do the same thing to go from the second to the third square.

11. **The correct answer is C.** The figures in a row are all rotations by a multiple of 90 degrees of each other.

12. **The correct answer is J.** The pattern across the rows is to remove the leftmost or bottom segment of the figure to go from the first to the second square. Then, do the same thing to go from the second to the third square.

13. **The correct answer is D.** The pattern across the rows is to start with a figure in the first square, divide it in half, and then shade half of it using diagonal line segments to get the figure in the second square. Then, to get the third square, shade the opposite portion of the figure from the second square using line segments in a different direction from those used in the second square.

14. **The correct answer is L.** The pattern across the rows is to start with a figure in the first square, and add something to it to get the second square. The third square is simply what you added in the second square.

15. **The correct answer is B.** The pattern across the rows is to start with a figure containing some line segments. To get the second square, remove those interior line segments to get an empty figure. To get the third square, put only the interior line segments that appear in the first square.

16. **The correct answer is N.** The pattern across the rows can be determined from the first to the third squares in this case. Here, the figure in the third square is the same as the one in the first square with the exception that the small shapes affixed to the ends of the line segments have opposite shading. The exercise does make a change from column one to column two, but it is not relevant to the third column.

17. **The correct answer is C.** The pattern across the rows is to insert the figure from the second square inside the figure in the first square and shade the region around it to get the figure in the third square.

18. **The correct answer is L.** The pattern across the rows is to insert the figure from the first square into the figure in the second square, and then turn the combined image upside down to arrive at the figure in the third square. In choice J, the zigzag line is rotated, but not turned upside down. In choice K, the triangle is rotated 90 degrees, but not turned upside down like the hexagon from the original matrix. In choice M, neither the zigzag nor the triangle have been turned upside down correctly. And choice N is incorrect because it gives us an equilateral triangle instead of a right triangle.

19. **The correct answer is D.** The pattern across the rows here is to remove the segment from column two from the shape in column one. In addition, the segment that is removed must be in the same orientation as shown in the second square. Choice A is incorrect because it subtracts the line segment from the right side of the shape, not the left side. Choice B is incorrect because it removes two lines of the hexagon instead of one. Choice C is incorrect because it adds a line segment to the hexagon instead of subtracting, and choice E is incorrect because it removes a line from the top instead of the hexagon instead of the lower left side.

20. **The correct answer is K.** The pattern across the rows is simply to place the shape from column one inside the shape from column two, and then reverse the shading. Choice J is incorrect because the size of the hexagon increased instead of staying the same. Choice L is incorrect because the circle should be solid and the hexagon transparent, not the other way around. Choice M is also incorrect for this reason, plus the size of the hexagon has been altered. Finally, choice N is incorrect because the hexagon in the middle of the circle has been rotated 60 degrees.

Paper Folding

1. A	3. C	5. B	7. D	9. A
2. N	4. N	6. K	8. M	10. J

1. **The correct answer is A.** The third fold in this exercise does not reach across far enough to be included in the hole punch, so the final hole pattern is only affected by the first two folds. As such, four sheets are being punched and the folds are perpendicular. So there are four holes in the shape of a square.

2. **The correct answer is N.** Six sheets are being punched. One sheet is missed since the second fold didn't overlap it. This explains the missing hole between the other three that have been punched.

3. **The correct answer is C.** Four sheets are being punched and the folds are all in the same direction. So, the holes line up along a single row.

4. **The correct answer is N.** Six sheets are being punched in the form of two parallel columns since the folds are made in perpendicular directions. One sheet is missed since the second fold didn't overlap it. This explains the missing hole between the other three that have been punched.

5. **The correct answer is B.** Eight sheets are being punched and so there are eight holes.

6. **The correct answer is K.** Only four sheets are being punched because there is no overlap between the second and third folds, so there are four holes.

7. **The correct answer is D.** Six sheets are being punched and the hole never reaches the leftmost edge of the square by the way the folds are being made. So, it cannot be choice C and hence, must be D.

8. **The correct answer is M.** Three sheets are being punched in parallel, diagonal folds, so the holes must align in a diagonal format.

9. **The correct answer is A.** Four sheets are being punched, so there are four holes, one in each corner, that are reflections of each other over the fold.

10. **The correct answer is J.** The only fold affecting where the holes will appear is the first one since the paper never reaches the top half of the square after subsequent folds. So there are two holes in the upper corners of the square.

NOTES

SCORE SHEET

Although your actual exam scores will not be reported as percentages, it might be helpful to convert your test scores to percentages so that you can see at a glance where your strengths and weaknesses lie. The numbers in parentheses represent the questions that test each skill.

Subject	# Correct ÷ # of questions	× 100 = _____ %
Reading		
Vocabulary/Word Relationships (1, 9, 12, 16, 18, 22, 24, 29, 31, 36, 38, 42, 45, 50)	_____ ÷ 14 = _____	× 100 = _____ %
Details/Main Idea/Structure (2, 6, 10, 14, 15, 17, 19, 20, 26, 27, 28, 30, 32, 33, 40, 41, 43, 44, 46, 48, 49)	_____ ÷ 21 = _____	× 100 = _____ %
Inference/Understanding (3, 4, 5, 7, 8, 11, 13, 21, 23, 25, 34, 35, 37, 39, 47)	_____ ÷ 15 = _____	× 100 = _____ %
TOTAL READING SKILLS	_____ ÷ 50 = _____	× 100 = _____ %
Written Expression		
Spelling and Capitalization (1, 2, 3, 4, 5, 6, 7, 8, 9, 10, 11, 15, 17, 19, 25, 35, 37, 38, 42, 43)	_____ ÷ 20 = _____	× 100 = _____ %
Punctuation (12, 13, 14, 18, 20, 21, 22, 23, 34, 36, 40, 44, 46, 47, 48)	_____ ÷ 15 = _____	× 100 = _____ %
Grammar (16, 24, 31, 45, 49)	_____ ÷ 5 = _____	× 100 = _____ %
Usage and Composition (26, 27, 28, 29, 30, 32, 33, 39, 41, 50)	_____ ÷ 10 = _____	× 100 = _____ %
TOTAL WRITTEN EXPRESSION SKILLS	_____ ÷ 50 = _____	× 100 = _____ %
Mathematics		
Arithmetic (1, 2, 3, 4, 5, 6, 7, 8, 9, 13, 15, 16, 19, 26, 27, 29, 33, 35, 39, 41, 42, 43, 44, 46, 47, 48, 49, 50)	_____ ÷ 28 = _____	× 100 = _____ %
Algebra (10, 18, 28, 36, 40)	_____ ÷ 5 = _____	× 100 = _____ %
Data Analysis (11, 12, 21, 22, 23, 24, 25, 30, 31)	_____ ÷ 9 = _____	× 100 = _____ %
Geometry and Measurement (14, 17, 20, 32, 34, 37, 38, 45)	_____ ÷ 8 = _____	× 100 = _____ %
TOTAL MATHEMATICS SKILLS	_____ ÷ 50 = _____	× 100 = _____ %
Ability		
Figure Classification (1, 2, 3, 4, 5, 6, 7, 8, 9, 10, 11, 12, 13, 14, 15, 16, 17, 18, 19, 20)	_____ ÷ 20 = _____	× 100 = _____ %
Figure Matrices (1, 2, 3, 4, 5, 6, 7, 8, 9, 10, 11, 12, 13, 14, 15, 16, 17, 18, 19, 20)	_____ ÷ 20 = _____	× 100 = _____ %
Paper Folding (1, 2, 3, 4, 5, 6, 7, 8, 9, 10)	_____ ÷ 10 = _____	× 100 = _____ %
TOTAL ABILITY SKILLS	_____ ÷ 50 = _____	× 100 = _____ %

Study Reference Guide

Subject	Chapter	Page
Reading	Chapter 5: Reading	192
Written Expression	Chapter 6: Language Composition and Expression	244
	Chapter 7: English Usage and Punctuation	
	Chapter 8: Capitalization and Spelling	
	Chapter 10: Synonyms and Antonyms	
Mathematics	Chapter 12: Basic Mathematics	388
	Chapter 13: Algebraic Thinking	
	Chapter 14: Geometry	
Ability	Chapter 16: Comparisons and Ability Questions	504

CHAPTER

HSPT® Diagnostic Test

HSPT® DIAGNOSTIC TEST

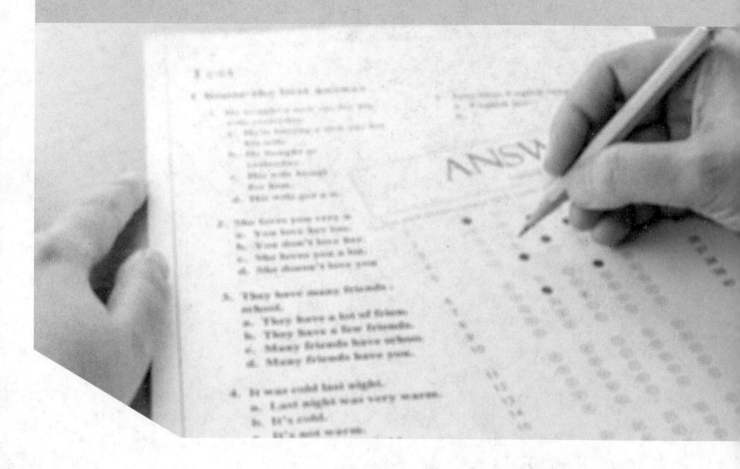

DIAGNOSTIC TEST:

This diagnostic test is designed to help you recognize your strengths and weaknesses. The questions cover information from all the different sections of the HSPT. Use the results to help guide and direct your study time.

ANSWER SHEETS: HSPT® DIAGNOSTIC TEST

Verbal Skills

1. Ⓐ Ⓑ Ⓒ Ⓓ
2. Ⓐ Ⓑ Ⓒ Ⓓ
3. Ⓐ Ⓑ Ⓒ Ⓓ
4. Ⓐ Ⓑ Ⓒ Ⓓ
5. Ⓐ Ⓑ Ⓒ Ⓓ
6. Ⓐ Ⓑ Ⓒ Ⓓ
7. Ⓐ Ⓑ Ⓒ Ⓓ
8. Ⓐ Ⓑ Ⓒ Ⓓ
9. Ⓐ Ⓑ Ⓒ Ⓓ
10. Ⓐ Ⓑ Ⓒ Ⓓ
11. Ⓐ Ⓑ Ⓒ
12. Ⓐ Ⓑ Ⓒ

13. Ⓐ Ⓑ Ⓒ
14. Ⓐ Ⓑ Ⓒ
15. Ⓐ Ⓑ Ⓒ
16. Ⓐ Ⓑ Ⓒ
17. Ⓐ Ⓑ Ⓒ
18. Ⓐ Ⓑ Ⓒ
19. Ⓐ Ⓑ Ⓒ
20. Ⓐ Ⓑ Ⓒ
21. Ⓐ Ⓑ Ⓒ
22. Ⓐ Ⓑ Ⓒ
23. Ⓐ Ⓑ Ⓒ Ⓓ
24. Ⓐ Ⓑ Ⓒ Ⓓ

25. Ⓐ Ⓑ Ⓒ Ⓓ
26. Ⓐ Ⓑ Ⓒ Ⓓ
27. Ⓐ Ⓑ Ⓒ Ⓓ
28. Ⓐ Ⓑ Ⓒ Ⓓ
29. Ⓐ Ⓑ Ⓒ Ⓓ
30. Ⓐ Ⓑ Ⓒ Ⓓ
31. Ⓐ Ⓑ Ⓒ Ⓓ
32. Ⓐ Ⓑ Ⓒ Ⓓ
33. Ⓐ Ⓑ Ⓒ Ⓓ
34. Ⓐ Ⓑ Ⓒ Ⓓ
35. Ⓐ Ⓑ Ⓒ Ⓓ
36. Ⓐ Ⓑ Ⓒ Ⓓ

37. Ⓐ Ⓑ Ⓒ Ⓓ
38. Ⓐ Ⓑ Ⓒ Ⓓ
39. Ⓐ Ⓑ Ⓒ Ⓓ
40. Ⓐ Ⓑ Ⓒ Ⓓ
41. Ⓐ Ⓑ Ⓒ Ⓓ
42. Ⓐ Ⓑ Ⓒ Ⓓ
43. Ⓐ Ⓑ Ⓒ Ⓓ
44. Ⓐ Ⓑ Ⓒ Ⓓ
45. Ⓐ Ⓑ Ⓒ Ⓓ
46. Ⓐ Ⓑ Ⓒ Ⓓ
47. Ⓐ Ⓑ Ⓒ Ⓓ
48. Ⓐ Ⓑ Ⓒ Ⓓ

49. Ⓐ Ⓑ Ⓒ Ⓓ
50. Ⓐ Ⓑ Ⓒ Ⓓ
51. Ⓐ Ⓑ Ⓒ Ⓓ
52. Ⓐ Ⓑ Ⓒ Ⓓ
53. Ⓐ Ⓑ Ⓒ Ⓓ
54. Ⓐ Ⓑ Ⓒ Ⓓ
55. Ⓐ Ⓑ Ⓒ Ⓓ
56. Ⓐ Ⓑ Ⓒ Ⓓ
57. Ⓐ Ⓑ Ⓒ Ⓓ
58. Ⓐ Ⓑ Ⓒ Ⓓ
59. Ⓐ Ⓑ Ⓒ Ⓓ
60. Ⓐ Ⓑ Ⓒ Ⓓ

Quantitative Skills

61. Ⓐ Ⓑ Ⓒ Ⓓ
62. Ⓐ Ⓑ Ⓒ Ⓓ
63. Ⓐ Ⓑ Ⓒ Ⓓ
64. Ⓐ Ⓑ Ⓒ Ⓓ
65. Ⓐ Ⓑ Ⓒ Ⓓ
66. Ⓐ Ⓑ Ⓒ Ⓓ
67. Ⓐ Ⓑ Ⓒ Ⓓ
68. Ⓐ Ⓑ Ⓒ Ⓓ
69. Ⓐ Ⓑ Ⓒ Ⓓ
70. Ⓐ Ⓑ Ⓒ Ⓓ
71. Ⓐ Ⓑ Ⓒ Ⓓ

72. Ⓐ Ⓑ Ⓒ Ⓓ
73. Ⓐ Ⓑ Ⓒ Ⓓ
74. Ⓐ Ⓑ Ⓒ Ⓓ
75. Ⓐ Ⓑ Ⓒ Ⓓ
76. Ⓐ Ⓑ Ⓒ Ⓓ
77. Ⓐ Ⓑ Ⓒ Ⓓ
78. Ⓐ Ⓑ Ⓒ Ⓓ
79. Ⓐ Ⓑ Ⓒ Ⓓ
80. Ⓐ Ⓑ Ⓒ Ⓓ
81. Ⓐ Ⓑ Ⓒ Ⓓ
82. Ⓐ Ⓑ Ⓒ Ⓓ

83. Ⓐ Ⓑ Ⓒ Ⓓ
84. Ⓐ Ⓑ Ⓒ Ⓓ
85. Ⓐ Ⓑ Ⓒ Ⓓ
86. Ⓐ Ⓑ Ⓒ Ⓓ
87. Ⓐ Ⓑ Ⓒ Ⓓ
88. Ⓐ Ⓑ Ⓒ Ⓓ
89. Ⓐ Ⓑ Ⓒ Ⓓ
90. Ⓐ Ⓑ Ⓒ Ⓓ
91. Ⓐ Ⓑ Ⓒ Ⓓ
92. Ⓐ Ⓑ Ⓒ Ⓓ
93. Ⓐ Ⓑ Ⓒ Ⓓ

94. Ⓐ Ⓑ Ⓒ Ⓓ
95. Ⓐ Ⓑ Ⓒ Ⓓ
96. Ⓐ Ⓑ Ⓒ Ⓓ
97. Ⓐ Ⓑ Ⓒ Ⓓ
98. Ⓐ Ⓑ Ⓒ Ⓓ
99. Ⓐ Ⓑ Ⓒ Ⓓ
100. Ⓐ Ⓑ Ⓒ Ⓓ
101. Ⓐ Ⓑ Ⓒ Ⓓ
102. Ⓐ Ⓑ Ⓒ Ⓓ
103. Ⓐ Ⓑ Ⓒ Ⓓ
104. Ⓐ Ⓑ Ⓒ Ⓓ

105. Ⓐ Ⓑ Ⓒ Ⓓ
106. Ⓐ Ⓑ Ⓒ Ⓓ
107. Ⓐ Ⓑ Ⓒ Ⓓ
108. Ⓐ Ⓑ Ⓒ Ⓓ
109. Ⓐ Ⓑ Ⓒ Ⓓ
110. Ⓐ Ⓑ Ⓒ Ⓓ
111. Ⓐ Ⓑ Ⓒ Ⓓ
112. Ⓐ Ⓑ Ⓒ Ⓓ

Reading

Comprehension

113. Ⓐ Ⓑ Ⓒ Ⓓ   121. Ⓐ Ⓑ Ⓒ Ⓓ   129. Ⓐ Ⓑ Ⓒ Ⓓ   137. Ⓐ Ⓑ Ⓒ Ⓓ   145. Ⓐ Ⓑ Ⓒ Ⓓ

114. Ⓐ Ⓑ Ⓒ Ⓓ   122. Ⓐ Ⓑ Ⓒ Ⓓ   130. Ⓐ Ⓑ Ⓒ Ⓓ   138. Ⓐ Ⓑ Ⓒ Ⓓ   146. Ⓐ Ⓑ Ⓒ Ⓓ

115. Ⓐ Ⓑ Ⓒ Ⓓ   123. Ⓐ Ⓑ Ⓒ Ⓓ   131. Ⓐ Ⓑ Ⓒ Ⓓ   139. Ⓐ Ⓑ Ⓒ Ⓓ   147. Ⓐ Ⓑ Ⓒ Ⓓ

116. Ⓐ Ⓑ Ⓒ Ⓓ   124. Ⓐ Ⓑ Ⓒ Ⓓ   132. Ⓐ Ⓑ Ⓒ Ⓓ   140. Ⓐ Ⓑ Ⓒ Ⓓ   148. Ⓐ Ⓑ Ⓒ Ⓓ

117. Ⓐ Ⓑ Ⓒ Ⓓ   125. Ⓐ Ⓑ Ⓒ Ⓓ   133. Ⓐ Ⓑ Ⓒ Ⓓ   141. Ⓐ Ⓑ Ⓒ Ⓓ   149. Ⓐ Ⓑ Ⓒ Ⓓ

118. Ⓐ Ⓑ Ⓒ Ⓓ   126. Ⓐ Ⓑ Ⓒ Ⓓ   134. Ⓐ Ⓑ Ⓒ Ⓓ   142. Ⓐ Ⓑ Ⓒ Ⓓ   150. Ⓐ Ⓑ Ⓒ Ⓓ

119. Ⓐ Ⓑ Ⓒ Ⓓ   127. Ⓐ Ⓑ Ⓒ Ⓓ   135. Ⓐ Ⓑ Ⓒ Ⓓ   143. Ⓐ Ⓑ Ⓒ Ⓓ   151. Ⓐ Ⓑ Ⓒ Ⓓ

120. Ⓐ Ⓑ Ⓒ Ⓓ   128. Ⓐ Ⓑ Ⓒ Ⓓ   136. Ⓐ Ⓑ Ⓒ Ⓓ   144. Ⓐ Ⓑ Ⓒ Ⓓ   152. Ⓐ Ⓑ Ⓒ Ⓓ

Vocabulary

153. Ⓐ Ⓑ Ⓒ Ⓓ   158. Ⓐ Ⓑ Ⓒ Ⓓ   163. Ⓐ Ⓑ Ⓒ Ⓓ   168. Ⓐ Ⓑ Ⓒ Ⓓ   173. Ⓐ Ⓑ Ⓒ Ⓓ

154. Ⓐ Ⓑ Ⓒ Ⓓ   159. Ⓐ Ⓑ Ⓒ Ⓓ   164. Ⓐ Ⓑ Ⓒ Ⓓ   169. Ⓐ Ⓑ Ⓒ Ⓓ   174. Ⓐ Ⓑ Ⓒ Ⓓ

155. Ⓐ Ⓑ Ⓒ Ⓓ   160. Ⓐ Ⓑ Ⓒ Ⓓ   165. Ⓐ Ⓑ Ⓒ Ⓓ   170. Ⓐ Ⓑ Ⓒ Ⓓ

156. Ⓐ Ⓑ Ⓒ Ⓓ   161. Ⓐ Ⓑ Ⓒ Ⓓ   166. Ⓐ Ⓑ Ⓒ Ⓓ   171. Ⓐ Ⓑ Ⓒ Ⓓ

157. Ⓐ Ⓑ Ⓒ Ⓓ   162. Ⓐ Ⓑ Ⓒ Ⓓ   167. Ⓐ Ⓑ Ⓒ Ⓓ   172. Ⓐ Ⓑ Ⓒ Ⓓ

Mathematics

175. Ⓐ Ⓑ Ⓒ Ⓓ	188. Ⓐ Ⓑ Ⓒ Ⓓ	201. Ⓐ Ⓑ Ⓒ Ⓓ	214. Ⓐ Ⓑ Ⓒ Ⓓ	227. Ⓐ Ⓑ Ⓒ Ⓓ
176. Ⓐ Ⓑ Ⓒ Ⓓ	189. Ⓐ Ⓑ Ⓒ Ⓓ	202. Ⓐ Ⓑ Ⓒ Ⓓ	215. Ⓐ Ⓑ Ⓒ Ⓓ	228. Ⓐ Ⓑ Ⓒ Ⓓ
177. Ⓐ Ⓑ Ⓒ Ⓓ	190. Ⓐ Ⓑ Ⓒ Ⓓ	203. Ⓐ Ⓑ Ⓒ Ⓓ	216. Ⓐ Ⓑ Ⓒ Ⓓ	229. Ⓐ Ⓑ Ⓒ Ⓓ
178. Ⓐ Ⓑ Ⓒ Ⓓ	191. Ⓐ Ⓑ Ⓒ Ⓓ	204. Ⓐ Ⓑ Ⓒ Ⓓ	217. Ⓐ Ⓑ Ⓒ Ⓓ	230. Ⓐ Ⓑ Ⓒ Ⓓ
179. Ⓐ Ⓑ Ⓒ Ⓓ	192. Ⓐ Ⓑ Ⓒ Ⓓ	205. Ⓐ Ⓑ Ⓒ Ⓓ	218. Ⓐ Ⓑ Ⓒ Ⓓ	231. Ⓐ Ⓑ Ⓒ Ⓓ
180. Ⓐ Ⓑ Ⓒ Ⓓ	193. Ⓐ Ⓑ Ⓒ Ⓓ	206. Ⓐ Ⓑ Ⓒ Ⓓ	219. Ⓐ Ⓑ Ⓒ Ⓓ	232. Ⓐ Ⓑ Ⓒ Ⓓ
181. Ⓐ Ⓑ Ⓒ Ⓓ	194. Ⓐ Ⓑ Ⓒ Ⓓ	207. Ⓐ Ⓑ Ⓒ Ⓓ	220. Ⓐ Ⓑ Ⓒ Ⓓ	233. Ⓐ Ⓑ Ⓒ Ⓓ
182. Ⓐ Ⓑ Ⓒ Ⓓ	195. Ⓐ Ⓑ Ⓒ Ⓓ	208. Ⓐ Ⓑ Ⓒ Ⓓ	221. Ⓐ Ⓑ Ⓒ Ⓓ	234. Ⓐ Ⓑ Ⓒ Ⓓ
183. Ⓐ Ⓑ Ⓒ Ⓓ	196. Ⓐ Ⓑ Ⓒ Ⓓ	209. Ⓐ Ⓑ Ⓒ Ⓓ	222. Ⓐ Ⓑ Ⓒ Ⓓ	235. Ⓐ Ⓑ Ⓒ Ⓓ
184. Ⓐ Ⓑ Ⓒ Ⓓ	197. Ⓐ Ⓑ Ⓒ Ⓓ	210. Ⓐ Ⓑ Ⓒ Ⓓ	223. Ⓐ Ⓑ Ⓒ Ⓓ	236. Ⓐ Ⓑ Ⓒ Ⓓ
185. Ⓐ Ⓑ Ⓒ Ⓓ	198. Ⓐ Ⓑ Ⓒ Ⓓ	211. Ⓐ Ⓑ Ⓒ Ⓓ	224. Ⓐ Ⓑ Ⓒ Ⓓ	237. Ⓐ Ⓑ Ⓒ Ⓓ
186. Ⓐ Ⓑ Ⓒ Ⓓ	199. Ⓐ Ⓑ Ⓒ Ⓓ	212. Ⓐ Ⓑ Ⓒ Ⓓ	225. Ⓐ Ⓑ Ⓒ Ⓓ	238. Ⓐ Ⓑ Ⓒ Ⓓ
187. Ⓐ Ⓑ Ⓒ Ⓓ	200. Ⓐ Ⓑ Ⓒ Ⓓ	213. Ⓐ Ⓑ Ⓒ Ⓓ	226. Ⓐ Ⓑ Ⓒ Ⓓ	

Language

239. Ⓐ Ⓑ Ⓒ Ⓓ	251. Ⓐ Ⓑ Ⓒ Ⓓ	263. Ⓐ Ⓑ Ⓒ Ⓓ	275. Ⓐ Ⓑ Ⓒ Ⓓ	287. Ⓐ Ⓑ Ⓒ Ⓓ
240. Ⓐ Ⓑ Ⓒ Ⓓ	252. Ⓐ Ⓑ Ⓒ Ⓓ	264. Ⓐ Ⓑ Ⓒ Ⓓ	276. Ⓐ Ⓑ Ⓒ Ⓓ	288. Ⓐ Ⓑ Ⓒ Ⓓ
241. Ⓐ Ⓑ Ⓒ Ⓓ	253. Ⓐ Ⓑ Ⓒ Ⓓ	265. Ⓐ Ⓑ Ⓒ Ⓓ	277. Ⓐ Ⓑ Ⓒ Ⓓ	289. Ⓐ Ⓑ Ⓒ Ⓓ
242. Ⓐ Ⓑ Ⓒ Ⓓ	254. Ⓐ Ⓑ Ⓒ Ⓓ	266. Ⓐ Ⓑ Ⓒ Ⓓ	278. Ⓐ Ⓑ Ⓒ Ⓓ	290. Ⓐ Ⓑ Ⓒ Ⓓ
243. Ⓐ Ⓑ Ⓒ Ⓓ	255. Ⓐ Ⓑ Ⓒ Ⓓ	267. Ⓐ Ⓑ Ⓒ Ⓓ	279. Ⓐ Ⓑ Ⓒ Ⓓ	291. Ⓐ Ⓑ Ⓒ Ⓓ
244. Ⓐ Ⓑ Ⓒ Ⓓ	256. Ⓐ Ⓑ Ⓒ Ⓓ	268. Ⓐ Ⓑ Ⓒ Ⓓ	280. Ⓐ Ⓑ Ⓒ Ⓓ	292. Ⓐ Ⓑ Ⓒ Ⓓ
245. Ⓐ Ⓑ Ⓒ Ⓓ	257. Ⓐ Ⓑ Ⓒ Ⓓ	269. Ⓐ Ⓑ Ⓒ Ⓓ	281. Ⓐ Ⓑ Ⓒ Ⓓ	293. Ⓐ Ⓑ Ⓒ Ⓓ
246. Ⓐ Ⓑ Ⓒ Ⓓ	258. Ⓐ Ⓑ Ⓒ Ⓓ	270. Ⓐ Ⓑ Ⓒ Ⓓ	282. Ⓐ Ⓑ Ⓒ Ⓓ	294. Ⓐ Ⓑ Ⓒ Ⓓ
247. Ⓐ Ⓑ Ⓒ Ⓓ	259. Ⓐ Ⓑ Ⓒ Ⓓ	271. Ⓐ Ⓑ Ⓒ Ⓓ	283. Ⓐ Ⓑ Ⓒ Ⓓ	295. Ⓐ Ⓑ Ⓒ Ⓓ
248. Ⓐ Ⓑ Ⓒ Ⓓ	260. Ⓐ Ⓑ Ⓒ Ⓓ	272. Ⓐ Ⓑ Ⓒ Ⓓ	284. Ⓐ Ⓑ Ⓒ Ⓓ	296. Ⓐ Ⓑ Ⓒ Ⓓ
249. Ⓐ Ⓑ Ⓒ Ⓓ	261. Ⓐ Ⓑ Ⓒ Ⓓ	273. Ⓐ Ⓑ Ⓒ Ⓓ	285. Ⓐ Ⓑ Ⓒ Ⓓ	297. Ⓐ Ⓑ Ⓒ Ⓓ
250. Ⓐ Ⓑ Ⓒ Ⓓ	262. Ⓐ Ⓑ Ⓒ Ⓓ	274. Ⓐ Ⓑ Ⓒ Ⓓ	286. Ⓐ Ⓑ Ⓒ Ⓓ	298. Ⓐ Ⓑ Ⓒ Ⓓ

ANSWER SHEETS: HSPT® DIAGNOSTIC TEST

VERBAL SKILLS

60 Questions—16 Minutes

Turn to the Verbal Skills section of your answer sheet to answer the questions in this section.

Directions: This test measures your performance on reasoning tasks involving the use of words. This ability is related to performance in language, reading, and social studies-related tasks.

Mark the answer you think is best for each problem.

1. Brown is to dirt as blue is to
   A. tree.
   B. sky.
   C. cloud.
   D. black.

2. Stove is to cook as bed is to
   A. run.
   B. sheet.
   C. sleep.
   D. laugh.

3. Glass is to window as wall is to
   A. house.
   B. beach.
   C. winter.
   D. car.

4. First is to last as beginning is to
   A. entrance.
   B. question.
   C. cup.
   D. end.

5. Dirty is to clean as interested is to
   A. bored.
   B. certain.
   C. silly.
   D. funny.

6. Hair is to head as leaves are to
   A. grow.
   B. green.
   C. tree.
   D. grass.

7. Finger is to hand as toe is to
   A. foot.
   B. nail.
   C. skin.
   D. knuckle.

8. Elevator is to lift as scale is to
   A. pound.
   B. machine.
   C. needle.
   D. weigh.

9. Bouquet is to vase as ice cube is to
   A. cold.
   B. bottle.
   C. tray.
   D. water.

10. Desk is to chair as jacket is to
    A. tie.
    B. pants.
    C. torso.
    D. elegant.

11. Bill is taller than Ingrid. Ingrid is taller than Charles. Charles is taller than Bill. If the first two statements are true, the third is

    A. true.

    B. false.

    C. uncertain.

12. The red car has a black roof. The blue car has a blue roof. All the cars are just one color. If the first two statements are true, the third is

    A. true.

    B. false.

    C. uncertain.

13. Alan has more books than Desmond. Liara has fewer books than Desmond. Alan has more books than Liara. If the first two statements are true, the third is

    A. true.

    B. false.

    C. uncertain.

14. Gerald has blond hair. Suzanne has blond hair. All the kids in Gerald's class have blond hair. If the first two statements are true, the third is

    A. true.

    B. false.

    C. uncertain.

15. All the vegetables in the soup are green. All the fruit in the salad is red. All the vegetables and fruit in the meal are green or red. If the first two statements are true, the third is

    A. true.

    B. false.

    C. uncertain.

16. Miles runs faster than Bea. Bea runs faster than Clarence. Miles runs faster than Clarence. If the first two statements are true, the third is

    A. true.

    B. false.

    C. uncertain.

17. A computer is more expensive than a chair. A chair is less expensive than an oven. A computer is more expensive than an oven. If the first two statements are true, the third is

    A. true.

    B. false.

    C. uncertain.

18. Grace ate more strawberries than Anna. Anna ate as many strawberries as Patrice. Grace ate more strawberries than Patrice. If the first two statements are true, the third is

    A. true.

    B. false.

    C. uncertain.

19. Dogs live longer than mosquitoes. Elephants live longer than dogs. Elephants live longer than mosquitoes. If the first two statements are true, the third is

    A. true.

    B. false.

    C. uncertain.

20. Shirley got a better grade on the math test than Yuri. Yuri got a better grade on the English test than Barry. Shirley got a better grade on the math test than Barry. If the first two statements are true, the third is

    A. true.

    B. false.

    C. uncertain.

21. Pablo is hungrier than Jann. Jann is as hungry as Kira. Kira is as hungry as Pablo. If the first two statements are true, the third is

    A. true.

    B. false.

    C. uncertain.

22. The brown horse is bigger than the white horse. The grey horse is bigger than the brown horse. The grey horse is smaller than the white horse. If the first two statements are true, the third is

    A. true.

    B. false.

    C. uncertain.

23. Which word does *not* belong with the others?

    A. Hammer

    B. Screwdriver

    C. Basket

    D. Wrench

24. Which word does *not* belong with the others?

    A. Watch

    B. Sing

    C. Talk

    D. Whisper

25. Which word does *not* belong with the others?

    A. Hopeful

    B. Perspective

    C. Positive

    D. Optimistic

26. Which word does *not* belong with the others?

    A. Cello

    B. Violin

    C. Guitar

    D. Trumpet

27. Which word does *not* belong with the others?

    A. Run

    B. Leap

    C. Sit

    D. Stroll

28. Which word does *not* belong with the others?

    A. Eraser

    B. Marker

    C. Pen

    D. Paint brush

29. Which word does *not* belong with the others?

    A. Earth

    B. Moon

    C. Venus

    D. Jupiter

30. Which word does *not* belong with the others?

    A. Oven

    B. Blender

    C. Refrigerator

    D. Television

31. Which word does *not* belong with the others?

    A. Milk

    B. Ham

    C. Butter

    D. Ice cream

32. Which word does *not* belong with the others?

    A. Snake

    B. Squirrel

    C. Mouse

    D. Rat

33. Which word does *not* belong with the others?

    A. Mustard

    B. Pepper

    C. Salsa

    D. Ketchup

34. Which word does *not* belong with the others?

    A. Florida

    B. Michigan

    C. New York

    D. Los Angeles

35. Which word does *not* belong with the others?

    A. Dress

    B. Sock

    C. Wallet

    D. Necklace

36. Which word does *not* belong with the others?

    A. Handlebars

    B. Seat

    C. Bicycle

    D. Wheels

37. Which word does *not* belong with the others?

    A. Dresser

    B. Clothing

    C. Suitcase

    D. Wardrobe

38. Which word does *not* belong with the others?

    A. Bulldozer

    B. Dump truck

    C. Backhoe

    D. Bus

39. An *artificial* tree is

    A. new.

    B. beautiful.

    C. natural.

    D. fake.

40. An *audible* hum is

    A. heard.

    B. quiet.

    C. melodic.

    D. unpleasant.

41. An *elementary* understanding is

    A. educational.

    B. basic.

    C. complex.

    D. perfect.

42. An *absurd* excuse is

    A. convincing.

    B. silly.

    C. weak.

    D. tired.

43. A *pungent* odor is

    A. strong.

    B. lovely.

    C. different.

    D. constant.

44. A *gradual* change is

    A. necessary.

    B. permanent.

    C. sudden.

    D. slow.

45. A *hilarious* story is

    A. troubling.

    B. long.

    C. dull.

    D. funny.

46. An *ignorant* opinion is

    A. smart.

    B. created.

    C. uninformed.

    D. popular.

47. A *jubilant* reaction is

    A. sad.

    B. controlled.

    C. thrilled.

    D. cruel.

48. A *sinister* plot is

    A. careful.

    B. evil.

    C. original.

    D. stylish.

49. A *misplaced* item is

    A. broken.

    B. simple.

    C. close.

    D. lost.

50. A *lucid* idea is

    A. clear.

    B. foolish.

    C. stupid.

    D. flawed.

51. A *humongous* hill is

    A. cluttered.

    B. dusty.

    C. huge.

    D. average.

52. Lavish means the *opposite* of

    A. plain.

    B. elegant.

    C. profitable.

    D. attractive.

53. Partial means the *opposite* of

    A. open.

    B. orderly.

    C. whole.

    D. normal.

54. Deteriorate means the *opposite* of

    A. liken.

    B. expect.

    C. improve.

    D. oppose.

55. Flair means the *opposite* of

    A. secret.

    B. unjust.

    C. darkness.

    D. inability.

56. Squander means the *opposite* of

    A. undo.

    B. save.

    C. approve.

    D. proceed.

57. Accurate means the *opposite* of

    A. mistaken.

    B. expected.

    C. useful.

    D. absent.

58. Escalate means the *opposite* of

    A. punctual.

    B. arise.

    C. obey.

    D. decrease.

59. Renounce means the *opposite* of

    A. discard.

    B. obvious.

    C. accept.

    D. redo.

60. Tumult means the *opposite* of

    A. calm.

    B. wild.

    C. turn.

    D. trouble.

QUANTITATIVE SKILLS

52 Questions—30 Minutes

Turn to the Quantitative Skills section of your answer sheet to answer the questions in this section.

> **Directions:** This test measures the ability to perform reasoning problems involving numbers and quantities. This ability is related to performance in mathematics, sciences, and other areas dealing with numbers.
>
> Mark the answer you think is best for each problem.

61. Look at this series: _____, 6, 10, 14, 18, ...
    What number should come first?

    A. 0

    B. 2

    C. 4

    D. 10

62. What number is 8 less than 3 cubed?

    A. 1

    B. 17

    C. 19

    D. 27

63. What is the sum of four squared and three cubed?

    A. 16

    B. 17

    C. 27

    D. 43

64. Look at this series: QXR SXT UXV _____ YXZ.
    What letter group should fill the blank in the middle of the series?

    A. WXV

    B. WXZ

    C. WXX

    D. WXY

65. Examine A, B, and C. Find the best answer.

    A. A and B each has more squares than C.

    B. A and C have the same number of squares.

    C. C has more squares than B.

    D. B and C each has fewer squares than A.

66. What number is twice $\frac{2}{3}$ of 24?

    A. 8

    B. 16

    C. 18

    D. 32

67. Look at this series: 81, 27, 9, 3, ...
    What number should come next?

    A. −3

    B. 0

    C. $\frac{1}{3}$

    D. 1

HSPT® DIAGNOSTIC TEST

68. Look at this series: 202, 200, 196, 190, 182, ...
What number should come next?

A. 170

B. 172

C. 176

D. 180

69. Examine A, B, and C. Choose the best answer.

    A. 8^2

    B. 9×7

    C. 67

A. C is less than A.

B. A, B, and C are all equal.

C. A is greater than B.

D. B is greater than A and C.

70. Examine A, B, and C. Choose the best answer.

A. The area of A and the area of C are equal, and the area of B is less than the area of C.

B. The area of C is less than the area of B, and the area of B is less than the area of A.

C. The area of C is less than the area of B, and the area of A is less than the area of B.

D. A, B, and C all have the same area.

71. Look at this series: A, B, A, BB, A, BBB, ...
What term should come next?

A. A

B. AA

C. BB

D. BBBB

72. Look at this series:
ARD, DAR, RDA, ARD, ...
What term should come next?

A. ARD

B. DAR

C. RAD

D. RDA

73. What number is 40% of the sum of 2.1 and 1.9?

A. 1.6

B. 4.0

C. 4.4

D. 16

74. Examine A, B, and C. Choose the best answer.

A. $(7 - 3)^2$

B. $7^2 - 3^2$

C. $(3 - 7)^2$

A. A = B and C < A

B. A = B = C

C. A = C and A < B

D. C < A < B

75. The product of 2 and what number, when subtracted from 1, leaves 5?

A. −3

B. −2

C. 6

D. 8

76. Look at this series: Z, YY, X, WW, V, ...
What term should come next?

A. T

B. TT

C. U

D. UU

77. Look at this series: 3, 4, 9, 6, 27, _____, 81, 10.
What term should fill in the blank?

A. 8

B. 18

C. 29

D. 36

78. Examine the square and find the best answer.

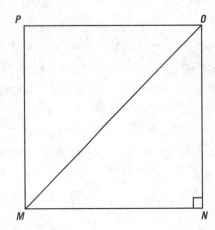

A. $\overline{MN}$ is equal to $\overline{MO}$.

B. $\overline{MO}$ minus $\overline{MN}$ is equal to $\overline{ON}$.

C. ∠OMP is greater than ∠ONM.

D. $\overline{MO}$ is greater than $\overline{MP}$.

79. Consider the diagram below and choose the best answer.

A. The sum of the measures of angles *AOB* and *DOC* is greater than the measure of angle *BOC*.

B. The sum of the measures of angles *DOC* and *COP* is greater than the sum of the measures of angles *AOB* and *POB*.

C. Angles *AOP* and *DOP* have the same measure.

D. The sum of the measures of angles *POC* and *COD* is less than 90 degrees.

80. Examine A, B, and C. Choose the best answer.

   A. 3^4

   B. 4^3

   C. 3×4

   A. A = C and B < A

   B. A = B = C

   C. C < B and B = A

   D. C < B and B < A

81. Look at this series: 28, 23, 18, 13, ...
What number should come next?

   A. 1

   B. 3

   C. 6

   D. 8

82. Examine A, B, and C. Choose the best answer.

   A. 6×10^2

   B. $\dfrac{6}{10}$

   C. 0.60

   A. B is equal to C

   B. A is less than B

   C. C is greater than A and B

   D. B is greater than A

83. Look at this series: $\dfrac{3}{4}$, $\dfrac{6}{16}$, $\dfrac{12}{64}$, ———, $\dfrac{48}{1024}$.

What term should fill in the blank?

   A. $\dfrac{24}{256}$

   B. $\dfrac{48}{256}$

   C. $\dfrac{24}{128}$

   D. $\dfrac{48}{128}$

84. One-third of what number leaves two less than $\dfrac{2}{3}$ of that number?

   A. $\dfrac{1}{3}$

   B. $\dfrac{2}{3}$

   C. 2

   D. 6

85. Look at the series: D2, G10, J50, ...
What term should come next?

   A. K500

   B. L60

   C. M100

   D. M250

86. Consider the following diagram in which the circle is centered at *O* and choose the best answer.

A. $\overline{BO}$ and $\overline{BA}$ have the same length.

B. $\overline{AO}$ is longer than $\overline{CO}$.

C. $\overline{BC}$ is longer than $\overline{EF}$.

D. The sum of the lengths of *AB* and *AO* is equal to the length of *BC*.

87. Look at the series: CY, DX, EW, ...

What term should come next?

A. FU

B. FV

C. GV

D. GY

88. One-fourth the sum of 1 and what number is one-half the sum of 2 and $\frac{1}{2}$?

A. $\frac{1}{5}$

B. $\frac{1}{4}$

C. 4

D. 5

89. Look at this series: 3, 4, 0, 8, −3, 16, ...
What two numbers should come next?

A. −6, 20

B. −6, 32

C. 0, 32

D. 3, 28

90. Examine A, B, and C. Choose the best answer.

A. 200% of 0.1

B. 50% of 1

C. 25% of 10

A. A > B and B = C

B. A = B and B < C

C. A < B and B < C

D. A > B and B > C

91. Examine figures A, B, and C. Choose the best answer.

A. The area of A equals the area of C, and the area of B is greater than the area of A.

B. The area of A is less than the area of B, and the area of B is less than the area of C.

C. The area of B is less than the area of C, and the area of C is less than the area of A.

D. A, B, and C all have the same area.

92. Look at this series: 0.5J, 1.2M, 1.9P, 2.6S, ...
What term should come next?

A. 3.1T

B. 3.3U

C. 3.3V

D. U3.3

93. Three-fourths of what number is $\frac{4}{3}$?

A. $\frac{1}{4}$

B. $\frac{9}{16}$

C. $\frac{3}{4}$

D. $\frac{16}{9}$

94. Look at this series: 7, 8, 10, 11, 13, 14, ...
What number should come next?

A. 14

B. 16

C. 17

D. 19

95. Examine A, B, and C. Choose the best answer.

A. Four times the square of 4

B. Half the cube of 4

C. Twice the cube of 3

A. A = B and B < C

B. A > C and C > B

C. C > B and B > A

D. A = B = C

96. Look at this series: 0.04, 0.20, 1, _____, _____,
125. What terms should fill in the two blanks?

A. 2, 10

B. 5, 25

C. 5, 50

D. 6, 30

97. Twice the sum of 4 and what number is the same as 4 times that number?

A. 2

B. 4

C. 6

D. 8

98. Examine A, B, and C. Choose the best answer.

A. $6(4 + 2)$

B. $(4 + 2)^2$

C. $(6 \times 4) + 2$

A. C is greater than B.

B. C is less than A and B.

C. A is less than B.

D. A, B, and C are all equal.

99. Look at this series: $1, \frac{3}{2}, \frac{5}{3}, \frac{7}{4}, \ldots$

What two terms should come next?

A. $\frac{9}{5}, \frac{11}{6}$

B. $\frac{8}{5}, \frac{9}{6}$

C. $\frac{8}{6}, \frac{9}{7}$

D. $\frac{10}{5}, \frac{14}{6}$

100. Examine A, B, and C. Choose the best answer.

A. 0.03×10^3

B. 0.003×10^4

C. 0.3×10^2

A. A = B = C

B. A < B < C

C. A = B and C > B

D. B > C and A > B

101. Look at this series: 2, 4, 7, 14, 17, 34, ...
What number should come next?

    A. 35

    B. 36

    C. 37

    D. 39

102. One-half of what number equals the product of 4 and that number?

    A. 0

    B. $\frac{1}{8}$

    C. $\frac{2}{3}$

    D. $\frac{3}{2}$

103. Examine A, B, and C. Choose the best answer.

    A.

    B.
    C.

    A. A, B, and C all have the same number of vertices.

    B. C and B have the same number of edges.

    C. A has two more edges than B.

    D. The number of vertices A has is equal to the sum of the number of vertices B and C have.

104. Look at this series: 3D, E8, 3F, G8, _____, _____, ...
What two terms should come next?

    A. 3H, I8

    B. H3, 8I

    C. H8, 3I

    D. 3I, J8

105. Look at this series: $\frac{2}{27}, \frac{3}{4}, \frac{2}{9}, \frac{4}{5}, \frac{2}{3}, \frac{5}{6}, \cdots$
What term should come next?

    A. $\frac{6}{7}$

    B. $\frac{7}{8}$

    C. 2

    D. 6

106. The sum of 6 and what number equals the square of the sum of 2 and 4?

    A. 6

    B. 14

    C. 30

    D. 32

107. Assume that $0 < z < 1$. Examine A, B, and C. Choose the best answer.

    A. $2z$

    B. z^2

    C. z^3

    A. $C < B < A$

    B. $A < B < C$

    C. $A < C < B$

    D. $B > A$ and $B > C$

108. Look at this series: 2, CC, 4, CCCC, 6, _____, ...
What term should come next?

    A. CCCCCCCC

    B. CCCCCC

    C. 8

    D. 12

109. Three less than what number equals one-half the square of 4?

   A. 5

   B. 7

   C. 11

   D. 19

110. Examine A, B, and C. Choose the best answer.

   A. $2 \div \dfrac{1}{10} \div 5$

   B. $2 \div \left(\dfrac{1}{10} \div 5\right)$

   C. $\left(2 \div \dfrac{1}{10}\right) \div 5$

   A. A = B = C

   B. A < B and B < C

   C. A < C and C < B

   D. A = C and A < B

111. Look at this series: 1.2, 2.1, 1.8, 2.7, 2.4, ... What two terms should come next?

   A. 2.1, 3.0

   B. 2.7, 1.8

   C. 2.9, 2.6

   D. 3.3, 3.0

112. The sum of twice a number and three times that number is five less than the square of 10. What is the number?

   A. 3

   B. 19

   C. 95

   D. 105

READING

62 Questions—25 Minutes

Comprehension

Turn to the Reading Comprehension section of your answer sheet to answer the questions in this section.

Directions: Read each passage carefully. Then, mark the answer you think is best for each question.

Questions 113–122 refer to the following passage.

In order to better understand what it is that makes people purchase particular items or be drawn to certain products, the business world conducts psychological research about buyer behavior. Researchers want to learn as much as they can about the actions that people take when they are in the purchasing process.
Line Much of market research revolves around uncovering the factors that influence how and why people make
5 purchasing decisions.

One of the ways in which companies conduct market research is through the use of surveys. A survey is a questionnaire that asks respondents for information, including their demographic characteristics. A survey might ask if a person is male or female, for instance. It might also ask for the individual's approximate age, income level, marital information, the number of persons living in the household, and the number
10 of children living at home. All of this information gives the company administering the survey a general profile or picture of the background of the person responding.

Then, depending on the type of products or services that the company specializes in, a survey will typically ask respondents about their behavioral patterns in a certain area. For example, a company that produces fabric softener might ask survey respondents if they own a washing machine or not, how often
15 they do the laundry, how many loads per week they do, or perhaps whether or not they use fabric softener.

As another example, a fast-food company might be interested in the types of food that people most frequently buy when they go through a drive-through. Or, they might ask if respondents prefer sandwiches with chicken or beef. They might inquire about what kinds of salad dressing a person eats most frequently.

All of this information is collected so that companies can track the behavior of buyers. Businesses want
20 to know about respondents' demographic characteristics in order to build a profile of the kind of person who most frequently buys their products or shops at their stores. If companies can track how their buyers make decisions, they can gain a much stronger understanding of the psychological motivations that drive people's purchases. They can also tailor their advertisements in order to attract the attention of their target customers by designing their ads to have the greatest appeal for potential buyers.

25 Market research involves more than administering questionnaires and surveys, however. Companies and corporate researchers can also investigate what colors and designs people find most appealing in product packaging. They can further inquire about the types of advertising and marketing messages that buyers are most likely to remember and respond to as they make their purchasing decisions.

Companies can also hold focus groups in which they ask groups of people about their preferences, opinions, or responses concerning different types of products—from food to cleaning supplies to electronics. Businesses collect the responses of these focus groups and use the data to construct advertisements and marketing campaigns in ways that are designed to be appealing, based on the focus groups' results. Though not as effective as surveys, focus groups are still a popular way to conduct market research.

Sometimes market researchers even ask buyers to test new products. They might ask a subject to use a certain new shampoo. The results of consumer tests such as these can influence whether a new product ever actually makes it onto the shelves for people to buy or not.

113. What is the passage mainly about?

   A. It focuses on how people make decisions concerning a company's products.

   B. It mainly discusses how advertisers test new products.

   C. It explains the various ways that companies conduct market research.

   D. It discusses people's preferences concerning their shopping decisions.

114. According to the passage, what is one of the main ways that companies collect market research information?

   A. Through the use of surveys

   B. Through the use of secret shoppers

   C. Through the use of role playing

   D. Through the use of psychological evaluations

115. As used in the passage, the word *demographic* in paragraph 2 most nearly means

   A. superior.

   B. problematic.

   C. likable.

   D. group.

116. Why does the author mention fabric softener in paragraph 3?

   A. To describe how many consumers make decisions concerning purchases

   B. To give an example of a product that might be the subject of market research

   C. To discuss the product that is the most common subject of market research

   D. To explain why buyers like the product based on historical market research

117. According to the passage, why do market research surveys collect demographic information?

   A. To be able to track customers' purchases with the company over time

   B. To keep careful records in a database so that the company can sell this information

   C. To compile information about people most likely to purchase the company's products

   D. To be able to tell why purchasers like certain colors better than other colors

118. According to the passage, companies hold focus groups to

   A. develop ideas for new products.

   B. collect data for constructing advertising campaigns.

   C. influence the people in the groups to buy new products.

   D. find out which products are the most marketable.

119. We can infer from the information provided in the passage that the author would most likely characterize market research as

   A. useful.

   B. invasive.

   C. untrustworthy.

   D. ingenious.

120. Which of the following pieces of information would make the discussion of product testing in the final paragraph clearer and more focused?

   A. How market researchers asked subjects to try the new shampoo

   B. The specific name of the new shampoo

   C. How many people the market researchers asked to try the new shampoo

   D. How market researchers follow up with a subject who uses the new shampoo

121. Based on the information provided in the passage, we can predict that readers who decide to become involved in market research will

   A. find the process of product testing exciting.

   B. make better informed decisions about the products they buy.

   C. help companies decide how to market their products.

   D. become mistrustful of the ways that products are marketed.

122. According to the passage, compared to surveys, focus groups are

   A. more popular forms of market research.

   B. completely useless forms of market research.

   C. superior forms of market research.

   D. less effective forms of market research.

Questions 123–132 refer to the following passage.

Whenever we hear the name of Napoleon mentioned, or see it printed in a book, it is usually in connection with a hard-fought victory on the battlefield. He certainly spent most of his life in the camp, and enjoyed the society of soldiers more than that of courtiers. The thunder of guns, the charge of cavalry, and the

Line flash of bayonets as they glittered in the sun, appealed to him with much the same force as music to more
5 ordinary folk. Indeed, he himself tells us that "the cries of the dying, the tears of the hopeless, surrounded my cradle from the moment of my birth."

We are apt to forget that this mighty conqueror, whom Carlyle calls "our last great man," had a childhood at all. He was born ... on the 15th August 1769 to be exact, in the little town of Ajaccio, the capital of picturesque Corsica. This miniature island rises a bold tree-covered rock in the blue waters of the Medi-
10 terranean, fifty miles west of the coast of Italy. It had been sold to France by the Republic of Genoa the previous year, but the inhabitants had fought for their independence with praiseworthy determination. Then civil war broke out, and the struggle finally ended three months before the birth of the boy who was to become the ruler of the conquering nation. The Corsicans had their revenge in time, although in a way very different from what they could have expected.

15 Letizia Bonaparte, Napoleon's mother, was as beautiful as she was energetic, and her famous son never allowed anyone to speak ill of her. "My excellent mother," said he, not long before his death, "is a woman of courage and of great talent ... she is capable of doing everything for me," and he added that the high position which he attained was due largely to the careful way in which she brought him up.

Napoleon was Letizia's fourth child, two having died in infancy, while Joseph, the surviving son, was
20 still unable to toddle when the latest addition to the family was in his cradle. His father was a happy-go-lucky kind of man of good ancestry, a lawyer by profession, who on the landing of the French had resigned the pen for the sword. He enlisted in the army raised by Pascal Paoli to defend the island, for the Corsicans were then a very warlike people and much sought after as soldiers, and it is supposed by some that he acted as Paoli's secretary. It is certain that the patriot showed him marked favor, which was never repaid.

—Excerpt from *The Story of Napoleon* by Harold F. B. Wheeler

123. The main contrast in the passage is between

  A. Napoleon's adult life and the person he was in his personal life.

  B. Napoleon's mother and Napoleon's father.

  C. what Napoleon said about his mother and how he actually treated her.

  D. the soldiers Napoleon commanded and the people in his family.

124. According to the passage, how many miles was Corsica from the west coast of Italy?

  A. 10

  B. 20

  C. 40

  D. 50

125. The passage states that Corsica was formerly the property of

  A. Ajaccio.

  B. the Republic of Genoa.

  C. France.

  D. Carlyle.

126. According to the passage, Napoleon's victories on the battlefield were generally

  A. easily won.

  B. difficult to achieve.

  C. few and far between.

  D. impossible to count.

127. In the last sentence of the final paragraph, "It is certain that the patriot showed him marked favor, which was never repaid," the word *patriot* refers to

  A. Napoleon's father.

  B. Napoleon Bonaparte.

  C. Letizia Bonaparte.

  D. Pascal Paoli.

128. As used in the passage, the word *apt* in paragraph 2 most nearly means:

  A. appropriate.

  B. clever.

  C. quick.

  D. right.

129. Based on the information provided in the passage, we can infer that the author would most likely compare Napoleon to

  A. his mother.

  B. his brother.

  C. other Corsicans.

  D. Carlyle.

130. Based on the information provided in the passage, what is the most likely explanation why Napoleon misrepresented his childhood?

  A. He wanted to present the idea that he was always a fierce warrior.

  B. He was embarrassed about his mother and father.

  C. He could not remember what his childhood was actually like.

  D. He was a weak soldier and wanted his enemies to think he was stronger than he was.

131. Based on the information provided in the passage, the "high position" mentioned in paragraph 3 most likely refers to a

  A. soldier.

  B. ruler.

  C. king.

  D. secretary.

132. The main idea of the passage is

  A. Napoleon was his parents' fourth child, and two of his siblings died in infancy.

  B. the years before Napoleon became a conqueror are not usually discussed.

  C. Napoleon spent most of his life on the battle-field where he won many battles.

  D. Napoleon was born on August 15, 1769, in the town of Ajaccio.

Questions 133–142 refer to the following passage.

Newspapers were once thought to have been first published in England in 1583 when Queen Elizabeth was monarch. What was believed to have been the first newspaper was called the *English Mercurie*, published in London by a man named Christopher Barker. However, this paper was actually a hoax perpetrated 200

Line years later by Philip Yorke and Thomas Birch. They submitted the newspaper they printed up to the Brit-
5   ish Museum in 1766, and it was soon accepted as historical fact. Ironically, the newspaper's purpose was to serve as a counterpoint to false reports!

The first real publications to have some sort of news-reporting purpose actually appeared in England in the 1600s. However, the main purpose of these papers was not to report current events: they were actually owned by various political parties, and these papers were generally intent on stimulating loyalty to a

10 particular political party or stirring outage against the opposing party.

While these papers varied quite a bit in the quality of their writing, there were some unusual consistencies when it came to their titles. References to Mercury and birds was an odd recurring theme in these titles, which included the *Scots Dove*, the *Parliament Kite*, the *Screech Owle*, the *Parliamentary Screech Owle*, *Mercurius Acheronticus*, *Mercurius Democritus*, and *Mercurius Mastix*. The implication was that

15 these papers reached the public with the latest news as quickly as a darting bird or an ancient Roman god best known for his incredible speed. Of course, in a modern age in which the latest news is released across the internet as soon as it occurs, these publications of more than 400 years ago were not nearly as on top of their times.

133. Which of the following is the best title for this passage?

A. "Mercury and Birds"

B. "The Speed of the Internet"

C. "The First 'Newspapers' in England"

D. "The Story of the *English Mercurie*"

134. The main purposes of England's first newspapers include

A. relaying current events.

B. discussing birds.

C. reporting on sporting events.

D. conveying political agendas.

135. The *English Mercurie* was unusual because it

A. discredited false reports.

B. was the first newspaper in England.

C. was not a real newspaper.

D. was accepted by the British Museum.

136. When the article says it is ironic that the purpose of the *English Mercurie* was to expose false stories, it is referring to the fact that the *English Mercurie*

A. was not published regularly.

B. exposed many false stories.

C. was never printed at all.

D. was a hoax.

137. Newspapers published during the 1600s are described as

A. inconsistent in quality.

B. entirely fake.

C. quickly delivered.

D. brilliantly written.

138. Of the following common characteristics of early English newspapers, the one that is not mentioned is

A. a title that references birds.

B. a title that references Mercury.

C. the presence of a political agenda.

D. the refusal to publish political attacks.

139. Based on how it's used in paragraph 1 of the passage, the word *perpetrated* most nearly means

A. committed.

B. continued.

C. covered.

D. related.

140. Based on the information provided in the passage, we can conclude that

A. the author does not consider any of the newspapers discussed in the passage to be proper newspapers.

B. the author believes that modern newspapers should be more like the ones discussed in the passage.

C. the author believes the internet is the only worthwhile place to obtain news today.

D. the author does not think there was any difference among the newspapers published during the 1600s.

141. We can infer from the information provided in the passage that the *English Mercurie* is like

A. a current events report on a television news channel.

B. a rare and precious jewel displayed in a museum.

C. a story that is too ridiculous to believe.

D. a man in a costume trying to convince people he is a monster.

142. According to the passage, which of the following words would have been least likely to be included in the title of a newspaper in 1600s England?

A. Eaglet

B. Falcon

C. Hen

D. Sparrow

HSPT® DIAGNOSTIC TEST

Questions 143–152 refer to the following passage.

Sound consists of three significant dimensions: speed, loudness, and frequency. Sound can travel through different media, such as air, for example. But it can also travel through water and even solids. After all, can you remember being inside a building but hearing a fire truck's siren outside? That is an example of how *Line* sound can travel through a solid. The sound travels through the solid matter of the building—its bricks 5 or limestone, for instance.

It can take sound longer to travel through liquids, and especially through solids, than it might take the same sound to travel through gases or the air. This explains why it sometimes seems as if you can hear a siren sooner when you are standing outside than you can when you are inside a building. This can also be what causes sounds to seem odd or modified when heard underwater.

10 Sound is made up of waves. This wave structure explains why the loudness of a sound can change as a person moves in relation to the sound. To go back to the siren example, as a fire truck drives closer to a building, the sound of its siren becomes louder. This increase in intensity has to do with the amplitude, or size, of the sound wave. As the fire truck moves away from the building, the sound of the siren becomes softer, since the listener is now farther away from the sound source.

15 Finally, the frequency of a sound makes the sound seem higher or lower in pitch. Only sounds that fall into a certain range are discernible by human hearing. That range is 20 to 20,000 hertz (Hz). Instrumental orchestras must tune before performing to make sure that their instruments are pitched at a specific frequency, so that the notes all match when the instruments play together. The tuning note that often sounds prior to an orchestra performance is an A. Usually, the frequency of this note is pitched right around 440 20 Hz. That is at the lower end of the frequency range that many human beings can hear.

143. What is the passage mainly about?

A. It focuses on how sound properties change because of position.

B. It discusses the properties associated with sound.

C. It explains ideas about why sounds become louder.

D. It talks generally about why pitches are used in certain ways for music.

144. As used in the passage, the word *media* in paragraph 1 most nearly means

A. substances.

B. artistic materials.

C. newspapers.

D. communication devices.

145. According to the passage, sound waves can take longer to travel through which of the following?

A. Air and gases

B. Liquids and solids

C. Air and liquids

D. Gases and solids

146. According to the passage, what causes an approaching fire truck's siren to first sound louder and then to become softer again?

A. The pitch of the siren as the truck moves past

B. The listener's location inside or outside a building

C. The frequency of the siren as the truck moves past

D. The proximity of the listener to the siren

147. Why does a siren seem to be heard sooner when a person is standing outside a building, according to the passage?

   A. The sound waves do not have to travel through the solid medium of a building.

   B. The sound waves do not have to travel through the liquid medium of a river.

   C. The person is physically more distant from the siren, so the siren is louder.

   D. The pitch of the siren sounds different to a listener outside the building.

148. Based on how it's used in the paragraph 2 of the passage, the word *modified* most nearly means

   A. changed.

   B. described.

   C. lost.

   D. clarified.

149. Based on how they're described in the passage, the way sound travels through a wall can best be compared to the way

   A. volume can be adjusted.

   B. clouds pass throughout the day.

   C. light travels through the atmosphere.

   D. liquid seeps through a cloth.

150. Based on the passage, we can say that a sound wave

   A. changes size as its source moves farther away.

   B. cannot be heard through solid material.

   C. is difficult to create in the right pitch.

   D. is more pleasant when heard from far away.

151. What is the author's purpose for discussing the musical note A in paragraph 4?

   A. To make the passage more interesting by including a reference to music

   B. To use it as an example of a sound at the lower end of sounds people can hear

   C. To illustrate how flawed human hearing can be

   D. To prove that certain animals have much better hearing than most people do

152. Based on the information in the passage, we can infer that compared to light, sound is more

   A. difficult to block.

   B. difficult to discern.

   C. common in everyday life.

   D. important to sense.

Vocabulary

Turn to the Vocabulary section of your answer sheet to answer the questions in this section.

> **Directions:** Choose the word that means the same or nearly the same as the underlined word.

153. an <u>articulate</u> speaker

   A. expressive

   B. boastful

   C. daring

   D. unusual

154. <u>curtail</u> the program

   A. begin

   B. appreciate

   C. enrich

   D. shorten

155. <u>lucrative</u> profession

   A. demanding

   B. profitable

   C. common

   D. exciting

156. great <u>elation</u>

   A. achievement

   B. joy

   C. interest

   D. appeal

157. a strong <u>adversary</u>

   A. effort

   B. support

   C. opponent

   D. attraction

158. <u>adjourn</u> the meeting

   A. discontinue

   B. organize

   C. direct

   D. schedule

159. effective <u>technique</u>

   A. discipline

   B. equipment

   C. instructor

   D. method

160. <u>amend</u> the rules

   A. create

   B. sketch

   C. change

   D. follow

161. <u>delete</u> the text

   A. enter

   B. write

   C. erase

   D. consider

162. a <u>sentimental</u> mood

   A. emotional

   B. bland

   C. normal

   D. serious

163. a <u>cordial</u> encounter

    A. brief

    B. friendly

    C. tense

    D. sudden

164. a <u>sluggish</u> movement

    A. boring

    B. quick

    C. easy

    D. slow

165. an <u>erroneous</u> explanation

    A. wrong

    B. unusual

    C. original

    D. timely

166. to <u>withhold</u> information

    A. reveal

    B. deny

    C. believe

    D. possess

167. a <u>frivolous</u> purchase

    A. necessary

    B. expensive

    C. silly

    D. smart

168. an <u>oppressive</u> government

    A. balanced

    B. fake

    C. controlling

    D. kind

169. a <u>valiant</u> decision

    A. foolish

    B. cowardly

    C. frightening

    D. brave

170. to <u>eliminate</u> waste

    A. expand

    B. remove

    C. revise

    D. create

171. a <u>lamentable</u> ending

    A. positive

    B. common

    C. final

    D. sad

172. a <u>slovenly</u> roommate

    A. neat

    B. punctual

    C. sloppy

    D. sleepy

173. a <u>wayward</u> kid

    A. naughty

    B. cute

    C. champion

    D. fast

174. a <u>vibrant</u> design

    A. dark

    B. bright

    C. unattractive

    D. gorgeous

MATHEMATICS

64 Questions—45 Minutes

Turn to the Mathematics Concepts section of your answer sheet to answer the questions in this section.

> **Directions:** Mark one answer—the answer you think is best—for each problem. You may use scratch paper when working on these problems.

175. Which number is fifty million thirty?

    A. 50,030

    B. 50,000,030

    C. 50,030,000

    D. 50,000,000,030

176. Complete the proportion: $\dfrac{5}{20} = \dfrac{\frac{1}{3}}{\Box}$

    A. $\dfrac{1}{4}$

    B. $\dfrac{3}{4}$

    C. $\dfrac{4}{3}$

    D. 4

177. Find the area of the triangle *ABC*:

    A. 28 square inches

    B. 42 square inches

    C. 56 square inches

    D. 84 square inches

178. To which of these is 0.05% equal?

    A. 0.0005

    B. $\dfrac{1}{200}$

    C. $\dfrac{1}{20}$

    D. 5

179. Fill in the blank with the appropriate symbol:

    $\dfrac{5}{8} \;\Box\; \dfrac{5}{9}$

    A. <

    B. >

    C. =

    D. ≡

180. The ratio of bathrooms to bedrooms in a mansion is 2:3. If there are 18 bedrooms, how many bathrooms are there?

    A. 9

    B. 12

    C. 15

    D. 21

181. Suppose a bag contains 7 tiles marked: A, X, K, B, E, E, M. If you select one tile from the bag without looking, what is the probability that you do *not* choose a vowel?

    A. $\dfrac{3}{7}$

    B. $\dfrac{4}{7}$

    C. 3

    D. 4

182. How many milliliters are in 5 liters?

    A. 5

    B. 500

    C. 1,000

    D. 5,000

183. Write 784 in expanded form, using exponents.

    A. $(7 \times 10^2) + (8 \times 10) + 4$

    B. $(7 \times 10^3) + (8 \times 10^2) + (4 \times 10)$

    C. $(7 \times 10^0) + (8 \times 10) + (4 \times 10)$

    D. None of the above

184. If *PQRS* is a parallelogram, what is the sum of the two topmost angles?

    A. 90

    B. 180

    C. 270

    D. 360

185. In the following expression, what is "3" called?

    $$(3x + 1)\,(x + 2)$$

    A. Coefficient

    B. Variable

    C. Expression

    D. Factor

186. A factory makes 200 cameras per day. How many days will it take the factory to make about 997 cameras?

    A. 5

    B. 11

    C. 53

    D. Not given

187. The ratio of 1 hour to 120 seconds is

    A. 6 to 24

    B. 18 to 1

    C. 30 to 1

    D. 120 to 1

188. Which is the shortest length?

    A. 90 millimeters

    B. 10 centimeters

    C. 10 inches

    D. 1.5 feet

189. What digit is in the ten thousandths place of the decimal 95,287.01364?

    A. 3

    B. 5

    C. 6

    D. 9

190. What is the mode of the data set 0, 0, 0, 1, 2, 3, 4?

    A. 0

    B. 1

    C. $1\frac{3}{7}$

    D. 2

191. A dog's toy box contains four tennis balls, five stuffed animals, three chew bones, and one rope. What is the probability that a dog chooses a tennis ball from the toy box?

    A. $\dfrac{1}{13}$

    B. $\dfrac{4}{13}$

    C. $\dfrac{5}{13}$

    D. $\dfrac{9}{13}$

192. Which of the following is a pair of reciprocals?

    A. $(12, -12)$

    B. $(0, 0)$

    C. $\left(3\dfrac{3}{4}, \dfrac{4}{15}\right)$

    D. $(5^2, 2^5)$

193. If a number is divisible by 12, it must also be divisible by which of the following?

    A. 6

    B. 10

    C. 18

    D. 24

194. What is the least common multiple of 12 and 18?

    A. 2

    B. 6

    C. 36

    D. 204

195. Compute:

$$4 \text{ hours } 12 \text{ minutes } 10 \text{ seconds}$$
$$- 1 \text{ hour } 58 \text{ minutes } 20 \text{ seconds}$$

    A. 2 hours 13 minutes 50 seconds

    B. 2 hours 47 minutes 30 seconds

    C. 3 hours 12 minutes 40 seconds

    D. 3 hours 46 minutes 10 seconds

196. What value of x makes this inequality true?

$$-3x > -1$$

    A. $\dfrac{1}{3}$

    B. 0

    C. 1

    D. 2

197. Fill in the box to make the statement true:

$$-1 - \square = 2$$

    A. −3

    B. −1

    C. 1

    D. 3

198. What is the circumference of this circle?

    A. 10π inches

    B. 20π inches

    C. 25π inches

    D. 100π inches

199. There are 60 minutes in one hour. To convert from hours to minutes, you would

    A. divide by 60.

    B. multiply by 60.

    C. subtract 60.

    D. add 60.

200. Which of these statements is false?

    A. $\dfrac{10 + 4}{2} = \dfrac{10}{2} + 4$

    B. $(4 + 6) - 2 = 4 + (6 - 2)$

    C. $\dfrac{3 \times 7}{4 \times 5} = \dfrac{3}{4} \times \dfrac{7}{5}$

    D. $5(8 - 2) = 5(8) - 5(2)$

201. There are 3 teaspoons in 1 tablespoon, and 8 tablespoons in 0.5 cup. How many teaspoons are in 1 cup?

    A. 16

    B. 24

    C. 48

    D. 64

202. Maria can paddle a kayak at a maximum speed of 8 miles per hour in still water. If she is paddling downstream with a current that has speed x miles per hour, what is her maximum speed?

   A. $8 + x$ miles per hour
   B. $8x$ miles per hour
   C. $8 - x$ miles per hour
   D. $x - 8$ miles per hour

203. How many sixths are in $6\frac{2}{3}$?

   A. $\frac{10}{9}$
   B. $\frac{26}{3}$
   C. 36
   D. 40

204. Which of these time durations does *not* equal the other three?

   A. 360 minutes
   B. 6 hours
   C. 2,160 seconds
   D. 0.25 day

205. Ken is deciding on materials to use for a fencing project. There are 6 different board patterns from which to choose, 3 different end posts, and 5 different types of wood. How many different combinations of board pattern, end post, and wood type are there from which to choose?

   A. 21
   B. 30
   C. 90
   D. 180

206. 100 inches = _____ yards

   A. $2\frac{7}{9}$
   B. $33\frac{1}{3}$
   C. 300
   D. 1,200

207. Which of these represents the ratio of 12 cats to 18 dogs?

   A. 2:3
   B. 3:2
   C. 4:9
   D. 18:12

208. Compute 0.04×0.04.

   A. 0.000016
   B. 0.0016
   C. 0.016
   D. 0.16

209. If $0 < x < 1$, then which of the following must be true?

   A. $x - \frac{1}{2} > 0$
   B. $2x > 1$
   C. $x^2 - 1 < 0$
   D. $1 - 2x < 0$

210. What is the median of this data set?
5, 0, 0, 10, 20

   A. 0
   B. 5
   C. 7
   D. 20

211. A side of a rhombus has a length of 5 inches. What is its perimeter?

   A. 10 inches
   B. 15 inches
   C. 20 inches
   D. Cannot be determined

212. What is 200% of $\frac{3}{5}$?

   A. $\frac{5}{6}$

   B. $1\frac{1}{5}$

   C. 12

   D. 120

213. Simplify: $12 - 3 \times 3 - 1$

   A. 2

   B. 3

   C. 18

   D. 26

214.

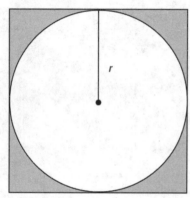

In the figure shown, the length of r is 3 centimeters. The area of the shaded portion of the square is approximately

   A. $5\frac{1}{4}$ sq. centimeters

   B. $7\frac{1}{6}$ sq. centimeters

   C. $7\frac{3}{4}$ sq. centimeters

   D. 10 sq. centimeters

215. Sandra buys two coffee mugs and four bags of coffee beans. If one coffee mug costs c dollars and one bag of coffee beans costs d dollars, what is the total cost of her purchase, in dollars?

   A. $c + d$

   B. $2cd$

   C. $2c + 4d$

   D. $8cd$

216. Consider the following line:

The length of XY is one-fourth the length of WZ; WX and YZ have the same length, and the length of WX is 3 meters. What is the length of WZ?

   A. 2 meters

   B. 4 meters

   C. 6 meters

   D. 8 meters

217. Simplify: $\frac{5}{8} \div 10 - 5 \times \frac{3}{8}$

   A. $-\frac{29}{16}$

   B. $-\frac{1}{4}$

   C. $\frac{3}{64}$

   D. $\frac{35}{8}$

218. If a is a nonzero number, which of these operations, when performed on a, will result in the number 0?

   A. Divide by 0.

   B. Multiply by the reciprocal of a.

   C. Multiply by $-a$.

   D. Subtract a.

219. What is the average of this list of numbers: 0.040, 0, 0.40, 4.00

    A. 0

    B. 0.22

    C. 1.11

    D. 1.48

220. If $a = -1$, $b = -\frac{1}{2}$, and $c = -2$, what is the value of $c(a - b)^2$?

    A. -1

    B. $-\frac{1}{2}$

    C. $\frac{1}{2}$

    D. 1

221. Solve for x: $3.7x - 1.2 = 58$

    A. 12

    B. 15.35

    C. 16

    D. 18.70

222. If Andrea spends $1\frac{3}{4}$ hours per day training for a marathon and she trains 5 days per week, how many hours does Andrea train for the marathon each week?

    A. $5\frac{1}{4}$

    B. $6\frac{1}{2}$

    C. $8\frac{3}{4}$

    D. 9

223. Alicia invests $2,000 and earns 8 percent interest on her investment in one year. What is the total amount of her investment after one year?

    A. $2,008

    B. $2,080

    C. $2,160

    D. $2,225

224. The time remaining for a video to come to its end is described by a time bar 4 inches long on the bottom of the monitor. If $\frac{1}{2}$ inch corresponds to 1 minute, 45 seconds, how long is the video?

    A. 10 minutes, 45 seconds

    B. 12 minutes, 30 seconds

    C. 14 minutes

    D. 16 minutes, 15 seconds

225. If it rains, there is a 30% chance that a school bus will run late. What is the probability that the school bus will not run late if it rains?

    A. 0.30

    B. 0.50

    C. 0.70

    D. 1.00

226. Felix earns $4,200 per month. He pays 22% in various taxes. Of the amount remaining, he invests 15% in different stocks. What amount of money remains, to the nearest dollar, after these amounts are subtracted?

    A. $2,646

    B. $2,785

    C. $3,276

    D. $3,425

227. Compute: $3\frac{3}{4} \div \frac{4}{3}$

    A. $2\frac{13}{16}$

    B. 3

    C. $3\frac{8}{9}$

    D. 5

228. For five weeks over the summer, Neera earned weekly paychecks at her part-time job. The amount of each paycheck was $101.65, $79.23, $84.67, $121.33, and $77.62. What was her average paycheck for those five checks?

    A. $92.90

    B. $94.16

    C. $99.47

    D. $101.30

229. Compute: $2 \div 0.004$

    A. 0.008

    B. 8

    C. 500

    D. 2,000

230. Which of these figures need *not* have a 90-degree angle?

    A. Rectangle

    B. Right triangle

    C. Square

    D. Parallelogram

231. Which of the following is *not* a factor of 36?

    A. 4

    B. 6

    C. 9

    D. 10

232. What is 40 reduced by 20%?

    A. 8

    B. 20

    C. 32

    D. 48

233. Find the area of the following figure.

    A. 48 square feet

    B. 52 square feet

    C. 78 square feet

    D. 82 square feet

234. Solve for b: $(b - 2)(b + 5) = 0$

    A. −2 and −5

    B. −2 and 5

    C. 2 and −5

    D. 2 and 5

235. If $xy - 7 = 56$, and $x = 7$, $y =$

    A. 3

    B. 7

    C. 9

    D. 12

236. Consider the following region:

Assume the following:

$\overline{PQ}$ is the radius of the inner semicircle and has measure 3 meters.

$\overline{PR}$ is the radius of the outer semicircle and has measure 8 meters.

Find the perimeter of the shaded region.

A. $(11\pi + 5)$ meters

B. $(11\pi + 10)$ meters

C. 21π meters

D. $(22\pi + 10)$ meters

237. The cost of a new sink is reduced from $350 to $275. By approximately what percentage has the price been reduced?

A. 21%

B. 27%

C. 35%

D. 75%

238. The square root of 141 is between

A. 11 and 12.

B. 20 and 22.

C. 41 and 100.

D. 70 and 71.

LANGUAGE

60 Questions—25 Minutes

Turn to the Language section of your answer sheet to answer the questions in this section.

Directions: In questions 239–277, look for errors in capitalization, punctuation, or usage. Mark the answer choice that contains the error. If you find no mistake, mark D on your answer sheet.

---

239. **A.** "I'm not sure who lives there," she said.
   B. Zach is a student here, isn't he?
   C. You cannot drive on this street. It is for pedestrian's only.
   D. *(No mistakes)*

240. **A.** He finished his homework on Friday so that he could relax all weekend.
   B. Who's in charge of graduation this year?
   C. Amy missed the bus she was late for school.
   D. *(No mistakes)*

241. **A.** Mr. Wolfe, who was my French teacher last year, is leading the trip to Paris.
   B. I don't like living in a small town. I prefer the city life.
   C. How many students in this class ride the bus to school?
   D. *(No mistakes)*

242. **A.** When we finished the hike, we were all very tired?
   B. "We parked the car behind the building," she said.
   C. If the weather is bad, we'll have to change our plans.
   D. *(No mistakes)*

243. **A.** Julia wrote their name in the book.
   B. The dog drank from its water bowl.
   C. That is not my book; it's hers.
   D. *(No mistakes)*

244. **A.** We shall now proceed into the next room.
   B. I cannot concieve of a better excuse.
   C. The teacher led the class into the auditorium.
   D. *(No mistakes)*

245. **A.** Will you stop shouting!
   B. Is that your cousin Gary?
   C. The night air is chilly, so be sure to wear a jacket.
   D. *(No mistakes)*

246. **A.** That is not mine; it is her's.
   B. Paul's brother is in my class this year, but Paul is in a different class.
   C. The dog's collar is brown; the cat's color is red.
   D. *(No mistakes)*

247. **A.** Jasmine likes apples; Davy prefers oranges.
   B. My dad is an artist; my mom is a lawyer.
   C. The bat actually flies; but the flying squirrel only glides.
   D. *(No mistakes)*

248. **A.** My little brother hates the taste of broccoli.
   B. This cantalope tastes really sweet.
   C. Spinach tastes better fresh than it does when it's boiled.
   D. *(No mistakes)*

249. **A.** How many of the *Star Wars* movies have you seen?

B. The first book of the *Lord of the Rings* trilogy is *The Fellowship of the Ring*.

C. My father read *Alice's Adventures in Wonderland* to me when I was a small child.

D. *(No mistakes)*

250. **A.** The best way to avoid mistakes is to do your homework slowly and carefully.

B. The boat rocked on the waves violently as the wind howled over the sea's surface.

C. That prettily dress is the nicest one in my closet.

D. *(No mistakes)*

251. **A.** The drummer beat out the rhythm of the song.

B. Having a well-developed conscience helps you to make the right decisions.

C. There is an embarrassing picture of me in that photo album!

D. *(No mistakes)*

252. **A.** The film crew included a director, a camera operator, actors and actresses, and a sound person.

B. The school orchestra has numerous musicians; cellists, violinists, brass players, woodwind players, and percussionists.

C. The artist works with paints, pencils, clay, metal, and many other tools and materials.

D. *(No mistakes)*

253. **A.** My parents are driving me to the play in they minivan.

B. Greta asked her sister for help with her homework.

C. My family is having Thanksgiving dinner at our house this year.

D. *(No mistakes)*

254. **A.** My favorite ice cream flavor is pistachio.

B. I keep my sissors in the same drawer as my pencils and erasers.

C. That dog may look vicious, but it is as gentle as a lamb.

D. *(No mistakes)*

255. **A.** "Listen," Francine began, "because I do not want to have to repeat myself."

B. The song "You're So Sweet" was playing the night my grandparents fell in love.

C. I started reading a story called "The Long, Long Night," but it was so long that I couldn't finish it before bedtime!

D. *(No mistakes)*

256. **A.** The glass broke; I used a plastic cup instead.

B. All of my clothing was dirty; I spent the day washing laundry.

C. The song was not very good; I changed the radio to a different station.

D. *(No mistakes)*

257. **A.** This is the chapter the teacher expects us to read tonight.

B. I would of called you but my phone was not working.

C. We talked of the good times we had when we were kids.

D. *(No mistakes)*

258. **A.** The cats are prowling through the night.

B. The stars are twinkling in the sky.

C. The trees leaves are falling.

D. *(No mistakes)*

259. **A.** At this school, we are committed to excellense.

B. That advertisement is trying to convince you to buy something you don't need.

C. Tyrese exceeds in every competition in which he competes.

D. *(No mistakes)*

260. **A.** My guitar string broke, so I need to take a trip to the music store to buy a new one.

   B. The temperature is too hot, so I am thinking about swimming instead of sitting on the sand.

   C. Bernie is organizing his books alphabetically by author, on the shelf.

   D. *(No mistakes)*

261. **A.** There is a noticeable flaw in this structure.

   B. Do you have an arguement you'd like to present?

   C. When you most feel like giving up, that is when you must persevere.

   D. *(No mistakes)*

262. **A.** If you are going to Lisa's house, please gave her this note for me.

   B. I wish you could have met Helga, because she would like you.

   C. They are studying for a test they are taking next week.

   D. *(No mistakes)*

263. **A.** Regardless of your plans, you still have to clean up your room.

   B. We would have gone to your party, but we thought it was going to be next week!

   C. I insure that you will have a good time.

   D. *(No mistakes)*

264. **A.** My brother (he's our family's worst backseat driver) is getting his first car.

   B. Those clouds (stratus and nimbostratus, I think) make the sky look ominous.

   C. That movie (which I was tricked into seeing) was much too scary for me.

   D. *(No mistakes)*

265. **A.** Do not run on the ice—it is very thin!

   B. Where is Janice going on vacation.

   C. This magazine is already two months old.

   D. *(No mistakes)*

266. **A.** We learned about president John F. Kennedy in history class.

   B. The senator participated in an important vote this morning.

   C. I am writing a letter to my congressperson.

   D. *(No mistakes)*

267. **A.** The only way to acheive anything is to try.

   B. I have a lot of respect for your mother.

   C. There is a small cemetery at the end of the street.

   D. *(No mistakes)*

268. **A.** My favorite novel is *Emma*.

   B. The movie *The Incredibles* is very funny!

   C. This song is called *Honey*.

   D. *(No mistakes)*

269. **A.** Either you like that color or you don't.

   B. The coach will choose either Tricia or me to be team captain.

   C. Neither Grace or Yuri was in class today.

   D. *(No mistakes)*

270. **A.** I spent the entire weekend worked.

   B. We went to the bowling alley, but it was closed.

   C. The day was incredibly cold, but the birds still sang.

   D. *(No mistakes)*

271. **A.** Will you stop talking so loudly?

   B. I cannot hear you!

   C. Is there no end to this day?

   D. *(No mistakes)*

272. **A.** Keith was born in Febuary.

   B. I think you misspelled that word.

   C. My sister is as mischievous as a pixie!

   D. *(No mistakes)*

273. A. She insisted on meeting you.

B. This is the first time we talked since a long time.

C. Iris has been building this birdhouse for two weeks.

D. *(No mistakes)*

274. A. First we're going to the movies; then we're going out to dinner.

B. Being selected to join the band will depend on how I perform at the audition.

C. I had the opportunity to go to the park on Saturday or Sunday, and I chose the later.

D. *(No mistakes)*

275. A. Today the weather is lovely, but tomorrow it is supposed to rain.

B. There are shrubs on the front lawn, and there are tall trees in the backyard.

C. Either I am going to study art or I am going to study music when I go to college.

D. *(No mistakes)*

276. A. If you want to get into the building, you will need to bring your id.

B. According to the American Medical Association, smoking is bad for you.

C. We're going to have a big celebration, and all of my aunts and uncles are coming to it!

D. *(No mistakes)*

277. A. I will check my calendar to see if I am free that day.

B. I am defiantly interested in hearing about your day.

C. I have no knowledge of what you are saying.

D. *(No mistakes)*

278. Choose the sentence that demonstrates correct usage.

A. The twins are asking her mother for permission to go to the party.

B. Cora and Luis are taking they dog to the veterinarian.

C. The group is naming itself The Community Cleaners.

D. The toys need new batteries so it can work again.

279. Choose the best word to join the thoughts together.

Alan and his family always visit the Statue of Liberty _____ they are in New York.

A. unless

B. until

C. whenever

D. after

280. Choose the sentence that demonstrates correct usage.

A. I am renewed my library card today.

B. I came to the dance a little late.

C. The teacher will stayed after school to tutor students.

D. The football team will traveled to another city for their next game.

281. Choose the word that best completes this sentence.

Lisette was in a bad mood, so she answered Marvin's question more _____ than she would have if she were feeling better.

A. abruptly

B. slowly

C. casually

D. horribly

282. Choose the sentence that demonstrates correct usage.

   A. Curtis rides his motorcycle to their job every day.

   B. Beatrice is washing the shirt they wore last night at the Laundromat.

   C. Han thinks I forgot his birthday, but I'm actually planning a surprise party for him!

   D. Glenda wants to visit her cousin Ralph, but she cannot remember its address.

283. Which of the following sentences offers the *least* support for the topic "Why we must recycle"?

   A. Recycling prevents air pollution by reducing the amount of new plastics factories produce.

   B. Recycling reduces global warming by cutting down on the release of carbon dioxide that occurs when producing aluminum.

   C. Recycling prevents water pollution by eliminating some of the garbage in landfills that releases contaminated material into ground water.

   D. Recycling is something that anyone can do simply by separating recyclable plastics, metals, and papers from non-recyclable trash.

284. Choose the sentence that demonstrates correct usage.

   A. Because she gets good grades, Anna is going to a great college.

   B. He was feeling ill, he stayed home from school today.

   C. Bryant still occupies the house in which he was born or so do I.

   D. She is my friend, then I did not hesitate to help her.

285. Choose the word that best completes this sentence.

   The cat found a warm stream of sunlight and laid herself down _____ it.

   A. beneath

   B. within

   C. between

   D. of

286. Choose the sentence that demonstrates correct usage.

   A. The shirts pattern is a little too garish for me.

   B. The moon's glow is particularly lovely tonight.

   C. The birds feathers only appear blue; there is no actual blue pigment in them.

   D. The books cover is starting to come apart from the binding.

287. Which of these expresses the idea most clearly?

   A. This picture does not fit this frame, so I'll have to get a new one.

   B. This picture does not fit this frame, a new frame I'll have to get.

   C. This picture does not fit this frame, so I'll have to get a new frame.

   D. So I'll have to get a new frame, this picture does not fit this frame.

288. Choose the sentence that demonstrates correct usage.

   A. The bird flew in the birdhouse.

   B. The firefighter went into save the puppy.

   C. I finished my project in two hour's time.

   D. I don't care for this brand of juice.

289. Choose the pair of sentences that best develops this topic sentence.

All high school students should perform mandatory community service.

A. High school students are generally irresponsible because they have too much free time on their hands. They are in dire need of things to keep them busy.

B. More and more people are living to advanced ages. High school students would perform an invaluable service by volunteering in senior citizen centers.

C. High school curricula should develop civic responsibility as well as academic proficiency. Mandatory community service would help achieve these noble aims.

D. Studies indicate that teenagers who participate in a diverse range of activities do well in college. High school curricula should therefore include more varied activities.

290. Choose the sentence that demonstrates correct usage.

A. Victoria did hers homework on Sunday night.

B. Tiana and Paolo are moving into her new house today.

C. This is not my book; it is your's.

D. We decided not to buy this house because it has a bad foundation.

291. Which of these expresses the idea most clearly?

A. The batteries in the remote control are dead I am going to have to replace them.

B. The batteries in the remote control are dead, so I am going to have to replace them.

C. So I am going to have to replace them, the batteries in the remote control are dead.

D. The batteries in the remote control are dead, so I am going to have to.

292. Choose the sentence that demonstrates correct usage.

A. To slowly work is to do a careful job.

B. The wind blew mighty during the storm.

C. The horse's mane flowed down its back beautifully.

D. The students grumbled when they learned loudly about the upcoming test.

293. Which sentence does *not* belong in the paragraph?

(1) Sometimes businesses in developing countries have not figured out the best ways to produce their goods. (2) FINE, an association of fair-trade networks, helps such companies run their businesses as responsibly as possible. (3) A business that receives fair trade approval meets certain standards regarding environmental concerns and fair treatment of their workers. (4) My local supermarket sells fair-trade coffee in aisle 7.

A. Sentence 1

B. Sentence 2

C. Sentence 3

D. Sentence 4

294. Choose the sentence that demonstrates correct usage.

A. I am going to the beach with Margaret and him.

B. If his wants his ball, he is going to have to look for it.

C. Garreth has the odd habit of talking about his-self in the third person.

D. What is her doing in the attic?

295. Which sentence does *not* belong in the paragraph?

(1) Doctors without Borders is a charitable organization that provides medical aid in troubled regions of the world. (2) "What would you like for your birthday this year?" Darren's mom asked. (3) "I have everything I could want," Darren replied. (4) "Maybe this year you could just make a donation to a worthy charity in my name."

A. Sentence 1

B. Sentence 2

C. Sentence 3

D. Sentence 4

296. Choose the sentence that demonstrates correct usage.

A. The spider spun its web intricate.

B. The sticker fell off the book because its glue was too drily.

C. The harp resounded lovely in the concert hall.

D. Writing a poem was a challenging task, but I performed it happily.

297. Which of the following sentences offers the *least* support to the topic "Why students should have after-school jobs"?

A. They can earn money for school supplies.

B. They can learn the value of having responsibilities.

C. They can get jobs close to their homes.

D. They can learn new skills on the job.

298. Choose the sentence that demonstrates correct usage.

A. If you have an moment, I'd like to talk to you.

B. Do you have a quarter I can borrow?

C. This glass has an crack in it.

D. Do you know a antonym of the word *loquacious*?

ANSWER KEYS AND EXPLANATIONS
Verbal Skills

1. B	13. A	25. B	37. B	49. D
2. C	14. C	26. D	38. D	50. A
3. A	15. C	27. C	39. D	51. C
4. D	16. A	28. A	40. A	52. A
5. A	17. C	29. B	41. B	53. C
6. C	18. A	30. D	42. B	54. C
7. A	19. A	31. B	43. A	55. D
8. D	20. C	32. A	44. D	56. B
9. C	21. B	33. B	45. D	57. A
10. B	22. B	34. D	46. C	58. D
11. B	23. C	35. C	47. C	59. C
12. B	24. A	36. C	48. B	60. A

1. **The correct answer is B.** This analogy is an object-characteristic relationship. Brown is the color of dirt; blue is the color of the sky.

2. **The correct answer is C.** This analogy is an object-purpose relationship. The purpose of a stove is to use it to cook; the purpose of a bed is to use it to sleep.

3. **The correct answer is A.** This analogy is a part-whole relationship. Glass is part of a window; a wall is part of a house.

4. **The correct answer is D.** This analogy is a sequence relationship. The first item in a series comes before the last item; the beginning of an event comes before the end.

5. **The correct answer is A.** This analogy is an antonym relationship. *Dirty* is the opposite of *clean*; *interested* is the opposite of *bored*.

6. **The correct answer is C.** This analogy is a part-whole relationship. Hair grows from the head; leaves grow from a tree.

7. **The correct answer is A.** This analogy is a part-whole relationship. A finger is a digit of the hand; a toe is a digit of the foot.

8. **The correct answer is D.** This analogy is an object-purpose relationship. Lifting is the purpose of an elevator; weighing is the purpose of a scale.

9. **The correct answer is C.** This analogy is an object-purpose relationship. A vase is used to contain a bouquet of flowers; an ice cube tray is used to contain ice cubes.

10. **The correct answer is B.** This analogy is an association relationship. A desk and a chair are included in a desk set; a jacket and pants are included in a suit set.

11. **The correct answer is B.** If Bill is taller than Ingrid, and she is taller than Charles, then Charles can't be taller than Bill. Therefore, the third statement is false.

12. **The correct answer is B.** Since we know that the red car is two colors because it has a black roof, all of the cars cannot be just one color. Therefore, the third statement is false.

13. **The correct answer is A.** Liara has the fewest books, so Alan must have more books than she does. Therefore, the third statement is true.

14. **The correct answer is C.** We do not know if Gerald and Suzanne are in the same class, or anything

about the other children in Gerald's class, so there is no way to know if the final statement is true.

15. **The correct answer is C.** We do not know if the only vegetables and fruits served at the meal are in the soup and salad, so there is no way to know if the third statement is true.

16. **The correct answer is A.** Clarence is the slowest runner, so Miles must be faster than him. Therefore, the third statement is true.

17. **The correct answer is C.** We can only compare the chair to the computer and oven since we know only that it is the least expensive item. There are no clues regarding whether an oven or a computer is more expensive, so there is no way to know if the third statement is true.

18. **The correct answer is A.** Anna ate the fewest strawberries, and since Patrice ate as many strawberries as she did, Grace has to have eaten more strawberries than Patrice. Therefore, the third statement is true.

19. **The correct answer is A.** All of the animals in question live longer than mosquitoes. Therefore, the third statement is true.

20. **The correct answer is C.** There is no true statement about how well Shirley did on the math test, so there is no way to determine if the third statement is true.

21. **The correct answer is B.** Pablo is the hungriest, so he must be hungrier than Kira. Therefore, the third statement is false.

22. **The correct answer is B.** The grey horse must be the biggest since it is bigger than the brown horse, which is bigger than the white horse. Therefore, the third statement is false.

23. **The correct answer is C.** A hammer, a screwdriver, and a wrench are all tools. A basket is not a tool, so it does not belong with the other three words.

24. **The correct answer is A.** To sing, to talk, and to whisper all involve using your voice. To watch requires using your eyesight, not your voice, so *watch* does not belong with the other three words.

25. **The correct answer is B.** The word *perspective* refers to a particular viewpoint. The other three words all reflect positive attitudes or qualities.

26. **The correct answer is D.** A cello, a violin, and a guitar are all stringed instruments. A trumpet is a brass instrument.

27. **The correct answer is C.** To run, leap, or stroll all involve movement. To sit does not.

28. **The correct answer is A.** A marker, a pen, and a paint brush all make marks. An eraser removes marks.

29. **The correct answer is B.** Earth, Venus, and Jupiter are all planets. The moon is not.

30. **The correct answer is D.** An oven, a blender, and a refrigerator are all appliances for storing or preparing food; a television has nothing to do with food.

31. **The correct answer is B.** Milk, butter, and ice cream are all dairy products. Ham is meat.

32. **The correct answer is A.** A squirrel, mouse, and rat are rodents. A snake is a reptile.

33. **The correct answer is B.** Mustard, salsa, and ketchup are all sauces; pepper is a spice.

34. **The correct answer is D.** Florida, Michigan, and New York are all states. Los Angeles is a city.

35. **The correct answer is C.** A dress, a sock, and a necklace are all things to wear. A wallet is not worn.

36. **The correct answer is C.** Handlebars, a seat, and wheels are all part of a bicycle. The bicycle is the object, itself.

37. **The correct answer is B.** A dresser, a suitcase, and a wardrobe are containers. Clothing is what is stored in those containers.

38. **The correct answer is D.** A bulldozer, a dump truck, and a backhoe are all construction vehicles. A bus is a transportation vehicle.

39. **The correct answer is D.** An artificial tree is fake.

40. **The correct answer is A.** An audible hum is heard.

41. **The correct answer is B.** An elementary understanding is basic.

4

42. **The correct answer is B.** An absurd excuse is silly.

43. **The correct answer is A.** A pungent odor is strong.

44. **The correct answer is D.** A gradual change is slow.

45. **The correct answer is D.** A hilarious story is funny.

46. **The correct answer is C.** An ignorant opinion is uninformed.

47. **The correct answer is C.** A jubilant reaction is thrilled.

48. **The correct answer is B.** A sinister plot is evil.

49. **The correct answer is D.** A misplaced item is lost.

50. **The correct answer is A.** A lucid idea is clear.

51. **The correct answer is C.** A humongous hill is huge.

52. **The correct answer is A.** *Lavish* means "extravagant"; the opposite is *plain*.

53. **The correct answer is C.** *Partial* means "incomplete"; the opposite is *whole*.

54. **The correct answer is C.** *Deteriorate* means "to worsen"; the opposite is to *improve*.

55. **The correct answer is D.** *Flair* means "skill"; the opposite is *inability*.

56. **The correct answer is B.** *Squander* means "to waste"; the opposite is to *save*.

57. **The correct answer is A.** *Accurate* means "correct"; the opposite is *mistaken*.

58. **The correct answer is D.** *Escalate* means "to increase"; the opposite is to *decrease*.

59. **The correct answer is C.** *Renounce* means "reject"; the opposite is *accept*.

60. **The correct answer is A.** *Tumult* means "commotion"; the opposite is *calm*.

 NOTES

Quantitative Skills

61. B	72. B	83. A	93. D	103. B
62. C	73. A	84. D	94. B	104. A
63. D	74. C	85. D	95. B	105. C
64. C	75. B	86. C	96. B	106. C
65. B	76. D	87. B	97. B	107. A
66. D	77. A	88. C	98. B	108. B
67. D	78. D	89. B	99. A	109. C
68. B	79. B	90. C	100. A	110. D
69. C	80. D	91. A	101. C	111. D
70. B	81. D	92. C	102. A	112. B
71. A	82. A			

61. **The correct answer is B.** The pattern is to add 4 to a term to get the next one in the series. Since you add 4 to 2 to get 6, the first term must be 2.

62. **The correct answer is C.** $3^3 - 8 = 27 - 8 = 19$

63. **The correct answer is D.** $4^2 + 3^3 = 16 + 27 = 43$.

64. **The correct answer is C.** This series consists of the letters of the alphabet in alphabetical order, beginning with the letter Q. The letter X appears in the middle of each set of three letters.

65. **The correct answer is B.** Count the number of squares in A, B, and C. The figures in A and C each have 11 squares, and the figure in B has 14 squares.

66. **The correct answer is D.** When solving a math problem expressed in words, look for key terms such as *twice* or *double* that indicate you will need to **multiply** a quantity by 2. Also be sure to recognize when when you see the word *of* in connection with a fraction, it also means to **multiply** a number by that fraction.

$$2 \times \left(\frac{2}{3} \times 24 \right) = 2 \times (16) = 32$$

67. **The correct answer is D.** The pattern is to divide a term by 3 to get the next term. So, the next term is $3 \div 3 = 1$.

68. **The correct answer is B.** The pattern in the series is to subtract 2 from the first term to get the second term, subtract 4 from the second term to get the third term, subtract 6 from the third term to get the fourth term, etc. So, to get the sixth term, subtract 10 from the fifth term, 182, to get 172.

69. **The correct answer is C.** Calculate the value of A and B. The value of A is 8×8, or 64. The value of B is 9×7, or 63. The only true statement is that A is greater than B.

70. **The correct answer is B.** The area of A is $(6)(10) = 60$ square inches. The area of B is $(6)(6) = 36$ square inches. The area of C is $\frac{1}{2}(6)(10) = 30$ square inches. So, the area of C is less than the area of B, and the area of B is less than the area of A.

71. **The correct answer is A.** The 1st, 3rd, 5th, etc., terms are all just "A." Since the term sought is the 7th one, it must be A.

72. **The correct answer is B.** This series consists of the three letters A-R-D in constant rotation. In each succeeding group of letters, the last letter of the previous group moves to the beginning of the group, and the other two letters move to the right, so the letter that was last in the previous group becomes the first letter of the next. After ARD, the

D must move to the beginning, and the next group must begin with D followed by AR.

73. **The correct answer is A.** The sum of 2.1 and 1.9 is 4.0. Forty percent of 4.0 is 4.0(0.04) = 1.6.

74. **The correct answer is C.** Note $(7 - 3)^2 = 4^2 = 16$, $7^2 - 3^2 = 49 - 9 = 40$, and $(3 - 7)^2 = 4^2 = 16$. So A = C and A < B.

75. **The correct answer is B.** Let x be the number. It satisfies the equation $1 - 2x = 5$. Solve for x:

$$1 - 2x = 5$$
$$-2x = 4$$
$$x = -2$$

76. **The correct answer is D.** The pattern is that each term involves the previous letter in the alphabet, and the 1st, 3rd, 5th, etc., terms use just one letter while the 2nd, 4th, 6th, etc., terms use two letters. Since the missing term is the 6th one, it must be UU.

77. **The correct answer is A.** The 3rd and 5th terms are obtained by multiplying the previous term by 3, while the 2nd, 4th, 6th, etc., terms are obtained by adding 2 to the previous term. Since the missing term is the 6th one, we add 2 to 6 to get 8.

78. **The correct answer is D.** The diagonal $\overline{MO}$ forms two right triangles. The hypotenuse of a right triangle is always its longest side, so $\overline{MO}$ must be greater than $\overline{MP}$.

79. **The correct answer is B.** Angles POC and POB both have measures of 45 degrees. So, the sum of the measures of angles DOC and POC is 105 degrees, while the sum of the measures of angles AOB and POB is 75 degrees.

80. **The correct answer is D.** Observe that $3^4 = 3 \times 3 \times 3 \times 3 = 81$, $4^3 = 4 \times 4 \times 4 = 64$, and $3 \times 4 = 12$. So, C < B < A.

81. **The correct answer is D.** The pattern in this series is formed by subtracting 5 from each number.

82. **The correct answer is A.** Calculate the value of A and B. The value of A is 6×10^2, or 6×100, which equals 600. The value of B is $6 \div 10$, or 0.60. Therefore, B is equal to C.

83. **The correct answer is A.** The pattern is to multiply the numerator of the previous term by 2 and the denominator by 4. Doing so here yields $\frac{12 \times 2}{64 \times 4} = \frac{24}{256}$.

84. **The correct answer is D.** Let x be the number. Then, x satisfies the equation $\frac{1}{3}x = \frac{2}{3}x - 2$. Solve for x:

$$\frac{1}{3}x = \frac{2}{3}x - 2$$
$$0 = \frac{1}{3}x - 2$$
$$2 = \frac{1}{3}x$$
$$x = 6$$

85. **The correct answer is D.** The pattern is to skip two letters from the previous term and to multiply the number portion of the previous term by 5. Doing so here yields M250.

86. **The correct answer is C.** The diameter is the longest chord of a circle. Since $\overline{BC}$ passes through the center, it is a diameter; since $\overline{EF}$ does not pass through the center, it is not a diameter. So, the length of BC is greater than the length of EF.

87. **The correct answer is B.** The pattern is that the first letter goes forward in the alphabet by one letter, and the second letter goes backward in the alphabet by one letter. Doing so here yields FV.

88. **The correct answer is C.** Let x be the number. Then, x satisfies the equation $\frac{1}{4}(1 + x) = \frac{1}{2}\left(2 + \frac{1}{2}\right)$. Solve for x:

$$\frac{1}{4}(1 + x) = \frac{1}{2}\left(2 + \frac{1}{2}\right)$$
$$\frac{1}{4}(1 + x) = \frac{1}{2}\left(\frac{5}{2}\right)$$
$$\frac{1}{4}(1 + x) = \frac{5}{4}$$
$$1 + x = 5$$
$$x = 4$$

89. **The correct answer is B.** The 3rd, 5th, etc., terms are obtained by subtracting 3 from the previous term, while the 2nd, 4th, 6th, etc., terms are

obtained by multiplying the previous term by 2. Since we are asked for the 7th and 8th terms, we subtract 3 from −3 to get −6 as the 7th term and multiply 16 by 2 to get 32 for the 8th term.

90. **The correct answer is C.**

    200% = 2, so 200% of 0.1 is 2(0.1) = 0.2.

    50% = 0.5, so 50% of 1 is 0.5(1) = 0.5.

    25% = 0.25, so 25% of 10 is 0.25(10) = 2.5.
    Therefore, A < B < C.

91. **The correct answer is A.** The area of the shaded region in A = 32 − 2(2) = 28 square inches. The area of the shaded region in B = 32 = 32 − 1 = 31 square inches. The area of the shaded region in C = 32 − 4(1) = 28 square inches.

    So, the area of A equals the area of C, and the area of B is greater than the area of A.

92. **The correct answer is C.** The pattern is to add 0.7 for the number portion and to skip two letters for the letter portion. Doing so yields 3.3V.

93. **The correct answer is D.** Remember, when you see the word *of* in connection with a fraction, it means you need to multiply the number that follows by that fraction. Let x be the number. Then, x must satisfy the equation $\frac{3}{4}x = \frac{4}{3}$.

    Solve for x:

    $$\frac{3}{4}x = \frac{4}{3}$$
    $$x = \frac{4}{3} \times \frac{4}{3}$$
    $$x = \frac{16}{9}$$

94. **The correct answer is B.** The pattern in this series is +1, +2, +1, +2, and so on. Adding 2 to 14 gives the sum 16.

95. **The correct answer is B.** Note:

    A: $4 \times 4^2 = 64$

    B: $\frac{1}{2}(4^3) = \frac{1}{2}(64) = 32$

    C: $2 \times 3^3 = 2 \times 27 = 54$

    So, A > C > B.

96. **The correct answer is B.** The pattern is to multiply by 5 to get the next term. Doing so here yields 1(5) = 5 for the 4th term and 5(5) = 25 for the 5th term.

97. **The correct answer is B.** Let x be the number. Then, x must satisfy the equation $2(x + 4) = 4x$. Solve for x:

    $$2(x+4) = 4x$$
    $$2x + 8 = 4x$$
    $$8 = 2x$$
    $$x = 4$$

98. **The correct answer is B.** Calculate the value of A, B, and C. The value of A is 6 × (4 + 2), or 6 × 6, which equals 36. The value of B is (4 + 2) × (4 + 2), or 6 × 6, which also equals 36. The value of C is (6 × 4) + 2, or 24 + 2, which equals 26. Therefore, C is less than A and B.

99. **The correct answer is A.** The pattern is to increase the numerator by 2 and the denominator by 1. Doing so here yields $\frac{9}{5}$ for the 5th term and $\frac{11}{6}$ for the 6th term.

100. **The correct answer is A.** For each of these expressions, the exponent on the 10 tells the number of places to the right to move the decimal point. In each case, moving the decimal point the indicated number of places results in the number 30. So, A = B = C.

101. **The correct answer is C.** The pattern in this series is ×2, +3, ×2, +3, and so on.

102. **The correct answer is A.** Remember, when you see the word *of* in connection with a fraction, it means you need to multiply the number that follows by that fraction. Let x be the number. Then, x must satisfy the equation $\frac{1}{2}x = 4x$. The only value of x that can make this true is $x = 0$.

103. **The correct answer is B.** The figures in C and B both have seven edges (i.e., a segment between two consecutive vertices).

104. **The correct answer is A.** The pattern is to alternate between 3 in the first slot and 8 in the second slot of a term for the number portion, and to

increase the letter portion by 1 each time. Doing so here yields the next two terms as being 3H and I8.

105. **The correct answer is C.** The 3rd and 5th terms are obtained by multiplying the previous term by 3, while the 2nd, 4th, 6th, etc., terms are obtained by adding 1 in the numerator and denominator of the previous term. Since we are asked for the 7th term, we multiply $\frac{2}{3}$ by 3 to get 2.

106. **The correct answer is C.** Let x be the number. Then, x must satisfy the equation $x + 6 = (2 + 4)^2$. Solve for x:

$$x + 6 = (2 + 4)^2$$
$$x + 6 = 6^2$$
$$x + 6 = 36$$
$$x = 30$$

107. **The correct answer is A.** Since $0 < z < 1$, it follows that multiplying both sides of $z < 1$ by z produces $z^2 < z$. Doing that again shows that $z^3 < z^2$. Since $z < 2z$, we see that $z^3 < z^2 < z < 2z$, so we know that C < B < A.

108. **The correct answer is B.** The 2nd, 4th, 6th, etc., terms are obtained by affixing two more C's to the previous term in that list. Doing so here yields CCCCCC.

109. **The correct answer is C.** Let x be the number. Then, x must satisfy the equation $x - 3 = \frac{1}{2} \times 4^2$.

Solve for x:

$$x - 3 = \frac{1}{2} \times 4^2$$
$$x - 3 = \frac{1}{2} \times 16$$
$$x - 3 = 8$$
$$x = 11$$

110. **The correct answer is D.** Using the order of operations, expressions A and C are equal:

$$2 \div \frac{1}{10} \div 5 = \left(2 \div \frac{1}{10}\right) \div 5$$
$$= 2 \times 10 \div 5$$
$$= 20 \div 5$$
$$= 4$$

Positioning the parentheses differently in B results in a different solution.

$$2 \div \left(\frac{1}{10} \div 5\right) = 2 \div \left(\frac{1}{10} \times \frac{1}{5}\right)$$
$$= 2 \div \left(\frac{1}{50}\right)$$
$$= 2 \times 50 = 100$$

So, A = C and A < B.

111. **The correct answer is D.** The pattern is to alternate between adding 0.9 and subtracting 0.3. Since we are asked for the 6th and 7th terms, we add 0.9 to 2.4 to get 3.3 for the 6th term. Then, subtract 0.3 from this to get 3.0 for the 7th term.

112. **The correct answer is B.** Let x be the number. Then, x satisfies the equation $2x + 3x = 10^2 - 5$. Solve for x:

$$2x + 3x = 10^2 - 5$$
$$5x = 100 - 5$$
$$5x = 95$$
$$x = 19$$

READING
Comprehension

113. C	121. C	129. C	137. A	145. B
114. A	122. D	130. A	138. D	146. D
115. D	123. A	131. B	139. A	147. A
116. B	124. D	132. B	140. A	148. A
117. C	125. B	133. C	141. D	149. D
118. B	126. B	134. D	142. C	150. A
119. A	127. D	135. C	143. B	151. B
120. D	128. C	136. D	144. A	152. A

113. **The correct answer is C.** The passage is mainly about the various ways that companies conduct market research. Choice A is incorrect because the passage explains how companies find out this information instead of how people make their decisions. The passage mainly describes various ways to conduct market research, so choices B and D can be eliminated.

114. **The correct answer is A.** In the beginning of the passage, the author explains that one of the main ways that companies conduct market research is through the distribution of surveys. The passage focuses on how market research is conducted, so choices C and D can be eliminated.

115. **The correct answer is D.** The second sentence in paragraph 2 uses *demographic* to refer to characteristics of a group. Gender and marital status are group characteristics mentioned in the sentence that follows, giving a clue as to the context. This eliminates *problematic* (choice B). Choices A and C also do not fit the context and can be eliminated.

116. **The correct answer is B.** The author mentions fabric softener in paragraph 3 to give an example of a product that might be the subject of market research. This example helps explain why a survey might contain certain types of questions.

117. **The correct answer is C.** The author states in paragraph 5 that companies ask for demographic information from survey respondents in order to understand what type of person is most likely to purchase their products. With this information, companies can build consumer profiles of potential customers.

118. **The correct answer is B.** According to information in paragraph 7, a main reason to hold focus groups is to collect data for constructing advertising campaigns. However, the passage never indicates that focus groups are held to develop ideas for new products (choice A), influence the people in the groups to buy new products (choice C), or find out which products are the most marketable (choice D).

119. **The correct answer is A.** This passage maintains a neutral tone, and since the author is never critical of market research and presents its purposes matter-of-factly, we can assume that the author would characterize market research as useful. The author never expresses opinions strong enough to justify the conclusions that market research is invasive (choice B), untrustworthy (choice C), or ingenious (choice D).

120. **The correct answer is D.** As written, the final paragraph does not present a clear idea of what product testing entails since there is no indication of what happens after the subject tries the new shampoo; choice D would clarify the product testing process. The way researchers went about approaching subjects (choice A), the name of the

shampoo (choice B), and the number of people asked to try the new shampoo (choice C) would not clarify this example intended to explain the purpose of product testing.

121. **The correct answer is C.** The passage focuses on how companies use market research to figure out the most effective ways to market their products, so choice C is the most logical answer. While choices A, B, and D are possible, they imply that the passage focuses on how market research affects the subjects involved, when it really focuses on how market research affects companies' marketing decisions.

122. **The correct answer is D.** According to paragraph 7, surveys are more effective than focus groups. This eliminates choice C, which suggests that the opposite of this is true. The popularity of particular forms of marketing research is not discussed in the passage, so there is no support for choice A. While focus groups are not as effective as surveys, choice B reaches an extreme conclusion that the passage simply does not support.

123. **The correct answer is A.** The passage draws a distinction between Napoleon's imposing reputation as a blood-thirsty conqueror and the fact that in his personal life he had a simple childhood and loved his mother. There is no contrast between Napoleon's father and mother in the passage, so choice B cannot be correct. Choice C is incorrect because the passage draws no contrast between how Napoleon spoke of his mother and how he treated her. The passage is not about the contrasts between people who were involved with Napoleon; it is about contrasts within Napoleon's personal story, so choice D is incorrect.

124. **The correct answer is D.** This information is given in the second paragraph: "He was born … on the 15th August 1769 to be exact, in the little town of Ajaccio, the capital of picturesque Corsica. This miniature island rises a bold tree-covered rock in the blue waters of the Mediterranean, fifty miles west of the coast of Italy."

125. **The correct answer is B.** This information can be found in paragraph 2, which states that Corsica

"…had been sold to France by the Republic of Genoa." Since Corsica was sold to France, France cannot be Corsica's former owner, so choice C is incorrect. Ajaccio is a town on Corsica, it is not the island's former owner, so choice A is incorrect. According to the passage, Carlyle is the name of a person, not the previous owner of Corsica, so choice D is incorrect.

126. **The correct answer is B.** The opening paragraph describes Napoleon's victories on the battlefield as "hard-fought," which supports choice B; if they were not difficult to achieve, he would not have had to fight so hard. This contradicts the answer in choice A. The passage implies that Napoleon fought many battles, which contradicts choice C. However, choice D is an extreme answer that the passage simply does not support.

127. **The correct answer is D.** In the final paragraph, the word *patriot* refers to Pascal Paoli. It does not refer to Napoleon's father (choice A), Napoleon himself (choice B), or Napoleon's mother (choice C).

128. **The correct answer is C.** While each answer choice can be used a synonym for *apt*, only *quick* makes sense in this context.

129. **The correct answer is C.** The author characterizes both Napoleon and Corsicans in general as "warlike," so choice C is the best answer. However, there is no indication that Napoleon's mother (choice A) or his brother Joseph (choice B) were much like Napoleon. There is no information at all about Carlyle aside from his opinion of Napoleon, so choice D does not make sense.

130. **The correct answer is A.** Napoleon had a reputation for being a fierce warrior, so it is likely that he misrepresented his childhood to support that reputation. The passage is clear about Napoleon's love for his mother, so choice B lacks strong support. There is no evidence that Napoleon simply could not remember his childhood, so choice C is not the best answer. The passage supports the idea that Napoleon was a fierce warrior, so choice D cannot be correct.

131. **The correct answer is B.** Earlier in the passage, Napoleon is identified as the future ruler of France, so the "high position" must refer to that. While he was a soldier, this is not as high a position as a ruler, so choice A is not the best answer. The passage only states that he was a ruler; it does not say that he was a king, so choice C is not the best answer either. Choice D seems to make the mistake that the person with the high position was Napoleon's father, not Napoleon, himself.

132. **The correct answer is B.** The passage is set up as an explanation of Napoleon's early years since they are not usually discussed. Choices A and D are just minor details in the passage. The detail in choice C is mentioned only to set up a discussion of Napoleon's life before he set foot on the battlefield.

133. **The correct answer is C.** The passage is focused mainly on the first purported papers in England, and since most of them did not function as modern newspapers do, the word *newspapers* is placed within quotes. While the titles of many of these papers referred to birds or Mercury, this is too minor a detail to serve as a fitting title, so choice A is not the best answer. The internet is mentioned only as a contrast to the newspapers of hundreds of years ago, so choice B would not be a fitting title. Only the first paragraph discussed the *English Mercurie*, and the best title should capture the idea of the whole passage, so choice D is not the best title.

134. **The correct answer is D.** The passage states that early newspapers in England were mostly intent on conveying the agenda of political parties. Choices A and C are purposes of today's newspapers, but these purposes are not discussed in the passage. While many of the titles of England's first papers referred to birds, there is no suggestion that the papers actually discussed birds, so choice B is incorrect.

135. **The correct answer is C.** According to the passage, the *English Mercurie* was a hoax, which means it was not real. This fact contradicts the conclusion in choice B. While it was supposedly a discredited false report, this is not what set it

apart from actual newspapers. While the British Museum did accept the *English Mercurie*, this is not the main factor that set it apart from other newspapers.

136. **The correct answer is D.** Irony is when an opposite occurs to humorous effect, and the fact that the *English Mercurie* was supposed to have exposed false stories when it, itself, was false, is ironic. While the fake newspaper was not published regularly, this is not necessarily ironic, so choice A is incorrect. It did not actually expose false stories either, so choice B is incorrect, too. However, the newspaper was printed, otherwise it could not be accepted by the British Museum, so choice C is incorrect.

137. **The correct answer is A.** According to paragraph 3, newspapers "varied quite a bit in the quality of their writing." This contradicts the conclusion in choice D. While the *English Mercurie* was entirely fake, these later newspapers were not, so choice B is incorrect. The passage indicates only that their titles were intended to emphasize the idea that these newspapers were quickly delivered to the public; it does not actually say that they really were all that quick, so choice C is not the best answer.

138. **The correct answer is D.** The passage indicates that many of these early English papers did publish attacks against political opponents, so choice D is incorrect. This fact also contradicts choice C. The passage states that many of the first English newspapers had titles that references birds or Mercury, so choices A and B are incorrect.

139. **The correct answer is A.** A hoax is something that is committed, so *committed* is the best answer. Choice B seems to have confused *perpetrated* with *perpetuated*. Choice C seems to have confused it with *permeated*. Choice D seems to have confused it with *pertained*.

140. **The correct answer is A.** The author seems to believe that a proper newspaper reports current events, and this is not the main purpose of any of the newspapers discussed in the passage. This contradicts choice B. The author states only that the internet delivers news quickly; there is no

implication that it delivers more credible news than the newspapers in 1600s England did. The author indicates that there are differences in the writing quality among the newspapers discussed in the passage, so choice D is incorrect.

141. **The correct answer is D.** The *English Mercurie* was a hoax, and choice D refers to another kind of hoax. Choice A is the opposite of that. While the *English Mercurie* was accepted by a museum, choice B fails to take the phoniness of the *English Mercurie* into account. Many people believed that the *English Mercurie* was really England's first newspaper, so choice C does not really capture what it is like.

142. **The correct answer is C.** Many of the titles of early English newspapers referenced fast birds of flight, and though a hen is a bird, it does not conjure images of speedy delivery. The birds referenced in the other answer choices do.

143. **The correct answer is B.** The passage is mainly about the various properties of sound. Choice A represents just one component of the passage, as does choice D. The author discusses the speed, loudness, and frequency of sound, so choice C can be eliminated.

144. **The correct answer is A.** Air is a medium, or intervening substance, through which sound is transmitted; therefore, in this context, *media* means "substances." Choices B, C, and D do not fit the context of the passage.

145. **The correct answer is B.** The passage explains in paragraph 2 that sound waves can take longer to move through liquids and solids than through gases or air, so choices A, C, and D can be eliminated.

146. **The correct answer is D.** The author describes how a siren gradually gets louder as it moves toward a building and then becomes softer again as it passes the building. This is because of the listener's proximity in relation to the siren's distance on a moving fire truck.

147. **The correct answer is A.** The passage mentions in paragraph 2 that a siren sometimes seems to be heard sooner when the listener is outside because the sound does not have to travel through the solid medium of a building. It takes longer for sound waves to travel through solids than through the air.

148. **The correct answer is A.** *Modified* means "changed." The other answer choices would not make sense if used in place of *modified* in the second paragraph of the passage.

149. **The correct answer is D.** A wall is a solid object and so is a cloth. The way volume can be adjusted does not compare to the passing of sound through a wall, so choice A is not the best answer. A day is not a solid object, so choice B is incorrect, and the atmosphere is not solid either, so choice C is incorrect as well.

150. **The correct answer is A.** The passage indicates that a sound wave is the size of a sound, and that as a source of noise moves farther away, it becomes more difficult to hear. This supports the conclusion in choice A. This fact also eliminates choice B. Musicians like those described in the passage create sounds in specific pitches, so choice C does not make much sense. Choice D is a matter of opinion and dependent on the sound in question, so it is not the best answer.

151. **The correct answer is B.** The author discusses the musical note of A in paragraph 4 only to use it as an example of a sound at the lower end of sounds people can hear. The author is less concerned with making the passage more interesting (choice A) or suggesting that human hearing is flawed (choice C). Since the passage never discusses the hearing of animals other than people, choice D is not the best answer.

152. **The correct answer is A.** Light cannot pass through walls, but sound can. Therefore, when compared to light, we can infer that sound is more difficult to block. There is no evidence to support the ideas that sound is more difficult to discern (choice B), common in everyday life (choice C), or important to sense (choice D) than light is.

Vocabulary

153. A	**158.** A	**163.** B	**167.** C	**171.** D
154. D	**159.** D	**164.** D	**168.** C	**172.** C
155. B	**160.** C	**165.** A	**169.** D	**173.** A
156. B	**161.** C	**166.** B	**170.** B	**174.** B
157. C	**162.** A			

153. **The correct answer is A.** *Expressive* is a synonym for *articulate*. Other synonyms include *eloquent*, *fluent*, and *well-spoken*.

154. **The correct answer is D.** *Shorten* is a synonym for *curtail*. Other synonyms include *limit*, *reduce*, and *curb*.

155. **The correct answer is B.** *Profitable* is the closest in meaning to the word *lucrative* among the four choices. Other synonyms include *productive*, *high-paying*, and *money-making*.

156. **The correct answer is B.** *Joy* is a synonym for the word *elation*. Other synonyms include *happiness*, *delight*, and *ecstasy*.

157. **The correct answer is C.** *Opponent* is a synonym for *adversary*. Other synonyms include *enemy*, *competitor*, and *rival*.

158. **The correct answer is A.** *Discontinue* is a synonym of *adjourn*. Other synonyms include *stop*, *finish*, and *suspend*.

159. **The correct answer is D.** *Method* is a synonym for the word *technique*. Other synonyms include *procedure* and *system*.

160. **The correct answer is C.** *Change* is a synonym for the word *amend*. Other synonyms include *alter* and *modify*.

161. **The correct answer is C.** *Erase* is a synonym for the word *delete*. Other synonyms include *remove* and *cancel*.

162. **The correct answer is A.** *Emotional* is a synonym for the word *sentimental*. Other synonyms include *maudlin* and *romantic*.

163. **The correct answer is B.** *Friendly* is a synonym for the word *cordial*. Other synonyms include *pleasant* and *warm*.

164. **The correct answer is D.** *Slow* is a synonym for the word *sluggish*. Other synonyms include *listless* and *slothful*.

165. **The correct answer is A.** *Wrong* is a synonym for the word *erroneous*. Other synonyms include *mistaken* and *invalid*.

166. **The correct answer is B.** *Deny* is a synonym for the word *withhold*. Other synonyms include *refuse* and *hold back*.

167. **The correct answer is C.** *Silly* is a synonym for the word *frivolous*. Other synonyms include *thoughtless* and *trivial*.

168. **The correct answer is C.** *Controlling* is a synonym for the word *oppressive*. Other synonyms include *cruel* and *harsh*.

169. **The correct answer is D.** *Brave* is a synonym for the word *valiant*. Other synonyms include *courageous* and *heroic*.

170. **The correct answer is B.** *Remove* is a synonym for the word *eliminate*. Other synonyms include *abolish* and *get rid of*.

171. **The correct answer is D.** *Sad* is a synonym for the word *lamentable*. Other synonyms include *terrible* and *appalling*.

172. **The correct answer is C.** *Sloppy* is a synonym for the word *slovenly*. Other synonyms include *messy* and *careless*.

173. **The correct answer is A.** *Naughty* is a synonym for the word *wayward*. Other synonyms include *unruly* and *disobedient*.

174. **The correct answer is B.** *Bright* is a synonym for the word *vibrant*. Other synonyms include *vivid* and *brilliant*.

Mathematics

175. B	188. A	201. C	214. C	227. A
176. C	189. C	202. A	215. C	228. A
177. B	190. A	203. D	216. D	229. C
178. A	191. B	204. C	217. A	230. D
179. B	192. C	205. C	218. D	231. D
180. B	193. A	206. A	219. C	232. C
181. B	194. C	207. A	220. B	233. D
182. D	195. A	208. B	221. C	234. C
183. A	196. B	209. C	222. C	235. C
184. B	197. A	210. B	223. C	236. B
185. A	198. A	211. C	224. C	237. A
186. A	199. B	212. B	225. C	238. A
187. C	200. A	213. A	226. B	

175. **The correct answer is B.** The ten million's place is the eighth digit from the right, and the tens place is the second digit from the right. So, the number is 50,000,030.

176. **The correct answer is C.** Solve for the box as follows:

First, put the fraction on the left side of the equation in lowest terms:

$$\frac{5}{20} = \frac{\frac{1}{3}}{\square}$$

$$\frac{1}{4} = \frac{\frac{1}{3}}{\square}$$

Then, get rid of the fraction on both sides of the equation by multiplying by the bottom terms of each: 4 on the left side and the $\square$ on the right side:

$$\frac{4}{1} \times \frac{1}{4} \times \square = \frac{\frac{1}{3}}{\square} \times \square \times \frac{4}{1}$$

This simplifies to the following:

$$1 \times \square = \frac{1}{3} \times \frac{4}{1}$$

Simplify further to get the final answer:

$$\square = \frac{4}{3}$$

177. **The correct answer is B.** The height is 6 inches and the base is 14 inches. The area is $\frac{1}{2}(6)(14) = 42$ square inches.

178. **The correct answer is A.**

$$0.05\% = \frac{0.05}{100} = 0.0005$$

179. **The correct answer is B.** Since the fractions have the same numerator, the one with the smaller denominator has the larger overall value. So, $\frac{5}{8} > \frac{5}{9}$.

180. **The correct answer is B.** Let x be the number of bathrooms. Set up and solve the proportion: $\frac{2}{3} = \frac{x}{18}$. Cross-multiply to get $36 = 3x$. Finally, dividing by 3 yields $x = 12$.

181. **The correct answer is B.** There are 4 tiles that are not vowels. Since each of the 7 tiles is equally likely to be chosen, the probability is $\frac{4}{7}$.

182. **The correct answer is D.** 1 liter = 1,000 milliliters. So, 5 liters = 5,000 milliliters.

183. **The correct answer is A.** The number 784 can be written as $(7 \times 10^2) + (8 \times 10) + 4$. The number 10^2 equals 100, so $7 \times 10^2 = 700$. The value of 8×10 is 80. Add the three numbers together to double check the result: $700 + 80 + 4 = 784$.

184. **The correct answer is B.** A property of parallelograms says that the sum of the measures of same-side interior angles is 180 degrees.

185. **The correct answer is A.** A number in front of a variable is called a coefficient.

186. **The correct answer is A.** The factory makes 200 cameras per day, so it would make 1,000 cameras in 5 days. It would take 5 days for the factory to make about 997 cameras.

187. **The correct answer is C.** The components of this problem must be stated in the same units. There are 60 minutes in an hour and 60 seconds in a minute. Therefore, 1 hour equals 60×60, or 3,600 seconds. The ratio of 3,600 to 120 is simplified to 30 to 1.

188. **The correct answer is A.** Note that 1.5 feet = 18 inches, and 90 millimeters = 9 centimeters. Since 10 centimeters is less than 10 inches, we have A < B < C < D.

189. **The correct answer is C.** The ten-thousandths place is four places after the decimal point. Here, that digit is 6.

190. **The correct answer is A.** The value that occurs most often in the data set is 0.

191. **The correct answer is B.** There are 13 toys total, 4 of which are tennis balls. So, the probability of the dog selecting one is $\frac{4}{13}$.

192. **The correct answer is C.** The reciprocal of a fraction is the fraction inverted. To find the answer, you would have to rewrite $3\frac{3}{4}$ as an improper

fraction, $\frac{15}{4}$. The fraction $\frac{15}{4}$ is the reciprocal of $\frac{4}{15}$.

193. **The correct answer is A.** Since 12 is divisible by 6, the number must also be divisible by 6.

194. **The correct answer is C.** The smallest number into which both 12 and 18 divide evenly is 36; this is the least common multiple.

195. **The correct answer is A.** Borrow 1 minute to perform the subtraction in the second's column, and then borrow 1 hour to perform the subtraction in the minute's column:

$$
\begin{array}{r}
^3\cancel{4}\ \text{hours} \quad ^{71}\cancel{12}\ \text{minutes} \quad ^{70}\cancel{10}\ \text{seconds} \\
-\quad 1\ \text{hour} \qquad\ 58\ \text{minutes} \qquad 20\ \text{seconds} \\
\hline
2\ \text{hours} \qquad 13\ \text{minutes} \qquad 50\ \text{seconds}
\end{array}
$$

196. **The correct answer is B.** Any number less than $\frac{1}{3}$ makes this inequality true.

197. **The correct answer is A.**

$-1 - (-3) = -1 + 3 = 2$

198. **The correct answer is A.** The diameter is 10 inches, so the circumference is 10π inches.

199. **The correct answer is B.** The conversion factor is $\cancel{x\ \text{hours}} \cdot \dfrac{60\ \text{minutes}}{1\ \cancel{\text{hour}}}$. So, you multiply by 60.

200. **The correct answer is A.** You must divide both numbers in the numerator by 2 when splitting into two fractions.

201. **The correct answer is C.** Since 8 tablespoons equals $\frac{1}{2}$ cup, it follows that 16 tablespoons equals 1 cup. So, there are 3(16) teaspoons = 48 teaspoons in 1 cup.

202. **The correct answer is A.** Since Maria is paddling downstream with the current, her speed is increased by the speed of the current by x miles per hour. So, her maximum speed would be $8 + x$ miles per hour.

203. **The correct answer is D.**

$$\frac{6\frac{2}{3}}{\frac{1}{6}} = \frac{20}{3} \div \frac{1}{6} = \frac{20}{3} \times 6 = 40$$

204. The correct answer is C. Note that 0.25 day = 0.25 × 24 = 6 hours, and 6 hours = 6 × 60 = 360 minutes, but 360 minutes = 360 × 60 = 21,600 seconds.

205. The correct answer is C. The number of combinations is 3 × 5 × 6 = 90.

206. The correct answer is A. Since 1 yard = 36 inches, we have

$$100 \text{ inches} \times \frac{1 \text{ yard}}{36 \text{ inches}} = \frac{100}{36} \text{ yards}$$

$$= 2\frac{7}{9} \text{ yards}$$

207. The correct answer is A. The ratio is $\frac{12}{18} = \frac{2}{3}$, which can be written as 2:3.

208. The correct answer is B. 0.04(0.04) = 0.0016

209. The correct answer is C. If you square a number that is between 0 and 1, the result is also between 0 and 1. Symbolically, this is written as $x^2 < 1$, which is equivalent to $x^2 - 1 < 0$.

210. The correct answer is B. Arrange the data in increasing order: 0, 0, 5, 10, 20. The median is the value in the middle, namely 5.

211. The correct answer is C. All four sides of a rhombus have the same length. The perimeter is 5(4) = 20 inches.

212. The correct answer is B. Since 200% is equal to 2, 200% of $\frac{3}{5}$ is $2\left(\frac{3}{5}\right) = \frac{6}{5} = 1\frac{1}{5}$.

213. The correct answer is A. To simplify, use the order of operations as shown:
12 − 3 × 3 − 1 = 12 − 9 − 1 = 3 − 1 = 2.

214. The correct answer is C. To find the area of the shaded portion, subtract the area of the circle from the area of the square. The area of the circle can be found using the formula A = πr^2. The area of the circle is therefore $\pi(3)^2$, or 3.14 × 9, which equals approximately 28.26 square centimeters.

The diameter of the circle is equal to the length of the side of the square. The radius of the circle measures 3 centimeters, so the diameter of the circle is twice that, or 6 centimeters. The area of the square can be found using the formula A =

s^2. The area of the square is 6 × 6, or 36 square centimeters.

The area of the shaded portion equals 36 − 28.26, or 7.74 square centimeters, which is closest to $7\frac{3}{4}$ square centimeters.

215. The correct answer is C. The cost of two coffee mugs is $2c$ dollars, and the cost of four bags of coffee beans is $4d$ dollars. The cost of her purchase is $2c + 4d$ dollars.

216. The correct answer is D. Label the given lengths as follows:

Note that $\frac{3}{4}$ of the length of WZ equals

3 m + 3 m = 6 m.

So, the length of WZ equals $\frac{4}{3}(6) = 8$ meters.

217. The correct answer is A. Use the order of operations:

$$\frac{5}{8} \div 10 - 5 \times \frac{3}{8} = \frac{5}{8} \times \frac{1}{10} - 5 \times \frac{3}{8}$$

$$= \frac{1}{16} - \frac{15}{8}$$

$$= \frac{1 - 30}{16}$$

$$= -\frac{29}{16}$$

218. The correct answer is D. For any number a, $a - a = 0$.

219. The correct answer is C.

$$\frac{0.040 + 0 + 0.40 + 4.00}{4} = \frac{4.44}{4} = 1.11$$

220. The correct answer is B.

$$-2\left(-1 - \left(-\frac{1}{2}\right)\right)^2 = -2\left(-\frac{1}{2}\right)^2 = -2\left(\frac{1}{4}\right) = -\frac{1}{2}$$

221. **The correct answer is C.** Solve the equation by isolating the variable x on one side:

$$3.7x = 58 + 1.2$$
$$3.7x = 59.2$$
$$x = \frac{59.2}{3.7}$$
$$x = 16$$

222. **The correct answer is C.**

$$1\frac{3}{4} \times 5 = 8\frac{3}{4} \text{ hours each week}$$

223. **The correct answer is C.** The amount of interest earned in one year is $2,000 \times 0.08$, or $160. The total value of Alicia's investment after one year is $2,000 + $160, or $2,160.

224. **The correct answer is C.** Let x be the length of the entire video. Solve the following proportion:

$$\frac{\frac{1}{2}\text{ inch}}{105 \text{ seconds}} = \frac{4 \text{ inches}}{x \text{ seconds}}$$
$$\frac{1}{2}x = 4(105)$$
$$x = 2(4)(105)$$
$$x = 840$$

Since there are 60 seconds in 1 minute,

$$840 \text{ seconds} = \frac{840}{60} = 14 \text{ minutes.}$$

225. **The correct answer is C.** The probability of a complement of an event is one minus the probability of the event. So, $1 - 0.3 = 0.7$ is the probability that the school bus will not run late.

226. **The correct answer is B.** The amount Felix pays in taxes is $(\$4,200)(0.22) = \$924$. The amount remaining after this is deducted is $4,200 - $924 = $3,276. Of this, he invests 15%, which is $(\$3,276)(0.15) = \$491.40$. So, the amount remaining is $3,276 - $491.40 = $2,784.60, which rounds to $2,785.

227. **The correct answer is A.**

$$3\frac{3}{4} \div \frac{4}{3} = \frac{15}{4} \div \frac{4}{3} = \frac{15}{4} \times \frac{3}{4} = \frac{45}{16} = 2\frac{13}{16}$$

228. **The correct answer is A.** To find the average, add the sum of the paychecks and divide by 5. The sum of the paychecks is $101.65 + $79.23 + $84.67 + $121.33 + $77.62, which equals $464.50. The average paycheck equals $464.50 ÷ 5, or $92.90.

229. **The correct answer is C.**

$$2 \div 0.004 = 2 \times \frac{1}{0.004}$$
$$= 2 \times \frac{1}{\frac{4}{1,000}}$$
$$= 2 \times \frac{1,000}{4}$$
$$= 500$$

230. **The correct answer is D.** A parallelogram need only have two pairs of parallel sides. The angles opposite congruent sides are congruent but need not have a measure of 90 degrees.

231. **The correct answer is D.** 36 cannot be divided evenly by 10.

232. **The correct answer is C.** 20% of 40 equals $40(0.2) = 8$. So 40 reduced by 20% is $40 - 8 = 32$.

233. **The correct answer is D.** The area of the triangle portion of the figure is $\frac{1}{2}(12)(5) = 30$ square feet. The area of the rectangle portion of the figure is $4(13) = 52$ square feet. So, the area of the figure is $30 + 52 = 82$ square feet.

234. **The correct answer is C.** Set each factor equal to zero and solve for b:

$b - 2 = 0$ has solution $b = 2$

$b + 5 = 0$ has solution $b = -5$

235. **The correct answer is C.** Substitute 7 into the equation for x. Then solve for y:

$$xy - 7 = 56$$
$$7y - 7 = 56$$
$$7y = 56 + 7$$
$$7y = 63$$
$$y = 9$$

236. The correct answer is B. The perimeter of the outer semicircle is $\frac{1}{2}\left(2\pi \cdot 8\right) = 8\pi$ meters, the perimeter of the inner semicircle is $\frac{1}{2}\left(2\pi \cdot 3\right) = 3\pi$ meters, and the two horizontal segments on the bottom of the figure each has a length of 5 meters. So, the perimeter of the entire figure is $(8\pi + 3\pi + 5 + 5) = (11\pi + 10)$ meters.

237. The correct answer is A. The percent reduction is $\frac{350 - 75}{350} = \frac{275}{350} \approx 0.21$, or about 21%.

238. The correct answer is A. Since $121 < 141 < 144$ and $\sqrt{121} = 11$ and $\sqrt{144} = 12$, it follows that $\sqrt{141}$ is between 11 and 12.

NOTES

Language

239. C	251. D	263. C	275. D	287. C
240. C	252. B	264. D	276. A	288. D
241. D	253. A	265. B	277. B	289. C
242. A	254. B	266. A	278. C	290. D
243. A	255. D	267. A	279. C	291. B
244. B	256. D	268. C	280. B	292. C
245. A	257. B	269. C	281. A	293. D
246. A	258. C	270. A	282. C	294. A
247. C	259. A	271. D	283. D	295. A
248. B	260. C	272. A	284. A	296. D
249. D	261. B	273. B	285. B	297. C
250. C	262. A	274. C	286. B	298. B

239. **The correct answer is C.** There should not be an apostrophe before the *s* in *pedestrians* because it is a plural noun, not a singular possessive noun.

240. **The correct answer is C.** Choice C is a run-on sentence. It contains two independent clauses joined with no punctuation. One way to correct this sentence would be to add a comma followed by a coordinating conjunction: Amy missed the bus, and she was late for school.

241. **The correct answer is D.** *No mistakes.* The sentences are correctly punctuated.

242. **The correct answer is A.** The sentence should end with a period because it is a statement, not a question.

243. **The correct answer is A.** Julia is just one person, so this sentence should have the singular pronoun *her*, not the plural *their*.

244. **The correct answer is B.** The correct spelling is *conceive*.

245. **The correct answer is A.** This is a question, not a declarative sentence, so it needs to end with a question mark.

246. **The correct answer is A.** There is a possessive pronoun error in the first sentence. The possessive form of *her* is *hers* without an apostrophe.

247. **The correct answer is C.** Either a semicolon or a conjunction such as *but* is used to join the clauses in a compound sentence. Both should not be used.

248. **The correct answer is B.** The correct spelling is *cantaloupe*.

249. **The correct answer is D.** *No mistakes.* All the sentences are capitalized correctly.

250. **The correct answer is C.** An adverb should modify a verb, yet in this sentence, the adverb *prettily* modifies the noun *dress*. The word should be written in its adjective form: *pretty*.

251. **The correct answer is D.** *No mistakes.* All the words in these sentences are spelled correctly.

252. **The correct answer is B.** The list in choice B is not introduced correctly; it should begin with an introductory word or a colon, not a semicolon.

253. **The correct answer is A.** The minivan belongs to the speaker's parents, so the sentence requires the possessive form of the pronoun *they*: *their*.

254. **The correct answer is B.** The correct spelling is *scissors*.

255. **The correct answer is D.** *No mistakes.* Each sentence uses quotations correctly.

256. **The correct answer is D.** *No mistakes.* Each sentence uses semicolons correctly.

257. **The correct answer is B.** There is a word choice error in this sentence. This sentence mistakenly uses the preposition *of* as a helping verb. It should have used *have* instead of *of*.

258. **The correct answer is C.** In this sentence, the leaves belong to the tree, so *trees* should be in its possessive form: *tree's*. Without the apostrophe, it is in its plural form.

259. **The correct answer is A.** There is a spelling error in this sentence. The correct spelling is *excellence*.

260. **The correct answer is C.** The comma in this sentence is unnecessary.

261. **The correct answer is B.** There is a spelling error in this sentence. The correct spelling is *argument*.

262. **The correct answer is A.** The introductory phrase of this complex sentence describes action that will take place in the future, but the verb *gave* is in the past tense in the second clause. The best fix would be to replace *gave* with *give*.

263. **The correct answer is C.** There is a word choice error in this sentence. *Insure* means to protect, but the writer clearly uses it to mean "guarantee." The author probably intended to use the word *ensure*.

264. **The correct answer is D.** *No mistakes.* There are no errors in parentheses use in these sentences.

265. **The correct answer is B.** This sentence is a question, so it should end with a question mark, not a period.

266. **The correct answer is A.** *President* is John F. Kennedy's title in this sentence, so it should be capitalized.

267. **The correct answer is A.** There is a spelling error in this sentence. The correct spelling is *achieve*.

268. **The correct answer is C.** Although the titles of novels and movies should be italicized, the titles of songs should be placed within quotations without italics. The song should be written as "Honey," not *Honey*.

269. **The correct answer is C.** This sentence uses an incorrect *neither/nor* construction. It should be written: "Neither Grace nor Yuri was in class today."

270. **The correct answer is A.** Although the sentence describes something that happened in the past (last weekend), it requires the present participle of *work* (*working*) to show that the speaker spent the entire weekend working.

271. **The correct answer is D.** *No mistakes.* Each sentence is punctuated correctly.

272. **The correct answer is A.** There is a spelling error in this sentence. The correct spelling is *February*.

273. **The correct answer is B.** There is a preposition error in this sentence. When describing a duration of time, the correct preposition to use is *for*, not *since*.

274. **The correct answer is C.** There is a word choice error in this sentence. *Later* means something that has happened beyond now; *latter* means the last thing mentioned, which is what this sentence requires.

275. **The correct answer is D.** *No mistakes.* Each sentence uses conjunctions correctly.

276. **The correct answer is A.** In this sentence, *id* is an acronym meaning identification, and acronyms need to be capitalized: ID.

277. **The correct answer is B.** There is a word choice error in this sentence. *Defiantly* means "rebelliously," which does not make much sense in this context. It's clear that the speaker intended to use *definitely*, which means "certainly."

278. **The correct answer is C.** This sentence demonstrates correct usage. The other answer choices contain incorrect pronoun choices.

279. **The correct answer is C.** The word *whenever* joins the thoughts together in a timeframe that is logical. Choices A, B, and C represent impossibilities.

280. **The correct answer is B.** Choice B is the only answer that does not have a verb-tense error. Choices A, C, and D describe actions that take place in the present or future, yet all choices use a past-tense verb.

281. **The correct answer is A.** When someone is in a bad mood, that person is likely to be impatient, and speaking abruptly or rudely is a sign of impatience. Choices B and C do not imply impatience

at all. Choice D may suggest something bad, such as a bad mood, but it would be odd to describe the way someone answered a question as "horribly."

282. **The correct answer is C.** Choice C is the only sentence without a pronoun error. Choice A matches the antecedent subject *Curtis* with the plural pronoun *their*. Choice B matches the singular antecedent *Beatrice* with the plural pronoun *they*. Choice D matches the human antecedent *Ralph* with the non-human pronoun *its*.

283. **The correct answer is D.** While choices A, B, and C describe great benefits of recycling, choice D focuses only on how easy it is to recycle. It does not support the topic as strongly as the other answer choices do.

284. **The correct answer is A.** Choice A is the only sentence that uses a conjunction correctly. The other sentences all contain conjunction errors. Choice B lacks any conjunction, so it is a comma splice. Choice C uses *or* instead of *and*, which makes the clauses seem like a choice even though they do not have that kind of relationship. Choice D uses the conjunction *then*, which makes it seem as though the clauses share a sequential relationship, when in reality they share a consequential relationship.

285. **The correct answer is B.** The preposition that makes the most sense is *within*. Lying beneath (choice A) a stream of sunlight would not be as warm as lying right within it. Since there is only one stream of sunlight, the cat cannot lie between it (choice C). "Lying of" (choice D) something does not make grammatical sense.

286. **The correct answer is B.** An apostrophe is needed to show possession, and choice B is the only one that uses an apostrophe correctly. Choices A, C, and D all need possessive nouns but feature plural nouns.

287. **The correct answer is C.** Only choice C is expressed clearly. It is unclear whether the speaker plans to get a new picture or a new frame in choice A. Choice B has awkward syntax and is a run-on. Switching the clauses renders the sentence confusing, so choice D is not the best answer.

288. **The correct answer is D.** Only choice D uses a preposition correctly. Choice A should use *into*, not *in*, since *in* is used to show a position, and *into* is used to show where something is going. Conversely, Choice B should use *in to*, as *to* is part of the infinitive "to save," not part of the preposition *into*. Choice C should use "hours' time," not "hour's time"; the apostrophe is needed after the *s* in the plural *hours*.

289. **The correct answer is C.** Both sentences tell us why community service is beneficial to high school students and support the argument that it should be mandatory. Choice A is a statement of opinion and a biased generalization. Choice B digresses into a narrow aspect of community service—the elderly—and fails to express why community service should be mandatory. Choice D does not specifically address or develop the statement introduced in the topic sentence.

290. **The correct answer is D.** Only choice D uses its pronoun correctly. Choice A uses the possessive pronoun *hers*, even though the word is not used to show possession. Choice B uses the singular pronoun *her*, even though "Tiana and Paolo" is a plural antecedent. Choice C uses an apostrophe in a pronoun that should not have one: *yours*.

291. **The correct answer is B.** Only choice B is expressed correctly. Choice A uses neither a punctuation-conjunction combination nor proper standalone punctuation (either a semi-colon or a dash), so it is a run-on. Choice C reverses the clauses, making it seem as though the batteries dying is a consequence of having to replace them. Choice D is a fragment since the sentence does not explain what the speaker must do.

292. **The correct answer is C.** Only choice C uses its adverb correctly. Choice A makes the mistake of using an adverb (*carefully*) to modify a noun (*job*). Choice B uses an adjective, *mighty*, to modify a verb, *blew*; but an adverb should modify a verb. Choice D misplaces the adverb *loudly*, making it seem as though it modifies *learned* instead of *grumbled*.

293. The correct answer is D. For the most part, this passage is informative and not personal, but sentence 4 shifts that purpose and tone with irrelevant information about the writer's local supermarket.

294. The correct answer is A. Only choice A uses its pronoun correctly. Choice B uses the possessive pronoun *his* when the non-possessive *he* should follow *If*. Choice C uses a non-existing pronoun (*hisself*); the correct reflexive pronoun is *himself*. Choice D uses the possessive pronoun *her* when the non-possessive *she* is required.

295. The correct answer is A. The paragraph is mostly a fictional dialogue between a boy and his mother. Sentence 1 supplies an informative detail roughly related to the topic Darren and his mother discuss. It does not belong in this paragraph.

296. The correct answer is D. Only choice D uses an adverb correctly. Choice A uses the adjective *intricate* to modify the verb *spun* when the adverb *intricately* is required. Choice B uses the adverb *drily* to modify the noun *glue*, but an adjective should be used to modify a noun. *Resounded* is a verb, and an adverb, not an adjective such as *lovely*, should modify a verb; therefore, choice C is incorrect.

297. The correct answer is C. Each answer choice supports the topic well except for choice C, which explains an approach to finding an after-school job rather than the value of having an after-school job.

298. The correct answer is B. Choice B is the only sentence that uses the correct article. Choices A and C are incorrect because *an* should be used only to indicate a word that begins with a vowel. Choice D is incorrect because *a* should be used to indicate a word that begins with a consonant, not a vowel such as the *a* at the beginning of *antonym*.

NOTES

ANSWERS: HSP® DIAGNOSTIC TEST

4

SCORE SHEET

Although your actual exam scores will not be reported as percentages, it might be helpful to convert your test scores to percentages so that you can see at a glance where your strengths and weaknesses lie. The numbers in parentheses represent the questions that test each skill.

Subject	# Correct ÷ # of questions	× 100 = _____ %
Verbal Analogies (1, 2, 3, 4, 5, 6, 7, 8, 9, 10)	_____ ÷ 10 = _____	× 100 = _____ %
Synonyms (39, 40, 41, 42, 43, 44, 45, 46, 47, 48, 49, 50, 51)	_____ ÷ 13 = _____	× 100 = _____ %
Logic (11, 12, 13, 14, 15, 16, 17, 18, 19, 20, 21, 22)	_____ ÷ 12 = _____	× 100 = _____ %
Verbal Classification/Word Knowledge (23, 24, 25, 26, 27, 28, 29, 30, 31, 32, 33, 34, 35, 36, 37, 38)	_____ ÷ 16 = _____	× 100 = _____ %
Antonyms (52, 53, 54, 55, 56, 57, 58, 59, 60)	_____ ÷ 9 = _____	× 100 = _____ %
TOTAL VERBAL SKILLS	_____ ÷ 60 = _____	× 100 = _____ %
Number Series/Sequences (61, 64, 67, 68, 71, 72, 76, 77, 81, 83, 85, 87, 89, 92, 94, 96, 99, 101, 104, 105, 108, 111)	_____ ÷ 22 = _____	× 100 = _____ %
Geometric Comparisons (63, 65, 70, 78, 79, 86, 91, 103)	_____ ÷ 8 = _____	× 100 = _____ %
Nongeometric Comparisons (69, 74, 80, 82, 95, 98, 100, 107, 110)	_____ ÷ 10 = _____	× 100 = _____ %
Number Manipulation/Reasoning (62, 66, 73, 75, 84, 88, 90, 93, 97, 102, 106, 109, 112)	_____ ÷ 12 = _____	× 100 = _____ %
TOTAL QUANTITATIVE SKILLS	_____ ÷ 52 = _____	× 100 = _____ %
Reading—Comprehension (113–152)	_____ ÷ 40 = _____	× 100 = _____ %
Reading—Vocabulary (153–174)	_____ ÷ 22 = _____	× 100 = _____ %
TOTAL READING SKILLS	_____ ÷ 62 = _____	× 100 = _____ %
Mathematics—Concepts (175–198)	_____ ÷ 24 = _____	× 100 = _____ %
Mathematics—Problem-Solving (199–238)	_____ ÷ 40 = _____	× 100 = _____ %
TOTAL MATHEMATICS SKILLS	_____ ÷ 64 = _____	× 100 = _____ %
Capitalization, Punctuation, Spelling, and Grammar (239–277)	_____ ÷ 39 = _____	× 100 = _____ %
Usage and Composition (278–298)	_____ ÷ 21 = _____	× 100 = _____ %
TOTAL LANGUAGE SKILLS	_____ ÷ 60 = _____	× 100 = _____ %

Study Reference Guide

Subject	Chapter	Page
Reading	Chapter 5: Reading	192
Written Expression	Chapter 6: Language Composition and Expression	244
	Chapter 7: English Usage and Punctuation	
	Chapter 8: Capitalization and Spelling	
	Chapter 9: Logic and Verbal Classification	
	Chapter 10: Synonyms and Antonyms	
	Chapter 11: Analogies	
Mathematics	Chapter 12: Basic Mathematics	388
	Chapter 13: Algebraic Thinking	
	Chapter 14: Geometry	
	Chapter 15: Series Reasoning	
Ability	Chapter 16: Comparisons and Ability Questions	504
Language	Chapter 7: English Usage and Punctuation	266
	Chapter 8: Capitalization and Spelling	

ANSWERS: HSPT® DIAGNOSTIC TEST

PART III
VERBAL SKILLS

CHAPTER

Reading

READING

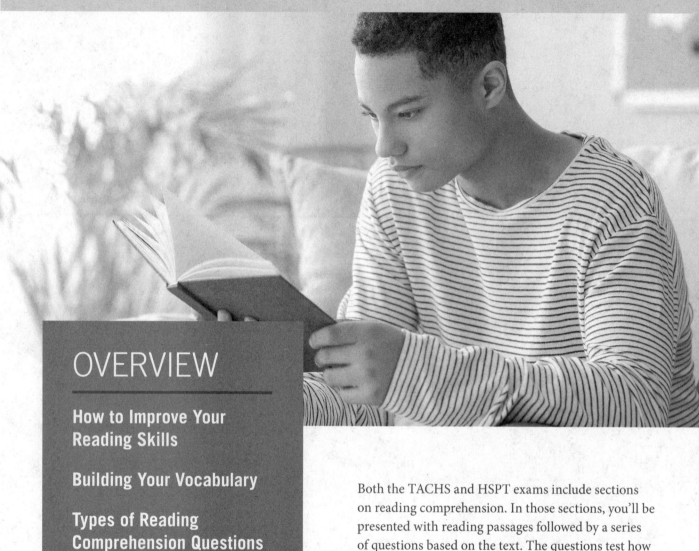

OVERVIEW

How to Improve Your Reading Skills

Building Your Vocabulary

Types of Reading Comprehension Questions

Summing It Up

Knowledge Check: Reading

Answer Keys and Explanations

TACHS   HSPT   ISEE   SSAT   SHSAT

Both the TACHS and HSPT exams include sections on reading comprehension. In those sections, you'll be presented with reading passages followed by a series of questions based on the text. The questions test how well you not only understand what you read on the surface but also interpret the passage's meaning and the author's intent. These questions also test how well you draw conclusions based on what you've read.

To do well on the reading comprehension sections of an exam, reading quickly is crucial—but so is comprehension. You won't be able to answer questions based on a passage if you don't allow yourself enough time to read it. Even if you can read the passage through once, you must have enough time left over to reread the selection for detailed questions.

HOW TO IMPROVE YOUR READING SKILLS

One of the best techniques for increasing your reading speed and comprehension is also one of the techniques that will help you improve your vocabulary—*reading*. The best way to increase your reading speed between now and the actual exam is to read as much as possible. Read everything in sight: newspapers, magazines, novels, billboards, nutrition labels, instruction manuals, etc. Push yourself to read the whole thing and give it your full attention as you read. Only by reading a complete work will you be able to properly analyze and understand it. If your mind wanders while you're reading, your comprehension is likely to wander, too.

To read with understanding, your eyes must occasionally stop on the page. Most people stop on each word because that is the way reading is taught in the early grades. But once you know how to read well, this method wastes a lot of time. The key to increasing your reading speed is to take in more words each time your eyes stop. If there's a line with ten words and you're able to read it by stopping only twice instead of ten times, you'll be reading approximately five times faster than you do now. As with most things in life, the only effective way to improve is with practice.

If you have a habit of softly speaking words as you read, break that habit now. This habit is called *subvocalizing*, and no matter how fast you can talk, you can read faster if you stop subvocalizing. Some people chew gum to stop subvocalizing. For others, just being aware of the habit is enough to help them correct it. Not only will it slow you down, but if you're reading aloud during your exam, the administrator may ask you to stop.

In building your reading speed, try moving your index finger or pencil tip underneath the line you are reading. Because your eyes tend to move as quickly as your pencil, you will not stop on every word. You will not regress (look back), and you will probably not subvocalize. However, what you might do is concentrate on your pencil and not on the reading passage. We recommend practicing this technique before trying it out on your test. Start with one finger or the point of your pencil at the second or third word in a line and stop before it hits the last word. Your peripheral vision (what you see at the edges) will pick up the first and last words in the lines, and you'll save time by not having to focus on them directly.

The following tips can improve performance on most reading comprehension passages. Experiment with how you approach passages and questions to discover what can compensate for your challenges on the subtest.

1. **Read actively:** Active reading means that you're summarizing what you're reading while you read, even asking questions, taking notes, or marking the text, if possible. After reading a paragraph, you should be able to recall its topic and purpose. Being able to do so will allow you not only to quickly return to relevant paragraphs based on the needs of a question but also to remember and understand the passage better. Active reading also means activating what you know about reading and writing to get what you need from a text. A well-written paragraph follows a particular structure. The first and last sentences of a paragraph (and a passage as a whole) often provide clear insight into topic and purpose.

2. **Work through questions strategically:** To perform well, nearly every reading comprehension test demands that you be thorough but efficient when reading passages and answering questions. You can avoid many of the typical time traps for test takers by following a set series of steps, as follows:

- Read the full question
- Make a prediction for the answer
- Read all answer choices
- Eliminate unsupported answers
- Find evidence for your choice

TIP

The reading comprehension section of the HSPT and TACHS exams requires that you read quickly and fully comprehend the text. The best way to increase your reading speed is to read as much as possible between now and the time of the exam.

3. **Be certain in your answers:** There's an excellent reason why the right answer is right and why each wrong answer is wrong; sometimes, this will come down to the details of the passage, and other times, it could come down to the specific wording of the answer. Sometimes, an answer can be true in the universal sense (known beyond the passage) but is not supported by the passage itself—in which case, it is incorrect. Regardless, you can be absolutely certain that your choice is correct if you have evidence from the passage to support it and evidence to eliminate other choices. If you can't be certain, then be aware that you're guessing. Remember, you should return to any questions you guessed on, time and test format permitting.

Here are a few other tips that will help you on the Reading section of the exam:

- Pay special attention to the first and last sentences of each paragraph, as they often state or reiterate the main idea.

- Reread the passage while giving attention to smaller details like point-of-view. Be alert for hints as to what the author finds important. Phrases such as "Note that...," "Of importance is...," and "Do not overlook..." give clues to what the writer is stressing.

- If the author quotes material from another source, be sure that you understand the quotation's purpose. Does the author agree or disagree with the quotation?

- Carefully read each question or incomplete statement and determine exactly what you need to look for. Watch for negatives or all-inclusive words such as *always, never, all, only, every, absolutely, completely, none, entirely,* and *no.*

- Read all the answer options. Avoid rushing to choose the first answer that appears correct. Eliminate the obviously incorrect choices first, then reread the remaining choices and refer to the passage, if necessary, to determine the *best* answer.

- Don't confuse a *true* answer with the *correct* answer—just because an answer is true doesn't mean it's the only true answer or that it's correct.

- Avoid involving personal or emotional judgments when finding your answers. Even if you disagree with the author, or spot a factual error in the passage, you must answer based on what's stated or implied in the text.

- Don't spend too much time on one question. If looking back at the passage doesn't help you figure it out, eliminate the wrong answers and choose from those that remain. Then, forget about it for the time being and move on.

Scan this QR code for more information about our reading comprehension method.

BUILDING YOUR VOCABULARY

Vocabulary and reading comprehension are closely related. You can't grow your vocabulary without reading, and you can't comprehend a text without a firm grasp of the words the author is using. To prepare yourself for the exam, you'll need a strong vocabulary. While reading can give you exposure to new and unfamiliar words, expanding your vocabulary requires *active reading*. Active reading involves more than just picking up a book or article and reading it over. There are a few additional steps you need to take.

Keep a Word Log

First off, read material that is more challenging. Check out magazines like *Scientific American*, *Newsweek*, *National Geographic*, and the like. Look over the *New York Times*, the *Washington Post*, the *Times of London*, and other well-regarded newspapers. You can even look ahead in some of your textbooks. The key is to find material with words that are new or unfamiliar to you.

Next, with pen in hand, write down the words that you don't understand. Instead of using a computer or mobile device, the act of writing something by hand actually helps you encode the word into your memory. Once you have a good list of unfamiliar words, look up the definitions in a dictionary. Focus on learning a few words at a time so that you can learn them well. Sometimes, it can be helpful to start with a learner's dictionary, which will define a word in simpler language and provide more examples of how to use it in a sentence. Write down the definitions for the unfamiliar words. You can even go back to where you originally

found the unfamiliar word and reread it to see how the now-familiar word is used.

Third, try to use the word yourself in a sentence or in conversation. Practice using the word by creating your own sentences and writing them down in a notebook. This will help you get a sense of how to use the word in different contexts while cementing the word and its meaning into your vocabulary. Take note of the contexts in which you often see or use a word. Getting familiar with the topics and situations in which certain words are used will help you feel more confident and self-assured when you integrate new words into your vocabulary.

When keeping your word log, be sure to write down the new words you have learned as well as the words you want to learn. When you document the definition for a new word, include details like the part of speech, as well as any synonyms and antonyms, and give an example of how the word can be used in a sentence. You can also study the roots, prefixes, and suffixes of words, so you can apply all you know whenever you encounter a word that's unfamiliar. If a word has more than one meaning, you should include those as well. Here is an example of what an entry might look like.

EXAMPLE:

ATTRITION: noun. 1. Sorrow for one's sins; 2. the act of wearing or grinding down by friction; 3. weakening or exhausting by constant harassment, abuse, or attack; 4. a reduction in numbers.

> **Synonyms:** corrosion, erosion, degradation
>
> **Antonyms:** buildup, growth, accumulation
>
> **Sentence:** The attrition rate among social workers is high, due mainly to the long hours, difficult work, and low pay.

If it's not possible to keep a paper log of new words, a mobile device can be a valuable tool for taking notes. When you're at the grocery store or on the bus and you see or hear a word that is unfamiliar, you can write it down and look it up later. Some devices will let you use a stylus, so you can still write by hand. Mobile devices also have access to a dictionary, whether it's through an app or a web browser. Lastly, such devices can give you access to reading material like online magazines and newspapers, books, and research papers, especially things you wouldn't normally have easy access to like English language newspapers from other countries.

Study Root Words, Prefixes, and Suffixes

You can actually increase your vocabulary—and your test score—by learning about the structure of words. This will help you figure out the meanings of unfamiliar words you come across in the verbal skills section of your exam. Knowing what the parts of words mean is the key to deciphering words you've never seen before.

English words have recognizable parts that most often come from Latin or Greek. Generally, there are three basic types of word parts:

1. **Roots** are the basic elements of a word that determine its meaning. Most derive from Latin and Greek and must be combined with prefixes, suffixes, or both.
2. **Prefixes** attach to the beginning of a root word to alter its meaning or to create a new word.
3. **Suffixes** attach to the end of a root word to change its meaning, help make it grammatically correct in context, or form a new word. Suffixes often indicate whether a word is a noun, verb, adjective, or adverb.

Sometimes, depending on the word, it can be difficult to parse out whether a word part is a prefix or a root word. However, the key takeaway here is that certain word parts carry meanings that are recognizable no matter what the word is. Knowing the meaning of part of a word can help you infer the meaning of the word.

To aid you in your learning, we've put together a compilation of frequently used root words, prefixes, and suffixes. This table is by no means comprehensive, but it should help you get started on breaking down some of the words you see most often.

COMMON ROOTS

Root	Meaning	Example
Aqu *Hydr*	Water	Aqueous, aquarium, hydrate, hydrotherapy
Aud	Hear	Auditory, audio, audible
Biblio	Book	Bibliophile, bibliography
Chrono	Time	Chronological, chronology
Chrom	Color	Monochromatic, chromosome
Circ	Round	Circle, circus
Geo	Earth	Geography, geomagnetic
Juris	Law	Jurisdiction, jurisprudence
Junct	Join	Conjunction, juncture
Log *Logue*	Speaking, speech	Epilogue, eulogy, dialogue
Photo	Light	Photosynthesis, photography, photon
Scribe	Write	Describe, prescribe, inscribe
Sect	Cut	Dissect, sector
Volve	Roll, turn	Involve, evolve, revolve

Scan this QR code to learn more about root words.

COMMON PREFIXES		
Prefix	**Meaning**	**Example**
Anti-	Against	Antifreeze, antibacterial
Bene-	Good	Benefit, benevolent
De-	Opposite	Deactivate, derail
Dis- *Dys-*	Not	Disagree, dysfunctional
En- *Em-*	Cover	Encode, embrace
Extra-	Beyond	Extraterrestrial, extracurricular
Fore-	Before	Forecast, forehead
Il- *Im-* *In-* *Ir-* *Non-* *Un-*	Not	Illegitimate, impossible, inexcusable, irregular, nonstop, nonsense, unable, undefined
Inter-	Between	Intergalactic, intermediary, interpret
Mis-	Wrongly	Mistake, misinterpret, misnomer
Over-	Over, more, too much	Overlook, oversee, overachieve, overcast
Pre-	Before	Prefix, prevent, predict, prehistoric, prejudice
Re-	Again	Revision, reimagine, return
Trans-	Across	Transatlantic, transverse, transport

COMMON SUFFIXES		
Suffix	**Meaning**	**Example**
-able *-ible*	Capable of; fit for	Agreeable, collectible
-al	Pertaining to	Logical, magical, criminal
-ance *-ence*	Indicating a state or condition; indicating a process or action	Clearance, ignorance, evidence, patience
-ent	Causing, promoting, or doing an action; one who causes or does something	Different, absorbent, student, agent, deterrent
-fy *-ize* *-ate* *-en*	Cause to be	Classify, diversify, realize, contextualize, create, communicate, awaken, sharpen
-ious *-ous*	Characterized by; full of	Nutritious, delicious, simultaneous, nervous
-ism	Belief, act	Catholicism, plagiarism
-ity	State or quality of being	Enmity, ability, responsibility
-less	Without	Homeless, restless, countless
-let	Small	Booklet, piglet
-or *-er* *-ist*	A person who is or does something	Benefactor, investigator, driver, teacher, narcissist, chemist
-ship	Position held	Friendship, citizenship, allyship, ownership
-tion *-sion* *-ment*	Action or instance of something	Liberation, concentration, admission, decision, achievement, bereavement
-y	Quality of	Thirsty, wintry

Let's take a look at the word *biography* and its parts. You know that a biography is something written about a person's life. How do the word parts tell you this? Well, the second part of the word, *graphy*, comes from a Greek word that means "writing." The first part of the word, *bio*, comes from Greek and means "life." Put them both together and you get *biography*, the story of a person's life. If you add the Latin word for "self"— *auto*—you get *autobiography*, a story you write about your own life. Think about some other words that use one or more of these parts, like *automobile*, *biochemistry*, and *autograph*.

Let's look at another example. For a word like *benefactor*, you can look over the list of prefixes and suffixes to find *bene-* (good) and the suffix *-or* (one who does) to break down the word: *bene-fact-or*. From the prefix, you know that this word means something good. From the suffix, you also know that the word refers to someone who does something. From that, you could arrive at the rough definition of someone who does something good. That definition strikes close to the actual definition, which is a person or thing that provides help or an advantage.

Different parts of words come together to form a variety of meanings, and as you study root words, prefixes, and suffixes, you'll start recognizing the patterns in the words you use most often. As you keep your log of unfamiliar words, try and track the root words, suffixes, and prefixes you encounter most. Once you begin to learn the word parts on the list, you'll be able to take apart unfamiliar words and infer their meaning from just the root word and the suffix or prefix. Knowing how to break a word into its root, suffix, and prefix can also help you determine what part of speech the word is, which in turn can help you eliminate incorrect answer options for certain questions.

Finally, don't forget to use the word list in Appendix A to expand your word horizons. As you make your way through the list, try to think of other words with the same parts. If you have time, check their meanings in a dictionary and take a look at the word origins in the entry so that you can add some new words to your ongoing word log.

TYPES OF READING COMPREHENSION QUESTIONS

This chapter details several types of questions you will encounter on the exam: main idea, primary purpose, applied meaning, statement agreement and inferences, supportive statements, and fact finding. The following questions demonstrate the kinds of tasks you will be asked to perform on the exam:

- What is the main idea of the passage?
- What is the primary purpose of the passage?
- What is the applied meaning of a term or phrase?
- Would the author agree with a statement about the passage?
- What can you infer from the passage?
- Is a statement supported by the passage?
- What information is or is not included in the passage?

Main Idea

Main idea questions ask you to think about the passage in its entirety. These questions often ask you to consider what a summary of the passage might look like. Main idea questions may look like the following:

"This passage is mainly about …"

"A good title for this passage would be …"

"The main idea of this passage is that …"

Correctly answering main idea questions shows that you read and understood the passage. When you're answering these questions, it's important to keep your focus on the passage overall. Even if the answer options are all accurate, in that they reflect facts or details presented in the passage, your goal is to pick the answer that provides the *best* overview of the passage in its entirety. In other words, consider the main idea a summary of the passage. Ask yourself, if you were to recount the passage to a friend so that they could understand what it's about without having to read it, what would you say?

As you read a passage, it's helpful to note ideas or themes that continually occur. If it's a single paragraph, you might look closely at the first and last sentences;

these sentences are most useful for determining the author's focus in a paragraph because they state the primary takeaways of the passage, what the author wants the reader to remember most. If you're reading a passage that consists of multiple paragraphs, it might be helpful to annotate the passage as you go, if possible. As you read, write down a word or a phrase next to each paragraph that summarizes the paragraph's main idea. Then, when you finish reading, you can review the ideas you jotted down next to each paragraph and draw a conclusion as to what the most important topic or theme is in the passage. Sometimes, it's helpful to choose an answer and then read the passage again to see if that answer holds true. Reading the passage a second time can help you focus on the themes and ideas being emphasized and helps you identify details or information that are less important to the passage as a whole.

Let's walk through an example of a main idea question.

EXAMPLE:

Using new tools and techniques, scientists, almost unnoticed, are remaking the world of plants. They have already
Line remodeled 65 sorts of flowers, fruits,
5 vegetables, and trees giving us, among other things, tobacco that resists disease, cantaloupes that are immune to the blight, and lettuce with crisper leaves. The chief new tool they are using is colchicine, an
10 anti-inflammatory drug that has astounding effects upon growth and heredity. It creates new varieties with astonishing frequency, whereas such mutations occur rarely in nature. Colchicine has thrown
15 new light on the fascinating jobs of plant hunters. The Department of Agriculture sends agents all over the world to find plants native to other lands that can be grown in the United States and that are
20 superior to those already here. Scientists

have crossed these foreign plants with those at home, thereby adding many desirable characteristics to our farm crops. The colchicine technique has drastically en-
25 hanced their work because hybrids can so often be made fertile and because it now takes so few generations of plants to build a new variety with the qualities desired.

Which title best expresses the ideas of the paragraph?

A. "Plant Growth and Heredity"
B. "The Dangers of Plant Diseases"
C. "Remodeling Plant Life"
D. "A More Abundant World"

The correct answer is C. The first sentence of the paragraph is the biggest clue as to what this passage is about: "remaking the world of plants." With that in mind, we could probably take a guess, without reading the passage, from the answer options available. The title "Remodeling Plant Life" captures the idea of remaking plants. That being said, we would want to reread the passage to confirm that it is the most fitting title. While the passage does address plant growth and heredity (choice A), the main idea seems to be crossing plants to form new crops, not necessarily the details of plant genetics. Similarly, though one of the reasons new varieties of plants are being bred is to make them resistant to disease, it is not the focal point of the passage (choice B). Finally, choice D is too broad and does not clue the reader into the topic of the passage.

Scan this QR code for a video on answering main idea questions.

Primary Purpose

Primary purpose questions are similar to main idea questions in that they require you to think about the topic or subject of the entire passage. However, the key difference here is understanding the author's intention. Like the main idea of a passage, the purpose of a passage is often revealed in its first and last sentences with the author's thesis statement or conclusion. However, these questions often go beyond main idea questions because they are concerned with not only *what* the author is saying but also *how* they say it and *why*. In other words, what type of writing is this and what is the author's purpose for writing it? In chapter 6, we elaborate on different types of writing and the purpose of each, which can also help you with this type of reading comprehension question.

VERBS THAT INDICATE PURPOSE	
Purpose	**Definition**
inform	providing information to educate a reader on a topic
persuade	convincing the reader to agree with an opinion or point of view
amuse	entertaining the reader with an interesting, inventive, or humorous topic
compare	showing the similarities or differences between ideas
describe	using the five senses to portray the characteristics or qualities of a topic
explain	making an idea or issue clearer through description or details
discuss	examining different angles or perspectives of a topic

When identifying the primary purpose, answer choices often rely on a series of key verbs that best summarize the purpose and form of the passage. For example, words such as *inform, persuade*, or *discuss* will typically head the sentences for each option and summarize what the

author's intentions behind the passage were. A solid understanding of commonly used key verbs and what they mean can help you on the exam.

Let's look at an example.

EXAMPLE:

John Patrick Rose began his career in 2014 with the launch of his introductory appliance repair program. When sales
Line skyrocketed in less than two weeks, his
5 instruction was in high demand. He began a weekly mentoring group for newly certified technicians, which only solidified his status as a vocational guru.

What is the primary purpose of this passage?

A. To advocate for appliance repair certification programs as a national standard
B. To discuss the life of John Patrick Rose and explore the perceived value behind his contributions to vocational education
C. To inform the reader about John Patrick Rose and his success in the field of appliance repair education
D. To encourage appliance repair persons to follow a mentor

The correct answer is C. This example illustrates the importance of understanding the key words. This passage does not advocate or discuss. It clearly informs. The passage provides solid facts about John Patrick Rose and his career as an appliance repair education guru.

The key to understanding primary purpose questions is understanding what words such as *provide, highlight, discuss, inform*, etc., mean and how they are used.

Applied Meaning

Applied meaning questions ask a reader to determine the meaning of a word or phrase in the context of the passage. These questions take advantage of how words may shift in definition depending on the situation in which they are used. Take, for instance, the word *restrained*. A violent prisoner may be restrained (bound) by guards. Alternatively, an individual may be restrained in how they communicate dissatisfaction (measured or controlled). Context can make all the difference.

Applied meaning questions will often take the following forms:

"In the first paragraph, the word _____ most likely means"

"The author most likely uses the phrase _____ in order to convey"

The best way to assess applied meaning questions is to return to the placement of the word or phrase in the passage, then read the sentence and the sentences before and after it. The word or phrase itself can oftentimes mean multiple things if read alone, but in the context of the passage, it will have a specific meaning.

EXAMPLE:

Hippos and humans have a long history with some of the earliest depictions of our interactions dating to around 4400 BCE in Egypt. At best, our relationship could be characterized as strained. Hippos have long had a reputation as one of the most dangerous animals in the world. They've been known to attack people near waterways and boats at random, sometimes resulting in the injury or death of passengers. Some sources estimate at least 500 deaths per year can be attributed to the aquatic mammal. However, despite their penchant for fierceness, hippos are also the victims of human aggression. To compensate for dwindling elephant populations, ivory poachers have turned to harvesting hippo teeth for income. Subsistence hunting and shrinking habitats have also impacted the hippo population, with a 2017 assessment labeling the animal as vulnerable to extinction. For centuries, both humans and hippos have threatened one another. It's safe to say that we would both be best served by maintaining a safe and respectful distance.

Line 5 and *10* markers appear in left margin.

The author uses the phrase "our relationship could be characterized as strained" to convey

A. the history of the species' interactions is filled with mutual tension.

B. humans have struggled to understand how hippos live.

C. both humans and hippos have injured one another.

D. humans have been plagued by hippos for thousands of years.

The correct answer is A. Essentially, the question asks for the meaning of the paragraph's second sentence. To understand the meaning, you need to understand not only the words used but also the supporting sentences to establish context. The strained relationship between humans and hippos, as explained by the author, is described in the paragraph as the result of the acts of aggression that have come from both sides. According to the passage, human poachers have hunted hippos for their ivory, and hippos have been known to attack boats filled with people. However, as this helps us understand the reason for the "strained relationship" between hippos and humans, it does not answer the question. Our understanding of the passage could lead us to select choice C, but the question wants us to assess the meaning of the phrase, not its cause.

With the exception of choice A, each answer option describes specific ways in which humans and hippos have interacted—some supported by the passage and some not. While some of these choices use words that could be synonyms for *strained*, the keywords of the original phrase are not represented. *Relationship*, *characterized*, and *strained* direct us to look for a general description of the species' tense history without offering information that goes beyond the words used. Choice A states, "the history of the species' interactions is filled with mutual tension." While the "tension" in question is the result of injuries caused by the two sides (choice C), no word in the original phrase can be contextually defined as meaning injury or aggression.

Statement Agreements and Inferences

Statement agreement questions will ask you to determine if the author or speaker of the passage would agree with a statement or how they might respond to a certain statement. The question may reference exact quotes from the passage or make an inference based on phrases found within the passage. The author or speaker will either agree with one of the answer options or they will not. An inference question requires similar thinking in that you must use the explicit information in the passage to come to a well-supported conclusion that aligns with the author's purpose.

Statement agreement and inference questions rely on your understanding of the primary purpose of the passage as well as your ability to understand relationships between details. Let's look at a passage and a statement agreement and inference question.

EXAMPLE:

America stands today at the opening of a second Space Age. Innovative NASA programs and American entrepreneurs together are transforming the space industry. These initiatives—both at NASA and in the private sector—are expanding the nation's opportunities for exploration and for the economic development of the solar system.

Line

5   Today's space economy extends some 36,000 kilometers (22,369 miles) from the surface of the Earth and includes an array of evidence-based technologies—satellite communications, global positioning satellites, and imaging satellites—on which our economy depends. These technologies are now an integral part of our economy, and they would not exist if not for the over 50 years of research, development, and investment in the enabling technologies by NASA

10   and other government agencies that seeded these efforts and allowed them to bloom. As we expand our activities in the solar system over the next decades, NASA programs and investments will provide the seed and soil that encourage economic development increasingly farther from Earth. The first signs of this are already visible.

The next era of space exploration will see governments pushing technological development

15   and the American private sector using these technologies as they expand their economic activities to new worlds. NASA's next objectives for exploration—visits to asteroids and Mars—are more complex than any previous space mission attempted. They will happen in the context of relatively smaller NASA budgets and an expanding commercial space economy. Teaming

with private-sector partners to develop keystone markets like low Earth orbit (LEO) transpor-
20 tation and technological capabilities like asteroid mining will help NASA achieve its mission
goals, help the space economy evolve to embrace new ambitions, and provide large economic
returns to the taxpayer through the stimulation and growth of new businesses and 21st-century
American jobs.

—Excerpt from "Emerging Space: The Evolving Landscape of 21st Century American
Spaceflight" as produced by the Office of the Chief Technologist at NASA

How might the author respond to news of a partnership between NASA and a private space exploration company for a future Mars mission?

- A. Criticize the private company for siphoning funds away from NASA's own research and
  exploration activities
- B. Express support for the partnership only if NASA has full control of any resulting
  technology
- C. Celebrate the partnership as a step toward achieving NASA's mission goals
- D. Contend that such partnerships distract from attempts to expand NASA's budget

The correct answer is C. This question requires your understanding of the purpose of the passage,
best summarized by the final sentence of the first paragraph, "These initiatives—both at NASA and
in the private sector—are expanding the nation's opportunities for exploration and for the economic
development of the solar system." Relevant to this question in particular are the positive framing
around the phrase "expanding the nation's opportunities" and the mention of both NASA and the
private sector. This can lead us to infer positive reception of any announcement that melds those
groups together. Choices A and D offer verbiage and ideas that run counter to the message of collaboration and partnership present throughout the passage. While choice B expresses support for
the partnership, it creates a condition for the support that misconstrues statements from the second
paragraph regarding "enabling technologies by NASA." Choice C expresses support and aligns with
a statement from the final paragraph of the passage, stating "Teaming with private-sector partners
[. . .] will help NASA achieve its mission goals."

Based on the passage, which of the following factors can one infer will likely support the future exploration of space?

- A. Dwindling funding for governmental space agencies
- B. Economic incentives from governments to encourage visits to asteroids and Mars
- C. An economy built on the technologies developed by NASA in the 20th century
- D. Government-supported technological development

The correct answer is D. The question asks that you use the details provided in the passage to infer
which activities will impact future space exploration. Choice A misrepresents a detail from the last
paragraph of the passage ("in the context of relatively smaller NASA budgets"). It infers a shrinking
budget instead of a "smaller" budget, assumes that this applies to all governmental space agencies,

and, in terms of the question, offers this as a supporting factor for space exploration, rather than it more likely having the opposite effect. Choices B and C offer similar misrepresentations of passage details and misalignment with the question's goal. No mention is made in the passage of direct incentives for exploration or similar measures, only that the technological development pursued by NASA can "provide the seed and soil that encourage economic development increasingly farther from Earth." For choice C, the technologies already developed by NASA are mentioned as having laid the groundwork for much of our modern economy; the emphasis on further development allows you to infer that such technology is insufficient for future needs. Only choice D presents a supporting factor for the future exploration of space. With "governments pushing technological development and the American private sector using these technologies," the expansion of "economic activities to new worlds" implies continued and future space exploration.

Supportive Statements

You will encounter questions on the exam that will ask you to locate specific information within the passage to determine whether a given statement is supported or not supported by the passage. These questions will likely present in several formats:

"Which of the following statements is supported by the passage?"

"Which of the following statements is *not* supported by the passage?"

Supportive statement questions require you to retain information provided in the passage and to return to its primary purpose once again. These are similar to statement agreement questions, where you must determine whether or not the author would agree with a given statement. However, those questions depend upon word choice and sentence structure, whereas supportive statement questions are strictly limited to the information provided in the passage. Let's look at an example.

EXAMPLE:

"The Party said that Oceania had never been in alliance with Eurasia. He, Winston Smith, knew that Oceania had been in alliance with Eurasia as short a time as four years ago. But where did that knowledge exist? Only in his own consciousness, which in any case must soon
Line   be annihilated. And if all others accepted the lie which the Party imposed — if all records told
5   the same tale — then the lie passed into history and became truth. 'Who controls the past,' ran the Party slogan, 'controls the future: who controls the present controls the past.' And yet the past, though of its nature alterable, never had been altered. Whatever was true now was true from everlasting to everlasting. It was quite simple. All that was needed was an unending series of victories over your own memory. 'Reality control', they called it: in Newspeak, 'doublethink.'"

—Excerpt from *1984*, by George Orwell

Which of the following statements is supported by the passage?

- **A.** Winston Smith had imagined the alliance between Oceania and Eurasia.
- **B.** The past is insignificant to the present.
- **C.** The Party created its own version of history.
- **D.** Ruling effectively requires brainwashing your constituents.

The correct answer is C. In this passage, the speaker is describing the tension between Winston Smith's memory about the past' specifically an alliance between Oceania and Eurasia, and how the Party has rewritten the past. Smith knows that there was an alliance between Oceania and Eurasia; the passage does not suggest that he imagined it as choice A erroneously indicates. It is clear that Smith's memory contradicts the version of reality presented by the Party, but the passage does not imply that Smith's memories, our memories generally, are incorrect. The passage discusses how the past is used to shape the present and future, so choice B is incorrect. There is no discussion of ruling effectively in this passage, so choice D is also incorrect.

Fact Finding

Fact finding questions require you to recall or locate specific details within the passage. Details are the facts and ideas in a passage that explain and support the main idea and the author's purpose. These sentences might offer examples, facts, statistics, quotations, further information, descriptions, or other details to convey the main idea and purpose.

Most times, you will be asked about the passage's content itself. For example, if the passage is informing you about five different types of pasta, a details question might ask, "Which of the following is *not* discussed as a type of pasta?" Or "In this passage, the author compares tortellini to…" It's your job to look back through the passage and choose the right answer based on the details provided (or not provided).

Sometimes, you'll get to one of these questions and you'll remember exactly what the passage said, making it easy for you to answer correctly. Even if you know the answer, you can return to the passage and skim to verify that what you remember about the passage is correct. Once you find evidence of the information the question is asking for, you can return back to the answer choices and mark the correct answer.

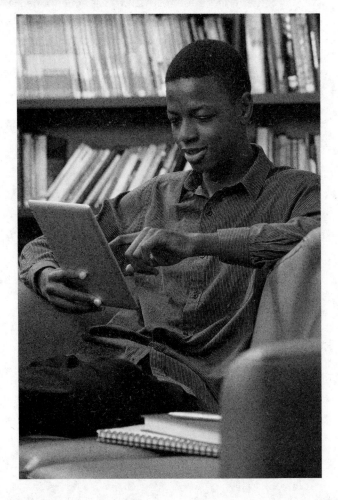

Let's look at an example.

EXAMPLE:

There are many signs by which people predict the weather. Some of these have a true basis, but many have not. There is, for example, no evidence that it is more likely to storm during one phase of the moon than during another. If it happens to rain on Easter, there is no reason

Line to think that it will rain for the next seven Sundays. The groundhog may or may not see his

5 shadow on Groundhog Day, but it probably won't affect the weather anyway.

Which of the following is *not* listed as a predictive weather phenomenon?

A. Rain on Easter

B. Phases of the moon

C. Pain in a person's joints

D. Groundhog's shadow

The correct answer is C. Older people complaining of pain in their joints as a sign of incoming bad weather is a common idea, but it's not mentioned anywhere in this paragraph. The author mentions rain on Easter (choice A) in the fourth sentence when talking about the superstition that rain on Easter means rain for seven more Sundays. The author references phases of the moon (choice B) in the third sentence—this is a quick mention, so you might've missed it the first time. The groundhog's shadow (choice D) is referenced near the end of the paragraph.

NOTES

SUMMING IT UP

- Both the TACHS and the HSPT include a reading comprehension section. Each test presents reading passages followed by a series of questions. The reading passages cover a wide range of topics and genres, so be prepared to encounter a variety of material.

- To do well on this section, you will need to be able to read quickly and actively, strategically work through questions, and be certain in your answers.

- To improve your reading skills, consider keeping a word log to study the roots, prefixes, and suffixes of words.

- There are many types of questions you can expect to see in the Reading section. The following six types of questions are the most common.

    1. Main Idea

        - What is the passage about?
        - Look to the beginnings and ends of passages, where the author will usually introduce and conclude with a summary of the passage.

    2. Primary Purpose

        - What is the primary purpose of the passage?
        - Look for key verbs like *advocate*, *discuss*, or *inform* at the beginning of the answer choices.
        - Pay attention to sentence structure in both the question and the answer choices.

    3. Applied Meaning

        - What is the applied meaning of a term or phrase? What does the word or phrase mean?
        - Look for terms like *most likely means* and *most likely uses the word/phrase*.
        - Read the sentence(s) around the word or phrase in question to help understand the context.

4. Statement Agreement and Inferences

   o   Would the author (or character, if a work of fiction) agree with a statement about the passage?

   o   Understanding the purpose of the passage is key in answering statement agreement questions correctly.

5. Supportive Statements

   o   Is a given statement supported by the passage?

   o   Look for questions like "Which of the following statements is/is *not* supported?"

   o   Answers to supportive statement questions rely on sentence structure or how the words are used in the question.

6. Fact Finding

   o   What information is included in the passage?

   o   You will be asked to determine what information is presented in the passage or to locate a specific detail.

   o   Answering these questions requires you to recall specific details or to skim the passage to determine the correct answer.

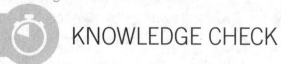

KNOWLEDGE CHECK

READING 1
40 Questions—28 Minutes

Directions: The following questions are based on several reading passages. Each passage is followed by a series of questions. Read each passage carefully, then answer the questions. You may reread the passage as often as you wish. When you have finished answering the set of questions based on a passage, go on to the next passage.

Questions 1–8 refer to the following passage.

The music of Mozart has had a significant impact on the world, and it still does to this day. Although Mozart died very young, at the age of 35, he wrote more compositions during his short lifetime than any other composer in history. He was so skilled as a musician that we find it difficult to comprehend the stories we hear of his talents today. His skill allowed him to leave a musical legacy that not only delighted audiences but had a great impact on the future of music as well.

Perhaps the most notable aspect of Mozart's career is how young he was when he started. From the time that Mozart was three years old, it was clear that he was extraordinarily gifted. He was considered a child <u>prodigy</u> because of his stunning musical talents. He began to play the piano at age three, and he composed his first music at the age of four. Mozart had an excellent ear for music, even at this very young age.

Mozart's efforts changed music in many ways. One of the most important changes that Mozart helped to contribute was expanding the different types of music that existed during his time. Before Mozart began composing, there was only one major form of music, known as the *sonata*. A sonata is a musical piece written for one or two solo instruments, consisting of three or four separate parts, called movements. At that time, composers wrote sonatas either for the violin or for the keyboard. The movements within these sonatas were also small, without much development.

Through his writing, Mozart greatly increased the types of music that were written and performed. He helped add forms such as symphonies, concertos, quartets, and trios. Mozart also wrote sonatas, but he added depth to the sonatas and gave them more structure. In part, he was able to do this because he had been exposed to many different types of music during his travels as a young boy. He combined the musical styles that he learned during his stays in Germany, France, Italy, and other regions in Austria.

Line

5

10

15

20

1. Which statement best reflects the main idea of the passage?

   A. Mozart started his musical career when he was extremely young: He learned to play the piano when he was only three years old.

   B. Mozart was an extremely talented musician and composer whose contributions have had a significant impact on music.

   C. Mozart greatly increased the types of music that were written and performed, adding symphonies, concertos, quartets, and trios to the sonata form that already existed.

   D. Mozart wrote a great number of musical works during his lifetime, but his music was not appreciated until after his death.

2. The underlined word *prodigy* in this context means a person

   A. with exceptional skills.

   B. who is slower than most.

   C. with a scientific mind.

   D. who shows great kindness.

3. Mozart's sonatas differed from sonatas written before his time because Mozart's sonatas were

   A. more entertaining than the previous sonatas.

   B. more structured and had more depth than the previous sonatas.

   C. composed more quickly than the previous sonatas.

   D. more difficult to play than the previous sonatas.

4. According to the passage, which statement is true of Mozart's compositions?

   A. No other composer in history has equaled his output.

   B. He wrote more symphonies than any other composer in history.

   C. His compositions all had at least three parts.

   D. All his compositions were sonatas.

5. According to the passage, what did Mozart accomplish before the age of 5?

   A. He learned to play the trumpet and piano.

   B. He composed a sonata for the violin and piano.

   C. He was introduced to the royal court in Vienna.

   D. He learned to play the piano and wrote his first composition.

6. According to the passage, a sonata is a musical composition for

   A. an orchestra with a piano solo.

   B. a stringed instrument and a woodwind.

   C. trios and quartets.

   D. one or two instruments.

7. According to the passage, as a boy, Mozart traveled through which countries outside of his homeland?

   A. England, France, and Italy

   B. France, Italy, and Germany

   C. Germany, Austria, and Italy

   D. Austria, France, and Italy

8. According to the passage, Mozart's travels as a young boy

   A. brought him fame and wealthy patrons.

   B. exposed him to disease, causing his death at the age of 35.

   C. exposed him to many different types of music.

   D. helped him learn several languages.

Questions 9–15 refer to the following passage.

When I was growing up during the Depression, I lived on a farm in New Jersey with my grandmother and grandfather. Aunt Frieda was my youngest aunt; she lived in New York City with her husband, my Uncle Stuart, and she frequently wrote letters to my grandmother and grandfather. My grandparents didn't

Line speak any English, so I always translated the correspondence for them from English into Italian.

5   One day, when I was about fifteen, I saw that the letters from my Aunt Frieda were coming written in Uncle Stuart's handwriting. I realized that Aunt Frieda wasn't really writing them, but I didn't say anything to my grandmother or grandfather because I didn't want to worry them. My grandmother was a real worrier, and I didn't want her to get upset, so I continued to read the letters to her as if they were coming from Aunt Frieda.

10   That went on for several weeks, until we had a visit from my Aunt Grace, who was Aunt Frieda's older sister. Aunt Grace told me that she had just visited Aunt Frieda. I asked my Aunt Grace what was wrong with Aunt Frieda, and Aunt Grace replied, "Your Aunt Frieda has had an eye operation. She's recuperating just fine, and she's planning a visit to see *Nana* very soon."

Shortly after that, I received a letter from Uncle Stuart informing me that he and Aunt Frieda were

15 coming to visit. On the day they arrived, the moment I saw their car, I said to my grandmother, "*Nana*, I have something to tell you about Aunt Frieda. Now I don't want to worry you—Aunt Frieda is fine, but she's had an operation on her eye. She went to the hospital in Philadelphia to have the surgery done."

My grandmother was beginning to get visibly upset, and I did my best to calm her down. We were all standing on the front porch when Aunt Frieda and Uncle Stuart drove up. When Aunt Frieda exited the car,

20 she was walking <u>gingerly</u>, like someone who couldn't see very well. I kept trying to keep my grandmother calm.

Nana behaved outwardly, but she cried silently to herself. When my Aunt Frieda got out of the car, all that my *Nana* said was, "Your own mother—you keep a secret from your own mother—your mother was supposed to be there by your side!" She kept repeating it over and over, but that was all she said.

25   I imagine that part of the reason why *Nana* would become so upset when she felt powerless was because she was accustomed to having everything go her way. Unlike my grandmother, my grandfather was a very quiet man who lived a routine, predictable life: he did his work, ate dinner, and went to bed. My grandmother, on the other hand, was absolutely in charge, and it was clear that she controlled the money, the decisions—she controlled everything. She was smart as a whip, too.

9. The underlined word *gingerly* in this context means

    A. confidently.

    B. cautiously.

    C. recklessly.

    D. naturally.

10. How is the author's grandfather different from his grandmother?

    A. His grandfather doesn't have many dreams, while his grandmother dreams often.

    B. His grandfather becomes sick easily, while his grandmother is very healthy.

    C. His grandfather tends to be controlling, while his grandmother is usually relaxed.

    D. His grandfather tends to be very quiet, while his grandmother gets easily agitated.

11. How did the author know that Aunt Frieda had stopped writing letters to his grandmother?

    A. His Aunt Grace told him that Aunt Frieda had stopped writing.

    B. Aunt Frieda's letters were written in Italian and not in English.

    C. His grandmother stopped receiving any letters from Aunt Frieda.

    D. The letters began coming in Uncle Stuart's handwriting.

12. From the passage, we can infer that the author considered *Nana* to be

    A. cut off from her children because she couldn't speak English.

    B. withdrawn and fearful of the outside world.

    C. the authority figure in the household.

    D. submissive to her husband's decisions.

13. When *Nana* sees Aunt Frieda, her main feeling is

    A. confusion because she did not know about the eye operation.

    B. relief because the operation was a success.

    C. anger because she had been tricked into thinking Frieda wrote the letters.

    D. powerlessness because Frieda did not tell her about the operation.

14. In the passage, the author regards *Nana* as someone who is

    A. fragile but easily soothed.

    B. intelligent but easily worried.

    C. intelligent but lacking in formal education.

    D. educated but easily deceived.

15. When the author asks Aunt Grace why Aunt Frieda is not writing the letters, the tone of Aunt Grace's answer is intended to be

    A. reassuring.

    B. consoling.

    C. alarming.

    D. distressing.

Questions 16–20 refer to the following passage.

On entering the amphitheater, new objects of wonder presented themselves. On a level spot in the center was a company of odd-looking personages playing at nine-pins. They were dressed in a quaint, out-landish fashion, some wore short doublets, others jerkins, with long knives in their belts, and most of them
Line had enormous breeches, of a type similar to that of the guide's. Their visages, too, were peculiar, one had a
5 large beard, broad face, and small piggish eyes. The face of another seemed to consist entirely of nose and was surmounted by a white sugar-loaf hat set off with a little red cock's tail. They all had beards of various shapes and colors. There was one who seemed to be the commander. He was a stout old gentleman, with a weather-beaten countenance; he wore a lace doublet, broad belt and hangar, high crowned hat and feather, red stockings, and high-heeled shoes with roses in them. The whole group reminded Rip of the figures in an
10 old <u>Flemish</u> painting, in the parlor of the village parson, which had been brought over from Holland at the time of the settlement.

What seemed particularly odd to Rip was that though these folks were evidently amusing themselves, yet they maintained the gravest faces, the most mysterious silence, and were the most melancholy party of pleasure he had ever witnessed. Nothing interrupted the stillness of the scene but the noise of the balls,
15 which, whenever they were rolled, echoed along the mountains like rumbling peals of thunder.

—from *Rip Van Winkle* by Washington Irving

16. Looking at this scene, the observer is apparently

    A. fascinated.

    B. frightened.

    C. repulsed.

    D. bored.

17. The underlined word *Flemish* possibly refers to

    A. something from the area near Holland.

    B. the village parson.

    C. a certain painter.

    D. an old-fashioned parlor.

18. The characters were probably playing

    A. a game like bowling.

    B. soccer.

    C. a type of baseball.

    D. golf.

19. The person observing all of this is

    A. Flemish.

    B. a parson.

    C. melancholic.

    D. Rip.

20. The observer was surprised that the

    A. men's beards were of so many shapes and colors.

    B. men appeared to be so serious while they were playing a game.

    C. leader was so stout.

    D. rolling balls sounded like thunder.

Questions 21–26 refer to the following passage.

Author Ben Wiens defines energy simply as "the ability to create a force over a distance some time in the future." The term energy, Wiens notes, was developed only about 200 years ago, by a scientist named Thomas Young. In Young's time, energy was thought to be the ability to do physical work, like the work that an axe can do when it comes down on a log with force and <u>severs</u> the log in two. In Young's time, according to Wiens, work was defined as "a force acting over a distance." When a person uses his energy to run, for instance, he is showing an example of a force acting over a distance.

As scientists began to research energy more carefully, they realized that energy was more than just the ability to do physical work. They started to see energy as the *potential* to do work as well. One scientist named James Prescott Joule believed that the ability to do work was stored within the molecules of matter. Joule stated in 1830 that molecules contained very small forms of energy. These forms of energy could not be seen by the naked eye, according to Joule, but they did exist.

In 1905, Albert Einstein made an important contribution to our study of energy. During Einstein's time, scientists knew that matter was made up of smaller parts, such as molecules and atoms. Einstein believed, however, that molecules and atoms were not the smallest parts of matter. He stated that molecules and atoms were made up of energy. He saw them as large groups of energy particles. Some of these energy particles were even able to transfer energy between different types of matter.

Thanks to Einstein's work, modern scientists developed a better understanding of energy. Since the time of Thomas Young, work had been recognized as force acting over a distance. Einstein showed that energy is the *ability to create* force over any distance. In other words, according to Wiens, energy is "the ability to do work sometime in the future." It is the stored potential to be able to complete work.

21. Which statement best reflects the main idea of the passage?

   A. Scientists once believed that molecules and energy were the smallest parts of matter, but now they believe that molecules and atoms themselves are made up of even smaller energy particles.

   B. Scientists once defined energy as the ability to do physical work, but they now define it as the stored potential to complete work at some time in the future.

   C. Because of the work of Albert Einstein, modern scientists now have a better understanding of energy than did earlier scientists.

   D. Our understanding of energy developed from the work of three scientists: Thomas Young, James Prescott Joule, and Albert Einstein.

22. The underlined word *severs* in the first paragraph means

   A. prepares.

   B. unites.

   C. splits.

   D. covers.

23. Which statement reflects a view shared by both James Prescott Joule and Albert Einstein?

   A. Molecules are the smallest parts of matter.

   B. Energy cannot be seen with the naked eye, so it does not exist.

   C. Energy is the ability to do physical work in the present moment.

   D. Molecules of matter are made up of energy.

24. According to the passage, Albert Einstein

    A. showed that energy is the ability to create force over any distance.

    B. showed that energy was made up of small particles called atoms.

    C. developed a way to view energy with the naked eye.

    D. developed the term "energy" about 200 years ago.

25. How did Albert Einstein's view of energy differ from that of Thomas Young?

    A. Einstein's view was more comprehensive than Young's because Einstein saw energy as the potential to be able to do work.

    B. Einstein's view was more concrete than Young's because Einstein saw energy as the ability to do physical work.

    C. Einstein's view was the opposite of Young's because Einstein saw energy as the ability to do physical work.

    D. Einstein's view was more developed than Young's because Einstein believed that molecules and atoms were the smallest parts of matter.

26. According to the passage, James Prescott Joule believed that the ability to do work

    A. could transfer between molecules.

    B. was constantly changing.

    C. was unable to be stored.

    D. was stored within matter.

Questions 27–31 refer to the following passage.

In 1911, an American named Hiram Bingham made a magnificent discovery in the Andes Mountains of Peru. Hidden deep in the Andean jungle and surrounded by mountain peaks lay the lost city of Machu Picchu, a sacred religious site built by the Inca Indians. Machu Picchu is located 43 miles northwest of a
Line Peruvian city called Cusco. Cusco was conquered by the Spanish in 1532, but no mention was made of the
5   remarkable city. Until Bingham's discovery in 1911, no one in the West knew that Machu Picchu even existed. Now, almost a century later, Machu Picchu is the best-known archeological site in South America.

Archeologists believe that when Machu Picchu was built around 1460, it was not built as a city. Instead, they believe, it was built as the royal estate of an Incan ruler named Pachacuti Inca Yupanqui. Machu Picchu doubled as the ruler's home and a religious retreat. It's located so high in the mountains—with an altitude of
10   8,000 feet—that it probably didn't have a military or host any major businesses.

Judging from the massive size of the "city," it must have housed many people during its day. Machu Picchu is made up of about 200 buildings. Most of these buildings were used as homes, but some were used as temples or for storage. Today, archeologists believe that about 1,200 people lived in the area of Machu Picchu and that most of these people were women, children, and priests.

27. Westerners learned of the existence of Machu Picchu after the site was discovered

   A. in 1911 by an American named Hiram Bingham.

   B. in 1420 by an Inca ruler named Pachacuti Inca Yupanqui.

   C. in 1532 by the Spanish, who conquered the Incas.

   D. in 1532 by an explorer named Cusco.

28. In this passage, Machu Picchu can best be described as

   A. a mythical city.

   B. the center of the Aztec Empire.

   C. the lost city of the Incan Empire.

   D. an example of Spanish colonization.

29. According to the passage, Machu Picchu is the

   A. largest archaeological site in South America.

   B. oldest archaeological site in South America.

   C. highest archaeological site in South America.

   D. most famous archaeological site in South America.

30. Archaeologists believe that the purpose of Machu Picchu was to serve as a

   A. home and religious retreat for the Incan ruler and his court.

   B. monastery exclusively for the use of Incan priests.

   C. fortress for Incan warriors.

   D. marketplace for traders from other parts of the Incan Empire.

31. Located near Machu Picchu, the city of Cusco was

   A. also lost, abandoned, and rediscovered like Machu Picchu.

   B. conquered by the Spanish.

   C. built around 1460.

   D. the burial site of Pachacuti Inca Yupanqui.

Questions 32–36 refer to the following passage.

Glutamate, or glutamic acid, is one of the amino acids present in our bodies. It serves as a neurotransmitter within the human body. As a neurotransmitter, glutamate works by sending signals to certain neurons, or nerve cells, located in the brain, spinal cord, and nervous system. Some researchers, such as Russell
Line Blaylock and James South, have argued that glutamate is not safe to eat when added to food. When present
5 in the blood in high levels, these researchers believe glutamate can destroy some types of brain cells.

How does this process of cell destruction occur? Neurotransmitters as a group fall into two types: those that *cause* nerve cells to act and those that *stop* nerve cells from acting. Glutamate is one of the neurotransmitters that cause nerve cells to act. Although glutamate is commonly used, it is normally present in the brain in very small amounts. When glutamate levels rise, nerve cells in the brain to become too active, lead-
10 ing to destruction of the cells.

Since glutamate is found naturally in the body, the brain has ways of keeping glutamate levels in the brain from rising too high. One of these ways is a system called the *blood-brain barrier*. The blood-brain barrier, writes Blaylock, protects the brain against moderate increases of glutamate. It stops working as well when faced with large amounts of glutamate, such as those that enter the bloodstream when a person eats
15 foods containing flavor enhancers.

Glutamate that is found naturally in foods does not pose as much of a risk of creating high levels of glutamate in the brain. This is because glutamate found naturally in foods occurs in its "bound" form, which means that it is bonded with other amino acids.

32. The title that best expresses the main idea of this selection is

A. "The Effect of Glutamate on the Brain."

B. "Glutamate as a Building Block of Cells."

C. "Glutamate: The Most Common Neurotransmitter."

D. "FDA Research on Glutamate."

33. How does excess glutamate in the brain destroy brain cells?

A. It slows down the activity of nerve cells in the brain.

B. It causes deterioration in the blood-brain barrier that protects the brain.

C. It causes nerve cells in the brain to become overactive.

D. It stops the hypothalamus from functioning.

34. Which type of glutamate does not pose much of a risk of creating high levels of glutamate in the brain?

A. Glutamate in its free form

B. Monosodium glutamate

C. Hydrolyzed vegetable protein

D. Glutamate that is bonded with other amino acids

35. As a neurotransmitter, glutamate

A. stops nerve cells from acting.

B. causes nerve cells to act.

C. creates a barrier protecting the brain.

D. slows down the brain's processing.

36. Glutamate in the brain

   A. helps strengthen the blood-brain barrier.

   B. blocks signals to nerve cells.

   C. is more potent in its bound form.

   D. is normally found in very small amounts.

Questions 37–40 refer to the following passage.

Janessa could not have had a tougher time falling asleep last night and woke up feeling exhausted. She has never been able to control the excitement she felt for an upcoming event, and she tossed and turned in bed until the sun rose that morning. Today was the day of her class trip to the Hopkins Planetarium. She *Line* did her best to shake off her tiredness and get ready for what she hoped would be a fun-filled day with her 5 friends.

After getting dressed, Janessa raced down the stairs and nearly tripped over Marmalade, the families' orange tabby cat, which could almost always be found sleeping at the foot of the staircase.

"Slow down Janessa, or you might trip and fall!" Janessa's mom said. "Sit down, catch your breath, and have some breakfast."

10 "Sorry mom, I'm just excited." Janessa replied. "I've been looking forward to our trip to the planetarium for weeks!" Janessa took her usual seat at the kitchen table and rocked back and forth with excitement as her mom prepared a plate with scrambled eggs, toast, and bacon, which she placed in front of Janessa.

"I know you're excited," said Janessa's mom. "What part are you looking forward to the most?"

"I'm SO glad you asked me that!" Janessa beamed. "I hear they have the best presentation on black holes 15 anywhere, and when they zoom in on the Milky Way solar system you can see HUNDREDS of stars and…" Janessa swung her hand wildly and knocked her plate onto the ground. It crashed, sending the uneaten food all over the floor.

Janessa's father came racing into the room. "What happened?" he asked.

"I think I got too excited…" Janessa replied. With that, her parents looked at each other and laughed.

20 "I tried to tell you, when people get too excited, they sometimes get careless," Janessa's mom said. Janessa's parents started cleaning up the mess.

"I know, I know… I just can't help it!" replied Janessa. "Dad, can you drive me to school? I can't wait to get there!"

Janessa's dad laughed and shook his head. "Some lessons are harder to learn than others," he said. "Ok, 25 let's get in the car."

Janessa and her father got in the car and headed toward the school. The whole ride over, Janessa talked about the things she's been learning about in science class: the layers of the earth, the planets, and photosynthesis. While her father paid careful attention to the road, Janessa spoke enthusiastically about her plans for her science project this year—a real working volcano—and got so excited that she gave herself the hiccups.

30 "Janessa, your mother and I tried to tell you—you have to try not to get too excited!"

"I know, I know…" Janessa said.

When Janessa arrived at school, she joined her classmates in the auditorium. Her teacher, Mrs. Ashton, had the students line up for the bus, but Janessa could hardly stand still. There was just one last thing before everyone could get on the bus and go to the planetarium. The teacher needed to collect the permission slips.

35 Janessa fished around in her pockets and came up empty. At that moment, she learned the lesson that her parents were trying to teach her that morning.

37. According to the story, why was Janessa so tired that morning?

A. She had a big test she was nervous about.

B. She felt sick and couldn't fall asleep.

C. She was too excited to sleep.

D. Her cat kept waking her up during the night.

38. When Janessa's father says, "Some lessons are harder to learn than others," he means

A. science is one of the most difficult subjects in school.

B. you must study hard to do well on class exams.

C. some students are smarter than others.

D. sometimes it takes a person a long while to learn something.

39. Janessa was learning all the following things in science class *except*

A. photosynthesis.

B. magnetism.

C. the layers of the Earth.

D. the planets.

40. What lesson did Janessa finally learn at the end of the story?

A. When someone gets too excited, they sometimes get careless and make mistakes.

B. When someone stays up too late and wakes up tired, they are always more forgetful.

C. When you don't eat a good breakfast in the morning, you're more likely to have accidents.

D. It's difficult to forgive someone when they make mistakes, so try not to make mistakes very often.

READING 2
40 Questions—28 Minutes

> **Directions:** The following questions are based on several reading passages. Each passage is followed by a series of questions. Read each passage carefully, then answer the questions. You may reread the passage as often as you wish. When you have finished answering the set of questions based on a passage, go on to the next passage.

Questions 1–4 refer to the following passage.

There used to be a saying in business that "if you make a better mousetrap, the world will beat a path to your door." This advice suggested to manufacturers that if they made a better product, the product would be destined to sell. Unfortunately, this piece of advice <u>erroneously</u> ignored the role that prices play in affecting what consumers buy. It turns out that that role is very important.

Line

5

In 1956, a better mousetrap *was* built by a company called the Pioneer Tool and Die Company. The mousetrap did not require the use of any bait (such as cheese), and it did not have any odor. It was a much higher quality product than the wooden mousetraps that households had been using. However, this mouse-trap did not sell very well, and the company eventually stopped producing it. The key reason why consum-ers failed to buy the mousetrap was its price. The product sold for $29.95, compared to $0.07 for a plain wooden mousetrap.

10

The Pioneer Tool and Die Company set a high price for their better mousetraps because the mousetraps had more advanced features than regular mousetraps. The company learned from this experience, however, that people really did not care about the "better" qualities that were built into Pioneer mousetraps. At least, consumers did not value these qualities enough to pay a higher price for them. It turns out that consumers were really only willing to pay about 7 cents for an ordinary wooden mousetrap. These ordinary mousetraps sold the best.

15

When consumers refused to buy Pioneer mousetraps, Pioneer took their mousetraps off the market. It received a strong message from consumers that consumers did not want expensive mousetraps with lots of bells and whistles. Instead, consumers preferred a simple mousetrap at a very inexpensive cost.

1. The underlined word *erroneously* in this context means

   A. bizarrely.

   B. mistakenly.

   C. wisely.

   D. quickly.

2. What happened to the expensive mousetraps produced by Pioneer Tool and Die Company?

   A. They were taken off the market.

   B. The company continues to produce them today.

   C. The company made them less expensive.

   D. The company made them easier to use.

3. Which is the most appropriate title for this passage?

   A. "A Cheaper Mousetrap"

   B. "A Successful Mousetrap"

   C. "An Electric Mousetrap"

   D. "A Better Mousetrap"

4. According to this passage, mousetraps preferred by consumers cost

   A. about $30.00.

   B. less than 10 cents each.

   C. 70 cents each.

   D. nothing, because they could be made at home.

Questions 5–9 refer to the following passage.

Nowadays, the compound fluoride is found inside most American homes. It is the main ingredient in most toothpastes and has been used by dentists to help prevent tooth decay. The fluoride that is now used in dental care was developed as a result of the discovery of an element known as fluorine.

Line

5   The discovery of fluorine began with the early work of Georg Bauer. Bauer was a German physician who studied the diseases of mine workers in the 1500s. In his work, Bauer described how a mineral known as "fluorspar" was used by miners in creating metal from ore. Fluorspar is a mineral found in nature in several different varieties. The purple version of fluorspar looks like amethyst, and the green version looks like emeralds.

10   In the 1600s and 1700s, scientists working with fluorspar saw that when the mineral was heated, it gave off a gas, which could create etchings in glass. However, it was not until 1771 that fluoric acid was discovered by a Swedish chemist named Carl Wilhelm Scheele. Once fluoric acid was discovered, the next step was to isolate the element fluorine. Many scientists unsuccessfully tried to isolate fluorine in dangerous experiments that cost some researchers their lives. The scientist who gets credit for isolating fluorine was a French chemist named Henri Moissan, who produced the element in 1886. Moissan's work was so signifi-

15   cant that he won the Nobel Prize in chemistry in 1906.

Fluorine is a highly destructive, pale yellow gas. It participates in reactions with almost all substances, including gold and platinum. It explodes when it is mixed with hydrogen, and it causes glass, metals, ceramics, carbon, and water to burn with a bright flame. Even the salts of fluorine, known as fluorides, are very dangerous and should never be touched, inhaled, or swallowed.

5. What does the author mean in paragraph 3 when noting that certain experiments designed to isolate fluorine "cost some researchers their lives?"

   A. Some researchers spent their entire lives trying to isolate fluorine.

   B. Some researchers spent a great deal of money trying to isolate fluorine.

   C. Some researchers died in these experiments to try to isolate fluorine.

   D. Some researchers took on large amounts of debt to fund the experiments.

6. Which mineral was most important to the discovery of fluorine?

   A. Diamond

   B. Floures

   C. Emerald

   D. Fluorspar

7. Which of the following conclusions can be drawn about flourides?

   A. It is safer for researchers to touch flourides than to breathe in their fumes.

   B. Researchers should remember that flourides are more harmful than fluorine gas.

   C. Researchers should ensure that flouride fumes are released into the laboratory.

   D. Researchers should avoid contact with fluoride compounds.

8. Which title best expresses the main idea of this passage?

   A. "The Development of Toothpaste"

   B. "The Discovery of Fluorine"

   C. "The Dangers of Scientific Experiments"

   D. "The Isolation of Chemical Elements"

9. In the passage, fluorine is described as an element

   A. that is dangerous and should be banned before it takes more lives.

   B. for which no practical use has ever been discovered.

   C. that is dangerous but also has practical uses.

   D. that is extremely rare and valuable to most nations.

Questions 10–15 refer to the following passage.

The Berlin Wall was built during the height of the Cold War, which was a period of tension between communist and democratic world powers. At that time, the city of Berlin was divided into two parts that sat in two different countries—East Germany and West Germany. East Germany, also known as the German
Line   Democratic Republic, had a Soviet-style communist government, and West Germany, also known as the
5   Federal Republic of Germany, had a democratic government. Between 1949 and 1961, over 2 million people escaped from East Berlin to the western parts of Germany to be free from an oppressive and invasive social-ist dictatorship. This created a so-called "brain drain," meaning that those with educations and specialized skills were leaving the country en masse. As a result, the Berlin Wall was built practically overnight on August 13th, 1961, to prevent East Germans from escaping East Berlin.

10   The wall was an imposing landmark. It was built of concrete right in the middle of the city and topped with barbed wire. It had a strip of "no man's land" in the center that was patrolled by attack dogs and included land mines and massive barriers. For 28 years, armed guards stood at this ominous border that symbolized the division between communism and democracy. During this period, more than 100,000 East German citizens tried to escape the Wall using such innovative methods as digging tunnels, ziplining, per-
15   forming suitcase contortion, and even flying hot air balloons. Tragically, more than 600 were not successful and lost their lives while attempting to escape.

Then, in 1989, all of that changed. Social unrest had been building for months in response to invasive spying by the East German secret police, known as the Stasi, as well as long wait times for domestic goods, and the government's threats of increasing violence against protesters. The East German government hoped
20   that loosening travel restrictions would help ease this unrest, so they planned to start offering citizens more freedoms over the course of a year. However, in a televised press conference on November 9th, 1989, upon being asked when East Germans would finally be able to travel to the other side of the Berlin Wall, a government official named Günter Schabowski mistakenly replied, "As far as I know, effective immedi-ately. . . without delay."

25   That very same night, thousands of East Germans flooded the six border crossings of the Berlin Wall. The border guards, who had no idea what had just been broadcast on national television, were over-whelmed by the size of the crowds and <u>flummoxed</u> as to what to do. One crossing in particular, Born-holmer Strasse, was located on a bridge. So many people gathered on this bridge that officials worried it would collapse; they were forced to open the gates and let the East Germans pour into West Berlin. Once
30   the gates were opened, it wasn't long before citizens and government alike started dismantling the wall and less than a year later, in October 1990, Germany was reunited as one country. In the end, it wasn't the Cold War or a big military display that brought down the Berlin Wall; instead, it was the sheer number of people who showed up to the border crossings, proving just how much power citizens can have when they band together.

10. According to the author, what caused the opening of the Berlin Wall?

    A. Large crowds following a mistaken announcement

    B. Loosened border restrictions in neighboring countries

    C. The Cold War between the Soviet Union and the United States

    D. Striking workers in Poland

11. Which statement is true, according to the passage?

    A. The building of the Berlin Wall led to the Cold War.

    B. The Berlin Wall was necessary to protect West Germany from communism.

    C. The number of skilled and educated citizens fleeing East Germany led to the erection of the Berlin Wall.

    D. Ronald Reagan helped negotiate the fall of the Berlin Wall.

12. As used in paragraph 4, the underlined word *flummoxed* most nearly means

    A. angered.

    B. anxious.

    C. confused.

    D. disorganized.

13. Bornholmer Strasse was the first crossing opened because

    A. the guards there had heard the announcement made by Günter Schabowski.

    B. more people gathered there than at any other crossing.

    C. the East German government planned for it to be the first crossing to open.

    D. officials were worried about the infrastructure of the Bornholmer Strasse bridge.

14. Which of the following was NOT a type of deterrent used to keep people from crossing the Berlin Wall?

    A. Armed guards

    B. Grenades

    C. Attack dogs

    D. Barbed wire

15. The wall was built in 1961 during a period of tension between democratic and communist world powers commonly known as

    A. the nuclear arms race.

    B. détente.

    C. the Red Scare.

    D. the Cold War.

Questions 16–21 refer to the following passage.

On 6 June 1822, French Canadian fur trade voyageur Alexis St. Martin was accidentally shot in the stomach at an American Fur Company store on Michigan's Mackinac Island. The blast left a gaping wound in St. Martin's abdomen. St. Martin eventually recovered from the gruesome accident, but the wound never *Line* closed completely, leaving a small permanent opening in his stomach wall. His surgeon, William Beau-
5 mont, began monitoring gastric secretions through this opening in St. Martin's body. Beaumont, who would later become known as the father of gastric physiology, would attach various types of food to a string and suspend them through the hole. Later he would pull out the string to see what portion of the food had been digested. During these experiments, Beaumont noticed that St. Martin's mood seemed to affect how quickly he digested food. When St. Martin was irritable, for instance, food broke down more slowly.

10 These early observations provided the first clues of crosstalk between the brain and the gut. Research-ers later called this communication system the gut–brain axis. Over the years, studies have revealed that the brain influences the gastrointestinal (GI) tract through several mechanisms. Yet, only recently have scien-tists recognized the importance of a third component to the gut–brain axis: the trillions of bacteria, viruses, archaea, and eukaryotes that make up the gut microbiome. In little more than a decade, researchers have
15 uncovered compelling associations between gut bacteria and a host of neurological disorders and psychiatric conditions. These include depression, anxiety, autism spectrum disorders (ASDs), and Parkinson's disease.

Most of the early research on the microbiome–gut–brain axis has been conducted in rodents. Germ-free mice—which are born in sterile conditions and free of all microorganisms—are popular for gut flora research because scientists can inoculate the mice with specific microbes and watch what happens. Ex-
20 periments with germ-free mice have yielded <u>intriguing</u> clues about the possible influence of the gut micro-biome on behavior and neurodevelopment. However, it is still unclear whether these findings are relevant to humans. Now, additional researchers are beginning to probe the connection in humans. Outside neurosci-ence, gut microbiome research in laboratory animals and humans is changing the way some environmental health scientists view the effects of environmental exposures on neurodevelopment and brain chemistry.
25 From the moment of birth—and possibly even earlier—our microbiomes begin to develop. There is evi-dence that a healthy gut microbiome is important for brain development.

16. The passage indicates that the reason germ-free mice are desirable for gut-microbiome experi-ments is because

   A. scientists can isolate different microbes and test what effects they have.

   B. mice microbiomes have a lot in common with human microbiomes.

   C. it's ethically questionable to experiment on humans.

   D. they share a lot of DNA with humans and can provide clues to our microbiomes.

17. As used in Paragraph 3, the underlined word *intriguing* most closely means

   A. boring.

   B. scientific.

   C. fascinating.

   D. secretive.

18. Based on the passage, which of the following statements most accurately captures the relevance of rodent gut-microbiome experiments to humans?

   A. Rodent gut-microbiome experiments can provide clues but scientists are still not certain how the results will apply to human health.

   B. Rodent gut-microbiome experiments can mimic the human microbiome with a high degree of accuracy.

   C. Experiments on germ-free mice artificially introduce microbes into the gut and are therefore not relevant to humans, who naturally host microbes.

   D. Findings from gut-microbiome experiments on rodents are not applicable to humans because of their vastly different brain size.

19. The passage mentions all the following components of the gut-microbiome except

   A. viruses.

   B. bacteria.

   C. algae.

   D. archaea.

20. The author's main purpose in providing the anecdote about Alexis St. Martin in the first paragraph is to

   A. show the history of microbiome experiments before discussing the present day.

   B. create a sense of drama that highlights the importance of the topic.

   C. cause the reader to feel pity for St. Martin, to make them care more about the topic.

   D. demonstrate the ethical issues that surround the microbiome experiments.

21. What would be the most appropriate title for this passage?

   A. "Gastric Physiology"

   B. "Gut Microbiomes and the Human Brain"

   C. "Do You Know What's in Your Gut?"

   D. "The Adventures of Alexis St. Martin"

Questions 22–26 refer to the following passage.

The history of modern pollution problems shows that most have resulted from negligence and ignorance. Humans have an appalling tendency to interfere with nature before all of the possible consequences of our actions have been studied in-depth. We produce and distribute radioactive substances, synthetic chemicals, and many other potent compounds before fully comprehending their effects on living organisms.
Line
5   Our education is dangerously incomplete.

It is often argued that the purpose of science is to move into unknown territory, to explore, and to discover. It can be said that similar risks have been taken before, and that these risks are necessary to technological progress. These arguments overlook an important element. In the past, risks taken in the name of scientific progress were restricted to a small place and a brief period of time. The effects of the processes we
10   now strive to master are neither localized nor brief. Air pollution covers vast urban areas. Ocean pollutants have been discovered in nearly every part of the world. Synthetic chemicals spread over huge stretches of forest and farmland may remain in the soil for decades. Radioactive pollutants will be found in the biosphere for generations. The size and persistence of these problems have grown with the expanding power of modern science.

15   One might also argue that the hazards of modern pollutants are small compared to the dangers associated with other human activity. No estimate of the actual harm done by smog, fallout, or chemical residues can obscure the reality that the risks are being taken before being fully understood. The importance of these issues lies in the failure of science to predict and control human intervention into natural processes. The true measure of the danger is represented by the hazards we will encounter if we enter the new age of
20   technology without first evaluating our responsibility to the environment.

22. According to the author, the major cause of pollution is the result of

   A. designing synthetic chemicals to kill living organisms.

   B. a lack of understanding of the history of technology.

   C. scientists who are too willing to move into unknown territory.

   D. changing our environment before understanding the effects of these changes.

23. The author believes that the risks taken by modern science are greater than those taken by earlier scientific efforts because

   A. the effects may be felt by more people for a longer period of time.

   B. science is progressing faster than ever before.

   C. technology has produced more dangerous chemicals.

   D. the materials used are more dangerous to scientists.

24. The author apparently believes that the problem of finding solutions to pollution depends on

   A. the removal of present hazards to the environment.

   B. the removal of all potential pollutants from their present uses.

   C. overcoming technical difficulties.

   D. the willingness of scientists to understand possible dangers before using new products in the environment.

25. The author seems to feel that the attitude of scientists toward pollution has been

   A. naïve.

   B. concerned.

   C. confused.

   D. nonchalant.

26. As used in paragraph 2, the underlined word *synthetic* most likely means

   A. new.

   B. unsafe.

   C. man-made.

   D. polluting.

Questions 27–31 refer to the following passage.

THE RHODORA

In May, when sea-winds pierced our solitudes,

I found the fresh Rhodora in the woods,

Spreading its leafless blooms in a damp nook,

Line   To please the desert and the sluggish brook.

5   The purple petals, fallen in the pool,

Made the black water with their beauty gay;

Here might the red-bird come his plumes to cool,

And court the flower that cheapens his array.

Rhodora! if the sages ask thee why

10   This charm is wasted on the earth and sky,

Tell them, dear, that if eyes were made for seeing,

Then Beauty is its own excuse for being:

Why thou wert there, O rival of the rose!

I never thought to ask, I never knew:

15   But, in my simple ignorance suppose

The self-same Power that brought me there brought you.

—Ralph Waldo Emerson

27. The poet is impressed with the beauty of

A. the sea.

B. the woods.

C. a bird.

D. a flower.

28. When the poet says that the flower cheapens the array of the red-bird, he means that the

A. bird gets nothing from the flower.

B. flower gets nothing from the bird.

C. color of the flower is brighter than that of the bird.

D. bird ruins the flower.

29. In saying "This charm is wasted on the earth and sky," the poet means that

A. the earth and sky do not appreciate beauty.

B. no one sees a flower that blooms deep in the woods.

C. wise men sometimes ask foolish questions.

D. the bird does not even notice the beauty of the flower.

30. The poet believes that

    A. flower petals pollute the water.

    B. red birds are garish.

    C. beauty exists for its own sake.

    D. sea-wind is refreshing.

31. The poet probably

    A. is an insensitive person.

    B. dislikes solitude.

    C. is a religious person.

    D. is ignorant.

Questions 32–35 are based on the following passage.

The kangaroo is found nowhere in the world but in Australasia. Ages ago, when that part of our earth was cut off from the Asian mainland, this fantastic animal from nature's past was also isolated. There are about two dozen species distributed throughout Australia, southward to Tasmania and northward to New
Line Guinea and neighboring islands. Some are no bigger than rabbits; some can climb trees. They are known
5 by a variety of picturesque names: wallabies, wallaroos, potoroos, boongaries, and paddymelons. But the kangaroo—the one that is Australia's national symbol—is the great gray kangaroo of the plains, fondly referred to as the Old Man throughout the continent. Other names include Boomer, Forester, and Man of the Woods. The smaller female, in Australian talk, is called a doe or a flyer. A baby kangaroo is known as a joey.

32. Kangaroos became isolated because

    A. Australia was cut off from the Asian mainland.

    B. they migrated to Tasmania and New Guinea.

    C. they spent most of their lives in trees.

    D. they did not play well with others.

33. Australasia is

    A. another name for Australia.

    B. an area that includes Australia and part of the continent of Asia.

    C. Australia and some surrounding islands to the north and south of it.

    D. all of the land in the Southern Hemisphere.

34. Which type of kangaroo is Australia's national symbol?

    A. The wallaby

    B. The Old Man

    C. The great gray kangaroo of the plains

    D. Grey Boomer

35. Which of the following would *not* be considered a picturesque name for the kangaroo?

    A. Potoroo

    B. Paddymelon

    C. Wallaby

    D. Man of the Woods

Questions 36–40 are based on the following passage.

For generations, historians and boat lovers have been trying to learn more about the brave ship that brought the Pilgrims to America. The task is a difficult one because *Mayflower* was such a common name for ships back in early seventeenth-century England that there were at least twenty of them when the Pilgrims left for the New World.

Line

5   An exact duplicate of the *Mayflower* has been built in England and given to the people of the United States as a symbol of goodwill and common ancestry linking Britons and Americans. The Pilgrims' *Mayflower* apparently was built originally as a fishing vessel. It seems to have been 90 feet long by 22 feet wide, displacing 180 tons of water. The duplicate measures 90 feet by 26 feet, displaces 183 tons of water, and has a crew of 21, as did the original vessel. The new *Mayflower* has no motor but travels faster than the old boat.

10   What happened to the historic boat? So far as can be told, the *Mayflower* went back to less colorful jobs and, not too many years later, was scrapped. What happened to the beams, masts, and planking is questionable. In the English city of Abingdon, there is a Congregational church that contains two heavy wooden pillars. Some say these pillars are masts from the *Mayflower*. A barn in the English town of Jordans seemed to be built on old ship timbers. Marine experts said these timbers were impregnated with salt and, if put

15   together, would form a vessel 90 feet by 22 feet. The man who owned the farm when the peculiar barn was built was a relative of the man who appraised the *Mayflower* when it was scrapped. It seems that the original *Mayflower* may still be doing service ashore while her duplicate sails the seas.

36. A long search was made for the Pilgrims' boat because it

   A. contained valuable materials.

   B. might still do sea service.

   C. has historical importance.

   D. would link Great Britain and America.

37. It has been difficult to discover what happened to the original *Mayflower* because

   A. many ships bore the same name.

   B. it was such a small vessel.

   C. the search was begun too late.

   D. it has become impregnated with salt.

38. The British recently had a duplicate of the *Mayflower* built because

   A. the original could not be located.

   B. they wanted to make a gesture of friendship.

   C. parts of the original could be used.

   D. historians recommended such a step.

39. Compared with the original *Mayflower*, the modern duplicate

   A. is longer.

   B. is identical.

   C. carries a larger crew.

   D. is somewhat wider.

40. When the author says that the original boat might still be doing service ashore, he means that

   A. it might be whole and intact somewhere.

   B. present-day buildings might include parts of it.

   C. it might be in a boat lover's private collection.

   D. it might be in the service of pirates.

ANSWER KEYS AND EXPLANATIONS
Reading 1

1. B	9. B	17. C	25. A	33. C
2. A	10. D	18. C	26. D	34. D
3. B	11. D	19. A	27. A	35. B
4. A	12. C	20. A	28. C	36. D
5. D	13. D	21. C	29. D	37. C
6. D	14. B	22. C	30. A	38. D
7. B	15. A	23. D	31. B	39. B
8. C	16. A	24. A	32. A	40. A

1. **The correct answer is B.** This main idea question requires you to locate the sentence that best describes the main point of the *entire* passage. This passage starts by describing Mozart's gifts as a musician and a composer, and then it explains his contribution to music. Choice B summarizes the main point clearly as it states: "Mozart was an extremely talented musician and composer whose contributions have a significant impact on music."

2. **The correct answer is A.** This question asks you to define the meaning of *prodigy*, a word that you may not be familiar with. When you are faced with unfamiliar words, you can use clues from the sentence to help you define the terms. If necessary, you can reread the part of the passage that the sentence was taken from to gain more clues about the meaning of the vocabulary word.

   The sentence that contains the word *prodigy* tells us that Mozart was highly musically talented. It is in paragraph 2, which describes how gifted he was as a child. The word *prodigy* must therefore mean "a child who is talented or gifted." Choice A comes closest to this meaning, so it is correct.

3. **The correct answer is B.** This is a compare-and-contrast question. It asks you to identify the difference between Mozart's sonatas and the sonatas that were written before his time. The answers to compare-and-contrast questions are often embedded directly in the text. If you look back to the part

of the passage that describes sonatas (paragraphs 3 and 4), you will find a sentence that explains how Mozart wrote sonatas: "Mozart also wrote sonatas, but he added depth to the sonatas and gave them more structure." This sentence describes the main difference between Mozart's sonatas and the sonatas that existed previously, which is reflected in choice B.

4. **The correct answer is A.** Paragraph 1 states that Mozart wrote more compositions than any other composer in history. The passage does not state how many symphonies he wrote compared to other composers, nor does it state the number of movements he included in his compositions, so we do not have enough information to determine if choices B and C are true. The passage does make it clear that Mozart wrote a variety of compositions, so choice D is false.

5. **The correct answer is D.** The passage states that Mozart learned to play the piano at the age of 3 and composed his first work at the age of 4. The passage does not indicate that he learned to play the trumpet, so choice A is incorrect. The passage does not state the nature of the composition, nor does the passage mention an introduction to the royal court, so choices B and C are also incorrect.

6. **The correct answer is D.** The passage states in paragraph 3 that a sonata is a composition for one or two solo instruments. There is no mention of the instruments listed in choices A and B. While

the passage indicates Mozart helped add forms such as quartets and trios, choice C is incorrect because the passage clearly says that sonatas were for one or two instruments, not three or four.

7. **The correct answer is B.** The last line of the passage states that Mozart "combined the musical styles that he learned during his stays in Germany, France, Italy, and other regions in Austria." England is not mentioned, so we can eliminate choice A. Although the passage does not specifically state that Mozart was born in Austria, the phrase "other regions in Austria," indicates that Mozart resided in a part of Austria, making choices C and D incorrect.

8. **The correct answer is C.** The passage states that Mozart's travels exposed him to many types of music, which helped him compose sonatas with more depth and structure. The passage does not support choices A, B, and D.

9. **The correct answer is B.** This vocabulary question asks you to identify the meaning of a word that you may or may not be familiar with. Use the context of the sentence to help you define the term. You may find it helpful to reread the paragraph that the sentence came from to get more clues about the meaning of *gingerly*. In this case, we're told that Aunt Frieda has recently had surgery on her eye. She is coming to visit her mother after the surgery. When she exits the car, she walks like someone who can't see very well. Someone who can't see very well would probably walk in a "careful" way, so we're looking for a word that has a meaning similar to *careful*. The word *cautiously* is close in meaning to *careful*, and it makes sense in the context of this sentence.

10. **The correct answer is D.** This compare and contrast question asks you to identify the difference between two of the characters in the passage. In the last paragraph of the passage, the author states that his grandfather was "a very quiet man who lived a routine, predictable life." We know that the author's grandmother, on the other hand, became upset very easily whenever things didn't go her way. Choice D summarizes this difference between the characters nicely.

11. **The correct answer is D.** This question concerns one specific detail from the passage. The correct answers to detail questions are given directly within the passage. If you can't remember the answer, you can find it by rereading the necessary part of the passage. At the beginning of paragraph 2, the author tells us that "One day, when I was about fifteen, I saw that the letters from my Aunt Frieda were coming written in Uncle Stuart's handwriting. I realized that Aunt Frieda wasn't really writing them . . . " The author knew that Aunt Frieda wasn't writing the letters because he could tell that the handwriting belonged to his Uncle Stuart.

12. **The correct answer is C.** The passage states that *Nana* controlled the family finances and made most of the decisions, so we can infer that she was the authority figure in the household. This eliminates choice D. Choice A is incorrect because, although she did not speak English, the author translated the letters from her children, so she was not cut off from them. While the author mentions that his grandmother was a worrier, this does not translate to the conclusion reached in choice B.

13. **The correct answer is D.** The author describes *Nana* as "crying inside" and feeling "powerless" when she sees Aunt Frieda. *Nana* is repeatedly saying that as a mother she should have been with her child at the hospital, so we can safely conclude that *Nana* felt powerless because Frieda did not tell her about the operation. While she may have felt confused (choice A) and later relieved (choice B), the author mentions that Nana felt powerless, so choice D is the better answer. Although it might make sense to suspect that *Nana* was also a little angry, she does not seem angry at the author about the deception regarding the letters, so choice C is incorrect.

14. **The correct answer is B.** When the letters started coming in Uncle Stuart's handwriting, the author did not inform Nana because she was easily

worried, as is noted in paragraph 2: "My grandmother was a real worrier, and I didn't want her to get upset…" At the end of the passage, the author remarks that she was also "smart as a whip," making choice B the best answer. The author does not reveal how much formal education she had, so choices C and D are incorrect.

15. **The correct answer is A.** Aunt Grace tells the author that Aunt Frieda is "recovering just fine," which is a reassuring statement. Choice B is incorrect because *console* means "to comfort another person at a time of grief, sorrow, or disappointment." Aunt Grace's words are not alarming, so we can eliminate choice C. Even though *Nana* later finds the news distressing, choice D is not the best answer because Aunt Grace's response is intended to be reassuring.

16. **The correct answer is A.** In the final paragraph, the passage states that germ-free mice are "popular for gut flora research because scientists can inoculate the mice with specific microbes and watch what happens." There are not enough details in the passage to support any of the other choices.

17. **The correct answer is C.** *Intriguing* means something like "arousing curiosity or interest." The only definition that comes close to this is choice C, *fascinating*.

18. **The correct answer is C.** This question is asking you to look for the exception: algae is never mentioned in the passage. While algae can be categorized as a eukaryote, which *is* mentioned, it is not a component of the gut microbiome indicated by the passage.

19. **The correct answer is A.** The anecdote discusses a historical example of a doctor performing an experiment and finding a connection between mood and the stomach, stating that "Beaumont noticed that St. Martin's mood seemed to affect how quickly he digested food." Just after providing the story, the author adds: "These early observations provided the first clues of crosstalk between the brain and the gut." Therefore, the author explicitly states why they have used this

anecdote, which is to set up the idea that doctors have historically noticed a brain-gut connection before diving into more current research on the topic.

20. **The correct answer is A.** Support for this answer can be found in the final paragraph, which states "experiments with germ-free mice have yielded intriguing clues about the possible influence of the gut microbiome on behavior and neurodevelopment. However, it is still unclear whether these findings are relevant to humans." Choice A basically restates this information in different words.

21. **The correct answer is C.** This passage focuses largely on gastrointestinal microbiomes and how scientists over the years have investigated the ways that the gut microbiome interacts with the brain. Consequently, the title "Gut Microbiomes and the Human Brain" does the best job of summarizing the main idea of the passage, which is what a good title should do. Choices A and C are not specific enough and choice D focuses on one small part of the passage (the story of Alexis St. Martin) without addressing the passage as a whole.

22. **The correct answer is C.** The word *severs* is found in the first paragraph of the passage. Here, we are presented with a definition of the term *energy*. We are told that the term *energy* was developed by a scientist named Thomas Young, who originally believed that energy was the ability to do physical work. Energy, Young thought, was like the work that an axe does when it comes down on a log and cuts the log into two pieces. The force of the axe acts on the log to break it in two. Therefore, we are looking for a word with a meaning similar to "cuts" or "breaks." The word *splits* reflects the action an axe takes when it divides a log in two.

23. **The correct answer is D.** To answer this question, you must identify a statement that reflects the views of *both* Joule and Einstein. The correct answer must express a belief shared by each scientist. If an answer choice contains the view of only one of the scientists, or neither of them, that choice will be incorrect. Choice D reflects a belief

that was held by both Joule and Einstein. Both scientists believed that molecules and atoms were made up of energy. Paragraph 2 tells us that Joule thought that "molecules contained very small forms of energy." Paragraph 3 tells us that Einstein thought that "molecules and atoms were made up of energy."

24. **The correct answer is A.** The last half of the passage is the place to look for the answer to this question. If we go back and reread paragraphs 3 and 4, we see that Einstein made two important discoveries that helped change our view of energy. First, as paragraph 3 tells us, he helped us understand that molecules and atoms were made up of large groups of energy particles. Second, as paragraph 4 states, Einstein broadened our definition of energy to "the ability to create force over any distance." This second discovery is mentioned in choice A. Choice B reflects the opposite of Einstein's view. Einstein did not show that energy was made up of atoms; on the contrary, he showed that molecules and atoms were made up of energy. Choice C is incorrect because the passage never states that Einstein invented a way to view energy with the naked eye. Choice D is false, based on the passage. Einstein did not develop the term *energy*. It is true that this term was developed about 200 years ago, as the passage tells us in paragraph 1, but it was developed by Thomas Young, not Einstein.

25. **The correct answer is A.** This question asks you to compare two views about energy that are given in the passage. The first view is that of Einstein, given toward the end of the passage. The second view is that of Thomas Young, given at the beginning of the passage. To answer the question, then, you must understand the difference between the two views.

The passage tells us in paragraph 1 that Young saw energy as the ability to do physical work. It then tells us in the last paragraph that Einstein saw energy as the stored potential to complete physical work. In other words, Young believed that energy was the ability to do work now, whereas Einstein

saw it as the ability to do work at some time in the future. Einstein's view is stated accurately only in choice A.

26. **The correct answer is D.** Paragraph 2 describes Joule's beliefs about the ability to do work. It states that Joule believed "the ability to do work was stored within the molecules of matter."

27. **The correct answer is A.** Paragraph 1 tells us that Machu Picchu was discovered by an American named Hiram Bingham in 1911, and that "until Bingham's discovery in 1911, no one in the West knew that Machu Picchu even existed." Therefore, we can conclude that Westerners learned about the site because of Bingham's discovery.

28. **The correct answer is C.** The passage focuses on the rediscovery of Machu Picchu, after it was lost to history for many centuries. It was not mentioned in Spanish accounts of the Inca, so choice D is incorrect. The term *mythical* refers to something that doesn't exist, thereby eliminating choice A. The Aztecs are not mentioned in the passage, so choice B cannot be correct. Therefore, it can best be described as the lost city of the Incan Empire.

29. **The correct answer is D.** The passage states that Machu Picchu is the most well-known archaeological site in South America. The passage does not compare or contrast it with other archaeological sites, so we are not given enough information to determine if it is the largest, oldest, or highest in altitude.

30. **The correct answer is A.** The passage states that archaeologists believe the site was used as both a home and religious retreat. The passage makes it clear that women and children also occupied Machu Picchu, so choice B is incorrect. The high altitude made it unlikely that it could have any military or business value, so choices C and D are incorrect as well.

31. **The correct answer is B.** The passage states that Cusco was conquered by the Spanish in 1532, though the Spanish apparently made no mention of Machu Picchu in their records. The passage does not state when Cusco was built or where Pachacuti Inca Yupanqui is buried.

32. **The correct answer is A.** The passage describes how glutamate works and how it can destroy certain types of brain cells. It addresses the impact of glutamate on the brain, so "The Effect of Glutamate on the Brain" is the best title. Choices B, C, and D aren't mentioned in the passage.

33. **The correct answer is C.** The correct answer can be found in the last sentence of paragraph two, which states "When levels of glutamate become high, this prompts nerve cells in the brain to become too active, which leads to destruction of the cells." Excess glutamate destroys brain cells by causing nerve cells in the brain to become too active.

34. **The correct answer is D.** Paragraph four tells us that glutamate found naturally in foods poses a low risk of causing high levels of glutamate in the brain. It goes on to explain that natural glutamate is bonded with other amino acids.

35. **The correct answer is B.** Paragraph 2 states that there are two types of neurotransmitters: those that *cause* nerve cells to act and those neurotransmitters that *stop* nerve cells from acting. Glutamate is one of the neurotransmitters that cause nerve cells to act.

36. **The correct answer is D.** Paragraph 2 states that glutamate is normally present in the brain in very small amounts.

37. **The correct answer is C.** The passage states that Janessa had a tough time falling asleep and woke up tired because she has never been able to control the excitement she feels for an upcoming event. There is no mention of an upcoming test, so choice A is incorrect. The story did not mention that Janessa was sick or that her cat kept her up that night, so choices B and D are also incorrect.

38. **The correct answer is D.** When Janessa's father said, "Some lessons are harder to learn than others," he was talking about what Janessa's mother had said—that when people get too excited, they sometimes get careless. He meant that sometimes people make mistakes multiple times before learning their lesson. There is no mention that he thinks science is the toughest subject in school, so choice A is incorrect. He also doesn't talk about studying hard to do well on exams, even if he thinks that's true, so choice B is incorrect. He also says nothing about some students being smarter than others, so choice C is also incorrect.

39. **The correct answer is B.** Use the information provided in the passage to answer this question. While riding in the car to school, Janessa talks to her father about the things she's learning in science class. The only topic she doesn't mention among the answer choices is magnetism.

40. **The correct answer is A.** At the end of the story, after checking her pockets for the trip permission slip and realizing she forgot it at home, Janessa finally realized the truth of what her parents were telling her that morning: if you get too excited, you may get careless and make mistakes, such as forgetting something. The lessons in the other answer choices may be important and worth learning, but they are not what Janessa finally realized when she discovered that she didn't have the trip permission slip.

Reading 2

1. B	9. C	17. C	25. D	33. C
2. A	10. A	18. A	26. C	34. C
3. D	11. C	19. B	27. D	35. D
4. B	12. C	20. C	28. C	36. C
5. C	13. D	21. A	29. B	37. A
6. D	14. B	22. D	30. C	38. B
7. D	15. D	23. A	31. C	39. D
8. B	16. B	24. D	32. A	40. B

1. **The correct answer is B.** To answer this question, it is helpful to first reread the paragraph that contains the sentence with the word *erroneously*. The sentence comes near the end of the first paragraph. Paragraph 1 tells us that some people used to believe that "if you build a better product, that product will definitely sell." It was discovered, however, that this idea was false. Sentence three of the paragraph tells us that the piece of advice was wrong because it "ignored the role that prices play in affecting what consumers buy." We are therefore looking for a definition of *erroneously* that means something like "incorrectly." *Mistakenly* best fits the definition that we're looking for.

2. **The correct answer is A.** Companies used to believe that people would always buy better products if those products were available on the market. This belief, however, turned out not to be true, as the Pioneer company learned. The Pioneer Tool and Die Company built a very high-quality mousetrap, but people wouldn't buy it because it was too expensive. The company therefore stopped producing or selling it.

3. **The correct answer is D.** The passage focuses on the fact that the Pioneer Tool and Die Company built a mousetrap that was better than others on the market. The most appropriate title among the choices then is "A Better Mousetrap." The other titles are not reflective of the focus of the passage. The mousetrap was not inexpensive, nor was it a

successful product, and the passage does not indicate if any of the features of the new mousetrap were powered by electricity.

4. **The correct answer is B.** The passage states that the mousetraps most consumers preferred cost about 7 cents each. Although it is possible that mousetraps could be made at home, the passage does not address that issue.

5. **The correct answer is C.** Paragraph 3 tells us that it was difficult to isolate fluorine because fluorine was very dangerous and destructive. The statement that it "cost some researchers their lives" tells us that certain researchers died during these destructive experiments.

6. **The correct answer is D.** This question is what is known as a detail question. It asks about a detail from the passage. The correct answer to detail questions will always be contained in the passage. In this case, paragraph 2 tells us that the discovery of fluorine began with a scientist named Georg Bauer, who first described a mineral known as "fluorspar." The third paragraph then tells us that scientists working with fluorspar saw that when the mineral was heated, it gave off a gas. It took years to isolate the element fluorine, but the process started with the research on fluorspar by Bauer.

7. **The correct answer is D.** This last paragraph of the passage lets us know that fluorides are

extremely dangerous and that they should never be touched, inhaled, or swallowed. The last paragraph is warning that fluorides could harm the human body upon contact. Choice D reflects this conclusion.

8. **The correct answer is B.** The passage deals primarily with the discovery and isolation of fluorine. The title "The Discovery of Florine" best expresses this main idea. While toothpaste and the dangers encountered by those experimenting with fluorine are details in the passage that contribute to the main idea, the titles in choices A and C do not reflect the emphasis of the passage. The title in choice D refers to chemical elements in general, not specifically fluorine.

9. **The correct answer is C.** The passage describes a practical use for fluorine as fluoride in toothpaste in the first paragraph and warns of its dangers in pure form in the last paragraph. This confirms the conclusion reached in choice C that while fluorine is dangerous, it has practical uses as well. This information eliminates choice B. The passage does not describe fluorine as an element that should be banned (choice A) or discuss the rarity or monetary value of fluorine (choice D).

10. **The correct answer is A.** This cause-and-effect question asks you to identify the factor that caused border guards to open the crossings in the Berlin Wall. To answer it, reread the paragraph that describes the opening of the wall. Paragraph 3 describes in detail how a mistaken TV announcement by a government official lead to crowds of East Germans swarming the border crossings. These crowds are what caused the border to open; soon after, the wall was dismantled.

11. **The correct answer is C.** The first paragraph mentions the idea of a "brain drain," which is when educated and skilled citizens move away from a place in large numbers. When so many East German citizens were leaving that officials worried about this issue, they put up the Berlin Wall in response. Ronald Reagan (choice D) is not mentioned at all and choice A does not make sense, as the Cold War had already started when the Berlin Wall was erected. Choice B is tricky because it reverses a concept from the passage; rather than the wall being erected to protect West Germany from communism, the East Germans built it to keep their citizens in and Western ideas out.

12. **The correct answer is C.** This question asks you to identify the meaning of a vocabulary term with which you might not be familiar based on the details given in the passage as context. In Paragraph 4, where the word *flummoxed* appears, the passage states: "The border guards, who had no idea what had just been broadcast on national television, were overwhelmed by the size of the crowds and flummoxed as to what to do." If the guards were both overwhelmed and didn't have enough information to know why it was happening or what to do, it would be safe to say that they were confused (choice C). Furthermore, there are no contextual details to support the conclusion that they were angered (choice A) or disorganized (choice D). While they might have been anxious (choice B) in such a chaotic situation, your task is to find the best answer for each question. Given the context, *confused* is a more accurate and specific answer than *anxious*.

13. **The correct answer is D.** This detail question is also a sneaky vocabulary question, since it relies on your understanding of the word *infrastructure*, meaning "the physical structure and organization of a particular facility or system." In this case, the passage discusses how the number of people gathered on the bridge at Bornholmer Strasse caused officials to worry about a collapse, forcing them to go along with the crowd's wishes. The passage specifically states that the guards had not heard Schabowski's announcement and that the opening did not go according to plan, so you can eliminate choices A and C. It may be possible that more people were gathered at Bornholmer Strasse than at any other crossing (choice B), but this conclusion is not supported by any details given in the passage.

5

14. **The correct answer is B.** Close reading reveals that grenades are never mentioned in the passage. However, land mines are, so if this question fooled you, make sure you're reading carefully and not confusing terms.

15. **The correct answer is D.** The term *Cold War* is mentioned in the first paragraph. This term refers to the period between roughly the end of World War II in 1945 and the fall of the Soviet Union in 1989. During this period, democratic world powers (led by the United States) and communist world powers (led by the Soviet Union) engaged in a conflict without ever reaching direct military confrontation.

16. **The correct answer is A.** In the final paragraph, the passage states that germ-free mice are "popular for gut flora research because scientists can inoculate the mice with specific microbes and watch what happens." There are not enough details in the passage to support any of the other choices.

17. **The correct answer is A.** Support for this answer can be found in the final paragraph, which states "experiments with germ-free mice have yielded intriguing clues about the possible influence of the gut microbiome on behavior and neurodevelopment. However, it is still unclear whether these findings are relevant to humans." Choice A basically restates this information in different words.

18. **The correct answer is C.** This question is asking you to look for the exception: algae is never mentioned in the passage. While algae can be categorized as a eukaryote, which *is* mentioned, it is not a component of the gut microbiome indicated by the passage.

19. **The correct answer is A.** The anecdote discusses a historical example of a doctor performing an experiment and finding a connection between mood and the stomach, stating that "Beaumont noticed that St. Martin's mood seemed to affect how quickly he digested food." Just after providing the story, the author adds: "These early observations provided the first clues of crosstalk between the brain and the gut." Therefore, the author explicitly states why they have used this anecdote, which is to set up the idea that doctors have historically noticed a brain-gut connection before diving into more current research on the topic.

20. **The correct answer is C.** *Intriguing* means something like "arousing curiosity or interest." The only definition that comes close to this is choice C, *fascinating*.

21. **The correct answer is C.** This passage focuses largely on gastrointestinal microbiomes and how scientists over the years have investigated the ways that the gut microbiome interacts with the brain. Consequently, the title "Gut Microbiomes and the Human Brain" does the best job of summarizing the main idea of the passage, which is what a good title should do. Choices A and C are not specific enough and choice D focuses on one small part of the passage (the story of Alexis St. Martin) without addressing the passage as a whole.

22. **The correct answer is D.** The second sentence of the paragraph describes the tendency to "interfere with nature" before the consequences of those actions are understood. Thus, we are making changes to the environment without fully understanding the consequences of those changes.

23. **The correct answer is A.** You can infer this answer from the third paragraph in which the author states that "The effects of the processes… are neither localized nor brief." In other words, the effects may be felt by more people for a longer period of time.

24. **The correct answer is D.** This answer can be inferred from the whole tone of the selection. We can assume from the tone that the author believes that the problem of finding solutions to pollution depends on the willingness of scientists to understand possible dangers before using new products in the environment. None of the other choices can be supported by the selection.

25. **The correct answer is D.** *Nonchalant* means "casually indifferent." Negligence and ignorance on the part of scientists certainly implies nonchalance.

26. **The correct answer is C.** *Synthetic* means "not natural" or man-made.

27. **The correct answer is D.** The poem is an ode to the flower.

28. **The correct answer is C.** The poet is saying that while the bird is splendid, the flower is even more beautiful. Therefore, we can conclude that he means that the color of the flower is brighter than that of the bird.

29. **The correct answer is B.** The flower blooms deep in the woods where, except for the occasional wanderer like himself, no one sees it.

30. **The correct answer is C.** The poem says that "Then beauty is its own excuse for being." This means that beauty exists for its own sake.

31. **The correct answer is C.** In saying "The self-same Power that brought me there brought you," the poet is expressing his faith in a Supreme Being that created man and nature. Based on this information, we can conclude that the poet is a religious person.

32. **The correct answer is A.** The passage states that when Australasia was cut off from the Asian mainland, the kangaroo "was also isolated."

33. **The correct answer is C.** The first paragraph tells us that kangaroos are found only in Australasia and that this part of the earth was cut off from the

Asian mainland. Specifically, kangaroos are found in Australia, Tasmania to the south, and New Guinea to the north.

34. **The correct answer is C.** The second to last sentence of the second paragraph makes this very clear: "Australia's national symbol…is the great gray kangaroo of the plains."

35. **The correct answer is D.** The word *picturesque* means "vivid." Potoroos, paddymelons, and wallabies are described as picturesque names for kangaroos. The only kangaroo moniker that is not on this list is the Man of the Woods.

36. **The correct answer is C.** Clues may be found in the first sentence of the first paragraph, which states that historians are trying to learn more about the *Mayflower*, and in the first sentence of the third paragraph, which describes the boat as historic.

37. **The correct answer is A.** The first paragraph explains how the name *Mayflower* was a very common name for ships in England during the early 1600s.

38. **The correct answer is B.** The first sentence of the second paragraph says that a duplicate of the *Mayflower* was "given to the people of the United States as a symbol of goodwill and common ancestry linking Britons and Americans."

39. **The correct answer is D.** The original *Mayflower* was 22 feet wide; the duplicate is 26 feet wide.

40. **The correct answer is B.** The author describes two buildings in England that may contain parts of the *Mayflower*.

NOTES

CHAPTER

Language Composition
and Expression

LANGUAGE COMPOSITION AND

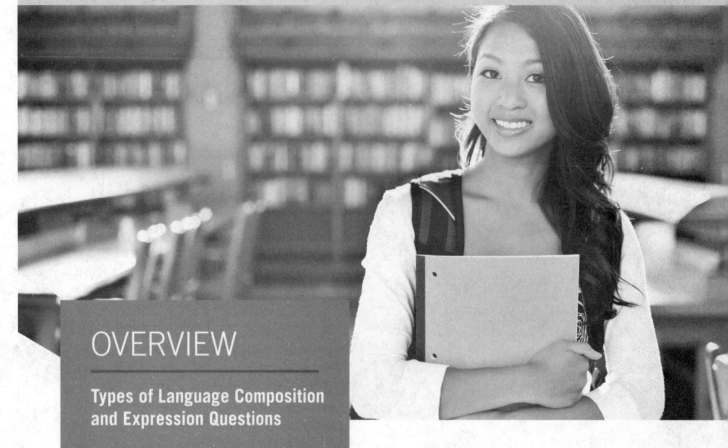

OVERVIEW

Types of Language Composition and Expression Questions

Audience and Purpose

Types of Writing

Organization

Summing It Up

Knowledge Check: Language Composition and Expression

Answer Key and Explanations

All of the Catholic high school entrance exams contain some kind of verbal section, but the way your verbal skills are tested varies greatly depending on which exam you're taking. Some exams rely only on your knowledge of synonyms and antonyms or analogies. Other exams ask you to find errors in grammar, punctuation, capitalization, and spelling. Sometimes, you may be required to think conceptually about a piece of writing by providing a topic sentence or by looking at the organization of a paragraph or essay. Some exams may require you to write an essay of your own. This range of tasks can make it difficult to prepare, but as long as you know what's on the exam you're taking, you can focus your energy on studying the right things.

TACHS   HSPT   ISEE   SSAT   SHSAT

EXPRESSION

On the English usage and language expression sections of the TACHS and HSPT exams, there are questions that are designed to test your potential for composition. Among these are questions that ask you to move a sentence to another location in the paragraph or to remove a sentence that does not belong. Other composition questions require you to identify topic sentences or choose the best development of topic sentences that are given.

In this chapter, we focus on global concepts and ideas related to composition, which generally refers to the writing process as well as the structure and development of a piece of writing. We'll talk about some fundamental principles of writing, like argument, organization, paragraph structure, and transitions. This will help you familiarize yourself with what a paragraph or passage should look like, which is critical for answering certain language composition and expression questions and will also be helpful on the reading comprehension portion of the exam. We'll also provide tips and tricks that apply directly to the question types you'll see on the exam.

TYPES OF LANGUAGE COMPOSITION AND EXPRESSION QUESTIONS

Composition questions make up only a small portion of the exam, but those few questions might be among the most difficult and time-consuming on the test. Expression questions typically test topic development and appropriateness. To prepare, you can familiarize yourself with some of the basic guidelines of composition and become familiar with the types of questions you'll encounter. First, we'll give an overview of what these questions look like. Then, we'll show how understanding the foundations of composition can help you better approach these questions.

Topic Development Questions

What do we mean by "development"? Topic development requires you to clearly understand the main point or idea of a paragraph or essay and then recognize additional information that logically expands upon or further clarifies that main point or idea. Topic development is much like finishing a story or an essay that someone else has started.

Topic development questions come in several forms. Here's an example of what this type of question might look like on your exam.

> **EXAMPLE:**

Choose the pair of sentences that best develops this topic sentence.

Plastic water bottles are one of the largest sources of plastic waste.

A. Styrofoam containers are a close second to plastic water bottles. Styrofoam never breaks down and releases toxic chemicals when exposed to sunlight.

B. Water is one of the most precious resources on the planet. We waste so much of it every day.

C. Most plastic water bottles end up in landfills while very few are recycled. A reusable water bottle made of glass or stainless steel is a more environmentally friendly choice.

D. Environmentalism has been around since the 1800s. Early environmentalists were followers of romanticism and wanted to preserve the beauty of nature for future generations.

The correct answer is C. The topic sentence prepares the reader for additional explanation about plastic waste. As such, the following sentences should elaborate on the idea of plastic waste by providing supporting evidence or details. Choice C does this by elaborating on why plastic water bottles are wasteful and providing an alternative option. Choice A shifts gears to focus on another source of waste: Styrofoam containers. While this is related, it does not follow through on the expectations of the topic sentence. Choice B focuses on water, not plastic water bottles. Again, while related to conservation, this is not the best choice for developing a topic sentence that focuses on plastic waste. Choice D focuses on environmentalism generally, which is a much bigger topic. This information might be helpful at the beginning of an essay on environmentalism at large but would be confusing if it followed the topic sentence we're given in this question.

Here are four tips that will help you tackle these questions on the exams:

1. If the question gives you a topic sentence and asks you to develop that sentence, your task is to choose the next two sentences that best develop the idea presented in the first sentence. You aren't just choosing some sentences that refer to the same subject presented in the topic sentence. You must choose the sentences that best expand upon or clarify the topic.

2. The question might give you an essay title and then ask that you choose a topic sentence that would best express the idea of that essay. You must choose a sentence that relates well to the subject presented by the title and that is broad enough to allow for further development of a paragraph.

3. If the question gives you a title and asks you to choose a sentence that belongs under that title, you must weed out the sentences that are related to but not entirely relevant to the topic.

4. The occasional answer choice "None of these" complicates your task and makes the question much more difficult. On the other questions, you know that one of the answers is the best solution to topic development, and you can use the process of elimination to improve your odds of landing on the correct response. When you're faced with a "None of these" response, you might not be able to use your skills to find the right answer. If you can't find the answer to one of these questions, just move on. Don't let it hold you up too long.

Appropriateness Questions

Questions that ask whether a particular sentence is appropriate to a specific paragraph are, in a way, asking you to perform the same skills you use in topic development but in reverse. With these questions, rather than choosing the best way to add to the information about a topic, you're asked to determine either the best placement of that information or whether the information belongs at all. Let's look at an example.

EXAMPLE:

Which sentence does NOT belong in the paragraph?

(1) Emily Brontë's *Wuthering Heights* tells the story of the Earnshaw and Linton families. (2) The story at first revolves around the relationship between Catherine Earnshaw and Heathcliff, a young, orphaned boy adopted by the Earnshaws. (3) However, Catherine and Heathcliff's romance is doomed due to his low social status. (4) Emily Brontë was also a poet and was even respected by Emily Dickinson. (5) The tension between love and social expectations is one of many important and powerful themes. (6) The novel has become a literary classic for its portrayal of pain and heartbreak that span generations.

A. Sentence 1
B. Sentence 2
C. Sentence 3
D. Sentence 4

The correct answer is D. Sentence 4 focuses on Emily Brontë as a person, not her book, *Wuthering Heights*. The topic sentence sets up expectations for the reader that the paragraph will focus on the book itself, not necessarily the author.

The key to answering this type of appropriateness question is to be able to identify what the main idea of the paragraph or passage is and to eliminate information that does not advance the main idea. Information that feels tangential or that introduces an unrelated idea is usually the culprit in these questions.

Similarly, you'll likely encounter questions where you'll be given a sentence and asked where it would work best in a paragraph or passage. This will require you to examine the sample paragraph and see what's missing or what could be expressed more thoroughly with the addition of another sentence. However, you may be given a sentence that is unrelated or does not really fit within the paragraph. In these scenarios, you'll want to select the answer "None of these" to indicate that the sentence does not belong in the paragraph. In these questions, your goal is to first identify the organization of the paragraph and then determine whether the sample sentence fits and where it belongs.

AUDIENCE AND PURPOSE

Now that we've covered the different types of questions, let's review some writing concepts that will help you answer these questions more effectively. First, we'll explore how every text has an audience and a purpose, which must be taken into consideration when you're revising or improving a sample paragraph.

As you're completing language composition and expression questions, you must remember that every piece of writing—whether it's a newspaper article, instruction manual, or nutrition label—has an **audience** and a **purpose**. The audience and purpose both determine which type of writing an author uses and how they structure their composition. When you encounter a sample passage on the exam, identifying the audience and purpose can help you answer specific questions about the passage's structure and topic.

A piece of writing is always written to a specific audience—a person or group of people who read that piece of writing. For example, when you're texting a friend, your friend is the audience for your text message. You and your friend likely know a lot about each other, so when you send messages, they are catered to what your friend cares about or finds interesting. What you know about your friend and the memories and experiences you've shared influence the way that you write to them. For example, if your friend likes playing video games, you might send them emoji related to their favorite games or send them memes that feature their favorite characters. If they are an especially close friend, the way you write may even include private jokes or phrases only they would understand. When you do these things, you are writing in a way that appeals to your audience.

Now, every piece of writing also has a purpose. The purpose is what the reader intends to accomplish with their piece of writing. When you text a friend, there's generally a reason or purpose for it. Perhaps you want to make them laugh or you want to confront them about something they did that you didn't like. Maybe you want to tell them about an awkward experience you had with someone at school or about a bad grade you got on a test. In order to accomplish your purpose, you make choices with the way that you write a text, like with the slang or the punctuation that you use or even the emoji you include.

Audience and purpose are integral to every piece of writing you read. On the exam, you'll be tested using many different types of writing, but no matter what type of writing it is, there is always an audience and a purpose. These influence the writer's decisions on

Scan this QR code to learn more about the role of audience and purpose in writing.

everything from the way they structure their writing to their use of an exclamation point at the end of a sentence. Being aware of the audience the author is writing to and why the author is writing in the first place can help you choose the correct answer when you're asked about how to improve or revise a sample sentence, paragraph, or passage on the exam.

TYPES OF WRITING

Here, we'll cover the diverse types of writing you can expect to see on the exam. The sample passages you encounter will cover a wide variety of genres and topics, so it's important to familiarize yourself with types of writing. An author will use different types of writing to best achieve their purpose. Does a composition tell a story or make a case for a particular point of view? Does it seek to inform or analyze?

Every piece of writing has a particular purpose, and the type of writing used is intrinsically tied to that purpose. There are four main types of writing: (1) narrative, (2) informative, (3) argumentative and persuasive, and (4) critical response. Luckily, these four main types will make up most, if not all, of the writing samples you'll encounter on the exam.

Narrative

Narrative writing tells a story. That story may be a work of fiction, such as a short story or novel, but it does not have to be. In fact, there are several forms of nonfictional narratives.

Nonfiction narratives are different from informative writing because narratives use all the elements that any story does: setting, people, and theme. Narrative writing focuses on bringing facts and details to life through descriptive and imaginative writing. For example, a history textbook is a piece of informative writing, and a biography is a piece of narrative writing. Any general American history textbook will contain details about Abraham Lincoln, the sixteenth president of the United States. The textbook will give details about Lincoln's actions and accomplishments in a straightforward manner, presenting facts and information without attempting to give the reader a detailed picture of what he was like. A biography, however, will attempt to show President Lincoln as a living, breathing person, giving readers a clear sense of what he was like by describing his personality and interests, as well as details of his life that may not be directly related to his actions and accomplishments.

Forms of Nonfictional Narratives

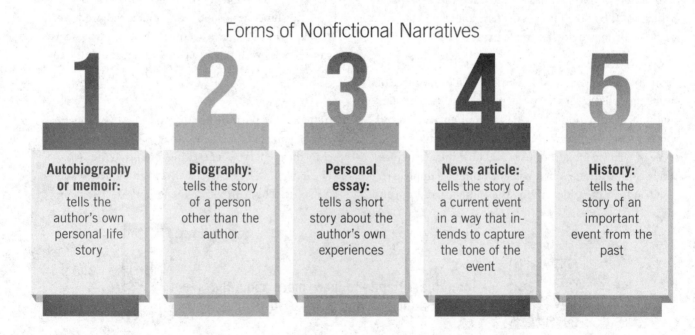

1

Autobiography or memoir: tells the author's own personal life story

2

Biography: tells the story of a person other than the author

3

Personal essay: tells a short story about the author's own experiences

4

News article: tells the story of a current event in a way that intends to capture the tone of the event

5

History: tells the story of an important event from the past

> **NOTE**
>
> Neutrality is the key to informative writing. This writing style merely presents the topic without taking a position on that topic.

Narrative writing can also be identified by its structure. It tends to be organized sequentially. In other words, events are described as they happened and not according to other organizational structures such as problem/solution, compare/contrast, or cause/effect, which we'll talk about more in the next section.

Because narrative writing seeks to both entertain and inform readers, its voice tends to be richer than that of an informative piece of writing. Narrative writing conveys mood as well as information. For example, if the story is a suspenseful one, the narration utilizes a suspenseful tone. Despite its similarities to the tone and structure of a fictional narrative, a nonfictional narrative must still adhere to the conventions of all nonfictional writing. It must be factual, well researched, and properly cited.

Informative

Unlike a narrative, informative writing is concerned with conveying information—it does so without the creativity of narrative writing. "Just the facts" is the motto of any informative composition, and teaching is its purpose. Informative writing uses an authoritative style without being too concerned with illustrating a specific mood. Creativity is much less important than ensuring that facts and details are clear and easy to understand.

Informative compositions are concerned with helping the reader understand an unfamiliar event, concept, process, or idea. Types of informative writing include:

- Summaries
- Instructions
- Encyclopedia articles
- Textbooks
- News reports that intend to convey facts and details only

- How-to articles
- Comparisons

Informative writing can be organized sequentially, but it might also use problem/solution, compare/contrast, or cause/effect structure, so it is easiest to identify by its straightforward style. An informative piece will usually include a thesis statement (more on this later in the chapter) that identifies the piece's purpose or main idea in the first paragraph. Evidence and details that support that statement follow while the concluding paragraph reinforces or sums up the purpose or main idea.

Unlike persuasive writing (which we'll get to next), informative writing is not concerned with gaining the reader's trust and acceptance. In other words, an informative composition is generally accepted as fact; however, note that acceptance can be undermined by sloppiness, which is why facts alone do not guarantee that an informative composition is effective. As is the case for all writing types, it must be well written, organized, cited, and documented.

Argumentative and Persuasive

Have you ever felt particularly passionate about an issue and tried to make a case for your point of view? Well, then you have basically done what writers of argumentative or persuasive compositions do. The word *argumentative* tends to have negative connotations associated with an angry person who likes to fight and contradict for the sake of contradicting. Adopting an angry tone is often not what a writer wants to do when composing an argumentative piece of writing because the real function of such writing is to persuade, not to fight or contradict. Consequently, there are a number of approaches to writing argumentative compositions, and choosing the right one often depends on the kind of audience the author wants to reach.

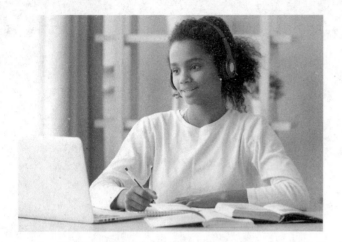

Some argumentative writing will present a case in order to persuade the audience, make a claim and argue for or against it, or consider two or more options and argue in favor of the better option. You may also be familiar with debate, which presents both sides of an issue and arrives at one position over the other. Similarly, a piece of satire pretends to argue in favor of a point that the author does not actually agree with in order to ridicule that point of view.

An argument can be written in a friendly and familiar style for, say, an audience of young readers, or it can be written using technical language for a very specific audience of educated adults. It may appeal to a reader's sense of right and wrong or logic. It may also play on the reader's emotions or intellect.

One of the keys to building a strong argument is identifying both the pros and cons of an issue. The issue will generally be clarified in the thesis statement while the body paragraphs may use a point/counterpoint structure to deal with the pros and cons of that issue. However, an argumentative composition may also utilize other organizational structures, such as problem/solution, compare/contrast, or cause/effect. Therefore, the best way to identify an argumentative composition is to figure out the piece's purpose. If the author is trying to persuade you to share their point of view, the piece is argumentative.

Critical Response

When a piece of writing conveys the author's reactions without necessarily trying to persuade the reader to do or think something, that piece is most likely a

critical response. A critical response is more analytical than expressly persuasive in nature. Nevertheless, the ultimate effect of a critical response may be persuasion, even though this is not its specific purpose. For example, after reading an analysis of a movie that identifies the movie's numerous weak points, you may decide to steer clear of that movie even if that is not the writer's express intention. But a good critical response is written from a perspective of objectivity. It evaluates a work on the work's own merit, using well-researched evidence to support its conclusions.

ORGANIZATION

On the exam, language expression questions typically test topic development and appropriateness. These two types of questions require you to understand how writing is structured so that you can identify the best topic sentence for a paragraph and determine whether a sentence is relevant to a passage overall. To answer these questions, it will be helpful to pay attention to how a passage is organized. When we refer to the organization of a text, we are talking about the order in which information appears. Ideas are generally presented in a specific order because that progression makes the most sense for the reader and helps the writer to advance or achieve their purpose for writing. In addition to overall structure and organization, paragraphs should also follow a general structure to make it easier for the reader to navigate the ideas presented, identify specific information, and anticipate what's coming next.

Most often, the passages you're working with for these questions will be informative, argumentative, or persuasive in nature. The sections that follow teach you how these types of writing are generally structured overall and at the paragraph level. We'll also walk through how to use this information in order to answer both topic development and appropriateness questions.

Structure of Ideas

When you are working with a sample passage on the exam, it's important that you understand how it is structured in order to identify any extra or unnecessary sentences or to reorganize a paragraph. Though readers generally expect information to be organized in certain

STRUCTURE OF A PASSAGE
There are many ways to organize a piece of writing.

1 **Cause/Effect:** explains processes and follows up with the results of those processes (appropriate for informative and argumentative writing)

2 **Compare/Contrast:** describes similarities and/or differences among ideas (appropriate for informative and argumentative writing)

3 **Description:** explains the characteristics of a topic (appropriate for critical responses and informative writing)

4 **Division/Classification:** groups ideas into categories (appropriate for informative writing)

5 **Problem/Solution:** presents a problem and explains how to solve that problem (appropriate for narrative, informative, and argumentative writing)

6 **Process:** presents information step by step (appropriate for informative writing)

7 **Sequential Order:** presents information in the order in which it occurred (appropriate for narrative and informative writing)

ways, it's important to note that individual paragraphs often serve specific functions in a passage. The passages you encounter on the exam will likely have an introduction, body, and conclusion. In longer pieces of writing, each of these will be its own paragraph(s). An introduction typically provides an overview of the topic being discussed and will include a thesis statement, which establishes the main idea or argument of the text. Body paragraphs develop the thesis statement in more detail with evidence and analysis that support the argument. A writer will use as many body paragraphs as needed to develop the topic and accomplish their purpose. Finally, the conclusion summarizes what was discussed and reiterates key points or examples from the body paragraph(s) as well as the significance of the topic overall.

In smaller passages, like those consisting of a single paragraph, you'll likely see a truncated version of this structure. The first sentence or two of a paragraph will be the introduction and thesis statement. The next few sentences will serve as the body and elaborate on the thesis statement with examples or explanation. The last sentence will function as a conclusion that wraps up the topic neatly.

Language composition and expression questions ask you to determine if the sequence of material in a passage could be improved or if there's an opportunity to add or delete sentences, depending on their relevance to the topic. If you need to quickly acquire information about the purpose of a passage or a specific paragraph, the title and first and last paragraphs (or even the first and last sentences) can summarize the topic. From there, you can eliminate answers that don't align with the purpose of the passage or a given question.

Thesis Statement

The thesis statement, or main claim, is the foundation of an argument. It is the central point the writer is trying to make, the thing that the writer is trying to persuade readers to believe.

Perhaps a writer is trying to convince readers that recycling is good for the environment. The thesis of that writer's argument would express this main claim in a clear, complete, declarative sentence, such as "Everyone should recycle." This thesis statement is really simple. A thesis can be a bit more complexly worded, say, for example, as "It is imperative that all global citizens recycle for the sake of the natural environment we all share." Whether simple or more complex, the thesis statement must maintain complete clarity. After all, it will be hard to persuade readers if the readers are not sure about what they are being persuaded to believe.

Because the thesis statement is so integral to the meaning and purpose of an argument, it is usually stated early in the piece—usually in the first paragraph, but in longer pieces, it may appear in the second or even third paragraph if the writer spends the first paragraph or two providing background information. On the reading comprehension portion of the exam, you are often asked to identify the main idea or primary purpose of a text. In a nutshell, these questions are asking you to identify the thesis statement of the text. If you know where to look for the thesis statement, then you can answer these questions more quickly and confidently. For language composition and expression questions, the thesis statement can help us determine whether or not a sentence is relevant to the topic at hand.

Because the thesis statement also gives a piece of writing structure and guidance, you can also identify information that does not belong. When you are deciding on whether a sentence belongs in a paragraph, you must evaluate it in relation to the thesis statement or main idea of the passage. Remember that for smaller passages consisting of a single paragraph, this is likely the first sentence.

Paragraph Structure

A paragraph is often structured in a way that helps advance the thesis statement of a piece of writing. The sentences in a paragraph generally go in the following order. Keep in mind that while a main idea and topic sentence are usually one sentence each, a writer will likely include multiple sentences of evidence and analysis to make the main idea stronger and to thoroughly develop the paragraph.

Main Idea/Topic Sentence: The first sentence should express and summarize the main idea or purpose of a paragraph. The topic sentence should tell you what the paragraph is about so that you know what to expect as you read. Think of topic sentences as signposts or markings that guide you through a piece of writing and tell you what's coming next. In longer pieces of writing with multiple paragraphs, the topic sentence helps to develop the central argument, known as the thesis statement.

Evidence: To develop the idea outlined in the topic sentence, a writer will provide supporting evidence in the form of examples, facts, statistics, and more. Think of supporting details as proof of the writer's main idea and purpose. Sometimes, the writer will present some evidence followed by analysis and then more evidence followed by more analysis. This is especially true if there is a lot of evidence to support the writer's point.

Analysis: This is where the writer explains the evidence itself, why the evidence is important, and how it proves the writer's point. A writer will try to anticipate additional explanation and context the reader might need to understand how the evidence supports the main idea of the paragraph.

Summary: Paragraphs often end with a summary of what was just discussed. This is where the writer reiterates their main idea to remind the reader of the most important takeaway from the paragraph. In a passage with several paragraphs, the last sentence of a paragraph usually summarizes what was just discussed while also functioning as a transition that prepares the reader for the next paragraph.

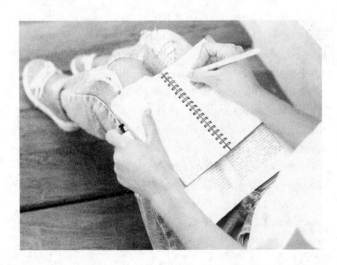

Let's look at a sample paragraph and break it down into parts:

EXAMPLE:

> If consumed too frequently, the delicious sugary beverage known as soda can be detrimental to one's dental health, especially if you don't practice good oral hygiene (**Main Idea**). In fact, people who drink soda on a daily basis and only brush their teeth once a day are far more likely to experience tooth decay (**Evidence**). This is because the sugar in soda interacts with the bacteria in your mouth and becomes highly acidic, causing cavities, erosion of enamel, and gum disease (**Analysis**). To combat the harmful effects of soda, practice good dental hygiene: rinse your mouth out with water after drinking a soda, brush your teeth twice a day, and floss (**Evidence**). These healthy habits can remove the bacteria on and in between your teeth while protecting your teeth from decay (**Analysis**). That way, you can still enjoy the carbonation and syrupy sweetness of soda in moderation while keeping your teeth clean and healthy (**Summary**).

The first sentence in this sample paragraph is the main idea. It introduces the topic and focus of the paragraph. From this sentence, we know that we'll be reading about the effect of soda on dental health. In the next sentence, we're presented with evidence of the detrimental effect that soda can have on one's dental health, which is that those who drink soda daily are more likely to have cavities. The following sentence explains why this is the case: The ingredients in soda can damage teeth. The fourth sentence provides examples of good dental hygiene, and the fifth sentence explains how these habits can mitigate the damage done by soda. Finally, the last sentence reiterates the main point of the paragraph, which is that you can still drink soda in moderation and keep your teeth clean.

If you remember that paragraphs are generally structured in this order—main idea, evidence, analysis, summary—then you can more efficiently identify the pieces that are missing or rearrange the sentences to be more effective in response to a sample question.

Transitions

Using transitional words and phrases is an effective way to clarify the selected organizational pattern of a text. Certain transitions are most appropriate for particular patterns.

TRANSITIONAL WORDS AND PHRASES

Organizational Patterns	Examples of Common Transitions
Cause/Effect	because, since, therefore, as a result, consequently, etc.
Compare/ Contrast	*To compare:* similarly, comparatively, just as, in the same way, correspondingly, likewise, etc.
	To contrast: however, but, conversely, in contrast, on the contrary, yet, on the other hand, nevertheless, in spite of, rather, instead, etc
Description	above, below, inside, outside, beside, etc.
Division/ Classification	the first type, the second variety, the third group, the fourth kind, etc.
Problem/ Solution	because, obviously, evidently, furthermore, in fact, in any case, since, for the same reason, etc.
Process	step one, step two, first, second, third, next, finally, as soon as, by the time, etc.
Sequential Order	first, next, then, later, meanwhile, the following year, etc.

As you read through a text, whether it consists of a single paragraph or a few paragraphs, pay attention to the transitions the writer uses. These are helpful indicators of the direction and structure of a text. For example, in writing that follows a cause-and-effect structure, the writer will need to use directional words that illustrate how one thing leads to another. When comparing and/or contrasting two things, a writer needs to make use of words that highlight similarities and/or differences. For a piece of writing that outlines or describes a process, using words that clearly indicate the steps of the process is helpful. When you see transition words, know that they are intended to guide you through the passage so that you understand the development of ideas.

Oftentimes, when you are asked to determine whether a sentence belongs in a paragraph, you can use transition words as a guide. While you can identify that a sentence is not on the same topic as the surrounding sentences, the writing style can help confirm this for you. Is there a clear connection between a specific sentence and the sentences that come before and after it? If there's no clear transition, for example, then it's possible that one of those sentences doesn't belong. Try reading the paragraph without the sentence that you suspect is off topic. Does the paragraph seem more logical and organized without the sentence in question? Do the sentences have clear transitions between them now that the extra sentence has been removed? If so, then you have probably identified the sentence that does not belong.

The Known-New Construct

Writers often create transitions between sentences or ideas using the known-new construct. The known-new construct first communicates what the reader knows (information that has already been presented) before introducing the reader to new information (information that has not yet been presented). In practice, writers will take the end of the previous sentence and rephrase it to become the subject of the next sentence. You'll also notice that writers deploy the known-new construct implicitly by using pronouns to refer back to information that has already been discussed. In other words, information that has been discussed in one sentence becomes the antecedent for a pronoun that is used in the next sentence.

Let's look at an example of the known-new construct in practice. In this example, we can see that the information at the end of one sentence (in bold) is restated as the subject (underlined) of the following sentence, and pronouns are used to refer back to material that has already been covered.

EXAMPLE:

(1) Climate change has resulted in unpredictable weather patterns, like more destructive storms and **more extreme drought conditions**. (2) The lack of precipitation has exacerbated the wildfire season for several states, including Colorado, Oregon, and **California**. (3) California had its largest fire season ever in 2020, **with close to 10,000 wildfires**. (4) These wildfires collectively **burned close to 4.5 million acres and destroyed over 10,000 structures**. (5) The widespread damage and destruction has prompted governors to **prioritize wildfire prevention and mitigation in state budgets**. (6) While this increase in spending is a good first step, more research into targeted environmental policies will be needed in the coming years.

Each sentence strategically builds off the previous one. Notice how the end of one sentence is rephrased to become the subject of the next sentence. The first sentence states that climate change has caused more extreme drought conditions. Then, "drought conditions" is rephrased as "lack of precipitation," which is the subject of the next sentence. In other words, information that was new in sentence 1 is now known information for sentence 2. Now, take a look at sentence 4: "These wildfires" refers back to the wildfires in California, which were mentioned in the previous sentence. Sentence 6 does something similar with "this increase in spending," referencing the budget priorities mentioned in the preceding sentence.

On the exam, you may be asked to identify a sentence that is out of place or where a sample sentence would be best positioned in a paragraph. Sentences in these examples are constructed so that they transition smoothly. Oftentimes, passages will follow the known-new construct to transition between sentences, which can make it easier to identify sentences that are out of place or to find the best position for a new sentence. Let's look at another example of the known-new construct in practice and how we can use it to decide which sentence would be best to add to a sample passage.

EXAMPLE:

(1) Younger plant owners prefer houseplants that require minimal care, like succulents or cacti. (2) Succulents come in a variety of styles, colors, and sizes, so there are plenty of options to choose from. (3) Cacti are a popular choice because they are easy to take care of and require so little water. (4) In fact, watering too frequently is the easiest way to kill your cactus. (5) Whether it's a classic aloe vera succulent or a prickly pear cactus, a houseplant can bring a touch of style and a sense of calm to any home.

Where would the sentence "Houseplants have risen drastically in popularity among young adults" work best?

A. Before sentence 1
B. Between sentence 2 and sentence 3
C. Between sentence 4 and sentence 5
D. After sentence 5

The correct answer is A. Look closely at the sample sentence. The first half of the sentence discusses how houseplants have risen in popularity, and the second half of the sentence explains that this increase in popularity has been among young adults. Using the known-new construct, we can find a sentence that begins with a phrase similar in meaning to "young adults." If we don't see a sentence like that, we can look for a sentence that begins with a pronoun that would refer back to young adults, like "they" or "this demographic." Now, notice the first few words of sentence 2: "Younger plant owners." This sentence would work as a follow-up to our sample sentence because it refers back to the idea of "young adults." Further, notice how the rest of the paragraph uses the known-new construct to create a deliberate sense of flow between sentences. Each sentence builds off the previous one by rephrasing known information in order to introduce new information to the reader. If you put the sample sentence from the question in any of the other locations, it would feel like an unrelated interruption because it does not create a deliberate connection between the sentence preceding or following it.

SUMMING IT UP

- Language composition and expression questions on the HSPT and TACHS use multiple-choice questions that ask you to move a sentence to another location in the paragraph, remove a sentence that does not belong, identify topic sentences, or choose the best development of topic sentences.

- Topic development requires that you be able to clearly understand the main point or idea and then recognize additional information that logically expands upon or further clarifies that main point or idea.

- Appropriateness questions ask you to choose which information does or does not belong or to determine where the best placement of that information might be.

- In preparation for the exam, you'll want to have a solid understanding of the audience and purpose for the texts that you read. These two principles guide every piece of writing, so any organizational or structural choices will always serve to advance the purpose of the text and make that purpose clear to the audience.

- You can expect to see several types of writing, such as narrative, argumentative/persuasive, informative, and critical response, in the sample passages on the exam.

- Knowing the organization of a text is critical for answering topic development and appropriateness questions. The organization of a text will depend on the audience, purpose, and type of writing involved but will typically include an introduction, body, and conclusion.

- You can generally expect passages to follow one of the following structures:
  - cause/effect
  - compare/contrast
  - description
  - division/classification
  - problem/solution
  - process
  - sequential order

- As part of organization, you should also know where to find the thesis statement of a passage, understand the general structure of body paragraphs, and identify how writers transition between ideas and paragraphs.

KNOWLEDGE CHECK

LANGUAGE COMPOSITION AND EXPRESSION
10 Questions—6 Minutes

Directions: For questions 1 and 2, choose the pair of sentences that best develops the topic sentence.

1. Salting highways in winter is undoubtedly helpful to the motorist, yet this practice may actually cause a great deal of harm.

   A. Salt works more quickly than chemical ice melters because it does not require heat to go into action. Salt mixed with sand offers especially good traction.

   B. While melting the ice and eliminating slippery conditions, the same salt eats into the road surface itself, creating dangerous potholes. Further, the salty runoff leaches into the soil and kills surrounding vegetation.

   C. A small amount of salt is a dietary necessity, especially in hot, dry climates. Large amounts of dietary salt, however, lead to water retention and high blood pressure.

   D. Salt is inexpensive because it occurs abundantly in nature. Highways in the Rocky Mountains should have good safety records because they are so close to Utah, a great source of salt.

2. Mesa Verde is a great flat-topped mountain that rises dramatically above the surrounding Colorado desert.

   A. In contrast to this desert, Mesa Verde is fertile and well-watered, a green oasis to which people have been drawn since ancient times. Within the sheer cliff walls of these canyons, nature has carved out vast caverns in soft sandstone rock.

   B. In 1275, a severe 24-year drought hit the Mesa Verde area. The Cliff Dwellers, hounded by their relentless enemies and forces they could not comprehend, abandoned their cities and fields and fled from Mesa Verde.

   C. At Mesa Verde, the Ancestral Puebloans found favorable growing conditions. The legends call them the *Anasazi*, the Ancient Ones or Ancient Enemies.

   D. Villages, towns, and ultimately great cities appeared on the mesa tops. Tools and implements became more diverse and elaborate.

Directions: For questions 3 and 4, choose the topic sentence that best fits the paragraph.

3. They set fires for many different reasons. Sometimes, a shopkeeper sees no way out of losing their business and sets fire to it to collect the insurance. Another type of arsonist wants revenge and sets fire to the home or shop of someone they feel has treated them unfairly.

   A. They don't look like criminals, but they cost the nation millions of dollars in property loss and sometimes loss of life.

   B. Arsonists of this type have even been known to help fight the fire.

   C. Arsonists are persons who set fires deliberately.

   D. Some arsonists just like the excitement of seeing the fire burn and watching the firefighters at work.

4. But you ought not to despise it, for it can help you and your family obtain many of the good things of life. It can buy an adequate diet, one of the basics of good health. It can make it easier for your children to secure an education. When necessary, it can provide medicine and medical care.

   A. Money can offer a great opportunity for you to help others.

   B. Money can be the means for a comfortable house, for travel, for good books, and for hobbies and recreation.

   C. Many people consider that amassing great wealth is a goal in itself.

   D. Certainly, money should not be your chief aim in life.

Directions: For questions 5 and 6, choose the sentence that does not belong in the paragraph.

5. (1) In a democratic state, people are allowed to have certain freedoms. (2) They can speak their views freely, even if these views are against the government. (3) Andrew Jackson, who served from 1829–1837, was the first president elected by the Democratic Party. (4) They can express their views freely in the media, such as newspapers. (5) Citizens are free to gather in groups to discuss political or religious issues. (6) They can form political parties, and they can elect the people they choose to govern them. (7) In a democratic state, no one can be arrested for expressing their views about politics. (8) The role of the government is to keep its citizens secure and to protect their freedoms.

   A. Sentence 2

   B. Sentence 3

   C. Sentence 4

   D. Sentence 5

6. (1) Hermit crabs are aquatic crustaceans that often dwell in saltwater reefs and near shorelines. (2) Hermit crabs typically protect their soft, curved abdomens from potential predators by wearing a shell, which is usually salvaged from sea snails or bivalves. (3) Other creatures that have shells include turtles and armadillos. (4) Did you know that hermit crabs have gills, which need to stay wet so they can breathe?

   A. Sentence 1

   B. Sentence 2

   C. Sentence 3

   D. Sentence 4

Directions: For questions 7–10, choose the best answer.

---

7. Where should the sentence, "Prior to the Civil War, the steamboat was the center of life in the thriving Mississippi towns," be placed in the paragraph below?

   (1) With the war came the railroads. (2) River traffic dwindled, and the white-painted vessels rotted at the wharves. (3) During World War I, the government decided to relieve rail congestion by reviving the long-forgotten waterways. (4) Today, steamers, diesels, and barges ply the Mississippi.

   A. Before sentence 1

   B. Between sentences 2 and 3

   C. Between sentences 3 and 4

   D. The sentence does not fit in this paragraph.

8. Where should the sentence, "It can damage the heart and also the blood vessels," be placed in the paragraph below?

   (1) Patients with the condition known as type 2 diabetes suffer from the same basic problem as patients with type 1 diabetes. (2) In short, their bodies are not able to use the sugar in their blood very effectively. (3) This blood sugar, known as glucose, becomes very high in patients with diabetes, and it can cause many problems. (4) People with type 2 diabetes usually have high blood pressure as well, which puts even more of a strain on the heart and circulatory system.

   A. Between sentences 1 and 2

   B. Between sentences 2 and 3

   C. Between sentences 3 and 4

   D. After sentence 4

9. Which of the following sentences best fits under the topic, "The Symbolic Use of Bears"?

   A. Dancing bears provide a comical form of entertainment at street fairs.

   B. Small children love to hug teddy bears because they are soft and warm.

   C. The bear has long been the symbol of Russia.

   D. None of these

10. Which topic is best for a one-paragraph theme?

    A. Development and Decline of the Whaling Industry

    B. The Effects of Automation Upon the Farming Industry

    C. The Advantage of Using a Heavier Baseball Bat

    D. None of these

ANSWER KEY AND EXPLANATIONS

1. B	**3.** C	**5.** B	**7.** A	**9.** C
2. A	**4.** D	**6.** C	**8.** C	**10.** C

1. **The correct answer is B.** The pair of sentences presented in choice B picks up where the topic sentence leaves off. The first sentence explains how the salt is helpful, and the second sentence gives examples of the harm caused by salt. While choice A amplifies the action of salt on ice and tells of its beneficial effects, the sentences in choice B better develop the topic sentence. Choices C and D do not develop the topic sentence at all.

2. **The correct answer is A.** The topic sentence introduces both Mesa Verde and the Colorado desert. The sentences in choice A flow naturally by contrasting Mesa Verde to the desert and then further describing Mesa Verde. While the sentences in choice C are good, a transitional sentence would be desirable to introduce the *Anasazi*, so choice C is not the best answer. Choices B and D do nothing to develop the topic sentence.

3. **The correct answer is C.** Most often, a definition makes a good topic sentence. "Arsonists are persons who set fires deliberately" sets a good reference point for the pronoun, *they*, which begins the next sentence. Neither choice A nor choice B can be the topic sentence since they both refer to antecedents that aren't there. Choice D would lead to very different paragraph development.

4. **The correct answer is D.** "Certainly, money should not be your chief aim in life" as a topic sentence sets up a nice contrast with the *but* that follows at the beginning of the second sentence. Choices A and B set up meaningless contrasts. Choice C makes a weak topic sentence, and it takes a broad perspective by mentioning "Many people," while the paragraph uses a more personal approach by addressing "you and your family." In addition, choice C leaves an unclear reference for the "it" that is not to be despised.

5. **The correct answer is B.** Although this paragraph discusses the types of freedoms associated with democracies, it does not address specific politicians, political events, or political parties. Sentence 3 provides information about a former president, noting that he was a prominent member of the Democratic Party, which is not the focus of this paragraph.

6. **The correct answer is C.** This is an informative passage about the hermit crab. Sentence 3 provides only tangential information about other animals that have shells, and therefore, it does not belong in the paragraph.

7. **The correct answer is A.** The organization of this paragraph is chronological. Because the third sentence discusses relief of rail congestion during World War I, it is clear that the war of the first sentence is the Civil War. Events prior to the Civil War should be mentioned before events that happened during the Civil War.

8. **The correct answer is C.** The topic sentence introduces the subject of type 2 diabetes and indicates that more information about this condition will follow. Elevated blood sugar levels and the resulting problems are mentioned in the second and third sentences, so a description of these problems would logically follow. Therefore, the sentence should be placed between sentences 3 and 4.

9. **The correct answer is C.** Choices A and B tell of actual uses of bears. Only choice C describes a bear as a symbol.

10. **The correct answer is C.** This is a limited topic that could be dealt with in one paragraph. The topic also lends itself to being one paragraph in a longer, more comprehensive essay. Choices A and B are much more involved and would require significant background information; neither topic could be covered adequately in a single paragraph.

NOTES

CHAPTER

**English Usage
and Punctuation**

ENGLISH USAGE AND PUNCTUATION

OVERVIEW

Grammar

Sentence Structure and Formation

Verb Tense

Conventions of Punctuation

Conventions of Usage

Agreement

Frequently Confused Words and Expressions

Knowledge Check: English Usage and Punctuation

Answer Keys and Explanations

The HSPT and the TACHS exams will test your expertise in language usage. The HSPT groups this subject with spelling, punctuation and capitalization, and composition in the Language Skills section. The TACHS tests this subject in the Language section.

Language usage includes a person's grasp of correct English and how it's used. Your expertise in this area is based on years of reading and hundreds of hours of classroom instruction on grammar. In answering language usage questions, you may have to consider problems of agreement, double negatives, and dangling modifiers. Word choice, punctuation, tense, and case may also affect which answer is best.

TACHS	HSPT	ISEE	SSAT	SHSAT

The sections that follow cover important topics in grammar, sentence structure, and punctuation. There will be a lot of rules to learn, but learning these rules will be helpful on multiple sections of the exam. This is especially true on the HSPT. Knowing grammatical rules will be essential on the Language Skills section of the exam but will also be helpful on the Verbal Skills section. For analogies and verbal classification questions, knowing the different parts of speech, verb tense, and parallel structure might help you pinpoint the correct answer.

As you study the rules in this chapter, try not to get too bogged down in grammar terminology. Instead, focus on the practical applications of the rules and how to identify and correct errors in usage. At the end of this chapter, you'll have a chance to practice what you've learned with a Knowledge Check.

GRAMMAR

The rules of grammar govern the ways in which **parts of speech** are organized in a sentence. There are rules concerning word endings, word order, and which words may be used together. You must know the parts of speech to follow the rules of grammar. Here, we'll provide a brief overview of the parts of speech, but in later sections of this chapter, we'll elaborate on the conventions that govern their usage.

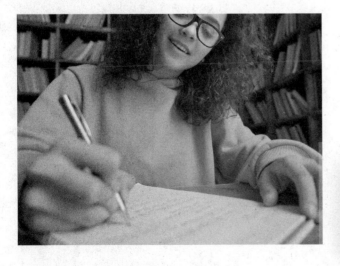

PARTS OF SPEECH

Type	Definition	Example
Noun	A person, place, thing, or idea	teacher, city, desk, democracy
Pronoun	Substitute for a noun	he, they, ours, those
Adjective	Describes a noun	warm, quick, tall, blue
Verb	Expresses action or a state of being	yell, interpret, feel, are
Adverb	Modifies a verb, an adjective, or another adverb	fast, slowly, friendly, well
Conjunction	Joins words, sentences, and phrases	for, and, nor, but, or, yet, so
Preposition	Shows position in time or space	in, during, after, behind

Nouns

A **noun** is a person, place, thing, or idea. There are different kinds of nouns:

- **Common nouns** are general, such as house, person, street, or city.
- **Proper nouns** are specific, such as White House, Fernando, Main Street, or New York.
- **Collective nouns** name groups like team, crowd, organization, or Congress.

Nouns have **cases**:

- A noun is in the **nominative** case when it is the subject of the sentence.

EXAMPLE:

Roberto joined the band.

- A noun is in the **objective** case when it is the direct object, indirect object, or object of the preposition.

> **EXAMPLES:**
>
> **Direct object:** She built a *treehouse.*
>
> **Indirect object:** Joel sent a message to *Marco.*
>
> **Object of the preposition:** The fairies danced around *Jasmine.*

- **Possessive** case is the form that shows possession.

> **EXAMPLE:**
>
> The *queen's* crown was filled with rubies.

Pronouns

A **pronoun** is a substitute for a noun. The **antecedent** of the pronoun is the noun that the pronoun replaces. A pronoun must agree with its antecedent in gender, person, and number. There are several kinds of pronouns:

- **Demonstrative pronoun:** this, that, these, those
- **Indefinite pronoun:** all, any, nobody
- **Interrogative pronoun:** who, which, what
- **Personal pronoun:** I, you, we, me, him, her, us, they

Scan this QR code for a video about nouns and verbs.

Adjectives

An **adjective** describes a noun. Adjectives can answer questions like:

- "Which one?"
- "What kind?"
- "How many?"

There are three uses of adjectives:

- A **noun modifier** is usually placed directly before the noun it describes.

> **EXAMPLE:**
>
> He is a *tall* man.

- A **predicate adjective** follows an inactive verb and modifies the subject.

> **EXAMPLES:**
>
> She is *happy.*
>
> I feel *terrible.*

- An **article** or **noun marker** points to a noun. The articles are *the, a,* and *an.*

> **EXAMPLE:**
>
> *The* teacher took *a* vacation to *an* island.

Verbs

A **verb** expresses action or a state of being. There are four major kinds of verbs: transitive, intransitive, linking, and auxiliary or helping verbs.

- **Transitive verbs** are action verbs and always have a direct object. In other words, there's something receiving the action of a transitive verb.

EXAMPLES:

The dog *broke* her tooth.

The teacher *discussed* the effects of the Black Death during the Middle Ages.

- **Intransitive verbs** are action verbs with no direct object. Some verbs can be either transitive or intransitive depending on their usage.

EXAMPLES:

The vase *broke*.

Miguel *cried*.

- **Linking verbs** indicate a state of being and have no action. These verbs serve to link the subject to additional descriptive information. Examples include *is, are, was, were, be, been, am, smell, taste, feel, look, seem, become,* and *appear*. Sometimes, the verbs listed here can be linking, auxiliary, or action verbs depending on their usage.

EXAMPLES:

I *am* here.

He *looks* nervous.

She *is* sick.

The food *tasted* delicious.

- **Auxiliary** or **helping verbs** are used with an infinitive or participle to create a verb phrase. Auxiliary verbs always need a primary verb to function. Examples of auxiliary verbs include all forms of the verbs *to be, to have, to do,* and *to keep*, as well as *can, could, may, might, must, ought to, shall, will, would,* and *should*.

EXAMPLES:

I *am having* a glass of water.

She *might go* to the store.

Alex *should study* harder.

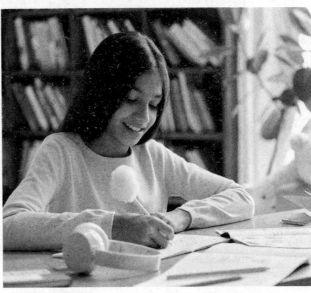

Adverbs

An **adverb** modifies a verb, an adjective, or another adverb and can answer questions like:

- "Why?"
- "How?"
- "Where?"
- "When?"
- "To what degree?"

Adverbs should not be used to modify nouns. Many adverbs are easy to identify because they end in *-ly*. But there are other adverbs that do not have this ending.

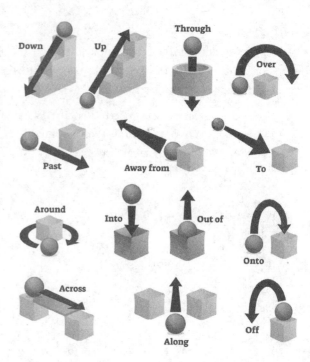

> **EXAMPLES:**
>
> He *quickly* jumped over the hole.
>
> I am doing *well*.
>
> The water swirled *clockwise* down the drain.

Conjunctions

A **conjunction** joins words, sentences, and phrases. The best way to remember the most common conjunctions is with the acronym **FANBOYS**: for, and, nor, but, or, yet, so.

Prepositions

A **preposition** shows position in time or space. Common prepositions are words like *around, in, over, under, during, after,* and *behind.* A preposition starts a **prepositional phrase** that usually shows the relationship between a noun or pronoun and the rest of the information in the sentence.

> **EXAMPLES:**
>
> The dog sleeps *under the bed*.
>
> She stood up *during the presentation*.
>
> *After the meeting*, Dr. Williams changed her policy.

> **EXAMPLES:**
>
> She *and* I went to the park.
>
> I wanted to play video games, *but* my mom said it was time to leave.
>
> Neither John *nor* his children wanted to move to the new city.

To learn more about adjectives and adverbs, scan this QR code.

SENTENCE STRUCTURE AND FORMATION

There are four different kinds of sentence structures in English:

1

SIMPLE SENTENCES: an independent clause

2

COMPOUND SENTENCES: two independent clauses joined together

3

COMPLEX SENTENCES: an independent clause and at least one dependent clause

4

COMPOUND-COMPLEX SENTENCES: at least two independent clauses and one dependent clause

Compound, complex, and compound-complex sentences can technically have as many clauses as you want, as long as they are connected and punctuated correctly. In this section, we will review some rules about sentence structure you will need in order to be successful on the TACHS and HSPT exams.

Fragments

Basic Rule

Every sentence must have a subject (something to do the action) and a verb or predicate (the action) and express a complete idea. When all those items are present, you get an **independent clause** (another way of saying "a complete sentence"). A group of words that is missing one of these elements is called a **sentence fragment** or an **incomplete sentence**. If a group of words has a subject and verb but doesn't express a complete thought, it's a **dependent clause**.

There are two ways to correct incomplete sentences:

1

Add the fragment to the sentence that precedes it or the sentence that follows.

❌ **Incorrect:** Zoologists and wildlife biologists study animals and other wildlife. Including how they interact with their ecosystems.

✔️ **Correct:** Zoologists and wildlife biologists study animals and other wildlife, including how they interact with their ecosystems.

ℹ️ **Explanation:** The fragment is added to the sentence that precedes it by inserting a comma.

❌ **Incorrect:** By studying animal behaviors. Wildlife biologists seek to understand how animals interact with their ecosystems.

✔️ **Correct:** By studying animal behaviors, wildlife biologists seek to understand how animals interact with their ecosystems.

ℹ️ **Explanation:** The fragment is added to the sentence that follows it by inserting a comma. (The fragment now serves as a prepositional phrase that modifies the rest of the sentence.)

Add a subject and verb to the fragment.

Incorrect: Considerable time studying animals in their natural habitats.

Correct: Wildlife biologists may spend considerable time studying animals in their natural habitats.

Explanation: A subject (*wildlife biologists*) and verb (*may spend*) are added to the fragment.

Run-Ons and Comma Splices

Basic Rule

You must use a period to separate complete sentences. When linking independent clauses, you can use either a semicolon or a comma and a coordinating conjunction. A **run-on sentence** occurs when a writer fails to use either end-stop punctuation to divide complete thoughts or suitable conjunctions to join two ideas. When two independent clauses are joined only by a comma, you have an error called a **comma splice**.

The following rules will help you avoid and fix run-on sentences and comma splices:

Divide the sentence using periods.

Incorrect: Zoologists need a bachelor's degree for entry-level positions a master's degree or Ph.D. is often needed for advancement.

Correct: Zoologists need a bachelor's degree for entry-level positions. A master's degree or Ph.D. is often needed for advancement.

Explanation: Inserting a period between *positions* and *A* corrects the run-on sentence by creating two independent clauses.

Create a compound sentence by joining independent clauses using a coordinating conjunction such as *and, but,* or *so.*

Incorrect: Zoologists need a bachelor's degree for entry-level positions, a master's degree is often needed for advancement.

Correct: Zoologists need a bachelor's degree for entry-level positions, but a master's degree is often needed for advancement. (Remember that a comma is required when you use a coordinating conjunction to join two independent clauses.)

Explanation: Adding a comma and the coordinating conjunction *but* eliminates the comma splice and connects the two independent clauses correctly.

Use a semicolon when ideas are closely related in meaning.

Incorrect: Zoologists and wildlife biologists study how animals and other wildlife interact with their ecosystems, these scientists work in offices, laboratories, or outdoors.

Correct: Zoologists and wildlife biologists study how animals and other wildlife interact with their ecosystems; these scientists work in offices, laboratories, or outdoors.

Explanation: Inserting a semicolon between the two independent clauses corrects the comma splice and creates a compound sentence.

4

Create a complex sentence by adding a subordinating conjunction—such as *because*, *although*, or *while*—making one of the independent clauses a dependent clause.

Incorrect: Zoologists need only a bachelor's degree for entry-level positions a master's degree is often needed for advancement.

Correct (option 1): Zoologists need only a bachelor's degree for entry-level positions although a master's degree is often needed for advancement.

Explanation: Adding the conjunction *although* between the two independent clauses corrects the run-on sentence by changing the second clause to a dependent clause and creating a complex sentence. Note: In general, commas are not required when the dependent clause follows the independent clause.

Correct (option 2): Although a master's degree is often needed for advancement, zoologists need only a bachelor's degree for entry-level positions.

Explanation: Adding the conjunction *although* and moving the second independent clauses corrects the run-on sentence by changing the first clause to a dependent clause and creating a complex sentence. Note: Commas are required when the dependent clause precedes the independent clause.

 Scan this QR code for a video on forming complex sentences.

Coordination and Subordination
Basic Rule

Coordinating and subordinating conjunctions are used to join phrases and clauses and form compound and complex sentences.

COMMON CONJUNCTIONS	
Coordinating conjunctions	**Subordinating conjunctions**
and, but, for, nor, or, so, yet	after, although, as, as if, because, before, even if, even though, if, if only, rather than, since, that, though, unless, until, when, where, whereas, wherever, whether, which, while

 TIP

For coordinating conjunctions, remember the acronym **FANBOYS:**

For
And
Nor
But
Or
Yet
So

Conjunctions connect ideas together. If you're using a comma to separate two complete sentences, you also need one of the FANBOYS.

Basic Rule of Coordinating Conjunctions

Coordinating conjunctions are used to add items to a list and join independent clauses to make compound sentences. With items in a list, the last item in the list should be preceded by a coordinating conjunction.

 Independent clauses: There was a Treaty of Paris signed in 1763. There was also one signed in 1783. There was another signed in 1919.

 Joined: There were Treaties of Paris signed in 1763, 1783, and 1919.

When two clauses are joined, if the second remains an independent clause, a comma must be used before the coordinating conjunction. The coordinating conjunction signals that each clause carries the same weight while also creating a relationship between the ideas (additive, contrasting, or causal).

 Independent clauses: There was a Treaty of Paris signed in 1763. There was also one signed in 1783.

 Joined: There was a Treaty of Paris signed in 1763, but there was another Treaty of Paris signed in 1783.

Basic Rule of Subordinating Conjunctions

Subordinating conjunctions are added to an independent clause to make it a dependent clause.

A dependent clause establishes a place, a time, a reason, a condition, a concession, or a comparison for the independent clause—some form of extra information that clarifies the action of the independent clause. Dependent clauses have a subject and a verb but don't express a complete thought—caused by the subordinating conjunction. Because of that, the clause needs (or *depends* on) an independent clause to be grammatically correct. This also means that dependent clauses are subordinate to the information in the independent clause—meaning they're less important (offering extra information) and preceded by a subordinating conjunction. Dependent clauses can come before or after an independent clause, but if they're before, they must be separated from the independent clause by a comma. Review the list of subordinating conjunctions to identify dependent clauses more quickly. Let's look at some examples of subordinating conjunctions used to create dependent clauses.

 Independent clauses: A tax on imported goods from another country is called a tariff. A tax on imported goods from another country to protect a home industry is called a protective tariff.

 Joined: A tax on imported goods from another country is called a tariff while a tax on imported goods from another country to protect a home industry is called a protective tariff.

 TIP

Remember that an independent clause is just a complete sentence. It has a subject and a verb and expresses a complete thought.

Here, the subordinating conjunction *while* was added to the second independent clause. The resulting dependent clause is then joined to the end of the first independent clause without using any punctuation.

A subordinating conjunction can also be used at the beginning of a sentence. The resulting dependent clause must be joined to an independent clause and separated by a comma.

 Independent clauses: A tax on imported goods from another country is called a tariff. A tax on imported goods from another country to protect a home industry is called a protective tariff.

 Joined: While a tax on imported goods from another country is called a tariff, a tax on imported goods from another country to protect a home industry is called a protective tariff.

Modifier Placement

A **modifier** is a word, phrase, or clause that adds detail to a sentence. In order to avoid confusion, modifiers should be placed as close as possible to the things they modify. Examples of different modifiers are underlined in the sentences below.

Example 1: <u>Within the field of marine biology</u>, employment is <u>highly</u> competitive.

 Explanation: The phrase "within the field of marine biology" modifies the subject of the sentence, which is *employment*. The word *highly* modifies our understanding of the competitive nature of finding employment.

 Example 2: The <u>abundant</u> supply of <u>marine</u> scientists far exceeds the demands, and the number of federal and state government jobs is <u>limited</u>.

 Explanation: *Abundant* modifies *supply*. *Marine* modifies *scientists*. *Limited* modifies our understanding of *the number of jobs*.

When the subject of a modifier is unclear or is not included in the sentence, it is considered a dangling modifier.

 Incorrect: Not realizing that the job title of marine biologist rarely exists, *marine biology* is a term recognized by most people. (What is the first phrase modifying?)

Possible revision: Not realizing that the job title of marine biologist rarely exists, most people recognize the term *marine biology*.

Misplaced modifiers occur when a modifier is poorly placed and doesn't express the writer's intent accurately.

 Incorrect: The term *marine biologist* is used to almost describe all of the disciplines and jobs that deal with the study of marine life, not just those that deal with the physical properties of the sea.

 Possible revision: The term *marine biologist* is used to describe almost all of the disciplines and jobs that deal with the study of marine life, not just those that deal with the physical properties of the sea.

On the exam, some questions will ask you to select the best sentence from several options. For these questions, you'll want to choose the sentence that is not only grammatically correct but also the clearest and most direct. In these sentences, there are often modifiers placed in strange or confusing places that make it difficult to figure out what the modifier is referring to and what the sentence means. The correct answer choice typically keeps the subject and verb close together, making it easy to identify *who* (subject) is doing *what* (verb), while also positioning modifiers closest to what they modify.

Parallel Structure

Parallel structure is the repetition of a grammatical form within a sentence. When things are parallel, they are moving in the same direction. Parallel structure is a hallmark of effective writing and is often used to emphasize ideas and present compared items in an equal light. Coordinating conjunctions are often used in parallel constructions.

 Nonparallel structure: As a child, George Washington Carver enjoyed reading, learned about plants, and he made art.

 Parallel structure: As a child, George Washington Carver enjoyed reading, learning about plants, and making art.

In the first sentence, "George Washington Carver enjoyed reading" leads the reader to expect that the next items in the list will also be **gerunds**, verbs that end in *-ing* and function as nouns. However, the next items in the list are not in the same form: "learned about plants" is in the past tense, while "he made art" is an independent clause. To resolve the issue with parallel structure, we need to pick one form of the word and stick to it. The easiest and most concise fix is to change the last two items to gerunds to match the first item, "reading."

Issues with parallel structure are most noticeable in lists of things. It's important to remember that parallel structure applies to other parts of speech as well. To be grammatically correct, items that are being compared should be the same part of speech and should be used correctly in the structure of the sentence.

VERB TENSE

Verb Tense

Basic Rule

Use the same verb tense whenever possible within a sentence or paragraph. Do not shift from one tense to another unless there is a valid reason for doing so.

 Incorrect: The Magna Carta *was* signed in 1215 by King John of England and *has been* the first document of its kind to limit the power of the British monarchy.

 Correct: The Magna Carta *was* signed in 1215 by King John of England and *was* the first document of its kind to limit the power of the British monarchy.

Naturally, different verb tenses have different forms, but you will see some overlap. For example, even though the sentences "He was tall" and "He was running" both use the verb "was," the former is a simple past tense verb while the latter is called the past progressive; it has a helping verb attached to the word

 CAUTION -

Different verb tenses have different forms, and there may be some overlap. It's important to select the choice that is the best for the passage.

running. Complete verbs can be individual words or consist of a helping verb (often a form of "to be," "to have," or "to do") and a main verb or a participle. Look out for those small verbs to decide which choice is best for the passage.

When to Use the Perfect Tenses

Basic Rule

Use *present perfect* for an action begun in the past and extended to the present.

1

Example: Scientists at NASA *have seen* an alarming increase in the accumulation of greenhouse gases.

Explanation: In this case, *scientists at NASA saw* would be incorrect. What they *have seen* (present perfect) began in the past and extends to the present.

Basic Rule

Use *past perfect* for an action begun and completed in the past before some other past action.

2

Example: Despite their preparations, Lewis and Clark *had never encountered* the kinds of challenges that awaited them before their expedition.

Explanation: In this case, *never encountered* would be incorrect. The action *had never encountered* (past perfect) is used because it is referring to events prior to their expedition.

Basic Rule

Use *future perfect* for an action begun at any time and completed in the future.

3

Example: When the American astronauts arrive, the Russian cosmonauts *will have been* on the International Space Station for six months.

Explanation: In this case, although both actions occur in the future, the Russian cosmonauts *will have been* on the space station before the American astronauts *arrive*. When there are two future actions, the action completed first is expressed in the future perfect tense.

Knowing when to choose between the simple (past, present, and future) and perfect tenses can be challenging as those choices often depend on the author's intended meaning. However, information presented in the sentence, like prepositional phrases or other modifiers, can help you decide which tense makes the most sense.

Tenses: Common Verbs

Refer to the following chart to familiarize yourself with some common verbs and their tenses.

COMMON VERBS AND THEIR TENSES						
Infinitive	Present	Past	Future	Present Perfect	Past Perfect	Future Perfect
to ask	ask	asked	will ask	have asked	had asked	will have asked
to be	am	was	will be	have been	had been	will have been
to become	become	became	will become	have become	had become	will have become
to begin	begin	began	will begin	have begun	had begun	will have begun
to come	come	came	will come	have come	had come	will have come
to do	do	did	will do	have done	had done	will have done
to eat	eat	ate	will eat	have eaten	had eaten	will have eaten
to feel	feel	felt	will feel	have felt	had felt	will have felt
to find	find	found	will find	have found	had found	will have found
to get	get	got	will get	have gotten	had gotten	will have gotten
to give	give	gave	will give	have given	had given	will have given
to go	go	went	will go	have gone	had gone	will have gone
to grow	grow	grew	will grow	have grown	had grown	will have grown
to have	have	had	will have	have had	had had	will have had
to hear	hear	heard	will hear	have heard	had heard	will have heard
to hide	hide	hid	will hide	have hidden	had hidden	will have hidden
to keep	keep	kept	will keep	have kept	had kept	will have kept
to know	know	knew	will know	have known	had known	will have known
to leave	leave	left	will leave	have left	had left	will have left
to like	like	liked	will like	have liked	had liked	will have liked
to look	look	looked	will look	have looked	had looked	will have looked
to make	make	made	will make	have made	had made	will have made
to meet	meet	met	will meet	have met	had met	will have met
to put	put	put	will put	have put	had put	will have put
to say	say	said	will say	have said	had said	will have said
to see	see	saw	will see	have seen	had seen	will have seen
to sleep	sleep	slept	will sleep	have slept	had slept	will have slept

COMMON VERBS AND THEIR TENSES

Infinitive	Present	Past	Future	Present Perfect	Past Perfect	Future Perfect
to speak	speak	spoke	will speak	have spoken	had spoken	will have spoken
to study	study	studied	will study	have studied	had studied	will have studied
to take	take	took	will take	have taken	had taken	will have taken
to think	think	thought	will think	have thought	had thought	will have thought
to walk	walk	walked	will walk	have walked	had walked	will have walked
to want	want	wanted	will want	have wanted	had wanted	will have wanted
to work	work	worked	will work	have worked	had worked	will have worked
to write	write	wrote	will write	have written	had written	will have written

*Note: For consistency, all verbs are conjugated in the first-person singular.

CONVENTIONS OF PUNCTUATION

Some questions on the TACHS and HSPT will test your knowledge of several key pieces of punctuation: commas, semicolons, em dashes, parentheses, colons, and apostrophes. Each punctuation mark has several uses, but not every rule is tested. The following sections prioritize the most common conventions that the TACHS and HSPT assess.

The Comma

Basic Rules

We use commas for a lot of things, but focus on separating the following:

- Independent clauses that are connected by a coordinating conjunction
- Introductory clauses and phrases
- Dependent and independent clauses
- Items in a series
- Nonessential and parenthetical elements
- Coordinate adjectives

Let's look at some examples:

- To separate independent clauses connected by a coordinating conjunction

EXAMPLE:

Toni Morrison's first novel, *The Bluest Eye*, was published in 1970, and it received a rave review from *The New York Times*.

- To set off introductory clauses and phrases

EXAMPLE:

The year after winning her Nobel Prize, Toni Morrison published the novel *Jazz*.

- To separate a leading dependent clause from an independent clause

EXAMPLE:

While she was praised for her writing style and range of emotion, Toni Morrison was also celebrated for the attention she drew to racial tension in the past and present of the United States.

- To separate nonessential and parenthetical elements from the main clause

EXAMPLES:

Toni Morrison, who won the Nobel Prize in Literature in 1993, was a Professor Emeritus at Princeton University.

Last night, Toni Morrison began her lecture, titled "The Future of Time: Literature and Diminished Expectations," with a meditation on the nature of time and the human perception of progress.

 TIP

Nonessential and parenthetical elements (commas, parentheses, or em dashes) provide extra information that is not necessary for the meaning or grammatical correctness of a sentence. While each of these punctuation marks serves a similar purpose, the difference between them is one of emphasis.

- To separate coordinate adjectives that precede the noun they describe

EXAMPLE:

Toni Morrison was rumored to be a fun, entertaining speaker.

- To separate three or more items in a list

EXAMPLE:

In a span of 15 years, Toni Morrison won a National Book Critics Circle Award, the Pulitzer Prize, and the Nobel Prize for Literature.

Commas and Adjective Order

When you have at least two adjectives describing a noun (e.g., "The tall, funny man" or "The cold and windy weather"), try separating the adjectives with a comma when their order can be reversed or when the conjunction *and* can be placed between them while still preserving the meaning of the phrase. If reversing the order or adding *and* disrupts the meaning of the phrase (e.g. "The giant hockey players" as "The hockey giant players" or "The giant and hockey players"), no comma is needed.

The Oxford Comma

If you pay attention to punctuation, it's likely you've noticed that not everyone puts the serial or Oxford comma before the *and* when separating three or more items in a list. In recent years, a lot of writing (especially online) has ignored the serial comma, but its absence or presence can affect what a sentence means. In 2018, a missing Oxford comma in a Maine labor law cost a dairy company in the state $5 million dollars in a lawsuit with its employees. Many standardized tests, such as the TACHS and HSPT, will operate with the assumption that the serial comma is essential for clear communication and will test on its use with their grammar questions.

The Semicolon

Basic Rules

A semicolon may be used to separate two complete ideas (independent clauses) in a sentence when the two ideas have a close relationship and are *not* connected with a coordinating conjunction.

> **EXAMPLE:**
>
> "Inalienable rights" are basic human rights that many believe cannot and should not be given up or taken away; life, liberty, and the pursuit of happiness are some of those rights.

The semicolon is often used between independent clauses connected by conjunctive adverbs such as *consequently, therefore, also, furthermore, for example, however, nevertheless, still, yet, moreover,* and *otherwise.*

> **EXAMPLE:**
>
> In 1867, critics thought William H. Seward foolish for buying the largely unexplored territory of Alaska for the astronomical price of $7 million; however, history has proven that it was an inspired purchase.

A word of caution: Do not use the semicolon between an independent clause and a phrase or subordinate clause.

> **Incorrect:** While eating ice cream for dessert; Clarence and Undine discussed their next business venture.
>
> **Correct:** While eating ice cream for dessert, Clarence and Undine discussed their next business venture.

Similar to serial commas, semicolons are used to separate items in a list when the items themselves contain commas.

> **EXAMPLE:**
>
> Some kinds of biologists study specific species of animals. For example, cetologists study marine mammals, such as whales and dolphins; entomologists study insects, such as beetles and butterflies; and ichthyologists study wild fish, such as sharks and lungfish.

The Em Dash

Basic Rules

Em dashes are used to set off parenthetical material that you want to emphasize. Dashes interrupt the flow of your sentence, thereby calling attention to the information they contain. An em dash always precedes the nonessential information, so the aside must start later in the sentence.

> **EXAMPLES:**
>
> Many consider Toni Morrison—winner of both the Pulitzer and Nobel Prizes in Literature—to be one of the greatest writers of her generation.
>
> ---
>
> Benjamin Franklin's many intellectual pursuits—from printmaking to politics—exemplify his eclectic personality.

Em dashes can also be used to rename a nearby noun. Typically, a comma would be used to set off this information, but since it includes commas already, use an em dash.

EXAMPLE:

> Benjamin Franklin—a printer, writer, inventor, and statesman—was the son of a soap maker.

An em dash also indicates a list, a restatement, an amplification, or a dramatic shift in tone or thought.

EXAMPLE:

> Eager to write for his brother's newspaper, young Benjamin began submitting letters to the editor under the pseudonym Silence Dogood—they were a hit!

Parentheses

Basic Rules

Just like commas and em dashes, parentheses separate nonessential (also called nonrestrictive or parenthetical) elements from the rest of the sentence. Parentheses indicate that the enclosed information is less important or more tangential to the surrounding sentence. Parentheses must always come in pairs.

EXAMPLES:

> Toni Morrison's novel *Beloved* (1987) was made into a movie in 1998.

> While at Princeton, Toni Morrison (the writer) established a special creative workshop for writers and performances called the Princeton Atelier.

The Colon

Basic Rule

The colon is used to precede a list, a long quotation, or a statement that illustrates or clarifies the earlier information.

EXAMPLES:

> There are only three nations that have successfully landed spacecraft on the moon: the Soviet Union, the United States, and China.

> In the United States, there are three branches of government: the Executive, the Legislative, and the Judicial.

Only use colons after independent clauses. Most commonly, that means that you won't use colons after a verb. Further, no introductory or connecting information should occur before or after a colon, such as *and* or *including*.

 Incorrect: The Louisiana Purchase included territory that would become: Montana, South Dakota, Nebraska, Kansas, Oklahoma, Arkansas, Louisiana, and Missouri.

 Correct: The Louisiana Purchase included territory that would become many of today's states: Montana, South Dakota, Nebraska, Kansas, Oklahoma, Arkansas, Louisiana, and Missouri.

The Apostrophe

Basic Rules

Apostrophes on the TACHS and HSPT exams will serve one of two purposes:

1

To indicate the possessive case *of nouns*: If the noun does not end in *s*—whether singular or plural—add an *'s*; if the noun ends in *s* simply add the *'*. Some writers like to add *'s* to all nouns, even those that already end in *s*, but the TACHS and HSPT will default to *s'*.

 Example 1: The impact of Allen Ginsberg's poem "Howl" on the cultural landscape of the United States cannot be overstated.

Example 2: A car's headlights are typically wired in parallel so that if one burns out the other will keep functioning.

Example 3: The women's club sponsored many charity events.

Example 4: Charles Mingus' skill as a jazz musician is widely recognized.

2

To indicate a *contraction*—the omission of one or more letters: Place the apostrophe exactly where the missing letters occur.

 Examples:

can't = cannot

it's = it is

we're = we are

Any question that asks you to choose *its* vs. *it's* will likely include the answer choice *its'* as well. You know that *its* is for singular possession and *it's* means *it is*. So, what's *its'*? Remember your apostrophe rules. A word with *s'* shows plural possession. But the word *it* is singular. You can't have a singular word with plural possession. *Its'* just isn't a word. When you see it, eliminate it.

⚠ **CAUTION**

Do not use apostrophes with possessive pronouns such as *yours*, *hers*, *ours*, *theirs*, and *whose*, which indicate possession already.

End-of-Sentence Punctuation

There are three types of punctuation used to end a sentence: the period, the question mark, and the exclamation mark.

1 A period is used at the end of a sentence that makes a statement.

Example: In 1620, the Pilgrims in Plymouth signed the Mayflower Compact.

2 A question mark is used after a direct question. A period is used after an indirect question.

Direct Question: Were *The Federalist Papers* written by James Madison, John Jay, or Alexander Hamilton?

Indirect Question: Professor Mahin wanted to know if you knew who wrote *The Federalist Papers*.

3 An exclamation mark is used after an expression that shows strong emotion or issues a command. It may follow a word, a phrase, or a sentence.

Example: Koko the gorilla knew more than 1,000 sign-language signs and could communicate with humans. Amazing!

Unnecessary Punctuation

Unnecessary punctuation can break a sentence into confusing and illogical fragments. Here are some common mistakes to look out for.

- Don't use a comma alone to connect independent clauses. This is called a **comma splice**.

Incorrect: Toni Morrison grew up in an integrated neighborhood, she did not become fully aware of racial divisions until she was in her teens.

Possible revision: Toni Morrison grew up in an integrated neighborhood and did not become fully aware of racial divisions until she was in her teens.

- Don't use a comma between compound elements that are not independent clauses.

Incorrect: In 1998, Oprah Winfrey, and Danny Glover starred in a film adaptation of Morrison's novel *Beloved*.

Possible revision: In 1998, Oprah Winfrey and Danny Glover starred in a film adaptation of Morrison's novel *Beloved*.

- Do not use an apostrophe when making a noun plural.

Incorrect: In 2006, *The New York Times Book Review* named *Beloved* the best American novel published in the last 25 year's.

Possible revision: In 2006, *The New York Times Book Review* named *Beloved* the best American novel published in the last 25 years.

7

CONVENTIONS OF USAGE
Pronouns
Basic Rules

Pronouns substitute for nouns in sentences. Every pronoun must have a clear **antecedent** (the noun that it replaces), have the same **number** as the antecedent (singular or plural), share the same perspective or **person** (1st, 2nd, or 3rd), and be in the proper pronoun **case** for its use in the sentence (subjective, objective, possessive).

> **EXAMPLES:**
>
> George Washington was born on February 22, 1732, in Pope's Creek, Virginia; *he* was the first American president.
>
> ---
>
> Did you know that Betsy Ross and George Washington both went to the same church? *It* was called Christ Church, and *it* was located in Philadelphia.

The following pronoun chart may prove useful:

PRONOUNS				
Number	Person	Subjective Case	Objective Case	Possessive Case
Singular	1st person	I	me	mine
	2nd person	you	you	yours
	3rd person	he, she, it, who	him, her, it, whom	his, hers, whose
Plural	1st person	we	us	ours
	2nd person	you	you	yours
	3rd person	they, who	them, whom	theirs, whose

A pronoun must agree in number with its antecedent, using a singular or plural pronoun of the correct person and case.

 Incorrect: George Washington was among the seven figures that were key to the formation of the United States government, the Founding Fathers, because them shaped and served the country's executive branch. (What is the antecedent for the marked pronoun? George Washington or Founding Fathers?)

 Correct: George Washington was among the seven figures that were key to the formation of the United States government, the Founding Fathers, because *he* shaped and served the country's executive branch. (The pronoun needs to be in the third-person singular in the subjective case in order to agree with the antecedent *George Washington*.)

Incorrect: George Washington issued two vetoes successfully during his two presidential terms. One was issued in his first term, and the other was issued after he left office. Congress was unable to overturn *it*. (What was Congress unable to overturn?)

 Correct: George Washington issued two vetoes successfully during his two presidential terms. One was issued in his first term, and the other was issued after he left office. Congress was unable to overturn *them*. (The pronoun needs to be third-person plural in the objective case to agree with the antecedent *two vetoes* and work with the grammar of the sentence.)

A pronoun uses the *subjective* case when it is the subject of the sentence or when it renames the subject as a subject complement.

 Incorrect: One story of the American flag's creation says George Ross, Robert Morris, and *him* asked Betsy Ross to sew the first flag.

 Correct: One story of the American flag's creation says George Ross, Robert Morris, and *he* asked Betsy Ross to sew the first flag. (*He* is part of the compound subject of the sentence.)

 Incorrect: *Him* is George Washington.

Correct: *He* is George Washington. (*He* renames the subject.)

If a pronoun is the object of a verb or preposition, it is placed in the *objective* case.

 Incorrect: Washington placed a lot of trust in Benedict Arnold. In 1780, George Washington gave command of West Point to *he*.

 Correct: Washington placed a lot of trust in Benedict Arnold. In 1780, George Washington gave command of West Point to *him*.

 Incorrect: Despite the fact that *us* turned in our American history paper late, our teacher gave Franklin and *I* an A grade.

 Correct: Despite the fact that *we* turned in our American history paper late, our teacher gave Franklin and *me* an A grade. (*We* is the subject of the dependent clause, and *me* is an object of the verb *gave*.)

Avoid ambiguity and confusion by making sure that the antecedent of the pronoun is clear. The presence of multiple nouns that share the same gender and number means that the sentence must clarify which antecedent is being referred to.

Incorrect: At the height of his career, Frank Lloyd Wright told an architectural scholar that *he* thought *his* work was improving. (Is Wright talking about his own work or the work of the scholar?)

 Correct: At the height of his career, Frank Lloyd Wright told an architectural scholar that he thought *his own* work was improving.

 Incorrect: Frank Lloyd Wright and his wife Olgivanna founded a school for aspiring artists in Spring Green, Wisconsin, where they could "learn by doing." (Does *they* refer to the Wrights or the artists?)

 Correct: Frank Lloyd Wright and his wife Olgivanna founded a school in Spring Green, Wisconsin, where aspiring artists could "learn by doing."

Possessive Determiners

When a pronoun expresses ownership, it is placed in the possessive case. An absolute possessive pronoun can stand on its own without needing a noun to follow it to be clear. Absolute possessive pronouns are *mine*, *yours*, *his*, *hers*, *its*, *ours*, and *theirs*.

 CAUTION

Some possessive determiners (*its*, *your*, *their*) and contractions (*it's*, *you're*, *they're*) are often confused. Remember that personal pronouns that express ownership never require an apostrophe.

 EXAMPLES:

The watch is *mine*.

That one is *his*.

Theirs are broken.

A possessive pronoun that identifies, specifies, or quantifies the noun it precedes is called a possessive determiner. Possessive determiners are *my*, *your*, *his*, *her*, *its*, *our*, and *their*.

EXAMPLES:

It's *my* watch.

That's *his* watch.

Their watches are broken.

AGREEMENT
Pronoun-Antecedent Agreement

A pronoun agrees with its antecedent in both person and number.

 Example: The archaeologists examined the fossilized bone with great care to make sure they didn't damage *it*.

Explanation: The antecedent of the pronoun *they* is archaeologists. The antecedent of the pronoun *it* is *bone*.

Remember to use a singular verb when you refer to indefinite pronouns such as *everyone, everybody, each, every, anyone, anybody, nobody, none, no one, one, either,* and *neither*. Some indefinite pronouns—*any, more, most, some*—will be singular or plural as dependent on usage. The pronouns *both, many, others,* and *several* will always need a plural verb for agreement.

EXAMPLES:

Although Union High School's male lacrosse players operate as a team, each knows it's *his* (not *their*) responsibility to arrive on time and in uniform.

Despite the fact that many of the women came from wealthy families, every woman who attended the Seneca Falls conference on women's rights risked *her* (not *their*) life and reputation.

Many of the protestors risked *their* jobs to fight for raising the minimum wage.

Subject-Verb Agreement
Basic Rule

A verb agrees in number with its subject. A singular subject takes a singular verb. A plural subject takes a plural verb.

A coral reef [S] is [V] an important part of the marine ecosystem.

My teacher [S] believes [V] that coral reefs [P] are [V] an important part of the marine ecosystem.

Let's take a look at an example.

 Example: Choose the correct verb: (is, am, are)

Booker T. Washington, Frederick Douglass, and W.E.B. DuBois _____ all important historical figures.

 Explanation: Remember that the verb must agree with the subject. Since the subject is plural—subjects joined by *and* are plural—a plural verb is needed. The correct response therefore should be: Booker T. Washington, Frederick Douglass, and W.E.B. DuBois *are* all important historical figures.

Sometimes, the subject comes after the verb, but the rule still applies.

 Example: Choose the correct verb: (is, are)

While the lecture has lasted two hours already, there _____ still three more speakers.

 Explanation: The correct choice is *are* since the subject *speakers* is plural and requires a plural verb.

There is one major exception to this rule. When the sentence is introduced by the word "there" and the verb is followed by a compound (double) subject, the first part of the subject dictates whether the verb should be singular or plural.

EXAMPLE:

There is one American astronaut in the shuttle and four Russian astronauts in the space station.

When compound subjects are joined by *either-or* or *neither-nor*, the verb agrees with the subject closest to the verb.

Example 1: Neither the violinist nor *the other musicians have had* much experience performing for an audience.

Example 2: Neither you nor *I am* willing to make the sacrifices required of a professional musician.

Explanation: In the first example, *musicians* (plural) is closest to the verb; in the second example, *I* (singular) is closest to the verb.

Sometimes, a word or a group of words may come between the subject and the verb. The verb still must agree with the simple subject, and the simple subject is never part of a prepositional phrase.

Example: Stephen King, the author of hundreds of best-selling novels, novellas, and short stories, *is* also a guitarist and singer in a band.

Explanation: The simple subject is *Stephen King*, a singular noun. The verb must be *is*.

ALERT

Test makers will often select verbs that are next to plural nouns but agree with a singular noun located earlier in the sentence. Work to identify which noun is performing the action, not just what's nearby.

Sometimes, you might encounter questions that are designed to misdirect you, especially for subject-verb agreement questions. For example, the verb in question might be placed next to a plural noun but agree with a singular noun located earlier in the sentence. Work to identify which noun is performing the action, not just what's nearby.

Example: Choose the correct verb: (was, were)

The causes of the deterioration of coral reefs _____ not known until recently.

Explanation: The simple subject is *causes*; "of the deterioration of coral reefs" is a prepositional phrase. Since the subject is plural, the plural verb *were* is required.

To learn more about subject-verb agreement, scan this QR code.

TIP

The third person singular of most verbs ends in "s." For other forms, consider the following: I, we speak (first person); you speak (second person); he, she, it speaks (third person singular). Examples: He runs. She jogs. It jumps. The man sees. Mary laughs. The child walks. They run.

Collective Nouns

Collective nouns present special problems. A **collective noun** names a group of people or things. Although usually singular in form, it is treated as either singular or plural according to the sense of the sentence:

- A *collective* is treated as singular when members of the group act, or are considered, as a unit.

EXAMPLE:

The citizens' *assembly is drafting* a petition that would seek to protect local aquifers from chemical run-off and hazardous waste.

- A *collective* is treated as plural when the members act, or are considered, as multiple individuals.

EXAMPLE:

After one of the longest and most fabled droughts in baseball history, the *Boston Red Sox have* finally overcome the "Curse of the Bambino" to win another World Series.

COMMON COLLECTIVE NOUNS			
assembly	commission	crowd	minority
association	committee	department	number
audience	company	family	pair
band	corporation	firm	press
board	council	group	public
cabinet	counsel	jury	staff
class	couple	majority	United States

FREQUENTLY CONFUSED WORDS AND EXPRESSIONS

The following pages review groups of words, phrases, and expressions that are similar in sound and/or meaning and are generally found to be confusing to students and adults alike. Misunderstanding what they mean or how they are used results in various usage problems. This section includes a brief list of some of the more commonly assessed words and phrases.

Words and Phrases

a is used before words that start with a consonant sound

an is used before words that start with a vowel sound

> Please give the baby *a* toy.
>
> He is *an* only child. We put up *a* united front. (*United* begins with a consonant sound—*y*.)
>
> We spent *an* hour together. (*Hour* begins with a vowel sound since the *h* is silent.)

---

accept means to receive or to agree to something

except means to exclude or excluding

> I'll *accept* the gift from you.
>
> Everyone *except* my uncle went home.
>
> My uncle was *excepted* from the group of losers.

---

advice means counsel (noun), opinion

advise means to offer advice (verb)

> Let me give you some free *advice*.
>
> I'd *advise* you to see your doctor.

---

affect means to influence (verb)

effect means to cause or bring about (verb) or a result (noun)

> The pollution can *affect* your health.
>
> The landmark decision will *effect* a change in the law.
>
> The *effect* of the storm could not be measured.

all ready means everybody or everything ready

already means previously

> They were *all ready* to write when the test began.
>
> They had *already* written the letter.

---

all together means everybody or everything together

altogether means completely

> The boys and girls stood *all together* in line.
>
> His action was *altogether* strange for a person of his type.

---

in is used to indicate inclusion, location, or motion within limits

into is used for motion toward one place from another

> The spoons are *in* the drawer.
>
> We were walking *in* the room.
>
> He was staring *into* space.
>
> She walked *into* the room.

---

it's is the contraction of *it is* or *it has*

its is a possessive pronoun meaning belonging to it

> *It's* a very difficult assignment.
>
> We tried to analyze *its* meaning.

---

lay means to put (a transitive verb)

lie means to recline (an intransitive verb)

LAY VS. LIE		
Tense	*To lay*	*To lie*
(present)	I lay the book back on the shelf.	I lie on the floor.
(past)	I laid the gift on the table.	I lay on my blanket at the beach.
(present perfect)	I have laid my phone somewhere.	I have lain about all day.

lets is third person singular present of *let*

let's is a contraction for *let us*

> He *lets* me park my car in his garage.
>
> *Let's* go home early today.

---

loose means not fastened or restrained, or not tight-fitting

lose means to mislay, to be unable to keep, to be defeated

> The dog got *loose* from the leash.
>
> Try not to *lose* your umbrella.

---

passed is the past tense of *to pass*

past means just preceding or an earlier time

> The week *passed* very quickly.
>
> The *past* week was a very exciting one.

---

principal means chief or main (adjective), or a leader, or a sum of money (noun)

principle means a fundamental truth or belief

> His *principal* support comes from the real estate industry.
>
> The *principal* of the school called a meeting of the faculty.
>
> He earned 10 percent interest on the *principal* he invested last year.
>
> As a matter *of principle*, he refused to register for the draft.

---

raise means to lift, to erect

raze means to tear down

rise means to get up, to move from a lower to a higher position, to increase in value

> The neighbors helped him *raise* a new barn.
>
> The demolition crew *razed* the old building.
>
> The price of silver will *rise* again this month.

set means to place something down (mainly)

sit means to seat oneself (mainly)

SET VS. SIT		
Tense	*To set*	*To sit*
(present)	He sets the mousetrap.	He sits.
(past)	He set the lamp on the table.	He sat on the chair.
(present perfect)	He has set the dishes for dinner.	He has sat on the couch for hours.

---

stationary means standing still

stationery means writing material

> In ancient times, people thought that the earth was *stationary*.
>
> We bought our school supplies at the *stationery* store.

---

than is used to express comparison

then is used to express time or a result or consequence

> Jim ate more *than* we could put on the large plate.
>
> I knocked on the door, and *then* I entered.
>
> If you go, *then* I will go, too.

---

their means belonging to them

there means in that place

they're is the contraction for *they are*

> We took *their* books home with us.
>
> Your books are over *there* on the desk.
>
> *They're* coming over for dinner.

though means although or as if

thought is the past tense of to think, or an idea (noun)

through means in one side and out another, by way of, finished

> *Though* he is my friend, I can't recommend him for this job.
>
> I *thought* you were serious!
>
> We enjoyed running *through* the snow.

to means in the direction of (preposition); it is also used before a verb to indicate the infinitive

too means very, also

two is the numeral 2

> We shall go *to* school.
>
> It is *too* hot today.
>
> We shall go, *too*.
>
> I ate *two* sandwiches for lunch.

weather refers to atmospheric conditions

whether introduces a choice; it should not be preceded by *of* or *as to*

> I don't like the *weather* in San Francisco.
>
> He inquired *whether* we were going to the dance.

well is an adverb (modifies a verb, adverb, or adjective) meaning in a good or proper manner

good is an adjective (modifies a noun) meaning favorable, pleasant, suitable, etc.

> I did *well* on my test.
>
> I received a *good* score on my test.

were is a past tense of *to be*

we're is a contraction of *we are*

where refers to place or location

> They *were* there yesterday.
>
> *We're* in charge of the decorations.
>
> *Where* are we meeting your brother?

who is a pronoun in the subjective case

whom is a pronoun in the objective case

> The man *who* stole my car was just seen at the supermarket.
>
> *Who* is at the door?
>
> For *whom* are you calling?
>
> *Whom* should I talk to about scheduling an appointment?

who's is the contraction for *who is* (or *who has*)

whose means of whom, implying ownership

> *Who's* the next batter?
>
> *Whose* notebook is on the desk?

your is a possessive, showing ownership

you're is a contraction for *you are*

> Please give him *your* notebook.
>
> *You're* very sweet.

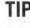 **TIP**

While the difference between *who* and *whom* has a minimal effect on your day-to-day life, it will potentially come up on the TACHS or HSPT exam. Try substituting *he* or *she* and *him* or *her* for the pronoun in the sentence. You may have to rearrange the sentence a bit to make this work. If *he* or *she* fits in place of the pronoun, you should use *who*. If *him* or *her* fits, you should use *whom*.

SUMMING IT UP

- The HSPT tests English usage in the Language Skills section along with spelling, punctuation and capitalization, and composition. The TACHS includes English usage in the Language section.

- The Standard English conventions reviewed in this chapter are keys to good writing. When you utilize proper sentence structure, grammar, and punctuation, your writing is stronger, clearer, and more focused. That is why the use of Standard English conventions is important for writing in high school, college, and in your future career.

- Knowing the parts of speech is critical for understanding the conventions and rules of grammar:

    - A **noun** is a person, place, thing, or idea.
    - A **pronoun** is a substitute for a noun.
    - An **adjective** describes a noun.
    - A **verb** expresses action or a state of being.
    - An **adverb** modifies a verb, an adjective, or another adverb.
    - A **conjunction** joins words, sentences, and phrases.
    - A **preposition** shows position in time or space.

- The following list summarizes the key conventions you need to remember to address most errors presented on the TACHS and HSPT exams:

    - **Sentence Structure and Formation**

        - **Fragments:** Every sentence must have a subject and a verb and express a complete idea.
        - **Run-Ons and Comma Splices:** Connect complete sentences with proper punctuation.
        - **Combining Independent Clauses:** Use periods, a comma + FANBOYS, or a semicolon; you can also make an independent clause dependent with a subordinating conjunction to link sentences.
        - **Combining Dependent and Independent Clauses:** Place a comma after a dependent clause at the beginning of a sentence.
        - **Misplaced Modifiers:** Place modifiers (adjectives, adverbs, prepositional phrases) as close to the word they're modifying as possible.

- **Parallel Structure:** Keep verbs and phrases in the same grammatical form when writing sentences.
- **Verb Tense:** Keep consistent verb tense within sentences and paragraphs unless otherwise justified.

○ **Punctuation**

- **Commas:** Separate independent clauses with a comma and FANBOYS; add a comma after an introductory phrase or leading subordinate clause; separate items in lists of three or more (including before the *and* before the final item); place commas around nonessential information to separate it from the main clause of a sentence.
- **Em dashes:** Indicate nonrestrictive or nonessential information with em dashes; these tangents, asides, and parenthetical statements follow em dashes and must be closed by another em dash—unless they finish the sentence.
- **Semicolons:** Separate related independent clauses and items in a list where the items have commas with a semicolon.
- **Colons:** Indicate the start of a list, a quotation, or emphasis with a colon; colons must be preceded by an independent clause.
- **Apostrophes:** Indicate possession with an *'s* (or just an apostrophe after a noun that ends in an *s*) or signal the contraction of two words into one (*they + are = they're*).
- **Parentheses:** Separate low-importance, nonessential information from the rest of the sentence with a pair of parentheses.
- **End-Stop Punctuation:** End statements and indirect questions with periods; use question marks to end direct questions; end statements that indicate strong emotion or commands with an exclamation point.

○ **Usage**

- **Pronouns:** Pronouns must agree in case, number, and gender (where applicable) with their antecedent (the word they replace); it must be clear to which antecedent a pronoun applies when multiple possible antecedents are present.
- **Subject-Verb Agreement:** A verb must agree with its subject in number, singular when the subject is singular, plural when the subject is plural; agreement occurs with the subject of a sentence—which may not be the word closest to the verb.
- **Confusing Words and Phrases:** Select the word or phrase most appropriate to the situation, relying on common expressions and correct word choice for frequently confused words.

KNOWLEDGE CHECK

ENGLISH USAGE
50 Questions—21 Minutes
Exercise 1

> **Directions:** In the following questions, choose which of the four sentences is constructed best. The answer keys and explanations follow Exercise 3.

1. **A.** It is the opinion of the commissioners that programs that include the construction of cut-rate municipal garages in the central business district is inadvisable.

   B. Having reviewed the material submitted, the program for putting up cut-rate garages in the central business district seemed likely to cause traffic congestion.

   C. The commissioners believe that putting up cut-rate municipal garages in the central business district is inadvisable.

   D. Making an effort to facilitate the cleaning of streets in the central business district, the building of cut-rate municipal garages presents the problem that it would encourage more motorists to come into the central city.

2. **A.** Since the report lacked the needed information, it was of no use to him.

   B. This report was useless to him because there were no needed information in it.

   C. Since the report did not contain the needed information, it was not real useful to him.

   D. Being that the report lacked the needed information, he could not use it.

3. **A.** In reviewing the typists' work reports, the job analyst found records of unusual typing speeds.

   B. It says in the job analyst's report that some employees type with great speed.

   C. The job analyst found that, in reviewing the typists' work reports, that some unusual typing speeds had been made.

   D. In the reports of typists' speeds, the job analyst found some records that are kind of unusual.

4. **A.** They do not ordinarily present these kind of reports in detail like this.

   B. A report of this kind is not hardly ever given in such detail as this one.

   C. This report is more detailed than what such reports ordinarily are.

   D. A report of this kind is not ordinarily presented in as much detail as this one is.

5. **A.** Elephants suck water through their long, flexible trunks and squirt it into their mouths.

   B. Every morning, Edwin talks to his parrot Rudy while getting dressed for school.

   C. The high school football teams practices diligently every morning during the playing season.

   D. Each year, everyone on the team go to the awards banquet.

6. **A.** If properly addressed, the letter will reach my mother and I.

   B. The letter had been addressed to myself and my mother.

   C. I believe the letter was addressed to either my mother or I.

   D. My mother's name, as well as mine, was on the letter.

7. **A.** The paper we use for this purpose must be light, glossy, and stand hard usage as well.

   B. Only a light and a glossy, but durable, paper must be used for this purpose.

   C. For this purpose, we want a paper that is light, glossy, but that will stand hard wear.

   D. For this purpose, paper that is light, glossy, and durable is essential.

8. **A.** This kind of worker achieves success through patience.

   B. Success does not often come to men of this type except they who are patient.

   C. Because they are patient, these sort of workers usually achieve success.

   D. This worker has more patience than any man in his office.

9. **A.** You have got to get rid of some of these people if you expect to have the quality of the work improve.

   B. The quality of the work would improve if they would leave fewer people do it.

   C. I believe it would be desirable to have fewer people doing this work.

   D. If you had planned on employing fewer people than this to do the work, this situation would not have arose.

10. **A.** It is quite possible that we shall reemploy anyone whose training fits them to do the work.

    B. It is probable that we shall reemploy those who have been trained to do the work.

    C. Such of our personnel that have been trained to do the work will be again employed.

    D. We expect to reemploy the ones who have had training enough that they can do the work.

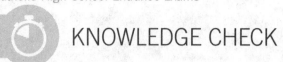

KNOWLEDGE CHECK

Exercise 2

> **Directions:** For questions 1–13, choose the word or group of words that should go into the blank to make a correct sentence.

1. All the boys and Joyce took _____ baseball gloves to the ball game.

   A. her

   B. their

   C. his

   D. our

2. Dana was the _____ person who dared go into the haunted house.

   A. most only

   B. onliest

   C. sole only

   D. only

3. Molly and Brandon always knew that _____ wanted to add a swimming pool to their family home.

   A. she

   B. he

   C. them

   D. they

4. If Duncan had joined the soccer team, he _____ been the star.

   A. should have

   B. could of

   C. would of

   D. might have

5. Even before the wind had stopped, the rain _____ down.

   A. was slowed

   B. has been slowing

   C. had been slowing

   D. had been slowed

6. Last week, I had lunch with the girl _____ won the English prize.

   A. who

   B. whom

   C. which

   D. what

7. In choosing between chocolate and vanilla ice cream, I like chocolate ice cream _____.

   A. most

   B. best

   C. better

   D. more better

8. The jury is depending _____ the witness' statements.

   A. about

   B. of

   C. upon

   D. from

9. I would bring Grandma to visit you, _____ I have no car.

   A. except
   B. while
   C. because
   D. moreover

10. The little girl next door _____ on her swings all day.

    A. swinged
    B. swang
    C. swung
    D. has swinged

11. Neither Kenneth nor Larry _____ book report.

    A. has completed their
    B. have completed their
    C. have completed his
    D. has completed his

12. We had just finished shoveling the driveway _____ the plow came through again.

    A. if
    B. until
    C. when
    D. than

13. You must wait for the election results until we _____ the ballots.

    A. had counted
    B. have counted
    C. are counting
    D. have had counted

Directions: For questions 14 and 15, make a complete sentence by choosing the words that should go into the blank.

---

14. After completing the lifesaving course, _____.

    A. and taking both the written and practical exams
    B. gaining months of practical experience as an apprentice
    C. you will be eligible to take the examination
    D. at the YMCA under the auspices of the Red Cross

15. Ella, a professional carpenter, _____.

    A. building is something that Ella really enjoys doing
    B. built her first bookcase when she was 20 years old
    C. her first serious building project will be a maple table and chair set
    D. at work Ella is learning how to build a residential cabin

Directions: For questions 16 and 17, select the sentence that means the same or most nearly the same as the underlined sentences.

16. The hiker was lost. A St. Bernard rescued him. It happened in the Alps.

    A. The hiker was rescued by a St. Bernard lost in the Alps.

    B. The lost Alpine hiker was rescued by a St. Bernard.

    C. The hiker in the lost Alps was rescued by a St. Bernard.

    D. In the Alps, the hiker was rescued by a lost St. Bernard.

17. Taxes are deducted from all wages. Workers who must work at night are paid overtime. The rate of tax to be withheld is fixed by law.

    A. The law requires that people who are paid overtime must pay taxes.

    B. According to the law, people who work at night must be paid overtime and deduct taxes.

    C. The tax rate on overtime pay is deducted from wages by law and is paid at night.

    D. By law, a fixed rate of taxes is deducted from all wages, including those paid overtime for night work.

Directions: For questions 18–20, choose the word or group of words that makes the second sentence have the same meaning as the underlined sentence.

18. The accident victim was not only frightened but also in pain.

    The accident victim was _____.

    A. neither frightened nor in pain

    B. both frightened and in pain

    C. either frightened or in pain

    D. only frightened, not in pain

19. I may go to the movies tomorrow if I babysit today.

    _____ babysitting today, I may go to the movies tomorrow.

    A. By

    B. While

    C. Until

    D. Once

20. <u>The criminal received consecutive sentences for his three crimes.</u>

    The criminal has to serve his sentences
    _____.

    A. all at once
    B. after a period of delay
    C. one at a time
    D. with no opportunity for parole

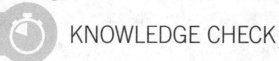

KNOWLEDGE CHECK

Exercise 3

Directions: For questions 1–8, look for errors in errors in punctuation or usage. Mark the answer choice that contains the error. If you find no mistake, choose D as your answer.

1. **A**. He got off of the horse.
   B. Your umbrella is better than mine.
   C. How could I be other than glad?
   D. *(No mistakes)*

2. **A**. No one was there except Charles.
   B. Your sample is the most satisfactory of all that I have seen.
   C. I couldn't hardly do it.
   D. *(No mistakes)*

3. **A**. There should be no secrets between you and me.
   B. I knew him to be the ringleader.
   C. Everyone has studied his lesson.
   D. *(No mistakes)*

4. **A**. There are a piano and a phonograph in the room.
   B. This is the man whom you interviewed last week.
   C. He is reported to be killed.
   D. *(No mistakes)*

5. **A**. I have met but one person.
   B. She is the tallest of the two girls.
   C. The child is able to shape the clay easily.
   D. *(No mistakes)*

6. **A**. I wish I were going to Mexico with you.
   B. Please borrow me five dollars until payday.
   C. The audience was enthusiastic.
   D. *(No mistakes)*

7. **A**. Because of the downpour, the carnival was postponed.
   B. He walks up and said "Hello."
   C. I already anticipate the good time I shall have at camp.
   D. *(No mistakes)*

8. **A**. The couple promised to renew they're wedding vows in Las Vegas every year.
   B. It's important to place all of your garbage in the proper recycling bins, in order to be environmentally responsible.
   C. Without a proper identification tag, it's difficult to determine whose piece of luggage this is.
   D. *(No mistakes)*

Directions: For questions 9–14, choose the answer that best describes the group of words.

9. The worst feature of my summer camp was the food the next worst was the latrine.

    A. Run-on sentence

    B. Complete sentence

    C. *Not* a complete sentence

10. The man with the wart on the end of his nose gave his seat to the old woman.

    A. Run-on sentence

    B. Complete sentence

    C. *Not* a complete sentence

11. Driving across the country in order to meet a deadline.

    A. Run-on sentence

    B. Complete sentence

    C. *Not* a complete sentence

12. Once upon a time in a corner of the kitchen lived a small black cricket and the cricket made a lot of noise which annoyed the woman who lived in the house and so the woman swept the cricket out the door.

    A. Run-on sentence

    B. Complete sentence

    C. *Not* a complete sentence

13. Bob and his brother, Ted, who is a Civil War buff, went to Gettysburg during summer vacation and studied the battlefield together.

    A. Run-on sentence

    B. Complete sentence

    C. *Not* a complete sentence

14. The strong wind suddenly increased to gale force and the sailboat to capsize.

    A. Run-on sentence

    B. Complete sentence

    C. *Not* a complete sentence

Directions: For questions 15–20, choose the sentence that is correctly written.

15. **A.** She had done much the people began to realize.

    B. When the people began to realize how much she had done.

    C. Soon the people began to realize how much she had done.

    D. The people began to realize and how much she had done.

16. **A**. Mounting the curb, the empty car crossed the sidewalk and came to rest against a building.

    B. The empty car mounts the curb, crossed the sidewalk, and will come to rest against a building.

    C. Mounting the curb when the empty car crosses the sidewalk and comes to rest against a building.

    D. The curb was mounted by the empty car and crossed the sidewalk and came to rest against a building.

17. **A**. I had forgotten my gloves realizing and returning to the theater.

    B. Because I will realize that I forgot my gloves, I returned to the theater.

    C. My gloves forgotten, realized, and returned to the theater.

    D. Realizing I had forgotten my gloves, I returned to the theater.

18. **A**. She learned that further practice will have had a good effect on her swimming ability.

    B. She learned that further practice would have a good effect on her swimming ability.

    C. Having learned and practiced had a good effect on her swimming ability.

    D. Learning and practicing to have a good effect on her swimming ability.

19. **A**. Assisting him his friend who lives in the next house.

    B. Assisting him and living in the next house his friend.

    C. His friend who lives in the next house assisting.

    D. He was assisted by his friend who lives in the next house.

20. **A**. The driver does all that it will be possible to do.

    B. The driver, having done all that was possible.

    C. The driver did all that it was possible to do.

    D. Doing all that is possible to do and driving.

ANSWER KEYS AND EXPLANATIONS
Exercise 1

1. C	3. A	5. A	7. D	9. C
2. A	4. D	6. D	8. A	10. B

1. **The correct answer is C.** Choice C presents the information in the most direct and concise manner. Choice A has an agreement error (should be *programs . . . are*). Choice B is incorrect because the program did not review the material. Choice D is totally garbled.

2. **The correct answer is A.** The sentence, "Since the report lacked the needed information, it was of no use to him" is constructed best. In choice B, the subject of the second clause is *information*, which is singular. In choice C, the adverb should be *really*. *Being that*, in choice D, is not an acceptable form.

3. **The correct answer is A.** The sentence "In reviewing the typists' work reports, the job analyst found records of unusual typing speeds" is constructed best. The indefinite pronoun *it* in choice B refers to nothing at all, so it means nothing. In choice C, the *that* after *found* should be omitted. Choice D uses colloquial language, which is unacceptable in Standard English.

4. **The correct answer is D.** The sentence "A report of this kind is not ordinarily presented in as much detail as this one is" is constructed best. Choice A contains an error of agreement (*these kind*). Choice B contains a double negative, *not hardly*. *What* is an extra word in choice C.

5. **The correct answer is A.** Remember, plural subjects require plural verb forms to be in proper agreement. The plural subject *elephants* requires the use of plural verbs: *suck* and *squirt*. Choice B is incorrect because *Rudy* is an appositive and should be set off in commas. Choice C is incorrect because *teams* is plural and would require the plural verb, *practice*. In choice D, *everyone* is a singular pronoun and would require the singular verb, *goes*.

6. **The correct answer is D.** Choices A and C use the subject-form pronoun, *I*, where the object-form, *me*, is required. In choice B, the object of the preposition *to* should be *me*, not *myself*. This leaves "My mother's name, as well as mine, was on the letter," in choice D as the sentence with the best construction.

7. **The correct answer is D.** The sentences in choices A, B, and C are not parallel in construction. All the words that modify *paper* should be in the same form. The sentence "For this purpose, paper that is light, glossy, and durable is essential" is the best.

8. **The correct answer is A.** As presented, "This kind of worker achieves success through patience" is constructed best. In choice B, *men* is the implied subject of the verb *are*. Inserting the subject into the phrase, you can see that it must read . . . *except to those (men) who are patient*. Choice C contains an error of agreement; to be correct, the phrase must read either *this sort of worker* or *these sorts of workers*. In choice D, the comparison is incomplete. It must read *than any other man*.

9. **The correct answer is C.** "I believe it would be desirable to have fewer people doing this work" is correct. Choice A is wordy. In choice B, the correct verb should be *have* in place of *leave*. In choice D, *arose* is incorrect; the correct form is *arisen*.

10. **The correct answer is B.** "It is probable that we shall reemploy those who have been trained to do the work" is correct. In choice A, *them* should be *him* because it refers to *anyone*, which is singular. Choices C and D are wordy and awkward. In addition, choice C uses the word *that* to refer to people, when the correct choice is *who*, to read *personnel who have been trained*.

Exercise 2

1. B	5. C	9. A	13. B	17. D
2. D	6. A	10. C	14. C	18. B
3. D	7. C	11. D	15. B	19. A
4. D	8. C	12. C	16. B	20. C

1. **The correct answer is B.** The subject is plural, and the object is plural; therefore, the possessive pronoun must be plural. The subject is in the third person, not the first, so *their*, not *our*, is the correct word.

2. **The correct answer is D.** *Only* is an exclusive term. It cannot be modified in any way.

3. **The correct answer is D.** This sentence requires a plural pronoun to replace the plural subject in this sentence, *Molly and Brandon*. The pronoun *they* is the correct choice.

4. **The correct answer is D.** *Of* is not an auxiliary verb, so choices B and C are automatically incorrect. *Might have* is more in tune with the nature of the sentence than *should have* (choice A).

5. **The correct answer is C.** To show that one past activity (the *slowing*) occurred before another past activity (the *stopping*) requires the *had been* construction (past perfect). *Had been slowed* (choice D) implies that an external force was working on the rain. *Had been slowing* more accurately describes the end of a storm.

6. **The correct answer is A.** *Who* is the subject of the verb *won*. (Think: *She* won the prize.) This eliminates *whom* (choice B). *Which* (choice C) may only be used to apply to things. *What* (choice D) is not a pronoun.

7. **The correct answer is C.** The comparison between two objects requires *more* or *better*. *More better* (choice D) is redundant and therefore incorrect. *Most* and *best* (choices A and B) refer to comparison among three or more objects.

8. **The correct answer is C.** The proper idiomatic use is *depend on* or *depend upon*.

9. **The correct answer is A.** In this sentence, *except* serves as a conjunction. *But* would fit into the blank in the same way. The other choices make no sense in the context of the sentence.

10. **The correct answer is C.** The past tense of *swing* is *swung*.

11. **The correct answer is D.** The construction *neither/nor* creates a singular subject (or object). Because the subject is singular, both the verb and the possessive pronoun must be singular as well. "Neither Kenneth nor Larry *has completed his* book report" is correct.

12. **The correct answer is C.** The sentence describes two activities in terms of their relationship in time. Only *when* makes sense.

13. **The correct answer is B.** A present activity that is dependent on a future activity requires that the future activity be stated in the present perfect, so *have counted* is correct.

14. **The correct answer is C.** The sentence fragment is nothing more than an introductory prepositional phrase. The completion must supply both subject and verb, and only "you will be eligible to take the examination" does that.

15. **The correct answer is B.** The correct answer must be in the proper tense. Since Ella is a professional carpenter, her first building project must have already occurred. *Built* is the correct past tense for this verb, which is appropriate for this sentence. The sentence should read, "Ella, a professional carpenter, built her first bookcase when she was 20 years old."

16. **The correct answer is B.** The correct answer must give correct information as to who was lost, where the hiker was lost, and how the hiker was rescued.

"The lost Alpine hiker was rescued by a St. Bernard" provides the necessary information. Choices A and D are confusing and sound like the dog was lost in the Alps. Choice C describes the Alps as lost, rather than the hiker.

17. **The correct answer is D.** The tax rate and the fact of withholding are established by law. Overtime pay is not established by law, but it does constitute wages subject to withholding. So, "By law, a fixed rate of taxes is deducted from all wages, including those paid overtime for night work" is correct.

18. **The correct answer is B.** The term *not only . . . but also* is inclusive. Which means that the accident victim was "both frightened and in pain."

19. **The correct answer is A.** The sentence is conditional and in reverse sequence: "I may do something tomorrow *if* I do something today." If you reverse the sentence, the correct answer becomes clear. "*By* doing something today, I may do something else tomorrow."

20. **The correct answer is C.** *Consecutive* means "one after the other." The word that means "all at the same time" is *concurrent*.

NOTES

Exercise 3

1. A	**5.** B	**9.** A	**13.** B	**17.** D
2. C	**6.** B	**10.** B	**14.** C	**18.** B
3. D	**7.** B	**11.** C	**15.** C	**19.** D
4. C	**8.** A	**12.** A	**16.** A	**20.** C

1. **The correct answer is A.** *Off of* is an unacceptable construction: He got off the horse.

2. **The correct answer is C.** *Hardly* is a negative word, so *couldn't hardly* is an unacceptable double negative. The correct version would be *I could hardly do it.*

3. **The correct answer is D.** *No mistakes.*

4. **The correct answer is C.** The activity began in the past (he *was* killed) and is completed in the present (is reported *now*). Therefore, the present perfect tense should be used. The sentence should read: "He is reported to *have been killed.*"

5. **The correct answer is B.** The comparison is between two girls; therefore, *taller,* not *tallest,* is correct.

6. **The correct answer is B.** To borrow something means to use or take it while planning to give it back. In this scenario, the one taking the money would be doing the borrowing and the one giving it would be lending. Therefore, the sentence requires the verb *lend.*

7. **The correct answer is B.** The two verbs should be in the same tense. He *walked* up and *said* "Hello."

8. **The correct answer is A.** *There, their,* and *there* are typically confused words. In this sentence, the possessive *their* is required.

9. **The correct answer is A.** The two complete, independent clauses must either be separated into two sentences or joined by a semicolon.

10. **The correct answer is B.** This sentence is complete.

11. **The correct answer is C.** This is not a complete sentence. It is a sentence fragment that either

needs a subject (*Juan was driving across the country in order to meet a deadline.*) or needs to be joined with an independent clause. (*Driving across the country in order to meet a deadline, Juan raced along in his red convertible.*)

12. **The correct answer is A.** There are actually three independent clauses here. The best correction would be to eliminate the first *and*, and to begin a second sentence with "The cricket." The second *and* should be eliminated and replaced by a comma.

13. **The correct answer is B.** This sentence is complete.

14. **The correct answer is C.** The sentence fragment, as organized, calls for a compound verb: *increased* to gale force and (try inserting) *caused* the sailboat to capsize.

15. **The correct answer is C.** The correctly written sentence is the following: "Soon the people began to realize how much she had done." Choice A is a run-on sentence. Choice B is a sentence fragment. In choice D, the *and* is superfluous.

16. **The correct answer is A.** The correctly written sentence is: "Mounting the curb, the empty car crossed the sidewalk and came to rest against a building." Choice B mixes tenses illogically. Choice C is a sentence fragment. In choice D, the curb crosses the street and comes to rest against the building.

17. **The correct answer is D.** The correctly written sentence is: "Realizing I had forgotten my gloves, I returned to the theater." No other choice makes sense.

18. **The correct answer is B.** The correctly written sentence is: "She learned that further practice would have a good effect on her swimming ability." Choice A confuses tenses; choices C and D are sentence fragments.

19. **The correct answer is D.** The correctly written sentence is: "He was assisted by his friend who lives in the next house." No other choice is a complete sentence.

20. **The correct answer is C.** The correctly written sentence is: "The driver did all that it was possible to do." Choice A confuses tenses; choices B and D are sentence fragments.

 NOTES

CHAPTER

Capitalization and Spelling

CAPITALIZATION AND SPELLING

OVERVIEW

Capitalization

Spelling

Summing It Up

Knowledge Check: Capitalization and Spelling

Answer Keys and Explanations

Capitalization and spelling rules are related to grammar, so the HSPT and the TACHS exams will test your knowledge of both. Unfortunately, understanding capitalization and spelling typically means memorizing a lot of rules, which isn't always super engaging. To help you review more dynamically, this chapter presents both capitalization and spelling rules in two different ways: as a set of reference tables and as a model to use the rules in context. This should help you to approach concepts from at least two different perspectives, break up your learning into digestible pieces, and ultimately, be able to actually apply the rules you learn to real-life contexts.

In capitalization and spelling questions, you are presented with a series of answer choices. Some of the choices contain words or sentences, but the last choice will always be "No Mistakes." You are asked to read the words or sentences and check for errors in capitalization and spelling, among other skills that will be tested, such as punctuation and usage. If you believe the text contains no errors, choose "No Mistakes."

TACHS   HSPT   ISEE   SSAT   SHSAT

CAPITALIZATION

Capitalization is important because it helps set apart proper nouns and titles from other words in a sentence. As an English skill, capitalization signals familiarity with the conventions of the language and adds clarity to written texts. Some rules, like the one governing that the first word of a sentence be capitalized, are likely already familiar to you. To help you understand some of the logic behind why things are capitalized, we've grouped capitalization rules into a few categories: title case, proper nouns, titles and honorifics, and general capitalization rules. Then, we'll look at a sample email that applies the capitalization rules we cover here. As you go through each of the following sections, take note of the rationale behind why certain things are capitalized and look for opportunities to identify these rules in real-word contexts. Use the reference tables included in this section to determine which rules are trickiest for you so that you can focus your study time accordingly. One good way to practice is by writing your own examples for each capitalization rule.

Title Case

There are numerous capitalization rules that specifically apply to title case. By title case, we mean the way that words should be presented to readers when they are part of a given title for something, like a book, movie, newspaper article, or anything else that receives a title.

TITLE CASE	
Rule	**Examples**
The first word, last word, and any major word in the title should be capitalized. Major words are typically considered nouns, pronouns, verbs, adjectives, adverbs, and some conjunctions.	• *A Midsummer Night's Dream* • "Missing Lawyer Found" • *Stranger Things* • *Mario Kart 8*
All prepositions remain lowercase in titles unless they are the first or last word of the title, regardless of the length of the preposition.	• *The Legend of Zelda* • *The Fault in Our Stars* • "Track Team Preps with Extra Practices for Tournament against Shaded Lake" • "Across the Universe" by The Beatles
Most conjunctions and articles also remain lowercase in titles, including *the, an, a, to, as, and, but, for, or,* and *nor.* As with prepositions, you can ignore this rule if it's the first or last word in the title.	• *Tristan and Isolde* • *The Good, the Bad, and the Ugly* • "A History of Aeronautics" • *But I'm Just a Kid!*
Title case should be used for subtitles and headlines. Email subject lines are also generally written in title case (as if they were headlines).	• *Frankenstein: The Modern Prometheus* • *Black Beauty: The Autobiography of a Horse* • "New Medicine Deemed Effective for Patients with Chronic Asthma" • Subject: Regarding the Vote on School Uniforms

Proper Nouns

Proper nouns are the most common place where capitalization is used. In English, no matter where in the sentence a proper noun is placed, it is always capitalized. Proper nouns can be identified by the way they take a general noun (*cat*, *school*) and give it a specific name (*Giorgio, Mountain View High School*), so you may also hear them called "proper names."

PROPER NOUNS	
Rule	**Examples**
Always capitalize a person or other being's proper name. This includes any initials and hyphenated names. Some have names that require more than one capital letter.	<ul><li>Barack Obama</li><li>Beyoncé Knowles-Carter</li><li>Michael J. Fox</li><li>This is my hamster, Mochi.</li><li>McKenzie O'Connell</li></ul>
In addition to the names of people, always capitalize the proper names of buildings, events (including holidays), places, words formed by referencing places, organizations, documents, individual deities, or anything else that can be represented by a specific name.	<ul><li>Empire State Building</li><li>Sundance Film Festival</li><li>Valentine's Day</li><li>Brazil</li><li>Brazilian</li><li>World Wildlife Fund</li><li>US Constitution</li><li>Shiva</li></ul>
If a proper noun gets long or contains prepositions, title case is often used. It is also not uncommon for such proper nouns to be represented by chosen acronyms, which also require capitalization.	<ul><li>Centers for Disease Control and Prevention (CDC)</li><li>Museum of Modern Art (MoMA)</li><li>American Society for the Prevention of Cruelty to Animals (ASPCA)</li></ul>
The pronoun *I* is treated like a proper noun—it always gets capitalized no matter where it falls in the sentence, including within contractions.	<ul><li>I went to the farmer's market.</li><li>Max will be here soon, so I need help.</li><li>I think I'm just tired.</li></ul>
A noun or adjective that is not regularly capitalized should still be capitalized when it is used as part of a proper name.	<ul><li>Have you met Uncle Casimiro?</li><li>This is my Grandma Velma.</li><li>Can Nurse Rick do it?</li><li>My truck's nickname is Big Betty.</li></ul>

Titles and Honorifics

If a person, group, or document can be referred to with a particular title, or if a title is used to show a position of honor, capitalization should be used. In these cases, you treat the title as if it were a proper noun. However, if the term does not apply to something or someone specific, then it should remain lowercased. Consider the following examples:

Amadou is the best man for the job. → I am the Best Man in Amadou's wedding.

I want to become a professor. → I asked Professor Smith-Loewen for an essay extension.

They haven't spoken to the senators. → Senator Hasad and Senator O'Brien wrote the bill.

Our club needs a constitution. → The Constitution grants everyone certain rights.

General Capitalization Rules

Other rules cannot be grouped together as neatly yet still represent important capitalization situations that one should learn.

GENERAL CAPITALIZATION RULES	
Rule	**Examples**
Capitalize the first word of a complete sentence, including the first sentence that comes after a greeting in a letter.	• Kelsie is a good friend. • We hate mushroom soup! • Are those for the party?
Capitalize the first word of a quotation if it contains a complete sentence. However, if the quoted material is not a complete sentence, do NOT capitalize the first word (unless it's a proper noun).	• Mr. Schutt said, "Please turn in your essays." • When the firefighter asked, "Are you hurt?" I was still in shock. • My mom said she needed to "have a think" about the situation. • These so-called "appleheads" are devoted fans of Fifi's Candy Apples. • When I asked Andre his favorite player, he said "Steph Curry."
Capitalize days of the week and months of the year, but do NOT capitalize the seasons.	• I'll see you next Wednesday. • My birthday is in June. • He'll fly out at the end of the summer. • The first day of winter is in December.
Points of the compass are capitalized when they refer to a specific place. When they are used as directions, they should remain lowercased.	• Head north on Monstera Ave., then the park is on the east side of the road. • Is there anything due west of here? • My grandpa is from the South.
The only school subjects that are regularly capitalized are languages and specific place names used as modifiers.	• Next year, I am taking German, biology, African dance, ancient philosophy, and English composition. • Does this book cover religion generally or East Asian religions specifically?
Acronyms and certain abbreviations are generally represented by capital letters.	• P.S. I love you! • I work at NASA. • The CDC recommends yearly flu shots. • Gia had to get a CT scan.
When opening a letter, capitalize the first and last words in the salutation. Remember to also capitalize any proper nouns or titles.	• Dear Dr. Hensley, • My dear Sir, • To Prof. Stanley on his Birthday:
When closing a letter, capitalize only the first word in the complimentary closing.	• Respectfully yours, • To your continued success, • Until we meet again,

CAPITALIZATION MODEL

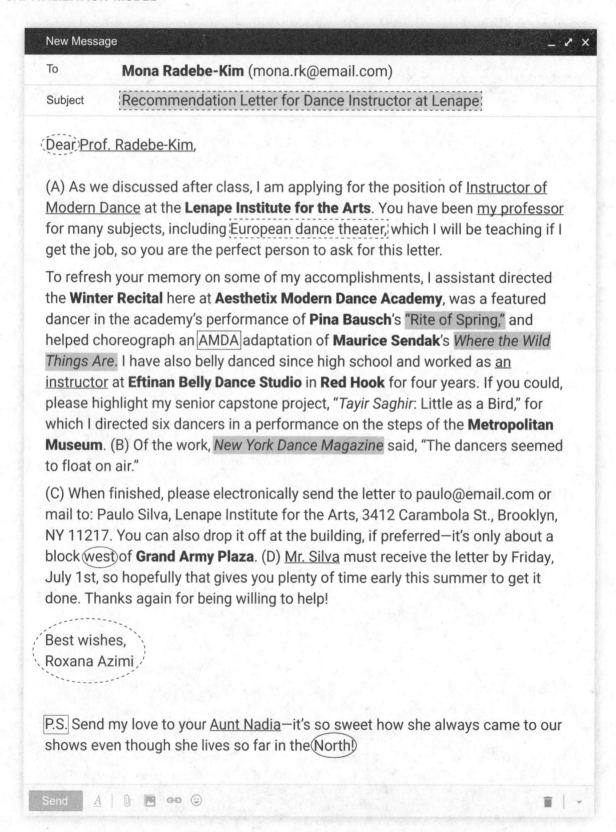

New Message   _ ↗ ×

To   **Mona Radebe-Kim** (mona.rk@email.com)

Subject   Recommendation Letter for Dance Instructor at Lenape

Dear Prof. Radebe-Kim,

(A) As we discussed after class, I am applying for the position of Instructor of Modern Dance at the **Lenape Institute for the Arts**. You have been my professor for many subjects, including European dance theater, which I will be teaching if I get the job, so you are the perfect person to ask for this letter.

To refresh your memory on some of my accomplishments, I assistant directed the **Winter Recital** here at **Aesthetix Modern Dance Academy**, was a featured dancer in the academy's performance of **Pina Bausch**'s "Rite of Spring," and helped choreograph an AMDA adaptation of **Maurice Sendak**'s *Where the Wild Things Are*. I have also belly danced since high school and worked as an instructor at **Eftinan Belly Dance Studio** in **Red Hook** for four years. If you could, please highlight my senior capstone project, "*Tayir Saghir*: Little as a Bird," for which I directed six dancers in a performance on the steps of the **Metropolitan Museum**. (B) Of the work, *New York Dance Magazine* said, "The dancers seemed to float on air."

(C) When finished, please electronically send the letter to paulo@email.com or mail to: Paulo Silva, Lenape Institute for the Arts, 3412 Carambola St., Brooklyn, NY 11217. You can also drop it off at the building, if preferred—it's only about a block west of **Grand Army Plaza**. (D) Mr. Silva must receive the letter by Friday, July 1st, so hopefully that gives you plenty of time early this summer to get it done. Thanks again for being willing to help!

Best wishes,
Roxana Azimi

P.S. Send my love to your Aunt Nadia—it's so sweet how she always came to our shows even though she lives so far in the North!

Send   *A* 🔗 🖼 🔗 ☺   🗑 | ▾

Title Case

In titles and subtitles, one should follow title case rules by capitalizing the first and last word of any title or subtitle as well as any important words. Prepositions and most conjunctions should remain lowercase.

Proper Names

Proper names of events, buildings, people, places, and organizations all require capitalization. As with title case, words like *for* and *the* can remain lowercase (Lenape Institute for the Arts). For hyphenated names, both names should be capitalized (Radebe-Kim). Note: General nouns (senior capstone project, performance) don't get capitalized, but proper names or titles given for such nouns ("*Tayir Saghir*: Little as a Bird", Winter Recital) do.

Titles for People

If a title applies to a specific person, it should be capitalized (Prof. Radebe-Kim). If the word is being used more generally, it should not be (my professor). Likewise, official job titles (Instructor of Modern Dance) should be capitalized when referring to a specific position or person but not when used more generally (an instructor). You should also capitalize a word that would not normally be capitalized if it acts like a title in a person's proper name (Aunt Nadia).

If the points of the compass refer to a specific place, they are capitalized; however, when used to give directions, they are not.

In acronyms and most abbreviations, like P.S., one should always use capital letters.

School subjects don't require capitalization unless they refer to specific languages or place names.

When opening and closing a letter, capitalize the first word and any titles or proper nouns.

Many formal subject lines follow title case, just like headlines do.

(A) Capitalize the first letter of any complete sentence, including the sentence that immediately follows your salutation. You also always capitalize *I* when it stands alone.

(B) If a quotation is a complete sentence, the first word inside the quotation should be capitalized.

(C) The city, state, and any street or building names should all be capitalized when formatting an address.

(D) Days of the week, months of the year, and holidays all need to be capitalized, but seasons do not.

SPELLING

Like capitalization, understanding spelling typically requires learning several rules. Additionally, spelling seems to be one of those skills that comes naturally to some, while others (regardless of intelligence level) may struggle more to pick it up. That said, as with capitalization, we have broken these rules into a series of categories to help you make sense of them. Then, you will have the opportunity to spellcheck an example email so you can apply your new understanding of these rules in context. We also encourage you to look in the dictionary for the spelling of words you encounter in your daily life as you practice for the exam—the more words with which you familiarize yourself, the better! Since some of these tips or rules will seem more familiar than others, remember to maximize your study time by concentrating first on those that seem less familiar.

Tips for Improving Your Spelling Skills

You can improve your spelling by keeping a list of words that you spell incorrectly or need to look up repeatedly. Add to this list whenever you find a word you can't spell. Set aside a few minutes to study spelling and write down each word correctly ten times. You can also type the words, but physically writing it out gives you time to concentrate on the spelling and apply it to memory. Let your hands get used to the feeling of spelling a difficult word correctly. Let your eye become accustomed to seeing a difficult word spelled correctly. Ask someone to read your list aloud to you on occasion and try writing them correctly or spelling them aloud. Frequent self-testing of problematic words should help you learn the correct spellings. On the day before the test, carefully read back over your list to refresh your memory.

Another way to improve your spelling is to develop mnemonic devices. A mnemonic device is a private clue that you create to help you remember something. For example, if you have trouble spelling the word *friend*, you might find it helpful to remember the sentence, "A friend is true to the *end*." This little sentence will help you remember to place the *i* before the *e*. If you have trouble distinguishing between *here* and *hear*, try a sentence like, "To listen is to hear with an ear." If you confuse the spellings *principle* and *principal*, remember (whether you believe it or not), "The princiPAL is your PAL." And finally, this cute mnemonic device might help you spell "misspells" correctly: "*Miss Pells* never *misspells*." When you have trouble spelling a word, try to invent your own mnemonic device, and you will have a built-in prompter when you encounter spelling questions on the exam.

Finally, you can use the list of 101 commonly misspelled words at the end of this section to familiarize yourself with their correct spellings in advance of your exam.

Spelling Rules

While there are many spelling rules, they can be divided based on which kinds of situations govern them; for instance, many rules concern what kind of suffix is affixed to the end of a word. Unfortunately, since English is tricky and borrows a lot from other languages, there are also exceptions to many of the rules. To help you identify exceptions, we have included the most common with examples when relevant.

TIP

If spelling is difficult for you, don't be discouraged. Many intelligent and creative people have had problems spelling, including highly regarded authors such as Agatha Christie, Ernest Hemingway, and Jane Austen. You can improve your spelling by using a dictionary each time you encounter a word you don't know and by testing yourself on words you often misspell.

Rules Related to Suffixes and Word Endings

A suffix describes a set of letters added to the end of all or part of a base word to create a new word. For instance, the suffix *-ical*, meaning "possessing the form of," can be added to base words like *method*, *magic*, and *nonsense* to make the words *methodical*, *magical*, and *nonsensical*.

RULES RELATED TO SUFFIXES AND WORD ENDINGS		
Rule	Exceptions (if applicable)	Examples
If a word ends in a *y* preceded by a vowel, keep the *y* when adding a suffix.		• day → days • attorney → attorneys • journey → journeyed • play → playing
If a word ends in a *y* preceded by a consonant, change the *y* to an *i* before adding a suffix.	To avoid creating a double *i*, retain the *y* when adding the suffixes *-ing* and *-ish*.	• silly → silliest • try → tries, tried, trying • fly → flying, flier • baby → babyish
If a word ends in a silent *e*, then the *e* is dropped before any suffix that begins with a vowel.	To retain the soft sounds of *c* and *g*, words ending in *ce* and *ge* often (but not always) retain *e* before the suffixes *-able* and *-ous*. Other exceptions: *canoeing, dyeing, acreage, mileage, rideable*	• dance → dancing • locate → location • use → using, usable • notice → noticeable • courage → courageous
Generally, retain a silent *e* before any suffix that begins with a consonant.	Some exceptions include the words *truly, duly, argument, wholly*, and *ninth*.	• care → careless, careful • late → lately • whole → wholesome • waste → wasteful • bore → boredom
One-syllable words that end in a single consonant preceded by a single vowel double the final consonant before any suffix beginning with a vowel, including *-y*.	Note that if the final consonant is preceded by two vowels, this rule doesn't apply. need → needing, needy	• drop → dropped, dropper • swim → swimmer, swimmingly • fit → fitted, fitting • mud → muddy, muddier • cut → cutting, cuttable
A word with two or more syllables that accents the last syllable and ends in a single consonant preceded by a single vowel doubles the final consonant before any suffix beginning with a vowel.	Remember, this rule does not apply if the accent is not on the last syllable. enter → entered, entering exhibit → exhibition	• begin → beginner • admit → admittance • control → controlling • commit → committed
A word ending in *-er* or *-ur* that is accented on the last syllable will double the *r* in the past tense. However, if the accent falls before the last syllable, the *r* will not be doubled.		• occur → occurred • prefer → preferred • transfer → transferred • answer → answered • offer → offered • differ → differed

RULES RELATED TO SUFFIXES AND WORD ENDINGS

Rule	Exceptions (if applicable)	Examples
When adding the suffix -*full* to the end of a noun, drop the final *l*.	In the rare case when adding -*full* to a word that is not a noun, keep the final *l*.	• wonder → wonderful • event → eventful • hope → hopeful • over → overfull
To pluralize a word, add -*s*. However, if it ends in -*s*, -*sh*, -*ch*, -*x*, or -*z*, spell it with an -*es* suffix.		• duck → ducks • meal → meals • box → boxes • crash → crashes
When pluralizing a word that ends with a consonant and *y*, change the *y* into an *i* and then add -*es*		• lady → ladies • canary → canaries • jelly → jellies • curry → curries

Rules Related to Prefixes and Word Beginnings

There are fewer rules governing prefixes, but they are still important to know. A prefix is a set of letters added to the beginning of all or part of a base word to create a new word. For instance, the prefix *de-*, meaning "away from, opposite of, off, or down" can be added to words like *escalate*, *activate*, and *sensitize* to make *deescalate*, *deactivate*, and *desensitize*.

RULES RELATED TO PREFIXES AND WORD BEGINNINGS

Rule	Examples
When *over-* is used as a prefix, the result is one word, not two.	• overcast • overcharge • overhear
All words with the prefix *self-* should be hyphenated.	• self-taught • self-control • self-defense
In general, prefixes will not change how a word is spelled. Simply attach the prefix to the word without a space between.	• anti + body → antibody • hyper + active → hyperactive • sub + marine → submarine
When attaching a prefix to a proper noun, add a hyphen before the proper noun.	• The pre-World War II landscape was different. • The protesters expressed anti-Walmart sentiments.
Some prefixes may create double letters—this is fine, and the double letter should be retained.	• un + necessary → unnecessary • mis + spell → misspell • re + education → reeducation

Rules Related to Grammar and Meaning

Some rules that pertain to spelling are also related to grammar, punctuation, and meaning. For instance, when two or more words sound the same but are spelled differently, misspelling them can also impact the grammatical correctness of one's sentence and make it unclear. Therefore, while it is important to memorize these rules for grammar purposes, thinking of them as spelling rules may also help you remember which form of a word to use and when. The following table contains some but not all of the grammar rules that you can also think of as spelling rules. For a challenge, see if you can think of any more.

RULES RELATED TO GRAMMAR AND MEANING	
Rule	**Examples**
Use *to* to show movement towards a particular location or reaching a particular state of being. Use *too* to mean "in addition," "also," or "to an excessive degree." Use *two* to represent the number 2.	• Are you going to the Billie Eilish concert? • No, I am too tired after such a long week. • Well, I still have two tickets, so if I give one to my friend, Tianna, maybe she can come, too.
Use *your* as the possessive form of *you*. Use *you're* as a contraction for *you are*.	• Who did your mother say was supposed to pick you up? • Dad, she said you're supposed to!
Whose is the possessive of *who*. *Who's* is the contraction for *who is*.	• Do you know who's ringing the doorbell? • It's probably the person whose car is parked in our driveway.
Its is the possessive of *it*. *It's* is the contraction for *it is*.	• Is that birthday card with its yellow envelope? • Yes, it's in the top drawer.
They're is the contraction for *they are*. *There* means *at that place*. *Their* is the possessive form of *they* or *them*.	• They're going to put their books over there. • The honeymooners said they're going to drive their Porsche along the beach in Italy when they get there.
To lose something means to misplace it. *Lose* is a verb. If something is loose, then it is not tight or secure. *Loose* is an adjective.	• Did you lose your wallet? • Yes, unfortunately, I think that pocket of my backpack came loose on the train.
All right, meaning "everything's correct," is two words. *Alright* is a different word that means "okay" or "fine."	• The camp counselor asked me if I needed help or if I was alright, and I told him that the decorations for the party were all right.
Already means "prior to some specified time." *All ready* means "completely ready."	• By the time I was all ready to go to the play, the tickets had already sold out.
Altogether means "entirely." *All together* means "in sum" or "collectively."	• There are altogether too many people to seat in this room when we are all together on holidays.

Other Spelling Rules

There are a few other rules that cannot easily be categorized, so it's best to just learn them independently.

OTHER SPELLING RULES	
Rule	**Examples**
The letter *q* is essentially always followed by *u*. Note: There are exceptions to this rule, but they are so rare that they don't impact much except word games.	• quiz • bouquet • acquire • quick • equate
Numbers from twenty-one to ninety-nine include a hyphen when spelled out.	• Two hundred and twenty-two • Eighty-five • Three thousand and thirty-eight
Percent is never hyphenated (*per-cent*), but it may be written as one word (*percent*) or two (*per cent*).	• I am 100 percent certain that I'm right. • This chart represents 7 per cent of our annual budget.
The sound expressed as *oi* differs depending on where it's found. If it occurs in the middle of a word, use *oi*. If it occurs at the end of a word, use *oy*.	• foil • avoid • annoy • boy
Generally, to express the sound *ch* at the beginning of a word, you use *ch*. However, to express this sound at the end of a word, you usually (but not always!) use *tch*. Some exceptions: *much, tchotchke, coach, march, branch, starch*	• childish • champion • chatty • stretch • clutch • wristwatch

The "*i* before *e* except after *c*" Trap

This is one of the most common spelling rules that people know, but it's also one of the most misleading. While it is generally true that in most English words, an *i* will come before an *e* except when the two letters follow *c* (*piece, ceiling, receipt, deceive, mischief*), there are enough exceptions to this rule to make it a confusing one. For instance, words that create an *ay* sound (*neighbor, sleigh, weigh, reign*) do not tend to follow this rule, nor do words that use the Germanic *ei* vowel sound (*either, neither, feisty, heist, heights*). Still, others are simply run-of-the-mill exceptions, like *foreign, seizure, weird, species, leisure, albeit, glacier, cueing*, and *science*, to name just a few. You can still consider this a useful rule of thumb when you aren't sure how to spell a word; just know that there are many more exceptions to this rule than some realize.

101 Commonly Misspelled Words

Recognizing a word that commonly gets misspelled and devoting time to learning the right way to spell it is another way to improve your overall spelling skills. In the process, you may notice patterns in your misspellings that also make it easier to recognize when a word might be tricky for you.

To help you find words you might like to practice, we have compiled the following list of 101 commonly misspelled words. If you don't know the meaning of a word, take this opportunity to practice looking it up in the dictionary.

acceptable	exhilarate	memento	playwright	rhythm
accidental	existence	millennium	precede	ridiculous
accommodate	extreme	miniature	principal	schedule
acquire	foreign	minuscule	principle	separate
amateur	gauge	mischievous	privilege	sergeant
apparent	grateful	misspell	questionnaire	subpoena
atheist	guarantee	nauseous	raspberry	supersede
believe	harass	necessary	receipt	surprise
calendar	height	neighbor	recommend	tableau
camouflage	hierarchy	noticeable	reference	tariff
cantaloupe	humorous	occasionally	refrigerator	threshold
cemetery	immediately	occurrence	relevant	tongue
changeable	independent	official	remembrance	vacuum
collectible	indispensable	omitted	rendezvous	weather
colonel	inoculate	pastime	renowned	weird
column	intelligence	perseverance	restaurant	welcome
commemorate	irresistible	personnel	rhyme	zeitgeist
committed	jewelry			
congratulations	judgment			
conscience	kernel			
definitely	leisure			
discipline	liaison			
dumbbell	library			
embarrass	license			
exceed	maneuver			

Test Yourself: Spelling

Directions: The following e-mail contains 30 different spelling errors. See if you can identify all 30 and determine the correct spelling for each, as if you were proofreading Rocco's email. For an extra challenge, time yourself.

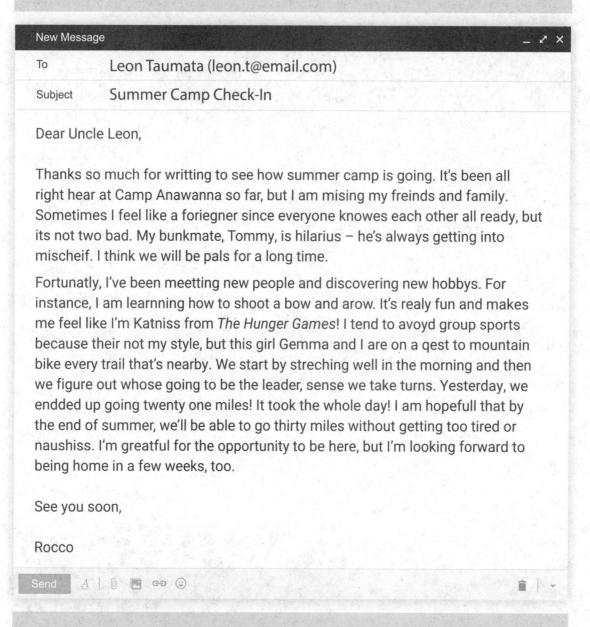

New Message   — ⟋ ✕

To   Leon Taumata (leon.t@email.com)

Subject   Summer Camp Check-In

Dear Uncle Leon,

Thanks so much for writting to see how summer camp is going. It's been all right hear at Camp Anawanna so far, but I am mising my freinds and family. Sometimes I feel like a foriegner since everyone knowes each other all ready, but its not two bad. My bunkmate, Tommy, is hilarius – he's always getting into mischeif. I think we will be pals for a long time.

Fortunatly, I've been meeting new people and discovering new hobbys. For instance, I am learnning how to shoot a bow and arow. It's realy fun and makes me feel like I'm Katniss from *The Hunger Games*! I tend to avoyd group sports because their not my style, but this girl Gemma and I are on a qest to mountain bike every trail that's nearby. We start by streching well in the morning and then we figure out whose going to be the leader, sense we take turns. Yesterday, we endded up going twenty one miles! It took the whole day! I am hopefull that by the end of summer, we'll be able to go thirty miles without getting too tired or naushiss. I'm greatful for the opportunity to be here, but I'm looking forward to being home in a few weeks, too.

See you soon,

Rocco

Send   A | 🖉 🖼 ⸺ 🙂   🗑 | ▾

Answer Key: Here are the correct spellings of the incorrectly spelled words, presented in the order they appear within the email: writing, alright, here, missing, friends, foreigner, knows, already, it's, too, hilarious, mischief, fortunately, meeting, hobbies, learning, arrow, really, avoid, they're, quest, stretching, who's, since, ended, twenty-one, hopeful, nauseous, grateful.

SUMMING IT UP

- The HSPT and the TACHS exams test your writing skills regarding capitalization and spelling.

- Keep track of words that are hard for you to spell so that you can get used to writing them out.

- Try coming up with your own mnemonic devices to remember the words you struggle with most.

- Remember that there are general capitalization rules as well as specific rules for title case, pronouns, and titles and honorifics.

- Spelling rules can be divided based on which kinds of situations govern them: There are spelling rules for word endings and suffixes as well as word beginnings and prefixes. There are also spelling rules that are tied to principles of grammar and meaning. Oftentimes, there are exceptions to these rules based on the sound of a word or its origins. Learn these rules and be aware of any exceptions you might encounter.

- Capitalization and spelling are best understood in context, so make sure you can apply each rule to your own example sentences.

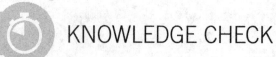

KNOWLEDGE CHECK

CAPITALIZATION
10 Questions—6 Minutes

> **Directions:** Among the following sentences, look for errors in capitalization. If you find no mistakes, mark D.

1. **A.** If a student wants to attend the museum field trip, they need to have a permission slip.
   B. Mrs. Beadle-Wright's request cannot be granted under any conditions.
   C. Charlie Little, who is a member of the prom committee, was asked to confer with principal Wu.
   D. *(No mistakes)*

2. **A.** Mariah is always willing to undertake difficult English assignments.
   B. The teacher entered the room and said, "your work must be completed today."
   C. The special project was assigned to Troy Salire and me.
   D. *(No mistakes)*

3. **A.** I find his study of the birds of North America to be fascinating.
   B. The doctor suggested that my grandfather go South for the winter to avoid frequent colds.
   C. Under the new rules, when do we revert to Eastern Standard Time?
   D. *(No mistakes)*

4. **A.** "If it rains on Friday," the boy mused, "the game may be played on Saturday instead."
   B. My Spanish teacher, Ms. Neff, sometimes gives us candy during games.
   C. Whenever I drive on a New York street, I watch for potholes.
   D. *(No mistakes)*

5. **A.** Every halloween, my mother takes a picture of my costume.
   B. Please submit an essay, two letters of recommendation, and the completed application form.
   C. The reporter asked the senator about the election results.
   D. *(No mistakes)*

6. **A.** Saul and his best friend Madison went to see *The Guiding Hand*, the newest movie at the Pekoe County Theater.
   B. After Nomi's physical examination, Dr. Pembroke said to her, "You are in excellent health."
   C. Aleck read the first seven chapters of the horror novel he purchased, *The sound of a ghost*, and couldn't sleep all night.
   D. *(No mistakes)*

7. **A.** Some students requested extra test-prep help before the important exam.

   B. The art teacher asked if anyone "Needed a brain break" after the standardized test.

   C. Heather recommended that the organization draft a new constitution.

   D. *(No mistakes)*

8. **A.** On their class trip to independence hall in Philadelphia, the students interviewed the actor who portrayed John Adams.

   B. Our tour guide said that the school is accredited by the Southern Association of Colleges and Schools.

   C. Please read the directions carefully, and hand in your test before the bell rings at 3:05.

   D. *(No mistakes)*

9. **A.** "When you finish your homework," my mom said, "please set the table for dinner."

   B. I was surprised to learn that Olive and Lucy are twins; they certainly don't look alike at all.

   C. I am always sad when the hummingbirds fly south for the winter.

   D. *(No mistakes)*

10. **A.** I have a job interview for the position of Managing Editor at a major newspaper.

    B. Niagara Falls consists of three different massive waterfalls on the Niagara River.

    C. Yolanda won homecoming queen at Adirondack Valley high school.

    D. *(No mistakes)*

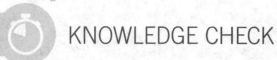

KNOWLEDGE CHECK

SPELLING
10 Questions—6 Minutes

> **Directions:** Look for errors in spelling. Choose the letter of the sentence that contains the error. No question contains more than one sentence with a spelling error. If you find no mistakes, mark D as your answer.

1. **A.** In the teacher's absence, the pupils had an eraser fight.
    B. The laws of apartheid prohibited marriage between people of different races.
    C. We may be haveing a fire drill this afternoon.
    D. (*No mistakes*)

2. **A.** The German foreign exchange student, Silke, taught us about how her family celebrates Oktoberfest.
    B. Galileo Galilei is credited with the discovary of Saturn.
    C. I screamed when my friend said she'd managed to acquire us two tickets to Coachella.
    D. (*No mistakes*)

3. **A.** Dakota's position in the chess match was not advantagous, and he was nervous.
    B. The welcome committee set up the registration booth by the entrance to the banquet hall.
    C. The manager, Rita, was eager to review her employee's recommendations for increasing company revenue.
    D. (*No mistakes*)

4. **A.** Meet me at the bus depot promptly at four.
    B. On Saturday, we will have dinner at a hip Thai restaurant.
    C. Have you ever booked accommodations on the Las Vegas Strip before?
    D. (*No mistakes*)

5. **A.** The shepherd would be lonely without his dog.
    B. The experiment served to confirm Marco's initial hypothesis.
    C. I was planning to pick Rafe up, but he allready found a ride.
    D. (*No mistakes*)

6. **A.** The golfer took a break after the nineth hole.
    B. Let me acquaint you with the new rules.
    C. The slugger wields a heavy bat.
    D. (*No mistakes*)

7. **A.** Biology is always a laboratory science.
    B. The short story is really a memoir.
    C. My neice will enter college in the fall.
    D. (*No mistakes*)

8. **A.** The currency of Mexico is the peso.
    B. The detective had the perfect disguise.
    C. Is there anything one can buy for a nickel anymore?
    D. (*No mistakes*)

9. **A.** Our senator is a staunch supporter of the president.

   B. What happened in the old house was a truly strange occurence.

   C. A surgeon must have steady hands.

   D. (*No mistakes*)

10. **A.** To grow crops in the desert, Paz must irrigate daily.

   B. Most convenience stores have very long hours.

   C. There was a lovly centerpiece on the table.

   D. (*No mistakes*)

ANSWER KEYS AND EXPLANATIONS

Capitalization

1. C	3. B	5. A	7. B	9. D
2. B	4. D	6. C	8. A	10. C

1. **The correct answer is C.** Principal Wu is a specific principal, so the *P* must be capitalized.

2. **The correct answer is B.** The direct quotation must begin with a capital *T*.

3. **The correct answer is B.** Do not capitalize compass points if they are simply directions—capitalization should only be used when these words are meant as place names.

4. **The correct answer is D.** *No mistakes.*

5. **The correct answer is A.** Holidays, along with days of the week and months of the year, should be capitalized, so the word *Halloween* should be capitalized.

6. **The correct answer is C.** Titles must follow title case capitalization rules. Consequently, the title of the novel should be *The Sound of a Ghost.*

7. **The correct answer is B.** The first word in a quotation should be capitalized only if the quotation forms a complete sentence. Here, the quotation is a fragment, so the first word in it should not be capitalized.

8. **The correct answer is A.** Independence Hall should be capitalized since it is the name of a building.

9. **The correct answer is D.** *No mistakes.*

10. **The correct answer is C.** The phrase "high school" is part of the proper name of the organization, so the words should be capitalized: Adirondack Valley High School.

Spelling

1. C	3. A	5. C	7. C	9. B
2. B	4. D	6. A	8. D	10. C

1. **The correct answer is C.** The correct spelling is *having.* Remember, a silent *e* at the end of a word is usually dropped before a suffix beginning with a vowel.

2. **The correct answer is B.** The correct spelling is *discovery.* Since the base word is *discover*, there is no reason to change the *e* to *a*.

3. **The correct answer is A.** The correct spelling is *advantageous.* Remember, words ending in *ce* and *ge* retain *e* before *-able* and *-ous* to maintain the soft sounds of *c* and *g*.

4. **The correct answer is D.** *No mistakes.*

5. **The correct answer is C.** *Already* is spelled with one *l*.

6. **The correct answer is A.** The correct spelling is *ninth.* This was mentioned as an exception to the rule stating that one should retain a silent *e* before any suffix that begins with a consonant.

7. **The correct answer is C.** The correct spelling is *niece,* as this word follows the "*i* before *e* except after *c*" rule.

8. **The correct answer is D.** *No mistakes.*

9. **The correct answer is B.** *Occurrence* is spelled with a double *r.* It is on the list of commonly misspelled words.

10. **The correct answer is C.** The correct spelling is *lovely.* Note that a silent *e* is usually kept before a suffix beginning with a consonant: love + ly = lovely.

NOTES

CHAPTER

Logic and Verbal
Classification

LOGIC AND VERBAL CLASSIFICATION

OVERVIEW

Logic

Verbal Classification

Summing It Up

Knowledge Check: Logic and Verbal Classification

Answer Keys and Explanations

>>

The HSPT exam will put your logical thinking and verbal reasoning skills to the test by presenting logic and verbal classification questions. Both question types appear within the HSPT Verbal Skills section.

Logic and verbal classification questions can seem a bit mystifying at first, but their goal is to test how you make observations, assess relationships between ideas, draw inferences, and come to conclusions.

Logic questions require you to extract indisputable information from a series of short sentences. Verbal classification questions will ask you to determine which of four words does not fit with the other three. Both types of questions test the same thing—your ability to draw conclusions from a given set of information.

TACHS   HSPT   ISEE   SSAT   SHSAT

HSPT® EXAM LOGIC

Logic questions on the HSPT take a slightly different form than other questions on the exam. In these questions, you're given a series of sentences. You are then asked to determine if—based on the truth of the other sentences—the final sentence is **A.** true, **B.** false, or **C.** uncertain. If it is not possible to determine whether the final sentence is true or false, then the correct answer is choice C.

Let's look at an example of an HSPT logic exam question:

> **EXAMPLE:**
>
> The black horse jumped over more hurdles than the spotted horse. The white horse jumped over more hurdles than the spotted horse. The white horse jumped over more hurdles than the black horse. If the first two statements are true, the third statement is.
>
>   **A.** true.
>
>   **B.** false.
>
>   **C.** uncertain.
>
> **The correct answer is C.** From the first two statements, we know that both the black horse and the white horse jumped over more hurdles than the spotted horse. The third statement suggests a relationship between the white horse and the black horse. However, since the first two statements do not offer any information about the comparative achievements of the black horse and the white horse, the third statement can be neither affirmed nor denied.

 TIP

Visualization and diagramming are valuable tools for understanding relationships. Try drawing out and labeling the relationships described by the sentences. If there's no room to draw, create a mental picture of the actions described by the sentences and then select the relevant answer.

When reading this type of question, you can assume that the first two statements are true, so all you need to determine is whether that makes the third statement true, false, or uncertain. You should have enough information from the first two statements to make this determination.

This type of question tests your ability to assess, categorize, and make enough sense of existing information to infer a conclusion. One of three situations will arise:

Based on the information in the first two statements, you're able to determine that the third statement is true.

Example: Tanisha is taller than Yusef. Yusef is taller than Zelma. Zelma is shorter than Tanisha.

Here, you have enough information to determine that Zelma is indeed shorter than Tanisha. The third statement is true.

Based on the information in the first two statements, you're able to determine that the third statement is false.

Example: Tanisha is taller than Yusef. Yusef is taller than Zelma. Zelma is taller than Tanisha.

Here, the first two sentences provide information that contradicts the third; they suggest that Zelma is actually shorter than Tanisha. Therefore, the third statement is false.

The details in the first two statements do not give you enough information to determine if the third statement is true or false—you are uncertain.

Example: Tanisha is taller than Yusef. Yusef is taller than Zelma. Sylvana is the tallest.

Here, you are not given any information about Sylvana in the first two statements, so you have no way of knowing if she is tallest. The third statement is uncertain.

The three statements will often give comparative information, so you need to be able to plot or visualize relationships as you go. Using a less than or greater than symbol can help you track and document information as you read each sentence.

Tracking the relationships in some way can be particularly helpful when dealing with uncertainty. While practicing, you'll see that there are a variety of reasons why the truth value of the third statements of HSPT Logic questions may be uncertain. The relationship between the final terms may not have been established by the first two statements (the horse example). Alternatively, a new term may have been introduced that was not previously stated or is only mentioned once (Sylvana in example 3). Sometimes, the third statement proposes a relationship that is plausible but not certain because of ambiguous language in the first two statements. Here is an example of the third case:

Alma is taller than Carlos. Forrest is shorter than Alma but is not shorter than Carlos. Forrest and Carlos are the same height. If the first two statements are true, then the third statement is

    A. true.

    B. false.

    C. uncertain.

Solution:

Let's breakdown the first two statements. The first establishes that Alma is taller than Carlos. You can track that more easily with the following notation:

Alma > Carlos

The second statement provides two clauses though. The first is as follows:

Forrest < Alma

With this, you know that Alma is taller than both Carlos and Forrest. But what about the relationship between Carlos and Forrest? The second clause provides a clue:

Forrest not < Carlos

But here you need to be careful of how you translate the "not" in the phrase. The statement would be written in the positive as follows:

Forrest ≥ Carlos

Notice that this does not strictly mean that Forrest is taller than Carlos. Nor does it mean that he is necessarily the same height. The particular phrasing creates the possibility for both situations: Forrest's height could be greater than OR equal to Carlos'. As such, are Forrest and Carlos the same height? With only the first two statements, it's possible, but you can't know for sure.

The correct answer is C. You can only state with certainty that Alma is taller than both Carlos and Forrest.

HSPT® EXAM VERBAL CLASSIFICATION

The Verbal Skills section of the HSPT also has Verbal Classification questions. In these questions, you are presented with four words and asked to determine which of the words does not fit with the other three. Here's an example:

EXAMPLE:

Which word does *not* belong with the others?

A. crack

B. cleave

C. split

D. pare

The correct answer is D. The first three words are synonyms. All refer to dividing something by opening it into two or more pieces. Choice D, on the other hand, refers to opening by peeling off the outer layer (to pare is to peel).

The key to answering this kind of question lies in determining the relationship among three of the words. You shouldn't have to work too hard to convince yourself which word is unrelated to the other three—when in doubt, trust your gut.

That said, understanding the variety of relationships exhibited in this question type will help you approach these questions with more confidence when they come up. There are many possible relationships; however, the three related words tend to share similarities that fall into one of four categories:

SYNONYMS: The three related words have essentially the same meaning. The correct answer will be a word that does not share that meaning.

EXAMPLE:

A. queasy

B. joyful

C. ecstatic

D. elated

The correct answer is A. Choice A is correct because it is not a synonym for happy.

DEGREES OF INTENSITY: The three related words represent three different intensities of the same idea. The correct answer will be a word that either does not relate to that idea or does not reflect a degree of intensity.

EXAMPLE:

A. cool

B. icy

C. freezing

D. icicle

The correct answer is D. Choice D is correct because even though it is thematically related, it is not a degree of intensity for the word *cold*.

PART OF SPEECH OR VERB TENSE: The

three related words are the same part of speech, meaning they are all nouns, adjectives, verbs, adverbs, etc. The correct answer will be a word that is not the same part of speech or that is in a different verb tense.

EXAMPLES:

A. scary
B. upsets
C. strange
D. quirky

The correct answer is B. Choice B is correct because it's a verb, not an adjective.

A. swims
B. speaks
C. jumped
D. rests

The correct answer is C. Choice C is correct because it is a past tense verb, not a present tense verb.

THEME: The subject matter of three of the

words is clearly related in some way, such as by where items can be found, how items are used, or any other relationship you can think of. Consequently, this is the least predictable type of question, but it may also be the easiest to spot. The correct answer will always be thematically unrelated to the others, even if it seems related in other ways.

EXAMPLE:

A. gymnastics
B. water polo
C. basketball
D. tennis racket

The correct answer is D. A tennis racket is a piece of sports equipment, not the name of a sport. Don't get distracted just because the correct answer is still related to sports generally, since the theme is "names of sports."

It *is* possible that the exam tests different relationships that aren't covered here, but don't stress! If you practice recognizing the types of relationships we have mentioned, you should still be well-primed to spot others.

SUMMING IT UP

- The HSPT exam tests different types of logic in its Verbal Skills section using logic and verbal classification questions.

  - Logic questions give you a series of sentences, then ask you to determine if—based on the truth of the other sentences—the final sentence is **A.** true, **B.** false, or **C.** uncertain. If it is not possible to determine whether the final sentence is true or false, then the correct answer is choice C.

  - Verbal Classification questions present you with four words. You must then determine which of the words doesn't fit with the other three.

LOGIC

10 Questions—3 Minutes

Directions: Choose the best answer.

1. George is older than Beatriz. Fred is younger than George. Beatriz is older than Fred. If the first two statements are true, the third statement is

   A. true.

   B. false.

   C. uncertain.

2. Group A sings higher than Group C. Group B sings lower than Group C. Group A sings higher than Group B. If the first two statements are true, the third statement is

   A. true.

   B. false.

   C. uncertain.

3. Percolator coffee is weaker than electric-drip coffee. Extractor coffee is stronger than electric-drip coffee. Percolator coffee is stronger than extractor coffee. If the first two statements are true, the third statement is

   A. true.

   B. false.

   C. uncertain.

4. Red kites fly higher than yellow kites. Purple balloons fly higher than red kites. Yellow kites fly higher than purple balloons. If the first two statements are true, the third statement is

   A. true.

   B. false.

   C. uncertain.

5. The New York team lost fewer games than the Boston team. The Boston team won more games than the Chicago team, but not as many games as the New York team. The Chicago team lost the fewest games. If the first two statements are true, the third statement is

   A. true.

   B. false.

   C. uncertain.

6. The history book has more pages than the poetry book, but fewer pages than the math book. The math book has more pages than the science book but fewer pages than the English book. The poetry book has the fewest pages. If the first two statements are true, the third statement is

   A. true.

   B. false.

   C. uncertain.

7. Diego reads faster than Amina. Lindsey reads slower than Diego, but not slower than Amina. Lindsey and Amina read at the same pace. If the first two statements are true, then the third statement is

   A. true.

   B. false.

   C. uncertain.

8. The widget factory sold more items than the gizmo factory sold. The gadget factory sold more items than the widget factory sold. The gizmo factory sold more items than the gadget factory sold. If the first two statements are true, then the third statement is

   A. true.

   B. false.

   C. uncertain.

9. Stefen has traveled to 16 countries. Wala'a has traveled to fewer countries than Stefen, but more than Natilla. Natilla has been to the fewest number of countries. If the first two statements are true, then the third statement is

   A. true.

   B. false.

   C. uncertain.

10. US Route 1 is longer than US Route 5. US Route 66 is fewer than 80 miles longer than US Route 1. US Route 66 is longer than US Route 5. If the first two statements are true, then the third statement is

    A. true.

    B. false.

    C. uncertain.

VERBAL CLASSIFICATION
10 Questions—3 Minutes

Directions: Choose the word that doesn't belong with the others.

1. Which word does *not* belong with the others?

   A. ceiling

   B. window

   C. floor

   D. wall

2. Which word does *not* belong with the others?

   A. orange

   B. apple

   C. cherry

   D. carrot

3. Which word does *not* belong with the others?

   A. emotion

   B. love

   C. anger

   D. disappointment

4. Which word does *not* belong with the others?

   A. destroy

   B. brick

   C. construct

   D. connect

5. Which word does *not* belong with the others?

   A. medicine

   B. healing

   C. therapy

   D. surgery

6. Which word does *not* belong with the others?

   A. city

   B. town

   C. village

   D. road

7. Which word does *not* belong with the others?

   A. bottle

   B. canteen

   C. cup

   D. plate

8. Which word does *not* belong with the others?

   A. smart phone

   B. console

   C. laptop

   D. tablet

9. Which word does *not* belong with the others?

   A. noun

   B. pronoun

   C. apostrophe

   D. verb

10. Which word does *not* belong with the others?

    A. glider

    B. skateboard

    C. bicycle

    D. scooter

ANSWER KEYS AND EXPLANATIONS

Logic

1. C	3. B	5. C	7. C	9. A
2. A	4. B	6. C	8. B	10. A

1. **The correct answer is C.** We know only that George is the oldest. There is no way to tell whether Beatriz is older than Fred or whether Fred is older than Beatriz.

2. **The correct answer is A.** Group A sings the highest of the three.

3. **The correct answer is B.** Extractor coffee is the strongest, electric drip comes next, and percolator is the weakest.

4. **The correct answer is B.** Purple balloons appear to fly higher than kites of either color.

5. **The correct answer is C.** We know for certain that the Chicago team *won* the fewest games, but without information about how many games were played, we have no knowledge of how many games the Chicago team *lost*.

6. **The correct answer is C.** The English book has the most pages, followed by the math book. The history book has more pages than the poetry book.

However, we do not have enough information to rank the science book; it might have more or fewer pages than the poetry book.

7. **The correct answer is C.** We know Diego reads faster than Amina and Lindsey, but we do not know how fast Amina and Lindsey read, only that Lindsey is not slower than Amina. Lindsey could read either faster or at the same pace.

8. **The correct answer is B.** The gadget factory sold more than the widget factory sold, and the widget factory sold more than the gizmo factory sold.

9. **The correct answer is A.** Wala'a traveled to more countries than Natilla did, but still not as many as Stefen did.

10. **The correct answer is A.** US Route 66 is longer than Route 1, which is longer than Route 5.

Verbal Classification

1. B	3. A	5. B	7. D	9. C
2. D	4. B	6. D	8. B	10. A

1. **The correct answer is B.** The window is transparent or, at the very least, translucent, and it is probably movable as well. All the other choices are solid, opaque, and fixed.

2. **The correct answer is D.** The carrot is a root vegetable. All the other choices are seed-bearing fruits.

3. **The correct answer is A.** The other three choices (*love*, *anger*, and *disappointment*) are all specific emotions.

4. **The correct answer is B.** *Brick* is the only noun; the rest are verbs.

5. **The correct answer is B.** *Medicine*, *therapy*, and *surgery* are all procedures leading to healing.

6. **The correct answer is D.** *City*, *town*, and *village* are all places one might live, whereas a road is simply an element of one of those places.

7. **The correct answer is D.** *Bottle*, *canteen*, and *cup* are all things used to hold water, but a plate holds food.

8. **The correct answer is B.** *Smart phones, laptops,* and *tablets* all have their own screens. A *console* needs to be connected to a screen.

9. **The correct answer is C.** The *apostrophe* is a punctuation mark. The others are all parts of speech.

10. **The correct answer is A.** *Gliders* fly through the air while *skateboards, bicycles*, and *scooters* roll on wheels.

NOTES

CHAPTER

Synonyms and Antonyms

SYNONYMS AND ANTONYMS

OVERVIEW

Tips for Answering Synonym Questions

Tips for Answering Antonym Questions

Summing It Up

Knowledge Check: Synonyms and Antonyms

Answer Keys and Explanations

Synonym and antonym questions test your understanding of words. A synonym for a word is a word that means something similar. For example, *chilly* is a synonym for *cold*. Both words mean the same thing. An antonym is the opposite of a word. For example, *hot* is an antonym for *cold*. *Hot* and *cold* are opposites. Both the HSPT and the TACHS test your ability to answer synonym questions, but only the HSPT tests your ability to answer antonym questions. On the HSPT, synonyms are tested in the Verbal Skills section and the Reading section under Vocabulary. On the TACHS, synonyms are tested in the Reading section under Vocabulary. On the HSPT, antonym questions appear on the Verbal Skills portion of the exam. Here, we'll cover strategies for answering both synonym and antonym questions.

TACHS   HSPT   ISEE   SSAT   SHSAT

TIPS FOR ANSWERING SYNONYM QUESTIONS

For synonym questions on the exam, you are asked to choose another word that has the same (or nearly the same) meaning as the word given. Each exam may indicate the synonym in a different fashion. For example, some exams will identify the word they want you to match by italicizing or capitalizing the word, then ask you to choose a synonym from the answer choices. Other exams will use the word in a sentence, usually identifying the synonym in question by italicizing, underlining, or capitalizing the word, and then ask you to select a matching synonym from the answer choices.

Here's a tip to use when choosing the answer for a synonym question: If the word is given in a sentence, try substituting the choices in the place of the indicated word. This process can help you find and check your answer. For example:

EXAMPLE:

The surface of the *placid* lake was smooth as glass.

    A. cold

    B. muddy

    C. deep

    D. calm

The correct answer is D. In this example, the word *calm* is the correct choice. The nice thing about a sentence example is that it provides contextual clues that make it easier to figure out the synonym's meaning. When you read that the lake was "smooth as glass" you can infer that while the lake *might* have been muddy, deep, or cold, it *must* have been calm. That makes choice D the best answer.

Sometimes, the italicized or underlined word has multiple meanings, which can make the contextual clues of the sentence even more important. Consider the following question:

EXAMPLE:

The camel is sometimes called the ship of the *desert*.

    A. abandon

    B. ice cream

    C. sandy wasteland

    D. leave

The correct answer is C. Here, the context in the sentence is crucial to the word's definition. Without the sentence, you would not know whether the word *desert* is to be pronounced *de-SERT*, which means to leave or to abandon, or *DES-ert*, which means a sandy wasteland. If you are not sure of your spelling, the sentence can also spare you the confusion of *desert* versus *dessert*, the latter of which is the last course of a meal.

On the other hand, the phrase or sentence might be of little or no use in helping you choose the correct synonym. The sentence might help you to determine the part of speech for the word in question, but not its meaning, as in the following example:

Scan this QR code for more information on synonyms.

The robbery suspect had a *sallow* complexion.

    A. ruddy

    B. pale

    C. pock-marked

    D. freckled

The correct answer is B. The sentence shows you the proper use of the word *sallow*. It is an adjective used to describe a complexion, but the sentence gives no clue that *sallow* means *pale*. You either know the meaning of the word or you must guess. When the given word isn't part of a sentence, or if the sentence doesn't help define the word, your best option may be to guess. Don't guess arbitrarily, however; first, you need to make sure there are no other clues that could lead you to the correct answer.

Perhaps you have seen the word used, but aren't sure what it means. Look carefully. Do you know the meaning of any part of the word? If you can associate the word with something else you've read or you know, you might be able to find the answer. An example:

EXAMPLE:

a <u>remedial</u> class

    A. instruction

    B. intermediate

    C. corrective

    D. isolated

The correct answer is C. Here, we see that *remedial* is an adjective, and class is the noun it modifies. Let's break down the word itself. Do you see the word *remedy* in *remedial*? You know

that a remedy is a cure or a correction for an ailment. If you combine all the information you now have, you can choose *corrective* as the word that most nearly means *remedial*.

Sometimes, you can find the correct answer to a synonym question by eliminating answers you know are wrong. If you can eliminate even one of the answers, you have a 33% chance (1 in 3) of choosing correctly, rather than a 25% chance (1 in 4). Eliminate two incorrect answers and you have a 50% chance of choosing correctly. For example:

EXAMPLE:

an <u>indestructible</u> fortress

    A. fancy.

    B. durable.

    C. poorly-made.

    D. well-made.

The correct answer is B. The first word you see when you look at *indestructible* is probably *destruct*, or maybe *destructible*. Something that is destructible is something that can be broken down or destroyed. Because *in-*, meaning "not," is a negative prefix, you should be looking for a negative word as your answer. By knowing that you're looking for a negative word, you can eliminate choice A, *fancy*. You may have heard the word *indestructible* used in reference to how something is made, so *poorly-made* (choice C) and *well-made* (choice D) may seem like alluring answers. However, consider the information you get from your prefix. If something is NOT destructible, then what is it? This line of thinking should reveal that choice B, durable, is the closest synonym for *indestructible*.

TIP

Make a habit of writing down unfamiliar words, reading them out loud, listening to their pronunciation, and using them in conversation. The more ways you use information (auditorily, visually, etc.), the more places your brain will store it, making it easier to recall when needed.

TIPS FOR ANSWERING ANTONYM QUESTIONS

Antonym questions are like synonym questions in that they test your understanding of words. Antonym questions, however, challenge you to demonstrate your mental flexibility as well as your verbal skills. The task in an antonym question is to define the indicated word and pick its *opposite*. However, in situations where there's no true opposite, you must choose the word or phrase that is most *nearly* opposite. Where there appears to be more than one opposite, you must choose the *best opposite*. You must resist choosing an associated word or phrase that is different in meaning but is not a true opposite. After defining a word, you must choose its *antonym*, not its *synonym*.

TIP

Use the prefix, root, and suffix of unknown words to uncover their meanings. As part of your prep, spend some time studying common Latin and Greek prefixes (*anti-, bi-, ex-*), roots (*dem-, liber-, omni-*), and suffixes (*-able, -cracy, -logy*) to increase your chances of understanding unfamiliar vocabulary.

Let's try an example.

EXAMPLE:

Inaudible means the *opposite* of

    A. invisible.

    B. bright.

    C. loud.

    D. clear.

The correct answer is C. You might not know the meaning of the word *inaudible*, but you may recognize some of the word's parts. You might know that the prefix *in-* typically means "not." You also might recognize a part of audio in the word, and you know that the *audio* of your TV is the sound. You might also see *-able* in *-ible* and thereby reconstruct "not sound-able" or "not heard." Recognizing this should help you see that *invisible* (choice A), meaning "not seen," is not the opposite of *inaudible*, nor is *bright* (choice B). A sound that is difficult could be described as unclear, so *clear* (choice D) may seem like the right answer; however, remember that you are asked to choose the best answer of your options. If something is loud, one would definitely be able to hear it, so choice C, *loud*, most accurately means the opposite of something that can't be heard.

ALERT

Antonym questions require you to choose the opposite of the indicated word. Keep this in mind as you read the possible answers.

This is the point at which your reasoning can easily lead you astray. If you associate the word *inaudible* with the sound coming from your TV, you might think, the opposite of "not heard" is "not seen" or *invisible* (choice A). However, *inaudible* and *invisible* are not true opposites. You might also associate "not heard" with "not seen" and choose *bright* (choice B) as the antonym; however, that too would also be incorrect. If you thought inaudible meant "hard to hear" and choose *clear* (choice D), this would not be a bad answer, but there is a better answer. The word *loud* is the better opposite word choice and is therefore the best answer.

Perhaps you are dealing with a single word that can be used as two different parts of speech and therefore has two entirely unrelated meanings. A *moor* (noun) is a boggy wasteland; to *moor* (verb) is to secure a ship or a boat in place; and the proper noun *Moor* refers to the Muslim conquerors of Spain.

Perhaps the word appears as different parts of speech with numerous meanings and shades of meaning within each of these. *Fancy* (noun) can mean inclination, love, notion, whim, taste, judgment, or imagination. *Fancy* (verb) can mean to like, to imagine, and to think. *Fancy* (adjective) can mean whimsical, ornamental, and extravagant. Your task is to choose one of the four choices that is opposite to one of the meanings of the word *fancy*.

Thankfully, there is a sound approach to handling antonym questions if you're not sure of the correct answer. After carefully reading the word and its four answer choices, run through the following four possibilities:

Possibility #1

You know the meaning of the word, but none of the answer choices seems correct.

- Perhaps you misread the word. Are there other words that look like the word in the question? For example, did you mistake *revelation* for *revaluation* or *compliment* for *complement*?

- Perhaps you read the word correctly but accented the wrong syllable. Some words have alternative pronunciations with vastly different meanings. Consider *DE-sert* and *des-ERT*.

Possibility #2

You do not know the meaning of the word, but it appears to contain prefix, suffix, or root clues. Examine those clues to deduce your answer. For example, the word *adaptable* contains the suffix *-able*, meaning "possessing the ability to," so if you are asked for its antonym, then you are looking for a word that means something like "unable to adapt."

Possibility #3

You do not know the meaning of the word and can see no clues, but you have a feeling that the word has some specific positive or negative connotation. Play your hunch and choose a word with the opposite connotation.

Possibility #4

You are stumped. There is no penalty for guessing on either the TACHS or the HSPT exam, so when all else fails, guess. If you can eliminate one or more of the choices, you improve your odds of guessing correctly. Eliminate choices wherever you can, choose from the remaining options, and move on. There's no need to waste time on a question for which you cannot figure out the answer.

All the previous suggestions can help you use clues to determine the meaning of words and find their synonyms or antonyms. But many questions give no clues at all. The best way to minimize the number of questions that you simply cannot answer is to learn as many vocabulary words as you can.

One way to increase your vocabulary is to work with a dictionary when preparing for your exam. When you run into a word that's unfamiliar, look it up. If you run across a word you don't know while doing the practice exams, circle the word and look it up later. Look up any new words you encounter in the reading passages, among answer choices, in the explanations, and in the chapters themselves. You can also consult Appendix B, which includes an extensive list of words along with their synonyms and antonyms. After defining a new word, write a sentence that creates a strong image. Your

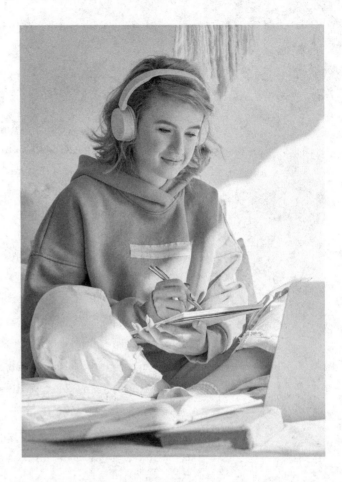

long-term memory excels with visual information, so creating images (especially those that are unique and stand out in your memory) will help you more easily store the word and its meaning for later use.

If you understand every word in this book, you are well on your way to a broad-based vocabulary and should be able to handle not only the synonym and antonym questions but the other verbal questions as well.

Scan this QR code for more information on antonyms.

SUMMING IT UP

- When choosing an answer for a synonym question, if the given word is in a sentence, try substituting the answer choices in the place of the indicated word.

- When the given word is in a sentence, there are several ways to select the best synonym.

- Look for contextual clues to determine which meaning of the word is being used.

- Determine which part of speech the word is, and look for an answer choice of the same part of speech.

- Antonym questions ask you to define the indicated word and choose its opposite—or the word or phrase that is most nearly opposite.

- When you think you know the meaning of the given word but can't find the answer, go back and check the following:

  - Did you misread the word?
  - Did you accent the wrong syllable?
  - Can the word be used as two different parts of speech?
  - Does the word have multiple meanings?

- When you don't know the meaning of a word, try to take the word apart. Look for prefixes, suffixes, and the root word.

- Before guessing, try to eliminate as many answer choices as possible. Consider connotation and the part of speech. If you must guess, eliminate answers that you know are wrong and concentrate on the others.

SYNONYMS
40 Questions—12 Minutes

Directions: For questions 1–20, choose the word that means ame as or about the same as the und lined word.

1. a display of <u>affluence</u>
   A. power
   B. wealth
   C. glibness
   D. junction

2. the <u>gloss</u> of her lips
   A. goblet
   B. shadow
   C. shine
   D. blush

3. a <u>wary</u> neighbor
   A. boastful
   B. cautious
   C. weak
   D. flexible

4. a thrilling <u>encounter</u>
   A. meeting
   B. bar
   C. ledge
   D. spaceship

5. to <u>concede</u> one's guilt
   A. hide
   B. invent
   C. admit
   D. contradict

6. to <u>merge</u> from hiding
   A. bury
   B. come out
   C. jo
   D. slow anger

7. to <u>teem</u> with humanity
   A. abound
   B. play
   C. group
   D. adolescent

8. to <u>permit</u> to attend
   A. discourage
   B. allow
   C. drive
   D. card

9. an <u>indifferent</u> politician
   A. confused
   B. involved
   C. charismatic
   D. neutral

10. a <u>recurrent</u> theme
    A. refined
    B. resultant
    C. electrifying
    D. returning

11. _____ verge of disaster
   A. boat
   B. force
   C. brink
   D. violence

12. to ponder deeply
   A. peruse
   B. think
   C. delay
   D. reveal

13. aspire to succeed
   A. hope
   B. breathe
   C. exhaust
   D. plot

14. an era of apathy
   A. mistake
   B. war
   C. place
   D. age

15. temerity to speak out
   A. fear
   B. nerve
   C. flutter
   D. cowardice

16. a feat of great renown
   A. body part
   B. celebration
   C. big meal
   D. achievement

17. zest for adventure
   A. enthusiasm
   B. fluency
   C. garment
   D. haste

18. a plaintive sound
   A. musical
   B. famous
   C. mournful
   D. patient

19. to view with consternation
   A. dismay
   B. telescope
   C. relief
   D. pretense

20. flagrant disobedience
   A. disguised
   B. glaring
   C. repeated
   D. perfumed

Directions: For questions 21–40, choose the word or phrase that has the same or nearly the same meaning as the underlined word or group of words.

21. The veracity of her story is without doubt.

    A. persistence

    B. truthfulness

    C. poetry

    D. horror

22. The drawings were completely identical.

    A. twin

    B. unclear

    C. breathtaking

    D. alike

23. In our cellar, we accumulate old clothes.

    A. affirm

    B. donate

    C. refurbish

    D. collect

24. This legislation will transform the railroad system.

    A. improve

    B. electrify

    C. change

    D. sell

25. Candy will gratify the child.

    A. satisfy

    B. fatten

    C. excite

    D. teach

26. The arena was girded with ribbons.

    A. protected

    B. established

    C. decorated

    D. encircled

27. How shall we quell the rebellion?

    A. begin

    B. cushion

    C. crush

    D. fire

28. His face looked pale and sickly.

    A. wan

    B. gabled

    C. paltry

    D. ponderous

29. The father was stern and impersonal with his children.

    A. gaudy

    B. gruff

    C. opinionated

    D. endeared

30. The meaning of the text was inscrutable to laymen.

    A. comprehensible

    B. loud

    C. mysterious

    D. enjoyable

31. Let us <u>hoist</u> the banner now.

    A. raise

    B. lower

    C. wave

    D. fold

32. The town took <u>drastic</u> measures to ensure its security.

    A. well-informed

    B. ill-advised

    C. haphazard

    D. extreme

33. The newscaster <u>alluded to</u> the weather forecast.

    A. changed

    B. complained about

    C. praised

    D. referred to

34. The strength of the cord <u>exceeds</u> government standards.

    A. surpasses

    B. equals

    C. challenges

    D. falls short of

35. The <u>austere</u> forest cabin appealed to the pioneers.

    A. simple

    B. sturdy

    C. extravagant

    D. hidden

36. I wish that you would stop <u>beating around the bush</u>.

    A. running in circles

    B. avoiding the subject

    C. cleaning up the dirt

    D. repeating the same thing over and over

37. I generally accept Jim's pronouncements with <u>a grain of salt</u>.

    A. some question

    B. criticism

    C. pleasure

    D. relief

38. That explanation is little more than <u>an old wives' tale</u>.

    A. a deliberate falsehood

    B. a half-truth

    C. feminist propaganda

    D. folklore

39. The medicine man shared his <u>tried and true</u> remedy with me.

    A. new and unusual

    B. tested and proven

    C. experimental

    D. unorthodox but effective

40. You should not <u>look a gift horse in the mouth</u>.

    A. question authority

    B. quibble over details

    C. expose yourself to danger

    D. be grateful for good fortune

ANTONYMS
30 Questions—19 Minutes

Directions: Choose the best answer.

1. Accelerate means the *opposite* of
   A. stop.
   B. slow.
   C. quicken.
   D. hasten.

2. Docile means the *opposite* of
   A. active.
   B. health.
   C. probable.
   D. teachable.

3. Candor means the *opposite* of
   A. frankness.
   B. doubt.
   C. deception.
   D. enthusiasm.

4. Nomadic means the *opposite* of
   A. secret.
   B. anonymous.
   C. stationary.
   D. famous.

5. Heed means the *opposite* of
   A. agree.
   B. ignore.
   C. listen.
   D. analyze.

6. Defy means the *opposite* of
   A. desire.
   B. embrace.
   C. fight.
   D. abscond.

7. Gorge means the *opposite* of
   A. duck.
   B. diet.
   C. stuff.
   D. valley.

8. Curtail means the *opposite* of
   A. curry.
   B. open.
   C. shorten.
   D. extend.

9. Initiate means the *opposite* of
   A. instruct.
   B. begin.
   C. terminate.
   D. invade.

10. Craven means the *opposite* of
    A. brave.
    B. greedy.
    C. hungry.
    D. nervous.

11. Clamor means the *opposite* of

    A. ugliness.

    B. beauty.

    C. silence.

    D. dishonor.

12. Rouse means the *opposite* of

    A. lull.

    B. alarm.

    C. complain.

    D. weep.

13. Credible means the *opposite* of

    A. believable.

    B. unbelievable.

    C. honorable.

    D. dishonorable.

14. Thorough means the *opposite* of

    A. around.

    B. circumvented.

    C. incomplete.

    D. inside.

15. Wooden means the *opposite* of

    A. iron.

    B. slippery.

    C. rubbery.

    D. green.

16. Succumb means the *opposite* of

    A. arrive.

    B. yield.

    C. eat.

    D. conquer.

17. Divert means the *opposite* of

    A. instruct.

    B. include.

    C. bore.

    D. amuse.

18. Admonish means the *opposite* of

    A. review.

    B. scare.

    C. praise.

    D. tease.

19. Diminish means the *opposite* of

    A. lessen.

    B. begin.

    C. complete.

    D. expand.

20. Brazen means the *opposite* of

    A. frozen.

    B. meek.

    C. rustproof.

    D. leaky.

21. Intent means the *opposite* of

    A. alfresco.

    B. busy.

    C. uninterested.

    D. shy.

22. Erode means the *opposite* of

    A. weaken.

    B. restore.

    C. combat.

    D. color.

23. Lavish means the *opposite* of

   A. filthy.

   B. elegant.

   C. squander.

   D. conserve.

24. Aloof means the *opposite* of

   A. sociable.

   B. humble.

   C. public.

   D. ignorant.

25. Elated means the *opposite* of

   A. on time.

   B. tardy.

   C. ideal.

   D. depressed.

26. Furnish means the *opposite* of

   A. dress.

   B. decorate.

   C. remove.

   D. polish.

27. Ostracize means the *opposite* of

   A. include.

   B. shun.

   C. hide.

   D. delight.

28. Exorbitant means the *opposite* of

   A. priceless.

   B. worthless.

   C. reasonable.

   D. straight.

29. Chastise means the *opposite* of

   A. dirty.

   B. cleanse.

   C. praise.

   D. straighten.

30. Profit means the *opposite* of

   A. gain.

   B. money.

   C. suffer.

   D. disgust.

ANSWER KEYS AND EXPLANATIONS

Synonyms

1.	B	9.	D	17.	A	25.	A	33.	D
2.	C	10.	D	18.	C	26.	D	34.	A
3.	B	11.	C	19.	A	27.	C	35.	A
4.	A	12.	B	20.	B	28.	A	36.	B
5.	C	13.	A	21.	B	29.	B	37.	A
6.	B	14.	D	22.	D	30.	C	38.	D
7.	A	15.	B	23.	D	31.	A	39.	B
8.	B	16.	D	24.	C	32.	D	40.	D

1. **The correct answer is B.** *Affluence* is a synonym for *wealth*. *Influence* is a synonym for *power* (choice A). *Glibness* (choice C) means being talkative in a smooth, somewhat insincere way. *Confluence* is a synonym for *junction* (choice D).

2. **The correct answer is C.** *Gloss* is brightness, polish, or shine.

3. **The correct answer is B.** To be *wary* means to be cautious or careful, particularly in dangerous situations.

4. **The correct answer is A.** An *encounter* is a face-to-face meeting.

5. **The correct answer is C.** To *concede* is to admit or to acknowledge.

6. **The correct answer is B.** To *emerge* is to come out. The word *emerge* is almost opposite to the word *merge*, which means "join."

7. **The correct answer is A.** To *teem* is to abound or to overflow. If you selected *group* (choice C), you might have been thinking about the homonym *team*. *Adolescent* (choice D) is incorrect because the word is *teem*, not *teen*.

8. **The correct answer is B.** The word *permit*, pronounced *per-MIT*, means allow. If the word were pronounced *PER-mit*, it would mean license (which is not offered as a choice), but in no event would it mean "discourage," "drive," or "card."

9. **The correct answer is D.** To be *indifferent* is to be neutral or disinterested in something.

10. **The correct answer is D.** That which is *recurrent* returns from time to time.

11. **The correct answer is C.** *Verge* means "brink or threshold."

12. **The correct answer is B.** To *ponder* is to think or to consider. *Peruse* (choice A) means "to read."

13. **The correct answer is A.** To *aspire* is to hope or to desire. To breathe is to respire.

14. **The correct answer is D.** An *era* is an age or period. Read carefully to avoid careless mistakes such as reading *err* or *area* and incorrectly selecting *mistake* (choice A) or *place* (choice C).

15. **The correct answer is B.** *Temerity* is audacity or nerve. *Timorousness* is timidity, fear, or cowardice.

16. **The correct answer is D.** A *feat* is an achievement. Beware of homonyms (words that sound the same) when choosing synonyms (words that mean the same).

17. **The correct answer is A.** *Zest* means "relish," "gusto," or "enthusiasm."

18. **The correct answer is C.** *Plaintive* means "mournful" or "melancholy."

19. **The correct answer is A.** *Consternation* is amazement or dismay that throws one into confusion.

10

20. **The correct answer is B.** *Flagrant* means glaring or conspicuously objectionable. The word meaning "perfumed" (choice D) is *fragrant*.

21. **The correct answer is B.** *Veracity* is truthfulness or accuracy. *Persistence* (choice A) would be a synonym for *tenacity*.

22. **The correct answer is D.** *Identical* means "same," "alike," or "exactly alike." Identical twins are genetically the same, but *twin* (choice A) is not a synonym for *identical*.

23. **The correct answer is D.** To *accumulate* is to collect or to amass.

24. **The correct answer is C.** To *transform* means "to change."

25. **The correct answer is A.** To *gratify* is to indulge, to please, or to satisfy.

26. **The correct answer is D.** *Girded* means "encircled."

27. **The correct answer is C.** To *quell* is to put down, to suppress, or to crush.

28. **The correct answer is A.** *Wan* means "pale, sickly, or feeble."

29. **The correct answer is B.** *Gruff* means "rough or stern."

30. **The correct answer is C.** Something that is *inscrutable* is mysterious or not easy to interpret.

31. **The correct answer is A.** To *hoist* is to raise or to lift.

32. **The correct answer is D.** *Drastic* means "extreme or severe."

33. **The correct answer is D.** To *allude* is to make indirect reference or to refer.

34. **The correct answer is A.** To *exceed* is to surpass.

35. **The correct answer is A.** Something that is *austere* is simple and not fancy in appearance and character.

36. **The correct answer is B.** *Beating around the bush* is talking about irrelevant topics or raising side issues to avoid addressing important issues in a given scenario.

37. **The correct answer is A.** When one takes something with *a grain of salt*, one does not accept it at face value but questions details, motives, or conclusions.

38. **The correct answer is D.** *An old wives' tale* is a story or explanation that has been handed down "from woman to woman" as an oral tradition until it becomes folklore.

39. **The correct answer is B.** *Tried and true* means "tested and proven."

40. **The correct answer is D.** This phrase conveys that one should accept a gift as a gift without questioning its value (checking the quality of its teeth). In other words, be grateful for your good fortune.

NOTES

Antonyms

1. B	7. B	13. B	19. D	25. D
2. A	8. D	14. C	20. B	26. C
3. C	9. C	15. C	21. C	27. A
4. C	10. A	16. D	22. B	28. C
5. B	11. C	17. C	23. D	29. C
6. B	12. A	18. C	24. A	30. C

1. **The correct answer is B.** To accelerate is to quicken or to hasten. Its best opposite is *slow*. *Accelerate* implies that the object was already in motion. *Stop* would be the opposite if the original word had meant "to put into motion" and not "to increase speed."

2. **The correct answer is A.** *Docile* means "calm and easily led." Of the choices offered, its best opposite is *active*.

3. **The correct answer is C.** *Candor* is frankness; its opposite is *deception*.

4. **The correct answer is C.** *Nomadic* means "wandering;" its opposite is *stationary, which means "staying in one place."* The other words have nothing to do with movement or lack of movement.

5. **The correct answer is B.** To heed means "to pay close attention to something." To ignore something is the opposite.

6. **The correct answer is B.** To defy is to challenge, and its opposite is *embrace*. In this case, *embrace* means "to accept." When reviewing answer options, try to think of all possible meanings for each word choice.

7. **The correct answer is B.** To gorge oneself is to overeat; the opposite is to diet. You could be forgiven for interpreting *gorge* as a landscape feature similar to a canyon, and therefore selecting *valley* as its opposite. However, if interpreted as a gorge in a landscape, the word *valley* would be closer to a synonym.

8. **The correct answer is D.** To curtail is to shorten; the opposite is to extend.

9. **The correct answer is C.** To initiate is to begin; its opposite is to end or to terminate.

10. **The correct answer is A.** *Craven* means "fearful" or "having a lack of courage." Being brave is the direct opposite of this.

11. **The correct answer is C.** *Clamor* is noise; its opposite is *silence*. You must read carefully. *Clamor* is not *glamour*.

12. **The correct answer is A.** To rouse is to awaken; to lull is to soothe and cause to sleep.

13. **The correct answer is B.** *Credible* means "believable;" its opposite is *unbelievable*. *Honorable* and *dishonorable* are choices designed to mislead you, under the assumption you will confuse *credible* with *creditable*. If you spot that connection, you can eliminate those choices, giving you a better chance of selecting the correct answer.

14. **The correct answer is C.** One meaning of *thorough* is to cover everything or all the important points; its opposite would be *incomplete*. *Circumvented* also implies lack of thoroughness but is not so clearly the opposite of *thorough*.

15. **The correct answer is C.** *Wooden* means "stiff and unbending"; its opposite, *rubbery*, means "flexible."

16. **The correct answer is D.** To succumb is to yield or to give in; the opposite is to conquer.

17. **The correct answer is C.** To divert is to amuse (think *diversion*); the opposite is to bore. To divert also means "to change the direction of," but no opposite to this meaning is offered.

18. **The correct answer is C.** To admonish means to criticize or reprimand; the opposite is to praise.

19. **The correct answer is D.** To diminish is to lessen. Therefore, the opposite is to expand. As with most antonym questions, one of the choices means the same (or nearly the same) as the word in question, in this case, *lessen* (choice A). This allows you to quickly eliminate at least one answer option.

20. **The correct answer is B.** *Brazen* means "bold or impudent"; its opposite is *meek*.

21. **The correct answer is C.** To be intent is to be engrossed or determined (think *intense*); the opposite is to be uninterested.

22. **The correct answer is B.** To *erode* means "to whither or wear away," often gradually over time. The opposite of this is to *restore*, meaning "to bring back to pristine condition."

23. **The correct answer is D.** To lavish is to spend profusely or to squander; the opposite is to conserve.

24. **The correct answer is A.** One who is aloof is distant or reserved; an opposite type of person is sociable. *Humble* (choice B) is tempting, but it is a better antonym for *arrogant*. The word *aloof* does not involve snobbery or arrogance, but rather a distant or nonsocial attitude, making *sociable* the best choice for an opposite.

25. **The correct answer is D.** *Elated* means "joyful" and "jubilant"; the opposite is *depressed*. Note that answer choices A and B are there to mislead you in case you mistakenly associate *elated* with lateness, rather than its actual meaning.

26. **The correct answer is C.** To furnish is to provide; its opposite is to remove.

27. **The correct answer is A.** To ostracize is to shut out or to exclude; the opposite is to include.

28. **The correct answer is C.** *Exorbitant* means "excessive"; its opposite is *reasonable*.

29. **The correct answer is C.** To chastise is to scold; the opposite is to praise.

30. **The correct answer is C.** To profit is to benefit; the opposite is to suffer.

NOTES

CHAPTER

Analogies

ANALOGIES

OVERVIEW

Types of Analogies

Tips for Answering Analogy Questions

Summing It Up

Knowledge Check: Analogies

Answer Key and Explanations

Verbal analogy questions on the HSPT will test your ability to see relationships between words and apply those relationships accordingly. It is a test of your ability to think things through clearly and logically.

Depending on the exam, verbal analogy questions might be presented in several different ways. On the HSPT exam, you are given two example words that are related to each other in a certain way. Then, you are given a third word and four answer choices to create a second word pair. Of the given answer choices, only one best expresses a relationship to the third word that is similar to that expressed between the first pair.

To answer the question, you need to look at the relationship of the paired words and apply it to the third word and the answer options. Consider the following example:

TACHS   HSPT   ISEE   SSAT   SHSAT

EXAMPLE:

Deer is to fawn as goat is to

A. chick.

B. sheep.

C. pup.

D. kid.

The correct answer is D. The word *deer* represents an adult stage of a *fawn*. To complete the analogy with *goat* as the first word, we need a term denoting a younger version of the animal in question: The word *kid* refers to a young goat.

Regardless of the form an analogy takes, the task is always the same: Define the relationships between words and then apply those relationships to a different set of words.

TYPES OF ANALOGIES

The Verbal Analogies subtest will depict a variety of relationships with its word pairs. The following table illustrates common types of relationships:

RELATIONSHIP	EXAMPLE
synonyms	ask : inquire
antonyms	long : short
homonyms	mail : male
location	Phoenix : Arizona
creator : creation	artist : painting
female : male	cow : bull
larger : smaller	lake : pond

RELATIONSHIP	EXAMPLE
noun : adjective	texture : coarse
cause : effect	negligence : accident
whole : part	chapter : paragraph
object : purpose or function	keyboard : type
object : user	camera : photographer
early stage : later stage	infant : adult
general : specific	vegetable : broccoli
more : less (degree)	arid : dry
verb : adjective	expand : large
measurement (e.g., time, distance, weight)	distance : mile
raw material : finished product	wood : bench
verb tense : verb tense	run : ran
singular noun : plural noun	child : children
subject pronoun : object pronoun	he : they
first-person pronoun : third-person pronoun	she : her
first-person pronoun : third-person pronoun	we : they
adjective : comparative adjective	good : better
adjective : superlative adjective	bad : worst

We've provided descriptions and sample questions for some of the most common analogy relationships: synonym/definition, antonyms, function/relationship, classification, and part-to-whole.

Synonym/Definition

Synonym analogies select words with the same or similar meanings. For example, *happy* and *glad* have the same meaning. The following synonym questions are similar to what you will see on your exam:

1. Interesting is to compelling as frightening is to
   A. scary.
   B. fear.
   C. monster.
   D. charming.

The correct answer is A. *Interesting* and *compelling* are synonyms, so we need a synonym for *frightening*. *Scary* is a synonym for *frightening*.

2. Enormous is to huge as muddy is to
   A. cavernous.
   B. clean.
   C. unclear.
   D. rocky.

The correct answer is C. Something that is *muddy* is clouded or *unclear*.

3. Cradle is to crib as car is to
   A. airplane.
   B. automobile.
   C. stroller.
   D. bed.

The correct answer is B. A *cradle* and a *crib* are synonyms for places a baby sleeps. The words *car* and *automobile* are also synonyms.

Antonyms

Antonyms are words that are opposite in meaning to the given word. For example, *cold* is the antonym for *hot*. The following antonym questions are similar to what you will see on your exam:

EXAMPLES:

1. Subtle is to overt as slow is to
   A. fast.
   B. quiet.
   C. sharp.
   D. bright.

The correct answer is A.
The opposite of *slow* is *fast*.

2. Long is to short as wide is to
   A. tall.
   B. large.
   C. small.
   D. narrow.

The correct answer is D. *Short* is the opposite of *long*, just as *wide* is the opposite of *narrow*.

3. Order is to chaos as discipline is to
   A. lawful.
   B. anarchy.
   C. fervor.
   D. containment.

The correct answer is B. *Chaos* is the opposite of *order*, just as *anarchy* is the opposite of *discipline*.

Classification and Function

Classification and function analogy questions will require you to create analogies that express that terms are of a similar type, overlap in category, or share a functional relationship—either those that fulfill the same function or express a specific function. The following questions are similar to what you will encounter on your exam:

EXAMPLES:

1. Canoe is to sailboat as manual is to
   A. flyer.
   B. play.
   C. textbook.
   D. story.

   The correct answer is C. A *canoe* and a *sailboat* are both watercrafts used for transportation, just as a *manual* and a *textbook* are both types of instructional books.

2. Candle is to flame as camera is to
   A. photo.
   B. portable.
   C. phone.
   D. flash.

   The correct answer is A. A *candle* produces a *flame* just as a *camera* produces a *photo*.

3. Rose is to tulip as silver is to
   A. metallic.
   B. ring.
   C. wood.
   D. gold.

   The correct answer is D. A *rose* and a *tulip* are both types of flowers, just as *silver* and *gold* are both types of metal.

4. Ceiling is to wall as television is to
   A. telephone.
   B. paper.
   C. monitor.
   D. floor.

   The correct answer is C. A *ceiling* and a *wall* are both used to support a building's structure. A *television* and a *monitor* are both devices used for viewing.

5. Argon is to gas as duck is to
   A. swan.
   B. avoid.
   C. shirk.
   D. bird.

   The correct answer is D. *Argon* is a type of *gas*, just as a *duck* is a type of *bird*.

6. Hospital is to clinic as doctor is to
   A. degree.
   B. medic.
   C. prescription.
   D. clerk.

   The correct answer is B. A *hospital* and a *clinic* are both medical facilities of greater and lesser degrees, just as a *doctor* and a *medic* are medical professionals of greater or lesser certification.

To learn more about analogies, scan this QR code.

Part-Whole

Part-Whole analogies (expressing either part-to-whole or whole-to-part relationships) compare a part of something to a whole or vice versa. The following part-whole questions are similar to what you will see on the actual exam:

1. Book is to page as clock is to

   A. time.

   B. watch.

   C. tower.

   D. hand.

   The correct answer is D. A *page* is part of a *book*, just as a *hand* is part of a *clock*.

2. Line is to sketch as finger is to

   A. hand.

   B. knuckle.

   C. digit.

   D. glove.

   The correct answer is A. A *line* is one part of a whole *sketch*. A *finger* is a part of a *hand*.

3. Los Angeles is to California as Houston is to

   A. Dallas.

   B. Hollywood.

   C. city.

   D. Texas.

   The correct answer is D. *Los Angeles* is a city in *California*, and *Houston* is a city in *Texas*.

TIPS FOR ANSWERING ANALOGY QUESTIONS

Here, we'll outline a few steps for how to answer an analogy question:

Step 1: The first step in tackling an analogy question is to define the first set of words. Most often, you will know the meanings of both words, but if you're not sure, make a guess and move on to the next step.

Step 2: Your next step will be to determine how those two words are related. Recall the different types of analogies we covered earlier in this chapter. As you look at the first two words in the analogy, it's important to get a clear understanding of how exactly the two words are related so that you know how to complete the pattern.

Step 3: Now, use process of elimination to arrive at the best answer. Look at the third word in the analogy question and the four answer choices available. Start by crossing off the answers that you know are incorrect. Ideally, you will find a word that has the same relationship to the third word that the first set has.

Step 4: If you have narrowed down the answers to two choices but can't decide which word best completes the analogy, then it's time to revisit the first pair of words and refine the relationship. Perhaps you initially believed the relationship was one of association, but upon closer inspection, you might realize that it is a cause-and-effect relationship.

Step 5: If you have refined the relationship further, then re-examine the answer choices. Now that you have a better understanding of the analogy, this might mean revisiting answer choices you initially eliminated as incorrect. Look for the answer that would best complete the relationship you've identified. If you're unsure but you've narrowed it down to two choices, consider guessing. However, depending on which exam you're taking, you may or may not be penalized for incorrect answers. If you are penalized for incorrect answers, then only guess if you are confident that one answer choice stands out as the best fit for the analogy. Otherwise, consider leaving the answer blank.

The process of answering an analogy question consists of the following five steps:

1 Define the initial terms.

2 Describe the initial relationship.

3 Eliminate incorrect answers.

4 Refine the initial relationship, if necessary.

5 Choose the best of the remaining answer choices.

Defining Relationships to Eliminate Incorrect answers

Let's look at how we can use the first and second steps to eliminate incorrect answer options. Remember, you should define the words first. Then, determine the relationship between them. As you undertake the second step, recall some of the analogies we covered earlier in this chapter. See if one relationship best describes the first pair of words in the analogy.

Let's continue with the *brim* is to hat example to illustrate this process.

> **EXAMPLE:**
>
> Brim is to hat as hand is to
>
> **A.** glove.
>
> **B.** finger.
>
> **C.** foot.
>
> **D.** arm.

The correct answer is D. *Hand* is certainly associated with *glove* (choice A), but in no way is a hand part of a glove. *Hand* and *finger*

(choice B) are certainly associated, and a *finger* is part of a *hand*. However, exercise caution here. Look again at the relationship of the first two words: *Brim* is a part of *hat*, or in other words, *hat* is the whole of which *brim* is a part. The relationship in choice B is the reverse of the relationship of the first two words. *Hand* is the whole and *finger* is the part. Your answer must maintain the same relationship in the same sequence as the original pair.

The relationship of *hand* and *foot* (choice C) is only one of association, not of part to whole. This answer is no more likely to be correct than choice A. In fact, because you have found two answers that have equal chances of being incorrect, you now know that neither of them is the answer you are looking for. There must be a best answer.

A *hand* is part of an *arm* in the same way that a *brim* is part of a *hat*. In other words, the *arm* is the whole of which a *hand* is a part in the same way that *hat* is the whole of which a *brim* is the part. Once you've spotted this, you're able to determine that *arm* is the best answer.

Identifying Parts of Speech to Determine Relationships

Earlier in this chapter, we included a table to summarize the relationships commonly used in analogy questions along with corresponding examples. For some analogy questions, your ability to determine (step 1) or refine (step 4) the relationship depends on your knowledge of parts of speech. Earlier in this book, we covered the different parts of speech, but knowing them will come in handy on multiple sections of the exam. For example, you may encounter an analogy with a noun and a corresponding adjective, like *sponge* and *absorbent* or *planet* and *round*. Some relationships will only consist of one part of speech, like object and user, which will both be nouns. Other relationships might contain an implied part of speech, like part-to-whole analogies, which will likely comprise pairs of nouns.

Let's look at a few examples where identifying parts of speech can help to determine or refine the relationship and arrive at the correct answer.

EXAMPLES:

1. Choose is to select as think is to
   A. contemplate.
   B. disagree.
   C. thought.
   D. careful.

The correct answer is A. These words will likely be familiar to you. The analogy presents a pair of verbs (*choose* and *select*) that are synonyms followed by another verb, *think*. This gives us direction when we go through the process of eliminating incorrect answers: While *thought* (choice C) can be both a noun and the past tense of *think*, it is not a synonym of *think*. *Contemplate* is both a verb and a synonym for *think*.

2. Goose is to geese as ox is to
   A. cow.
   B. oxen.
   C. elk.
   D. horns.

The correct answer is B. In this example, the correct answer should be a plural noun, since *goose* is the singular noun and *geese* is the plural form. *Ox* is a singular noun, and its irregular plural form is *oxen*.

3. Rabbit is to soft as cactus is to
   A. cacti.
   B. prickly.
   C. desert.
   D. green.

The correct answer is B. *Rabbit* is a noun and *soft* is an adjective, so the correct answer must be an adjective that corresponds to the noun *cactus*. That leaves us with two options: *prickly* or *green*. Since the original analogy involves an adjective that describes the texture or feel of a rabbit, we would select the option that describes the texture or feel of a cactus. The best answer that completes the analogy is *prickly*.

 TIP

If multiple answer choices seem correct, try to refine the initial relationship (step 4). This can help you eliminate incorrect answers and choose the word that fits best.

Using Parts of Speech to Refine the Relationship

Sometimes, you might be confronted with multiple answer choices that could each be correct. In this scenario, it likely means that your initial understanding of the analogy was too broad. To narrow your options further, you'll need to go back and refine the relationship between the first two words. Let's walk through an example of this scenario.

Consider an analogy that begins "letter is to word." Initially, you will probably think, "A letter is part of a word; therefore, the relationship is that of part-to-whole." If the relationship of the third word to any of the choices is also part-to-whole, then all is well. However, suppose the question looks like this

EXAMPLE:

Letter is to word as song is to

A. story.

B. music.

C. note.

D. orchestra.

The correct answer is C. Three choices offer an association relationship; however, you should attempt to refine your understanding of the relationship to be as specific as possible. No choice offers a whole of which a song might be a part (such as an opera). Therefore, you must return to the original pair of words and consider other relationships between *letter* and *word*. If *letter* refers to "written communication," rather than "letter of the alphabet," then a *word* is part of a *letter* and the relationship of the first to the second is the whole to a part. Then, the answer becomes clear: A *song* is the whole of which *note* is the part. The relationship of *song* and *note* is the same as that of *letter* and *word*.

TIP

Turn the analogy pairs into sentences to help see the connection. Then, fit the answer pairs into the same sentence until you find the one that works best.

Common Pitfalls in Answering Analogy Questions

Analogy questions also present many opportunities for error. Here are some of the most common pitfalls to avoid:

- **Reversal of sequence of the relationship:**
  - Part to whole is *not* the same as whole-to-part.
  - Cause-and-effect is *not* the same as effect to its cause.
  - Smaller to larger is *not* the same as larger to smaller.
  - Action to object is *not* the same as object to action.

- **Confusion of relationship:**
  - Part-to-part (*geometry* to *calculus*) with part-to-whole (*algebra* to *mathematics*)
  - Cause-and-effect (*fire* to *smoke*) with association (*hurricane* to *typhoon*)
  - Degree (*drizzle* to *downpour*) with antonyms (*dry* to *wet*)
  - Association (*walk* to *limp*) with synonyms (*eat* to *consume*)

- **Grammatical inconsistency:** The grammatical relationship of the first two words must be retained throughout the analogy. A wrong analogy would be *imprisoned* is to *convict* as *cage* is to *parrot*. While the meaningful relationship exists, the analogy is not parallel in construction. A correct analogy of this sort would have to read *prison* is to *convict* as *cage* is to *parrot*, or *imprisoned* is to *convict* as *caged* is to *parrot*. In analogy questions, you must create a pair that is grammatically consistent with the first pair, as well as being correct in definition and meaning.

- **Concentration on the meanings of words instead of on their relationships:** In this type of error, you see *gear* to *transmission*, and you think of *car* as the common relationship instead of spotting the part-to-part relationship; gears are part of the transmission. When looking for an analogy for the word *piston*, and the list of answers includes *car* and *engine*, you might pick *car* when the better answer is *engine*.

Remember: The key to answering analogy questions lies in the relationship between the first two words.

If you struggle with finding the relationship between the words of the initial pair, you might find it useful to mentally reverse their order. If this works, remember to mentally reverse the order of the third and fourth terms as well to maintain the relationship in your answer.

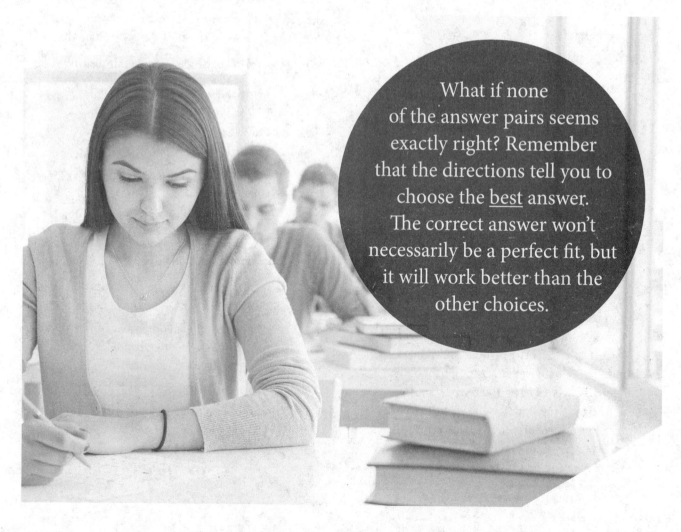

What if none of the answer pairs seems exactly right? Remember that the directions tell you to choose the <u>best</u> answer. The correct answer won't necessarily be a perfect fit, but it will work better than the other choices.

SUMMING IT UP

- Analogies are a test of your ability to identify logical relationships between words.
- Study and learn the different types of analogy questions, with an emphasis on the following analogies: synonym/definition, antonym, classification and function, and part-to-whole.
- Follow the steps: define the initial terms, describe the initial relationship, eliminate incorrect answers, refine the initial relationship, and choose the best answer.
- Take note of common pitfalls in answering analogy questions:
  - Maintain the sequence of the original pair of words.
  - Avoid misidentifying similar types of relationships between words (e.g., cause-and-effect vs. association).
  - Maintain grammatical consistency across the pairs of words.
  - Focus on the relationship between words instead of their individual meanings.

KNOWLEDGE CHECK

ANALOGIES
30 Questions—9 Minutes

Directions: In the following questions, the first two words are related to each other in a certain way. The third and fourth words must be related to each other in the same way. Choose a word from among the four choices that is related to the third word in the same way that the second word is related to the first.

1. Gasoline is to petroleum as sugar is to
   A. sweet.
   B. oil.
   C. plant.
   D. cane.

2. Fly is to spider as mouse is to
   A. cat.
   B. rat.
   C. rodent.
   D. trap.

3. Volcano is to crater as chimney is to
   A. smoke.
   B. fire.
   C. flue.
   D. stack.

4. Petal is to flower as fur is to
   A. coat.
   B. rabbit.
   C. warm.
   D. hairy.

5. Retreat is to advance as timid is to
   A. bold.
   B. cowardly.
   C. fearful.
   D. shy.

6. Ledger is to accounts as journal is to
   A. pen.
   B. territory.
   C. book.
   D. observations.

7. Picture is to see as speech is to
   A. view.
   B. enunciate.
   C. hear.
   D. soliloquize.

8. Soprano is to high as bass is to
   A. guitar.
   B. bad.
   C. low.
   D. fish.

9. Addition is to addend as subtraction is to

   A. difference.

   B. sum.

   C. subtrahend.

   D. minus.

10. Famine is to hunger as drought is to

    A. thirst.

    B. water.

    C. starvation.

    D. desert.

11. Acute is to chronic as temporary is to

    A. persistent.

    B. sick.

    C. pretty.

    D. narrow.

12. Sleeves are to shirt as legs are to

    A. shoes.

    B. slacks.

    C. hats.

    D. closets.

13. Chariot is to charioteer as automobile is to

    A. passenger.

    B. engine.

    C. motor.

    D. driver.

14. Team is to league as player is to

    A. piano.

    B. team.

    C. tournament.

    D. football.

15. Honor is to citation as speeding is to

    A. citation.

    B. hurry.

    C. race.

    D. stop.

16. Stethoscope is to doctor as hose is to

    A. water.

    B. firefighter.

    C. firetruck.

    D. hydrant.

17. *Hamlet* is to Shakespeare as telephone is to

    A. Bell.

    B. telegraph.

    C. smartphone.

    D. talk.

18. Distracting is to noise as soothing is to

    A. medicine.

    B. music.

    C. volume.

    D. bleeding.

19. Year is to calendar as hour is to

    A. decade.

    B. minute.

    C. clock.

    D. month.

20. Superior is to inferior as skilled is to

    A. technical.

    B. unskilled.

    C. exterior.

    D. informed.

21. Words are to books as notes are to

    A. songs.
    B. letters.
    C. pianos.
    D. fragrances.

22. Pungent is to odor as shrill is to

    A. whisper.
    B. sound.
    C. piercing.
    D. shriek.

23. Present is to birthday as reward is to

    A. accomplishment.
    B. medal.
    C. punishment.
    D. money.

24. Mouse is to mammal as lizard is to

    A. fish.
    B. scale.
    C. camouflage.
    D. reptile.

25. Sky is to ground as ceiling is to

    A. floor.
    B. roof.
    C. top.
    D. plaster.

26. Food is to nutrition as light is to

    A. watt.
    B. bulb.
    C. electricity.
    D. vision.

27. Actor is to play as musician is to

    A. guitarist.
    B. performer.
    C. instrument.
    D. concert.

28. Square is to triangle as cube is to

    A. circle.
    B. line.
    C. ball.
    D. pyramid.

29. Abacus is to calculator as propeller is to

    A. jet.
    B. airplane.
    C. mathematics.
    D. flight.

30. Dizziness is to vertigo as fate is to

    A. adversity.
    B. order.
    C. destiny.
    D. pride.

11

ANSWER KEY AND EXPLANATIONS

1. D	6. D	11. A	16. B	21. A	26. D
2. A	7. C	12. B	17. A	22. B	27. D
3. C	8. C	13. D	18. B	23. A	28. D
4. B	9. C	14. B	19. C	24. D	29. A
5. A	10. A	15. A	20. B	25. A	30. C

1. **The correct answer is D.** The relationship is that of the product to its source. *Gasoline* comes from *petroleum*; *sugar* comes from *cane*. Although you could argue that sugar also comes from a plant, cane is a more direct and specific relationship, much like the relationship between gasoline and petroleum.

2. **The correct answer is A.** The relationship is that of the eaten to the eater. The *fly* is eaten by the *spider*; the *mouse* is eaten by the *cat*. Refine this analogy to eating in order to solve it. If you were to consider only catching, then you would not be able to distinguish between the cat and the trap.

3. **The correct answer is C.** The relationship is functional. The *crater* contains the vent(s) for a *volcano*; the *flue* is the vent for a *chimney*.

4. **The correct answer is B.** The relationship is that of part-to-whole. A *petal* is part of a *flower*; *fur* is part of a *rabbit*. *Fur* might be part of a *coat*, but it is not a necessary part, so *rabbit* makes a better analogy.

5. **The correct answer is A.** The relationship is that of antonyms. *Retreat* is the opposite of *advance*; *timid* is the opposite of *bold*.

6. **The correct answer is D.** This analogy involves a functional relationship. A *ledger* stores and maintains accounts for *businesses*. A *journal* stores and maintains observations for *individuals*.

7. **The correct answer is C.** This is another variety of object-to-action relationship. You *see* a *picture*; you *hear* a *speech*.

8. **The correct answer is C.** The relationship is that of synonyms or definition. A *soprano* voice is *high*; a *bass* voice is *low*. While *bass* has multiple meanings, you must define the word in context of the relationship among the first two words.

9. **The correct answer is C.** The relationship is that of the whole to a part. The *addend* is one term of an *addition* problem; the *subtrahend* is one term of a *subtraction* problem.

10. **The correct answer is A.** This is a cause-and-effect relationship: *Famine* causes *hunger*, and *drought* causes *thirst*.

11. **The correct answer is A.** The relationship is that of antonyms. *Acute* means sudden and short; *chronic* means always present. *Temporary* is the opposite of *persistent*.

12. **The correct answer is B.** This is a part-to-whole relationship—*sleeves* are a part of a *shirt*. *Legs*, therefore, must be a part of the correct answer. Review the answer choices: *legs* are a part of *slacks*, which completes the analogy.

13. **The correct answer is D.** The relationship is that of object and actor. The *charioteer* drives the *chariot*; the *driver* drives the *automobile*. You must consider the action in this analogy in order to differentiate between *driver* and *passenger*.

14. **The correct answer is B.** The relationship is that of the part to the whole. The *team* is part of the *league*; the *player* is part of the *team*.

15. **The correct answer is A.** This analogy is probably more difficult than any you you might encounter on the exam. The trick lies in the fact that *citation* has two distinct meanings. The relationship is that of cause-to-effect. When you are to be *honored*, you receive a *citation*, which is a formal document

describing your achievements. When you are stopped for *speeding*, you receive a *citation*, which is an official summons to appear in court.

16. **The correct answer is B.** The relationship is that of an object to its user. A *stethoscope* is used by a *doctor* and a *hose* is used by a *firefighter*.

17. **The correct answer is A.** This is a creation-creator relationship. *Shakespeare* is the creator (author) of *Hamlet*; the *telephone* is an invention of Alexander Graham *Bell*.

18. **The correct answer is B.** The relationship is that of effect to its cause. *Noise* is *distracting*; *music* is *soothing*.

19. **The correct answer is C.** This is a functional relationship. *Years* are measured on a *calendar*; *hours* are measured on a *clock*.

20. **The correct answer is B.** The relationship is one of antonyms. *Superior* is the opposite of *inferior*, and *skilled* is the opposite of *unskilled*.

21. **The correct answer is A.** This is a part-whole relationship. *Words* are parts of *books*; *notes* are parts of *songs*.

22. **The correct answer is B.** The relationship is that of an adjective to the noun it modifies. An *odor* may be described as *pungent*, though there are many other adjectives you could use. A sound may be described as *shrill*, though certainly not all sounds are shrill. *Shriek* is not the best answer because it is is always a *shrill* sound.

23. **The correct answer is A.** This is a purpose relationship. The purpose of a *present* is to celebrate a *birthday*; the purpose of a *reward* is to celebrate an *accomplishment*.

24. **The correct answer is D.** The relationship is one of classification. A *mouse* is a *mammal*; a *lizard* is a *reptile*.

25. **The correct answer is A.** The relationship is one of antonyms. *Sky* is the opposite of *ground*; *ceiling* is the opposite of *floor*.

26. **The correct answer is D.** The relationship is that of cause-and-effect. *Food* promotes *nutrition*; *light* promotes *vision*.

27. **The correct answer is D.** This analogy highlights a part-to-whole relationship. An *actor* is a part of a *play* performance, and a *musician* is a part of a *concert* performance.

28. **The correct answer is D.** You might loosely state the relationship as four is to three. A *square* is a four-sided plane figure in relation to a *triangle*, which is a three-sided plane figure. A *cube* is a solid figure based on a square; a *pyramid* is a solid figure based on a triangle.

29. **The correct answer is A.** The relationship is sequential. An *abacus* is an earlier, more primitive *calculator*; a *propeller* is an earlier, less sophisticated means of propulsion than a *jet*.

30. **The correct answer is C.** The relationship is that of synonyms. *Vertigo* is *dizziness*; *destiny* is *fate*.

NOTES

PART IV
QUANTITATIVE AND NONVERBAL SKILLS

CHAPTER

Basic Mathematics

BASIC MATHEMATICS

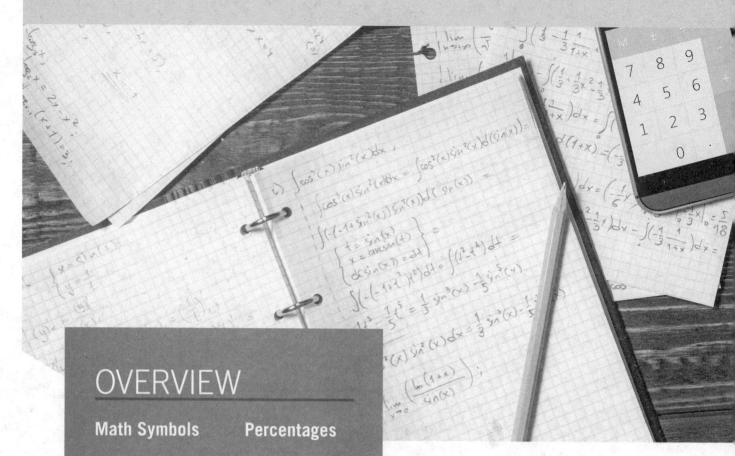

OVERVIEW

Whether you love it or hate it, math is always a part of your life. Sometimes, you might feel as though you are just not good at math or that you're not a math person. While it may not be your favorite subject, sometimes, you just have to figure out which parts of math you enjoy. Other times, it might be a matter of needing to review some fundamental concepts so that you can feel more confident and prepared going into more advanced mathematics. It's important that you get comfortable with math because you will find mathematics questions on all

TACHS   HSPT   ISEE   SSAT   SHSAT

scholastic aptitude and achievement tests, including the Catholic high school entrance exams. On the HSPT, math questions include the categories of Mathematics and Quantitative Skills. On the TACHS, the category is called Math.

In the sections that follow, we have condensed eight years of mathematics classes into a comprehensive review that touches on most topics covered in the exams. If you find that you're having difficulties with a specific topic, talk with a teacher or refer to your mathematics textbooks. These chapters will help most by illuminating what you *don't* know, so you can focus some of your test-prep time on reinforcing your skills in problem areas. The explanations that accompany the mathematics exercises can help you understand the processes involved in finding the correct answers. For extra practice, complete the Test Yourself exercises and Knowledge Checks in each of these three chapters. Work through the exercises carefully, and pay close attention to your accuracy and speed as you work. Note which problems are difficult as well as those that are easy for you. After you complete each chapter, you'll know exactly which areas you need to strengthen. In

Appendix C, we've also included a list of important formulas and other information, so feel free to reference that information as needed.

First, we'll look at math symbols and types of numbers, including whole numbers and signed numbers. We'll also discuss properties and how the order of operations should guide your calculations. Then, we'll focus on decimals, fractions, and percentages and how to convert between them. Finally, we'll cover ratios, proportions, probability, and measurement conversions to illustrate some real-world applications of the concepts we've covered here.

MATH SYMBOLS

Math is a language, with terms, meanings, structure, and symbols. To succeed at math, you need to understand the language. Often, the symbols used in equations can be the biggest challenge, so we'll start there. Some, if not all, of these symbols are already familiar to you, but it's worth reviewing the symbols that go beyond addition and subtraction. We've included a list of math symbols and their meanings for easy reference.

Symbol	Meaning	Function	Example
+	Plus sign	Addition	$5 + 3 = 8$
−	Minus sign	Subtraction	$5 - 3 = 2$
×	Times sign	Multiplication	$5 \times 3 = 15$
·	Multiplication dot	Multiplication	$5 \cdot 3 = 15$
÷	Division	Division	$10 \div 5 = 2$
/	Division slash	Division	$10/5 = 2$
.	Period	Decimal point	5.3, 7.25
%	Percent	$5\% = 5/100 = 0.05$	$0.5 = 50\%$ $1.25 = 125\%$

MATH SYMBOLS (table title)

MATH SYMBOLS			
Symbol	**Meaning**	**Function**	**Example**
$<$	Strict inequality	Less than	$3 < 5$
$\leq$	Inequality	Less than or equal to	$5 \leq 5, 4 \leq 5$
$>$	Strict inequality	Greater than	$5 > 3$
$\geq$	Inequality	Greater than or equal to	$5 \geq 5, 5 \geq 4$
$()$	Parentheses	Solve within first	$3 + (2 + 1) + 2 = 3 + 3 + 2 = 8$
$[]$	Brackets	Solve within first	$3 + [2 + 1] + 2 = 3 + 3 + 2 = 8$
x^y	Power	Exponent	$3^2 = 3 \times 3 = 9$ $3^3 = 3 \times 3 \times 3 = 27$
$\sqrt{}$	Square root	$\sqrt{a} \cdot \sqrt{a} = a$	$\sqrt{9} = 3, \sqrt{16} = 4$
π	Pi constant	Ratio between the circumference of a circle and its diameter	$c = \pi \times d$ $\pi = \dfrac{c}{d}$
$\angle$	Angle	Formed by two rays	$\angle CDE = 45°$
$\measuredangle$	Measured angle	Formed by two rays	$\angle DEF = 60°$
$\llcorner$	Right angle	Right angle $= 90°$	$a = 90°$
$°$	Degree	A circle $= 360°$, $\frac{1}{2} = 180°$	$a = 45°$
$!$	Factorial	$n! = 1 \times 2 \times 3 \times 4 \times ... \times n$	$4! = 1 \times 2 \times 3 \times 4 = 24$

TYPES OF NUMBERS

In math, various terms exist to describe the array of numbers used for counting and calculations. The ability to distinguish between whole numbers, integers, and rational and irrational numbers can keep you from selecting incompatible answer choices on the relevant subtests.

Whole Numbers and Integers

Starting with one of the most basic terms, **whole numbers** are simply numbers that are not decimals or fractions. They are always positive and include zero. An **integer** is any whole number not only including zero but also negative numbers—excluding negative decimals and fractions.

Some examples of whole numbers are as follows:

1, 2, 3, 50, 75, 100

Some examples of integers are as follows:

0, 1, 3, 42, 197, –2, –30, –212

Some examples of numbers that are NOT integers:

$\dfrac{3}{4}$, 0.14, –11.3, 56.0035

Rational and Irrational Numbers

A **rational number** is any number that results from dividing two integers. For example, $\dfrac{1}{3}, \dfrac{3}{5}, -\dfrac{7}{3}$ are all rational numbers. That means any number that has a terminating or repeating decimal, including no decimal, is rational. Here are some examples of rational numbers and what makes them so:

$$1 = \frac{1}{1} = \frac{2}{2} = \frac{-5}{-5} = \frac{0.354}{0.354} = \frac{10,000}{10,000}$$

$$-2 = \frac{-2}{1} = \frac{14}{-7} = \frac{-10}{5} = \frac{-40,000}{20,000}$$

$$5.25 = \frac{5.25}{1} = \frac{-10.5}{-2} = \frac{21}{4} = \frac{525,000}{100,000}$$

$$0.\overline{3} = \frac{1}{3} = \frac{30}{90} = \frac{400}{1,200}$$

 NOTE

The line over a decimal $0.\overline{3} = 0.3333333...$ means that it is a repeating decimal, going on forever.

The term *rational* is derived from *ratio*. In other words, any rational number is essentially the ratio of one integer to another or one integer divided by another integer. Each of these examples is expressed as a ratio. $\frac{-5}{-5}$ is equivalent to 1, just as $\frac{14}{-7}$ is equivalent to –2. The third example, 5.25, is a terminating decimal, so it is a rational number. The fourth example, $0.\overline{3}$, is a repeating decimal, so it can also be expressed as a ratio. We'll talk a bit more about ratios later on in this chapter.

Irrational numbers are numbers that have nonterminating, nonrepeating decimals. The most widely known irrational number is pi (π), or 3.1415926535897932384 62643383279 and on and on. The following are other irrational numbers:

$$\sqrt{2} = 1.41421356237...$$
$$\sqrt{3} = 1.73205080756...$$

Signed Numbers

We'll use a number line to talk about signed numbers. The number line exists on both sides of zero. Each positive number to the right of zero has a negative counterpart to the left of zero. The number line below shows the location of some pairs of numbers (+4, –4; +2, –2; +1, –1).

Because each number of a pair is located the same distance from zero (though in different directions), each has the same **absolute value**. Absolute value is symbolized by placing two vertical bars—one on each side of the number.

$$|+4| = |-4| = 4$$

The absolute value of +4 equals the absolute value of –4. Both are equivalent to 4. If you think of absolute value as the distance from zero, regardless of direction, it makes sense. The absolute value of any number, positive or negative, is expressed as a positive number.

Addition of Signed Numbers

When we add two oppositely signed numbers having the same absolute value, the sum is zero.

$$(+10) + (-10) = 0$$
$$(-1.5) + (+1.5) = 0$$
$$(-0.010) + (+0.010) = 0$$
$$\left(+\frac{3}{4}\right) + \left(-\frac{3}{4}\right) = 0$$

If one of the two oppositely signed numbers is greater in absolute value, the sum is equal to the amount of that excess and carries the same sign as the number having the greater absolute value.

$$(+2) + (-1) = +1$$
$$(+8) + (-9) = -1$$
$$(-2.5) + (+2.0) = -0.5$$
$$\left(-\frac{3}{4}\right) + \left(+\frac{1}{2}\right) = -\frac{1}{4}$$

Subtraction of Signed Numbers

Subtraction is the operation that finds the difference between two numbers, including the difference between signed numbers. When subtracting signed numbers, it can be helpful to refer to a number line.

-5 -4 -3 -2 -1 0 1 2 3 4 5

For example, if we wish to subtract +2 from +5, we can use the number line to see that the difference is +3. We give the sign to the difference that represents the direction we are moving along the number line from the number being subtracted to the number from which you are subtracting. In this case, because we are subtracting +2 from +5, we count three units in a positive direction from +2 to +5 on the number line.

When subtracting signed numbers:

- The distance between the two numbers gives you the absolute value of the difference.
- The direction you move from the number being subtracted to get to the number from which you are subtracting gives you the sign of the difference.

EXAMPLES:

Subtract –3 from +5.

Solution:

Distance on the number line between –3 and +5 is 8 units.

Direction is from negative to positive, a positive direction.

Answer is +8.

Subtract –6 from –8.

Solution:

Distance on number line between –6 and –8 is 2 units.

Direction is from –6 to –8, a negative direction.

Answer is –2.

Subtract +1.30 from –2.70.

Solution:

Distance between +1.30 and –2.70 on the number line is 4.0.

Direction is from +1.30 to –2.70, a negative direction.

Answer is –4.0.

A quick way to subtract signed numbers accurately involves placing the numbers in columns, reversing the sign of the number being subtracted and then adding the two. In other words, change the sign of the number being subtracted and follow the rules for addition.

 TIP

To easily subtract signed numbers, change the sign of the number being subtracted and follow the rules for addition.

EXAMPLES:

Subtract +26 from +15.

Solution:

$$+15 = +15$$
$$- \ +26 = -26$$
$$= -11$$

Subtract −35 from +10.

Solution:

$$+10 = +10$$
$$- \ - 35 = +35$$
$$= +45$$

Notice that in each of the examples, we found the correct answer by reversing the sign of the number being subtracted and then adding.

Multiplication of Signed Numbers

Signed numbers are multiplied as any other numbers would be, with the following exceptions:

The product of two negative numbers is positive.

$$(-3) \times (-6) = +18$$

The product of two positive numbers is positive.

$$(+3.05) \times (+6) = +18.30$$

The product of a negative and positive number is negative.

$$\left(+4\frac{1}{2}\right) \times (-3) = -13\frac{1}{2}$$
$$(+1) \times (-1) \times (+1) = -1$$

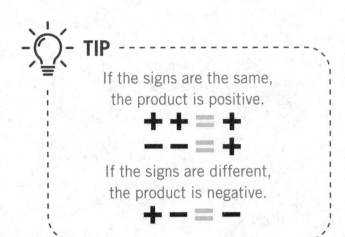

TIP

If the signs are the same, the product is positive.

$$+ \ + = +$$
$$- \ - = +$$

If the signs are different, the product is negative.

$$+ \ - = -$$

Division of Signed Numbers

As with multiplication, the division of signed numbers requires you to observe three simple rules:

When dividing a positive number by a negative number, the result is negative.

$$(+6) \div (-3) = -2$$

When dividing a negative number by a positive number, the result is negative.

$$(-6) \div (+3) = -2$$

When dividing a negative number by a negative number or a positive number by a positive number, the result is positive.

$$(-6) \div (-3) = +2$$
$$(+6) \div (+3) = +2$$

MEAN, MEDIAN, AND MODE

Now that we've covered the types of numbers you'll encounter in math problems, let's take a look at some of the applications and uses of numbers in different real-world contexts. Statistics, for instance, is all about numerical data. Have you ever had a teacher ask the class how many students did their homework every day last month? That is a statistic: Out of the 26 students in the class, eight of them did all their homework last month. When you have a set of data points, like how often each student did homework over that month,

To learn more about finding the mean, scan this QR code.

you would have a data set of 26 numbers—one for each student—that is written as:

{1, 2, 3, 4, 5, 6, 7, 8, 9, 10, 11, 12, 13, 14, 15, 16, 17, 18, 19, 20, 21, 22, 23, 24, 25, 26}

Notice that the data points are between those squiggly brackets (which is the actual name for those, though they are generally referred to as *brackets*). Now, imagine that data set was made up of 26 random numbers. That could easily become confusing, especially when you have one hundred pieces of data, or 1,000, or 50,000. This is where the central tendency terms come in handy; they can help you organize, summarize, and describe the data in front of you. There are three central tendency terms you'll likely encounter on your exam: mean, median, and mode.

Mean

The first term, **mean**, may be the one you are most familiar with, as it's another word for average. Average means typical or middle, which is exactly what the mean is. We find the mean by adding the numbers in the set of data, then dividing by the number of terms in that set. In the example above, we would find the mean by adding the data together $(1 + 2 + 3 + 4 + \ldots)$ and dividing that sum by the number of data points in the set.

$$\frac{351}{26} = 13.5$$

Your average then is 13.5. You can do this with any data set, and you do not have to put all the data points in order. Just add, then divide.

Median

Median is another method to help make sense of a data set. Unlike the mean, the **median** is looking for the

middle number in your data set, and not the average, although the two may be very close or even equal. To find the median, you must put all the data points in order.

{7, 8, 9, 10, 11}

In this data set, the median, or the number that is in the middle, is 9. If you have an odd number of digits or data points, put them in order and find the one right in the middle.

Now, let's use the data set from earlier:

{1, 2, 3, 4, 5, 6, 7, 8, 9, 10, 11, 12, 13, 14, 15, 16, 17, 18, 19, 20, 21, 22, 23, 24, 25, 26}

You already know the median is the digit that appears right in the middle of the data set. In this case though, we have an even number of data points, and that means the median is two digits. If you have two numbers as the median, take those two and find the mean of the two. That is, when you have two numbers as the median, then the mean is exactly in the middle. For this data set, the median is {13, 14}.

$$13 + 14 = 27 \qquad 27 \div 2 = 13.5$$

The mean of those two numbers is 13.5, which is the median for the larger data set.

Mode

Mode is a bit different from the previous two. While the mean seeks the average of a data set and the median seeks the middle digit in a data set when it's written in order, the **mode** is the piece of data that shows up most often in a data set.

Let's take a data set where 26 students estimated how many hours per day they spend on social media. That would be written out as {5, 7, 8, 1, 4, 2, 5, 3, 9, 6, 5, 6, 5, 5, 4, 1, 7, 8, 2, 9, 2, 8, 5, 7, 4, 0}. That's a mess, so just like we did for finding the median, let's put this in order:

{0, 1, 1, 2, 2, 2, 3, 4, 4, 4, 5, 5, 5, 5, 5, 5, 6, 6, 7, 7, 7, 8, 8, 8, 9, 9}

Now, count how many times each number comes up.

$$0 = 1$$

$$1 = 2$$

2 = 3

3 = 1

4 = 3

5 = 6

6 = 2

7 = 3

8 = 3

9 = 2

Looking at this information, we see that the number 5 appears six times. That means the mode of that data set is 5. When would this be helpful information? If you want to show a trend (like hours spent on social media), knowing which value appears most frequently tells you which is the most popular. In this case, five hours a day on social media is the most common occurrence in the data set.

Let's find the mode for another set of data: This time, we'll examine how many pages each student reads at home every night. Your data set is {3, 3, 4, 4, 4, 5, 5, 7, 7, 7, 8, 8, 9, 11, 11, 12, 12, 12, 12, 12, 12, 12, 17, 23}. Counting the frequency for each number in the set, 12 is the number that occurs most often, meaning more students read 12 pages each night than any other amount.

Another practical application would be if you have several kinds of trading cards that you're hoping to sell. If you keep track of which kind of trading card sells the most, that's the mode. Looking at the mode would tell you which cards are purchased most often and which ones don't sell as well. If this becomes your business, knowing which trading cards sell the best can help you know what to keep in stock more often and what to stock less often.

To learn more about median and mode, scan this QR code.

Test Yourself 1

Find the mean, median, and mode for the number set provided. The answers will follow.

{37, 46, 49, 11, 40, 32, 3, 39, 6, 47, 40, 4, 35}

1. Mean =
2. Median =
3. Mode =

{31, 1, 20, 43, 21, 39, 31, 25, 31, 9, 28, 36, 28, 18, 12, 21, 29, 41, 28, 27, 31}

4. Mean =
5. Median =
6. Mode =

{12, 22, 7, 35, 3, 30, 12, 7, 13, 24, 12, 1, 11, 3, 17, 15}

7. Mean =
8. Median =
9. Mode =

Answers:
1. 29.92
2. 37
3. 40
4. 26.19
5. 28
6. 31
7. 14
8. 12
9. 12

PROPERTIES

When studying math, it's important to understand how properties describe the behavior of numbers in certain situations. Properties in math are rules that have been proven over time. They may seem like common sense, and for the most part, they are. Knowing properties can help simplify the process of solving problems because you can count on the fact that certain things will always be true. Become thoroughly familiar with the rules in this section, and commit to memory as many properties and rules as possible.

Here's a list of properties, with definitions and examples. You may need to refer back to this section as we get into more advanced math, like solving algebraic equations.

- **Commutative Property:** in addition and multiplication, order does not affect outcome.
  - $7 + 8 = 8 + 7$
  - $3 \times 5 = 5 \times 3$
  - $2(6) = 6(2)$

- **Distributive Property:** given an equation, $a(b + c)$, you can distribute the value a to the values inside the parentheses.
  - $7(2 + 8) = 7 \times 2 + 7 \times 8 = 14 + 56 = 70$

- **Associative Property:** in addition and multiplication, changing how numbers are grouped will not change the result.
  - $2(5 \times 4) = 5(2 \times 4) = 4(2 \times 5)$
  - $3 + (5 + 2) = 2 + (3 + 5) = 5 + (2 + 3)$

- **Identity Property:** any number added to zero will not change; any number multiplied by 1 will not change.
  - $15 + 0 = 15$
  - $15 \times 1 = 15$

- **Reflexive Property:** a number is always equal to itself.
  - $a = a$
  - $2 = 2$
  - $\pi = \pi$

- **Symmetric Property:** if $a = b$, then $b = a$.
  - If $x = 10$, then $10 = x$

- **Transitive Property:** if $a = b$ and $b = c$, then $a = c$.
  - If $a = b$ and $b = 3 + 4$, then $a = 3 + 4$

- **Substitution Property:** if $a = b$, then a can be substituted for b.
  - If $a = 7$ and $b = 7$, then $a + 3 = 10$ and $b + 3 = 10$

- **Additive Identity:** any variable added to zero will remain unchanged.
  - $x + 0 = x$

- **Multiplicative Property of Zero:** any number multiplied by zero equals zero.
  - $1 \times 0 = 0$
  - $4,962 \times 0 = 0$

- **Multiplicative Inverse:** any number multiplied by its reciprocal will equal 1.
  - $2 \times \dfrac{1}{2} = 1$
  - $2 \times \dfrac{1}{12} = 1$

ORDER OF OPERATIONS

One of the most important things to know when solving math problems is where to start. You will often encounter problems that have a series of operations to perform. Fortunately, there are rules to explain what goes first. We call these rules the **order of operations**. The order of operations ensures that, by solving operations in this order, you'll always be able to arrive at the same correct solution. At this stage of mathematics, there are only four rules to know. They are as follows:

1. Solve operations within parentheses first.
2. Solve operations with exponents and square roots next.
3. Solve multiplication and division from left to right.
4. Solve addition and subtraction from left to right.

TIP

Remember your order of operations with the acronym **PEMDAS:**

P Parentheses

E Exponents (and Square Roots)

M Multiplication

D Division

A Addition

S Subtraction

Some students use the mnemonic device "**P**lease **e**xcuse **m**y **d**ear **A**unt **S**ally."

These rules inform where you should start when solving a math problem. In short, solve anything in parentheses first, going from hardest to easiest. As you go through problems using the order of operations, carefully follow each step to make sure you don't skip a step or forget anything along the way.

Let's look at a few examples.

- $(7 \times 2) + (8 - 2) = (14) + (6) = 20$ (Solve within the parentheses before adding)
- $4^3 + (5 + 1) =$ (Parentheses first)

  $4^3 + 6 = 64 + 6$ (Exponent, then addition)

- $6 - 8 \div 2 + 3 =$ (No multiplication, so start with division)

  $6 - 4 + 3 = 5$ (Addition and subtraction from left to right)

- $\sqrt{81} \times 5^2 - 45 \div 9 + 14 =$ (No parentheses, so start with exponents and square roots)

  $9 \times 25 - 45 \div 9 + 14 =$ (Now solve multiplication and division from left to right)

  $225 - 5 + 14 = 234$ (Now solve addition and subtraction from left to right)

We just demonstrated the order of operations discussed here. As you go through these chapters on mathematics, you will come across other rules concerning order of operations. Refer back to this section as needed.

Test Yourself 2

Put the following equations into standard form. The answers will follow.

1. $(8 \times 2) + (9 - 2) - \sqrt{144} \div 2^2$
2. $10 + 5^2 - (7 \times 3) + 1$
3. $\sqrt{9} \div 1 + (6^2 \div 4) - 10$
4. $10 \times 3 + (11 - 2) \div 3$
5. $4^3 + 6 - (4 \times 7) \div 2$

Answers:

1. 20
2. 15
3. 2
4. 33
5. 56

 Scan this QR code to watch a video about the order of operations.

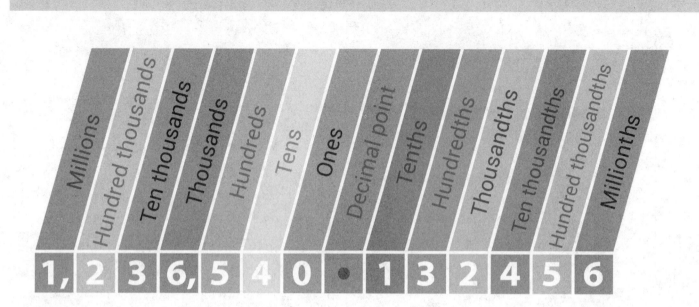

DECIMALS

So far, we've talked extensively about whole numbers and integers, but in math, you'll frequently be working with parts of numbers in the form of decimals, fractions, and percentages. First, we'll address decimals, and then we'll move on to fractions and percentages.

When a number is written in **decimal** form, everything to the left of the decimal point is a whole number, and everything to the right of the decimal point represents a part of the whole (a tenth, hundredth, thousandth, and so on). If you can count money or make change, then you already have experience with decimals. The most important step when writing decimals is placing the decimal point. The whole system is based on its location. The chart shows places for the number **1,236,540.132456**.

Place value refers to the specific value of a digit in a decimal number. For example, in the decimal number 1,236,540.132456:

The digit 1 is in the "millions" place.

The digit 2 is in the "hundred thousands" place.

The digit 3 is in the "ten thousands" place.

The digit 6 is in the "thousands" place.

The digit 5 is in the "hundreds" place.

The digit 4 is in the "tens" place.

The digit 0 is in the "ones" place.

The digit 1 is in the "tenths" place.

The digit 3 is in the "hundredths" place.

The digit 2 is in the "thousandths" place.

The digit 4 is in the "ten thousandths" place.

The digit 5 is in the "hundred thousandths" place.

The digit 6 is in the "millionths" place.

As such, you could express the numbers to the left of the decimal point as $1,000,000 + 200,000 + 36,000 + 500 + 40 + 0$. You could express the numbers to the right of the decimal point as

$$\frac{1}{10} + \frac{3}{100} + \frac{2}{1000} + \frac{4}{10,000} + \frac{5}{100,000} + \frac{6}{1,000,000}.$$

Adding zeros to the end of a decimal number does not change its value. For example, the decimal number 0.5 is the same as 0.50 or 0.5000. But adding a zero to the front (the left) of the number will change the number's value. For example, 0.5 means "five tenths," but 0.05 means "five hundredths."

When adding or subtracting decimals, you need to keep the decimal points in line. After you have lined up the decimal points, proceed with the problem the same way as with whole numbers while maintaining the location of the decimal point.

EXAMPLES:

Add 36.08 + 745 + 4.362 + 58.6 + 0.0061.

Solution:

$$
\begin{array}{r}
36.08 \\
745. \\
4.362 \\
58.6 \\
+\quad 0.0061 \\
\hline
844.0481
\end{array}
$$

To keep track of the decimal places, you can also fill in the spaces with zeros.

$$
\begin{array}{r}
036.0800 \\
745.0000 \\
004.3620 \\
058.6000 \\
+\quad 000.0061 \\
\hline
844.0481
\end{array}
$$

Subtract 7.928 from 82.1.

Solution:

$$
\begin{array}{r}
82.1 \\
-\quad 7.928 \\
\hline
74.172
\end{array}
\quad \text{or} \quad
\begin{array}{r}
82.100 \\
-\quad 7.928 \\
\hline
74.172
\end{array}
$$

When multiplying decimals, ignore the decimal points until you reach the product. The placement of the decimal point depends on the sum of the places to the right of the decimal point in both the multiplier and number being multiplied.

$$
\begin{array}{r}
1.482 \\
\times\ 0.16 \\
\hline
8892 \\
14820 \\
\hline
0.23712
\end{array}
$$

   1.482   (3 places to the right of decimal point)
  × 0.16   (2 places to the right of decimal point)
  8892
14820
0.23712 (5 places to the right of decimal point)

You cannot divide by a decimal because a decimal itself is a ratio. If the divisor is a decimal, you must move the decimal point to the right until the divisor becomes a whole number. Count the number of spaces you moved the decimal point in the divisor to the right, and move the decimal point in the dividend (the number being divided) the same number of spaces to the right. The decimal point in the answer should be directly above the decimal point in the dividend.

$$
0.06\overline{)4.212} = 70.2
$$

Decimal point moves two spaces to the right.

Test Yourself 3

Write the answers to the following problems in the space provided. The answers will follow.

1. 1.52 + 0.389 + 42.9 =

2. 84 − 1.9 =

3. 18 ÷ 0.3 =

4. 1.5 × 0.9 =

5. 7.55 ÷ 5 =

Answers:

1. 44.809

2. 82.1

3. 60

4. 1.35

5. 1.51

To watch a video about decimals, scan this QR code.

FACTORS AND MULTIPLES

Before we can start working with fractions, we need to understand factors and multiples. A **factor** is a number that can be divided into a whole number evenly without leaving a remainder. The factors of any integer include 1 as well as the integer itself. Figuring out whether one number is a factor of another requires you to divide that number by another number. For example, to determine what numbers are factors of 4, we would divide 4 by the numbers in question: 1, 2, and 4 all divide into 4 evenly, without a remainder. In contrast, 3 is not a factor of 4 because when you divide 4 by 3 you do not end up with a whole number: $4 \div 3 = 1\frac{1}{3}$. Because 3 cannot be divided evenly into 4, it is not a factor of 4.

Keep in mind these basic rules about factors:

Complementing factors are **multiples**. If f is a factor of n, then n is a multiple of f. For example, 8 is a multiple of 2 for the same reason that 2 is a factor of 8: because 8 ÷ 2 = 4, which is an integer.

A **prime number** is a positive integer that is divisible by only two positive integers: itself and 1. Zero (0) and 1 are not considered prime numbers; 2 is the first prime number. Here are all the prime numbers less than 50:

2 3 5 7
11 13 17 19
23 29
31 37
41 43 47

As you can see, factors, multiples, and divisibility are different aspects of the same concept.

Greatest Common Factor

In order to solve problems with fractions, you'll need to be able to determine the greatest common factor. The term **greatest common factor** (or GCF) refers to the largest number that can be factored into two numbers cleanly (that is, without a remainder). For example, the greatest common factor of 10 and 15 is 5. For 10 and 20, the GCF is 10. How did we get those answers? Let's look at a pair of numbers.

> **EXAMPLE:**
>
> Find the GCF for (12, 8)
>
> **Solution:**
> Factors for 12: 1, 2, 3, 4, 6, 12
>
> Factors for 8: 1, 2, 4, 8
>
> The common factors—the factors common to both sets of numbers—for 12 and 8 are 1, 2, and 4. The greatest (largest) of the group is 4, so that's your answer.

Divisibility Rules

RULE 1:

Any integer is a factor of itself.

RULE 2:

1 and –1 are factors of all integers (except 0).

RULE 3:

The integer zero (0) has no factors and is not a factor of any integer.

RULE 4:

A positive integer's largest factor (other than itself) will never be greater than one half the value of the integer.

EXAMPLE:

Find the GCF for (28, 56)

Solution:

Factors for 28: 1, 2, 4, 7, 14, 28

Factors for 56: 1, 2, 4, 7, 14, 28, 56

The greatest common factor the two numbers share is 28, which is your answer.

 TIP

Don't be confused by the term "Greatest Common Divisor," as a divisor and a factor have the same meaning. They are both numbers that can divide into something.

There may be number pairs, like (7, 13), that don't have anything other than 1 in common. When this happens, the numbers are relatively prime. Remember that a prime number is a number that is only divisible by itself and 1.

What about problems with more than two numbers to factor? That just means you add another group of factors to choose from.

EXAMPLE:

Find the GCF for (28, 56, 84)

Solution:

Factors for 28: 1, 2, 4, 7, 14, 28

Factors for 56: 1, 2, 4, 7, 14, 28, 56

Factors for 84: 1, 2, 3, 4, 6, 7, 12, 14, 21, 28, 42, 84

The greatest common factor the three numbers share is still 28, which is your answer.

Test Yourself 4

Find the greatest common factor for each group of numbers. The answers will follow.

1. (20, 75)	6. (13, 117)
2. (14, 35)	7. (15, 25)
3. (5, 13)	8. (6, 21)
4. (30, 150)	9. (4, 12)
5. (12, 78)	10. (24, 64)

Answers:

1. 5	6. 13
2. 7	7. 5
3. 1	8. 3
4. 30	9. 4
5. 6	10. 8

 Scan this **QR code** for more information on how to find the greatest common factor and least common multiple.

Least Common Multiple

In addition to using the greatest common factor, solving problems with fractions will also require you to find the least common multiple. The **least common multiple** (LCM) is the smallest whole number into which each number in the list divides evenly. For example, the GCF of {18, 36, 63} is 9, and the LCM of {18, 36, 63} is 504.

Both factors and multiples will be essential for simplifying and converting fractions; however, factors are used much more frequently than multiples, as you are usually aiming to simplify fractions. Finding the least common multiple is helpful when you need to add or subtract fractions with different denominators, as you'll need each to have the same denominator in order to add them together. However, you will likely use the greatest common factor to reduce or simplify the end result.

FRACTIONS

A **fraction** is a part of a whole. For instance, there are 10 dimes in each dollar, so one dime is one-tenth of a dollar—one of ten equal parts. The fraction to represent one-tenth is written $\frac{1}{10}$. The top number of a fraction is called the **numerator**, and the bottom number is called the **denominator**. The denominator tells you how many equal parts the object or number is divided into, and the numerator tells how many of those parts we are concerned with.

$$\frac{3}{4} \begin{matrix} \leftarrow \text{numerator} \rightarrow \\ \leftarrow \text{denominator} \rightarrow \end{matrix} \frac{7}{8}$$

A **proper fraction** is one in which the numerator is less than the denominator. An **improper fraction** is one in which the numerator is the same as or greater than the denominator. $\frac{3}{5}$ is a proper fraction, but $\frac{5}{3}$ is an improper fraction. Sometimes, you will see a whole number and a fraction together. This is called a **mixed number**. $2\frac{3}{5}$ is an example of a mixed number.

Let's look at a few examples of how to express parts of a whole as fractions.

EXAMPLE:

Divide a baseball game, a football game, and a hockey game into convenient numbers of parts. Write a fraction to answer each equation.

1. If a pitcher played two innings, how much of the whole baseball game did he play?
2. If a quarterback played three quarters of a football game, how much of the whole game did he play?
3. If a goalie played two periods of a hockey game, how much of the whole game did he play?

Solution 1:

A baseball game has nine parts (each an inning). The pitcher pitched two innings. Therefore, he played $\frac{2}{9}$ of the game. The denominator represents the nine parts the game is divided into; the numerator represents the two parts we are concerned with.

Solution 2:

Similarly, there are four quarters in a football game, and a quarterback playing three of those quarters plays in $\frac{3}{4}$ of the game

Solution 3:

There are three periods in hockey, and the goalie played in two of them. Therefore, he played in $\frac{2}{3}$ of the game.

Reciprocals

When working with fractions (or any numbers), you may need to find a fraction's reciprocal. Finding a reciprocal comes down to flipping something over. Defined, a reciprocal is $\frac{1}{x}$ where x is the number in question. For example, the reciprocal of $5 = \frac{1}{5}$ or 0.2 as a decimal. Let's see a few more.

EXAMPLES:

$$17 = \frac{1}{17}$$

$$100 = \frac{1}{100}$$

$$42 = \frac{1}{42}$$

One thing to think about with a whole number is that 17 is the same as $\frac{17}{1}$. Keep that in mind not only with reciprocals but any time you have a mix of whole numbers and fractions.

Finding the reciprocal of a fraction requires flipping the numerator and denominator. For example, to find the reciprocal of $\frac{4}{5}$, you flip the fraction over to get $\frac{5}{4}$. Let's look at a few more examples.

Scan this QR code to watch a video about fractions.

EXAMPLES:

$$\frac{1}{8} = \frac{8}{1} = 8$$

$$\frac{2}{10} = \frac{10}{2} = 5$$

$$\frac{1}{0.25} = \frac{0.25}{1} = 0.25$$

The rule of thumb with reciprocals is to divide by one for whole numbers and to flip the numerator and denominator for fractions.

Test Yourself 5

Write the reciprocals to the following problems in the space provided. The answers will follow.

1. $72 =$
2. $\frac{1}{2} =$
3. $0.65 =$
4. $\frac{3}{36} =$
5. $-6 =$

Answers:

1. $\frac{1}{72}$
2. 2
3. $\frac{20}{13}$
4. 12
5. $\frac{1}{-6}$

Equivalent Fractions

Fractions having different denominators and numerators might represent the same amount. These are equivalent fractions.

For example, divide the following circle into two equal parts. Write a fraction to indicate how much of the circle is shaded.

$$\frac{1 \text{ shaded}}{2 \text{ parts}} = \frac{1}{2} \text{ of the circle is shaded.}$$

The circle below is divided into four equal parts. Write a fraction to indicate how much of the circle is shaded.

$$\frac{2 \text{ shaded}}{4 \text{ parts}} = \frac{2}{4} \text{ of the circle are shaded.}$$

This circle is divided into eight equal parts. Write a fraction to indicate how much of the circle is shaded.

$$\frac{4 \text{ shaded}}{8 \text{ parts}} = \frac{4}{8} \text{ of the circle are shaded.}$$

In each circle, the same amount was shaded. This shows that there is more than one way to indicate one half of something.

The fractions $\frac{1}{2}$, $\frac{2}{4}$, and $\frac{4}{8}$ that you wrote are *equivalent fractions* because they all represent the same amount. Notice that the denominator is twice as large as the numerator in every case. Any fraction you write that has a denominator that is exactly twice as large as the numerator will be equivalent to $\frac{1}{2}$.

EXAMPLES:

Write other fractions equivalent to $\frac{1}{2}$.

Solution:

Any fraction that has a denominator that is twice as large as the numerator: $\frac{3}{6}$, $\frac{5}{10}$, $\frac{6}{12}$, $\frac{32}{64}$, etc.

Write other fractions equivalent to $\frac{1}{4}$.

Solution:

Any fraction that has a denominator that is four times as large as the numerator: $\frac{2}{8}$, $\frac{4}{16}$, $\frac{5}{20}$, $\frac{15}{60}$, etc.

Write other fractions equivalent to $\frac{2}{3}$.

Solution:

Any fraction that has a denominator that is one and one-half times as large as the numerator: $\frac{4}{6}$, $\frac{10}{15}$, $\frac{14}{21}$, $\frac{16}{24}$, etc.

When you cannot divide the numerator and denominator of a fraction evenly by the same whole number (other than 1), the fraction is in its simplest form. In the examples above, $\frac{1}{2}$, $\frac{1}{4}$, and $\frac{2}{3}$ are in their simplest forms. To write equivalent fractions where the numerator is not 1 requires one more step.

EXAMPLE:

What is the equivalent fraction for $\frac{4}{5}$ using 10 as a denominator?

Solution:

Each $\frac{1}{5}$ is equivalent to $\frac{2}{10}$; therefore, $\frac{4}{5}$ is equivalent to $\frac{8}{10}$.

The quickest way to find an equivalent fraction is to divide the denominator of the fraction you want by the denominator you know. Take the result and multiply it by the numerator of the fraction you know. This becomes the numerator of the equivalent fraction.

EXAMPLES:

Rename $\frac{3}{8}$ as an equivalent fraction having 16 as a denominator.

Solution:

$$\frac{3}{8} = \frac{6}{16} \quad (16 \div 8 = 2; \ 2 \times 3 = 6)$$

Rename $\frac{3}{4}$ as equivalent fractions having 8, 12, 24, and 32 as denominators.

Solution:

$$\frac{3}{4} = \frac{6}{8} \quad (8 \div 4 = 2; \ 2 \times 3 = 6)$$

$$\frac{3}{4} = \frac{9}{12} \quad (12 \div 4 = 3; \ 3 \times 3 = 9)$$

$$\frac{3}{4} = \frac{18}{24} \quad (24 \div 4 = 6; \ 6 \times 3 = 18)$$

$$\frac{3}{4} = \frac{24}{32} \quad (32 \div 4 = 8; \ 8 \times 3 = 24)$$

Simplifying Fractions

A fraction can be simplified to its lowest terms if its numerator and denominator share a common factor. Here are a few simple examples:

$$\frac{6}{9} = \frac{(3)(2)}{(3)(3)} = \frac{2}{3}$$

(you can "cancel" or factor out the common factor 3)

$$\frac{21}{35} = \frac{(7)(3)}{(7)(5)} = \frac{3}{5}$$

(you can factor out the common factor 7)

Before you perform any operation with a fraction, always check to see if you can simplify it first. By reducing a fraction to its lowest terms, you will also simplify whatever operation you perform on it.

Mixed Numbers and Improper Fractions

As noted earlier, a **mixed number** consists of a whole number along with a simple fraction. The number $4\frac{2}{3}$ is an example of a mixed number. Before combining fractions, you might need to convert mixed numbers to improper fractions. Recall that an improper fraction is a fraction where the numerator is larger than the denominator. To convert, follow these three steps:

1. Multiply the denominator of the fraction by the whole number.

2. Add the product to the numerator of the fraction.

3. Place the sum over the denominator of the fraction.

For example, here's how to convert the mixed number $4\frac{2}{3}$ to an improper fraction:

$$4\frac{2}{3} = \frac{(3)(4) + 2}{3} = \frac{14}{3}$$

To add or subtract mixed numbers, you can convert each one to an improper fraction, then find their lowest common denominator and combine them. Alternatively, you can add together the whole numbers, and add together the fractions separately. To perform multiple operations, always perform multiplication and division before you perform addition and subtraction.

A fraction that has a numerator greater than the denominator is an **improper fraction**. Examples of improper fractions include $\frac{3}{2}$, $\frac{12}{7}$, and $\frac{9}{5}$. Improper fractions can also be in their simplest forms when the numerator and denominator cannot be divided evenly by a number other than 1.

Improper fractions can be represented as mixed numbers and vice versa. Below are a few examples of how to rename a mixed number as an improper fraction.

EXAMPLE:

Rename $2\frac{1}{4}$ as an improper fraction.

Solution:

The whole number 2 contains 8 fourths. Add $\frac{1}{4}$ to it to write the equivalent fraction $\frac{9}{4}$.

Another way to solve this problem is to multiply the denominator of the fraction by the whole number and add the numerator.

EXAMPLE:

Rename $2\frac{1}{4}$ as an improper fraction.

Solution:

$4 \times 2 = 8 + 1 = 9$; combined with the denominator, the result is $\frac{9}{4}$.

To rename an improper fraction as a mixed number, proceed backward.

EXAMPLE:

Rename $\frac{9}{4}$ as a mixed number.

Solution:

Divide the numerator by the denominator and use the remainder (R) as the fraction numerator:

$9 \div 4 = 2\text{ R}1$ or $9 \div 4 = 2\frac{1}{4}$.

Adding and Subtracting Fractions

To add fractions with the same denominators, add the numerators and keep the common denominator.

EXAMPLE:

Add $\frac{1}{4} + \frac{3}{4} + \frac{3}{4}$.

Solution:

When the denominators are the same, add the numerators to arrive at the answer, $\frac{7}{4}$ or simplify $1\frac{3}{4}$.

To find the difference between two fractions with the same denominators, subtract the numerators, leaving the denominators alone.

EXAMPLE:

Find the difference between $\dfrac{7}{8}$ and $\dfrac{3}{8}$.

Solution:

$\dfrac{7}{8} - \dfrac{3}{8} = \dfrac{4}{8}$ simplified, $\dfrac{4}{8} = \dfrac{1}{2}$.

To add or subtract fractions with different denominators, you must first find the **lowest common denominator**, also known as the least common multiple. A common denominator is a number that can be divided by the denominators of all the fractions in the problem without a remainder. Finding the lowest common denominator is important to ensure that you have the simplest fraction. As you go through the upcoming exercises, review the section on factors and multiples to understand how to find the lowest common denominator.

EXAMPLE:

Find a common denominator for $\dfrac{1}{4}$ and $\dfrac{1}{3}$.

Solution:

Multiply the denominators to get $4 \times 3 = 12$.

12 can be divided by both 4 and 3:

$\dfrac{1}{4}$ is equivalent to $\dfrac{3}{12}$

$\dfrac{1}{3}$ is equivalent to $\dfrac{4}{12}$

We can now add the fractions because we have written equivalent fractions with a common denominator.

Therefore:

$$\frac{3}{12} + \frac{4}{12} = \frac{7}{12}$$

$$\frac{1}{4} + \frac{1}{3} = \frac{7}{12}$$

Seven-twelfths is in its simplest form because 7 and 12 do not have a whole number (other than 1) by which they are both divisible.

EXAMPLE:

Add $\dfrac{3}{8}$, $\dfrac{5}{6}$, $\dfrac{1}{4}$, and $\dfrac{2}{3}$.

Solution:

Find a number into which all denominators will divide evenly. For 8, 6, 4, and 3, the lowest common denominator is 24. Now convert each fraction to an equivalent fraction having a denominator of 24:

$\dfrac{3}{8} = \dfrac{9}{24}$ ($24 \div 8 = 3$; $3 \times 3 = 9$)

$\dfrac{5}{6} = \dfrac{20}{24}$ ($24 \div 6 = 4$; $4 \times 5 = 20$)

$\dfrac{1}{4} = \dfrac{6}{24}$ ($24 \div 4 = 6$; $6 \times 1 = 6$)

$\dfrac{2}{3} = \dfrac{16}{24}$ ($24 \div 3 = 8$; $8 \times 2 = 16$)

Now add the fractions:

$$\frac{9}{24} + \frac{20}{24} + \frac{6}{24} + \frac{16}{24} = \frac{51}{24}$$

The answer, $\dfrac{51}{24}$, is an improper fraction: The numerator is greater than the denominator. To rename the answer to a mixed number, divide the numerator by the denominator and express the remainder as a fraction.

$$\frac{51}{24} = 51 \div 24 = 2\frac{3}{24} = 2\frac{1}{8}$$

Multiplying and Dividing Fractions

When multiplying fractions, multiply numerators by numerators and denominators by denominators.

$$\frac{3}{5} \times \frac{4}{7} \times \frac{1}{5} = \frac{3 \times 4 \times 1}{5 \times 7 \times 5} = \frac{12}{175}$$

Try to work with numbers that are as small as possible. You can make numbers smaller by dividing out common factors. Do this by dividing the numerator of any one fraction and the denominator of any one fraction by the same number.

$$\frac{\overset{1}{\cancel{3}}}{\underset{2}{\cancel{4}}} \times \frac{\overset{1}{\cancel{2}}}{\underset{3}{\cancel{9}}} = \frac{1 \times 1}{2 \times 3} = \frac{1}{6}$$

In this case, we divided the numerator of the first fraction and the denominator of the second fraction by 3, while the denominator of the first fraction and the numerator of the second fraction were divided by 2.

To divide by a fraction, multiply by the reciprocal of the divisor.

$$\frac{3}{16} \div \frac{1}{8} = \frac{3}{\underset{2}{\cancel{16}}} \times \frac{\overset{1}{\cancel{8}}}{1} = \frac{3}{2} = 1\frac{1}{2}$$

Test Yourself 6

Divide out common factors wherever possible and express your answers in the simplest form. The answers will follow.

1. $\dfrac{4}{5} \times \dfrac{3}{6} =$

2. $\dfrac{2}{4} \times \dfrac{8}{12} \times \dfrac{7}{1} =$

3. $\dfrac{3}{4} \div \dfrac{3}{8} =$

4. $\dfrac{5}{2} \div \dfrac{3}{6} =$

5. $\dfrac{8}{9} \times \dfrac{3}{4} \times \dfrac{1}{2} =$

Answers:

1. $\dfrac{2}{5}$

2. $2\dfrac{1}{3}$

3. 2

4. $\dfrac{15}{3} =$

5. $\dfrac{1}{3}$

PERCENTAGES

A **percentage** (%) is a fraction or decimal number written in a different form. The decimal number 0.25 is written as 25%. A percentage expressed as a fraction is the number divided by 100. The last syllable of the word *percent*, *-cent*, is the name we give to one hundredth of a dollar. Think of the word *century*, which is 100 years. Both share the root *cent*. As an example, there are 100 cents in a dollar. One percent of $1.00, then, is one cent. Using decimal notation, we can write one cent as $0.01, five cents as $0.05, twenty-five cents as $0.25, and so forth. Instead of saying that 25 cents is equal to 25 hundredths of a dollar, we use the word percent.

The information in this section will help you understand the relationship between decimals, fractions, and percentages and convert numbers from one form to another.

Converting Between Decimals, Fractions, and Percentages

1. To change a decimal to a percentage, add the % sign and multiply by 100.

   Example: $0.25 = 0.25\% \times 100 = 25\%$

2. The fraction bar in a fraction means "divided by." To change a fraction to a decimal, follow through on the division.

   Example: $\dfrac{4}{5} = 4 \div 5 = 0.8$

3. To change a fraction to a percentage, multiply by 100 and add the percent sign (%).

   Example: $\dfrac{1}{4} \times 100 = 25\%$

4. To change a percentage to a decimal, remove the percent sign (%) and divide the number by 100.

   Example: $25\% = \dfrac{25}{100} = 0.25$

5. To change a percentage to a fraction, remove the % sign and use that number as your numerator, with 100 as your denominator.

   Example: $25\% = \dfrac{25}{100} = \dfrac{1}{4}$

Percentage is not limited to comparing other numbers to 100. You can divide any number into hundredths and talk about percentage.

EXAMPLE:

Find 1% of 200.

Solution:

1% of 200 is 1/100, or 0.01, of 200.
Using decimal notation, we can calculate one percent of 200 by multiplying 200 by 0.01:

$200 \times 0.01 = 2$

Similarly, we can find a percentage of any number we choose by multiplying it by the correct decimal notation. For example:

Five percent of 50: $0.05 \times 50 = 2.5$

Three percent of 150: $0.03 \times 150 = 4.5$

Ten percent of 60: $0.10 \times 60 = 6$

Not all percentage measurements are between one percent and 100 percent. You might need to consider less than one percent of something, especially if that something is very large.

For example, if you were handed a book 1,000 pages long and told to read one percent of it in five minutes, how much would you have to read?

$1000 \times 0.01 = 10$ pages

Quite an assignment! You might bargain to read one half of one percent or one-tenth of one percent in the five minutes allotted to you.

Using decimal notation, we write one-tenth of one percent as 0.001, the decimal number for one thousandth. If you remember that a percent is one hundredth of

something, you can see that one tenth of that percent is equivalent to one thousandth of the whole.

In percent notation, one tenth of one percent is 0.1%. On high school entrance exams, students often mistakenly think that 0.1% is equal to 0.1. As you know, 0.1% is equal to 0.001.

Here are some common percentage and fractional equivalents you should remember:

- Ten percent (10%) is one tenth $\left(\dfrac{1}{10} \right)$ or 0.10.
- Twelve and one-half percent (12.5%) is one eighth $\left(\dfrac{1}{8} \right)$ or 0.125.
- Twenty percent (20%) is one fifth $\left(\dfrac{1}{5} \right)$ or 0.20.
- Twenty-five percent (25%) is one quarter $\left(\dfrac{1}{4} \right)$ or 0.25.
- Thirty-three and one-third percent $\left(33\dfrac{1}{3}\% \right)$ is one third $\left(\dfrac{1}{3} \right)$ or $0.33\overline{3}$.
- Fifty percent (50%) is one half $\left(\dfrac{1}{2} \right)$ or 0.50.
- Sixty-six and two-thirds percent $\left(66\dfrac{2}{3}\% \right)$ is two thirds $\left(\dfrac{2}{3} \right)$ or $0.66\overline{6}$.

TIP

When multiplying by percentages, students frequently mix up 0.1 and 0.1%. If you are trying to find 0.1% of something, you must multiply by 0.001, not 0.1, to get the correct answer.

Scan this QR code to learn more about percents.

Test Yourself 7

Rename each fraction, first as a decimal and then as a percent. The answers will follow.

1. $\dfrac{2}{4} =$

2. $\dfrac{7}{8} =$

3. $\dfrac{5}{6} =$

4. $\dfrac{3}{4} =$

5. $\dfrac{2}{3} =$

6. $\dfrac{3}{5} =$

7. $\dfrac{4}{10} =$

8. $\dfrac{1}{4} =$

9. $\dfrac{2}{5} =$

10. $\dfrac{1}{8} =$

Answers:

1. $0.5 = 50\%$

2. $0.875 = 87\dfrac{1}{2}\%$

3. $0.833 = 83\dfrac{1}{3}\%$

4. $0.75 = 75\%$

5. $0.666 = 66\dfrac{2}{3}\%$

6. $0.60 = 60\%$

7. $0.40 = 40\%$

8. $0.25 = 25\%$

9. $0.40 = 40\%$

10. $0.125 = 12\dfrac{1}{2}\%$

Percentages over 100%

Sometimes, we are concerned with more than 100% of something. When things are growing, or increasing in size or amount, we may want to compare their new size to the size they once were. For example, suppose we measured the heights of three plants to be 6 inches, 9 inches, and 12 inches one week and discover a week later that the first plant is still 6 inches tall, but the second and third ones are now 18 inches tall.

The 6-inch plant grew zero percent because it didn't grow at all. The second plant added 100% to its size. It doubled in height. The third plant added 50% to its height.

We can also say:

The first plant is 100% of its original height.

The second plant grew to 200% of its original height.

The third plant grew to 150% of its original height.

Solving Percentage Problems

A question involving percentages might involve one of these three tasks:

- Finding the percentage of a number
- Finding a number when a percentage is given
- Finding what percentage one number is of another

Regardless of the task, three distinct values are involved: the part, the whole, and the percentage. Often, the problem will give you two of the three numbers, and your job is to find the missing value. To work with percentages, use the following formula:

$$\text{percentage} = \frac{\text{part}}{\text{whole}} \times 100$$

Once again, knowing any two of those values allows you to determine the third.

Finding the Percentage

30 is what percent of 50?

In this question, 50 is the whole, and 30 is the part. Your task is to find the missing percent:

$$\text{percentage} = \frac{30}{50} \times 100$$
$$= 60\%$$

Finding the Part

What number is 25% of 80?

In this question, 80 is the whole, and 25 is the percentage. Your task is to find the part:

$$25\% = \frac{\text{part}}{80} \times 100$$

In this situation, it can be helpful to change the percentage into its decimal form (.25), which then lets you drop the 100 from the equation or to represent the percentage as a fraction, in this case $\frac{25}{100}$. That gives us a new form of the equation:

$$\frac{25}{100} = \frac{\text{part}}{80}$$

To solve for the missing part, cross multiply 25 with 80 and 100 with the missing part. That yields the following:

$$100(\text{part}) = 25(80)$$
$$100(\text{part}) = 2000$$
$$\text{part} = \frac{2000}{100}$$
$$\text{part} = 20$$

25% of 80 is 20. Because of the values used, there are any number of ways you could have come to that solution faster, by simplifying the left fraction to $\frac{1}{4}$ or calculating $80 \div 4$ or $80 \times .25$, but it's important that you see the full process. Let's look at how you can streamline your work in the next example.

Finding the Whole

75% of what number is 150?

In this question, 150 is the part, and 75 is the percentage. Your task is to find the whole. Here's the streamlined equation:

$$\frac{75}{100} = \frac{150}{\text{whole}}$$

Here, you can simplify the fraction on the left to $\frac{3}{4}$ and then cross multiply:

$$\frac{3}{4} = \frac{150}{\text{whole}}$$
$$\text{whole}(3) = 150(4)$$

Then, multiply the two diagonally situated numbers you know: $150 \times 4 = 600$. Finally, divide 600 by 3, which equals 200. 75% of 200 is 150.

$$\text{whole} = 200$$

Percent Increase and Decrease

You've likely encountered the concept of percent change with investment interest, sales tax, and discount pricing. Percent change always relates to the value before the change.

 TIP

You can find a percentage with the following equation:

$\text{percentage} = \left(\dfrac{part}{whole} \right) \times 100$. That equation can be flipped around algebraically to find

that $part = whole \times \left(\dfrac{percentage}{100} \right)$ or $whole = part \div \left(\dfrac{percentage}{100} \right)$.

Here are two examples:

10 increased by what percent is 12?

The amount of the increase is 2.

Compare the change (2) to the original number (10).

The change in percent is $\frac{2}{10}$, or 20%.

Example:

12 decreased by what percent is 10?

The amount of the decrease is 2.

Compare the change (2) to the original number (12).

The change is $\frac{2}{12}$, or $\frac{1}{6}$ (or 16.66%).

Notice that the percent increase from 10 to 12 (20%) is not the same as the percent decrease from 12 to 10 (16.66%). That's because the original number (before the change) is different in the two questions.

Percent-change problems typically involve tax, interest, profit, discount, or weight. In handling these problems, you might need to calculate more than one percent change.

Let's look at an example problem.

EXAMPLE:

A computer originally priced at $500 is discounted by 10%, then by another 10%. What is the price of the computer after the second discount, to the nearest dollar?

A. $400

B. $405

C. $425

D. $450

Solution:

The correct answer is B. After the first 10% discount, the price was $450 ($500 minus 10% of $500). After the second discount, which is calculated based on the $450 price, the price of the computer is $405 ($450 minus 10% of $450).

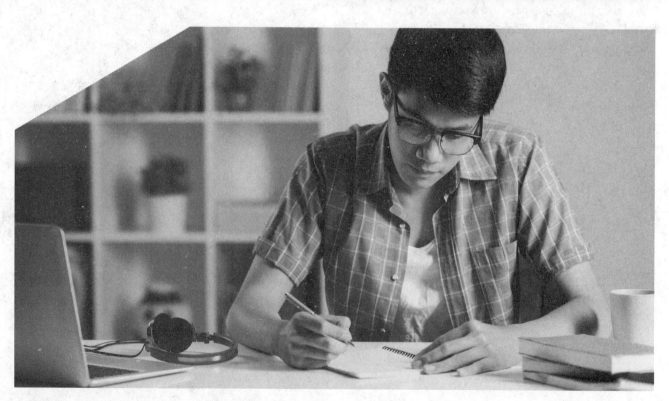

RATIOS AND PROPORTIONS

A **ratio** expresses proportion or comparative size—the size of one quantity relative to the size of another. Write a ratio by placing a colon (:) between the two numbers. Read the colon as the word "to." For example, read the ratio 3:5 as "3 to 5." As with fractions, you can reduce ratios to lowest terms by canceling common factors. For example, given a menagerie of 28 pets that includes 12 cats and 16 dogs:

The ratio of cats to dogs is 12:16, or 3:4 ("3 to 4").

The ratio of dogs to cats is 16:12, or 4:3 ("4 to 3").

The ratio of cats to the total number of pets is 12:28, or 3:7 ("3 to 7").

The ratio of dogs to the total number of pets is 16:28, or 4:7 ("4 to 7").

Another way to think about a ratio is as a fraction. A **proportion** is an equation relating two ratios; it is expressed by equating two fractions, say $\frac{1}{2} = \frac{4}{8}$. Another way of saying that two ratios (or fractions) are equivalent is to say that they are *proportionate*. For example, the ratio 12:16 is proportionate to the ratio 3:4. Similarly, the fraction $\frac{12}{16}$ is proportionate to the fraction $\frac{3}{4}$.

Proportions are formulated when one ratio is known and one of the two quantities in an equivalent ratio is unknown. They arise when changing units of measurement or scaling up a ratio, like in a recipe, among other applications. Since you can express any ratio as a fraction, you can set two equivalent ratios (also called proportionate ratios) equal to each other as fractions. The ratio 16:28 is proportionate to the ratio 4:7 because $\frac{16}{28} = \frac{4}{7}$.

If one of the four terms is missing from the equation (the proportion), you can solve for the missing term using the same method that you learned for solving percent problems:

1. Simplify the known fraction, if possible.
2. Cross-multiply the numbers you know.
3. Divide the product by the third number you know.

For example, if the ratio 10:15 is proportionate to 14:x, you can find the missing number by first setting up the following proportion:

$$\frac{10}{15} = \frac{14}{x}$$

Reading the ratio 10:15 as a fraction, simplify it to $\frac{2}{3}$.

$$\frac{2}{3} = \frac{14}{x}$$

Then, cross multiply the numbers you know: $3 \times 14 = 42$. Finally, divide by the third number you know: $42 \div 2 = 21$. The ratio 10:15 is equivalent to the ratio 14:21.

You'll often encounter proportion problems as word problems. Word problems will require you to parse out the numbers and then set up the ratios so that they are proportionate in order to solve for the missing term. Let's look at a sample problem.

EXAMPLE:

Suppose there are 2 hockey sticks for every 5 pucks in the storage locker room. If the last count was 60 pucks, how many hockey sticks are in the storage room?

Solution:

Let h denote the number of hockey sticks in the storage room. Here, we know that there are 2 hockey sticks for every 5 pucks. We know that there's a total of 60 pucks, but we don't know how many hockey sticks there are. However, because the number of hockey sticks is proportional to the number of pucks, we can scale up the ratio we do know to solve for the number of hockey sticks.

Set up the proportion as follows:

$$\frac{2}{5} = \frac{h}{60}$$
$$5h = 120$$
$$h = 24$$

Test Yourself 9

Write each problem as a ratio. The answers will follow.

1. If Imani can read 10 pages in 15 minutes, how long does it take her to read 40 pages?

2. At an elementary school, there are 17 students to every 1 teacher. There are a total of 425 students. How many teachers are there?

3. At an aquarium, there are 14 penguins for every 2 octopi. If there are 8 octopi, how many penguins are there?

4. The local grocery store has three times as many cashiers as janitors. If there are 21 cashiers, how many janitors are there?

5. For every day of rain in Los Angeles, there are 7 days of sunshine. If there were 315 days of sunshine, how many days of rain were there?

Answers:

1. 60 minutes
2. 25 teachers
3. 56 penguins
4. 7 janitors
5. 45 days of rain

PROBABILITY

Probability refers to the statistical chances of an event occurring (or not occurring). By definition, probability ranges from 0 to 1. Probability is never negative, and it is never greater than 1.

Here's the basic formula for determining probability:

$$\text{Probability} = \frac{\text{number of desired outcomes}}{\text{total possible outcomes}}$$

Probability can be expressed as a fraction, a percent, or a decimal number.

Determining Probability (Single Event)

Probability plays an integral role in games of chance. In the throw of a single die, for example, the probability of rolling a 5 is "one in six," or $\frac{1}{6}$, or 16.66%. Of course, the probability of rolling any other number is the same. A standard deck of 52 playing cards contains 12 face cards. The probability of selecting a face card from a full deck is $\frac{12}{52}$ or $\frac{3}{13}$. The probability of selecting a queen from a full deck is $\frac{1}{13}$.

Determining Probability (Two Events)

To determine probability involving two or more events, you must distinguish probabilities involving **independent** events from an event that is **dependent** on another one.

Two events are independent if neither event affects the probability that the other will occur. The events may involve the random selection of one object from *each of two or more groups*. Or they may involve the random selection of one object from a group, then *replacing* it and selecting again (as in a "second round" or "another turn" of a game).

In either scenario, to find the probability of two events BOTH occurring, multiply together their individual probabilities:

probability of event 1 occurring

×

probability of event 2 occurring

=

probability of both events occurring

For example, assume that you randomly select one letter from each of two sets: {A, B} and {C, D, E}. The probability of selecting A and C $= \frac{1}{2} \times \frac{1}{3} = \frac{1}{6}$.

To calculate the probability that two events will NOT BOTH occur, subtract the probability of both events occurring from 1.

EXAMPLE:

If you randomly select one candy from a jar containing two cherry candies, two licorice candies, and one peppermint candy, what is the probability of selecting a cherry candy?

A. $\frac{1}{6}$

B. $\frac{1}{3}$

C. $\frac{2}{5}$

D. $\frac{3}{5}$

The correct answer is C. There are two ways among five possible occurrences that a cherry candy will be selected. Thus, the probability of selecting a cherry candy is $\frac{2}{5}$.

For dependent probability, two distinct events might be related in that one event affects the probability of the other one occurring—for example, randomly selecting one object from a group, then selecting a second object from the same group without replacing the first selection. Removing one object from the group increases the odds of selecting any particular object from those that remain.

For example, assume that you randomly select one letter from the set {A, B, C, D}. Then, from the remaining three letters, you select another letter. What is the probability of selecting both A and B? To answer this question, you need to consider each of the two selections separately.

In the first selection, the probability of selecting either A or B is $\frac{2}{4}$. But the probability of selecting the second of the two is $\frac{1}{3}$. Why? Because after the first selection, only *three* letters remain from which to select. Since the question asks for the chances of selecting both A and B (as opposed to either one), multiply the two individual probabilities: $\frac{2}{4} \times \frac{1}{3} = \frac{2}{12}$, or $\frac{1}{6}$.

EXAMPLE:

A gaming die is a cube with numbers 1–6 on its faces, each number on a different face. In a roll of two gaming dice, what is the probability that the two numbers facing up will total 12?

A. $\dfrac{1}{64}$

B. $\dfrac{1}{36}$

C. $\dfrac{1}{12}$

D. $\dfrac{1}{9}$

The correct answer is B. The only two-number combination on the dice that can total 12 is 6 + 6. The probability of rolling 6 on each die is $\dfrac{1}{6}$. Accordingly, the probability of rolling 6 on both dice is $\dfrac{1}{6} \times \dfrac{1}{6} = \dfrac{1}{36}$.

MEASUREMENT CONVERSIONS

A common real-world application of ratios and proportions is converting measurements from one form to another. While the U.S. has its own standard system of measurement, most of the world uses the metric system. As you've probably noticed, some things are commonly expressed in standard units, like miles per hour in speed limits or two cups of flour in a recipe. If you run track or cross country, you've probably tried a 100-meter dash or a 5K, which are metric units. Because we see both systems used in different parts of daily life, it's helpful to know how to convert between the two systems.

Measurement conversions are also helpful when you want to convert from one unit of measurement to another within the same system. For example, you wouldn't say that you've walked 5,280 feet to the grocery store. Instead, you would express that distance as a mile, since there are 5,280 feet in a mile. Conceptually, we can better understand longer distances in terms of larger units rather than smaller units. If you're solving

a problem and you notice that the figure could be more efficiently expressed in a different unit, you'll want to convert that figure to the most practical unit.

On the exam, you might be expected to know certain common conversions. For example, knowing how many feet are in a yard or a mile would be advantageous. You should also know how many cups are in a pint, pints in a quart, quarts in a gallon, and so on. Similarly, knowing that the metric system operates on powers of ten will allow you to quickly convert from millimeters to meters or from meters to kilometers. Some conversions, however, are less intuitive, especially when going from the U.S. system to the metric system and vice versa. For example, converting from Fahrenheit to Celsius when discussing temperature requires you to memorize the formula: $(F - 32) \times 5 \div 9 = C$. In more complex conversions, you'll likely be given the necessary conversion factors. Here, we'll cover the basics for how to perform common unit conversions.

METRIC SYSTEM MEASUREMENTS		
Prefix	**Power**	**Meaning**
kilo	10^3	1,000
hecto	10^2	100
deca	10^1	10
Base Unit	10^0	1
deci	10^{-1}	0.1
centi	10^{-2}	0.01
milli	10^{-3}	0.001
micro	10^{-6}	0.000001
nano	10^{-9}	0.000000001

Let's start with the metric system. Since the metric system is based on powers of 10, converting units expressed in the metric system is a matter of appropriately moving the decimal point. For example, 300 cm = 3 m because 1 cm = 10^{-2} m. The exponent indicates the number of decimal places we're working with and whether those places are bigger than one or smaller than one. Positive exponents indicate big numbers greater than one, while negative exponents indicate much smaller parts of numbers that are less than one. (We'll cover this concept in more detail in the next chapter.) In this case, therefore, multiplying both sides by 300 yields the result.

Likewise, 400 dm = 40 m since 1 dm = 10^{-1} m. In both cases, note that the conversion only involved moving the decimal point to the *left* the number of places indicated by the power without the negative sign (2 and 1, respectively). This is always true when converting a unit lower on the table to one higher up. The exact opposite is true if you are converting a unit higher on the table to one lower. For instance, 2 km = 200 hm because 1 km = 100 hm.

Converting units in the U.S. customary system is slightly more involved only because the units are not based on powers of 10. Here, the key is to set up products of fractions that show the original units canceling and the new units remaining in the final product. For example, to convert 3.5 feet to inches, we use the conversion factor 1 foot = 12 inches in the following computation:

$$3.5 \text{ feet} = \frac{3.5 \text{ feet}}{1} \times \frac{12 \text{ inches}}{1 \text{ foot}} = \frac{3.5 \text{ feet}}{1} \times \frac{12 \text{ inches}}{1 \text{ foot}} = (3.5) \times (12) \text{ inches} = 42 \text{ inches}$$

This works because the fraction $\frac{12 \text{ inches}}{1 \text{ foot}} = 1$.

Here's a list of common conversions for reference:

- 1 foot = 12 inches
- 1 yard = 3 feet = 36 inches
- 1 mile = 5,280 feet
- 1 lb. = 16 oz
- 1 ton = 2,000 lb.

- 1 gallon = 4 quarts = 16 cups
- 1 cup = 8 ounces

Converting units of speed involves making *two* conversions—one for the numerator and one for the denominator. For example, to convert 85 miles per hour to *feet per minute*, we use the conversion factors 1 mile = 5,280 feet and 1 hour = 60 minutes and perform the following computation:

$$\frac{85 \text{ miles}}{1 \text{ hour}} = \frac{85 \text{ miles}}{1 \text{ hour}} \times \frac{5,280 \text{ feet}}{1 \text{ mile}} \times \frac{1 \text{ hour}}{60 \text{ minutes}} = \frac{85 \times 5,280}{60} \text{ feet per minute}$$

You can also convert between the metric and U.S. systems, but you will need to use established conversion factors (like 1 m ≈ 3.28 feet) to do so. In this case, you'll likely be given the necessary conversion factors.

Test Yourself 10

Solve each conversion problem. The answers will follow.

1. Keisha's doctor says she should be drinking 11.5 cups of water per day. How many ounces of water should she drink per day?

2. Haziel is 5 feet, 8 inches tall. How tall is she in inches?

3. Angel's dad drives 15 miles to work one way. What is the length of his commute in feet?

4. Ian's dog weighed in at 67 pounds at the vet. What is the dog's weight in ounces?

5. Afi's hair is 400 millimeters long. How long is her hair in meters?

Answers:

1. 92 ounces
2. 68 inches
3. 158,400 feet
4. 1,072 ounces
5. 0.4 meter

SUMMING IT UP

- If you are having difficulties with any mathematics topic, talk with a teacher or refer to any of your math textbooks.

- Use the exercises in this chapter to determine what you DON'T know well and concentrate your study on those areas.

- Review the math symbols covered in this chapter so that you're prepared when you encounter them in math problems.

- Know the different types of numbers: whole numbers, integers, rational numbers, irrational numbers, and signed numbers.

- Using central tendency terms—mean, median, and mode—can help you summarize and describe a set of data.

- Properties describe how numbers behave in consistent and predictable ways, which simplifies the process of solving math problems. These will be especially important for solving algebraic equations.

- When solving equations, use the mnemonic device "Please excuse my dear Aunt Sally" to remember the order of operations:

  - Parentheses
  - Exponents (and Square Roots)
  - Multiplication
  - Division
  - Addition
  - Subtraction

- Decimals represent parts of numbers: Everything to the left of a decimal point is a whole number and everything to the right of a decimal point represents a part of the whole.

- A factor is a number that can be divided into a whole number evenly without leaving a remainder. Multiples are similar to factors in that they are whole numbers into which a number can be divided evenly. Being able to determine the greatest common factor and least common multiple of a set of numbers is important for solving problems with fractions.

- A fraction is a part of a whole and consists of both a numerator and a denominator. Proper fractions are those in which the numerator is smaller than the denominator and improper fractions are those in which the numerator is greater than the denominator.

- Percentages are fractions or decimals written in a different form. They represent parts of numbers, and you can convert between percentages, fractions, and decimals. Percentage problems may require you to find the percentage, the part, the whole, or the percent increase or decrease.

- Ratios express the size of one quantity relative to the size of another. Proportions are equations relating two ratios, expressed by equating two fractions.

- Questions centered on probability may ask you to calculate the odds of performing a certain task by dividing the number of ways it could happen by the total number of possible outcomes. Similar questions might require you to identify patterns and determine relationships to anticipate the next item in a series.

- Make sure you are familiar with common, everyday conversions, like feet to a mile, ounces in a pound, quarts in a gallon, etc. Also, remember that the metric system is based on powers of 10, which should simplify the process of conversions. For conversions between the U.S. system and the metric system, you will likely be given the conversion factors on the exam.

KNOWLEDGE CHECK

BASIC MATHEMATICS
50 Questions—40 Minutes

Directions: In the following questions, work out each problem and mark the letter that corresponds to the correct answer. The answers will follow.

1. $(-12) + (+4) =$

   A. -16

   B. -8

   C. $+8$

   D. $+16$

2. $(-22) - (-18) =$

   A. -30

   B. -4

   C. $+6$

   D. $+13$

3. Adam scored 84, 65, 76, 76, 92, 75, and 85 on his math tests. What was his median grade?

   A. 75

   B. 76

   C. 80

   D. 84

4. Six girls sold the following numbers of boxes of cookies: 42, 35, 28, 30, 24, 27. What was the mean number of boxes sold?

   A. 26

   B. 29

   C. 30

   D. 31

5. In the expression, $166 \div 42 + (17 \times 2) - 7^2$, what operation will you perform first to simplify?

   A. $166 \div 42$

   B. $42 + (17 \times 2)$

   C. -7^2

   D. 17×2

6. $6 \times 4 \div 8 + 8^2 \div 2 - 5 =$

   A. -30

   B. 20

   C. 24

   D. 30

7. $(17 - 10 \div 5) + 6 \times 3$

   A. 0

   B. 14

   C. 33

   D. 40

8. $144 \div 12 + (-4 + 1) \times -10 =$

   A. -42

   B. 9

   C. 36

   D. 42

9. $(6 \times 10 \div 15) - (3^2 + 12) =$

   A. −35

   B. −15

   C. 5

   D. 12

10. $-2(64 \div 2^3) + 10 - 3^2 =$

    A. −15

    B. −15

    C. 10

    D. 12

11. $3.41 + 5.6 + 0.873 =$

    A. 4.843

    B. 9.883

    C. 15.264

    D. 17.743

12. $3.7 \overline{)2,339.86}$

    A. 62.34

    B. 63.24

    C. 632.4

    D. 642.3

13. $\$59.60 \div \$0.40 =$

    A. 0.149

    B. 1.49

    C. 14.9

    D. 149

14. $0.3 \times 0.08 =$

    A. 0.0024

    B. 0.024

    C. 0.240

    D. 2.40

15. The greatest common factor of 24 and 12 is

    A. 2

    B. 4

    C. 6

    D. 12

16. The greatest common factor of 10 and 25 is

    A. 2

    B. 5

    C. 10

    D. 25

17. The greatest common factor of 6 and 9 is

    A. 2

    B. 3

    C. 6

    D. 9

18. The least common multiple of 4 and 14 is

    A. 14

    B. 16

    C. 28

    D. 56

19. $\dfrac{8}{15} \times \dfrac{3}{4} =$

    A. $\dfrac{1}{5}$

    B. $\dfrac{3}{10}$

    C. $\dfrac{2}{5}$

    D. $\dfrac{3}{5}$

20. $\frac{3}{4} + \frac{3}{8} =$

A. $\frac{7}{8}$

B. $\frac{8}{9}$

C. $1\frac{1}{8}$

D. $1\frac{3}{8}$

21. $45,286$

$\times \quad 4\frac{1}{5}$

A. $190,021\frac{1}{5}$

B. $190,201\frac{1}{5}$

C. $190,202\frac{2}{5}$

D. $190,234$

22. $4\frac{1}{3} \overline{\smash{\big)}\, \frac{1}{4}}$

A. $\frac{3}{52}$

B. $\frac{5}{52}$

C. $\frac{12}{52}$

D. $17\frac{1}{3}$

23. $\frac{1}{9} \times \frac{2}{3} \times \frac{7}{8} =$

A. $\frac{6}{108}$

B. $\frac{7}{108}$

C. $\frac{12}{52}$

D. $\frac{14}{27}$

24. $8\frac{1}{6}$

$-5\frac{2}{3}$

A. $2\frac{1}{3}$

B. $2\frac{1}{2}$

C. $3\frac{1}{6}$

D. $3\frac{2}{3}$

25. $3\frac{1}{4}$

$4\frac{1}{8}$

$+4\frac{1}{2}$

A. $11\frac{5}{8}$

B. $11\frac{3}{4}$

C. $11\frac{7}{8}$

D. 12

26. $5\dfrac{1}{4} \times 2\dfrac{2}{7} =$

A. $10\dfrac{3}{28}$

B. 11

C. $11\dfrac{4}{7}$

D. 12

27. $\dfrac{3}{4}\overline{\smash{\big)}\,\dfrac{9}{16}}$

A. $\dfrac{27}{64}$

B. $\dfrac{7}{16}$

C. $\dfrac{5}{8}$

D. $\dfrac{3}{4}$

28. $\begin{aligned}10\dfrac{2}{3}\\-9\dfrac{1}{2}\\\hline\end{aligned}$

A. $\dfrac{13}{32}$

B. $1\dfrac{1}{6}$

C. $1\dfrac{1}{3}$

D. $1\dfrac{1}{2}$

29. 10% of 32 =

A. 3

B. 3.2

C. 3.5

D. 4

30. 8 is 25% of what number?

A. 16

B. 24

C. 32

D. 40

31. 12 is what percent of 24?

A. 12%

B. 24%

C. 30%

D. 50%

32. 20% of 360 =

A. 72

B. 75

C. 80

D. 90

33. 5 is what percent of 60?

A. 8

B. $8\dfrac{1}{3}\%$

C. $8\dfrac{2}{3}\%$

D. 9

34. A smartphone originally priced at $1,200 is discounted by 10%, then by another 10%. What is the price of the smartphone after the second discount, to the nearest dollar?

A. $960

B. $972

C. $978

D. $980

35. A library contains 600 books on arts and crafts. If this is 2% of the total number of books on the shelves, how many books does the library own?

    A. 12,000

    B. 30,000

    C. 60,000

    D. 120,000

36. During a sale, the price of a computer was discounted from $750 to $600. By what percent was the price decreased?

    A. 15%

    B. 20%

    C. 25%

    D. 30%

37. Maurice sold 24 health club memberships this week. If he sold 18 club memberships last week, his sales this week are what percent higher than his sales last week?

    A. 18%

    B. 24%

    C. 25%

    D. $33\frac{1}{3}$%

38. Duncan purchases $500 worth of cryptocurrency. The cryptocurrency's value rises by 20% during the first week, but then falls by 20% during the following week. What is the net percent change in the cryptocurrency's value?

    A. The value remains the same.

    B. The value increases by 2%.

    C. The value decreases by 4%.

    D. The value decreases by 1%.

39. A recipe for 6 quarts of punch calls for $\frac{3}{4}$ cups of sugar. How much sugar is needed for 9 quarts of punch?

    A. $\frac{5}{8}$ of a cup

    B. $\frac{7}{8}$ of a cup

    C. $1\frac{1}{8}$ cups

    D. $2\frac{1}{4}$ cups

40. A house plan uses the scale $\frac{1}{4}$ inch = 1 foot, and in the drawing the living room is 7 inches long. If the scale changes to 1 inch = 1 foot, what will the length of the living room be in the new drawing?

    A. 18 inches

    B. 28 inches

    C. 30 inches

    D. 36 inches

41. The scale of a certain map is 4 inches = 32 miles. The number of inches that would represent 80 miles is

    A. 8

    B. 12

    C. 10

    D. 16

42. A recipe calls for $1\frac{1}{2}$ cups of sugar. It is necessary to make eight times the recipe for a church supper. If 2 cups of sugar equal 1 pound, how many pounds of sugar will be needed to make the recipe?

   A. 4
   B. 6
   C. 8
   D. 10

43. Suppose you roll a fair 6-sided die three times in succession and record the result each time. What is the probability that you do NOT roll three 5s?

   A. $\frac{1}{216}$

   B. $\frac{125}{216}$

   C. $\frac{35}{36}$

   D. $\frac{215}{216}$

44. A recipe calls for basil, thyme, and oregano in a ratio of 4:2:3. If 12 ounces of oregano are use, how much basil is used?

   A. 12 ounces
   B. 14 ounces
   C. 16 ounces
   D. 18 ounces

45. A vase contains 14 carnations and 11 daisies. If two flowers are selected at random without replacement, what is the probability of selecting two daisies?

   A. $\frac{11}{25} \times \frac{10}{25}$

   B. $\frac{11}{25} \times \frac{11}{25}$

   C. $\frac{11}{14} \times \frac{10}{14}$

   D. $\frac{11}{25} \times \frac{10}{24}$

46. How many yards of ribbon will it take to make 45 badges if each badge uses 4 inches of ribbon?

   A. 5
   B. 9
   C. 11
   D. 15

47. If an inch of wire costs $0.20, how much will 5.25 feet of wire cost?

   A. $0.87
   B. $2.40
   C. $12.60
   D. $63.00

48. A bag of sugar weighs 2.5 kg. What is its weight in grams?

   A. 25 grams
   B. 250 grams
   C. 2,500 grams
   D. 25,000 grams

49. A car is driving 60 mph. What is the speed of the car in feet per minute?

   A. 4,000
   B. 4,500
   C. 5,000
   D. 5,280

50. If one pound equals 16 ounces, how many pounds are in 820 ounces?

   A. $48\frac{1}{2}$

   B. $51\frac{1}{4}$

   C. 54

   D. $56\frac{1}{2}$

ANSWER KEY AND EXPLANATIONS

1. B	11. B	21. B	31. D	41. C
2. B	12. C	22. A	32. A	42. B
3. B	13. D	23. B	33. B	43. D
4. D	14. B	24. B	34. B	44. C
5. D	15. D	25. C	35. B	45. D
6. D	16. B	26. D	36. B	46. A
7. C	17. B	27. D	37. D	47. C
8. D	18. C	28. B	38. C	48. C
9. A	19. C	29. B	39. C	49. D
10. A	20. C	30. C	40. B	50. B

1. **The correct answer is B.** When adding two numbers of unlike sign, subtract and assign the sign of the larger number.

2. **The correct answer is B.** Minus negative becomes plus positive. The problem then reads:

$$(-22) + (+18) = -4.$$

3. **The correct answer is B.** Rewrite these 7 scores in order from least to greatest: 65, 75, 76, 76, 84, 85, 92. The median, or middle value, is 76.

4. **The correct answer is D.** To find the mean, add all the numbers and divide the sum by the number of terms.

$$42 + 35 + 28 + 30 + 24 + 27 = 186$$

$$186 \div 6 = 31$$

5. **The correct answer is D.** Remember PEMDAS, the mnemonic device for remembering the order of operations, and you will know that the first step is to solve what is inside the parentheses first. 17 × 2 is the expression inside the parentheses, so it is the first thing you should solve.

6. **The correct answer is D.** Remember the order of operations as you solve the problem:

$$6 \times 4 \div 8 + 8^2 \div 2 - 5$$
$$6 \times 4 \div 8 + 64 \div 2 - 5$$
$$24 \div 8 + 64 \div 2 - 5$$
$$3 + 64 \div 2 - 5$$
$$3 + 32 - 5$$
$$35 - 5$$
$$= 30$$

7. **The correct answer is C.** Remember the order of operations as you work through the problem:

$$(17 - 10 \div 5) + 6 \times 3$$
$$(17 - 2) + 6 \times 3$$
$$15 + 6 \times 3$$
$$15 + 18$$
$$= 33$$

8. **The correct answer is D.** Remember the order of operations as you solve the problem:

$$144 \div 12 + (-4 + 1) \times -10$$
$$144 \div 12 + (-3) \times -10$$
$$12 + (-3) \times -10$$
$$12 + 30$$
$$= 42$$

9. **The correct answer is A.** Remember the order of operations as you work through the problem:

$$(6 \times 10 \div 15) - (3^3 + 12)$$
$$(6 \times 10 \div 15) - (27 + 12)$$
$$(60 \div 15) - (27 + 12)$$
$$4 - (27 + 12)$$
$$4 - (39)$$
$$= -35$$

10. **The correct answer is A.** Remember the order of operations as you proceed through the problem:

$$-2(64 \div 2^3) + (10 - 3^2) =$$
$$-2(64 \div 8) + (10 - 9)$$
$$-2(8) + (10 - 9)$$
$$-16 + (10 - 9)$$
$$-16 + 1$$
$$= -15$$

11. **The correct answer is B.**

$$\begin{array}{r} 3.410 \\ 5.600 \\ +\,0.873 \\ \hline 9.883 \end{array}$$

12. **The correct answer is C.**

$$\begin{array}{r} 63\,2.39 \approx 632.4 \\ 3.7\overline{)2339.8\,60} \\ \underline{222} \\ 119 \\ \underline{111} \\ 88 \\ 74 \\ \hline 146 \\ \underline{111} \\ 350 \\ \underline{333} \\ \hline 17 \end{array}$$

13. **The correct answer is D.**

$$\begin{array}{r} 1\,49 \\ \$0.40\overline{)\$59.60} \\ \underline{40} \\ 19\,6 \\ \underline{16\,0} \\ 3\,60 \\ 3\,60 \end{array}$$

14. **The correct answer is B.** Add up the places to the right of the decimal point to get 0.024.

15. **The correct answer is D.** The greatest number by which both 12 and 24 can be divided is 12.

16. **The correct answer is B.** The greatest number by which both 10 and 25 can be divided is 5.

17. **The correct answer is B.** The greatest number by which both 6 and 9 can be divided is 3.

18. **The correct answer is C.** The lowest multiple that both 4 and 14 share is 28.

19. **The correct answer is C.**

$$\frac{\cancel{8}^2}{\cancel{15}_5} \times \frac{\cancel{3}^1}{4_1} = \frac{2}{5}$$

20. **The correct answer is C.**

$$\frac{3}{4} = \frac{6}{8}$$
$$+ \frac{3}{8} = \frac{3}{8}$$
$$\overline{\frac{9}{8} = 1\frac{1}{8}}$$

21. **The correct answer is B.**

$$\frac{1}{5} = 0.20$$

$$\begin{array}{r} 45{,}286 \\ \times 4.20 \\ \hline 905{,}720 \\ 181{,}144 \\ \hline 190{,}201.20 = 190{,}201\frac{1}{5} \end{array}$$

22. **The correct answer is A.**

$$\frac{1}{4} \div 4\frac{1}{3} = \frac{1}{4} \div \frac{13}{3} = \frac{1}{4} \times \frac{3}{13} = \frac{3}{52}$$

23. **The correct answer is B.**

$$\frac{1}{9} \times \frac{\cancel{2}^1}{3} \times \frac{7}{\cancel{8}_4} = \frac{7}{108}$$

24. **The correct answer is B.**

$$8\frac{1}{6} = 7\frac{7}{6}$$
$$-5\frac{2}{3} = 5\frac{4}{6}$$
$$\overline{2\frac{3}{6} = 2\frac{1}{2}}$$

25. **The correct answer is C.**

$$3\frac{1}{4} = 3\frac{2}{8}$$
$$4\frac{1}{8} = 4\frac{1}{8}$$
$$+\ 4\frac{1}{2} = 4\frac{4}{8}$$
$$\overline{\quad\quad\quad 11\frac{7}{8}}$$

26. **The correct answer is D.**

$$5\frac{1}{4} \times 2\frac{2}{7} = \frac{^3\cancel{21}}{\cancel{4}_1} \times \frac{^4\cancel{16}}{7_1} = \frac{12}{1} = 12$$

27. **The correct answer is D.**

$$\frac{9}{16} \div \frac{3}{4} = \frac{^3\cancel{9}}{\cancel{16}_4} \times \frac{^1\cancel{4}}{\cancel{3}_1} = \frac{3}{4}$$

28. **The correct answer is B.**

$$10\frac{2}{3} = 10\frac{4}{6}$$
$$-\ 9\frac{1}{2} = 9\frac{3}{6}$$
$$\overline{\quad\quad\quad 1\frac{1}{6}}$$

29. **The correct answer is B.** Convert 10% to a decimal, 0.10, and multiply the total amount by the decimal to find the answer: $32 \times 0.10 = 3.2\%$.

30. **The correct answer is C.** Remember that you can't divide by a decimal, so if the divisor is a decimal, you must move the decimal point to the right until the divisor becomes a whole number. As such, we must first divide 8 by 25: $8 \div 25 = 0.32$. Then, move the decimal point two places to the right, which gives you 32.

31. **The correct answer is D.** If we express our part and our whole as a fraction, 12 would be the numerator and 24 would be the denominator. In this form, we can see that 12 is a common factor, and we can convert our simplest fraction to a percentage: $\frac{12}{24} = \frac{1}{2} \times 100 = 50\%$.

32. **The correct answer is A.** Start by converting the percentage to a decimal: 0.20. Then, multiply 360 by the decimal: $360 \times 0.20 = 72$.

33. **The correct answer is B.** If we express our part and our whole as a fraction, 5 would be the numerator and 60 would be the denominator. In this form, we can see that 5 is a common factor, so we can simplify the fraction to $\frac{1}{12}$. We can then convert this fraction to a percentage by multiplying by 100: $\frac{1}{12} \times 100 = 8.33\%$ or $8\frac{1}{3}\%$.

34. **The correct answer is B.** After the first 10% discount, the price was $1,080 ($1,200 minus 10% of $120). After the second discount, which is calculated based on the $1,080 price, the price of the computer is $972 ($1,080 minus 10% of $1,080).

35. **The correct answer is B.** The library has 30,000 volumes. If 600 books is 2% of the library's total collection, we can set up a proportion problem to solve for the whole:

$$\frac{2}{100} = \frac{600}{x}$$
$$2x = 60,000$$
$$x = 30,000$$

36. **The correct answer is B.** The total discount was $150, so we need to determine what percentage of the original price, $750, that $150 is. We can set up a proportion that allows us to find the percentage:

$$\frac{x}{100} = \frac{150}{750}$$
$$750x = 150(100)$$
$$750x = 15000$$
$$\frac{750x}{750} = \frac{15000}{750}$$
$$x = 20$$

37. **The correct answer is D.** The original number is 18, and the difference between the two numbers is $24 - 18 = 6$, which is $\frac{1}{3}$ of the original number, or $33\frac{1}{3}\%$.

38. **The correct answer is C.** First, the cryptocurrency rises by 20% ($0.2 \times \$500 = \$100$), so the value is: $\$500 + \$100 = \$600$. Then, it falls by 20% ($0.2 \times \$600 = \$120$), so the final value is: $\$600 - \$120 = \$480$. The difference from the original price is: $\$500 - \$480 = \$20$. Knowing the difference, set up

a proportion problem to determine the percentage of decrease:

$$\frac{20}{500} = \frac{x}{100}$$
$$2000 = 500x$$
$$\frac{2000}{500} = \frac{500x}{500}$$
$$4 = x$$

39. **The correct answer is C.** First, find out how much sugar one quart of punch needs.

$$\frac{3}{4} \text{ cups} \div 6 = \frac{3}{4} \div \frac{6}{1} = \frac{1\!\!\!/ 3}{4} \times \frac{1}{6_2} = \frac{1}{8}$$

For 9 quarts of punch:

$$9 \times \frac{1}{8} = \frac{9}{8} = 1\frac{1}{8}$$

40. **The correct answer is B.** $\frac{1}{4}$ inch = 1 foot, so 1 inch = 4 foot and the living room is $7 \times 4 = 28$ feet long. When the scale changes to 1 inch = 1 foot, the 28-foot living room will be 28 inches on the new drawing.

41. **The correct answer is C.** 4 inches = 32 miles; therefore, 1 inch = $32 \div 4 = 8$ miles. 80 miles would be represented by 10 inches.

42. **The correct answer is B.**

$1\frac{1}{2}$ cups sugar $\times 8 = 12$ cups sugar

12 cups $\div$ 2 cups per pound = 6 pound of sugar

43. **The correct answer is D.** The three rolls are independent of each other, and each has 6 possible outcomes. As such, there are $(6)(6)(6) = 216$ possible three-roll outcomes. There is only one way to get all 5s. The probability of NOT getting three 5s is $\frac{215}{216}$.

44. **The correct answer is C.** Basil and oregano have a part-to-part ratio of 4:3. Set up a proportion to solve for the amount of basil needed:

$$\frac{4}{3} = \frac{x}{12}$$
$$48 = 3x$$
$$\frac{48}{3} = \frac{3x}{3}$$
$$16 = x$$

45. **The correct answer is D.** There are 11 daisies of 25 flowers total that could be chosen in the first selection, so the probability of selecting a daisy is $\frac{11}{25}$. Once this flower is removed, there are 24 remaining in the vase, 10 of which are daisies. The probability of choosing a second daisy is $\frac{10}{24}$. Since the selections are performed in succession, we multiply the probabilities. Therefore, the probability of randomly selecting two daisies is $\frac{11}{25} \times \frac{10}{24}$.

46. **The correct answer is A.** 45 badges $\times$ 4 inches each = 180 inches needed. There are 36 inches in one yard. 180 inches $\div$ 36 = 5 yards of ribbon needed.

47. **The correct answer is C.** If 1 inch of wire costs $0.20, 1 foot costs 12($0.20) = $2.40. Therefore, 5.25 feet of wire cost ($2.40)(5.25) = $12.60.

48. **The correct answer is C.** Remember that the prefix *kilo* means 1,000, so a kilogram is a thousand grams. Accordingly, 2.5 kilograms is 2,500 grams.

49. **The correct answer is D.** Because the car is traveling 60 mph, you know that the car is traveling 1 mile per minute, as there are 60 minutes in an hour. Since you already know that 1 mile is 5,280 feet, you have the answer: 5,280 feet per minute.

50. **The correct answer is B.** Set up a proportion to calculate this conversion problem:

$$\frac{1lb.}{16oz.} = \frac{x}{820oz.}$$
$$820 = 16x$$
$$\frac{820}{16} = \frac{16x}{16}$$
$$51\frac{1}{4} = x$$

CHAPTER

Algebraic Thinking

ALGEBRAIC THINKING

OVERVIEW

Expressions and Equations

Distance, Rate, and Time Problems

Work Problems

Summing It Up

Knowledge Check: Mathematics

Answer Key and Explanations

If you are finishing the eighth grade this year, you might not have had a formal algebra class yet. However, you may be familiar with algebraic terms and expressions, and you have probably solved simple equations. Algebra is essentially the manipulation of mathematical symbols in order to find unknown information. Algebraic thinking is essential for understanding how both numbers and variables can be used together, allowing you to logically solve real-world problems.

This chapter will review the skills you have acquired so far and will show you the kinds of questions you can expect to find on a high school entrance examination. First, we'll discuss how to solve equations. Then, we'll look at two common applications of algebra in the form of word problems.

TACHS   HSPT   ISEE   SSAT   SHSAT

EXPRESSIONS AND EQUATIONS

Fundamentally, algebra is the manipulation of mathematical symbols. More than likely, your familiarity with the field stems from solving for unknowns by applying various rules and procedures. First, we'll discuss how to put an equation into standard form and how to use other types of notation, like scientific notation and factorials. Then, we'll cover the basics of how to solve an equation.

So far, you've already seen plenty of expressions: at least two values with some math operator used between them. Algebraic expressions, however, are usually used to form **equations,** which set two expressions equal to one another. When we're talking about algebraic expressions, know that a **term** is any coefficient, variable, or combination of a coefficient and a variable. In equations, at least one of the terms will be a **variable**—a letter such as x or y that represents a number that can *vary*. It does not need an exponent, but if it has one, it must be a non-negative exponent. A **coefficient** is the number that multiplies with a variable, such as the 2 in $2y$.

Standard Form

Standard form is something you've been using since you learned how to write numbers. Write the number one hundred: 100. That is standard form—the usual way you'd write a number. In addition to being the way you've written numbers all your life, standard form is also an agreed-upon method of writing an equation. The standard form for equations has a couple of rules you need to know.

1. Always set an equation = 0
   Example: $x = 7$ should have everything on the left of the equal sign, and 0 on the right:
   $x - 7 = 0$ is standard form

2. Work from the highest exponent
   Example: $7x^3 + 3x^6 - 5 + 4x^2$ should start with the highest exponent: $3x^6 + 7x^3 + 4x^2 - 5$

By writing equations in standard form, it is easier to locate information because it is presented in a consistent order. When an equation is in standard form, you'll know what to expect and how to proceed with isolating and solving for the variable.

Test Yourself 1

Put the following equations into standard form. The answers will follow.

1. $x + 7 = 49$
2. $x = 4y$
3. $ab = 14c$
4. $4x^3 + 17x^5 - 2 - 4x^9 = -12$
5. $3x + 4y + 5 = 17 + x$

Answers:

1. $x - 42 = 0$
2. $x - 4y = 0$
3. $ab - 14c = 0$
4. $-4x^9 + 17x^5 + 4x^3 + 10 = 0$
5. $2x + 4y - 12 = 0$

Scientific Notation

While standard form helps to present information in a predictable way, it is not as useful for equations with extremely large or small numbers. Instead, you will want to use **scientific notation**, a system for writing extremely large or extremely small numbers more efficiently. For example, the number 380,000,000 is written in standard form. However, writing all of those zeros over and over again can be time consuming. In scientific notation, an integer or decimal number between 1 and 10 is written to the power of 10, which eliminates the need to include all those zeros. We can use scientific notation to express 380,000,000 as 3.8×10^8. Ultimately, scientific notation makes working with very large and small numbers more manageable and convenient.

To explain how we used scientific notation to write 380,000,000 as 3.8×10^8, let's work backwards. First, we start with a value between 1 and 10. In this case, we are using 3.8, the first non-zero digits of the larger value.

To go from 3.8 to 380,000,000, you need to shift the decimal 8 places to the right. The number of places to the right of the decimal point is expressed as the exponent in scientific notation. Here, the exponent is 8. In contrast, a negative exponent would signify a fractional number, since we would be moving that many decimal places to the left instead of the right. Now that we know the exponent is 8, we can write our very large number in scientific notation: 3.8×10^8.

Here are some more examples of how to write numbers in scientific notation.

EXAMPLES:

Write 4 million in scientific notation.

Solution:

4,000,000

Move the decimal point to the left six times to get to a number between 1 and 10.

4.000000

Multiply 4 by 10 to the power of the number of zeros to the right of the decimal point.

4×10^6

Write 735 trillion in scientific notation.

Solution:

735,000,000,000,000

Move the decimal to get a number between 1 and 10.

7.35000000000000

Multiply 7.35 by 10 to the number of digits to the right of the decimal point.

7.35×10^{14}

EXAMPLE:

Write 32,570,000,000 in scientific notation.

Solution:

Move the decimal point to the right until you have a number between 1 and 10.

3.2570000000

Multiply by 10 to the power of the number of digits to the right of the decimal point.

3.257×10^{10}

You can also use scientific notation to write out very small numbers like 0.00000000000092. The two key differences between solving this compared to the very large numbers are that you are moving the decimal point to the right to get a value between 1 and 10 and your exponent is negative.

9.2×10^{-13}

When the number is negative, be sure to make the scientific notation negative.

EXAMPLES:

−42,000,000

Solution:
$−4.2 \times 10^7$

−0.00000000065

Solution:
$−6.5 \times 10^{-10}$

Moving the decimal point to the left gives a positive exponent. Moving the decimal to the right gives a negative exponent. Whether the number itself is positive or negative, the exponent's sign does not change.

$$5 \times 4 = 20$$
$$20 \times 3 = 60$$
$$60 \times 2 = 120$$
$$120 \times 1 = 120$$

Let's try a few questions.

Test Yourself 2

Write the following numbers in scientific notation. The answers will follow.

1. 20,000,000,000
2. 5,150,000,000,000,000,000
3. 3,420
4. 0.00000008
5. −0.0000000000005

EXAMPLES:

$3! =$

Solution:

Write out the factorial and solve:

$3 \times 2 \times 1 = 6$

$4! =$

Solution:

Write out the factorial and solve:

$4 \times 3 \times 2 \times 1 = 12 \times 2 = 24$

Answers:

1. 2×10^{10}
2. 5.15×10^{18}
3. 3.42×10^{3}
4. -8×10^{-8}
5. -5×10^{-13}

Factorials

Like scientific notation, factorials are a type of notation used to more efficiently present information. Factorials denote when to multiply an integer by all the integers that come before it on a number line. To indicate a factorial, you would use the integer in question followed by an exclamation point:

$$5! = 5 \times 4 \times 3 \times 2 \times 1 = 120$$

In this example, we break down five factorial. Let's solve the example:

To watch a video about factorials, scan this QR code.

EXAMPLE:

$8! =$

Solution:

Write out the factorial and solve:

$8 \times 7 \times 6 \times 5 \times 4 \times 3 \times 2 \times 1 =$

We can multiply pairs of numbers:

$56 \times 30 \times 12 \times 2 =$

$1,680 \times 24 = 40,320$

$10! =$

Solution:

Write out the factorial and solve (again, multiply paired numbers):

$10 \times 9 \times 8 \times 7 \times 6 \times 5 \times 4 \times 3 \times 2 \times 1 =$

$90 \times 56 \times 30 \times 12 \times 2 = 3,628,800$

When adding factorials, it's not enough to add the numbers. Rather, you need to solve the factorials, then add those numbers together to make a new factorial. What happens if you just add the two factorials together? Let's look at the previous example.

That's a big difference, so remember to solve the factorials before adding. Fortunately, the same rule applies for subtraction, multiplication, and division. As such, you can put this step at the top of the order of operations discussed in the previous chapter. Here are some sample problems.

You will notice the answer is not written as a factorial. Remember, solving a factorial does not itself create a new factorial. Let's look at another example.

EXAMPLES:

$2! + 3! =$ Solve each factorial

Solution:

$(2 \times 1) + (3 \times 2 \times 1) =$

$2 + 6 = 8$

$7! + 4! =$

Solution:

$(7 \times 6 \times 5 \times 4 \times 3 \times 2 \times 1) + (4 \times 3 \times 2 \times 1) =$

$5,040 + 24 = 5,064$

What happens if you just add the two factorials together? Let's look at the previous example.

EXAMPLE:

$7! + 4! \neq 11!$

Solution:

$11! = 11 \times 10 \times 9 \times 8 \times 7 \times 6 \times 5 \times$
$4 \times 3 \times 2 \times 1 = 39,916,800$

That's a big difference, so remember to solve the factorials before adding. Fortunately, the same rule applies for subtraction, multiplication, and division. As such, you can put this step at the top of the order of operations discussed in the previous chapter. Here are some sample problems.

EXAMPLE:

$4! - 3! =$

Solution:

$(4 \times 3 \times 2 \times 1) - (3 \times 2 \times 1) =$

$24 - 6 = 18$

$6! - 2! =$

Solution:

$(6 \times 5 \times 4 \times 3 \times 2 \times 1) \times (2 \times 1) =$

$720 \times 2 = 1,440$

$\dfrac{6!}{4!} = \dfrac{6 \times 5 \times 4 \times 3 \times 2 \times 1}{4 \times 3 \times 2 \times 1}$

Fortunately, we have common factors in the numerator and denominator.

$\dfrac{6 \times 5 \times \cancel{4 \times 3 \times 2 \times 1}}{\cancel{4 \times 3 \times 2 \times 1}} =$

$6 \times 5 = 30$

Test Yourself 3

Write the answers to the following problems in the space provided. The answers will follow.

1. $9! =$
2. $3! + 7! =$
3. $6! - 3! =$
4. $3! \times 7! =$
5. $7! \div 4! =$

Answers:

1. 362,880
2. 5,046
3. 714
4. 30,240
5. 210

Solving an Equation Using the Four Basic Operations

Now that we've discussed the different forms of notation you'll encounter in algebra problems, let's move on to equations. To find the value of a variable (such as x), you must **solve the equation**. To solve any equation containing only one variable, your goal is always the same: isolate the variable on one side of the equation. To accomplish this, you may need to perform one or more of the following operations on both sides, depending on the equation:

- Add or subtract the same term on both sides.
- Multiply or divide both sides by the same term.
- Clear fractions by cross-multiplication.
- Clear radicals by raising both sides to the same power (exponent).

Whatever operation you perform on one side of an equation you must also perform on the other side. Otherwise, the two sides will not be equal. Performing any of these operations on *both* sides does not change the equality; it just restates the equation in a different form.

To isolate the variable and solve an equation, you'll need to know the properties we covered in the previous chapter, specifically the distributive, commutative, associative, and identity properties. Knowing these will be critical to solving algebra problems. If you're a little fuzzy on what these are, review them and make sure that you fully understand what they look like in practice before moving on to solving equations.

To find the value of the variable (to solve for x), you may need to either add a term to both sides of the equation or subtract a term from both sides. Here are two examples:

Adding the same number to both sides:

$x - 2 = 5$

$x - 2 + 2 = 5 + 2$

$x = 7$

Subtracting the same number from both sides:

$$\frac{3}{2} - x = 12$$

The objective is to isolate the variable x. To do this, like terms must be combined.

$$\frac{3}{2} - \frac{3}{2} - x = 12 - \frac{3}{2}$$

$$-x = 10\frac{1}{2} \text{ (divide by } -1 \text{ to make the variable positive)}$$

$$x = -10\frac{1}{2}$$

The first system isolates x by adding 2 to both sides. The second system isolates x by subtracting $\frac{3}{2}$ from both sides. As we saw in the example, solving for x also required dividing both sides by -1 to make the variable positive. Let's look at some more examples of equations where we need to multiply or divide both sides of the equation by the same term in order to isolate the variable:

Multiplying both sides by the same number:

$$\frac{x}{2} = 14$$

$$2 \times \frac{x}{2} = 14 \times 2$$

$$x = 28$$

Dividing both sides by the same number:

$$3x = 18$$

$$\frac{3x}{3} = \frac{18}{3}$$

$$x = 6$$

The first system isolates x by multiplying both sides by 2. The second system isolates x by dividing both sides by 3. If the variable appears on both sides of the equation, first perform whatever operation is required to position the variable on just one side—either the left or the right. The next system positions both x-terms on the left side by subtracting $2x$ from both sides:

$$16 - x = 9 + 2x$$

$$16 - x - 2x = 9 + 2x - 2x$$

$$16 - 3x = 9$$

Now that x appears on just one side, the next step is to isolate it by subtracting 16 from both sides and then dividing both sides by -3:

$$16 - 3x = 9$$

$$16 - 16 - 3x = 9 - 16$$

$$-3x = -7$$

$$\frac{-3x}{-3} = \frac{-7}{-3}$$

$$x = \frac{7}{3}$$

Let's look at an example multiple-choice question similar to what you will see on the actual exam.

EXAMPLES:

For what value of x does $2x - 6$ equal $x - 9$?

Solution:

First, write the verbal description as the equation $2x - 6 = x - 9$. Then, position both x-terms on the same side. To place them both on the left side, subtract x from both sides. Then, combine x-terms:

$$2x - 6 - x = 9 - x$$

$$x - 6 = -9$$

Finally, isolate x by adding 6 to both sides:

$$x - 6 + 6 = -9$$

$$x = -3$$

Equations with fractional coefficients are solved in the same way as those with integer coefficients—don't be intimidated because they look more complex! Just treat them as you would any rational expression. Let's walk through a couple of examples.

EXAMPLES:

Solve for x:

$$\frac{2}{3}x - \frac{3}{2} = 3 - \frac{5}{6}x$$

Solution:

Gather the x-terms on the left side and constant terms on the right. Then, proceed as follows:

$$\frac{2}{3}x - \frac{3}{2} = 3 - \frac{5}{6}x$$

$$\frac{2}{3}x + \frac{5}{6}x = 3 + \frac{3}{2}$$

$$\frac{9}{6}x = \frac{9}{2}$$

$$x = 3$$

Solve for x:

$$\frac{3}{4}\left(\frac{9}{2} - 2x\right) - 3\left(\frac{4}{3}x + 2\right) = -1$$

Solution:

This example may look complicated, but it is just testing your knowledge of working with rational expressions. First, apply the distributive property to simplify the left side. Then, take the constant terms to the right side and solve as follows:

$$\frac{3}{4}\left(\frac{9}{2} - 2x\right) - 3\left(\frac{4}{3}x + 2\right) = -1$$

$$\frac{27}{8} - \frac{3}{2}x - 4x - 6 = -1$$

$$\left(-\frac{3}{2} - 4\right)x = -1 + 6 - \frac{27}{8}$$

$$-\frac{11}{2}x = \frac{13}{8}$$

$$x = -\frac{2}{11}\left(\frac{13}{8}\right)$$

$$x = -\frac{13}{44}$$

Test Yourself 4

Solve the following equations for x. The answers will follow.

1. $x + 13 = 25$
2. $4x = 84$
3. $x - 5 = 28$
4. $x \div 9 = 4$
5. $3x + 2 = 14$
6. $\frac{x}{4} - 2 - 4 = 0$
7. $10x - 27 = 73$
8. $2x \div 4 = 13$
9. $8x + 9 = 81$
10. $2x \div 11 = 6$

Answers:

1. $x = 12$
2. $x = 21$
3. $x = 33$
4. $x = 36$
5. $x = 4$
6. $x = 24$
7. $x = 10$
8. $x = 26$
9. $x = 9$
10. $x = 33$

Scan this QR code to watch a video about working with variables.

DISTANCE, RATE, AND TIME PROBLEMS

On the high school entrance examinations, you might be presented with word problems that require you to parse out relevant information and set up an equation to solve for one or more variables. An incredibly common real-world application of equations can be seen in the formula used for calculating distance, rate, and time. The skills we've discussed here and in the last chapter, especially fractions, should prepare you for these problems, but we're going to break down each type of word problem below.

The basic formula used in solving problems for distance is $D = RT$ (Distance = Rate × Time).

Use this formula when you know rate (speed) and time.

To find rate, use $R = \dfrac{D}{T}$ (Rate = Distance ÷ Time).

To find time, use $T = \dfrac{D}{R}$ (Time = Distance ÷ Rate).

Let's look at an example.

EXAMPLE:

A driver is traveling from Denver, Colorado, to Laramie, Wyoming. The distance between these two cities is 128 miles. If the driver goes straight there without stopping and drives at a rate of 60 mph the entire time, how long will it take to get to Laramie?

Solution:

Here, we are given two of the variables we need: rate and distance. This means we need to solve for time. To solve for time, we'll use $T = \dfrac{D}{R}$ and plug in the values we know. We know that the driver is traveling at a rate of 60 mph. We also know that the drive is 128 miles total.

If we plug the values into our formula, we get $T = \dfrac{128}{60}$. If we divide 128 miles by 60 mph, we get 2.13 hours. Note that this isn't the same as 2 hours and 13 minutes, but we generally know that it will take the driver a little over 2 hours to make the drive.

Depending on how this problem might be set up on the exam and what the answer choices are, you might want to take the extra step of calculating this figure to the minute just to be extra sure that you have the right answer. To calculate the exact number of minutes in 2.13 hours, we need to set up a proportion problem:

$$\frac{2.13hrs}{1hr} = \frac{x}{60\min}$$

Here, we set 1 hour equal to 60 minutes, and we've set 2.13 hours equal to x minutes. Now, we can set up an equation by cross-multiplying:

$2.13(60) = x$

$x = 127.8$ minutes, or 2 hours and 8 minutes

Let's look at a more complex example.

EXAMPLE:

Two hikers start walking from the city line at different times. The second hiker, whose speed is 4 miles per hour, starts 2 hours after the first hiker, whose speed is 3 miles per hour. Determine the amount of time and distance that will be consumed before the second hiker catches up with the first.

Solution 1:

The first hiker has a 2-hour head start and is walking at a rate of 3 miles per hour. This means that Hiker 1 is 6 miles from the city line when Hiker 2 starts.

$$\text{Rate} \times \text{Time} = \text{Distance}$$

Subtracting 3 miles per hour from 4 miles per hour gives us 1 mile per hour, or the difference in the rates of speed of the two hikers. In other words, Hiker 2 gains 1 mile on Hiker 1 in every hour.

Because there is a 6-mile difference to cut down, and this difference is cut down at a rate of 1 mile every hour, Hiker 2 will need 6 hours to overtake Hiker 1. In this time, Hiker 2 will have traveled $4 \times 6 = 24$ miles. Hiker 1 will have been walking 8 hours, which, when factoring in the 2-hour head start, computes as $8 \times 3 = 24$ miles.

Solution 2:

One excellent way to solve word problems is to organize all of the data in a chart. For distance problems, make columns for Rate, Time, and Distance and separate lines for each moving object. In the problem about the two hikers, the chart technique works like this:

Step 1: Draw the chart.

	Rate	×	Time	=	Distance
Hiker 1					
Hiker 2					

Step 2: Since the problem states that Hiker 1 is traveling at 3 miles per hour and Hiker 2 is traveling at 4 miles per hour, enter these two figures in the Rate column.

	Rate	×	Time	=	Distance
Hiker 1	3 mph				
Hiker 2	4 mph				

Step 3: The problem does not tell us how long each hiker traveled, but it does say that Hiker 1 started 2 hours before Hiker 2. Therefore, if we use the unknown x to represent the number of hours Hiker 2 traveled, we can set Hiker 1's time as $x + 2$. Enter these two figures in the Time column.

	Rate	×	Time	=	Distance
Hiker 1	3 mph	$x + 2$			
Hiker 2	4 mph	x			

Step 4: Using the formula $D = R \times T$, we can easily find each hiker's distance by multiplying the figures for rate and time already in the chart.

For Hiker 1: $3(x + 2) = 3x + 6$

For Hiker 2: $4(x) = 4x$

	Rate	×	Time	=	Distance
Hiker 1	3 mph	$x + 2$	$3x + 6$
Hiker 2	4 mph	x	$4x$

Step 5: When the two hikers meet, each will have covered the same distance. Using this information, we can set up an equation:

Distance covered by Hiker 1		Distance covered by Hiker 2
$3x + 6$	$=$	$4x$

Solving this equation for x, we find that $x = 6$. This means that Hiker 1 has walked for $6 + 2 = 8$ hours when Hiker 2 catches up.

Step 6: Because Hiker 1 started 2 hours earlier than Hiker 2, Hiker 2 will have walked for 6 hours to catch up to Hiker 1.

Step 7: Using this information, we can determine that Hiker 1 walked 8 hours at 3 miles per hour to cover 24 miles. Hiker 2 walked for 6 hours at 4 miles per hour to cover the same 24 miles.

Let's try one more example.

EXAMPLE:

The same two hikers start walking toward each other along a road connecting two cities that are 60 miles apart. Their speeds are the same as in the preceding example, 3 and 4 miles per hour, respectively. How much time will elapse before they meet?

Solution 1:

In each hour of travel toward each other, the hikers will cut down a distance equal to the sum of their speeds, $3 + 4 = 7$ miles per hour. To meet, they must cut down 60 miles, and at 7 miles per hour this would be:

$$\frac{D}{R} = T \quad \text{or} \quad \frac{60}{70} = 8\frac{4}{7} \text{ hours}$$

Solution 2:

In this problem, we know that the distance traveled by Hiker 1 plus the distance traveled by Hiker 2 equals 60 miles. We also know that the two hikers will have been traveling for the same length of time when they meet. Therefore, we set up an equation to represent this information and solve for x to find the time that will have elapsed before the two hikers meet:

$$3x + 4x = 60$$
$$7x = 60$$
$$x = 8\frac{4}{7}$$

The problem might also have asked: "How much distance must the slower hiker cover before the two hikers meet?" In such a case, we should go through the same steps plus one additional step:

The time consumed before meeting was $8\frac{4}{7}$ hours. To find the distance covered by the slower hiker, we multiply Hiker 1's rate by the time elapsed:

$$R \times T = D \qquad 3 \times 8\frac{4}{7} = 25\frac{5}{7}$$

Test Yourself 5

Solve the following problems. The answers and explanations will follow.

1. A sailor on leave drove to Yosemite Park from home at 60 miles per hour. On the trip home, the sailor's rate was 10 miles per hour less, and the trip took 1 hour longer. How far is the sailor's home from the park?

2. Two cars leave a restaurant at the same time and travel along a straight highway in opposite directions. At the end of 3 hours, they are 300 miles apart. Find the rate of the slower car if one car travels at a rate 20 miles per hour faster than the other.

Answers:

1. **The correct answer is 300 miles.**

	Rate	×	Time	=	Distance
Going	60 mph		x		$60x$
Return	50 mph		$x + 1$		$50x + 50$

Let x = time of trip at 60 mph

The distances are equal.

$$60x = 50x + 50$$

$$10x = 50$$

$$x = 5$$

$R \times T = D$; 60 mph × 5 hours = 300 miles

2. The correct answer is 40 miles per hour.

	Rate ×	Time =	Distance
Slow Car	x	3	$3x$
Fast Car	$x + 20$	3	$3x + 60$

Let x = rate of slower car

$$\leftarrow \frac{3x + 60 + 3x}{300 \text{ miles}} \rightarrow$$

$$3x + 3x + 60 = 300$$

$$6x = 240 \text{ mph}$$

$$x = 40 \text{ mph}$$

WORK PROBLEMS

Another type of problem you might encounter is a work problem. The aim of a work problem is to predict how long it will take to complete a job if the number of workers increases or decreases. Work problems may also involve determining how fast pipes can fill or empty tanks. In solving pipe and tank problems, you must think of the pipes as workers.

In most work problems, a job is broken into several parts, each representing a fractional portion of the entire job. For each part represented, the numerator should represent the time actually spent working, while the denominator should represent the total time the worker needs to do the job alone. The sum of all the individual fractions must be 1 if the job is completed. The easiest way to understand this procedure is to carefully study the examples that follow. By following the step-by-step solutions, you will learn how to make your own fractions to solve the practice problems that follow and the problems you may find on your exam.

 To learn more about rate problems, scan this QR code and watch the video.

EXAMPLE:

If A does a job in 6 days, and B does the same job in 3 days, how long will it take the two of them, working together, to do the job?

Solution:

Step 1: Write the fractions as follows.

$$\frac{\text{Time actually spent}}{\text{Time needed to do entire job alone}} \quad \overset{A}{\underset{}{\frac{x}{6 \text{ days}}}} + \overset{B}{\underset{}{\frac{x}{3 \text{ days}}}} = 1$$

The variable x represents the amount of time each worker will work when both work together. The number 1 represents the completed job.

Step 2: Multiply all the terms by the same number (in this case, 6) in order to clear the fractions and work with whole numbers.

$$x + 2x = 6$$

Step 3: Solve for x.

$$3x = 6$$

$$x = 2 \text{ days}$$

Working together, A and B will get the job done in 2 days.

EXAMPLE:

A and B, working together, do a job in $4\frac{1}{4}$ days. If B works alone, B can do the job in 10 days. How long would it take A to do the job working alone?

Solution:

Step 1: Write the fractions as follows.

$$\frac{\text{Time actually spent}}{\text{Time needed to do entire job alone}} \quad \overset{A}{\frac{4.5 \text{ days}}{x \text{ days}}} + \overset{B}{\frac{4.5 \text{ days}}{10 \text{ days}}} = 1$$

Step 2: Multiply all the terms by $10x$ to clear the fractions.

$$45 + 4.5x = 10x$$

Step 3: Solve for x.

$$45 = 5.5x$$

$$x = 8\frac{2}{11} \text{ or } 8.18 \text{ days}$$

It would take A nearly $8\frac{2}{11}$ days to do the job alone.

EXAMPLE:

One pipe can fill a pool in 20 minutes, a second pipe can fill the pool in 30 minutes, and a third pipe can fill it in 10 minutes. How long would it take the three pipes together to fill the pool?

Solution:

Step 1: Treat the pipes as workers and write the fractions as follows:

$$\frac{\text{Time actually spent}}{\text{Time needed to do entire job alone}} \quad \overset{A}{\frac{x}{20 \text{ min.}}} + \overset{B}{\frac{x}{30 \text{ min.}}} + \overset{C}{\frac{x}{10 \text{ min.}}} = 1$$

Step 2: Multiply all terms by 60 to clear the fractions.

$$3x + 2x + 6x = 60$$

Step 3: Solve for x.

$$11x = 60$$

$$x = 5\frac{5}{11} \text{ min}$$

If the water flows from all three pipes at once, it will take $5\frac{5}{11}$ minutes to fill the pool.

EXAMPLE:

If A can do a job in 6 days that B can do in $5\frac{1}{2}$ days and C can do in $2\frac{1}{5}$ days, how long would the job take if A, B, and C were working together?

Solution:

Step 1: This example is similar to the first example we presented in this section. While the number of workers is greater, the procedure to solve the problem is the same.

$$\frac{\text{Time actually spent}}{\text{Time needed to do entire job alone}} \quad \overset{A}{\frac{x}{6 \text{ days}}} + \overset{B}{\frac{x}{5.5 \text{ days}}} + \overset{C}{\frac{x}{2.2 \text{ days}}} = 1$$

Convert all the decimals to fractions:

$$\frac{x}{6} + \frac{2x}{11} + \frac{5x}{11} = 1$$

Remember that 1 represents the completed job regardless of the number of days involved.

Step 2: Multiply all terms by 66 to clear the fractions.

$$11x + 12x + 30x = 66$$

Step 3: Solve for x.

$$53x = 66$$

$$x = 1.245 \text{ days}$$

A, B, and C all working together at their usual rates would get the job done in about $1\frac{1}{4}$ days.

Test Yourself 6

Solve the following work problems. Answers and explanations will follow.

1. John can complete a paper route in 20 minutes. Steve can complete the same route in 30 minutes. How long will it take them to complete the route if they work together?

2. Mr. Powell can mow his lawn twice as fast as his son Rick can. Together they do the job in 20 minutes. How many minutes would it take Mr. Powell to do the job alone?

Answers:

1. **The correct answer is 12 minutes.**

$$\frac{\text{Time actually spent}}{\text{Time needed to do entire job alone}} \quad \overset{\text{John}}{\frac{x}{20}} + \overset{\text{Steve}}{\frac{x}{30}} = 1$$

Multiply all terms by 60 to clear the fractions.

$$3x + 2x = 60$$

$$5x = 60$$

$$x = 12$$

2. **The correct answer is 30 minutes.**

It takes Mr. Powell x minutes to mow the lawn. Rick alone will take twice as long or $2x$ minutes.

$$\frac{\text{Time actually spent}}{\text{Time needed to do entire job alone}} \quad \overset{\text{Mr. Powell}}{\frac{20}{x}} + \overset{\text{Rick}}{\frac{20}{2x}} = 1$$

Multiply all terms by $2x$ to clear the fractions.

$$40 + 20 = 2x$$

$$60 = 2x$$

$$x = 30 \text{ minutes}$$

SUMMING IT UP

- If you are having difficulties with any mathematics topic, talk with a teacher or refer to your math textbook.

- Use the exercises in this chapter to determine what you DON'T know well and concentrate your study on those areas.

- Review the properties of mathematics covered in the previous chapter, as these will be important for knowing how to isolate the variable in an equation.

- Knowing how to put an equation into standard form, along with other types of notation like scientific notation and factorials, is essential for being able to solve equations.

- To isolate the variable and solve an equation, you might need to perform one of four basic operations:

  1. Add or subtract the same term on both sides.
  2. Multiply or divide both sides by the same term.
  3. Clear fractions by cross-multiplication.
  4. Clear radicals by raising both sides to the same power (exponent).

- To solve problems for distance, rate, or time, remember the formula $D = RT$ (Distance = Rate × Time). This formula can be used and rearranged to solve for any of the variables, as long as you know the other two.

- To solve work problems, remember that you'll need to set up fractions that reflect the relationship of different parts: The numerator should represent the time actually spent working, while the denominator should represent the total time the worker needs to do the job alone. The sum of all the individual fractions must be 1 if the job is completed.

ALGEBRAIC THINKING
25 Questions—20 Minutes

> **Directions:** In the following questions, work out each problem on scratch paper or in the margins. Then, mark the letter that corresponds to the correct answer.

1. Solve the following problem for b:
   $5b + 3 = 4b + 19$

   A. 4

   B. 10

   C. 12

   D. 16

2. Solve the equation for y:
   $3(2y + 4) = 8y$

   A. 2

   B. 3

   C. 4

   D. 6

3. Solve for x:
   $\frac{x}{2} + 3 = 15$

   A. 18

   B. 20

   C. 22

   D. 24

4. If $y + 2 > 10$, then y must be

   A. smaller than 10.

   B. smaller than 8.

   C. greater than 8.

   D. equal to 0.

5. Solve the following for x:
   $\frac{4}{x+5} = \frac{5}{x+7}$

   A. -1

   B. 0

   C. 3

   D. 4

6. If $x - y = 5$ and $x + 3y = 21$, what is the value of y?

   A. 4

   B. 5

   C. 8

   D. 9

7. Solve for x:
   $5(2x - 1) = 4(3x - 2)$

   A. $\frac{13}{2}$

   B. $\frac{1}{2}$

   C. $\frac{3}{2}$

   D. 3

8. $9.87 \times 10^{-1} =$

   A. 0.00987

   B. 0.0987

   C. 0.987

   D. 9,870

9. $4,400,000 =$

   A. 4.4×10^{-2}

   B. 4.4×10^{3}

   C. 4.4×10^{6}

   D. 4.4×10^{5}

10. $0.000623 =$

    A. 6.23×10^{-3}

    B. 6.23×10^{-4}

    C. 6.23×10^{-2}

    D. 6.23×10^{4}

11. $6! - 5! =$

    A. 8

    B. $6!$

    C. $19 \times 18 \times 17 \times 16 \times 15 \times 14$

    D. 600

12. $30 \times 6! =$

    A. 8

    B. $19 \times 18 \times 17 \times 16 \times 15 \times 14$

    C. 640

    D. $6!$

13. $19! \div 13! =$

    A. 8

    B. $6!$

    C. $19 \times 18 \times 17 \times 16 \times 15 \times 14$

    D. 500

14. Put this equation into standard form: $ab = 2c$

    A. $ab - 2c = 0$

    B. $ab + 2c = 0$

    C. $2a + 2b + 2c = 0$

    D. $2abc = 0$

15. Put this equation into standard form:
    $2x + 3y + 4 = 12$

    A. $24x - 36y + 48 = 0$

    B. $2x - 3y = 8$

    C. $2x + 3y - 8 = 0$

    D. $2x - 3y + 8 = 0$

16. Put this equation into standard form: $x - 10 = 24$

    A. $x = 34$

    B. $0 = x - 34$

    C. $x - 10 - 24 = 0$

    D. $x - 34 = 0$

17. Put this equation into standard form: $2y = -x$

    A. $-2y - x = 0$

    B. $2y = -x$

    C. $y = \dfrac{-x}{2}$

    D. $2y + x = 0$

18. Put this equation into standard form:
    $2x^{3} + 5x^{4} + 7x^{5} + 12 = -13$

    A. $2x^{3} + 5x^{4} + 7x^{5} - 1 = 0$

    B. $7x^{5} + 5x^{4} + 2x^{3} - 1 = 0$

    C. $7x^{5} + 2x^{3} + 5x^{4} - 1 = 0$

    D. $-1 - 7x^{5} + 5x^{4} + 2x^{3} = 0$

19. Put this equation into standard form:
    $4x + 3y + 2 = 13 + x$

    A. $3x - 11 = -3y$

    B. $3x + 3y - 11 = 0$

    C. $3x + 3y + 11 = 0$

    D. $3x + 11 = 3y$

20. One boy skied the length of a 4.6-mile trail in just under 14 minutes. His average speed was approximately

   A. 15 miles per hour.

   B. 20 miles per hour.

   C. 25 miles per hour.

   D. 30 miles per hour.

21. Three workers of about equal efficiency were assigned to work on a car. One worker worked on the car full time but was always assisted by one of the other workers. The work took 4 weeks to complete. If the full-time worker needed to complete the job alone, how many weeks would the car have been in the shop?

   A. 2 weeks

   B. 4 weeks

   C. 6 weeks

   D. 8 weeks

22. If a plane travels 1,000 miles in 5 hours 30 minutes, what is its average speed in miles per hour?

   A. $181\frac{9}{11}$

   B. $191\frac{1}{5}$

   C. 200

   D. 215

23. Two cars start from the same point at the same time. One drives north at 20 miles an hour, and the other drives south on the same straight road at 36 miles an hour. How many miles apart are they after 30 minutes?

   A. Fewer than 10

   B. Between 10 and 20

   C. Between 20 and 30

   D. Between 30 and 40

24. Two cars are 550 miles apart and traveling toward each other on the same road. If one travels at 50 miles per hour, the other travels at 60 miles per hour, and they both leave at 1:00 p.m., what time will they meet?

   A. 4:00 p.m.

   B. 4:30 p.m.

   C. 5:45 p.m.

   D. 6:00 p.m.

25. If a vehicle is to complete a 20-mile trip at an average rate of 30 miles per hour, it must complete the trip in

   A. 20 minutes.

   B. 30 minutes.

   C. 40 minutes.

   D. 50 minutes.

ANSWER KEY AND EXPLANATIONS

1. D	**6.** A	**11.** D	**16.** D	**21.** D
2. D	**7.** C	**12.** D	**17.** D	**22.** A
3. D	**8.** C	**13.** C	**18.** B	**23.** C
4. C	**9.** C	**14.** A	**19.** B	**24.** D
5. C	**10.** B	**15.** C	**20.** B	**25.** C

1. **The correct answer is D.** Separate variables on one side and numbers on the other. Remember to always do the same thing to both sides of the equation:

$$5b + 3 = 4b + 19$$
$$5b + 3 - 3 = 4b + 19 - 3$$
$$5b = 4b + 16$$
$$5b - 4b = 4b + 16 - 4b$$
$$b = 16$$

2. **The correct answer is D.** First, we can distribute the 3 in order to simplify the equation:

$$3(2y + 4) = 8y$$
$$6y + 12 = 8y$$

Then, we can isolate the variable and divide both sides by 2:

$$12 = 2y$$
$$y = 6$$

3. **The correct answer is D.**

$$\frac{x}{2} + 3 = 15$$
$$\frac{x}{2} = 15 - 3$$
$$\frac{x}{2} = 12$$
$$x = 12 \times 2$$
$$x = 24$$

4. **The correct answer is C.**

$$y + 2 > 10$$
$$y > 10 - 2$$
$$y > 8$$

5. **The correct answer is C.** Solve the proportion for x in the following manner:

$$5(x + 5) = 4(x + 7)$$
$$5x + 25 = 4x + 28$$
$$5x - 4x = 28 - 25$$
$$x = 3$$

6. **The correct answer is A.** The question asks for the value of y, so solve the first equation for x:

$$x - y = 5$$
$$x - y + y = 5 + y$$
$$x = 5 + y$$

Now, replace x in the second equation with this result, and solve the second equation for y:

$$x + 3y = 21$$
$$(5 + y) + 3y = 21$$
$$5 + 4y = 21$$
$$5 + 4y - 5 = 21 - 5$$
$$4y = 16$$
$$\frac{4y}{4} = \frac{16}{4}$$
$$y = 4$$

7. **The correct answer is C.** First, distribute the 5 on the left side of the equation and the 4 on the right side of the equation:

$$5(2x - 1) = 4(3x - 2)$$
$$10x - 5 = 12x - 8$$

Then, subtract $10x$ from both sides, and add 8 to both sides.

$$10x - 5 = 12x - 8$$
$$-5 = 2x - 8$$
$$3 = 2x$$

Finally, divide each side by 2:

$$\frac{3}{2} = \frac{2x}{2}$$
$$\frac{3}{2} = x$$

8. **The correct answer is C.** Since the exponent is -1, move the decimal point to the left one place: $9.87 \times 10^{-1} = 0.987$.

9. **The correct answer is C.** To put 4,400,000 in scientific notation, move the decimal six places to the left: 4.4×10^6.

10. **The correct answer is B.** Since 0.000623 is a very small number, we move the decimal place in 6.23 to the left four places, so our exponent is negative: 6.23×10^{-4}.

11. **The correct answer is D.** $6! = 6 \times 5 \times 4 \times 3 \times 2 \times 1 = 720$. $5! = 5 \times 4 \times 3 \times 2 \times 1 = 120$. Therefore, $6! - 5! = 600$.

12. **The correct answer is D.** 30 is equal to 6×5, and $4! = 4 \times 3 \times 2 \times 1$. Therefore, the whole expression becomes $6 \times 5 \times 4 \times 3 \times 2 \times 1$, which is the same as $6!$

13. **The correct answer is C.** When you write this as a fraction and expand the terms, $13!$ cancels out of both the top and bottom. This leaves all of the numbers that are in the top but not in the bottom: $19 \times 18 \times 17 \times 16 \times 15 \times 14$.

14. **The correct answer is A.** To put the equation in standard form, you must set the equation to 0 by subtracting $2c$ from both sides: $ab - 2c = 0$

15. **The correct answer is C.** Set the equation to zero by subtracting 12 from both sides, giving you $2x + 3y - 8 = 0$.

16. **The correct answer is D.** You might be tempted to solve this equation, but remember that you are being asked to put the equation into standard form. To do so, subtract 24 from both sides, and you'll end up with $x - 34 = 0$.

17. **The correct answer is D.** In order to set the equation to 0, you must add x to both sides. This will get you $2y + x = 0$.

18. **The correct answer is B.** Remember that you must set the equation to 0 and you must arrange the exponents from greatest to smallest. This gives you $7x^5 + 5x^4 + 2x^3 - 1 = 0$.

19. **The correct answer is B.** Subtract x from both sides, which gives you $3x$ on the left side. Then, subtract 13 from both sides, and you'll end up with $3x + 3y - 11 = 0$.

20. **The correct answer is B.** The formula for determining rate is $\frac{D}{T}$. The distance skied is 4.6 miles. The time, just under 14 minutes, is approximately 0.25 hour.

$4.6 \div 0.25 = 18.4$ miles per hour

Because he skied the distance in slightly less than 0.25 hour, his average speed was very close to 20 miles per hour.

21. **The correct answer is D.** You do not have to calculate this problem. If you read carefully, you will see that 2 workers worked full time and the work took 4 weeks. If only one worker (half the number) had worked, the job would have taken twice the time or 8 weeks.

22. **The correct answer is A.**

5 hours, 30 minutes $= 5\frac{1}{2}$ hours

1,000 miles $\div \, 5\frac{1}{2}$ hours $= 1,000 \div \frac{11}{2} =$

$1,000 \times \frac{2}{11} = 181\frac{9}{11}$ miles per hour

23. **The correct answer is C.** One car went 20 mph for $\frac{1}{2}$ hour = 10 miles. The other went 36 mph for $\frac{1}{2}$ hour = 18 miles. Because they went in opposite directions, add the two distances to find the total number of miles apart: $10 + 18 = 28$.

24. **The correct answer is D.** The cars are traveling toward each other, so the distance between them is being reduced at $60 + 50$ or 110 miles per hour. At a rate of 110 miles per hour, 550 miles will be covered in 5 hours. If both cars left at 1:00 p.m., they should meet at 6:00 p.m.

25. **The correct answer is C.** Note that a 20-mile trip at 60 mph (which is 1 mile per minute) would take 20 minutes. Because the vehicle is traveling half as fast (30 miles per hour), the 20-mile trip should take twice as long or 40 minutes.

NOTES

CHAPTER

Geometry

GEOMETRY

OVERVIEW

Perimeter, Area, and Volume

Angles

Coordinate Geometry

Summing It Up

Knowledge Check: Geometry

Answer Key and Explanations

Roughly translated from Greek as "to measure the earth," geometry deals with the properties of figures and space. Its real-world applications are practically everywhere, ranging from fine arts and classical architecture to intricate LEGO sculpture and video animation, from cooking to space travel, and from interior design to criminal forensic re-creations. Objects can fit together and work together because of the compatibility and predictability of their shapes. Geometry is the math that makes sure they fit and work together.

Geometry questions focus your attention on matters of distance, shape, and size of geometric figures—whether lines, angles, or solids. First, we'll discuss how to find the area and perimeter of plane figures and the volume of solid figures. Then, we'll cover the different types of angles as well as the relationships between pairs of angles. Finally, we'll provide a basic overview of coordinate geometry, which involves plotting and identifying coordinates on a grid.

TACHS   HSPT   ISEE   SSAT   SHSAT

PERIMETER, AREA, AND VOLUME

In geometry problems, you'll be asked to find the perimeter, area, and volume of various geometric figures. Before we dive into these concepts, you should know the difference between plane figures and solid figures, which encompass the shapes of most everyday objects. **Plane figures** are flat, two-dimensional figures that have both length and width. Examples of these include triangles, squares, rectangles, circles, and a variety of other shapes. **Solid figures** are figures that have both length and width but also possess a third dimension: depth, also referred to as height. Examples of solid figures include cubes, spheres, pyramids, and so on.

There are formulas unique to each figure to help you determine its perimeter, area, or volume. First, we'll cover how to determine the perimeter of a plane figure. Next, we'll explain how to determine the area of a plane figure. Finally, we'll examine how to determine the volume of three-dimensional solid figures.

Perimeter of Plane Figures

The **perimeter** of a plane figure is the distance around the outside. To find the perimeter of a polygon (a plane figure bounded by line segments), add the lengths of the sides. When you are using a formula to determine the perimeter of a specific shape, the formula will be adjusted to account for the unique features of that shape, but generally, finding perimeter involves adding up the distance of its sides or the outer edges.

First, we'll discuss how to find the perimeter of **quadrilaterals**, shapes that have four sides. A rectangle is a type of quadrilateral, and in rectangles, opposite sides are equal. The longer side is considered the length of the rectangle, while the shorter side is considered the width. To find the perimeter of a rectangle, you would use the formula $2(l + w)$. In this formula, you're adding up the values for two of the four sides and then doubling it to arrive at the perimeter of a rectangle. You can also add up the lengths of all the sides, since opposite sides are equal, and arrive at the same result.

$P = 2(3 + 5)$ $P = 3 + 5 + 3 + 5$
$P = 16$ in. $P = 16$ in.

A square is also a type of quadrilateral, but it has four sides of equal length. As such, finding the perimeter of a square only requires you to know the length of one side. The formula for finding the perimeter of a square is $P = 4s$.

In this square, we're shown that each side is 5 inches. To find the perimeter, we either multiply the length of one side by four or add the lengths of each side.

$P = 4s$ $P = 5 + 5 + 5 + 5$
$P = 4(5)$ $P = 20$ in.
$P = 20$ in.

A triangle is a three-sided shape. All triangles share a few universal properties:

- The base of a triangle is always perpendicular to its height.
- The sum of the lengths of any two sides of a triangle must be larger than the length of its third side.
- The measures of the three angles in any triangle must be 180°.

We'll elaborate on some of these concepts later on when we discuss finding the area of a triangle and working with angles.

Finding the perimeter of a triangle requires you to add up the lengths of its sides. Unlike other shapes, there is no formula involved in determining the perimeter of a triangle. In the triangle shown, we're given the length of each of its sides, which we can add up to determine the perimeter.

$P = 4$ cm $+ 6$ cm $+ 5$ cm
$P = 15$ cm

A circle is a perfectly round figure. Every circle is named by a point labeled at its center. In the figure shown, the circle has a center point C. This refers to circle C.

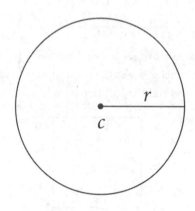

Extending from point C is a line that reaches to the edge of the circle. This line is called the **radius** of the circle. (The plural of radius is radii.) A circle's radius is represented by the lowercase letter r.

The radius is important because it is used in many circle measurements. Therefore, you need to know what a radius is—and be able to distinguish it from the second key component of a circle, the diameter.

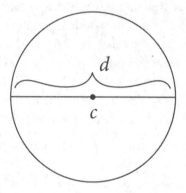

A **diameter** is essentially twice the length of a radius because it runs through the center of the circle and touches two points on the circle's edge. A circle's diameter is represented by the lowercase letter d.

The perimeter of a circle is called the **circumference**. The formula for the circumference of a circle is πd or $2\pi r$. Pi (π) is a mathematical value equal to approximately 3.14, or $\frac{22}{7}$. It is the ratio of a circle's circumference to its diameter, so pi (π) is frequently used in calculations involving circles.

 NOTE -

Many different lines can run across a circle and touch two points on its edge, but only those that run through the circle's center are diameters. All of a circle's diameters have equal length, and, because they all run through the center point, they are the longest possible lines on the circle.

The formulas for finding the circumference of a circle are both equivalent. However, depending on what information you are given about a circle, one formula might be more useful. For example, if you are given the diameter of a circle, you would use the πd formula, in which d stands for diameter. If you only know the radius, then you would plug in the length of the radius in $2\pi r$. Because the radius of a circle is always half of its diameter, both of these formulas are equivalent.

In the example shown, we're given the radius of the circle: 3 feet. To find the circumference, plug the radius into the $2\pi r$ formula and calculate.

$$C = 2 \times 3 \times \pi = 6\pi$$

Perimeter problems on the exam will likely ask you to apply these formulas to a real-world context. For example, you might be asked to find the perimeter of a given space, or you might be asked to determine the length of one side if you know the length of another side and the perimeter. Alternatively, you could be given a shape that looks unfamiliar but actually comprises other shapes, like rectangles or squares, or has pieces cut out of it. In these scenarios, you can still use what you know about finding the perimeter—like the fact that opposite sides are always equal in quadrilaterals—to answer the question. Knowing the formulas for finding the perimeter of the shapes we've covered will help you prepare for different scenarios you might encounter on the exams. We've included a table that provides an overview of the different shapes and their corresponding perimeter formulas.

Scan this QR code for a video on circles.

PERIMETER FORMULAS FOR PLANE FIGURES

Plane Figure	Illustration	Formula
Rectangle		$P = 2(l + w)$
Square		$P = 4s$
Triangle		Add up the three lengths of the triangle.
Circle		$P = 2\pi r = \pi d$

1. Find the perimeter.

2. Find the circumference.

3. Find the perimeter.

4. Find the perimeter.

5. Find the perimeter.

Answers:

1. $P = 6 + 5 + (6 - 2) + 8 + 2 + (8 + 5)$
   $P = 38$ inches

2. $C = 2\pi r$
   $C = 2 \times \pi \times 7$
   $C = 14\pi$ centimeters

3. $P = 3 + 3 + 3 + 3 + 3 + 3 + 3 + 3$
   $P = 24$ centimeters

4. $P = 8 + 8 + 6 = 22$ feet

5. $P = 1 + 1 + 1 + 1 = 4$ inches

Area of Plane Figures

While perimeter is the distance around a figure, **area** measures the space inside a figure, the space a plane figure occupies. Because you are multiplying a unit by itself, you are squaring the unit. Therefore, area is always measured in square units. Like perimeter, the formulas for finding the area of different shapes vary depending on the shape's features. While finding the perimeter of a figure requires you to add sides together or to multiply sides by 2 or 4, finding the area requires you to multiply one side by another side.

To find the area of a rectangle, multiply the length of the rectangle by its width.

$A = lw$

$A = 9$ ft. $\times$ 3 ft.

$A = 27$ sq. ft.

Notice that the area is expressed in square feet. This is because we multiplied feet by feet, thereby arriving at square feet (or feet squared).

Recall that four sides of a square are the same length. You find the area of a square by squaring the length of one side, which is the same as multiplying the square's length by its width.

$A = s^2$

$A = 4$ in. $\times$ 4 in.

$A = 16$ sq. in.

Remember that the base of a triangle is always perpendicular to its height. The base is the bottom of the triangle. The height of a triangle is the length of the segment from the base to the vertex (corner) opposite of the base. To find the area of a triangle, multiply the base by the height. Then, multiply by one half, which is equivalent to dividing by 2.

$A = \frac{1}{2}bh$

$A = \frac{1}{2}(9 \times 5)$

$A = \frac{1}{2}(45)$

$A = 22.5$ sq. in

ALERT

Don't confuse the two formulas for calculating the circumference and the area of circles. A good way to keep them straight is to remember the square in πr^2. It should remind you that area must be in square units.

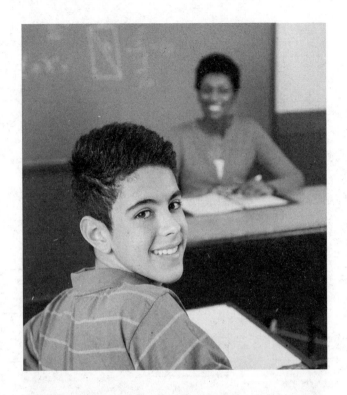

For circles, remember the difference between radius and diameter: A radius is a line that extends from the center of the circle to the edge of the circle. A diameter runs through the center of the circle and touches two points on the circle's edge. The diameter is always twice the length of the radius.

You find the area of a circle by squaring the radius and multiplying it by π. You may leave the area in terms of pi unless you are told what value to assign π.

$A = \pi r^2$

$A = \pi (4 \text{ cm})^2$

$A = 16\pi \text{ sq. cm}$

Like perimeter questions, area questions will likely be situated within a real-world application. For example, you might be asked to determine the area of a space based on its perimeter or vice versa, or you might need to figure out how much paint or carpeting is required to cover a specific area. Remember that area is always expressed in square units, and do your best to differentiate between area and perimeter formulas for a given shape. If you accidentally use a perimeter formula to determine area or vice versa, you'll find yourself confused when none of the answer options match your calculation. Here, we've included a table of plane figures and their corresponding area formulas.

AREA FORMULAS FOR PLANE FIGURES

Plane Figure	Illustration	Formula
Rectangle		$A = lw$
Square		$A = s^2$
Triangle		$A = \dfrac{1}{2}bh$
Circle		$A = \pi r^2$

Test Yourself 2

Find the area of each figure. The answers will follow.

1.

2.

3.

4.

5.

6.

7.

8.

9.

10.

Answers:

1. $A = lw$

   $A = 8 \times 4 = 32$ sq. ft.

2. $A = \dfrac{1}{2}bh$

   $A = \dfrac{1}{2}(7 \times 8)$

   $A = \dfrac{1}{2}(56) = 28$ sq. in.

3. $A = s^2$

   $A = 1^2 = 1$ sq. mi.

4. $A = \dfrac{1}{2}bh$

   $A = \dfrac{1}{2}(5 \times 3)$

   $A = \dfrac{1}{2}(15) = 7\dfrac{1}{2}$ sq. yds.

5. $A = \pi r^2$

   $A = \pi 2^2$

   $A = 4\pi$ sq. cm.

6. $A = lw$

   $A = 12 \times 6 + (12 - 8) \times 6$

   $A = 12 \times 6 + 4 \times 6$

   $A = 72 \times 24 = 96$ sq. yds.

7. $A = lw$

   $A = 10 \times 8 = 80$ sq. yds.

   $A = \dfrac{1}{2}bh$

   $A = \dfrac{1}{2}(10 \times 3) = \dfrac{1}{2}(30)$

   $A = 15$ sq. yds.

   $80 + 15 = 95$ sq. yds.

8. $A = \pi r^2$

   $A = \pi 6^2$

   $A = 36\pi$ sq. ft.

9. $A = \dfrac{1}{2}bh$

   $A = \dfrac{1}{2}(26 \times 2) = \dfrac{1}{2}(52)$

   $A = 26$ sq. ft.

10. $A = lw$

    $A = 6 \times 5 + 20 \times (17 - 5)$

    $A = 6 \times 5 + 20 \times 12$

    $A = 30 + 240 = 270$ sq. m.

Volume of Solid Figures

Plane figures are two-dimensional, so you can only determine their perimeter and their area. Solid figures, however, have a third dimension, which gives them depth. As such, you can find their **volume**, or the measure of the space within a figure considering these three dimensions. Like perimeter and area, the formula for volume varies depending on the shape of the figure, but generally, it is each of its dimensions—the length, width, and height (depth) of the figure—multiplied together.

When discussing the volume of solid figures, you'll likely encounter the term **base**, which refers to the face on which the figure rests—the area of the two-dimensional version of the figure. Although area is calculated differently depending on the solid, the formula for finding a shape's volume is generally its area formula times its height. Volume is always expressed in cubic units because you are multiplying a unit by itself twice.

A rectangular solid is the three-dimensional version of a rectangle. The volume of a rectangular solid is length × width × height.

$V = lwh$

$V = (10 \text{ in.}) \, (6 \text{ in.}) \, (5 \text{ in.})$

$V = 300 \text{ cu. in.}$

A cube is the three-dimensional version of a square. The volume of a cube is the cube of one side—the measurement of one side to the third power.

$V = s^3$

$V = (3 \text{ ft.})^3$

$V = 27 \text{ cu. ft.}$

A cylinder is the three-dimensional version of a circle, and it resembles a tube. In calculating its volume, use the formula for finding the area of circle but also multiply by height, since the shape has a third dimension. The height is the distance between the top and bottom circles. In other words, the volume of a cylinder is the area of the circular base (πr^2) times the height.

$V = \pi r^2 h$

$V = \pi (4 \text{ in.})^2 \, (5 \text{ in.})$

$V = \pi(16)(5) = 80\pi \text{ cu. in.}$

When encountering volume problems on the exam, prepare for questions that ask you to calculate the volume of everyday objects, typically containers like a can or a box. We've included a table with the volume formulas for the shapes we've covered here.

VOLUME FORMULAS FOR SOLID FIGURES		
Plane Figure	**Illustration**	**Formula**
Rectangular Solid		$V = lwh$
Cube		$V = s^3$
Cylinder		$C = \pi r^2 h$

Test Yourself 3

Find the volume of each figure. The answers will follow.

1.

6 in.

2 in.

2.

4 in.

3 in.

8 in.

3.

4 yd.

4 yd.

4 yd.

Answers:

1. $V = \pi r^2 h$

   $V = \pi \times 2^2 \times 6$

   $V = \pi \times 4 \times 6$

   $V = 24\pi$ cubic inches

2. $V = lwh$

   $V = 8 \times 3 \times 4$

   $V = 96$ cubic inches

3. $V = s^3$

   $V = 4 \times 4 \times 4$

   $V = 64$ cubic yards

ANGLES

Angles are classified according to their "size" measured using degrees. Angles are usually named by letters, and the notation ($m\angle A$) is used to denote the measure of angle A. The line that extends in only one direction from a point is called a **ray.** Lines, rays, or line segments meet at a point called the **vertex.**

The sum of angles and the types of angles you're working with will vary. For the shapes we covered in the previous section, the sum of the angles are as follows:

The sum of the angles of a triangle is 180°.

50°

90°   40°

The sum of the angles of a rectangle is 360°.

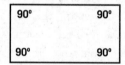

90°   90°

90°   90°

The sum of the angles of a circle is 360°.

80°

100°   140°

40°

The sum of the angles of a polygon of n sides is $(n - 2)180°$.

$$(8 - 2)(180°) = 6 \times 180° = 1{,}080°$$

135°   150°

135°   120°

135°   120°

135°   150°

Knowing the different types of angles and the relationships between them will be important for solving geometry questions on the exam. Use the angle terminology table to help you navigate these terms.

Let's look at a few examples to better understand the relationships between pairs of angles and how different angles are formed by intersecting lines. We'll start with a **right angle**.

The name of this angle is ∠ABC. Notice the small square in the corner where lines *AB* and *BC* intersect. This square indicates that this is a right angle, which means that m∠ABC = 90°. When two lines meet to form a right angle, they are said to be **perpendicular** to each other, as indicated by the symbol ⊥. Therefore, $\overrightarrow{BA} \perp \overrightarrow{BC}$.

An angle that measures less than 90° is called an **acute** angle. An angle that measures more than 90° but less than 180° is called an **obtuse** angle.

Acute Angle   **Obtuse Angle**

A **straight angle** measures 180°. ∠XYZ in the following figure is a straight angle.

Two or more angles whose measures add up to 180° are called **supplementary**. In the next figure, ∠DEG forms a straight line and therefore measures 180°. ∠DEF and ∠FEG are supplementary angles; their measures add up to 180°.

ANGLE TERMINOLOGY

Term	Definition
Acute Angle	An angle with measure between 0 and 90 degrees.
Right Angle	An angle with measure of 90 degrees.
Obtuse Angle	An angle with measure between 90 and 180 degrees.
Straight Angle	An angle with measure of 180 degrees.
Complementary Angles	Two angles with measures that add up to 90 degrees.
Supplementary Angles	Two angles with measures that add up to 180 degrees.
Congruent Angles	Two angles with the same measure.
Vertical Angles	A pair of opposite angles formed by intersecting lines.
Adjacent Angles	Two angles that have a common side and a common vertex but do not overlap in any way.

Two angles are called **complementary** angles when their measurements add up to 90° (a right angle). In the next figure, m∠ABC = 90°. ∠ABE and ∠CBE are complementary because their measurements add up to 90°. You also know that m∠ABD = 90° because ∠ABD and ∠ABC are **adjacent angles** and combine to form a straight line, which measures 180°.

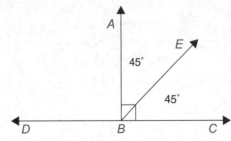

Rules about angles formed by intersecting lines

1

VERTICAL ANGLES:

Vertical angles (angles across the vertex from each other and formed by the same two lines) are equal in degree measure or congruent (≅). In other words, they're the same size.

2

ADJACENT ANGLES:

If adjacent angles combine to form a straight line, their degree measures total 180. In fact, a straight line is actually a 180° angle.

3

PERPENDICULAR LINES:

If two lines are perpendicular (⊥) to each other, they intersect at right (90°) angles.

4

THE SUM OF ANGLES:

The sum of all angles formed by the intersection of two (or more) lines at the same point is 360°, regardless of how many angles are involved.

In geometry, the set of points that makes up a flat surface is referred to as a **plane**. When two lines in the same plane never meet, no matter how far they are extended, they are called **parallel lines** and are indicated by the symbol ∥. If two parallel lines are intersected by a third line, eight angles are formed. A line that intersects two parallel lines is called a **transversal**. If a transversal intersects two parallel lines perpendicularly (at a 90° angle), all eight angles that are formed are right angles (90°). Otherwise, some angles are acute, while others are obtuse. This figure illustrates parallel lines intersected by a transversal line:

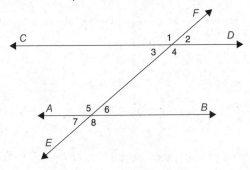

As noted earlier, angles that are equal in degree measure are called **congruent angles** (the symbol ≅ indicates congruency). In the figure, you can see that eight angles have been formed. The four acute angles (∠2, ∠3, ∠6, and ∠7) are congruent, and the four obtuse angles (∠1, ∠4, ∠5, and ∠8) are also congruent. Each pair of angles that are opposite each other in relation to a vertex (for example, ∠2 and ∠3) are called **vertical angles**. Vertical angles are always congruent.

Four angles formed by two intersecting lines add up to 360° in measure. In the same figure, m∠1 + m∠2 + m∠3 + m∠4 = 360°. (The same holds true for angles 5, 6, 7, and 8.) In the figure, the measure of any one of the four acute angles plus the measure of any obtuse angle equals 180°. If you know the measure of any one angle, you can determine the measure of all seven other angles. For example, if m∠2 = 30°, then ∠3, ∠6, and ∠7 each measures 30° as well, while ∠1, ∠4, ∠5, and ∠8 each measures 150°.

A geometry question might involve nothing more than intersecting lines and the angles they form. To handle this type of question, remember the four basic rules about angles formed by intersecting lines.

Test Yourself 4

Identify the size of the unlabeled angle in each figure. The answers will follow.

Answers:

1. 80°	**5.** 140°
2. 240°	**6.** 120°
3. 90°	**7.** 180°
4. 55°	**8.** 50°

COORDINATE GEOMETRY

Finding points on a plane is the study of **coordinate geometry**. A grid is commonly used to do this. The grid is divided into four sections. Each section is called a **quadrant**. The two number lines that divide the grid into quadrants are called the **x-axis** (the horizontal axis) and the **y-axis** (the vertical axis). The center of the grid, where the two axes meet, is called the **origin**. Any point on the plane has two coordinates that indicate its location relative to the axes. The points that are drawn on the grid are identified by **ordered pairs.** In ordered pairs, the x-coordinate is always written first. The ordered pair for the origin, in the middle of the grid, is (0, 0).

The quadrants of a grid are named in counterclockwise order, beginning with the first quadrant in the upper right corner. For any point in the first quadrant, the coordinates are positive. The quadrant in the top left is called the second quadrant. For any point in the second quadrant, the x-coordinate is negative but the y-coordinate is positive. The quadrant in the lower left is called the third quadrant. In the third quadrant, both coordinates are negative. The quadrant in the lower right is called the fourth quadrant, and in the fourth quadrant, the x-coordinate is positive, and the y-coordinate is negative.

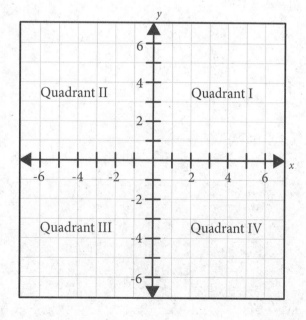

On the following graph, the x-coordinate of point A is 3. The y-coordinate of point A is 2. The coordinates of point A are given by the ordered pair (3, 2). Point B has coordinates (–1, 4). Point C has coordinates (–4, –3). Point D has coordinates (2, –3).

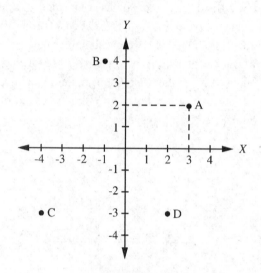

To graph a point whose coordinates are given, first locate the x-coordinate on the x-axis, then from that position move vertically the number of spaces indicated by the y-coordinate.

To graph (4, –2), locate 4 on the x-axis, then move –2 spaces vertically (2 spaces down, since the number is negative) to find the given point.

The point at which the x-axis and the y-axis meet has coordinates (0, 0) and is called the origin. Any point on the y-axis has 0 as its x-coordinate. Any point on the x-axis has 0 as its y-coordinate.

Test Yourself 5

Solve each graph. The answers will follow.

1. In the graph below, the coordinates of point A are

2. The coordinates of point P on the graph are

3. Which point might possibly have the coordinates (2,–3)?

4. The point with the coordinate (3, 0) is

5. Which point is named by the ordered pair (5, 1)?

To learn more about coordinate geometry, scan this QR code.

Answers:

1. **The correct answer is (3, –1).** A vertical line through A meets the *x*-axis at 3; therefore, the *x*-coordinate is 3. A horizontal line through A meets the *y*-axis at –1; therefore, the *y*-coordinate is –1. The coordinates of point A are (3, –1).

2. **The correct answer is (–3, 2).** Point P has coordinates $x = -3$ and $y = 2$.

3. **The correct answer is point C.** Start by moving in a positive direction along the *x*-axis. Then, you must move along the *y*-axis in a negative direction. The actual number of spaces you move is irrelevant, since point C is the only possible answer.

4. **The correct answer is point C.** Again, make your moves in order. First, move in the positive direction along the *x*-axis. Because the second coordinate is 0, make no move on the *y*-axis. Point C is your answer.

5. **The correct answer is point B.** Because both coordinates are positive numbers, the point must be located in the upper-right quadrant of the graph. Location along the *x*-axis is always stated first, so the correct answer is point B.

SUMMING IT UP

- If you are having difficulties with any mathematics topic, talk with a teacher or refer to any of your math textbooks.

- Use the exercises in this chapter to determine what you DON'T know well, and concentrate your study on those areas.

- Know the difference between perimeter, area, and volume.

  - Perimeter is the distance around the outside of a shape.

  - Area measures the space inside a two-dimensional plane figure, like a rectangle or circle.

  - Volume measures the space inside a three-dimensional solid figure, like a cube or a cylinder, and is the product of the figure's area and its height.

- Memorize the formulas for determining perimeter, area, and base, as these may not be given to you on the test. The formulas are also listed in Appendix C.

- Angles are measured in degrees. Lines, rays, or line segments form angles and meet at a point called the vertex. Know the different types of angles—right, obtuse, acute, and straight angles—as well as the relationships formed between pairs of angles—complementary, supplementary, congruent, vertical, and adjacent angles.

- Coordinate geometry requires you to find points on a plane. On the exam, you may be required to graph the points of an ordered pair or to determine the value of an ordered pair using the x- and y-coordinates plotted on a graph.

KNOWLEDGE CHECK

GEOMETRY
25 Questions—20 Minutes

> **Directions:** In the following questions, work out each problem and mark the letter that corresponds to the correct answer. The answers will follow.

1. Suppose two sides of a triangle measure 4 cm and 8 cm and that the perimeter of the triangle is 17 cm. What is the length of the triangle's third side?

   A. 4 cm

   B. 5 cm

   C. 8 cm

   D. 12 cm

2. Two rectangular boards, each measuring 5 feet by 3 feet, are placed together to make one large board. How much shorter will the perimeter be if the two long sides are placed together than if the two short sides are placed together?

   A. 2 feet

   B. 4 feet

   C. 6 feet

   D. 8 feet

3. Nine square tiles, each with an area of 25 square centimeters, have been arranged to form a larger square. What is the perimeter of the large square?

   A. 60 centimeters

   B. 100 centimeters

   C. 150 centimeters

   D. 220 centimeters

4. What is the circumference of a circle with radius 9?

   A. 6π

   B. 9π

   C. 18π

   D. 81π

5. What is the area of this triangle?

   A. 5

   B. 11

   C. 12

   D. 24

6. A square has an area of 49 square inches. The number of inches in its perimeter is

   A. 7

   B. 14

   C. 28

   D. 98

7. If circle *F* has an area of 36π, what is its diameter?

   A. 6

   B. 12

   C. 36

   D. 72

8. A roll of carpeting will cover 224 square feet of floor space. How many rolls are needed to carpet a room 36' × 8' and another 24' × 9'?

   A. 2.25

   B. 2.50

   C. 4.25

   D. 4.50

h=4

r=2

9. What is the volume of this cylinder?

   A. 16

   B. 16π

   C. 32

   D. 32π

10. What is the volume of a cube with a side of length 5 in.?

    A. 25 in.^{3}

    B. 125 in.^{3}

    C. 150 in.^{3}

    D. 225 in.^{3}

11. The number of cubic feet of soil needed for a flower box 3 feet long, 8 inches wide, and 1 foot deep is

    A. 2

    B. $4\frac{2}{3}$

    C. 12

    D. 24

12. The formula for the volume of a cylinder is $V = \pi r^2 h$. What is the volume of a cylinder with a radius of 5 ft. and a height of 3 ft.?

    A. 15π ft.^{3}

    B. 45π ft.^{3}

    C. 60π ft.^{3}

    D. 75π ft.^{3}

13. If $a + b = 200°$, and $c + d + e + f = 140°$, what is the number of degrees in angle g?

    A. 10°

    B. 20°

    C. 30°

    D. 45°

14.

    In this figure, what is the value of $a + b$?

    A. 60

    B. 90

    C. 120

    D. 140

15.

    Find the value of x in this figure:

    A. 60

    B. 85

    C. 90

    D. 110

16. What is the measure of ∠A?

    A. 20°

    B. 50°

    C. 70°

    D. 90°

17.

In the figure shown, line *l* is perpendicular to line *m*. One angle formed by line *l* and line *q* has a measure of 130°, as shown. What is the degree measure of *a*?

    A. 25°

    B. 65°

    C. 130°

    D. 155°

18.

Lines *RS* and *TU* intersect at point *V*. If angle *RVT* has a measure of 35°, what is the measure of angle *SVU*?

    A. 35°

    B. 45°

    C. 70°

    D. 145°

19.

In triangle *ABC*, what is the value of *x*?

    A. 40

    B. 60

    C. 80

    D. 100

20.

What is the value of *x* in the diagram below?

    A. 25

    B. 45

    C. 70

    D. 90

21. Which point shown below corresponds to (8, 3)?

    A. Point F

    B. Point G

    C. Point H

    D. Point J

22.

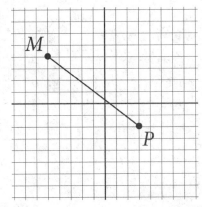

What are the coordinates of point M?

A. (5, 4)

B. (–5, 4)

C. (5, –4)

D. (–5, –4)

23.

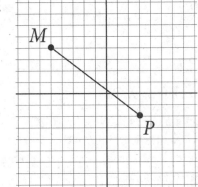

What are the coordinates of point *P*?

A. (3, 2)

B. (–3, 2)

C. (3, –2)

D. (–3, –2)

24.

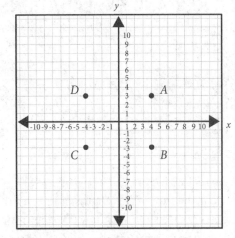

Points A, B, C, and D are shown on the coordinate plane. Which point is located at (4, –3)?

A. Point *A*

B. Point *B*

C. Point *C*

D. Point *D*

25.

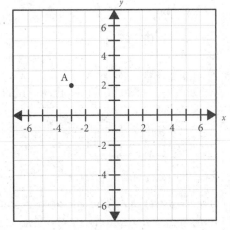

Which statement about the figure is true?

A. The coordinates of point *A* are (–3, –2).

B. The coordinates of point *A* are (3, 2).

C. Point *A* is located in quadrant II.

D. Point *A* is located in quadrant IV.

ANSWER KEY AND EXPLANATIONS

1. B	6. C	11. A	16. D	21. D
2. B	7. B	12. D	17. D	22. B
3. A	8. A	13. B	18. A	23. C
4. D	9. B	14. C	19. B	24. B
5. C	10. B	15. B	20. A	25. C

1. **The correct answer is B.** The perimeter of a triangle is the sum of the lengths of its sides. If the perimeter is given and we know the lengths of two sides, and the missing side has a length of x, then:

$$P = x + y + z$$
$$17 = x + 4 + 8$$
$$17 = x + 12$$
$$5 = x$$

2. **The correct answer is B.** Perimeter of a rectangle $= 2l + 2w$. If the two long sides are together, the perimeter will be $5 + 3 + 3 + 5 + 3 + 3 = 22$.

   If the two short sides are together, the perimeter will be $3 + 5 + 5 + 3 + 5 + 5 = 26$.

   Therefore, $26 - 22 = 4$ feet shorter

3. **The correct answer is A.** The side of each square $= \sqrt{25}$ or 5 cm. Aligned to form a large square, the tiles form three rows and three columns, each column and row with side $5 \times 3 = 15$. The perimeter $= 15 \times 4 = 60$.

4. **The correct answer is C.** The formula for the circumference of a circle is $C = 2\pi r$, so the circumference of a circle with radius 9 is $C = 2\pi(9) = 18\pi$.

5. **The correct answer is C.** This triangle includes a height, 3, and a base, 8. The height given corresponds to the base, since the height starts at the corner opposite the base and stretches down to the base. Apply the formula for the area of a triangle.

$$A = \frac{1}{2}bh$$
$$= \frac{1}{2}(8)(3)$$
$$= \frac{1}{2}(24)$$
$$= 12$$

6. **The correct answer is C.**

   Area of a square $= s^2$

   $49 = 7^2$

   One side $= 7$ inches

   $P = 4s$

   $P = 4 \times 7" = 28$ inches

7. **The correct answer is B.** We know that $A = \pi r^2$, where r represents the radius. In this problem, we're given the area, so we can plug it into the formula and solve for r:

$$36\pi = \pi r^2$$
$$\frac{36\pi}{\pi} = \frac{\pi r^2}{\pi}$$
$$36 = r^2$$
$$6 = r$$

   The radius equals 6, so the diameter must equal 6×2, or 12.

8. **The correct answer is A.**

   First room:

   36 ft. $\times$ 8 ft. = 288 sq. ft.

   Second room:

   24 ft. $\times$ 9 ft. $= \dfrac{216 \text{ sq. ft.}}{504 \text{ sq. ft.}}$

   $504 \div 224 = 2.25$ rolls needed

9. **The correct answer is B.** First, find the area of the base by using the formula for the area of a circle. Since the radius is 2, the area of the base is:

$$A = \pi r^2$$
$$= \pi(2)^2$$
$$= 4\pi$$

Now, find the volume of the cylinder by multiplying the area of the base times the height:

$$4\pi \times 4 = 16\pi$$

10. **The correct answer is B.** The formula for the volume of a cube is s^3, in which s is the length of a side of the cube. Therefore, the volume of a cube with a side of 5 in. in length equals 5^3, which equals $5 \times 5 \times 5$, or 125 in³.

11. **The correct answer is A.** Rename 8 in. as $\frac{2}{3}$ ft. so that all measurements are in the same unit. Then multiply $l \times w \times h$.

$$3 \text{ ft.} \times \frac{2}{3} \text{ft.} \times 1 \text{ ft.} = 2 \text{ cubic ft.}$$

12. **The correct answer is D.** You've been given the formula for a cylinder, so the only thing to do is to be sure you plug the values in all the right places. You've been asked for the volume, V, and you've been given the radius ($r = 5$) and the height ($h = 3$). Plug in those values and solve for V:

$$V = \pi r^2$$
$$= \pi(5^2)3$$
$$= \pi(25)(3)$$
$$= 75\pi$$

13. **The correct answer is B.** The sum of the angles of a circle equals 360°. Angles a through f total 340°. Angle g must be 20°.

14. **The correct answer is D.** In this question, we are presented with supplementary angles, angles that form a straight line. We know that the measures of angles lying on a straight line add up to 180°. Thus:

$$a + b + 40° = 180°$$
$$a + b = 180° - 40°$$
$$a + b = 140°$$

15. **The correct answer is B.** The sum of the interior angles of any quadrilateral equals 360°. In this case, we are given the measures of three interior angles, and are asked to find the measure of the fourth angle:

$$360° = 110° + 40° + 40°$$
$$360° = 275° + x$$
$$360° - 275° = 275° - 275 + x$$
$$85° = x$$

16. **The correct answer is D.** To answer this question, it's important to remember that the sum of the measures of the angles inside a triangle always equals 180°. In this case,

$$\angle A + 70° + 20° = 180°$$
$$\angle A + 90° = 180°$$
$$\angle A = 180° - 90°$$
$$= 90°$$

17. **The correct answer is C.** Lines l and m are parallel, and line q intersects these two parallel lines, so it is a transversal. Recall that certain angles are congruent when two parallel lines are intersected by a transversal. In this case, the obtuse angle that measures 130° and the angle with the measure of a degrees are congruent. Therefore, you know it measures 130°.

18. **The correct answer is A.** Vertical angles, formed when two lines intersect each other, are always equal to each other. Angles RVT and SVU are vertical angles, so their measures are equal. Therefore, if angle RVT has a measure of 35°, the measure of angle SVU is 35° as well.

19. **The correct answer is B.** The sum of the measures of the interior angles of a triangle is 180°. Therefore, $x = 180 - 80 - 40 = 60$.

20. **The correct answer is A.** The angle between the 110° angle and the 45° angle forms a vertical angle with the $x°$ angle and its measure is therefore equal to $x°$. The three angles form a straight line, so the sum of their measures is 180°. As such, $x + 45 + 110 = 180$, so that $x = 25$.

21. **The correct answer is D.** In reading a graph, always read along the horizontal axis first. The point that corresponds to the coordinates (8, 3) is point J.

22. **The correct answer is B.** The numbers themselves are the same throughout all four choices—the only difference is whether they are negative or positive. When a point is in quadrant II, the *x*-coordinate is negative and the *y*-coordinate is positive. Therefore, the coordinates of point *M* are (–5, 4).

23. **The correct answer is C.** When a point is in quadrant IV, the *x*-coordinate is positive and the *y*-coordinate is negative. Therefore, the coordinates of point *P* are (3, –2).

24. **The correct answer is B.** The ordered pair (*x*, *y*) gives the location of a point. Starting at the origin, (0, 0), the *x*-coordinate tells you the number of units to move to the right (if it's positive) or to the left (if it's negative). The *y*-coordinate tells you the number of units to move up (if it's positive) or down (if it's negative). Therefore, the point (4, –3) is 4 units to the right and 3 units down from the origin. Point B is located at (4, –3).

25. **The correct answer is C.** The quadrants are named in counterclockwise order beginning with quadrant I in the upper right corner. Point A is located in quadrant II.

NOTES

CHAPTER

Series Reasoning

SERIES REASONING

OVERVIEW

Number Series

Letter Series

Mixed Series

Tips for Answering Series Questions

Summing It Up

Knowledge Check: Series Reasoning

Answer Keys and Explanations

Series reasoning questions crop up on the HSPT exam. These questions are in the Sequence section. Series reasoning questions—symbol series, number series, letter series, or mixed—test your ability to reason without words. These questions can be challenging, fun, or sometimes very frustrating.

Series questions are a lot like analogy questions, which, as you hopefully remember, ask you to find the relationships between words. In series questions, you must determine the relationship between a series of symbols, numbers, or letters, and then choose the next item for the series.

This chapter gives you some in-depth instruction in working with series questions by showing you how to complete number and letter series. These are the most

TACHS   HSPT   ISEE   SSAT   SHSAT

common kinds of series questions you'll encounter on the HSPT exam. The information and practice you get in this chapter will help you develop your own methods and strategies for solving these types of questions. What's more, you can use those same strategies to solve mixed series and even symbol series questions.

All series reasoning questions require the same concentration, the same logical thinking, and the same flexibility of approach. With any series reasoning question, you run the risk of working out a sequence only to find that the answer you would choose to complete the sequence is not among the choices. Don't be discouraged! Go back and determine what other relationship is reasonable.

NUMBER SERIES

Number series questions measure your ability to think numerically and recognize the relationship among numbers in a series. Even though this type of task might be new and unfamiliar to you, the actual mathematics of number series questions is not complicated. The problems involve nothing more than simple arithmetic and a few other mathematical concepts. What the questions do require of you is concentration; you must be able to see how the numbers in a series are related so that you can supply the next number in that series. You must be flexible enough in your thinking so that if the first pattern you consider for a series turns out to be invalid, you can try a different pattern.

There is a system with which to approach number series questions. First, look hard at the series. The pattern might be obvious to you right away. A series such as 1, 2, 3, 1, 2, 3, 1 . . . should not require much time to identify. As you can see, the sequence 1, 2, 3 is repeating. The next number in the series must be 2. You might also instantly recognize the pattern of a simple series into which one number periodically intrudes. An example of such a series is 1, 2, 15, 3, 4, 15, 5 . . . . The number 15 appears after each set of two numbers in a +1 series. The next number in this series is 6, followed by 15. Can you see why?

Test Yourself 1

Here are five series questions that you should be able to answer by inspection. Choose the number that should come next in the series. The answers follow on the next page.

1. 12, 10, 13, 10, 14 . . .
   A. 9
   B. 10
   C. 14
   D. 15

2. 6, 21, 36, 6, 21 . . .
   A. 6
   B. 21
   C. 36
   D. 51

3. 9, 1, 9, 3, 9 . . .
   A. 4
   B. 5
   C. 6
   D. 8

4. 5, 8, 5, 8, 5 . . .
   A. 5
   B. 6
   C. 8
   D. 9

5. 10, 9, 8, 7, 6 . . .
   A. 4
   B. 5
   C. 6
   D. 7

Answers:

1. **The correct answer is B.** The series is a +1 series with the number 10 inserted after each step of the series.

2. **The correct answer is C.** The sequence 6, 21, 36 repeats itself without changing.

3. **The correct answer is B.** This is a +2 series, with the number 9 appearing before each member of the series.

4. **The correct answer is C.** In this series, the sequence 5, 8 repeats.

5. **The correct answer is B.** This is a descending series; each number is one less than the one before it. This is called a -1 series.

Sometimes, you might find that your ear is more adept than your eye. You might be able to "hear" a pattern or "feel" a rhythm more easily than you can "see" it. If you cannot immediately spot a pattern, try saying the series softly to yourself. First, read through the series. If that does not help, try accenting the printed numbers and speaking the missing intervening numbers even more softly. Try grouping the numbers within the series into twos or threes. After grouping, try accenting the last number or the first. If you read aloud 2, 4, 6, 8, 10, you will hear that the next number is 12. Likewise, if you see the series 31, 32, 33, 32, 33, 34, 33, and you group that series this way: 31, 32, 33/ 32, 33, 34/ 33 . . ., you will feel the rhythm. This is a mini-series consisting of three numbers. Each mini-series begins with a number one higher than the first number of the previous mini-series. The next number of the above series is 34, then 35, and then the next step will be 34, 35, 36.

Test Yourself 2

You might be able to answer the next five series questions by inspection. If you cannot, try sounding them out. The answers will follow.

1. 1, 2, 5, 6, 9, 10, 13 . . .

   A. 14
   B. 15
   C. 16
   D. 17

2. 2, 3, 4, 3, 4, 5, 4 . . .

   A. 3
   B. 4
   C. 5
   D. 6

3. 10, 10, 12, 14, 14, 16 . . .

   A. 16
   B. 18
   C. 20
   D. 22

4. 1, 2, 3, 2, 2, 3, 3, 2, 3 . . .

   A. 1
   B. 2
   C. 3
   D. 4

5. 22, 20, 18, 20, 18, 16, 18 . . .

   A. 14
   B. 16
   C. 18
   D. 20

Answers:

1. **The correct answer is A.** If you pair the numbers, you can whisper the bracketed "missing numbers" to determine the pattern; 1, 2, [3, 4,] 5, 6, [7, 8,] 9, 10, [11, 12,] 13

   The next number to read aloud is 14, followed by a whispered 15, 16, and then aloud again for 17.

2. **The correct answer is C.** If you group the numbers into threes and read them aloud, accenting either the first or last number of each group, you should feel that each group of three begins and ends with a number one higher than the previous group.

   Read <u>2</u>, 3, 4/ <u>3</u>, 4, 5/ <u>4</u>, 5, 6; or 2, 3, <u>4</u>/ 3, 4, <u>5</u>/ 4, 5, <u>6</u>.

3. **The correct answer is B.** Once more, group the numbers into threes. This time, be certain to accent the third number in each group in order to sense the rhythm, and thereby the pattern, of the series:

   10, 10, 12/ 14, 14, 16/ 18 . . .

4. **The correct answer is D.** In this series, the rhythm emerges when you accent the first number in each group:

   <u>1</u>, 2, 3/ <u>2</u>, 2, 3/ <u>3</u>, 2, 3/ <u>4</u>, 2, 3.

5. **The correct answer is B.** Consider the first three terms 22, 20, 18. To obtain the second set of three terms, subtract 2 from the first three terms. Then, when moving to the third set of three terms, subtract 2 from the second set, and so on.

If you cannot hear the pattern of a series, the next step is to mark the degree and direction of change between the numbers. Most series progress by either + (plus) or − (minus) or a combination of both directions, so first try marking your changes in terms of + and −. If you cannot make sense of a series in terms of + and −, try × (times) and ÷ (divided by). You may mark the changes between numbers right on your exam or scratch paper, but be sure to mark the letter of the answer on your answer sheet when you figure it out.

Scan this QR code to watch a video on series reasoning.

Test Yourself 3

Try this next set of practice questions. If you cannot "see" or "hear" the pattern, mark the differences between the numbers to establish the pattern. Then, continue the pattern to determine the next number of the series. The answers will follow.

1. 9, 10, 12, 15, 19, 24 . . .

   A. 25
   B. 29
   C. 30
   D. 31

2. 35, 34, 31, 30, 27, 26 . . .

   A. 22
   B. 23
   C. 24
   D. 25

3. 16, 21, 19, 24, 22, 27 . . .

   A. 20
   B. 25
   C. 29
   D. 32

4. 48, 44, 40, 36, 32, 28 . . .

   A. 24
   B. 26
   C. 26
   D. 27

5. 20, 30, 39, 47, 54, 60 . . .

   A. 65
   B. 66
   C. 68
   D. 70

Answers:

1. **The correct answer is C.** The pattern here is that a number is added to each number in the series to get the next number. The "added" number starts with 1 and increases by 1 for each successive addition; 9 *(+ 1)*, 10 *(+ 2)*, 12 *(+ 3)*, 15 *(+ 4)*, 19 *(+ 5)*, 24 *(+ 6)*, 30 . . .

2. **The correct answer is B.** The pattern for this series is to first subtract 1, then subtract 3, and then repeat this alternating pattern; 35 *(– 1)*, 34 *(– 3)*, 31 *(– 1)*, 30 *(– 3)*, 27 *(– 1)*, 26 *(– 3)*, 23 . . .

3. **The correct answer is B.** The pattern in this series is to add 5, then subtract 2; 16 (+ 5), 21 *(– 2)*, 19 (+ 5), 24 *(– 2)*, 22 (+ 5), 27 *(– 2)*, 25 . . .

4. **The correct answer is A.** This series simply subtracts 4 to get each new member.

5. **The correct answer is A.** This series begins by adding 10, after which each successive addition is 1 less than the previous addition; 20 (+ 10), 30 (+ 9), 39 (+ 8), 47, (+ 7), 54 (+ 6), 65 . . .

Arithmetical series such as those just discussed might be interrupted by a number that appears periodically or by repetition of numbers according to a pattern. For example: 3, 6, 25, 9, 12, 25, 15, 18, 25 . . . and 50, 50, 35, 40, 40, 35, 30, 30, 35 . . . . In these cases, you must search a bit harder to spot both the arithmetic pattern and the pattern of repetition. When choosing your answer, you must be alert to the interruption point in the pattern.

Test Yourself 4

Choose the number that should come next in the series. Do not repeat a number that has already been repeated, but do not forget to repeat before continuing the arithmetical pattern if repetition is called for at this point in the series. The answers will follow.

1. 10, 13, 13, 16, 16, 19 . . .

   A. 16
   B. 19
   C. 21
   D. 22

2. 2, 4, 25, 8, 16, 25, 32 . . .

   A. 25
   B. 32
   C. 48
   D. 64

3. 80, 80, 75, 75, 70, 70 . . .

   A. 60
   B. 65
   C. 70
   D. 75

4. 35, 35, 32, 30, 30, 27 . . .

   A. 25
   B. 26
   C. 27
   D. 28

5. 76, 70, 12, 65, 61, 12 . . .

   A. 12
   B. 54
   C. 55
   D. 58

Answers:

1. **The correct answer is B.** The series pattern here is to add 3, repeat that number, then add 3 again, repeat *that* number, and continue; 10 (+ 3), 13 (repeat), 13 (+ 3), 16 (repeat), 16 (+ 3), 19 (repeat), 19 . . .

2. **The correct answer is D.** This series pattern includes an extraneous number that is repeated periodically. Specifically, 25 repeats itself every third number. The complete pattern is to multiply each number by 2, but insert 25 as every third entry; 2 (× 2), 4 (× 2), 25, 8 (× 2), 16 (× 2), 25, 32 (× 2), 64 . . .

3. **The correct answer is B.** This pattern repeats each number once, and then subtracts 5; 80 (repeat), 80 (– 5), 75 (repeat), 75 (– 5), 70 (repeat), 70 (– 5), 65 . . .

4. **The correct answer is A.** This series contains three repeated steps: repeat the first number, subtract 3, then subtract 2. The pattern starts again by repeating the last number; 35 (repeat), 35 (– 3), 32 (– 2), 30 (repeat), 30 (– 3), 27 (– 2), 25 . . .

5. **The correct answer is D.** This series starts by subtracting 6 from the initial number, and each successive subtraction is one less than the prior number. In addition, the number 12 is repeated every third number in the series; 76 (– 6), 70 (– 5), 12, 65 (– 4), 61 (– 3), 12, 58 . . .

LETTER SERIES

In the letter series section of your exam, each question consists of letters arranged according to a definite pattern. You must discover what that pattern is and then use that knowledge to determine which one of the four options completes the series. Letter series questions might be simple alphabetical progressions or intricate combinations that alternate between forward and backward steps.

Because each question is based on the twenty-six letters of the alphabet, it is a good idea to write the alphabet in your booklet as you work. In addition, it is well worth your time to assign a number to each letter, jotting down the numbers from one to twenty-six directly under the letters. The seconds spent doing this might save you precious minutes as you work through the letter series.

There is more than one method of attack for letter series questions. You may solve these problems by inspection whenever possible. If that fails, try numerical analysis.

Inspection

The first line of attack should always be inspection; this is the quickest and easiest approach. Look at the letters. Are they progressing in normal or reverse alphabetical order? Are the letters consecutive, or do they skip one or more letters between terms? Are certain letters repeated?

Test Yourself 5

Here are some series that you should be able to solve by inspection only. The answers will follow.

1. d b f b h b j b l b
   A. b
   B. m
   C. n
   D. o

2. a b c c d e f f g h i
   A. f
   B. j
   C. k
   D. i

3. gij jlm mop
   A. prq
   B. prs
   C. rst
   D. qur

Answers:

1. **The correct answer is C.** The even terms of the sequence are always "b." The other terms start with "d" and skip a letter each time. So, the odd terms are d, f, h, j, l, n, . . .

2. **The correct answer is D.** This is also a consecutive alphabetical progression, but here, the third letter of each set repeats. Thus, we have abcc deff ghii. Because only one *i* is given in the original series, the next letter must be the second *i* needed to complete the third set.

3. **The correct answer is B.** This is a bit more difficult, but with the grouping already done for you, you should be able to solve it by inspection. The pattern is as follows: From the first letter, skip one, then let the next letter in sequence follow immediately. Start each new three-letter sequence with the last letter of the previous sequence. The missing sequence begins with the *p* of the previous sequence, skips one letter to *r*, then continues immediately with *s*.

Numerical Analysis

If inspection does not make the answer apparent, try a numerical analysis of the series. Assign each letter in the series a numerical value according to its position in the alphabet. Write the direction and degree of difference between letters. Once you have done this, you will find yourself with a pattern of pluses and minuses like those you utilized in number series.

Test Yourself 6

Here are some series that you should be able to solve by inspection only. The answers will follow.

1. c d b e f d g h f i j

   A. h
   B. k
   C. f
   D. l

2. a b d g k p

   A. q
   B. u
   C. w
   D. v

3. mpt jmq gjn dgk

   A. cfj
   B. bei
   C. kos
   D. adhr

Answers:

a	b	c	d	e	f	g	h	i	j	k	l	m	n	o	p	q	r	s	t	u	v	w	x	y	z
1	2	3	4	5	6	7	8	9	10	11	12	13	14	15	16	17	18	19	20	21	22	23	24	25	26

1. **The correct answer is A.**

c		d		b		e		f		d		g		h		f		i		j		h
3		4		2		5		6		4		7		8		6		9		10		8
	+1		−2		+3		+1		−2		+3		+1		−2		+3		+1		−2	

Now it is obvious that the series progresses by the formula +1 −2 +3. According to this pattern, the next letter must be 10 (−2), or 8, which corresponds to the letter *h*.

2. **The correct answer is D.**

a		b		d		g		k		p		v
1		2		4		7		11		16		22
	+1		+2		+3		+4		+5		+6	

The progression is obvious once placed into a format showing the numerical translation of the alphabet. The numeric difference between each member of the series starts with 1 and increases by 1 with each letter.

3. **The correct answer is D.**

m		p		t		j		m		q		g		j		n		d		g		k		a		d		h
13		16		20		10		13		17		7		10		14		4		7		11		1		4		8
	+3		+4		−10		+3		+4		−10		+3		+4		−10		+3		+4		−10		+3		+4	

This series has three steps; the pattern is +3, +4, −10. This series could be seen as groups of three, three in this instance; watch for questions in which the letters are pre-grouped for you.

MIXED SERIES

With mixed series, you must once again ask yourself, "What's happening?" How are the numbers progressing? Up or down? What about the letters? Are changes occurring in the relationships of numbers to letters? According to what pattern?

Test Yourself 7

Choose the answer that will continue the pattern or sequence or that should fill in the blank in the series. The answers will follow.

1. RA_1T_2 RA_3T_4 RA_1T_2 RA_4T_5 _____

    A. RA_5T_6

    B. RA_5T_4

    C. RA_1T_2

    D. R_1AT_2

2. $L^2M_2N^2$ $O_3P^3Q_3$ $R^2S_2T^2$ _____ $X^2Y_2Z^2$

    A. $U_4V^4W_4$

    B. $T_3U^3V_3$

    C. $U^3V_3W^3$

    D. $V^4W_3X^4$

Answers:

1. **The correct answer is C.** A good solid look at the groupings within the series shows that the unit RA_1T_2 intervenes between the other units of the series. With no further information on which to base any other features of the series, you can determine that RA_1T_2 is the correct answer.

2. **The correct answer is A.** The first thing that becomes clear in this mixed series is that the letters form a simple alphabetical progression. You can immediately narrow your choices to A and C. On the basis of the information given, there is no way to know whether the numbers in the missing unit should be 3s or 4s, but we do have information about their position with relation to the letters. The 2s are grouped by a pattern that goes superscript, subscript, superscript. We are given only one group in which the numbers are not 2s, and the pattern in this case is subscript, superscript, subscript—the opposite of the groups with 2s. Because there is evidence of possible alternation of patterns—and we have already determined that we need to choose between choice A or C—the best choice is A, in which the pattern of the numbers is subscript, superscript, subscript.

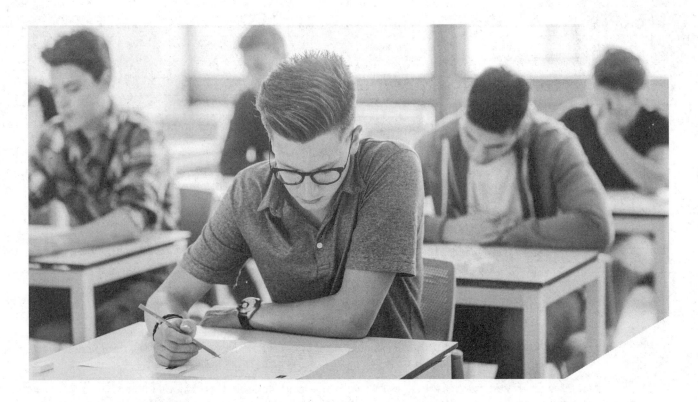

TIPS FOR ANSWERING SERIES QUESTIONS

- Tackle the questions that seem easiest for you first. Questions generally tend to be arranged in order of difficulty, with the easiest questions first, but problems that seem easy for some people might be more difficult to others, and vice versa. Quickly answer the questions that require little of your time, and leave yourself extra time for the more difficult questions.

- When you skip a question, mark or note the question in some way and leave its answer space blank. When you return to a question that you have skipped, be sure to mark its answer in the correct space. The time you spend checking to make sure that your question and answer numbers are alike is time well spent.

- Follow the procedures outlined in this chapter. First, look for an obvious pattern. Second, sound out the series; if necessary, group the numbers or letters and sound out again. Third, write the direction and amount of change between the numbers or letters.

- If you solve any problems in your test booklet or on scratch paper, be sure to mark the letter of the correct answer on your answer sheet. All answers must be marked on the answer sheet.

- If none of the answers given fits the rule you have figured out, try again. Try to figure out a rule that makes one of the four answers a correct one.

- Do not spend too much time on any one question. If a question seems impossible, skip it and come back to it later. A fresh look will sometimes help you find the answer. If you still cannot figure out the answer, guess. Remember that there is no penalty for a wrong answer on the HSPT exam.

- Keep track of time. Because there is no penalty for a wrong answer on the HSPT exam, you will want to answer every question. Leave yourself time to go back to the questions you skipped so that you can give them a second look. On the HSPT exam, if you are not finished as the time limit approaches, mark random answers for the remaining questions.

SUMMING IT UP

- Series questions are in the Sequence category of the HSPT exam under Quantitative Skills.

- In series questions, you must determine the relationship among a series of numbers, letters, and symbols. Then, choose the next item for the series.

- For series of symbols, pay attention to the differences between shapes. Focus on what is black and white, what is shaded, what shapes are used, etc.

- First, read through the series. If that does not help, try accenting the printed numbers and speaking the missing intervening numbers even more softly. Try grouping the numbers within the series into twos or threes. After grouping, try accenting the last number or the first.

- It is a good idea to keep a copy of the alphabet in front of you as you work. In addition, it is well worth your time to assign a number to each letter, jotting down the numbers from 1 to 26 directly under the letters to which they correspond.

- Study and practice the series reasoning question tactics in this chapter. Remember to answer the easiest questions first and return back to any questions you skipped, time permitting. Follow the system described in this chapter—look, sound, and group series items. Don't spend too much time on any one question, and keep track of time.

SERIES REASONING
32 Questions—16 Minutes
Exercise 1

Directions: Choose the number that should come next or that should fill in the blank in the series. The answer keys and explanations appear after Exercise 3.

---

1. 75, 75, 72, 72, 69, 69, . . .

   A. 63

   B. 66

   C. 68

   D. 69

2. 12, 16, 21, 27, 31, . . .

   A. 33

   B. 35

   C. 36

   D. 37

3. 22, 24, 12, 26, 28, 12, . . .

   A. 12

   B. 30

   C. 34

   D. 36

4. 13, 22, 32, 43, _____, 68

   A. 53

   B. 54

   C. 55

   D. 56

5. $4, 2, 1, \dfrac{1}{2}, \dfrac{1}{4}, \ldots$

   A. 0

   B. $\dfrac{1}{8}$

   C. $\dfrac{3}{8}$

   D. $\dfrac{1}{16}$

6. 100, 81, _____, 49, 36

   A. 60

   B. 64

   C. 65

   D. 75

7. 32, 25, 86, 32, 25, . . .

   A. 5

   B. 32

   C. 68

   D. 86

8. 51, 51, 30, 47, 47, 30, 43, . . .

   A. 30

   B. 41

   C. 43

   D. 45

9. 3 3 9 | 15 15 21 | 27 27 _____

   A. 1

   B. 27

   C. 30

   D. 33

10. 95 90 86 | 83 78 74 | 71 _____ 62

    A. 60

    B. 66

    C. 68

    D. 70

11. 1 5 1 | 2 6 2 | 3 _____ 3

    A. 0

    B. 3

    C. 4

    D. 7

12. 50 52 48 | 35 37 33 | _____ 14 10

    A. 9

    B. 11

    C. 12

    D. 15

13. 39 40 80 | 10 11 22 | 17 18 _____

    A. 9

    B. 33

    C. 36

    D. 38

14. 36 12 4 | 63 21 7 | _____ 36 12

    A. 72

    B. 85

    C. 97

    D. 108

Exercise 2

Directions: Choose the letter or group of letters that should come next or that should fill in the blank in the series.

1. n n o p p q r r s
   - A. t
   - B. u
   - C. s
   - D. r

2. a j e b u q i y e p a
   - A. k
   - B. d
   - C. f
   - D. w

3. d e f d g h i g j k l j m n o
   - A. j
   - B. m
   - C. n
   - D. o

4. a c d a a c d b a c d c a c
   - A. a
   - B. b
   - C. c
   - D. d

5. a d h l b e i m c f j
   - A. l
   - B. m
   - C. n
   - D. o

6. z a z c z f z j z
   - A. g
   - B. o
   - C. z
   - D. s

7. hat | mat | rat | bat | _____
   - A. jat
   - B. qat
   - C. pat
   - D. uat

8. mnp | hik | bce | _____ | kln
   - A. uvx
   - B. gij
   - C. rqp
   - D. xyz

9. ZWT WTQ TQN _____ NKH
   - A. PNL
   - B. NLJ
   - C. MJG
   - D. QNK

10. ABC IRS GNO DHI
    - A. BDG
    - B. FKL
    - C. EJK
    - D. NTZ

KNOWLEDGE CHECK

Exercise 3

Directions: Choose the answer that will continue the pattern or sequence or that should fill in the blank in the series.

1. $STPR_1$ STP_1R_2 $STPR_3$ _____ $STPR_5$

   A. $STPR_4$

   B. STP_4R_5

   C. $ST_1P_2R_3$

   D. STP_2R_3

2. $F^1G_2H^3I_4G_6H^7I_8J^9H_4I^5J_6K^7I^3J_4K^5L_6$ _____

   A. $J^7K_8L^9M_{10}$

   B. $M^5N_6O^7P_8$

   C. $J^8K_9L^{10}M_{11}$

   D. $K^1L_3M^5N_9$

3. $D_4F_6H_8E_5G_7I_9$ _____ $K_{11}M_{13}O_{15}P_{16}R_{18}T_{20}$

   A. $J_{10}K_{11}L_{12}$

   B. $J_{10}L_{12}N_{14}$

   C. $J_{10}L_{11}N_{12}$

   D. $J_{10}K_{12}L_{14}$

4. $R^2D^2R^2D_2R_2D_2R_2D^2D^2R^2$ _____

   A. D_2R_2

   B. R^2D_2

   C. D^2R_2

   D. D. D_2R^2

5.

6.

7.

8.

ANSWER KEYS AND EXPLANATIONS

Exercise 1

1. B	4. C	7. D	10. B	13. C
2. C	5. B	8. C	11. D	14. D
3. B	6. B	9. D	12. C	

1. **The correct answer is B.** The pattern is: repeat the number, –3; repeat the number, –3; repeat the number, –3. The next number must be 69 – 3 = 66.

2. **The correct answer is C.** The pattern repeats in groups of three; +4, +5, +6; +4, +5, +6. The next number must be 31 + 5, which is 36.

3. **The correct answer is B.** The basic pattern is a simple +2. The number 12 is inserted after each two terms of the series.

4. **The correct answer is C.** The numbers are large, but the progression is simple. If you mark the differences between numbers, you will recognize: +9, +10, +11, supply the +12 term, then continue with +13 to get the final number shown in the series.

5. **The correct answer is B.** This is a simple ÷2 series.

6. **The correct answer is B.** This series consists of the squares of the whole numbers in descending order.

7. **The correct answer is D.** This series follows no mathematical rule. You must solve it by inspection. The sequence 32, 25, 86 simply repeats.

8. **The correct answer is C.** The basic pattern is: repeat the number, –4; repeat the number, –4. The number 30 appears each time after the repeat and before the –4.

9. **The correct answer is D.** The entire series pattern is repeat, +6, +6; repeat, +6, +6. To answer the

question, it is enough to recognize that the pattern within each segment of the series is: repeat, +6, +6.

10. **The correct answer is B.** Within each segment of the series, the pattern is –5, –4, –3. In the final segment, 71 – 5 = 66, and 66 – 4 = 62.

11. **The correct answer is D.** You might see the pattern within each segment as +4, –4, or you might recognize by inspection or vocalization that each segment is simply a step up from the previous one.

12. **The correct answer is C.** Within each segment, the pattern is +2, –4. Because there is no overall pattern for the series, you must establish the pattern in the first two segments, then apply it in reverse to determine the first term in the last segment. Since the second term is two higher than the first, you can subtract 2 from the second term to determine the first.

13. **The correct answer is C.** The pattern is +1, ×2.

14. **The correct answer is D.** In the first two segments, you can establish that the pattern is ÷3. When you reach the third segment, multiply the second term by 3 to achieve the number that when divided by 3 equals 36.

Exercise 2

1. A	3. B	5. C	7. C	9. D
2. A	4. D	6. B	8. A	10. C

1. **The correct answer is A.** This pattern alternates double and single letters in alphabetical order: nn o pp q rr s tt. The next letter must be *t* to maintain the pattern.

2. **The correct answer is A.** In this series, each set of two letters is a vowel followed by a consonant that contains the sound of the vowel with which it is paired: aj eb uq iy ep a. The only consonant offered that contains the sound of *a* is *k*.

3. **The correct answer is B.** This series is an alphabetical progression of four-letter sequences where each fourth letter repeats the first letter of each sequence: defd ghig jklj mno. The missing letter is therefore the *m* needed to complete the fourth set.

4. **The correct answer is D.** This pattern consists of the letters *acd* followed by consecutive letters of the alphabet, starting with *a*. Thus: acda acdb acdc acd. The next letter must be *d*.

5. **The correct answer is C.** The best way to visualize this pattern is to assign the letters of the alphabet numbers from 1 to 26. This series then becomes:

   a d h l b e i m c f j n
   1 4 8 12 2 5 9 13 3 6 10 14
   +3 +4 +4 −10 +3 +4 +4 −10 +3 +4 +4

   The last number must be 10 + 4, which is 14, corresponding to the letter *n*. If you look at the numbers corresponding to each letter in each group of 4, you may notice that each item is one number higher than the group before.

6. **The correct answer is B.** Starting at the beginning of the alphabet, the space between even letters increases by one with each new letter:

   a   c   f   j   o
        +2   +3   +4   +5

   The letter *z* is a constant between each term. The next step in this series must be five letters after *j*, which is *o*.

7. **The correct answer is C.** In this series, each set of three letters makes a word composed of a consonant plus *at*: hat, mat, rat, bat. The next segment, therefore, must consist of a consonant plus *at* that may be combined to form an English word.

8. **The correct answer is A.** The easiest way to solve this series is to verify the numerical relationship within segments. In each instance, the sequence is +1, +2. The only option that satisfies this sequence is $u + 1 = v + 2 = x$.

9. **The correct answer is D.** To visualize the sequence, use the numbered alphabet you wrote for yourself in your notes. From *Z*, skip two letters back to *W*, and from *W* skip two more to *T*. In the next group, the procedure is exactly the same, and in each of the following groups as well. In addition, note that each succeeding group begins with the middle letter of the group before it. Thus, the missing group begins with the *Q* in the middle of the preceding group, continues with the skip of two back to *N*, and concludes with the further skip back to *K*.

10. **The correct answer is C.** It is very important to have written the entire alphabet and to have assigned each letter its numerical equivalent in order to choose the answer to this question.

    ABC I R S G N O D H I E J K
    1 2 3 9 18 19 7 14 15 4 8 9 5 10 11
    ×2 +1 ×2 +1 ×2 +1 ×2 +1 ×2 +1

    Here, it is necessary to figure out the relationship in groups other than the first one, then confirm that the relationship of the first three letters is not simple alphabetical succession. Notice that no group of three bears any external relationship to any other group of three letters. Only the relationship within a group of three will determine the correct answer. Only choice C satisfies the ×2, +1 formula.

Exercise 3

1. D	3. B	5. B	7. C
2. A	4. C	6. D	8. B

1. **The correct answer is D.** In all groupings, the letters are the same. You might assume that the answer choice will contain those same letters. When there is only one subscript number, it is at the end. When there are two, they follow the last and the next-to-last letter. Your best guess, if you can find reasonable choices to fit, is that the number pattern appears to alternate: one number, two numbers, one number, two numbers. Choices B and D might fit into this pattern. Then, look for the rationale for the numbers themselves. The numbers of the second group add to make the number of the third. Because the numbers of choice D add to make the number in the final group, this is the most logical choice.

2. **The correct answer is A.** By inspection, you can find the pattern of the letters. Each succeeding group of four picks up with the second letter of the preceding group and proceeds in alphabetical order. This means the next group must start with *J*, which narrows your answer choices to A or C. Now look at the numbers. Within each set of four, the numbers go in order, but there seems to be no rule by which numbers are assigned to succeeding groups. You must look for a pattern of some sort. Note that even numbers always appear as subscripts and odd numbers are always superscripts. Now you know why choice A is the correct answer.

3. **The correct answer is B.** Some series questions are easier than others. The numbers that follow the letters are the numbers assigned to the letters according to their position in the alphabet. Immediately, you may narrow the correct answer possibility to choices A and B, since the numbers in choices C and D do not match their positions in the alphabet. Now look at the pattern of the letters.

In each group, there is a skip-one pattern. Because choice A gives letters in sequence, the correct answer must be B.

4. **The correct answer is C.** In the first four groupings, the 2s position themselves in all possible combinations around the *R* and the *D*. The fifth group reverses the positions of *R* and *D* and appears to begin anew the circuit of 2s around the letters. The final group, then, should continue the rotation of the 2s, following in the same manner as when the letters were in their original position. Thus, the second *D R* should have the 2s placed in the same manner as the second *R D*—the first 2 at the top and the second 2 at the bottom.

5. **The correct answer is B.** As the pattern progresses, in each succeeding frame an additional circle is darkened. Thus, in the first, none; in the second, one; in the third, two; and in the fourth, three. Because three circles have already been darkened in the fourth frame, the frame must be completed with undarkened circles, horizontal as in all frames.

6. **The correct answer is D.** Because frames one and three are identical, you must assume that the pattern is of alternating identities and that frames two and four must also be identical.

7. **The correct answer is C.** In the first three frames, the farthest-right figure is always a U shape. In the first frame, the next-to-last figure is upended; in the second frame, an additional figure is upended, reading from right to left; in the third frame, three figures are upended. Logically, as the series progresses, the fourth frame should include the four left-hand figures upended, with only the farthest right maintaining its position as a U.

8. **The correct answer is B.** The darkened figures seem to be following no particular pattern within themselves, but they do seem to be alternating frames with the undarkened figures. The positions of the undarkened arrows in the first and third frames are identical. There is no reason to expect their positions to change the next time they appear in the series. With the alternating dark, light pattern, the undarkened arrows are due to appear in the next frame, and only choice B maintains their same position as in the two previous appearances.

NOTES

CHAPTER

Comparisons and
Ability Questions

COMPARISONS AND ABILITY QUESTIONS

OVERVIEW

Geometric Comparisons

Nongeometric Comparisons

Ability Questions

Summing It Up

Knowledge Check: Comparisons and Ability

Answer Key and Explanations

The comparison questions in the Quantitative Skills section of the HSPT and the Ability questions on the TACHS require a little bit of mathematical skill, a lot of patience, and some logical thinking. With such careful thinking required, it's important to take adequate time to study the mechanics of each question type and practice.

In this chapter, we'll cover strategies for how to approach geometric comparisons, nongeometric comparisons, and ability questions. For geometric comparisons, closely examine the given shape(s) and then compare the statements presented to you. For nongeometric comparisons, be sure to perform all the operations listed, and then work through each statement strategically, determining whether each statement is true or false. While ability questions test a few different skills, you'll need to know how to visualize the holes punched into a folded piece of paper and how to identify patterns among figures.

GEOMETRIC COMPARISONS

Geometric comparison questions ask you to compare values among multiple objects. You may be asked to compare multiple shapes, their total areas, their shaded areas, side numbers, patterns, and other traits. Much like the series exercises in Chapter 15, geometric comparisons require your complete focus to spot the pattern(s) among the figures in the question. Some will be easier than others, but don't expect that they are all going to be the same. That said, let's look at a few problems and identify techniques to help you solve them.

EXAMPLE:

Examine A, B, and C and find the best answer.

A. A is more shaded than B.

B. B is more shaded than A and less shaded than C.

C. A and B are equally shaded and less shaded than C.

D. A, B, and C are equally shaded.

SOLUTION:

The correct answer is C. This question asks how much of each circle is shaded. Note that all three circles are divided into eight segments. Count the number of shaded segments in each circle and write it down. If you've counted accurately, you'll notice you have written the following: A 4, B 4, C 5. Regardless of the pattern, two circles have the same number of spaces shaded, while the third has one more wedge filled in.

Now, read each statement and mark true or false next to each one. Choice A is false because both A and B have four shaded segments. The statement in choice B is only partially true: B is less shaded than C but not more shaded than A. Therefore, choice B is false. Choice C is true: A and B are equally shaded (four each) and both are less shaded than C, which has five shaded segments. Check choice D in case you have made an error. Choice D says that all are equally shaded, which is false.

 TIP

Carefully examine each shape to identify what element(s) change between each item and the next: measurement of a side, number of sides, how much of a shape is shaded, and whether there is a pattern in the shapes.

ALERT

Make sure you look at each figure carefully. Without careful examination, an optical illusion could give you the wrong first impression.

EXAMPLE:

The pie is divided into sixteen equal portions. Study the pie and find the best answer.

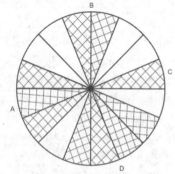

A. A plus D equals B plus C.

B. D minus A equals B minus C.

C. C minus D equals A.

D. B equals A plus C.

SOLUTION:

The correct answer is C. Begin by counting the pie wedges in each portion; write the number of wedges next to the letter: A (1), B (3), C (3), D (2). Now perform the arithmetic for each statement.

A. $1 + 2 = 3 + 3$; $3 = 6$—false

B. $2 - 1 = 3 - 3$; $1 = 0$—false

C. $3 - 2 = 1$—true

D. $3 = 1 + 3$; $3 = 4$—false

NONGEOMETRIC COMPARISONS

Nongeometric comparison questions test your ability to spot patterns with numbers or equations. Some might give you equations to solve, while others might give you a set of values. The object is to compare the values and equations against the response options. Like geometric comparisons, it is easier to actually see how it works than to try to explain all of the possible variations. Let's look at a couple of nongeometric comparison questions.

EXAMPLE:

Examine A, B, and C and find the best answer.

  A. $(5 \times 4) - 10$

  B. $(3 \times 6) + 4$

  C. $(8 \times 3) - 6$

A. $B = C > A$

B. $B > C > A$

C. $A > C$

D. $C > A > B$

SOLUTION:

Start by performing the operations in A, B, and C.

  A: $(5 \times 4) - 10 = 20 - 10 = 10$

  B: $(3 \times 6) + 4 = 18 + 4 = 22$

  C: $(8 \times 3) - 6 = 24 - 6 = 18$

Now you can substitute these numbers for the letters in the four statements and choose the correct one.

Choice A: 22 is equal to 18 and greater than 10—this is false, 22 is greater than 18.

Choice B: 18 is greater than 10 but less than 22—this is true, 10 is less than 18, which is less than 22.

Choice C: 10 is greater than 18—this is false, 10 is not greater than 18.

Choice D: 10 is less than 18 but more than 22—this is false, 10 is not greater than 22.

The correct answer is B. We know this because each portion of the statement in choice B is true; 18 is greater than 10, and 18 is less than 22.

EXAMPLE:

Examine A, B, and C and find the best answer.

  A. 4^3

  B. 3^4

  C. $(3 \times 4)(4)$

A. $A > B > C$

B. $A = B > C$

C. $B > A > C$

D. $A = C < B$

SOLUTION:

First, perform the operations.

  A: $4^3 = 4 \times 4 \times 4 = 64$

  B: $3^4 = 3 \times 3 \times 3 \times 3 = 81$

  C: $(3 \times 4)(4) = 12 \times 4 = 48$

Substitute the numbers in the statements.

Choice A: 64 is greater than 81, which is greater than 48—false, 64 is less than 81.

Choice B: 64 equals 81, which is greater than 48—false, 64 is not equal to 81.

Choice C: 48 is smaller than 81, which is greater than 64—true, 81 is greater than both 64 and 48.

Choice D: 64 is equal to 48, which is smaller than 81—false, 64 is not equal to 48.

The correct answer is C. As soon as you hit a falsehood in an answer, no matter what comes before or after, that answer cannot be true.

You will have a chance to practice more geometric and nongeometric comparison questions in the Knowledge Check at the end of this chapter.

ABILITY QUESTIONS

If you are taking the TACHS, your reasoning abilities will be assessed in the Ability section of the exam. Questions in this section will assess the reasoning abilities you've developed through your experiences both in and out of school. This section will also test your ability to reason using spatial and figure-based content. Unlike math or language arts questions, ability questions will highlight how well you use your reasoning skills to solve problems that you may or may not have learned in the classroom.

Ability questions come in three different formats: paper folding, figure classification, and figure matrices. Let's explore each of these question types.

Paper Folding

Paper folding questions test how well you can visualize what happens when holes are punched in a folded piece of paper. For these problems, you see a flat square piece of paper that folds one, two, or three times. You will observe each fold, presented in a sequence of folds and ending with a hole punch.

To successfully solve these problems, always assume that the paper fold is toward the front (toward you). The broken lines you will see indicate the original position of the paper prior to that fold, and the solid lines indicate the final position of the folded paper.

After the last fold, one or more holes will be added to the paper. You must then mentally unfold the paper and determine the position of the holes as they would appear on the original square piece of paper. Select the answer choice that matches your mental image of the original paper with the appropriate hole placement.

In the answer choices, punched holes are based on an imaginary grid of 4 rows and 4 columns of circles, or in a 5 x 5 grid, as shown:

These two grids represent the possible positions of the final holes; no partial holes will appear in the final answer.

There are only four main type of folds:

1. A horizontal fold that occurs one-eighth, one-fourth, one-third, or one-half from the top or bottom edge of the square paper.

2. A vertical fold that occurs one-eighth, one-fourth, one-third, or one-half from the right or left edge of the square paper.

3. A fold along one of the two main diagonals of the square piece of paper.

4. A fold along a diagonal connecting the midpoints of adjacent sides.

The location in which the holes will appear is determined by the fold. If the paper folds vertically, then the holes will line up horizontally, and vice versa. After the first fold, the paper may fold one or two more times. The four types of folds are used in a wide variety of combinations, producing many different patterns of holes in the end product.

Paper folding questions can be quite difficult to follow, especially when there are multiple folds. However, there are some key details to watch out for that will help you eliminate answer choices.

1. It's important to **keep track of the layers of paper that result from each fold**; different parts of the folded paper following a fold can have a different number of layers—it depends on where the fold creates an overlap.

2. **Look at the symmetry of the first fold**. The unfolding step is the opposite of that initial fold. Any position with a hole on one side of the line of symmetry will result in hole appearing in the corresponding position on the other side of the line of symmetry. You should immediately discard any answer choice that does not have that line of symmetry. You can see this in the following diagram:

16

TIP

When dealing with paper folding questions, it helps to mentally divide the original square piece of paper into four congruent squares, or quarters (also called *quadrants*).

3. **Remember that the number of holes in the result is directly related to the number of overlapping layers and the location of folds.** The number of layers of paper that overlap in the position where the hole was punched will affect the number of holes punched. A hole punched along a fold will result in two holes; if a hole is punched on an unfolded section, then it will result in one hole, not two.

Let's see these strategies in action by walking through two paper folding problems.

EXAMPLE:

Determine the final hole pattern resulting from this sequence of folds and a hole punch.

SOLUTION:

The first fold divides the paper square in half from right to left, thereby producing two layers throughout the entire folded construct. Then, the paper folds in half from right to left, producing *four* layers throughout. Finally, the paper folds in half from top to bottom. All told, the entire folded construct comprises *eight* layers.

Now, the hole appears near the fold, going through all eight layers. Therefore, when you mentally unfold the paper you see eight holes. But where are they located?

If we mentally unfold the paper one step at a time, we first see that reversing the final fold reveals holes in these two positions:

Then, reversing the middle fold yields holes in four positions, as shown here:

Finally, reversing the very first fold shows holes in eight positions, as shown:

This last image is the final answer.

Scan this QR code to watch a video on paper folding.

Let's try the next problem:

EXAMPLE:

Determine the final hole pattern resulting from this sequence of folds and hole punch.

SOLUTION:

For the first step, the fold line is the diagonal line connecting the top left and bottom right corners of the square piece of paper. The triangle formed below that line folds toward the bottom right corner. Visually, you can see that it divides the paper in two; however, you also know enough about geometry to realize that this is what happens when you fold a piece of paper in half—you get two equal halves.

In the second step (second square in the image), the triangle created in step one is folded in half again, this time moving the bottom left corner to the top right corner. Keep track of how many layers are now present in the triangle (there are four).

In the third step, we see that two holes have been punched through the folded paper—one through the center of the right edge, and another just below that. Now you need to

mentally unfold the paper to see where the holes appear across the entire sheet of paper. You must unfold the paper in the reverse order of your initial folds. Undoing the second fold will cause the holes to reflect to the center and right of the bottom edge. Undoing the large diagonal fold will then reflect all four holes to the top-left part of the page, as shown here.

Yes, paper folding questions require a lot of concentration and mental gymnastics. But with practice, you will learn to do the folds in your head just as easily as if you had the paper in your hands. So, grab a stack of construction paper and a hole punch and start practicing.

Figure Classification

In figure classification questions, three figures appear together that share some type of similarity. You must review the answer choices to find a figure that shares that similarity.

The following are some common ways in which the figures might be similar:

- The number of line segments or points that make up the figures may be similar. The figures could all have the same number, or have an even or an odd number of points or segments, etc. They may even increase or decrease in a pattern from one figure to the next.

 ALERT -

For geometric questions based on figures or images, you may be told that all angles that *look like* 90 degree angles *are* 90 degree angles or that all lines that *look* straight *are* straight. In other words, you are allowed to assume a figure or angle is geometrically perfect, even though the actual image may not meet that standard.

- The alignment of the line segments that make up the figures may be the same. They may be parallel or perpendicular.

- The objects may be symmetrical, like a reflection across certain lines or rotations.

- The nature of the shapes must be considered, including dotted vs. solid borders or the type of shape (e.g., triangle, square, pentagon, and so on).

- The alignment and/or nature of shapes inside other shapes must be examined.

- The shaded portion of figures appearing across a row or down a column can be a factor, including the direction or slant of any shading lines.

If you have shapes within shapes, be sure to closely examine any relationships there. For example, let's look at a couple of TACHS-style figure classification problems and walk through how to determine which answer is correct.

EXAMPLES:

Determine which answer exhibits the same characteristic as the three shapes shown here.

SOLUTION:

All three figures possess the following characteristics:

- The outer figure comprises dashed line segments.

- The inner figure comprises solid line segments.

- The number of sides of the figure inside is *one less* than the number of segments the outer figure comprises.

The correct answer is C. Choices A and D violate all three conditions, while choices B and E violate the first two conditions. Only choice C possesses all three characteristics exhibited in the original figures.

Determine which of the answer choices exhibits the same characteristic as the three shown:

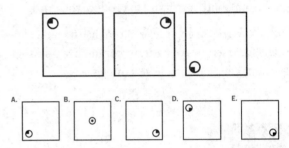

SOLUTION:

All three figures possess these characteristics:

- There is a circle in different corners of the square.

- Each circle has one quarter shaded.

- The shaded portion corresponds to the location of that circle in the square—for example, the circle in the upper-right corner has the upper-right quarter shaded.

The correct answer is E. Choices A and D violate the first condition because those corners of the square already have a circle in them in one of the three given figures. In choice B, the circle is not in a corner. Choice C violates the third condition.

Figure Matrices

Figure matrices questions present you with a 3-by-3 matrix of figures. Most often, the figure in the bottom right square will be missing. You need to determine which of the answer choices is the figure that completes the matrix. The figures are related either by row or by column.

The matrix uses the same pattern to produce the two complete rows or columns. The goal is to determine this pattern and apply it to identify the missing figure.

Just as with figure classification problems, the patterns can emerge in a variety of ways. For instance, there could be a change between adjacent entries in number, size, or position. Or, the pattern could add or remove a figure from another column to produce the third.

Once you work through several problems, you will get the feel for the types of patterns commonly assessed on the exam. Let's look at a few examples.

EXAMPLES:

Determine which of the answer choices fits into the missing square so that either all three rows or all three columns exhibit the same pattern:

SOLUTION:

The correct answer is C. You can see the pattern repeating across the rows in this matrix. For both rows 1 and 2, the figure remains the same, but the number of dots contained within it decreases by one as you move from left to right in that row. As such, the answer choice that should fill in

the missing cell is a triangle containing no dots. Choices A and E contain the correct number of points (none) but are not the same shape as the one used in the third row. Choices B and D contain the wrong number of points.

Determine which of the answer choices you should insert into the missing square so that either all three rows or all three columns exhibit the same pattern.

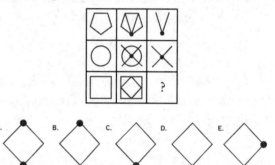

SOLUTION:

The correct answer is D. The pattern appears across rows in this matrix. In rows 1 and 2, you start with an empty figure and add something to it to get the second cell. To get the third cell, you mentally erase the original figure, leaving only the portion added in the second cell. As such, the answer choice that should fill in the missing cell is the diamond inserted inside the original square in the third row. Also, there are no shaded vertices on this diamond. All the other answer choices have vertices darkened, but those are not part of the added element in the second cell of row 3.

You will have more opportunities to familiarize yourself with ability questions in the practice tests for the TACHS in Part 4. Be sure to read the explanations carefully—they can help you to understand the logic behind these question types and prepare you mentally for test day.

SUMMING IT UP

- Comparison questions are in the Quantitative Skills section of the HSPT exam. You will get questions on geometric and nongeometric comparisons.

- Geometric comparisons require careful observation and counting to solve correctly.

- To solve nongeometric comparison questions, follow these three steps:

  1. Perform all the operations in the question.

  2. Work through all the answer choices one by one, and eliminate each statement that is false.

  3. When you think you have found the correct answer, continue until you have tried each answer choice.

- The TACHS Ability section includes three question types:

  1. **Paper folding**, which tests how well you can visualize what happens when you punch a hole in a folded piece of paper

  2. **Figure classification**, in which you must choose a figure that shares a similarity with three images presented in the question

  3. **Figure matrices**, which present a 3 × 3 matrix that you must complete by choosing the correct figure based on the pattern established in the matrix

⏱ KNOWLEDGE CHECK

COMPARISONS AND ABILITY
15 Questions—9 Minutes

Directions: For questions 1–5, examine A, B, and C and choose the best answer.

1. A   B   C

A. B and C have the same number of dots.

B. A has fewer dots than B but more dots than C.

C. C has more dots than A.

D. B has more dots than A and C, which have the same number of dots.

2. The distance from X to Y is one inch.

A. Lines A, B, and C are of equal length.

B. Line A is longer than lines B and C, which are of equal length.

C. Line B is shorter than line A but longer than line C.

D. Line A is shorter than line C.

3.   A   B   C

A. C has more rings than A.

B. A has the same number of rings as B.

C. B and C have the same number of rings, which are more rings than A.

D. B has fewer rings than either A or C.

4.   A   B   C

A. C has more corners than A.

B. B has the same number of corners as C and more corners than A.

C. A has fewer corners than B.

D. A, B, and C all have the same number of corners.

5.   A   B   C

A. C is more shaded than B, which is more shaded than A.

B. C is more shaded than A, which is not less shaded than B.

C. B and C are equally shaded.

D. A and B are equally shaded.

Directions: For questions 6 and 7, examine the image shown and choose the best answer.

6.

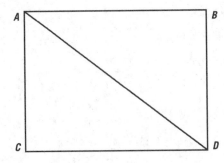

A. *AB* is equal to *CD*, which is longer than *AD*.

B. *BD* is shorter than *AC*.

C. *CD* is longer than *AD*.

D. *AC* is equal to *BD*.

7.

A. C plus D minus A equals B.

B. B plus D equals C.

C. A plus B equals C.

D. C minus D equals A plus B.

Directions: For questions 8–15, examine A, B, and C and choose the best answer.

8. **A.** 30% of 30

  B. 25% of 40

  C. 20% of 50

A. A = B = C

B. A = C > B

C. A = B < C

D. B = C > A

9. **A.** (4 + 8) × 10

  B. (8 + 10) × 4

  C. (4 + 10) × 8

A. A > B < C

B. A = C > B

C. C > A, which is less than B

D. A = B = C

10.
    A. $(12 - 4) - 6$
    B. $(12 - 6) - 4$
    C. $12 - (6 - 4)$

A. C > A > B
B. C = A > B
C. A = B = C
D. A = B < C

11.
    A. $\frac{2}{3}$ of 27
    B. $\frac{2}{5}$ of 10
    C. $\frac{3}{7}$ of 28

A. B > A > C
B. B > C < A
C. B < C > A
D. A > C > B

12.
    A. $\frac{2}{5}$%
    B. $\frac{2}{5}$
    C. 0.04

A. B > A > C
B. A < C < B
C. A = C < B
D. A = B = C

13.
    A. $(8 \div 2) \times 12$
    B. $(15 \div 3) \times 10$
    C. $(22 \div 1) \times 4$

A. A > B < C
B. C > A > B
C. A = B < C
D. C > A < B

14.
    A. 160%
    B. $\sqrt{256}$
    C. 4^2

A. A = B = C
B. B = C < A
C. C > B > A
D. A < C = B

15. Both x and y are positive integers
    A. $7(x + 2y)$
    B. $7x + 2y$
    C. $7(x + 2y) + 2x$

A. C > B < A
B. B < C < A
C. A = B < C
D. C > A < B

ANSWER KEY AND EXPLANATIONS

1. C	4. C	7. A	10. D	13. D
2. D	5. A	8. D	11. D	14. D
3. B	6. D	9. A	12. B	15. A

1. **The correct answer is C.** A has 10 dots, B has 12 dots, and C has 11 dots. 11 is greater than 10, so C has more dots than A. Test the other statements, and you will find them all false.

2. **The correct answer is D.** A straight line is the shortest distance between two points, so line A is the shortest line. Only choice D reflects this fact.

3. **The correct answer is B.** Each of the three figures has five rings, so any statement that speaks of more or fewer rings must be incorrect. Choice B does not mention figure C, but the statement regarding the other points is true, and therefore choice B is true.

4. **The correct answer is C.** Figures A and C are hexagons with 6 sides and 6 corners. Figure B is an octagon with 8 sides and 8 corners. The statement in choice C that figure A has fewer corners than figure B is correct.

5. **The correct answer is A.** C is exactly half shaded, B is somewhat less than half shaded, and A is sparsely shaded. That is exactly the statement made in choice A.

6. **The correct answer is D.** In a rectangle, parallel sides are equal in length. Therefore, AB is equal to CD, and AC is equal to BD. This eliminates choice B. AD is a hypotenuse. The hypotenuse is always the longest leg of a right triangle, which means AD cannot be shorter than any other line segment. This means choices A and C are incorrect.

7. **The correct answer is A.** Do the arithmetic to prove which choice is true. $60 + 10 - 30 = 40$. In other words, 40 equals 40. The only choice that proves to be true is choice A.

8. **The correct answer is D.** Start by doing the arithmetic. For A, 30% of 30 = 9; for B, 25% of 40 = 10, and for C, 20% of 50 = 10. Therefore, B and C are equal, and both are greater than A.

9. **The correct answer is A.** Do the arithmetic. For A, $12 \times 10 = 120$; for B, $18 \times 4 = 72$, and for C, $14 \times 8 = 112$. 120 is greater than 72, which is smaller than 112.

10. **The correct answer is D.** Do the arithmetic. For A, $8 - 6 = 2$; for B, $6 - 4 = 2$; and for C, $12 - 2 = 10$. A and B equal each other at 2, which is less than the 10 of C.

11. **The correct answer is D.** Do the math. For A, $\frac{2}{3}$ of 27 = 18; for B, $\frac{2}{5}$ of 10 = 4; and for C, $\frac{3}{7}$ of 28 = 12. 18 is greater than 12, which is greater than 4. After examining each answer choice, only choice D proves to be true as it states that A is greater than C, which is greater than B.

12. **The correct answer is B.** Convert all quantities to decimals. For A, $\frac{2}{5}\% = 0.4\% = 0.004$. For B, $\frac{2}{5} = 0.4$ and we are already given the decimal value of C. Checking against each of the answer options, choice B is correct in stating A < C < B.

13. **The correct answer is D.** Do the arithmetic. For A, $4 \times 12 = 48$; for B, $5 \times 10 = 50$; and for C, $22 \times 4 = 88$. Choice D correctly states that C > A < B, or 88 is greater than 48, which is less than 50.

14. **The correct answer is D.** Convert all quantities to decimals. For A, 160% = 1.6. Both B and C equal 16. Therefore, choice D is correct in stating A < C = B.

15. **The correct answer is A.** You could substitute numerical values for x and y and arrive at the correct answer, but it is unnecessary to work with numbers. Simply perform the algebraic multiplications to make your comparisons.

A: $7(x + 2y) = 7x + 14y$;

B: $7x + 2y = 7x + 2y$;

C: $7(x + 2y) + 2x = 7x + 14y + 2x = 9x + 14y$.

The resulting expressions make it easy to see that $9x + 14y$ is greater than $7x + 2y$, which is smaller than $7x + 14y$. That is what choice A states: C is greater than B, which is smaller than A.

PART V
PRACTICE TESTS

TACHS PRACTICE TEST 1

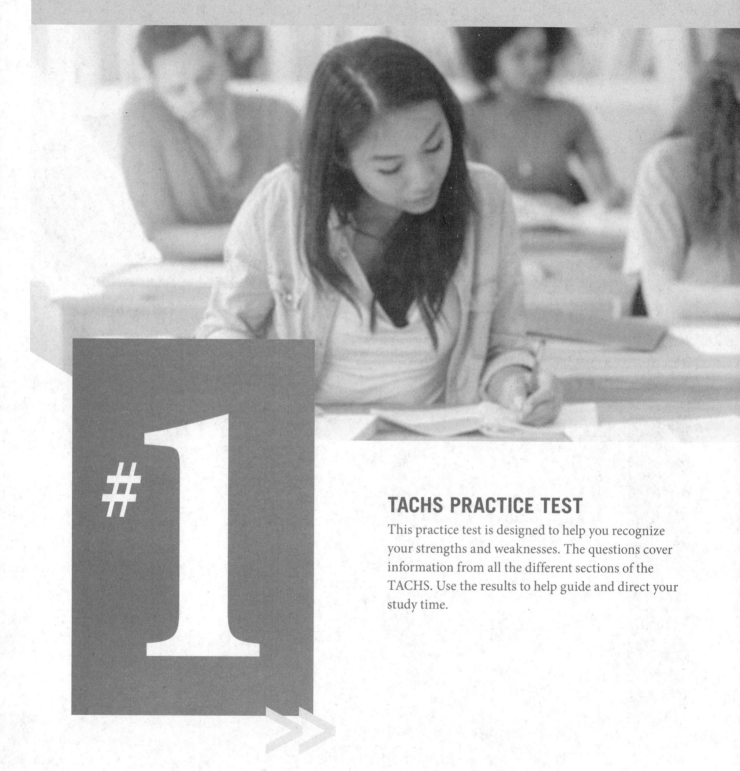

#1

TACHS PRACTICE TEST

This practice test is designed to help you recognize your strengths and weaknesses. The questions cover information from all the different sections of the TACHS. Use the results to help guide and direct your study time.

ANSWER SHEETS: TACHS PRACTICE TEST 1

Reading

1. Ⓐ Ⓑ Ⓒ Ⓓ	11. Ⓐ Ⓑ Ⓒ Ⓓ	21. Ⓐ Ⓑ Ⓒ Ⓓ	31. Ⓐ Ⓑ Ⓒ Ⓓ	41. Ⓐ Ⓑ Ⓒ Ⓓ
2. Ⓙ Ⓚ Ⓛ Ⓜ	12. Ⓙ Ⓚ Ⓛ Ⓜ	22. Ⓙ Ⓚ Ⓛ Ⓜ	32. Ⓙ Ⓚ Ⓛ Ⓜ	42. Ⓙ Ⓚ Ⓛ Ⓜ
3. Ⓐ Ⓑ Ⓒ Ⓓ	13. Ⓐ Ⓑ Ⓒ Ⓓ	23. Ⓐ Ⓑ Ⓒ Ⓓ	33. Ⓐ Ⓑ Ⓒ Ⓓ	43. Ⓐ Ⓑ Ⓒ Ⓓ
4. Ⓙ Ⓚ Ⓛ Ⓜ	14. Ⓙ Ⓚ Ⓛ Ⓜ	24. Ⓙ Ⓚ Ⓛ Ⓜ	34. Ⓙ Ⓚ Ⓛ Ⓜ	44. Ⓙ Ⓚ Ⓛ Ⓜ
5. Ⓐ Ⓑ Ⓒ Ⓓ	15. Ⓐ Ⓑ Ⓒ Ⓓ	25. Ⓐ Ⓑ Ⓒ Ⓓ	35. Ⓐ Ⓑ Ⓒ Ⓓ	45. Ⓐ Ⓑ Ⓒ Ⓓ
6. Ⓙ Ⓚ Ⓛ Ⓜ	16. Ⓙ Ⓚ Ⓛ Ⓜ	26. Ⓙ Ⓚ Ⓛ Ⓜ	36. Ⓙ Ⓚ Ⓛ Ⓜ	46. Ⓙ Ⓚ Ⓛ Ⓜ
7. Ⓐ Ⓑ Ⓒ Ⓓ	17. Ⓐ Ⓑ Ⓒ Ⓓ	27. Ⓐ Ⓑ Ⓒ Ⓓ	37. Ⓐ Ⓑ Ⓒ Ⓓ	47. Ⓐ Ⓑ Ⓒ Ⓓ
8. Ⓙ Ⓚ Ⓛ Ⓜ	18. Ⓙ Ⓚ Ⓛ Ⓜ	28. Ⓙ Ⓚ Ⓛ Ⓜ	38. Ⓙ Ⓚ Ⓛ Ⓜ	48. Ⓙ Ⓚ Ⓛ Ⓜ
9. Ⓐ Ⓑ Ⓒ Ⓓ	19. Ⓐ Ⓑ Ⓒ Ⓓ	29. Ⓐ Ⓑ Ⓒ Ⓓ	39. Ⓐ Ⓑ Ⓒ Ⓓ	49. Ⓐ Ⓑ Ⓒ Ⓓ
10. Ⓙ Ⓚ Ⓛ Ⓜ	20. Ⓙ Ⓚ Ⓛ Ⓜ	30. Ⓙ Ⓚ Ⓛ Ⓜ	40. Ⓙ Ⓚ Ⓛ Ⓜ	50. Ⓙ Ⓚ Ⓛ Ⓜ

Written Expression

1. Ⓐ Ⓑ Ⓒ Ⓓ Ⓔ	11. Ⓐ Ⓑ Ⓒ Ⓓ	21. Ⓐ Ⓑ Ⓒ Ⓓ	31. Ⓐ Ⓑ Ⓒ Ⓓ	41. Ⓐ Ⓑ Ⓒ Ⓓ
2. Ⓙ Ⓚ Ⓛ Ⓜ Ⓝ	12. Ⓙ Ⓚ Ⓛ Ⓜ	22. Ⓙ Ⓚ Ⓛ Ⓜ	32. Ⓙ Ⓚ Ⓛ Ⓜ	42. Ⓙ Ⓚ Ⓛ Ⓜ
3. Ⓐ Ⓑ Ⓒ Ⓓ Ⓔ	13. Ⓐ Ⓑ Ⓒ Ⓓ	23. Ⓐ Ⓑ Ⓒ Ⓓ	33. Ⓐ Ⓑ Ⓒ Ⓓ	43. Ⓐ Ⓑ Ⓒ Ⓓ
4. Ⓙ Ⓚ Ⓛ Ⓜ Ⓝ	14. Ⓙ Ⓚ Ⓛ Ⓜ	24. Ⓙ Ⓚ Ⓛ Ⓜ	34. Ⓙ Ⓚ Ⓛ Ⓜ	44. Ⓙ Ⓚ Ⓛ Ⓜ
5. Ⓐ Ⓑ Ⓒ Ⓓ Ⓔ	15. Ⓐ Ⓑ Ⓒ Ⓓ	25. Ⓐ Ⓑ Ⓒ Ⓓ	35. Ⓐ Ⓑ Ⓒ Ⓓ	45. Ⓐ Ⓑ Ⓒ Ⓓ
6. Ⓙ Ⓚ Ⓛ Ⓜ Ⓝ	16. Ⓙ Ⓚ Ⓛ Ⓜ	26. Ⓙ Ⓚ Ⓛ Ⓜ	36. Ⓙ Ⓚ Ⓛ Ⓜ	46. Ⓙ Ⓚ Ⓛ Ⓜ
7. Ⓐ Ⓑ Ⓒ Ⓓ Ⓔ	17. Ⓐ Ⓑ Ⓒ Ⓓ	27. Ⓐ Ⓑ Ⓒ Ⓓ	37. Ⓐ Ⓑ Ⓒ Ⓓ	47. Ⓐ Ⓑ Ⓒ Ⓓ
8. Ⓙ Ⓚ Ⓛ Ⓜ Ⓝ	18. Ⓙ Ⓚ Ⓛ Ⓜ	28. Ⓙ Ⓚ Ⓛ Ⓜ	38. Ⓙ Ⓚ Ⓛ Ⓜ	48. Ⓙ Ⓚ Ⓛ Ⓜ
9. Ⓐ Ⓑ Ⓒ Ⓓ Ⓔ	19. Ⓐ Ⓑ Ⓒ Ⓓ	29. Ⓐ Ⓑ Ⓒ Ⓓ	39. Ⓐ Ⓑ Ⓒ Ⓓ	49. Ⓐ Ⓑ Ⓒ Ⓓ
10. Ⓙ Ⓚ Ⓛ Ⓜ Ⓝ	20. Ⓙ Ⓚ Ⓛ Ⓜ	30. Ⓙ Ⓚ Ⓛ Ⓜ	40. Ⓙ Ⓚ Ⓛ Ⓜ	50. Ⓙ Ⓚ Ⓛ Ⓜ

Mathematics

1. Ⓐ Ⓑ Ⓒ Ⓓ
2. Ⓙ Ⓚ Ⓛ Ⓜ
3. Ⓐ Ⓑ Ⓒ Ⓓ
4. Ⓙ Ⓚ Ⓛ Ⓜ
5. Ⓐ Ⓑ Ⓒ Ⓓ
6. Ⓙ Ⓚ Ⓛ Ⓜ
7. Ⓐ Ⓑ Ⓒ Ⓓ
8. Ⓙ Ⓚ Ⓛ Ⓜ
9. Ⓐ Ⓑ Ⓒ Ⓓ
10. Ⓙ Ⓚ Ⓛ Ⓜ

11. Ⓐ Ⓑ Ⓒ Ⓓ
12. Ⓙ Ⓚ Ⓛ Ⓜ
13. Ⓐ Ⓑ Ⓒ Ⓓ
14. Ⓙ Ⓚ Ⓛ Ⓜ
15. Ⓐ Ⓑ Ⓒ Ⓓ
16. Ⓙ Ⓚ Ⓛ Ⓜ
17. Ⓐ Ⓑ Ⓒ Ⓓ
18. Ⓙ Ⓚ Ⓛ Ⓜ
19. Ⓐ Ⓑ Ⓒ Ⓓ
20. Ⓙ Ⓚ Ⓛ Ⓜ

21. Ⓐ Ⓑ Ⓒ Ⓓ
22. Ⓙ Ⓚ Ⓛ Ⓜ
23. Ⓐ Ⓑ Ⓒ Ⓓ
24. Ⓙ Ⓚ Ⓛ Ⓜ
25. Ⓐ Ⓑ Ⓒ Ⓓ
26. Ⓙ Ⓚ Ⓛ Ⓜ
27. Ⓐ Ⓑ Ⓒ Ⓓ
28. Ⓙ Ⓚ Ⓛ Ⓜ
29. Ⓐ Ⓑ Ⓒ Ⓓ
30. Ⓙ Ⓚ Ⓛ Ⓜ

31. Ⓐ Ⓑ Ⓒ Ⓓ
32. Ⓙ Ⓚ Ⓛ Ⓜ
33. Ⓐ Ⓑ Ⓒ Ⓓ
34. Ⓙ Ⓚ Ⓛ Ⓜ
35. Ⓐ Ⓑ Ⓒ Ⓓ
36. Ⓙ Ⓚ Ⓛ Ⓜ
37. Ⓐ Ⓑ Ⓒ Ⓓ
38. Ⓙ Ⓚ Ⓛ Ⓜ
39. Ⓐ Ⓑ Ⓒ Ⓓ
40. Ⓙ Ⓚ Ⓛ Ⓜ

41. Ⓐ Ⓑ Ⓒ Ⓓ
42. Ⓙ Ⓚ Ⓛ Ⓜ
43. Ⓐ Ⓑ Ⓒ Ⓓ
44. Ⓙ Ⓚ Ⓛ Ⓜ
45. Ⓐ Ⓑ Ⓒ Ⓓ
46. Ⓙ Ⓚ Ⓛ Ⓜ
47. Ⓐ Ⓑ Ⓒ Ⓓ
48. Ⓙ Ⓚ Ⓛ Ⓜ
49. Ⓐ Ⓑ Ⓒ Ⓓ
50. Ⓙ Ⓚ Ⓛ Ⓜ

Ability

Figure Classification

1. Ⓐ Ⓑ Ⓒ Ⓓ Ⓔ   5. Ⓐ Ⓑ Ⓒ Ⓓ Ⓔ   9. Ⓐ Ⓑ Ⓒ Ⓓ Ⓔ   13. Ⓐ Ⓑ Ⓒ Ⓓ Ⓔ   17. Ⓐ Ⓑ Ⓒ Ⓓ Ⓔ
2. Ⓙ Ⓚ Ⓛ Ⓜ Ⓝ   6. Ⓙ Ⓚ Ⓛ Ⓜ Ⓝ   10. Ⓙ Ⓚ Ⓛ Ⓜ Ⓝ   14. Ⓙ Ⓚ Ⓛ Ⓜ Ⓝ   18. Ⓙ Ⓚ Ⓛ Ⓜ Ⓝ
3. Ⓐ Ⓑ Ⓒ Ⓓ Ⓔ   7. Ⓐ Ⓑ Ⓒ Ⓓ Ⓔ   11. Ⓐ Ⓑ Ⓒ Ⓓ Ⓔ   15. Ⓐ Ⓑ Ⓒ Ⓓ Ⓔ   19. Ⓐ Ⓑ Ⓒ Ⓓ Ⓔ
4. Ⓙ Ⓚ Ⓛ Ⓜ Ⓝ   8. Ⓙ Ⓚ Ⓛ Ⓜ Ⓝ   12. Ⓙ Ⓚ Ⓛ Ⓜ Ⓝ   16. Ⓙ Ⓚ Ⓛ Ⓜ Ⓝ   20. Ⓙ Ⓚ Ⓛ Ⓜ Ⓝ

Figure Matrices

1. Ⓐ Ⓑ Ⓒ Ⓓ Ⓔ   5. Ⓐ Ⓑ Ⓒ Ⓓ Ⓔ   9. Ⓐ Ⓑ Ⓒ Ⓓ Ⓔ   13. Ⓐ Ⓑ Ⓒ Ⓓ Ⓔ   17. Ⓐ Ⓑ Ⓒ Ⓓ Ⓔ
2. Ⓙ Ⓚ Ⓛ Ⓜ Ⓝ   6. Ⓙ Ⓚ Ⓛ Ⓜ Ⓝ   10. Ⓙ Ⓚ Ⓛ Ⓜ Ⓝ   14. Ⓙ Ⓚ Ⓛ Ⓜ Ⓝ   18. Ⓙ Ⓚ Ⓛ Ⓜ Ⓝ
3. Ⓐ Ⓑ Ⓒ Ⓓ Ⓔ   7. Ⓐ Ⓑ Ⓒ Ⓓ Ⓔ   11. Ⓐ Ⓑ Ⓒ Ⓓ Ⓔ   15. Ⓐ Ⓑ Ⓒ Ⓓ Ⓔ   19. Ⓐ Ⓑ Ⓒ Ⓓ Ⓔ
4. Ⓙ Ⓚ Ⓛ Ⓜ Ⓝ   8. Ⓙ Ⓚ Ⓛ Ⓜ Ⓝ   12. Ⓙ Ⓚ Ⓛ Ⓜ Ⓝ   16. Ⓙ Ⓚ Ⓛ Ⓜ Ⓝ   20. Ⓙ Ⓚ Ⓛ Ⓜ Ⓝ

Paper Folding

1. Ⓐ Ⓑ Ⓒ Ⓓ Ⓔ   3. Ⓐ Ⓑ Ⓒ Ⓓ Ⓔ   5. Ⓐ Ⓑ Ⓒ Ⓓ Ⓔ   7. Ⓐ Ⓑ Ⓒ Ⓓ Ⓔ   9. Ⓐ Ⓑ Ⓒ Ⓓ Ⓔ
2. Ⓙ Ⓚ Ⓛ Ⓜ Ⓝ   4. Ⓙ Ⓚ Ⓛ Ⓜ Ⓝ   6. Ⓙ Ⓚ Ⓛ Ⓜ Ⓝ   8. Ⓙ Ⓚ Ⓛ Ⓜ Ⓝ   10. Ⓙ Ⓚ Ⓛ Ⓜ Ⓝ

READING

50 Questions—35 Minutes

Turn to the Reading section of your answer sheet to answer the questions in this section.

Directions: This is a test of how well you understand what you read.

- Read the passages below and answer the questions.

- Four answers are given for each question. You must choose the answer that you think is better than the others.

Questions 1–4 are based on the following passage.

PASSAGE 1

Mrs. Rachel Lynde lived just where the Avonlea main road dipped down into a little hollow, fringed with alders and ladies' eardrops and traversed by a brook that had its source away back in the woods of the old Cuthbert place; it was reputed to be an intricate, headlong brook in its earlier course through those
Line
woods, with dark secrets of pool and cascade; but by the time it reached Lynde's Hollow it was a quiet, well-
5 conducted little stream, for not even a brook could run past Mrs. Rachel Lynde's door without due regard for decency and decorum; it probably was conscious that Mrs. Rachel was sitting at her window, keeping a sharp eye on everything that passed, from brooks and children up, and that if she noticed anything odd or out of place she would never rest until she had ferreted out the whys and wherefores thereof.

There are plenty of people in Avonlea and out of it, who can attend closely to their neighbor's business
10 by dint of neglecting their own; but Mrs. Rachel Lynde was one of those capable creatures who can manage their own concerns and those of other folks into the bargain.

—from *Anne of Green Gables* by Lucy Maud Montgomery

1. From line 8 of the passage, the word *ferreted* most likely means

   A. avoided.

   B. stopped.

   C. completed.

   D. uncovered.

2. Where does the brook start?

   J. Avonlea

   K. The Cuthbert Place

   L. Lynde's Hollow

   M. The source is unknown.

3. Which of these words best describes Mrs. Rachel Lynde?

   A. Mean

   B. Curious

   C. Sneaky

   D. Helpful

4. From the passage, you can infer that

   J. Avonlea is a large city.

   K. people in Avonlea live in fear of Mrs. Lynde.

   L. Avonlea is a place where people have many secrets.

   M. Avonlea is located near the woods.

Questions 5–10 are based on the following passage.

PASSAGE 2

The Moon was but a Chin of Gold

The Moon was but a Chin of Gold
A Night or two ago—
And now she turns Her perfect Face
Upon the World below—

Line
5   Her Forehead is of Amplest Blonde—
Her Cheek—a Beryl hewn—
Her Eye unto the Summer Dew
The likest I have known—

Her Lips of Amber never part—
10 But what must be the smile
Upon Her Friend she could confer
Were such Her Silver Will—

And what a privilege to be
But the remotest Star—
15 For Certainly She take Her Way
Beside Your Palace Door—

Her Bonnet is the Firmament—
The Universe—Her Shoe—
The Stars—the Trinkets at Her Belt—
20 Her Dimities—of Blue—

—Emily Dickinson

5. The poet believes that the moon

A. is really a person.

B. is made of stone.

C. is beautiful.

D. only comes out in summer.

6. The first stanza describes

J. how the moon changes.

K. the change of the seasons.

L. the location of the moon in the sky.

M. the poet's own face.

7. The poet likely

A. dislikes the outdoors.

B. only goes out at night.

C. studies astronomy.

D. is interested in fashion.

8. In saying "The Universe—Her Shoe—/The Stars— the Trinkets at Her Belt," the poet means that the moon is

J. old-fashioned.

K. cold and unfeeling.

L. the most important part of the sky.

M. not as beautiful today as it once was.

9. Based on the passage, *firmament* most likely means

A. Earth.

B. top.

C. head.

D. sky.

10. The tone of this poem is

J. whimsical.

K. comic.

L. realistic.

M. sad.

Questions 11–16 are based on the following passage.

PASSAGE 3

Take a book, leave a book. That's the idea behind "little free libraries," which are small birdhouse-like structures that contain bookshelves. These miniscule libraries are meant to be free community resources, letting neighbors share books they don't need anymore, or pick up a new book to read.

Line
5   These small libraries don't require a library card or a special password for access. Usually, they are simple wooden cabinets (with a door to protect the books from the elements) that can be opened by anyone who comes along. Borrowing books is done on the honor system, in the hopes that the community will help maintain the library by adding to it and returning books when they're done. Many public areas like parks and beaches are starting to see these little libraries pop up.

11. Which of these sayings is best illustrated by this passage?

A. Birds of a feather flock together.

B. You have to give a little to get a little.

C. Opportunity knocks.

D. Necessity is the mother of invention.

12. As used in sentence 3, *miniscule* most likely means

J. free.

K. underground.

L. tiny.

M. secret.

13. Based on the passage, those likely to use the little free libraries are people who

A. read books online.

B. want to read a variety of books.

C. hate reading.

D. already have library cards.

14. The purpose of the library's door is to keep

J. rain out.

K. thieves out.

L. children out.

M. books from falling.

15. The passage is intended to be

A. humorous.

B. persuasive.

C. informative.

D. personal.

16. As used in the passage, the phrase "honor system" is another way of saying which of the following?

J. All users are responsible for their own use of the library.

K. People who don't return books will be caught.

L. There is a security camera built into the library.

M. Only nice people can use the library.

Questions 17–22 are based on the following passage.

PASSAGE 4

The seasonal comings and goings of birds have excited the attention and wonder of all sorts of people in all ages and places. The oracles of Greece and the augurs of Rome wove them into ancient mythology. They are spoken of in the Books of Job and Jeremiah.

Line
5   Nevertheless, it has been difficult for many to believe that small birds, especially, are capable of migratory journeys. Aristotle was convinced that the birds that wintered in Greece were not new arrivals but merely Greece's summer birds in winter dress. According to a belief persisting in some parts of the world to this day, swallows and swifts do not migrate but spend the winter in hibernation. (Swifts and swallows do migrate, just as most other Northern Hemisphere birds do.) Another old and charming, but untrue, legend enlists the aid of the stork in getting small birds to and from winter quarters: Small birds are said
10 to hitch rides on the European stork's back.

    It is clear why Northern Hemisphere birds fly south in the fall; they go to assure themselves of food and a more favorable climate for the winter months. It is also clear where most of the migrants come from and where they go. Years of bird-banding have disclosed the routes of the main migratory species.

    But there are other aspects of migration that remain, for all our powers of scientific investigation, as
15 puzzling and mysterious to modern man as to the ancients. Why do migrant birds come north each spring? Why don't they simply stay in the warm tropics the whole twelve months of the year? What determines the moment of departure for north or south? Above all, how do birds—especially species like the remarkable golden plover, which flies huge distances directly across trackless ocean wastes—find their way?

17. Which of the following is the best title for this selection?

    A. "The Solution of an Ancient Problem"

    B. "Mysterious Migrations"

    C. "The Secret of the Plover"

    D. "Aristotle's Theory"

18. Bird-banding has revealed

    J. the kinds of food birds eat.

    K. why the birds prefer the tropics in the summer.

    L. why birds leave at a certain time.

    M. the routes taken by different types of birds.

19. Swallows and swifts

    A. remain in Greece all year.

    B. change their plumage in winter.

    C. hibernate during the winter.

    D. fly south for the winter.

20. The article proves that

    J. nature still has secrets that man has not discovered.

    K. the solutions of Aristotle are accepted by modern science.

    L. we live in an age that has lost all interest in bird lore.

    M. man has no means of solving the problems of bird migration.

21. How was it once believed small birds were able to migrate long distances?

    A. African swallows brought hollow coconuts for small birds to ride in.

    B. Small birds rode in the mouths of European storks.

    C. Small birds were in a constant state of migration due to their short flight ranges.

    D. European storks allowed small birds to ride on their backs.

22. The main reason birds migrate is

   J. for vacation.

   K. to assure a good food supply and favorable climate.

   L. to satisfy their need to expand their habitat.

   M. so they can find potential mates.

Questions 23–28 are based on the following passage.

PASSAGE 5

If you are asked the color of the sky on a fair day in summer, your answer will most probably be "blue." This answer is only partially correct. Blue sky near the horizon is not the same kind of blue as it is straight overhead. Look at the sky some fine day and you will find that the blue sky near the horizon is slightly *Line* greenish. As your eye moves upward toward the zenith, you will find that the blue changes into pure blue 5 and finally shades into a violet-blue overhead.

   Have you heard the story of a farmer who objected to the color of the distant hills in the artist's picture? He said to the artist, "Why do you make those hills blue? They are green. I've been over there and I know!" The artist asked him to do a little experiment. "Bend over and look at the hills between your legs." As the farmer did this, the artist asked, "Now what color are the hills?" The farmer looked again, then he 10 stood up and looked. "By gosh, they turned blue!" he said. It is quite possible that you have looked at many colors that you did not really recognize. Sky is not just blue; it is many kinds of blue. Grass is not plain green; it may be one of several varieties of green. A red-brick wall frequently is not pure red. It may vary from yellow-orange to violet-red in color, but to the unseeing eye it is just red brick.

23. Which title best expresses the ideas of this passage?

   A. "The Summer Sky"

   B. "Artists vs. Farmers"

   C. "Recognizing Colors"

   D. "Blue Hills"

24. At the zenith, the sky is usually

   J. violet-blue.

   K. violet-red.

   L. greenish-blue.

   M. yellow-orange.

25. The author suggests that

   A. farmers are color-blind.

   B. perceived color varies.

   C. brick walls should be painted pure red.

   D. some artists use poor color combinations.

26. The word *zenith* in paragraph 1 probably refers to

   J. a color.

   K. a point directly overhead.

   L. a point on the horizon.

   M. the hills.

27. The artist's experiment with the farmer shows that

   A. farmers cannot tell the difference between colors.

   B. artists use hypnosis to change other people's perception.

   C. glancing at something and really seeing it can change how we perceive our environment.

   D. artists like to make fun of people.

28. What should people do to understand the different shades of color?

    J. Become artists

    K. Look at more works of art

    L. Stop trusting their own eyes

    M. Open themselves to new perspectives

Questions 29–34 are based on the following passage.

PASSAGE 6

In a stressed-out world, yoga has become one of the most popular wellness practices around. It involves using a combination of body stretches, deep breathing techniques, and meditation to help practitioners achieve a state of inner well-being. People who practice yoga often report feeling less stressed, having lower blood pressure, and feeling more in tune with their bodies.

    Yoga has its roots in ancient India, where it originated around the 5th century BCE as a type of philosophical meditation practice. The name comes from the Sanskrit word *yuj*, which means "to join" or "to unite." Historically, yoga has been used as a way to achieve an equilibrium between body and mind.

    It wasn't until the late 1900s that yoga began to take hold in the West, when Indian *gurus*, or *yogis*, began to introduce the practice as a form of meditation. One of the most notable figures in this introduction was Swami Vivekananda, who brought Hindu culture to Chicago in 1893. In the 1980s, the practice of yoga truly caught on as a form of physical exercise, instead of philosophical meditation, and became popular as a type of body-mind workout.

29. Based on the passage, the term yogi likely describes a(n)

    A. novice yoga practitioner.

    B. yoga expert.

    C. Indian ruler.

    D. Sanskrit speaker.

30. How did yoga become popular in the modern era?

    J. It was framed as exercise.

    K. It was a major philosophical trend in the West.

    L. Gurus were considered celebrities in the West.

    M. People became more interested in ancient Indian philosophy.

31. In paragraph 2, *equilibrium* most likely means

    A. yoga.

    B. breathing.

    C. balance.

    D. history.

32. All the following benefits of yoga are mentioned in the passage *except*

    J. stress relief.

    K. physical fitness.

    L. low blood pressure.

    M. increased intelligence.

33. As a practice, yoga originated in

    A. the United States.

    B. India.

    C. Europe.

    D. China.

34. Around when did yoga likely originate?

    J. 500 BCE

    K. 1893 CE

    L. 1900 CE

    M. 1980 CE

Questions 35–40 are based on the following passage.

PASSAGE 7

Benjamin Franklin, one of the most prominent "founding fathers" in American history, is often credited with proposing that the new United States adopt the turkey as its national symbol. Instead of the turkey, the founders selected the majestic bald eagle, and Ben Franklin's sponsorship of the humble turkey has
Line become a bit of humorous lore over the centuries.

5   The only problem with this story? It's not actually true. Although he is credited with championing the turkey while the national symbol was being selected, Franklin did not suggest at the time that it should take its place on the new country's national seal. Rather, he thought that the eagle design on the national seal *looked* like a turkey, and he discussed this and wrote a milder endorsement of the turkey in a later letter to his daughter:

10   "For the Truth the Turkey is in Comparison a much more respectable Bird, and withal a true original Native of America."

    Yet over the years, the myth has persisted, and the image of Ben Franklin standing among the signers of the Constitution, passionately debating the nobility of the Great American turkey, has captured the American imagination in a way that few stories do.

35. Based on the information in the passage, the author refers to the turkey as "humble" because

    A. there are fewer turkeys than bald eagles in the United States.

    B. turkeys' personalities are different from bald eagles.

    C. turkeys are seen as less noble than bald eagles.

    D. turkeys were less expensive than bald eagles.

36. As used in the first sentence of paragraph 1, what does the word *prominent* most likely mean?

    J. Foolish

    K. Oldest

    L. Underrated

    M. Famous

37. The story about Ben Franklin and the turkey has likely survived because

    A. people find it humorous.

    B. the United States later voted to adopt the turkey as its symbol.

    C. the bald eagle turned out to be an unpopular choice.

    D. people agree with Ben Franklin.

38. In the third sentence of paragraph 2, *championing* most likely means

    J. winning.

    K. representing.

    L. racing.

    M. bringing.

39. Why did people think Ben Franklin supported the turkey as the national symbol?

    A. He gave a passionate speech about it in Congress.

    B. His letter about turkeys was taken out of context.

    C. His daughter told everyone he supported the turkey over the eagle.

    D. His fellow founding fathers spread it as a rumor.

40. An appropriate title for this passage would be

    J. "How the Bald Eagle Became the National Bird."

    K. "Ben Franklin: A Biography."

    L. "Letters from Ben Franklin."

    M. "The Myth of the Great American Turkey."

Questions 41–46 are based on the following passage.

PASSAGE 8

You might not think of Hollywood stars as having much in common with inventors, but one American celebrity was both. Actress Hedy Lamarr, who appeared in more than 30 films between 1930 and 1950, was also a well-known "tinkerer" whose inventions have helped make modern innovations possible.

Line   Lamarr was born in Austria but moved to the United States in the late 1930s to pursue a movie career.
5   She appeared in famous films like *Samson and Delilah* and went on to star in films alongside some of the biggest movie actors of the time, like Clark Gable and Bob Hope. Throughout her burgeoning Hollywood career, she kept up her lifelong hobby of taking things apart and tinkering with them and devised new ways to approach engineering. The millionaire Howard Hughes became one of the earliest supporters of her inventing career when she developed ways to streamline his fleet of airplanes.

10   Her biggest invention came during World War II when Lamarr worked on a coded form of radio communication which was used to guide Allied torpedoes to their targets. After the war, her contribution was largely forgotten—until her patented work ended up forming the basis for Bluetooth®, GPS, Wi-Fi®, and other wireless forms of communication in the late 20th century and early 21st century. Although Lamarr, who passed away in 2000, is still best known for her glamorous on-screen career, she was truly a mother of
15   modern technology. Lamarr was posthumously elected into the National Inventors Hall of Fame in 2014.

41. Who helped Hedy Lamarr's inventing career?

   A. Clark Gable

   B. Bob Hope

   C. Howard Hughes

   D. No one because she was never able to get investors.

42. In the third sentence of paragraph 2, the word *burgeoning* most likely means

   J. growing.

   K. stalled.

   L. unsatisfying.

   M. miraculous.

43. How did Lamarr's World War II-era technology lead to modern inventions?

   A. She worked with engineers to develop new communication technology.

   B. Her airplane designs are used now by the airline industry.

   C. Her patents were used by modern inventors to develop communication technology.

   D. She quit Hollywood and devoted the rest of her life to being an inventor.

44. What was the original purpose of the coding that eventually helped create Bluetooth® and Wi-Fi®?

   J. Building a better airplane

   K. Guiding military torpedoes

   L. Improving film equipment

   M. Developing GPS

45. In the last sentence of the passage, the word *posthumously* most likely means

   A. collectively.

   B. before long.

   C. gratefully.

   D. after death.

46. Based on the passage, which of the following was true?

   J. All Hollywood celebrities have secret other careers.

   K. Hedy Lamarr had a more complex career than most people realize.

   L. Hedy Lamarr was a much better actress than inventor.

   M. Most modern inventions were first developed during World War II.

PASSAGE 9

The most famous baseball card doesn't have Babe Ruth on it, or Jackie Robinson, or any of the other players you might think of when you think about baseball greats. Instead, the most valuable baseball card in the world has the picture and name of someone you may never have heard of: Honus Wagner.

Line

5 Honus Wagner was a shortstop who played for the Pittsburgh Pirates for twenty-one seasons, from 1897 to 1917. But although his career was long, that's not why his baseball card has become so notorious. At the turn of the century, most baseball cards featured Major League Baseball players and were produced by tobacco companies as promotions for cigarettes. Honus Wagner objected to having his picture used to sell tobacco, and he refused to allow the American Tobacco Company to continue producing his card (known as the "T206 Honus Wagner"). By then, experts estimate, no more than 200 Honus Wagner cards

10 had been distributed.

Since then, the price tag for this rare card has grown exponentially: in 2016, one of the few remaining Wagner cards sold at auction for $3.12 million—making it the most expensive baseball card in the world.

47. Why are Honus Wagner cards so valuable?

A. Wagner became the baseball player with the longest career.

B. They are the most common baseball card.

C. Wagner went on to become the greatest baseball player in history.

D. Only a very small number were ever produced.

48. What was the original purpose of baseball cards?

J. To promote baseball players

K. To promote a holiday

L. To promote Major League Baseball

M. To promote tobacco products

49. Today, there are how many T206 Honus Wagner cards in existence?

A. More than 200

B. None

C. Fewer than 200

D. Exactly 200

50. In the first sentence of paragraph 3, the word *exponentially* most likely means that the card's value increased

J. quickly.

K. slowly.

L. not at all.

M. more than anyone had expected.

WRITTEN EXPRESSION
50 Questions—30 Minutes

Turn to the Written Expression section of your answer sheet to answer the questions in this section.

Directions: This is a test of how well you can find mistakes in writing. For questions 1–25, choose the answer with the same letter as the line containing the mistake in spelling, capitalization, or punctuation. When there is no mistake, choose the last answer choice.

1. A. involvment
   B. bologna
   C. organic
   D. matador
   E. (*No mistakes*)

2. J. redemption
   K. commitee
   L. claustrophobic
   M. malleable
   N. (*No mistakes*)

3. A. pseudonym
   B. placate
   C. anonymous
   D. suspishus
   E. (*No mistakes*)

4. J. retreave
   K. famished
   L. belligerent
   M. mnemonic
   N. (*No mistakes*)

5. A. compensate
   B. expression
   C. judgment
   D. fragile
   E. (*No mistakes*)

6. J. precious
   K. leverage
   L. credence
   M. beleivable
   N. (*No mistakes*)

7. A. flail
   B. appreshiate
   C. cognition
   D. statistics
   E. (*No mistakes*)

8. J. reccomendation
   K. cemetery
   L. finesse
   M. repetition
   N. (*No mistakes*)

9. A. ailment
   B. onerous
   C. pretense
   D. manadgement
   E. (*No mistakes*)

10. J. competetive
    K. symbol
    L. cringe
    M. careening
    N. (*No mistakes*)

11. **A.** Lake Huron,

   B. one the of the great lakes of north America,

   C. runs from Michigan in the United States to Ontario, a province in Canada.

   D. (*No mistakes*)

12. **J.** Every morning without fail, Jackie purchases a copy of her favorite newspaper,

   K. *The Beaverton Telegraph*, from Henri,

   L. the local Merchant at the corner drugstore by the train station.

   M. (*No mistakes*)

13. **A.** Shu watched her Dad's favorite movie,

   B. *The Last City in the World*,

   C. on her laptop as she lay on her living room couch.

   D. (*No mistakes*)

14. **J.** Duncan and his friend Jaden went to the local pet store,

   K. Oakville Furry Friends,

   L. and purchased a Rare spotted rabbit with the money he saved from his after-school job.

   M. (*No mistakes*)

15. **A.** Reina's Dentist, Dr. Larissa Guerrero,

   B. told Reina that she is going to need to have

   C. her wisdom teeth removed next week.

   D. (*No mistakes*)

16. **J.** Rosa has not yet received her ticket for the concert

   K. at the convention center next weekend,

   L. but she is really looked forward to going next Tuesday.

   M. (*No mistakes*)

17. **A.** This morning, Edsen hid his new headphones,

   B. which he will buy from the music store at the mall,

   C. from his younger sister Stephanie.

   D. (*No mistakes*)

18. **J.** After he watching the new episode

   K. of *Creature Hunters* on television,

   L. Rafi felt that the ending was too predictable.

   M. (*No mistakes*)

19. **A.** What are the most valuable life lessons

   B. that you have learned during

   C. your years in junior high school!

   D. (*No mistakes*)

20. **J.** Boris asked his best friend Keisha,

   K. (Can I borrow four quarters?),

   L. while they waited at the laundromat on Clarke Avenue.

   M. (*No mistakes*)

21. **A.** The Empire State Building,

   B. located in the heart of New York City,

   C. is one of the most famous skyscrapers in the world?

   D. (*No mistakes*)

22. **J.** After Diego's senior year of high school,

   K. he plans to attend Georgetown university,

   L. and major in computer science.

   M. (*No mistakes*)

23. **A.** Aysha's European vacation last summer

   B. included stops at the canals of Venice, the Eiffel Tower in Paris,

   C. and Buckingham Palace in London.

   D. (*No mistakes*)

24. **J.** Mikhaila was terrified, of roller, coasters
    K. and refused to even walk by one or look up
    L. whenever she was at a carnival or amusement park.
    M. (*No mistakes*)

25. **A.** Louis memorized the quickest way
    B. to get to their piano teachers house:
    C. take a right on Meadow Road and a left on Crasset Avenue.
    D. (*No mistakes*)

Directions: For questions 26–30, choose the best way of expressing the idea.

---

26. **J.** Drowned out by the fire trucks and their noise outside, no one can hear the value of hard work, dedication, and passion, the parts that discussed pursuing a goal, when Radhika's award acceptance speech reached the most important parts.

    K. The most important parts of Radhika's award acceptance speech, the parts that discussed the value of hard work, dedication, and passion when pursuing a goal, were drowned out by the noise from the fire trucks outside.

    L. The most important parts of the fire trucks outside was the noise delivered from the trucks that discussed Sheila's award acceptance speech, which contained parts about the value of pursuing a goal—including hard work, dedication, and passion.

    M. When pursuing a goal, like Radhika did during the noise from the fire trucks outside, she showed hard work, dedication, and passion, which drowned out her important parts for the award acceptance speech and her values discussed.

27. **A.** Party punch was Finn's nice enough bringing to the graduation celebration, and everyone loved his secret ingredient—pineapple juice, crowd-favorite limes, fruit punch, cherries.

    B. Everybody loves graduation party secret ingredients, and Finn was nice enough to bring some of his to the party punch that was a crowd favorite, which contained limes, fruit punch, and pineapple juice.

    C. Finn was nice enough to bring some of his crowd-favorite party punch, which was loved by everyone at the graduation celebration; it contained limes, fruit punch, cherries, and his secret ingredient—pineapple juice.

    D. Was Finn, a crowd favorite at graduation celebrations, nice enough to bring his limes, fruit punch, cherries, and his secret ingredient—pineapple juice—to the contained party punch?

28. **J.** Completing the required certification exams will help you earn a degree in teaching and finish college, so you can plan after high school to get interested in pursuing a career as a teacher.

K. Teachers are interested in pursuing a career, so plan finishing required certification exams and earn a degree after high school in college teaching, if you are as well.

L. College teachers who finished high school complete the required certification exams, earn a pursuit in teaching careers, and finish college degrees in teaching.

M. If you're interested in pursuing a career as a teacher, your plan after high school should be to finish college, earn a degree in teaching, and complete the required certification exams.

29. **A.** Karina, who was running for student body president of Lakeville High School, promised her fellow students that there would be free snacks available every day in the cafeteria if she were elected.

B. Who was Karina running for? Student body president, where free snacks would be available every day at Lakeville high school if elected, which she promised her fellow students every day in the cafeteria.

C. Every student body president in the cafeteria offered free available snacks every day, and Karina promised to run for her fellow students and for Lakeville High School.

D. The president of the cafeteria promised that free Lakeville High School snacks would be available every day for student body presidents and their fellow students, if Karina ran.

30. **J.** The winning gasoline-powered engine used old cooking oil and an ingenious new method for usable and environmentally friendly fuel, to win and develop the science competition.

K. The engine of the gasoline-powered science competition was the winner who developed and ingenious and environmentally friendly new method for converting usable old cooking oil.

L. The winner of the science competition developed an ingenious new method for converting old cooking oil into usable and environmentally friendly fuel for gasoline-powered engines.

M. The science competition winner was an ingenious new method for converting gasoline-powered engines into old and usable cooking oil that is environmentally friendly.

Directions: For questions 31–50, choose the best answer based on the following paragraphs. You may see additional errors beyond those in the underlined words and phrases of the paragraphs.

(1) Do you know what's commonly accepted as the very first printed book? (2) The Gutenberg Bible <u>will be considered</u> to be the first major printed book in the world. (3) It was created in Europe in the mid-15th century using movable metal type. (4) Today, it is among the most valuable books in existence. (5) Fewer than 50 copies of the Gutenberg Bible are known to exist in the entire world.

31. What is the best way to write the underlined portion of sentence 2?

   A. were considered

   B. is considered

   C. it's considered

   D. (*No change*)

32. Choose the best last sentence to add to this paragraph.

   J. The Gutenberg Bible sure is one rare book!

   K. What other books are as old as the Gutenberg Bible?

   L. Do you have books that are important to you?

   M. The Gutenberg Bible sure is a large book!

(1) Spelunking, also known as "caving," is an intense and exciting physical activity that's popular around the world. (2) Spelunking involves the exploration of caves and cave systems, which presents a variety of challenges, not the least of which is the absence of natural light and the risk of unknown conditions. (3) Safety is an obvious issue for spelunkers, as <u>falling rock's</u>, extreme temperature shifts, unexpected falls, and even extreme exhaustion are concerns, not to mention getting lost. (4) Typical gear used during spelunking includes a headlamp, hardhat, water bottle, boots, and rock climbing equipment. (5) However, if you're experienced and follow safety protocols, cave exploration can be a wonderful pastime that tests your mental and physical abilities.

33. Choose the best first sentence to add to this paragraph.

   A. Diamonds are often found in caves throughout the world.

   B. Is there any place darker than inside a cave at night?

   C. There was a large volcano eruption in 2015.

   D. Have you ever heard of spelunking?

34. What is the best way to write the underlined portion of sentence 3?

   J. falling rocks

   K. falling's rock's

   L. falling rocks'

   M. (*No change*)

(1) What do you know about the humble ladybug! (2) Well, you may be unaware of the wide variety of colors and patterns that ladybugs, or lady beetles, can be found sporting. (3) There are actually over 6,000 species of ladybug that have been found in nature, with the most common being either red, orange, or yellow in color. (4) The number and color of spots found on the wing covers of ladybugs can also vary wildly. (5) Ladybugs are widely considered to be useful creatures, as they typically eat a variety of crop-ravaging insects, such as Aphids.

35. What is the best way to write the underlined portion of sentence 1?

   A. ladybug.
   B. ladybug?
   C. ladybug;
   D. (*No change*)

36. What is the best way to write the underlined portion of sentence 5?

   J. aphid
   K. Aphid's
   L. aphids
   M. (*No change*)

(1) Is there an author whose very Name stirs up eerie chills and dark, moody Victorian settings like Edgar Allan Poe does? (2) Poe was a 19th century American author whose work is often categorized in the Gothic artistic genre. (3) Many of their works focus on death and the afterlife, and the sad darkness that often dwells deep in the human heart. (4) Among his most famous works is "The Raven," a poem in which a raven pays a nighttime visit to a lovelorn man who is slowly spiraling into madness as he laments the loss of his great love. (5) Did you know that Poe is widely considered to be the "father" of detective fiction, which would later give rise to such literary luminaries as Sir Arthur Conan Doyle and his most famous character, Sherlock Holmes?

37. What is the best way to write the underlined portion of sentence 1?

   A. whose very name
   B. who's very Name
   C. who is very name
   D. (*No change*)

38. What is the best way to write the underlined portion of sentence 3?

   J. their work
   K. his works
   L. its works
   M. (*No change*)

(1) Have you ever flown high in the sky without being on an airplane? (2) It may sound scary, but many hot air balloon <u>detractors</u> do just that whenever they feel an urge to soar high above the ground. (3) Hot air balloons are relatively simple in construction, and include a fabric "balloon," full of heated air, an on-board heat source (typically an open flame), and a basket. (4) Heating the volume of <u>air inside; the balloon</u> reduces the density of the air, as compared with the colder ambient air, thus making it more buoyant. (5) The record for the highest hot air balloon flight is currently a staggering 68,986 feet, and took place in India.

39. What is the best way to write the underlined portion of sentence 2?

 A. inventors

 B. collaborators

 C. enthusiasts

 D. (*No change*)

40. What is the best way to write the underlined portion of sentence 4?

 J. air inside the balloon

 K. air inside, the balloon

 L. air inside. The balloon

 M. (*No change*)

(1) Few man-made structures are as iconic and instantly recognizable as the Golden Gate Bridge, in San Francisco. (2) The colossal structure, which officially opened in 1937, connects Marin County to Northern San Francisco. (3) The Golden Gate Bridge is a <u>suspension bridge</u>, which means that the load-bearing portion of its construction is hung below vertically suspended suspension cables. (4) The Golden Gate Bridge is approximately 4,200 feet in length, and had been the longest suspension bridge span in the world until 1964. (5) Currently, the longest suspension bridge in the world is the Akashi Kaikyo Bridge in Japan.

41. Choose the best final sentence to add to this paragraph.

 A. San Francisco also has some of the most scenic parks in the country.

 B. The Akashi Kaikyo Bridge is 6,532 feet long.

 C. San Francisco is one of the most expensive cities to live in America.

 D. New York City is also home to several famous bridges.

42. What is the best way to write the underlined portion of sentence 3?

 J. Suspension Bridge

 K. Suspension bridge

 L. suspension Bridge

 M. (*No change*)

(1) It's hard to argue with the notion that giant sequoias are among the most ancient and majestic living organisms on Earth. (2) These gigantic trees have been known to live for thousands of years; the oldest known example of a giant sequoia is over 3,500 years old. (3) They are also widely considered to be not only the largest trees but also the largest living organisms (by volume) in the <u>entire World</u>. (4) Giant sequoias have been known to reach heights of over 300 feet in height and over 25 feet in diameter. (5) Although <u>it is only</u> found in small patches in California, giant sequoias have made a lasting impression on the entire world.

43. What is the best way to write the underlined portion of sentence 3?

    A. Entire World

    B. Entire world

    C. entire world

    D. (*No change*)

44. What is the best way to write the underlined portion of sentence 5?

    J. he was

    K. they are

    L. we were

    M. (*No change*)

(1) Did you know that the first state in America to ratify the Constitution of the <u>United-States</u> is also one of the smallest? (2) Delaware, which has earned the nickname "The First State," is ranked 49th out of 50 states in terms of overall land area. (3) Only Rhode Island, also among the first Thirteen Colonies that would eventually form the United States of America, is smaller. (4) Interestingly, while a colony Rhode Island was the first to officially renounce <u>it's</u> allegiance to the British Crown. (5) This goes to show that you don't have to be a particularly large state to be an influential one!

45. What is the best way to write the underlined portion of sentence 1?

    A. United States

    B. united-states

    C. United, States

    D. (*No change*)

46. What is the best way to write the underlined portion of sentence 4?

    J. It's

    K. it is

    L. its

    M. (*No change*)

(1) The United States is chock full of <u>unique roadside attractions curious tourist sites and curious exhibits</u>. (2) The state of North Carolina is no exception, and if you find yourself travelling through the western part of the state with some time to spare, you may want to check out the American Museum of the House Cat. (3) This quirky little museum is entirely dedicated to the furry feline pet, and <u>youll find</u> over 10,000 cat-related objects to discover and enjoy during your visit here. (4) There is a wide array of objects on display, from statues and figurines to paintings, dolls, glassware, toys, and much more. (5) The objects range in age and obscurity—some are modern and easy-to-find objects, and some are quite rare and old, dating back to 600 BC!

47. What is the best way to write the underlined portion of sentence 1?

    A. unique roadside attractions—curious tourist sites—and curious exhibits

    B. unique roadside attractions, curious tourist sites, and curious exhibits

    C. unique roadside attractions. Curious tourist sites. And curious exhibits

    D. (*No change*)

48. What is the best way to write the underlined portion of sentence 3?

    J. you'll find

    K. you well find

    L. youll' find

    M. (*No change*)

(1) Few events in American history have so radically altered the concept and scope of the United States as the Louisiana Purchase did. (2) This agreement with France in 1803 <u>allow</u> the United States to officially acquire land that spans fifteen current states, including parts of Oklahoma, Iowa, Kansas, Arkansas, and Missouri, to name but a few. (3) In return for the land acquired under the Louisiana Purchase, France received fifty million francs and had a sizable portion of its debt to the United States cancelled. (4) Negotiation of the Louisiana Purchase Treaty between France and the United States was difficult <u>at times. With criticism</u> arising on both sides during the process. (5) However, it's hard to imagine what life in present-day United States would be like without the land that was acquired during this seminal negotiation.

49. What is the best way to write the underlined portion of sentence 2?

    A. allowing

    B. allowance

    C. allowed

    D. (*No change*)

50. What is the best way to write the underlined portion of sentence 4?

    J. times; with criticism

    K. times with; criticism

    L. times, with criticism

    M. (*No change*)

MATHEMATICS

50 Questions—40 Minutes

Turn to the Mathematics section of your answer sheet to answer the questions in this section. Do not use a calculator.

> **Directions:** Four answers are given for each problem. Choose the best answer.

1. Which of the following is *not* a factor of 20?

   A. 3

   B. 4

   C. 5

   D. 10

2. The fraction $\frac{2}{3}$ is approximately which of the following?

   J. 0.23

   K. 0.67

   L. $\frac{3}{2}$

   M. 23.67

3. Which of the following is *not* a prime number?

   A. 3

   B. 9

   C. 13

   D. 19

4. Which of the following is a multiple of 3?

   J. 29

   K. 39

   L. 49

   M. 89

5. What is the product of 43 and 100?

   A. 0.43

   B. 57

   C. 143

   D. 4,300

6. What is the difference between $\frac{7}{8}$ and $\frac{1}{2}$?

   J. $\frac{3}{8}$

   K. $\frac{6}{8}$

   L. $\frac{3}{4}$

   M. $\frac{6}{2}$

7. What is the sum of
   $(6 - 1) + (1 \times 5) + (10 \div 2) + (2.5 + 2.5)$?

   A. 15

   B. 20

   C. 25

   D. 125

8. Which of the following is *not* a multiple of 6?

   J. 72

   K. 112

   L. 186

   M. 246

9. Which of the following is the equivalent of
   $3 - (-6)$?

   A. −9

   B. −3

   C. 3

   D. 9

10. What is the least common multiple of
    6, 12, and 72?

    J. 6

    K. 12

    L. 36

    M. 72

11. Jeff has 6 notebooks in his locker. Maggie has
    in her locker twice as many notebooks as Jeff.
    Darnell has in his locker twice as many notebooks
    as Maggie and Jeff combined. How many note-
    books does Darnell have stuffed into his locker?

    A. 12

    B. 18

    C. 24

    D. 36

12. Baxter needed to replenish his supply of bottled
    water. The water dispenser in his kitchen holds 14
    gallons of water. Baxter buys his water one half-
    gallon at a time at his local grocery store. How
    many half-gallon water purchases will Baxter need
    to make to fill his water dispenser?

    J. 7

    K. 14

    L. 21

    M. 28

13. Dae currently has $50 set aside to purchase a TV
    that costs $300. She earns $25 per week babysit-
    ting. How many weeks will it take her to earn
    enough money to buy the TV?

    A. 7

    B. 8

    C. 10

    D. 12

14. Izzy's scooter gets 50 miles per gallon, and the
    scooter's gas tank holds 3 gallons of gasoline.
    If the gas tank in Izzy's scooter is $\frac{2}{3}$ full, how
    many miles can Izzy expect to travel before the
    tank is empty?

    J. 75

    K. 100

    L. 150

    M. 175

15. The rim on a basketball goal is 10 feet from the
    floor. If Maxim made 6 baskets, what is the sum
    of the distances that the ball would travel between
    the rim and the floor below?

    A. 60 feet

    B. 70 feet

    C. 160 feet

    D. Not given

16. Two hundred million, one hundred seventy-three
    thousand, sixty-three =

    J. 2,173,063

    K. 20,173,063

    L. 200,173,063

    M. 200,173,630

17. Seventeen million, sixty thousand, thirty-four =

    A. 17,634

    B. 1,760,034

    C. 17,060,034

    D. 17,600,034

18. 0.5% is equal to

    J. 0.005

    K. 0.05

    L. 0.5

    M. $\frac{1}{2}$

19. A group of 6 people raised $690 for charity. Lupita raised 35% of the total. What was the amount raised by the other 5 people in her group combined?

    A. $241.50

    B. $445.50

    C. $448.50

    D. $449.50

20. If a pie is divided into 20 parts, what percent is one part of the whole pie?

    J. 0.5%

    K. 2.0%

    L. 5%

    M. 20%

21. Two angles of a triangle are 45° and 75°. What is the measure of the third angle?

    A. 35°

    B. 45°

    C. 60°

    D. 180°

22.

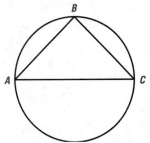

Isosceles $\triangle ABC$ is inscribed in a circle that has a diameter of 10 centimeters. The area of the triangle is

    J. 12.5 sq. cm.

    K. 25 sq. cm.

    L. 50 sq. cm.

    M. 78.5 sq. cm.

23. The volume of a small warehouse measuring 75 feet long, 50 feet wide, and 30 feet high is

    A. 112,500 feet.

    B. 112,500 square feet.

    C. 112,500 cubic feet.

    D. 1,112,500 cubic feet.

24. A department store marks up its clothing 80% over cost. If it sells blue jeans for $14, how much did the store pay for them?

    J. $1.12

    K. $7.78

    L. $11.20

    M. $17.50

25. The monthly finance charge on Aldo's charge account is $1\frac{1}{2}\%$ on the unpaid amount up to $500 and 1% on the unpaid amount over $500. What would Aldo's finance charge be on an unpaid amount of $750?

    A. $1.00

    B. $10.00

    C. $22.50

    D. $100.00

26. What is the sum of $(8 \times 10^2) + (6 \times 10) + 2$ and $(5 \times 10^3) + (2 \times 10^2) + (8 \times 10) + 9$?

    J. 6,041

    K. 6,151

    L. 50,041

    M. 51,151

27. The set of common factors for 30 and 24 is

    A. {1,2,3,6}.

    B. {1,2,3,4,6}.

    C. {1,2,4,6}.

    D. {1,2,4,6,12}.

28. If the scale on a blueprint is $\frac{1}{4}$ inch = 1 foot, give the blueprint dimensions of a room that is actually 29 feet long and 23 feet wide.

    J. $7\frac{1}{2}" \times 5\frac{1}{4}"$

    K. $6\frac{3}{4}" \times 6"$

    L. $7\frac{1}{4}" \times 5\frac{1}{2}"$

    M. $7\frac{1}{4}" \times 5\frac{3}{4}"$

29. A scalene triangle has

    A. no equal sides.

    B. two equal sides.

    C. two equal sides and one right angle.

    D. three equal sides.

30. On a recent trip, the Alonso family drove at an average speed of 55 miles per hour. If the trip took $5\frac{1}{2}$ hours, how many miles did they drive?

    J. 302.5

    K. 312.5

    L. 320.5

    M. 320.75

31. Audrey and Maira volunteer each month to drive meals to elderly people. The first month they volunteered, they delivered a total of 60 meals. The next month they delivered $33\frac{1}{3}$ percent more than they did the first month. The third month they delivered twice as many meals as the first two months combined. How many meals did the two girls deliver in the third month?

    A. 80

    B. 90

    C. 160

    D. 280

32. If Rohaan earns $7.50 per hour, how many 40-hour weeks will he need to work to earn enough to buy a new computer system that costs $1,350?

    J. 3

    K. 4

    L. $4\frac{1}{2}$

    M. $12\frac{1}{2}$

33. Denver wants to wallpaper their bedroom. Each roll of wallpaper covers 75 square feet of wall space. Their room has four walls that are 10 feet high and 15 feet wide. How many rolls of wallpaper will Denver need to cover all four of their walls?

    A. 2

    B. 8

    C. 16

    D. 20

34. An amateur bowler practices daily and bowls four games per day. Today, his scores were 189, 243, 202, and 198. What was his average score?

J. 200

K. 208

L. 212

M. 220

35. Gee-Whiz electronics company exports 400,000 electronic devices each year. Gee-Whiz wants to merge with Go Electro, a new electronics company that exports 1,900 electronic devices each month. After the merger, how many electronic devices will the new company export per year?

A. 35,233

B. 401,900

C. 422,800

D. 6,333,333

36. If 8 lb., 12 oz. of fruit were to be divided among eight people, how much would each receive?

J. 10.5 oz.

K. 13.5 oz.

L. 1 lb., 1.5 oz.

M. 2.0 lb.

37. Two sisters, Cecilia and Marisol, both run the same marathon. Cecilia finishes with a time of 2 hours 12 minutes 38 seconds and Marisol finishes with a time of 3 hours 2 minutes 24 seconds. What is the time difference between their finishes?

A. 48 min. 56 sec.

B. 49 min. 46 sec.

C. 1 hr. 26 min. 12 sec.

D. 1 hr. 51 min. 22 sec.

38. The drawing of a wheel in a book is done at $\frac{1}{16}$ scale. If the drawing is 1.8 inches in diameter, what is the wheel's diameter?

J. 0.1125 inch

K. 24 inches

L. 28.8 inches

M. 32 inches

39. If Elias runs M miles in T hours, his speed is

A. M/T.

B. $M + T$.

C. $M - T$.

D. MT.

40. If there are x rooms in a house and each have y square feet, how many total square yards are in the house?

J. $\dfrac{xy}{144}$

K. $\dfrac{xy}{9}$

L. $9xy$

M. $144xy$

Directions: Use the charts provided to answer each question.

Yards

41. The city recently held a football skills competition at Barton Park. Based on the information in the chart above, which competitor passed the football the shortest distance?

A. Claire

B. Bradley

C. Megan

D. Tommy

42. Based on the information in the chart above, which competitor passed 4 more yards than he/she kicked the football?

J. Claire

K. Bradley

L. Megan

M. Tommy

Use the following chart for Questions 43 and 44:

Recyclable Materials

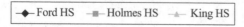

43. The City School District sponsored a week-long recycling campaign in which the three city high schools collected items to be recycled. The chart indicates the results of the campaign as measured in hundreds of pounds. Based on the information in the chart above, which of the high schools collected the most cans and paper products combined?

A. Ford HS

B. Holmes HS

C. King HS

D. Holmes HS and King HS

44. Based on the information in the preceding chart, what was the total weight of all plastics collected in the campaign?

J. 800 pounds

K. 1,600 pounds

L. 2,400 pounds

M. 6,900 pounds

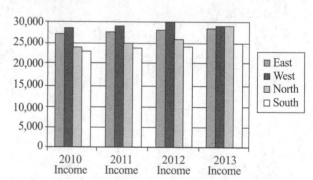

45. The bar graph illustrates per capita income by region in thousands of dollars. According to the data, which region experienced the most income growth from 2010 to 2013?

A. East

B. West

C. North

D. South

Directions: For the following questions, estimate the answer in your head. No scratch work is allowed. Do not try to compute exact answers.

46. The closest estimate of 6,544 – 3,466 is _____.

    J. 1,000

    K. 2,000

    L. 3,000

    M. 4,000

47. The closest estimate of 82,122 ÷ 4,055 is

    _____.

    A. 20

    B. 200

    C. 2,000

    D. 20,000

48. The average class size at Kennedy High School is 31 students. There are 30 classes in session at any one time. About how many Kennedy High students are in class at any given time?

    J. 800

    K. 900

    L. 1,000

    M. Not given

49. The closest estimate of 3,988 + 2,177 is _____.

    A. 5,000

    B. 5,500

    C. 6,000

    D. 6,500

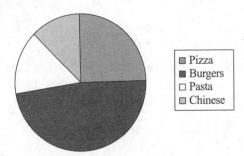

**Favorite Foods of New York
High School Seniors**

50. According to the chart above, about what percent of New York high school seniors prefer burgers?

    J. 15%

    K. 25%

    L. 33%

    M. 50%

ABILITY

50 Questions—32 Minutes

Figure Classification

Turn to the Ability section of your answer sheet to answer the questions in this section.

Directions: In questions 1–20, the first three figures are alike in certain ways. Choose the answer choice that corresponds to the first three figures.

1.

A.   B.   C.   D.   E.

2.

J.   K.   L.   M.   N.

3.

A.   B.   C.   D.   E.

4.

J.   K.   L.   M.   N.

5.

A.   B.   C.   D.   E.

6.

J.   K.   L.   M.   N.

7.

J.   K. L. M. N.

8.

TACHS PRACTICE TEST 1

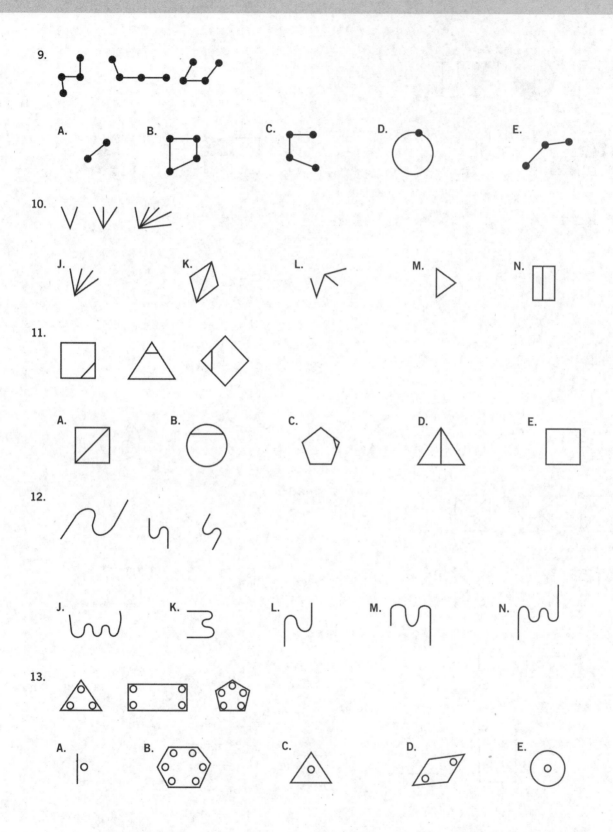

9.

A.   B.   C.   D.   E.

10.

J.   K.   L.   M.   N.

11.

A.   B.   C.   D.   E.

12.

J.   K.   L.   M.   N.

13.

A.   B.   C.   D.   E.

14.

J.   K.   L.   M.   N.

15.

A.   B.   C.   D.   E.

16.

J.   K.   L.   M.   N.

17.

A.   B.   C.   D.   E.

18.

J.   K.   L.   M.   N.

19.

20.

Figure Matrices

Directions: In questions 1–20, find the figure that completes the matrix.

1.

2.

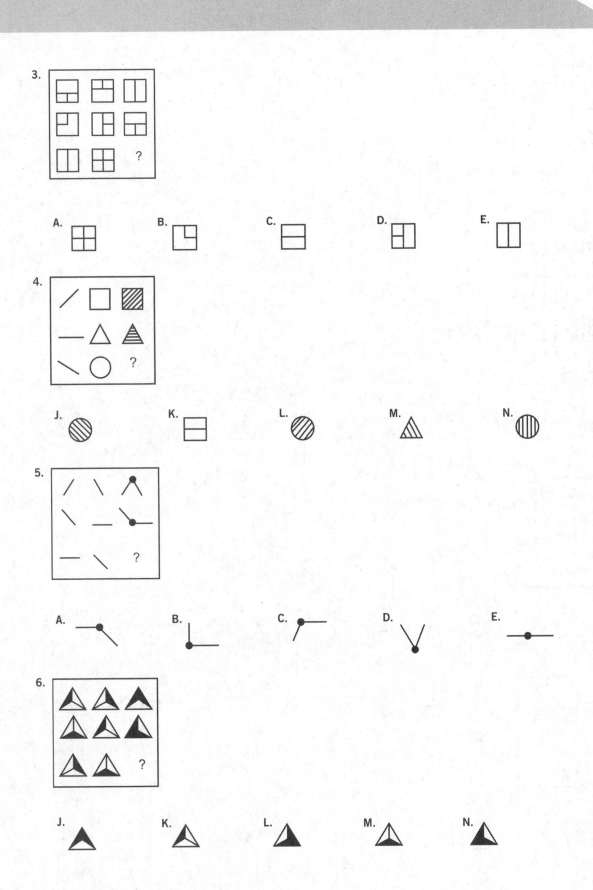

3.

A. B. C. D. E.

4.

J. K. L. M. N.

5.

A. B. C. D. E.

6.

J. K. L. M. N.

7.

A. B. C. D. E.

8.

J. K. L. M. N.

9.

A. B. C. D. E.

10.

J. K. L. M. N.

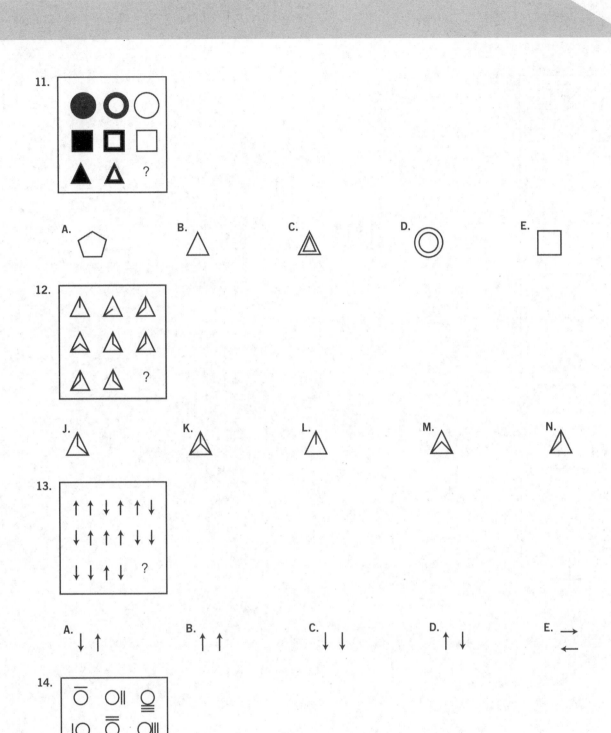

11.

A. B. C. D. E.

12.

J. K. L. M. N.

13.

A. B. C. D. E.

14.

J. K. L. M. N.

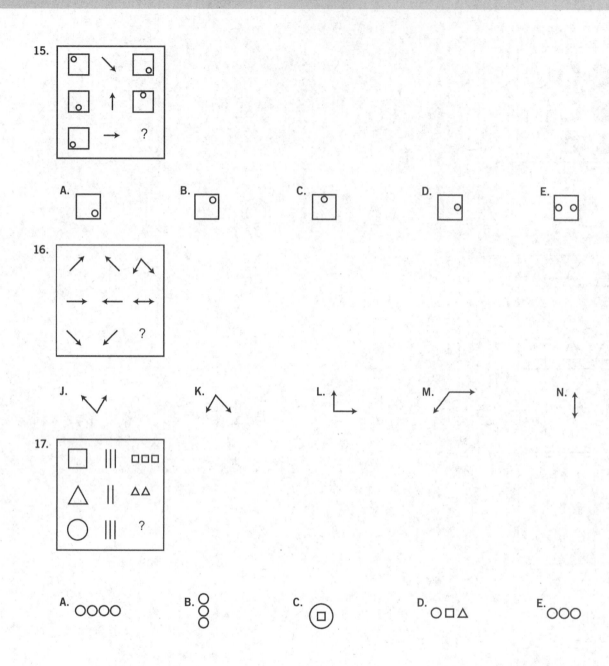

15.

A.

B.

C.

D.

E.

16.

J.

K.

L.

M.

N.

17.

A.

B.

C.

D.

E.

18.

J.   K.   L.   M.   N.

19.

A.   B.   C.   D.   E.

20.

J.   K.   L.   M.   N.

Paper Folding

Directions: In questions 1–10, look at the top row to see how a square piece of paper is folded and where holes are punched into it. Then look at the bottom row to decide which answer choice shows how the paper will look when it is completely unfolded.

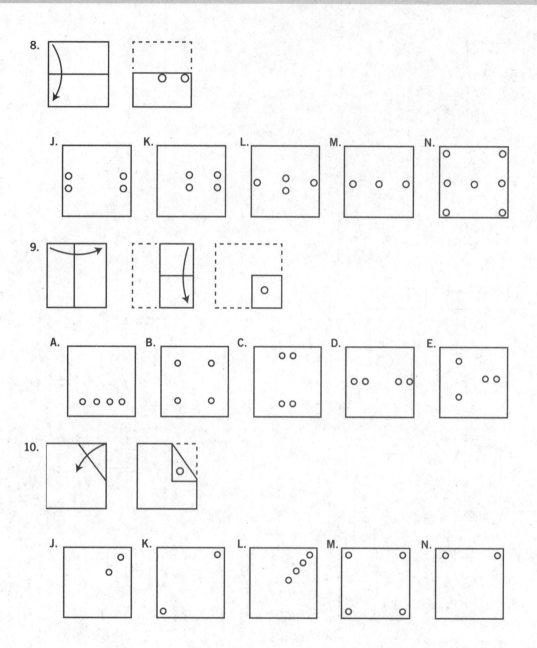

8.

J. K. L. M. N.

9.

A. B. C. D. E.

10.

J. K. L. M. N.

ANSWER KEYS AND EXPLANATIONS
Reading

1. D	11. B	21. D	31. C	41. C
2. K	12. L	22. K	32. M	42. J
3. B	13. B	23. C	33. B	43. C
4. M	14. J	24. J	34. J	44. K
5. C	15. C	25. B	35. C	45. D
6. J	16. J	26. K	36. M	46. K
7. C	17. B	27. C	37. A	47. D
8. L	18. M	28. M	38. K	48. M
9. D	19. D	29. B	39. B	49. C
10. J	20. J	30. J	40. M	50. J

1. **The correct answer is D.** The passage tells you that Mrs. Lynde is interested in knowing all that happens near her house, and the phrase "whys and wherefores" can clue you in that *ferreted* means "uncovered." Choice A doesn't fit because Mrs. Lynde is characterized as someone who wants to be in the know. Choice B is incorrect because there is no information that suggests she's against what is happening, just that she wants to know what is happening. Choice C is incorrect as there is no indication that Mrs. Lynde seeks to "complete" anything, even though she is observant and interested in obtaining information.

2. **The correct answer is K.** The passage tells you that the brook "had its source away back in the woods of the old Cuthbert place." Although the passage mentions that the town is Avonlea (choice J), there is not enough information to tell you that the brook starts in the town. The passage also suggests the brook runs past Lynde's Hollow (choice L), but it does not start there.

3. **The correct answer is B.** The author paints Mrs. Lynde as someone who wants to know exactly what is going on in her neighborhood, saying that nothing gets past her without investigation. The clearest support for choice B is this sentence: "Mrs. Rachel Lynde was one of those capable creatures

who can manage their own concerns and those of other folks into the bargain." The passage does not suggest Mrs. Lynde is spiteful about her neighbors (choice A), nor does it say that Mrs. Lynde intends to help her neighbors (choice D); there is merely the statement that she can "manage" the concerns of others. Finally, there is not enough information to suggest that she is sneaky (choice C) about seeking information; rather, the passage says that Mrs. Lynde is open about her interest in neighborhood happenings.

4. **The correct answer is M.** The only information that the reader is given about Avonlea is that people live there and that the main road is located near the woods, so choice M is the choice best supported by the passage.

5. **The correct answer is C.** The poet is using figurative language to describe the moon, so she does not likely believe that the moon is made of stone (choice B) or is actually a person (choice A). Although the poet describes the moon in terms of "Summer Dew," there is not enough to suggest that the poet really believes that the moon is only present during the summer (choice D).

6. **The correct answer is J.** By mentioning that the moon is different now than it was two days ago and that it now appears bigger ("now she turns Her

perfect Face / Upon the World below"), the poet is describing the moon's phases over time. Although summer is mentioned later in the poem, it is in relation to the moon, not any other seasons (choice K). Choice L is incorrect because there is no information to suggest where the moon is located in the sky. Choice M is incorrect because the poet is using figurative language about the moon, not a literal description of her own face.

7. **The correct answer is C.** Because the poet gives such a detailed description of the moon, you can infer that she has spent a lot of time observing the night sky, making choice A unlikely. Observing the moon does require nighttime observation, but there is nothing to suggest that the poet goes out only at night (choice B). Further, there is no indication that the author is interested in fashion (choice D).

8. **The correct answer is L.** By suggesting that the rest of the sky simply accessorizes the moon, the poet is declaring the moon the most important part of the sky. Early in the last stanza, the word *bonnet* appears and may suggest something old-fashioned (choice J), but such an inference depends on information beyond the quoted lines. Stanzas 2 and 3 do suggest that the moon is cold (choice K), but this is not related to the quoted lines in question. At no point does the poet indicate that she thinks the moon's beauty is fading (choice M).

9. **The correct answer is D.** In this stanza, the poet is describing things that can be found in the sky ("Universe," "Stars"). That should clue you in that *firmament* is also something that can be found in the sky.

10. **The correct answer is J.** The poet creates a fanciful image of the moon as a beautiful woman. She is not making fun of the moon or using jokes (choice K), nor is she describing the moon literally (choice L) or with sadness (choice M).

11. **The correct answer is B.** The first sentence of the passage essentially summarizes the concept described in choice B.

12. **The correct answer is L.** The previous sentence calls the libraries "small" and "little," so it is likely that *miniscule* is a synonym for these words.

13. **The correct answer is B.** The passage describes how people can get rid of their own books and read the ones that others donate. People who read online (choice A), who hate reading (choice C), or who prefer going to the public library (choice D) are less likely to need or want this type of library.

14. **The correct answer is J.** Paragraph 2 says that the door protects the books from "the elements," which includes weather events like rain.

15. **The correct answer is C.** The author presents information about the libraries and their purpose using a neutral tone, so there's no humor (choice A) or personal narrative (choice D) in the passage. The author also does not take a specific stance on little free libraries, so it is not meant to be persuasive (choice B).

16. **The correct answer is J.** "Honor system" means that there is nothing in place to make sure that people don't steal the books, so choice J is the best answer. The idea is that people will leave books as well as take them and return the books they borrow, but if they do not, there are no security systems, like a camera, (choice L) to make sure that everyone is using the library correctly. Although one may assume that an honor system only works if people are "nice," this is not a condition that can be enforced, so choice M is incorrect.

17. **The correct answer is B.** The topic of the passage is bird migration and the mystery it has posed throughout the ages, so choice B is the best reflection of this primary theme.

18. **The correct answer is M.** The last sentence of paragraph 3 clearly states that "years of bird-banding have disclosed the routes of the main migratory species."

19. **The correct answer is D.** The migratory patterns of swallows and swifts is stated within the parentheses in the second paragraph: They fly south for the winter.

20. **The correct answer is J.** The final paragraph emphasizes that nature still holds some secrets as humans still have many questions about different aspects of migration.

21. **The correct answer is D.** Despite evidence, some people still believe that small birds travel by piggybacking on European storks!

22. **The correct answer is K.** Birds migrate during the winter to find reliable food sources in a warmer climate. Choice M may seem correct because many birds do mate during migration; however, mating is not the primary purpose of bird migration.

23. **The correct answer is C.** The topic of the passage is how people recognize, or perceive, colors. Only choice C addresses this main topic.

24. **The correct answer is J.** Sentence 5 states that toward the zenith the sky is "pure blue" and "shades into a violet-blue."

25. **The correct answer is B.** You should be able to discern that color perception varies from the passage, but if not, you can eliminate the other answers as illogical.

26. **The correct answer is K.** The phrase "moves up toward the zenith" should lead you to the correct answer.

27. **The correct answer is C.** Answers A, B, and D are all illogical, so you can use a process of elimination here.

28. **The correct answer is M.** The experiment with the farmer demonstrates how shifting to a new perspective can help you change how you see things.

29. **The correct answer is B.** The passage tells you that yoga originated in India and that it was brought to the West. A novice (choice A) would not likely be spreading yoga, and though *yogis* are described as Indian, there is nothing to suggest that they are rulers (choice C). Although the original word *yoga* does come from Sanskrit, there is not enough information to suggest that *yogis* were Sanskrit speakers (choice D) specifically.

30. **The correct answer is J.** In paragraph 3, the passage states that in the 1980s, yoga became popular as a type of exercise.

31. **The correct answer is C.** *Equilibrium* is a synonym for *balance*.

32. **The correct answer is M.** Choices J, K, and L are all listed as physical benefits of yoga, but increased intelligence (choice M) is not one of the health benefits included in the passage.

33. **The correct answer is B.** In paragraph 2, it states that yoga originated in India.

34. **The correct answer is J.** According to the passage, yoga first emerged in India in the 5th century BCE. Choices K, L, and M are all dates mentioned in the passage, but they refer to events occurring after yoga had already spread beyond India.

35. **The correct answer is C.** The word *humble* is used here to show a difference between the eagle (which was ultimately chosen) and the underdog recommendation, the turkey. There is not enough information in the passage to draw conclusions about the turkey and eagle populations (choice A), turkey and eagle personalities (choice B), or the price of each kind of bird (choice D).

36. **The correct answer is M.** *Prominent* means "noticeable" or "famous."

37. **The correct answer is A.** The author presents the turkey as a humorous symbol, playing up the differences between it and the bald eagle to suggest that the humor in the story is what has helped it survive this long.

38. **The correct answer is K.** *Championing* means to represent or sponsor something. Choice J may seem correct because the term champion is associated with winning; however, that passage makes it clear that Franklin was not successful in supporting the turkey.

39. **The correct answer is B.** Though the popular story suggests he always wanted the turkey to be a national symbol, Benjamin Franklin compared the turkey to the bald eagle much later in life; there is no evidence that he supported the turkey at the time of the debate (choice A). The letter discussing

the turkey was sent to Franklin's daughter, but the passage does not say that she had anything to do with the story being repeated (choice C). There is also no evidence that Franklin's peers started the rumor (choice D).

40. **The correct answer is M.** Of the options, choice M best represents the entire passage, not just portions of it.

41. **The correct answer is C.** Clark Gable (choice A) and Bob Hope (choice B) were fellow actors, but they did not affect Lamarr's inventing career. The passage states that Howard Hughes *did* support her inventing career, making choice D incorrect.

42. **The correct answer is J.** The word *burgeoning* means "expanding" or "growing."

43. **The correct answer is C.** Paragraph 3 states that Lamarr's patents and her work eventually helped scientists develop new technologies. There is no indication that Lamarr personally worked on these newer inventions (choice A). Although the passage mentions Lamarr working on airplanes (choice B), there is no information in the passage that suggests her airplane designs are still in use. The passage also says that her inventing career was

"largely forgotten" in favor of her acting career, so choice D is incorrect.

44. **The correct answer is K.** As stated in paragraph 2, Lamarr's invention was originally used for military purposes during World War II.

45. **The correct answer is D.** *Posthumously* means "after death." If you didn't know this, you could still use the dates given in the passage as context clues to figure it out: Lamarr died in 2000 but was elected into the National Inventors Hall of Fame in 2014, 14 years later.

46. **The correct answer is K.** Only choice K is supported by the passage.

47. **The correct answer is D.** There were fewer cards available, which makes the ones that were produced more valuable. This is the only answer supported by the passage.

48. **The correct answer is M.** The second paragraph states that the baseball cards were produced by tobacco companies as a promotion for cigarettes.

49. **The correct answer is C.** The passage says that "no more than 200" cards had been produced and distributed, and that there are "few remaining" now.

50. **The correct answer is J.** *Exponentially* means "expanding at a steady and rapid rate."

NOTES

Written Expression

1. A	11. B	21. C	31. B	41. B
2. K	12. L	22. K	32. J	42. M
3. D	13. A	23. D	33. D	43. C
4. J	14. L	24. J	34. J	44. K
5. E	15. A	25. B	35. B	45. A
6. M	16. L	26. K	36. L	46. L
7. B	17. B	27. C	37. A	47. B
8. J	18. J	28. M	38. K	48. J
9. D	19. C	29. A	39. C	49. C
10. J	20. K	30. L	40. J	50. L

1. **The correct answer is A.** The correct spelling is *involvement*.

2. **The correct answer is K.** The correct spelling is *committee*.

3. **The correct answer is D.** The correct spelling is *suspicious*.

4. **The correct answer is J.** The correct spelling is *retrieve*.

5. **The correct answer is E.** *No mistakes.*

6. **The correct answer is M.** The correct spelling is *believable*.

7. **The correct answer is B.** The correct spelling is *appreciate*.

8. **The correct answer is J.** The correct spelling is *recommendation*.

9. **The correct answer is D.** The correct spelling is *management*.

10. **The correct answer is J.** The correct spelling is *competitive*.

11. **The correct answer is B.** In this sentence, *North America* is a proper noun and should be capitalized.

12. **The correct answer is L.** As written, *merchant* is a common noun that should be set in lowercase.

13. **The correct answer is A.** Although the name of Shu's father is a proper noun that should be capitalized, the word *dad* is a common noun that should be lowercased.

14. **The correct answer is L.** The word *rare* is a common noun. There is no need to capitalize it.

15. **The correct answer is A.** Although the name of Reina's dentist (Dr. Larissa Guerrero) is a proper noun that must be capitalized, the word *dentist* is a common noun that should be written in lowercase.

16. **The correct answer is L.** As written, the action of Rosa "looking forward" to the concert is still occurring, so it should not be written in the past tense.

17. **The correct answer is B.** Edsen already has the new headphones since he hid them this morning. Consequently, the act of purchasing them from the music store should be written in the past tense: *had bought* should replace *will buy*.

18. **The correct answer is J.** If Rafi was able to comment on the ending of the new episode of *Creature Hunters*, then he has already watched the episode. Thus, "he watching" must become the past tense "he watched."

19. **The correct answer is C.** The sentence is a question, as indicated by it beginning with the word *what*. It should be punctuated with a question mark (?).

20. The correct answer is K. Quotes, including dialogue spoken by people in a sentence, should always be set in quotation marks: Boris asked his best friend Keisha, "Can I borrow four quarters?" while they waited at the laundromat on Clarke Avenue.

21. The correct answer is C. The sentence is a statement of fact and should end with a period (.), not a question mark.

22. The correct answer is K. The name of a university, such as *Georgetown University*, is a proper noun that should be capitalized.

23. The correct answer is D. *No mistakes.*

24. The correct answer is J. The sentence contains incorrectly placed commas that introduce awkward pauses. None of the commas in choice J should be there.

25. The correct answer is B. Since the house belongs to the piano teacher, an apostrophe should be added to show possession: teacher's.

26. The correct answer is K. This answer choice most clearly and effectively conveys the ideas in this sentence. The other answer choices make the sentence more awkward or confusing.

27. The correct answer is C. While the other answer choices are scattered and disorganized, choice C clearly conveys the thoughts contained within this sentence.

28. The correct answer is M. This choice best shows the logical and chronological progression of ideas for those interested in pursuing a career as a teacher.

29. The correct answer is A. Choice A clearly expresses the information as intended in this sentence. The other choices are confusing and awkwardly written.

30. The correct answer is L. This choice is expressed with the greatest clarity.

31. The correct answer is B. The Gutenberg Bible is a singular noun, and since the consideration here is current, the correct verb form would be *is considered*. Choice A incorrectly utilizes a future tense. Choice C incorrectly uses the contraction *it's* (it is).

32. The correct answer is J. This paragraph discusses characteristics of the Gutenberg Bible, currently ending with the fact that less than 50 copies are known to exist. Choice J is correct because it helps reinforce the notion that the Gutenberg Bible is rare.

33. The correct answer is D. The focus of this paragraph is spelunking; therefore, Choice D most effectively introduces this core topic.

34. The correct answer is J. The sentence as written inappropriately contains a possessive form of *rock*. Choice J removes the apostrophe to correctly create the plural *rocks*.

35. The correct answer is B. Because this sentence begins with *what*, it is a question. It should end in a question mark (?), as shown in choice B.

36. The correct answer is L. *Aphids* is a common noun and should only be capitalized when it begins a sentence. The plural is also correct here, so you can eliminate choice J.

37. The correct answer is A. Choice A both uses the correct form of the adjective and correctly places the common noun *name* in lowercase.

38. The correct answer is K. As written, the underlined portion of the sentence utilizes the incorrect pronoun form. The antecedent, *Edgar Allen Poe*, is a singular masculine noun and requires the singular pronoun *his*, which choice K uses.

39. The correct answer is C. As written, the word choice doesn't make logical sense. "Detractors" avoid using or supporting something, so they wouldn't use hot air balloons when they feel the urge to soar above the ground. Choice C correctly fixes the problem because "enthusiasts" would be the ones to happily use hot air balloons.

40. The correct answer is J. As written, the underlined portion of the sentence contains superfluous punctuation, as semicolons are used to join independent clauses, which we do not have here. There is no internal punctuation required at this point in the sentence.

41. The correct answer is B. This paragraph currently ends by discussing the world's longest suspension bridge, but then doesn't mention the length. Choice B provides this missing information.

42. **The correct answer is M.** *No change.* The sentence is correct as written; "suspension bridge" is a common noun and should be capitalized only when used at the beginning of a sentence.

43. **The correct answer is C.** The words *entire* and *world* are common nouns and should not be capitalized in this sentence.

44. **The correct answer is K.** In this sentence, giant sequoias are being discussed generally, so a plural pronoun and verb form are required.

45. **The correct answer is A.** "United States," a proper noun, should not be hyphenated. Choice A correctly removes the hyphenation.

46. **The correct answer is L.** Currently, the sentence incorrectly includes the contraction *it's* ("it is"). The possessive adjective *its* should be used instead.

47. **The correct answer is B.** Items in a list need to be separated by commas.

48. **The correct answer is J.** Contractions such as *you'll* require the proper placement of an apostrophe, as shown in choice J.

49. **The correct answer is C.** The past tense of the verb *to allow* is required here, as this action occurred in the past.

50. **The correct answer is L.** As written, the period creates a sentence fragment and is incorrect. Choice L fixes this problem.

 NOTES

Mathematics

1. A	11. D	21. C	31. D	41. A
2. K	12. M	22. K	32. L	42. L
3. B	13. C	23. C	33. B	43. A
4. K	14. K	24. K	34. K	44. L
5. D	15. A	25. B	35. C	45. C
6. J	16. L	26. K	36. L	46. L
7. B	17. C	27. A	37. B	47. A
8. K	18. J	28. M	38. L	48. K
9. D	19. C	29. A	39. A	49. C
10. M	20. L	30. J	40. K	50. M

1. **The correct answer is A.** 20 cannot be divided evenly by 3.

2. **The correct answer is K.** $\frac{2}{3}$ is the same as 0.67, rounded to the nearest hundredth.

3. **The correct answer is B.** 9 is divisible by three numbers: 1, 3, and 9. Since 9 is evenly divisible by a number other than 1 or itself, it is not a prime number.

4. **The correct answer is K.** 3 multiplied by 13 is 39. None of the other choices is evenly divisible by 3.

5. **The correct answer is D.** The term *product* means to multiply; $43 \times 100 = 4,300$.

6. **The correct answer is J.** $\frac{7}{8} - \frac{1}{2}$ is the same as $\frac{7}{8} - \frac{4}{8}$, which equals $\frac{3}{8}$.

7. **The correct answer is B.** $(6 - 1 = 5) + (1 \times 5 = 5) + (10 \div 2 = 5) + (2.5 + 2.5 = 5) = 5 + 5 + 5 + 5 = 20$

8. **The correct answer is K.** Dividing 112 by 6 gives 18 remainder 4. Therefore, 112 is not a multiple of 6.

9. **The correct answer is D.** Subtracting a negative is the same as adding a positive. $3 - (-6) = 3 + 6 = 9$

10. **The correct answer is M.** 72 is the lowest number of which 6, 12, and 72 are all factors.

11. **The correct answer is D.** Jeff has 6 notebooks. Maggie has 2×6 notebooks. Jeff and Maggie combined have 18 notebooks. Darnell has 2×18, or 36, notebooks.

12. **The correct answer is M.** Baxter needs two half-gallons for each gallon, or $2 \times 14 = 28$.

13. **The correct answer is C.** Since Dae already has $50, she must earn $250 to be able to purchase the $300 TV. Divide $250 by $25 (the amount earned per week) to see that it will take her 10 weeks to earn this money.

14. **The correct answer is K.** A full tank would go 150 miles, since 3×50 equals 150 miles. Izzy's tank is only two-thirds full, so she can only drive a two-thirds of that distance, or 100 miles:

$$\frac{2}{3} \times 150 = 100$$

15. **The correct answer is A.** There would be 6 trips from rim to floor, so 6×10 feet = 60 feet.

16. **The correct answer is L.** Remember, the hundreds place will not be mentioned if its value is zero.

17. **The correct answer is C.** Notice that the 6 is in the ten thousands place.

18. **The correct answer is J.** 1% = 0.01; one-half of l percent is written as 0.005.

19. **The correct answer is C.** One person raised 35% of $690, or $241.50 ($690 × 0.35 = $241.50). Subtract that amount from the total to get the amount raised by the others, which is $448.50 (690 − $241.50 = $448.50).

20. **The correct answer is L.** The whole pie is 100%. Since each slice is $\frac{1}{20}$ of the entire pie, divide 100% by 20 to get 5% (100 ÷ 20 = 5%).

21. **The correct answer is C.** The sum of the angles of a triangle is always 180°. As such, the missing value x can be obtained by subtracting the total of the known values (45° and 75° = 120°) from 180°. Choice C is correct, since 180° − 120° = 60°.

22. **The correct answer is K.** Note that the base of the triangle is the same as the diameter of the circle. Because ΔABC is isosceles, its altitude is the same length as the radius of the circle. Use the formula for the area of a triangle, and substitute the correct values:

$$A = \frac{1}{2}bh$$
$$= \frac{1}{2} \times 10 \times 5$$
$$= 25 \text{ sq. cm.}$$

23. **The correct answer is C.** These measurements describe a large rectangular room 30 feet high. Use the formula $V = l \times w \times h$ to find the volume:

$$V = 75 \text{ feet} \times 50 \text{ feet} \times 30 \text{ feet}$$
$$V = 112{,}500 \text{ cubic feet}$$

Choices A and B use the wrong units. Volume is always measured in *cubic* units.

24. **The correct answer is K.** A store markup of 100% would exactly double the price. An 80% markup almost doubles the price. The $14 jeans are priced at almost double their cost to the store, which means their original cost would have been near $7. By estimation, the best answer is choice K. To figure precisely, remember that an 80% markup is the equivalent of multiplying the cost by 180%, or 1.80.

$$\text{cost} \times 1.80 = 14.00$$
$$\text{cost} = 14.00 \div 1.80$$
$$\text{cost} = \$7.78$$

25. **The correct answer is B.** The finance charge will be the sum of $1\frac{1}{2}$% of $500, plus 1% of $250. You can write this as follows: (0.015 × 500) + (0.01 × 250) = 7.50 + 2.50 = $10.00

You can estimate the answer if you remember that percent means "hundredths of." One hundredth of $500 is $5.00; one hundredth of $250 is $2.50. The only answer near this sum is choice C, $10.00. Choices A and D could result from a misplaced decimal point.

26. **The correct answer is K.** Calculate the first expression as $(8 \times 10^2) + (6 \times 10) + 2 = 862$, and then calculate the second expression to get $(5 \times 10^3) + (2 \times 10^2) + (8 \times 10) + 9 = 5{,}289$. Add the two results together to arrive at 6,151.

27. **The correct answer is A.** The set of factors for 24 is:

{1,2,3,4,6,8,12,24}

The set of factors for 30 is:

{1,2,3,5,6,10,15,30}

Only four numbers appear in both sets. As such, the set of common factors is {1,2,3,6}, choice A.

28. **The correct answer is M.** For the length, 29 feet would be represented by 29 units of $\frac{1}{4}$ inch, resulting in $\frac{29}{4}$, or $7\frac{1}{4}$, inches. For the width, 23 feet would be represented by 23 units of $\frac{1}{4}$ inch, resulting in $\frac{23}{4}$, or $5\frac{3}{4}$, inches.

29. **The correct answer is A.** A scalene triangle has no equal sides.

30. **The correct answer is J.**

Distance = Rate × Time
$$= 55 \text{ mph} \times 5\frac{1}{2} \text{ hours}$$
$$= 55 \text{ mph} \times 5.5 \text{ hours}$$
$$= 302.5 \text{ miles}$$

31. **The correct answer is D.** 60 meals in the first month plus $33\frac{1}{3}$ percent more meals in the second month (60 + 20 = 80) equals 140 meals. In the third month, they delivered 2 × 140, or 280 meals.

32. **The correct answer is L.** $7.50 × 40 = $300.
$1,350 ÷ $300 = 4.5, or $4\frac{1}{2}$ weeks.

33. **The correct answer is B.** The total amount of wall space is equal to $10 × 15 × 4$, or 600 square feet. Divide by the capacity of each roll of wallpaper (75 square feet) to arrive at $600 ÷ 75 = 8$ rolls.

34. **The correct answer is K.** The average is $\frac{189 + 243 + 202 + 198}{4} = 208$.

35. **The correct answer is C.** Go Electro produces 1,900 devices per month; multiply this by 12 to find the annual number of devices they will add to the output, which is 22,800 devices per year. Add that amount to the current output (400,000) to calculate the new annual output, which is 422,800 devices.

36. **The correct answer is L.** You do not have to calculate this answer. If eight people share equally of 8 pounds and some ounces of fruit, each person would receive 1 pound and a few ounces. Only choice L is possible.

37. **The correct answer is B.** This is a subtraction problem. You must find the difference between the lengths of time required to finish the race. As with other problems involving units of measurement, you must work carefully.

    3 hr. 2 min. 24 sec.
    − 2 hr. 12 min. 38 sec.

Because 38 seconds is larger than 24 seconds, and 12 minutes is larger than 2 minutes, borrow from the minutes' column and the hour column and rewrite the problem as follows:

    2 hr. 61 min. 84 sec.
    − 2 hr. 12 min. 38 sec.
    0 hr. 49 min. 46 sec.

38. **The correct answer is L.** If the drawing is at a $\frac{1}{16}$ scale, then the drawing is $\frac{1}{16}$ the size of the actual wheel. Therefore, multiply the size of the drawing by 16 to arrive at choice K, or $1.8 × 16 = 28.8$ inches.

39. **The correct answer is A.** This problem asks you to find speed, also called rate. Rate is found by dividing the distance traveled (M) by the time required (T). The choice in which distance is divided by time is A.

40. **The correct answer is K.** There are 9 square feet in 1 square yard. So, y square feet equals $\frac{y}{9}$ square yards. Since there are x rooms with the same area, multiply this by x to get $x\left(\frac{y}{9}\right) = \frac{xy}{9}$ square yards.

41. **The correct answer is A.** The grey horizontal bars indicate how far each competitor passed the football, and each vertical line represents 4 feet. Claire passed for only 27 yards.

42. **The correct answer is L.** Megan passed for 36 yards and kicked 32 yards.

43. **The correct answer is A.** Ford HS collected 900 pounds of cans and 500 pounds of paper products, for a combined total of 1,400 pounds of can/paper recyclables. Holmes HS and King HS had can/paper totals of 1,100 pounds and 1,000 pounds, respectively.

44. **The correct answer is L.** Each of the three schools collected 800 pounds of plastics, totaling $800 × 3 = 2,400$ pounds.

45. **The correct answer is C.** The income in the North grew from about $24,000 to nearly $29,000, the most of any region.

46. **The correct answer is L.** 6,544 − 3,466 is approximately 6,500 − 3,500, or 3,000.

47. **The correct answer is A.** 82,122 ÷ 4,055 is approximately 80,000 ÷ 4,000, or 20.

48. **The correct answer is K.** 31 × 30 is approximately 30 × 30, or 900.

49. **The correct answer is C.** 3,988 + 2,177 is approximately 4,000 + 2,000, or 6,000.

50. **The correct answer is M.** About half, or 50 percent, chose burgers.

Ability

Figure Classification

1. A	5. A	9. C	13. B	17. B
2. J	6. L	10. J	14. M	18. L
3. E	7. E	11. C	15. E	19. C
4. M	8. K	12. L	16. L	20. N

1. **The correct answer is A.** Each figure has a small circle connected by a segment to a vertex (a corner) of the shape. For all the other choices, the segment bisects one side of the figure, rather than connecting at a vertex.

2. **The correct answer is J.** Each figure has a regular polygon inscribed in a circle. When used in a mathematical context, *inscribed* means that one figure is placed within another in such a manner that it touches at as many points as possible. The number of vertices (a.ka. corners) of the shape inscribed in the circle increases by one each time. Thus, the correct answer must be a hexagon inscribed in a circle.

3. **The correct answer is E.** Each square has segments splitting two adjacent sides.

4. **The correct answer is M.** Each shape is $\frac{1}{4}$ shaded.

5. **The correct answer is A.** Each figure consists of two parallel lines.

6. **The correct answer is L.** Each circle has two radii that form an approximately 90-degree angle.

7. **The correct answer is E.** In each of the figures, there are three circles placed on intersection points to form a triangle. It does not matter that some of the triangles contain two segments of the figure while others contain only one.

8. **The correct answer is K.** Each figure is a rectangle.

9. **The correct answer is C.** Each figure consists of four small circles connected by means of three segments.

10. **The correct answer is J.** Each figure consists of segments meeting at a single point.

11. **The correct answer is C.** Each figure consists of a polygon with a segment drawn to form a triangle at one of its vertices.

12. **The correct answer is L.** Each figure is a curve that changes direction exactly twice.

13. **The correct answer is B.** Each figure is a polygon with a circle at each of its vertices.

14. **The correct answer is M.** Each of these figures is shaded with vertical stripes.

15. **The correct answer is E.** Each of these figures is a rectangle.

16. **The correct answer is L.** Each figure is split in half by an internal line to form two equal parts.

17. **The correct answer is B.** Each figure is a polygon.

18. **The correct answer is L.** Each of the examples is a closed figure with six sides.

19. **The correct answer is C.** Each of the example figures is bisected by a single line in one direction and filled with multiple segments perpendicular to that line.

20. **The correct answer is N.** The example figures include a circle and two irregular shapes. The answer choices do not include any irregular shapes, but they do include one circle, choice N.

Figure Matrices

1. B	5. A	9. E	13. A	17. E
2. M	6. L	10. L	14. K	18. K
3. C	7. B	11. B	15. A	19. C
4. J	8. J	12. M	16. J	20. J

1. **The correct answer is B.** Moving through the matrix from right to left rotates the shape clockwise by 90 degrees. Moving from top to bottom adds another segment to the image.

2. **The correct answer is M.** The third image in each row is just a combination of the first two images in that row. Notice that none of the images are rotated from one cell to the next, which makes choice M a better option than choice L.

3. **The correct answer is C.** The internal segments in the last square in each row are those that appear in one of the previous two images, but not both.

4. **The correct answer is J.** The third image in each row is obtained as follows: take the shape from the second position in the row, then shade it using segments parallel to the segment in the first position in the row.

5. **The correct answer is A.** The third image in each row is just the first two images in the row joined with a circle.

6. **The correct answer is L.** The shading in the third column combines shading for the sections that are shaded in the first and second columns.

7. **The correct answer is B.** The solid segments in the third column are those that are not solid in either the first or second columns.

8. **The correct answer is J.** Moving left to right adds a segment that continues the current pattern in a clockwise manner. Similarly, moving top to bottom adds a segment that continues the pattern in a counterclockwise manner. Using either approach produces the correct answer.

9. **The correct answer is E.** Moving left to right across a row, the image rotates 90 degrees

clockwise at each step. Moving top to bottom, a new segment is added at each step.

10. **The correct answer is L.** The image in the last position of each row is simply the previous two images in the row placed over each other.

11. **The correct answer is B.** Shapes are the same within a single row, and shading style is the same throughout a single column.

12. **The correct answer is M.** The internal segments in each triangle in the third column are visible based on the following rule: a segment is visible if it is visible in either the first or second triangles in the row, but not both.

13. **The correct answer is A.** Within each row, a move from the first to second image consists of reversing the first arrow and leaving the second arrow alone. Moving from the second to third column reverses both arrows.

14. **The correct answer is K.** A move from left to right consists of adding an extra segment and rotating the segments to the right by 90 degrees. A move from top to bottom is a rotation of 90 degrees counterclockwise.

15. **The correct answer is A.** The image in the first column is transformed by moving the circle in the direction indicated by the arrow in the second column; that arrow indicates both a vertical and horizontal movement. In the third row, the arrow does not indicate any vertical movement, only horizontal, so the circle needs to be at the bottom of the figure.

16. **The correct answer is J.** The first two arrows in each row are reversed and joined to form the last image in the row.

17. **The correct answer is E.** The third figure in each row is multiple smaller versions of the first figure, and the number of smaller figures is determined by the number of segments in the second cell. The figures in the last column are placed side by side, which makes choice E a better option than choice B.

18. **The correct answer is K.** The figures in the middle of each row include all elements of the figures on both sides. Any elements not in the first column appear in the third.

19. **The correct answer is C.** The third figure in each row consists of the first figure placed inside the second figure.

20. **The correct answer is J.** The second figure in each row includes a polygon with various small shapes, circles, or line segments inside. The third figure in the row consists of the contents of that polygon. The first figure in each row (i.e., the entire first column) has no relation to the rest of the figures.

NOTES

Paper Folding

1. A	3. A	5. E	7. D	9. B
2. M	4. J	6. K	8. K	10. J

1. **The correct answer is A.** The second fold has no effect on the result since it does not overlap the only hole. The result needs to have two holes, at the centers of the bottom and left edges.

2. **The correct answer is M.** Unfolding the paper will result in each of the two holes being reflected first vertically and then horizontally. The hole near the center becomes four arranged around the center of the page, and the hole in the corner reflects to each of the other corners as well.

3. **The correct answer is A.** The hole on the bottom edge will be reflected to the center of the right edge, and the hole on the left edge will be reflected to the center of the top edge.

4. **The correct answer is J.** Each of the three holes on the folded page will reflect vertically across the center of the page.

5. **The correct answer is E.** When the last fold is undone, the two holes will reflect upward to become four, all still on the bottom half of the full page. Undoing the original fold will cause each of these four to reflect vertically upward again,

creating two columns of four holes immediately on either side of the page center.

6. **The correct answer is K.** Each of the two holes on the folded page will reflect horizontally across the vertical fold.

7. **The correct answer is D.** The horizontal row of two holes centered vertically in the page will reflect across the fold to become a vertical row of two holes centered horizontally in the page.

8. **The correct answer is K.** The two holes reflect over the fold onto the upper half of the page. Since they are near the fold, they will be near the fold on the other side as well.

9. **The correct answer is B.** The single hole in the center of the quarter-page will first reflect upward to be in the center of the upper-right quadrant. These two holes will then reflect across the vertical fold and end up in the centers of the lower-left and upper-left quadrants, respectively.

10. **The correct answer is J.** The small folded flap will, when unfolded, reflect the hole over the diagonal line and nearer to the corner.

NOTES

SCORE SHEET

Although your actual exam scores will not be reported as percentages, it might be helpful to convert your test scores to percentages so that you can see at a glance where your strengths and weaknesses lie. The numbers in parentheses represent the questions that test each skill.

Subject	# Correct ÷ # of questions	× 100 = _____ %
Reading		
Vocabulary/Word Relationships: (1, 9, 12, 16, 18, 22, 24, 29, 31, 35, 36, 38, 42, 45, 50)	_____ ÷ 15 = _____	× 100 = _____ %
Details/Main Idea/Structure (2, 6, 10, 14, 15, 17, 19, 20, 26, 27, 28, 30, 32, 33, 34, 39, 40, 41, 43, 44, 48, 49)	_____ ÷ 22 = _____	× 100 = _____ %
Inference/Understanding (3, 4, 5, 7, 8, 11, 13, 21, 23, 25, 37, 46, 47)	_____ ÷ 13 = _____	× 100 = _____ %
TOTAL READING SKILLS	_____ ÷ 50 = _____	× 100 = _____ %
Written Expression		
Spelling and Capitalization (1, 2, 3, 4, 5, 6, 7, 8, 9, 10, 11, 12, 13, 14, 15, 36, 37, 42, 43)	_____ ÷ 19 = _____	× 100 = _____ %
Punctuation (19, 20, 21, 22, 23, 24, 25, 34, 35, 40, 45, 46, 48, 50)	_____ ÷ 14 = _____	× 100 = _____ %
Grammar (16, 17, 18, 31, 38, 44)	_____ ÷ 6 = _____	× 100 = _____ %
Usage and Composition (26, 27, 28, 29, 30, 32, 33, 39, 41, 47, 49)	_____ ÷ 11 = _____	× 100 = _____ %
TOTAL WRITTEN EXPRESSION SKILLS	_____ ÷ 50 = _____	× 100 = _____ %
Mathematics		
Arithmetic (1, 2, 3, 4, 5, 6, 7, 8, 9, 10, 11, 12, 13, 14, 15, 16, 17, 18, 19, 25, 26, 27, 30, 33, 35, 36, 37, 46, 47, 48, 49)	_____ ÷ 31 = _____	× 100 = _____ %
Algebra (24, 31, 32, 39, 40)	_____ ÷ 5 = _____	× 100 = _____ %
Data Analysis (34, 41, 42, 43, 44, 45, 50)	_____ ÷ 7 = _____	× 100 = _____ %
Geometry and Measurement (20, 21, 22, 23, 28, 29, 38)	_____ ÷ 7 = _____	× 100 = _____ %
TOTAL MATHEMATICS SKILLS	_____ ÷ 50 = _____	× 100 = _____ %
Ability		
Figure Classification (1, 2, 3, 4, 5, 6, 7, 8, 9, 10, 11, 12, 13, 14, 15, 16, 17, 18, 19, 20)	_____ ÷ 20 = _____	× 100 = _____ %
Figure Matrices (1, 2, 3, 4, 5, 6, 7, 8, 9, 10, 11, 12, 13, 14, 15, 16, 17, 18, 19, 20)	_____ ÷ 20 = _____	× 100 = _____ %
Paper Folding (1, 2, 3, 4, 5, 6, 7, 8, 9, 10)	_____ ÷ 10 = _____	× 100 = _____ %
TOTAL ABILITY SKILLS	_____ ÷ 50 = _____	× 100 = _____ %

TACHS PRACTICE TEST 2

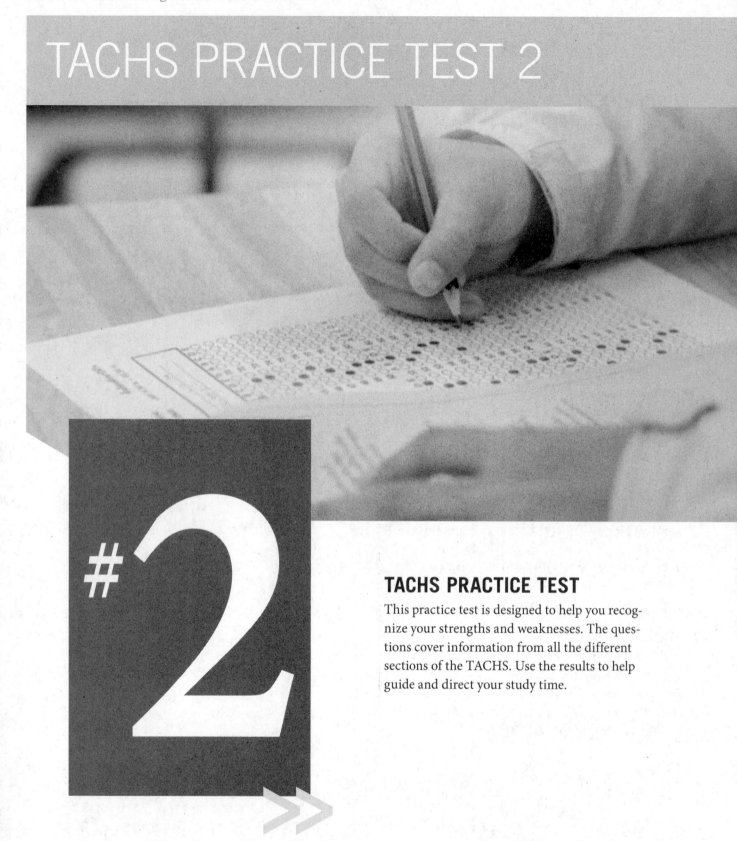

 # 2

TACHS PRACTICE TEST

This practice test is designed to help you recognize your strengths and weaknesses. The questions cover information from all the different sections of the TACHS. Use the results to help guide and direct your study time.

ANSWER SHEETS: TACHS PRACTICE TEST 2

Reading

1. Ⓐ Ⓑ Ⓒ Ⓓ   11. Ⓐ Ⓑ Ⓒ Ⓓ   21. Ⓐ Ⓑ Ⓒ Ⓓ   31. Ⓐ Ⓑ Ⓒ Ⓓ   41. Ⓐ Ⓑ Ⓒ Ⓓ

2. Ⓙ Ⓚ Ⓛ Ⓜ   12. Ⓙ Ⓚ Ⓛ Ⓜ   22. Ⓙ Ⓚ Ⓛ Ⓜ   32. Ⓙ Ⓚ Ⓛ Ⓜ   42. Ⓙ Ⓚ Ⓛ Ⓜ

3. Ⓐ Ⓑ Ⓒ Ⓓ   13. Ⓐ Ⓑ Ⓒ Ⓓ   23. Ⓐ Ⓑ Ⓒ Ⓓ   33. Ⓐ Ⓑ Ⓒ Ⓓ   43. Ⓐ Ⓑ Ⓒ Ⓓ

4. Ⓙ Ⓚ Ⓛ Ⓜ   14. Ⓙ Ⓚ Ⓛ Ⓜ   24. Ⓙ Ⓚ Ⓛ Ⓜ   34. Ⓙ Ⓚ Ⓛ Ⓜ   44. Ⓙ Ⓚ Ⓛ Ⓜ

5. Ⓐ Ⓑ Ⓒ Ⓓ   15. Ⓐ Ⓑ Ⓒ Ⓓ   25. Ⓐ Ⓑ Ⓒ Ⓓ   35. Ⓐ Ⓑ Ⓒ Ⓓ   45. Ⓐ Ⓑ Ⓒ Ⓓ

6. Ⓙ Ⓚ Ⓛ Ⓜ   16. Ⓙ Ⓚ Ⓛ Ⓜ   26. Ⓙ Ⓚ Ⓛ Ⓜ   36. Ⓙ Ⓚ Ⓛ Ⓜ   46. Ⓙ Ⓚ Ⓛ Ⓜ

7. Ⓐ Ⓑ Ⓒ Ⓓ   17. Ⓐ Ⓑ Ⓒ Ⓓ   27. Ⓐ Ⓑ Ⓒ Ⓓ   37. Ⓐ Ⓑ Ⓒ Ⓓ   47. Ⓐ Ⓑ Ⓒ Ⓓ

8. Ⓙ Ⓚ Ⓛ Ⓜ   18. Ⓙ Ⓚ Ⓛ Ⓜ   28. Ⓙ Ⓚ Ⓛ Ⓜ   38. Ⓙ Ⓚ Ⓛ Ⓜ   48. Ⓙ Ⓚ Ⓛ Ⓜ

9. Ⓐ Ⓑ Ⓒ Ⓓ   19. Ⓐ Ⓑ Ⓒ Ⓓ   29. Ⓐ Ⓑ Ⓒ Ⓓ   39. Ⓐ Ⓑ Ⓒ Ⓓ   49. Ⓐ Ⓑ Ⓒ Ⓓ

10. Ⓙ Ⓚ Ⓛ Ⓜ   20. Ⓙ Ⓚ Ⓛ Ⓜ   30. Ⓙ Ⓚ Ⓛ Ⓜ   40. Ⓙ Ⓚ Ⓛ Ⓜ   50. Ⓙ Ⓚ Ⓛ Ⓜ

Written Expression

1. Ⓐ Ⓑ Ⓒ Ⓓ Ⓔ   11. Ⓐ Ⓑ Ⓒ Ⓓ   21. Ⓐ Ⓑ Ⓒ Ⓓ   31. Ⓐ Ⓑ Ⓒ Ⓓ   41. Ⓐ Ⓑ Ⓒ Ⓓ

2. Ⓙ Ⓚ Ⓛ Ⓜ Ⓝ   12. Ⓙ Ⓚ Ⓛ Ⓜ   22. Ⓙ Ⓚ Ⓛ Ⓜ   32. Ⓙ Ⓚ Ⓛ Ⓜ   42. Ⓙ Ⓚ Ⓛ Ⓜ

3. Ⓐ Ⓑ Ⓒ Ⓓ Ⓔ   13. Ⓐ Ⓑ Ⓒ Ⓓ   23. Ⓐ Ⓑ Ⓒ Ⓓ   33. Ⓐ Ⓑ Ⓒ Ⓓ   43. Ⓐ Ⓑ Ⓒ Ⓓ

4. Ⓙ Ⓚ Ⓛ Ⓜ Ⓝ   14. Ⓙ Ⓚ Ⓛ Ⓜ   24. Ⓙ Ⓚ Ⓛ Ⓜ   34. Ⓙ Ⓚ Ⓛ Ⓜ   44. Ⓙ Ⓚ Ⓛ Ⓜ

5. Ⓐ Ⓑ Ⓒ Ⓓ Ⓔ   15. Ⓐ Ⓑ Ⓒ Ⓓ   25. Ⓐ Ⓑ Ⓒ Ⓓ   35. Ⓐ Ⓑ Ⓒ Ⓓ   45. Ⓐ Ⓑ Ⓒ Ⓓ

6. Ⓙ Ⓚ Ⓛ Ⓜ Ⓝ   16. Ⓙ Ⓚ Ⓛ Ⓜ   26. Ⓙ Ⓚ Ⓛ Ⓜ   36. Ⓙ Ⓚ Ⓛ Ⓜ   46. Ⓙ Ⓚ Ⓛ Ⓜ

7. Ⓐ Ⓑ Ⓒ Ⓓ Ⓔ   17. Ⓐ Ⓑ Ⓒ Ⓓ   27. Ⓐ Ⓑ Ⓒ Ⓓ   37. Ⓐ Ⓑ Ⓒ Ⓓ   47. Ⓐ Ⓑ Ⓒ Ⓓ

8. Ⓙ Ⓚ Ⓛ Ⓜ Ⓝ   18. Ⓙ Ⓚ Ⓛ Ⓜ   28. Ⓙ Ⓚ Ⓛ Ⓜ   38. Ⓙ Ⓚ Ⓛ Ⓜ   48. Ⓙ Ⓚ Ⓛ Ⓜ

9. Ⓐ Ⓑ Ⓒ Ⓓ Ⓔ   19. Ⓐ Ⓑ Ⓒ Ⓓ   29. Ⓐ Ⓑ Ⓒ Ⓓ   39. Ⓐ Ⓑ Ⓒ Ⓓ   49. Ⓐ Ⓑ Ⓒ Ⓓ

10. Ⓙ Ⓚ Ⓛ Ⓜ Ⓝ   20. Ⓙ Ⓚ Ⓛ Ⓜ   30. Ⓙ Ⓚ Ⓛ Ⓜ   40. Ⓙ Ⓚ Ⓛ Ⓜ   50. Ⓙ Ⓚ Ⓛ Ⓜ

Mathematics

1. Ⓐ Ⓑ Ⓒ Ⓓ   11. Ⓐ Ⓑ Ⓒ Ⓓ   21. Ⓐ Ⓑ Ⓒ Ⓓ   31. Ⓐ Ⓑ Ⓒ Ⓓ   41. Ⓐ Ⓑ Ⓒ Ⓓ

2. Ⓙ Ⓚ Ⓛ Ⓜ   12. Ⓙ Ⓚ Ⓛ Ⓜ   22. Ⓙ Ⓚ Ⓛ Ⓜ   32. Ⓙ Ⓚ Ⓛ Ⓜ   42. Ⓙ Ⓚ Ⓛ Ⓜ

3. Ⓐ Ⓑ Ⓒ Ⓓ   13. Ⓐ Ⓑ Ⓒ Ⓓ   23. Ⓐ Ⓑ Ⓒ Ⓓ   33. Ⓐ Ⓑ Ⓒ Ⓓ   43. Ⓐ Ⓑ Ⓒ Ⓓ

4. Ⓙ Ⓚ Ⓛ Ⓜ   14. Ⓙ Ⓚ Ⓛ Ⓜ   24. Ⓙ Ⓚ Ⓛ Ⓜ   34. Ⓙ Ⓚ Ⓛ Ⓜ   44. Ⓙ Ⓚ Ⓛ Ⓜ

5. Ⓐ Ⓑ Ⓒ Ⓓ   15. Ⓐ Ⓑ Ⓒ Ⓓ   25. Ⓐ Ⓑ Ⓒ Ⓓ   35. Ⓐ Ⓑ Ⓒ Ⓓ   45. Ⓐ Ⓑ Ⓒ Ⓓ

6. Ⓙ Ⓚ Ⓛ Ⓜ   16. Ⓙ Ⓚ Ⓛ Ⓜ   26. Ⓙ Ⓚ Ⓛ Ⓜ   36. Ⓙ Ⓚ Ⓛ Ⓜ   46. Ⓙ Ⓚ Ⓛ Ⓜ

7. Ⓐ Ⓑ Ⓒ Ⓓ   17. Ⓐ Ⓑ Ⓒ Ⓓ   27. Ⓐ Ⓑ Ⓒ Ⓓ   37. Ⓐ Ⓑ Ⓒ Ⓓ   47. Ⓐ Ⓑ Ⓒ Ⓓ

8. Ⓙ Ⓚ Ⓛ Ⓜ   18. Ⓙ Ⓚ Ⓛ Ⓜ   28. Ⓙ Ⓚ Ⓛ Ⓜ   38. Ⓙ Ⓚ Ⓛ Ⓜ   48. Ⓙ Ⓚ Ⓛ Ⓜ

9. Ⓐ Ⓑ Ⓒ Ⓓ   19. Ⓐ Ⓑ Ⓒ Ⓓ   29. Ⓐ Ⓑ Ⓒ Ⓓ   39. Ⓐ Ⓑ Ⓒ Ⓓ   49. Ⓐ Ⓑ Ⓒ Ⓓ

10. Ⓙ Ⓚ Ⓛ Ⓜ   20. Ⓙ Ⓚ Ⓛ Ⓜ   30. Ⓙ Ⓚ Ⓛ Ⓜ   40. Ⓙ Ⓚ Ⓛ Ⓜ   50. Ⓙ Ⓚ Ⓛ Ⓜ

Ability

Figure Classification

1. Ⓐ Ⓑ Ⓒ Ⓓ Ⓔ   5. Ⓐ Ⓑ Ⓒ Ⓓ Ⓔ   9. Ⓐ Ⓑ Ⓒ Ⓓ Ⓔ   13. Ⓐ Ⓑ Ⓒ Ⓓ Ⓔ   17. Ⓐ Ⓑ Ⓒ Ⓓ Ⓔ

2. Ⓙ Ⓚ Ⓛ Ⓜ Ⓝ   6. Ⓙ Ⓚ Ⓛ Ⓜ Ⓝ   10. Ⓙ Ⓚ Ⓛ Ⓜ Ⓝ   14. Ⓙ Ⓚ Ⓛ Ⓜ Ⓝ   18. Ⓙ Ⓚ Ⓛ Ⓜ Ⓝ

3. Ⓐ Ⓑ Ⓒ Ⓓ Ⓔ   7. Ⓐ Ⓑ Ⓒ Ⓓ Ⓔ   11. Ⓐ Ⓑ Ⓒ Ⓓ Ⓔ   15. Ⓐ Ⓑ Ⓒ Ⓓ Ⓔ   19. Ⓐ Ⓑ Ⓒ Ⓓ Ⓔ

4. Ⓙ Ⓚ Ⓛ Ⓜ Ⓝ   8. Ⓙ Ⓚ Ⓛ Ⓜ Ⓝ   12. Ⓙ Ⓚ Ⓛ Ⓜ Ⓝ   16. Ⓙ Ⓚ Ⓛ Ⓜ Ⓝ   20. Ⓙ Ⓚ Ⓛ Ⓜ Ⓝ

Figure Matrices

1. Ⓐ Ⓑ Ⓒ Ⓓ Ⓔ   5. Ⓐ Ⓑ Ⓒ Ⓓ Ⓔ   9. Ⓐ Ⓑ Ⓒ Ⓓ Ⓔ   13. Ⓐ Ⓑ Ⓒ Ⓓ Ⓔ   17. Ⓐ Ⓑ Ⓒ Ⓓ Ⓔ

2. Ⓙ Ⓚ Ⓛ Ⓜ Ⓝ   6. Ⓙ Ⓚ Ⓛ Ⓜ Ⓝ   10. Ⓙ Ⓚ Ⓛ Ⓜ Ⓝ   14. Ⓙ Ⓚ Ⓛ Ⓜ Ⓝ   18. Ⓙ Ⓚ Ⓛ Ⓜ Ⓝ

3. Ⓐ Ⓑ Ⓒ Ⓓ Ⓔ   7. Ⓐ Ⓑ Ⓒ Ⓓ Ⓔ   11. Ⓐ Ⓑ Ⓒ Ⓓ Ⓔ   15. Ⓐ Ⓑ Ⓒ Ⓓ Ⓔ   19. Ⓐ Ⓑ Ⓒ Ⓓ Ⓔ

4. Ⓙ Ⓚ Ⓛ Ⓜ Ⓝ   8. Ⓙ Ⓚ Ⓛ Ⓜ Ⓝ   12. Ⓙ Ⓚ Ⓛ Ⓜ Ⓝ   16. Ⓙ Ⓚ Ⓛ Ⓜ Ⓝ   20. Ⓙ Ⓚ Ⓛ Ⓜ Ⓝ

Paper Folding

1. Ⓐ Ⓑ Ⓒ Ⓓ Ⓔ   3. Ⓐ Ⓑ Ⓒ Ⓓ Ⓔ   5. Ⓐ Ⓑ Ⓒ Ⓓ Ⓔ   7. Ⓐ Ⓑ Ⓒ Ⓓ Ⓔ   9. Ⓐ Ⓑ Ⓒ Ⓓ Ⓔ

2. Ⓙ Ⓚ Ⓛ Ⓜ Ⓝ   4. Ⓙ Ⓚ Ⓛ Ⓜ Ⓝ   6. Ⓙ Ⓚ Ⓛ Ⓜ Ⓝ   8. Ⓙ Ⓚ Ⓛ Ⓜ Ⓝ   10. Ⓙ Ⓚ Ⓛ Ⓜ Ⓝ

READING

50 Questions—35 Minutes

Turn to the Reading section of your answer sheet to answer the questions in this section.

Directions: This is a test of how well you understand what you read.

- Read the passages below and answer the questions.
- Four answers are given for each question. You must choose the answer that you think is better than the others.

Questions 1–6 are based on the following passage.

PASSAGE 1

My people are the people of Elu, the capital village of Ohafia in southeast Nigeria. Ours is a warrior tradition. We keep the tradition today primarily in name, but the warrior image is an important part of our identity, passed down through the generations.

Line
5
We learn the tradition of the warrior through the process of many rituals, each taught to us by our elders, who ensure that our identity is maintained. I remember the first step of my manhood, when I reached the age of eight and was finally ready for the *nnu nnu mbu*, a ritual that proves that you are ready to enter the world of men. It is a sweltering morning, and my family has been preparing for the ceremony since dawn. My father is absorbed in the task of dressing me in a fine costume befitting the occasion, and he looks down upon me with pride as he completes his final touches and prepares me for show.

10
My father is beaming, and I feel his pride lift me as I move into the street to start the process of visiting others in the village who will honor me for my efforts. My chest swells and I hear my heart pounding in my ears, the blood rushing, as one by one I visit the huts of my kinfolk, receiving gifts of money and yams from each as they greet me. Some of the family members from my mother's line are introduced to me during this ceremony for the first time. I feel the strength that comes with knowing that I am emerging into manhood.

1. How does the author's father feel about his son?

   A. He is confused by his son's behavior.

   B. He pays little attention to his son.

   C. He is proud of his son's accomplishments.

   D. He feels shamed by the actions of his son.

2. What happens when the author meets his mother's family?

   J. His family members urge him to continue his target practice.

   K. Some of his family members pretend that they do not know him.

   L. He receives gifts of money and yams from the family members.

   M. His family members come together to meet him in the village square.

3. From the passage, we can infer that

    A. the author's father was never proud of him before.

    B. the author and his father have a new way to bond.

    C. the author is closer to his father's family than his mother's family.

    D. the author is not interested in taking the warrior identity.

4. The village that the author lives in is

    J. Ohafia.

    K. Nigeria.

    L. Elu.

    M. unknown.

5. Based on the passage, we can conclude that the author

    A. still has further rituals to complete.

    B. is considered fully a man in his village.

    C. will move in with his mother's relatives.

    D. will soon be leaving his village.

6. Which of the following would be the best title for this passage?

    J. "Life in My Village"

    K. "My Journey into Manhood"

    L. "The Warrior Culture"

    M. "Money, Yams, and Manhood"

Questions 7–10 are based on the following passage.

PASSAGE 2

Barrett had always dreamed of opening a photography studio. As soon as he finished photography school, he rented a small space in a strip mall just off the highway. For the first few years, he barely made ends meet. He took just enough photos to pay for rent and materials.

Line Barrett knew his business was not going to be successful if he continued to do business the way he had
5 since he opened his studio. He researched several business strategies before he made his decision. Barrett advertised a month-long special in the newspaper. He decided to reduce his standard pricing by one third for the entire month. He knew this was a calculated risk, but it was one he felt he had to take.

7. The phrase "made ends meet" is another way of saying which of the following?

    A. Opened the doors

    B. Took nice pictures

    C. Took care of customers

    D. Balanced the budget

8. If Barrett was struggling financially, why did he reduce his prices?

    J. He hoped to increase the number of customers.

    K. He was giving up.

    L. He was paying too many taxes.

    M. His research was faulty.

9. From the passage, we can infer that Barrett is

    A. lazy.

    B. unsuccessful.

    C. ambitious.

    D. not a good photographer.

10. Why is reducing his prices a risk?

    J. He might take just as many photos but make less money.

    K. He doesn't understand how business works.

    L. His rent and materials costs will go up.

    M. His research recommended against reducing prices.

Questions 11–16 are based on the following passage.

Passage 3

History is full of "accidental inventions"—ingenious advances that were initially unintended but eventually served to benefit mankind in a variety of unique ways. Let's take a closer look at a few of these items, as well as their curious origins.

Line
5   Many of us take for granted having a microwave to cook and reheat food quickly. However, individuals were without this useful appliance until 1945 when an engineer named Percy Spencer accidentally cooked a chocolate bar in his pocket while tinkering with a magnetron for a radar-building project. This unexpected event led Spencer down an experimental path that ultimately resulted in the creation of the microwave oven.

Penicillin is an antibiotic used to treat a wide array of infections and is widely considered one of the most essential medications in the world today. But did you know that its discovery was due to a careless
10 mistake by a scientist? In 1928, Alexander Fleming, a Scottish scientist, noticed a unique mold strain on a Petri dish that was mistakenly left open on a lab table, a mold strain that inhibited the growth of bacteria surrounding it. Rigorous scientific testing of the strange new mold followed, leading to one of the most significant scientific and medical advances in history.

It's clear that scientific curiosity, when in the capable hands of an innovative thinker, can lead an in-
15 dividual down a path to greatness. But sometimes that path contains an unexpected detour, possibly due to a completely unforeseen mistake or accident, and the result changes history forever.

11. Based on the information in the passage, what do the microwave oven and penicillin have in common?

  A. Both the microwave and penicillin are essential inventions.

  B. Both required the work of professional inventors to create them.

  C. Both inventions are the direct result of an accident or mistake.

  D. Both would have eventually been invented, even if the accidents mentioned in the passage didn't occur.

12. As used in the passage, "an unexpected detour," most likely refers to

  J. a change in a driving route that leads to a new road.

  K. an unintended event leading to an innovation.

  L. an unlikely inventor who becomes famous.

  M. a world-changing invention that changes science.

13. As used in the passage, the word *inhibited* most likely means

  A. accelerated.

  B. shy.

  C. introverted.

  D. prevented.

14. An example of an accidental invention given in the passage is

  J. radar.

  K. the microwave.

  L. the Petri dish.

  M. bubble gum.

15. Which of the following would be the best title for this passage?

  A. "Innovative Thinkers in Modern Science"

  B. "Happy Accidents"

  C. "Careless Mistakes"

  D. "Scientific Innovations of the 20th Century"

16. Which of the following is a lesson one can learn from the passage?

    J. Be very careful when doing scientific research.

    K. Hide your mistakes.

    L. Don't be afraid to make mistakes.

    M. Every accident can change modern medicine.

Questions 17–22 are based on the following passage.

Passage 4

With the increased use of email and instant messaging, experts have struggled to make any substantial conclusions regarding the effects electronic communication has on computer users' social skills. Some experts in fields such as communications argue that email and instant messaging have increased the social
Line skills of computer users because people now communicate with each other more frequently than ever before.
5   Others, however, maintain that computer users can hide behind their anonymity, thus allowing them to take on false personality traits and characteristics. Such experts further contend that the more communication takes place via email and instant messaging, the less effective communication becomes in face-to-face settings. Experts on both sides of the debate do, however, agree that the frequency of communications has increased since the advent of electronic correspondence and that this alone should have some positive ef-
10 fect on the communication skills of computer users. After all, the adage says that practice makes perfect.

17. Which of the following would be the best title for the passage above?

    A. "The Problems with Email and Instant Messaging"

    B. "The Electronic Communications Revolution"

    C. "The Possible Effects of Electronic Communication on Communication Skills of Computer Users"

    D. "The Debate Over Instant Communications and Its Effects on Email"

18. The phrase "practice makes perfect" in the last sentence refers to which of the following?

    J. The increased frequency of electronic communication

    K. Public speaking engagements

    L. Practice with computer software

    M. Research conducted by experts in the field

19. How does anonymity decrease social skills?

    A. It prevents people from communicating at all.

    B. It lets people hide without working on their real-life communication skills.

    C. It means that people will grow mistrustful of everyone else.

    D. It decreases the frequency of communication.

20. Which of the following most affects electronic communication skills?

    J. Frequency of use

    K. Email

    L. Instant messaging

    M. Face-to-face conversation

21. Which of the following is seen as a drawback of electronic communication?

A. Anonymity

B. Bad grammar

C. Bullying

D. Forgetting how to talk face-to-face

22. As used in the passage, the word *adage* most likely means

J. expert.

K. dance.

L. saying.

M. book.

Questions 23–28 are based on the following passage.

PASSAGE 5

The reality TV craze that began bombarding viewers in the United States two decades ago apparently is here to stay, at least for several more years. Strangely, though, some people who watch reality TV still have not caught on to the fact that there is little to no reality in reality television shows. Producers and direc-
Line tors often direct reality show stars to say particular things or act in a particular manner. Filming stops
5 frequently to re-shoot certain scenes or pieces of dialogue between cast members. The dramatic arguments and intense fistfights might seem improvised but are actually scripted in great detail. The public, though, is still largely unaware of the many staged, contrived shows that are advertised as reality.

23. Which of the following is the main idea of the passage?

A. Reality shows are the most popular shows on TV.

B. Reality shows lure watchers through fancy advertising slogans and cute stars.

C. Reality TV consists of very little reality.

D. Reality show cast members usually become big stars and famous celebrities.

24. The author of the passage above is most likely a(n)

J. reality show winner.

K. reality show producer.

L. critic of reality TV.

M. executive from a TV network.

25. The author would most likely say that reality shows are

A. authentic.

B. deceptive.

C. fleeting.

D. fantastic.

26. The passage presents all of the following as evidence that reality shows are not real, *except* that

J. producers convince the stars to act a certain way.

K. scenes are re-shot as necessary.

L. stars are expected to keep details secret.

M. shows are tightly scripted, not improvised.

27. Based on the passage, what do reality TV shows and regular TV shows most likely have in common?

    A. Cast members are sworn to secrecy.

    B. Both types of shows are staged.

    C. People expect both to be fake.

    D. Both types of shows are advertised as reality.

28. As used in the passage, the word *bombarding* most likely means

    J. shielding.

    K. flooding.

    L. attacking

    M. endangering.

Questions 29–36 are based on the following passage.

PASSAGE 6

While the Europeans were still creeping cautiously along their coasts, Polynesians were making trips between Hawaii and New Zealand, a distance of 3,800 miles, in frail canoes. These fearless sailors of the Pacific explored every island in their vast domain without even the simplest of navigational tools.

Line   In the daytime, the Polynesians guided their craft by the position of the sun, the trend of the waves and 5 wind, and the flight of seabirds. At night, they used stars during long trips between island groups. Youths studying navigation learned to view the heavens as a cylinder on which the highways of navigation were marked. An invisible line bisected the sky from the North Star to the Southern Cross.

In addition to single canoes, the Polynesians often used twin canoes for transpacific voyages. The two boats were fastened together by canopied platforms that shielded passengers from sun and rain. Such 10 crafts were remarkably seaworthy and could accommodate 60 to 80 people, in addition to water, food, and domestic animals. Some of these vessels had as many as three masts.

These Pacific *mariners* used paddles to propel and steer their canoes. The steering paddle was so important that it was always given a personal name. Polynesian legends not only recite the names of the canoe and the hero who discovered a new island but also the name of the steering paddle he used.

29. Which title is best for this selection?

    A. "European Sailors"

    B. "The History of the Pacific Ocean"

    C. "The Study of Navigation"

    D. "Early Polynesian Navigation"

30. The Polynesians made trips to

    J. New Zealand.

    K. the Atlantic.

    L. the Southern Cross.

    M. Europe.

31. The word *mariner* means

    A. propeller.

    B. seaman.

    C. paddle.

    D. navigation.

32. This passage suggests that the Polynesians

    J. trained seabirds to guide their canoes.

    K. had seen a line in the sky that was invisible to others.

    L. used a primitive telescope to view the heavens.

    M. were astronomers as well as explorers.

33. The steering paddle was

    A. sometimes named after a Polynesian village.

    B. made from wood found floating in the ocean.

    C. always given a personal name.

    D. often replaced between journeys.

34. Of what use were dual canoes?

    J. They were primarily fishing vessels.

    K. They could carry passengers, food, and cargo.

    L. The chief and his family used them as leisure boats.

    M. They served as troop transport boats during times of war.

35. Based on the passage, we can infer that

    A. the Polynesians were skilled navigators.

    B. Polynesian canoes would often get lost on the Pacific Ocean.

    C. navigators could see invisible objects.

    D. they were afraid of traveling far from home.

36. What information do Polynesian legends state when referring to explorers?

    J. Route information, name of the Polynesian village, number of days

    K. Captain's log entries, weather, cargo brought home

    L. Name of the canoe, hero who discovered a new island, name of the steering paddle he used

    M. Type of wood used for the paddle, name of the paddle, name of the canoe

Questions 37–42 are based on the following passage.

PASSAGE 7

Was Phileas Fogg rich? Undoubtedly. But those who knew him best could not imagine how he had made his fortune, and Mr. Fogg was the last person to whom to apply for the information. He was not lavish, nor, on the contrary, avaricious; for, whenever he knew that money was needed for a noble, useful, or benevolent *Line* purpose, he supplied it quietly and sometimes anonymously. He was, in short, the least communicative of *5* men. He talked very little, and seemed all the more mysterious for his taciturn manner. His daily habits were quite open to observation; but whatever he did was so exactly the same thing that he had always done before, that the wits of the curious were fairly puzzled.

    Had he travelled? It was likely, for no one seemed to know the world more familiarly; there was no spot so secluded that he did not appear to have an intimate acquaintance with it. He often corrected, with *10* a few clear words, the thousand conjectures advanced by members of the club as to lost and unheard-of travellers, pointing out the true probabilities, and seeming as if gifted with a sort of second sight, so often did events justify his predictions. He must have travelled everywhere, at least in the spirit.

    It was at least certain that Phileas Fogg had not absented himself from London for many years.

—Around the World in Eighty Days by Jules Verne

37. As used in the passage, the word *avaricious* most likely means

    A. generous.

    B. wealthy.

    C. stingy.

    D. mean.

38. Phileas Fogg can best be described as

    J. reserved.

    K. unhappy.

    L. sociable.

    M. brave.

39. Based on the passage, which statement is true?

   A. Phileas Fogg is secretive.

   B. Phileas Fogg is knowledgeable about the world.

   C. Phileas Fogg is a world traveler.

   D. Phileas Fogg is unable to afford travel.

40. As used in the passage, the phrase *second sight* most likely means

   J. psychic ability.

   K. good eyesight.

   L. intelligence.

   M. experience.

41. The overall tone of the passage is

   A. lighthearted.

   B. somber.

   C. critical.

   D. harsh.

42. Based on the passage, we can infer that the author will be telling a story about Phileas Fogg's

   J. wealth.

   K. friends.

   L. travels.

   M. reputation.

Questions 43–46 are based on the following passage.

PASSAGE 8

Up until the 1970s, the Brontosaurus was one of the most popular dinosaurs around, right alongside the Tyrannosaurus Rex. It was easily identified by its four legs, large cylindrical body, long neck, swooping tail, and small head. It even made it into pop culture, appearing in cartoons like *The Flintstones*, The Bronto-

Line saurus was one of the most prominent "thunder lizards." So what changed?

5   It turns out the Brontosaurus may never have existed at all. Paleontologist O.C. Marsh was attempting to reconstruct an Apatosaurus skeleton in 1877 when he mistakenly attached the skull of a Camarasaurus to the Apatosaurus's body and believed he'd discovered a new dinosaur altogether—which he christened the Brontosaurus. Over the years, the Brontosaurus grew in popularity, but some paleontologists remained unconvinced. Eventually, the skull mistake was identified and corrected as a result of the work of paleon-

10 tologists at the Carnegie Museum—and suddenly, the mighty Brontosaurus was no more.

43. Which of the following is the main idea of the passage?

   A. Mistakes can create decades of "conventional wisdom" that eventually turn out to be untrue.

   B. We don't know as much about dinosaurs as we think we do.

   C. All dinosaur-related discoveries are suspect.

   D. The Brontosaurus was very popular.

44. Who was most responsible for the myth of the Brontosaurus?

   J. *The Flintstones*

   K. Carnegie Museum

   L. O.C. Marsh

   M. None of these

45. A good title for this passage might be

   A. "Finding the Apatosaurus."

   B. "What Happened to the Brontosaurus?"

   C. "Paleontology Today."

   D. "Return of the Brontosaurus."

46. According to the passage, what kind of skull was attached to the wrong body?

   J. Brontosaurus

   K. Tyrannosaurus Rex

   L. Camarasaurus

   M. Apatosaurus

Questions 47–50 are based on the following passage.

PASSAGE 9

Tom presented himself before Aunt Polly, who was sitting by an open window in a pleasant rearward apartment, which was bedroom, breakfast-room, dining-room, and library, combined. The balmy summer air, the restful quiet, the odor of the flowers, and the drowsing murmur of the bees had had their effect, and
Line she was nodding over her knitting—for she had no company but the cat, and it was asleep in her lap. Her
5 spectacles were propped up on her gray head for safety. She had thought that of course Tom had deserted long ago, and she wondered at seeing him place himself in her power again in this intrepid way. He said: "Mayn't I go and play now, aunt?"

"What, a'ready? How much have you done?"

"It's all done, aunt."

10 "Tom, don't lie to me—I can't bear it."

"I ain't, aunt; it is all done."

Aunt Polly placed small trust in such evidence. She went out to see for herself; and she would have been content to find twenty percent of Tom's statement true. When she found the entire fence whitewashed, and not only whitewashed but elaborately coated and recoated, and even a streak added to the ground, her
15 astonishment was almost unspeakable.

—from *The Adventures of Tom Sawyer* by Mark Twain

47. As used in the passage, the word *balmy* most likely means

  A. chilly.

  B. chaotic.

  C. hostile.

  D. pleasant.

48. What has Aunt Polly asked Tom to do?

  J. Clean the house

  K. Go outside

  L. Help with knitting

  M. Paint the fence

49. From the passage it is clear that

  A. Aunt Polly trusts Tom.

  B. Aunt Polly does not believe Tom.

  C. Tom always does what he's asked.

  D. Tom enjoys painting.

50. In the phrase "such evidence," the author is conveying what tone?

  J. Sarcastic

  K. Optimistic

  L. Angry

  M. Excited

WRITTEN EXPRESSION
50 Questions—30 Minutes

Turn to the Written Expression section of your answer sheet to answer the questions in this section.

Directions: This is a test of how well you can find mistakes in writing.

- For the questions with mistakes in spelling, capitalization, and punctuation, choose the answer with the same letter as the line containing the mistake.

- For the questions with mistakes in usage and expression, choose the answer with the same letter as the line containing the mistake, or choose the word, phrase, or sentence that is better than the others.

- When there is no mistake or no change needed, select the last answer choice.

---

1. A. dictionery
   B. tragic
   C. vintage
   D. surprise
   E. *(No mistakes)*

2. J. vacation
   K. discovery
   L. collide
   M. patience
   N. *(No mistakes)*

3. A. fortress
   B. obtane
   C. complete
   D. interview
   E. *(No mistakes)*

4. J. invention
   K. coffee
   L. perswade
   M. employer
   N. *(No mistakes)*

5. A. disscuss
   B. manager
   C. exam
   D. advisory
   E. *(No mistakes)*

6. J. fortune
   K. traffic
   L. intrude
   M. messinger
   N. *(No mistakes)*

7. A. referee
   B. amature
   C. against
   D. believe
   E. *(No mistakes)*

8. J. cancellashun
   K. invest
   L. remark
   M. mall
   N. *(No mistakes)*

9. A. wander

B. mygrate

C. functional

D. disappear

E. (No mistakes)

10. J. mountain

K. progress

L. batter

M. profit

N. (No mistakes)

11. A. Lourdes is going to College

B. at Outback University, which

C. is located in Australia.

D. (No mistakes)

12. J. The Mississippi river travels southward

K. toward the Gulf of Mexico

L. and passes through many states along the way.

M. (No mistakes)

13. A. Jovan couldn't wait to have lunch

B. at the new Chinese Restaurant

C. on the corner of Ridge Street and Dey Road.

D. (No mistakes)

14. J. Anthony and I are planning a nice dinner at the steak restaurant

K. to celebrate valentine's day; we're planning to watch

L. the movie *Shrek* after dinner.

M. (No mistakes)

15. A. You just can't beat a cold drink

B. or a few scoops of Ben and Jerry's

C. on a scorching-hot Summer day.

D. (No mistakes)

16. J. Mrs. Samson said that Archie,

K. her sister's third cousin, used to

L. live across the street from Taylor Swift.

M. (No mistakes)

17. A. The astronauts aboard the Apollo rocket

B. said that the moon looked much different in Space

C. than it did from on the ground.

D. (No mistakes)

18. J. Angel's so smart because he reads *Time* magazine

K. and the Newspaper in the morning

L. before he even gets to school.

M. (No mistakes)

19. A. Saoirse accompanied her mother

B. on a visit to father O'Reilly to

C. thank him for visiting her brother in the hospital.

D. (No mistakes)

20. J. The Dirt Road that wound through the woods

K. was just a few miles from Interstate 95,

L. which led to many major eastern cities.

M. (No mistakes)

Directions: For questions 21 and 22, choose the best way of expressing the idea.

21. **A.** Dario liked to tinker in his workshop and often came up with new product ideas.

    B. Dario, who liked to tinker in his workshop; he often came up with new product ideas.

    C. In his workshop, Dario liked to tinker, where he often came up with new product ideas.

    D. Often coming up with new product ideas, Dario liked to tinker in his workshop where he was.

22. **J.** The Garmin's house, their summer house in Maine, was built all month with a new bedroom by the carpenter.

    K. In Maine, a summer house of the Garmin's, the carpenter spent all month building it—a new bedroom.

    L. The carpenter spent all month building a new bedroom for the Garmins' summer house in Maine.

    M. A summer house, which is the Garmin's, had a new bedroom built onto it by the carpenter, who spent all month building it.

Directions: For questions 23–50, choose the best answer based on the following paragraphs. You may see additional errors beyond those in the underlined words and phrases of the paragraphs.

(1) Among the many scenic and storied lighthouses that still exist across the United States, there's one that stands above the rest—literally. (2) Cape Hatteras Lighthouse is America's tallest lighthouse, a 210-foot striped beacon to sailors and their sea vessels <u>since they were</u> first constructed in 1870. (3) It's located in a town called Buxton, on Hatteras Island—one of several islands that make up the Outer Banks along the coast of North Carolina. (4) <u>Obviously,</u> the current Cape Hatteras lighthouse is not the original; the original lighthouse was destroyed in 1862, during the Civil War. (5) Although the Cape Hatteras Lighthouse is the tallest in America, it currently ranks only 29th tallest in the world—it's dwarfed by the mammoth 436-foot Jeddah Lighthouse in Saudi Arabia.

23. What is the best way to write the underlined part of sentence 2?

    A. when she was

    B. when he were

    C. since it was

    D. *(No change)*

24. What is the best way to write the underlined part of sentence 4?

    J. Therefore,

    K. Interestingly,

    L. In contrast,

    M. *(No change)*

(1) Like many Impressionist painters working in France during the mid-to-late 19th century, Edgar Degas attempted to capture a fleeting moment in time on canvas. (2) Defined as an artistic movement in which painters tried to recreate the changing light and colors of a particular place and time, Impressionism featured heavy dabs of color painted with <u>bold, swift</u> strokes and subject matter rooted in nature. (3) Instead of painting the garden parties and floral landscapes embraced by his contemporaries, Degas preferred to paint a wide spectrum of human subjects. (4) Although best known for his depiction of <u>dancers especially</u> behind-the-scenes glimpses of ballerinas rehearsing or warming up backstage, he also painted everyday scenes of working-class Parisian life at racetracks and cafes.

25. What is the best way to write the underlined part of sentence 2?

    A. bold swift

    B. bold; swift

    C. bold, Swift

    D. *(No change)*

26. What is the best way to write the underlined part of sentence 4?

    J. dancers. Especially

    K. dancers, especially

    L. dancers: especially

    M. *(No change)*

(1) When we think of the fastest members of the animal kingdom, mammals often come to mind. (2) <u>Indeed,</u> cheetahs can sprint at over 70 mph, and greyhounds have been clocked at 46 mph. (3) A more unlikely candidate, however, claims the title of the fastest creature on the <u>Planet</u>—the peregrine falcon. (4) After soaring high above its prey, the peregrine falcon plunges into a hunting dive with ever-increasing velocity and speeds topping 200 mph. (5) Known as the *stoop*, this dizzying maneuver not only makes the peregrine falcon a highly effective predator, but also allows this bird of prey to attain record speeds during its free-falling descent.

27. What is the best way to write the underlined part of sentence 2?

    A. Nonetheless,

    B. Conversely,

    C. Subsequently,

    D. *(No change)*

28. What is the best way to write the underlined part of sentence 3?

    J. Galaxy

    K. planet

    L. Hemisphere

    M. *(No change)*

(1) Described as the most famous diamond in the world, the Hope Diamond is housed in the <u>Smithsonian Natural History museum</u> in Washington, D.C. (2) The Hope Diamond was formed about 1.1 billion years ago and was first discovered in India during the seventeenth century. (3) Pear-shaped and uncommonly large, the diamond is the size of a walnut with a brilliant, deep-blue color attributed to traces of boron found within its crystal structure. (4) Since its founding, the diamond has frequently changed hands as it traveled from India to France and Britain before reaching its final destination in the United States. (5) Legends of a supposed curse on those who have worn or owned the Hope Diamond <u>abound</u>, but these stories of troubles and misfortune have never been proven.

29. What is the best way to write the underlined part of sentence 1?

A. Smithsonian Natural History Museum

B. Smithsonian natural history museum

C. smithsonian natural history museum

D. *(No change)*

30. What is the best way to write the underlined part of sentence 5?

J. abounds

K. abounded

L. a bound

M. *(No change)*

(1) There are few more economically challenging events in American history than the Great Depression. (2) The Great Depression, which followed the stock market crash of 1929 and lasted until 1941, adversely affected the entire global economy. (3) <u>Million's</u> of people lost their jobs and livelihoods as a result of the Great Depression, and thousands of banks and tens of thousands of business failed during this time period. (4) It is estimated that the national <u>Unemployment Rate</u> in the United States rose to 25% or more, depending on analytical metrics used. (5) No demographic group was spared from this crisis—rich and poor, urban and rural dwellers, and young and old were all hit hard by this tragic event.

31. What is the best way to write the underlined portion of sentence 3?

A. Millions

B. millions

C. Millions'

D. *(No change)*

32. What is the best way to write the underlined portion of sentence 4?

J. Unemployment rate

K. unemployment rate

L. unemployment Rate

M. *(No change)*

(1) Few treats are as beloved among individuals both young and old as s'mores. (2) This popular and delicious snack, often made around campfires, typically consists of marshmallow and chocolate sandwiched between two graham crackers. (3) To make a classic s'more, the <u>marshmallow; is heated</u> over a fire and smashed against the chocolate covered graham cracker, and the chocolate melts from the heat of the marshmallow. (4) Once the other graham cracker is placed over the marshmallow and chocolate this gooey treat is ready to enjoy. (5) There's even a nationally recognized "National S'Mores Day."

33. What is the best way to write the underlined portion of sentence 3?

    A. marshmallow. Is heated

    B. marshmallow is heated

    C. marshmallow is, heated

    D. (*No change*)

34. Choose the best final sentence to add to this paragraph.

    J. My favorite snack is popcorn covered in lots of melted butter.

    K. Some people prefer eating trail mix when camping.

    L. The commemorative day occurs on August 10th of each year.

    M. Do you enjoy campfires?

(1) A trip to <u>new york city</u> would not be complete without a visit to Central Park. (2) This sprawling oasis in the heart of the Big Apple consists of approximately 843 acres of <u>lawns, lakes, trees, and walkways.</u> (3) The initial design for the current incarnation of Central Park was conceptualized by famed landscape architect Frederick Law Olmstead. (4) Did you know that Central Park is the most visited park in the United States? (5) The park receives approximately 40 million visitors each year, and individuals from all over the world flock to the park to check out its beauty.

35. What is the best way to write the underlined portion of sentence 1?

    A. New York city

    B. New York City

    C. New york city

    D. (*No change*)

36. What is the best way to write the underlined portion of sentence 2?

    J. lawns lakes. Trees and walkways

    K. lawns lakes trees and walkways

    L. lawns; lakes trees; and walkways

    M. (*No change*)

(1) Plenty of time and attention is given to the largest and most impressive bodies of water on Earth, including the major oceans and Great Lakes. (2) However, have you ever heard of Roe River? (3) Roe River, which runs between the Missouri River and Giant Springs in Great Falls, Montana, is recognized by the <u>(Guinness Book of World Records)</u> as the world's shortest river. (4) Roe River is a humble 201 feet at its longest constant point, and ranges approximately 6-8 feet in depth. (5) In contrast, the <u>shortest</u> river in the world is the Amazon River, which runs for a staggering 4,345 miles.

37. What is the best way to write the underlined portion of sentence 3?

    A. *Guinness Book of World Records*

    B. "Guinness Book of World Records"

    C. Guinness Book of World Records

    D. (*No change*)

38. What is the best way to write the underlined portion of sentence 5?

    J. coldest

    K. ugliest

    L. longest

    M. (*No change*)

(1) Root beer, a popular and tasty North American beverage, has an interesting history. (2) This soft drink, which <u>will be traditionally made</u> using the root of the sassafras tree for years, was actually used for medicinal purposes by indigenous Native American people. (3) Following the Food and Drug Administration (FDA) ban of sassafras in commercial food and beverage products in 1960, many root beers started to be made using artificial flavoring. (4) Today, there is a wide variety of commercially available variants of root beer, and it is now produced in every state in <u>America?</u> (5) Although its origins can be traced to North America, where root beer's popularity is greatest, root beer is currently produced and sold in countries throughout Europe and Asia.

39. What is the best way to write the underlined portion of sentence 2?

A. have being traditionally making

B. is being traditionally make

C. has traditionally been made

D. (*No change*)

40. What is the best way to write the underlined portion of sentence 4?

J. America.

K. America;

L. America

M. (*No change*)

(1) It's a sad truth of history that collectively we often learn from mistakes. (2) The issues of worker safety <u>besides</u> employer accountability came under focus following the experience of the "Radium Girls." (3) The Radium Girls were a group of female <u>factory worker</u> who were tasked with painting watch dials in the early 20th century. (4) Although they were originally told that the paint was completely harmless, it actually contained deadly amounts of radium. (5) The incident helped to advance the labor rights movement, and in the wake of the unfortunate event industrial safety standards across the nation were improved.

41. What is the best way to write the underlined portion of sentence 2?

A. and

B. or

C. within

D. (*No change*)

42. What is the best way to write the underlined portion of sentence 3?

J. factory work

K. factory workers

L. factory working

M. (*No change*)

(1) One of the <u>worlds</u> most popular and widely played board games is also one of the oldest in existence. (2) Backgammon is a game played by two opponents in which pieces are moved based on dice rolls and the winner is the player who is able to remove all of their pieces from the board first. (3) The precise origin of the game is difficult to ascertain, but research suggests that versions of the game have existed for at least 5,000 years, stemming back to ancient Persia. (4) Today, scientists <u>is investigating</u> the implementation of computer software and artificial intelligence to challenge the best human players at the game.

43. What is the best way to write the underlined portion of sentence 1?

A. worlds'

B. World's

C. world's

D. (*No change*)

44. What is the best way to write the underlined portion of sentence 4?

J. are investigating

K. they're investigating

L. won't investigate

M. (*No change*)

(1) Harvard University, in Cambridge, Massachusetts <u>was established</u> in 1636, and originally primarily served to train clergymen. (2) The university is named after John Harvard, an English minister and one of the original benefactors of the university. (3) Each year, tens of thousands of elite students study and train across the university's eleven separate academic units. (4) Among Harvard's illustrious graduates are eight US presidents, more than 100 Nobel laureates, and several billionaires.

45. Choose the best first sentence to add to this paragraph.

A. Where do you plan to go to college after you graduate from high school?

B. Did you know that one of the most prestigious universities in the United States is also the oldest?

C. What are some good reasons for deciding to earn a college degree?

D. Do you live close to Cambridge Massachusetts, in the northeastern region of the United States?

46. What is the best way to write the underlined portion of sentence 1?

J. will be established

K. will establish

L. will be establishing

M. (*No change*)

(1) People all around the world enjoy eating garlic. (2) It's a popular addition to <u>sauces, soups; and stews,</u> and its flavor and aroma is unmistakable for any other food. (3) However, did you know that eating garlic also has a variety of health <u>benefits!</u> (4) It has been argued that regularly consuming garlic as part of a healthy diet can combat illnesses like colds and the flu, and can even reduce the risk of heart disease. (5) Garlic also contains a wealth of vitamins and nutrients including vitamin C, vitamin B6, selenium, and fiber.

47. What is the best way to write the underlined portion of sentence 2?

A. sauces; soups and stews

B. sauces. Soups and stews

C. sauces, soups, and stews

D. (*No change*)

48. What is the best way to write the underlined portion of sentence 3?

J. benefits;

K. benefits.

L. benefits?

M. (*No change*)

(1) One of the most famous obelisks in the world is the <u>Washington monument</u>, located at the National Mall in Washington, DC. (2) An obelisk is a towering, four-sided narrow monument that tapers as it rises and is topped with a pyramid-like structure. (3) The Washington Monument stands approximately 554 feet tall and is comprised of marble, bluestone gneiss, and granite. (4) It's currently the <u>world's; tallest,</u> obelisk and stone structure, and was built to commemorate George Washington, the first President of the United States. (5) However, it's not the world's oldest obelisk, as examples from Ancient Egypt are still standing tall.

49. What is the best way to write the underlined portion of sentence 1?

   A. Washington Monument
   B. washington monument
   C. "Washington Monument"
   D. (*No change*)

50. What is the best way to write the underlined portion of sentence 4?

   J. world's, tallest
   K. world's tallest
   L. world's tallest;
   M. (*No change*)

MATHEMATICS

50 Questions—40 Minutes

Turn to the Mathematics section of your answer sheet to answer the questions in this section.

Directions: Read each question carefully, then solve the problem to find the correct answer.

---

1. The number 0.003 can also be represented by which of the following?

   A. $\dfrac{3}{10,000}$

   B. $\dfrac{3}{1,000}$

   C. $\dfrac{3}{100}$

   D. $\dfrac{3}{10}$

2. Which of the following is the equivalent of 3^3?

   J. 3×3

   K. $3 \times 3 \div 3$

   L. 27

   M. 30

3. What is the sum of $\dfrac{1}{2} + \dfrac{2}{4} + \dfrac{3}{3}$?

   A. 1

   B. 2

   C. $2\dfrac{1}{2}$

   D. 3

4. What is the sum of $(3 \times 3) + (4 \times 4) + (5 \times 5)$?

   J. 24

   K. 50

   L. 60

   M. 345

5. Which of the following represents the reduced form for 1.6?

   A. $1\dfrac{6}{10}$

   B. $1\dfrac{3}{5}$

   C. $\dfrac{16}{10}$

   D. $\dfrac{32}{20}$

6. Which of the following is a prime number?

   J. 27

   K. 28

   L. 29

   M. 30

7. The fraction $\dfrac{8}{4}$ can be reduced to which of the following?

   A. 84

   B. $\dfrac{1}{2}$

   C. $\dfrac{4}{8}$

   D. 2

8. Which of the following is the product of 16 and 4?

   J. 2

   K. 4

   L. 20

   M. 64

9. Which of the following is the equivalent of 6^7?

   A. 6×7

   B. $7 \times 6 \times 6 \times 6 \times 6 \times 6 \times 6$

   C. $6 \times 6 \times 6 \times 6 \times 6 \times 6 \times 6$

   D. $(6 + 6) \times 7$

10. The fraction $2\frac{6}{1,000}$ can be expressed as a decimal by which of the following?

    J. 0.0026

    K. 2.006

    L. 26.1000

    M. 26,000.000

11. Ruliann's accountant's fee for preparing a tax report for a customer is 40% more than his closest competitor. If the competitor charges $300, what is this accountant's fee?

    A. $360

    B. $400

    C. $420

    D. $500

12. Carl has collected 27 of the 32 available Captain Cosmos comic books, 19 of the 24 available Galactic General comic books, and 21 of the 23 available Larry the Laser comic books. If Carl wanted to acquire the missing comics from each series he collects, how many comic books would he need to buy?

    J. 7

    K. 67

    L. 79

    M. Not given

13. The school library recently relocated to a new building on campus. There are many new book-shelves in the new library. Each bookshelf holds 245 books. The library has 12 bookshelves that are 100 percent full and one bookshelf that is $\frac{4}{5}$ full. How many books are in the new library?

    A. 2,940

    B. 2,989

    C. 3,136

    D. 294,000

14. Anatoli's digital camera normally holds 200 images. If Anatoli sets his camera to take extra-high-quality pictures, his camera holds only 40 pictures. Anatoli has already saved 100 normal images on his camera, but he wants to take as many pictures as possible of the sunset over the bay. How many extra-high-quality pictures can Anatoli hold on his camera in addition to the 100 normal images he's already saved?

    J. 10

    K. 20

    L. 30

    M. 40

15. If Jasmine spends $3\frac{1}{4}$ hours per day practicing piano and she practices 4 days per week, how many hours does Jasmine practice piano each week?

   A. $12\frac{1}{4}$

   B. $12\frac{3}{4}$

   C. 13

   D. 14

16. A centimeter is what part of a kilometer?

   J. $\dfrac{1}{100,000}$

   K. $\dfrac{1}{10,000}$

   L. $\dfrac{1}{1,000}$

   M. $\dfrac{1}{100}$

17. Find the area of a rectangle with a length of 176 feet and a width of 79 feet.

   A. 13,304 sq. ft.

   B. 13,804 sq. ft.

   C. 13,854 sq. ft.

   D. 13,904 sq. ft.

18. Mr. Loewen makes a weekly salary of $250 plus 7% commission on his sales. What will his income be for a week in which he made sales totaling $1,250?

   J. $87.50

   K. $267.50

   L. $327.50

   M. $337.50

19. Complete the following statement:
   $3(\underline{\hspace{1cm}} \times 4) - 20 = 280$.

   A. 5

   B. 5×2

   C. 5^2

   D. 5^3

20. Find the area of a triangle whose dimensions are: $b = 14$ inches, $h = 20$ inches.

   J. 140 sq. in.

   K. 208 sq. in.

   L. 280 sq. in.

   M. 288 sq. in.

Directions: For questions 21–40, read each problem and find the answer.

21. If $x = 2\frac{2}{5}$, the reciprocal of x equals

    A. $\frac{5}{12}$

    B. $\frac{5}{4}$

    C. $\frac{12}{5}$

    D. $\frac{5}{2}$

22. The product of $\frac{7}{16}$ and a number x is 1. The number is

    J. 1

    K. $1\frac{7}{16}$

    L. $\frac{16}{7}$

    M. $\frac{31}{14}$

23. $\dfrac{\frac{1}{x}+1}{1+\frac{1}{x}}$ is equivalent to

    A. 1

    B. $\frac{1}{x}$

    C. $\frac{1}{x}+2$

    D. $1 + x$

24. $\dfrac{\frac{5}{12}-\frac{7}{24}}{\frac{1}{2}-\frac{3}{8}} =$

    J. $\frac{1}{2}$

    K. $\frac{3}{8}$

    L. 1

    M. 8

25. In the formula $L = \frac{3}{4}bxh$, if $b = 2$, $x = 7$, and $h = \frac{1}{2}$, L equals

    A. $\frac{21}{8}$

    B. $\frac{21}{4}$

    C. $\frac{21}{2}$

    D. $\frac{7x}{4}$

26.

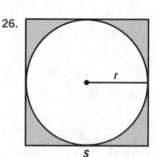

The square above has a side 4" long. The area of the shaded portion is approximately

    J. $\frac{22}{7}$ sq. in.

    K. $3\frac{3}{7}$ sq. in.

    L. $4\frac{3}{7}$ sq. in.

    M. 16 sq. in.

27. The ratio of teachers to students in a certain school is 1:14. If there are fourteen teachers in the school, how many students are there?

    A. 14

    B. 176

    C. 196

    D. 206

28. Evaluate $\dfrac{10^4}{100^5}$.

   J. $\dfrac{1}{10}$

   K. $\dfrac{1}{1,000}$

   L. $\dfrac{1}{100,000}$

   M. $\dfrac{1}{1,000,000}$

29. If x is an odd whole number, which of the following also represents an odd number?

   A. $2x + 1$

   B. $x - 2$

   C. $4x - 3$

   D. All of the above

30. The sum of 4 hours 17 minutes, 3 hours 58 minutes, 45 minutes, and 7 hours 12 minutes is

   J. 14 hours, 50 minutes

   K. 15 hours, 32 minutes

   L. 16 hours, 12 minutes

   M. 17 hours, 32 minutes

31. If every car that travels along Highway 27 has four wheels, and there are 72 cars driving on Highway 27, how many wheels are touching the road on Highway 27?

   A. 54

   B. 108

   C. 144

   D. 288

32. Ted can text 30 characters in 10 seconds. How many characters can Ted text in 2 minutes?

   J. 300

   K. 360

   L. 600

   M. 3,600

33. Aunt Noelle has 7 dozen antique ornaments for her Christmas tree. She anticipates needing a total of 200 ornaments to finish decorating her tree. How many ornaments should Aunt Noelle purchase at the antique fair to reach her goal of 200 antique ornaments for her tree?

   A. 84

   B. 96

   C. 116

   D. 124

34. Darrius and Roxanne are planning to paint the concession stand at school. They have four walls to paint. Each wall is exactly the same size. The walls are each 12 feet long and 10 feet high. How many square feet of walls should they plan to paint if they are going to paint all four walls?

   J. 120 sq. ft.

   K. 240 sq. ft.

   L. 480 sq. ft.

   M. 1,200 sq. ft.

35. The penguins at the zoo eat 36,500 pounds of fish each year. How many pounds of fish do the penguins eat each day?

   A. 100

   B. 365

   C. 1,000

   D. Not given

Use the following chart for Questions 36 and 37:

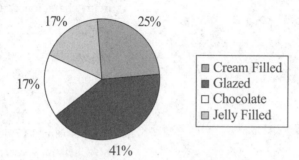

36. At Doodle's Donuts, the most popular item on the menu is Doodle's Dozen. The chart shows the typical distribution of donuts in each Doodle's Dozen that is sold. According to the chart, the single most widely consumed donut in Doodle's Dozen is which of the following?

    J. Cream Filled

    K. Glazed

    L. Chocolate

    M. Jelly Filled

37. Based on the information in the chart, Doodle's Dozen includes three of which type of donut?

    A. Cream Filled

    B. Glazed

    C. Chocolate

    D. Jelly Filled

Use the following graph for Questions 38 and 39:

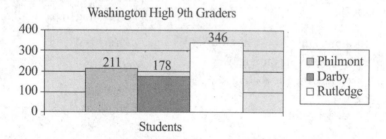

38. The chart above shows the feeder schools from which current ninth graders at Washington High School came. If these are the only feeder schools that sent students to the ninth grade at Washington High School, which school sent the largest percentage of current Washington ninth graders?

    J. Philmont

    K. Darby

    L. Rutledge

    M. Not given

39. Based on the information in the chart above, Washington High School currently has how many ninth graders?

    A. 178

    B. 211

    C. 346

    D. 735

40. The pie chart below illustrates the number and types of portraits at the Hudson Museum. Based on the information in the chart, which of the following is true of the number of portraits in the museum?

The Hudson Museum Portraits

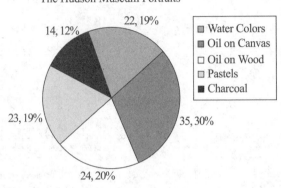

J. There are fewer than 100 portraits.

K. There are 100 portraits.

L. There are more than 100 portraits.

M. Not given

Directions: For the following questions, estimate the answer in your head. No scratch work is allowed. Do *NOT* try to compute exact answers.

---

41. The closest estimate of 46,922 + 32,090 is _____ .

A. 70,000

B. 75,000

C. 80,000

D. 85,000

42. The closest estimate of 7,988 ÷ 397 is _____ .

J. 20

K. 25

L. 200

M. 220

43. Tamir decides to skate along the boardwalk at the local beach. He can skate at 6 miles per hour. If the boardwalk is 15 miles long, how long did it take him to complete the trip?

A. 90 minutes

B. 120 minutes

C. 150 minutes

D. 180 minutes

44. Coach Lefebvre has a total of 653 wins in her career, and she has coached for 40 years. About how many wins has she averaged per year?

J. 13

K. 16

L. 19

M. 24

45. The closest estimate of $148 + 153.5 + 146 + 154.1 + 151 + 145.9 + 149 + 153 + 152.5 + 147.75$ is _____ .

   A. 1,375

   B. 1,400

   C. 1,500

   D. 1,575

46. $\frac{17}{30}$ is greater than

   J. $\frac{7}{8}$

   K. $\frac{9}{20}$

   L. $\frac{9}{11}$

   M. $\frac{22}{25}$

47. One millimeter equals what part of a meter?

   A. $\frac{1}{100}$

   B. $\frac{1}{1,000}$

   C. $\frac{1}{10,000}$

   D. $\frac{1}{100,000}$

48. A baseball team won 18 games, which was 40% of its season. How many games did the team lose?

   J. 25

   K. 27

   L. 32

   M. 45

49. If $-2 < q < -1$, which of the following is true?

   A. $q =$

   B. $q > -1$

   C. $q > 0$

   D. $q > -2$

50. Which pair of values for x and $\square$ will make the following statement true?

$$2x \,\square\, 8$$

   J. $(-3, >)$

   K. $(0, <)$

   L. $(4, >)$

   M. $(6, <)$

ABILITY

50 Questions—32 Minutes

Figure Classification

Turn to the Ability section of your answer sheet to answer the questions in this section.

Directions: In questions 1–20, the first three figures are alike in certain ways. Choose the answer choice that corresponds to the first three figures.

1.

   A.   B.   C.   D.   E.

2.

   J.   K.   L.   M.   N.

3.

   A.   B.   C.   D.   E.

4.

   J.   K. L. M. N.

5.

A.　　　B.　　　C.　　　D.　　　E.

6.

J.　　　K.　　　L.　　　M.　　　N.

7.

A.　　　B.　　　C.　　　D.　　　E.

8.

J.　　　K.　　　L.　　　M.　　　N.

9.

A.　　　B.　　　C.　　　D.　　　E.

10.

J.　　　K.　　　L.　　　M.　　　N.

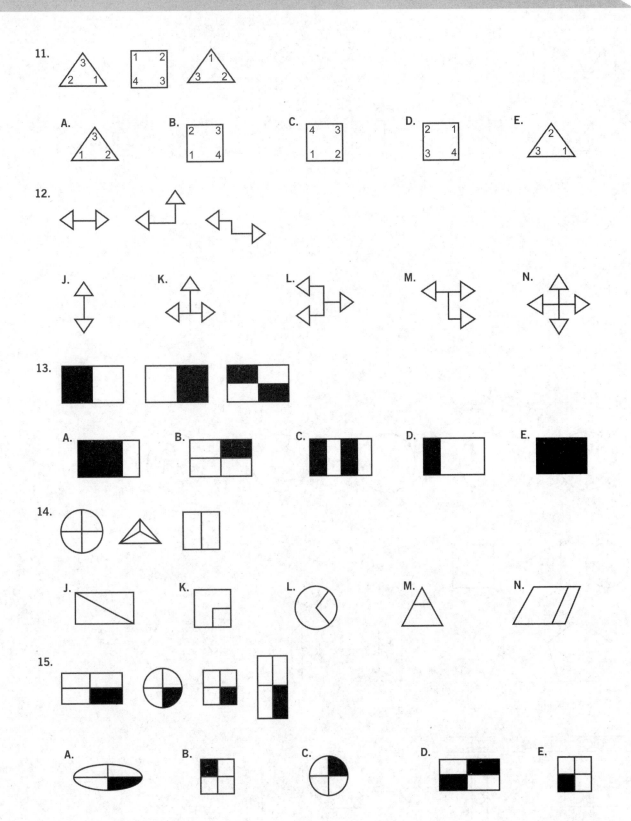

11.

12.

13.

14.

15.

Figure Matrices

Directions: In questions 1–20, find the figure that completes the matrix.

1.

A.

B.

C.

D.

E.

2.

J.

K.

L.

M.

N.

3.

A.

B.

C.

D.

E.

4.

J.   K.   L.   M.   N.

5.

A.   B.   C.   D.   E.

6.

J.   K.   L.   M.   N.

7.

A.   B.   C.   D.   E.

8.

J.   K.   L.   M.   N.

9.

A.   B.   C.   D.   E.

10.

J.   K.   L.   M.   N.

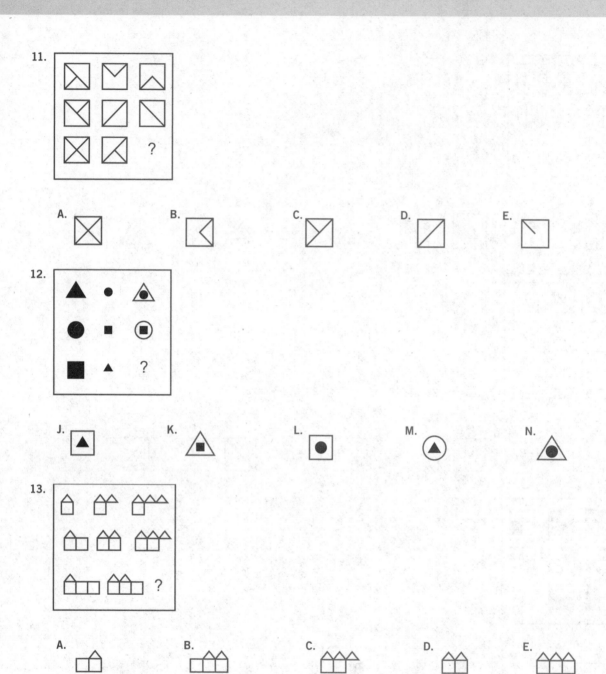

11.

A.

B.

C.

D.

E.

12.

J.

K.

L.

M.

N.

13.

A.

B.

C.

D.

E.

14.

J.   K.   L.   M.   N.

15.

A.   B.   C.   D.   E.

16.

J.   K.   L.   M.   N.

17.

A.

B.

C.

D.

E.

18.

J.

K.

L.

M.

N.

19.

A.

B.

C.

D.

E.

20.

J.

X X

K.

X X X

L. ☐

X X X

M. ☐

X X

N. ☐

Paper Folding

Directions: In questions 1–10, look at the top row to see how a square piece of paper is folded and where holes are punched into it. Then look at the bottom row to decide which answer choice shows how the paper will look when it is completely unfolded.

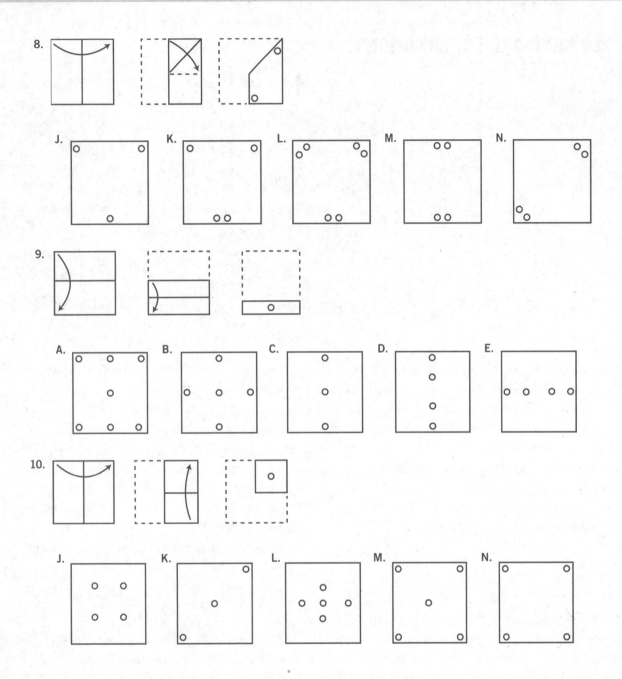

ANSWER KEYS AND EXPLANATIONS
Reading

1. C	11. C	21. A	31. B	41. A
2. L	12. K	22. L	32. M	42. L
3. B	13. D	23. C	33. C	43. A
4. L	14. K	24. L	34. K	44. L
5. A	15. B	25. B	35. A	45. B
6. K	16. L	26. L	36. L	46. L
7. D	17. C	27. B	37. C	47. D
8. J	18. J	28. K	38. J	48. M
9. C	19. B	29. D	39. B	49. B
10. J	20. J	30. J	40. J	50. J

1. **The correct answer is C.** The passage shows that the author's father is proud of his son's accomplishments. In paragraph 3, the fact that he is "beaming" indicates that he is happy and has a positive expression on his face.

2. **The correct answer is L.** To answer a "detail" question like this one, you might go back and refresh your memory by re-reading the part of the passage that describes what happened when the author met his mother's family. In paragraph 4, we are told that the author received gifts of money and yams from the family members who greeted him.

3. **The correct answer is B.** We can infer from the passage that the author is able to relate to his father in a new way now that he has entered manhood. Because the author does not discuss his relationship with his father before this ceremony, we don't have enough information to conclude that the father was not proud of his son before this (choice A). Nor do we have enough information for choice C to be a logical inference from this passage. Choice D is incorrect because the author is clearly very proud and honored to be taking part in this family tradition.

4. **The correct answer is L.** In the first sentence, the author identifies the village of Elu, which is the

capital of a region (Ohafia) and part of the country Nigeria.

5. **The correct answer is A.** In the second paragraph, the author refers to "many rituals" and calls this particular ritual the "first step," suggesting that there are others yet to come. At the end of the passage, he uses the phrase "emerging into manhood," which also suggests that the process is not yet complete.

6. **The correct answer is K.** The passage is about the process of this particular ritual as one step in the author's path. "My Journey into Manhood" is the title that best embraces the main idea of the passage. Choices J and L are too broad, and choice M is too narrow, given that the money and yams are one small part of the ceremony.

7. **The correct answer is D.** The phrase "made ends meet" is a common way of saying that a budget is balanced. In other words, when people make ends meet, they are making their money last long enough to pay all expenses. The last sentence of the first paragraph gives the context clue about the phrase.

8. **The correct answer is J.** Barrett knew he needed more customers, and the first paragraph indicates that he had just enough customers to balance his budget; it is implied that he was not making much,

if any, profit. In order to increase his profit, he needed more paying customers.

9. **The correct answer is C.** *Ambitious* means "having a desire to be successful," and based on the information given about how Barrett is implementing changes to to make his business more successful, the reader can infer that he is ambitious. There is not enough information in the passage to justify the other options.

10. **The correct answer is J.** If Barrett's strategy to attract customers doesn't work, then he will be doing the same amount of work while making a fraction of the money. He would need to bring in more customers than usual for the strategy to pay off. The passage says that Barrett had put time into researching business strategies, so choices K and M are incorrect. There is nothing in the passage to suggest that his costs will increase (choice L).

11. **The correct answer is C.** The main idea of the passage is an exploration of accidental inventions—"ingenious advances that were initially unintended but eventually served to benefit mankind." The passage illustrates this topic by providing two examples—the microwave oven and penicillin, both described as inventions that are the direct result of an accident or mistake. The passage describes penicillin as essential but does not describe the microwave that way, so choice A is incorrect. Choices B and D are incorrect because there is no indication that a "professional inventor" was required or that both the microwave and penicillin would have eventually been invented, even if the accidents mentioned in the passage hadn't occurred.

12. **The correct answer is K.** As described in the passage, the phrase "an unexpected detour" refers to a line of scientific curiosity by an innovative thinker (like Spencer or Fleming) that is disrupted by an unintended event but ultimately leads to a new innovation. For example, Fleming's unexpected detour led to the discovery of penicillin.

13. **The correct answer is D.** *Inhibited* can mean "shy," but given the context, it's apparent that *inhibited* is being used as a verb, so choices B and C are

incorrect. The best meaning of *inhibited* in this case is "prevented," given that penicillin is referred to as an "antibiotic," meaning it prevents bacteria and disease.

14. **The correct answer is K.** The second paragraph of the passage focuses on Percy Spencer's accidental discovery of the microwave.

15. **The correct answer is B.** A title for this passage should include the idea that some accidents happen to be lucky. The title "Happy Accidents" (choice B) does exactly that. All the rest are either too generic or too incomplete to be the correct answer.

16. **The correct answer is L.** The passage talks about how some accidents can spark creativity—not necessarily that all accidents are good or will lead to unexpected discoveries, but that they should be embraced when they do. In other words, don't be afraid to make mistakes.

17. **The correct answer is C.** "The Possible Effects of Electronic Communication on Communication Skills of Computer Users" is the best title because the passage directly addresses the social skills of computer users and the ways that those skills are affected by communicating electronically, via email and instant messaging.

18. **The correct answer is J.** The phrase implies that the more something is practiced by someone, the better that person becomes at whatever they practice. The next-to-last sentence mentions increased communications, so it is implied that "practice makes perfect" refers to that increase in communications.

19. **The correct answer is B.** If someone is hiding their communication flaws behind an anonymous name or persona, the passage suggests that they are avoiding working on their own true communication skills.

20. **The correct answer is J.** With the phrase "practice makes perfect," the author is suggesting that the more people interact online, the better they'll get. Therefore, frequency affects electronic

communication skills more than any one type of communication.

21. **The correct answer is A.** For this question, you have to rely on the passage itself. The passage discusses the idea that the possibility of "hiding behind [one's] anonymity" online causes people to change their personalities. Neither choice B nor choice C is mentioned in the passage, so you can eliminate those. The passage also doesn't say that people will forget how to communicate face-to-face (just that these skills may decline), so choice D is incorrect as well.

22. **The correct answer is L.** An adage is a motto or old saying.

23. **The correct answer is C.** There is very little that can be considered real about reality TV. The author contends that this is because producers and directors have a huge influence on the things that are filmed and televised, meaning it couldn't possibly be an accurate reflection of real-life events.

24. **The correct answer is L.** Someone who criticizes and points out flaws or weaknesses in something can be considered a critic of that thing.

25. **The correct answer is B.** The entire passage is about how "reality" shows don't contain much reality, so it is unlikely that the author would describe reality tv as authentic (choice A) or fantastic (choice D). The author states that reality shows are likely here to stay, so it would also be odd to call them fleeting (choice C).

26. **The correct answer is L.** The passage does not mention that reality TV stars are instructed to keep the details of the show secret. Remember to base your answer specifically on what is in the passage, not on what you may know or believe from outside sources.

27. **The correct answer is B.** The author debunks reality TV shows by calling them "staged," so it's likely that this is what the two types of shows would have in common.

28. **The correct answer is K.** *Bombarding* can mean "attacking" or "hitting," but in this context, it's more likely to mean "flooding," as the author does

not seem to be arguing that reality TV is harmful or dangerous to the viewers.

29. **The correct answer is D.** This passage focuses on Polynesian navigators' ability to guide their canoes without the benefit of charts or navigational tools, so the correct answer is the title that highlights this focus, "Early Polynesian Navigation."

30. **The correct answer is J.** The first paragraph states that the Polynesians made trips to New Zealand and Hawaii.

31. **The correct answer is B.** *Mariner* means "sailor" or "seaman."

32. **The correct answer is M.** The passage makes it clear that Polynesian navigators used the sun and stars to find their way, meaning they must have studied the movements of the stars. Therefore, the passage suggests that the Polynesians were astronomers as well as explorers.

33. **The correct answer is C.** The steering paddle was such an integral part of each journey that it was always given a personal name.

34. **The correct answer is K.** Dual canoes were often used for transpacific journeys because they could carry cargo such as food, water, and domestic animals, as well as passengers.

35. **The correct answer is A.** Polynesian navigators were skilled in using the sun and stars, as well as tidal trends and seabirds to guide their crafts.

36. **The correct answer is L.** The last sentence in the passage indicates that Polynesian legends state the name of the canoe, the hero who discovered a new island, and the name of the steering paddle used.

37. **The correct answer is C.** The context words here are *on the contrary* and *lavish*, so you know the correct choice will be the opposite of *lavish*. *Stingy* is the only option that fits this context.

38. **The correct answer is J.** The passage describes Phileas Fogg as avoiding talking to others, even when it comes to his own stories. *Reserved*, or detached, fits the characterization the best out of the options given. *Sociable* (choice L) means the opposite of how Fogg is presented in the passage,

so it is incorrect. *Unhappy* (choice K) and *brave* (choice M) are not supported by the passage.

39. **The correct answer is B.** The passage is concerned with trying to illustrate Phileas Fogg, but it presents conflicting information (he is wealthy but not greedy, he can answer complicated questions but doesn't seem to have left town, etc.), so there aren't many things that can be said definitively about Phileas Fogg. The only option that can be verified by the passage is that Phileas Fogg is very "familiar" with the world.

40. **The correct answer is J.** The author is humorously suggesting that Phileas Fogg must have special insight or psychic abilities in order to know the things he knows without having left the city recently.

41. **The correct answer is A.** The author/narrator is presenting information about Phileas Fogg in a comic way. The author is not especially critical of or harsh on Phileas Fogg but instead describes him and adds humorous theories ("second sight") about why he is the way he is and why he knows what he does.

42. **The correct answer is L.** The passage mentions Phileas Fogg's wealth, but it comes to focus on his travel (or apparent lack thereof). That context, along with the given title of the work from which the passage came, can help you infer that the author will continue talking about Phileas Fogg's travels.

43. **The correct answer is A.** Although the passage describes the popularity of the Brontosaurus (choice D), it is mainly about how our knowledge about the dinosaur has changed since O.C. Marsh's mistake was discovered.

44. **The correct answer is L.** The reference to *The Flintstones* television show (choice J) merely provided a cultural representation of the Brontosaurus, and the Carnegie Museum (choice K) helped correct the mistake.

45. **The correct answer is B.** Only the title "What Happened to the Brontosaurus?" does a good job of representing the main idea of the passage.

46. **The correct answer is L.** The second paragraph states that Marsh "mistakenly attached the skull of a Camarasaurus to the Apatosaurus's body."

47. **The correct answer is D.** The author is using positive, mild adjectives to describe the "restful" atmosphere, so you can infer that the adjective *balmy* is similarly positive. Because it's summer, choice A is incorrect. *Restful* makes choice B incorrect, and *hostile* (choice C) means "opposed or antagonistic," which does not accurately describe the atmosphere.

48. **The correct answer is M.** Although the author doesn't describe Tom's actual task until the final paragraph, the steps outlined describe painting. "Whitewashing" and "coating and recoating" are the key context words that tell you what Tom has been working on.

49. **The correct answer is B.** That Aunt Polly "would have been content to find twenty percent of Tom's statement true" suggests that she didn't expect any of it to be true. There is no information in the passage to suggest that Tom likes painting or that he always does what he's asked—and in fact, Aunt Polly's doubt suggests that he does not.

50. **The correct answer is J.** Although the author uses the word *evidence*, he is using it to suggest that, to Aunt Polly, Tom's word is the *opposite* of evidence.

Written Expression

1. A	11. A	21. A	31. A	41. A
2. N	12. J	22. L	32. K	42. K
3. B	13. B	23. C	33. B	43. C
4. L	14. K	24. K	34. L	44. J
5. A	15. C	25. D	35. B	45. B
6. M	16. M	26. K	36. M	46. M
7. B	17. B	27. D	37. A	47. C
8. J	18. K	28. K	38. L	48. L
9. B	19. B	29. A	39. C	49. A
10. N	20. J	30. M	40. J	50. K

1. **The correct answer is A.** The correct spelling is *dictionary*.

2. **The correct answer is N.** *(No mistakes)*

3. **The correct answer is B.** The correct spelling is *obtain*.

4. **The correct answer is L.** The correct spelling is *persuade*.

5. **The correct answer is A.** The correct spelling is *discuss*.

6. **The correct answer is M.** The correct spelling is *messenger*.

7. **The correct answer is B.** The correct spelling is *amateur*.

8. **The correct answer is J.** The correct spelling is *cancellation*.

9. **The correct answer is B.** The correct spelling is *migrate*.

10. **The correct answer is N.** *(No mistakes)*

11. **The correct answer is A.** The word *college* is capitalized only when included in a proper noun such as Boston College or Ithaca College.

12. **The correct answer is J.** The word *river* is capitalized when included as part of a proper noun such as "Mississippi River."

13. **The correct answer is B.** Although the name of a country's cuisine is capitalized, the word *restaurant* is not capitalized unless it is used to begin a sentence or is part of a proper name.

14. **The correct answer is K.** Holidays, because they are proper nouns, should be capitalized.

15. **The correct answer is C.** Names of seasons are not proper nouns and do not need capitalization.

16. **The correct answer is M.** *(No mistakes)*

17. **The correct answer is B.** *Space* needs no capitalization because it is a common noun, but related terms such as *Haley's Comet* or *Jupiter* should be capitalized because they are proper nouns.

18. **The correct answer is K.** The word *newspaper* is a common noun and would be capitalized only as part of a proper noun such as the "Baltimore Newspaper Publishing Company."

19. **The correct answer is B.** Words like *father* or *sister* require capitalization when used as part of (or in place of) a person's name, as in the cases of "Father Dowling" or "Sister Wendy."

20. **The correct answer is J.** Names of streets, roads, or avenues are to be capitalized, as in "Abbey Road" or "Penny Lane," but not when used as common nouns like "the dirt road" or "the winding country lane."

21. **The correct answer is A.** Choice A expresses the idea clearly with the correct punctuation.

22. **The correct answer is L.** Choice L most efficiently and effectively expresses the ideas in this sentence, without the unnecessary wordiness, redundancy, and confusion that makes the other choices incorrect.

23. **The correct answer is C.** As written, the underlined portion of the sentence incorrectly uses the plural pronoun *they* to replace the singular noun, *Cape Hatteras Lighthouse*. Choice C correctly uses the singular pronoun *it* to replace the singular noun.

24. **The correct answer is K.** As written, the passage makes an incorrect assumption that information about Cape Hatteras Lighthouse not being the original would be obvious to the reader. *Interestingly* (choice K) would be a more effective way to begin this sentence, given the context of the passage.

25. **The correct answer is D.** *(No change).* Both the words *bold* and *swift* are adjectives modifying the noun *strokes*. Since two adjectives are used together to modify one noun, the two adjectives must be separated with a comma.

26. **The correct answer is K.** Commas are needed to separate the phrase "especially behind-the-scenes glimpses of ballerinas rehearsing or warming up backstage" from the remainder of the sentence.

27. **The correct answer is D.** *(No change).* The word *Indeed* signifies that a similar idea to what was presented in the first sentence will follow in the next sentence. Choices A and B both suggest information that opposes what has already been stated, and choice C would indicate a cause-and-effect relationship.

28. **The correct answer is K.** The word *planet* is a common noun and would need capitalization only if used as part of a name, such as "Dwarf Planet Institute."

29. **The correct answer is A.** The word *museum* by itself is a common noun, but it requires capitalization when used as part of a proper noun naming a specific place. The other answer choices are incorrect since all four words in the name of the Smithsonian Natural History Museum must be capitalized.

30. **The correct answer is M.** *(No change).* No change is necessary to the sentence since the plural noun *Legends* takes a plural verb. Furthermore, the verb should be in present tense to match the rest of the sentence, ruling out choice K.

31. **The correct answer is A.** As written, the sentence contains an incorrect possessive form of *millions*. A possessive form is not required here, so choice A is correct. Choice B fails to capitalize the word, which should be done because it's at the beginning of a sentence. Choice C provides a possessive plural form that's incorrect for this sentence.

32. **The correct answer is K.** The underlined portion of the sentence incorrectly capitalizes these words. Choice K fixes this problem by using the correct lowercase form of "unemployment rate." Choices J and L also use incorrect capitalization, given the context of this sentence.

33. **The correct answer is B.** The sentence as written contains incorrect internal punctuation. A semicolon should be used to separate two independent clauses, which we don't have here. No internal punctuation is needed in this part of the sentence.

34. **The correct answer is L.** This paragraph ends with a statement about "National S'Mores Day" but doesn't provide any information about when it is. Choice L follows up on this thought by providing the date and is the most logical final sentence for this paragraph.

35. **The correct answer is B.** New York City is a proper noun, and it should always be capitalized.

36. **The correct answer is M.** *(No change).* Items in a simple list should be separated by commas, which the sentence as written does.

37. **The correct answer is A.** Book titles, like the *Guinness Book of World Records*, should always be italicized.

38. **The correct answer is L.** When looking to determine the appropriate word choice, context matters. We're told that the underlined word stands *in contrast* to the main topic of the paragraph—the

Roe River, the shortest river in the world. The logical contrast to the shortest river is the longest river, and the fact that we're told the length of the Amazon River is a good indication that *longest* is the correct word choice.

39. **The correct answer is C.** As written, the sentence incorrectly uses the future tense for an activity that has already been occurring. Choice C corrects this error.

40. **The correct answer is J.** As written, the sentence ends in a question mark, although no question is being posed; instead, it is a declaration that should end with a period.

41. **The correct answer is A.** Here, we're looking at two clearly related issues, and *besides* would indicate something "other than," which does not logically fit. The word *besides* should be replaced by the conjunction *and*.

42. **The correct answer is K.** As written, the singular noun *worker* is incorrect when referring to a group of people. The plural *workers* should be used instead.

43. **The correct answer is C.** As written, the plural form of the word *worlds* is incorrect; the possessive form is required, making the word *world's*.

44. **The correct answer is J.** The passage currently uses the incorrect verb form of "to be" since the singular *is* does not fit with the plural *scientists*. Choice J corrects the problem and uses the appropriate plural form *are*.

45. **The correct answer is B.** This paragraph focuses on Harvard University and discusses both its age and its "illustrious graduates." The best option to introduce this topic is choice B, which supports this focus by showing that Harvard is one of the oldest and most prestigious universities in the United States.

46. **The correct answer is M.** (*No change*). Since Harvard University's establishment in 1636 clearly occurred in the past, the correct verb form required here is the past tense.

47. **The correct answer is C.** The items in this list should each be separated by commas.

48. **The correct answer is L.** The sentence currently uses an exclamation point as end punctuation, which is incorrect because an exclamation point should only be used when expressing surprise or heightened emotion. Instead, since the sentence poses a question, it should end in a question mark.

49. **The correct answer is A.** Proper nouns like "Washington Monument" should always be capitalized. Quotation marks are not needed when referring to a proper noun that isn't part of the name of a poem or short story or piece of dialog.

50. **The correct answer is K.** As written, the sentence contains inappropriate internal punctuation and creates awkward pauses. No punctuation is needed at the underlined portion of this sentence.

Mathematics

1. B	11. C	21. A	31. D	41. C
2. L	12. M	22. L	32. K	42. J
3. B	13. C	23. A	33. C	43. C
4. K	14. K	24. L	34. L	44. K
5. B	15. C	25. B	35. A	45. C
6. L	16. J	26. K	36. K	46. K
7. D	17. D	27. C	37. A	47. B
8. M	18. M	28. M	38. L	48. K
9. C	19. C	29. D	39. D	49. D
10. K	20. J	30. L	40. L	50. K

1. **The correct answer is B.** The third place to the right of the decimal is thousandths.

2. **The correct answer is L.**
    $$3 \times 3 \times 3 = 3 \times 9 = 27$$

3. **The correct answer is B.**
    $$\frac{1}{2} + \frac{2}{4} + \frac{3}{3} = \frac{1}{2} + \frac{1}{2} + 1 = 1 + 1 = 2$$

4. **The correct answer is K.**
    $$(3 \times 3) + (4 \times 4) + (5 \times 5) = 9 + 16 + 25 = 50$$

5. **The correct answer is B.** $1.6 = 1\frac{6}{10}$, which must be reduced to $1\frac{3}{5}$.

6. **The correct answer is L.** 29 is divisible only by 1 and 29.

7. **The correct answer is D.** $\frac{8}{4}$ can be reduced to $\frac{2}{1}$, or 2.

8. **The correct answer is M.** The term *product* is a clue to multiply. So $16 \times 4 = 64$.

9. **The correct answer is C.** $6 \times 6 \times 6 \times 6 \times 6 \times 6 \times 6$; 6^7 means that 6 is multiplied by itself 7 times.

10. **The correct answer is K.** The number 2.006 is the same as $2\frac{6}{1,000}$.

11. **The correct answer is C.** 40% of $300 is $120. So, the accountant's fee is $420.

12. **The correct answer is M.** $32 - 27 = 5$, $24 - 19 = 5$, and $23 - 21 = 2$. There are $5 + 5 + 2 = 12$ comic books that Carl needs to buy; 12 is not an answer choice.

13. **The correct answer is C.** $12 \times 245 = 2,940$ books on the 100 percent full book shelves. The fraction $\frac{4}{5}$ is the same as 80%, so 80% of 245, or 0.8×245, equals 196. $2,940 + 196 = 3,136$ books.

14. **The correct answer is K.** 100 normal images is the same as $\frac{1}{2}$, or 50 percent, of the 200 high-quality images. If $\frac{1}{2}$ of the memory is already used, then only $\frac{1}{2}$ of the camera's memory is still available. $\frac{1}{2}$ of 40 extra-high-quality images the camera normally would hold is 20.

15. **The correct answer is C.** $4 \times 3\frac{1}{4} = 13$ hours each week.

16. **The correct answer is J.** There are 100,000 centimeters in a kilometer. Each centimeter is $\frac{1}{100,000}$ of a kilometer.

17. **The correct answer is D.**

$$\text{Area} = \text{length} \times \text{width}$$
$$= 176 \text{ ft.} \times 79 \text{ ft.}$$
$$= 13{,}904 \text{ sq. ft.}$$

18. **The correct answer is M.** Mr. Loewen's total income is equal to 7% of his sales plus $250. 7% of his sales is $1,250 × 0.07 = $87.50 + $250 = $337.50.

19. **The correct answer is C.**

$$3(y \times 4) - 20 = 280$$
$$3(y \times 4) = 280 + 20$$
$$3(y \times 4) = 300$$
$$4y = 100$$
$$y = 25 \text{ or } 5^2$$

You can check your calculations by plugging your answer into the original equation.

$$3(5^2 \times 4) - 20 = 3(25 \times 4) - 20$$
$$= 3(100) - 20$$
$$= 300 - 20$$
$$= 280$$

20. **The correct answer is J.** The area of a triangle is found by using the formula:

$$A = \frac{1}{2}bh$$

Since the base = 14 and the height = 20,

$$A = \frac{1}{2} \times 14 \times 20$$

$A = 140$ sq. in.

21. **The correct answer is A.** Convert x to an improper fraction and then flip it over to get the reciprocal: $x = 2\frac{2}{5} = \frac{12}{5}$, so the reciprocal is $\frac{5}{12}$.

22. **The correct answer is L.** The product of any number and its reciprocal is 1. Therefore, $\frac{7}{16} \times \frac{16}{7} = 1$. Even if you didn't know this rule, you could have

examined the answers and eliminated choice K because that product was greater than 1 and choice M because its product was less than 1. Choice J is easily eliminated because any number multiplied by 1 is equal to itself.

23. **The correct answer is A.** This problem looks much harder than it really is. The numerator of this complex fraction is the same as the denominator. When numerator and denominator are equivalent, the fraction is equal to 1.

24. **The correct answer is L.** First, simplify the numerator:

$$\frac{5}{12} - \frac{7}{24} = \frac{10}{24} - \frac{7}{24}$$
$$= \frac{3}{24}$$
$$= \frac{1}{8}$$

Next, simplify the denominator:

$$\frac{1}{2} - \frac{3}{8} = \frac{4}{8} - \frac{3}{8} = \frac{1}{8}$$

So,

$$\frac{\frac{5}{12} - \frac{7}{24}}{\frac{1}{2} - \frac{3}{8}} = \frac{\frac{1}{8}}{\frac{1}{8}} = 1.$$

25. **The correct answer is B.** This is a problem in which you must substitute the values given into the formula. After you do that, you can solve.

$$L = \frac{3}{4} \times 2 \times 7 \times \frac{1}{2}$$

$$\frac{3 \times 2 \times 7 \times 1}{4 \times 2} = \frac{42}{8} = \frac{21}{4}$$

Choices A and C are the result of forgetting to multiply one of the numbers in the numerator. Choice D is an outlier.

26. **The correct answer is K.** The area of the shaded portion is equal to the area of the square minus the area of the circle. The length of the side of the square is equal to the diameter of the circle.

Therefore, using $\frac{22}{7}$ for pi:

$$4'' \times 4'' - \left(\pi 2^2\right) = 16 \text{ sq. in.} - \frac{88}{7} \text{ sq. in.}$$
$$= 3\frac{3}{7} \text{ sq. in.}$$

If you selected choice L, $4\frac{3}{7}$, check your skills in subtracting fractions from whole numbers.

27. **The correct answer is C.** For each teacher, there are 14 students. Because there are 14 teachers, there must be $14 \times 14 = 196$ students.

28. **The correct answer is M.**

$$\frac{10^4}{100^5} = \frac{10^4}{\left(10^2\right)^5}$$
$$= \frac{10^4}{10^{10}}$$
$$= \frac{1}{10^6}$$
$$= \frac{1}{1,000,000}$$

29. **The correct answer is D.** In the whole number system, every other number is odd and every other number is even. If x is odd, $x + 1$ is even, $x + 2$ is odd, $x + 3$ is even, and so forth. Also, if x is odd, $x - 1$ is even, $x - 2$ is odd, and $x - 3$ is even. If an even or odd number is doubled, the outcome is even. Therefore, if x is odd, $2x + 1$ is odd, $x - 2$ is odd, and $4x - 3$ is odd.

30. **The correct answer is L.** Arrange the periods of time in columns and add as you would add whole numbers.

$$\begin{array}{r} 4 \text{ hr.} \quad 17 \text{ min.} \\ 3 \text{ hr.} \quad 58 \text{ min.} \\ 45 \text{ min.} \\ +7 \text{ hr.} \quad 12 \text{ min.} \\ \hline 14 \text{ hr.} \; 132 \text{ min.} \end{array}$$

We know there are 60 minutes in each hour. Therefore, 132 minutes equal 2 hours 12 minutes. The correct answer for this addition is 16 hours 12 minutes. When working with units that measure time, volume, and length, it is usually best to represent the answer using as many larger units as possible. That's why 16 hours 12 minutes is preferable to 14 hours 132 minutes as an answer.

31. **The correct answer is D.** If there are 72 cars with 4 wheels each, or 72×4, then there are 288 wheels touching the road.

32. **The correct answer is K.** Two minutes equals $2 \times 60 = 120$ seconds. In this amount of time, Ted can text $30 \times 12 = 360$ characters.

33. **The correct answer is C.** Seven dozen is $7 \times 12 = 84$ ornaments. Subtract that amount from the desired number of ornaments to get $200 - 84 = 116$ ornaments still to be purchased.

34. **The correct answer is L.** Each wall is 12×10, or 120 square feet. Four walls of 120 square feet is $4 \times 120 = 480$ square feet.

35. **The correct answer is A.** $36,500 \div 365$ days in a year is 100 pounds of fish each day.

36. **The correct answer is K.** Forty-one percent of the donuts consumed are glazed.

37. **The correct answer is A.** Twenty-five percent of a dozen, or 12, equals 3. The chart shows that cream-filled donuts represent 25% of the Doodle's Dozen.

38. **The correct answer is L.** Because Rutledge sent more students to Washington High than the other two schools, it represents the largest percentage.

39. **The correct answer is D.** $211 + 178 + 346 = 735$.

40. **The correct answer is L.** There are more than 100 portraits. By adding the values (not the percentages) of each section, it can be determined that there are $14 + 22 + 35 + 24 + 23 = 118$ portraits.

41. **The correct answer is C.** $46,922 + 32,090$ is approximately $47,000 + 32,000$, which equals 79,000. 79,000 is approximately 80,000, so choice C is the closest estimate among the answer choices.

42. The correct answer is J. $7,988 \div 397$ is approximately $8,000 \div 400 = 20$.

43. The correct answer is C. Distance equals rate × time, so $15 = 6x$. Therefore, it takes Rick $\frac{15}{6} = 2.5$ hours, which equals $2.5(60) = 150$ minutes.

44. The correct answer is K. $40 \times 16 = 640$, which is an approximation of 653.

45. The correct answer is C. $148 + 153.5 + 146 + 154.1 + 151 + 145.9 + 149 + 153 + 152.5 + 147.75$ is approximately 150 added 10 times, or 1,500.

46. The correct answer is K. Note that $\frac{17}{30}$ is only slightly larger than $\frac{15}{30}$ or $\frac{1}{2}$. Choices J, L, and M are much closer in value to 1 than to $\frac{1}{2}$.

47. The correct answer is B. One thousand millimeters equals 1 meter. So, 1 millimeter is $\frac{1}{1,000}$ meter.

48. The correct answer is K. If 18 games constituted 40% of the season, the season was $18 \div 0.40$, or 45 games long. If the team won 18 games, it lost $45 - 18$, or 27 games.

49. The correct answer is D. The inequality should be conceptualized as "q is between –2 and –1." Because q must be closer to 0 than –2, it is *larger* than –2.

50. The correct answer is K. If $x = 0$, then $2x < 8$ because $2(0) = 0$, which is less than 8. None of the other pairs results in a true statement.

NOTES

Ability

Figure Classification

1. B	5. C	9. C	13. C	17. A
2. J	6. L	10. N	14. J	18. J
3. E	7. B	11. B	15. A	19. E
4. M	8. J	12. J	16. L	20. J

1. **The correct answer is B.** Each figure is a square divided vertically into two equal parts.

2. **The correct answer is J.** Each figure consists of two shapes that differ only in size, with one nested inside the other.

3. **The correct answer is E.** Each figure contains two triangles.

4. **The correct answer is M.** Each square contains a rectangle and two circles.

5. **The correct answer is C.** Each figure consists of three line segments in the same configuration but in different states of rotation. Choices A, B, and E are all reflections of the original figures, not rotations. Choice C is the only figure that has the correct configuration of line segments to match the originals.

6. **The correct answer is L.** Each figure consists of a single circle connected directly to multiple squares via line segments. Although choice K includes a circle and two squares, one of the squares is not connected directly to the circle. Therefore, the figure shown in choice L is the best match.

7. **The correct answer is B.** Each figure is a polygon with an additional segment inside that is parallel to one of the sides.

8. **The correct answer is J.** The number of circles in each figure is equal to the number of horizontal line segments.

9. **The correct answer is C.** Each figure has both horizontal and vertical lines of symmetry. This means that you can fold the image vertically or horizontally and the two halves will match exactly.

The figure in choice C is the only image that will fold symmetrically in both directions.

10. **The correct answer is N.** The number of horizontal segments in each figure is one more than the number of vertical segments.

11. **The correct answer is B.** The numbers in each figure are arranged so that they increase in a clockwise direction.

12. **The correct answer is J.** Each figure contains exactly two triangles.

13. **The correct answer is C.** Exactly half of each figure is shaded.

14. **The correct answer is J.** Each figure is split into equal-sized parts.

15. **The correct answer is A.** The bottom-right corner of each shade is shaded.

16. **The correct answer is L.** Each figure is split into equal sized parts. The number of these parts is equal to the number of sides of the outer shape.

17. **The correct answer is A.** The figure rotates clockwise a quarter-turn. Choice A is the same figure and is rotated a quarter-turn.

18. **The correct answer is J.** Regardless of the how many dots there are, the dots must be equally spaced around the circle's perimeter.

19. **The correct answer is E.** A dashed line divides each shape into two equal parts (the resulting parts must have the same area).

20. **The correct answer is J.** All lines are oriented horizontally. Even numbers of dots are empty while odd numbers of dots are filled.

Figure Matrices

1. C	5. C	9. A	13. E	17. C
2. K	6. N	10. L	14. L	18. N
3. E	7. A	11. E	15. B	19. C
4. K	8. M	12. J	16. M	20. K

1. **The correct answer is C.** Moving left to right, add one vertical and one horizontal line per step.

2. **The correct answer is K.** The third image in each row is a combination of the first two images in that row.

3. **The correct answer is E.** The third image in each row is a combination of the first two images in that row.

4. **The correct answer is K.** In each row, the first image is split into the second and third images. The second contains only the circle from the left side, and the third contains only the circle from the right side.

5. **The correct answer is C.** Moving from left to right, the arrows rotate clockwise. Moving top to bottom, the arrows rotate counterclockwise.

6. **The correct answer is N.** Each row has a different internal pattern, while each column has a different orientation of triangle.

7. **The correct answer is A.** In the last row, the circle is always in the bottom row of the image. In the last column, the circle is always in the middle column.

8. **The correct answer is M.** The third image in each row nests the second figure inside the first image. Note also that each row has a specific slant for the internal lines, which makes choice M a better option than choice L.

9. **The correct answer is A.** The last image in each row consists of the segments that are shown in either the first image or second image but not both.

10. **The correct answer is L.** The third image in each row is shaded as follows: a section is shaded only if it is not shaded in either of the first two images in the row.

11. **The correct answer is E.** The last image in each row consists of the segments shown in the first image but not in the second image.

12. **The correct answer is J.** The third image in each row is the second image set inside a hollow version of the first image.

13. **The correct answer is E.** Moving from top to bottom, each row adds a square. Moving left to right, each column adds a triangle.

14. **The correct answer is L.** The third image in each contains the second image set on top of the first image.

15. **The correct answer is B.** The empty section in the third column is filled in both of the two previous columns.

16. **The correct answer is M.** The third image in each row is the second image split into equal parts. The number of parts is determined by the number of segments in the first column.

17. **The correct answer is C.** The third image in each row consists of the shape from the second image filled using segments parallel to the segment in the first image.

18. **The correct answer is N.** The shape in the last column is the shape from the first column but with dots positioned at the ends of the lines depicted in the second column. Therefore, the last shape will be a hexagon surrounded by seven dots. There will be three dots on the top half of the hexagon and four on the bottom. Thus choice N is better than choice M.

19. **The correct answer is C.** From left to right, the second figure rotates one of the arrows 180 degrees; the third figure then rotates both arrows 180 degrees and shades the unshaded parts and vice versa.

20. **The correct answer is K.** From left to right, add an "X" and remove a square block for each step. From top to bottom, remove two square blocks and one "X" for each step.

Paper Folding

1. D	3. E	5. A	7. D	9. D
2. J	4. K	6. K	8. L	10. J

1. **The correct answer is D.** Both holes are reflected across the vertical fold. The one near the center line remains near the center line, while the one in the top corner ends up in the opposite top corner.

2. **The correct answer is J.** Each hole is reflected across the diagonal fold, moving toward the opposite corner a distance that is equal to its original distance from the fold.

3. **The correct answer is E.** Unfolding the second fold reflects both holes across the vertical fold, resulting in four holes on the bottom half of the paper. Each of these is then reflected across the horizontal fold to the top half of the paper, for a total of eight holes.

4. **The correct answer is K.** All of the folds are horizontal; therefore, when unfolding, the hole in the corner only moves vertically, and remains along the right edge of the page.

5. **The correct answer is A.** The hole on the right edge is first reflected diagonally to the bottom edge of the page. Both holes are then reflected diagonally again, ending up on the top and left sides of the page.

6. **The correct answer is K.** All three holes are reflected diagonally from the bottom right part of the page to the top left.

7. **The correct answer is D.** The hole is first reflected horizontally to the right edge of the page. Both holes are then reflected vertically just over the horizontal center line.

8. **The correct answer is L.** When the second fold is undone, the hole on the top right is reflected over the diagonal, still remaining in the top right corner. The three holes on the right side of the page are then reflected over the center vertical line, creating a mirror image of them on the left side of the page.

9. **The correct answer is D.** All of the folds are horizontal; therefore, when unfolding, the hole in the center only moves vertically, and remains in the center of the page.

10. **The correct answer is J.** The hole in the top-right quadrant of the page is first reflected to the bottom-right quadrant, and then these are reflected into the top-left and bottom-left quadrants. They all remain in the center of their respective quadrants.

SCORE SHEET

Although your actual exam scores will not be reported as percentages, it might be helpful to convert your test scores to percentages so that you can see at a glance where your strengths and weaknesses lie. The numbers in parentheses represent the questions that test each skill.

Subject	# Correct ÷ # of questions	× 100 = _____ %
Reading		
Vocabulary/Word Relationships (7, 13, 22, 28, 29, 37, 40, 47)	_____ ÷ 8 = _____	× 100 = _____ %
Details/Main Idea/Structure (2, 4, 6, 11, 14, 15, 17, 19, 20, 21, 23, 26, 27, 30, 31, 32, 34, 43, 44, 45, 46, 48)	_____ ÷ 22 = _____	× 100 = _____ %
Inference/Understanding (1, 3, 5, 8, 9, 10, 12, 16, 18, 24, 25, 33, 35, 36, 38, 39, 41, 42, 49, 50)	_____ ÷ 20 = _____	× 100 = _____ %
TOTAL READING SKILLS	_____ ÷ 50 = _____	× 100 = _____ %
Written Expression		
Spelling and Capitalization (1, 2, 3, 4, 5, 6, 7, 8, 9, 10, 11, 12, 13, 14, 15, 16, 17, 18, 19, 20, 29, 32, 35, 49)	_____ ÷ 24 = _____	× 100 = _____ %
Punctuation (25, 26, 31, 33, 36, 40, 43, 47, 48, 50)	_____ ÷ 10 = _____	× 100 = _____ %
Grammar (23, 30, 39, 42, 44, 46)	_____ ÷ 6 = _____	× 100 = _____ %
Usage and Composition (21, 22, 24, 27, 28, 34, 37, 38, 41, 45)	_____ ÷ 10 = _____	× 100 = _____ %
TOTAL WRITTEN EXPRESSION SKILLS	_____ ÷ 50 = _____	× 100 = _____ %
Mathematics		
Arithmetic (1, 2, 3, 4, 5, 6, 7, 8, 9, 10, 11, 12, 13, 14, 15, 18, 24, 27, 28, 30, 31, 32, 33, 35, 41, 42, 43, 44, 45, 46, 48)	_____ ÷ 31 = _____	× 100 = _____ %
Algebra (19, 21, 22, 23, 25, 29, 49, 50)	_____ ÷ 8 = _____	× 100 = _____ %
Data Analysis (36, 37, 38, 39, 40)	_____ ÷ 5 = _____	× 100 = _____ %
Geometry and Measurement (16, 17, 20, 26, 34, 47)	_____ ÷ 6 = _____	× 100 = _____ %
TOTAL MATHEMATICS SKILLS	_____ ÷ 50 = _____	× 100 = _____ %
Ability		
Figure Classification (1, 2, 3, 4, 5, 6, 7, 8, 9, 10, 11, 12, 13, 14, 15, 16, 17, 18, 19, 20)	_____ ÷ 20 = _____	× 100 = _____ %
Figure Matrices (1, 2, 3, 4, 5, 6, 7, 8, 9, 10, 11, 12, 13, 14, 15, 16, 17, 18, 19, 20)	_____ ÷ 20 = _____	× 100 = _____ %
Paper Folding (1, 2, 3, 4, 5, 6, 7, 8, 9, 10)	_____ ÷ 10 = _____	× 100 = _____ %
TOTAL ABILITY SKILLS	_____ ÷ 50 = _____	× 100 = _____ %

NOTES

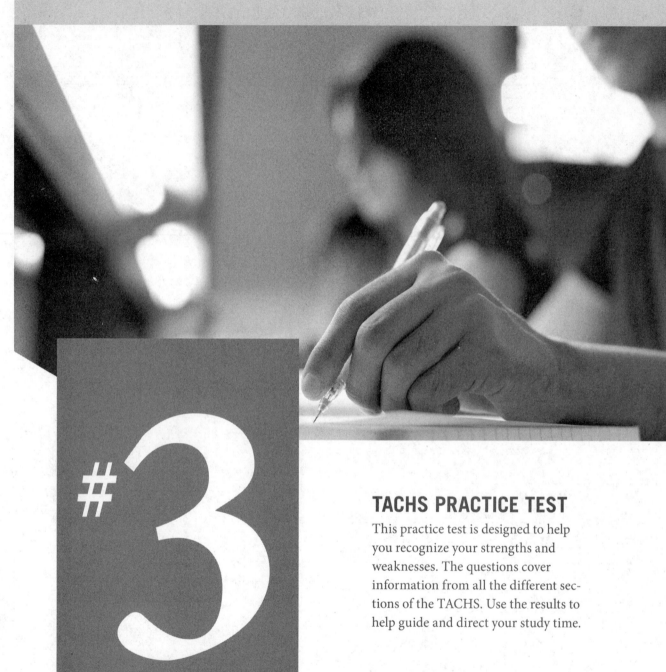

TACHS PRACTICE TEST 3

TACHS PRACTICE TEST

This practice test is designed to help you recognize your strengths and weaknesses. The questions cover information from all the different sections of the TACHS. Use the results to help guide and direct your study time.

ANSWER SHEETS: TACHS PRACTICE TEST 3

Reading

1. Ⓐ Ⓑ Ⓒ Ⓓ	11. Ⓐ Ⓑ Ⓒ Ⓓ	21. Ⓐ Ⓑ Ⓒ Ⓓ	31. Ⓐ Ⓑ Ⓒ Ⓓ	41. Ⓐ Ⓑ Ⓒ Ⓓ
2. Ⓙ Ⓚ Ⓛ Ⓜ	12. Ⓙ Ⓚ Ⓛ Ⓜ	22. Ⓙ Ⓚ Ⓛ Ⓜ	32. Ⓙ Ⓚ Ⓛ Ⓜ	42. Ⓙ Ⓚ Ⓛ Ⓜ
3. Ⓐ Ⓑ Ⓒ Ⓓ	13. Ⓐ Ⓑ Ⓒ Ⓓ	23. Ⓐ Ⓑ Ⓒ Ⓓ	33. Ⓐ Ⓑ Ⓒ Ⓓ	43. Ⓐ Ⓑ Ⓒ Ⓓ
4. Ⓙ Ⓚ Ⓛ Ⓜ	14. Ⓙ Ⓚ Ⓛ Ⓜ	24. Ⓙ Ⓚ Ⓛ Ⓜ	34. Ⓙ Ⓚ Ⓛ Ⓜ	44. Ⓙ Ⓚ Ⓛ Ⓜ
5. Ⓐ Ⓑ Ⓒ Ⓓ	15. Ⓐ Ⓑ Ⓒ Ⓓ	25. Ⓐ Ⓑ Ⓒ Ⓓ	35. Ⓐ Ⓑ Ⓒ Ⓓ	45. Ⓐ Ⓑ Ⓒ Ⓓ
6. Ⓙ Ⓚ Ⓛ Ⓜ	16. Ⓙ Ⓚ Ⓛ Ⓜ	26. Ⓙ Ⓚ Ⓛ Ⓜ	36. Ⓙ Ⓚ Ⓛ Ⓜ	46. Ⓙ Ⓚ Ⓛ Ⓜ
7. Ⓐ Ⓑ Ⓒ Ⓓ	17. Ⓐ Ⓑ Ⓒ Ⓓ	27. Ⓐ Ⓑ Ⓒ Ⓓ	37. Ⓐ Ⓑ Ⓒ Ⓓ	47. Ⓐ Ⓑ Ⓒ Ⓓ
8. Ⓙ Ⓚ Ⓛ Ⓜ	18. Ⓙ Ⓚ Ⓛ Ⓜ	28. Ⓙ Ⓚ Ⓛ Ⓜ	38. Ⓙ Ⓚ Ⓛ Ⓜ	48. Ⓙ Ⓚ Ⓛ Ⓜ
9. Ⓐ Ⓑ Ⓒ Ⓓ	19. Ⓐ Ⓑ Ⓒ Ⓓ	29. Ⓐ Ⓑ Ⓒ Ⓓ	39. Ⓐ Ⓑ Ⓒ Ⓓ	49. Ⓐ Ⓑ Ⓒ Ⓓ
10. Ⓙ Ⓚ Ⓛ Ⓜ	20. Ⓙ Ⓚ Ⓛ Ⓜ	30. Ⓙ Ⓚ Ⓛ Ⓜ	40. Ⓙ Ⓚ Ⓛ Ⓜ	50. Ⓙ Ⓚ Ⓛ Ⓜ

Written Expression

1. Ⓐ Ⓑ Ⓒ Ⓓ Ⓔ	11. Ⓐ Ⓑ Ⓒ Ⓓ	21. Ⓐ Ⓑ Ⓒ Ⓓ	31. Ⓐ Ⓑ Ⓒ Ⓓ	41. Ⓐ Ⓑ Ⓒ Ⓓ
2. Ⓙ Ⓚ Ⓛ Ⓜ Ⓝ	12. Ⓙ Ⓚ Ⓛ Ⓜ	22. Ⓙ Ⓚ Ⓛ Ⓜ	32. Ⓙ Ⓚ Ⓛ Ⓜ	42. Ⓙ Ⓚ Ⓛ Ⓜ
3. Ⓐ Ⓑ Ⓒ Ⓓ Ⓔ	13. Ⓐ Ⓑ Ⓒ Ⓓ	23. Ⓐ Ⓑ Ⓒ Ⓓ	33. Ⓐ Ⓑ Ⓒ Ⓓ	43. Ⓐ Ⓑ Ⓒ Ⓓ
4. Ⓙ Ⓚ Ⓛ Ⓜ Ⓝ	14. Ⓙ Ⓚ Ⓛ Ⓜ	24. Ⓙ Ⓚ Ⓛ Ⓜ	34. Ⓙ Ⓚ Ⓛ Ⓜ	44. Ⓙ Ⓚ Ⓛ Ⓜ
5. Ⓐ Ⓑ Ⓒ Ⓓ Ⓔ	15. Ⓐ Ⓑ Ⓒ Ⓓ	25. Ⓐ Ⓑ Ⓒ Ⓓ	35. Ⓐ Ⓑ Ⓒ Ⓓ	45. Ⓐ Ⓑ Ⓒ Ⓓ
6. Ⓙ Ⓚ Ⓛ Ⓜ Ⓝ	16. Ⓙ Ⓚ Ⓛ Ⓜ	26. Ⓙ Ⓚ Ⓛ Ⓜ	36. Ⓙ Ⓚ Ⓛ Ⓜ	46. Ⓙ Ⓚ Ⓛ Ⓜ
7. Ⓐ Ⓑ Ⓒ Ⓓ Ⓔ	17. Ⓐ Ⓑ Ⓒ Ⓓ	27. Ⓐ Ⓑ Ⓒ Ⓓ	37. Ⓐ Ⓑ Ⓒ Ⓓ	47. Ⓐ Ⓑ Ⓒ Ⓓ
8. Ⓙ Ⓚ Ⓛ Ⓜ Ⓝ	18. Ⓙ Ⓚ Ⓛ Ⓜ	28. Ⓙ Ⓚ Ⓛ Ⓜ	38. Ⓙ Ⓚ Ⓛ Ⓜ	48. Ⓙ Ⓚ Ⓛ Ⓜ
9. Ⓐ Ⓑ Ⓒ Ⓓ Ⓔ	19. Ⓐ Ⓑ Ⓒ Ⓓ	29. Ⓐ Ⓑ Ⓒ Ⓓ	39. Ⓐ Ⓑ Ⓒ Ⓓ	49. Ⓐ Ⓑ Ⓒ Ⓓ
10. Ⓙ Ⓚ Ⓛ Ⓜ Ⓝ	20. Ⓙ Ⓚ Ⓛ Ⓜ	30. Ⓙ Ⓚ Ⓛ Ⓜ	40. Ⓙ Ⓚ Ⓛ Ⓜ	50. Ⓙ Ⓚ Ⓛ Ⓜ

Mathematics

1. Ⓐ Ⓑ Ⓒ Ⓓ
2. Ⓙ Ⓚ Ⓛ Ⓜ
3. Ⓐ Ⓑ Ⓒ Ⓓ
4. Ⓙ Ⓚ Ⓛ Ⓜ
5. Ⓐ Ⓑ Ⓒ Ⓓ
6. Ⓙ Ⓚ Ⓛ Ⓜ
7. Ⓐ Ⓑ Ⓒ Ⓓ
8. Ⓙ Ⓚ Ⓛ Ⓜ
9. Ⓐ Ⓑ Ⓒ Ⓓ
10. Ⓙ Ⓚ Ⓛ Ⓜ

11. Ⓐ Ⓑ Ⓒ Ⓓ
12. Ⓙ Ⓚ Ⓛ Ⓜ
13. Ⓐ Ⓑ Ⓒ Ⓓ
14. Ⓙ Ⓚ Ⓛ Ⓜ
15. Ⓐ Ⓑ Ⓒ Ⓓ
16. Ⓙ Ⓚ Ⓛ Ⓜ
17. Ⓐ Ⓑ Ⓒ Ⓓ
18. Ⓙ Ⓚ Ⓛ Ⓜ
19. Ⓐ Ⓑ Ⓒ Ⓓ
20. Ⓙ Ⓚ Ⓛ Ⓜ

21. Ⓐ Ⓑ Ⓒ Ⓓ
22. Ⓙ Ⓚ Ⓛ Ⓜ
23. Ⓐ Ⓑ Ⓒ Ⓓ
24. Ⓙ Ⓚ Ⓛ Ⓜ
25. Ⓐ Ⓑ Ⓒ Ⓓ
26. Ⓙ Ⓚ Ⓛ Ⓜ
27. Ⓐ Ⓑ Ⓒ Ⓓ
28. Ⓙ Ⓚ Ⓛ Ⓜ
29. Ⓐ Ⓑ Ⓒ Ⓓ
30. Ⓙ Ⓚ Ⓛ Ⓜ

31. Ⓐ Ⓑ Ⓒ Ⓓ
32. Ⓙ Ⓚ Ⓛ Ⓜ
33. Ⓐ Ⓑ Ⓒ Ⓓ
34. Ⓙ Ⓚ Ⓛ Ⓜ
35. Ⓐ Ⓑ Ⓒ Ⓓ
36. Ⓙ Ⓚ Ⓛ Ⓜ
37. Ⓐ Ⓑ Ⓒ Ⓓ
38. Ⓙ Ⓚ Ⓛ Ⓜ
39. Ⓐ Ⓑ Ⓒ Ⓓ
40. Ⓙ Ⓚ Ⓛ Ⓜ

41. Ⓐ Ⓑ Ⓒ Ⓓ
42. Ⓙ Ⓚ Ⓛ Ⓜ
43. Ⓐ Ⓑ Ⓒ Ⓓ
44. Ⓙ Ⓚ Ⓛ Ⓜ
45. Ⓐ Ⓑ Ⓒ Ⓓ
46. Ⓙ Ⓚ Ⓛ Ⓜ
47. Ⓐ Ⓑ Ⓒ Ⓓ
48. Ⓙ Ⓚ Ⓛ Ⓜ
49. Ⓐ Ⓑ Ⓒ Ⓓ
50. Ⓙ Ⓚ Ⓛ Ⓜ

Ability

Figure Classification

1. Ⓐ Ⓑ Ⓒ Ⓓ Ⓔ   5. Ⓐ Ⓑ Ⓒ Ⓓ Ⓔ   9. Ⓐ Ⓑ Ⓒ Ⓓ Ⓔ   13. Ⓐ Ⓑ Ⓒ Ⓓ Ⓔ   17. Ⓐ Ⓑ Ⓒ Ⓓ Ⓔ

2. Ⓙ Ⓚ Ⓛ Ⓜ Ⓝ   6. Ⓙ Ⓚ Ⓛ Ⓜ Ⓝ   10. Ⓙ Ⓚ Ⓛ Ⓜ Ⓝ   14. Ⓙ Ⓚ Ⓛ Ⓜ Ⓝ   18. Ⓙ Ⓚ Ⓛ Ⓜ Ⓝ

3. Ⓐ Ⓑ Ⓒ Ⓓ Ⓔ   7. Ⓐ Ⓑ Ⓒ Ⓓ Ⓔ   11. Ⓐ Ⓑ Ⓒ Ⓓ Ⓔ   15. Ⓐ Ⓑ Ⓒ Ⓓ Ⓔ   19. Ⓐ Ⓑ Ⓒ Ⓓ Ⓔ

4. Ⓙ Ⓚ Ⓛ Ⓜ Ⓝ   8. Ⓙ Ⓚ Ⓛ Ⓜ Ⓝ   12. Ⓙ Ⓚ Ⓛ Ⓜ Ⓝ   16. Ⓙ Ⓚ Ⓛ Ⓜ Ⓝ   20. Ⓙ Ⓚ Ⓛ Ⓜ Ⓝ

Figure Matrices

1. Ⓐ Ⓑ Ⓒ Ⓓ Ⓔ   5. Ⓐ Ⓑ Ⓒ Ⓓ Ⓔ   9. Ⓐ Ⓑ Ⓒ Ⓓ Ⓔ   13. Ⓐ Ⓑ Ⓒ Ⓓ Ⓔ   17. Ⓐ Ⓑ Ⓒ Ⓓ Ⓔ

2. Ⓙ Ⓚ Ⓛ Ⓜ Ⓝ   6. Ⓙ Ⓚ Ⓛ Ⓜ Ⓝ   10. Ⓙ Ⓚ Ⓛ Ⓜ Ⓝ   14. Ⓙ Ⓚ Ⓛ Ⓜ Ⓝ   18. Ⓙ Ⓚ Ⓛ Ⓜ Ⓝ

3. Ⓐ Ⓑ Ⓒ Ⓓ Ⓔ   7. Ⓐ Ⓑ Ⓒ Ⓓ Ⓔ   11. Ⓐ Ⓑ Ⓒ Ⓓ Ⓔ   15. Ⓐ Ⓑ Ⓒ Ⓓ Ⓔ   19. Ⓐ Ⓑ Ⓒ Ⓓ Ⓔ

4. Ⓙ Ⓚ Ⓛ Ⓜ Ⓝ   8. Ⓙ Ⓚ Ⓛ Ⓜ Ⓝ   12. Ⓙ Ⓚ Ⓛ Ⓜ Ⓝ   16. Ⓙ Ⓚ Ⓛ Ⓜ Ⓝ   20. Ⓙ Ⓚ Ⓛ Ⓜ Ⓝ

Paper Folding

1. Ⓐ Ⓑ Ⓒ Ⓓ Ⓔ   3. Ⓐ Ⓑ Ⓒ Ⓓ Ⓔ   5. Ⓐ Ⓑ Ⓒ Ⓓ Ⓔ   7. Ⓐ Ⓑ Ⓒ Ⓓ Ⓔ   9. Ⓐ Ⓑ Ⓒ Ⓓ Ⓔ

2. Ⓙ Ⓚ Ⓛ Ⓜ Ⓝ   4. Ⓙ Ⓚ Ⓛ Ⓜ Ⓝ   6. Ⓙ Ⓚ Ⓛ Ⓜ Ⓝ   8. Ⓙ Ⓚ Ⓛ Ⓜ Ⓝ   10. Ⓙ Ⓚ Ⓛ Ⓜ Ⓝ

READING

50 Questions—35 Minutes

Turn to the Reading section of your answer sheet to answer the questions in this section.

Directions: This is a test of how well you understand what you read.

- Read the passages below and answer the questions.

- Four answers are given for each question. You must choose the answer that you think is better than the others.

Questions 1–6 are based on the following passage.

PASSAGE 1

Charlie finally decided that he had had enough of city life. He made up his mind that he was tired of riding the subway an hour to work every day, tired of living in a tiny apartment, and tired of not seeing the sunrise and sunset. Charlie gathered his family around the dinner table and informed them of his desire
Line to escape the concrete jungle permanently. After a few hours, Charlie persuaded his wife and two kids to
5 give the country life a try.

Two weeks after Charlie made his decision, the family moved into a ranch house in rural Texas. On the day the family moved in, Charlie's youngest, Laurie, got stung by a small scorpion. Only a few hours later, Charlie's wife began sneezing uncontrollably and developed red, watery eyes. Charlie's son found a rattlesnake in the shed shortly thereafter. Before the movers unloaded half the furniture from the truck,
10 Charlie was on the phone with a realtor back in New York City.

1. In sentence 1 of paragraph 2, what does the word *rural* mean?

   A. Western

   B. In the country

   C. Primitive

   D. Scenic

2. Why did Charlie call his realtor before he was even unpacked in Texas?

   J. He was upset with the view from his porch.

   K. He wanted to double-check the price of his new house.

   L. The country life wasn't what he hoped for, and he was ready to move back to the city.

   M. He was disappointed in the movers.

3. All of these contributed to Charlie's decision to move back to New York City *except*

   A. a rattlesnake.

   B. a scorpion.

   C. the realtor.

   D. illness.

4. The phrase "concrete jungle" refers to

   J. Texas.

   K. Charlie's job.

   L. the city.

   M. the country.

5. What can we infer about Charlie's family's move to Texas?

    A. They did not consider potential drawbacks of life in Texas.

    B. They did not want to move to Texas in the first place.

    C. They never planned to stay in Texas permanently.

    D. They will move back to New York while Charlie stays in Texas.

6. When did Charlie make the decision to move back to New York City?

    J. Two weeks after moving

    K. The same day they moved in

    L. Before they left New York City

    M. After their furniture was unpacked

Questions 7–12 are based on the following passage.

Passage 2

In the nineteenth century, a wave of liberalism swept across Europe. Liberals—those who advocated liberalism—heavily favored liberty, equality, and natural rights for citizens of European nations. Specifically, liberals hoped to win for citizens such things as voting rights and equal protection under the law. Ironically, the vast majority of liberals sought these rights for men only and not for women.

    Standing in the way of liberal reform were the wealthy nobles, aristocrats, and the monarchs seated precariously on the thrones of Europe. The nobility felt threatened by liberalism because nobles held nearly all political power in early nineteenth-century Europe. Because they held all the power, the common man had virtually no say in the government. The nobles knew that their political positions would be in jeopardy if the common citizens could choose government officials. Ultimately, liberalism proved too strong a force for the aristocracy to defeat.

7. What was the nobles' greatest fear about common citizens winning the right to vote?

    A. Citizens didn't know how to vote.

    B. Citizens might not exercise their right to vote.

    C. Nobles may not get the right to vote.

    D. Citizens probably would elect people who had not been the power-holding nobles prior to elections, thus leaving the nobles with little or no power.

8. Based on context clues in paragraph 2, the word *monarchs* probably means which of the following?

    J. Commoners

    K. Kings and queens

    L. Jesters

    M. Judges

9. In sentence 4 of paragraph 1, the word *ironically* is used to show that

    A. nobles would prevent the liberals from getting rights.

    B. liberals did not really want voting rights and equal protection.

    C. nobles wanted the same things as the liberals wanted.

    D. liberals were not fully practicing what they preached.

10. The passage suggests that

J. the aristocrats had a strong grip on political power in the nineteenth century.

K. the liberals could be defeated if the aristocrats and monarchs united.

L. although the nobles had political power, they were still vulnerable.

M. the common man now holds all political power in Europe.

11. This passage would most likely appear in

A. a persuasive article.

B. a history textbook.

C. both of these.

D. neither of these.

12. From the last sentence of the passage, we can infer that

J. Europe eventually embraced voting rights and equal protection under the law.

K. the nobles would lose power but become powerful again later.

L. Europe would embrace voting rights for women.

M. the liberals would become aristocrats after they took power.

Questions 13–18 are based on the following passage.

PASSAGE 3

Among the famous Seven Wonders of the Ancient World, do you know which one is truly the most ancient? It's the Great Pyramid of Giza, and curiously enough, it's also the only one of the Wonders that still exists and remains largely unscathed by the ravages of time. Let's explore this architectural marvel and discover
Line what makes this structure a truly wonderful monument to human capability.
5   Based on extensive research by Egyptologists, it's believed that the Great Pyramid of Giza was built around 2560 BC as a tomb for the Egyptian Pharaoh Khufu of the fourth dynasty. Pyramids commonly served as majestic resting places for dead royalty in Ancient Egypt, but the Great Pyramid of Giza is truly in a class all its own. Its initial height is a staggering 481 feet, the world's tallest man-made structure for nearly 4,000 years. The pyramid contains a series of chambers and levels for its "royal residents," and it
10   is just one of several pyramids that make up the Giza pyramid complex in Cairo, which also includes the Great Sphinx, cemeteries, and an industrial complex. This grand structure is estimated to include more than 2.3 million blocks of limestone and granite (some blocks weighing upwards of 50 tons), likely excavated from nearby quarries, and set with nearly half a million tons of mortar. Although there is a great amount of disagreement among experts regarding how the Egyptians built the pyramid so long ago, one
15   thing that is hardly in dispute is that it is truly a magnificent and awe-inspiring piece of human history.

13. Based on the information in the passage, the author refers to the Great Pyramid of Giza as "truly in a class all its own" because

 A. there were no other pyramids located anywhere near it.

 B. the pyramid is taller than the others created at the time.

 C. you'll likely only learn about the pyramid in a classroom.

 D. the original designers had a great deal of formal education.

14. As used in sentence 2 of paragraph 1, what does the word *unscathed* likely mean?

 J. Gigantic

 K. Modern

 L. Not new

 M. Unharmed

15. The Great Pyramid of Giza was originally meant to be a(n)

 A. tourist attraction.

 B. tomb for a pharaoh.

 C. housing complex.

 D. industrial complex.

16. All of the following materials help make up the structure of the Great Pyramid of Giza *except*

 J. mortar.

 K. limestone.

 L. granite.

 M. steel.

17. Which of the following is true of the Great Pyramid of Giza?

 A. It contains the Great Sphinx.

 B. It is the last surviving Wonder of the Ancient World.

 C. It is a naturally occurring structure.

 D. It is clear how the pyramid was built.

18. Which of the following describes how the author feels about the Great Pyramid of Giza?

 J. Bored

 K. Impressed

 L. Surprised

 M. Skeptical

PASSAGE 4

As Margie strolled through the mall, a muscular young man handed her a pamphlet advertising a brand-new workout facility across town. Margie took the pamphlet; she had been pondering a new fitness routine. She read as she walked past store after store. On her way through the department store at the end of the *Line* mall, she stopped and browsed the fitness equipment in the store. Margie was convinced that she needed 5 to do something to help herself feel better, have more energy, and generally lead a healthier life.

After much thought, Margie decided that an expensive exercise apparatus eventually would turn into an expensive clothes rack in her bedroom. Margie also decided that the new workout facility would be better than the exercise equipment. However, she wondered if a facility on the other side of town would actually deter her from working out regularly. Margie ultimately decided to spend a fraction of the money 10 she would have spent otherwise, and she purchased small set of weights and some workout videos.

19. What was Margie's true feeling about purchasing the expensive exercise equipment?

   A. She was afraid she wouldn't know how to use the equipment.

   B. She wanted to hang clothes somewhere other than in her closet.

   C. She feared that she wouldn't use the equipment enough to justify the price.

   D. She didn't think the equipment would fit anywhere except in her bedroom.

20. Based on context clues, what does the word *deter* mean in paragraph 2 of the passage?

   J. Allow

   K. Include

   L. Encourage

   M. Discourage

21. Based on the passage, we can infer that Margie will

   A. go back and buy the expensive apparatus.

   B. likely not stick to her new routine.

   C. join the gym across town.

   D. be more likely to stick to her new routine.

22. Margie's new fitness routine is most inspired by

   J. the pamphlet.

   K. her health.

   L. the department store.

   M. the young man.

23. What makes Margie decide against the new workout facility?

   A. She feels intimidated by the young man with the pamphlet.

   B. It is less effective than weights and a workout video.

   C. She lives too far away from the gym.

   D. It costs too much money.

24. Based on the information in the passage, Margie is

   J. impulsive.

   K. frustrated.

   L. thoughtful.

   M. unhappy.

Questions 25–30 are based on the following passage.

PASSAGE 5

The camp director stood in front of the staff late Friday evening to address her camp counselors. The counselors had been working for two weeks without a break and faced another two weeks of the same routine before camp was to be dismissed for the summer. The counselors directed or participated in activities like

Line
5 swimming and arts and crafts with the campers for 12 or 14 hours every day. In addition, the counselors made themselves available to the campers for one-on-one attention, including giving advice and just listening. The counselors poured themselves into their jobs.

The director looked at the face of each counselor and smiled. She knew how much of themselves they invested in making the camp a success. She said, "When my hands get chapped from hard work and exposure to the elements, I rub aloe vera lotion on them to help them relax and refresh. In that same spirit,

10 I want to give you all some proverbial aloe vera for the soul—you get tomorrow off!"

25. Which of the following most likely describes the counselors?

   A. Unruly

   B. Disinterested

   C. Exhausted

   D. Confused

26. When the director tells the counselors that she wants to give them "some proverbial aloe vera for the soul," she means that she wants to

   J. give each of them their own jars of aloe vera lotion.

   K. help them feel relaxed and refreshed after a day off.

   L. hint to the counselors that their skin looks dry and they should try some lotion.

   M. insist that they apply aloe vera when working with campers.

27. Why did the director give the counselors a day off?

   A. She doesn't need them for the next day's activities.

   B. They are overworked, and the director knows they need a break.

   C. They are terrible at doing their jobs.

   D. The campers want the counselors to have a day off.

28. The director can be described as

   J. sympathetic.

   K. heartless.

   L. lazy.

   M. energetic.

29. Based on the passage, how long is the camp in session by the end of the summer?

   A. 2 weeks

   B. 4 weeks

   C. 12 weeks

   D. 16 weeks

30. Which of the following is *not* one of the counselors' duties?

   J. Giving advice

   K. Directing activities

   L. Listening to campers

   M. Providing medical care

PASSAGE 6

Scholars often trace the birth of modern science back to the work of an English philosopher named Sir Francis Bacon. Before Bacon's time, scientific theories as we know them did not exist. Instead, the ideas that were considered to be knowledge were based upon faith, and most came from the philosophies of the
Line church. Bacon was very opposed to this approach to knowledge. He disliked the notion that knowledge
5 could be based simply on beliefs or on the ideas of the church. He searched for a way of developing knowledge that he felt was more reliable.

Bacon was very interested in the facts that we could gain from simply observing what goes on around us in the physical world. He believed that observing the physical world would produce much more reliable knowledge than simply making up knowledge based on beliefs. In 1620, Bacon published a book containing
10 his ideas on the importance of developing knowledge through observation of nature. This book, called *The New Organon*, created a foundation for what is now known as "empirical" science, or science that comes from observing that which can be perceived through our senses.

Bacon's approach came to be known by the name *inductivism*. Inductivism is the idea that a person can develop theories about science by observing events. In the inductivist approach, the scientist views a series of
15 repeating events and draws a general conclusion from these events. The scientist takes this conclusion to be true because it is based on experience. A scientist using the inductivist approach might conclude, for instance, that "all swans are white," based solely on the fact that all swans that he has previously observed are white.

31. Which of the titles below best captures the main idea of this selection?

   A. "Understanding the Scientific Method"

   B. "Bacon and the Development of Science"

   C. "Testing Hypotheses and Theories"

   D. "The History of Sir Francis Bacon"

32. Why did Sir Francis Bacon search for a way to develop knowledge based on observing the physical world?

   J. He believed that knowledge based on observing similar, repeated events was unreliable.

   K. He believed that knowledge based on the principle of inductivism was unreliable.

   L. He believed that knowledge based on faith, or the ideas of the church, was unreliable.

   M. He believed that knowledge based on the principle of falsification was unreliable.

33. Bacon's approach to science was known as

   A. inductivism.

   B. positivism.

   C. radicalism.

   D. relativism.

34. Before Bacon, scientific knowledge was based on

   J. concepts from astronomy.

   K. rigorous testing.

   L. legal precepts.

   M. the ideas of the church.

35. Bacon's book, *The New Organon*, focused on

   A. refining knowledge that is based on personal beliefs.

   B. developing knowledge perceived through the senses.

   C. revising the ideas of political leaders of Bacon's time.

   D. practicing strict scientific discipline in the church.

36. Which of the following would Bacon be most likely to accept as scientific knowledge?

   J. Ideas based on church doctrine

   K. Untested philosophical concepts

   L. Theories based on empirical facts

   M. A hypothesis based on opinion

37. Inductivist theories are developed from

   A. observing events.

   B. scientific mistakes.

   C. ongoing debates.

   D. experimental competitions.

38. Based on the context clues in paragraph 2, the word *foundation* most likely means

   J. charity.

   K. support.

   L. method.

   M. physical structure.

Questions 39–44 are based on the following passage.

PASSAGE 7

In the not-too-distant past, recycling meant dividing materials into separate containers so that they could be recycled with like materials: cans and bottles with other cans and bottles, paper with paper, etc. Since the 1990s, however, a new and innovative recycling trend has emerged—one that makes the process more
Line manageable for people who want to be environmentally conscious but want an easier way to do it.
5   As a solution, single-stream recycling was developed in the late 1990s in California. In it, recyclables stay together in one container—cans, plastic bottles, paper, glass, cardboard—and are sent to a facility that parses out each material type and packages them for separate recycling. The recyclable materials are still separated from regular garbage like Styrofoam® and food waste, but the process is simplified. This type of single-stream recycling encourages people to recycle more because they spend less time separating out
10   recyclables from regular trash. The efficiency has led to many towns and cities across the country adopting single-stream recycling processes to replace the old dual-stream facilities. As of 2013, more than 100 million Americans used single-stream recycling programs.

39. Based on the context clues in the passage, what does *like* (sentence 1) mean?

   A. Enjoy

   B. Similar

   C. As if

   D. None of the above

40. Which of the following is the best way to describe single-stream recycling?

   J. Unsuccessful

   K. Growing

   L. Expensive

   M. Old-fashioned

41. Which of these titles best expresses the main idea of the selection?

   A. "Simplifying the Streams in Recycling"

   B. "The Wide World of Recycling"

   C. "Living a Sustainable Life in the 21st Century"

   D. "Recycling Since 2013"

42. As used in paragraph 2, the word *parses* most likely means

   J. decides.

   K. understands.

   L. separates.

   M. finishes.

43. What is the main difference between single-stream recycling and dual-stream recycling?

A. The amount of processing done by the recycling facilities

B. The types of materials that are recyclable

C. The quantity of garbage sent to landfills

D. The amount of work consumers need to do at the start of the process

44. Which of these is *not* a recyclable material, according to the passage?

J. Glass

K. Cardboard

L. Styrofoam

M. Plastic bottles

Questions 45–50 are based on the following passage.

PASSAGE 8

There was nothing of the giant in the aspect of the man who was beginning to awaken on the sleeping porch of a Dutch Colonial house in that residential district of Zenith known as Floral Heights.

His name was George F. Babbitt. He was forty-six years old now, in April, 1920, and he made nothing in particular, neither butter nor shoes nor poetry, but he was nimble in the calling of selling houses for more than people could afford to pay.

His large head was pink, his brown hair thin and dry. His face was babyish in slumber, despite his wrinkles and the red spectacle-dents on the slopes of his nose. He was not fat but he was exceedingly well fed; his cheeks were pads, and the unroughened hand which lay helpless upon the khaki-colored blanket was slightly puffy. He seemed prosperous, extremely married and unromantic; and altogether unromantic appeared this sleeping-porch, which looked on one sizable elm, two respectable grass-plots, a cement driveway, and a corrugated iron garage. Yet Babbitt was again dreaming of the fairy child, a dream more romantic than scarlet pagodas by a silver sea.

—from *Babbitt* by Sinclair Lewis

45. George Babbitt is a

A. real estate salesman.

B. poet.

C. shoemaker.

D. teacher.

46. The description of George Babbitt suggests that he is

J. very young.

K. physically fit.

L. wealthy.

M. giant.

47. Based on the passage, we can infer that Babbitt

A. has no interest in imaginary things.

B. has a richer inner life than one would expect.

C. has no friends or family.

D. has a special interest in the sea.

48. The author uses the phrase "unroughened hand" to suggest that Babbitt

J. is a hard worker.

K. does not do manual labor.

L. is healthy.

M. has a lot of wealth.

49. What common saying best sums up the passage?

   A. Appearances can be deceiving.

   B. Judge not lest you be judged.

   C. Money makes the world go 'round.

   D. When life gives you lemons, make lemonade.

50. The neighborhood that George Babbitt lives in is called

   J. Dutch Colony.

   K. Zenith.

   L. Floral Heights.

   M. None of the above

WRITTEN EXPRESSION
50 Questions—30 Minutes

Turn to the Written Expression section of your answer sheet to answer the questions in this section.

Directions: This is a test of how well you can find mistakes in writing.

- For the questions with mistakes in spelling, capitalization, and punctuation, choose the answer with the same letter as the **line** containing the mistake.

- For the questions with mistakes in usage and expression, choose the answer with the same letter as the **line** containing the mistake, or choose the word, phrase, or sentence that is better than the others.

- When there is no mistake or no change needed, choose the last answer choice.

1. A. ocean
   B. calculer
   C. trench
   D. minute
   E. *(No mistakes)*

2. J. transport
   K. attitude
   L. sinse
   M. evaluate
   N. *(No mistakes)*

3. A. receive
   B. fault
   C. liquid
   D. lable
   E. *(No mistakes)*

4. J. notebook
   K. famine
   L. zebra
   M. knolledge
   N. *(No mistakes)*

5. A. destination
   B. declare
   C. mischief
   D. concquer
   E. *(No mistakes)*

6. J. liquid
   K. scrumptious
   L. agregate
   M. conspicuous
   N. *(No mistakes)*

7. A. finished
   B. relyable
   C. chrome
   D. disappoint
   E. *(No mistakes)*

8. J. credible
   K. starlight
   L. venom
   M. accelerate
   N. *(No mistakes)*

9. **A.** initiate
   B. simply
   C. govenor
   D. decline
   E. *(No mistakes)*

10. **J.** monstrous
    K. protection
    L. fields
    M. decieve
    N. *(No mistakes)*

11. **A.** To find my dog, rover, I
    B. sailed across the ocean
    C. to the Johnson's farm.
    D. *(No mistakes)*

12. **J.** The king's jet flew
    K. over the Andes Mountains
    L. and beyond the river.
    M. *(No mistakes)*

13. **A.** The New York Jets' kicker and
    B. the Dallas cowboys' punter
    C. are actually Atlanta Falcons fans.
    D. *(No mistakes)*

14. **J.** President Jefferson once lived
    K. in the famous Virginia Home
    L. known as Monticello.
    M. *(No mistakes)*

15. **A.** For christmas last year,
    B. mom and dad gave me
    C. a coat just like Jamie's.
    D. *(No mistakes)*

16. **J.** The Basketball Coach sent
    K. the injured basketball player
    L. to see Dr. Moore.
    M. *(No mistakes)*

17. **A.** Dr. Jose Sandoz had never
    B. expect to see his cousin
    C. Jules at his office last Monday.
    D. *(No mistakes)*

18. **J.** How many times did a.j.
    K. take a bite of Andre's ice cream
    L. when Andre was talking to Molly?
    M. *(No mistakes)*

19. **A.** The leading candy company,
    B. Sweet Tooth, inc., just announced
    C. a new candy bar called O Yum.
    D. *(No mistakes)*

20. **J.** I can't remember if California
    K. is the biggest State
    L. or if Texas is the biggest.
    M. *(No mistakes)*

Directions: For questions 21 and 22, choose the best way of expressing the idea.

21. **A.** At Shara's office, with incredible food, there was great music, as well as there being an exciting midnight countdown—the New Year's Eve party was an amazing event.

   B. There was incredible food. There was great music. There was an exciting countdown. At midnight, at Shara's office. There was a New Year's Eve party, an amazing event.

   C. The New Year's Eve party at Shara's office was an amazing event, with incredible food, great music, and an exciting midnight countdown.

   D. What an event, an amazing event. There was a party at Shara's office, a New Year's Eve party. There was lots of stuff that made it a great event. There was food, incredible food. Great music that was really great to listen to. And, there was an exciting countdown, at midnight it happened.

22. **J.** To understand advanced calculus, Mr. Johnson has an uncanny knack for teaching his students.

   K. Mr. Johnson has an uncanny knack for teaching his students to understand advanced calculus.

   L. An uncanny knack for teaching his students, Mr. Johnson has to understand advanced calculus.

   M. For teaching his students to understand advanced calculus, Mr. Johnson has an uncanny knack.

Directions: For questions 23–50, choose the best answer based on the following paragraphs. You may see additional errors beyond those in the underlined words and phrases of the paragraphs.

(1) Although <u>seventy-one</u> percent of the earth's surface is covered with water, freshwater makes up less than three percent of this total. (2) Access to safe drinking water has improved over the last decade; however, many people around the world still lack a reliable supply. (3) To ensure that clean water is available for current and future <u>populations water</u> conservation strategies and practices are essential. (4) These efforts must consider the sustainability of the water supply so that freshwater is not removed more quickly than it can be replaced by an ecosystem. (5) Water conservation policies must also focus on delivering safe drinking water efficiently and preserving freshwater habitats for local wildlife.

23. What is the best way to write the underlined part of sentence 1?

   A. seventy one
   B. seventyone
   C. seventy, one
   D. *(No change)*

24. What is the best way to write the underlined part of sentence 3?

   J. populations, water
   K. populations—water
   L. populations. Water
   M. *(No change)*

(1) Today's vloggers aren't just aimless and meandering individuals who have more free time on their hands than motivation and ambition. (2) As sources of media entertainment shift from corporate studios and major networks to creative individuals with cameras, vloggers represent burgeoning and evolving media brands. (3) Some of the most popular vlogs and <u>there</u> creators are now multi-million-dollar empires, with legions of loyal fans and followers. (4) The entertainment landscape has truly <u>changed; according</u> to a recent study by the Interactive Advertising Bureau, more people watch original internet video content than primetime network television. (5) This trend, spurred on by lightning-quick advances in technology, could hardly have been predicted just a few decades ago.

25. What is the best way to write the underlined part of sentence 3?

  A. their

  B. they are

  C. they're

  D. *(No change)*

26. What is the best way to write the underlined part of sentence 4?

  J. changed according

  K. changed, according

  L. changed? According

  M. *(No change)*

(1) Located 67 miles west of Key West, Florida, the Dry Tortugas are a remote collection of seven small islands, or keys, encompassing about 143 acres. (2) All of the keys' shorelines are affected by erosion; over the years, islands have disappeared and reappeared following strong storms. (3) Visitors arrive by seaplane or boat to visit Dry Tortugas National Park, which <u>included</u> all the islands and the surrounding waters and is known for its clear blue waters, brilliant coral reefs, varied marine and bird life, and the former military fortress, Fort Jefferson. (4) Some of the keys are larger <u>then</u> others. (5) Loggerhead Key, Garden Key, and Bush Key make up more than ninety percent of the Dry Tortugas, while other keys are merely sand bars rising out of the sea.

27. What is the best way to write the underlined part of sentence 3?

  A. includes

  B. had included

  C. has been including

  D. *(No change)*

28. What is the best way to write the underlined part of sentence 4?

  J. as opposed to

  K. regardless of

  L. than

  M. *(No change)*

(1) For many <u>Commuters</u>, being locked in gridlock traffic on crowded highways is a common frustration. (2) In the not-so-distant future, however, our daily commute to work, school, and other activities might involve flying instead of driving. (3) Developed after years of experimentation, the Skycar is the most promising flying car model to date. (4) Reaching speeds of 400 mph, the Skycar has a range of 900 miles and is fully automated using Global Positioning System (GPS) satellites. (5) Although their high costs now make them impractical, flying cars could cost about $60,000 each if <u>they are</u> eventually mass produced. (6) Flying cars taking to the open skies may finally move from the realm of science fiction to everyday reality.

29. What is the best way to write the underlined part of sentence 1?

   A. commuter
   B. commuters'
   C. commuters
   D. (No change)

30. What is the best way to write the underlined part of sentence 5?

   J. their
   K. there
   L. it's
   M. (No change)

(1) There aren't many national monuments in the United States as ominously named as Devil's Tower. (2) This unmistakable rock formation, technically a butte, will be located in the Bear Lodge Mountains in northeastern Wyoming. (3) A butte, derived from the French word that means "small hill," is a lone hill that is characterized by steep vertical sides and a flat peak. (4) Devil's Tower is made of Igneous Rock and is approximately 867 feet from its base to its summit. (5) Hundreds of thousands of tourists come to visit Devil's Tower annually, and the tower holds the distinction of being the first declared United States National Monument, having achieved this status in 1906.

31. What is the best way to write the underlined portion of sentence 2?

   A. was located
   B. is located
   C. wasn't located
   D. (No change)

32. What is the best way to write the underlined portion of sentence 4?

   J. igneous rock
   K. Igneous rock
   L. igneous Rock
   M. (No change)

(1) When people discuss the most memorable presidents in United States history, Millard Fillmore tends not to enter the construction. (2) Fillmore, the 13th President of the United States, entered the office in 1850 as a member of the Whig party. (3) Fillmore became president following the death of his predecessor, Zachary Taylor. (4) Among Fillmore's achievements was their involvement in getting the Compromise of 1850 passed, which helped forge a temporary compromise between slave states and free states. (5) Following his presidency, Fillmore and his wife, whom he married after retiring from politics, devoted themselves to philanthropic and social pursuits.

33. What is the best way to write the underlined portion of sentence 1?

   A. conversation
   B. combination
   C. conservation
   D. (No change)

34. What is the best way to write the underlined portion of sentence 4?

   J. our involvement
   K. her involvement
   L. his involvement
   M. (No change)

(1) A variety of artistic <u>movements; have</u> taken the spotlight in the cultural landscape of the United States over the years. (2) Among those is the Hudson River School, which began to rise in popularity and prominence in the mid-19th century. (3) The Hudson River School, whose genesis occurred in the Hudson River Valley of New York, was characterized by stunning landscape designs that were heavily influenced by 18th century European romanticism. (4) Artists who are recognized as prominent members of the Hudson River School include <u>Frederic Edwin Church—Asher Durand—and Thomas Cole</u>. (5) Fine examples of this artistic movement are part of permanent collections in museums and galleries across the country, and many pieces have become highly collectible and exceedingly valuable over the years.

35. What is the best way to write the underlined portion of sentence 1?

   A. movements have

   B. movements. Have

   C. movements—have

   D. (*No change*)

36. What is the best way to write the underlined portion of sentence 4?

   J. Frederic Edwin Church, Asher Durand, and Thomas Cole

   K. Frederic Edwin Church; Asher Durand, and Thomas Cole

   L. "Frederic Edwin Church," "Asher Durand," and "Thomas Cole"

   M. (*No change*)

(1) Tic-tac-toe is a popular but relatively simple <u>(game)</u>, and it has a long history that includes a valuable life lesson. (2) A game that is traditionally played by children using paper and pencil, versions of this game can be traced back to <u>Ancient Egypt</u>. (3) During a game of tic-tac-toe, one player selects Xs and one player select Os, and they proceed to place markers in a 3x3 grid until one player gets three markers in a row and wins. (4) More often than not, the grid is filled with Xs and Os and neither player gets 3 markers in a row; when this occurs, the game ends in a draw. (5) Some claim that tic-tac-toe is a metaphor for life: some battles between opponents are futile and the best possible outcome is a tie, where no one wins and no one loses.

37. What is the best way to write the underlined portion of sentence 1?

   A. "game"

   B. *game*

   C. game

   D. (*No change*)

38. What is the best way to write the underlined portion of sentence 2?

   J. Ancient egypt

   K. ancient Egypt

   L. ancient egypt

   M. (*No change*)

(1) Many of us are <u>aware of or familiar with</u> the term "pug-ugly," but how much do you know about this popular dog breed? (2) Pugs are actually one of the world's oldest dog breeds, having originated in ancient China as early as 550 BC. (3) Pugs <u>were originally bred</u> to be companion animals for China's elite ruling families, and were brought to Europe in the 16th century, after which they spread to the entire world and grew in popularity. (4) Despite prominent appearances in movies, television shows, and commercials worldwide, opinion seems to be split between those who find pugs adorable and those who consider them unattractive. (5) Perhaps one of the primary jobs that pugs have today is to remind us of the phrase that states "beauty is in the eye of the beholder."

39. What is the best way to write the underlined portion of sentence 1?

    A. familiar with

    B. aware of and familiar with

    C. aware with and familiar of

    D. (*No change*)

40. What is the best way to write the underlined portion of sentence 3?

    J. will be originally bred

    K. is originally bred

    L. will one day originally be bred

    M. (*No change*)

(1) What do you know about the <u>avocado!</u> (2) Interestingly, what we commonly refer to as avocadoes are actually the fruit from an avocado tree, and they are actually big berries that each contain a prominent seed in the middle. (3) Commercially available avocadoes in the United States typically come from Mexico, California, and Peru, and are harvested before they are ripe. (4) Once they are dark and soft to the touch, avocadoes are ready to be eaten, and despite their high fat levels, they actually pack quite a nutritional punch. (5) An average avocado is rich in a wide array of vitamins and minerals, including vitamin B, vitamin K, vitamin C, potassium, and lutein.

41. What is the best way to write the underlined portion of sentence 1?

    A. avocado.

    B. avocado;

    C. avocado?

    D. (*No change*)

42. Choose the best last sentence to add to this paragraph.

    J. That's one healthy vegetable!

    K. That's one nutritious fruit!

    L. You should take a multivitamin every day!

    M. What's your favorite food?

(1) Have you ever said a palindrome out loud? (2) Palindromes are curious creations, and refer to words and phrases that read the same <u>forwards and sideways</u>, like *Anna* or *racecar*. (3) Although the modern word *palindrome* was coined by an English playwright in the 17th century, palindromes <u>unfortunately</u> date back to 79 AD, in ancient Greece. (4) If you're ever on the hunt for an extra-long palindrome, the *Guinness Book of World Records* places the Finnish word *saippuakivikauppias*, meaning "lye dealer," as the world's longest everyday palindromic word.

43. What is the best way to write the underlined portion of sentence 2?

    A. forwards and backwards

    B. upside down and right-side up

    C. diagonally and sideways

    D. (*No change*)

44. What is the best way to write the underlined portion of sentence 3?

    J. actually

    K. accidentally

    L. jokingly

    M. (*No change*)

(1) If you've ever been to Lancaster County, Pennsylvania, you may have come across a group of <u>Amish person</u>. (2) Amish people, who are popularly characterized by their simple style of clothing and lifestyle as well as rejection of various modern technologies, immigrated to Pennsylvania in the early 18th century. (3) Jakob Ammann, a Swiss leader of the Anabaptist religion, is commonly recognized as the <u>Founder and Namesake</u> of the Amish religious movement. (4) Recent census studies suggest that there are approximately 250,000 Amish people currently living in the United States, and this population is growing at a far faster rate than other demographic groups within the country.

45. What is the best way to write the underlined portion of sentence 1?

A. Amish individual

B. Amish people

C. Amish worker

D. (*No change*)

46. What is the best way to write the underlined portion of sentence 3?

J. founder and Namesake

K. Founder and namesake

L. founder and namesake

M. (*No change*)

(1) Have you ever wondered about the inspiration behind the dark, gothic castle that's featured prominently in *Dracula*? (2) Bran Castle, a national monument and fortress that lies on the border of Wallachia and Transylvania, is popularly referred to as "Dracula's Castle." (3) The castle, perched on top of a hill and <u>designed. In</u> the medieval architectural style, has a wealth of rooms, chambers, and secret passages. (4) Despite its nickname, Bran Castle is just one of many locations that have been linked to the legend of Dracula, and was never described as the home of the character in the book. (5) Today, Bran Castle is <u>an unpopular</u> tourist attraction, and many tourists from all over the world come annually for a visit.

47. What is the best way to write the underlined portion of sentence 3?

A. designed, in

B. designed; in

C. designed in

D. (*No change*)

48. What is the best way to write the underlined portion of sentence 5?

J. a confusing

K. a popular

L. an aromatic

M. (*No change*)

(1) If you've ever paid a visit to Buckingham Palace in London, England, you may have noticed the distinctive Queen's Guard, clad in red coats and large fur hats. (2) Many people are familiar with the daily Changing the Guard ceremony, a popular tourist spectacle that includes one regiment of soldiers marching to replace the regiment currently on duty, which lasts approximately <u>45 years</u>. (3) These cavalry and infantry soldiers are charged with protecting the official residences of the royal family in the United Kingdom. (4) Those interested in becoming a member of the Queen's Guard must go through a rigorous <u>application interview and training</u> process.

49. What is the best way to write the underlined portion of sentence 2?

    A. 45 minutes

    B. 45 weeks

    C. 45 months

    D. (*No change*)

50. What is the best way to write the underlined portion of sentence 4?

    J. "application interview and training"

    K. application interview; and training

    L. application, interview, and training

    M. (*No change*)

MATHEMATICS

50 Questions—40 Minutes

Turn to the Mathematics section of your answer sheet to answer the questions in this section.

Directions: For questions 1–5, four answers are given for each problem. Choose the best answer.

---

1. According to the bar graph below, what was the approximate income of Southerners in 2013?

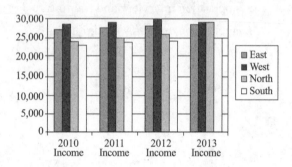

   A. $25,000

   B. $26,000

   C. $27,000

   D. $28,000

Use the following chart for Questions 2 and 3:

2. The pie chart below illustrates the proposed budget for a new company opening soon around the corner. Based on the information in the chart, what will be the most expensive part of running the new company?

   J. Advertising

   K. Office Supplies

   L. Salaries

   M. Rent & Utilities

3. Which two items in the proposed budget when added together equal the amount spent on salaries?

   A. Advertising and Office Supplies

   B. Rent & Utilities and Office Supplies

   C. Advertising and Salaries

   D. Advertising and Rent & Utilities

Use the following chart for Questions 4 and 5:

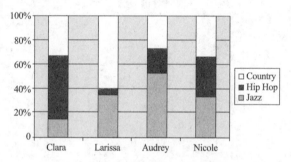

4. The chart above represents the music collections of four high school seniors. Based on the information in the chart, which of the girls has a music collection composed of approximately 60 percent country music?

   J. Clara

   K. Larissa

   L. Audrey

   M. Nicole

5. Based on the information in the chart, if all four collections are the same size, which girl seems to prefer jazz to both hip hop and country music?

A. Clara

B. Larissa

C. Audrey

D. Nicole

Directions: For questions 6–10, estimate the answer in your head. No scratch work is allowed. Do *not* try to compute exact answers.

---

6. According to the chart, if 200 students were surveyed, about how many prefer pizza?

Favorite Foods of Millstone University Students

J. 20

K. 25

L. 50

M. Not given

7. Most half-hour television shows are actually 23 minutes long once commercial time is deducted. If this is true, approximately how many seconds of commercials do viewers see in one half-hour show?

A. 300

B. 400

C. 500

D. 600

8. The closest estimate of
43 + 71 + 19 + 68 + 11 + 29 is _____ .

J. 200

K. 210

L. 240

M. 300

9. The closest estimate of
63,977 ÷ 7,991 is _____ .

A. 8

B. 80

C. 256

D. Not given

10. The closest estimate of
414 – 289 – 106 + 89 + 277 is _____ .

J. 300

K. 400

L. 500

M. 600

Directions: For questions 11–15, four answers are given for each problem. Choose the best answer.

11. The combination of which two portrait types make up half of the entire collection?

The Hudson Museum Portraits

- ■ Water Colors
- ■ Oil on Canvas
- □ Oil on Wood
- □ Pastels
- ■ Charcoal

22, 19%
14, 12%
23, 19%
35, 30%
24, 20%

A. Oil on Canvas and Oil on Wood

B. Water Colors and Oil on Canvas

C. Charcoal and Pastels

D. Pastels and Water Colors

Use the following chart for Questions 12 and 13:

12. The chart above shows the number of yards serviced by Morris and Angelo, each of whom runs a small lawn-care business. Based on the information in the chart, what is the busiest season for lawn care?

J. Spring

K. Summer

L. Fall

M. Winter

13. Based on the information in the chart, which of the following statements is true?

A. Morris experienced a bigger decline in business from the summer to the winter than did Angelo.

B. Angelo experienced a bigger decline in business from the summer to the winter than did Morris.

C. Angelo and Morris experienced the same decline in business from the summer to the winter.

D. Neither Morris nor Angelo experienced a decline in business from the summer to the winter.

Use the following chart for Questions 14 and 15:

Kensington Athletic Club Members

- □ Golf
- ■ Tennis
- ■ Jogging

Men 40–50	Men 50–60	Women 40–50	Women 50–60
22	63	31	71
44		44	
65	44	90	44
	27		20

14. The chart above illustrates the members of the Kensington Athletic Club between the ages of 40 and 60 and the sports in which they currently participate. Based on the information in the chart, which sport becomes the most popular as both men and women grow older?

J. Golf

K. Tennis

L. Jogging

M. Not enough information available

15. Based on the information in the chart, which sport currently has the most total members participating in it?

A. Golf

B. Tennis

C. Jogging

D. Not enough information available

Directions: For questions 16–20, estimate the answer in your head. No scratch work is allowed. Do *not* try to compute exact answers.

---

16. At Morning Dew Café, a plain bagel has 250 calories, and a glass of orange juice has 160 calories. A king-sized jelly donut with chocolate icing and sprinkles has about 740 calories, and a large soda has about 255 calories. Roughly how many bagel–juice combos would it take to equal the number of calories in the donut and large soda?

J. $1\frac{1}{2}$

K. 2

L. $2\frac{1}{2}$

M. 3

17. The closest estimate of 385 − (2.9 × 15.8) is _____.

A. 337

B. 355

C. 360

D. 415

18. George earns $10 per week. How many weeks will it take him to earn about $255?

J. 25

K. 52

L. 144

M. Not given

19. The closest estimate of 7.1 × 7.9 is _____ .

A. 49

B. 56

C. 63

D. 70

20. The closest estimate of 221.8 ÷ 9.989 is _____ .

J. 11

K. 12

L. 20

M. 22

Directions: For questions 21–50, read each problem and find the answer.

21. $(6 \times 2) + (7 \times 3) =$

    A. $(6 \times 7) + (2 \times 3)$

    B. $(7 - 6) + (3 - 2)$

    C. $(7 \times 3) + (6 \times 2)$

    D. $(7 \times 3) \times (6 \times 2)$

22. Which of the following will substitute for x and make the statement below true?

    $56 - (7 - x) = 53$

    J. 1

    K. 2

    L. 3

    M. 4

23. An angle that is greater than 90° and less than 180° is a(n)

    A. acute angle.

    B. right angle.

    C. reflex angle.

    D. obtuse angle.

24.

    What was the average temperature on the afternoon shown in the above graph?

    J. 20°

    K. 24°

    L. 25°

    M. 30°

25. Mr. Ramos has agreed to borrow $3,500 for one year at 10% interest. What is the total amount he will pay back to the bank?

    A. $350

    B. $3,675

    C. $3,700

    D. $3,850

26. Which of the following statements is true?

    J. $4 \times 5 < 4 \times 1 + 6$

    K. $87 + 3 < 30$

    L. $2^5 = 2 \times 5$

    M. $\dfrac{1}{4} < \dfrac{1}{5}$

27. If one angle of a triangle measures 115°, then the sum of the other two angles is

A. 65°

B. 75°

C. 195°

D. 245°

28. At 20 miles per hour, how long does it take to travel 1 mile?

J. 1 min.

K. 2 min.

L. 3 min.

M. 4 min.

29. Approximate the circumference of a circle whose radius is 21 feet. (Use $\pi = \dfrac{22}{7}$.)

A. 65.94 feet

B. 132 feet

C. 153 feet

D. 1,769.4 feet

30. Nikolai made $8.80 per hour this summer selling hot dogs at the baseball stadium. If union rules require that each stadium employee receive a raise of between 10% and 20% each year, what is the acceptable range for Nikolai's hourly wage next summer?

J. $8.80 to $9.00

K. $9.04 to $9.52

L. $9.68 to $10.56

M. $10.57 to $11.4

31.

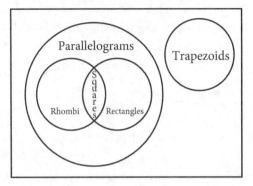

From the diagram above, we know that

A. all trapezoids are parallelograms.

B. some rhombi are parallelograms.

C. some rectangles are rhombi.

D. all parallelograms are rectangles.

32. How many 2-inch tiles would have to be put around the outside edge of a 4-foot × 12-foot rectangle to completely frame the rectangle?

J. 32

K. 36

L. 192

M. 196

33. A certain highway intersection has had *A* accidents over a ten-year period, resulting in *B* deaths. What is the yearly average death rate for the intersection?

A. $A + B - 10$

B. $\dfrac{B}{10}$

C. $10 - \dfrac{A}{B}$

D. $\dfrac{AB}{12}$

34. Which point is named by the ordered pair (–4, 4)?

J. Point A

K. Point B

L. Point C

M. Point D

35. What are the coordinates of point *P* on the graph?

A. $\left(-2\frac{1}{2}, 0\right)$

B. $\left(0, -3\frac{1}{2}\right)$

C. $\left(0, -2\frac{1}{2}\right)$

D. $\left(-1, -2\frac{1}{2}\right)$

36. On a blueprint, 2 inches represents 24 feet. How long must a line be to represent 72 feet?

J. 4 inches

K. 6 inches

L. 12 inches

M. 36 inches

37. A store puts a pair of $14 jeans on sale at a 25% discount. What is the new selling price?

A. $3.50

B. $10.50

C. $13.65

D. $13.75

38.

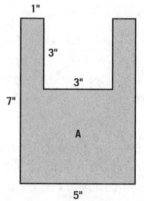

The area of figure A is

J. 19 sq. in.

K. 26 sq. in.

L. 30 sq. in.

M. 44 sq. in.

39. A boy of *M* years old has a brother six years older and a sister four years younger. The combined age of the three is

A. $M + 10$

B. $3M + 2$

C. $3M - 2$

D. $2M - 6$

40. Event A occurs every 14 minutes and event B every 12 minutes. If they both occur at 1:00 p.m., when will be the next time that both occur together?

J. 1:48 p.m.

K. 2:12 p.m.

L. 2:24 p.m.

M. 3:48 p.m.

41. The ratio of six inches to six feet is

A. 1:6

B. 12:1

C. 1:12

D. 24:1

42. Event A occurs every 4 years, event B every 11 years, and event C every 33 years. If they last occurred together in 1950, what is the next year they will occur simultaneously?

J. 1983

K. 2082

L. 3402

M. 6804

43.

Two drivers, Piper and Kip, begin at point C simultaneously. Piper drives from C to B to A. Kip drives directly to A at 50 mph. How fast must Piper drive to get to A first?

A. Less than 50 mph

B. Less than 60 mph

C. Less than 70 mph

D. More than 70 mph

44.

The graph above shows

J. *x* increasing faster than *y*.

K. *y* increasing faster than *x*.

L. *x* increasing as fast as *y*.

M. no relationship between *x* and *y*.

45. In the number 6,000,600,000, there are

A. 6 billions and 6 hundred thousands.

B. 6 millions and 6 thousands.

C. 6 billions and 6 millions.

D. 6 millions and 60 thousands.

46. One of the scales used in drawing topographic maps is 1:24,000. On a scale of this sort, 1 inch on the map would equal how much distance on the ground?

J. 1 inch

K. 2,000 feet

L. 24,000 feet

M. 1 mile

47. If 'A' number of people each make 'L' things, the total number of things made is

A. A/L

B. $A + L$

C. $A - L$

D. AL

48.

Based upon the graph above, what is the cost per item if 400 items are manufactured?

J. < $20

K. $20

L. $28

M. $40

49.

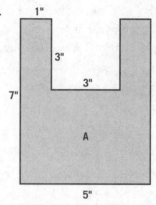

Note: In the figure above, assume that any angle which appears to be a right angle *is* a right angle.

The perimeter of figure A is

A. 19 in.

B. 23 in.

C. 24 in.

D. 30 in.

50. Of 27 people in a certain group, 15 are men and 12 are women. In the simplest form, what is the ratio of men to women?

J. 15:12

K. 12:15

L. 5:4

M. 27:12

ABILITY

50 Questions—32 Minutes

Figure Classification

Turn to the Ability section of your answer sheet to answer the questions in this section.

Directions: In questions 1–20, the first three figures are alike in certain ways. Choose the answer choice that corresponds to the first three figures.

1.

A. B. C. D. E.

2.

J. K. L. M. N.

3.

A. B. C. D. E.

4.

J. K. L. M. N.

5.

A. B. C. D. E.

12.

J. K. L. M. N.

13.

A. B. C. D. E.

14.

J. K. L. M. N.

15.

A. B. C. D. E.

16.

J. K. L. M. N.

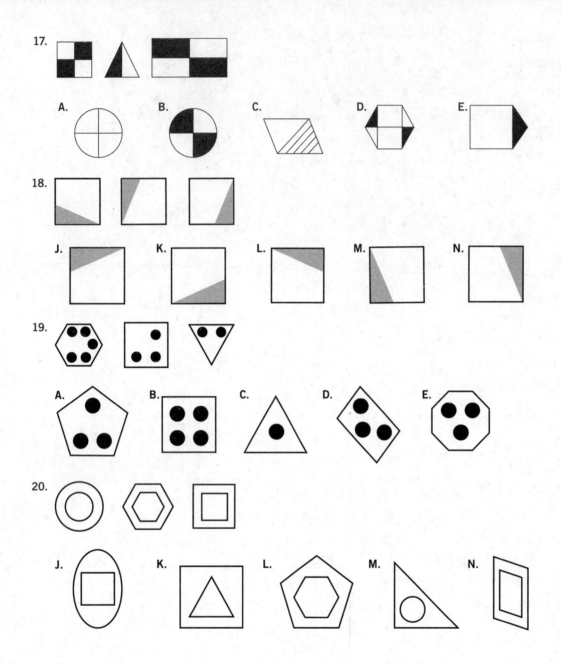

Figure Matrices

Directions: In questions 1–20, find the figure that completes the matrix.

1.

A. → B. ↑ C. ← D. ↓ E. ↗

2.

J. K. L. ○○○ M. N. ||

3.

A. B. ○ C. △ D. □ E.

4.

J. K. L. M. N.

5.

A. B. C. D. E.

6.

J. K. L. M. N.

7.

A. B. C. D. E.

8.

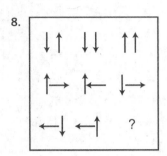

J. →↓

K. ←↓

L. ↑↑

M. →↑

N. ←↑

9.

A. ○—■

B. □—●

C. ■—●

D. ●—■

E. ○—□

10.

J.

K.

L.

M.

N.

11.

A.

B.

C.

D.

E. >

12.

J.

K.

L.

M.

N.

13.

A.

B.

C.

D.

E.

14.

J.

K.

L.

M.

N.

15.

A. ∞ B. △ (house shape) C. ϕ D. ⊕ (circle with vertical line through) E. ϙ

16.

J. ⊕ K. ⊕ (crosshatched) L. ⊕ M. ○ N. ⊕ (crosshatched)

17.

A. trapezoid with 2 dots B. trapezoid with 2 dots C. trapezoid with 1 dot D. trapezoid with 2 dots E. trapezoid with 2 dots

18.

J.   K.   L.   M.   N.

19.

A.   B.   C.   D.   E.

20.

J.   K.   L.   M.   N.

Paper Folding

Directions: In questions 1–10, look at the top row to see how a square piece of paper is folded and where holes are punched into it. Then, look at the bottom row to decide which answer choice shows how the paper will look when it is completely unfolded.

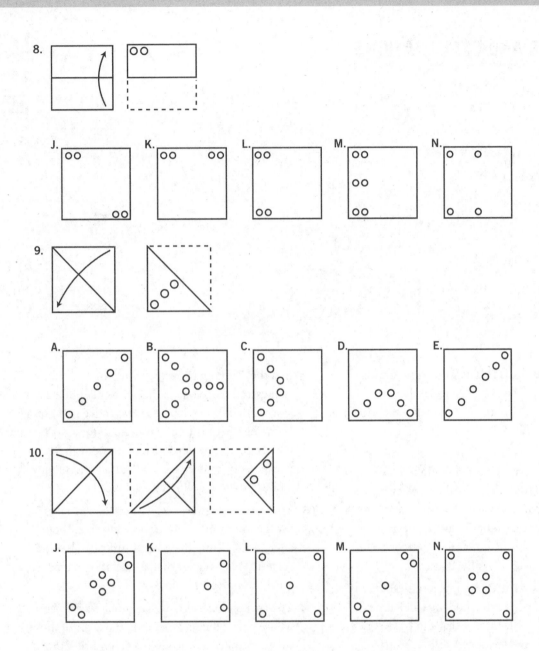

ANSWER KEYS AND EXPLANATIONS
Reading

1. B	11. B	21. D	31. B	41. A
2. L	12. J	22. K	32. L	42. L
3. C	13. B	23. C	33. A	43. D
4. L	14. M	24. L	34. M	44. L
5. A	15. B	25. C	35. B	45. A
6. K	16. M	26. K	36. L	46. L
7. D	17. B	27. B	37. A	47. B
8. K	18. K	28. J	38. L	48. K
9. D	19. C	29. B	39. B	49. A
10. L	20. M	30. M	40. K	50. L

1. **The correct answer is B.** The word *rural* means "in the country." The last sentence of the first paragraph gives the context clue when it mentions "the country life."

2. **The correct answer is L.** Charlie likely realized he had made a hurried, rash decision to move from the city to the country without weighing the downsides. It makes sense for Charlie's character that he then made a similarly hurried decision to immediately call his realtor and try to move back once those downsides became clear.

3. **The correct answer is C.** Finding a rattlesnake, a scorpion stinging his child, and his wife's illness all convinced Charlie to move back to New York City. The realtor is someone Charlie calls *after* he has made the decision to leave.

4. **The correct answer is L.** "Concrete jungle" is a common term used to refer to cities, and here the author is using it as a stand-in for New York City, which Charlie wants to leave behind. He hasn't yet moved to the country (choice M) in Texas (choice J) when he uses the term, and there is no indication that he's unhappy with his job, so the process of elimination can be useful here even if you aren't familiar with the term.

5. **The correct answer is A.** That Charlie and his family want to move back to New York suggests that they had not expected things like poisonous snakes and scorpions, or his wife's allergies. The story is told from Charlie's perspective so we don't know whether his family wanted to move to Texas (choice B), if they never planned to stay there permanently (choice C), or that they would move while Charlie stays in Texas (choice D).

6. **The correct answer is K.** The context phrases "on the day the family moved in," "only a few hours later," and "before the movers unloaded half the furniture" all suggest that the decision happened quickly, on the same day.

7. **The correct answer is D.** The nobles were people whose power didn't depend on the favor of those they controlled and exploited. They knew that if given the chance, common citizens would most likely elect candidates with whom they had something in common.

8. **The correct answer is K.** The reference to thrones in the first sentence of the second paragraph is the context clue that *monarchs* is synonymous with "kings and queens."

9. **The correct answer is D.** This sentence is meant to show that the liberals were not practicing what they preached since they were calling for equal rights but would not apply those rights equally to all people.

10. **The correct answer is L.** The first sentence of paragraph 2 uses the word *precarious*, or fragile, to describe the nobles' collective hold on political power, so choices J and K are incorrect. The passage focuses on the nineteenth century, so we have no way to know whether the common man holds the most power in Europe now (choice M).

11. **The correct answer is B.** The author presents information without taking a specific stand or offering their own personal opinions, so this text would fit in a textbook but not a persuasive article.

12. **The correct answer is J.** The last sentence of the passage tells the reader that the aristocracy could not defeat liberalism, suggesting that the liberals' ideals became the law of the land. There is not enough information to determine whether the nobles would eventually regain power (choice K), whether Europe would allow women to vote as well as men (choice L), or whether liberals would eventually turn into aristocrats themselves (choice M).

13. **The correct answer is B.** The passage mentions that there were other pyramids in Egypt then goes on to say that the Great Pyramid of Giza was set apart from all other structures at the time because it was the tallest.

14. **The correct answer is M.** The passage mentions that the Great Pyramid of Giza is the only one of the Seven Wonders that still exists despite the ravages of time. The word *unharmed* comes closest to conveying this.

15. **The correct answer is B.** The second sentence of paragraph 2 states that pyramids were resting places for dead royalty, like pharaohs.

16. **The correct answer is M.** The second paragraph describes the limestone and granite blocks that make up the pyramid, as well as the mortar that held them together as part of the architecture. Steel is never mentioned.

17. **The correct answer is B.** The second sentence of the passage states that the Great Pyramid is the only one of the Seven Wonders of the Ancient World that still exists. The Great Sphinx is part of the pyramid complex but is not the Great Pyramid

itself, so choice A is incorrect. The passage contradicts choices C and D.

18. **The correct answer is K.** The author describes the pyramid as a "marvel," a "wonderful monument to human capability," and a "magnificent and awe-inspiring piece of human history," all of which convey that they are *impressed* by the Great Pyramid.

19. **The correct answer is C.** Margie had a feeling that after a while, she would stop using the equipment for exercise. The line about the "expensive clothes rack" is a metaphor for exercise equipment that is not used for exercising. The passage does not support any of the other answer choices.

20. **The correct answer is M.** Based on context clues, the word *deter* means "discourage." Margie initially considered the new workout facility but wondered if its location on the other side of town would make her less likely to go regularly.

21. **The correct answer is D.** In the passage, Margie gives careful thought to the fitness routine that will work best for her and has carefully weighed a series of options. Based on her logic, we can infer that in buying small weights and videos that she can do at home, she has made the choice that she is most likely to follow through on.

22. **The correct answer is K.** The last sentence of the first paragraph says that Margie wants a new fitness routine to feel better and have more energy, suggesting that this is what is driving her to pick a new fitness routine. Although the pamphlet (choice J) handed to her by the young man (choice M) does help her make the decision, she had already been considering a new fitness routine at that point.

23. **The correct answer is C.** Paragraph 2 clearly states that Margie is worried that the distance of the advertised workout facility could deter her from working out.

24. **The correct answer is L.** Throughout the passage, Margie shows that she is putting a lot of thought and consideration into her decision. If she were impulsive (choice J), she would likely have joined

the gym or bought the equipment right away. We don't have enough information in the passage to conclude that she is frustrated (choice K) or unhappy (choice M).

25. **The correct answer is C.** Paragraph 1 describes the counselors' grueling and demanding schedule. It would be reasonable to expect people to be tired, or *exhausted*, after a schedule like the one described. The director's appreciation of "how much of themselves they invested" suggests that the counselors are the opposite of unruly (choice A) or disinterested (choice B), and there is no evidence to suggest that they are confused (choice D) either.

26. **The correct answer is K.** *Proverbial* is an adjective to describe something that comes from a proverb or idiom, and it can be used to introduce metaphorical concepts as well. The director uses "proverbial aloe vera" as a metaphor for something that would relax and refresh the way her aloe vera lotion does, like a day off would for the counselors. A metaphor is symbolic and representative, so it shouldn't be interpreted literally, as in choices J, L, and M.

27. **The correct answer is B.** Paragraph 1 gives enough context for paragraph 2 that it should be clear that the director wants the counselors to have a day off as a reward for their hard work. There is nothing in the passage to suggest she doesn't need them the following day (choice A) or that the campers wanted her to make this decision (choice D). The passage contradicts choice C.

28. **The correct answer is J.** The director understands what the counselors are doing and sees that they need a break, so she is being *sympathetic* to the counselors' needs.

29. **The correct answer is B.** Paragraph 1 says that the counselors have been working for two weeks already, and that there are two more weeks before the camp is dismissed for the summer, so that's four total weeks.

30. **The correct answer is M.** The passage does not make any mention of the counselors providing medical care to the campers, but giving advice

(choice J), directing activities (choice K), and listening to campers (choice L) are all included in the first paragraph.

31. **The correct answer is B.** The passage spends about an equal amount of time discussing the development of science and Sir Francis Bacon's contributions to it. The title "Bacon and the Development of Science" best reflects this balance.

32. **The correct answer is L.** To answer this cause-and-effect question, you must identify why Francis Bacon chose to look for a new approach to knowledge. Paragraphs 2 and 3 tell us that before Bacon's time, knowledge was based on the beliefs of the church and that Bacon did not like the idea of basing knowledge only on faith or belief. The final sentence of paragraph 2 notes that Bacon "searched for a way of developing knowledge that he felt was more reliable," suggesting that he considered faith-based knowledge unreliable.

33. **The correct answer is A.** Paragraph 4 tells us that Bacon's approach came to be known by the name *inductivism*.

34. **The correct answer is M.** According to paragraph 2, scientific knowledge before Bacon's time was based on religious ideas and the doctrine of the church.

35. **The correct answer is B.** The answer to this question is found in paragraph 3. *The New Organon*, published in 1620, became the foundation for what we know today as the "empirical" sciences. It addressed how to develop knowledge gained from observing that which can be perceived through the senses, like hearing and sight.

36. **The correct answer is L.** To answer this inference question, you must draw on information given in the passage to make a logical deduction. Bacon did not support scientific ideas based on church doctrine. He advocated that science should be based on empirical research, or what could be observed through the senses.

37. **The correct answer is A.** The second sentence of paragraph 4 tells us that inductivism is the idea

that theories about science can be developed from observing events.

38. **The correct answer is L.** Although *foundation* can have multiple meanings, like a physical structure underneath a building (choice M), a charitable organization (choice J), or support for an idea (choice K), the author is talking about a concept, so *method* is the most likely intended meaning.

39. **The correct answer is B.** While *like* has several meanings, in this context it is showing a comparison between different types of materials, so *similar* is the most logical option.

40. **The correct answer is K.** Since this type of recycling was developed in the 1990s, more than 100 million people have started using it. This suggests the opposite of *unsuccessful* (choice J). The passage also calls this recycling "innovative," so *old-fashioned* (choice M) seems unlikely. The passage never addresses the cost of the program (choice L).

41. **The correct answer is A.** The passage is about how single-stream recycling is replacing a dual-stream process. The title "Simplifying the Streams in Recycling" best reflects this main topic. All of the other options are not specific enough to reflect the main topic of the passage.

42. **The correct answer is L.** *Parse* means to "pull apart" or "analyze." The word *separates* is closest in meaning to *parses*.

43. **The correct answer is D.** The difference between single-stream recycling and dual-stream recycling, as outlined in the passage, is that the materials are packaged differently before the recyclable materials even get to the facility. While it may be true that single-stream recycling changes the amount of processing done at the recycling facilities (choice A), the main focus of the passage is that single-stream recycling requires less work for consumers who want to recycle.

44. **The correct answer is L.** The passage mentions Styrofoam as an item treated as regular garbage,

while glass (choice J), cardboard (choice K), and plastic bottles (choice M) are all mentioned as recyclable materials.

45. **The correct answer is A.** The passage states that Babbitt sells houses to people for more than they can afford to pay. It specifically says that he is not gifted with poetry (choice B) or making things (choice C), and there is no mention that he is a teacher (choice D) either.

46. **The correct answer is L.** In the fourth sentence of paragraph 3, it states that Babbitt "seemed prosperous," which is a synonym for *wealthy*.

47. **The correct answer is B.** The author presents a specific physical picture of what Babbitt is like and then uses that to contrast with the "fairy child" in his dreams. This contrast between the ordinary (Babbitt and his surroundings) and the extraordinary (his "romantic" dream) is best matched by choice B. His dream disproves choice A. The passage suggests that Babbitt is "extremely married," so there is not enough evidence to suggest that he has no loved ones (choice C). While his dream is compared to "scarlet pagodas by a silver sea," the author does not imply that Babbitt is actually dreaming about the sea (choice D).

48. **The correct answer is K.** The image of rough hands is frequently associated with hard physical labor, and the author is trying to show that Babbitt does not have a physically taxing job.

49. **The correct answer is A.** Much of the passage is spent describing the reality of how Babbitt looks, including an observation that he seems "unromantic." Yet his dreams are "more romantic than scarlet pagodas by a silver sea." This contrast is best described by choice A—the others don't suit the passage's themes.

50. **The correct answer is L.** The first sentence states that Floral Heights is a district (or neighborhood) of the town of Zenith. The phrase "Dutch Colonial" describes the house where George is sleeping.

Written Expression

1. B	11. A	21. C	31. B	41. C
2. L	12. M	22. K	32. J	42. K
3. D	13. B	23. D	33. A	43. A
4. M	14. K	24. J	34. L	44. J
5. D	15. A	25. A	35. A	45. B
6. L	16. J	26. M	36. J	46. L
7. B	17. B	27. A	37. C	47. C
8. N	18. J	28. L	38. K	48. K
9. C	19. B	29. C	39. A	49. A
10. M	20. K	30. M	40. M	50. L

1. **The correct answer is B.** The correct spelling is *calculator.*

2. **The correct answer is L.** The correct spelling is either *sense* or *since.*

3. **The correct answer is D.** The correct spelling is *label.*

4. **The correct answer is M.** The correct spelling is *knowledge.*

5. **The correct answer is D.** The correct spelling is *conquer.*

6. **The correct answer is L.** The correct spelling is *aggregate.*

7. **The correct answer is B.** The correct spelling is *reliable.*

8. **The correct answer is N.** *No mistakes.*

9. **The correct answer is C.** The correct spelling is *governor.*

10. **The correct answer is M.** The correct spelling is *deceive.*

11. **The correct answer is A.** The name "Rover" should be capitalized because a name is a proper noun.

12. **The correct answer is M.** *No mistakes.*

13. **The correct answer is B.** The Dallas Cowboys is the name of a professional team and, as with names of other professional organizations

(including the New York Jets and the Atlanta Falcons), *Cowboys* should be capitalized because it is a proper noun.

14. **The correct answer is K.** In this sentence, *home* simply means a house and is not part of a title. Therefore, *home* is a common noun and needs no capitalization.

15. **The correct answer is A.** Holidays are proper nouns and should be capitalized.

16. **The correct answer is J.** As used in this sentence, "basketball coach" is a common noun. If "coach" were included in a title like "Coach Van Gundy" or "Coach Parcells," then it would be capitalized.

17. **The correct answer is B.** Because the action in the sentence occurred in the past, the correct form of the verb in choice B is the past tense *expected.*

18. **The correct answer is J.** Even though these initials are an abbreviation, they should be capitalized because A.J. is a person's name, so it's a proper noun.

19. **The correct answer is B.** The abbreviation "Inc." is short for "Incorporated," which is part of the official name of a business organization and must be capitalized as a proper noun.

20. **The correct answer is K.** The word *state* is a common noun; the names of states—Texas or New

York, for example—are proper nouns and should be capitalized.

21. **The correct answer is C.** Choice C most efficiently and effectively expresses the ideas in this sentence without the unnecessary wordiness, redundancy, and confusion that makes the other choices incorrect.

22. **The correct answer is K.** Although some of the alternate answer choices come close to expressing the main idea of the sentence, choices J and L lead us to the incorrect conclusion that Mr. Johnson needs to learn advanced calculus instead of teaching the subject to his students. Choice M is simply a less clear rearrangement of the correct answer.

23. **The correct answer is D.** *No change.* Since hyphens are needed when spelling out longer numbers above twenty, the word can stay as is.

24. **The correct answer is J.** In this sentence, the subject "water conservation strategies and practices" and the verb "are" follow a long introductory phrase. The introductory clause must be set off with a comma to link it to the main part of the sentence that follows.

25. **The correct answer is A.** As written, the underlined portion of the sentence incorrectly uses the adverb *there*. The adjective *their* is required here to refer to the vlog creators.

26. **The correct answer is M.** *No change.* As written, the sentence correctly uses a semicolon to join these two independent clauses.

27. **The correct answer is A.** Since the passage is written in the present tense, a present tense verb is needed. The past tense verb *included* must be changed to the present tense *includes* to agree with the rest of the passage.

28. **The correct answer is L.** The word *then* should be replaced with the word *than* in this sentence. Using *then* indicates a sequence of events while *than* introduces a comparison of unequal items.

29. **The correct answer is C.** The word *commuters* is not a proper noun, so it does not need capitalization. Choice A is incorrect since a plural form of the noun is needed, and choice B shows the plural

possessive version of the word *commuter*, which is not needed in this sentence.

30. **The correct answer is M.** *No change.* No change is needed because the phrase "they are" refers back to the subject of the sentence, "flying cars." *Their* (choice J) and *there* (choice K) are commonly confused with the correct answer because they sound very similar.

31. **The correct answer is B.** As written, the sentence incorrectly uses future tense for the underlined verbs. Since Devil's Tower is currently in this location, it should be written in the present tense: *is located*.

32. **The correct answer is J.** Common nouns and the adjectives used to describe them should be lowercased unless they appear at the beginning of a sentence. Choice J correctly leaves both terms in lowercase.

33. **The correct answer is A.** When trying to select the appropriate word choice in a sentence, one must understand the context. Here, we are looking for a word that refers to people discussing memorable presidents. *Conversation* is the word that best fits this activity.

34. **The correct answer is L.** As written, the sentence contains an incorrect pronoun. Instead of *their* in place of the singular antecedent "Millard Fillmore," this sentence construction requires the possessive pronoun *his*.

35. **The correct answer is A.** As written, the semicolon in the sentence is incorrectly placed. Semicolons should be used to separate connected independent clauses, which we do not have here. In fact, no internal sentence punctuation is needed here.

36. **The correct answer is J.** This simple list of names should be separated by commas, as choice J correctly does.

37. **The correct answer is C.** As written, the underlined portion of the sentence incorrectly includes parentheses. Parentheses are reserved for additional information or asides, which is not what we have here. This information is part of the regular

narrative flow of the sentence and requires no special treatment.

38. **The correct answer is K.** As used in the sentence, *ancient* is an adjective and should be lowercased, while *Egypt* is a proper noun and should be capitalized. Choice K correctly handles this. The other choices make incorrect use of capitalization and lowercase.

39. **The correct answer is A.** The phrases "aware of" and "familiar with" are close enough in meaning that using both would be redundant. Choice A selects just one of the two options. Choice B merely replaces the conjunction *or* with *and*, which does not solve the problem of redundancy. Choice C jumbles the words so that the prepositions are incorrect.

40. **The correct answer is M.** *No change.* Since the original breeding of pugs is something that had occurred in the past, the correct verb form here is the past plural.

41. **The correct answer is C.** The question-word *what* at the beginning clues you in that this sentence is a question. Choice C correctly punctuates the sentence with a question mark.

42. **The correct answer is K.** The primary topic of this paragraph is the avocado, which we are told is a fruit that possesses a variety of healthy properties. Therefore, the best sentence to sum these ideas up is "That's one nutritious fruit!" Choice J incorrectly calls the avocado a vegetable, while choices L and M stray from the main topic.

43. **The correct answer is A.** There are context clues available in this sentence to help us determine what the right word choices are here. We are looking to determine the directions that palindromes can be read. The examples provided (*Anna* and *racecar*) tell us that they are the same forwards and backwards.

44. **The correct answer is J.** The only logical choice here is to use the adverb *actually*. As written, there's no logical justification for using the adverb *unfortunately*, as there's nothing unfortunate going on in this sentence. There is also no justification for using *accidentally* (choice K) since nothing accidental is being referred to. Since no jokes are being made, *jokingly* (choice L) doesn't fit either.

45. **The correct answer is B.** The sentence as written contains a logical error—you can't have a group consisting of one Amish "person." "Amish people" corrects this error. Choices A and C also incorrectly use singular nouns.

46. **The correct answer is L.** Despite referring to a specific person, these two underlined words are common nouns and should be in lowercase.

47. **The correct answer is C.** As written, the two sentences separated by a period are fragments. These two fragments should be joined into one cohesive sentence with no internal punctuation. Choice A adds a comma, and choice B adds a semicolon, but neither are appropriate here.

48. **The correct answer is K.** The sentence as written is illogical—an "unpopular" tourist attraction does not get many tourists from all over the world, as Bran Castle does. A better adjective to describe a well-visited tourist attraction is *popular*. Neither *confusing* (choice J) nor *aromatic* (choice L) are logical descriptions of the castle.

49. **The correct answer is A.** The only answer choice that contains a time period that can occur daily is choice A, 45 minutes.

50. **The correct answer is L.** This list of steps for applying to become a member of the Queen's Guard should be separated by commas.

Mathematics

1. A	11. A	21. C	31. C	41. C
2. L	12. K	22. M	32. M	42. K
3. B	13. B	23. D	33. B	43. D
4. K	14. J	24. J	34. M	44. L
5. C	15. C	25. D	35. C	45. A
6. L	16. L	26. K	36. K	46. K
7. B	17. A	27. A	37. B	47. D
8. L	18. J	28. L	38. K	48. J
9. A	19. B	29. B	39. B	49. D
10. K	20. M	30. L	40. L	50. L

1. **The correct answer is A.** According to the bar graph, the approximate income of Southerners (the white bar) in 2013 was $25,000.

2. **The correct answer is L.** The money that will be spent on salaries represents 45% of the entire budget—more than any other single category of expenditure.

3. **The correct answer is B.** When added together, Rent & Utilities plus Office Supplies (31% + 14% = 45%) equals Salaries (45%).

4. **The correct answer is K.** Each horizontal band on the chart equals 20%. Even though the white portion (country music) of Larissa's column starts at the 40% mark, it is easy to see that it occupies 3 bands. Since 3 times 20 equals 60, Larissa's collection includes 60% country.

5. **The correct answer is C.** Audrey's collection consists of approximately 50% jazz, 20% hip hop, and 30% country.

6. **The correct answer is L.** About one fourth, or 25 percent, chose pizza. $200 \times 0.25 = 50$.

7. **The correct answer is B.** Subtract 23 minutes from 30 to determine how many minutes of commercials are seen; $30 - 23 = 7$. Seven minutes is 7×60 seconds = 420 seconds, which is about 400.

8. **The correct answer is L.** The original addition problem of $43 + 71 + 19 + 68 + 11 + 29$ can be approximated to $40 + 70 + 20 + 70 + 10 + 30$, which is 240.

9. **The correct answer is A.** $63,977 \div 7,991$ is approximately $64,000 \div 8000$, which is 8. Since this is a division problem, you could drop the zeros from the estimates on both figures, and you would still arrive at the correct answer; $64 \div 8 = 8$.

10. **The correct answer is K.** $414 - 289 - 106 + 89 + 277$ is approximately $400 - 300 - 100 + 100 + 300 = 400$.

11. **The correct answer is A.** Oil on Canvas and Oil on Wood make up 59 of the 118 portraits, or 50 percent of the portraits.

12. **The correct answer is K.** Morris had 28 lawns in the summer, and Angelo had 30 lawns in the summer.

13. **The correct answer is B.** Angelo experienced a bigger decline in business from the summer to the winter than Morris did; Angelo's business went from 30 lawns in the summer to 6 lawns in the winter, a difference of 24, whereas Morris' business went from 28 to 7 in the same period, a difference of only 21.

14. **The correct answer is J.** The number of members who play golf in the older-age category is much more than the number of members who play golf in the younger-age category. This holds true for both men and women.

15. **The correct answer is C.** A total of 202 members currently participate in jogging, whereas 187 members participate in golf and 176 members participate in tennis.

16. **The correct answer is L.** It would take roughly $2\frac{1}{2}$ combos of approximately 400 calories to equal the approximately 1,000 calories of the donut-soda combo.

17. **The correct answer is A.** 385 – (2.9 × 15.8) is approximately equal to 385 – (3 × 16) = 385 – 48 = 337.

18. **The correct answer is J.** If you revised the $255 to $250, it is easy to recognize that 10 goes into 250 exactly 25 times. It would take about 25 weeks to earn $255.

19. **The correct answer is B.** 7.1 × 7.9 is approximately 7 × 8, which is 56.

20. **The correct answer is M.** 221.8 ÷ 9.989 is approximately 222 ÷ 10. 222 ÷ 10 is 22.2, or about 22.

21. **The correct answer is C.** The order in which numbers are added does not affect the sum, but changing the signs does. Choice A has the operational symbols correct but has incorrectly transposed the numbers in the parentheses. Choice B changes the signs within the parentheses from multiplication to subtraction, and choice D changes the operator between the two sets of parentheses from addition to multiplication. As such, both choices are incorrect.

22. **The correct answer is M.** We want the amount in the parentheses to be equal to 3. This can only be accomplished if the value of x is equal to 4.

23. **The correct answer is D.** An angle that is greater than 90° and less than 180° is an obtuse angle.

24. **The correct answer is J.** The average temperature over the 6 hours graphed can be found by adding the temperatures and dividing by the number of hours: 10° + 20° + 20° + 30° + 20° + 20°= 120° ÷ 6 = 20°.

25. **The correct answer is D.** He will pay back $3,500 plus 10% interest. Ten percent of $3,500 is $350;

when added to the original amount borrowed, the result is $3,500 + $350 = $3,850.

26. **The correct answer is K.** Each option must be examined. Choice K is true because 87 divided by 3 equals 29, and 29 is less than 30. Choice J is false because 4 times 5 is 20, which is not less than 4 × 1 + 6, which equals 10. Choice L is false because 2^5 equals 32, which does not equal 2 × 5, or 10. Choice M is false because $\frac{1}{4}$ is greater than (not less than) $\frac{1}{5}$.

27. **The correct answer is A.** The sum of the angles of a triangle is 180°. Therefore, the sum of the other two angles must be 180° – 115° = 65°.

28. **The correct answer is L.** Because Distance = Rate × Time, it follows that Time = Distance ÷ Rate. Therefore, Time = $\frac{1}{20}$ of an hour = 3 minutes. Or, because 60 mph is 1 mile per minute, 20 mph is 1 mile every 3 minutes.

29. **The correct answer is B.** Use the formula circumference (C) = π × diameter. We are told the radius is 21 feet, so the diameter is twice that, or 42 feet.

$C = π × 21 × 2$

$C = π × 42$

$C = \frac{22}{7} × 42$

$C = 132$ feet

30. **The correct answer is L.** Start with Nikolai's salary this year: $8.80. Next year, he will have to earn at least 10% more, but less than 20% more. So you need to find 10% of $8.80 and 20% of $8.80. Since "per cent" means "out of 100" and "of" means "multiply," you can rewrite "10% of $8.80" like this:

$$\frac{10}{100} × 8.80 = \frac{10}{100} × \frac{8.80}{1} = \frac{88}{100} = 0.88$$

A 10% raise equals another $0.88 per hour. If you add $0.88 to $8.80, you get $9.68. You can rewrite the second term, "20% of $8.80," in a similar way:

$$\frac{20}{100} \times 8.80 = \frac{20}{100} \times \frac{8.80}{1} = \frac{176}{100} = 1.76$$

A 20% raise equals another $1.76 per hour. If you add $1.76 to $8.80, you get $10.56. The range is therefore $9.68 to $10.56.

31. **The correct answer is C.** Careful study of the Venn diagram shows overlap of the circles enclosing rectangles and rhombi, so some rectangles are rhombi just as those same rhombi are rectangles. The other statements should read as follows: No trapezoids are parallelograms; all rhombi are parallelograms; and some parallelograms are rectangles, or all rectangles are parallelograms.

32. **The correct answer is M.** Each tile is 2 inches wide, so there are 6 tiles per foot. 12 feet × 6 = 72 tiles across each length. Each width equals 4 feet × 6, or 24 tiles. Each corner needs 1 extra tile, so add 4 more tiles.

12 ft. = 72 tiles

4 ft. = 24 tiles

$$(2 \times 72) + (2 \times 24) + 4 = 144 + 48 + 4$$
$$= 196$$

Hence, 196 tiles.

33. **The correct answer is B.** The number of accidents is irrelevant to the question. B deaths occurred in 10 years, so each year, an average of one tenth of B deaths occurred.

34. **The correct answer is M.** Point D is in the upper left quadrant. First read to the left along the negative x-axis, then read up on the y-axis.

35. **The correct answer is C.** Because point P has not moved along the x-axis, the x-coordinate is 0. Moving down on the y-axis, point P is located

at $-2\frac{1}{2}$. As such, the coordinates for point P are expressed as $\left(0, -2\frac{1}{2}\right)$.

36. **The correct answer is K.** If 2 inches equal 24 feet, 1 inch equals 12 feet. A line representing 72 feet, therefore, must be 6 inches long (72 ÷ 12 = 6).

37. **The correct answer is B.** Start by determining the amount of the price reduction:

25% of $14 = $14 × 0.25 = $3.50

Next, subtract the reduction from the original price to obtain the reduced price:

$14 – $3.50 = $10.50 (new price)

38. **The correct answer is K.** The area is most easily found by multiplying the length of the figure by its width, and then subtracting the area of the small 3" × 3" square.

(7" × 5") – (3" × 3") = area
35 sq. in. – 9 sq. in. = 26 sq. in.

39. **The correct answer is B.** The boy's age is M years. His older brother is $M + 6$ years old, and his younger sister is $M – 4$ years old. Adding the three ages together:

$$M + (M + 6) + (M – 4) = 3M + 2$$

40. **The correct answer is L.** This problem requires two steps. First, find the smallest number divisible by both 14 and 12 (the least common multiple, or LCM). Second, add the number to 1:00 and rename it as time of day. The LCM of 14 and 12 is 84. Both events will occur simultaneously 84 minutes (1 hour 24 minutes) past 1:00, or 2:24 p.m.

41. **The correct answer is C.**

    Step 1. To find the correct ratio, write it as:

    $$\frac{6 \text{ inches}}{6 \text{ feet}}$$

    Step 2. Rewrite each quantity in inches.

    $$\frac{6 \text{ inches}}{72 \text{ inches}}$$

    Step 3. Simplify the ratio.

    $$\frac{6}{72} = \frac{1}{12} = 1:12$$

42. **The correct answer is K.** Here, three events occur periodically, so we must find the LCM of 4, 11, and 33 and add that number to 1950. That year will be the next common occurrence. The LCM of 4, 11, and 33 is 132, so 1,950 + 132 = 2,082.

43. **The correct answer is D.** This is a two-step problem. First, find the length of the hypotenuse, so you know how far Kip is driving.

    $$(AC)^2 = (AB)^2 + (BC)^2$$
    $$= (40)^2 + (30)^2$$
    $$= 1,600 + 900$$
    $$(AC) = \sqrt{2,500} = 50 \text{ miles}$$

    This tells you that Kip is driving 50 miles at 50 miles per hour (mph). Kip will get there in 1 hour. Piper is driving 70 miles. To get there first, Piper must drive faster than 70 miles per hour.

44. **The correct answer is L.** This graph contains a line that has points with coordinates (1, 1), (2, 2), (3, 3), and (4, 4). From one point to another, the value of the x-coordinate changes just as much as the value of the y-coordinate. This line is at a 45° angle from the x-axis and will be created whenever the x- and y-coordinates are equal.

45. **The correct answer is A.** The first 6 is in the billions place; the second is in the hundred-thousands place. If you had trouble with this problem, review how to read numbers and determine place values.

46. **The correct answer is K.** A scale of 1:24,000 means that 1 inch on the map equals 24,000 inches on the ground. 24,000 inches equals 2,000 feet (24,000 ÷ 12 = 2,000).

47. **The correct answer is D.** This is a *literal problem* requiring you to "think without numbers." Creating mental pictures might help you solve this type of problem. If each person in a group makes L number of things, the group's output will be the product of the number of people in the group and the number of things each makes. Choice D represents the product and is the correct answer.

48. **The correct answer is J.** Find 400 on the horizontal axis. Draw a vertical line upward until you touch the line. Move horizontally from this point on the line to the vertical axis. Note that you touch the vertical axis at a point that would be below the $20 line. Therefore, it must be less than $20.

49. **The correct answer is D.** To find the perimeter, we add up the dimensions of all the sides. Note that there are some parts that have not been assigned measurements, so we should infer that because each of the angles is an assumed right angle, then the those sides are the same as those corresponding sides whose measurements have been designated. Beginning at the bottom and moving clockwise, the dimensions are:

    5" + 7" + 1" + 3" + 3" + 3" + 1" + 7"

    The sum of these lengths is 30 inches.

50. **The correct answer is L.** The ratio of men to women is 15:12, but this ratio must be expressed in simplest form. Because 15 and 12 have 3 as a common factor, divide both figures by 3 to obtain the ratio expressed correctly as 5:4.

Ability

Figure Classification

1. B	5. B	9. E	13. C	17. B
2. L	6. J	10. L	14. K	18. L
3. E	7. E	11. A	15. C	19. D
4. M	8. K	12. N	16. L	20. N

1. **The correct answer is B.** Each of the figures is an oval.

2. **The correct answer is L.** Each figure consists of a triangle and a square conjoined along one full side of the square.

3. **The correct answer is E.** Each figure contains two parallel arrows pointing in opposite directions.

4. **The correct answer is M.** Each figure has exactly one-third of its segments shaded.

5. **The correct answer is B.** The number of dots in the circle is equal to the number of vertical segments.

6. **The correct answer is J.** Each figure can be transformed to any of the others by rotating it.

7. **The correct answer is E.** Each figure is a regular polygon where all but one side has been given a thick border.

8. **The correct answer is K.** Each figure consists of three copies of the same shape joined at a single point.

9. **The correct answer is E.** In each figure, there are two arrows pointing away from a pair of parallel segments.

10. **The correct answer is L.** Each figure is a quadrilateral (it has four sides).

11. **The correct answer is A.** Each figure consists of an S-shaped part along with a straight segment.

12. **The correct answer is N.** Each figure contains two different shapes joined by a single point.

13. **The correct answer is C.** The three given figures are all triangles.

14. **The correct answer is K.** The three given figures are all circles or ovals.

15. **The correct answer is C.** Each of the three given figures is bisected by a line segment.

16. **The correct answer is L.** Each of the figures has six sides.

17. **The correct answer is B.** Each of the given figures has half its area shaded in black.

18. **The correct answer is L.** The example figures are all identical, apart from being rotated in 90 degree increments. The second figure has been rotated 90 degrees from the first figure. The third figure has been rotated 270 degrees from the first figure. The only rotation missing is 180 degrees.

19. **The correct answer is D.** The number of dots equals the number of sides of each shape, minus one.

20. **The correct answer is N.** Each figure features a smaller version of itself nested inside its outer shape.

Figure Matrices

1. B	5. A	9. C	13. D	17. A
2. L	6. L	10. K	14. J	18. M
3. D	7. D	11. C	15. E	19. B
4. N	8. J	12. N	16. L	20. L

1. **The correct answer is B.** Moving from left to right rotates the arrow clockwise. Moving from top to bottom rotates the arrow counterclockwise.

2. **The correct answer is L.** The third image in each row is created as follows: rotate the second image (the line) 90 degrees and add three of the first image shape alongside the line. This means that the vertical line in the third row should rotate to a horizontal line, and three circles should be added. The only choice that shows a horizontal line with 3 circles is choice L.

3. **The correct answer is D.** The first image in a row is made up of both a small and large shape. The second image in the row is the small one by itself, and the third image in the row is the large one by itself. It could also be said, more simply, that the larger shape from the first figure appears as the third figure when moving left to right.

4. **The correct answer is N.** The third triangle in each row has sides that obey the following rule: a side is solid if the corresponding side is solid in either the first or second image in the row.

5. **The correct answer is A.** The third image in each row consists of the first two images in the row placed atop one another, with their intersection shaded in. The third image in each row preserves the angle of the first two images. The missing image is shown in choice A.

6. **The correct answer is L.** Moving from column to column changes dashed segments to solid and vice versa, and also changes the number of dashes that make up each dashed segment. For the third column, that number is four.

7. **The correct answer is D.** The last image in each column consists of those segments that the

first and second images in the row both have in common.

8. **The correct answer is J.** Moving from the first to second image in each row, the first arrow remains the same while the second arrow is reversed. Moving from the second to the third image in each row, both arrows are reversed.

9. **The correct answer is C.** Images that are horizontally adjacent to each other are horizontal reflections of each other, so the third image in each row is identical to the first image in the row. Which row an image is in determines whether neither end is shaded (first row), only the square is shaded (second row), or both the square and the circle are shaded (third row).

10. **The correct answer is K.** In the third square in each row, a corner is shaded only if it is not shaded in either of the first two squares in the row.

11. **The correct answer is C.** The images in each column rotate by 90 degrees clockwise as you move from top to bottom.

12. **The correct answer is N.** The columns differ in the pattern inside each shape; for the third column, the pattern includes both horizontal and vertical segments. Each row consists of a square, a triangle, and a circle, so the missing image must be a circle.

13. **The correct answer is D.** Starting with the first image in a row, obtain the third image in the row by mentally erasing any parts that appear in the second image.

14. **The correct answer is J.** The third column consists of triangles, and the third row consists of three copies of a shape put together.

15. **The correct answer is E.** The third image in a row is formed by moving the first two images in the row towards each other until they touch.

16. **The correct answer is L.** Moving from top to bottom adds a horizontal stripe while moving from left to right adds a vertical stripe.

17. **The correct answer is A.** Moving left to right, the rule is to subtract one dot and rotate the shape 180 degrees for each step.

18. **The correct answer is M.** Multiply the figure from the first box and use it to fill the second box to get the figure for box three.

19. **The correct answer is B.** Center the lines from the second figure inside the first figure to get the figure for box three.

20. **The correct answer is L.** Use a dot to join the line segments from the first and second figures in a row to get the third figure.

NOTES

Paper Folding

1. A	3. C	5. B	7. D	9. E
2. N	4. M	6. J	8. L	10. J

1. **The correct answer is A.** Both holes reflect upward across the horizontal. The one near the center line remains near the center line while the one in the bottom-left corner ends up in the top-left corner.

2. **The correct answer is N.** Each hole reflects across the diagonal fold. The hole in the bottom-right corner ends up in the top-left corner while the one on the right edge ends up on the top edge.

3. **The correct answer is C.** The single hole is punched near the bottom edge in the middle of its quadrant. Unfolding the second fold reflects the hole to the top of the paper, also along the edge and in the middle of its quadrant. Unfolding the first fold results in the two holes reflecting to the left side of the sheet, resulting in a total of four holes.

4. **The correct answer is M.** The hole reflects along the second diagonal fold onto the center of the left edge of the page, and then the two holes reflect onto the centers of the right and top edges, respectively.

5. **The correct answer is B.** The holes in the corners are unaffected by the unfolding. The hole near the center of the page reflects up and to the right towards the top-right corner of the page.

6. **The correct answer is J.** Both holes are on the bottom edge, an area which is not involved in any of the folds.

7. **The correct answer is D.** The hole is centered in the left half of the page. When reflected across the vertical fold, it ends up in the center of the right half of the page.

8. **The correct answer is L.** From the top-left corner, the two holes reflect onto the bottom-left corner.

9. **The correct answer is E.** The holes extending from the bottom-left corner to the center of the page reflect across the diagonal fold. They form the other half of the line that continues from the center of the page to the top-right corner.

10. **The correct answer is J.** After unfolding the second fold, the two holes reflect towards the bottom-left of the page, remaining below the long diagonal fold. They then reflect just across the long diagonal, forming two parallel lines of four holes each.

NOTES

SCORE SHEET

Although your actual exam scores will not be reported as percentages, it might be helpful to convert your test scores to percentages so that you can see at a glance where your strengths and weaknesses lie. The numbers in parentheses represent the questions that test each skill.

Subject	# Correct ÷ # of questions	× 100 = _____ %
Reading		
Vocabulary/Word Relationships (1, 4, 8, 14, 20, 38, 39, 42, 48)	_____ ÷ 9 = _____	× 100 = _____ %
Details/Main Idea/Structure (3, 6, 7, 11, 15, 16, 17, 29, 30, 31, 33, 34, 35, 37, 41, 43, 44, 45, 49, 50)	_____ ÷ 20 = _____	× 100 = _____ %
Inference/Understanding (2, 5, 9, 10, 12, 13, 18, 19, 21, 22, 23, 24, 25, 26, 27, 28, 32, 36, 40, 46, 47)	_____ ÷ 21 = _____	× 100 = _____ %
TOTAL READING SKILLS	_____ ÷ 50 = _____	× 100 = _____ %
Written Expression		
Spelling and Capitalization (1, 2, 3, 4, 5, 6, 7, 8, 9, 10, 11, 12, 13, 14, 15, 16, 18, 19, 20, 25, 29, 30, 32, 38, 46)	_____ ÷ 25 = _____	× 100 = _____ %
Punctuation (23, 24, 26, 35, 36, 37, 41, 47, 50)	_____ ÷ 9 = _____	× 100 = _____ %
Grammar (17, 27, 31, 34, 40)	_____ ÷ 5 = _____	× 100 = _____ %
Usage and Composition (21, 22, 28, 33, 39, 42, 43, 44, 45, 48, 49)	_____ ÷ 11 = _____	× 100 = _____ %
TOTAL WRITTEN EXPRESSION SKILLS	_____ ÷ 50 = _____	× 100 = _____ %
Mathematics		
Arithmetic (8, 9, 10, 16, 17, 18, 19, 20, 21, 25, 26, 36, 37, 45, 50)	_____ ÷ 15 = _____	× 100 = _____ %
Algebra (22, 30, 33, 34, 35, 39, 40, 42, 44, 47)	_____ ÷ 10 = _____	× 100 = _____ %
Data Analysis (1, 2, 3, 4, 5, 6, 7, 11, 12, 13, 14, 15, 24, 48)	_____ ÷ 14 = _____	× 100 = _____ %
Geometry and Measurement (23, 27, 28, 29, 31, 32, 38, 41, 43, 46, 49)	_____ ÷ 11 = _____	× 100 = _____ %
TOTAL MATHEMATICS SKILLS	_____ ÷ 50 = _____	× 100 = _____ %
Ability		
Figure Classification (1, 2, 3, 4, 5, 6, 7, 8, 9, 10, 11, 12, 13, 14, 15, 16, 17, 18, 19, 20)	_____ ÷ 20 = _____	× 100 = _____ %
Figure Matrices (1, 2, 3, 4, 5, 6, 7, 8, 9, 10, 11, 12, 13, 14, 15, 16, 17, 18, 19, 20)	_____ ÷ 20 = _____	× 100 = _____ %
Paper Folding (1, 2, 3, 4, 5, 6, 7, 8, 9, 10)	_____ ÷ 10 = _____	× 100 = _____ %
TOTAL ABILITY SKILLS	_____ ÷ 50 = _____	× 100 = _____ %

HSPT® PRACTICE TEST 4

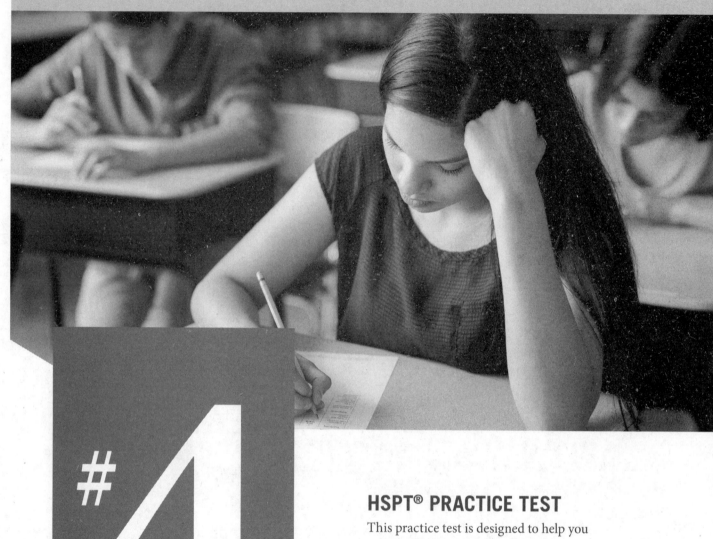

#4

HSPT® PRACTICE TEST

This practice test is designed to help you recognize your strengths and weaknesses. The questions cover information from all the different sections of the HSPT. Use the results to help guide and direct your study time.

>>

ANSWER SHEETS: HSPT® PRACTICE TEST 4

Verbal Skills

1. Ⓐ Ⓑ Ⓒ Ⓓ
2. Ⓐ Ⓑ Ⓒ Ⓓ
3. Ⓐ Ⓑ Ⓒ Ⓓ
4. Ⓐ Ⓑ Ⓒ Ⓓ
5. Ⓐ Ⓑ Ⓒ Ⓓ
6. Ⓐ Ⓑ Ⓒ Ⓓ
7. Ⓐ Ⓑ Ⓒ Ⓓ
8. Ⓐ Ⓑ Ⓒ Ⓓ
9. Ⓐ Ⓑ Ⓒ Ⓓ
10. Ⓐ Ⓑ Ⓒ Ⓓ
11. Ⓐ Ⓑ Ⓒ
12. Ⓐ Ⓑ Ⓒ

13. Ⓐ Ⓑ Ⓒ
14. Ⓐ Ⓑ Ⓒ
15. Ⓐ Ⓑ Ⓒ
16. Ⓐ Ⓑ Ⓒ
17. Ⓐ Ⓑ Ⓒ
18. Ⓐ Ⓑ Ⓒ
19. Ⓐ Ⓑ Ⓒ
20. Ⓐ Ⓑ Ⓒ
21. Ⓐ Ⓑ Ⓒ Ⓓ
22. Ⓐ Ⓑ Ⓒ Ⓓ
23. Ⓐ Ⓑ Ⓒ Ⓓ
24. Ⓐ Ⓑ Ⓒ Ⓓ

25. Ⓐ Ⓑ Ⓒ Ⓓ
26. Ⓐ Ⓑ Ⓒ Ⓓ
27. Ⓐ Ⓑ Ⓒ Ⓓ
28. Ⓐ Ⓑ Ⓒ Ⓓ
29. Ⓐ Ⓑ Ⓒ Ⓓ
30. Ⓐ Ⓑ Ⓒ Ⓓ
31. Ⓐ Ⓑ Ⓒ Ⓓ
32. Ⓐ Ⓑ Ⓒ Ⓓ
33. Ⓐ Ⓑ Ⓒ Ⓓ
34. Ⓐ Ⓑ Ⓒ Ⓓ
35. Ⓐ Ⓑ Ⓒ Ⓓ
36. Ⓐ Ⓑ Ⓒ Ⓓ

37. Ⓐ Ⓑ Ⓒ Ⓓ
38. Ⓐ Ⓑ Ⓒ Ⓓ
39. Ⓐ Ⓑ Ⓒ Ⓓ
40. Ⓐ Ⓑ Ⓒ Ⓓ
41. Ⓐ Ⓑ Ⓒ Ⓓ
42. Ⓐ Ⓑ Ⓒ Ⓓ
43. Ⓐ Ⓑ Ⓒ Ⓓ
44. Ⓐ Ⓑ Ⓒ Ⓓ
45. Ⓐ Ⓑ Ⓒ Ⓓ
46. Ⓐ Ⓑ Ⓒ Ⓓ
47. Ⓐ Ⓑ Ⓒ Ⓓ
48. Ⓐ Ⓑ Ⓒ Ⓓ

49. Ⓐ Ⓑ Ⓒ Ⓓ
50. Ⓐ Ⓑ Ⓒ Ⓓ
51. Ⓐ Ⓑ Ⓒ Ⓓ
52. Ⓐ Ⓑ Ⓒ Ⓓ
53. Ⓐ Ⓑ Ⓒ Ⓓ
54. Ⓐ Ⓑ Ⓒ Ⓓ
55. Ⓐ Ⓑ Ⓒ Ⓓ
56. Ⓐ Ⓑ Ⓒ Ⓓ
57. Ⓐ Ⓑ Ⓒ Ⓓ
58. Ⓐ Ⓑ Ⓒ Ⓓ
59. Ⓐ Ⓑ Ⓒ Ⓓ
60. Ⓐ Ⓑ Ⓒ Ⓓ

Quantitative Skills

61. Ⓐ Ⓑ Ⓒ Ⓓ
62. Ⓐ Ⓑ Ⓒ Ⓓ
63. Ⓐ Ⓑ Ⓒ Ⓓ
64. Ⓐ Ⓑ Ⓒ Ⓓ
65. Ⓐ Ⓑ Ⓒ Ⓓ
66. Ⓐ Ⓑ Ⓒ Ⓓ
67. Ⓐ Ⓑ Ⓒ Ⓓ
68. Ⓐ Ⓑ Ⓒ Ⓓ
69. Ⓐ Ⓑ Ⓒ Ⓓ
70. Ⓐ Ⓑ Ⓒ Ⓓ
71. Ⓐ Ⓑ Ⓒ Ⓓ

72. Ⓐ Ⓑ Ⓒ Ⓓ
73. Ⓐ Ⓑ Ⓒ Ⓓ
74. Ⓐ Ⓑ Ⓒ Ⓓ
75. Ⓐ Ⓑ Ⓒ Ⓓ
76. Ⓐ Ⓑ Ⓒ Ⓓ
77. Ⓐ Ⓑ Ⓒ Ⓓ
78. Ⓐ Ⓑ Ⓒ Ⓓ
79. Ⓐ Ⓑ Ⓒ Ⓓ
80. Ⓐ Ⓑ Ⓒ Ⓓ
81. Ⓐ Ⓑ Ⓒ Ⓓ
82. Ⓐ Ⓑ Ⓒ Ⓓ

83. Ⓐ Ⓑ Ⓒ Ⓓ
84. Ⓐ Ⓑ Ⓒ Ⓓ
85. Ⓐ Ⓑ Ⓒ Ⓓ
86. Ⓐ Ⓑ Ⓒ Ⓓ
87. Ⓐ Ⓑ Ⓒ Ⓓ
88. Ⓐ Ⓑ Ⓒ Ⓓ
89. Ⓐ Ⓑ Ⓒ Ⓓ
90. Ⓐ Ⓑ Ⓒ Ⓓ
91. Ⓐ Ⓑ Ⓒ Ⓓ
92. Ⓐ Ⓑ Ⓒ Ⓓ
93. Ⓐ Ⓑ Ⓒ Ⓓ

94. Ⓐ Ⓑ Ⓒ Ⓓ
95. Ⓐ Ⓑ Ⓒ Ⓓ
96. Ⓐ Ⓑ Ⓒ Ⓓ
97. Ⓐ Ⓑ Ⓒ Ⓓ
98. Ⓐ Ⓑ Ⓒ Ⓓ
99. Ⓐ Ⓑ Ⓒ Ⓓ
100. Ⓐ Ⓑ Ⓒ Ⓓ
101. Ⓐ Ⓑ Ⓒ Ⓓ
102. Ⓐ Ⓑ Ⓒ Ⓓ
103. Ⓐ Ⓑ Ⓒ Ⓓ
104. Ⓐ Ⓑ Ⓒ Ⓓ

105. Ⓐ Ⓑ Ⓒ Ⓓ
106. Ⓐ Ⓑ Ⓒ Ⓓ
107. Ⓐ Ⓑ Ⓒ Ⓓ
108. Ⓐ Ⓑ Ⓒ Ⓓ
109. Ⓐ Ⓑ Ⓒ Ⓓ
110. Ⓐ Ⓑ Ⓒ Ⓓ
111. Ⓐ Ⓑ Ⓒ Ⓓ
112. Ⓐ Ⓑ Ⓒ Ⓓ

Reading

Comprehension

113. Ⓐ Ⓑ Ⓒ Ⓓ	121. Ⓐ Ⓑ Ⓒ Ⓓ	129. Ⓐ Ⓑ Ⓒ Ⓓ	137. Ⓐ Ⓑ Ⓒ Ⓓ	145. Ⓐ Ⓑ Ⓒ Ⓓ
114. Ⓐ Ⓑ Ⓒ Ⓓ	122. Ⓐ Ⓑ Ⓒ Ⓓ	130. Ⓐ Ⓑ Ⓒ Ⓓ	138. Ⓐ Ⓑ Ⓒ Ⓓ	146. Ⓐ Ⓑ Ⓒ Ⓓ
115. Ⓐ Ⓑ Ⓒ Ⓓ	123. Ⓐ Ⓑ Ⓒ Ⓓ	131. Ⓐ Ⓑ Ⓒ Ⓓ	139. Ⓐ Ⓑ Ⓒ Ⓓ	147. Ⓐ Ⓑ Ⓒ Ⓓ
116. Ⓐ Ⓑ Ⓒ Ⓓ	124. Ⓐ Ⓑ Ⓒ Ⓓ	132. Ⓐ Ⓑ Ⓒ Ⓓ	140. Ⓐ Ⓑ Ⓒ Ⓓ	148. Ⓐ Ⓑ Ⓒ Ⓓ
117. Ⓐ Ⓑ Ⓒ Ⓓ	125. Ⓐ Ⓑ Ⓒ Ⓓ	133. Ⓐ Ⓑ Ⓒ Ⓓ	141. Ⓐ Ⓑ Ⓒ Ⓓ	149. Ⓐ Ⓑ Ⓒ Ⓓ
118. Ⓐ Ⓑ Ⓒ Ⓓ	126. Ⓐ Ⓑ Ⓒ Ⓓ	134. Ⓐ Ⓑ Ⓒ Ⓓ	142. Ⓐ Ⓑ Ⓒ Ⓓ	150. Ⓐ Ⓑ Ⓒ Ⓓ
119. Ⓐ Ⓑ Ⓒ Ⓓ	127. Ⓐ Ⓑ Ⓒ Ⓓ	135. Ⓐ Ⓑ Ⓒ Ⓓ	143. Ⓐ Ⓑ Ⓒ Ⓓ	151. Ⓐ Ⓑ Ⓒ Ⓓ
120. Ⓐ Ⓑ Ⓒ Ⓓ	128. Ⓐ Ⓑ Ⓒ Ⓓ	136. Ⓐ Ⓑ Ⓒ Ⓓ	144. Ⓐ Ⓑ Ⓒ Ⓓ	152. Ⓐ Ⓑ Ⓒ Ⓓ

Vocabulary

153. Ⓐ Ⓑ Ⓒ Ⓓ	158. Ⓐ Ⓑ Ⓒ Ⓓ	163. Ⓐ Ⓑ Ⓒ Ⓓ	168. Ⓐ Ⓑ Ⓒ Ⓓ	173. Ⓐ Ⓑ Ⓒ Ⓓ
154. Ⓐ Ⓑ Ⓒ Ⓓ	159. Ⓐ Ⓑ Ⓒ Ⓓ	164. Ⓐ Ⓑ Ⓒ Ⓓ	169. Ⓐ Ⓑ Ⓒ Ⓓ	174. Ⓐ Ⓑ Ⓒ Ⓓ
155. Ⓐ Ⓑ Ⓒ Ⓓ	160. Ⓐ Ⓑ Ⓒ Ⓓ	165. Ⓐ Ⓑ Ⓒ Ⓓ	170. Ⓐ Ⓑ Ⓒ Ⓓ	
156. Ⓐ Ⓑ Ⓒ Ⓓ	161. Ⓐ Ⓑ Ⓒ Ⓓ	166. Ⓐ Ⓑ Ⓒ Ⓓ	171. Ⓐ Ⓑ Ⓒ Ⓓ	
157. Ⓐ Ⓑ Ⓒ Ⓓ	162. Ⓐ Ⓑ Ⓒ Ⓓ	167. Ⓐ Ⓑ Ⓒ Ⓓ	172. Ⓐ Ⓑ Ⓒ Ⓓ	

Mathematics

Concepts

175. Ⓐ Ⓑ Ⓒ Ⓓ   180. Ⓐ Ⓑ Ⓒ Ⓓ   185. Ⓐ Ⓑ Ⓒ Ⓓ   190. Ⓐ Ⓑ Ⓒ Ⓓ   195. Ⓐ Ⓑ Ⓒ Ⓓ

176. Ⓐ Ⓑ Ⓒ Ⓓ   181. Ⓐ Ⓑ Ⓒ Ⓓ   186. Ⓐ Ⓑ Ⓒ Ⓓ   191. Ⓐ Ⓑ Ⓒ Ⓓ   196. Ⓐ Ⓑ Ⓒ Ⓓ

177. Ⓐ Ⓑ Ⓒ Ⓓ   182. Ⓐ Ⓑ Ⓒ Ⓓ   187. Ⓐ Ⓑ Ⓒ Ⓓ   192. Ⓐ Ⓑ Ⓒ Ⓓ   197. Ⓐ Ⓑ Ⓒ Ⓓ

178. Ⓐ Ⓑ Ⓒ Ⓓ   183. Ⓐ Ⓑ Ⓒ Ⓓ   188. Ⓐ Ⓑ Ⓒ Ⓓ   193. Ⓐ Ⓑ Ⓒ Ⓓ   198. Ⓐ Ⓑ Ⓒ Ⓓ

179. Ⓐ Ⓑ Ⓒ Ⓓ   184. Ⓐ Ⓑ Ⓒ Ⓓ   189. Ⓐ Ⓑ Ⓒ Ⓓ   194. Ⓐ Ⓑ Ⓒ Ⓓ

Problem Solving

199. Ⓐ Ⓑ Ⓒ Ⓓ   207. Ⓐ Ⓑ Ⓒ Ⓓ   215. Ⓐ Ⓑ Ⓒ Ⓓ   223. Ⓐ Ⓑ Ⓒ Ⓓ   231. Ⓐ Ⓑ Ⓒ Ⓓ

200. Ⓐ Ⓑ Ⓒ Ⓓ   208. Ⓐ Ⓑ Ⓒ Ⓓ   216. Ⓐ Ⓑ Ⓒ Ⓓ   224. Ⓐ Ⓑ Ⓒ Ⓓ   232. Ⓐ Ⓑ Ⓒ Ⓓ

201. Ⓐ Ⓑ Ⓒ Ⓓ   209. Ⓐ Ⓑ Ⓒ Ⓓ   217. Ⓐ Ⓑ Ⓒ Ⓓ   225. Ⓐ Ⓑ Ⓒ Ⓓ   233. Ⓐ Ⓑ Ⓒ Ⓓ

202. Ⓐ Ⓑ Ⓒ Ⓓ   210. Ⓐ Ⓑ Ⓒ Ⓓ   218. Ⓐ Ⓑ Ⓒ Ⓓ   226. Ⓐ Ⓑ Ⓒ Ⓓ   234. Ⓐ Ⓑ Ⓒ Ⓓ

203. Ⓐ Ⓑ Ⓒ Ⓓ   211. Ⓐ Ⓑ Ⓒ Ⓓ   219. Ⓐ Ⓑ Ⓒ Ⓓ   227. Ⓐ Ⓑ Ⓒ Ⓓ   235. Ⓐ Ⓑ Ⓒ Ⓓ

204. Ⓐ Ⓑ Ⓒ Ⓓ   212. Ⓐ Ⓑ Ⓒ Ⓓ   220. Ⓐ Ⓑ Ⓒ Ⓓ   228. Ⓐ Ⓑ Ⓒ Ⓓ   236. Ⓐ Ⓑ Ⓒ Ⓓ

205. Ⓐ Ⓑ Ⓒ Ⓓ   213. Ⓐ Ⓑ Ⓒ Ⓓ   221. Ⓐ Ⓑ Ⓒ Ⓓ   229. Ⓐ Ⓑ Ⓒ Ⓓ   237. Ⓐ Ⓑ Ⓒ Ⓓ

206. Ⓐ Ⓑ Ⓒ Ⓓ   214. Ⓐ Ⓑ Ⓒ Ⓓ   222. Ⓐ Ⓑ Ⓒ Ⓓ   230. Ⓐ Ⓑ Ⓒ Ⓓ   238. Ⓐ Ⓑ Ⓒ Ⓓ

Language

239. Ⓐ Ⓑ Ⓒ Ⓓ 251. Ⓐ Ⓑ Ⓒ Ⓓ 263. Ⓐ Ⓑ Ⓒ Ⓓ 275. Ⓐ Ⓑ Ⓒ Ⓓ 287. Ⓐ Ⓑ Ⓒ Ⓓ

240. Ⓐ Ⓑ Ⓒ Ⓓ 252. Ⓐ Ⓑ Ⓒ Ⓓ 264. Ⓐ Ⓑ Ⓒ Ⓓ 276. Ⓐ Ⓑ Ⓒ Ⓓ 288. Ⓐ Ⓑ Ⓒ Ⓓ

241. Ⓐ Ⓑ Ⓒ Ⓓ 253. Ⓐ Ⓑ Ⓒ Ⓓ 265. Ⓐ Ⓑ Ⓒ Ⓓ 277. Ⓐ Ⓑ Ⓒ Ⓓ 289. Ⓐ Ⓑ Ⓒ Ⓓ

242. Ⓐ Ⓑ Ⓒ Ⓓ 254. Ⓐ Ⓑ Ⓒ Ⓓ 266. Ⓐ Ⓑ Ⓒ Ⓓ 278. Ⓐ Ⓑ Ⓒ Ⓓ 290. Ⓐ Ⓑ Ⓒ Ⓓ

243. Ⓐ Ⓑ Ⓒ Ⓓ 255. Ⓐ Ⓑ Ⓒ Ⓓ 267. Ⓐ Ⓑ Ⓒ Ⓓ 279. Ⓐ Ⓑ Ⓒ Ⓓ 291. Ⓐ Ⓑ Ⓒ Ⓓ

244. Ⓐ Ⓑ Ⓒ Ⓓ 256. Ⓐ Ⓑ Ⓒ Ⓓ 268. Ⓐ Ⓑ Ⓒ Ⓓ 280. Ⓐ Ⓑ Ⓒ Ⓓ 292. Ⓐ Ⓑ Ⓒ Ⓓ

245. Ⓐ Ⓑ Ⓒ Ⓓ 257. Ⓐ Ⓑ Ⓒ Ⓓ 269. Ⓐ Ⓑ Ⓒ Ⓓ 281. Ⓐ Ⓑ Ⓒ Ⓓ 293. Ⓐ Ⓑ Ⓒ Ⓓ

246. Ⓐ Ⓑ Ⓒ Ⓓ 258. Ⓐ Ⓑ Ⓒ Ⓓ 270. Ⓐ Ⓑ Ⓒ Ⓓ 282. Ⓐ Ⓑ Ⓒ Ⓓ 294. Ⓐ Ⓑ Ⓒ Ⓓ

247. Ⓐ Ⓑ Ⓒ Ⓓ 259. Ⓐ Ⓑ Ⓒ Ⓓ 271. Ⓐ Ⓑ Ⓒ Ⓓ 283. Ⓐ Ⓑ Ⓒ Ⓓ 295. Ⓐ Ⓑ Ⓒ Ⓓ

248. Ⓐ Ⓑ Ⓒ Ⓓ 260. Ⓐ Ⓑ Ⓒ Ⓓ 272. Ⓐ Ⓑ Ⓒ Ⓓ 284. Ⓐ Ⓑ Ⓒ Ⓓ 296. Ⓐ Ⓑ Ⓒ Ⓓ

249. Ⓐ Ⓑ Ⓒ Ⓓ 261. Ⓐ Ⓑ Ⓒ Ⓓ 273. Ⓐ Ⓑ Ⓒ Ⓓ 285. Ⓐ Ⓑ Ⓒ Ⓓ 297. Ⓐ Ⓑ Ⓒ Ⓓ

250. Ⓐ Ⓑ Ⓒ Ⓓ 262. Ⓐ Ⓑ Ⓒ Ⓓ 274. Ⓐ Ⓑ Ⓒ Ⓓ 286. Ⓐ Ⓑ Ⓒ Ⓓ 298. Ⓐ Ⓑ Ⓒ Ⓓ

VERBAL SKILLS

60 Questions—16 Minutes

Turn to the Verbal Skills section of your answer sheet to answer the questions in this section.

Directions: Mark the answer you think is best for each problem.

1. Lobster is to ocean as scorpion is to
   - A. zoo.
   - B. desert.
   - C. sting.
   - D. animal.

2. Tea is to leaves as coffee is to
   - A. caffeine.
   - B. hot.
   - C. drink.
   - D. beans.

3. Sombrero is to hat as poodle is to
   - A. furry.
   - B. obedient.
   - C. dog.
   - D. white.

4. Dozen is to gross as inch is to
   - A. foot.
   - B. meter.
   - C. measurement.
   - D. ruler.

5. Tall is to short as quick is to
   - A. athlete.
   - B. speedy.
   - C. slow.
   - D. race.

6. Slice is to pie as piece is to
   - A. water.
   - B. air.
   - C. pudding.
   - D. puzzle.

7. Mold is to clay as carve is to
   - A. bag.
   - B. wood.
   - C. slice.
   - D. artist.

8. Bee is to falcon as trout is to
   - A. shark.
   - B. gerbil.
   - C. aquarium.
   - D. fisherman.

9. Monkey is to mouse as rhinoceros is to
   - A. ram.
   - B. snake.
   - C. turtle.
   - D. goose.

10. Snail is to slimy as rabbit is to
    - A. carrot.
    - B. hop.
    - C. furry.
    - D. smart.

11. Syrah is younger than Myriam. Radja is younger than Syrah. Myriam is younger than Radja. If the first two statements are true, the third is

    A. true.
    B. false.
    C. uncertain.

12. Last week, Antonio ate more nachos than Kevin. Kevin ate fewer nachos than Patricia. Patricia ate more nachos than Antonio. If the first two statements are true, the third is

    A. true.
    B. false.
    C. uncertain.

13. Frieda is thirstier than Paulo. Gus is thirstier than Frieda. Paulo drank more water than Gus. If the first two statements are true, the third is

    A. true.
    B. false.
    C. uncertain.

14. Nareen did better than Tariq in the school-wide spelling bee. Tariq did not win the school-wide spelling bee. Nareen came in last place in the school-wide spelling bee. If the first two statements are true, the third is

    A. true.
    B. false.
    C. uncertain.

15. Poplar trees grow faster than myrtle trees. Willow trees grow faster than poplar trees. Myrtle trees grow faster than willow trees. If the first two statements are true, the third is

    A. true.
    B. false.
    C. uncertain.

16. Iron costs more than aluminum. Iron costs less than copper. Copper costs more than aluminum and iron. If the first two statements are true, the third is

    A. true.
    B. false.
    C. uncertain.

17. Eric swims faster than Marco. Carrie swims faster than Eric. Marco swims faster than Carrie. If the first two statements are true, the third is

    A. true.
    B. false.
    C. uncertain.

18. All the carrots in Bob's garden are orange. All the tomatoes in Bob's garden are red. All the vegetables in Bob's garden are either orange or red. If the first two statements are true, the third is

    A. true.
    B. false.
    C. uncertain.

19. Arianna is the tallest child in the orange classroom. Jake is the shortest child in the green classroom. Jake is shorter than Arianna. If the first two statements are true, the third is

    A. true.
    B. false.
    C. uncertain.

20. During the past month, Sadie downloaded more songs than Roxy. Roxy downloaded more songs than Henry. Henry downloaded more songs than Sadie. If the first two statements are true, the third is

    A. true.
    B. false.
    C. uncertain.

21. Which word does *not* belong with the others?

    A. Kettle

    B. Pot

    C. Spoon

    D. Pan

22. Which word does *not* belong with the others?

    A. Baseball

    B. Archery

    C. Football

    D. Soccer

23. Which word does *not* belong with the others?

    A. Scissor

    B. Knife

    C. Wrench

    D. Saw

24. Which word does *not* belong with the others?

    A. Glass

    B. Cement

    C. Construction worker

    D. Brick

25. Which word does *not* belong with the others?

    A. Pencil

    B. Book

    C. Newspaper

    D. Website

26. Which word does *not* belong with the others?

    A. Dragon

    B. Harmful

    C. Lion

    D. Tiger

27. Which word does *not* belong with the others?

    A. Throw

    B. Catch

    C. Ball

    D. Pitch

28. Which word does *not* belong with the others?

    A. Firefighter

    B. Police officer

    C. Comedian

    D. Problem solver

29. Which word does *not* belong with the others?

    A. Biscuit

    B. Calzone

    C. Taco

    D. Pizza

30. Which word does *not* belong with the others?

    A. Eel

    B. Pony

    C. Seahorse

    D. Whale

31. Which word does *not* belong with the others?

    A. Chisel

    B. Shovel

    C. Spoon

    D. Spatula

32. Which word does *not* belong with the others?

    A. Ladder

    B. Stairs

    C. Mountain

    D. Waterfall

33. Which word does *not* belong with the others?

    A. Winning

    B. Sorrow

    C. Fear

    D. Joy

34. Which word does *not* belong with the others?

    A. Cosmetics

    B. Groceries

    C. Fulfillment

    D. Clothing

35. Which word does *not* belong with the others?

    A. Contemporary

    B. List

    C. Enjoyable

    D. Extend

36. Which word does *not* belong with the others?

    A. Eggs

    B. Oysters

    C. Walnuts

    D. Tomatoes

37. An *anomalous* event is

    A. disgraceful.

    B. formless.

    C. irregular.

    D. threatening.

38. A *courteous* gentleman is

    A. quiet.

    B. sleeping.

    C. energetic.

    D. polite.

39. A *spacious* environment is

    A. ugly.

    B. roomy.

    C. loud.

    D. confusing.

40. A *loquacious* speaker is

    A. talkative.

    B. confident.

    C. humorous.

    D. quiet.

41. A *deft* performer is

    A. clumsy.

    B. bashful.

    C. untalented.

    D. skillful.

42. A *venerable* judge is

    A. angry.

    B. tired.

    C. honored.

    D. untrustworthy.

43. A *fecund* cornfield is

    A. barren.

    B. delicious.

    C. fruitful.

    D. spare.

44. A *cantankerous* customer is

    A. disagreeable.

    B. thoughtful.

    C. pleasant.

    D. informed.

45. A *caustic* remark is

   A. scathing.

   B. comical.

   C. meaningful.

   D. clever.

46. A *collaborative* effort is

   A. exclusive.

   B. cooperative.

   C. individual.

   D. difficult.

47. A *bombastic* speech is

   A. boring.

   B. destructive.

   C. grandiose.

   D. plain.

48. A *rancorous* employee is

   A. tall.

   B. loyal.

   C. swift.

   D. resentful.

49. A *contentious* meeting is

   A. crowded.

   B. wistful.

   C. wasteful.

   D. combative.

50. An *erudite* professor is

   A. confused.

   B. educated.

   C. loud.

   D. tough.

51. A *prominent* leader is

   A. noticeable.

   B. intelligent.

   C. effective.

   D. hidden.

52. Diligent means the *opposite* of

   A. generous.

   B. focused.

   C. passive.

   D. mournful.

53. Industrious means the *opposite* of

   A. idle.

   B. excessive.

   C. annoying.

   D. reasonable.

54. Intelligible means the *opposite* of

   A. agreeable.

   B. fluent.

   C. cheerful.

   D. inarticulate.

55. Denigrate means the *opposite* of

   A. ruminate.

   B. decorate.

   C. approve.

   D. dismiss.

56. Frugal means the *opposite* of

   A. odorous.

   B. wasteful.

   C. colorful.

   D. silly.

57. Altruistic means the *opposite* of

    A. extended.

    B. truthful.

    C. charitable.

    D. selfish.

58. Oblivious means the *opposite* of

    A. aware.

    B. ignorant.

    C. overweight.

    D. comical.

59. Beguile means the *opposite* of

    A. connect.

    B. adorn.

    C. repel.

    D. improvise.

60. Mollify means the *opposite* of

    A. gladden.

    B. aggravate.

    C. shrink.

    D. soften.

QUANTITATIVE SKILLS

52 Questions—30 Minutes

Turn to the Quantitative Skills section of your answer sheet to answer the questions in this section.

Directions: Mark the answer you think is best for each problem.

---

61. What number is 3 more than 20% of 40?

    A. 5

    B. 8

    C. 9

    D. 11

62. Look at this series: 32, 39, 46, 53, ... What number should come next?

    A. 59

    B. 60

    C. 61

    D. 68

63. What number is $\frac{3}{4}$ of $\sqrt{256}$?

    A. 6

    B. 12

    C. 15

    D. 20

64. Examine A, B, and C and find the best answer.

A.   B.   C.

    A. A plus C is less than B.

    B. C is equal to A.

    C. A is greater than C.

    D. C is less than B and greater than A.

65. Examine A, B, and C and find the best answer.

    A. 0.625

    B. $\frac{4}{7}$

    C. 0.297 × 2.1

    A. B is less than A but greater than C.

    B. A and C are equal and greater than B.

    C. C is greater than A and B.

    D. B is less than A and C.

66. What number is 5 cubed divided by 5?

    A. 15

    B. 25

    C. 75

    D. 125

67. Look at this series: 10, 12, 6, ___, 4, 6, 3. What number should fill in the blank in the middle of the series?

    A. 5

    B. 8

    C. 9

    D. 10

68. Examine A, B, and C and find the best answer.

A.   B.   C.

    A. A is more shaded than B.

    B. B and C are equally shaded.

    C. C is less shaded than either A or B.

    D. A and C are both less shaded than B.

69. Look at this series: 1, 4, 11, _____ , 21, 24, 31. What number should fill the blank in the middle of the series?

　A. 3

　B. 14

　C. 20

　D. 22

70. Examine A, B, and C and find the best answer.

　　A. 10% of 80

　　B. 80% of 10

　　C. 1% of 8

　A. B is greater than A or C.

　B. A, B, and C are equal.

　C. A is equal to B and smaller than C.

　D. A is greater than C.

71. What number is 4 more than $\frac{2}{3}$ of 39?

　A. 12

　B. 15

　C. 26

　D. 30

72. Look at this series: 56, 51, 47, 48, 43, 39, 40, ... What three numbers come next?

　A. 36, 37, 32

　B. 36, 31, 32

　C. 35, 31, 32

　D. 34, 30, 31

73. What number subtracted from 30 leaves 7 more than $\frac{3}{5}$ of 25?

　A. 8

　B. 15

　C. 22

　D. 23

74. What number is 7 less than $\frac{1}{4}$ of 64?

　A. 4

　B. 9

　C. 18

　D. 23

75. Elliot bought 23 party hats and paid $14.95. How much was each hat?

　A. $0.45

　B. $0.54

　C. $0.65

　D. $0.89

76. Look at this series: 821, 812, 804, 797, ... What number should come next?

　A. 791

　B. 788

　C. 787

　D. 778

77. Examine A, B, and C and find the best answer.

A.   B.   C.

　A. A has more circles than B.

　B. B and C have the same number of circles.

　C. B and C each have more circles than A.

　D. A and C each have fewer circles than B.

78. Examine A, B, and C and find the best answer.

A.   B.   C.

A. C is more shaded than B.

B. A and C are equally shaded, and both are more shaded than B.

C. B is more shaded than A and less shaded than C.

D. A, B, and C are equally shaded.

79. Look at this series: 95, 99, _____ , 107, 111. What number should fill the blank in the middle of the series?

A. 98

B. 103

C. 104

D. 106

80. What number divided by 4 is $\frac{1}{5}$ of 100?

A. 20

B. 80

C. 200

D. 400

81. Look at this series: 1, V, 6, X, ... What number should come next?

A. XV

B. 11

C. 10

D. IX

82. Examine A, B, and C and find the best answer.

A.   B.   C.

A. A and B are each shaded more than C.

B. A, B, and C are equally shaded.

C. C is more shaded than A.

D. B is shaded less than C, which is shaded less than A.

83. $\frac{1}{2}$ of what number is 7 times 3?

A. 5

B. 20

C. 21

D. 42

84. Examine A, B, and C and find the best answer.

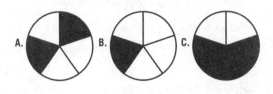

A.   B.   C.

A. A, B, and C are equally shaded.

B. B is less shaded than C and more shaded than A.

C. A is more shaded than B or C.

D. C is more shaded than A.

85. What number added to 6 is 3 times the product of 5 and 2?

A. 4

B. 16

C. 24

D. 30

86. Look at this series: 50, 48, 52, 50, 54, 52, ...
What number should come next?

A. 50

B. 54

C. 56

D. 58

87. Examine A, B, and C and find the best answer.

A. 125%

B. 1.25

C. $\dfrac{25}{2}$

A. A is greater than C, and C is greater than B.

B. A and B are equal, and both are less than C.

C. A and C are equal, and both are greater than B.

D. A, B, and C are all equal.

88. Six factorial (6!) falls between which two numbers?

A. 335 and 380

B. 340 and 560

C. 580 and 625

D. 700 and 725

89. Look at this series: 12, 14, 28, _____, 60. What number should fill the blank in this series?

A. 16

B. 19

C. 30

D. 40

90. Alexei's father got a $33 discount on a new trumpet that normally sells for $150. What percentage was the discount?

A. 13%

B. 18%

C. 22%

D. 31%

91. Examine the triangle and find the best answer.

A. *AD* is greater than *CD*.

B. *BA* and *AD* are each less than *BC*.

C. *AB* is equal to *BC*.

D. *AB* is equal to *AC* plus *BC*.

92. What number multiplied by 3 is 5 less than 29?

A. 6

B. 8

C. 21

D. 24

93. Look at this series: 23, 29, 32, 38, 41, _____, 50.
What number should fill the blank in this series?

A. 42

B. 47

C. 48

D. 51

94. Examine A, B, and C and find the best answer.

A. $(10 \div 5) \times 10$

B. $(5 \div 1) \times 4$

C. $(20 \div 5) \times 5$

A. A is equal to B, which is equal to C.

B. A is equal to B and less than C.

C. B is equal to C and less than A.

D. C is greater than A and B.

95. Look at this series: 100, 101, 91, 92, 82, ...
What two numbers should come next?

A. 72, 73

B. 72, 74

C. 83, 73

D. 84, 74

96. Examine the cube and find the best answer.

A. *CF* is greater than *CB*.

B. *EF* is less than *AB*.

C. *CB* is equal to *CE*.

D. *CF* is greater than *AB*.

97. Examine A, B, and C, and choose the best answer.

A. $\frac{1}{2}$ of $\frac{2}{3}$

B. $\frac{3}{4}$ of 1

C. $\frac{1}{2}$ of $\frac{3}{2}$

A. A < B < C

B. A = B < C

C. A = B = C

D. A < B = C

98. Examine A, B, and C. Choose the best answer if $1 < x < y$ and x and y are whole numbers.

A. xy

B. y^2

C. x^2

A. A is less than B and B is less than C.

B. C is less than A and A is less than B.

C. B is less than A and A is less than C.

D. C is less than B and B is less than A.

99. Look at this series: 14, 28, 32, 64, 68, ...
What number should come next?

A. 76

B. 78

C. 132

D. 136

100. Look at this series: 1, 3, 7, 13, 21, ...
What number comes next?

A. 22

B. 29

C. 31

D. 42

101. Look at this series: A24, C28, E18, G22, ...
What term comes next?

A. F20

B. H26

C. I12

D. J14

102. Examine the graph and find the best answer.

A. B plus C minus A equals D.

B. C minus A minus B equals D.

C. C plus D equals A plus B.

D. D minus B equals A plus C.

103. What number is 2 less than $\frac{3}{5}$ of 10?

A. 2

B. 4

C. 6

D. 8

104. Look at this series: 4, 16, 5, 25, 6, ...
What number should come next?

A. 6

B. 20

C. 30

D. 36

105. Examine A, B, and C and find the best answer.

A. 5^2

B. 4^3

C. 2^4

A. A > B > C

B. B > A > C

C. A = B = C

D. B > A = C

106. Look at this series: 10, $7\frac{1}{2}$, 5, $2\frac{1}{2}$, ...
What number should come next?

A. 0

B. $\frac{1}{2}$

C. $1\frac{1}{2}$

D. 2

107. Look at this series: AA, A1, BA, B1, CA, ...
What term should come next?

A. CB

B. C1

C. DA

D. D1

108. Look at this series: 26, 30, 28, 27, 31, 29, 28, ...
What three numbers should come next?

A. 32, 38, 24

B. 32, 30, 25

C. 32, 30, 29

D. 24, 26, 27

109. $\frac{1}{3}$ of what number added to 6 is 2 times 9?

A. 3

B. 12

C. 18

D. 36

110. Examine the parallelogram and find the best answer.

- **A.** The perimeter of the parallelogram is 10 inches.
- **B.** The area of the parallelogram is 5 square inches.
- **C.** The area of triangle *ABD* is greater than the area of triangle *ACD*.
- **D.** The perimeter of triangle *BAC* is equal to the perimeter of the parallelogram.

111. What number is 10 more than $\frac{4}{9}$ of 27?

- **A.** 2
- **B.** 12
- **C.** 22
- **D.** 37

112. What number is 11 more than 5 squared?

- **A.** 1
- **B.** 14
- **C.** 21
- **D.** 36

READING
62 Questions—25 Minutes

Comprehension

Turn to the Reading Comprehension section of your answer sheet to answer the questions in this section.

> **Directions:** Read each passage and review the associated questions, then reread—if necessary—to find the correct answer.

Questions 113–122 refer to the following passage.

Contrary to what we may have heard, not all fats we eat are bad for a person's health. It is certainly wise to be cautious about how much fat one eats: Many nutritionists recommend that people restrict fat intake to about 30 percent of our total daily calories. Research now shows, however, that it is also important to be
Line sure that a person integrate enough of the good fats in their diet to achieve optimal nutrition.

5   The fats that are particularly important for us belong to a group of fats that scientists call "essential fatty acids." These fats are termed "essential" because they are so vital to a person's health. Scientists have determined that there are two types of essential fatty acids that we humans must get from our diets: omega-3 and omega-6 fatty acids.

    According to nutrition author Clara Felix, scientists now believe that we should consume at least one
10 gram of omega-3 fatty acids for every 3 grams of omega-6 fatty acids that we eat. Although most people tend to eat enough omega-6 fats, the American diet falls short when it comes to omega-3 fats. The best way to balance out our diets, Felix recommends, is to reduce the amount of omega-6 oils we are eating while at the same time increasing the amount of omega-3 fat.

    Those hoping to improve the balance in their fatty acid consumption should start by first limiting the
15 amount of salad dressing and margarine they eat, as well as baked goods such as breads, muffins, cakes, and donuts. Next, they should increase omega-3 fats by adding more flaxseed oil and olive oil into their diet, as well as more walnuts and fish. The fish that provide the greatest sources of omega-3 fats, according to Felix, are herring, mackerel, salmon, sardines, trout, tuna, and whitefish.

113. Which of the following is true about Clara Felix?

    A. She has conducted experiments on dietary fat.

    B. She is a medical doctor.

    C. She has written works about nutrition.

    D. She has a degree in biology.

114. What is the author's opinion about omega-6 fatty acids?

    A. We should consume more of them.

    B. We get plenty of them in our diets already.

    C. We should not consume them in our diets.

    D. They are difficult to find in common foods.

115. This passage mainly focuses on how to

    A. lose weight by consuming less dietary fat.

    B. eliminate bad fats from our diet.

    C. improve nutrition by consuming more Omega-3.

    D. analyze the importance of fat in the diet.

116. According to the passage, nutritionists recommend that we limit our consumption of fats to

    A. around 30 calories a day.

    B. a little more than 30 ounces a day.

    C. about 30 percent of total ounces of food consumed every day.

    D. about 30 percent of total calories consumed every day.

117. According to the passage, good sources of omega-3 fats include

    A. bread, salmon, and walnuts.

    B. olive oil, margarine, and sardines.

    C. salads, sardines, and white fish.

    D. olive oil, walnuts, and sardines.

118. As used in the passage, the word *optimal* in paragraph 1 most nearly means

    A. disadvantageous.

    B. ideal.

    C. expensive.

    D. limiting.

119. We can infer from the passage that the author would most likely characterize the average American diet as

    A. falling short on the consumption of good fats.

    B. falling short on the consumption of bad fats.

    C. ideally balanced compared to other countries.

    D. balanced in terms of consumption of good versus bad fats.

120. Which of the following pieces of information would make the results of Clara Felix's research clearer and more focused?

    A. The school at which Clara Felix studied

    B. How far the American diet falls short on omega-6 fats

    C. How far the American diet falls short on omega-3 fats

    D. Recipes for incorporating more good fats into our diets

121. Based on the information provided in the passage, we can predict that readers who follow the author's advice will

    A. eat more margarine.

    B. increase their consumption of bad fats.

    C. increase their consumption of good fats.

    D. eat an average amount of muffins and cakes.

122. According to the passage, compared to omega-3 fatty acids, the average American most likely

    A. consumes more omega-6 fatty acids.

    B. consumes fewer omega-6 fatty acids.

    C. consumes an equal amount of omega-6 fatty acids.

    D. does not consume omega-6 fatty acids.

Questions 123–132 refer to the following passage.

Few people have seen the world from the vantage point of John Amatt. Some of those who have didn't live to tell about it.

Amatt was a leader and climber on a 1982 Canadian expedition to Mount Everest, which is the tallest
Line   mountain in the world at 29,028 feet. This was the first Canadian expedition to Mount Everest. In the end,
5   it successfully placed two Canadian climbers on the summit of the great mountain. The journey to that goal, however, was fraught with danger.

The trip started with 16 Canadian climbers and 24 sherpas, expert mountain guides who live in the Himalayas in Nepal. By the end of the trip, ten weeks later, only two Canadians and four sherpas made it to the top of the mountain. One Canadian and three sherpas had lost their lives in avalanche accidents
10   during the early part of the trip. The accidents almost caused the climb to be called off, but the team chose to press on.

In his book, *Straight to the Top and Beyond*, Amatt describes how his experiences during the Everest expedition helped his team to learn from their setbacks. In Amatt's view, such an impactful experience of loss helped the team to strengthen their perspective on the reality of what they were up against. It also
15   inspired them to approach their challenges with clarity and humbleness. He believes that one of the greatest lessons the team took from the experience was the importance of taking the risks that they faced more seriously. This lesson ultimately helped make the Everest expedition a success.

123. The main contrast in the article is between

   A. the work of the Canadians and the work of the sherpas.

   B. those who have seen the world from Mount Everest and those who have not.

   C. the success of the expedition and the losses it faced.

   D. John Amatt and less successful climbers.

124. According to the passage, how many sherpas reached the top of Mount Everest with the Canadian expedition?

   A. 2

   B. 4

   C. 6

   D. 24

125. The passage states that the expedition led by John Amatt was the

   A. first expedition to scale Mount Everest.

   B. only successful expedition to scale Mount Everest.

   C. first Canadian expedition to scale Mount Everest.

   D. last expedition that Amatt led up Mount Everest.

126. In his book, Amatt states that his team learned several lessons from their setbacks and challenges, including how to approach their efforts with

   A. indifference.

   B. pride.

   C. ambition.

   D. humility.

127. In the following sentence from the last paragraph, "It also inspired them to approach their challenges with clarity and humbleness," the word *it* refers to the

   A. experience of loss cited in sentence 2 of the last paragraph.
   B. experiences of Amatt's expedition cited in sentence 1 of the last paragraph.
   C. book written by Amatt cited in sentence 1 of the last paragraph.
   D. accidents cited in sentence 4 of the last paragraph.

128. As used in paragraph 2, the word *summit* most nearly means

   A. peak.
   B. success.
   C. climb.
   D. step.

129. Based on the information provided in the passage, we can infer that the author would most likely compare John Amatt to a

   A. professional athlete who attempts to cheat if there is an opportunity to get away with it.
   B. runner who had to stop mid race due to a severely swollen ankle.
   C. restaurant owner who hired a manager to run the daily business for him.
   D. swimmer who overcame treacherous conditions to successfully swim the English Channel.

130. Based on the information provided in the passage, Amatt most likely titled his book *Straight to the Top and Beyond* because

   A. Amatt climbed higher than any other climber had done before in history.
   B. Amatt did not climb Mount Everest alone; instead, he went with sherpas and other Canadian climbers.
   C. the book describes both his climb to the top of Mount Everest and the lessons he learned from the adversity he faced.
   D. Amatt was flown by helicopter straight to the top of Mount Everest and beyond.

131. Based on the information provided in the passage, the "experience of loss" mentioned in paragraph 4 most likely refers to

   A. time wasted while climbing Mount Everest.
   B. lives lost during the climb up Mount Everest.
   C. the equipment the climbers lost during the treacherous storm that hit Mount Everest.
   D. the fact that Amatt failed to reach the top of Mount Everest.

132. The main idea of the passage is to

   A. tell the story of John Amatt's experience and lessons learned through his success and adversity as a climber.
   B. warn readers against mountain climbing due to the potential dangers and perils of the activity.
   C. tell the history of mountain climbing in Canada in the 20th century.
   D. provide the history of attempts to climb Mount Everest, one of the most famous mountains in the entire world.

Questions 133–142 refer to the following passage.

The dark and the sea are full of dangers to the fishermen of Norway. A whale might come and destroy the floating chain of corks that edges the nets, break it, and carry it off. Or a storm might come suddenly, un-expectedly, out of the night. The sea seems to turn somersaults. It opens and closes immense caverns with
Line terrible clashes, chasing boats and fishermen who must flee from their nets and the expected catch. Then
5 the fishermen might lift their nets as empty as they set them. At other times, the herring might come in such masses that the lines break from the weight when lifted, and the fishermen must return home empty-handed, without line, nets, or herring.

But often the nets are full of herring that shine and glisten like silver. Once in a while, a couple of fishermen will venture in their boats along the net lines to see whether the herring are coming, and when
10 the corks begin to bob and jerk as if something were hitting the nets to which they are attached, they then know that the herring are there. The nets are being filled, and all the fishermen sit in quiet excitement. They dare only to whisper to each other, afraid to disturb, and quite overcome by the overwhelming generosity of the sea. Eyes shine with happy anticipation; hands folded in thanks. Then muscles strain with power. It is as though the strength of the body doubled. They can work day-and-night without thoughts of weari-
15 ness. They need neither food nor rest; the thought of success keeps their vigor up almost endlessly. They will take food and rest when it is all over.

133. Which is the best title for this passage?

A. "Hard Work in Norway"

B. "The Perils and Rewards of Fishing"

C. "Risky Business"

D. "The Generosity of the Sea"

134. The difficulties faced by the Norwegian fishermen include

A. whales eating the herring they'd caught.

B. the difficulty of being very calm.

C. interference by rough seas.

D. the jerking of the corks.

135. At the first indication that herring are entering the nets, the fishermen

A. try not to frighten the fish away.

B. strain every muscle to haul in the catch.

C. collect the nets quickly.

D. row quickly along the edge of the nets.

136. When the article says that the sea "opens and closes immense caverns," it is referring to

A. caves along the shoreline.

B. deep holes in the ocean floor.

C. dangerous large boulders that get rolled around.

D. hollow pockets beneath very high waves.

137. The fishermen are described as

A. strong, angry, and excitable.

B. skillful, religious, and impatient.

C. patient, brave, and grateful.

D. surly, hardworking, and cautious.

138. Of the following, the one that is not mentioned as posing a problem to the fishermen is

A. destruction of the nets.

B. theft of the nets by other fishermen.

C. too large a catch.

D. whales.

139. The author of the passage would most likely compare the sea in Norway mentioned in the passage to

- **A.** a peaceful and tranquil pond.
- **B.** a fun-filled car ride.
- **C.** a dark and dangerous storm.
- **D.** an informative historical trip through nature.

140. Based on the information provided in the passage, we can conclude that the life of a fisherman is

- **A.** filled with danger and hard work, with peaks of satisfying success.
- **B.** lucrative and fun, with occasional moments of quiet solitude.
- **C.** serious and hilarious, with temporary moments of enjoyable weather.
- **D.** rapidly disappearing in today's technology-focused modern society.

141. From the information provided in the passage, we can infer that a net without herring to a Norwegian fisherman is like

- **A.** a lost baseball.
- **B.** a store without a manager.
- **C.** a salesman without a sale.
- **D.** lightning striking a tree.

142. According to the passage, which of the following items might *not* be found on a Norwegian fishing boat?

- **A.** Lines
- **B.** Lantern
- **C.** Nets
- **D.** Fisherman

Questions 143–152 refer to the following passage.

In caffeine-fueled cultures across the globe, it has never been easier to enjoy a great cup of coffee, regardless of where you may find yourself. Coffee has become one of the most profitable—and revered—businesses in the world, with ever-increasing numbers of coffee house openings, some of which proclaim to make
Line and serve the best cup of coffee around. While individual coffee tastes and preferences are as varied as the
5   number of bean varieties that exist, it would be hard to find a coffee more interesting—or expensive—than kopi luwak.

Kopi luwak is also referred to as civet coffee, and for good reason. These prized beans are harvested from the digested remains of coffee cherries that have been eaten by Asian palm civets, small squirrel-like creatures that inhabit Southeast Asia. The vast majority of kopi luwak is produced in the islands of Java,
10   Bali, Sumatra, Sulawesi, and the Philippines. Many coffee experts proclaim that civets naturally select only the best, most fleshy coffee cherries to consume—and ultimately eliminate—and that during the digestion process, a process of fermentation occurs within the civets that diminishes the coffee bean's natural acidity, reduces bitterness, and ultimately leads to a smoother and more satisfying beverage.

After the civets consume the fruity pulp of the coffee cherries, they excrete the remains, which are then
15   collected for cleaning and roasting. Because of the unique conditions in which the beans are obtained, their limited supply, and its prized taste, kopi luwak is widely recognized as one of the most expensive and rare coffees in the world. Prices have been known to go as high as several hundred dollars or more for a pound of beans. As a result, farmers and harvesters, keen on profiting from the prized droppings, have taken to extreme methods to increase supply, including trapping and caging these creatures in overcrowded civet
20   farms, which have raised concerns regarding the welfare and safety of these animals. Unsavory merchants have also taken to selling inferior beans under the kopi luwak name in an effort to turn a profit.

While kopi luwak has its critics, and not everyone believes this process yields a superior cup of coffee, there are certainly enough people who either greatly enjoy the beans or are at least curious enough to try it to ensure that the harvesting of kopi luwak remains a profitable enterprise. One could argue that when
25   it comes to kopi luwak the old adage, "there's no accounting for taste," is on full display.

143. Which title best expresses the main idea of this passage?

   A. "Kopi Luwak: A Prized Cup of Coffee"

   B. "Exploring the Life of the Civet"

   C. "Discover How Coffee is Made"

   D. "What's Your Favorite Beverage?"

144. What bodily process helps kopi luwak achieve its distinct flavor?

   A. Respiration

   B. Digestion

   C. Perspiration

   D. Circulation

145. Based on the final sentence of the passage, the word *adage* most nearly means a

   A. warning.

   B. saying.

   C. joke.

   D. secret code.

146. According to the passage, kopi luwak can most likely be found in all the following places *except*

   A. Java.

   B. Sumatra.

   C. Bali.

   D. Nicaragua.

147. Which of the following happens to coffee beans during the fermentation process within civets?

    A. The color changes.

    B. The thickness diminishes.

    C. The bitterness decreases.

    D. The sweetness increases.

148. Based on how they're described in the passage, unsavory kopi luwak merchants can best be compared to a

    A. restaurant accidentally serving you a hamburger when you really ordered a pizza.

    B. contractor finishing a building project three weeks ahead of schedule.

    C. salesman selling cheaply made smart phones and pretending they're more expensive iPhones.

    D. science teacher helping his student earn a passing score on the midterm exam.

149. Based on the passage, we can say that the source for creating kopi luwak, the Asian palm civet, is

    A. unnecessary.

    B. essential.

    C. uneventful.

    D. disagreeable.

150. The author's purpose for including the adage "there's no accounting for taste" at the end of the passage is to

    A. highlight the notion that it's hard to explain why different people like different things, even if they're unappealing.

    B. discuss the fact that most people enjoy the taste of coffee and are willing to pay almost anything to have it.

    C. highlight the fact that coffee growing is a business, and that an accounting department is required to run the business.

    D. assert the notion that everyone enjoys the taste of kopi luwak coffee, which explains its high price.

151. As used in paragraph 1, the word *revered* most nearly means

    A. unpopular.

    B. admired.

    C. unethical.

    D. combined.

152. Based on the information in the passage, we can infer that compared to the kopi luwak, the process of collecting traditional coffee beans is more

    A. time consuming.

    B. expensive.

    C. uncommon.

    D. common.

Vocabulary

Turn to the Vocabulary section of your answer sheet to answer the questions in this section.

Directions: Choose the word closest in meaning to the underlined word in the question.

153. a <u>pioneer</u> in her industry

   A. expert

   B. last person

   C. first person

   D. novice

154. a <u>plausible</u> explanation

   A. phony

   B. truthful

   C. easy

   D. reasonable

155. gave <u>sage</u> advice

   A. wise

   B. optimistic

   C. angry

   D. strange

156. a plaque <u>commemorating</u> the war

   A. describing

   B. honoring

   C. depicting

   D. ending

157. <u>decipher</u> the code

   A. cover up

   B. discover

   C. read

   D. translate

158. his <u>blasé</u> attitude

   A. unconcerned

   B. unusual

   C. uninformed

   D. unhappy

159. <u>apprehended</u> the suspect

   A. interrogated

   B. arrested

   C. arranged

   D. released

160. to <u>forfeit</u> the game

   A. win

   B. lose

   C. surrender

   D. complete

161. need to build <u>stamina</u>

   A. skills

   B. patience

   C. immunity

   D. endurance

162. a <u>lucrative</u> business

   A. failing

   B. profitable

   C. brand new

   D. long term

163. a standing <u>ovation</u>

   A. review

   B. applause

   C. appointment

   D. idea

164. a mountain <u>panorama</u>

   A. view

   B. photograph

   C. trail

   D. terrain

165. a <u>conscientious</u> worker

   A. indiscreet

   B. quick

   C. careful

   D. experienced

166. a <u>voracious</u> eater

   A. picky

   B. tasteful

   C. indiscriminate

   D. insatiable

167. a <u>haven</u> for like-minded people

   A. vacation

   B. sanctuary

   C. house

   D. trap

168. a purely <u>mercenary</u> decision

   A. academic

   B. scientific

   C. financial

   D. emotional

169. the regional <u>dialect</u>

   A. cuisine

   B. accent

   C. history

   D. geography

170. an <u>eccentric</u> millionaire

   A. cruel

   B. shrewd

   C. strange

   D. reputable

171. at the <u>pivotal</u> moment

   A. incorrect

   B. essential

   C. last

   D. worst

172. a sense of <u>foreboding</u>

   A. contentment

   B. optimism

   C. agony

   D. dread

173. an <u>elite</u> squad

   A. exclusive

   B. experienced

   C. large

   D. diverse

174. she acted <u>aloof</u>

   A. foolish

   B. alone

   C. unfriendly

   D. excited

MATHEMATICS
64 Questions—45 Minutes

Concepts

Turn to the Mathematics Concepts section of your answer sheet to answer the questions in this section.

Directions: Read each question carefully, then solve the problem to find the correct answer.

---

175. 19 inches is closest to

    A. 1 foot

    B. 2 feet

    C. 3 feet

    D. 4 feet

176. There are 3 feet in 1 yard. Therefore, to convert from feet to yards, you would

    A. add 3.

    B. subtract 3.

    C. multiply by 3.

    D. divide by 3.

177. If x and y are two different numbers, then their average will always be

    A. greater than both x and y.

    B. smaller than both x and y.

    C. between x and y.

    D. equal to either x or y.

178. 1 inch is equal to 2.54 centimeters. Which answer best describes the number of centimeters in 7 inches?

    A. Exactly 7

    B. More than 7

    C. Less than 7

    D. Exactly 14

179. If the measures of all the angles in a triangle are added, what is the sum?

    A. 180° °

    B. 200°

    C. 360°

    D. 540

180. How many centimeters are in 1 meter?

    A. 0.1

    B. 1

    C. 10

    D. 100

181. If there are 16 cups in 1 gallon, which expression shows the number of cups in x gallons?

    A. $\dfrac{x}{16}$

    B. $x + 16$

    C. $x \times 16$

    D. $x - 16$

182. Which of the following is *not* a quadrilateral?

    A. Square

    B. Trapezoid

    C. Triangle

    D. Rectangle

183. To the nearest tenth, 63.594 is written

    A. 63.5

    B. 63.59

    C. 63.6

    D. 64

184. As a fraction, 0.24 is

A. $\dfrac{24}{1,000}$

B. $\dfrac{6}{25}$

C. $\dfrac{1}{4}$

D. $\dfrac{100}{24}$

185. How many integers are between $\dfrac{33}{7}$ and 8.001?

A. 3

B. 4

C. 5

D. 6

186. Which of the following is true?

A. $a \div (b + c) = \dfrac{a}{b} + \dfrac{a}{c}$

B. $a(x + b) = ax + b$

C. $a(x + b) = a(x) + ab$

D. $a \div b = b\left(\dfrac{1}{a}\right)$

187. It is possible to have a right triangle that is also

A. equilateral.

B. equiangular.

C. obtuse.

D. isosceles.

188. The perimeter of the rectangle is

A. 2

B. 7

C. 14

D. 18

189. Find the median of the following list:
1, 2, 3, 9, 10

A. 3

B. 4

C. 5

D. 6

190. If there is a 20% chance of rain on a certain day, what is the percent chance that it will NOT rain that day?

A. 20%

B. 40%

C. 80%

D. 90%

191. The average of –2, 0, 2, and 4 is

A. 0

B. 1

C. 2

D. 4

192. A boy M years old has a brother six years older and a sister four years younger. The combined age of the three is

A. M + 10

B. 3M + 2

C. 3M – 2

D. 2M – 6

193. Simplify: $3(-2)^3$

A. –216

B. –24

C. –18

D. 1

194. The measure of angle A is

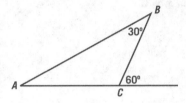

A. 15°

B. 20°

C. 30°

D. 35°

195. Which of the following is a pair of reciprocals?

A. (3, –3)

B. $\left(3\frac{1}{3}, \frac{3}{10}\right)$

C. $(2^3, 3^2)$

D. (0, 1)

196. The circumference of this circle is

A. 32π

B. 16

C. 8π

D. 4

197. The ratio of 3 yards to 18 inches is

A. 3 to 18

B. 1 to 6

C. 3 to 2

D. 6 to 1

198. The square root of 198 is between

A. 98 and 100

B. 90 and 100

C. 19 and 20

D. 14 and 15

Problem Solving

199. George earns $10 per week. How many weeks will it take him to earn about $255?

A. 25

B. 40

C. 52

D. 144

200. ΔABC is similar to ΔDBE. The length of AB is

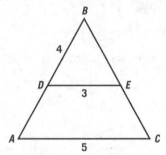

A. $6\frac{1}{3}$

B. $6\frac{2}{3}$

C. $8\frac{1}{3}$

D. $8\frac{2}{3}$

201. Mr. Allen paid $542.40 for his telephone bills last year. How much did he pay, on average, per month?

    A. $45.20

    B. $46.20

    C. $54.20

    D. $55.20

202. Simplify: $(-2) \cdot (-4) \cdot (3) \cdot (-1)$

    A. -24

    B. -4

    C. 12

    D. 24

203. Solve: $4\frac{1}{8} - 2\frac{2}{3} =$

    A. $2\frac{13}{24}$

    B. $2\frac{11}{24}$

    C. $1\frac{13}{24}$

    D. $1\frac{11}{24}$

204. If $-5 + 4x = 21$, $x =$

    A. 4

    B. 5.75

    C. 6.5

    D. 8.5

205. Solve: $3\frac{1}{3} \times 3\frac{3}{4} \times \frac{2}{5} =$

    A. $9\frac{1}{4}$

    B. 6

    C. 5

    D. $4\frac{2}{5}$

206. If $a = 6$ and $b = 3$, then $7a - 3b =$

    A. 7

    B. 9

    C. 32

    D. 33

207. If $N\%$ of 60 is 24, $N =$

    A. 40

    B. 84

    C. 125

    D. 150

208. If $10x - 3 = 2x + 4$, then x equals

    A. $\frac{6}{7}$

    B. $\frac{7}{8}$

    C. $\frac{8}{7}$

    D. $\frac{9}{8}$

209. The ratio of $\frac{3}{4}$ to $\frac{5}{2}$ is

    A. 10 to 3

    B. 15 to 8

    C. 3 to 10

    D. 8 to 15

210. Solve: 65.14×0.093

    A. 6.05802

    B. 6.06502

    C. 605.602

    D. 605.802

211. 26.80, 26.86, 26.92, 26.98, ...
    What number should come next in this sequence?

    A. 26.02

    B. 26.04

    C. 27.02

    D. 27.04

212. Solve: $72,528 \times 109$

    A. 1,377,032

    B. 1,378,032

    C. 7,805,452

    D. 7,905,552

213. How many boards $1\frac{1}{3}$ feet long can be cut from a board $9\frac{1}{2}$ feet long?

    A. 6

    B. 7

    C. 8

    D. 9

214. Solve for x: $3x + 3 < 9 + x$

    A. $x = 6$

    B. $x > 3$

    C. $x < 3$

    D. $x > 6$

215. Solve: $0.602 + 4.2 + 5.03 =$

    A. 9.644

    B. 9.802

    C. 9.832

    D. 10.441

216. Solve: $28\overline{)54,900}$

    A. 1,642 R16

    B. 1,858 R12

    C. 1,868 R20

    D. 1,960 R20

217. Solve: If $\sqrt{x + 36} = 10$, then $x =$

    A. 64

    B. 56

    C. −16

    D. −4

218. A basket contains 2 red balls and 3 green balls. If a person reaches in without looking and randomly chooses one of the balls, what is the probability that the ball chosen is red?

    A. $\frac{1}{5}$

    B. $\frac{1}{4}$

    C. $\frac{2}{5}$

    D. $\frac{3}{4}$

219. If Katie is half of her brother's age, and her brother is 10 years old, in how many years will Katie be 12 years old?

    A. 5

    B. 7

    C. 10

    D. 12

220. A movie ticket normally costs $12, but there is a 25% discount on Wednesday afternoons. How much do 3 movie tickets cost on Wednesday afternoon?

    A. 12

    B. 27

    C. 31

    D. 48

221. If Caleb has the option between 2 pairs of pants and 3 shirts, how many different outfits can he create?

    A. 2

    B. 3

    C. 5

    D. 6

222. A TV that normally costs $600 is advertised as being on sale for 50% off. You also have a 10% off coupon that will be applied to the sale price. What will be the final price of the TV?

A. $240

B. $270

C. $300

D. $540

223. The average of 10 and what other number is equal to 18?

A. 10

B. 18

C. 20

D. 26

224. Each square foot of a sheet of rubber weighs 17 ounces. If you cut out a rectangle from this sheet that is 16 inches long and 18 inches wide, how much would it weigh?

A. 17 ounces

B. 22 ounces

C. 29 ounces

D. 34 ounces

225. If Kai is 7 months older than Hunter, and Hunter is 3 months younger than Paul, then Kai is how much older than Paul?

A. 2 months

B. 3 months

C. 4 months

D. 10 months

226. If Yadira can mow a lawn in x hours, what part of the lawn can she mow in 2 hours?

A. $\dfrac{2}{x}$

B. $\dfrac{x}{2}$

C. $\dfrac{1}{2}$

D. $\dfrac{1}{x}$

227. A movie theater sold 130 student tickets at $1.25 each and 340 adult tickets at $1.90 each. How much was collected?

A. $708.50

B. $798.50

C. $808.50

D. $818.50

228. Bettina has $10 less than four times the amount Tim has. If Bettina has $88, how much does Tim have?

A. $48

B. $24.50

C. $22

D. $16

229. The formula $F = \dfrac{9}{5}C + 32$ converts temperature from Centigrade to Fahrenheit. What is the Fahrenheit temperature for 85° Centigrade?

A. 192°

B. 185°

C. 175°

D. 130°

230. If the 5% sales tax on a snowmobile was $42, what was the price of the snowmobile not including the tax?

A. $640

B. $680

C. $820

D. $840

231. Mr. Symon paid $58.50 interest on a loan that had a 6% simple interest rate. How much did he borrow?

A. $410

B. $898

C. $951

D. $975

232. If a flagpole has a shadow 56 feet long when a 6-foot man's shadow is 14 feet long, what is the height of the flagpole?

   A. 20 feet

   B. 24 feet

   C. 28 feet

   D. 32 feet

233. If the perimeter of a rectangular region is 50 units, and the length of one side is 7 units, what is the area of the rectangular region?

   A. 124 square units

   B. 126 square units

   C. 252 square units

   D. 291 square units

234. If 18 is added to an integer, and the result is $\frac{5}{4}$ of the integer, what is the integer?

   A. −18

   B. 24

   C. 36

   D. 72

235. Four years ago, Jin's father was 5 times as old as Jin. How old is Jin's father now if Jin is 12?

   A. 36

   B. 40

   C. 44

   D. 56

236. What is the cost of carpeting a square room that is 27 feet by 27 feet if the carpet costs $11 per square yard?

   A. $594

   B. $729

   C. $891

   D. $8,019

237. What is the volume of this rectangular solid?

   A. 90 cu. in.

   B. 140 cu. in.

   C. 160 cu. in.

   D. 180 cu. in.

238. If the tax rate is $3.62 per $100, how much tax must be paid on a home assessed at $25,000?

   A. $80.50

   B. $90.50

   C. $805

   D. $905

LANGUAGE

60 Questions—25 Minutes

Turn to the Language section of your answer sheet to answer the questions in this section.

> **Directions:** In questions 239–267, look for errors in capitalization, punctuation, or usage. Mark the answer choice that contains the error. If you find no mistake, mark D on your answer sheet.

239. A. Gus couldn't swim to the end of the lake and back without stopping.

B. What time are you going to the chess club meeting today!

C. Can you please make me pancakes for breakfast tomorrow morning?

D. *(No mistakes)*

240. A. Nayleen watched her favorite movie, star wars, with her cousin.

B. Kareef just finished reading his new favorite novel, *To the End and Back.*

C. The *Hammondville Tribune* just published an article on national tax reform.

D. *(No mistakes)*

241. A. Raymond took his overdue book back on the library.

B. Carmine had a new set of art supplies to work with at home.

C. The bookstore had a new shipment of novels to organize.

D. *(No mistakes)*

242. A. The thunderbolt struck with tremendous force!

B. What is the best route to get to the courthouse?

C. How tall is the giraffe in the Cincinnati Zoo?

D. *(No mistakes)*

243. A. Were you surprised by how difficult the exam questions were?

B. Blaine was surprised by how difficult the exam questions were?

C. Do you know where the final science exam is taking place today?

D. *(No mistakes)*

244. A. The watchmaker's items for sale were displayed in his case.

B. Silence filled the club as the singer jumped onto the stage.

C. Alison took us new dog for a walk around the block.

D. *(No mistakes)*

245. A. However, we couldn't predict that the rainstorm would be as bad as it was.

B. Sharee was by far the tallest student in her homeroom;

C. The clown completed an impressive juggling display for the kids.

D. *(No mistakes)*

246. A. My favorite uncle lives in Jackson Hole, Wyoming.

B. Our class took a trip to the Lincoln Memorial in Washington, DC.

C. The statue of Liberty is one of the most famous tourist attractions in New York City.

D. *(No mistakes)*

247. **A.** Jazmine walked cautious down the slippery staircase.

   B. Did you see the way Isaiah ran through the hallway?

   C. The tiger cage at the zoo was full of lurking animals.

   D. *(No mistakes)*

248. **A.** Trevor had a notebook headphones and a sandwich in his backpack.

   B. The biggest dog in the dog park, Bruno, scared the other dogs.

   C. We took a wrong turn at the edge of the woods and needed to look at a map.

   D. *(No mistakes)*

249. **A.** Do you think Janelle should lend her friend Myriam she jacket?

   B. The roar of the crowd, louder than the band's playing, was tremendous.

   C. Emma asked her friend Ryan, "Can I please borrow a jacket?"

   D. *(No mistakes)*

250. **A.** Lebron was excited to see the new action movie; at his neighborhood theater.

   B. Cameron met his first cousin, Lebron, at the movie theater on Tuesday.

   C. Can Sheila join her friends for an afternoon at the movies on Tuesday?

   D. *(No mistakes)*

251. **A.** Beverly couldn't remember the combination to her locker.

   B. There was a mysterious sound coming from Daphnes closet.

   C. Doug accidentally left his phone on his desk at work.

   D. *(No mistakes)*

252. **A.** Simon always gets nervous when he drives across the Golden Gate Bridge.

   B. If you could visit any country in the world, which one would you choose?

   C. Darnelle couldn't, believe, his luck as he, listened to the lotto numbers being called.

   D. *(No mistakes)*

253. **A.** Does anyone know what's being served for lunch in the cafeteria today?

   B. Katora was the first to finish the marathon; Shana was the runner-up.

   C. The nearest gas station, in Pinedale, also sells coffee and hot dogs.

   D. *(No mistakes)*

254. **A.** Kija had always wondering why cookies never lasted long in his house.

   B. Parrots are an expensive but rewarding type of pet.

   C. Hanna couldn't decide what type of dress to wear to work today.

   D. *(No mistakes)*

255. **A.** Carissa's new blog received a surprising amount of traffic.

   B. No one was ever able to pass Mrs. Hudson's easy final exam.

   C. This is possibly the longest elevator ride in history.

   D. *(No mistakes)*

256. **A.** People often wonder how they can lose weight as quickly as possible?

   B. The final exam, which covered geometry, was the hardest exam this year.

   C. Cecille won the 8th grade science fair this year; Sharon won an honorable mention.

   D. *(No mistakes)*

257. **A.** Amelia has always dreamed of visiting the Louvre Museum in Paris.

B. Mika's favorite painting in the museum was create by Renoir.

C. Harold purchased a new laptop from the computer store on Airedale Road.

D. *(No mistakes)*

258. **A.** Have you ever visited the Guggenheim Museum in New York City?

B. Freida asked Archie, *Are you certain you can't make it to my party?*

C. Can anyone pick up Jenna from the airport this evening?

D. *(No mistakes)*

259. **A.** Can Lawrence finish his chores and make it to work on time?

B. Francine got two toppings on her yogurt—strawberries and sprinkles.

C. Crystal had to decide whether she wanted to eat either chicken and steak.

D. *(No mistakes)*

260. **A.** Patrice has never enjoyed lying out on a hot beach.

B. Melissa has decided to ride her bicycle to work today.

C. Tomorrow, Caroline went to the senior prom at her school.

D. *(No mistakes)*

261. **A.** Janice purchased a magazine, two cans of soda, and a bagel from the store.

B. Shirelle went to the post office to purchase some stamps!

C. Francine manages the pet store where Candy purchased her iguana.

D. *(No mistakes)*

262. **A.** Joey couldn't tell which spices were in his mother's chili.

B. Do you know that woman who is standing in the stage?

C. Antonia's new phone was faster and thinner than her old one.

D. *(No mistakes)*

263. **A.** The new bridge was built over the sprawling lake.

B. Vincent had to duck under the table to retrieve his pencil.

C. Larissa arrived before breakfast was over and missed her chance to eat.

D. *(No mistakes)*

264. **A.** I think that peanut butter or chocolate make an excellent combination.

B. The French toast was just too burnt to eat and was thrown away.

C. Harrison couldn't wait to get home and check his email.

D. *(No mistakes)*

265. **A.** Jovan kept his head below water so he wouldn't get his hair wet.

B. If there are any onions on the plate, I won't be eating them.

C. The gym was too crowded for Andy to work out comfortably.

D. *(No mistakes)*

266. **A.** The picnic basket was closed, but the ants had found their way into it.

B. Lilith can only go to the baseball game tomorrow but she finishes her homework first.

C. There was no space in the lot for Juan to park his new car.

D. *(No mistakes)*

267. A. The electric drill is an indispensable tool in Sydney's tool kit.

B. Hassan wondered if he had the discipline needed to compete on the wrestle team.

C. Jacqui went to the mall to purchase some new jewelry.

D. *(No mistakes)*

Directions: For questions 268–277, look for mistakes in spelling only.

---

268. A. Damon thought the long wait for a table was unacceptable.

B. Claire was well aware of the affect of exhaustion on her daily routine.

C. Daniel helped his good friend through a challenging dilemma.

D. *(No mistakes)*

269. A. Johann asked his tutor for some advise on studying for the midterm exam.

B. The debate team got into a heated argument about the debate rules.

C. Amy was a conscientious worker who could always be counted on by others.

D. *(No mistakes)*

270. A. Kiernan tripped while going up the auditorium stairs and was embarrassed.

B. Cyril considered himself to be the best skateboarder in existence.

C. Hikers were not aloud to go to the top of the steep mountain.

D. *(No mistakes)*

271. A. Her mentor's presents in the classroom made Lisa nervous during her presentation.

B. The keys to success in life are different for everyone.

C. The carnival workers had to stay at the fairgrounds late.

D. *(No mistakes)*

272. A. Charles always considered himself someone with good judgment.

B. Jann always remembered to seperate the recyclables from the trash.

C. Marcia couldn't wait to get her new driver's license.

D. *(No mistakes)*

273. A. Sherman was intrigued but afraid to visit a foreign country.

B. Natalia was grateful for the help she got while building her tree house.

C. Casey was dissapointed by his score during the bowling team competition.

D. *(No mistakes)*

274. A. Xavier occasionally felt the need to call his aunt on the phone.

B. Marie didn't find the plot of the television show beleivable.

C. Ellen knew that being on the elite chess team was a privilege.

D. *(No mistakes)*

275. A. The comic book store on Vantage Road sold a variety of colectible items.

B. Lucy took a humorous approach to his award acceptance speech.

C. Myrna took some aspirin and felt an immediate effect.

D. *(No mistakes)*

276. **A.** Matt was two tired to go to the concert after work on Friday.

B. Lorraine almost fell asleep during the committee meeting.

C. Olive took a yacht ride during her vacation in Greece.

D. *(No mistakes)*

277. **A.** Gemma's family had an adorable miniature poodle for a pet.

B. The work crew took their lunch brake in the nearby park.

C. Our neighbor never seemed to take care of his lawn.

D. *(No mistakes)*

Directions: In questions 278–288, look for errors and mark the sentence that demonstrates correct usage.

---

278. **A.** Will the hockey team beat her high score during today's game?

B. Beatriz lent her new earmuffs to her best friend, Natasha.

C. Everyone is waiting to get his copy of the new suspense novel.

D. Jennice wore the new earrings it got at the mall last Thursday.

279. **A.** The faculty at Eden View High School have their annual meeting this afternoon.

B. The members of the chorus left her instruments in the concert hall during the break.

C. Darian teased our sister until they laughed uncontrollably during dinner.

D. The golden retriever pulled off our collar and ran across the empty field.

280. **A.** Tyrone decided to eating dinner at the Thai restaurant.

B. The new hybrid car was released for sale next year.

C. We decided to go hiking through the woods on our vacation.

D. The deer frolicked through the meadow and stop by the river.

281. **A.** Barb worked on her science project day and night, by the time her life depended on it.

B. Only if Arielle is the best lacrosse player on the team, she never brags.

C. Before Lucinda discovered the spider under her bed, she ran out of the room.

D. Jimmy completed as much of his homework on his own as possible before asking for help.

282. **A.** We all went together to the end-of-summer party at Summers house.

B. The table's had a wobbly leg and shook horribly.

C. Clarice checked out the selection of skirt's at the department store.

D. The parade of cars honked loudly in the rush hour traffic.

283. **A.** Louis hates it when people talk beyond the movie and cause a disruption.

B. Darren layered the roast beef and mustard between two pieces of bread.

C. Sylvia leaned her umbrella among the coat rack in the hallway.

D. The new chairs had to be returned because they didn't fit about the table.

284. A. The Robinson family took her family photo every Thanksgiving.

 B. The bookcase fell on her side when Jack leaned against it.

 C. Chiara's classmates sent her a beautiful get-well-soon card.

 D. The leaves made a beautiful display when he fell to the ground.

285. A. Bogdan always handles his job responsibilities capable.

 B. The snail slow slithered across the freshly mown lawn.

 C. The French vanilla wedding cake was decorated beautiful.

 D. Gianna was greeted coolly by the strangers at the art gallery.

286. A. Can you meet Fabian at his house during the presentation starts?

 B. Derek wasn't allowed to eat his dessert because after he finished dinner.

 C. Sam will breathe a huge sigh of relief after the final exam is over.

 D. Jayden won the debate competition because he was more convincing because anyone else.

287. A. Mandy approached the edge of the slippery diving board very carefully.

 B. Tamryn absentminded left her water bottle at the gym last night.

 C. Phillip tiptoed quiet through the crowded library and went to the water fountain.

 D. The athletes hungry devoured the pizza after today's practice.

288. A. I'd never been to a lecture at the university and was excited to go.

 B. She wanted to get a ice cream cone after dinner tonight.

 C. Bonnie bought her daughter an new purse for her birthday.

 D. Can someone lend Vera a umbrella so she doesn't get wet on her way home?

289. Choose the pair of sentences that best develops this topic sentence:

"A healthy diet and exercise can improve your brain function."

A. Folks who eat a lot of lean protein and low-fat meals tend to live longer. Working out makes people look better and improves their self-confidence.

B. Do you maintain a healthy diet and get regular exercise? If so, then you're part of a growing group of health-conscious people.

C. Individuals who eat a diet rich in vitamins do better on tests of intelligence. People who work out more than twice a week have been shown to have a better memory than people who don't.

D. There is no reason not to try and improve your diet and get some regular exercise. There's no better time than now to live a healthier and more active life!

290. Choose the word that best completes this sentence.

Sharrod, who was late for his meeting, moved _____ through the train station in order to get to his office.

A. briskly

B. slowly

C. casually

D. jokingly

291. Which of the following sentences offers the *least* support for the topic "Why the town of Willowbrook Needs a Library"?

A. Every town surrounding Willowbrook has its own library.

B. The children of Willowbrook need a place to borrow books.

C. There's a retail bookstore located in the town's mall.

D. Towns with libraries have a better educated citizenry.

292. Choose the word that best completes this sentence.

Phineas had to carefully parallel park his car _____ an SUV and a pickup truck.

A. beneath

B. between

C. beyond

D. but

293. Which of these expresses the idea most clearly?

A. Who were packing for a weekend getaway in the country, put their camping gear and picnic basket, Quinlan and Tiffany into the back of their car.

B. Put their camping gear and picnic basket, Quinlan and Tiffany, who were packing for a weekend getaway in the country into the back of their car.

C. Into the back of their car for a weekend getaway in the country, who were Quinlan and Tiffany packing for? Put their camping gear and picnic basket.

D. Quinlan and Tiffany, who were packing for a weekend getaway in the country, put their camping gear and picnic basket into the back of their car.

294. Choose the best word to join the thoughts together.

The cleaning crew had the unfortunate task of cleaning up the street _____ the busy parade was finished.

- **A.** since
- **B.** while
- **C.** until
- **D.** after

295. Which of these expresses the idea most clearly?

- **A.** Many pastry chefs feel that it's best to use room temperature eggs when baking, as it creates a fluffier, lighter, and more flavorful final product.
- **B.** A fluffier, lighter, and more flavorful final product, when baking, as it creates—many pastry chefs feel that room temperature eggs it's best to use.
- **C.** That it's best to use room temperature eggs when baking, many pastry chefs create a fluffier, lighter, and more flavorful final product as it creates.
- **D.** When baking as it creates, many pastry chefs create a fluffier, lighter, and more flavorful final product and feel that it's best to use room temperature eggs.

296. Which sentence does *not* belong in the paragraph?

(1) Snakes are fascinating and diverse creatures that also move in interesting ways. (2) Without legs, they utilize their muscles and scales to help them get around. (3) Earthworms move in a similar way. (4) Snakes push off of whatever surface they are laying upon to propel themselves forward.

- **A.** Sentence 1
- **B.** Sentence 2
- **C.** Sentence 3
- **D.** Sentence 4

297. Which of the following sentences would best fit at the end of this paragraph?

(1) Giraffes are tall, herbivorous mammals that typically live in savannahs and open woodlands. (2) They tend to avoid contact with other animals and use their immense height to feed in places where other animals can't. (3) Fully grown giraffes tend to range between 14 and 18 feet in height.

- **A.** Giraffes are often found in zoos.
- **B.** Giraffes truly are gentle giants.
- **C.** Few get the change to ride a giraffe.
- **D.** Who doesn't love a funny giraffe?

298. Which of the following sentences offers the *least* support for the topic "College Should Be Free for Everybody"?

- **A.** Too many students deal with excessive student loans after graduating from college.
- **B.** College tuition helps to fund a variety of campus upgrades, innovations, and events.
- **C.** Some people feel that choosing a major while in college is too limiting and unfair.
- **D.** More students than ever before are deciding to skip going to college and start their own businesses.

ANSWER KEYS AND EXPLANATIONS

Verbal Skills

1. B	13. C	25. A	37. C	49. D
2. D	14. B	26. B	38. D	50. B
3. C	15. B	27. C	39. B	51. A
4. A	16. A	28. D	40. A	52. C
5. C	17. B	29. A	41. D	53. A
6. D	18. C	30. B	42. C	54. D
7. B	19. C	31. A	43. C	55. C
8. A	20. B	32. D	44. A	56. B
9. A	21. C	33. A	45. A	57. D
10. C	22. B	34. C	46. B	58. A
11. B	23. C	35. B	47. C	59. C
12. C	24. C	36. D	48. D	60. B

1. **The correct answer is B.** This analogy shows a creature-habitat relationship. Lobsters live in the ocean, and scorpions live in the desert.

2. **The correct answer is D.** This is a product-source relationship. Tea is made from tea leaves, and coffee is made from coffee beans.

3. **The correct answer is C.** This is an example-object relationship. A sombrero is a type of hat, and a poodle is a type of dog.

4. **The correct answer is A.** This analogy is a measurement-range relationship. Twelve dozens make up a gross, and twelve inches make up a foot.

5. **The correct answer is C.** This is an opposite relationship. The opposite of tall is short, and the opposite of quick is slow.

6. **The correct answer is D.** This is a part-whole relationship. A slice is a part of a pie, and a piece is part of a puzzle.

7. **The correct answer is B.** This is an object-process relationship. Molding is a process to shape and transform clay, and carving is a process to shape and transform wood.

8. **The correct answer is A.** This is a movement/transportation relationship. Bees and falcons both

fly to get around. Trout and sharks both swim to get around.

9. **The correct answer is A.** This is a common characteristic relationship. Monkeys and mice both have tails. Rhinoceroses and rams both have distinctive horns.

10. **The correct answer is C.** This is a tactile characteristic relationship. Snails are slimy to the touch, and rabbits are furry to the touch.

11. **The correct answer is B.** Based on the information we're told, Myriam *must* be older than Radja, since we know that Myriam is older than Syrah and Syrah is older than Radja.

12. **The correct answer is C.** Although we know that both Antonio and Patricia ate more nachos than Kevin, we don't know by *how much* more, and therefore cannot determine if Antonio or Patricia ate more nachos.

13. **The correct answer is C.** Although we are told how thirsty these individuals are, we are given no information regarding how much water they may or may not have drank.

14. **The correct answer is B.** We know that there's no way that Nareen could have come in last place in

the school-wide spelling bee because we're told that they did better than Tariq. Therefore, choice B is correct.

15. **The correct answer is B.** If the first two statements are true, myrtle trees grow the least fast of the three types of trees. Therefore, the third statement must be false.

16. **The correct answer is A.** If the first two statements are true, copper is the most expensive of the three metals.

17. **The correct answer is B.** We know from the first two statements that Carrie swims the fastest, so the third statement must be false.

18. **The correct answer is C.** The first two statements give information about Bob's carrots and tomatoes. Information about any other vegetables in Bob's garden cannot be determined.

19. **The correct answer is C.** Despite the fact that Jake is the shortest child in the green classroom, he could *still* be taller than Arianna (and everyone else in the orange classroom). Therefore, choice C is correct.

20. **The correct answer is B.** If the first two statements are true, both Sadie and Roxy downloaded more music than Henry, so the third statement is false.

21. **The correct answer is C.** Choices A, B, and D are all kitchen tools that are designed to be heated on the stove. Choice C is not meant to be heated on the stove.

22. **The correct answer is B.** Choices A, C, and D are all team sports. *Archery* (choice B) is a solo sport.

23. **The correct answer is C.** The common feature among choices A, B, and D is that they are all tools designed to cut. A *wrench* (choice C) is not designed to cut.

24. **The correct answer is C.** Choices A, B, and D are all types of building equipment. A *construction worker* (choice C) may work in building but does not share the characteristic of being a type of building equipment.

25. **The correct answer is A.** Choices B, C, and D are all things that can be read. A *pencil* (choice A) is something that can be written with, not read.

26. **The correct answer is B.** *Dragon*, *lion*, and *tiger* are all nouns. Although they may all be harmful, *harmful* (choice B) is an adjective, not a noun.

27. **The correct answer is C.** *Catch*, *throw*, and *pitch* are all verbs. Although you can throw, catch, and pitch a ball, *ball* (choice C) is incorrect because it is a noun, not a verb.

28. **The correct answer is D.** The common feature among a *firefighter*, *police officer*, and *comedian* is that they are all types of jobs. Someone may be a *problem solver* (choice D) while solving a specific problem, but it's not a job type.

29. **The correct answer is A.** Although they are all types of food, *calzone*, *taco*, and *pizza* all end with vowels; *biscuit* (choice A) ends with a consonant.

30. **The correct answer is B.** Although they are all living creatures, an *eel*, *seahorse*, and *whale* are all found in the water, while a *pony* (choice B) is found on the land.

31. **The correct answer is A.** The common feature among a *shovel*, *spoon*, and *spatula* is that they are all designed to scoop or pick up things, while a *chisel* (choice A) is designed to chip away at things.

32. **The correct answer is D.** *Ladders*, *stairs*, and *mountains* are all things that you climb, while a *waterfall* (choice D) is generally not.

33. **The correct answer is A.** *Sorrow*, *fear*, and *joy* are all types of emotions. *Winning* (choice A) may bring positive emotions, but it itself is not a type of emotion.

34. **The correct answer is C.** The common feature among *cosmetics*, *groceries*, and *clothing* is that they are all things that can be directly purchased; *fulfillment* (choice C) cannot be directly purchased.

35. **The correct answer is B.** *Contemporary*, *enjoyable*, and *extend* are all multi-syllabic words, which means that they have more than one syllable. *List* is a one-syllable word.

36. **The correct answer is D.** *Eggs*, *oysters*, and *walnuts* are all types of foods that have a shell. *Tomatoes* (choice D) do not have a shell.

37. **The correct answer is C.** An *anomalous* event is irregular.

38. **The correct answer is D.** A *courteous* gentleman is polite.

39. **The correct answer is B.** A *spacious* environment is roomy.

40. **The correct answer is A.** A *loquacious* speaker is talkative.

41. **The correct answer is D.** A *deft* performer is skillful.

42. **The correct answer is C.** A *venerable* judge is honored.

43. **The correct answer is C.** A *fecund* cornfield is fruitful.

44. **The correct answer is A.** A *cantankerous* customer is disagreeable.

45. **The correct answer is A.** A *caustic* remark is scathing.

46. **The correct answer is B.** A *collaborative* effort is cooperative.

47. **The correct answer is C.** A *bombastic* speech is grandiose.

48. **The correct answer is D.** A *rancorous* employee is resentful.

49. **The correct answer is D.** A *contentious* meeting is combative.

50. **The correct answer is B.** An *erudite* professor is educated.

51. **The correct answer is A.** A *prominent* leader is noticeable.

52. **The correct answer is C.** *Diligent* means the opposite of *passive*.

53. **The correct answer is A.** *Industrious* means the opposite of *idle*.

54. **The correct answer is D.** *Intelligible* means the opposite of *inarticulate*.

55. **The correct answer is C.** *Denigrate* means the opposite of *approve*.

56. **The correct answer is B.** *Frugal* means the opposite of *wasteful*.

57. **The correct answer is D.** *Altruistic* means the opposite of *selfish*.

58. **The correct answer is A.** *Oblivious* means the opposite of *aware*.

59. **The correct answer is C.** *Beguile* means the opposite of *repel*.

60. **The correct answer is B.** *Mollify* means the opposite of *aggravate*.

NOTES

Quantitative Skills

61. D	**72.** C	**83.** D	**93.** B	**103.** B
62. B	**73.** A	**84.** A	**94.** A	**104.** A
63. B	**74.** B	**85.** C	**95.** C	**105.** B
64. C	**75.** C	**86.** C	**96.** D	**106.** A
65. D	**76.** A	**87.** B	**97.** D	**107.** B
66. B	**77.** C	**88.** D	**98.** B	**108.** C
67. B	**78.** D	**89.** C	**99.** D	**109.** D
68. D	**79.** B	**90.** C	**100.** C	**110.** A
69. B	**80.** B	**91.** A	**101.** C	**111.** C
70. D	**81.** B	**92.** B	**102.** A	**112.** D
71. C	**82.** C			

61. **The correct answer is D.** Start by finding 20% of 40; $0.20 \times 40 = 8$. Then, add 3 to get $8 + 3 = 11$.

62. **The correct answer is B.** The pattern in this series is created by adding 7 to each number.

63. **The correct answer is B.** The square root of 256 is 16. Multiply by $\frac{3}{4} \times 16 = 12$.

64. **The correct answer is C.** Determine the amount of money for A, B, and C. Then, test the given alternatives see which is correct.

65. **The correct answer is D.** A is 0.625; B is 0.571; and C is 0.6237. Clearly B is less than both A and C, which are not equal.

66. **The correct answer is B.** The cube of 5 is 125. 125 divided by 5 = 25.

67. **The correct answer is B.** The pattern in this series is +2, ÷, +2, ÷, and so on. Since $6 + 2 = 8$, and $8 \div 2 = 4$, the missing term is 8.

68. **The correct answer is D.** Determine how much of each box is shaded. Then, test each alternative to see which is correct.

69. **The correct answer is B.** The pattern in this series is +3, +7, +3, +7, and so on.

70. **The correct answer is D.** Determine the amounts for A, B, and C. Here, A = 8, B = 8, and C = 0.08.

When you test each alternative to see which is correct, you see that choice D is the correct answer: A is greater than C.

71. **The correct answer is C.** Start by finding $\frac{2}{3}$ of 39:
$$\frac{2}{3} \times 39 = 26$$
Then, add 4 to find your answer: $26 + 4 = 30$.

72. **The correct answer is C.** The pattern in this series is −5, −4, +1, −5, −4, +1, ... So, the next three numbers in the series are 35, 31, 32.

73. **The correct answer is A.** Start this problem from the end and work backward:
$$\frac{3}{5} \times \frac{25}{1} = 15$$
$$15 + 7 = 22$$

The number you're looking for is found by setting up an equation.
$$30 - x = 22$$
$$x = 30 - 22$$
$$x = 8$$

74. **The correct answer is B.** $\frac{1}{4}$ of 64 is 16, and 7 less than 16 is 9.

75. The correct answer is C. Finding the answer is as simple as dividing the total cost by the number of hats.

$$
\begin{array}{r}
0.65 \\
23\overline{)\$14.95} \\
-13.80 \\
\hline
1.15 \\
-1.15 \\
\hline
.00
\end{array}
$$

76. The correct answer is A. The pattern in this series is −9, −8, −7, −6, and so on.

77. The correct answer is C. Count the circles in A, B, and C. Test each alternative to find the one that is true. You will see that B has 12 circles and C has 13 circles—both of which are more than A, which has only 10 circles.

78. The correct answer is D. Determine how much of each figure is shaded. Then test each alternative to find the one that is true. In this case, A, B, and C each have 3 parts shaded, so they're equally shaded.

79. The correct answer is B. The pattern in this series is created by adding 4 to each number. $99 + 4 = 103$.

80. The correct answer is B. Determine $\frac{1}{5}$ of 100: $\frac{1}{5} \times \frac{100}{1} = 20$. Multiply this result by 4 to find the answer; $20 \times 4 = 80$.

81. The correct answer is B. The pattern in this series is +4, +1, +4, +1, and so on. Also, whenever 1 is added, the result is expressed as an Arabic numeral; whenever 4 is added, the result is expressed as a Roman numeral.

82. The correct answer is C. Each circle is divided into five equal parts. Circle B has the fewest shaded wedges, while figure C has the most.

83. The correct answer is D. First, find 7 times 3; $7 \times 3 = 21$. Double this result to find the answer: $2 \times 21 = 42$.

84. The correct answer is A. Each box is shaded by $\frac{1}{2}$. Therefore, only A can be true.

85. The correct answer is C. Figure this problem from the end and work forward:

$$
\begin{aligned}
5 \times 2 &= 10 \\
3 \times 10 &= 30 \\
6 + x &= 30 \\
x &= 30 - 6 = 24
\end{aligned}
$$

86. The correct answer is C. The pattern in this series is −2, + 4, −2, +4, and so on.

87. The correct answer is B. 125% = 1.25, so A and B are equal. But $\frac{25}{2} = 12.5$, which is greater than A and B. So, A and B are both less than C.

88. The correct answer is D. With factorials, you multiply whole numbers from 1 to the given number. In this case, $1 \times 2 \times 3 \times 4 \times 5 \times 6$.

89. The correct answer is C. The pattern in this series is +2, ×, +2, ×, and so on.

90. The correct answer is C. To find the answer, you need to enter the information you have into the percent change formula.

$$
\frac{\% \ change}{100} = \frac{33}{150}
$$

Then cross-multiply and solve for the percent change (p).

$$
\frac{p \times 150}{100 \times 33} = \frac{150p}{3,300} \ \text{ or } 150p = 3,300
$$

$$
\frac{150p}{150} = \frac{3,300}{150}
$$

$$
p = 22
$$

91. The correct answer is A. The line drawn from point A to the base of triangle ABD divides this triangle into two right triangles, one of which is ACD. AD is the hypotenuse of this right triangle whose length must be greater than the length CD, a leg of ACD.

92. The correct answer is B. Begin by subtracting 5 from 29. This number divided by 3 will provide the answer:

$$
\begin{aligned}
29 - 5 &= 24 \\
24 \div 3 &= 8
\end{aligned}
$$

93. **The correct answer is B.** The pattern in this series is +6, +3, +6, +3, and so on.

94. **The correct answer is A.** Determine the amounts for A, B, and C. Then choose the best alternative. Be sure to do the operations in the parentheses first when figuring.

95. **The correct answer is C.** The pattern in this series is +1, −10, +1, −10, and so on.

96. **The correct answer is D.** Because the figure is a cube, all edges and sides are equal. When a diagonal line is drawn across one side, like $\overline{CE}$, it forms a hypotenuse of a right triangle whose length is longer than the length of either of its sides ($\overline{CE}$ and $\overline{EF}$). Because the sides of the cube are all equal, $\overline{CF}$ must also be longer than $\overline{AB}$.

97. **The correct answer is D.** The value of A is $\frac{1}{2} \times \frac{2}{3} = \frac{1}{3}$, B is $\frac{3}{4} \times 1 = \frac{3}{4}$, and C is $\frac{1}{2} \times \frac{2}{3} = \frac{3}{4}$. B and C are equal, and A is less than these.

98. **The correct answer is B.** Since $x < y$, multiplying both sides by x gives $x^2 < xy$. So, C is less than A. Likewise, since $x < y$, multiplying both sides by y gives $xy < y^2$. A is less than B.

99. **The correct answer is D.** The pattern in this series is $\times$, +4, $\times$, +4, and so on.

100. **The correct answer is C.** The pattern here is +2, +4, +6, +8, and so on. The next term should be 21 + 10 = 31.

101. **The correct answer is C.** The pattern for the letters in this series is made by using every other letter starting with A. The pattern for the numbers is +4, −10, +4, −10, and so on.

102. **The correct answer is A.** Determine the values for each bar in the graph by using the number scale to the left. Then choose the correct alternative. Choice A is correct because 2 + 10 − 4 = 8 or 12 − 4 = 8.

103. **The correct answer is B.** This can be set up as an algebraic equation to solve for x:

$$x = \frac{3}{5}(10) - 2$$
$$x = 6 - 2$$
$$x = 4$$

104. **The correct answer is A.** The pattern in this series is created by taking numbers in sequential order (4, 5, 6, and so on) and following each number with its square. The last number in the series is 6, so $6^2 = 36$, choice A.

105. **The correct answer is B.** Determine the amounts for A, B, and C. Then, decide which alternative is true.

A. $5^2 = 25$

B. $4^3 = 64$

C. $2^4 = 16$

So, B is greater than A, which is greater than C.

106. **The correct answer is A.** The pattern in this series is created by subtracting $2\frac{1}{2}$ from each number.

107. **The correct answer is B.** Each letter is paired with A, and then with 1. C has already been paired with A, so the next term should be C1.

108. **The correct answer is C.** The pattern in this series is +4, −2, −1, +4, −2, −1, and so on.

109. **The correct answer is D.** This can be set up as an algebraic equation if you're solving for x:

$$6 + \frac{1}{3}x = 2 \times 9$$
$$6 + \frac{1}{3}x = 18$$
$$\frac{1}{3}x = 12$$
$$x = 36$$

110. **The correct answer is A.** Test each of the alternatives to find the true one. To find the perimeter, add the length of all four sides together: 2 + 3 + 2 + 3 = 10.

111. **The correct answer is C.** This can be set up as an algebraic equation if you're solving for x:

$$x = \frac{4}{9}(27) + 10$$
$$x = 12 + 10$$
$$x = 22$$

112. **The correct answer is D.** 5 squared is 25, and 11 more than 25 is 36.

Reading

Comprehension

113. C	121. C	129. D	137. C	145. B
114. B	122. A	130. C	138. B	146. D
115. C	123. C	131. B	139. C	147. C
116. D	124. B	132. A	140. A	148. C
117. D	125. C	133. B	141. C	149. B
118. B	126. D	134. C	142. B	150. A
119. A	127. A	135. A	143. A	151. B
120. C	128. A	136. D	144. B	152. D

113. **The correct answer is C.** In paragraph 3, we are told that Felix is a "nutrition author," which means that she has written works on the subject of nutrition. The passage never tells us that Felix has conducted experiments on fats (choice A), that she is a medical doctor (choice B), or that she has a degree in biology (choice D). We cannot draw these conclusions without specific information from the passage, so each of these choices can be eliminated.

114. **The correct answer is B.** In paragraph 3, we are told that "most people tend to eat enough omega-6 fats," so we can infer that these fats are common in American diets.

115. **The correct answer is C.** Paragraphs 2 and 3 focus on the need for more omega-3 fats in the diet and foods that are good sources for omega-3 fats. Choice D is incorrect because, although the first two paragraphs mention the overall need for fats in the diet, the passage deals specifically with reducing omega-6 and increasing omega-3, making this answer too general.

116. **The correct answer is D.** The first paragraph states that a person should restrict intake of fats to 30 percent of the total number of calories they consume every day.

117. **The correct answer is D.** Olive oil, walnuts, and sardines are three of the foods specifically mentioned in the last paragraph as good sources of omega-3 fats. Choice C is incorrect because, although salads are generally healthy, the passage does not say that they are good sources of omega-3 fats. Choices A and B are incorrect because the passage specifically states that nutritionists recommend limiting consumption of salad dressing, margarine, bread, and other baked goods.

118. **The correct answer is B.** The author is advocating for an increase in the amount of good fats humans consume, as this would help improve people's nutrition levels. Thus, the best adjective to describe the positive influence that an increased consumption of good fats would have on the American diet is *ideal*.

119. **The correct answer is A.** The passage mentions that "the American diet falls short when it comes to omega-3 fats." Since omega-3 is an essential fatty acid (good fat), we can infer from the passage that the author would most likely characterize the average American diet as falling short on the consumption of good fats.

120. **The correct answer is C.** Clara Felix's research mentions that the American diet falls short on omega-3 fats but does not mention how far short. Providing this information would help readers understand how critical and drastic this issue is, and how much effort would be required to balance their fat consumption.

121. **The correct answer is C.** The primary purpose of the passage is to educate readers on the value of increasing their consumption of good fats as part of a healthy, nutritionally optimal diet. Therefore, readers who follow the author's advice will likely increase their consumption of good fats.

122. **The correct answer is A.** The passage states: "Although most people tend to eat enough omega-6 fats, the American diet falls short when it comes to omega-3 fats." You can infer from this information that the average American consumes more omega-6 fatty acids than omega-3 acids.

123. **The correct answer is C.** Paragraph 2 tells us that while the expedition was successful in placing six climbers at the summit of Mount Everest, it had to overcome many challenges and setbacks. The next two paragraphs describe those challenges and their effect on the climbers.

124. **The correct answer is B.** Paragraph 3 states that two Canadians and four sherpas made it to the top of Mount Everest. Choice C is incorrect, as it refers to the total number of climbers who made it to the top, including both the Canadians and the sherpas guiding them.

125. **The correct answer is C.** The second paragraph states that this was the first Canadian expedition to Mount Everest, making choice C the correct answer. Choice D is incorrect, because the passage does not give us any information on whether this was the last expedition that Amatt led up Mount Everest.

126. **The correct answer is D.** The last paragraph mentions that the expedition inspired Amatt's team to approach their challenges with "humbleness," which is another way of saying *humility*. Humility is the opposite of *pride* (choice B) and it is unlikely they would be *indifferent* (choice A) if they are humbled by the risks of the expedition. While the team was definitely *ambitious* (choice C), this wasn't a result of their setbacks and challenges.

127. **The correct answer is A.** The word *it* refers back to the second sentence of the paragraph, which cites the experience of loss that Amatt and his team encountered. The noun *experience* is

singular, so it agrees with the singular pronoun *it*. Choice B is incorrect because the noun *experiences* in the first sentence is plural, and it would not use the singular pronoun *it*. Choices C and D do not make sequential sense.

128. **The correct answer is A.** The passage recounts John Amatt's successful climb to the top—or peak—of the great mountain.

129. **The correct answer is D.** According to the information provided in the passage, John Amatt overcame great adversity to successfully complete a physical challenge. The scenario that most closely compares to this is a swimmer who overcame treacherous conditions to successfully swim the English Channel.

130. **The correct answer is C.** Based on the information provided in the passage, the most likely explanation why Amatt titled his book *Straight to the Top and Beyond* is because the book describes both his climb to the top of Mount Everest and the lessons he learned from the adversity he faced during the experience.

131. **The correct answer is B.** The experience of loss referenced in paragraph 4 most likely refers to the climbers and sherpas who lost their lives during the climb, as mentioned in paragraph 3. There is no mention of wasted time (choice A) or lost equipment (choice C). Amatt successfully made it to the top of Mount Everest, so choice D is incorrect.

132. **The correct answer is A.** This passage focuses on John Amatt, a Canadian climber; his 1982 expedition to the top of Mount Everest; and the lessons he learned through overcoming adversity and loss as a climber. The passage does not attempt to warn readers against mountain climbing (choice B), tell the history of Canadian mountain climbing (choice C), or provide the history of attempts to climb Mount Everest (choice D).

133. **The correct answer is B.** The first paragraph speaks of the perils of fishing; the second speaks about its rewards.

134. **The correct answer is C.** The middle of the first paragraph discusses the problems created by rough seas. No other choice is mentioned as a difficulty.

135. **The correct answer is A.** In the middle of paragraph 2, we learn that when fishermen note that herring are entering the nets, they sit in quiet excitement so as not to frighten the fish away. They row along the net earlier in order to find out if the net is filling and haul in the nets later, when they are full.

136. **The correct answer is D.** This phrase represents a powerful metaphor. Picture huge waves rising over empty space and crashing down upon fishermen and boats.

137. **The correct answer is C.** All the other choices include at least one trait that is not ascribed to these fishermen.

138. **The correct answer is B.** One might add honesty to the fishermen's traits. Theft is not mentioned as a problem. If you had forgotten about the whales, reread the first sentence.

139. **The correct answer is C.** The first paragraph of the passage describes the sea as dark and dangerous, unpredictable and unexpected. The answer choice that most resembles this description is a dark and dangerous storm (choice C).

140. **The correct answer is A.** The author of the passage paints a specific portrait of life as a fisherman in Norway, one "full of dangers" on the high seas, with fisherman constantly working, muscles straining, working "day-and-night without a thought of weariness" to handle the bounty of herring. The choice that best captures this portrait is choice A.

141. **The correct answer is C.** For a Norwegian fisherman, a net without herring is disappointing and a threat to one's professional livelihood. Similarly, a salesman without a sale would also be disappointed and worry about their professional livelihood, so this is the correct answer.

142. **The correct answer is B.** All of the items listed among the answer choices are mentioned as being a part of a fisherman's life on a Norwegian fishing boat except a lantern (choice B).

143. **The correct answer is A.** This passage is about kopi luwak coffee, how it's made, and why it's such a prized and expensive beverage. The title that best expresses the main idea of this passage is "Kopi Luwak: A Prized Cup of Coffee."

144. **The correct answer is B.** The passage explicitly mentions that "these prized beans are harvested from the digested remains of coffee cherries that have been eaten by Asian palm civets," so choice B is correct.

145. **The correct answer is B.** The word *adage* appears in the final sentence of the passage in reference to the phrase "there's no accounting for taste." Scanning the answer choices, this phrase is most closely a saying (choice B) rather than a warning (choice A), joke (choice C), or secret code (choice D).

146. **The correct answer is D.** The passage mentions that "the vast majority of kopi luwak is produced in the islands of Java, Bali, Sumatra, Sulawesi, and the Philippines." The only option not mentioned in the passage is Nicaragua (choice D).

147. **The correct answer is C.** The passage discusses some of the properties of the fermentation process, and how the coffee beans are changed. This includes a reduction in the bitterness of the coffee beans (choice C). The other choices are not mentioned in the passage.

148. **The correct answer is C.** In the passage, we are told that some unsavory coffee merchants have "taken to selling inferior beans under the kopi luwak name in an effort to turn a profit." The comparison among the answer choices that most closely resembles this unethical behavior is a salesman selling cheaply made smart phones and pretending they're more expensive iPhones.

149. **The correct answer is B.** According to the passage, in order to create kopi luwak coffee beans, they're "harvested from the digested remains of coffee cherries that have been eaten by Asian palm civets, small squirrel-like creatures that inhabit

Southeast Asia." Therefore, we can conclude that the Asian palm civet is *essential* to the process.

150. **The correct answer is A.** The author of the passage is making the point that even though kopi luwak beans are made through a possibly strange and unique process that some people would find unappetizing, the beans are still highly prized by some and are expensive—which highlights the notion that it's hard to explain why different people like different things, even if they're unappealing.

151. **The correct answer is B.** Paragraph 1 discusses how profitable and successful the coffee industry has been in recent years, with new businesses opening all around the globe. The answer choice that best highlights the fact that this is a revered business is *admired* (choice B). Choices A and C would indicate that the business is not thriving or healthy, so they are incorrect. Choice D does not make sense given the context of the passage.

152. **The correct answer is D.** We are told in the passage that the process of creating kopi luwak coffee beans is a "unique" process that yields a "limited supply" of beans—therefore, we can infer that compared to harvesting kopi luwak, the process of collecting traditional coffee beans is more common.

NOTES

Vocabulary

153. C	**158.** A	**163.** B	**167.** B	**171.** B
154. D	**159.** B	**164.** A	**168.** C	**172.** D
155. A	**160.** C	**165.** C	**169.** B	**173.** A
156. B	**161.** D	**166.** D	**170.** C	**174.** C
157. D	**162.** B			

153. **The correct answer is C.** A *pioneer* is a person who is the first (or among the first) to do or accomplish something. Although it is possible to be an expert (choice A) in an industry, or even a novice (choice D), this is not the same as being a pioneer (which is a commonly used expression). A person who is the last person (choice B) in an industry would be the opposite of a pioneer.

154. **The correct answer is D.** *Plausible* means "reasonable" or "possible."

155. **The correct answer is A.** *Sage* means "wise" or "knowledgeable."

156. **The correct answer is B.** *Commemorate* means "to honor something or someone."

157. **The correct answer is D.** To decipher something is to translate it into an understandable format. *Discover* (choice B) is close because it's similar in meaning to *understanding*, but *translate* is a better answer.

158. **The correct answer is A.** *Blasé* means "nonchalant," "carefree," or "unconcerned."

159. **The correct answer is B.** To apprehend someone is to arrest or detain them. A suspect can certainly be interrogated (choice A) or even released (choice D), but that does not mean the same thing. It makes no sense to say the suspect was arranged (choice C).

160. **The correct answer is C.** To forfeit means to surrender (as in a sports game) or to submit to a penalty. *Lose* (choice B) is close because a forfeit can be a type of loss, but *surrender* is a more direct meaning of the word.

161. **The correct answer is D.** *Stamina* can mean "endurance," "strength," or "resilience."

162. **The correct answer is B.** *Lucrative* means "profitable," "rewarding," or "well-compensated."

163. **The correct answer is B.** An ovation is a round of applause after a performance.

164. **The correct answer is A.** A panorama describes a broad physical view, usually an outdoor landscape.

165. **The correct answer is C.** To be conscientious about something means to work diligently or carefully at it.

166. **The correct answer is D.** To be voracious means that you consume things (often eating food or reading books) in a "greedy," "hungry," or "insatiable" way.

167. **The correct answer is B.** A haven is a place of "refuge," or "sanctuary," where someone is safe or happy. It is possible you may go to a house (choice C) that is a haven for your vacation (choice A), but *sanctuary* is a far more accurate choice. A haven should not be a trap (choice D).

168. **The correct answer is C.** If someone is making a mercenary decision, they are making it based on monetary needs or financial concerns. An emotional decision (choice D) is the opposite of a mercenary decision.

169. **The correct answer is B.** A dialect is a specific accent or manner of speaking that is often specific to a region or demographic.

170. **The correct answer is C.** *Eccentric* describes someone or something that is "unusual," "strange," or "unconventional."

171. **The correct answer is B.** *Pivotal* means "essential" or "crucial." It does not tell the reader anything about when a moment occurs but rather, how

important it is, so choice C is incorrect. *Pivotal* also does not indicate whether the moment was good or bad, so choices A and D are incorrect.

172. **The correct answer is D.** If something is foreboding, it brings with it a sense of "dread" or something bad to come. *Agony* is too strong of a word to fit with *foreboding*.

173. **The correct answer is A.** *Elite* means "exclusive," "top," or "privileged." It's a subset chosen from a larger group.

174. **The correct answer is C.** *Aloof* can mean "stand-offish" or "distant." It doesn't always have negative connotations, but it can mean "unfriendly." *Aloof* does not mean "foolish" (choice A) or "excited" (choice D). *Aloof* implies exclusivity, which can be connected to being alone (choice B). But one does not say someone "acted alone" (choice B) as a way of describing a person's mannerr.

NOTES

Mathematics

Concepts

175. B	180. D	185. B	190. C	195. B
176. D	181. C	186. C	191. B	196. C
177. C	182. C	187. D	192. C	197. D
178. B	183. C	188. D	193. B	198. D
179. A	184. B	189. A	194. C	

175. **The correct answer is B.** 19 inches is between 1 and 2 feet, but it is closer to 2 feet (24 inches) than to 1 foot (12 inches).

176. **The correct answer is D.** Since each group of 3 feet only counts for 1 yard, you need to figure out how many groups of 3 feet you can make. This is the same as dividing by 3.

177. **The correct answer is C.** The average of two different numbers is the number that falls exactly halfway between the two on a number line.

178. **The correct answer is B.** To convert from inches to centimeters, multiply the number of inches by 2.54. The product of 7×2.54 must be more than 14, so the only possible correct answer is choice B.

179. **The correct answer is A.** The angles in any triangle always add up to 180°.

180. **The correct answer is D.** A meter contains 100 centimeters.

181. **The correct answer is C.** Each gallon contains 16 cups, so the number of gallons needs to be multiplied by 16 to obtain the number of cups.

182. **The correct answer is C.** A quadrilateral is defined as a figure with four sides. A triangle has only three sides.

183. **The correct answer is C.** This problem requires you to "round off" the given number to the place one digit to the right of the decimal point, which immediately eliminates choices B and D. Since the digits in the hundredths place (and beyond) are more than 5, the figure must be rounded upward. Choice A would be the result if you erroneously rounded down.

184. **The correct answer is B.** The digits 2 and 4 end in the hundredths place. This means $0.24 = \frac{24}{100}$. When simplified to simplest form, $\frac{24}{100} = \frac{6}{25}$.

185. **The correct answer is B.** $\frac{33}{7}$ is about 4.7; so, 5, 6, 7, and 8 are between $\frac{33}{7}$ and 8.001.

186. **The correct answer is C.** The distributive property makes choice C true.

187. **The correct answer is D.** By definition, an isosceles triangle is any triangle with two equal sides. Therefore, it is the only possible answer.

188. **The correct answer is D.** The perimeter of a rectangle is the sum of all four sides: $7 + 7 + 2 + 2 = 18$.

189. **The correct answer is A.** If there are an odd number of values in a sorted list, the median is the value that is exactly in the middle. In this case, the 3 is in the middle.

190. **The correct answer is C.** The percent chance of something not happening is always 100 minus the chance of it happening. Since there is a 20% chance of rain, the chance that it will not rain is 100 - 20, or 80%.

191. **The correct answer is B.** The average of a list of numbers is the sum of the numbers divided by how many there are. $-2 + 0 + 2 + 4 = 4$, and $4 \div 4 = 1$.

192. **The correct answer is B.** A boy M years old has a brother six years older and a sister four years younger. The combined age of the three is $M + (M + 6) + (M - 4) = 3M + 2$

193. **The correct answer is B.** Always start with the operations in the parentheses first:

$$(-2)^3 = (-2) \times (-2) \times (-2)$$
$$(-2)^3 = -8$$

Then continue with the operations outside the parentheses:

$$3 \times (-8) = -24$$

Remember, multiplying a negative by a positive results in a negative, but a negative times a negative equals a positive number.

194. **The correct answer is C.** A straight line represents a "straight angle" of 180°. An angle of 60° is given, so $m\angle C$ must be 120° to complete the line. All the angles in a triangle added together equal 180°, therefore:

$$m\angle A + m\angle B + m\angle C = 180°$$
$$m\angle A + 30° + 120° = 180°$$
$$m\angle A = 180° - 150°$$
$$m\angle A = 30°$$

NOTES

195. **The correct answer is B.** The reciprocal of a fraction is the fraction "reversed." To find the answer, you would have to rename $3\frac{1}{3}$ as an improper fraction: $3\frac{1}{3} = \frac{10}{3}$; $\frac{10}{3}$ is the reciprocal of $\frac{3}{10}$.

196. **The correct answer is C.** The formula for finding the circumference of a circle is π times the diameter. The diameter is 2 times the radius. In this case, $2 \times 4 = 8$ is the diameter. Therefore:

$$C = d\pi$$
$$C = 8\pi$$

197. **The correct answer is D.** The components of this problem must be stated in the same units. Therefore, 3 yards = 108 inches. The ratio of 108 to 18 is simplified to 6 to 1.

198. **The correct answer is D.** First, determine the value of the squared numbers: $14^2 = 196$; $15^2 = 225$. This shows us that the square root of 198 must fall between 14 and 15.

Problem Solving

199. D	207. A	215. C	223. D	231. D
200. B	208. B	216. D	224. D	232. B
201. A	209. C	217. A	225. C	233. B
202. A	210. A	218. C	226. A	234. D
203. D	211. D	219. D	227. C	235. C
204. C	212. D	220. B	228. B	236. C
205. C	213. B	221. D	229. B	237. D
206. D	214. C	222. B	230. D	238. D

199. **The correct answer is A.** $10 per week is about $500 per year, so it would take about 25 weeks to earn $255.

200. **The correct answer is B.** Figures are "similar" when their corresponding angles are equal, and their corresponding sides are in proportion.

$$\frac{4}{AB} = \frac{3}{5}$$
$$3AB = 20$$
$$AB = \frac{20}{3} = 6\frac{2}{3}$$

201. **The correct answer is A.** There are 12 months in 1 year. If $542.40 is the total amount paid in a year, the average amount paid per month is $542.40 ÷ 12 = $45.20.

202. **The correct answer is A.** Multiply the numbers as you would whole numbers. Then, since there are an odd number of negative signs, affix a negative sign to the product. Doing so yields $(-2) \cdot (-4) \cdot (3) \cdot (-1) = -24$.

203. **The correct answer is D.** Rename the fractions of the equation with a common denominator.

$$4\frac{1}{8} - 2\frac{2}{3} = \frac{33}{8} - \frac{8}{3}$$
$$= \frac{99}{24} - \frac{64}{24}$$
$$= \frac{35}{24}$$
$$= 1\frac{11}{24}$$

204. **The correct answer is C.** Solve for x:

$$-5 + 4x = 21$$
$$4x = 21 + 5$$
$$4x = 26$$
$$x = \frac{26}{4}$$
$$x = 6.5$$

205. **The correct answer is C.** Before multiplying, rename the mixed numbers as improper fractions:

$$3\frac{1}{3} \times 3\frac{3}{4} \times \frac{2}{5} = \frac{10}{3} \times \frac{15}{4} \times \frac{2}{5}$$
$$= \frac{300}{60} = 5$$

206. **The correct answer is D.** Replace the letters with the given numbers and solve:

$$7a - 3b =$$
$$7(6) - 3(3) =$$
$$42 - 9 = 33$$

207. **The correct answer is A.**

$$N\% \times 60 = 24$$
$$N\% = \frac{24}{60}$$
$$N\% = \frac{2}{5}$$
$$N\% = 0.4$$
$$N\% = 40$$

208. **The correct answer is B.** Solve for *x*:

$$10x - 3 = 2x + 4$$
$$10x - 2x = 4 + 3$$
$$8x = 7$$
$$x = \frac{7}{8}$$

209. **The correct answer is C.** To determine ratios, multiply the first numerator by the second denominator and the first denominator by the second numerator. Then reduce:

$$\frac{3}{4} \text{ to } \frac{5}{2}$$

6 to 20

3 to 10

210. **The correct answer is A.** When solving this problem, remember that the number of decimal places to the right of the decimal point in the answer should equal the total number of places to the right of the decimal points in the two factors being multiplied.

$$
\begin{array}{r}
65.14 \\
\times 0.093 \\
\hline
19542 \\
586260 \\
\hline
6.05802
\end{array}
$$

211. **The correct answer is D.** The pattern in this sequence is formed by adding 0.06 to each number.

212. **The correct answer is D.**

$$
\begin{array}{r}
72,528 \\
\times \quad 109 \\
\hline
652\,752 \\
000\,00 \\
7\,252\,8 \\
\hline
7,905,552
\end{array}
$$

213. **The correct answer is B.** Convert the mixed numbers into improper fractions. Reduce, then divide the total length of the board by the length into which it will be cut.

$$9\frac{1}{2} \div 1\frac{1}{3} = \frac{19}{2} \div \frac{4}{3}$$
$$= \frac{19}{2} \times \frac{3}{4}$$
$$= \frac{57}{8}$$
$$= 7\frac{1}{8}$$

Though $\frac{1}{8}$ of a board is left, only 7 full-size boards can be made.

214. **The correct answer is C.**

$$3x + 3 < 9 + x$$
$$3x - x < 9 - 3$$
$$2x < 6$$
$$x < \frac{6}{2}$$
$$x < 3$$

215. **The correct answer is C.** When adding decimal numbers, line up the decimal points.

$$
\begin{array}{r}
0.602 \\
4.200 \\
+5.030 \\
\hline
9.832
\end{array}
$$

216. The correct answer is D.

$$
\begin{array}{r}
1{,}960 \\
28\overline{)54{,}900} \\
\underline{28\phantom{{,}900}} \\
269 \\
\underline{252} \\
170 \\
\underline{168} \\
20
\end{array}
$$

217. The correct answer is A.

$$\sqrt{x+36} = 10$$
$$x + 36 = 10^2$$
$$x + 36 = 100$$
$$x = 100 - 36$$
$$x = 64$$

218. The correct answer is C. The probability is the number of red balls over the total number of balls in the basket.

219. The correct answer is D. Since her brother is 10, Katie herself is half of 10, or 5 years old. She will be 12 in 7 years, since $5 + 7 = 12$.

220. The correct answer is B. 25% of $12 is $3, so each ticket will cost $9. Three tickets will cost $9 \times 3 =$ $27.

221. The correct answer is D. Each pair of pants can be matched up with 3 different shirts, so there are $2 \times 3 = 6$ different outfits.

222. The correct answer is B. 50% of $600 is $300, so the sale price is $600 - $300 = $300. The coupon is for 10% of $300, or $30. The final price will be $300 - $30 = $270.

223. The correct answer is D. The average of two numbers is half their sum. If the average is 18, their sum must be 36. The second number must then be $36 - 10 = 26$.

224. The correct answer is D. There are $16 \times 18 = 288$ square inches of rubber. Each square foot is 144 square inches, so that is $288 \div 144 = 2$ square feet. Since each square foot weighs 17 ounces, the total weight is $17 \times 2 = 34$ ounces.

225. The correct answer is C. Since Paul is 3 months older than Hunter, Paul is 3 months closer to Kai than Hunter is, and $7 - 3 = 4$.

226. The correct answer is A. This problem is solved by using ratios. The relationship between part of the lawn and the whole lawn is the same as the relationship between the time it takes to mow part of the lawn and the time it takes to mow the whole lawn.

227. The correct answer is C. This involves multiplication and addition.

Student
tickets $130 \times \$1.25 =$ $162.50
Adult
tickets $340 \times \$1.90 = +$ $646.00
Total = $808.50

228. The correct answer is B.
First, add $10 to Bettina's $88:

$$\$88 + \$10 = \$98$$

Then, divide by 4:

$$\$98 \div 4 = \$24.50$$

229. The correct answer is B. Replace the C in the formula with 85 and solve:

$$F = \frac{9}{5}(85) + 32 = 153 + 32$$
$$= 185$$

230. The correct answer is D. This can be set up as an algebraic equation. If n equals the price of the snowmobile, 5% of n equals $42, or

$$0.05n = \$42$$
$$n = \$42 \div 0.05$$
$$n = \$840$$

231. The correct answer is D. This can be set up as an algebraic equation. If n is the amount Mr. Symon borrowed:

$$6\%(n) = 58.50$$
$$n = \frac{58.50}{6\%}$$
$$= \frac{58.50}{0.06}$$
$$= 975$$

232. The correct answer is B. This problem is solved using ratios:

$$\frac{n}{6} = \frac{56}{14}$$
$$336 = 14n$$
$$\frac{336}{14} = n$$
$$24 = n$$

233. The correct answer is B. By definition, opposite sides of a rectangle are equal to each other. Because of this, if one side is 7 units, the opposite side is also 7 units. Consequently, 14 units account for two sides (7 + 7). The other two sides are each equal to (50 – 14) ÷ 2, or 18 units. Area is length times width—in this case: 7 × 18 = 126 square units.

234. The correct answer is D. Solve this as an algebraic equation with n as the unknown integer:

$$n + 18 = \frac{5}{4}n$$
$$18 = \frac{5}{4}n - n$$
$$18 = \frac{1}{4}n$$
$$72 = n$$

235. The correct answer is C. Because Jin is now 12, four years ago he was 8. His father was then 5 times older, or 40. Now, 4 years later, Jin's father is 44.

236. The correct answer is C. The area to be carpeted is (27 × 27) = 729 square feet. Since there are 9 square feet in one yard, this is equivalent to 81 square yards, and since it costs $11 per square yard, the total cost is (81 × 11) = $891.

237. The correct answer is D.

$$V = lwh$$
$$V = 18 \times 2 \times 5$$
$$V = 180 \text{ cu. in.}$$

238. The correct answer is D. First, determine how many times 25,000 can be divided by 100:

$$25,000 \div 100 = 250$$

For *every* $100 in 25,000, $3.62 must be paid in taxes: 250 × 3.62 = $905.00.

Language

239. B	251. B	263. C	275. A	287. A
240. A	252. C	264. A	276. A	288. A
241. A	253. D	265. A	277. B	289. C
242. D	254. A	266. B	278. B	290. A
243. B	255. B	267. B	279. A	291. C
244. C	256. A	268. B	280. C	292. B
245. B	257. B	269. A	281. D	293. D
246. C	258. B	270. C	282. D	294. D
247. A	259. C	271. A	283. B	295. A
248. A	260. C	272. B	284. C	296. C
249. A	261. B	273. C	285. D	297. B
250. A	262. B	274. B	286. C	298. B

239. **The correct answer is B.** This is a question and should thus end in a question mark (the word *what* at the beginning is a clue).

240. **The correct answer is A.** The names of movies, like *Star Wars*, should be capitalized.

241. **The correct answer is A.** The preposition *on* is incorrect—the book goes back *to* the library.

242. **The correct answer is D.** *No mistakes.*

243. **The correct answer is B.** This simple, declarative statement is not a question, so it should end with a period instead of a question mark.

244. **The correct answer is C.** The use of the pronoun *us* is incorrect. A possessive pronoun, such as *our*, *her*, or *their*, should be used in its place..

245. **The correct answer is B.** This sentence incorrectly ends with a semicolon, which is internal sentence punctuation, not end-of-sentence punctuation.

246. **The correct answer is C.** The Statue of Liberty is a proper noun and should be capitalized.

247. **The correct answer is A.** The adjective *cautious* should be an adverb (*cautiously*) since it's describing how the action of the sentence (*walked*) is being performed.

248. **The correct answer is A.** The items in the list in this sentence need to be separated by commas.

249. **The correct answer is A.** The pronoun *she* could modify the name *Janelle*, but in this case, one needs to show possession, so *she* should be changed to *her*.

250. **The correct answer is A.** This sentence contains a semicolon, which creates an awkward pause. Semicolons should be used to connect two independent clauses, which we do not have here.

251. **The correct answer is B.** The noun *Daphnes* should be in the possessive form (*Daphne's*), as ownership of the closet is being shown here.

252. **The correct answer is C.** This sentence contains inappropriate commas, which create awkward pauses in the sentence. The sentence does not need internal punctuation as written.

253. **The correct answer is D.** *No mistakes.*

254. **The correct answer is A.** The verb *wondering* should be *wondered* as the action began in the past.

255. **The correct answer is B.** The adjective *easy* in this sentence is illogical, as we are told that no one has ever been able to pass it. A more appropriate adjective would be *difficult* or *challenging*.

256. **The correct answer is A.** This simple declarative statement, which is not a question, should end with a period, not a question mark.

257. **The correct answer is B.** In this sentence, the verb *create* does not agree with the adverb *was*, and should be in the past-tense, *created*.

258. **The correct answer is B.** The dialogue in this sentence should be set in quotation marks, not italicized: "Are you certain you can't make it to my party?"

259. **The correct answer is C.** The sentence as written is illogical—a choice between two items, and the use of the word *either*, indicates that the correct article to use is *or*, not *and*.

260. **The correct answer is C.** Since we are told that the action in this sentence will occur in the future ("tomorrow"), the verb should be set in the future tense: "will go" or "will be going."

261. **The correct answer is B.** This simple sentence does not contain any pointed emotion or surprise, so it should end in a period, not an exclamation point.

262. **The correct answer is B.** The preposition *in* does not make sense in this sentence, as you can't stand inside of a stage. The correct preposition here is "on."

263. **The correct answer is C.** The sentence as written is illogical—if Larissa arrived "before" breakfast was over, she shouldn't have missed her chance to eat. A more appropriate preposition here would be *after*.

264. **The correct answer is A.** When two things are described as an excellent "combination," they should be joined by the conjunction *and* not *or*.

265. **The correct answer is A.** The incorrect preposition is used in this sentence. If Jovan didn't want to get his hair wet, he must have kept his hair "above" the water, not "below."

266. **The correct answer is B.** This sentence contains an error in preposition choice. Since a conditional activity (going to the baseball game) is dependent on the completion of another activity (finishing

her homework), the preposition *if* is a more appropriate choice: Lilith can only go to the baseball game tomorrow if she finishes her homework first.

267. **The correct answer is B.** The sentence contains an error in adjective usage. *Wrestle* should be changed to *wrestling*.

268. **The correct answer is B.** The correct spelling is *effect*.

269. **The correct answer is A.** The correct spelling is *advice*.

270. **The correct answer is C.** The correct spelling is *allowed*.

271. **The correct answer is A.** The correct spelling is *presence*.

272. **The correct answer is B.** The correct spelling is *separate*.

273. **The correct answer is C.** The correct spelling is *disappointed*.

274. **The correct answer is B.** The correct spelling is *believable*.

275. **The correct answer is A.** The correct spelling is *collectible*.

276. **The correct answer is A.** The correct spelling is *too*.

277. **The correct answer is B.** The correct spelling is *break*.

278. **The correct answer is B.** This sentence demonstrates correct usage. The other answer choices contain incorrect pronoun choices.

279. **The correct answer is A.** This sentence demonstrates correct usage. The other answer choices contain incorrect pronoun choices.

280. **The correct answer is C.** This sentence demonstrates correct usage. The other answer choices contain incorrect verb forms.

281. **The correct answer is D.** This sentence demonstrates correct usage. The other answer choices contain conjunction errors. Choice A should use *as if*, rather than *by the time*. Choice B should use *Although* instead of *Only if*, and choice C should use *When* in place of *Before*.

282. **The correct answer is D.** This sentence demonstrates correct usage. The other answer choices contain incorrect possessive noun forms.

283. **The correct answer is B.** This sentence demonstrates correct usage. The other answer choices contain incorrect preposition choices. Choice A should use *about* rather than *beyond*; choice C should use *on* rather than *among*, and Choice D should use *around* rather than *about*.

284. **The correct answer is C.** This sentence demonstrates correct usage. The other answer choices contain incorrect pronoun choices.

285. **The correct answer is D.** This sentence demonstrates correct usage. The other answer choices contain adverb errors. Proper adverb choices would have been *capably* (choice A); *slowly* (choice B); and *beautifully* (choice C).

286. **The correct answer is C.** This sentence demonstrates correct usage. The other answer choices contain conjunction or preposition errors. Choice A should use *when* instead of *during*; choice B should eliminate the word *because*; and Choice D should use *than* rather than *because*.

287. **The correct answer is A.** This sentence demonstrates correct usage. The other answer choices contain adverb errors. The correct adverb choice would have been *absentmindedly* (choice B), *quietly* (choice C), and *hungrily* (choice D).

288. **The correct answer is A.** This sentence demonstrates correct usage. The other answer choices contain incorrect articles (*a* versus *an*).

289. **The correct answer is C.** These two sentences best support the topic sentence that a healthy diet and exercise can improve your brain functioning.

290. **The correct answer is A.** We are told in the sentence that Sharrod is late for a meeting, so it follows that he would move briskly through the train station.

291. **The correct answer is C.** Mentioning that there's a retail bookstore located in the town's mall offers the least support for why the town of Willowbrook needs a library.

292. **The correct answer is B.** This is the best word choice to complete this sentence: "Phineas had to carefully parallel park his car *between* an SUV and a pickup truck."

293. **The correct answer is D.** This version of the sentence expresses the ideas most clearly.

294. **The correct answer is D.** This is the best word choice to complete this thought: "The cleaning crew had the unfortunate task of cleaning up the street *after* the busy parade was finished."

295. **The correct answer is A.** This version of the sentence expresses the ideas most clearly.

296. **The correct answer is C.** This sentence veers off topic from the main subject of the paragraph (snakes) and does not belong.

297. **The correct answer is B.** This sentence best captures the two main ideas of the paragraph, that giraffes are gentle and quite tall creatures.

298. **The correct answer is B.** This sentence provides no direct support for the idea that college should be free for everybody; in fact, it could be used to argue against the topic.

SCORE SHEET

Although your actual exam scores will not be reported as percentages, it might be helpful to convert them so you can better visualize your strengths and weaknesses. The numbers in parentheses represent the question numbers testing each skill.

Subject	# Correct ÷ # of questions	× 100 = _____ %
Verbal Analogies (1–10)	_____ ÷ 10 = _____	× 100 = _____ %
Synonyms (37–51)	_____ ÷ 15 = _____	× 100 = _____ %
Logic (11–20)	_____ ÷ 10 = _____	× 100 = _____ %
Verbal Classification (21–36)	_____ ÷ 16 = _____	× 100 = _____ %
Antonyms (52–60)	_____ ÷ 9 = _____	× 100 = _____ %
TOTAL VERBAL SKILLS	_____ ÷ 60 = _____	× 100 = _____ %
Number Series (62, 67, 69, 72, 76, 79, 81, 86, 89, 93, 95, 99, 100, 101, 104, 106, 107, 108)	_____ ÷ 18 = _____	× 100 = _____ %
Geometric Comparisons (68, 77, 78, 82, 84, 91, 96, 102, 110)	_____ ÷ 9 = _____	× 100 = _____ %
Nongeometric Comparisons (64, 65, 70, 87, 94, 97, 98, 105)	_____ ÷ 8 = _____	× 100 = _____ %
Number Manipulation (61, 63, 66, 71, 73, 74, 75, 80, 83, 85, 88, 90, 92, 103, 109, 111, 112)	_____ ÷ 17 = _____	× 100 = _____ %
TOTAL QUANTITATIVE SKILLS	_____ ÷ 52 = _____	× 100 = _____ %
Reading—Comprehension (113–152)	_____ ÷ 40 = _____	× 100 = _____ %
Reading—Vocabulary (153–174)	_____ ÷ 22 = _____	× 100 = _____ %
TOTAL READING SKILLS	_____ ÷ 62 = _____	× 100 = _____ %
Mathematics—Concepts (175–198)	_____ ÷ 24 = _____	× 100 = _____ %
Mathematics—Problem Solving (199–238)	_____ ÷ 40 = _____	× 100 = _____ %
TOTAL MATHEMATICS SKILLS	_____ ÷ 64 = _____	× 100 = _____ %
Punctuation and Capitalization (239, 240, 242, 243, 245, 246, 248, 250, 252, 253, 256, 261)	_____ ÷ 12 = _____	× 100 = _____ %
Usage (241, 244, 247, 249, 251, 254, 255, 257, 258, 259, 260, 262–267, 278–288)	_____ ÷ 28 = _____	× 100 = _____ %
Spelling (268–277)	_____ ÷ 10 = _____	× 100 = _____ %
Composition (289–298)	_____ ÷ 10 = _____	× 100 = _____ %
TOTAL LANGUAGE SKILLS	_____ ÷ 60 = _____	× 100 = _____ %

NOTES

HSPT® PRACTICE TEST 5

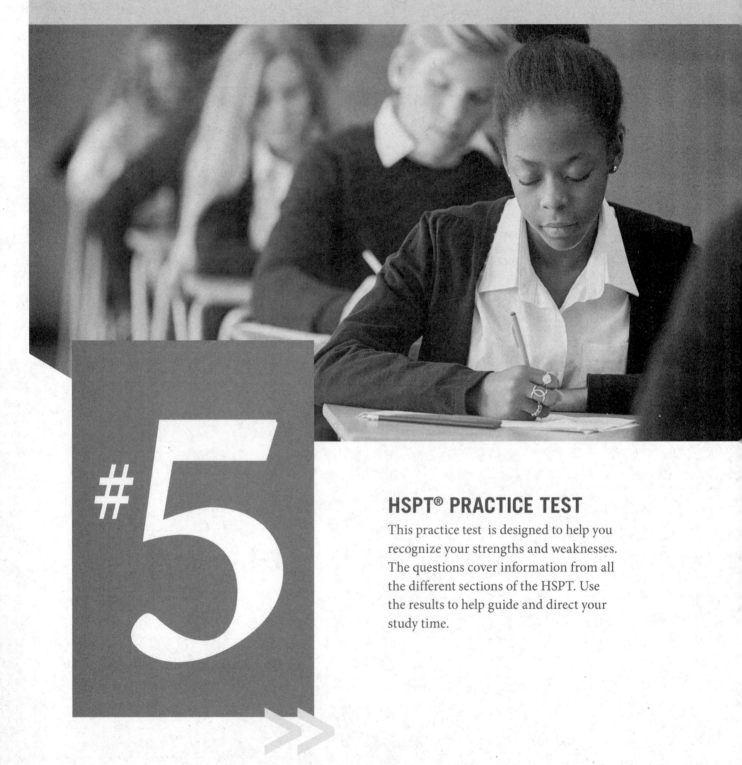

#5

HSPT® PRACTICE TEST

This practice test is designed to help you recognize your strengths and weaknesses. The questions cover information from all the different sections of the HSPT. Use the results to help guide and direct your study time.

ANSWER SHEETS: HSPT® PRACTICE TEST 5

Verbal Skills

1. Ⓐ Ⓑ Ⓒ Ⓓ
2. Ⓐ Ⓑ Ⓒ Ⓓ
3. Ⓐ Ⓑ Ⓒ Ⓓ
4. Ⓐ Ⓑ Ⓒ Ⓓ
5. Ⓐ Ⓑ Ⓒ Ⓓ
6. Ⓐ Ⓑ Ⓒ Ⓓ
7. Ⓐ Ⓑ Ⓒ Ⓓ
8. Ⓐ Ⓑ Ⓒ Ⓓ
9. Ⓐ Ⓑ Ⓒ Ⓓ
10. Ⓐ Ⓑ Ⓒ Ⓓ
11. Ⓐ Ⓑ Ⓒ
12. Ⓐ Ⓑ Ⓒ

13. Ⓐ Ⓑ Ⓒ
14. Ⓐ Ⓑ Ⓒ
15. Ⓐ Ⓑ Ⓒ
16. Ⓐ Ⓑ Ⓒ
17. Ⓐ Ⓑ Ⓒ
18. Ⓐ Ⓑ Ⓒ
19. Ⓐ Ⓑ Ⓒ
20. Ⓐ Ⓑ Ⓒ
21. Ⓐ Ⓑ Ⓒ Ⓓ
22. Ⓐ Ⓑ Ⓒ Ⓓ
23. Ⓐ Ⓑ Ⓒ Ⓓ
24. Ⓐ Ⓑ Ⓒ Ⓓ

25. Ⓐ Ⓑ Ⓒ Ⓓ
26. Ⓐ Ⓑ Ⓒ Ⓓ
27. Ⓐ Ⓑ Ⓒ Ⓓ
28. Ⓐ Ⓑ Ⓒ Ⓓ
29. Ⓐ Ⓑ Ⓒ Ⓓ
30. Ⓐ Ⓑ Ⓒ Ⓓ
31. Ⓐ Ⓑ Ⓒ Ⓓ
32. Ⓐ Ⓑ Ⓒ Ⓓ
33. Ⓐ Ⓑ Ⓒ Ⓓ
34. Ⓐ Ⓑ Ⓒ Ⓓ
35. Ⓐ Ⓑ Ⓒ Ⓓ
36. Ⓐ Ⓑ Ⓒ Ⓓ

37. Ⓐ Ⓑ Ⓒ Ⓓ
38. Ⓐ Ⓑ Ⓒ Ⓓ
39. Ⓐ Ⓑ Ⓒ Ⓓ
40. Ⓐ Ⓑ Ⓒ Ⓓ
41. Ⓐ Ⓑ Ⓒ Ⓓ
42. Ⓐ Ⓑ Ⓒ Ⓓ
43. Ⓐ Ⓑ Ⓒ Ⓓ
44. Ⓐ Ⓑ Ⓒ Ⓓ
45. Ⓐ Ⓑ Ⓒ Ⓓ
46. Ⓐ Ⓑ Ⓒ Ⓓ
47. Ⓐ Ⓑ Ⓒ Ⓓ
48. Ⓐ Ⓑ Ⓒ Ⓓ

49. Ⓐ Ⓑ Ⓒ Ⓓ
50. Ⓐ Ⓑ Ⓒ Ⓓ
51. Ⓐ Ⓑ Ⓒ Ⓓ
52. Ⓐ Ⓑ Ⓒ Ⓓ
53. Ⓐ Ⓑ Ⓒ Ⓓ
54. Ⓐ Ⓑ Ⓒ Ⓓ
55. Ⓐ Ⓑ Ⓒ Ⓓ
56. Ⓐ Ⓑ Ⓒ Ⓓ
57. Ⓐ Ⓑ Ⓒ Ⓓ
58. Ⓐ Ⓑ Ⓒ Ⓓ
59. Ⓐ Ⓑ Ⓒ Ⓓ
60. Ⓐ Ⓑ Ⓒ Ⓓ

Quantitative Skills

61. Ⓐ Ⓑ Ⓒ Ⓓ
62. Ⓐ Ⓑ Ⓒ Ⓓ
63. Ⓐ Ⓑ Ⓒ Ⓓ
64. Ⓐ Ⓑ Ⓒ Ⓓ
65. Ⓐ Ⓑ Ⓒ Ⓓ
66. Ⓐ Ⓑ Ⓒ Ⓓ
67. Ⓐ Ⓑ Ⓒ Ⓓ
68. Ⓐ Ⓑ Ⓒ Ⓓ
69. Ⓐ Ⓑ Ⓒ Ⓓ
70. Ⓐ Ⓑ Ⓒ Ⓓ
71. Ⓐ Ⓑ Ⓒ Ⓓ

72. Ⓐ Ⓑ Ⓒ Ⓓ
73. Ⓐ Ⓑ Ⓒ Ⓓ
74. Ⓐ Ⓑ Ⓒ Ⓓ
75. Ⓐ Ⓑ Ⓒ Ⓓ
76. Ⓐ Ⓑ Ⓒ Ⓓ
77. Ⓐ Ⓑ Ⓒ Ⓓ
78. Ⓐ Ⓑ Ⓒ Ⓓ
79. Ⓐ Ⓑ Ⓒ Ⓓ
80. Ⓐ Ⓑ Ⓒ Ⓓ
81. Ⓐ Ⓑ Ⓒ Ⓓ
82. Ⓐ Ⓑ Ⓒ Ⓓ

83. Ⓐ Ⓑ Ⓒ Ⓓ
84. Ⓐ Ⓑ Ⓒ Ⓓ
85. Ⓐ Ⓑ Ⓒ Ⓓ
86. Ⓐ Ⓑ Ⓒ Ⓓ
87. Ⓐ Ⓑ Ⓒ Ⓓ
88. Ⓐ Ⓑ Ⓒ Ⓓ
89. Ⓐ Ⓑ Ⓒ Ⓓ
90. Ⓐ Ⓑ Ⓒ Ⓓ
91. Ⓐ Ⓑ Ⓒ Ⓓ
92. Ⓐ Ⓑ Ⓒ Ⓓ
93. Ⓐ Ⓑ Ⓒ Ⓓ

94. Ⓐ Ⓑ Ⓒ Ⓓ
95. Ⓐ Ⓑ Ⓒ Ⓓ
96. Ⓐ Ⓑ Ⓒ Ⓓ
97. Ⓐ Ⓑ Ⓒ Ⓓ
98. Ⓐ Ⓑ Ⓒ Ⓓ
99. Ⓐ Ⓑ Ⓒ Ⓓ
100. Ⓐ Ⓑ Ⓒ Ⓓ
101. Ⓐ Ⓑ Ⓒ Ⓓ
102. Ⓐ Ⓑ Ⓒ Ⓓ
103. Ⓐ Ⓑ Ⓒ Ⓓ
104. Ⓐ Ⓑ Ⓒ Ⓓ

105. Ⓐ Ⓑ Ⓒ Ⓓ
106. Ⓐ Ⓑ Ⓒ Ⓓ
107. Ⓐ Ⓑ Ⓒ Ⓓ
108. Ⓐ Ⓑ Ⓒ Ⓓ
109. Ⓐ Ⓑ Ⓒ Ⓓ
110. Ⓐ Ⓑ Ⓒ Ⓓ
111. Ⓐ Ⓑ Ⓒ Ⓓ
112. Ⓐ Ⓑ Ⓒ Ⓓ

Reading

Comprehension

113. Ⓐ Ⓑ Ⓒ Ⓓ   121. Ⓐ Ⓑ Ⓒ Ⓓ   129. Ⓐ Ⓑ Ⓒ Ⓓ   137. Ⓐ Ⓑ Ⓒ Ⓓ   145. Ⓐ Ⓑ Ⓒ Ⓓ

114. Ⓐ Ⓑ Ⓒ Ⓓ   122. Ⓐ Ⓑ Ⓒ Ⓓ   130. Ⓐ Ⓑ Ⓒ Ⓓ   138. Ⓐ Ⓑ Ⓒ Ⓓ   146. Ⓐ Ⓑ Ⓒ Ⓓ

115. Ⓐ Ⓑ Ⓒ Ⓓ   123. Ⓐ Ⓑ Ⓒ Ⓓ   131. Ⓐ Ⓑ Ⓒ Ⓓ   139. Ⓐ Ⓑ Ⓒ Ⓓ   147. Ⓐ Ⓑ Ⓒ Ⓓ

116. Ⓐ Ⓑ Ⓒ Ⓓ   124. Ⓐ Ⓑ Ⓒ Ⓓ   132. Ⓐ Ⓑ Ⓒ Ⓓ   140. Ⓐ Ⓑ Ⓒ Ⓓ   148. Ⓐ Ⓑ Ⓒ Ⓓ

117. Ⓐ Ⓑ Ⓒ Ⓓ   125. Ⓐ Ⓑ Ⓒ Ⓓ   133. Ⓐ Ⓑ Ⓒ Ⓓ   141. Ⓐ Ⓑ Ⓒ Ⓓ   149. Ⓐ Ⓑ Ⓒ Ⓓ

118. Ⓐ Ⓑ Ⓒ Ⓓ   126. Ⓐ Ⓑ Ⓒ Ⓓ   134. Ⓐ Ⓑ Ⓒ Ⓓ   142. Ⓐ Ⓑ Ⓒ Ⓓ   150. Ⓐ Ⓑ Ⓒ Ⓓ

119. Ⓐ Ⓑ Ⓒ Ⓓ   127. Ⓐ Ⓑ Ⓒ Ⓓ   135. Ⓐ Ⓑ Ⓒ Ⓓ   143. Ⓐ Ⓑ Ⓒ Ⓓ   151. Ⓐ Ⓑ Ⓒ Ⓓ

120. Ⓐ Ⓑ Ⓒ Ⓓ   128. Ⓐ Ⓑ Ⓒ Ⓓ   136. Ⓐ Ⓑ Ⓒ Ⓓ   144. Ⓐ Ⓑ Ⓒ Ⓓ   152. Ⓐ Ⓑ Ⓒ Ⓓ

Vocabulary

153. Ⓐ Ⓑ Ⓒ Ⓓ   158. Ⓐ Ⓑ Ⓒ Ⓓ   163. Ⓐ Ⓑ Ⓒ Ⓓ   168. Ⓐ Ⓑ Ⓒ Ⓓ   173. Ⓐ Ⓑ Ⓒ Ⓓ

154. Ⓐ Ⓑ Ⓒ Ⓓ   159. Ⓐ Ⓑ Ⓒ Ⓓ   164. Ⓐ Ⓑ Ⓒ Ⓓ   169. Ⓐ Ⓑ Ⓒ Ⓓ   174. Ⓐ Ⓑ Ⓒ Ⓓ

155. Ⓐ Ⓑ Ⓒ Ⓓ   160. Ⓐ Ⓑ Ⓒ Ⓓ   165. Ⓐ Ⓑ Ⓒ Ⓓ   170. Ⓐ Ⓑ Ⓒ Ⓓ

156. Ⓐ Ⓑ Ⓒ Ⓓ   161. Ⓐ Ⓑ Ⓒ Ⓓ   166. Ⓐ Ⓑ Ⓒ Ⓓ   171. Ⓐ Ⓑ Ⓒ Ⓓ

157. Ⓐ Ⓑ Ⓒ Ⓓ   162. Ⓐ Ⓑ Ⓒ Ⓓ   167. Ⓐ Ⓑ Ⓒ Ⓓ   172. Ⓐ Ⓑ Ⓒ Ⓓ

Mathematics

Concepts

175. Ⓐ Ⓑ Ⓒ Ⓓ   180. Ⓐ Ⓑ Ⓒ Ⓓ   185. Ⓐ Ⓑ Ⓒ Ⓓ   190. Ⓐ Ⓑ Ⓒ Ⓓ   195. Ⓐ Ⓑ Ⓒ Ⓓ

176. Ⓐ Ⓑ Ⓒ Ⓓ   181. Ⓐ Ⓑ Ⓒ Ⓓ   186. Ⓐ Ⓑ Ⓒ Ⓓ   191. Ⓐ Ⓑ Ⓒ Ⓓ   196. Ⓐ Ⓑ Ⓒ Ⓓ

177. Ⓐ Ⓑ Ⓒ Ⓓ   182. Ⓐ Ⓑ Ⓒ Ⓓ   187. Ⓐ Ⓑ Ⓒ Ⓓ   192. Ⓐ Ⓑ Ⓒ Ⓓ   197. Ⓐ Ⓑ Ⓒ Ⓓ

178. Ⓐ Ⓑ Ⓒ Ⓓ   183. Ⓐ Ⓑ Ⓒ Ⓓ   188. Ⓐ Ⓑ Ⓒ Ⓓ   193. Ⓐ Ⓑ Ⓒ Ⓓ   198. Ⓐ Ⓑ Ⓒ Ⓓ

179. Ⓐ Ⓑ Ⓒ Ⓓ   184. Ⓐ Ⓑ Ⓒ Ⓓ   189. Ⓐ Ⓑ Ⓒ Ⓓ   194. Ⓐ Ⓑ Ⓒ Ⓓ

Problem Solving

199. Ⓐ Ⓑ Ⓒ Ⓓ   207. Ⓐ Ⓑ Ⓒ Ⓓ   215. Ⓐ Ⓑ Ⓒ Ⓓ   223. Ⓐ Ⓑ Ⓒ Ⓓ   231. Ⓐ Ⓑ Ⓒ Ⓓ

200. Ⓐ Ⓑ Ⓒ Ⓓ   208. Ⓐ Ⓑ Ⓒ Ⓓ   216. Ⓐ Ⓑ Ⓒ Ⓓ   224. Ⓐ Ⓑ Ⓒ Ⓓ   232. Ⓐ Ⓑ Ⓒ Ⓓ

201. Ⓐ Ⓑ Ⓒ Ⓓ   209. Ⓐ Ⓑ Ⓒ Ⓓ   217. Ⓐ Ⓑ Ⓒ Ⓓ   225. Ⓐ Ⓑ Ⓒ Ⓓ   233. Ⓐ Ⓑ Ⓒ Ⓓ

202. Ⓐ Ⓑ Ⓒ Ⓓ   210. Ⓐ Ⓑ Ⓒ Ⓓ   218. Ⓐ Ⓑ Ⓒ Ⓓ   226. Ⓐ Ⓑ Ⓒ Ⓓ   234. Ⓐ Ⓑ Ⓒ Ⓓ

203. Ⓐ Ⓑ Ⓒ Ⓓ   211. Ⓐ Ⓑ Ⓒ Ⓓ   219. Ⓐ Ⓑ Ⓒ Ⓓ   227. Ⓐ Ⓑ Ⓒ Ⓓ   235. Ⓐ Ⓑ Ⓒ Ⓓ

204. Ⓐ Ⓑ Ⓒ Ⓓ   212. Ⓐ Ⓑ Ⓒ Ⓓ   220. Ⓐ Ⓑ Ⓒ Ⓓ   228. Ⓐ Ⓑ Ⓒ Ⓓ   236. Ⓐ Ⓑ Ⓒ Ⓓ

205. Ⓐ Ⓑ Ⓒ Ⓓ   213. Ⓐ Ⓑ Ⓒ Ⓓ   221. Ⓐ Ⓑ Ⓒ Ⓓ   229. Ⓐ Ⓑ Ⓒ Ⓓ   237. Ⓐ Ⓑ Ⓒ Ⓓ

206. Ⓐ Ⓑ Ⓒ Ⓓ   214. Ⓐ Ⓑ Ⓒ Ⓓ   222. Ⓐ Ⓑ Ⓒ Ⓓ   230. Ⓐ Ⓑ Ⓒ Ⓓ   238. Ⓐ Ⓑ Ⓒ Ⓓ

Language

239. Ⓐ Ⓑ Ⓒ Ⓓ   251. Ⓐ Ⓑ Ⓒ Ⓓ   263. Ⓐ Ⓑ Ⓒ Ⓓ   275. Ⓐ Ⓑ Ⓒ Ⓓ   287. Ⓐ Ⓑ Ⓒ Ⓓ

240. Ⓐ Ⓑ Ⓒ Ⓓ   252. Ⓐ Ⓑ Ⓒ Ⓓ   264. Ⓐ Ⓑ Ⓒ Ⓓ   276. Ⓐ Ⓑ Ⓒ Ⓓ   288. Ⓐ Ⓑ Ⓒ Ⓓ

241. Ⓐ Ⓑ Ⓒ Ⓓ   253. Ⓐ Ⓑ Ⓒ Ⓓ   265. Ⓐ Ⓑ Ⓒ Ⓓ   277. Ⓐ Ⓑ Ⓒ Ⓓ   289. Ⓐ Ⓑ Ⓒ Ⓓ

242. Ⓐ Ⓑ Ⓒ Ⓓ   254. Ⓐ Ⓑ Ⓒ Ⓓ   266. Ⓐ Ⓑ Ⓒ Ⓓ   278. Ⓐ Ⓑ Ⓒ Ⓓ   290. Ⓐ Ⓑ Ⓒ Ⓓ

243. Ⓐ Ⓑ Ⓒ Ⓓ   255. Ⓐ Ⓑ Ⓒ Ⓓ   267. Ⓐ Ⓑ Ⓒ Ⓓ   279. Ⓐ Ⓑ Ⓒ Ⓓ   291. Ⓐ Ⓑ Ⓒ Ⓓ

244. Ⓐ Ⓑ Ⓒ Ⓓ   256. Ⓐ Ⓑ Ⓒ Ⓓ   268. Ⓐ Ⓑ Ⓒ Ⓓ   280. Ⓐ Ⓑ Ⓒ Ⓓ   292. Ⓐ Ⓑ Ⓒ Ⓓ

245. Ⓐ Ⓑ Ⓒ Ⓓ   257. Ⓐ Ⓑ Ⓒ Ⓓ   269. Ⓐ Ⓑ Ⓒ Ⓓ   281. Ⓐ Ⓑ Ⓒ Ⓓ   293. Ⓐ Ⓑ Ⓒ Ⓓ

246. Ⓐ Ⓑ Ⓒ Ⓓ   258. Ⓐ Ⓑ Ⓒ Ⓓ   270. Ⓐ Ⓑ Ⓒ Ⓓ   282. Ⓐ Ⓑ Ⓒ Ⓓ   294. Ⓐ Ⓑ Ⓒ Ⓓ

247. Ⓐ Ⓑ Ⓒ Ⓓ   259. Ⓐ Ⓑ Ⓒ Ⓓ   271. Ⓐ Ⓑ Ⓒ Ⓓ   283. Ⓐ Ⓑ Ⓒ Ⓓ   295. Ⓐ Ⓑ Ⓒ Ⓓ

248. Ⓐ Ⓑ Ⓒ Ⓓ   260. Ⓐ Ⓑ Ⓒ Ⓓ   272. Ⓐ Ⓑ Ⓒ Ⓓ   284. Ⓐ Ⓑ Ⓒ Ⓓ   296. Ⓐ Ⓑ Ⓒ Ⓓ

249. Ⓐ Ⓑ Ⓒ Ⓓ   261. Ⓐ Ⓑ Ⓒ Ⓓ   273. Ⓐ Ⓑ Ⓒ Ⓓ   285. Ⓐ Ⓑ Ⓒ Ⓓ   297. Ⓐ Ⓑ Ⓒ Ⓓ

250. Ⓐ Ⓑ Ⓒ Ⓓ   262. Ⓐ Ⓑ Ⓒ Ⓓ   274. Ⓐ Ⓑ Ⓒ Ⓓ   286. Ⓐ Ⓑ Ⓒ Ⓓ   298. Ⓐ Ⓑ Ⓒ Ⓓ

VERBAL SKILLS

60 Questions—16 Minutes

Turn to the Verbal Skills section of your answer sheet to answer the questions in this section.

Directions: Read each question carefully, then consider all options and mark the correct answer.

1. Which word does *not* belong with the others?

   A. Oven

   B. Toaster

   C. Cook

   D. Microwave

2. Which word does *not* belong with the others?

   A. Run

   B. Walk

   C. Jog

   D. Sneaker

3. Red is to pink as black is to

   A. beige.

   B. white.

   C. dark.

   D. gray.

4. Isabella reads faster than Ethan. Karen reads faster than Isabella. Karen reads more slowly than Ethan. If the first two statements are true, the third is

   A. true.

   B. false.

   C. uncertain.

5. *Create* most nearly means

   A. destroy.

   B. despise.

   C. discover.

   D. invent.

6. Youth is to young as age is to

   A. people.

   B. parents.

   C. grandmother.

   D. old.

7. Which word does *not* belong with the others?

   A. Quality

   B. Honesty

   C. Sincerity

   D. Integrity

8. Sand is to beach as soil is to

   A. earth.

   B. plants.

   C. water.

   D. farm.

9. Which word does *not* belong with the others?

   A. Day

   B. Time

   C. Month

   D. Hour

10. A *salamander* is a(n)

    A. amphibian.

    B. hammock.

    C. spice.

    D. fish.

11. *Arrogant* most nearly means

   A. poised.

   B. superior.

   C. fragrant.

   D. haughty.

12. North is to south as left is to

   A. west.

   B. down.

   C. right.

   D. sideways.

13. One is to two as three is to

   A. two.

   B. five.

   C. six.

   D. thirty.

14. Which word does *not* belong with the others?

   A. Figure

   B. Number

   C. Add

   D. Letter

15. Dylan is taller than Peter. Peter is shorter than John. Dylan is taller than John. If the first two statements are true, the third is

   A. true.

   B. false.

   C. uncertain.

16. A *mature* peach is

   A. ripe.

   B. rotten.

   C. yellow.

   D. green.

17. *Gossamer* most nearly means

   A. beautiful.

   B. delicate.

   C. eerie.

   D. supernatural.

18. *Coddle* most nearly means

   A. handle.

   B. embrace.

   C. pamper.

   D. love.

19. Books are to libraries as rides are to

   A. carnivals.

   B. fun.

   C. roller coaster.

   D. bookstore.

20. Choir is to director as team is to

   A. sport.

   B. coach.

   C. player.

   D. athlete.

21. *Diversify* most nearly means

   A. vary.

   B. oppose.

   C. change.

   D. strengthen.

22. Liam is more intelligent than George. Sam is more intelligent than Ralph. Liam is more intelligent than Ralph. If the first two statements are true, the third is

   A. true.

   B. false.

   C. uncertain.

23. A *superficial* wound is

    A. serious.

    B. deep.

    C. facial.

    D. shallow.

24. Jackie can throw a javelin farther than Elsa. Liandra can throw a javelin farther than Shelley but not as far as Jackie. Shelley won the javelin-throwing contest. If the first two sentences are true, the third is

    A. true.

    B. false.

    C. uncertain.

25. A *bellicose* general is

    A. peaceful.

    B. combative.

    C. understanding.

    D. weak.

26. A *sadistic* remark is

    A. sad.

    B. silly.

    C. hurtful.

    D. sudden.

27. Which word does *not* belong with the others?

    A. College

    B. University

    C. School

    D. Dormitory

28. *Truncate* most nearly means

    A. pack.

    B. cut.

    C. sound.

    D. transport.

29. A *facetious* game show host is

    A. serious.

    B. intelligent.

    C. humorous.

    D. boring.

30. An *indigent* person is

    A. delicate.

    B. intelligent.

    C. indignant.

    D. needy.

31. Table is to leg as automobile is to

    A. wheel.

    B. axle.

    C. door.

    D. fuel.

32. Which word does *not* belong with the others?

    A. Dungeon

    B. Residence

    C. Dwelling

    D. Domicile

33. Bishop's house is the largest on his street. Terrence and Arianna both live on Oakville Lane, but Arianna's house is much larger than Terrence's house. Arianna and Bishop live on the same street. Arianna's house is the largest on Oakville Lane. If the first three sentences are true, the fourth is

    A. true.

    B. false.

    C. uncertain.

34. Which word does *not* belong with the others?

    A. Prison

    B. Jail

    C. Reformatory

    D. Punishment

35. Refuse means the *opposite* of

    A. reheat.

    B. accept.

    C. reveal.

    D. organized.

36. Ink is to pen as paint is to

    A. canvas.

    B. bucket.

    C. wall.

    D. brush.

37. Acquire means the *opposite* of

    A. solo.

    B. buy.

    C. release.

    D. collect.

38. River A is wider than River B. River B is narrower than River C. River A is wider than River C. If the first two statements are true, the third is

    A. true.

    B. false.

    C. uncertain.

39. Scant means the *opposite* of

    A. sparse.

    B. scoundrel.

    C. abundant.

    D. straight.

40. Pinnacle means the *opposite* of

    A. bridge.

    B. base.

    C. wall.

    D. rummy.

41. Team is to captain as office is to

    A. secretary.

    B. accountant.

    C. staff.

    D. manager.

42. Which word does *not* belong with the others?

    A. Window

    B. Drape

    C. Shade

    D. Curtain

43. Corpulent means the *opposite* of

    A. bulky.

    B. singular.

    C. company.

    D. slender.

44. Naive means the *opposite* of

    A. rural.

    B. dull.

    C. sophisticated.

    D. funny.

45. Which word does *not* belong with the others?

    A. Fez

    B. Turban

    C. Glove

    D. Derby

46. Which word does *not* belong with the others?

    A. Gallery

    B. Audience

    C. Congregation

    D. Podium

47. *Pledge* most nearly means

    A. promise.
    B. beg.
    C. join.
    D. obey.

48. Depression is the *opposite* of

    A. incline.
    B. valley.
    C. hill.
    D. oppression.

49. Grapes cost more than apples but less than pineapples. Oranges cost more than apples but less than lemons. Apples cost the least of the fruits. If the first two statements are true, the third is

    A. true.
    B. false.
    C. uncertain.

50. Which word does *not* belong with the others?

    A. Oak
    B. Elm
    C. Maple
    D. Fir

51. Diminish is the *opposite* of

    A. trim.
    B. augment.
    C. decorate.
    D. decrease.

52. Jay's batting average is better than Michael's. Michael's batting average is higher than Paulo's. Jay's batting average is lower than Paulo's. If the first two statements are true, the third is

    A. true.
    B. false.
    C. uncertain.

53. Abandon is the *opposite* of

    A. abdicate.
    B. keep.
    C. maintain.
    D. encourage.

54. Which word does *not* belong with the others?

    A. Flexible
    B. Feasible
    C. Supple
    D. Malleable

55. A is northeast of B. C is southwest of D, but northwest of A. C is north of B. If the first two statements are true, the third is

    A. true.
    B. false.
    C. uncertain.

56. Which word does *not* belong with the others?

    A. Leather
    B. Cotton
    C. Wool
    D. Fur

57. Which word does *not* belong with the others?

    A. Zipper
    B. Button
    C. Snap
    D. Seam

58. *Dwindle* most nearly means

    A. shrink.
    B. ooze.
    C. leak.
    D. spoil.

59. Which word does *not* belong with the others?

    A. Oxygen

    B. Water

    C. Helium

    D. Gold

60. David ran faster than Sophia. Ron ran faster than George but not as fast as David. Sophia was the fastest runner.

    A. true.

    B. false.

    C. uncertain.

Quantitative Skills

52 Questions—30 Minutes

Turn to the Quantitative Skills section of your answer sheet to answer the questions in this section.

Directions: Read each question carefully, then solve the problem to find the correct answer.

61. Look at this series: 23, 22, 20, 19, 16, 15, 11, ...
What number should come next?

  A. 13

  B. 10

  C. 7

  D. 6

62. Examine A, B, C, and D, then find the best answer.

  A. A is longer than C but shorter than D.

  B. C is shorter than A minus D.

  C. B and D together are longer than A.

  D. C plus D is longer than A plus B.

63. Examine A, B, and C and find the best answer.

  A. $(5 + 8)^2$

  B. $5^2 + 8^2$

  C. $2(5) + 2(8)$

  A. A equals B, and C is less than A.

  B. A equals B, and B equals C.

  C. B is less than C, and C is less than A.

  D. C is less than B, and B is less than A.

64. What number is 5 less than 60% of 40?

  A. 19

  B. 20

  C. 24

  D. 29

65. Look at this series: 50, 52, 48, 50, 46, 48, 44, ...
What number should come next?

  A. 38

  B. 40

  C. 46

  D. 48

66. Look at this series: A+ B−, C+ D−, E+ ....
What are the next three terms?

  A. F−, G+ H−

  B. F+, G+ H+

  C. G, H+ H

  D. F, G, H

67. What number is 2 times the average of {6, 12, 4, 41, 7}?

  A. 12

  B. 14

  C. 28

  D. 30

68. Look at this series: 42, 40, 38, 35, 32, 28, 24, ...
What two numbers should come next?

  A. 21, 18

  B. 20, 14

  C. 19, 14

  D. 18, 16

69. Look at this series: 34, 41, 43, 50, 52, ...
    What is the next number in the series?

    A. 54

    B. 59

    C. 61

    D. 68

70. Examine the triangle and find the best answer.

    A. *AB* is equal to *AC*.

    B. *m∠B* is greater than *m∠C*.

    C. *AB* minus *AC* is equal to *BC*.

    D. $m\angle A + m\angle B = m\angle C$.

71. What number times $\frac{2}{3}$ equals 6 times 4?

    A. 16

    B. 32

    C. 36

    D. 48

72. What number divided by $\frac{1}{4}$ is 3 less than 79?

    A. 304

    B. 298

    C. 20.5

    D. 19

73. Examine A, B, and C and find the best answer.

    A. B is less shaded than A.

    B. B and C are equally shaded.

    C. A and B are both less shaded than C.

    D. A and C are both more shaded than B.

74. What is the reciprocal of $3\frac{5}{8}$?

    A. $5\frac{8}{3}$

    B. $\frac{64}{16}$

    C. $\frac{8}{15}$

    D. $\frac{8}{29}$

75. Examine A, B, and C and find the best answer.

    A. 0.875

    B. 0.33×2.6

    C. $\frac{7}{8}$

    A. A, B, and C are all equal.

    B. B is greater than C.

    C. B is less than A.

    D. A is greater than C.

76. The number that is 6 less than 69 is the product of 7 and what other number?

    A. 10

    B. 9

    C. 8

    D. 6

77. Examine A, B, and C and find the best answer.

   A. $\frac{1}{5}$ of 20

   B. $\frac{1}{4}$ of 24

   C. $\frac{1}{8}$ of 32

   A. B is equal to C.

   B. A is less than B and equal to C.

   C. A plus C equals B.

   D. B minus A equals C.

78. Examine A, B, and C and find the best answer.

   A. Figure A is less shaded than both figures B and C.

   B. Figures A and C are equally shaded, and are more shaded than figure B.

   C. Figure B is more shaded than figure A, but not as shaded as figure C.

   D. All three figures are shaded equally.

79. Look at this series: 8, 16, 9, 18, 11, _____, 15, 30.... What number should fill the blank in this series?

   A. 32

   B. 22

   C. 19

   D. 7

80. Find the greatest common factor for (42, 39).

   A. 13

   B. 6

   C. 5

   D. 3

81. Look at this series: A1, B1, B2, C1, C2, C3, D1, D2, ... What term should come next?

   A. E1

   B. E3

   C. D3

   D. D4

82. By how much does the average of 12, 87, 72, and 41 exceed 25?

   A. 78

   B. 53

   C. 28

   D. 25

83. Look at this series: 24, 25, 23, 24, 21, 22, 18, ... What number should come next?

   A. 27

   B. 23

   C. 21

   D. 19

84. Examine A, B, C, and D and find the best answer.

   A.   B.   C.   D.

   A. A has fewer paddles than B but more than D.

   B. A and D together are equal to B and C together.

   C. B has fewer paddles than A and C together.

   D. B has more paddles than C and D together.

85. Look at this series: 1, 3, 7, 15, 31, ... What number comes next?

   A. 32

   B. 42

   C. 54

   D. 63

86. How many pints in 17 quarts? How many gallons is 17 quarts?

    A. 8.5 pts., 6 gal.

    B. 34 pts., 5.75 gal.

    C. 34 pts., 6.25 gal.

    D. 68 pts., 8.5 gal.

87. Examine A, B, and C and find the best answer.

    A. 62

    B. 26

    C. $(2 \times 6)(6 \times 2)$

    A. $A + B = C$

    B. $C - B = A$

    C. A = B and both are smaller than C.

    D. C is greater than either A or B.

88. Examine A, B, C, and D and find the best answer.

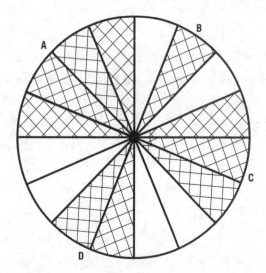

    A. A is equal to C, which is smaller than D.

    B. C is greater than B but equal to A.

    C. A is greater than B, which is less than C.

    D. D is greater than A.

89. What number added to 30 is 3 times the product of 8 and 4?

    A. 39

    B. 63

    C. 66

    D. 93

90. Examine A, B, and C, and choose the best answer.

    A. 4 more than the square of 3

    B. 4 less than the square of 4

    C. 4 more than the cube of 2

    A. $A < B < C$

    B. $A = B > C$

    C. $A = B = C$

    D. $A > B = C$

91. Look at this series: 0.125, 0.250, 0.375, 0.500, ... What number should come next?

    A. 0.620

    B. 0.625

    C. 0.728

    D. 0.875

92. Examine A, B, and C and find the best answer.

    A.   B.   C.

    A. C is more shaded than A.

    B. A and B are equally shaded and are more shaded than C.

    C. A is less shaded than B and more shaded than C.

    D. A and C are equally shaded.

93. Look at this series: $\frac{1}{1}, \frac{1}{2}, \frac{1}{4}, \frac{1}{7}, \frac{1}{11}, \dots$
What term should come next?

A. $\frac{1}{13}$

B. $\frac{1}{14}$

C. $\frac{1}{15}$

D. $\frac{1}{16}$

94. What number divided by $\frac{3}{4}$ yields a quotient that is equal to the divisor?

A. $\frac{9}{16}$

B. $\frac{5}{8}$

C. $\frac{7}{16}$

D. $\frac{3}{4}$

95. Examine A, B, and C and find the best answer.

A. 0.8

B. 80%

C. $\frac{8}{10}$%

A. B is greater than A or C.

B. A is greater than B plus C.

C. A, B, and C are equal.

D. C is smaller than both A and B.

96. Examine the figure and find the best answer.

A. Line segment A is shorter than line segment D, which is longer than line segment C.

B. Line segment B is shorter than line segment A, which is longer than line segment D.

C. Line segment C is longer than line segment D, which is longer than line segment B.

D. Line segment B plus line segment C together equal the length of line segment D.

97. Look at this series: 81, 9, 64, 8, _____ , 7, 36.
What number should fill the blank in this series?

A. 9

B. 49

C. 56

D. 63

98. Find the mean, median, and mode for {2, 7, 4, 5, 9, 32, 25, 17, 3, 9, 28}

A. Mean = 12.8, median = 9, mode = 9

B. Mean = 14.6, median = 21, mode = 2

C. Mean = 15.75, median = 7, mode = 5

D. Mean = 23.5, median = 32, mode = 18

99. Look at this series: 1, 3, 3, 9, 9, 27, 27, ...
What three numbers should come next?

A. 81, 81, 729

B. 81, 81, 243

C. 27, 81, 81

D. 27, 36, 36

100. If $\frac{3}{8}$ of a number is 9, then $83\frac{1}{3}$% of the number is

    A. 14

    B. 20

    C. 27

    D. 54

101. Examine the figure and choose the best answer.

    A. Angle B plus angle C equals a right angle.

    B. Angle A is greater than angle C, which is smaller than angle B.

    C. Angle B minus angle C equals angle A.

    D. Angle A is equal to angle C.

102. Convert 27,840,000,000 to scientific notation.

    A. $2,784 \times 10^7$

    B. 278.4×10^8

    C. 27.84×10^9

    D. 2.784×10^{10}

103. Look at this series: −19, −14, −12, −7, −5, ...
What number should come next?

    A. −1

    B. 0

    C. 1

    D. 5

104. What number when subtracted from 75 is twice the sum of 9 and 3?

    A. 24

    B. 51

    C. 61

    D. 99

105. Look at this series: 0.2, 0.1, 0.05, 0.025, ...
What number should come next?

    A. 0.00625

    B. 0.0025

    C. 0.0125

    D. 0.055

106. What number is 12 less than $\frac{5}{8}$ of 96?

    A. 48

    B. 56

    C. 60

    D. 65

107. Examine A, B, and C and find the best answer.

    A. A is equal to C.

    B. B is greater than A and less than C.

    C. A is not greater than C, which is not greater than B.

    D. A plus B is not greater than C.

108. Look at this series: VI, IX, 12, 15, XVIII, ...
What term should come next?

    A. XXI

    B. 21

    C. XXII

    D. 22

109. Look at this series: $\dfrac{16}{2}, \dfrac{8}{2}, \dfrac{8}{4}, \dfrac{8}{8}, \dfrac{8}{16}, \ldots$
What number should come next?

A. $\dfrac{16}{16}$

B. $\dfrac{4}{8}$

C. $\dfrac{16}{32}$

D. $\dfrac{8}{32}$

110. Examine A, B, and C and find the best answer.

   A. 100% of 95

   B. 100% of 195%

   C. 95% of 100

A. B is greater than A.

B. C is greater than A plus B.

C. A and C are equal and are greater than B.

D. A and C are equal and are smaller than B.

111. What number decreased by 40% of itself is 90?

A. 36

B. 60

C. 145

D. 150

112. Look at this series: 26, 18, 18, 12, 12, 8, 8, ...
What two numbers should come next?

A. 7, 7

B. 8, 6

C. 6, 6

D. 6, 4

READING

62 Questions—25 Minutes

Comprehension

Turn to the Reading Comprehension section of your answer sheet to answer the questions in this section.

Directions: Read each passage and review the associated questions, then reread—if necessary—to find the correct answer.

Questions 113–122 refer to the following passage.

Our planet Earth is divided into seven separate layers. The outer layer is called the crust and appears to be approximately twenty miles thick. Next in line are the four layers of the mantle. These layers <u>vary</u> in thickness from 250 to 1,000 miles. The <u>remaining</u> two layers are divided into the outer core and inner
Line
5 core. The thickness of the outer core has been determined to be <u>slightly</u> more than 1,200 miles, while that of the inner core is slightly less than 800 miles. Scientists calculate the location and depth of these layers by measuring and studying the speed and direction of earthquake waves. They have also determined that both temperature and pressure are much greater at the core than at the crust.

113. The thickest portion of the earth is its

    A. crust.

    B. outer core.

    C. mantle.

    D. inner core.

114. The earth has how many separate layers?

    A. Two

    B. Four

    C. Seven

    D. Twenty

115. Which of the following is correct?

    A. No two sets of earthquake waves ever travel in the same direction.

    B. Earthquakes usually travel in the same direction.

    C. Earthquake waves travel at different speeds.

    D. Earthquake waves travel at the same speed but in different directions.

116. You would expect to find the kind of information in this passage in

    A. an encyclopedia.

    B. a science book.

    C. neither an encyclopedia nor a science book.

    D. both an encyclopedia and a science book.

117. Moving from the surface to the center of the earth, in which order would you pass through the layers?

    A. Crust, outer core, mantle, inner core

    B. Outer core, inner core, crust, mantle

    C. Outer core, crust, inner core, mantle

    D. Crust, mantle, outer core, inner core

118. The word *vary*, as underlined and used in this passage, most nearly means

    A. stabilize.

    B. increase.

    C. range.

    D. arbitrate.

119. Which of the following is correct?

    A. Scientists know the exact thickness of the crust.

    B. Scientists believe they know the thickness of the crust.

    C. The thickness of the crust cannot be determined.

    D. Scientists cannot agree on the thickness of the crust.

120. In comparing the core with the crust, you would find that at the core there is

    A. less pressure and lower temperature.

    B. greater pressure, but lower temperature.

    C. higher temperature, but less pressure.

    D. higher temperature and greater pressure.

121. The word *slightly*, as underlined and used in this passage, most nearly means

    A. scarcely.

    B. considerably.

    C. a little.

    D. at least.

122. The word *remaining*, as underlined and used in this passage, most nearly means

    A. previous.

    B. outer.

    C. last.

    D. prior.

Questions 123–132 refer to the following passage.

The man is in <u>utter</u> darkness. Only the wavering beam of light from his flashlight pierces the blackness. The air, damp and cold, smells of dank, unseen, decaying material.

The man stumbles over stones and splashes into a hidden puddle. He bangs into a cold rocky wall.
Line The flashlight cocks upward, and suddenly, the air is filled with the flutter of thousands of wings and the
5 piping of tiny animal wails. He ducks, startled, then grins. He's found what he's looking for—bats!

This man is a spelunker, another name for someone who explores caves for the fun of it. Spelunkers enjoy crawling on their stomachs in narrow, rocky tunnels far below the surface of the earth.

Spelunkers have discovered new caves. Some have formed clubs, sharing safety knowledge, developing new techniques, and teaching novices.
10 Spelunkers believe that Earth's inner spaces are as exciting as the universe's outer spaces.

123. The first two paragraphs of this passage describe a cave's

    A. rocks.

    B. depth.

    C. atmosphere.

    D. streams.

124. What effect does the first paragraph have on the passage?

    A. It emphasizes that spelunking is full of unknowns.

    B. It shows that the spelunker is terrified of bats.

    C. It contrasts bats and spelunkers.

    D. It sets up a persuasive argument.

125. The author of this passage is most likely a

    A. spelunker.

    B. cave scientist.

    C. medical doctor.

    D. magazine writer.

126. The cave the man was exploring was probably

    A. large and dry.

    B. deep underground.

    C. near the surface.

    D. dangerous.

127. According to this passage, what made the bats start flying about?

    A. The spelunker

    B. The damp and cold air

    C. The flashlight

    D. The sudden noise

128. The man ducked when the bats flew because he was

    A. angry.

    B. afraid.

    C. surprised.

    D. hurt.

129. The word *utter*, as underlined and used in this passage, most nearly means

    A. bovine.

    B. unspeakable.

    C. oppressive.

    D. great.

130. According to this passage, spelunkers ignore

    A. safety rules.

    B. light.

    C. discomfort.

    D. other spelunkers.

131. Which title is best for this passage?

    A. "Batty about Bats"

    B. "Spelunkers—Underground Explorers"

    C. "Inner Space"

    D. "The Life of a Spelunker"

132. According to this passage, which word would most nearly describe spelunkers?

    A. Experimental

    B. Cautious

    C. Antisocial

    D. Adventurous

Even adventurous eaters may have very little experience encountering the kohlrabi, also known as the turnip cabbage or German turnip. Often misidentified as a root vegetable because of its bulbous, root-like appearance, kohlrabi is both a resilient crop and a <u>protean</u> menu ingredient—it can be eaten raw or cooked
Line and serves as an excellent addition to a wide array of recipes. Many of its fans insist that it deserves a wider
5 audience and more attention than it currently receives.

This versatile—but largely unknown—vegetable is a member of the *Brassica oleracea* species, which also includes broccoli, kale, cauliflower, and Brussels sprouts. This may not come as a surprise to those who have eaten kohlrabi, as the taste is similar to these other vegetables. Kohlrabi grows above ground and comes in both green and purple colors. Among the many <u>varietals</u> are the White Danube, Purple Danube,
10 White Vienna, and Purple Vienna, perhaps a reflection of the vegetable's popularity in Germanic regions.

Need a few more reasons to give kohlrabi a try? This hearty vegetable is a great addition to salads, stews, and slaws, and also packs a nutrient-rich punch—it's an excellent source of vitamin C, vitamin B, potassium, and fiber and helps promote good muscle and nerve function, vision and digestive health, bone strength, and more. The next time you're doing some meal planning, think beyond the usual ingredients
15 and consider adding kohlrabi.

133. The author's opinion on kohlrabi as a food is most likely

A. pessimistic.

B. cautious.

C. enthusiastic.

D. curious.

134. Which is the best title for this passage?

A. "Consider Kohlrabi"

B. "Exploring German Foods"

C. "Mix Up Your Menu"

D. "A Brand New Vegetable"

135. The word *protean*, as underlined and used in this passage, most nearly means

A. delicious.

B. versatile.

C. expensive.

D. nutritious.

136. According to the passage, kohlrabi is a good source of

A. calories.

B. energy.

C. spice.

D. potassium.

137. What is the most logical explanation for the author's statement regarding kohlrabi's popularity in Germanic regions?

A. The Danube and Vienna are in Germanic regions.

B. The author of the passage is from Germany.

C. German-speaking countries often lead the world in new food trends.

D. It's well known that Germans love eating vegetables.

138. The word *varietal*, as underlined and used in this passage, most nearly means the

    A. flavor of kohlrabi.

    B. price of kohlrabi.

    C. use of kohlrabi.

    D. type of kohlrabi.

139. According to the passage, the main reason kohlrabi is often mistaken as a root vegetable is its

    A. taste.

    B. color.

    C. appearance.

    D. name.

140. Kohlrabi is *not* in the same vegetable species as

    A. turnips.

    B. broccoli.

    C. kale.

    D. cauliflower.

141. All the following are mentioned in the passage as benefits of kohlrabi *except*

    A. muscle and nerve function.

    B. heart health.

    C. vision and digestive health.

    D. bone strength.

142. Most likely, the author's purpose in writing this passage is to

    A. compare kohlrabi with other vegetables.

    B. get people interested in trying kohlrabi.

    C. convince individuals to cook more.

    D. promote a healthy vegetarian lifestyle.

Questions 143–152 refer to the following passage.

Most music today has some kind of electronic element. Whether it's pop, rock, hip-hop, techno, dance, country, or any other musical genre, electronic instrumentation using synthesizers and computers is an increasingly common feature of the musical soundscape. That's why it's such a surprise that so many people
Line have never heard of the Grammy-winning electronic music pioneer Wendy Carlos, who is one of the most
5 influential composers of the modern age.

One of the instruments that Carlos helped make famous was the Moog synthesizer. Back in 1968, she released an album called *Switched-On Bach* on which she translated the music of classical composer Johann Sebastian Bach for the Moog. Few people had used electronic sounds to compose music before that point, so hearing Bach in this new way made Carlos a sensation. Furthermore, the success of the album made the Moog
10 synthesizer one of the <u>definitive</u> sounds of the 1970s, as everyone who's anyone started using it in their music. Later, producers like the Italo-disco legend Giorgio Moroder and the German band Kraftwerk would help popularize genres centered on the synthesizer sound, creating a ripple effect that still <u>resonates</u> today; everyone from Jay-Z to Coldplay has made modern songs directly influenced by these early electronic sounds.

Many music historians would argue that without Wendy Carlos' early influence, music might sound com-
15 pletely different today. In the 1980s, Carlos went on to lend her signature electronic compositions to films like Stanley Kubrick's *The Shining* and Disney's *Tron*, and she has continued making electronic music well into the 21st century. In 2005, for her contributions to both electronic music and various social issues, Carlos was awarded a Lifetime Achievement Award by the Society for Electro-Acoustic Music in the United States.

143. This passage is intended to

   A. persuade.

   B. inform.

   C. amuse.

   D. critique.

144. According to this passage, Wendy Carlos is best known for her contributions to

   A. film.

   B. television.

   C. music.

   D. computer science.

145. One place we can see Wendy Carlos' influence on music today is through the

   A. use of computer-based beats in rap music.

   B. numerous music schools she founded.

   C. continued popularity of Johann Sebastian Bach.

   D. many bands she started.

146. Which group can we be sure has at one time had members who liked Wendy Carlos' electronic music?

   A. Film producers

   B. TV producers

   C. Computer scientists

   D. Teenagers

147. This passage notes that Wendy Carlos "translated the music of classical composer Johann Sebastian Bach for the Moog." What would be an example of an equivalent idea of translation?

   A. A medical interpreter in the US translating what a doctor had said for a Japanese speaker.

   B. A dance company creating a hip-hop dance version of a famous ballet.

   C. A friend saying "I'm fine" but actually being very angry.

   D. A film using closed captioning to show what someone speaking another language is saying.

148. According to the passage, another artist, Giorgio Moroder, was famous for producing

   A. disco music.

   B. hip-hop music.

   C. opera music.

   D. country music.

149. As used in paragraph 2, the underlined term *definitive* most nearly means

   A. disappointing.

   B. quintessential.

   C. forgotten.

   D. mysterious.

150. As used in paragraph 2, the underlined term *resonates* most nearly describes something that

   A. sounds unpleasant.

   B. sounds pleasant.

   C. becomes irrelevant.

   D. remains relevant.

151. This passage suggests that not everyone who is influential is

   A. well-known.

   B. comfortable being famous.

   C. a positive influence.

   D. successful.

152. Which is the best title for this passage?

   A. "Wendy Carlos: Electronic Music Icon"

   B. "The Rise of Disco Music"

   C. "Electronic Music in American Society"

   D. "The Power of the Moog"

Vocabulary

Turn to the Vocabulary section of your answer sheet to answer the questions in this section.

Directions: Choose the answer that's closest in meaning to the underlined word in the question.

---

153. a new <u>perspective</u>

   A. receptacle

   B. sight

   C. picture

   D. view

154. <u>impair</u> his vision

   A. test

   B. weaken

   C. improve

   D. destroy

155. strong business <u>acumen</u>

   A. intelligence

   B. speed

   C. flexibility

   D. confusion

156. <u>subjugate</u> the enemy

   A. confront

   B. bargain with

   C. trick

   D. overpower

157. to <u>reproach</u>

   A. approach

   B. praise

   C. blame

   D. steal

158. to be <u>elated</u>

   A. happy

   B. akin

   C. moved

   D. upset

159. his <u>brusque</u> manner

   A. foreign

   B. subtle

   C. soft

   D. abrupt

160. <u>depress</u> the key

   A. put away

   B. insert

   C. turn

   D. push down

161. <u>quench</u> your thirst

   A. end

   B. increase

   C. continue

   D. decrease

162. a famous <u>exploit</u>

   A. crime

   B. deed

   C. reputation

   D. game

163. a <u>precipitous</u> incline

    A. gradual

    B. steep

    C. unavoidable

    D. delicate

164. an interesting <u>chronicle</u>

    A. fairy tale

    B. record

    C. time

    D. item

165. that <u>amiable</u> soul

    A. casual

    B. honest

    C. fine

    D. likable

166. her <u>astute</u> mind

    A. shrewd

    B. careful

    C. stupid

    D. astounding

167. to <u>sever</u> contact

    A. cut

    B. maintain

    C. seek

    D. establish

168. the <u>eminent</u> man

    A. wicked

    B. destitute

    C. ancient

    D. outstanding

169. to <u>terminate</u> a contract

    A. end

    B. enter

    C. make

    D. determine

170. to <u>hinder</u> someone

    A. assist

    B. follow

    C. impede

    D. slight

171. a spirit of <u>contention</u>

    A. debate

    B. content

    C. inquiry

    D. calm

172. to <u>concede</u> defeat

    A. suspect

    B. admit

    C. realize

    D. refuse

173. to <u>forego</u> his rights

    A. usurp

    B. insure

    C. insist on

    D. give up

174. your <u>canny</u> guess

    A. uncertain

    B. mistaken

    C. clever

    D. insincere

MATHEMATICS

64 Questions—45 Minutes

Concepts

Turn to the Mathematics Concepts section of your answer sheet to answer the questions in this section.

Directions: Read each question carefully, then solve the problem to find the correct answer.

---

175. Which of these is the longest length?

    A. 17 inches

    B. 2 feet

    C. 0.5 yards

    D. 14 centimeters

176. Which of the following is *not* a parallelogram?

    A. Rhombus

    B. Square

    C. Rectangle

    D. Triangle

177. Three numbers are added together, and the sum is divided by three. What is the result called?

    A. Mean

    B. Median

    C. Mode

    D. Probability

178. Two objects are weighed on a scale at the same time. One object has a weight of x pounds, and the other has a weight of y pounds. What is their combined weight, in pounds?

    A. $x + y$

    B. xy

    C. $\dfrac{x}{y}$

    D. $2x + 2y$

179. What is the sum of the measures of the angles in a square?

    A. 90

    B. 180

    C. 270

    D. 360

180. How many variables are there in the equation $\dfrac{m}{n} + 2p = 5$?

    A. 0

    B. 1

    C. 3

    D. 5

181. In which of the following types of triangles are all the sides the same length?

    A. Equilateral

    B. Isosceles

    C. Scalene

    D. Right

182. How many centimeters are in 2 meters?

    A. 2

    B. 50

    C. 100

    D. 200

183. There are 8 ounces in a cup, and 2 cups in a pint. How many ounces are in a pint?

   A. 6

   B. 8

   C. 10

   D. 16

184. Three hundred twenty-six million, nine hundred thousand, six hundred nineteen can be expressed numerically as

   A. 3,269,619

   B. 32,690,619

   C. 326,900,619

   D. 326,960,019

185. A number is changed if

   A. 0 is added to it.

   B. 1 is subtracted from it.

   C. it is divided by 1.

   D. it is multiplied by 1.

186. In the number 4,000,400,000, there are

   A. 4 billions and 4 hundred thousands.

   B. 4 millions and 4 thousands.

   C. 4 billions and 4 millions.

   D. 4 millions and 40 thousands.

187. Which is the longest time?

   A. 1,440 minutes

   B. 25 hours

   C. $\frac{1}{2}$ day

   D. 3,600 seconds

188. Find the average of 3, 5, 1, 2, and 9.

   A. 1

   B. 3

   C. 4

   D. 9

189. Find the median of 3, 5, 1, 2, and 9.

   A. 1

   B. 3

   C. 4

   D. 9

190. A contest is held in which two winners are chosen. If 8 people enter the contest, what is each person's probability of being one of the winners?

   A. $\frac{1}{4}$

   B. $\frac{1}{2}$

   C. $\frac{8}{8}$

   D. $\frac{4}{2}$

191. Which of the following has the same value as $1\frac{3}{4}\%$?

   A. 0.0175

   B. $\frac{7}{40}$

   C. $\frac{7}{4}$

   D. 1.75

192. What is the total number of degrees found in angles A and C in the triangle below?

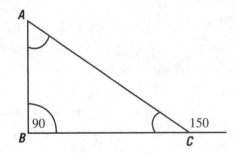

   A. 60°

   B. 90°

   C. 100°

   D. 180°

193. If $x > 9$, then

    A. $x^2 > 80$

    B. $x^2 - 2 = 47$

    C. $x^2 < 65$

    D. $x^2 - 2 < 90$

194. Any number that is divisible by both 3 and 4 is also divisible by

    A. 8

    B. 9

    C. 12

    D. 16

195. Which symbol belongs in the circle? 0.023 O 0.0086

    A. >

    B. <

    C. =

    D. ≅

196. The greatest common factor of 50 and 10 is

    A. 1

    B. 5

    C. 10

    D. 25

197. What number belongs in the box?

$$+ 5 + \square = -3$$

    A. −8

    B. −3

    C. +3

    D. +8

198. The area of the circle is

    A. 3π sq. cm.

    B. 6π sq. cm.

    C. 9π sq. cm.

    D. 36π sq. cm.

Problem Solving

199. The ratio of 3 quarts to 3 gallons is

    A. 3:1

    B. 1:4

    C. 6:3

    D. 4:1

200. Which pair of values for x and $\square$ will make the following statement true?

$$2x \, \square \, 8$$

    A. (6, <)

    B. (4, >)

    C. (0, <)

    D. (−3, >)

201. How many fifths are there in $4\frac{1}{4}$?

    A. $\frac{4}{85}$

    B. $\frac{17}{20}$

    C. 20

    D. $21\frac{1}{4}$

202. A wheel is divided into 12 wedges of equal size, numbered from 1 through 12. If the pointer is spun counterclockwise, what is the probability that it will land on an even number?

    A. 0

    B. $\frac{1}{4}$

    C. $\frac{1}{2}$

    D. 1

203. If Izzy is x years old now and her sister is 3 years younger, then what age will her sister be 5 years from now?

    A. $x + 5$ years

    B. $x + 3$ years

    C. $x + 2$ years

    D. 8 years

204. Which of the following statements is true?

    A. $7 \times 11 > 78$

    B. $6 + 4 < 10.5$

    C. $8 - 3 = 7 + 4$

    D. $16 \div 2 > 9$

205.

$\overline{AB} \cup \overline{BC}$

    A. $\overline{BD}$

    B. $\overline{BC}$

    C. $\overline{AD}$

    D. $\overline{AC}$

206. Solve: $2.01 \div 1.02 =$

    A. 0.507

    B. 1.97

    C. 2.0001

    D. 3.03

207. Simplify: $-2[3 - 2(1 - 5) - 6]$

    A. -28

    B. -10

    C. 22

    D. 34

208. What is 140% of 70?

    A. 9.8

    B. 98

    C. 150

    D. 9,800

209. Solve: $6 \div \dfrac{1}{3} + \dfrac{2}{3} \times 9 =$

    A. $\dfrac{2}{3}$

    B. 24

    C. 54

    D. 168

210. If $x = -3$, $y = 5$, and $z = -2$, the value of $x(y - z)^2$ is

    A. -147

    B. -27

    C. 27

    D. 147

211. Seven is to 21 as $\dfrac{2}{3}$ is to

    A. 1

    B. $\dfrac{4}{3}$

    C. 2

    D. 3

212. The mean of $-10, 6, 0, -3,$ and 22 is

    A. -6

    B. -3

    C. 2

    D. 3

213. Solve for x: $x^2 + 5 = 41$

    A. ± 6

    B. ± 7

    C. ± 8

    D. ± 9

214. Find the area of a rectangle with a length of 168 feet and a width of 82 feet.

    A. 13,306 sq. ft.

    B. 13,706 sq. ft.

    C. 13,776 sq. ft.

    D. 13,856 sq. ft.

215. Solve: $63 \div \frac{1}{9} =$

    A. 7

    B. 56

    C. 67

    D. 567

216. Solve: $72.61 \div 0.05 =$

    A. 1.45220

    B. 14.522

    C. 145.220

    D. 1,452.20

217. Increased by 150%, the number 72 becomes

    A. 170

    B. 180

    C. 188

    D. 206

218. Consider this list of numbers: 2, 5, 5, 6, 7. Which of the following is true?

    A. The mean is greater than the median.

    B. The mode is greater than the mean.

    C. The mean, median, and mode are all equal.

    D. The median is greater than the mode and the mean.

219. A class is voting for a class president and a class vice president. If there are 10 students running for president, and 7 students running for vice president, how many different combinations of president and vice president are possible?

    A. 17

    B. 70

    C. 77

    D. 170

220. A rectangle has a length of $x + 3$, and a width of $x - 1$. If $x = 2$, what is the perimeter of the rectangle?

    A. 10

    B. 12

    C. 18

    D. 21

221. If Michael studies for his math test, there is an 80% chance he will get an A. If he studies, what is the probability that he will not get an A?

    A. 10%

    B. 20%

    C. 50%

    D. 80%

222. The ratio of teachers to students at St. John Bosco Academy is 1:12. If there are 16 teachers in the school, how many students are there?

    A. 16

    B. 176

    C. 192

    D. 202

223. The legend on a trail map indicates that 1.2 inches represents 50 feet. How many feet does 6 inches represent?

    A. 200

    B. 250

    C. 360

    D. 400

224. A department store marks up its clothing 75% over cost. If it sells yoga pants for $17, how much did the store pay for them?

A. $1.12

B. $9.71

C. $11.20

D. $17.50

225.

Note: In the figure above, assume that any angle which appears to be a right angle *is* a right angle. The perimeter of the figure above is

A. 38 in.

B. 38 sq. in.

C. 46 sq. in.

D. 60 in.

226. The area of the figure above is

A. 104 sq. in.

B. 120 sq. in.

C. 240 sq. in.

D. 276 sq. in.

227. The charge for a long-distance call was $1.56 for the first 3 minutes and $0.22 for each additional minute. What was the total charge for a 16-minute call?

A. $2.86

B. $4.42

C. $5.08

D. $5.80

228. The winner of a race received $\frac{1}{3}$ of the total purse. The third-place finisher received $\frac{1}{3}$ of the winner's share. If the winner's share was $2,700, what was the total purse?

A. $900

B. $1,800

C. $2,700

D. $8,100

229. As a train departs from station A, it has 12 empty seats, 14 seated passengers, and 4 standing passengers. At the next stop, 8 passengers get off, 13 passengers get on, and everyone on the train takes a seat. How many empty seats are there?

A. 1

B. 2

C. 3

D. 4

230. In order to increase revenues, a municipality considers raising its sales tax from 5% to 8%. How much more will it cost to buy a $250 television set if the 8% sales tax is approved?

A. $7.50

B. $10

C. $12.50

D. $15.50

231.   5 gallons 2 quarts 1 pint
−1 gallon 3 quarts
_____

A. 2 gallons 6 quarts 2 pints

B. 3 gallons 3 quarts 1 pint

C. 4 gallons 2 quarts 1 pint

D. 4 gallons 9 quarts 1 pint

232. The number of landline phones in Adelaide, Australia, is 48,000. If this represents 12.8 phones per 100 persons, the population of Adelaide to the nearest thousand is

    A. 128,000

    B. 375,000

    C. 378,000

    D. 556,000

233. A carpenter needs four boards, each 2 feet 9 inches long. If wood is sold only by the foot, how many feet must he buy?

    A. 9

    B. 10

    C. 11

    D. 12

234. A square has an area of 49 sq. in. The number of inches in its perimeter is

    A. 7

    B. 28

    C. 35

    D. 98

235. Aluminum bronze consists of copper and aluminum, usually in the ratio of 10:1 by weight. If an object made of this alloy weighs 77 pounds, how many pounds of aluminum does it contain?

    A. 7

    B. 7.7

    C. 10

    D. 70

236. Mr. Szuta makes a weekly salary of $175 plus 8% commission on his sales. What will his income be for a week in which he makes sales totaling $1,025?

    A. $257

    B. $260.50

    C. $264

    D. $267

237. A house was valued at $83,000 and insured for 80% of that amount. Find the yearly premium if it is figured at $0.45 per $100 of value.

    A. $83.80

    B. $252.63

    C. $298.80

    D. $664

238. A group left on a trip at 8:50 a.m. and reached its destination at 3:30 p.m. How long, in hours and minutes, did the trip take?

    A. 3 hours 10 minutes

    B. 4 hours 40 minutes

    C. 5 hours 10 minutes

    D. 6 hours 40 minutes

LANGUAGE

60 Questions—25 Minutes

Turn to the Language section of your answer sheet to answer the questions in this section.

Directions: In questions 239–267, look for errors in capitalization, punctuation, or usage. Mark the answer choice that contains the error. If there are no mistakes, mark D on your answer sheet.

239. **A.** Alexis hit a home run "her tenth one this year" to win the championship game.
  B. Rhianna spent all of her savings on a new couch for her living room.
  C. When should people start thinking about college and the future?
  D. *(No mistakes)*

240. **A.** Demma read the *daily cryer* newspaper each morning.
  B. Mr. Judson prepared the annual quarterly report for his presentation.
  C. Stelth ordered the cod entrée from the restaurant's expansive menu options.
  D. *(No mistakes)*

241. **A.** This year's corn maze was extremely difficult to figure out.
  B. Have you ever seen someone run as fast as Casper can!
  C. There were not enough pockets to hold Dorota's stuff.
  D. *(No mistakes)*

242. **A.** The greedy lion ate an entire sirloin steak in just a few seconds.
  B. Sari yearned to travel to America and see the grand canyon.
  C. Have you ever cooked a turkey for Thanksgiving?
  D. *(No mistakes)*

243. **A.** Where in the world did you leave your gloves?
  B. The dog licked its chops after the meal.
  C. "Oh, that's terrible!" Sally cried.
  D. *(No mistakes)*

244. **A.** Detroit is the center of the automobile industry.
  B. Governor Jiemenez was an officer in the Navy.
  C. Their making a terrible mistake.
  D. *(No mistakes)*

245. **A.** How is your cold?
  B. The rabbit got sick and died.
  C. Who's book is this?
  D. *(No mistakes)*

246. **A.** That is a pretty dress, isn't it, Noah?
  B. How old is your pet, Alfie?
  C. Why are you so tired?
  D. *(No mistakes)*

247. **A.** Katie's final exam grade was the highest in her geometry class.
  B. Anderson's favorite movie of all time is *Toy Story*.
  C. Moshe thinks the Bronx Zoo were his favorite place to visit.
  D. *(No mistakes)*

248. **A.** Don told us where he'd bought his coat.

 B. What's your name, little girl?

 C. Yellowstone is run by the National Park Service.

 D. *(No mistakes)*

249. **A.** How are you, Sebastian?

 B. I'm fine, thank you.

 C. Did you notice that Jayden left early?

 D. *(No mistakes)*

250. **A.** Ross felt butterflies in his stomach before the interview.

 B. A trip to Chicago in the spring is an absolutely wonderful idea.

 C. Mia purchased; a gigantic piñata for; her birthday party on Sunday.

 D. *(No mistakes)*

251. **A.** Will, you're parents are very nice.

 B. Esther's family is buying a boat.

 C. My father is a textbook publisher.

 D. *(No mistakes)*

252. **A.** What is the matter with Angel's leg?

 B. The first show is at 2:30, isn't it?

 C. How much is your plane ticket?

 D. *(No mistakes)*

253. **A.** The award was given jointly to Olivia and I.

 B. John asked if he might go home early.

 C. Cats and dogs sometimes play well together.

 D. *(No mistakes)*

254. **A.** The explosion at the "fireworks factory" was unbelievably loud.

 B. Frederico has basil and cilantro growing on his kitchen windowsill.

 C. Kevin knew it was time to change the water in the aquarium tank.

 D. *(No mistakes)*

255. **A.** She and I consider ourselves to be best friends.

 B. Do you know which of the spellings of *too* means *also*?

 C. There is a narrow path beside the railroad track.

 D. *(No mistakes)*

256. **A.** We would have called you if we'd known.

 B. May I open my eyes now?

 C. My brother-in-law lives in Long Beach, California.

 D. *(No mistakes)*

257. **A.** Actually, ice hockey is exciting to watch.

 B. Minato plays guitar almost as well like Ruliann.

 C. Does Fabiola like to talk to Mason?

 D. *(No mistakes)*

258. **A.** Ken will graduate from Stanford this June.

 B. Jude is learning Kira to draw.

 C. Before we knew it, the class was over.

 D. *(No mistakes)*

259. **A.** When will you know what the assignment is?

 B. You should of seen the crowd at Paul's yesterday.

 C. Josue will be stationed at Fort Benning, Georgia.

 D. *(No mistakes)*

260. **A.** Unfortunately, the rug delivery was delayed by six days.

 B. The bright lights in the auditorium gave Yasmine a headache.

 C. Please include your (complete name) on the application form.

 D. *(No mistakes)*

261. **A.** We have already sold too many tickets.

 B. If I knew the answer, I would be rich now.

 C. The artist works less hours than the carpenter.

 D. *(No mistakes)*

262. A. Everyone must sign their name on the register.

   B. I am all ready, but the taxi is not here yet.

   C. I do not believe that I have only two choices.

   D. *(No mistakes)*

263. A. If you don't know the answer, don't raise your hand.

   B. The baby is playing in her crib.

   C. Jeff is the taller of my three sons.

   D. *(No mistakes)*

264. A. Neither Wesley nor Liz has made the honor roll.

   B. I have much more free time than you.

   C. Everyone wants to have his own way.

   D. *(No mistakes)*

265. A. Piper loved all the natural light that flooded into her new apartment.

   B. Marianna has packed her, favorite novel, for a day at the beach.

   C. Jessica happily ordered coffee and pecan pie for dessert.

   D. *(No mistakes)*

266. A. The sun set at 5:15 this afternoon.

   B. Lacey set the table for dinner yesterday.

   C. Please set those books over there, Vera.

   D. *(No mistakes)*

267. A. The horse ran swiftly and won the race.

   B. I feel badly that I cannot attend your wedding.

   C. Most birds and some people fly south for the winter.

   D. *(No mistakes)*

Directions: In questions 268–278, mark the sentence that demonstrates <u>correct</u> usage.

---

268. A. Perry stacked the bundle of envelopes on the desk in his office.

   B. There was an empty parking spot next to super-market entrance.

   C. Painting that hung on Regina's bedroom wall fell to the floor.

   D. Shawn did not make single noise for fear of waking up his brother

269. A. Brendan placed his new bowling trophy on his bedroom dresser.

   B. Have our ever seen a comet race across the night sky?

   C. What is the best time for they to pick you up for the dance?

   D. Sharlene couldn't wait for its book to arrive in the mail.

270. A. The newborn puppy scampered timid through the house.

   B. Bevyn waited nervously for the midterm exam to begin.

   C. Haven sat anxious in traffic, late for their first day of work.

   D. I will happy take that last slice of chocolate cream cake.

271. A. Matthew didn't think it was fair when his parents took away him skateboard.

   B. Harvey was never able to improve our grade in chemistry this year.

   C. The squirmy pile of puppies jumped excitedly from its bed.

   D. Have you seen the way Carrie had her hair styled yesterday?

272. A. He decided to wear leather jacket to his first day of school.

B. Lucy went to store and purchased a bag of peanuts.

C. The New York City is my favorite place to visit.

D. I wanted to get a pizza for dinner, but I had no money.

273. A. Can you believed how tired Heidi was during her speech in class?

B. Will you be gone to the antique fair at the church this weekend?

C. Celeste is determined to finish reading her mystery novel today.

D. The store having a sale on light bulbs and cooking utensils today.

274. A. The lightning bolt crackled and shot across the rain-filled sky?

B. Nadine was really nervous about her upcoming dental appointment?

C. Will Douglas rally and come from behind to win the game?

D. Did you pick up the mail yet.

275. A. Marcel was short on time, yet he decided to skip a visit to the mall.

B. Grady was a real connoisseur of both vintage automobiles or motorcycles.

C. Zuri really wanted to go to the hair salon today, but she was too busy.

D. Melissa wanted either sushi and tacos for dinner after work.

276. A. The happy crowd booed their favorite band as they took the stage.

B. Congrats on your big win today!

C. The boring beige dress had plenty of zing!

D. The guest speaker yelled "oops!" when he walked effortlessly to the podium.

277. A. Tanisha went outside of the library to get out of the rain.

B. Brianna sat in the chair and put her feet carefully beyond the desk.

C. Lamonte climbed the ladder and stood on top of the roof.

D. Fabian reclined on the ground and looked down at the night sky.

278. A. Belle didn't not borrow the library book, as she didn't have her library card.

B. Lucas couldn't go to the movies tonight, so he binge-watched his favorite sci-fi series.

C. Angelina was grounded for her poor grades, so she couldn't not got to the party.

D. Did you see the parrot that Eddie didn't have on his shoulder at the park?

Directions: For questions 279–288, look for mistakes in spelling only.

279. **A.** Clarence Darrow was a distinguished trial lawyer.
   B. Apparantly, Suzy couldn't find her umbrella.
   C. Orion will be married next Wednesday.
   D. *(No mistakes)*

280. **A.** Are you sure you can complete the assignment on time?
   B. The entire crew worked very efficently.
   C. Brie went to the library yesterday.
   D. *(No mistakes)*

281. **A.** It occured to me that I should write home.
   B. "What a dreadful comparison," Ida remarked.
   C. Dana's temperature was back to normal yesterday.
   D. *(No mistakes)*

282. **A.** Rashaad is eligible for the committee.
   B. Discussion and argument are not the same thing.
   C. The chemist anayzed the solution in his laboratory.
   D. *(No mistakes)*

283. **A.** My brother's going out for athletics next year.
   B. "This is a small token of my esteem," he told his teacher.
   C. Mary dropped her handkerchief in the corridor.
   D. *(No mistakes)*

284. **A.** Tyler noticed a mispelled word in the book he just purchased.
   B. The steering committee couldn't wait to vote on the new referendum.
   C. The inn was unable to accommodate the large group of tourists.
   D. *(No mistakes)*

285. **A.** The schedule is posted on the bulletin board in the hall.
   B. Althea discribed the play with sweeping gestures.
   C. Occasionally our class runs over into the next period.
   D. *(No mistakes)*

286. **A.** Serena perfers to sit by the door.
   B. Joy has a very agreeable personality.
   C. We struggle with ourselves to overcome our faults.
   D. *(No mistakes)*

287. **A.** Did you hear the announcement about the picnic?
   B. While the initial cost is high, the maintenance is low.
   C. Hwan's coat is similar to mine.
   D. *(No mistakes)*

288. **A.** Alexander said it was not neccessary to read all of the plays.
   B. It's disappointing to have missed the picture.
   C. The original order was difficult to decipher.
   D. *(No mistakes)*

Directions: For questions 289–298, review the text and look for errors in composition.

289. Choose the best word or words to join the thoughts together.

I left my books at school; _____ I won't be able to do my homework.

A. therefore,

B. nevertheless,

C. however,

D. None of these

290. Choose the best word or words to join the thoughts together.

That area is experiencing great economic hardship; _____ its unemployment rate is very high.

A. for example,

B. in contrast,

C. suprisingly,

D. None of these

291. Choose the group of words that best completes this sentence.

After a hard day at work, _____

A. sleep was something Chaya did very well.

B. Chaya slept very well.

C. Chaya slept well afterwards.

D. sleeping was what Chaya did.

292. Which of these sentences expresses the idea most clearly?

A. Tom, every morning at breakfast, the paper he liked to read.

B. At breakfast every morning it was the paper that Tom liked to read.

C. At breakfast, reading the paper was what Tom liked to do every morning.

D. Tom liked to read the paper every morning at breakfast.

293. Which of these expresses the idea most clearly?

A. In order to hear her favorite musician perform, 50 miles it was that she drove.

B. She drove 50 miles in order to hear her favorite musician perform.

C. She drove, in order to hear her favorite musician perform, 50 miles.

D. Her favorite musician performed, and she drove 50 miles in order to hear him perform.

294. Which of these best fits under the topic "History of the Automobile"?

A. Cars require a great deal of attention and care in order to prevent problems from developing.

B. The legal driving age varies from one state to another.

C. The invention of the automobile cannot be credited to any one person.

D. None of these

295. Which of these sentences expresses the idea most clearly?

A. His brother, and Stuart, were eager to experience—never on an airplane voyaging in the skies.

B. Stuart and his brother had never been on an airplane, and they were eager to experience their first voyage in the skies.

C. Voyage in the skies? Eager Stuart and his brother haven't. They've never been on an airplane.

D. Never on an airplane, never voyaging—in the skies—Stuart or his brother have never had this eager experience.

296. Which sentence does *not* belong in the paragraph?

(1) Everyone in the class was looking forward to the Halloween party. (2) Five students had difficulty with their math homework from the previous day. (3) Each student had prepared a snack to bring. (4) The costumes included four ghosts, five space creatures, and two pumpkins.

A. Sentence 1
B. Sentence 2
C. Sentence 3
D. Sentence 4

297. Which topic is best for a one-paragraph theme?

A. How to Open Your Own Business
B. Child Psychology
C. The Geography of Asia and Africa
D. None of these

298. Where should the sentence, "The government has set up laws restricting or forbidding the hunting of certain animals," be placed in the paragraph below?

(1) Many animal species are now becoming or have recently become extinct. (2) Both government and private efforts are being made to protect those species currently in danger. (3) It has also attempted to educate the public about the problem.

A. Between sentences 1 and 2
B. Between sentences 2 and 3
C. After sentence 3
D. The sentence does not fit in this paragraph.

ANSWER KEYS AND EXPLANATIONS
Verbal Skills

1. C	13. C	25. B	37. C	49. A
2. D	14. C	26. C	38. C	50. D
3. D	15. C	27. D	39. C	51. B
4. B	16. A	28. B	40. B	52. B
5. D	17. B	29. C	41. D	53. B
6. D	18. C	30. D	42. A	54. B
7. A	19. A	31. A	43. D	55. A
8. D	20. B	32. A	44. C	56. B
9. B	21. A	33. B	45. C	57. D
10. A	22. C	34. D	46. D	58. A
11. D	23. D	35. B	47. A	59. B
12. C	24. C	36. D	48. C	60. B

1. **The correct answer is C.** Ovens, toasters, and microwave ovens are all types of appliances that are used for cooking. *Cook* (choice C) does not share this common characteristic with the other words.

2. **The correct answer is D.** The common feature among three of the answer choices is that they're all verbs—*run*, *walk*, and *jog*. *Sneaker* (choice D) is a noun, not a verb.

3. **The correct answer is D.** This is a cause-effect relationship. The effect of adding white to or lightening red is pink; the effect of adding white to or lightening black is gray.

4. **The correct answer is B.** Because the first two statements are true, and Karen reads faster than Isabella, she must also read faster than Ethan.

5. **The correct answer is D.** *Create* means "to bring into existence" or to "invent."

6. **The correct answer is D.** The analogy illustrates a noun-adjective relationship.

7. **The correct answer is A.** *Quality* is a general classification. The other choices are examples of good qualities.

8. **The correct answer is D.** The analogy establishes a part-whole relationship. Sand is part of the beach; soil is part of a farm.

9. **The correct answer is B.** *Time* is a general classification. The other choices are measures of time.

10. **The correct answer is A.** A *salamander* is an amphibian resembling a lizard.

11. **The correct answer is D.** *Arrogant* means "proud" or "haughty."

12. **The correct answer is C.** The first part of the analogy establishes opposite directions. The opposite direction of left is right (choice C).

13. **The correct answer is C.** The analogy establishes a part-whole relationship. One is half of two; three is half of six.

14. **The correct answer is C.** *Add* is a function. The others are general classifications of symbols.

15. **The correct answer is C.** From the first two statements, it is only certain that Peter is the shortest of the three boys. The relationship between Dylan and John cannot be determined.

16. **The correct answer is A.** A mature fruit is one that is tender and sweet, or ripe.

17. **The correct answer is B.** Other synonyms for *gossamer* are "insubstantial," "fragile," or "tenuous."

18. **The correct answer is C.** *Coddle* means "to treat with extreme care," or "pamper."

19. **The correct answer is A.** The first part of the analogy establishes a type of item (books) and a place where they're usually found (libraries). Rides are a type of item that are usually found in carnivals.

20. **The correct answer is B.** The analogy establishes an object-purpose relationship. The purpose of a director is to lead a choir; the purpose of a coach is to lead a team.

21. **The correct answer is A.** *Diversify* means "to make or become more varied."

22. **The correct answer is C.** The first two statements indicate no relationship between Liam and Ralph; therefore, the third statement is uncertain.

23. **The correct answer is D.** A superficial wound is a shallow or surface wound.

24. **The correct answer is C.** Although Shelley cannot throw a Javelin farther than Liandra, we are not told who took part in the javelin-throwing contest, so we cannot be certain who won.

25. **The correct answer is B.** Someone who is *bellicose* is eager to fight, or combative.

26. **The correct answer is C.** A *sadistic* remark is intended to inflict pain, or to be hurtful.

27. **The correct answer is D.** A dormitory is only one part of a school, university, or college.

28. **The correct answer is B.** *Truncate* means "to shorten or to cut off."

29. **The correct answer is C.** Someone who is facetious is clever and humorous.

30. **The correct answer is D.** An indigent person is impoverished, or needy.

31. **The correct answer is A.** The analogy establishes a part-whole relationship. A leg is a part of a table on which the table rests; a wheel is a part of a car on which the car rests.

32. **The correct answer is A.** A dungeon is a place where people may be forced to stay. The other choices are places in which people choose to live.

33. **The correct answer is B.** We are told early on that "Bishop's house is the largest on his street." We are also told that "Arianna and Bishop live on the same street." Therefore, even though Arianna's house is much larger than Terrence's house, it is false that Arianna's house is the largest on Oakville Lane, since Bishop's house is the largest on his street, and he lives on the same street as Arianna.

34. **The correct answer is D.** *Punishment* is a general classification. The other choices describe specific types or places of punishment.

35. **The correct answer is B.** *Refuse* means to decline; the opposite is *accept*.

36. **The correct answer is D.** The analogy establishes an object-user relationship. Ink is used in a pen when applied; paint is used on a brush when applied.

37. **The correct answer is C.** *Acquire* means "to gain possession of;" the opposite is *release*.

38. **The correct answer is C.** Though the first two statements are considered true, they do not provide any information as to the direct relationship between rivers A and C.

39. **The correct answer is C.** *Scant* means "meager;" the opposite is *abundant*.

40. **The correct answer is B.** *Pinnacle* means "peak;" the opposite is *base*.

41. **The correct answer is D.** The analogy establishes a part-whole relationship. The captain is the part of a team that guides the team; the manager is the part of an office that guides the office.

42. **The correct answer is A.** A window may be covered by the other three choices.

43. **The correct answer is D.** *Corpulent* means "fat;" the opposite is *slender*.

44. **The correct answer is C.** *Naive* means "lacking experience or knowledge;" the opposite is *sophisticated*.

45. **The correct answer is C.** A glove is a hand covering; all the other choices are head coverings.

46. **The correct answer is D.** A podium is positioned at the front of an auditorium or theater. The other choices represent those who face the podium.

47. **The correct answer is A.** To pledge is to promise.

48. **The correct answer is C.** A depression is a low spot or a hollow; the opposite is a hill.

49. **The correct answer is A.** Because the first two statements are true, and all the fruits cost more than apples, apples must cost the least.

50. **The correct answer is D.** A fir tree is an evergreen; all of the other trees are deciduous, which means they lose their leaves.

51. **The correct answer is B.** *Diminish* means "to decrease;" the opposite is *augment*.

52. **The correct answer is B.** Because the first two statements are true, Jay's batting average must be higher than Paulo's.

53. **The correct answer is B.** *Abandon* means "to give up;" the opposite is *keep*.

54. **The correct answer is B.** *Feasible* is an attribute of abstract things or ideas. The other choices are generally attributes applied to concrete objects regarding texture or firmness.

55. **The correct answer is A.** Because the first two statements are true and C is north of A, it must also be north of B.

56. **The correct answer is B.** Cotton is a vegetable product; leather, wool, and fur are animal products.

57. **The correct answer is D.** A seam is a type of closing. The other choices are things for opening and closing.

58. **The correct answer is A.** *Dwindle* means "to grow smaller."

59. **The correct answer is B.** Oxygen, helium, and gold are elements; water is a compound of hydrogen and oxygen.

60. **The correct answer is B.** Because the first two statements are true, and the third statement is in direct opposition to the first, it cannot be true.

NOTES

Quantitative Skills

61. B	72. D	83. D	93. D	103. B
62. C	73. C	84. B	94. A	104. B
63. D	74. D	85. D	95. D	105. C
64. A	75. C	86. C	96. A	106. A
65. C	76. B	87. D	97. B	107. C
66. A	77. B	88. C	98. A	108. A
67. C	78. B	89. C	99. B	109. D
68. C	79. B	90. D	100. B	110. C
69. B	80. D	91. B	101. B	111. A
70. D	81. C	92. D	102. D	112. C
71. C	82. C			

61. **The correct answer is B.** If you write the direction and amount of change between the numbers of the series, you see that the pattern of the series is –1, –2, –1, –3, –1, –4, ... The next step is –1; 11 – 1 = 10.

62. **The correct answer is C.** The relationships are clearly visible. Just read and examine carefully.

63. **The correct answer is D.** Evaluate each separately:

    A. = $(5 + 8)^2 = 13^2 = 169$

    B. = $5^2 + 8^2 = 25 + 64 = 89$

    C. = $2(5) + 2(8) = 10 + 16 = 26$

    So, C is less than B, and B is less than A.

64. **The correct answer is A.** Start by calculating 60% of 40, which equals 24. Then subtract five, to get 24 – 5 = 19.

65. **The correct answer is C.** The pattern is +2, –4, +2, –4, and so on. The next step is 44 + 2 = 46.

66. **The correct answer is A.** The letters in each term move forward by one, and the + and – alternate. The next three terms are F–, G+ H–.

67. **The correct answer is C.** Add the numbers within the brackets and divide by 5 to get the average; 6 + 12 + 4 + 41 + 7 = 70 ÷ 5 = 14. The question asks for twice that amount, so multiply to get the final answer; 14 × 2 = 28.

68. **The correct answer is C.** The series so far is: –2, –2, –3, –3, –4, –4. Next should come –5, –5, which, when applied to the last number in the series, results in 24 – 5 = 19, and 19 – 5 = 14.

69. **The correct answer is B.** The pattern is to add 7, then add 2, add 7, then add 2. So, the next number is 52 + 7 = 59.

70. **The correct answer is D.** Angle C is a right angle (90°). The three angles of a triangle must add up to 180°. Therefore, the sum of the other two angles is equal to 90°.

71. **The correct answer is C.**

$$6 \times 4 = 24$$

$$\frac{2}{3}x = 24$$

$$x = 24\left(\frac{3}{2}\right)$$

$$x = 36$$

72. **The correct answer is D.** Let x denote the number. Then, translate the number sentence into the equation $\dfrac{x}{\frac{1}{4}} = 79 - 3$.

Solve as follows:

$$\frac{x}{\frac{1}{4}} = 79 - 3$$

$$4x = 76$$

$$x = 19$$

73. **The correct answer is C.** Count the shaded areas, taking note of the fact that some areas are larger than others. Then choose your answer by inspection and careful reading. If it is visually easier, you could also count the non-shaded areas, noting that fewer non-shaded area means more shaded areas.

74. **The correct answer is D.** The first thing to do with this question is to convert $3\frac{5}{8}$ to an improper fraction. $(3 \times 8) + 5 = 29$, so we get the improper fraction $\frac{29}{8}$. The reciprocal of $\frac{29}{8}$ is $\frac{8}{29}$.

75. **The correct answer is C.** Doing the math, B = 0.858. The decimal form of C = 0.875, which makes it equal to A. Now, you can see that there is only one true statement.

76. **The correct answer is B.** First, perform the subtraction, and then divide by 7; $69 - 6 = 63 \div 7 = 9$.

77. **The correct answer is B.** Start by calculating the three fraction problems; A is 4, B is 6, and C is 4. Now just be careful when reviewing the answer options.

78. **The correct answer is B.** Each of the figures is divided into eight equal wedges. By counting the shaded wedges, we see that figure A and figure C both have five wedges shaded, while figure B has only four.

79. **The correct answer is B.** Sometimes, you must shift gears. Most series are based upon addition and subtraction but not all. You cannot make sense of this series if you stick to the + 8 with which you probably started out. The relationship between 9 and 18 and between 15 and 30 should make you think of multiplication.

The series follows the pattern of: ×2, −7, ×2, −7, ×2, −7, ... The next step would be 11 × 2 = 22. Since we are provided with the next term in the series, we can confirm the answer: 22 − 7 = 15.

80. **The correct answer is D.** Find the factors for both numbers.

42: 1, 2, 3, 6, 7, 14, 21   39: 1, 3, 13

The only shared factor besides 1 is 3.

81. **The correct answer is C.** Each letter is repeated a number of times that increases by one for each letter. A is repeated once, B is repeated twice, C is repeated three times. D should be repeated four times, so the next term is D3.

82. **The correct answer is C.** First find the average; $12 + 87 + 72 + 41 = 212 \div 4 = 53$. Next, determine how much this figure exceeds 25 by subtracting; $53 - 25 = 28$.

83. **The correct answer is D.** The series +1, −2, +1, −3, +1, −4 now continues with +1, so add $18 + 1 = 19$.

84. **The correct answer is B.** Read each answer choice, and then count and reason carefully. There is no special trick for this kind of question, apart from being alert and following the question closely.

85. **The correct answer is D.** Each term is double the previous term, plus 1. Since $2 \times 31 = 62$, the next term is $62 + 1 = 63$.

86. **The correct answer is C.** There are two pints in a quart, and four quarts in a gallon. To find the number of pints, multiply $17 \times 2 = 34$. To find the number of gallons, divide $17 \div 4 = 6.25$. Be certain that both terms in your answer choice are correct.

87. **The correct answer is D.** By completing the last of the three options, (2 × 6) (6 × 2), we are left with $12 \times 12 = 144$. Since 144 is greater than the other numbers, the only correct answer is choice D.

88. **The correct answer is C.** By counting the shaded wedges corresponding to each letter, you can see that section A has four wedges, while section C has three, D has two, and B has one.

89. **The correct answer is C.** First, find the product of $8 \times 4 = 32$. Multiply this product by 3 and

then subtract 30 to get the result; $32 \times 3 = 96$, and $96 - 30 = 66$.

90. **The correct answer is D.** The values of each expression are $A = 3^2 + 4 = 13$, $B = 4^2 - 4 = 12$, $C = 2^3 + 4 = 12$. A is greater than B and C, which are equal.

91. **The correct answer is B.** The series may be interpreted as a repetition of $+0.125$ or as increasing decimals of $\frac{1}{8}, \frac{2}{8}, \frac{3}{8}$, and so on. Taking the figure from the end of the series, we find that $0.500 + 0.125 = 0.625$.

92. **The correct answer is D.** Count, then read carefully. If you find it visually confusing to count the dark squares, it may be easier to count the white squares and subtract from the total number of squares, which is 15.

93. **The correct answer is D.** The denominator increases by 1, then 2, then 3, then 4. For the next term, the denominator should increase by 5, resulting in $11 + 5 = 16$.

94. **The correct answer is A.** The easiest way to find the solution is to try out each of the answers.

$$\frac{9}{16} \div \frac{3}{4} = \frac{9}{16} \times \frac{4}{3} = \frac{3}{4}; \frac{5}{8} \div \frac{3}{4} = \frac{5}{6};$$
$$\frac{7}{16} \div \frac{3}{4} = \frac{7}{12}; \frac{3}{4} \div \frac{3}{4} = 1.$$

95. **The correct answer is D.** 0.8 and 80% are equal, but $\frac{8}{10}$% is only 0.008.

96. **The correct answer is A.** The order of the lengths of the line segments, shortest to longest, is B, C, A, D. Only choice D requires more information, but the sum of both sides is $8 + 17 = 25$, which is not equal to the length of line segment D, so choice D is incorrect.

97. **The correct answer is B.** You should see quite readily that the series is based on squares followed by their positive number square roots in descending order. The missing number is the square of 7, which is 49.

98. **The correct answer is A.** The mean is also the average; combine the data points, then divide the sum by the number of data points to get an average, or mean, of 12.8. For the median, put the data points in order and identify the data point in the middle of the set, which is 9. For mode, find the data point that appears most often within the set, which is also 9.

99. **The correct answer is B.** After you look beyond the first two numbers, you can see that the progression is multiply by 3, repeat the number, multiply by 3, repeat the number, multiply by 3, repeat the number. We pick up the series at $27 \times 3 = 81$. Then repeat the number 81. Then, $81 \times 3 = 243$.

100. **The correct answer is B.** If $\frac{3}{8} x = 9$, then $3x = 72$ and $x = \frac{72}{3}$. So, $x = 24$. $83\frac{1}{3}$%, or $\frac{5}{6}$, of $24 = 20$.

101. **The correct answer is B.** The size of the angle is easily read on the arc of the protractor. $A = 70°$, $B = 60°$, and $C = 50°$. A right angle is $90°$. Now, plug the angle sizes into the statements to find the answer.

102. **The correct answer is D.** To convert a number to scientific notation, move the decimal point to the left until you have a number between 1 and 10; for 27,840,000,000 we get 2.784. Count how many spaces you move to the decimal point (ignoring the commas), and that becomes your exponent; in this case it's 10. Then multiply your first number by 10 raised to your exponent.

$$2.784 \times 10^{10} = 27{,}840{,}000{,}000$$

103. **The correct answer is B.** Don't be thrown by the negative numbers. The series is: $+5, +2, +5, +2$. Next comes $+5$, so $-5 + 5 = 0$.

104. **The correct answer is B.** Let x represent the number. We translate the number sentence into the following equation:

$75 - x = 2(9 + 3)$. Solve for x, as follows:

$$75 - x = 2(12)$$
$$75 - x = 24$$
$$75 - 24 = x$$
$$51 = x$$

105. **The correct answer is C.** This is a ÷ 2 series. The decimals make it a bit confusing. The next number in the series would be .0025 ÷ 2 = 0.0125

106. **The correct answer is A.** First, calculate $\frac{5}{8}$ of 96, which equals 60. Then, subtract 12 to get the final answer; 60 − 12 = 48.

107. **The correct answer is C.** A is 21¢, B is 28¢, and C is 25¢. Replace letters with money amounts and you will see that choice C is the only true statement.

108. **The correct answer is A.** The progress of the series is +3, so the next value is 18 + 3 = 21. However, in the small segment that we see, the series alternates two Roman numerals and two Arabic numbers. Having no reason to suppose that this alternation will change later in the series, we must assume that the next entry will be a Roman numeral. Hence, XXI is the correct form for the next number in the series.

109. **The correct answer is D.** This is a ÷2 series, which you might find somewhat hard to visualize in the fraction form. Rename the improper fractions as whole numbers to make this clear:

$$\frac{16}{2} = 8; \frac{8}{2} = 4; \frac{8}{4} = 2; \frac{8}{8} = 1; \frac{8}{16} = \frac{1}{2}$$

Picking up the series where it leaves off, the correct answer is $\frac{8}{16} \div 2$, or $\frac{8}{32}$.

$$\frac{8}{16} \div 2 = \frac{8}{16} \times \frac{1}{2} = \frac{8}{32}$$

110. **The correct answer is C.** A is 95, B is 1.95, and C is 95. Work with the numbers instead of the letters to find the answer.

111. **The correct answer is A.** This is another instance in which it is easiest to try out the answers. Multiply each answer choice by 40%. In this case, however, 40% of 150 is 60, and when we decrease 150 by 40%, we arrive at the desired answer, 150 − 60 = 90. Because the first choice works, there is no reason to continue. Choices B and C, being less than 90, could not possibly be correct. If you wanted to be doubly sure (and if you had spare time), you could try 40% of 145 = 58, and continue with 145 − 58 = 87, which is not 90.

112. **The correct answer is C.** The pattern being established is as follows: −8, repeat the number, −6, repeat the number, −4, repeat the number. Logically, the next step is −2, repeat the number; 8 − 2 = 6. Then, repeat the 6.

NOTES

Reading

Comprehension

113. C	121. C	129. D	137. A	145. A
114. C	122. C	130. C	138. D	146. A
115. C	123. C	131. B	139. C	147. B
116. D	124. A	132. D	140. A	148. A
117. D	125. D	133. C	141. B	149. B
118. C	126. B	134. A	142. B	150. D
119. B	127. C	135. B	143. B	151. A
120. D	128. C	136. D	144. C	152. A

113. **The correct answer is C.** Sentences 3 and 4 say the mantle has four layers, all of which are between 250 and 1,000 miles thick, so the combined layers of the mantle, at minimum, would be 1,750 miles thick. This minimum is larger than the other layers. Sentence 6 says the outer core (choice B) is a little over 1,200 miles thick, and the inner core (choice D) is slightly less than 800 miles. The crust (choice A) is only about 20 miles thick.

114. **The correct answer is C.** The answer is in sentence 1: "Our planet Earth is divided into seven separate layers."

115. **The correct answer is C.** This is an inference question. Based on sentence 7, we know that both the speed and direction of earthquake waves vary. We do not know from this information if choice A is true, so we must assume that C is the best answer.

116. **The correct answer is D.** Because of the nature of the information, it would be found in both an encyclopedia and a science book.

117. **The correct answer is D.** This answer is determined by the entire passage, which describes the layers in order. The answer can be verified by eliminating choices A, B, and C.

118. **The correct answer is C.** *Vary* most closely means "range." To stabilize means "to steady," so choice A is incorrect. Choice B may be tempting because

the thickness does increase, but *increase* is not a synonym for *vary*. Choice D is incorrect because to arbitrate means "to judge."

119. **The correct answer is B.** This is an inference question. Though not specifically stated, the answer can be assumed based on sentence 2 and the phrase "appears to be."

120. **The correct answer is D.** The last sentence of the paragraph states that "both temperature and pressure are much greater at the core than at the crust."

121. **The correct answer is C.** In this passage, *slightly* most nearly means "a little."

122. **The correct answer is C.** *Remaining* most closely means "last."

123. **The correct answer is C.** This answer may be verified by eliminating choices A, B, and D. Though rocks are mentioned, they are only a part of the entire description.

124. **The correct choice is A.** The author uses specific imagery—a dark, scary cave—to show what kind of environment spelunkers face. There is no mention of bats in the first paragraph, so there is no indication that the man is afraid of bats (choice B), and there is no information to compare bats with spelunkers (choice C). This is an informative passage, so choice D is incorrect as well.

125. **The correct answer is D.** This answer may be verified by eliminating choices A, B, and C. One clue to the answer is in the way the passage is written—without technical terms and in the third person.

126. **The correct answer is B.** The cave the man was exploring was probably deep underground. This is an inference question. The answer may be verified by eliminating the other choices.

127. **The correct answer is C.** This is the most specific, direct answer, though the other choices may have been indirectly related. The answer is found in paragraph 2, where the flashlight is mentioned immediately before the bats suddenly begin to fly about.

128. **The correct answer is C.** In paragraph 2, sentence 4 states: "He ducks, startled, then grins." The key context word is *startled*, which is a synonym for "surprised," so choice C is the best option.

129. **The correct answer is D.** *Utter* most nearly means "great."

130. **The correct answer is C.** Spelunkers ignore *discomfort*. In the course of the passage, the author refers to "decaying" smells, banging into a "cold rocky wall," and crawling through narrow passage "on their stomachs." Yet the author also describes these spelunking activities as fun and exciting. In paragraph 4, the author specifically refers to spelunkers forming clubs, which makes choice D incorrect. In the same paragraph, he mentions that spelunkers share safety tips, which eliminates choice A. Although the author does mention the darkness as a major feature of spelunking, he does not ignore it, but rather brings a light with him, making choice B incorrect.

131. **The correct answer is B.** A good title for this passage would be "Spelunkers—Underground Explorers." Though the author mentions bats, the passage concentrates on the more general topic of spelunkers, so choice A is not the best option. Choices C and D are too broad.

132. **The correct answer is D.** According to this passage, *adventurous* is the word that would most

nearly describe spelunkers. The answer may be verified by eliminating the other choices.

133. **The correct answer is C.** This passage provides positive information about kohlrabi, and based on the optimistic tone, readers can determine that the author's opinion on kohlrabi as a food is most likely enthusiastic, choice C.

134. **The correct answer is A.** This passage is a persuasive piece that highlights the many merits of this vegetable in an effort to get readers to try it. Therefore, "Consider Kohlrabi" (choice A) would be the best title for this passage.

135. **The correct answer is B.** *Protean* means "mutable and adaptable." As used in the passage, *protean* is used to describe the type of menu ingredient that "can be eaten raw or cooked and is an excellent addition to a wide array of recipes." This description attempts to portray kohlrabi as a versatile ingredient, making choice B the correct answer.

136. **The correct answer is D.** According to the passage, kohlrabi is a good source of vitamin C, vitamin B, fiber, and *potassium*. There is no mention of kohlrabi being a source of calories, energy, or spice, so choices A, B, and C are incorrect.

137. **The correct answer is A.** The author mentions "the vegetable's popularity in Germanic regions" in the same sentence as the types of kohlrabi (White Danube, Purple Danube, White Vienna, and Purple Vienna). The most likely scenario is that these names are of Germanic origin, making choice A the correct answer.

138. **The correct answer is D.** Within the passage, the word varietal is used to introduce the White Danube, Purple Danube, White Vienna, and Purple Vienna—each a *type* of kohlrabi. Therefore, choice D is correct.

139. **The correct answer is C.** According to the passage, the main reason why kohlrabi is often mistaken as a root vegetable is its bulbous, root-like appearance. The kohlrabi's taste (choice A), color (choice B), and name (choice D) have nothing to do with its being mistaken for a root vegetable.

140. The correct answer is A. Kohlrabi is a member of the *Brassica oleracea* species, which also includes broccoli (choice B), kale (choice C), cauliflower (choice D), and Brussels sprouts. There is no mention of it being in the same species as turnips, so choice A is correct.

141. The correct answer is B. In the passage, the only item among the answer choices that's *not* mentioned as a benefit of kohlrabi is heart health, making choice B the correct answer.

142. The correct answer is B. This passage is an enthusiastic piece of writing that is in full support of giving kohlrabi a try. It discusses a wide array of kohlrabi's benefits and positive characteristics, and it suggests trying kohlrabi "the next time you're doing some meal planning." Therefore, choice B is correct.

143. The correct answer is B. This passage describes its subject in a matter-of-fact, straightforward way, which means that *inform* is the most apt choice. While the argument might persuade (choice A) someone to believe Wendy Carlos was an interesting figure, this is not the main purpose of the passage. Furthermore, there is no attempt to amuse the reader (choice C) or to critique Carlos or her music (choice D).

144. The correct answer is C. Close reading of the passage should make it clear that while Carlos did create soundtracks for film (choice A) and use computers (choice D) in her electronic compositions, her primary influence was on the world of music. Television (choice B) is never mentioned in the passage.

145. The correct answer is A. This question is asking you to make an inference based on the information provided in the passage. We know from the details given that Wendy Carlos had a huge influence on today's music and that she was known for using computers and electronic instruments. You may also have spotted the reference to Jay-Z and know that he is a rapper. By paying attention to these context clues, it should be clear that the use of computer-based beats in rap is a clear example

of Carlos' influence on later music. Even when the context makes things clear, ensure that the other answers aren't more logical; neither choice B nor choice D is supported by the passage, and Bach is famous enough that he would have likely remained popular even without Carlos' influence (choice C).

146. The correct answer is A. To answer this question, you have to consider the details you've been given to make a logical inference. Paragraph 3 states that Wendy Carlos was asked to make music for film soundtracks, so we can be certain that film producers were interested in her music. None of the other answers can be supported by the passage.

147. The correct answer is B. Every answer given provides an example of something either being translated or needing translation—your job is to figure out which matches the context used in the passage. The passage describes Carlos taking Bach's original music and creating an electronic version of the same compositions using a Moog synthesizer. The answer that best matches is choice B, since a dance company taking a famous choreographer's ballet and doing a hip-hop interpretation of it would be a very similar act of translation. Reading between the lines of what someone is saying (choice C) and making something understandable across language barriers (choices A and D) are two different concepts of translation that are valid but which do not match the context here.

148. The correct answer is A. The passage states that Giorgio Moroder was an "Italo-disco legend" who also helped make synthesizer music popular, so you can infer that this means he was known for disco music.

149. The correct answer is B. Something that is definitive can also be described as quintessential, meaning "an ideal example of something." Contextually, the passage is saying that the Moog synthesizer sound was typical of 1970s music and recognizable as such.

150. The correct answer is D. If something resonates with the current times, that means it is still relevant today. You may have heard *resonate* used to refer to sound, making choices A and B seem potentially correct. However, remember to always consider the context in which a word is used, since neither they nor choice C would make sense in context.

151. **The correct answer is A.** The first paragraph clearly states that "many people have never heard of the Grammy-winning electronic music pioneer Wendy Carlos, who is one of the most influential composers of the modern age," so the passage suggests that not everyone who is influential is well-known.

152. **The correct answer is A.** A good title for this passage might be "Wendy Carlos: Electronic Music Icon." This theme occurs throughout the passage. Choices B and D focus on small details of the passage that do not encompass the main point, while choice C is too vague.

NOTES

Vocabulary

153. D	**158.** A	**163.** B	**167.** A	**171.** A
154. B	**159.** D	**164.** B	**168.** D	**172.** B
155. A	**160.** D	**165.** D	**169.** A	**173.** D
156. D	**161.** A	**166.** A	**170.** C	**174.** C
157. C	**162.** B			

153. **The correct answer is D.** *Perspective* means "aspect," "attitude," or "view."

154. **The correct answer is B.** To impair is to spoil, damage, or weaken.

155. **The correct answer is A.** *Acumen* refers to a "keen intelligence."

156. **The correct answer is D.** To subjugate means to dominate or overpower.

157. **The correct answer is C.** *Reproach* means to condemn, chide, or blame.

158. **The correct answer is A.** To be elated is to be jubilant, exhilarated, or happy.

159. **The correct answer is D.** *Brusque* means curt, blunt, or abrupt.

160. **The correct answer is D.** To depress something is to squash, flatten, or push down.

161. **The correct answer is A.** To quench is to allay, stifle, or end.

162. **The correct answer is B.** An exploit is an escapade, deed, or venture.

163. **The correct answer is B.** A precipitous incline is steep.

164. **The correct answer is B.** A chronicle is an account, a history, or a record of something.

165. **The correct answer is D.** To be an amiable person means to be likeable.

166. **The correct answer is A.** The meaning of the word *astute* is to be keen, shrewd, or clever.

167. **The correct answer is A.** *Sever* means "divide," "split," or "cut."

168. **The correct answer is D.** *Eminent* means "distinguished," "important," or "outstanding."

169. **The correct answer is A.** To terminate is to end, cancel, or stop something.

170. **The correct answer is C.** To hinder means to obstruct, interfere, or impede something.

171. **The correct answer is A.** To be in contention means to be in strife, discord, or debate.

172. **The correct answer is B.** To concede means to admit, allow, or acknowledge.

173. **The correct answer is D.** The word *forego* means "concede," "give up," or "relinquish."

174. **The correct answer is C.** If something is canny, that means it is clever.

Mathematics

Concepts

175. B	180. C	185. B	190. A	195. A
176. D	181. A	186. A	191. A	196. C
177. A	182. D	187. B	192. B	197. A
178. A	183. D	188. C	193. A	198. C
179. D	184. C	189. B	194. C	

175. **The correct answer is B.** You don't have to do any deep calculating to find the answer here; just note that 2 feet is 24 inches, 0.5 yards is 1.5 feet or 18 inches, and, since a centimeter is smaller than an inch, 14 centimeters is certainly smaller than 17 inches. Therefore, 2 feet (choice B) is the largest.

176. **The correct answer is D.** A parallelogram has four sides, with each pair of opposite sides being parallel. A rhombus, square, and rectangle all satisfy these conditions. A triangle, however, only has three sides.

177. **The correct answer is A.** The mean, or average, of a set of numbers is their sum divided by how many numbers are in the set.

178. **The correct answer is A.** The weight of a set of objects will always be the sum of the weights of the individual objects.

179. **The correct answer is D.** Each angle in a square is a right angle, or 90 degrees. Four of these add up to 360 degrees.

180. **The correct answer is C.** The variables are the unknown values represented as letters. There are three variables in this equation: m, n, and p.

181. **The correct answer is A.** An equilateral triangle is one in which all the sides are the same length, and all the angles are the same size (think "equal").

182. **The correct answer is D.** Each meter is 100 centimeters, so 2 meters is 200 centimeters.

183. **The correct answer is D.** A pint is 2 cups, so it contains 8 + 8 = 16 ounces.

184. **The correct answer is C.** The millions begin with the seventh digit to the left of the decimal place. Because you need 326 million, you can immediately eliminate choices A and B. Read on to the thousands place, and you will see it is 900 thousand. You need look no further for the correct answer.

185. **The correct answer is B.** A number is changed if 1 is subtracted from it. You should know this answer instantly. If you do not, try out each option.

186. **The correct answer is A.** The first 4 is in the billion's place; the second, in the hundred-thousand's place. If you had trouble with this problem, review how to read numbers and determine place values.

187. **The correct answer is B.** You should recognize immediately that $\frac{1}{2}$ day is shorter than 25 hours and that 3,600 seconds is far shorter than 1,440 minutes. Narrowing down to the first two choices, you probably know that there are 1,440 minutes in a day. If you do not know this, multiply 24 by 60 to see for yourself.

188. **The correct answer is C.** To find the average, or mean, add the digits in the set, then divide by the number of digits. So, 3 + 5 + 1 + 2 + 9 = 20, and 20 ÷ 5 = 4.

189. **The correct answer is B.** In order, the numbers are 1, 2, 3, 5, 9. The median is the middle number.

190. **The correct answer is A.** The probability is the number of winners divided by the total number of contestants. In this case, that is the fraction $\frac{2}{8}$ which reduces to $\frac{1}{4}$.

191. **The correct answer is A.**

$$1\frac{3}{4}\% = 1.75\% = 0.0175$$

192. **The correct answer is B.** Since the sum of the angles of a triangle always equals 180° and m∠B = 90°, angles A and C together must equal 90°. Do not allow yourself to be diverted by extra information. m∠C of the triangle is equal to 30°, so m∠A = 60°, but this knowledge is irrelevant to the question being asked. Avoid wasting time on unnecessary calculations.

193. **The correct answer is A.** $9^2 = 81$. Because x is greater than 9, x^2 would have to be greater than 81, which also makes it greater than 80. As such, choice A is the correct option.

194. **The correct answer is C.** Many numbers are divisible by either 3 or 4 but not by both. All numbers that are divisible by both 3 and 4 are also divisible by their multiple, 12.

195. **The correct answer is A.** Compare the digit in the hundredths place; 0.023 is greater than 0.0086.

196. **The correct answer is C.** The *greatest* common factor of 50 and 10 is 10 itself. 1 and 5 are also common factors, but they are smaller.

197. **The correct answer is A.** For the sum to be smaller than the given number of an addition problem, the missing number must be negative.

198. **The correct answer is C.** The formula for determining the area of a circle is πr^2. Since $r = 3$, the formula can be expressed as $3^2\pi = 9\pi$ sq. cm.

NOTES

Problem Solving

199. B	207. B	215. D	223. B	231. B
200. C	208. B	216. D	224. B	232. B
201. D	209. B	217. B	225. D	233. C
202. C	210. A	218. C	226. A	234. B
203. C	211. C	219. B	227. B	235. A
204. B	212. D	220. B	228. D	236. A
205. D	213. A	221. B	229. C	237. C
206. B	214. C	222. C	230. A	238. D

199. **The correct answer is B.** Three gallons contain 12 quarts. The ratio is 3:12, or, in simplest form, 1:4.

200. **The correct answer is C.** For this question, you must try out all of the answer options. If $x = 0$, then $2x < 8$ because $2(0) < 8$. None of the other pairs results in a true statement.

201. **The correct answer is D.**

$$4\frac{1}{4} \div \frac{1}{5} = \frac{17}{4} \div \frac{1}{5}$$
$$= \frac{17}{4} \times 5$$
$$= \frac{85}{4}$$
$$= 21\frac{1}{4}$$

202. **The correct answer is C.** When determining probability, find the number of desired outcomes (what you want to happen) and divide it by the number of all possible outcomes (all the things that could happen). There are six even numbers (2, 4, 6, 8, 10, and 12), and there are 12 numbers overall. Therefore, the probability that the pointer will land on an even number is $\frac{6}{12}$ or $\frac{1}{2}$. Note that you can use the process of elimination to eliminate choices A and D because a probability of 0 means something can never happen; a probability of 1 means something will always happen. Also, don't worry about the counterclockwise reference; the probability is the same no matter the direction in which you spin the pointer.

203. **The correct answer is C.** Izzy's age now $= x$. Her sister's age now is $x - 3$. In 5 years, her sister's age will be $x - 3 + 5$, or, in simplest form, $x + 2$.

204. **The correct answer is B.** For this question, you must perform the calculation for each answer option. However, this is a good problem to do in your head. For example, in the correct answer, choice B, you can quickly see that $6 + 4 < 10.5$ is the same as $10 < 10.5$.

205. **The correct answer is D.** The union of the two adjacent line segments creates one continuous line segment.

206. **The correct answer is B.**

$$\begin{array}{r} 1.970 \\ 1.02\overline{)2.01000} \\ \underline{1\ 02} \\ 99\ 0 \\ \underline{91\ 8} \\ 7\ 20 \\ \underline{7\ 14} \\ 60 \end{array}$$

207. **The correct answer is B.** Use the order of operations:

$$-2\left[-2\left(1-5\right)-6\right] =$$
$$-2\left[-2\left(-4\right)-6\right] =$$
$$-2\left[3+8-6\right] =$$
$$-2\left[11-6\right] =$$
$$-2[5] = -10$$

208. **The correct answer is B.** This is a good problem to do in your head. Note that 10% of 70 is 7. It then follows that 140% is 14×7, or 98.

209. **The correct answer is B.** Bracket the multiplication and division first, then solve the problem.

$$\left(6 \div \frac{1}{3}\right) + \left(\frac{2}{3} \times 9\right)$$
$$= 18 + 6$$
$$= 24$$

210. **The correct answer is A.** Substitute in the values of x, y, and z and simplify using the order of operations:

$$x(y - z)^2 = -3(5 - (-2))^2$$
$$= -3(7)^2$$
$$= -3(49)$$
$$= -147$$

211. **The correct answer is C.** Seven is one-third of 21, and $\frac{2}{3}$ is one-third of 2.

212. **The correct answer is D.** To find the average, find the sum of the addends and divide that sum by the number of addends.

$$-10 + 6 + 0 - 3 + 22 = 15$$
$$15 \div 5 = 3$$

213. **The correct answer is A.**

$$x^2 + 5 = 41$$
$$x^2 = 41 - 5$$
$$x^2 = 36$$
$$x = \pm 6$$

214. **The correct answer is C.**

Area = length × width
Area = 168 ft. × 82 ft.
Area = 13,776 sq. ft.

215. **The correct answer is D.**

$$63 \div \frac{1}{9} = 63 \times \frac{9}{1} = 567$$

This is a good answer to estimate. By dividing a number by $\frac{1}{9}$, you are, in effect, multiplying it by 9. Only one of the suggested answers is close.

216. **The correct answer is D.** Move the decimal point of the divisor two places to the right; do the same for the dividend. Then divide by 0.5. Since $0.5 = \frac{1}{2}$, you could choose to divide by $\frac{1}{2}$ or multiply by 2.

217. **The correct answer is B.** This is a tricky question. It doesn't ask for 150% of 72, but rather to increase 72 by 150%. Because 150% of 72 = 108, we add 72 and 108 for the correct answer. Careful reading is an important factor in test success.

218. **The correct answer is C.** The mean is $(2 + 5 + 5 + 6 + 7) \div 5 = 5$. The median is the number in the middle, which is 5. The mode is the number that appears most often, which is also 5.

219. **The correct answer is B.** For each of the 10 possible presidents, there are 7 possible vice presidents. Therefore, the total number of combinations is $10 \times 7 = 70$.

220. **The correct answer is B.** Since $x = 2$, the length is $2 + 3 = 5$, and the width is $2 - 1 = 1$. The perimeter is $5 + 5 + 1 + 1 = 12$. We are not told what units are being used.

221. **The correct answer is B.** The probability that he will not get an A is 100% minus the probability that he will get an A. That is, $100\% - 80\% = 20\%$.

222. **The correct answer is C.** For each teacher, there are 12 students. Because there are 16 teachers, there must be 12×16, or 192, students.

223. **The correct answer is B.**

Set up a proportion:

$$\frac{1.2 \text{ inches}}{50 \text{ feet}} = \frac{6 \text{ inches}}{x \text{ feet}}$$

Solve for x, as follows:
$$1.2x = (6)(50)$$
$$1.2x = 300$$

$$x = \frac{300}{1.2} = 250$$

224. **The correct answer is B.** A store markup of 100% would exactly double the price. A 75% markup almost doubles the price. The $17 pants are priced at almost double their cost to the store. By estimation, the best answer is A. To figure precisely, remember that a 75% markup is the equivalent of multiplying the cost by 175%, or 1.75.

$$\text{cost} \times 1.75 = 17.00$$
$$\text{cost} = 17.00 \div 1.75$$
$$\text{cost} = \$9.71$$

225. **The correct answer is D.** To find the perimeter, we add up the dimensions of all the sides. Note that there are some parts that have not been assigned measurements, so we should infer that they are the same as those corresponding parts whose measurements have been designated because we are told to assume that there are right angles in the figure. Beginning at the bottom and moving clockwise, the dimensions are:

$$10'' + 14'' + 2'' + 6'' + 6'' + 6'' + 2'' + 14''$$

These equal 60 inches. If you selected choice A, C, or D, you failed to add up all the segments. Also, you should have rejected choices C and D because a perimeter is a linear measurement, and would not be expressed in square inches.

226. **The correct answer is A.** The area is most easily found by multiplying the length of the figure by its width, and then subtracting the area of the small 6" × 6" square.

$$(14'' \times 10'') - (6'' \times 6'') = \text{area}$$
$$140 \text{ sq. in.} - 36 \text{ sq. in.} = 104 \text{ sq. in.}$$

227. **The correct answer is B.** A 16-minute call would cost $1.56 for the first 3 minutes, plus 22¢ for each of the 13 additional minutes. The total cost is found as follows: $1.56 + 13(0.22) = $1.56 + $2.86 = $4.42.

228. **The correct answer is D.** You only need to read the first and third sentences to solve this problem. The information in the second sentence is not relevant to the problem. The winner received $\frac{1}{3}$ of the total, or $2,700. Thus, the total purse was $2,700 × 3 = $8,100.

229. **The correct answer is C.** Number of seats = 12 + 14 = 26

Number of passengers at station A = 14 + 4 = 18
Number of passengers at next stop = 18 − 8 + 13 = 23
Number of empty seats = 26 − 23 = 3

230. **The correct answer is A.** Raising the sales tax from 5% to 8% is a raise of 3%. The dollar amount is found by calculating 3% of $250 = 0.03 × $250 = $7.50.

231. **The correct answer is B.** Borrow a gallon and add it to 2 quarts. Rewrite the problem.

    4 gallons 6 quarts 1 pint
− 1 gallon 3 quarts 0 pints
    3 gallons 3 quarts 1 pint

232. **The correct answer is B.** By knowing how many phones are in Adelaide (48,000) and how many serve each group of 100 in the population (12.8), we can find how many groups of 100 are in the population. 48,000 phones ÷ 12.8 phones per 100 of population = 3,750 groups of 100 in the population. Therefore, 3,750 × 100 = 375,000 people.

233. **The correct answer is C.** Four boards, each 2'9" long, total 11 feet. The carpenter must buy 11 feet of wood.

234. **The correct answer is B.**

$$\text{Area of a square} = s^2$$
$$49 = 7^2$$
$$\text{one side} = 7 \text{ inches}$$
$$P = 4s$$
$$P = 4 \times 7'' = 28 \text{ inches}$$

235. **The correct answer is A.** Copper and aluminum in the ratio of 10:1 means 10 parts copper to 1 part aluminum.

Let x = weight of aluminum, then $10x$ = weight of copper

$$10x + x = 77$$
$$11x = 77$$
$$x = 7$$

236. The correct answer is A. His total income is equal to 8% of his sales plus $175. First, calculate 8% of his sales; $1,025 × 0.08 = $82. This commission must be added to his weekly salary, so $82 + $175 = $257.

237. The correct answer is C. The amount for which the house was insured is 80% of $83,000, or $66,400. The insurance is calculated at 45¢ per hundred, or $4.50 per thousand of value. Because we are insuring 66.4 thousands in value, 66.4 × $4.50 per thousand equals the yearly premium of $298.80.

238. The correct answer is D. First convert to a 24-hour clock.

3:30 p.m. = 15:30

15:30	14:90		
− 8:50	− 8:50		
	6:40	=	6 hours 40 minutes

To subtract a greater number of minutes from a lesser number of minutes, "borrow" 60 minutes from the hour to enlarge the lesser number, as shown in the second column.

NOTES

Language

239. A	251. A	263. C	275. C	287. D
240. A	252. D	264. D	276. B	288. A
241. B	253. A	265. B	277. C	289. A
242. B	254. A	266. D	278. B	290. A
243. D	255. D	267. B	279. B	291. B
244. C	256. D	268. A	280. B	292. D
245. C	257. B	269. A	281. A	293. B
246. D	258. B	270. B	282. C	294. C
247. C	259. B	271. D	283. D	295. B
248. D	260. C	272. D	284. A	296. B
249. D	261. C	273. C	285. B	297. D
250. C	262. A	274. C	286. A	298. B

239. **The correct answer is A.** The part of the sentence that is set in quotation marks is done so incorrectly. This additional piece of information about Alexis should be set in parentheses.

240. **The correct answer is A.** The names of newspapers are both capitalized and italicized: *Daily Cryer.*

241. **The correct answer is B.** This sentence is a question and should end with a question mark.

242. **The correct answer is B.** The proper names of places are capitalized: Grand Canyon.

243. **The correct answer is D.** *No mistakes.*

244. **The correct answer is C.** The word *Their* is incorrect in this context. The word should be *They're* (they are).

245. **The correct answer is C.** The word *Who's* (who is) is incorrect in this context. The word should be *Whose.*

246. **The correct answer is D.** *No mistakes.*

247. **The correct answer is C.** The adjective *were* is plural, and does not agree with the singular subject of the sentence, *Moshe.*

248. **The correct answer is D.** *No mistakes.*

249. **The correct answer is D.** *No mistakes.*

250. **The correct answer is C.** The semicolons in this sentence are incorrect and create awkward pauses. Semicolons should be used for joining related independent clauses, which we do not have here.

251. **The correct answer is A.** The word *you're* (you are) is incorrect in this context. The word should be *your.*

252. **The correct answer is D.** *No mistakes.*

253. **The correct answer is A.** The object of the preposition *to* is Olivia and *me.*

254. **The correct answer is A.** There is no need to set *fireworks factory* in quotes, and they should be removed from this sentence.

255. **The correct answer is D.** *No mistakes.*

256. **The correct answer is D.** *No mistakes.*

257. **The correct answer is B.** The word *like* relates two or more things, while *as well as* compares two or more things. In this sentence, we are comparing Minato's ability to Ruliann's, so *as well as* is correct.

258. **The correct answer is B.** The word *learning* is incorrect in this context. The word should be *teaching.*

259. **The correct answer is B.** The word *of* is incorrect in this context. The word should be *have.*

260. **The correct answer is C.** There is no need to set *complete name* in parentheses, as it's a primary and essential component of the sentence, and not an aside or tangential information.

261. **The correct answer is C.** The number of hours can be counted—therefore, *fewer* is the correct word.

262. **The correct answer is A.** *Everyone* is singular. The pronoun must be singular as well. Either *his* or *her* would be correct.

263. **The correct answer is C.** There are three, so the comparative term must be *tallest*.

264. **The correct answer is D.** *No mistakes.*

265. **The correct answer is B.** As written, the commas create unnecessary pauses in the sentence and should be removed.

266. **The correct answer is D.** *No mistakes.*

267. **The correct answer is B.** "I feel bad" is the correct usage. "I feel badly" would be correct if something were wrong with the speaker's hands.

268. **The correct answer is A.** This sentence demonstrates correct usage. The other answer choices are missing articles, which result in awkward sentences.

269. **The correct answer is A.** This sentence demonstrates correct usage. The other answer choices contain incorrect pronouns.

270. **The correct answer is B.** This sentence demonstrates correct usage. The other answer choices contain incorrect adverbs.

271. **The correct answer is D.** This sentence demonstrates correct usage. The other answer choices contain pronoun errors.

272. **The correct answer is D.** This sentence demonstrates correct usage. The other answer choices incorrectly contain missing or extra articles.

273. **The correct answer is C.** This sentence demonstrates correct usage. The other answer choices contain errors in verb tense.

274. **The correct answer is C.** This sentence demonstrates correct usage. The other answer choices use incorrect end punctuation.

275. **The correct answer is C.** This sentence demonstrates correct usage. The other answer choices contain incorrect conjunction choices.

276. **The correct answer is B.** This sentence demonstrates correct usage. The other answer choices contain incorrect choices of interjections.

277. **The correct answer is C.** This sentence demonstrates correct usage. The other answer choices contain incorrect preposition choices.

278. **The correct answer is B.** This sentence demonstrates correct usage. The other answer choices contain incorrect negatives or double negatives, which lead to illogical sentences.

279. **The correct answer is B.** The correct spelling is *apparently.*

280. **The correct answer is B.** The correct spelling is *efficiently.*

281. **The correct answer is A.** The correct spelling is *occurred.*

282. **The correct answer is C.** The correct spelling is *analyzed.*

283. **The correct answer is D.** *No mistakes.*

284. **The correct answer is A.** The correct spelling of the word is *misspelled.*

285. **The correct answer is B.** The correct spelling is *described.*

286. **The correct answer is A.** The correct spelling is *prefers.*

287. **The correct answer is D.** *No mistakes.*

288. **The correct answer is A.** The correct spelling is *necessary.*

289. **The correct answer is A.** *Therefore* indicates the cause-and-effect relationship of the two clauses.

290. **The correct answer is A.** The second clause provides an example.

291. **The correct answer is B.** The subject (*Chaya*) must follow the introductory phrase. The use of *afterward* makes choice C redundant.

292. **The correct answer is D.** This sentence expresses the idea most clearly.

293. The correct answer is B. The second clause offers the reason she drove 50 miles.

294. The correct answer is C. The invention of the automobile belongs in a discussion of the automobile's history.

295. The correct answer is B. This choice most clearly and succinctly presents the ideas provided here.

296. The correct answer is B. Sentences 1, 3, and 4 all concern preparation for the Halloween party.

297. The correct answer is D. All these topics are too broad for a one-paragraph theme.

298. The correct answer is B. The given sentence should be placed before sentence 3, because it refers to a singular noun and sentence 2 contains a plural noun. By placing this sentence between sentences 2 and 3, the paragraph makes sense.

 NOTES

SCORE SHEET

Although your actual exam scores will not be reported as percentages, it might be helpful to convert them so you can better visualize your strengths and weaknesses. The numbers in parentheses represent the question numbers testing each skill.

Subject	# Correct ÷ # of questions	× 100 = _____ %
Verbal Analogies (3, 6, 8, 12, 13, 19, 20, 31, 36, 41)	_____ ÷ 10 = _____	× 100 = _____ %
Synonyms (5, 10, 11, 16, 17, 18, 21, 23, 25, 26, 28, 29, 30, 47, 58)	_____ ÷ 15 = _____	× 100 = _____ %
Logic (4, 15, 22, 24, 33, 38, 49, 52, 55, 60)	_____ ÷ 10 = _____	× 100 = _____ %
Verbal Classification (1, 2, 7, 9, 14, 27, 32, 34, 42, 45, 46, 50, 54, 56, 57, 59)	_____ ÷ 16 = _____	× 100 = _____ %
Antonyms (35, 37, 39, 40, 43, 44, 47, 48, 51, 53)	_____ ÷ 9 = _____	× 100 = _____ %
TOTAL VERBAL SKILLS	_____ ÷ 60 = _____	× 100 = _____ %
Number Series (61, 65, 66, 68, 69, 79, 81, 83, 85, 91, 93, 97, 99, 103, 105, 108, 109, 112)	_____ ÷ 18 = _____	× 100 = _____ %
Geometric Comparisons (62, 70, 73, 78, 84, 88, 92, 96, 101)	_____ ÷ 9 = _____	× 100 = _____ %
Nongeometric Comparisons (63, 75, 77, 87, 90, 95, 107, 110)	_____ ÷ 8 = _____	× 100 = _____ %
Number Manipulation (64, 67, 71, 72, 74, 76, 80, 82, 86, 89, 94, 98, 100, 102, 104, 106, 111)	_____ ÷ 17 = _____	× 100 = _____ %
TOTAL QUANTITATIVE SKILLS	_____ ÷ 52 = _____	× 100 = _____ %
Reading—Comprehension (113–152)	_____ ÷ 40 = _____	× 100 = _____ %
Reading—Vocabulary (153–174)	_____ ÷ 22 = _____	× 100 = _____ %
TOTAL READING SKILLS	_____ ÷ 62 = _____	× 100 = _____ %
Mathematics—Concepts (175–198)	_____ ÷ 24 = _____	× 100 = _____ %
Mathematics—Problem Solving (199–238)	_____ ÷ 40 = _____	× 100 = _____ %
TOTAL MATHEMATICS SKILLS	_____ ÷ 64 = _____	× 100 = _____ %
Punctuation and Capitalization (239, 240, 241, 242, 243, 246, 248, 249, 252, 256, 265, 256)	_____ ÷ 12 = _____	× 100 = _____ %
Usage (244, 245, 247, 250, 251, 253, 254, 255, 257–264, 267–278)	_____ ÷ 28 = _____	× 100 = _____ %
Spelling (279–288)	_____ ÷ 10 = _____	× 100 = _____ %
Composition (289–298)	_____ ÷ 10 = _____	× 100 = _____ %
TOTAL LANGUAGE SKILLS	_____ ÷ 60 = _____	× 100 = _____ %

HSPT® PRACTICE TEST 6

#6

HSPT® PRACTICE TEST

This practice test is designed to help you recognize your strengths and weaknesses. The questions cover information from all the different sections of the HSPT. Use the results to help guide and direct your study time.

ANSWER SHEETS: HSPT® PRACTICE TEST 6

Verbal Skills

1. Ⓐ Ⓑ Ⓒ Ⓓ   13. Ⓐ Ⓑ Ⓒ   25. Ⓐ Ⓑ Ⓒ Ⓓ   37. Ⓐ Ⓑ Ⓒ Ⓓ   49. Ⓐ Ⓑ Ⓒ Ⓓ

2. Ⓐ Ⓑ Ⓒ Ⓓ   14. Ⓐ Ⓑ Ⓒ   26. Ⓐ Ⓑ Ⓒ Ⓓ   38. Ⓐ Ⓑ Ⓒ Ⓓ   50. Ⓐ Ⓑ Ⓒ Ⓓ

3. Ⓐ Ⓑ Ⓒ Ⓓ   15. Ⓐ Ⓑ Ⓒ   27. Ⓐ Ⓑ Ⓒ Ⓓ   39. Ⓐ Ⓑ Ⓒ Ⓓ   51. Ⓐ Ⓑ Ⓒ Ⓓ

4. Ⓐ Ⓑ Ⓒ Ⓓ   16. Ⓐ Ⓑ Ⓒ   28. Ⓐ Ⓑ Ⓒ Ⓓ   40. Ⓐ Ⓑ Ⓒ Ⓓ   52. Ⓐ Ⓑ Ⓒ Ⓓ

5. Ⓐ Ⓑ Ⓒ Ⓓ   17. Ⓐ Ⓑ Ⓒ   29. Ⓐ Ⓑ Ⓒ Ⓓ   41. Ⓐ Ⓑ Ⓒ Ⓓ   53. Ⓐ Ⓑ Ⓒ Ⓓ

6. Ⓐ Ⓑ Ⓒ Ⓓ   18. Ⓐ Ⓑ Ⓒ   30. Ⓐ Ⓑ Ⓒ Ⓓ   42. Ⓐ Ⓑ Ⓒ Ⓓ   54. Ⓐ Ⓑ Ⓒ Ⓓ

7. Ⓐ Ⓑ Ⓒ Ⓓ   19. Ⓐ Ⓑ Ⓒ   31. Ⓐ Ⓑ Ⓒ Ⓓ   43. Ⓐ Ⓑ Ⓒ Ⓓ   55. Ⓐ Ⓑ Ⓒ Ⓓ

8. Ⓐ Ⓑ Ⓒ Ⓓ   20. Ⓐ Ⓑ Ⓒ   32. Ⓐ Ⓑ Ⓒ Ⓓ   44. Ⓐ Ⓑ Ⓒ Ⓓ   56. Ⓐ Ⓑ Ⓒ Ⓓ

9. Ⓐ Ⓑ Ⓒ Ⓓ   21. Ⓐ Ⓑ Ⓒ Ⓓ   33. Ⓐ Ⓑ Ⓒ Ⓓ   45. Ⓐ Ⓑ Ⓒ Ⓓ   57. Ⓐ Ⓑ Ⓒ Ⓓ

10. Ⓐ Ⓑ Ⓒ Ⓓ   22. Ⓐ Ⓑ Ⓒ Ⓓ   34. Ⓐ Ⓑ Ⓒ Ⓓ   46. Ⓐ Ⓑ Ⓒ Ⓓ   58. Ⓐ Ⓑ Ⓒ Ⓓ

11. Ⓐ Ⓑ Ⓒ   23. Ⓐ Ⓑ Ⓒ Ⓓ   35. Ⓐ Ⓑ Ⓒ Ⓓ   47. Ⓐ Ⓑ Ⓒ Ⓓ   59. Ⓐ Ⓑ Ⓒ Ⓓ

12. Ⓐ Ⓑ Ⓒ   24. Ⓐ Ⓑ Ⓒ Ⓓ   36. Ⓐ Ⓑ Ⓒ Ⓓ   48. Ⓐ Ⓑ Ⓒ Ⓓ   60. Ⓐ Ⓑ Ⓒ Ⓓ

Quantitative Skills

61. Ⓐ Ⓑ Ⓒ Ⓓ   72. Ⓐ Ⓑ Ⓒ Ⓓ   83. Ⓐ Ⓑ Ⓒ Ⓓ   94. Ⓐ Ⓑ Ⓒ Ⓓ   105. Ⓐ Ⓑ Ⓒ Ⓓ

62. Ⓐ Ⓑ Ⓒ Ⓓ   73. Ⓐ Ⓑ Ⓒ Ⓓ   84. Ⓐ Ⓑ Ⓒ Ⓓ   95. Ⓐ Ⓑ Ⓒ Ⓓ   106. Ⓐ Ⓑ Ⓒ Ⓓ

63. Ⓐ Ⓑ Ⓒ Ⓓ   74. Ⓐ Ⓑ Ⓒ Ⓓ   85. Ⓐ Ⓑ Ⓒ Ⓓ   96. Ⓐ Ⓑ Ⓒ Ⓓ   107. Ⓐ Ⓑ Ⓒ Ⓓ

64. Ⓐ Ⓑ Ⓒ Ⓓ   75. Ⓐ Ⓑ Ⓒ Ⓓ   86. Ⓐ Ⓑ Ⓒ Ⓓ   97. Ⓐ Ⓑ Ⓒ Ⓓ   108. Ⓐ Ⓑ Ⓒ Ⓓ

65. Ⓐ Ⓑ Ⓒ Ⓓ   76. Ⓐ Ⓑ Ⓒ Ⓓ   87. Ⓐ Ⓑ Ⓒ Ⓓ   98. Ⓐ Ⓑ Ⓒ Ⓓ   109. Ⓐ Ⓑ Ⓒ Ⓓ

66. Ⓐ Ⓑ Ⓒ Ⓓ   77. Ⓐ Ⓑ Ⓒ Ⓓ   88. Ⓐ Ⓑ Ⓒ Ⓓ   99. Ⓐ Ⓑ Ⓒ Ⓓ   110. Ⓐ Ⓑ Ⓒ Ⓓ

67. Ⓐ Ⓑ Ⓒ Ⓓ   78. Ⓐ Ⓑ Ⓒ Ⓓ   89. Ⓐ Ⓑ Ⓒ Ⓓ   100. Ⓐ Ⓑ Ⓒ Ⓓ   111. Ⓐ Ⓑ Ⓒ Ⓓ

68. Ⓐ Ⓑ Ⓒ Ⓓ   79. Ⓐ Ⓑ Ⓒ Ⓓ   90. Ⓐ Ⓑ Ⓒ Ⓓ   101. Ⓐ Ⓑ Ⓒ Ⓓ   112. Ⓐ Ⓑ Ⓒ Ⓓ

69. Ⓐ Ⓑ Ⓒ Ⓓ   80. Ⓐ Ⓑ Ⓒ Ⓓ   91. Ⓐ Ⓑ Ⓒ Ⓓ   102. Ⓐ Ⓑ Ⓒ Ⓓ

70. Ⓐ Ⓑ Ⓒ Ⓓ   81. Ⓐ Ⓑ Ⓒ Ⓓ   92. Ⓐ Ⓑ Ⓒ Ⓓ   103. Ⓐ Ⓑ Ⓒ Ⓓ

71. Ⓐ Ⓑ Ⓒ Ⓓ   82. Ⓐ Ⓑ Ⓒ Ⓓ   93. Ⓐ Ⓑ Ⓒ Ⓓ   104. Ⓐ Ⓑ Ⓒ Ⓓ

Reading

Comprehension

113. Ⓐ Ⓑ Ⓒ Ⓓ   121. Ⓐ Ⓑ Ⓒ Ⓓ   129. Ⓐ Ⓑ Ⓒ Ⓓ   137. Ⓐ Ⓑ Ⓒ Ⓓ   145. Ⓐ Ⓑ Ⓒ Ⓓ

114. Ⓐ Ⓑ Ⓒ Ⓓ   122. Ⓐ Ⓑ Ⓒ Ⓓ   130. Ⓐ Ⓑ Ⓒ Ⓓ   138. Ⓐ Ⓑ Ⓒ Ⓓ   146. Ⓐ Ⓑ Ⓒ Ⓓ

115. Ⓐ Ⓑ Ⓒ Ⓓ   123. Ⓐ Ⓑ Ⓒ Ⓓ   131. Ⓐ Ⓑ Ⓒ Ⓓ   139. Ⓐ Ⓑ Ⓒ Ⓓ   147. Ⓐ Ⓑ Ⓒ Ⓓ

116. Ⓐ Ⓑ Ⓒ Ⓓ   124. Ⓐ Ⓑ Ⓒ Ⓓ   132. Ⓐ Ⓑ Ⓒ Ⓓ   140. Ⓐ Ⓑ Ⓒ Ⓓ   148. Ⓐ Ⓑ Ⓒ Ⓓ

117. Ⓐ Ⓑ Ⓒ Ⓓ   125. Ⓐ Ⓑ Ⓒ Ⓓ   133. Ⓐ Ⓑ Ⓒ Ⓓ   141. Ⓐ Ⓑ Ⓒ Ⓓ   149. Ⓐ Ⓑ Ⓒ Ⓓ

118. Ⓐ Ⓑ Ⓒ Ⓓ   126. Ⓐ Ⓑ Ⓒ Ⓓ   134. Ⓐ Ⓑ Ⓒ Ⓓ   142. Ⓐ Ⓑ Ⓒ Ⓓ   150. Ⓐ Ⓑ Ⓒ Ⓓ

119. Ⓐ Ⓑ Ⓒ Ⓓ   127. Ⓐ Ⓑ Ⓒ Ⓓ   135. Ⓐ Ⓑ Ⓒ Ⓓ   143. Ⓐ Ⓑ Ⓒ Ⓓ   151. Ⓐ Ⓑ Ⓒ Ⓓ

120. Ⓐ Ⓑ Ⓒ Ⓓ   128. Ⓐ Ⓑ Ⓒ Ⓓ   136. Ⓐ Ⓑ Ⓒ Ⓓ   144. Ⓐ Ⓑ Ⓒ Ⓓ   152. Ⓐ Ⓑ Ⓒ Ⓓ

Vocabulary

153. Ⓐ Ⓑ Ⓒ Ⓓ   158. Ⓐ Ⓑ Ⓒ Ⓓ   163. Ⓐ Ⓑ Ⓒ Ⓓ   168. Ⓐ Ⓑ Ⓒ Ⓓ   173. Ⓐ Ⓑ Ⓒ Ⓓ

154. Ⓐ Ⓑ Ⓒ Ⓓ   159. Ⓐ Ⓑ Ⓒ Ⓓ   164. Ⓐ Ⓑ Ⓒ Ⓓ   169. Ⓐ Ⓑ Ⓒ Ⓓ   174. Ⓐ Ⓑ Ⓒ Ⓓ

155. Ⓐ Ⓑ Ⓒ Ⓓ   160. Ⓐ Ⓑ Ⓒ Ⓓ   165. Ⓐ Ⓑ Ⓒ Ⓓ   170. Ⓐ Ⓑ Ⓒ Ⓓ

156. Ⓐ Ⓑ Ⓒ Ⓓ   161. Ⓐ Ⓑ Ⓒ Ⓓ   166. Ⓐ Ⓑ Ⓒ Ⓓ   171. Ⓐ Ⓑ Ⓒ Ⓓ

157. Ⓐ Ⓑ Ⓒ Ⓓ   162. Ⓐ Ⓑ Ⓒ Ⓓ   167. Ⓐ Ⓑ Ⓒ Ⓓ   172. Ⓐ Ⓑ Ⓒ Ⓓ

Mathematics

Concepts

175. Ⓐ Ⓑ Ⓒ Ⓓ
176. Ⓐ Ⓑ Ⓒ Ⓓ
177. Ⓐ Ⓑ Ⓒ Ⓓ
178. Ⓐ Ⓑ Ⓒ Ⓓ
179. Ⓐ Ⓑ Ⓒ Ⓓ

180. Ⓐ Ⓑ Ⓒ Ⓓ
181. Ⓐ Ⓑ Ⓒ Ⓓ
182. Ⓐ Ⓑ Ⓒ Ⓓ
183. Ⓐ Ⓑ Ⓒ Ⓓ
184. Ⓐ Ⓑ Ⓒ Ⓓ

185. Ⓐ Ⓑ Ⓒ Ⓓ
186. Ⓐ Ⓑ Ⓒ Ⓓ
187. Ⓐ Ⓑ Ⓒ Ⓓ
188. Ⓐ Ⓑ Ⓒ Ⓓ
189. Ⓐ Ⓑ Ⓒ Ⓓ

190. Ⓐ Ⓑ Ⓒ Ⓓ
191. Ⓐ Ⓑ Ⓒ Ⓓ
192. Ⓐ Ⓑ Ⓒ Ⓓ
193. Ⓐ Ⓑ Ⓒ Ⓓ
194. Ⓐ Ⓑ Ⓒ Ⓓ

195. Ⓐ Ⓑ Ⓒ Ⓓ
196. Ⓐ Ⓑ Ⓒ Ⓓ
197. Ⓐ Ⓑ Ⓒ Ⓓ
198. Ⓐ Ⓑ Ⓒ Ⓓ

Problem Solving

199. Ⓐ Ⓑ Ⓒ Ⓓ
200. Ⓐ Ⓑ Ⓒ Ⓓ
201. Ⓐ Ⓑ Ⓒ Ⓓ
202. Ⓐ Ⓑ Ⓒ Ⓓ
203. Ⓐ Ⓑ Ⓒ Ⓓ
204. Ⓐ Ⓑ Ⓒ Ⓓ
205. Ⓐ Ⓑ Ⓒ Ⓓ
206. Ⓐ Ⓑ Ⓒ Ⓓ

207. Ⓐ Ⓑ Ⓒ Ⓓ
208. Ⓐ Ⓑ Ⓒ Ⓓ
209. Ⓐ Ⓑ Ⓒ Ⓓ
210. Ⓐ Ⓑ Ⓒ Ⓓ
211. Ⓐ Ⓑ Ⓒ Ⓓ
212. Ⓐ Ⓑ Ⓒ Ⓓ
213. Ⓐ Ⓑ Ⓒ Ⓓ
214. Ⓐ Ⓑ Ⓒ Ⓓ

215. Ⓐ Ⓑ Ⓒ Ⓓ
216. Ⓐ Ⓑ Ⓒ Ⓓ
217. Ⓐ Ⓑ Ⓒ Ⓓ
218. Ⓐ Ⓑ Ⓒ Ⓓ
219. Ⓐ Ⓑ Ⓒ Ⓓ
220. Ⓐ Ⓑ Ⓒ Ⓓ
221. Ⓐ Ⓑ Ⓒ Ⓓ
222. Ⓐ Ⓑ Ⓒ Ⓓ

223. Ⓐ Ⓑ Ⓒ Ⓓ
224. Ⓐ Ⓑ Ⓒ Ⓓ
225. Ⓐ Ⓑ Ⓒ Ⓓ
226. Ⓐ Ⓑ Ⓒ Ⓓ
227. Ⓐ Ⓑ Ⓒ Ⓓ
228. Ⓐ Ⓑ Ⓒ Ⓓ
229. Ⓐ Ⓑ Ⓒ Ⓓ
230. Ⓐ Ⓑ Ⓒ Ⓓ

231. Ⓐ Ⓑ Ⓒ Ⓓ
232. Ⓐ Ⓑ Ⓒ Ⓓ
233. Ⓐ Ⓑ Ⓒ Ⓓ
234. Ⓐ Ⓑ Ⓒ Ⓓ
235. Ⓐ Ⓑ Ⓒ Ⓓ
236. Ⓐ Ⓑ Ⓒ Ⓓ
237. Ⓐ Ⓑ Ⓒ Ⓓ
238. Ⓐ Ⓑ Ⓒ Ⓓ

Language

239. Ⓐ Ⓑ Ⓒ Ⓓ   251. Ⓐ Ⓑ Ⓒ Ⓓ   263. Ⓐ Ⓑ Ⓒ Ⓓ   275. Ⓐ Ⓑ Ⓒ Ⓓ   287. Ⓐ Ⓑ Ⓒ Ⓓ

240. Ⓐ Ⓑ Ⓒ Ⓓ   252. Ⓐ Ⓑ Ⓒ Ⓓ   264. Ⓐ Ⓑ Ⓒ Ⓓ   276. Ⓐ Ⓑ Ⓒ Ⓓ   288. Ⓐ Ⓑ Ⓒ Ⓓ

241. Ⓐ Ⓑ Ⓒ Ⓓ   253. Ⓐ Ⓑ Ⓒ Ⓓ   265. Ⓐ Ⓑ Ⓒ Ⓓ   277. Ⓐ Ⓑ Ⓒ Ⓓ   289. Ⓐ Ⓑ Ⓒ Ⓓ

242. Ⓐ Ⓑ Ⓒ Ⓓ   254. Ⓐ Ⓑ Ⓒ Ⓓ   266. Ⓐ Ⓑ Ⓒ Ⓓ   278. Ⓐ Ⓑ Ⓒ Ⓓ   290. Ⓐ Ⓑ Ⓒ Ⓓ

243. Ⓐ Ⓑ Ⓒ Ⓓ   255. Ⓐ Ⓑ Ⓒ Ⓓ   267. Ⓐ Ⓑ Ⓒ Ⓓ   279. Ⓐ Ⓑ Ⓒ Ⓓ   291. Ⓐ Ⓑ Ⓒ Ⓓ

244. Ⓐ Ⓑ Ⓒ Ⓓ   256. Ⓐ Ⓑ Ⓒ Ⓓ   268. Ⓐ Ⓑ Ⓒ Ⓓ   280. Ⓐ Ⓑ Ⓒ Ⓓ   292. Ⓐ Ⓑ Ⓒ Ⓓ

245. Ⓐ Ⓑ Ⓒ Ⓓ   257. Ⓐ Ⓑ Ⓒ Ⓓ   269. Ⓐ Ⓑ Ⓒ Ⓓ   281. Ⓐ Ⓑ Ⓒ Ⓓ   293. Ⓐ Ⓑ Ⓒ Ⓓ

246. Ⓐ Ⓑ Ⓒ Ⓓ   258. Ⓐ Ⓑ Ⓒ Ⓓ   270. Ⓐ Ⓑ Ⓒ Ⓓ   282. Ⓐ Ⓑ Ⓒ Ⓓ   294. Ⓐ Ⓑ Ⓒ Ⓓ

247. Ⓐ Ⓑ Ⓒ Ⓓ   259. Ⓐ Ⓑ Ⓒ Ⓓ   271. Ⓐ Ⓑ Ⓒ Ⓓ   283. Ⓐ Ⓑ Ⓒ Ⓓ   295. Ⓐ Ⓑ Ⓒ Ⓓ

248. Ⓐ Ⓑ Ⓒ Ⓓ   260. Ⓐ Ⓑ Ⓒ Ⓓ   272. Ⓐ Ⓑ Ⓒ Ⓓ   284. Ⓐ Ⓑ Ⓒ Ⓓ   296. Ⓐ Ⓑ Ⓒ Ⓓ

249. Ⓐ Ⓑ Ⓒ Ⓓ   261. Ⓐ Ⓑ Ⓒ Ⓓ   273. Ⓐ Ⓑ Ⓒ Ⓓ   285. Ⓐ Ⓑ Ⓒ Ⓓ   297. Ⓐ Ⓑ Ⓒ Ⓓ

250. Ⓐ Ⓑ Ⓒ Ⓓ   262. Ⓐ Ⓑ Ⓒ Ⓓ   274. Ⓐ Ⓑ Ⓒ Ⓓ   286. Ⓐ Ⓑ Ⓒ Ⓓ   298. Ⓐ Ⓑ Ⓒ Ⓓ

VERBAL SKILLS

60 Questions—16 Minutes

Turn to the Verbal Skills section of your answer sheet to answer the questions in this section.

Directions: Read each question carefully, then consider all options and mark the correct answer.

---

1. Which word does *not* belong with the others?

   A. One

   B. Three

   C. Fourth

   D. Nine

2. Arouse is to pacify as agitate is to

   A. smooth.

   B. ruffle.

   C. understand.

   D. ignore.

3. Henri is a much better juggler than Jerome. Francine is a better juggler than Jerome. Francine is a better juggler than Henri. If the first two statements are true, the third is

   A. true.

   B. false.

   C. uncertain.

4. Query means the *opposite* of

   A. argument.

   B. answer.

   C. square.

   D. loner.

5. *Impair* most nearly means

   A. direct.

   B. improve.

   C. stimulate.

   D. weaken.

6. Which word does *not* belong with the others?

   A. Rotate

   B. Revolve

   C. Spin

   D. Planet

7. If the wind is *variable*, it is

   A. shifting.

   B. mild.

   C. chilling.

   D. steady.

8. Egg is to beat as potato is to

   A. yam.

   B. bake.

   C. eye.

   D. mash.

9. If you *obstruct* the entrance to a building, you

   A. block it.

   B. enter it.

   C. leave it.

   D. cross it.

10. The red balloon is higher in the sky than the green balloon. The yellow balloon is higher in the sky than the red balloon. The green balloon is higher in the sky than the yellow balloon. If the first two statements are true, the third is

    A. true.

    B. false.

    C. uncertain.

11. Which word does *not* belong with the others?

    A. Blended

    B. Stirred

    C. Mixing

    D. Whisked

12. Cause means the *opposite* of

    A. affect.

    B. result.

    C. question.

    D. accident.

13. Game is to play as lemonade is to

    A. blast.

    B. drink.

    C. tart.

    D. cold.

14. Which word does *not* belong with the others?

    A. Tent

    B. Igloo

    C. Cabin

    D. Cave

15. Pepper is the shaggiest dog in the obedience school class. Pretzel is a dachshund. Pepper and Pretzel are in the same obedience school class. If the first two statements are true, the third is

    A. true.

    B. false.

    C. uncertain.

16. Camera is to lens as lightbulb is to

    A. filament.

    B. lamp.

    C. bright.

    D. watts.

17. *Revenue* most nearly means

    A. taxes.

    B. income.

    C. expenses.

    D. produce.

18. Which word does *not* belong with the others?

    A. Trapeze

    B. Wedge

    C. Lever

    D. Pulley

19. Which word does *not* belong with the others?

    A. Joy

    B. Sadness

    C. Tears

    D. Glee

20. Wendy jumps rope faster than Bozhou but slower than Inez. Dave jumps faster than Inez but slower than Deepti. Bozhou is the slowest jumper in the group. If the first two statements are true, the third is

    A. true.

    B. false.

    C. uncertain.

21. If a machine has *manual* controls, it is

    A. self-acting.

    B. simple.

    C. hand-operated.

    D. handmade.

22. *Marshy* most nearly means

    A. swampy.

    B. sandy.

    C. wooded.

    D. rocky.

23. Seal is to fish as bird is to

   A. wing.

   B. minnow.

   C. worm.

   D. snail.

24. Profit means the *opposite* of

   A. ratio.

   B. gross.

   C. net.

   D. loss.

25. Rest means the *opposite* of

   A. sleep.

   B. activity.

   C. wake.

   D. speak.

26. Which word does *not* belong with the others?

   A. Wind

   B. Gale

   C. Hurricane

   D. Zephyr

27. All people eaters are purple. No yetis eat people. No yetis are purple. If the first two statements are true, the third is

   A. true.

   B. false.

   C. uncertain.

28. A *churlish* old cat is

   A. small.

   B. tired.

   C. surly.

   D. energetic.

29. If a judge rules that a piece of evidence is *immaterial*, that means it is

   A. unclear.

   B. unimportant.

   C. unpredictable.

   D. missing.

30. Green books are heavier than red books but not as heavy as orange books. Orange books are lighter than blue books, but not as light as yellow books. Yellow books are heavier than green books. If the first two statements are true, the third is

   A. true.

   B. false.

   C. uncertain.

31. Shoe is to leather as highway is to

   A. passage.

   B. road.

   C. trail.

   D. asphalt.

32. Mend means the *opposite* of

   A. give back.

   B. change.

   C. destroy.

   D. clean.

33. Abstract means the *opposite* of

   A. art.

   B. absurd.

   C. sculpture.

   D. concrete.

34. A computer that does not *function* does not

   A. operate.

   B. finish.

   C. stop.

   D. overheat.

35. Which word does *not* belong with the others?

    A. Vitamin E

    B. Protein

    C. Meat

    D. Calcium

36. On an alien planet, all Totos are either green-eyed Yahoos or blue-tailed Gogos. All blue-tailed Gogos have brown eyes and red noses. Some Totos have red noses. If the first two statements are true, the third is

    A. true.

    B. false.

    C. uncertain.

37. A *cacophony* of sirens is

    A. loud.

    B. pleasant.

    C. melodic.

    D. helpful.

38. Which word does *not* belong with the others?

    A. Stag

    B. Monkey

    C. Bull

    D. Ram

39. Taste is to tongue as touch is to

    A. finger.

    B. eye.

    C. feeling.

    D. borrow.

40. Discord means the *opposite* of

    A. reward.

    B. record.

    C. harmony.

    D. music.

41. Which word does *not* belong with the others?

    A. Aroma

    B. Odor

    C. Scent

    D. Fumes

42. Which word does *not* belong with the others?

    A. Ride

    B. Creep

    C. Shuffle

    D. Run

43. *Fatal* most nearly means

    A. accidental.

    B. deadly.

    C. dangerous.

    D. beautiful.

44. Terry has won more races than Cleo. Cleo has won more races than Luis. Terry has won fewer races than Luis. If the first two statements are true, the third is

    A. true.

    B. false.

    C. uncertain.

45. Which word does *not* belong with the others?

    A. Glass

    B. Screen

    C. Brick

    D. Lattice

46. If the packages were kept in a *secure* place, the place was

    A. distant.

    B. safe.

    C. convenient.

    D. secret.

47. Garish means the *opposite* of

   A. dull.

   B. damp.

   C. nice.

   D. closed.

48. Horse is to foal as mother is to

   A. mare.

   B. son.

   C. stallion.

   D. father.

49. Which word does *not* belong with the others?

   A. Gelatin

   B. Tofu

   C. Gum

   D. Cracker

50. *Counterfeit* most nearly means

   A. mysterious.

   B. false.

   C. unreadable.

   D. priceless.

51. The thruway has more lanes than the parkway. The parkway has fewer lanes than the highway. The thruway has more lanes than the highway. If the first two statements are true, the third is

   A. true.

   B. false.

   C. uncertain.

52. Dog is to flea as horse is to

   A. rider.

   B. mane.

   C. fly.

   D. shoe.

53. The foghorn that sounded *intermittently* sounded

   A. constantly.

   B. annually.

   C. using intermediaries.

   D. at intervals.

54. Which word does *not* belong with the others?

   A. Greek

   B. Acrylic

   C. Latin

   D. Arabic

55. Diverse means the *opposite* of

   A. definite.

   B. understandable.

   C. similar.

   D. boring.

56. Finder is to reward as repenter is to

   A. religion.

   B. sin.

   C. absolution.

   D. contrition.

57. Which word does *not* belong with the others?

   A. Bend

   B. Explode

   C. Shatter

   D. Burst

58. The grocery store is south of the drugstore, which is between the gas station and the dry cleaner. The bookstore is north of the gas station. The grocery store is north of the dry cleaner. If the first two statements are true, the third is

   A. true.

   B. false.

   C. uncertain.

59. *Deception* most nearly means

    A. secrets.

    B. fraud.

    C. mistrust.

    D. hatred.

60. Which word does *not* belong with the others?

    A. Cotton

    B. Linen

    C. Silk

    D. Nylon

QUANTITATIVE SKILLS

52 Questions—30 Minutes

Turn to the Quantitative Skills section of your answer sheet to answer the questions in this section.

Directions: Read each question carefully, then solve the problem to find the correct answer.

61. Look at this series: 2, 4, __, 16, 32. What number should fill in the blank in the middle of the series?

A. 5

B. 6

C. 8

D. 12

62. What number is double the average of 4, 9, and 17?

A. 6

B. 8

C. 10

D. 20

63. What number is 20 more than $\frac{1}{4}$ of 48?

A. 20

B. 32

C. 48

D. 68

64. Look at this series: 3, 4, 8, 9, 13, 14, ... What number comes next?

A. 15

B. 16

C. 18

D. 20

65. Examine A, B, and C and find the best answer.

A. 50% of 20

B. 20% of 50

C. 5% of 200

A. A, B, and C are equal

B. A is greater than B and less than C.

C. A is greater than C.

D. A is less than B.

66. Examine A, B, and C, and find the best answer.

A   B   C

A. A, B, and C are equally shaded.

B. A is more shaded than B.

C. C is shaded more than A or B.

D. C is shaded less than A.

67. What number is 5 less than 9^2?

A. 5

B. 13

C. 76

D. 86

68. Examine A, B, and C and find the best answer.

A. $4 + (3 \times 2)$

B. $(4 + 3) \times 2$

C. $(3 + 2) \times 4$

A. A is greater than B and C.

B. B is greater than A and C.

C. C is less than A and B.

D. C is greater than A and B.

69. What number subtracted from 22 leaves 3 more than half of 26?

A. 6

B. 13

C. 16

D. 19

70. Examine the square and find the best answer.

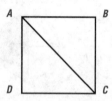

A. *AB*, *BC*, and *AC* are all equal.

B. *AC* is greater than *CD*.

C. *AC* and *AB* are equal.

D. *BC* is greater than *AD*.

71. Look at this series: 3, 6, 8, 16, 18, ...
What number should come next?

A. 18

B. 20

C. 36

D. 38

72. What number is 7 more than half of 14?

A. 0

B. 7

C. 14

D. 21

73. Look at this series: A, B, B, A, B, B, A, B, ...
What should the next three terms of this series be?

A. B, A, B

B. A, A, A

C. B, B, A

D. A, A, B

74. Examine A, B, and C and find the best answer.

A. 6^2

B. 5^2

C. 3^2

A. $A < B < C$

B. $A = B < C$

C. $A > B > C$

D. $A = B = C$

75. Look at this series: $2\frac{1}{2}$, 4, $5\frac{1}{2}$, 7, ...
What number should come next?

A. $7\frac{1}{2}$

B. 8

C. $8\frac{1}{2}$

D. 9

76. Look at this series: 67, 73, ___, 85, 91.
What number should fill in the blank?

A. 78

B. 79

C. 80

D. 81

77. Examine the triangle and find the best answer.

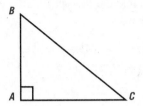

   A. *AB* is equal to *BC*.
   B. *AC* is equal to *BC*.
   C. *BC* is greater than *AB*.
   D. *BC* is less than *AC*.

78. Look at this series: Z5, Y7, X9, W11, ...
   What term should come next?

   A. T12
   B. S12
   C. U13
   D. V13

79. What number can be averaged with 10 to get 12?

   A. 10
   B. 12
   C. 14
   D. 16

80. How many nickels are equal to three quarters and two dimes?

   A. 5
   B. 18
   C. 19
   D. 20

81. Look at this series: 2, 0, 2, 0, 0, 2, 0, 0, 0, 2, ...
   What should the next four terms be?

   A. 0, 0, 0, 0
   B. 0, 0, 0, 2
   C. 0, 2, 0, 2
   D. 2, 2, 2, 2

82. What number is seven more than $\frac{1}{3}$ of 12^2?

   A. 42
   B. 48
   C. 55
   D. 57

83. Look at this series: 9, 7, 8, 6, 7, 5, 6, ...
   What number should come next?

   A. 4
   B. 5
   C. 6
   D. 7

84. How many millimeters are in 355 meters?

   A. 3,550
   B. 35,000
   C. 355,000
   D. 3,550,000

85. Look at this series: A, BB, CCC, DDDD, ...
   What term should come next?

   A. EEEE
   B. EEEEE
   C. E
   D. EEE

86. Examine A, B, and C and choose the best answer.

   A. 50% of 30
   B. 25% of 60
   C. 10% of 100

   A. A = B = C
   B. A = B > C
   C. A < B = C
   D. A < B < C

87. Look at this series: __, 5, 9, 12, 16, 19.
What number should fill in the blank?

A. 1

B. 2

C. 3

D. 4

88. What is half of a quarter of six squared?

A. 1.5

B. 3

C. 4.5

D. 6

89. Look at this series: 1, 4, 7, 10, 13, ...
If the pattern continues, what number will *not* eventually appear?

A. 16

B. 18

C. 19

D. 22

90. Examine the square and the rectangle and find the best answer.

A. The area of the square is greater than the area of the rectangle.

B. The perimeter of the square is greater than the perimeter of the rectangle.

C. The area of the square is equal to the area of the rectangle.

D. The perimeter of the square is equal to the perimeter of the rectangle.

91. Look at this series: 1, 2, 4, 8, 16, 32, ...
Which term of this series will be the first to exceed 100?

A. 7th

B. 8th

C. 9th

D. 10th

92. What number is 75% of the median of {1, 2, 3, 3, 4, 5, 6, 9, 9, 14, 17, 20}?

A. $\dfrac{11}{3}$

B. $\dfrac{13}{4}$

C. $\dfrac{28}{6}$

D. $\dfrac{33}{8}$

93. Examine the parallelogram and choose the best answer.

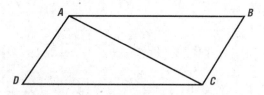

A. *AD* is greater than *BC*.

B. *CD* is less than *AB*.

C. The area of the parallelogram is equal to the area of triangle *ABC*.

D. The perimeter of triangle *ABC* is equal to the perimeter of triangle *ADC*.

94. Look at this series: ABC, CDE, EFG, GHI, ...
What term should come next?

A. IJK

B. JKL

C. HIJ

D. GIJ

95. What is the reciprocal of $\frac{18}{5} \div 3$?

   A. $\frac{4}{7}$

   B. $\frac{5}{6}$

   C. $\frac{12}{10}$

   D. $\frac{18}{15}$

96. Examine A, B, and C and choose the best answer.

   A. $(3 + 2) \div 5$

   B. $(3 + 1) \div 4$

   C. $(2 + 4) \div 3$

   A. A is equal to B and less than C.

   B. A is equal to C.

   C. B is equal to C.

   D. C is less than A and B.

97. The square of what number is equal to 7 more than the square of 3?

   A. 3

   B. 4

   C. 9

   D. 16

98. Look at this series: 13, 24, 35, 46, ... What number comes next?

   A. 52

   B. 53

   C. 56

   D. 57

99. What number is 5 less than half the average of 7, 9, and 26?

   A. 1

   B. 2

   C. 3

   D. 4

100. Examine the rectangles A, B, and C and choose the best answer.

   A. The shading in A is greater than the shading in B.

   B. The shading is the same in all three rectangles.

   C. The shading in C is more than the shading in A and B.

   D. The shading in B is less than the shading in C.

101. Look at this series: 0, –2, –4, –6, –12, –14, –28, ... What number should come next?

   A. –30

   B. –26

   C. –20

   D. 26

102. There are on average 27.5 students for every teacher, and eight teachers per principal. How many students are there if the district has 14 principals?

   A. 3,020.5

   B. 3,080

   C. 3,120

   D. 3,200.5

103. Examine the cube and choose the best answer.

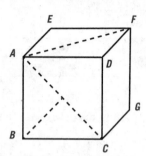

   A. *AC* is equal to *DF*.

   B. *AC* is equal to *AF*.

   C. *CG* is equal to *AF*.

   D. *AE* is equal to *AC*.

104. Examine A, B, and C, and find the best answer in terms of how much white (unshaded area) is visible in the figure.

   A. A > B < C

   B. A < B > C

   C. A < B < C

   D. A > B > C

105. Examine A, B, and C and choose the best answer.

   A. $\frac{3}{4}$

   B. $\frac{5}{8}$

   C. $\frac{3}{8}$

   A. A < B < C

   B. B < C < A

   C. C < A < B

   D. C < B < A

106. What is $\frac{1}{3}$ of the largest two-digit number?

   A. 3

   B. 9

   C. 33

   D. 99

107. Look at this series: 4, __, 10, __, 16. If the pattern is to add the same number for each step, what two numbers are missing?

   A. 6 and 13

   B. 6 and 12

   C. 7 and 12

   D. 7 and 13

108. Which series has a pattern that uses both addition and multiplication?

   A. 2, 3, 6, 7, 14, 15, 30

   B. 1, 2, 4, 8, 16, 32, 64

   C. 2, 4, 6, 8, 10, 12, 14

   D. 8, 7, 6, 5, 4, 3, 2

109. Examine the circle, square, and triangle, and choose the best answer.

   A. All the shapes have an equal area.

   B. The area of the square is equal to the area of the triangle, and greater than the area of the circle.

   C. The area of the triangle is equal to the area of the circle.

   D. The area of the square is greater than the area of the triangle.

110. Examine A, B, and C and choose the best answer.

A. 6 more than $\frac{1}{3}$ of 21

B. 2 less than $\frac{1}{2}$ of 26

C. 5 more than $\frac{1}{4}$ of 100

A. C > A > B
B. A > B = C
C. A = B = C
D. A > B > C

111. The variable x is the average of 10, 10, and 11. The best answer would state that

A. x is less than 10.
B. x is between 10 and 11.
C. x is between 11 and 12.
D. x is greater than 12.

112. Examine A, B, and C and choose the best answer.

A. 3 dimes and 17 pennies

B. 4 dimes and 2 nickels

C. 2 quarters

A. A < B = C
B. A = B < C
C. A < B < C
D. A = B = C

READING

62 Questions—25 Minutes

Comprehension

Turn to the Reading Comprehension section of your answer sheet to answer the questions in this section.

Directions: Read each passage and review the associated questions, then reread—if necessary—to find the correct answer.

Questions 113–122 refer to the following passage.

Early in the nineteenth century, American youth were playing a game, somewhat like the English game of rounders, that contained all the elements of modern baseball. It was neither scientifically planned nor skillfully played, but it furnished considerable excitement for players and spectators alike. The playing field was

Line
5   a sixty-foot square with goals, or bases, at each of its four corners. A pitcher stationed himself at the center of the square, and a catcher and an indefinite number of fielders supported the pitcher and completed the team. None of these players, usually between 8 and 20 on a side, covered the bases. The batter was ruled out for balls caught on the fly or on the first bounce, and a base runner was out if he was hit by a thrown ball while off base. The bat was nothing more than a stout paddle with a two-inch-thick handle. The ball was apt to be an <u>impromptu</u> affair composed of a bullet, cork, or metal slug tightly wound with wool yarn and

10 string. With its simple equipment and only a few rules, this game steadily increased in popularity during the first half of the century.

113. Which of the following titles best expresses the main idea of the selection?

    A. "Baseball Rules"

    B. "An English Game"

    C. "Baseball's Predecessor"

    D. "American Pastimes"

114. The rules of this game required

    A. 8 fielders.

    B. a pitcher, a catcher, and one fielder for each base.

    C. 20 fielders.

    D. no specific number of players.

115. The shape of the playing field was

    A. oblong.

    B. irregular.

    C. square.

    D. subject to no rules.

116. The game was

    A. scientifically planned.

    B. exciting for the players but boring to watch.

    C. boring for the players but exciting to watch.

    D. like an English game called "rounders."

117. The underlined word *impromptu*, as used in this passage, most nearly means

    A. proven.

    B. unavoidable.

    C. improvised.

    D. argued about.

118. This passage roughly places the playing of this game between the years of

    A. 1900 to 1950.

    B. 1800 to 1850.

    C. 1700 to 1750.

    D. 1760 to 1790.

119. This selection suggests that

    A. the game continued growing in its popularity.

    B. the game was dangerous.

    C. baseball originated in the United States.

    D. the game required skilled players.

120. According to the author, the popularity of this game was based largely upon

    A. the excitement of watching skillful players.

    B. the low cost of equipment.

    C. the fact that none of the players covered the bases.

    D. it being a new, strictly American game.

121. Based on the passage, we can infer that the game is different from modern baseball in that

    A. the game in the passage includes four bases.

    B. the game in the passage is more like rounders.

    C. baseball is nothing like the game in the passage.

    D. baseball is more organized and has more official rules.

122. The writer of this selection

    A. disdains this game because of its unprofessional aspects.

    B. is nostalgic for days when games were simpler.

    C. presents a factual report.

    D. admires the ingenuity of American youth.

Questions 123–132 refer to the following passage.

Nuclear power is generated is through a process known as nuclear fission. The term *fission* means "to split," as nuclear fission occurs when an atom absorbs an extra neutron, or an atomic particle that has no electrical charge. If an atom is hit by a neutron traveling at high speed, the atom will split into two or more
Line parts. Two types of atoms that release considerable energy when split are uranium and plutonium. When
5 uranium or plutonium atoms are split, they release a great deal of energy. They also release more neutrons, which causes the splitting process to continue. This continued splitting process is known as a nuclear chain reaction. It is the process that enables nuclear fission to create power.

Most nuclear reactors today use uranium as the main element in the fission process. Uranium is found naturally in the earth and is extracted through mining. When natural uranium is first mined, it contains
10 two components known as Uranium-235 and Uranium-238. The first component, Uranium-235, creates large amounts of energy in a nuclear reaction and can therefore be used for the fission process. The second component, Uranium-238, cannot be used in the fission process and must be discarded. However, most natural uranium is made up of 99.3 percent U-238 and only 0.07 percent U-235. Before the uranium is used in nuclear reactions, then, it first goes through a process known as enrichment. The <u>enriched</u> uranium
15 contains much more of the usable U-235 than natural uranium—about 4 or 5 percent.

123. When natural uranium is first mined, how much of it is usable in a nuclear reactor?

   A. 0.07 percent

   B. 4 percent

   C. 96 percent

   D. 99. 3 percent

124. In a nuclear chain reaction, what causes the nuclear splitting process to continue?

   A. The neutrons released when uranium or plutonium atoms are split

   B. The energy released when uranium or plutonium atoms are split

   C. The radioactive waste produced when uranium or plutonium atoms are split

   D. The fuel rods used to house the fission process, during which uranium atoms are split

125. All the following statements are true according to the passage *except*

   A. plutonium atoms release a lot of energy when split.

   B. natural uranium does not contain enough usable U-235.

   C. nuclear fission is an entirely natural process.

   D. power is created by a nuclear chain reaction.

126. The underlined word *enriched*, as used in this passage, most nearly means

   A. weakened.

   B. strengthened.

   C. wealthier.

   D. lightened.

127. A neutron is a particle that has

   A. a negative electrical charge.

   B. a positive electrical charge.

   C. no electrical charge.

   D. an alternating electrical charge.

128. What do the elements uranium and plutonium have in common?

   A. They both contain atoms that split very easily.

   B. They do not possess any neutrons.

   C. They both are enriched by one another.

   D. They both have a positive electrical charge.

129. A nuclear chain reaction is the process that creates

   A. enriched uranium.

   B. nuclear reactors.

   C. an electrical charge.

   D. nuclear power.

130. How many uranium components are found in uranium in its natural state?

   A. None

   B. One

   C. Two

   D. Four

131. The author's purpose in writing this selection was most probably to

   A. warn people of the dangers of nuclear power.

   B. explain how nuclear power is created.

   C. promote the benefits of nuclear power.

   D. explore alternatives to fossil fuels.

132. Which of the following titles best expresses the main idea of this passage?

   A. "The Discovery of Nuclear Fission"

   B. "The Uses of Nuclear Fission"

   C. "The Process of Nuclear Fission"

   D. "The Varieties of Nuclear Fission"

Questions 133–142 refer to the following passage.

Have you ever wondered about the origins of the humble and unassuming fortune cookie? Many people have been introduced to these curious little treats at the <u>cessation</u> of a meal at a Chinese restaurant—after eating, your waiter or waitress brought you a small plate with fortune cookies for your table on it. You'd
Line
then carefully select a cookie, crack it open, and read your fortune on the small slip of paper inside while
5   eating the cookie. These intriguing slips of paper may contain a wise saying, a prophecy, or even a good luck phrase and numbers. Whether or not that slip of paper truly holds your fortune is best left to fate to decide. For many, their first experience with fortune cookies left an <u>indelible</u> mark on their memories. But where do these cookies come from?

Believe it or not, the origins of the fortune cookie are as mysterious as the messages found inside of
10   them. Traditional fortune cookies were handmade, and claims as to who invented it are varied and far-reaching, spanning countries across the globe—folks in the United States, Japan, and China all claim to have invented the fortune cookie. Variations of the fortune cookie go back at least as far as 19th-century Japan, although they didn't resemble the modern cookies many people recognize today. Some even claim that the roots of the fortune cookie go back as far as the late 17th century in Romania, where "note pies"
15   were commonly served as part of elegant royal feasts. Others declare that Japanese mooncakes from the Ming revolution, which contained hidden messages, are the direct ancestors of modern fortune cookies. Regarding the origins of the fortune cookie, only one thing seems certain—the dispute as to who invented them may never be definitively settled.

Today's fortune cookies, typically made with vanilla, butter, flour, sugar, and sesame oil, are often
20   manufactured by huge machines—a big change from traditional cookies. Approximately 3 billion fortune cookies are made worldwide every year, and they are always a welcome sight at meals, gatherings, and special events. We may not always be able to predict the future, but hopefully we'll always have fortune cookies around to help us get a glimpse of what's in store for us.

133. Which of the following titles best expresses the main idea of this passage?

   A. "Fortune Cookies: A Mysterious Treat with Mysterious Origins"

   B. "What is Your Favorite Treat after a Good Meal?"

   C. "An Exploration of Hidden Messages and Secret Codes"

   D. "A History of the World's Most Popular and Beloved Cookie"

134. The underlined word *cessation*, as used in this passage, most nearly means

   A. ending.

   B. beginning.

   C. climax.

   D. middle.

135. The best word to sum up the author's beliefs regarding the origins of the fortune cookie is

   A. obvious.

   B. unclear.

   C. traceable.

   D. humorous.

136. The author refers to modern, machine-made fortune cookies as "a big change from traditional cookies" because

   A. no one knows who invented traditional fortune cookies.

   B. traditional fortune cookies were larger and had different ingredients.

   C. traditional fortune cookies were made by hand.

   D. traditional fortune cookies tasted better.

137. The word *indelible*, as used in this passage, most nearly means

  A. inedible.

  B. brief.

  C. unimaginable.

  D. unforgettable.

138. Based on the information in the passage, can we conclude that fortune cookies are the author's favorite cookie?

  A. Yes, the author says that this is his or her favorite type of cookie.

  B. Yes, that's the only reason the author would write this passage.

  C. No, there's not enough information in the passage to determine this.

  D. No, the author most likely prefers another type of cookie.

139. According to the information in the passage, all the following ingredients make up the modern fortune cookie *except*

  A. vanilla.

  B. cinnamon.

  C. butter.

  D. flour.

140. According to the information in the passage, all the following are possible things you'd find in a fortune cookie fortune *except* a

  A. funny riddle.

  B. wise saying.

  C. prophecy.

  D. good luck phrase.

141. What is the author's most likely purpose for writing this passage?

  A. To practice writing an investigative essay

  B. To confess his or her obsession with fortune cookies

  C. To inform readers about the origin of fortune cookies

  D. To persuade readers to eat more fortune cookies

142. According to the information in the passage, fortune cookies were potentially invented in which of the following places?

  A. Thailand

  B. Brazil

  C. Bali

  D. Japan

Questions 143–152 refer to the following passage.

By the mere age of 25, Orson Welles had already distinguished himself in multiple areas of the entertainment field. He'd founded his own theater group called the Mercury Theatre that not only produced dramas for the stage but also crafted celebrated radio plays. He'd inadvertently executed one of history's most noteworthy

Line hoaxes when many people mistook his radio production of H.G. Welles's novel *The War of the Worlds*, a

5 thrilling tale about a Martian invasion, for an actual news report. However, despite his multiple achievements and <u>claims to fame</u>, even Welles must have been surprised by the outcome of his very first foray into the world of cinema. When the 25-year old wrote, directed, and starred in *Citizen Kane* for RKO Pictures, he made what is often considered to be the greatest film of all time because of its innovative storytelling, superb acting, and experimental filmmaking techniques. Perhaps most incredible of all is the fact that

10 audiences did not embrace *Citizen Kane* eagerly when it was first released. In fact, the film ultimately lost money for RKO. Of course, for the man who once said, "I have always been more interested in experiment than in accomplishment," such financial failure could not have mattered much.

143. Orson Welles was a

   A. filmmaker.

   B. film critic.

   C. film studio chief.

   D. film teacher.

144. Orson Welles's version of *The War of the Worlds* is a

   A. novel.

   B. radio play.

   C. stage play.

   D. film.

145. By his statement, "I have always been more interested in experiment, than in accomplishment," Orson Welles implies that he

   A. thought that every artist should be mainly focused on trying new things.

   B. was afraid that people might find out how little money *Citizen Kane* made.

   C. preferred making original art to being thought of as successful.

   D. knew that his work was too experimental but did not care.

146. The phrase "claims to fame," as used in the passage, most nearly means

   A. arguments for success.

   B. noteworthy achievements.

   C. statements about popularity.

   D. maintains celebrity.

147. Orson Welles formed the Mercury Theatre

   A. when he was 25-years old.

   B. in order to perform *The War of the Worlds*.

   C. for RKO Pictures.

   D. before he made *Citizen Kane*.

148. Orson Welles

   A. was extremely creative.

   B. was the greatest artist ever.

   C. produced more successful work than failures.

   D. respected everyone who made great art.

149. Critics who praised *Citizen Kane* did not

   A. think Orson Welles deserved so much credit for making the film.

   B. give any other film as much praise as they showered on *Citizen Kane*.

   C. care that few people went to see the film.

   D. convince many people to see the film when it was released.

150. Based on this passage, Orson Welles would probably *not* choose to

   A. act in a stage play.

   B. write a movie script.

   C. direct a radio play.

   D. paint a picture.

151. In the first sentence, the writer uses "mere" to describe Orson Welles's age because

   A. Welles was very inexperienced when he made *Citizen Kane*.

   B. most people thought Welles was too old to make *Citizen Kane*.

   C. 25 is a relatively young age at which to make such an important film.

   D. Welles had just turned 25 when he made his first film.

152. *Citizen Kane* was probably popular with film critics because they

   A. always appreciated films like *Citizen Kane*.

   B. appreciated its many impressive qualities.

   C. liked the other films Orson Welles had made.

   D. thought Orson Welles was a good actor.

Vocabulary

Turn to the Vocabulary section of your answer sheet to answer the questions in this section.

> **Directions:** Choose the answer that's closest in meaning to the underlined word in the question.

153. tedious work

    A. technical

    B. interesting

    C. tiresome

    D. confidential

154. to rescind an order

    A. revise

    B. cancel

    C. misinterpret

    D. confirm

155. a histrionic reaction

    A. confusing

    B. impressive

    C. dramatic

    D. productive

156. the problem of indigence

    A. poverty

    B. corruption

    C. intolerance

    D. laziness

157. a vindictive person

    A. prejudiced

    B. unpopular

    C. petty

    D. revengeful

158. unsatisfactory remuneration

    A. payment

    B. summary

    C. explanation

    D. estimate

159. a deficient program

    A. excellent

    B. inadequate

    C. demanding

    D. interrupted

160. a detrimental influence

    A. favorable

    B. lasting

    C. harmful

    D. restraining

161. accurate information

    A. correct

    B. good

    C. ample

    D. useful

162. to amplify one's remarks

    A. soften

    B. simplify

    C. enlarge

    D. repeat

163. to be legally <u>competent</u>

   A. expert

   B. ineligible

   C. accused

   D. able

164. a <u>shrewd</u> comment

   A. clever

   B. boring

   C. tired

   D. meaningless

165. a <u>relevant</u> article

   A. applicable

   B. controversial

   C. miscellaneous

   D. recent

166. an office <u>manual</u>

   A. laborer

   B. handbook

   C. typewriter

   D. handle

167. a computational <u>device</u>

   A. calculator

   B. adder

   C. mathematician

   D. machine

168. a <u>conventional</u> test

   A. agreeable

   B. public

   C. large-scale

   D. ordinary

169. the subject of <u>controversy</u>

   A. annoyance

   B. debate

   C. envy

   D. review

170. a <u>diplomatic</u> person

   A. well-dressed

   B. tactful

   C. domineering

   D. tricky

171. an <u>irate</u> student

   A. irresponsible

   B. untidy

   C. insubordinate

   D. angry

172. <u>durable</u> paint

   A. cheap

   B. long-lasting

   C. easily applied

   D. quick-drying

173. an intense <u>skirmish</u>

   A. conversation

   B. conflict

   C. meal

   D. package

174. the <u>inception</u> of the program

   A. beginning

   B. discussion

   C. rejection

   D. purpose

MATHEMATICS
64 Questions—45 Minutes

Concepts

Turn to the Mathematics Concepts section of your answer sheet to answer the questions in this section.

Directions: Read each question carefully, then solve the problem to find the correct answer.

175. Which of the following could be a valid measurement for the speed at which a car is moving?

    A. 6 minutes
    B. 5 miles per hour
    C. 17 kilometers
    D. 14 pounds per inch

176. If there are five numbers, all of which are between 4 and 9, which of the following *cannot* be the average of these numbers?

    A. 3
    B. 4
    C. 5
    D. 6

177. It is possible for a scalene triangle to also be

    A. right.
    B. equilateral.
    C. isosceles.
    D. equiangular.

178. Which of the following is true?

    A. $a(b + c) = ab + c$
    B. $a + (b + c) = ab + ac$
    C. $(a + b) + c = a + (b + c)$
    D. $ab + ac = a + bc$

179. Which of these is a unit of volume?

    A. Square inches
    B. Seconds
    C. Pounds
    D. Cubic centimeters

180. If the radius of a circle is 3, what is its diameter?

    A. 1.5
    B. 3
    C. 6
    D. 9

181. Which of the following is the best unit of measure to use for the weight of a pencil?

    A. Ounces
    B. Pounds
    C. Tons
    D. Kilometers

182. Which of the following is a quadrilateral?

    A. Circle
    B. Pentagon
    C. Triangle
    D. Rhombus

183. If there are 2.54 centimeters in an inch, which of the following is closest to the number of centimeters in 10 inches?

    A. 20
    B. 25
    C. 30
    D. 35

184. If there are y kilometers in a mile, which expression represents the number of kilometers in k miles?

   A. ky

   B. $k + y$

   C. $y \div k$

   D. $k \div y$

185. To multiply a number by 100, move the decimal point

   A. one place to the right.

   B. two places to the left.

   C. three places to the right.

   D. two places to the right.

186. Which of these is a correctly written scientific notation?

   A. $0.038 = 3.8 \times 10^{-2}$

   B. $0.38 = 3.8 \times 10^{-2}$

   C. $380 = 3.8 \times 10^{3}$

   D. $3,800 = 3.8 \times 10^{2}$

187. Which of the following is true?

   A. $8 \leq 6$

   B. $6 \geq 6$

   C. $0.080 > 0.08$

   D. $15 < 8$

188. If two angles in a triangle are measured at 48° and 92°, what is the size of the third angle?

   A. 30°

   B. 40°

   C. 140°

   D. 180°

189. Evaluate: $3\frac{1}{2} + 2\frac{1}{4} - 1\frac{3}{4}$

   A. $1\frac{3}{5}$

   B. $2\frac{1}{2}$

   C. $3\frac{3}{4}$

   D. 4

190. A squirrel collected 165 acorns over the course of a 30-day month. On average, how many acorns did it collect per day?

   A. 3.9

   B. 4.1

   C. 5.5

   D. 6.2

191. A book was sold for $14.70, which was 30% off its regular price. What is its regular price?

   A. $16

   B. $17

   C. $19

   D. $21

192. There are 5,280 feet in a mile, and 3 feet in a yard. How many yards are in half a mile?

   A. 750

   B. 770

   C. 800

   D. 880

193. Consider this list of numbers: 3, 5, 9, 9, 2, 7, 1. Find the median and mode of the list. What is the average of the median and mode?

   A. 4

   B. 5

   C. 6

   D. 7

194. Simplify: $2\frac{2}{3} \times 4\frac{1}{4}$

   A. $10\frac{1}{3}$

   B. $10\frac{3}{4}$

   C. $11\frac{1}{3}$

   D. $11\frac{2}{3}$

195. What is the greatest common factor of 24 and 40?

   A. 4

   B. 8

   C. 10

   D. 16

196. The square root of 60 is between

   A. 5 and 6.

   B. 6 and 7.

   C. 7 and 8.

   D. 8 and 9.

197. Using a standard 6-sided number cube, what is the probability of rolling an even number?

   A. 25%

   B. 50%

   C. 75%

   D. 100%

198. What is the length of the hypotenuse in the triangle?

   A. 4

   B. 5

   C. 6

   D. 7

Problem Solving

Turn to the Mathematics Problem Solving section of your answer sheet to answer the questions in this section.

Directions: Read each question carefully, then solve the problem to find the correct answer.

199. Which set of numbers has a median of 13?

  A. 10, 12, 14, 15

  B. 12, 13, 14, 15, 16

  C. 10, 12, 12, 13, 13

  D. 9, 10, 15, 16

200. The perimeter of this shape is

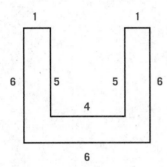

  A. 34

  B. 36

  C. 37

  D. 39

201. In a base-five system of numeration, what are the next three counting numbers after $43_{(5)}$?

  A. $44_{(5)}, 45_{(5)}, 50_{(5)}$

  B. $44_{(5)}, 45_{(5)}, 46_{(5)}$

  C. $44_{(5)}, 50_{(5)}, 52_{(5)}$

  D. $44_{(5)}, 100_{(5)}, 101_{(5)}$

202. Which one of the following is *not* equal to $62\frac{1}{2}\%$?

  A. $\frac{10}{16}$

  B. $\frac{5}{8}$

  C. 0.625

  D. 62.5

203. Solve: $12 - 2\frac{3}{16} =$

  A. $10\frac{13}{16}$

  B. $10\frac{3}{16}$

  C. $9\frac{13}{16}$

  D. $9\frac{3}{16}$

204. If $5(1 - 2x) + 25 = 0$, then $x =$ _____ .

  A. -3

  B. 3

  C. 15

  D. 20

205. Solve: $2\frac{1}{2} + 7\frac{2}{3} + \frac{3}{4} =$

  A. $10\frac{1}{4}$

  B. $10\frac{11}{12}$

  C. $11\frac{1}{2}$

  D. $11\frac{7}{12}$

206. Solve: $6.41\overline{)3.6537}$

A. 67

B. 57

C. 0.57

D. 0.47

207. If $A = 3$, $B = 2$, and $C = 6$, find $\dfrac{3ABC}{2A}$.

A. $4\dfrac{1}{6}$

B. $4\dfrac{1}{2}$

C. 16

D. 18

208. Simplify: $4\dfrac{2}{5} \times 2\dfrac{3}{11}$

A. $1\dfrac{117}{125}$

B. $6\dfrac{1}{2}$

C. $8\dfrac{6}{55}$

D. 10

209. If $\dfrac{5}{6}x = 30$, then $x =$

A. 20

B. 25

C. 36

D. 42

210. The product of 11 and 12 is 3 more than N. What is N?

A. 126

B. 129

C. 132

D. 135

211. Solve for x: $2.5x + 12.5 = 30$

A. 7

B. 9

C. 17

D. 70

212. Add in base 5:

$$143_{(5)}$$
$$+\quad 33_{(5)}$$

A. $131_{(5)}$

B. $221_{(5)}$

C. $231_{(5)}$

D. $241_{(5)}$

213. $\dfrac{3 \times 8}{6 \times 5} =$

A. $\dfrac{1}{6}$

B. $\dfrac{2}{3}$

C. $\dfrac{3}{4}$

D. $\dfrac{4}{5}$

214. What does 493 look like written out in expanded form using exponents?

A. $(4 \times 10^2) + (9 \times 10) + 3$

B. $(4 \times 10^3) + (9 \times 10^2) + (3 \times 10)$

C. $(4 \times 10^1) + (9 \times 10) + 3$

D. None of the above

215. Solve: $\dfrac{1\frac{3}{4} - \frac{1}{8}}{\frac{1}{8}} =$

 A. 12

 B. 13

 C. 14

 D. 15

216. $(3+4)^3 =$

 A. 21

 B. 91

 C. 343

 D. 490

217. Find the area of a triangle with the dimensions $b = 12'$, $h = 14'$.

 A. 24 sq. ft.

 B. 42 sq. ft.

 C. 84 sq. ft.

 D. 168 sq. ft.

218. If the average of 10, x, and 20 is equal to 30, what is the value of x?

 A. 10

 B. 20

 C. 60

 D. 80

219. If the three sides of a triangle have lengths $x + 1$, $2x$, and $3x - 2$, what is the perimeter of the triangle in terms of x?

 A. $6x - 1$

 B. $6x$

 C. $5x + 3$

 D. $x + 7$

220. Sally is 3 years older than Jim, and Jim is 2 years younger than Kate. Sally is 12 years old. How old is Kate?

 A. 9

 B. 10

 C. 11

 D. 12

221. The ratio of boys to girls in Mr. Castillo's class is 2:3. If there are 12 girls in the class, how many boys are there?

 A. 4

 B. 6

 C. 8

 D. 10

222. A $35 shirt is on sale for 20% off. How much is the sale price?

 A. $14

 B. $20

 C. $28

 D. $35

223. If the square has a perimeter of 40, what is the area of the circle?

 A. 2π

 B. 15π

 C. 20π

 D. 25π

224. A board is 7 feet 8 inches long. A piece measuring 2 feet 10 inches is cut from one end. What is the remaining length of the board?

    A. 4 feet 10 inches

    B. 5 feet

    C. 5 feet 2 inches

    D. 5 feet 3 inches

225. Ruriko bought 3 boxes of pencils for $2.50 each, and 2 large erasers for $1.75 each. How much did she spend altogether?

    A. $4.25

    B. $9.80

    C. $10.75

    D. $11.00

226. A bag contains both cherry and lemon-flavored candies. If the bag contains 50 candies altogether, and the ratio of cherry to lemon candies is 4:1, how many lemon candies are in the bag?

    A. 10

    B. 20

    C. 30

    D. 40

227. A bag contains 3 blue chips, 5 green chips, and 6 red chips. If a chip is chosen at random from this bag, what is the probability that it is *not* green?

    A. $\frac{1}{3}$

    B. $\frac{5}{14}$

    C. $\frac{3}{7}$

    D. $\frac{9}{14}$

228. The perimeter of a rectangular garden is 120 feet. The length of the garden is 20 feet. What is the area of the garden, in square feet?

    A. 140

    B. 700

    C. 800

    D. 2,400

229. Two thirds of a number added to half the same number equals 14. What is the number?

    A. 6

    B. 9

    C. 10

    D. 12

230. Silver costs $17 per ounce. What is the cost of 3 pounds of silver?

    A. $792

    B. $794

    C. $816

    D. $1,078

231. Charles is $x + 3$ years old, and his sister Jenna is $2x + 1$ years old. If Jenna is 13, how old is Charles?

    A. 6

    B. 7

    C. 8

    D. 9

232. The population of a certain sample of bacteria doubles every 3 days. If there are 126 bacteria on a Monday morning, how many will there be on Wednesday morning of the following week?

    A. 936

    B. 1,008

    C. 1,134

    D. 1,200

233. On a certain day, there is a 25% chance of rain and a 30% chance of snow. What is the probability that it neither rains nor snows?

A. 45%

B. 55%

C. 65%

D. 75%

234. Admission to a museum is $3 for children and $7 for adults. On a certain day, the museum had 80 adult visitors. If they earned a total of $851 that day, how many children visitors did they have?

A. 61

B. 80

C. 97

D. 102

235. Giorgio has $40, and he wants to buy a game that costs $38.50 before a 6% sales tax. How much more money does he need?

A. $0.81

B. $1.20

C. $1.55

D. $1.98

236. A store puts $17 pants on sale at a 20% discount. What is the new selling price?

A. $3.40

B. $12.65

C. $13.60

D. $16.80

237. What is the difference between $(4 \times 10^3) + 6$ and $(2 \times 10^3) + (3 \times 10) + 8$?

A. 55,968

B. 10,213

C. 3,765

D. 1,968

238.

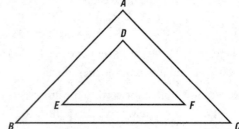

In the figure above, the sides of $\triangle ABC$ are respectively parallel to the sides of $\triangle DEF$. If the complement of $\angle A$ is 40°, then the complement of $\angle D$ is

A. 20°

B. 40°

C. 50°

D. 60°

LANGUAGE
60 Questions—25 Minutes

Turn to the Language section of your answer sheet to answer the questions in this section.

> **Directions:** In questions 239–267, look for errors in capitalization, punctuation, or usage. Then, mark the answer choice containing that error. If there is no error, mark D on your answer sheet.

239. **A.** We had swum across the lake before the sun rose.
   B. Clearly visible on the desk were those letters he claimed to have mailed yesterday.
   C. John Kennedy effected many executive reforms during the tragically few years that he served as president of the United States.
   D. *(No mistakes)*

240. **A.** The waiter brought a salad two steaks and a glass of iced tea to the corner table.
   B. Everyone looked forward to the circus; each year, a new venue was chosen to host the spectacle.
   C. Can we please stop making such a big deal about leaving the sleeping bag in the car?
   D. *(No mistakes)*

241. **A.** Rather than go with Jordan, he decided to stay at home.
   B. Each of the nurses were scrupulous about personal cleanliness.
   C. His education had filled him with anger against those who he believed had hurt or humiliated him.
   D. *(No mistakes)*

242. **A.** Neither tears nor protests effected their parents' decision.
   B. Being able to trust one's sources is indispensable for the investigative reporter.
   C. When you go to the library tomorrow, please take this book to the librarian who sits in the reference room.
   D. *(No mistakes)*

243. **A.** It's not good to have too much cholesterol in your diet.
   B. Eno waited for his favorite newspaper, *The Haverford Courier*, to be delivered.
   C. Frieda ate Muriel's signature dish, Eggplant Lasagna, on Sunday night.
   D. *(No mistakes)*

244. **A.** If you prepare systematically and diligently for the examination, one can be confident of passing it.
   B. Sequoia was so uninterested in the baseball game that she yawned unashamedly.
   C. If he had thought to arrange an appointment, his reception might have been more friendly.
   D. *(No mistakes)*

245. **A.** Mahala, Gracie, and Birthe are members of the swim team.
   B. Kanna and Margie are the school's best pitchers.
   C. My favorite zoo exhibit is the snake house.
   D. *(No mistakes)*

246. **A.** Are you familiar with the benefits of owning life insurance.
   B. What can you say about such a decorated soccer player?
   C. The steam from the subway grate made the entire platform hazy.
   D. *(No mistakes)*

247. A. Do not make a choice that changed the meaning of the original sentence.

B. I would appreciate your treating me as if I were your sister.

C. The contract should not have been awarded to the secretary's nephew.

D. (No mistakes)

248. A. There is a fantastic miniature golf course in Ocean City, Maryland.

B. At the time, the titanic was the largest passenger liner ever built.

C. Zaima must have her wisdom teeth removed by a dentist.

D. (No mistakes)

249. A. You must explain that, in the United States, there is no government interference with the arts.

B. Failure to pay back loans is a major issue for banks.

C. The former Soviet Union was unsuccessful in curbing youth's "addiction" to hard rock and heavy metal music.

D. (No mistakes)

250. A. The driver was fined for driving more than 200 miles per hour.

B. The lady looked well in her new boots.

C. Neither the manager nor the employees want to work overtime.

D. (No mistakes)

251. A. The *Santa Maria* was the larger of Christopher Columbus's three ships.

B. His speech is so precise that it seems affected.

C. The door opens and in walk Rusul and Neka.

D. (No mistakes)

252. A. His testimony today is different from that of yesterday.

B. If you had studied the problem carefully, you would have found the solution more quickly.

C. The flowers smelled so sweet that the whole house was perfumed.

D. (No mistakes)

253. A. Band practice is every other Tuesday.

B. Charlotte and Ksenia are planning a Memorial Day tribute with the local Firefighters.

C. The deadline for signing up for soccer is next Friday.

D. (No mistakes)

254. A. Thanking someone in advance is an unacceptable modern practice.

B. I like Burns's poem, "To a Mountain Daisy."

C. Venetian blinds—called that even though they probably did not originate in Venice, are no longer used in most homes.

D. (No mistakes)

255. A. You see, you did mail the letter to yourself!

B. Your introduction to your new classmates has been a pleasant experience, has it not.

C. During the broadcast, you are expected to stand, to salute, and to sing the fourth stanza of "America the Beautiful."

D. (No mistakes)

256. A. Participation in active sports produces both release from tension as well as physical well-being.

B. One of those clerks is responsible for these errors.

C. None of the rocks that form the solid crust of our planet is more than two billion years old.

D. (No mistakes)

257. **A.** We all prefer those other kinds of candy.

   B. The law prescribes when, where, and to whom the tax should be paid.

   C. Everything would have turned out well if only she had waited.

   D. *(No mistakes)*

258. **A.** Yesterday they laid their uniforms aside with the usual end-of-season regret.

   B. Levi told Dakota that he were sure he had seen it.

   C. He decided to be guided by the opinion of whoever spoke first.

   D. *(No mistakes)*

259. **A.** While driving through the mountain pass, the breathtaking scenes awed the travelers.

   B. I do not understand why Mother should object to my playing the piano at the party.

   C. My experience in South Africa taught me that the climate there is quite different from ours.

   D. *(No mistakes)*

260. **A.** Learning to speak a foreign language fluently requires practice.

   B. Buzzing around the picnic basket, a bumblebee flew into Laine's open mouth.

   C. It would be interesting to compare the interior of one of the pyramids in Mexico with that of one in Egypt.

   D. *(No mistakes)*

261. **A.** "We are still gathering information on the landslide," reports a government official, adding that "all efforts will be made to update the public in a timely fashion."

   B. Statistics tell us, "that heart disease kills more people than any other illness."

   C. According to a report released by the Department of Agriculture, the labor required to produce a bushel of wheat in 1830 was three hours.

   D. *(No mistakes)*

262. **A.** His written work has been done in so careless a manner that I refuse to read it.

   B. I never feel badly if, after trying hard, I fail to win a prize; the effort gives me satisfaction.

   C. Despite living in New York City their entire lives, neither Alexander nor Nadia had ever visited the Statue of Liberty.

   D. *(No mistakes)*

263. **A.** My landlord does not approve of my sending that letter to the local rent control agency.

   B. My artist friend and myself were the only guests in the gallery to truly appreciate the abstract paintings on display.

   C. The messenger will have gone to the airport before the package arrives at the shipping room.

   D. *(No mistakes)*

264. **A.** Due to the impending snowstorm, we will go directly home instead of stopping for ice cream.

   B. The eraser was lost after it had lain alongside the typewriter for weeks.

   C. Please distribute these newly arrived booklets among all the teachers in the building.

   D. *(No mistakes)*

265. **A.** The lecture was interrupted by the whirring sound of the street-repair machinery right outside the window.

   B. Mandated school courses include mathematics, literature, history, and science; optional subjects include drama, marching band, and coding.

   C. The pupil's account of his lateness is incredible, I will not give him a classroom pass.

   D. *(No mistakes)*

266. **A.** Winter came before the archaeologists could do anything more than mark out the burial site.

   B. Since her concentration was disrupted by the loud noise, Ola decided to wash her hair.

   C. Let's you and me settle the matter between ourselves.

   D. *(No mistakes)*

267. **A.** I recommend that you participate in all the discussions and heed the council of your elders.

B. Upon graduation from the training course, my friend will be assigned to a permanent position.

C. He finally realized that the extra practice had had a visible effect on his accuracy at the foul line.

D. *(No mistakes)*

Directions: For questions 268–277, look for mistakes in spelling only.

---

268. **A.** A novocaine shot promises only transient pain in place of agony from prolonged drilling.

B. I will join the theater party next week if I am able to locate a responseble babysitter.

C. That painting is so valuable that it is described as priceless.

D. *(No mistakes)*

269. **A.** Anthony thinks downhill skiing is absolutely exhilarating.

B. Nala understood that being successful on the gymnastic team would require great disipline.

C. Gloria knew she wanted a red convertible immediately after getting her license.

D. *(No mistakes)*

270. **A.** Camila and Ben listened to the announcer on the radio as they drove back from the party.

B. The first game of the year was marred by what appeared to be unprofessional refereeing.

C. I went to the museum, but remained unimpressed throughout the tour.

D. *(No mistakes)*

271. **A.** The eager young politician stood at the street corner handing out political pamphlets.

B. If you do not watch your eating habits in a foreign country, you may return with an intestinal paresite.

C. My childhood heroes were mainly cartoon characters.

D. *(No mistakes)*

272. **A.** Begin to descend into the cave by way of the staircase just beyond the huge copper beech tree.

B. Admissible evidence is evidence that has been collected in entirely legal ways.

C. Since our army is so outnumbered, we might as well conceed defeat and limit our casualties.

D. *(No mistakes)*

273. **A.** The scavengers desecrated many native graves.

B. Be sure you enter your figures in a straight column.

C. Even an exorbitant charge does not guarantee that the doctor will perform a thorough examination.

D. *(No mistakes)*

274. **A.** The prologue to the play greatly enhanced its meaning.

B. All students in attendance today will join together for an assembly program and a physical education class.

C. The error on the scoreboard was immediately noticable to all.

D. *(No mistakes)*

275. **A.** The union and management agreed that the reccomendation of the arbitrator would be binding.

B. Parallel lines never meet.

C. Drinking and driving often culminate in a tragic accident.

D. *(No mistakes)*

276. **A.** The hospital issued a daily bulletin regarding the movie star's medical condition.

B. Please do not interrup my telephone conversation.

C. The newest soft contact lenses allow for extended wear.

D. *(No mistakes)*

277. **A.** The manufacturer's reply was terse but cordial.

B. Every student who was questioned gave a similar explanation.

C. The writer has created a clever psuedonym for himself.

D. *(No mistakes)*

Directions: In questions 278–288, choose the sentence that demonstrates correct usage.

---

278. **A.** We all hope there are no onions on our pizzas when it arrive.

B. All the tables in the furniture showroom have our tops dusted daily.

C. Mohammed has an amazing collection of books displayed in its bookshelf.

D. Will Diane remember to bring her famous pie to the reception dinner?

279. **A.** Derrick placed his new pair of scissor's in the kitchen drawer.

B. Amelia's new cat ran nervously under her living room couch.

C. Will we ever get to finally see Richards new play?

D. I want to buy the same headphone's that Leland has.

280. **A.** Joshua knows that he'll need a great grade on the final to pass the class.

B. The chess team is facing an opponent that he'll never faced before.

C. The cleaning crew said that it'll be willing to work late this weekend.

D. Can we ask Aya how she'll knew that it would rain yesterday?

281. **A.** Little bit of patience can go a long way when working with a team.

B. What are the benefits to eating healthy diet every day?

C. I rented umbrella to keep us out of the sun this afternoon.

D. I just couldn't believe how long the movie was.

282.
A. All of Wilma's video games were alphabetized in her entertainment unit.

B. Victor gathered all the cupcakes and put sprinkles on his tops.

C. Edwin set the antique globe upon us newly varnished wooden desk.

D. Will we ever see lasting improvements in their environment?

283.
A. Chris has a surprising number of room's in his new house.

B. Lucy went to the flower shop's in search of a new orchid.

C. Will Ed's prediction about the outcome of the game come true?

D. We have yet to see Daphne's reach her full potential in class.

284.
A. Hildy purchased too lavender vases from the florist shop.

B. Lucas spent to years working on earning his degree.

C. Kimmie is looking forward too her gymnastics meet tomorrow.

D. There were way too many people in the crowded elevator.

285.
A. The millionaire lavish flaunted his incredible wealth.

B. Chenille careful diced two carrots for the salad.

C. Our new house cat sat lazy on the back of the sofa.

D. The player took a really long time to make the free throw.

286.
A. Would you like to add an onion to the pot of chili?

B. Will there be opening act at the concert this weekend?

C. Keys hung on the hook by the front door.

D. Nearest highway rest stop was about five miles away.

287.
A. Shea knows that she isn't eat the cake, but she did anyway.

B. Terence sprained his ankle and don't be able to run on Friday.

C. Unfortunately, Abraham can't make it to the charity auction.

D. Let's make a list of who they're coming to the gala in March.

288.
A. The paw's of the alley cat had extremely sharp claws.

B. Martin's treadmill was used only a handful of times.

C. Margot tablet ran out of battery power at the worst time.

D. Chloe's placed the boxes in her basement for storage

Directions: For questions 289–298, follow the individual instructions.

289. Choose the best word or words to join the thoughts together.

The soldiers will not come home _____ the war is over.

A. while

B. since

C. before

D. None of these

290. Choose the best word(s) to join the thoughts together.

We enjoyed the movie _____ the long wait in line.

A. during

B. despite

C. because of

D. None of these

291. Choose the word that best completes this sentence.

Donte, a responsible security guard, could not leave his post _____ his shift replacement arrived each night.

A. however

B. because

C. until

D. but

292. Which of these expresses the idea most clearly?

A. In tropical waters you can swim and see colorful fish in glass-bottomed boats.

B. You can see glass-bottomed fish swimming among coral reefs and colorful boats in tropical waters.

C. In tropical waters you often can see glass-bottomed boats, colorful fish, and coral reefs swimming.

D. From glass-bottomed boats you can see colorful fish swimming in tropical waters among the coral reefs.

293. Which of these expresses the idea most clearly?

A. Backgammon is a complex game, and you must change strategies often to learn it well.

B. Though backgammon is easy to learn, it's a complex game that requires frequent shifts in strategy at the highest levels.

C. To learn to play backgammon, you must shift complex strategies easily.

D. You must easily learn to shift strategies to play the complex game of backgammon well.

294. Choose the pair of sentences that best develops this topic sentence.

"For cities, computers came along at just the right moment."

A. Cities were growing larger and spreading farther. People found they couldn't gather facts fast enough to make needed decisions.

B. The computer is a mass of complex parts and flashing lights. However, it is still just a machine made by humans to serve humans.

C. The most unusual use for computers lately has been in the supermarket. At the wave of a wand, the computer can read what a person has bought.

D. The computer aids business by storing information. It is able to provide this information almost as soon as a problem comes up.

295. Which of the following sentences offers *least* support to the topic "The Need to Protect the Bald Eagle"?

A. In flight, the bald eagle is beautiful.

B. Today, it enjoys the full protection of the law and seems to be slowly increasing.

C. It is so plentiful that it is seen as a dangerous rival to the fishing industry.

D. The game laws of Alaska are under local jurisdiction.

296. Which of these best fits under the topic "The Squid—A Master of Disguise"?

A. Because the squid is shy, it is often misunderstood.

B. Little sacs of pigment enable the squid to change its color and evade predators.

C. In reality they're adaptable, intelligent, and, oftentimes, even beautiful.

D. They propel themselves backward by squirting water out of a nozzle located near their heads.

297. Which sentence does *not* belong in the paragraph?

(1) Intense religious zeal was the main reason for the Crusades, but it was not the only reason. (2) The Crusades weakened feudalism. (3) Businessmen saw good opportunities to set up new markets in the East. (4) Some knights hoped to win military glory, and many just sought adventure.

A. Sentence 1

B. Sentence 2

C. Sentence 3

D. Sentence 4

298. Where should the sentence "Man is learning." be placed in the paragraph below?

(1) His past experiences have taught him well. (2) He imports ladybugs to destroy aphids. (3) He irrigates, fertilizes, and rotates his crops.

A. Before sentence 1

B. Between sentences 1 and 2

C. Between sentences 2 and 3

D. The sentence does not fit in this paragraph.

ANSWER KEYS AND EXPLANATIONS
Verbal Skills

1. C	13. B	25. B	37. A	49. D
2. A	14. D	26. A	38. B	50. B
3. C	15. C	27. C	39. A	51. C
4. B	16. A	28. C	40. C	52. C
5. D	17. B	29. B	41. D	53. D
6. D	18. A	30. C	42. A	54. B
7. A	19. C	31. D	43. B	55. C
8. D	20. A	32. C	44. B	56. C
9. A	21. C	33. D	45. C	57. A
10. B	22. A	34. A	46. B	58. C
11. C	23. C	35. C	47. A	59. B
12. B	24. D	36. A	48. B	60. D

1. **The correct answer is C.** *Fourth* is an ordinal number. The other three are cardinal numbers.

2. **The correct answer is A.** *Arouse* and *pacify* are antonyms, as are *agitate* and *smooth*. *Ruffle* is a synonym for *agitate*.

3. **The correct answer is C.** If the first two statements are true, then the only thing we can be certain of is that both Francine and Henri are better jugglers than Jerome. It is uncertain if Francine is a better juggler than Henri, or vice versa.

4. **The correct answer is B.** A query is a question, which is the opposite of *answer*.

5. **The correct answer is D.** To impair is to damage or to weaken.

6. **The correct answer is D.** All other choices are synonyms of the word *spin*. A planet (choice D) is something that spins, but it is not a synonym for the word.

7. **The correct answer is A.** That which is variable is changeable, fluctuating, or shifting.

8. **The correct answer is D.** The relationship is that of object to an action. When one beats an egg, one vigorously mixes up the egg's substance to prepare it for a certain type of cooking application. When one mashes a potato, one performs an analogous act upon the potato. Baking a potato (choice B) prepares it for eating, but the act of baking is not analogous to the act of beating. If *mash* were not offered as a choice, *bake* might have served as the answer. Always choose the best answer available, even if it seems like more than one is feasible.

9. **The correct answer is A.** To obstruct is to clog or to block.

10. **The correct answer is B.** The green balloon is lower in the sky than the red balloon. Since the yellow balloon is higher in the sky than the red balloon, the green balloon cannot be higher than the yellow balloon, so the third statement must be false.

11. **The correct answer is C.** The common feature among three of the answer choices is that they're all in the past tense. *Mixing* (choice C) is in the present tense.

12. **The correct answer is B.** The result is the product of a cause. A synonym for *result* is *effect*. Do not confuse *effect* with *affect*, which means "to influence."

13. **The correct answer is B.** The first part of the analogy establishes a noun (*game*) and a verb that is typically used with it (*play*). Lemonade is a beverage that one typically drinks (choice B).

14. **The correct answer is D.** A cave is a naturally occurring shelter that might be used as a dwelling place. All the other choices are man-made.

15. **The correct answer is C.** Pretzel, the dachshund, is clearly less shaggy than Pepper and so could be in the same dog obedience class, but there is no information to suggest that Pretzel even goes to obedience school.

16. **The correct answer is A.** The first part of the analogy establishes an item (*camera*) and a part that it comprises (*lens*). A lightbulb is an item and a filament (choice A) is part of it.

17. **The correct answer is B.** *Revenue* means "income." Taxes produce revenue, but they are not in themselves revenue.

18. **The correct answer is A.** A trapeze is a short horizontal bar that gymnasts and aerialists swing from and upon which they perform. All the other choices are tools that make work easier.

19. **The correct answer is C.** Tears may well come as a sign of emotion. All the other choices are emotions themselves.

20. **The correct answer is A.** From fastest to slowest jumper we have: Deepti—Dave—Inez—Wendy—Bozhou.

21. **The correct answer is C.** *Manual,* as opposed to *automatic* or *mechanical,* means "hand-operated."

22. **The correct answer is A.** *Marshy* means "boggy" or "swampy."

23. **The correct answer is C.** The relationship is that of actor to object or, if you like, eater to eaten. A seal eats fish; a bird eats worms.

24. **The correct answer is D.** *Loss* is the opposite of *profit.*

25. **The correct answer is B.** Activity is motion. Rest is freedom from activity.

26. **The correct answer is A.** *Wind* is the general term for air in motion. All the other choices are descriptions of winds based upon wind speed.

27. **The correct answer is C.** All people eaters are purple, but it does not necessarily follow that all things purple eat people. We cannot tell whether there are some yetis that are purple even though they do not eat people.

28. **The correct answer is C.** *Churlish* most nearly means "surly."

29. **The correct answer is B.** The word *immaterial* means "unimportant."

30. **The correct answer is C.** From the heaviest to the lightest books, we are told the order is: blue, orange, green, and red. Although we are told that orange books are not as light as yellow books, we cannot tell whether yellow books are heavier or lighter than the green books.

31. **The correct answer is D.** A shoe is made of leather; a highway is made of asphalt.

32. **The correct answer is C.** To mend is to repair, which is the opposite of *destroy.*

33. **The correct answer is D.** *Concrete* means "specific" or "particular." *Abstract* means "general" or "theoretical."

34. **The correct answer is A.** To function is to operate or to work.

35. **The correct answer is C.** Meat is food. All the other choices are nutrients found in food.

36. **The correct answer is A.** Because all Totos are either green-eyed Yahoos or blue-tailed Gogos, it is reasonable to assume that some are blue-tailed Gogos. Because all blue-tailed Gogos have red noses, we can safely assume that some Totos, at least those that are blue-tailed Gogos, have red noses.

37. **The correct answer is A.** A cacophony is a collection of loud or harsh noises.

38. **The correct answer is B.** *Monkey* is the general term describing a whole class of primates, regardless of gender. All the other choices are specifically male animals.

39. **The correct answer is A.** You taste with your tongue, but touch with your finger.

40. **The correct answer is C.** *Discord* means "deep disagreement." Music may be either harmonious (when the notes complement one another) or discordant (when the notes "disagree").

41. **The correct answer is D.** *Fumes* are gas, smoke, or vapor emanations. The other choices describe the smell of fumes.

42. **The correct answer is A.** *Riding* is a passive act; an animal or machine does the transporting. All the other choices are active ways to move from one place to another.

43. **The correct answer is B.** *Fatal* means "causing death" or "deadly."

44. **The correct answer is B.** Terry has won the most races of all.

45. **The correct answer is C.** A *brick* is opaque. All the other choices are translucent.

46. **The correct answer is B.** *Secure* means "safe," as in "not exposed to danger."

47. **The correct answer is A.** *Garish* means "gaudy" and "glaring," the opposite of *dull*.

48. **The correct answer is B.** This is a sequential relationship. A foal is the child of a horse, just as a son is the child of a mother.

49. **The correct answer is D.** Crackers are hard and crunchy in their texture, while all of the other foods listed are soft.

50. **The correct answer is B.** That which is counterfeit is an "imitation made with intent to defraud," and is therefore false.

51. **The correct answer is C.** All you know is that the thruway and the highway have more lanes than the parkway.

52. **The correct answer is C.** In this actor-and-object relationship, the actor serves as an irritant to the object. Thus, a flea irritates a dog; a fly irritates a *horse.*

53. **The correct answer is D.** The word *intermittently* means "recurring from time to time."

54. **The correct answer is B.** *Acrylic* means a type of paint, and is not a language like the other choices.

55. **The correct answer is C.** *Diverse* means "different," so its antonym would be *similar.*

56. **The correct answer is C.** The finder seeks and receives a reward; the repenter seeks and receives absolution (from sin, choice B). Contrition (choice D) is the feeling the repenter must have in order to repent. *Religion (choice A)* may be associated with *repentance* but without the same essential actor-to-object relationship.

57. **The correct answer is A.** When an object bends, it changes shape or orientation but remains intact. All other choices imply the breaking apart of an object.

58. **The correct answer is C.** We are told only relative positions regarding north and south, with no information about the concrete positions of these establishments. We cannot tell from this information exactly where the grocery store is in relation to the dry cleaner.

59. **The correct answer is B.** *Deception* means "fraud" or "subterfuge."

60. **The correct answer is D.** *Nylon* is a synthetic fiber; all other choices are natural

Quantitative Skills

61. C	72. C	83. A	93. D	103. B
62. D	73. A	84. C	94. A	104. C
63. B	74. C	85. B	95. B	105. D
64. C	75. C	86. B	96. A	106. C
65. A	76. B	87. B	97. B	107. D
66. C	77. C	88. C	98. D	108. A
67. C	78. D	89. B	99. B	109. B
68. D	79. C	90. C	100. C	110. A
69. A	80. C	91. B	101. A	111. B
70. B	81. A	92. D	102. B	112. A
71. C	82. C			

61. **The correct answer is C.** The pattern in this series is made by multiplying each number by 2, and $2 \times 4 = 8$.

62. **The correct answer is D.** To find the average, add the numbers and divide the total by 3: $\frac{4 + 9 + 17}{3} = 10$. So, double the average is 20.

63. **The correct answer is B.** Start by finding $\frac{1}{4}$ of 48: $\frac{1}{4} \times 48 = 12$. Add 20 to this to get $12 + 20 = 32$.

64. **The correct answer is C.** The pattern here is +1, +4, +1, +4, and so on; $14 + 4 = 18$.

65. **The correct answer is A.** First find each number. A = 10, B = 10, and C = 10. All three are equal, so choice A is correct.

66. **The correct answer is C.** Examine the shading in each circle: A is $\frac{1}{4}$ shaded, B is $\frac{3}{8}$ shaded, and C is $\frac{1}{2}$ shaded. Now examine the answers. Only C is true, since $\frac{1}{4} < \frac{3}{8} < \frac{1}{2}$.

67. **The correct answer is C.** Since $9^2 = 81$, subtract 5 to get $81 - 5 = 76$.

68. **The correct answer is D.** Find each value. A is $4 + (3 \times 2) = 10$, B is $(4 + 3) \times 2 = 14$, and C is $(3 + 2) \times 4 = 20$. C is the largest, so the answer is D.

69. **The correct answer is A.** Half of 26 is 13, and 3 more than that is 16. The number that leaves 16 when subtracted from 22 is 6.

70. **The correct answer is B.** *AB*, *BC*, *CD*, and *AD* are all equal since they are the sides of a square. *AC* is greater than any of these, since it is the hypotenuse of a right triangle whose legs are the sides of the square.

71. **The correct answer is C.** The pattern in this series is ×2, +2, ×2, +2, and so on. Apply this pattern to the series to get $18 \times 2 = 36$.

72. **The correct answer is C.** First, find half of 14; $\frac{1}{2} \times 14 = 7$. Then add 7 to get the answer to the question; $7 + 7 = 14$.

73. **The correct answer is A.** The pattern in the series is one A, followed by two Bs. To continue this pattern, the next three terms need to be B, A, B.

74. **The correct answer is C.** Find each value: A is $6^2 = 36$, B is $5^2 = 25$, and C is $3^2 = 9$. They are in order from largest to smallest, so A > B > C.

75. **The correct answer is C.** Each number is $1\frac{1}{2}$ more than the previous number. The next number is $7 + 1\frac{1}{2} = 8\frac{1}{2}$.

76. **The correct answer is B.** Each number in the series is 6 more than the previous number, so the missing number must be 73 + 6 = 79. To check your answer, see if the next number matches the series; 79 + 6 = 85.

77. **The correct answer is C.** This is a right triangle, and *BC* is the hypotenuse. The hypotenuse is the longest side of any right triangle, so *BC* is greater than both other sides.

78. **The correct answer is D.** The letter in each term is one place in the alphabet earlier than the letter in the previous term. The number is two more than the number in the previous term. The next term that follows this pattern is V13.

79. **The correct answer is C.** The average of two numbers is their sum divided by 2. If the answer is 12, that means the sum of the two numbers must be 24, since 24 ÷ 2 = 12. To get a sum of 24 from 10, you need to add 14.

80. **The correct answer is C.** Each quarter is worth 5 nickels, so three quarters is worth 3 × 5 = 15 nickels. Each dime is worth 2 nickels, so two dimes is worth 2 × 2 = 4 nickels. The total is 15 + 4 = 19 nickels.

81. **The correct answer is A.** The number of zeros following each "2" increases by one for each step. Next, there should be four zeros.

82. **The correct answer is C.** The square of 12 is 144. One third of 144 is 48, so add 7 to get 55.

83. **The correct answer is A.** The pattern is −2, +1, −2, +1, and so on. The next term is 6 − 2 = 4.

84. **The correct answer is C.** There are 1,000 millimeters in one meter. Multiply 1,000 by 355 to get your answer.

85. **The correct answer is B.** Each term in the series advances by one letter and increases the number of times that letter is repeated by one. The next term is the letter E repeated 5 times.

86. **The correct answer is B.** Find each value. A is 15, B is 15, and C is 10, so A = B > C.

87. **The correct answer is B.** The pattern is +4, +3, +4, +3, and so on. Since the first increase shown (from 5 to 9) is +4, the one before that should have been +3, and 2 + 3 = 5.

88. **The correct answer is C.** $6^2 = 36$, a quarter of that is 36 ÷ 4 = 9, and half of that is 9 ÷ 2 = 4.5.

89. **The correct answer is B.** The pattern is +3, +3, +3, and so on. The series continues with 16, 19, 22, skipping over 18.

90. **The correct answer is C.** The square has a perimeter of 6 + 6 + 6 + 6 = 24 and an area of 6 × 6 = 36. The rectangle has a perimeter of 2 × 3 + 2 × 12 = 30, and an area of 3 × 12 = 36. Both figures have an area of 36, making choice C the correct answer.

91. **The correct answer is B.** The pattern is ×2, ×2, ×2, and so on. After 32, the series continues with 64, 128, and 256, so the first term to exceed 100 would be 128, the 8th term.

92. **The correct answer is D.** When you have an even number of data points in a set, you will find the median between the two center data points. In this case, it falls between 5 and 6, so 5.5 is the median. Multiply that by 75% to get 4.125, which converts to $4\frac{1}{8}$, or $\frac{33}{8}$.

93. **The correct answer is D.** The parallelogram is split into two identical triangles by the diagonal *AC*. Since these triangles are identical, they have the same perimeter.

94. **The correct answer is B.** Each term starts with the last letter of the previous term and also includes the next two letters. The next term should start with I and also include J and K.

95. **The correct answer is B.** Remember to flip the divisor; $\frac{18}{5} \times \frac{1}{3} = \frac{18}{15} = \frac{6}{5}$. Then, flip your result to get the reciprocal.

96. **The correct answer is A.** Start by finding the values of the 3 expressions; A is (3 + 2) ÷ 5 = 1, B is (3 + 1) ÷ 4 = 1, and C is (2 + 4) ÷ 3 = 2. So, A and B are equal, but they are less than C.

97. **The correct answer is B.** The square of 3 is $3^2 = 9$, and 7 more than this is 9 + 7 = 16. The question asks for "the square of what number," so you need

to find the square root of 16; $4^2 = 16$, so the answer is 4 (choice B). Careful reading is paramount!

98. **The correct answer is D.** The pattern is +11, +11, +11, and so on. The next term is $46 + 11 = 57$.

99. **The correct answer is B.** The average of 7, 9, and 26 is $(7 + 9 + 26) \div 3 = 14$. Half of this average is $14 \div 2 = 7$, and 5 less than 7 is 2.

100. **The correct answer is C.** In A, half the rectangle is shaded. In B, 6 of the 12 squares are shaded, equal to one half. In C, $\frac{3}{5}$ of the rectangle is shaded, which is greater than one half, so C is the correct answer.

101. **The correct answer is A.** The pattern is -2, $\times 2$, -2, $\times 2$, and so on. The next term is $-28 - 2 = -30$.

102. **The correct answer is B.** For this, we use order of operations, starting within the parentheses: $(27.5 \times 8) \times 14 = 220 \times 14 = 3{,}080$.

103. **The correct answer is B.** All sides of a cube are the same. This means that the diagonals shown, *AF* and *AC*, are equal.

104. **The correct answer is C.** Each image is divided into seven parts: the center, and six triangular point sections. Figure B has the least visible white, since only two of the point sections are not shaded. Figure C has only the center hexagon unshaded, meaning it is more shaded than Figure A, which has the same amount of white visible as Figures B and C combined.

105. **The correct answer is D.** Since B and C have the same denominator, and B has a larger numerator, you can immediately see that C < B. The fraction in A is $\frac{3}{4} = \frac{6}{8}$, and therefore B < A, meaning choice D is correct.

106. **The correct answer is C.** The largest two-digit number is 99 (the next number, 100, has three digits). Take $\frac{1}{3}$ of 99 to get 33, choice C.

107. **The correct answer is D.** The jump from 4 to 10 is 6, and this must be equal to adding the same number twice. Therefore, the pattern must be +3, +3, +3, and so on. The same logic can be used observing the second gap in the series. The missing terms are $4 + 3 = 7$, and $10 + 3 = 13$.

108. **The correct answer is A.** The pattern in choice A is $+1$, $\times 2$, $+1$, $\times 2$. The pattern in choice B is $\times 2$, $\times 2$, $\times 2$. The pattern in choice C is $+2$, $+2$, $+2$. The pattern in choice D is -1, -1, -1. Only choice A involves both addition and multiplication.

109. **The correct answer is B.** Since the answer options all deal with areas, first calculate the area of each figure. The area of the square is $3 \times 3 = 9$, and the area of the triangle is $\frac{1}{2} \times 6 \times 3 = 9$. Since the circle fits inside the square, we know it has a smaller area, so there is no need to calculate the circle's actual area. Reading each of the answer options, choice B is the only one that fits the conditions.

110. **The correct answer is A.** Start by calculating values; $\frac{1}{3}$ of 21 is 7, and 6 more than 7 is 13. Similarly, B is 2 less than 13, or 11, and C is 5 more than 25, or 30. Once you have the values, plug them into the answer options, and you will find that C (30) is greater than A (13), which is greater than 11, as stated in choice A.

111. **The correct answer is B.** You might be able to do this one in your head. An average of 10, 10, and 11 is going to be more than 10, its lowest term, and less than 11, its highest term. As such, it is logical that the average would be between 10 and 11. In fact, the average of 10, 10, and 11 is $(10 + 10 + 11) \div 3$, or $31 \div 3$. This equals $10\frac{1}{3}$, which is indeed between 10 and 11.

112. **The correct answer is A.** The value of A is 30 cents + 17 cents = 47 cents, B is 40 cents + 10 cents = 50 cents, and C is 50 cents. Plugging these values into the answer choices shows that A (47 cents) is less than B (50 cents), which is equal to C (also 50 cents), making choice A correct.

Reading

Comprehension

113. C	**121.** D	**129.** D	**137.** D	**145.** C
114. D	**122.** C	**130.** C	**138.** C	**146.** B
115. C	**123.** A	**131.** B	**139.** B	**147.** D
116. D	**124.** A	**132.** C	**140.** A	**148.** A
117. C	**125.** C	**133.** A	**141.** C	**149.** D
118. B	**126.** B	**134.** A	**142.** D	**150.** D
119. A	**127.** C	**135.** B	**143.** A	**151.** C
120. B	**128.** A	**136.** C	**144.** B	**152.** B

113. **The correct answer is C.** The selection is about a game that appears to be an early version of modern baseball, so choice C is the best option. The paragraph is not actually about baseball, so choices A and D are incorrect. The article also mentions that the game is "somewhat like" the English game of rounders, but calling it "An English Game" would be misleading, making choice B incorrect.

114. **The correct answer is D.** There were "usually between 8 and 20 players." The number of players was not fixed by rule. In fact, according to the last sentence, there were very few rules.

115. **The correct answer is C.** One of the few rules defined the playing field as a 60-foot square.

116. **The correct answer is D.** The first sentence tells us that the game was similar to the English game of rounders. The second sentence assures us that the game was exciting for both players and spectators.

117. **The correct answer is C.** *Impromptu* means "improvised" or "made up on-the-spot." The ball is described as a bullet, cork, or metal slug wound with yarn and string, which matches the meaning of *impromptu* very well.

118. **The correct answer is B.** The nineteenth century consists of the years in the 1800s. The game is placed in the early nineteenth century, from 1800 on. Its popularity increased throughout the first half of the century, so it clearly was played at least until 1850—and probably beyond.

119. **The correct answer is A.** See the last sentence of the passage, in which the author specifically says the game "steadily increased in popularity." None of the other choices are supported in the selection.

120. **The correct answer is B.** The simple, improvised equipment made this a low-cost pastime. The players were not exceptionally skillful, and the game was only an American adaptation of an English game, so choices A and C are incorrect. Choice C is not singled out as an attraction of the game, so it not a good choice.

121. **The correct answer is D.** The first sentence says that the game had "all the elements of modern baseball," but then the second sentence says that this game was not "scientifically planned nor skillfully played." Modern baseball is an organized sport, so this suggests the main difference between the two. Choice A is incorrect because modern baseball also includes four bases. Choice B is incorrect because we don't know enough about rounders from the passage to make this determination. Choice C is incorrect because the passage explicitly says that many elements are similar between this game and baseball.

122. **The correct answer is C.** The writer of the passage expresses no feeling whatsoever. This is nothing more than a clear, factual report. There are no specific opinions about this game or baseball (choice A), about whether this time period was better than

now (choice B), or about the people who invented this game (choice D).

123. **The correct answer is A.** The answer to this detail question can be found by rereading paragraph two of the passage, which discusses the percentage of usable uranium found in natural uranium when it is first mined. The passage tells us that most natural uranium contains only 0.07 percent of the usable type of uranium, which is known as U-235.

124. **The correct answer is A.** This question is a "cause and effect" question. In this case, you're asked to identify what causes the nuclear splitting process to continue in a chain reaction. The answer to this question can be found in the first paragraph of the passage. Here, we are told that the release of neutrons that occurs during fission causes the nuclear splitting process to continue. Choice A pinpoints the cause as "the neutrons released" when uranium and plutonium atoms are split.

125. **The correct answer is C.** According to the passage, nuclear fission occurs after uranium is enriched, and atoms are split—not as a natural process. Choices A, B, and D are all specifically mentioned as facts in the passage.

126. **The correct answer is B.** The passage states that the process of enrichment makes the uranium contain a higher percentage of U-235. Enriched uranium is therefore a more powerful type of uranium, so the word *strengthened* is the correct answer.

127. **The correct answer is C.** Paragraph 1 states that a neutron is an atomic particle with no electrical charge.

128. **The correct answer is A.** Paragraph 1 states that two types of atoms that split very easily are found in uranium and plutonium.

129. **The correct answer is D.** Paragraph 1 states that a nuclear chain reaction is the process that creates power, making choice D the correct answer. Choice B is incorrect, because a nuclear reactor is a device in which nuclear power is created. Nuclear chain reactions do not create reactors, but instead take place *within* nuclear reactors.

130. **The correct answer is C.** Paragraph 2 states that natural uranium contains two components, Uranium-235 and Uranium-238.

131. **The correct answer is B.** The author explains the process of nuclear fission and uranium's role in that process. Choices A and C are incorrect, because the author doesn't offer any personal opinions regarding the dangers or benefits of nuclear power. Choice D is incorrect because the author does not discuss nuclear power as an alternative to fossil fuels.

132. **The correct answer is C.** The passage focuses almost entirely on the process of nuclear fission and how it creates nuclear power. The passage does not explore or expand upon the ways in which nuclear power may be employed, so choice B is incorrect. Choices A and D imply information that is not addressed in the passage.

133. **The correct answer is A.** The purpose of the passage is to inform readers about the history of the fortune cookie, and the mystery that surrounds its origins. Therefore, the most appropriate title for this passage would be: "Fortune Cookies: A Mysterious Treat with Mysterious Origins." The other choices are too general for this passage.

134. **The correct answer is A.** The word *cessation* is used to describe the point at which fortune cookies come during the meal, and the author mentions that the cookies are served "after eating." Therefore, it most nearly means "ending."

135. **The correct answer is B.** The author states that "regarding the origins of the fortune cookie, only one thing seems certain—the dispute as to who invented them may never be definitively settled." Therefore, *unclear* is the best word to sum up the author's beliefs regarding the origins of the fortune cookie.

136. **The correct answer is C.** The author refers to modern, machine-made fortune cookies as "a big change from traditional cookies" because traditional cookies were made by hand, as mentioned in the second paragraph.

137. **The correct answer is D.** The word *indelible* is used in the passage to describe the lasting memory one's first experience with a fortune cookie can provide.

138. **The correct answer is C.** It may be true that the fortune cookie is the author's favorite cookie, but there's not enough information in the passage to determine this.

139. **The correct answer is B.** The only option that is not explicitly mentioned in the passage is cinnamon.

140. **The correct answer is A.** The only option that is not explicitly stated in the passage as something you could potentially find in a fortune cookie is a funny riddle.

141. **The correct answer is C.** This is an informative piece of writing regarding the fortune cookie and its origins, and the author's most likely purpose in writing this passage is to inform readers about the origin of the fortune cookie.

142. **The correct answer is D.** The passage explicitly states that Japan is one of the places where individuals claim the fortune cookie was invented.

143. **The correct answer is A.** According to the passage, Orson Welles wrote and directed films, which means he was a filmmaker. Film critics offer educated opinions on films, and this isn't among the numerous jobs mentioned in the passage. Therefore, choice B is incorrect. While Welles worked for the film studio RKO Pictures, the passage offers no evidence that he ran that studio, so choice C is incorrect. There is no evidence in the passage that Welles taught film either, so choice D is wrong as well.

144. **The correct answer is B.** According to the passage, Orson Welles's version of *The War of the Worlds* was a radio play. Although H.G. Wells's original version of the story was a novel, Orson Welles's version was not, so choice A is incorrect. While Welles did produce plays for the stage, there is no evidence in the passage to support the idea that he made a version of *The War of the Worlds* for the stage, so choice C is incorrect too. There have been film versions of *The War of the Worlds*,

but the passage never suggests that Orson Welles made any of them, so choice D is incorrect.

145. **The correct answer is C.** Experimentation is often an important element of original art. In addition, the passage uses the words *innovative* and *experimental* to describe Welles's work, making choice C the most logical interpretation of Welles's statement. Welles was only talking about himself when he made this statement; he was not talking about *all* artists, so choice A lacks support. While it is true that *Citizen Kane* did not make much money, Welles's statement does not seem to support the idea that he was afraid that people would find this out, so choice B is not a strong answer. Choice D implies that Welles was uncomfortable with how experimental his work was, but nothing in the statement supports that conclusion.

146. **The correct answer is B.** The idiom "claims to fame" means "noteworthy achievements," and the fact that this phrase follows mention of Welles's noteworthy achievements supports this interpretation of the phrase. While a claim can be an argument, and fame can signify success, the phrase "claims to fame" does not mean "arguments for success" in this context, as choice A suggests. Choices C and D make similar misinterpretations.

147. **The correct answer is D.** The passage suggests that Welles formed the Mercury Theatre before making *Citizen Kane*. However, it only mentions making *Citizen Kane* as something Welles did when he was 25, so choice A lacks support. While the Mercury Theatre did perform *The War of the Worlds*, choice B implies that performing that play was the specific reason Welles started the theater in the first place, and the passage does not support that conclusion. RKO Pictures made movies, not radio plays for the Mercury Theatre, so choice C is wrong.

148. **The correct answer is A.** Welles's ability to act in, write, and direct films—including stage radio and theater plays—is sufficient evidence of his extreme creativity. However, not everyone may agree with the extreme statement in choice B, so this answer is not as strong as choice A is. There is simply not

enough evidence in the passage to support choices C and D.

149. **The correct answer is D.** The passage suggests that while most critics loved *Citizen Kane*, relatively few people actually went to see the movie, and this supports the conclusion in choice D, since it is a critic's job to either convince people to see a film or dissuade them from seeing a film. There is no evidence in the passage that supports choices A or B. And it's a critics job to persuade readers to see a movie or stay home, so choice C is incorrect.

150. **The correct answer is D.** While the passage provides ample evidence that Orson Welles worked in stage, film, and radio, there is no evidence that he was also a painter, so choice D is the best answer.

151. **The correct answer is C.** The word *mere* means "basic," and the author uses it to indicate that 25 was a relatively young age at which to make a film

as important as *Citizen Kane*. However, the fact that Kane had so much success in radio or on the stage by the time he was 25 makes choice A an unlikely answer. Choice B mistakes the meaning of the word *mere* for its opposite. And *mere* does not mean "recent," as assumed in choice D.

152. **The correct answer is B.** The passage discusses *Citizen Kane's* impressive qualities directly, mentioning its "innovative storytelling, superb acting, and experimental filmmaking techniques." The innovative and experimental nature of the film suggests that there were no others like *Citizen Kane*, so choice A is incorrect. *Citizen Kane* was Welles's first film, so choice C cannot be true. Choice D describes only one quality of *Citizen Kane* that may have impressed film critics, so it is not as strong an answer as choice B.

NOTES

Vocabulary

153. C	158. A	163. D	167. D	171. D
154. B	159. B	164. A	168. D	172. B
155. C	160. C	165. A	169. B	173. B
156. A	161. A	166. B	170. B	174. A
157. D	162. C			

153. **The correct answer is C.** *Tedious* means "monotonous," "boring," or 'tiresome."

154. **The correct answer is B.** *Rescind* means "to take back," "to revoke," or "to cancel."

155. **The correct answer is C.** *Histrionic* refers to something or someone who is "dramatic."

156. **The correct answer is A.** Indigence is destitution or poverty. The word that means "laziness" is *indolence.*

157. **The correct answer is D.** *Vindictive* means "eager to get even," or "revengeful."

158. **The correct answer is A.** *Remuneration* means "compensation," "reward," or "payment."

159. **The correct answer is B.** *Deficient* means "lacking," "incomplete," or "inadequate."

160. **The correct answer is C.** *Detrimental* means "causing damage," or "harmful."

161. **The correct answer is A.** *Accurate* means "precise," or "correct."

162. **The correct answer is C.** To *amplify* is "to make larger or stronger," "to develop more fully," or "enlarge upon, as with details and examples."

163. **The correct answer is D.** To be competent is to be able, sufficient, permissible, or authorized.

164. **The correct answer is A.** *Shrewd* refers to something or someone that is "clever."

165. **The correct answer is A.** *Relevant* means "related to the matter at hand," or "applicable."

166. **The correct answer is B.** A manual is a book of instructions, or a handbook.

167. **The correct answer is D.** A device is a machine devised for a specific purpose. Be careful to define *only* the underscored word. A calculator (choice A) is a "computational device," but that is not the correct answer to the question.

168. **The correct answer is D.** *Conventional* means "customary," "usual," or "ordinary."

169. **The correct answer is B.** *Controversy* is "difference of opinion," "argument," or "debate."

170. **The correct answer is B.** *Diplomatic* means "tactful when dealing with people."

171. **The correct answer is D.** *Irate* means "angry."

172. **The correct answer is B.** *Durable* means "long-lasting, even under conditions of hard use."

173. **The correct answer is B.** *Skirmish* refers to a conflict.

174. **The correct answer is A.** *Inception* means "the beginning."

Mathematics

Concepts

175. B	180. C	185. D	190. C	195. B
176. A	181. A	186. A	191. D	196. C
177. A	182. D	187. B	192. D	197. B
178. C	183. B	188. B	193. D	198. B
179. D	184. A	189. D	194. C	

175. **The correct answer is B.** Units of speed are of the form x per y, where x is distance, and y is time. In choice B, x is miles and y is one hour.

176. **The correct answer is A.** The average of a set of numbers can never be outside of the range of values of the original numbers.

177. **The correct answer is A.** A scalene triangle has 3 sides that are all different. It is possible to also have a right angle in such a triangle. On the other hand, it is not possible for the triangle to be equilateral (choice B) since that means all 3 sides are the same. It cannot be isosceles (choice C) because that means that 2 sides are the same. Nor can it be equiangular (choice D) since that means all 3 angles are the same, which can only happen in an equilateral triangle.

178. **The correct answer is C.** This is the associative property of addition.

179. **The correct answer is D.** Volume units are cubed measurements of space occupied (or enclosed) by a substance or object.

180. **The correct answer is C.** The diameter of a circle is double its radius, so $2 \times 3 = 6$.

181. **The correct answer is A.** A pencil weighs much less than a pound (choice B) or a ton (choice C), so ounces are the most appropriate unit of measure from among the choices we are given. Kilometers (choice D) measure distance, not weight.

182. **The correct answer is D.** A quadrilateral must have 4 sides. A circle (choice A) does not have any sides, a pentagon (choice B)

has 5, and a triangle (choice C) has 3. Only the rhombus has 4 sides, making it a quadrilateral.

183. **The correct answer is B.** The number of centimeters in 10 inches is $2.54 \times 10 = 25.4$, which is closest to 25.

184. **The correct answer is A.** If each mile is equal to y kilometers, then k miles consists of y kilometers added to itself k times, or ky kilometers.

185. **The correct answer is D.** When multiplying by 10, 100, 1,000, etc., move the decimal point one place to the right for each zero in the multiplier. For this example, 100 has two zeros, so the decimal point would be moved two places to the right.

186. **The correct answer is A.** When working with scientific notation, the exponent represents the number of places the decimal point moves in the multiplier. If the exponent of 10 is positive, the decimal point moves to the right; if negative, it moves to the left.

187. **The correct answer is B.** The symbol $\geq$ means "greater than or equal to," and 6 is equal to 6.

188. **The correct answer is B.** The sum of the two angles given is $48° + 92° = 140°$. The angles in a triangle always add up to $180°$, so the third angle must be $180° - 140° = 40°$.

189. **The correct answer is D.** Converting each mixed number to a fraction makes the expression $\frac{7}{2} + \frac{9}{4} - \frac{7}{4}$. The common denominator is 4, so this turns into $\frac{14}{4} + \frac{9}{4} - \frac{7}{4} = \frac{16}{4} = 4$.

190. **The correct answer is C.** If the total is 165, and the number of days is 30, the average per day is 165 ÷ 30 = 5.5 acorns collected per day.

191. **The correct answer is D.** The sale price, $14.70, is 30% off the regular price, so it is equal to 70% of the regular price. To compute the number that 14.70 is 70% of, calculate 14.70 ÷ 0.7 = 21. The regular price is $21.

192. **The correct answer is D.** To find the number of yards in a mile, divide by 3 to get 5,280 ÷ 3 = 1,760 yards. The question asks for the yards in half a mile, so 1,760 ÷ 2 = 880 yards. Be sure to review each answer to verify you have included all the steps the question asks for.

193. **The correct answer is D.** To find the median, put the list in order: 1, 2, 3, 5, 7, 9, 9. The median is 5, since it is in the middle of the list. The mode is the number that appears most often, which is 9. The average of 5 and 9 is (5 + 9) ÷ 2 = = 7.

194. **The correct answer is C.** First, convert the mixed numbers into improper fractions; $2\frac{2}{3} = \frac{8}{3}$, and

$4\frac{1}{4} = \frac{17}{4}$. The product is $\frac{8}{3} \times \frac{17}{4} = \frac{136}{12}$. Dividing the top and bottom by 4 reduces this fraction to $\frac{34}{3}$, which is equal to $11\frac{1}{3}$.

195. **The correct answer is B.** The prime factorization of 24 is 2 × 2 × 2 × 3, and the prime factorization of 40 is 2 × 2 × 2 × 5. They have 2 × 2 × 2 in common, so the greatest common factor is 8.

196. **The correct answer is C.** $7^2 = 49$, and $8^2 = 64$. 60 is between 49 and 64, so the square root of 60 is greater than 7 and less than 8.

197. **The correct answer is B.** The numbers on a standard number cube are 1, 2, 3, 4, 5, and 6. Three of these (2, 4, 6) are even, and there are six numbers altogether. Therefore, the probability of rolling an even number is $\frac{3}{6} = \frac{1}{2}$, or 50%.

198. **The correct answer is B.** By the Pythagorean Theorem, the square of the hypotenuse must be equal to $3^2 + 4^2 = 9 + 16 = 25$. Therefore, the hypotenuse itself must be 5.

NOTES

Problem Solving

199. A	**207.** D	**215.** B	**223.** D	**231.** D
200. A	**208.** D	**216.** C	**224.** A	**232.** B
201. D	**209.** C	**217.** C	**225.** D	**233.** A
202. D	**210.** B	**218.** C	**226.** A	**234.** C
203. C	**211.** A	**219.** A	**227.** D	**235.** A
204. B	**212.** C	**220.** C	**228.** C	**236.** C
205. B	**213.** D	**221.** C	**229.** D	**237.** D
206. C	**214.** A	**222.** C	**230.** C	**238.** B

199. **The correct answer is A.** When there are an even number of terms, the median of a list is the average of the two middle numbers. In answer A, the two middle numbers are 12 and 14, and the median of these is 13. Answer B has a average of 14, answer C has a median of 12, and answer D has a median of 12.5 (the average of 10 and 15).

200. **The correct answer is A.** The perimeter is the sum of the lengths of all the sides. The lengths of all sides are included in the figure, so they only need to be added. There are three sides of length 6, two of length 5, two of length 1, and one of length 4. These numbers have a sum of 34.

201. **The correct answer is D.** The base-five system uses only five symbols: 1, 2, 3, 4, and 0. Because of this, the other three alternatives are eliminated.

202. **The correct answer is D.** For choice D to be equal, it would need the percent symbol after it. $62\frac{1}{2}\%$ is actually equal to 0.625 (choice C).

203. **The correct answer is C.** When subtracting fractional numbers, you must first rename the numbers with a common denominator.

$$12 - 2\frac{3}{16} = \frac{192}{16} - \frac{35}{16}$$
$$= \frac{157}{16}$$
$$= 9\frac{13}{16}$$

204. **The correct answer is B.** Solve for x:

$$5(1 - 2x) + 25 = 0$$
$$5 - 10x + 25 = 0$$
$$30 - 10x = 0$$
$$30 = 10x$$
$$3 = x$$

205. **The correct answer is B.** Convert the mixed numbers into improper fractions, then find the common denominator and add:

$$2\frac{1}{2} + 7\frac{2}{3} + \frac{3}{4} = \frac{5}{2} + \frac{23}{3} + \frac{3}{4}$$
$$= \frac{30}{12} + \frac{92}{12} + \frac{9}{12}$$
$$= \frac{131}{12}$$
$$= 10\frac{11}{12}$$

206. **The correct answer is C.**

$$
\begin{array}{r}
0.57 \\
6.41\overline{)3.6537} \\
3205 \\
\hline
4487 \\
4487 \\
\hline
0
\end{array}
$$

207. The correct answer is D. Replace the letters in the problem with the given numbers.

$$\frac{3ABC}{2A} = \frac{3 \times 3 \times 2 \times 6}{2 \times 3}$$
$$= \frac{108}{6}$$
$$= 18$$

208. The correct answer is D. Convert the mixed numbers to improper fractions and then multiply:

$$4\frac{2}{5} \times 2\frac{3}{11} = \frac{22}{5} \times \frac{25}{11}$$
$$= \frac{550}{55}$$
$$= 10$$

209. The correct answer is C.

$$\frac{5}{6}x = 30$$
$$x = \frac{30}{1} \cdot \frac{6}{5}$$
$$x = \frac{180}{5}$$
$$x = 36$$

210. The correct answer is B. Set this problem up as an algebraic equation.

$$11 \times 12 = N + 3$$
$$132 = N + 3$$
$$132 - 3 = N$$
$$129 = N$$

211. The correct answer is A.

$$2.5x + 12.5 = 30$$
$$2.5x = 30 - 12.5$$
$$2.5x = 17.5$$
$$x = \frac{17.5}{2.5}$$
$$x = 7$$

212. The correct answer is C.

$$143_{(5)}$$
$$+33_{(5)}$$
$$\overline{231_{(5)}}$$

213. The correct answer is D. Multiply and simplify:

$$\frac{3 \times 8}{6 \times 5} = \frac{24}{30} = \frac{4}{5}$$

214. The correct answer is A. Choice A is 493, choice B is 4,930, and choice C is 133.

215. The correct answer is B. Simplify the numerator of the fraction, then divide.

$$\frac{1\frac{3}{4} - \frac{1}{8}}{\frac{1}{8}} = \frac{1\frac{6}{8} - \frac{1}{8}}{\frac{1}{8}}$$
$$= \frac{1\frac{5}{8}}{\frac{1}{8}} = 1\frac{5}{8} \times \frac{8}{1}$$
$$= \frac{13}{8} \times \frac{8}{1} = 13$$

216. The correct answer is C. First perform the operation within the parentheses. To cube a number, multiply it by itself two times.

$$(3 + 4)^3 = (7)^3 = 7 \times 7 \times 7 = 343$$

217. The correct answer is C. The formula for the area of a triangle is $A = \frac{1}{2}bh$. Plug in the numbers:

$$A = \frac{1}{2} \times 12 \times 14$$
$$A = 84 \text{ sq. ft.}$$

218. The correct answer is C. If the average of 3 numbers is 30, the sum of the numbers must be $3 \times 30 = 90$. Since the two numbers given, 10 and 20, have a sum of 30, the remaining number must be $90 - 30 = 60$.

219. The correct answer is A. The perimeter of a triangle is the sum of the lengths of its sides. Here, the sum is $(x + 1) + (2x) + (3x - 2) = 6x - 1$.

220. **The correct answer is C.** Sally is 12, and that is 3 years older than Jim, so Jim is $12 - 3 = 9$. Jim is 2 years younger than Kate, so Kate is $9 + 2 = 11$.

221. **The correct answer is C.** Since the ratio of boys to girls is 2:3, there are $\frac{2}{3}$ as many boys as girls, and $\frac{2}{3} \times 12 = 8$.

222. **The correct answer is C.** Start by calculating the amount of the discount; 20% of $35 is $7. Then subtract the discount from the regular price to get the final answer; $35 - $7 = $28.

223. **The correct answer is D.** If the perimeter of the square is 40, each side must have a length of 10. From the placement of the circle within the square, we can assume that the circle's diameter is equal to the length of a side of the square, or 10. The radius of the circle is equal to half of the diameter, so it is 5. The area of the circle is therefore $\pi \times 5^2$, or 25π.

224. **The correct answer is A.** Starting with 7 feet 8 inches and subtracting 2 feet leaves 5 feet 8 inches. Subtracting an additional 10 inches means that the remaining length is 2 inches less than 5 feet, which is 4 feet 10 inches.

225. **The correct answer is D.** The pencils cost $3 \times $2.50 = 7.50. The erasers cost $2 \times $1.75 = 3.50. In total, Ruriko spent $7.50 + $3.50 = $11.

226. **The correct answer is A.** The ratio of cherry to lemon candies being 4:1 means that for each group of 5 candies, 4 of them are cherry and 1 is lemon. There are 10 groups of 5 in the bag, since $50 \div 5 = 10$. Each of these groups contains only a single lemon candy, so there are 10 lemon candies.

227. **The correct answer is D.** There are total of $3 + 5 + 6 = 14$ chips, and $3 + 6 = 9$ of them are not green. The probability of a randomly chosen chip not being green is $\frac{9}{14}$. Choice B is the probability that it *will* be green.

228. **The correct answer is C.** The length is 20 feet, so the two 20-foot sides make up 40 feet of the 120-foot perimeter. This leaves 80 feet, which must come from the other two sides. These other two sides must each be 40 feet. So, the dimensions of the garden are 20 feet by 40 feet. Therefore, its area is $20 \times 40 = 800$ square feet.

229. **The correct answer is D.** The description given can be translated into the equation $\frac{2}{3}x + \frac{1}{2}x = 14$, where x is the unknown number. Using a common denominator of 6, the left side of the equation is equal to $\frac{7}{6}x$. Multiplying both sides of the equation by $\frac{6}{7}$ gives $x = 12$.

230. **The correct answer is C.** There are 16 ounces in a pound, so 3 pounds is $16 \times 3 = 48$ ounces. Each ounce costs $17, so 48 ounces costs $17 \times 48 = $816.

231. **The correct answer is D.** Since Jenna's age is given as both $2x + 1$ and 13, the equation $2x + 1 = 13$ must hold. The solution to this equation is $x = 6$. Charles is then $x + 3 = 6 + 3 = 9$ years old.

232. **The correct answer is B.** Nine days pass between Monday morning and the Wednesday morning of the following week. In other words, there are three 3-day periods in that time, so the population will double 3 times. $2 \times 126 = 252$, $2 \times 252 = 504$, and $2 \times 504 = 1,008$.

233. **The correct answer is A.** Rain and snow have a combined $25\% + 30\% = 55\%$ chance of happening. All the probabilities must add up to 100%, so the chance of neither happening is $100\% - 55\% = 45\%$ (choice A).

234. **The correct answer is C.** The 80 adults account for $80 \times $7 = 560. Since $851 - $560 = 291, the children must account for $291. Each child admission is $3, so the number of children must have been $291 \div 3 = 97$.

235. **The correct answer is A.** Start by calculating the amount of sales tax; 6% of $38.50 is $2.31. This means the total cost will be $38.50 + $2.31 = $40.81. Christopher already has $40, so he needs $0.81 more.

236. **The correct answer is C.** Reduce the $17 price by 20%.

20% of $17 = $17 × 0.20 = $3.40

$17.00 − 3.40 = $13.60 (new price)

Choice A is the amount of the 20% reduction, which needs to be subtracted from the original price. Choice B is a reduction of $4.35, which is not correct. Choice D indicates a reduction of only 20 cents, when it should be 20%.

237. **The correct answer is D.**

$(4 \times 10^3) + 6 = 4{,}006$

$(2 \times 10^3) + (3 \times 10) + 8 = 2{,}038$

The difference is 1,968.

238. **The correct answer is B.** If the sides are parallel, the angles are congruent, and would both have a complement of 40°.

NOTES

Language

239. D	251. A	263. B	275. A	287. C
240. A	252. D	264. A	276. B	288. B
241. B	253. B	265. C	277. C	289. C
242. A	254. C	266. D	278. D	290. B
243. C	255. B	267. A	279. B	291. C
244. A	256. A	268. B	280. A	292. D
245. D	257. D	269. B	281. D	293. B
246. A	258. B	270. D	282. A	294. A
247. A	259. A	271. B	283. C	295. C
248. B	260. D	272. C	284. D	296. B
249. D	261. B	273. D	285. D	297. B
250. B	262. B	274. C	286. A	298. A

239. **The correct answer is D.** *No mistakes.*

240. **The correct answer is A.** This sentence contains a list of items that need to be separated by commas: " … a salad, two steaks, and a glass of iced tea to the corner table."

241. **The correct answer is B.** Each of the nurses, one at a time, *was* scrupulous, meaning "careful." If you selected choice C, you may not have realized that *who,* rather than *whom,* is correctly the subject of the clause "who had hurt or humiliated him."

242. **The correct answer is A.** *Effect* is a noun meaning "result," while *affect* is a verb meaning "to influence."

243. **The correct answer is C.** *Eggplant lasagna* is not a proper noun and shouldn't be capitalized unless it's at the beginning of a sentence—even then, only the first word would be capitalized.

244. **The correct answer is A.** Maintain a consistent voice and point-of-view throughout a sentence. "If *you* prepare, *you* can be confident." The statement, "If *one* prepares, *one* can be confident" would also be correct.

245. **The correct answer is D.** *No mistakes.*

246. **The correct answer is A.** This sentence is a question and therefore needs to be punctuated with a question mark.

247. **The correct answer is A.** In this sentence, there is a change in verb tense that renders it nonsensical. The choice that you have not yet made (future tense) cannot have already changed (past tense) the meaning of the sentence.

248. **The correct answer is B.** The name of a ship, such as the *Titanic,* is a proper noun and should be capitalized.

249. **The correct answer is D.** *No mistakes.*

250. **The correct answer is B.** It is unlikely that the new boots made the lady look healthy; they made her look *good,* that is, fashionable.

251. **The correct answer is A.** Three ships are being compared, so the superlative, *largest,* must be used. Choice C might sound awkward, but both verbs are in the present tense, and the sentence is correct.

252. **The correct answer is D.** *No mistakes.*

253. **The correct answer is B.** *Firefighters* isn't a proper noun and thus should not be capitalized.

254. **The correct answer is C.** Em dashes—used to set apart amplifying but extraneous information—must be used in pairs (the comma after *Venice* should be replaced by a dash).

255. **The correct answer is B.** This direct question should end with a question mark.

256. **The correct answer is A.** "Both" requires two objects connected by "and." Sports produce both release from tension *and* physical well-being.

257. **The correct answer is D.** *No mistakes.*

258. **The correct answer is B.** *Were* is the past tense plural form of *was*. Since *he* is singular, *were* is incorrect.

259. **The correct answer is A.** The breathtaking scenes did not drive, but that is what the sentence implies. The "travelers" must be cast as the subject of the sentence. "While driving, the travelers were awed by . . . " In answer B, the upper-case M in *Mother* is correct because in this case, *mother* is used as a proper noun.

260. **The correct answer is D.** *No mistakes.*

261. **The correct answer is B.** There is no direct quote here, so quotation marks are inappropriate, as is the comma following *us*.

262. **The correct answer is B.** Feeling "badly" refers to one's sense of touch. When referring to health or emotions, one feels "bad."

263. **The correct answer is B.** The correct subject of the sentence is "my artist friend and *I*." The reflexive *myself* is used only when someone reflects back on themselves, for instance, "I was beside myself with grief."

264. **The correct answer is A.** It is poor form to begin a sentence with "due to." The correct introduction to such an explanatory statement is "because of." In choice B, the past participle of the verb *to lie* is *lain*, so this sentence is correct.

265. **The correct answer is C.** This error is called a comma splice. The cure is to create two sentences with a period at the end of the first, or to join the two independent clauses with a semicolon or conjunction.

266. **The correct answer is D.** *No mistakes.*

267. **The correct answer is A.** A council is a group; *counsel*, the required word, means "advice."

268. **The correct answer is B.** The correct spelling is *responsible*.

269. **The correct answer is B.** The correct spelling is *discipline*.

270. **The correct answer is D.** *No mistakes.*

271. **The correct answer is B.** The correct spelling is *parasite*.

272. **The correct answer is C.** The correct spelling is *concede*.

273. **The correct answer is D.** *No mistakes.*

274. **The correct answer is C.** The correct spelling is *noticeable*.

275. **The correct answer is A.** The correct spelling is *recommendation*.

276. **The correct answer is B.** The correct spelling is *interrupt*.

277. **The correct answer is C.** The correct spelling is *pseudonym*.

278. **The correct answer is D.** This sentence demonstrates correct usage. The other answer choices contain incorrect pronouns.

279. **The correct answer is B.** This sentence demonstrates correct usage. The other answer choices contain incorrect possessive noun forms.

280. **The correct answer is A.** This sentence demonstrates correct usage. The other answer choices contain incorrect contractions that don't fit, given the context of the sentence.

281. **The correct answer is D.** This sentence demonstrates correct usage. The other answer choices have missing articles, which result in awkward sentences.

282. **The correct answer is A.** This sentence demonstrates correct usage. The other answer choices contain incorrect pronouns.

283. **The correct answer is C.** This sentence demonstrates correct usage. The other answer choices contain incorrect possessive noun forms.

284. **The correct answer is D.** This sentence demonstrates correct usage. The other answer choices contain incorrect forms of the homonyms *too, two,* and *to.*

285. **The correct answer is D.** This sentence demonstrates correct usage. The other answer choices are missing correct adverb forms.

286. **The correct answer is A.** This sentence demonstrates correct usage. The other answer choices have missing articles, which result in awkward sentences.

287. **The correct answer is C.** This sentence demonstrates correct usage. The other answer choices contain incorrect contractions.

288. **The correct answer is B.** All other choices exhibit incorrect use of the possessive apostrophe.

289. **The correct answer is C.** The point is that the soldiers are busy fighting a war and won't return until it's over.

290. **The correct answer is B.** Choice A represents an impossibility, and choice C is highly improbable. If the movie is very good, one might consider it to have been worth the wait.

291. **The correct answer is C.** *Until* is the correct choice. : "Donte, a responsible security guard, could not leave his post until his shift replacement arrived each night."

292. **The correct answer is D.** "Glass-bottomed fish" and "coral reefs swimming" make no sense at all,

so choices B and C are incorrect. Choice A has a misplaced modifier—the *fish* are not in the glass-bottom boats; readers would be watching the fish from the boats.

293. **The correct answer is B.** Choices A and C are incorrect, as they suggest that changing strategies is part of the learning process. Choice D is totally garbled, and contradicts itself by stating that one "must easily learn" a "complex game." The statement made by choice B is more reasonable.

294. **The correct answer is A.** The growth of cities and the information explosion define the moment at which computers were needed.

295. **The correct answer is C.** The threat that the bald eagle poses to the fishing industry counters (i.e., argues against) the need to protect the bird.

296. **The correct answer is B.** Changing one's color is a means for disguise. None of the other choices address the squid's ability to hide itself in this manner.

297. **The correct answer is B.** Sentences 1, 3, and 4 present reasons for the Crusades. Sentence 2, however, presents an effect of the Crusades, rather than a reason for their existence.

298. **The correct answer is A.** This sentence serves as a topic sentence and provides a subject. All the other sentences begin with pronouns referring to "man" and offer examples to bolster the topic sentence.

SCORE SHEET

Although your actual exam scores will not be reported as percentages, it might be helpful to convert them so you can better visualize your strengths and weaknesses. The numbers in parentheses represent the question numbers testing each skill.

Subject	# Correct ÷ # of questions	× 100 = _____ %
Analogies (2, 8, 13, 16, 23, 31, 39, 48, 52, 56)	_____ ÷ 10 = _____	× 100 = _____ %
Synonyms (5, 7, 9, 17, 21, 22, 28, 29, 34, 37, 43, 46, 50, 53, 59)	_____ ÷ 15 = _____	× 100 = _____ %
Logic (3, 10, 15, 20, 27, 30, 36, 44, 51, 58)	_____ ÷ 10 = _____	× 100 = _____ %
Verbal Classification (1, 6, 11, 14, 18, 19, 26, 35, 38, 41, 42, 45, 49, 54, 57, 60)	_____ ÷ 16 = _____	× 100 = _____ %
Antonyms (4, 12, 24, 25, 32, 33, 40, 47, 55)	_____ ÷ 9 = _____	× 100 = _____ %
TOTAL VERBAL SKILLS	_____ ÷ 60 = _____	× 100 = _____ %
Number Series (61, 64, 71, 73, 75, 76, 78, 81, 83, 85, 87, 89, 91, 94, 98, 101, 107, 108)	_____ ÷ 18 = _____	× 100 = _____ %
Geometric Comparisons (66, 70, 77, 90, 93, 100, 103, 104, 109)	_____ ÷ 9 = _____	× 100 = _____ %
Nongeometric Comparisons (65, 68, 74, 86, 96, 105, 110, 112)	_____ ÷ 8 = _____	× 100 = _____ %
Number Manipulation (62, 63, 67, 69, 72, 79, 80, 82, 84, 88, 92, 95, 97, 99, 102, 106, 111)	_____ ÷ 17 = _____	× 100 = _____ %
TOTAL QUANTITATIVE SKILLS	_____ ÷ 52 = _____	× 100 = _____ %
Reading—Comprehension (113–152)	_____ ÷ 40 = _____	× 100 = _____ %
Reading—Vocabulary (153–174)	_____ ÷ 22 = _____	× 100 = _____ %
TOTAL READING SKILLS	_____ ÷ 62 = _____	× 100 = _____ %
Mathematics—Concepts (175–198)	_____ ÷ 24 = _____	× 100 = _____ %
Mathematics—Problem Solving (199–238)	_____ ÷ 40 = _____	× 100 = _____ %
TOTAL MATHEMATICS SKILLS	_____ ÷ 64 = _____	× 100 = _____ %
Punctuation and Capitalization (239, 240, 243, 245, 246, 248, 249, 253, 254, 255, 261, 265)	_____ ÷ 12 = _____	× 100 = _____ %
Usage (241, 242, 244, 247, 250, 251, 252, 256, 257, 258, 259, 260, 262, 263, 264, 266, 267, 278-288)	_____ ÷ 28 = _____	× 100 = _____ %
Spelling (268–277)	_____ ÷ 10 = _____	× 100 = _____ %
Composition (289–298)	_____ ÷ 10 = _____	× 100 = _____ %
TOTAL LANGUAGE SKILLS	_____ ÷ 60 = _____	× 100 = _____ %

NOTES

ANSWERS: HSPT® PRACTICE TEST 6

PART VI
APPENDIXES

APPENDIX A: WORD LIST

WORD LIST

The following is a list of words you can review in order to improve and expand your vocabulary. Consider documenting some of these in your word log and studying the roots, prefixes, and suffixes as relevant. Expanding your vocabulary will help you on the verbal skills sections of the exam. The words included here are arranged in alphabetical order.

A

abbreviate (verb) to make briefer, to shorten. *Because time was running out, the speaker had to abbreviate his remarks.* **abbreviation** (noun).

abrasive (adjective) irritating, grinding, rough. *The manager's rude, abrasive way of criticizing the workers was bad for morale.* **abrasion** (noun).

abridge (verb) to shorten, to reduce. *The Bill of Rights is designed to prevent Congress from abridging the rights of Americans.* **abridgment** (noun).

absolve (verb) to free from guilt, to exonerate. *The criminal jury absolved Mr. Callahan of the murder of his neighbor.* **absolution** (noun).

abstain (verb) to refrain, to hold back. *After his heart attack, William was warned by his doctor to abstain from smoking, drinking, and overeating.* **abstinence** (noun), **abstemious** (adjective).

accentuate (verb) to emphasize, to stress. *The overcast skies and chill winds only accentuate our gloomy mood.* **accentuation** (noun).

acrimonious (adjective) biting, harsh, caustic. *The election campaign became acrimonious, as the candidates traded insults and accusations.* **acrimony** (noun).

adaptable (adjective) able to be changed to be suitable for a new purpose. *Some scientists say that the mammals outlived the dinosaurs because they were more adaptable to a changing climate.* **adapt** (verb), **adaptation** (noun).

adulation (noun) extreme admiration. *The young actress received great adulation from critics and fans following her performance on Broadway.* **adulate** (verb), **adulatory** (adjective).

adversary (noun) an enemy or opponent. *When Germany became an American ally, the United States lost a major adversary.* **adversarial** (adjective).

adversity (noun) misfortune. *It's easy to be patient and generous when things are going well, but true character is revealed in times of adversity.* **adverse** (adjective).

aesthetic (adjective) relating to art or beauty. *Mapplethorpe's photos have been attacked on moral grounds, but no one questions their aesthetic value—they are beautiful.* **aestheticism** (noun).

aggressive (adjective) forceful, energetic, and attacking. *Some believe that a football player needs a more aggressive style of play than a soccer player.* **aggression** (noun).

alacrity (noun) promptness, speed. *The alacrity of her arrival caught him entirely by surprise—he still hadn't gotten dinner ready.* **alacritous** (adjective).

allege (verb) to state without proof. *Some have alleged that Foster was murdered, but all the evidence points to suicide.* **allegation** (noun).

alleviate (verb) to make lighter or more bearable. *Although no cure for AIDS has been found, doctors are able to alleviate the suffering of those with the disease.* **alleviation** (noun).

ambiguous (adjective) having two or more possible meanings. *The phrase, "Let's table that discussion" is ambiguous; some think it means, "Let's discuss it now," while others think it means, "Let's save it for later."* **ambiguity** (noun).

ambivalent (adjective) having two or more contradictory feelings or attitudes; uncertain. *She was ambivalent toward her impending marriage; at times she was eager to go ahead, while at other times she wanted to call it off.* **ambivalence** (noun).

amiable (adjective) likable, agreeable, friendly. *He was an amiable lab partner, always smiling, on time, and ready to work.* **amiability** (noun).

amicable (adjective) friendly, peaceable. *They remained amicable despite their divorce.*

amplify (verb) to enlarge, expand, or increase. *The students asked the teacher to amplify his explanation.* **amplification** (noun).

anachronistic (adjective) outside the proper time. *Shakespeare's reference in* Julius Caesar *to "the clock striking twelve" is anachronistic, since there were no striking timepieces in ancient Rome.* **anachronism** (noun).

anarchy (noun) absence of law or order. *For several months after the Nazi government collapsed, anarchy ruled Germany.* **anarchic** (adjective).

anomaly (noun) something different or irregular. *Tiny Pluto, orbiting next to the giants Jupiter, Saturn, and Neptune, had long appeared to be an anomaly.* **anomalous** (adjective).

antagonism (noun) hostility, conflict, opposition. *As more and more reporters investigated the Watergate scandal, antagonism between Nixon and the press increased.* **antagonistic** (adjective), **antagonize** (verb).

antiseptic (adjective) fighting infection; extremely clean. *Open wounds should be washed with an antiseptic solution.*

apathy (noun) lack of interest, concern, or emotion. *Tom's apathy toward his job could be seen in his sloppy work and his overall poor attitude.* **apathetic** (adjective).

arable (adjective) able to be cultivated for growing crops. *Rocky New England has relatively little arable farmland.*

arbiter (noun) someone able to settle disputes; a judge or referee. *The public is the ultimate arbiter of financial value; it decides what sells and what doesn't.*

arbitrary (adjective) based on random or merely personal preference. *Both computers cost the same and had the same features, so in the end, my decision was arbitrary.*

arcane (adjective) little-known, mysterious, obscure. *Eliot's* Waste Land *is filled with arcane lore, including quotations in Latin, Greek, French, German, and Sanskrit.* **arcana** (noun, plural).

ardor (noun) a strong feeling of passion, energy, or zeal. *The young revolutionary proclaimed his convictions with an ardor that excited the crowd.* **ardent** (adjective).

arid (adjective) very dry; boring and meaningless. *The arid climate of Arizona makes farming difficult. Some find the law fascinating, but for me, it's an arid subject.* **aridity** (noun).

ascetic (adjective) practicing strict self-discipline for moral or spiritual reasons. *The so-called Desert Fathers were hermits who lived an ascetic life of fasting, study, and prayer.* **asceticism** (verb).

assiduous (adjective) working with care, attention, and diligence. *Although Karen is not a naturally gifted math student, by assiduous study she managed to earn an A in trigonometry.* **assiduity** (noun).

astute (adjective) observant, intelligent, and shrewd. *The reporter's years of experience in Washington and his personal acquaintance with many political insiders made him an astute commentator on politics.*

atypical (adjective) not typical; unusual. *In* Hyde Park on Hudson, *Bill Murray, best known as a comic actor, gave an atypical dramatic performance.*

audacious (adjective) bold, daring, adventurous. *Her plan to cross the Atlantic single-handedly in a 12-foot sailboat was audacious, if not reckless.* **audacity** (noun).

audible (adjective) able to be heard. *Although she whispered, her voice was picked up by the microphone, and her words were audible throughout the theater.* **audibility** (noun).

auspicious (adjective) promising good fortune; propitious. *The news that a team of British climbers had reached the summit of Everest seemed an auspicious sign for the reign of newly crowned Queen Elizabeth II.* **auspice** (noun).

authoritarian (adjective) favoring or demanding blind obedience to leaders. *Despite Americans' belief in democracy, the American government has supported authoritarian regimes in other countries.* **authoritarianism** (noun).

B

belated (adjective) delayed past the proper time. *She called her mother on January 5th to offer a belated "Happy New Year."*

belie (verb) to present a false or contradictory appearance. *Lena Horne's youthful appearance belied her long, distinguished career in show business.*

benevolent (adjective) wishing or doing good. *In old age, Carnegie used his wealth for benevolent purposes, donating large sums to found schools and libraries.* **benevolence** (noun).

berate (verb) to scold or criticize harshly. *The judge angrily berated the two lawyers for their unprofessional behavior.*

bereft (adjective) lacking or deprived of something. *Bereft of parental love, orphans sometimes grow up insecure.*

bombastic (adjective) inflated or pompous in style. *Old-fashioned bombastic political speeches don't work on television, which demands a more intimate style of communication.* **bombast** (noun).

bourgeois (adjective) middle class or reflecting middle-class values. *The Dadaists of the 1920s produced art deliberately designed to offend bourgeois art collectors, with their taste for respectable, refined, uncontroversial pictures.* **bourgeois** (noun).

buttress (noun) something that supports or strengthens; a projecting structure of masonry or wood. *The endorsement of the American Medical Association is a powerful buttress for the claims made about this new medicine. The buttress on the south wall of the Medieval castle was crumbling.* **buttress** (verb).

C

camaraderie (noun) a spirit of friendship. *Spending long days and nights together on the road, the members of a traveling theater group develop a strong sense of camaraderie.*

candor (noun) openness, honesty, frankness. *In his memoir about the Vietnam War, former defense secretary McNamara described his mistakes with remarkable candor.* **candid** (adjective).

capricious (adjective) unpredictable, whimsical. *The pop star has changed her image so many times that each new transformation now appears capricious rather than purposeful.* **caprice** (noun).

carnivorous (adjective) meat-eating. *The long, dagger-like teeth of the Tyrannosaurus make it obvious that it was a carnivorous dinosaur.* **carnivore** (noun).

carping (adjective) unfairly or excessively critical; querulous. *New York is famous for its demanding critics, but none is harder to please than the carping John Simon, said to have single-handedly destroyed many acting careers.* **carp** (verb).

catalytic (adjective) bringing about, causing, or producing some result. *The conditions for revolution existed in America by 1765; the disputes about taxation that arose later were the catalytic events that sparked the rebellion.* **catalyze** (verb), **catalyst** (noun).

caustic (adjective) burning, corrosive. *No one was safe when the satirist H. L. Mencken unleashed his caustic wit.*

censure (noun) blame, condemnation. *The news that the senator had harassed several women brought censure from feminists around the world.* **censure** (verb).

chaos (noun) disorder, confusion, chance. *The first moments after the explosion were chaos: no one was sure what happened and the area was filled with people screaming.* **chaotic** (adjective).

circuitous (adjective) winding or indirect. *We drove to the cottage by a circuitous route so we could see as much of the surrounding countryside as possible.*

circumlocution (noun) speaking in a roundabout way; wordiness. *Legal documents often contain circumlocutions that make them difficult to understand.*

circumscribe (verb) to define by a limit or boundary. *The original role of the executive branch was clearly circumscribed, but that role has greatly expanded over time.* **circumscription** (noun).

circumvent (verb) to get around. *When James was caught speeding, he tried to circumvent the law by offering the police officer a bribe.*

clandestine (adjective) secret, surreptitious. *As a member of the underground, Balas took part in clandestine meetings to discuss ways of sabotaging the Nazi forces.*

cloying (adjective) overly sweet or sentimental. *The deathbed scenes in the novels of Dickens are famously cloying; as Oscar Wilde said, "One would need a heart of stone to read the death of Little Nell without dissolving into tears . . . of laughter."*

cogent (adjective) forceful and convincing. *The committee members were won over to the project by the cogent arguments of the chairman.* **cogency** (noun).

cognizant (adjective) aware, mindful. *Cognizant of the fact that it was getting late, the master of ceremonies decided to cut part of his speech.* **cognizance** (noun).

cohesive (adjective) sticking together, unified. *An effective military unit must be a cohesive team with all its members working together for a common goal.* **cohere** (verb), **cohesion** (noun).

collaborate (verb) to work together. *To create a truly successful movie, the director, writers, and actors must collaborate closely.* **collaboration** (noun), **collaborative** (adjective).

colloquial (adjective) informal in language; conversational. *Some of Shakespeare's expressions—such as his use of thou and thee—sound overly formal today, but they were colloquial English in his time.*

competent (adjective) having the skill and knowledge needed for a specific task; capable. *Any competent lawyer can draw up a will.* **competence** (noun).

complacent (adjective) smug, self-satisfied. *Until recently, American automakers were complacent, believing that they would continue to be successful with little effort.* **complacency** (noun).

composure (noun) calm, self-assurance. *The company's president managed to keep his composure during his speech even when the teleprompter broke down, leaving him without a script.* **composed** (adjective).

conciliatory (adjective) seeking agreement, compromise, or reconciliation. *As a conciliatory gesture, the union leaders agreed to postpone a strike and to continue negotiations with management.* **conciliate** (verb), **conciliation** (noun).

concise (adjective) expressed briefly and simply; succinct. *Less than a page long, the Bill of Rights is a concise statement of the freedoms enjoyed by all Americans.* **concision** (noun).

condescending (adjective) having an attitude of superiority toward another; patronizing. *"What a cute little car,"* *she remarked in a condescending tone, "I suppose it's the nicest one someone like you could afford!"* **condescension** (noun), **condescend** (verb).

condolence (noun) pity for someone else's sorrow or loss; sympathy. *After the sudden death of Princess Diana, thousands of condolences were sent to her family by mail.* **condole** (verb).

confidant (noun) someone entrusted with another's secrets. *No one knew about Jane's engagement, except Sarah, her confidant.* **confide** (verb), **confidential** (adjective).

conformity (noun) agreement with or adherence to custom or rule. *Conformity was common in my high school: everyone dressed the same, talked the same, and listened to the same music.* **conform** (verb), **conformist** (noun, adjective).

consensus (noun) general agreement among a group. *Traditional voting isn't used among Quakers; instead, discussion continues until a consensus is formed among the entire group.*

consolation (noun) relief or comfort in sorrow or suffering. *Although we miss our dog very much, it is a consolation to know that she died quickly and without suffering.* **console** (verb).

consternation (noun) shock, amazement, dismay. *When a voice in the back of the church shouted out, "I know why they shouldn't be married!" the entire gathering was thrown into consternation.*

consummate (verb) to complete, finish, or perfect. *The deal was consummated with a handshake and the payment of the agreed-upon fee.* **consummate** (adjective), **consummation** (noun).

contaminate (verb) to make impure. *Chemicals dumped in a nearby forest had seeped into the soil and contaminated the local water supply.* **contamination** (noun).

contemporary (adjective) modern, current; from the same time. *I prefer old-fashioned furniture rather than contemporary styles. The composer Vivaldi was practically Bach's contemporary.* **contemporary** (noun).

contrite (adjective) sorry for past misdeeds. *The public is often willing to forgive celebrities involved in scandal so long as they appear contrite.* **contrition** (noun).

conundrum (noun) a riddle, puzzle, or problem. *The question of why an all-powerful, all-loving God allows evil to exist is a conundrum pondered by philosophers since the beginning of time.*

convergence (noun) the act of coming together or becoming more like one another. *A remarkable example of evolutionary convergence can be seen in the shark and dolphin, two sea creatures that developed from different origins to become very similar in form.* **converge** (verb).

convoluted (adjective) twisting, complicated, intricate. *Tax law has become so convoluted that it's easy to accidentally violate it.* **convolute** (verb), **convolution** (noun).

corroborating (adjective) supporting with evidence; confirming. *A passerby who witnessed the crime gave corroborating testimony about the presence of the accused.* **corroborate** (verb), **corroboration** (noun).

corrosive (adjective) eating away, gnawing, or destroying. *Years of poverty and hard work had a corrosive effect on her health.* **corrode** (verb), **corrosion** (noun).

credulity (noun) willingness to believe, even with little evidence. *Con artists fool people by taking advantage of their credulity.* **credulous** (adjective).

criterion (noun) a standard of measurement or judgment. *In choosing a design for the new taxicabs, reliability will be our main criterion.* **criteria** (plural).

critique (noun) a critical evaluation. *The editor gave a detailed critique of the manuscript, explaining its strengths and weaknesses.* **critique** (verb).

culpable (adjective) deserving blame, guilty. *Although he committed the crime, because he was mentally ill, he should not be considered culpable for his actions.* **culpability** (noun).

cumulative (adjective) made up of successive additions. *Smallpox was eliminated only through the cumulative efforts of several generations.* **accumulation** (noun), **accumulate** (verb).

curtail (verb) to shorten. *The opening round of the golf tournament was curtailed by thunderstorms.*

D

debased (adjective) lowered in quality, character, or esteem. *The quality of TV journalism has been debased by the popularity of tabloid-style talk shows.* **debase** (verb).

debunk (verb) to expose as false or worthless. *Magician James Randi loves to debunk psychics, mediums, clairvoyants, and others who claim supernatural powers.*

decorous (adjective) having good taste; proper, appropriate. *Prior to her visit to Buckingham Palace, the young woman was instructed to demonstrate the most decorous behavior.* **decorum** (noun).

decry (verb) to criticize or condemn. *The workers continued to decry the lack of safety in their factory.*

deduction (noun) a logical conclusion based on a process of elimination. *Given what's known about the effects of greenhouse gases on atmospheric temperature, scientists have made several deductions about the likelihood of their contribution to global warming.* **deduce** (verb).

delegate (verb) to give authority or responsibility. *The president delegated the vice president to represent the administration at the peace talks.* **delegate, delegation** (noun).

deleterious (adjective) harmful. *Thirty years ago, scientists proved that working with asbestos could be deleterious to one's health by causing cancer and other diseases.*

delineate (verb) to outline or describe. *Naturalists had long theorized about evolution, but Darwin was the first to delineate a process—natural selection—by which evolution occurred.* **delineation** (noun).

demagogue (noun) a leader who plays dishonestly on the prejudices and emotions of his followers. *Senator Joseph McCarthy was a demagogue who used the paranoia of the anti-Communist 1950s as a means for seizing fame and power in Washington.* **demagoguery** (noun).

demure (adjective) modest or shy. *The demure heroines of Victorian fiction have given way to today's stronger, more opinionated, and more independent female characters.*

denigrate (verb) to criticize or belittle. *The firm's new president tried to explain his plans for improving the company without appearing to denigrate the work of his predecessor.* **denigration** (noun).

depose (verb) to remove from office, especially from a throne. *Iran was once ruled by a monarch called the Shah who was deposed in 1979.*

derelict (adjective) neglecting one's duty. *The train crash was blamed on a derelict switchman who fell asleep on the job.* **dereliction** (noun).

derivative (adjective) taken from or inspired by another source. *When a person first writes poetry, their poems are often derivative of whatever poet they enjoy reading most.* **derivation** (noun), **derive** (verb).

desolate (adjective) empty, lifeless, and deserted; hopeless, gloomy. *Robinson Crusoe was shipwrecked and had to survive alone on a desolate island. Mary Lincoln was left desolate after the murder of her husband.* **desolation** (noun).

destitute (adjective) very poor. *Years of rule by a dictator who stole the wealth of the country left the people of the Philippines destitute.* **destitution** (noun).

deter (verb) to discourage from acting. *The best way to deter crime is to ensure that criminals will receive swift and certain punishment.* **deterrence** (noun), **deterrent** (adjective).

detractor (noun) someone who belittles or disparages. *Neil Diamond has many detractors who consider his music boring, inane, and melodramatic.* **detract** (verb).

deviate (verb) to depart from a standard or norm. *Having agreed upon a spending budget for the company, we mustn't deviate from it; if we do, we may run out of money.* **deviation** (noun).

devious (adjective) tricky, deceptive. *The CEO's devious financial tactics were designed to enrich his firm while confusing or misleading government regulators.*

didactic (adjective) intended to teach; instructive. *The children's TV show* Sesame Street *is designed to be both entertaining and didactic.* **didacticism** (noun).

diffident (adjective) hesitant, reserved, shy. *Someone with a diffident personality should pursue a career that requires little public contact.* **diffidence** (noun).

diffuse (verb) to spread out, to scatter. *The red dye quickly became diffused through the water, turning it a very pale pink.* **diffusion** (noun).

digress (verb) to wander from the main path or the main topic. *My high school biology teacher loved to digress from science lectures into personal anecdotes about his college adventures.* **digression** (noun), **digressive** (adjective).

dilatory (adjective) delaying, procrastinating. *The lawyer used various dilatory tactics, hoping that his opponent would get tired of waiting for a trial and drop the case.*

diligent (adjective) working hard and steadily. *Through diligent efforts, the townspeople were able to clear the debris from the disaster site in a matter of days.* **diligence** (noun).

diminutive (adjective) unusually small, tiny. *Children are fond of Shetland ponies because their diminutive size makes them easy to ride.* **diminution** (noun).

discern (verb) to detect, notice, or observe. *I could discern the shape of a whale off the starboard bow, but it was too far away to determine its size or species.* **discernment** (noun).

disclose (verb) to make known; to reveal. *Election laws require candidates to disclose the names of those who contribute large sums of money to their campaigns.* **disclosure** (noun).

discomfit (verb) to frustrate, thwart, or embarrass. *Discomfited by the interviewer's unexpected question, Peter could only stammer in reply.* **discomfiture** (noun).

disconcert (verb) to confuse or embarrass. *When the hallway bells began to ring halfway through her lecture, the speaker was disconcerted and didn't know what to do.* **disconcerted** (noun).

discredit (verb) to cause disbelief in the accuracy of some statement or the reliability of a person. *Many believe in extraterrestrials, even though reports of "alien encounters" have been thoroughly discredited among scientists.*

discreet (adjective) showing good judgment in speech and behavior. *Be discreet when discussing confidential business matters; for example, don't talk among strangers in an elevator.* **discretion** (noun).

discrepancy (noun) a difference or variance between two or more things. *The discrepancies between the two witnesses' stories show that one of them must be lying.* **discrepant** (adjective).

disdain (noun) contempt, scorn. *The professor could not hide his disdain for students who were perpetually late to class.* **disdain** (verb), **disdainful** (adjective).

disingenuous (adjective) pretending to be candid, simple, and frank. *When Texas billionaire H. Ross Perot ran for president, many considered his downhome style disingenuous.*

disparage (verb) to speak disrespectfully about, to belittle. *Many political ads today both praise their own candidate and disparage their opponent.* **disparagement** (noun), **disparaging** (adjective).

disparity (noun) difference in quality or kind. *There's often a disparity in the types of assets held by the rich and poor.* **disparate** (adjective).

disregard (verb) to ignore, to neglect. *If you don't write a will, when you die, your survivors may disregard your wishes about how your property should be handled.* **disregard** (noun).

disruptive (adjective) causing disorder, interrupting. *When the senator spoke at our college, angry demonstrators picketed, heckled, and engaged in other disruptive activities.* **disrupt** (verb), **disruption** (noun).

dissemble (verb) to pretend, to simulate. *When the police questioned her about the crime, she dissembled innocence.*

dissipate (verb) to spread out or scatter. *The windows and doors were opened, allowing the smoke that filled the room to dissipate.* **dissipation** (noun).

dissonance (noun) lack of music harmony; lack of agreement between ideas. *Much modern music is characterized by dissonance, which many listeners find hard to enjoy.* **dissonant** (adjective).

diverge (verb) to move in different directions. *Be careful not to diverge too far from the marked path.* **divergence** (noun), **divergent** (adjective).

diversion (noun) a distraction or pastime. *The game on his phone was a welcome diversion during the two hours he spent in the waiting room.* **divert** (verb).

divination (noun) the art of predicting the future. *In ancient Greece, people wanting to know their fate would visit the priests at Delphi, supposedly skilled at divination.* **divine** (verb).

divisive (adjective) causing disagreement or disunity. *Throughout history, race has been the most divisive issue in American society.*

divulge (verb) to reveal. *The people who count the votes for the Oscar awards are under strict orders not to divulge the names of the winners.*

dogmatic (adjective) holding firmly to a set of beliefs with little or no basis. *Believers in Marxist doctrine tend to be dogmatic and ignore evidence that contradicts their beliefs.* **dogmatism** (noun).

dominant (adjective) greatest in importance or power. *Television quickly became a dominant influence in American culture.* **dominate** (verb), **domination** (noun).

dubious (adjective) doubtful, uncertain. *Despite the chairman's attempts to convince the committee members that his plan would succeed, most of them remained dubious.* **dubiety** (noun).

durable (adjective) long lasting. *Denim is a popular material for work clothes because it's strong and durable.* **durability** (noun).

duress (noun) compulsion or restraint. *Fearing the police might beat him, he confessed to the crime under duress.*

E

eclectic (adjective) drawn from many sources; varied, heterogeneous. *The Mellon family art collection is an eclectic one, including works from ancient Greek and Mesopotamia.* **eclecticism** (noun).

efficacious (adjective) able to produce a desired effect. *Though thousands of people today are taking herbal supplements to treat depression, researchers haven't yet proved them efficacious.* **efficacy** (noun).

effrontery (noun) shameless boldness. *The sports world was shocked when a professional basketball player had the effrontery to choke his head coach during practice.*

effusive (adjective) pouring forth one's emotions freely. *Having won the Oscar for Best Actress, Sally Field gave an effusive acceptance speech.* **effusion** (noun).

egotism (noun) excessive concern with oneself; conceit. *Robert's egotism was so great that all he could talk about was the importance—and brilliance—of his own opinions.* **egotistic** (adjective).

egregious (adjective) obvious, conspicuous, flagrant. *It's hard to imagine how the editor could allow such an egregious error to go to print.*

elated (adjective) excited and happy; exultant. *When the Miami Dolphins' last, desperate pass was intercepted, elated Philadelphia Eagle's fans began to celebrate.* **elate** (verb), **elation** (noun).

elliptical (adjective) very terse or concise in writing or speech; difficult to understand. *Rather than speak plainly, she hinted at her meaning through a series of nods, gestures, and elliptical half sentences.*

elusive (adjective) hard to capture, grasp, or understand. *Though everyone thinks they know what "justice" is, it's a concept that proves quite elusive to definition.*

embezzle (verb) to steal money or property that has been entrusted to your care. *The treasurer embezzled thousands of dollars by writing phony checks on the company bank account.* **embezzlement** (noun).

emigrate (verb) to leave one's place or country to settle elsewhere. *Millions of Irish emigrated to the New World in the wake of the Irish famines of the 1840s.* **emigrant** (noun), **emigration** (noun).

eminent (adjective) noteworthy, famous. *Vaclav Havel was an eminent author before he was elected president of the Czech Republic.* **eminence** (noun).

emissary (noun) someone who represents another. *To avoid a military showdown, former President Jimmy Carter was sent as an emissary to Korea to negotiate a settlement.*

emollient (noun) something that softens or soothes. *She used a soothing cream as an emollient for her dry, work-roughened hands.* **emollient** (adjective).

empathy (noun) imaginative sharing of the feelings, thoughts, or experiences of another. *It's easy for a parent to have empathy for their own children.* **empathetic** (adjective).

empirical (adjective) based on experience or personal observation. *Although many people believe in ESP, scientists have found no empirical evidence of its existence.* **empiricism** (noun).

emulate (verb) to imitate or copy. *The British band Oasis admitted their desire to emulate their idols, the Beatles.* **emulation** (noun).

encroach (verb) to go beyond acceptable limits; to trespass. *Robert Moses continually encroached on the powers of other government leaders by seizing undue authority.* **encroachment** (noun).

enervate (verb) to reduce the energy or strength of someone or something. *Extended exposure to the sun enervated the shipwrecked crew, leaving them too weak to spot the passing vessel.*

engender (verb) to produce, to cause. *Countless disagreements over the proper use of national forests have engendered feelings of hostility between ranchers and environmentalists.*

enhance (verb) to improve in value or quality. *New kitchen appliances will enhance your house and increase the amount of money you'll make when you sell it.* **enhancement** (noun).

enmity (noun) hatred, hostility, ill will. *Long-standing enmity, like that between the Protestants and Catholics in Northern Ireland, is difficult to overcome.*

enthrall (verb) to enchant or charm. *The Swedish singer Jenny Lind enthralled American audiences in the nineteenth century with her beauty and talent.*

ephemeral (adjective) quickly disappearing; transient. *Stardom in pop music is ephemeral; many of the top acts of ten years ago have been forgotten about today.*

equanimity (noun) calmness of mind, especially under stress. *Franklin Roosevelt faced the great crises of his presidency—the Depression and the Second World War—with equanimity and humor.*

eradicate (verb) to destroy completely. *American society has failed to eradicate poverty despite decades of effort.*

espouse (verb) to take up as a cause; to adopt. *Some politicians in America today will openly espouse racism, while others behave and speak in racially prejudiced ways.*

euphoric (adjective) a feeling of extreme happiness and well-being; elation. *One often feels euphoric during the early days of a love affair.* **euphoria** (noun).

evanescent (adjective) vanishing like a vapor; fragile and transient. *The moment would have been evanescent had it not been captured on film.*

exacerbate (verb) to make worse or more severe. *The roads in our town already have too much traffic; building a new shopping mall will exacerbate the problem.*

exasperate (verb) to irritate or annoy. *Sharon was exasperated by the yelling of her neighbors' children while trying to study.*

exculpate (verb) to free from blame or guilt. *When someone else confessed to the crime, the previous suspect was exculpated.* **exculpation** (noun), **exculpatory** (adjective).

exemplary (adjective) worthy to serve as a model. *The Baldrige Award is given to a company with exemplary standards of excellence in products and service.* **exemplar** (noun), **exemplify** (verb).

exonerate (verb) to free from blame. *Although the truck driver was at first a suspect in the bombing, later evidence exonerated him.* **exoneration** (noun), **exonerative** (adjective).

expansive (adjective) broad and large; to speak openly and freely. *It was a large tract of land on an expansive ranch in Texas.* **expand** (verb), **expansion** (noun).

expedite (verb) to carry out promptly. *As the flood waters rose, the governor ordered state agencies to expedite their rescue efforts.*

expertise (noun) skill, mastery. *The software company was eager to hire new graduates with programming expertise.*

expiate (verb) to atone for. *The president's apology to the survivors of the notorious Tuskegee experiments was an attempt to expiate the nation's guilt over their mistreatment.* **expiation** (noun).

expropriate (verb) to seize ownership of. *When the Communists came to power in China, they expropriated most businesses and turned them over to government-appointed managers.* **expropriation** (noun).

extant (adjective) currently in existence. *Of the seven ancient Wonders of the World, only the pyramids of Egypt are still extant.*

extenuate (verb) to make less serious. *Jeanine's guilt is extenuated by the fact that she was only twelve when she committed the theft.* **extenuating** (adjective), **extenuation** (noun).

extol (verb) to greatly praise. *At the party convention, speaker after speaker rose to extol the virtues of their candidate for the presidency.*

extricate (verb) to free from a difficult or complicated situation. *Much of the humor in the TV show* I Love Lucy *comes in watching Lucy try to extricate herself from her own problems.* **extricable** (adjective).

extrinsic (adjective) not an innate part or aspect of something; external. *The high price of old baseball cards is due to extrinsic factors like the nostalgia felt by baseball fans for the stars of their youth rather than the inherent value of the cards themselves.*

exuberant (adjective) wildly joyous and enthusiastic. *As the final seconds of the game ticked away, the fans of the winning team began an exuberant celebration.* **exuberance** (noun).

F

facile (adjective) easy; shallow or superficial. *One-minute political commercials favor candidates with facile opinions rather than serious, thoughtful solutions.* **facilitate** (verb), **facility** (noun).

fallacy (noun) an error in fact or logic. *It's a fallacy to think that "natural" means "healthy"; after all, the deadly poison arsenic is a completely natural compound.* **fallacious** (adjective).

felicitous (adjective) pleasing, fortunate, apt. *The sudden blossoming of the dogwood trees on the morning of Matt's wedding seemed a felicitous sign of good luck.* **felicity** (noun).

feral (adjective) wild. *The dump was inhabited by a pack of feral dogs that escaped from their owners.*

fervent (adjective) full of intense feeling; ardent, zealous. *In the days immediately following his religious conversion, his piety was at its most fervent.* **fervid** (adjective), **fervor** (noun).

flagrant (adjective) obviously wrong; offensive. *Nixon was forced to resign the presidency after a series of flagrant crimes against the U.S. Constitution.* **flagrancy** (noun).

flamboyant (adjective) colorful, showy, or elaborate. *At Mardi Gras, partygoers compete in a display of the most wild and flamboyant outfits.*

florid (adjective) flowery, fancy; reddish. *The ballroom looked magnificent with its florid decoration.*

foppish (adjective) one who is foolishly vain in dress or appearance. *The foppish character of the 1890s wore bright-colored spats and a top hat; in the 1980s, he wore fancy suspenders and a shirt with a contrasting collar.* **fop** (noun).

formidable (adjective) awesome, impressive, or frightening. *According to his plaque in the Baseball Hall of Fame, pitcher Tom Seaver turned the New York Mets "from lovable losers into formidable foes."*

fortuitous (adjective) lucky, fortunate. *Although the mayor claimed credit for the falling crime rate, there were several fortuitous trends behind it.*

fractious (adjective) troublesome, unruly. *Members of the British Parliament are often fractious, shouting insults and sarcastic questions during debates.*

fragility (noun) easily broken; delicacy, weakness. *Because of their fragility, few stained-glass windows from the early Middle Ages have survived.* **fragile** (adjective).

fraternize (verb) to associate with on friendly terms. *Although baseball players aren't supposed to fraternize with opponents, players from opposing teams often chat before games.* **fraternization** (noun).

frenetic (adjective) chaotic, frantic. *The floor of the stock exchange, filled with traders shouting and gesturing, is a scene of frenetic activity.*

frivolity (noun) lack of seriousness; levity. *The frivolity of the Mardi Gras carnival contrasts with the seriousness of the religious season that follows.* **frivolous** (adjective).

frugal (adjective) spending little. *We bought a frugal dinner with our last few dollars: a loaf of bread and some slices of cheese.* **frugality** (noun).

fugitive (noun) someone trying to escape. *When two prisoners broke out of the local jail, police were warned to keep an eye out for the fugitives.* **fugitive** (adjective).

G

gargantuan (adjective) huge, colossal. *The Great Wall of China was one of the most gargantuan building projects ever undertaken.*

genial (adjective) friendly, gracious. *A good host welcomes all visitors in a warm and genial fashion.*

grandiose (adjective) overly large, pretentious, or showy. *Among Hitler's grandiose plans for Berlin was a gigantic building with a dome several times larger than any ever built.* **grandiosity** (noun).

gratuitous (adjective) given freely or without cause. *Since her opinion was not requested, her harsh criticism of his singing seemed a gratuitous insult.*

gregarious (adjective) one who enjoys the company of others; sociable. *Naturally gregarious, Emily is a popular member of several clubs and a sought-after lunch companion.*

guileless (adjective) without cunning; innocent or naïve. *Deborah's guileless personality and total honesty made it hard for her to survive in the harsh world of politics.*

gullible (adjective) easily fooled. *When the sweepstakes entry form arrived bearing the message, "You may be a winner!" my gullible neighbor tried to claim a prize.* **gullibility** (noun).

H

hackneyed (adjective) without originality, trite. *The phrase "no pain, no gain" used to be clever, but now it's so overused that it seems hackneyed.*

haughty (adjective) overly proud. *The fashion model strode down the runway, her hips thrust forward and a haughty expression on her face.* **haughtiness** (noun).

hedonist (noun) one who pursues pleasure as their chief purpose. *Having inherited great wealth, he chose to live the life of a hedonist, traveling the world in luxury.* **hedonism** (noun), **hedonistic** (adjective).

heinous (adjective) evil, hateful. *The massacre by Pol Pot of more than a million Cambodians is one of the twentieth century's most heinous crimes.*

hierarchy (noun) an ordered ranking of people, ideas, or things. *A cabinet secretary ranks just below the president and vice president in the hierarchy of the executive branch.* **hierarchical** (adjective).

hypocrisy (noun) a false pretense of virtue. *When the sexual misconduct of the television preacher was exposed, his followers were shocked by his hypocrisy.* **hypocritical** (adjective).

I

iconoclast (noun) someone who attacks traditional beliefs or institutions. *Comedian Stephen Colbert enjoys his reputation as an iconoclast, though people in power often resent his satirical jabs.* **iconoclasm** (noun), **iconoclastic** (adjective).

idiosyncratic (adjective) peculiar to an individual; eccentric. *Cyndi Lauper sings pop music in an idiosyncratic style, mingling high-pitched whoops and squeals with throaty gurgles.* **idiosyncrasy** (noun).

idolatry (noun) the worship of a person, thing, or institution as a god. *In Communist China, Chairman Mao was the subject of widespread praise and idolatry.* **idolatrous** (adjective).

impartial (adjective) fair, equal, unbiased. *If a judge is not impartial, then all her rulings are questionable.* **impartiality** (noun).

impeccable (adjective) flawless. *The crooks printed impeccable counterfeit tickets that were impossible to distinguish from the real thing.*

impetuous (adjective) acting hastily or impulsively. *Stuart's resignation was an impetuous act; he did it without thinking and soon regretted the decision.* **impetuosity** (noun).

impinge (verb) to encroach upon, touch, or affect. *You have a right to do whatever you want, so long as your actions don't impinge on the rights of others.*

implicit (adjective) understood without being openly expressed; implied. *Although the restaurant does not have a dress code, there's an implicit rule that you should dress in business casual attire.*

impute (verb) to attribute; to pass onto someone else. *Although Helena's comments embarrassed me, I don't impute her for any ill will; I don't think she realized what she was saying.* **imputation** (noun).

inarticulate (adjective) unable to speak or express oneself clearly and understandably. *A skilled athlete may be an inarticulate public speaker, as demonstrated by many post-game interviews.*

incisive (adjective) clear and direct expression. *Franklin settled the debate with a few incisive remarks that perfectly summarized the issue at hand.*

incompatible (adjective) unable to exist together; conflicting. *The Bluetooth speaker was incompatible with my phone, so we had to use an old radio.* **incompatibility** (noun).

inconsequential (adjective) of little importance. *When the vase was delivered, it was a slightly different shade of gray than expected, but the difference was inconsequential.*

incontrovertible (adjective) impossible to question. *The fact that Alexandra's fingerprints were the only ones on the murder weapon made her guilt seem incontrovertible.*

incorrigible (adjective) impossible to manage or reform. *Lou is an incorrigible trickster, constantly playing practical jokes despite frequent complaints.*

incremental (adjective) increasing gradually by small amounts. *Although the initial cost of the Medicare program was small, the incremental expenses have been relentless.* **increment** (noun).

incriminate (verb) to give evidence of guilt. *The fifth amendment to the Constitution says no one is required to reveal information that would incriminate themselves.* **incriminating** (adjective).

incumbent (noun) someone who occupies an office or position. *It is often difficult for a challenger to win a seat from an incumbent member of Congress.* **incumbency** (noun), **incumbent** (adjective).

indeterminate (adjective) not definitely known. *The college plans to enroll an indeterminate number of students; class sizes will depend on the number of applicants who accept their offers.* **determine** (verb).

indifferent (adjective) unconcerned, apathetic. *The mayor's small proposed budget for education suggests his indifference to the needs of our school system.* **indifference** (noun).

indistinct (adjective) unclear, uncertain. *We could see boats on the water, but in the thick morning fog their shapes were indistinct.*

indomitable (adjective) unable to be conquered or controlled. *The world admired the indomitable spirit of Nelson Mandela, who remained courageous despite years of imprisonment.*

induce (verb) to cause. *The doctor administered a medication that was supposed to induce labor in the pregnant patient.* **induction** (noun).

ineffable (adjective) difficult to describe or express. *He gazed in silence at the sunrise over the Taj Mahal, his eyes reflecting an ineffable sense of wonder.*

inevitable (adjective) impossible to avoid. *Once the Japanese attacked Pearl Harbor, American involvement in World War II was inevitable.* **inevitability** (noun).

inexorable (adjective) unable to be deterred; relentless. *It's difficult to imagine how the mythic character of Oedipus could have avoided his evil destiny; his fate appears inexorable.*

ingenious (adjective) showing cleverness and originality. *The Post-it note is an ingenious solution to a common problem—how to mark papers without spoiling them.* **ingenuity** (noun).

inherent (adjective) naturally part of something. *Compromise is inherent to democracy, since not everyone gets his or her way.* **inhere** (verb), **inherence** (noun).

innate (adjective) inborn, native. *Not everyone who takes lessons becomes a fine musician, which shows that music requires some innate talent as well as training.*

innocuous (adjective) harmless, inoffensive. *I'm surprised Melissa was offended by my innocuous joke.*

inoculate (verb) to prevent a disease by infusing with a disease-causing organism. *Pasteur found he could prevent rabies by inoculating patients with the virus itself.* **inoculation** (noun).

insipid (adjective) flavorless, uninteresting. *Some TV shows are so insipid that you can watch them while reading and not miss a thing.* **insipidity** (noun).

insolence (noun) an attitude or behavior that is bold and disrespectful. *Some feel that news reporters who shout questions at the president are behaving with insolence.* **insolent** (adjective).

insular (adjective) narrow or isolated in attitude or viewpoint. *Americans are famous for their insular beliefs that nothing important has ever happened outside of their country.* **insularity** (noun).

insurgency (noun) uprising, rebellion. *The insurgency of angry townspeople bordered on revolution as they flooded the streets in protest.* **insurgent** (adjective).

integrity (noun) honesty, uprightness; soundness, completeness. *"Honest Abe" Lincoln was a model of political integrity. Inspectors examined the building and found no reason to doubt its structural integrity.*

interlocutor (noun) someone taking part in a dialogue or conversation. *Annoyed by constant questions from the crowd, the speaker challenged his interlocutor directly.* **interlocutory** (adjective).

interlude (noun) a break or interruption. *The two most dramatic scenes in* King Lear *are separated, strangely, by comic interludes starring the king's jester.*

interminable (adjective) endless or seemingly endless. *Addressing the United Nations, Castro announced "we will be brief" before delivering an interminable four-hour speech.*

intransigent (adjective) unwilling to compromise. *Despite the mediator's attempts to suggest a fair solution, the two parties were intransigent and wanted a showdown.* **intransigence** (noun).

intrepid (adjective) fearless and resolute. *Only an intrepid traveler is willing to undertake the long and dangerous trip by sled to the South Pole.* **intrepidity** (noun).

intrusive (adjective) forcing a way in; unwelcome. *The legal requirement of a search warrant is supposed to protect Americans from intrusive searches by police.* **intrude** (verb), **intrusion** (noun).

intuitive (adjective) known directly, without apparent thought or effort. *An experienced chess player has an intuitive sense of the best move, even if they can't explain it.* **intuit** (verb), **intuition** (noun).

inundate (verb) to flood; to overwhelm. *As soon as the playoff tickets went on sale, eager fans inundated the box office with orders.*

invariable (adjective) unchanging, constant. *When writing a book, it was her invariable habit to rise at 6 a.m. and work at her desk from 7 to 12.* **invariability** (noun).

inversion (noun) turned backward, inside-out, or upside-down; reversed. *Latin poetry often features an inversion of word order, like the first line of Virgil's* Aeneid: *"Arms and the man I sing."* **invert** (verb), **inverted** (adjective).

inveterate (adjective) persistent, habitual. *It's notoriously difficult for an inveterate gambler to stop on their own accord.* **inveteracy** (noun).

invigorate (verb) to give energy to; to stimulate. *As her car climbed the mountain road, Lucinda felt invigorated by the clear air and cool breezes.*

invincible (adjective) impossible to conquer or overcome. *For three years, at the height of his career, boxer Mike Tyson seemed invincible.*

inviolable (adjective) impossible to undo or trespass upon. *In the president's remote hideaway at Camp David guarded by the Secret Service, his privacy is inviolable.*

irrational (adjective) unreasonable. *Richard knew that his fear of insects was irrational, but he was unable to overcome it.* **irrationality** (noun).

irresolute (adjective) uncertain how to act, indecisive. *The line in the ice cream shop grew as the irresolute child wavered between her two favorite flavors.* **irresolution** (noun).

J

jeopardize (verb) to put in danger. *Terrorist attacks jeopardize fragile peace not only in the Middle East but also right here at home.* **jeopardy** (noun).

juxtapose (verb) to compare side by side. *Juxtaposing the two editorials revealed the enormous differences in the writers' opinions.* **juxtaposition** (noun).

L

languid (adjective) without energy; slow, sluggish, listless. *The hot, humid weather of late August can make anyone feel languid.* **languish** (verb), **languor** (noun).

latent (adjective) not currently obvious or active; hidden. *Although he only committed a minor crime, the psychiatrist said it's likely he's always had a latent potential for violence.* **latency** (noun).

laudatory (adjective) giving praise. *Ads for the movie were filled with laudatory comments from critics.*

lenient (adjective) mild, soothing, or forgiving. *The judge was known for his lenient disposition, and he rarely imposed long jail sentences.* **leniency** (noun).

lethargic (adjective) lacking energy; sluggish. *Visitors to the zoo are often surprised that the lions appear so lethargic; in the wild, however, lions sleep up to 18 hours a day.* **lethargy** (noun).

liability (noun) an obligation or debt; a weakness or drawback. *The insurance company had a liability of millions of dollars after the town was destroyed by a tornado.* **liable** (adjective).

lithe (adjective) flexible and graceful. *The ballet dancer was lithe as a cat.*

longevity (noun) length of life; durability. *The reduction in early deaths from infectious diseases is responsible for most of the increase in human longevity over the past two centuries.*

lucid (adjective) clear and understandable. *Hawking's* A Short History of the Universe *is a lucid explanation of modern scientific theories about the origin of the universe.* **lucidity** (noun).

lurid (adjective) shocking, gruesome. *The newspapers were filled with lurid stories about his crimes.*

M

malediction (noun) a curse. *In the fairy tale "Sleeping Beauty," the princess is trapped in a death-like sleep because of the malediction uttered by an angry witch.*

malevolence (noun) hatred, ill will. *Critics say that Iago, the villain in Shakespeare's* Othello, *seems to exhibit malevolence with no understandable motivation.* **malevolent** (adjective).

malinger (verb) to pretend incapacity or illness to avoid a duty or work. *During the labor dispute, hundreds of employees malingered and forced the company to slow production.*

malleable (adjective) susceptible to change from outside pressures. *Gold is useful because it's so malleable. A child's personality is malleable and deeply influenced by their upbringing.* **malleability** (noun).

mandate (noun) order, command. *The new policy of using only organic produce in the restaurant went into effect as soon as the manager issued the mandate.* **mandate** (verb), **mandatory** (adjective).

maturation (noun) the process of becoming fully grown or developed. *Free markets in former Communist nations are likely to operate smoothly only after a long period of maturation.* **mature** (adjective and verb), **maturity** (noun).

mediate (verb) to reconcile differences between two parties. *During the baseball strike, both the players and club owners were willing to have the president mediate the dispute.* **mediation** (noun).

mediocrity (noun) the state of being middling or poor in quality. *The New York Mets finished in ninth place in 1968, but won the World Championship in 1969, going from horrible to great in a single year and skipping mediocrity.* **mediocre** (adjective).

mercurial (adjective) changing quickly and unpredictably. *The mercurial personality of Robin Williams made him perfect for the role of the ever-changing genie in* Aladdin.

meticulous (adjective) careful with details. *Repairing an old watch requires a meticulous craftsman.*

mimicry (noun) imitation, aping. *The continued popularity of Elvis Presley has given rise to a class of entertainers who make a living through mimicry of "The King."* **mimic** (noun and verb).

misconception (noun) a mistaken idea; misunderstanding. *Columbus sailed west with the misconception that he would reach the shores of Asia.* **misconceive** (verb).

mitigate (verb) to make less severe; to relieve. *Wallace certainly committed the assault, but the verbal abuse he'd received helps explain his behavior and mitigate his guilt.* **mitigation** (noun).

modicum (noun) a small amount. *The plan for your new business is well-designed; with a modicum of luck, you should be successful.*

mollify (verb) to soothe or calm; to appease. *Sam tried to mollify the angry customer with a full refund.*

morose (adjective) gloomy, sullen. *After Chuck's girlfriend dumped him, he laid around the house for days feeling morose.*

mundane (adjective) everyday, ordinary, commonplace. *Moviegoers in the 1930s liked the glamorous films of Fred Astaire as they provided an escape from the mundane problems of the Great Depression.*

munificent (adjective) very generous; lavish. *Ted Turner's billion-dollar donation to the United Nations was one of the most munificent acts of charity in history.* **munificence** (noun).

mutable (adjective) likely to change. *A politician's reputation can be highly mutable, as seen in the case of Harry Truman, who was mocked during his lifetime but revered after his death.*

N

narcissistic (adjective) showing excessive love for oneself; egoistic. *Andre's room, decorated with photos of himself and sports trophies he's won, suggests a narcissistic personality.* **narcissism** (noun).

nocturnal (adjective) of the night; active at night. *Travelers on the Underground Railroad escaped from slavery to the North with a series of nocturnal flights.*

nonchalant (adjective) appearing to be unconcerned. *Unlike other players who pumped their fists when announced, John took the field with a nonchalant wave of his hand.* **nonchalance** (noun).

nondescript (adjective) without distinctive qualities; drab. *The bank robber's clothes were nondescript; none of the witnesses could remember their color or style.*

notorious (adjective) famous, especially for evil actions or qualities. *Warner Brothers produced a series of movies about notorious gangsters such as John Dillinger and Al Capone.* **notoriety** (noun).

novice (noun) beginner. *Lifting your head before finishing your swing is a typical novice golf mistake.*

nuance (noun) a subtle difference or quality. *At first glance, Monet's paintings of waterlilies all look alike; the closer one looks, however, the more nuance one sees.*

nurture (verb) to nourish or help to grow. *The money given by the National Endowment for the Arts helps nurture local arts organizations throughout the country.* **nurture** (noun).

O

obdurate (adjective) unwilling to change; stubborn, inflexible. *Despite many pleas, the governor was obdurate in his refusal to grant clemency to the convicted murderer.*

objective (adjective) dealing with observable facts rather than opinions or interpretations. *When a legal case involves a shocking crime, it may be hard for a judge to remain objective in his ruling.*

oblivious (adjective) unaware, unconscious. *Karen practiced her oboe with complete concentration, oblivious to the noise and activity around her.* **oblivion** (noun), **obliviousness** (noun).

obscure (adjective) little known; hard to understand. *Mendel was an obscure monk until his scientific work was finally discovered decades after his death.* **obscure** (verb), **obscurity** (noun).

obsessive (adjective) haunted or preoccupied by an idea or feeling. *His concern with cleanliness became so obsessive that he washed his hands twenty times a day.* **obsess** (verb), **obsession** (noun).

obsolete (adjective) no longer current; old-fashioned. *W. H. Auden said that his ideal landscape would include water wheels, wooden grain mills, and other forms of obsolete machinery.* **obsolescence** (noun).

obstinate (adjective) stubborn, unyielding. *Drug abuse remains as obstinate as ever.* **obstinacy** (noun).

obtrusive (adjective) overly prominent. *Philip should sing more softly; his voice is so obtrusive that the other singers can barely be heard over him.* **obtrude** (verb), **obtrusion** (noun).

ominous (adjective) foretelling evil. *Ominous black clouds gathered on the horizon.* **omen** (noun).

onerous (adjective) heavy, burdensome. *The hero Hercules was ordered to clean the Augean Stables, one of several onerous tasks now known as "the labors of Hercules."* **onus** (noun).

opportunistic (adjective) eagerly seizing chances as they arise. *When Princess Diana died suddenly, opportunistic publishers were quick to release books about her life and death.* **opportunism** (noun).

opulent (adjective) rich, lavish. *The mansion of newspaper tycoon William Randolph Hearst is famous for its opulent decor.* **opulence** (noun).

ornate (adjective) highly decorated, elaborate. *Baroque architecture is often highly ornate, featuring surfaces covered with detailed carvings, sinuous curves, and painted scenes.*

ostentatious (adjective) overly showy, pretentious. *To show off his wealth, the billionaire threw an ostentatious party featuring a full orchestra and famous singer.*

ostracize (verb) to exclude from a group. *In biblical times, those who suffered from the disease of leprosy were ostracized from the community and forced to live alone.* **ostracism** (noun).

P

pallid (adjective) pale; dull. *Working all day in the coal mine had given him a pallid complexion. The new musical offers only pallid entertainment; it's lifeless, the acting is dull, and the story is beyond absurd.*

parched (adjective) very dry; thirsty. *After two months without rain, the crops were shriveled and parched by the sun.* **parch** (verb).

pariah (noun) outcast. *Accused of robbery, he became a pariah; his neighbors stopped talking to him, and people he'd considered friends no longer called.*

partisan (adjective) reflecting strong allegiance to a specific political party or cause. *The vote on the president's budget was strictly partisan: Every member of his party voted yes.* **partisan** (noun).

pathology (noun) disease or the study of disease; extreme abnormality. *Some people believe that high rates of crime are symptoms of an underlying social pathology.* **pathological** (adjective).

pellucid (adjective) very clear; transparent; easy to understand. *The water in the mountain stream was cold and pellucid. Thanks to the professor's pellucid explanation, I finally understand relativity theory.*

penitent (adjective) feeling sorry for past sins or crimes. *Having grown penitent, he wrote a long letter of apology asking forgiveness.*

penurious (adjective) extremely frugal; stingy. *Haunted by memories of poverty, he lived in penurious fashion, driving a 12-year-old car and wearing only the cheapest clothes.* **penury** (noun).

perceptive (adjective) quick to notice, observant. *With his perceptive intelligence, Holmes was the first to notice the importance of this clue.* **perceptible** (adjective), **perception** (noun).

perfidious (adjective) disloyal, treacherous. *Although one of the most talented generals of the American Revolution, Benedict Arnold is remembered as a perfidious betrayer of his country.* **perfidy** (noun).

perfunctory (adjective) unenthusiastic, routine, or mechanical. *When the play opened, the actors sparkled, but by the thousandth night, their performance had become perfunctory.*

permeate (verb) to spread through or penetrate. *Little by little, the smell of gas from the broken pipe permeated the house.*

persevere (adjective) to continue despite difficulties. *Although several of her teammates dropped out of the marathon, Gail persevered.* **perseverance** (noun).

perspicacity (noun) keenness of observation or understanding. *Journalist Murray Kempton was famous for the perspicacity of his comments on social and political issues.* **perspicacious** (adjective).

peruse (verb) to examine or study. *Carol perused the contract carefully before signing.* **perusal** (noun).

pervasive (adjective) spreading throughout. *As news of the disaster reached the town, a pervasive sense of gloom could be felt.* **pervade** (verb).

phlegmatic (adjective) sluggish and unemotional in temperament. *It was surprising to see Tom, who's normally so phlegmatic, acting upbeat and excited.*

placate (verb) to soothe or appease. *The waiter tried to placate the angry customer with the offer of a free dessert.* **placatory** (adjective).

plastic (adjective) able to be molded or reshaped. *Because it is highly plastic, clay is an easy material for beginning sculptors to use.*

plausible (adjective) apparently believable. *According to the judge, the defense attorney's argument was both powerful and plausible.* **plausibility** (noun).

polarize (verb) to separate into opposing groups or forces. *The abortion debate has polarized the American people for years, with no shortage of extreme views.* **polarization** (noun).

portend (verb) to indicate a future event; to forebode. *According to folklore, a red sky at dawn portends a day of stormy weather.*

potentate (noun) a powerful ruler. *The Tsar of Russia was one of the last hereditary potentates of Europe.*

pragmatism (noun) a belief in approaching problems through practical rather than theoretical means. *Roosevelt's approach to the Great Depression was based on pragmatism: "Try something," he said, and "if it doesn't work, try something else."* **pragmatic** (adjective).

preamble (noun) an introductory statement. *The preamble to the Constitution begins with the famous line, "We the people of the United States of America..."*

precocious (adjective) mature at an unusually early age. *Picasso was so precocious as an artist that, at nine, he is said to have painted better than his teacher.* **precocity** (noun).

predatory (adjective) living by killing and eating other animals; exploiting others for personal gain. *The tiger is the largest predatory animal native to Asia. Microsoft has been accused of predatory business practices.* **predation** (noun), **predator** (noun).

predilection (noun) a liking or preference. *Kennedy had a predilection for spy novels that helped him escape from his presidential duties.*

predominant (adjective) greatest in numbers or influence. *Although hundreds of religions are practiced in India, the predominant faith is Hinduism.* **predominance** (noun), **predominate** (verb).

prepossessing (adjective) attractive. *Smart, lovely, and talented, she has all the prepossessing qualities that mark a potential movie star.*

presumptuous (adjective) going beyond the limits of courtesy or appropriateness. *The senator winced when the presumptuous young staffer addressed him as "Chuck."* **presume** (verb), **presumption** (noun).

pretentious (adjective) claiming excessive value or importance. *For a shoe salesman to call himself a "Personal Foot Apparel Consultant" seems awfully pretentious.* **pretension** (noun).

procrastinate (verb) to put off, to delay. *If you habitually procrastinate, try never touching a piece of paper without either filing it, responding to it, or throwing it out immediately.* **procrastination** (noun).

profane (adjective) impure, unholy. *It is inappropriate and rude to use profane language in a church.* **profane** (verb), **profanity** (noun).

proficient (adjective) skillful, adept. *Only a proficient artist could sketch a scene of such complexity.* **proficiency** (noun).

proliferate (verb) to increase or multiply. *Over the past twenty-five years, tech companies have proliferated in northern California, Massachusetts, and Seattle.* **proliferation** (noun), **prolific** (adjective).

prominence (noun) the quality of standing out; fame. *Barack Obama rose to political prominence after his keynote address at the 2004 Democratic National Convention.* **prominent** (adjective).

promulgate (verb) to make public, to declare. *Lincoln signed the proclamation that freed the slaves in 1862, but he waited several months to promulgate it.*

propagate (verb) to cause to grow; to foster. *The school was propagated by its original founder and continues to grow even after his death.* **propagation** (noun).

propriety (noun) appropriateness. *The principal questioned the propriety of the discussion the teacher had with her students about another instructor's gambling addiction.*

prosaic (adjective) everyday, ordinary, unremarkable. *"Paul's Case" tells the story of a boy who longs to escape from the prosaic life of a clerk into a world of wealth, glamor, and beauty.*

protagonist (noun) the main character in a story or play; the main supporter of an idea. *Leopold Bloom is the protagonist of James Joyce's great novel Ulysses.*

provocative (adjective) likely to stimulate emotions, ideas, or controversy. *The demonstrators began the provocative act of chanting obscenities at police.* **provoke** (verb), **provocation** (noun).

proximity (noun) closeness, nearness. *Neighborhood residents were angry over the proximity of the sewage plant to the local school.* **proximate** (adjective).

prudent (adjective) wise, cautious, practical. *A prudent investor will avoid putting all their money into a single investment.* **prudence** (noun), **prudential** (adjective).

pugnacious (adjective) combative, bellicose, truculent; ready to fight. *Ty Cobb, the pugnacious Detroit Tigers outfielder, got into his fair share of brawls both on and off the field.* **pugnacity** (noun).

punctilious (adjective) concerned with proper forms of behavior and manners. *A punctilious dresser like James would rather skip the party altogether than wear the wrong color tie.* **punctilio** (noun).

pundit (noun) someone who offers opinions in an authoritative style. *The Sunday morning talk shows are filled with pundits, each with their own theory about the week's political news.*

punitive (adjective) inflicting punishment. *The jury awarded the plaintiff one million dollars in punitive damages, hoping to teach the defendant a lesson.*

purify (verb) to make pure, clean, or perfect. *The new plant is supposed to purify the drinking water provided to everyone in the nearby towns.* **purification** (noun).

Q

quell (verb) to quiet, to suppress. *It took a huge number of police officers to quell the rioting.*

querulous (adjective) complaining, whining. *The nursing home attendant needed a lot of patience to care for the three querulous, unpleasant residents on his floor.*

R

rancorous (adjective) expressing bitter hostility. *Many Americans are disgusted by recent political campaigns, which seem more rancorous than ever before.* **rancor** (noun).

rationale (noun) an underlying reason or explanation. *Looking at the sad faces of his employees, it was hard for the company president to explain the rationale for closing the business.*

raze (verb) to destroy; demolish. *The old Coliseum will soon be razed to make room for a new hotel.*

reciprocate (verb) to give and take mutually. *If you'll watch my children tonight, I'll reciprocate by taking care of yours tomorrow.* **reciprocity** (noun).

reclusive (adjective) withdrawn from society. *During the last years of her life, actress Greta Garbo led a reclusive existence, rarely appearing in public.* **recluse** (noun).

reconcile (verb) to make consistent or harmonious. *It's always wise to reconcile individual differences before starting a group project.* **reconciliation** (noun).

recrimination (noun) a retaliatory accusation. *After the governor called his opponent unethical, he was met with recriminations of his own guilt.* **recriminate** (verb), **recriminatory** (adjective).

recuperate (verb) to regain health after an illness. *Although Marie left the hospital two days after her operation, it took her a few weeks to fully recuperate.* **recuperation** (noun), **recuperative** (adjective).

redoubtable (adjective) inspiring respect, awe, or fear. *Johnson's knowledge, experience, and personal clout made him a redoubtable political opponent.*

refurbish (verb) to fix up; renovate. *It took three days' work by a team of carpenters, painters, and decorators to completely refurbish the apartment.*

refute (verb) to prove false. *The company invited reporters to visit their plant to refute charges of unsafe working conditions.* **refutation** (noun).

relevance (noun) connection to the matter at hand; pertinence. *Testimony in a criminal trial may be admitted only if it has clear relevance to the question of guilt or innocence.* **relevant** (adjective).

remedial (adjective) serving to remedy, cure, or correct some condition. *Affirmative action is a remedial step to help minority members overcome past discrimination.* **remediation** (noun), **remedy** (verb).

remorse (noun) a painful sense of guilt over wrongdoing. *In Poe's story* The Tell-Tale Heart, *a murderer is driven insane by remorse over his crime.* **remorseful** (adjective).

remuneration (noun) pay. *In a civil lawsuit, the attorney often receives part of the financial settlement as remuneration.* **remunerate** (verb), **remunerative** (adjective).

renovate (verb) to renew by repairing or rebuilding. *The television program* This Old House *shows how skilled craftspeople renovate houses.* **renovation** (noun).

renunciation (noun) the act of rejecting or refusing something. *King Edward VII's renunciation of the throne was driven by his taboo desire to marry an American divorcée.* **renounce** (verb).

replete (adjective) filled abundantly. *Graham's book is replete with wonderful stories and deep insights.*

reprehensible (adjective) deserving criticism or censure. *Pete Rose's misdeeds were reprehensible, but not all fans agree he should be banned from the Hall of Fame.* **reprehend** (verb), **reprehension** (noun).

repudiate (verb) to reject, to renounce. *After it became known that Duke had been a leader of the Ku Klux Klan, most Republican leaders repudiated him.* **repudiation** (noun).

reputable (adjective) having a good reputation; respected. *Find a reputable auto mechanic by asking your friends for recommendations based on their own experiences.* **reputation** (noun), **repute** (noun).

resilient (adjective) able to recover from difficulty. *A professional athlete must be resilient, able to lose a game one day and come back the next with confidence and enthusiasm.* **resilience** (noun).

resplendent (adjective) glowing, shining. *In late December, midtown New York is resplendent with holiday lights and decorations.* **resplendence** (noun).

responsive (adjective) reacting quickly and appropriately. *The new director of the Internal Revenue Service has promised to make the agency more responsive to public complaints.* **respond** (verb), **response** (noun).

restitution (noun) return of something to its original owner; repayment. *Some Native American leaders are lobbying for the U.S. government to make restitution for the lands taken from them.*

revere (verb) to admire deeply, to honor. *Millions of people around the world revered Mother Teresa for her saintly generosity.* **reverence** (noun), **reverent** (adjective).

rhapsodize (verb) to praise in a wildly emotional way. *That critic is such a huge fan of Toni Morrison that she will surely rhapsodize over the writer's next novel.* **rhapsodic** (adjective).

S

sagacious (adjective) discerning, wise. *Only a leader as sagacious as Nelson Mandela could have united South Africa so successfully and peacefully.* **sagacity** (noun).

salvage (verb) to save from wreck or ruin. *After the hurricane destroyed her home, she was able to salvage only a few of her belongings.* **salvage** (noun), **salvageable** (adjective).

sanctimonious (adjective) showing false or excessive piety. *The sanctimonious prayers of the TV preacher were interspersed with requests that the viewers send him money.* **sanctimony** (noun).

scapegoat (noun) someone who bears the blame for others' acts; someone hated for no apparent reason. *Although Buckner's error was only one reason the Red Sox lost, many fans made him the scapegoat, booing him mercilessly.*

scrupulous (adjective) acting with extreme care; painstaking. *Disney theme parks are famous for their scrupulous attention to small details.* **scruple** (noun).

scrutinize (verb) to study closely. *The lawyer scrutinized the contract, searching for any sentence that could pose a risk for her client.* **scrutiny** (noun).

secrete (verb) to emit; to hide. *Glands in the mouth secrete saliva to aid in digestion.*

sedentary (adjective) static; unmoving. *When Officer Samson was given a desk job, she had trouble getting used to sedentary work after years on the street.*

sequential (adjective) arranged in an order or series. *The courses for the chemistry major are sequential; you must take them in order, since each course builds on the previous ones.* **sequence** (noun).

serendipity (noun) the act of lucky, accidental discoveries. *Great inventions sometimes come through deliberate research and hard work and others through pure serendipity.* **serendipitous** (adjective).

servile (adjective) like a slave or servant; submissive. *The tycoon demanded that his underlings behave in a servile manner, agreeing quickly with everything he said.* **servility** (noun).

simulated (adjective) imitating something else; artificial. *High-quality simulated gems must be examined under a magnifying glass to be distinguished from real ones.* **simulate** (verb), **simulation** (noun).

solace (verb) to comfort or console. *There was little the rabbi could say to solace the husband after his wife's death.* **solace** (noun).

spontaneous (adjective) happening without plan. *When the news of Kennedy's assassination broke, people everywhere gathered in a spontaneous effort to share their shock and grief.* **spontaneity** (noun).

spurious (adjective) false, fake. *The so-called Piltdown Man, supposed to be the fossil of a primitive human, turned out to be spurious, although who created the hoax is still uncertain.*

squander (verb) to use up carelessly; to waste. *Those who had made donations to the charity were outraged to learn that its director had squandered millions on fancy dinners and first-class travel.*

stagnate (verb) to become stale through lack of movement or change. *Having had no contact with the outside world for generations, Japan's culture gradually stagnated.* **stagnant** (adjective), **stagnation** (noun).

staid (adjective) sedate, serious, and grave. *This college is not a "party school"; the students work hard and the campus has a staid reputation.*

stimulus (noun) something that excites a response or provokes an action. *The arrival of merchants and missionaries from the West provided a stimulus for change in Japanese society.* **stimulate** (verb).

stoic (adjective) showing little feeling, even in response to pain or sorrow. *A soldier must respond to the death of his comrades in stoic fashion, since the fighting will not stop for his grief.* **stoicism** (noun).

strenuous (adjective) requiring energy and strength. *Hiking the foothills of the Rockies may be easy, but climbing higher peaks is strenuous exercise.*

submissive (adjective) accepting the will of others; humble, compliant. *At the end of A Doll's House, Nora leaves her husband and abandons her role as a submissive housewife.*

substantiate (verb) verified or supported by evidence. *The charge that Nixon had helped to cover up crimes was substantiated by his comments about it on a series of audio tapes.* **substantiated** (adjective), **substantiation** (noun).

sully (verb) to soil, stain, or defile. *Nixon's misdeeds as president did much to sully the reputation of the American government.*

superficial (adjective) on the surface only; without depth or substance. *Her wound was superficial and required only a light bandage.* **superficiality** (noun).

superfluous (adjective) more than is needed, excessive. *Once you've won the debate, don't keep talking; superfluous arguments will only bore and annoy the audience.*

suppress (verb) to put down or restrain. *As soon as the unrest began, thousands of helmeted police were sent into the streets to suppress the riots.* **suppression** (noun).

surfeit (noun) an excess. *Most Americans have a surfeit of food on Thanksgiving Day.* **surfeit** (verb).

surreptitious (adjective) done in secret. *Because Iraq avoided weapons inspections, many believed it had a surreptitious weapons development program.*

surrogate (noun) a substitute. *When the congressman died in office, his wife was named to serve the rest of his term as a surrogate.* **surrogate** (adjective).

sustain (verb) to keep up, to continue; to support. *Because of fatigue, he was unable to sustain the effort needed to finish the marathon.*

T

tactile (adjective) relating to the sense of touch. *The thick brush strokes and gobs of color give the paintings of van Gogh a strongly tactile quality.* **tactility** (noun).

talisman (noun) an object supposed to have magical effects or qualities. *Superstitious people sometimes carry a rabbit's foot, a lucky coin, or some other talisman.*

tangential (adjective) touching lightly; only slightly connected or related. *My travels to South America were of only tangential interest to the students in my African-American history class.* **tangent** (noun).

tedium (noun) boredom. *For most people, watching the Weather Channel for 24 hours would be sheer tedium.* **tedious** (adjective).

temerity (noun) boldness, rashness, excessive daring. *Only someone who didn't understand the danger would have the temerity to try to climb Everest without a guide.* **temerarious** (adjective).

temperance (noun) moderation or restraint in feelings and behavior. *Most professional athletes practice temperance in their personal habits; too much eating or drinking, they know, can harm their performance.* **temperate** (adjective).

tenacious (adjective) clinging, sticky, or persistent. *Tenacious in pursuit of her goal, she applied for the grant unsuccessfully four times before it was finally approved.* **tenacity** (noun).

tentative (adjective) subject to change; uncertain. *A firm schedule has not been established, but the Super Bowl has been given the tentative date of February 3.*

terminate (verb) to end, to close. *The Olympic Games terminate with a grand ceremony attended by athletes from every participating country.* **terminal** (noun), **termination** (noun).

terrestrial (adjective) of the earth. *The movie Close Encounters of the Third Kind tells the story of the first contact between beings from outer space and terrestrial humans.*

therapeutic (adjective) curing or helping to cure. *Hot-water spas were popular in the nineteenth century among the sickly, who believed that soaking in the water had therapeutic effects.* **therapy** (noun).

timorous (adjective) fearful, timid. *The cowardly lion approached the throne of the wizard with a timorous look on his face.*

toady (noun) someone who flatters a superior in hopes of gaining favor; a sycophant. *"I can't stand a toady!" declared the movie mogul. "Give me someone who'll tell me the truth—even if it costs him his job!"* **toady** (verb).

tolerant (adjective) accepting, enduring. *San Franciscans have a tolerant attitude about lifestyles: "Live and let live" seems to be their motto.* **tolerate** (verb), **toleration** (noun).

toxin (noun) poison. *Insecticides are powerful toxins used to kill insects, but many are now banned in the United States because of the risk they pose to human health.* **toxic** (adjective).

tranquility (noun) freedom from disturbance or turmoil; calm. *She moved from New York City to rural Vermont seeking the tranquility of country life.* **tranquil** (adjective).

transgress (verb) to go past limits; to violate. *No one could fathom why the honor student transgressed by shoplifting hundreds of dollars of merchandise from his favorite clothing store.* **transgression** (noun).

transient (adjective) passing quickly. *Long-term visitors to this hotel pay a different rate than transient guests who stay for just a day or two.* **transience** (noun).

transitory (adjective) quickly passing. *Public moods tend to be transitory; people may be anxious and angry one*

month but relatively content and optimistic the next. **transition** (noun).

translucent (adjective) letting some light pass through. *Panels of translucent glass let daylight into the room while maintaining privacy.*

transmute (verb) to change in form or substance. *In the Middle Ages, the alchemists tried to discover ways to transmute metals such as iron into gold.* **transmutation** (noun).

treacherous (adjective) untrustworthy or disloyal; dangerous or unreliable. *Nazi Germany proved to be a treacherous ally, first signing a peace pact with the Soviet Union, then invading. Be careful crossing the rope bridge; parts are badly frayed and treacherous.* **treachery** (noun).

tremulous (adjective) trembling or shaking; timid or fearful. *Never having spoken in public before, he began his speech in a tremulous, hesitant voice.*

trite (adjective) boring because of over-familiarity; hackneyed. *Her letters were filled with trite expressions, like "all's well that ends well" and "so far so good."*

truculent (adjective) aggressive, hostile, belligerent. *Hitler's truculent behavior in demanding more territory for Germany made it clear that war was inevitable.* **truculence** (noun).

truncate (verb) to cut off. *The poor copying job truncated the playwright's manuscript: The last page ended in the middle of a scene, halfway through the first act.*

turbulent (adjective) agitated or disturbed. *The night before the championship match, Serena Williams was unable to sleep, her mind turbulent with fears and hopes.* **turbulence** (noun).

U

unheralded (adjective) little known, unexpected. *In a year of big-budget, much-hyped mega-movies, this unheralded foreign film has surprised everyone with its popularity.*

unpalatable (adjective) distasteful, unpleasant. *Although I agree with the candidate on many issues, I can't vote for her because I find her position on capital punishment unpalatable.*

unparalleled (adjective) with no equal; unique. *Tiger Woods's victory in the Masters golf tournament by a full twelve strokes was an unparalleled accomplishment.*

unstinting (adjective) giving freely and generously. *Eleanor Roosevelt was much admired for her unstinting efforts on behalf of the poor.*

untenable (adjective) impossible to defend. *The theory that this painting is a genuine van Gogh became untenable when the artist who painted it came forth.*

untimely (adjective) out of the natural or proper time. *The untimely death of a youthful Princess Diana seemed far more tragic than Mother Teresa's death of old age.*

unyielding (adjective) firm, resolute, obdurate. *Despite criticism, former governor Mario Cuomo was unyielding in his opposition to capital punishment as he vetoed several death penalty bills.*

usurper (noun) someone who takes a place or possession without the right to do so. *Kennedy's most devoted followers tended to regard later presidents as usurpers, holding the office they felt he or his brothers should have held.* **usurp** (verb), **usurpation** (noun).

utilitarian (adjective) purely of practical benefit. *The design of the Model T car was simple and utilitarian, lacking the luxuries found in later models.*

utopia (noun) an imaginary, perfect society. *Those who founded the Oneida community dreamed that it could be a kind of utopia—a prosperous state of freedom and harmony.* **utopian** (adjective).

V

validate (verb) to officially approve or confirm. *The election of the president is validated when the members of the Electoral College meet to confirm the choice of the voters.* **valid** (adjective), **validity** (noun).

variegated (adjective) spotted with different colors. *The brilliant, variegated appearance of butterflies makes them popular among collectors.* **variegation** (noun).

venerate (verb) to admire or honor. *In Communist China, Chairman Mao Zedong was venerated as an almost godlike figure.* **venerable** (adjective), **veneration** (noun).

verdant (adjective) green with plant life. *Southern England is famous for its verdant countryside filled with gardens and small farms.*

vestige (noun) a trace or remainder. *Today's tiny Sherwood Forest is the last vestige of a woodland that once covered most of England.* **vestigial** (adjective).

vex (verb) to irritate, annoy, or trouble. *It vexes me that she never helps with any chores around the house.* **vexation** (noun).

vicarious (adjective) experienced through someone else's actions by way of the imagination. *Great literature broadens our minds by giving us vicarious participation in the lives of other people.*

vindicate (verb) to confirm, justify, or defend. *Lincoln's Gettysburg Address was intended to vindicate the objectives of the Union in the Civil War.*

virtuoso (noun) someone very skilled, especially in an art. *Vladimir Horowitz was one of the great piano virtuosos of the twentieth century.* **virtuosity** (noun).

vivacious (adjective) lively, sprightly. *The role of Maria in* The Sound of Music *is usually played by a charming, vivacious young actress.* **vivacity** (noun).

volatile (adjective) quickly changing; fleeting, transitory; prone to violence. *Public opinion is notoriously volatile; a politician who is very popular one month may be voted out of office the next.* **volatility** (noun).

W

whimsical (adjective) based on a capricious, carefree impulse or idea; fanciful, playful. *Dave Barry's* Book of Bad Songs *is filled with goofy jokes typical of his whimsical sense of humor.* **whim** (noun).

Z

zealous (adjective) filled with eagerness, fervor, or passion. *A crowd of the candidate's most zealous supporters greeted her at the airport with banners, signs, and a marching band.* **zeal** (noun), **zealot** (noun), **zealotry** (noun).

APPENDIX B: LIST OF SYNONYMS

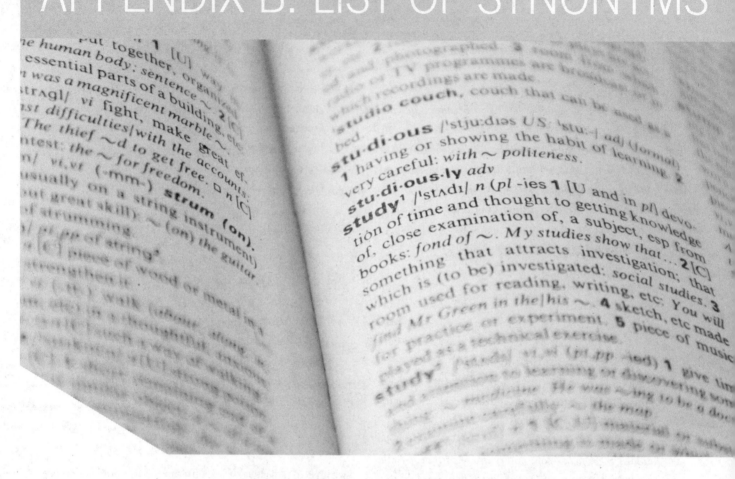

LIST OF SYNONYMS AND ANTONYMS

The following is a list of synonyms and antonyms. Studying the words on this list will you help you prepare for synonym and antonym questions on the exam. The words included here are listed in alphabetical order.

A

abbreviate
Synonyms—shorten, make concise
Antonyms—lengthen, elongate (to make longer)

abrasive
Synonyms—harsh, rough, irritating
Antonyms—smooth, soft, soothing

abstain
Synonyms—refrain, give up, hold back
Antonyms—give in, indulge (to allow oneself to partake or participate)

acclaim
Synonyms—praise, approve, applaud
Antonyms—blame, condemn, censure (to criticize)

accumulate
Synonyms—acquire, gain, hoard
Antonyms—diminish, give away, squander (to waste)

accuse
Synonyms—challenge, blame, incriminate (to attribute responsibility)
Antonyms—forgive, exonerate (to free from guilt)

adaptable
Synonyms—flexible, changeable
Antonyms—inflexible, rigid

adept
Synonyms—skillful, proficient, competent
Antonyms—inexperienced, incompetent, unskillful

adhere
Synonyms—attach, stick, follow, uphold
Antonyms—detach, disengage, reject

adversary
Synonyms—enemy, opponent, foe, nemesis (an arch enemy)
Antonyms—friend, collaborator, ally (one who collaborates)

adverse
Synonyms—bad, negative
Antonyms—good, positive

aggressive
Synonyms—combative, belligerent (hostile)
Antonyms—peaceful, conciliatory (easily makes amends)

agitate
Synonyms—irritate, anger, upset, stir
Antonyms—soothe, calm, pacify (to calm)

agreeable
Synonyms—pleasant, likeable, delightful
Antonyms—mean, unkind, unpleasant

ambiguous
Synonyms—unclear, vague
Antonyms—clear, straightforward

ambitious
Synonyms—determined, driven, motivated
Antonyms—lazy, unmotivated, unenthusiastic

ambivalent
Synonyms—indecisive, wishy-washy, unsure
Antonyms—decided, determined, sure

amplify
Synonyms—expand, heighten, enlarge
Antonyms—decrease, minimize, diminish

animated
Synonyms—energetic, lively, spirited
Antonyms—lazy, sluggish, depressed

animosity
Synonyms—hostility, resentment, hatred
Antonyms—kindness, friendliness, warmth, compassion (caring)

anomalous
Synonyms—odd, inconsistent, irregular, unusual
Antonyms—commonplace, ordinary, normal, regular

anonymous
Synonyms—nameless, unknown, unidentified
Antonyms—identified, known, recognized

antagonize
Synonyms—irritate, bother, annoy
Antonyms—help, aid, soothe

apathy
Synonyms—indifference, unconcern, disregard (lack of interest)
Antonyms—interest, concern

arbitrary
Synonyms—random, chance, inconsistent
Antonyms—steady, unchanging, reliable, predictable

arid
Synonyms—dry, barren, parched (lacking water)
Antonyms—humid, soaked, well-watered

attentive
Synonyms—interested, observant, aware
Antonyms—unaware, unconcerned, neglectful

astute
Synonyms—quick-witted, intelligent, smart
Antonyms—inept, foolish, slow-witted

atypical
Synonyms—not normal, uncommon, unnatural
Antonyms—normal, regular, common, typical

audacious
Synonyms—outrageous, bold, daring
Antonyms—meek, mild, quiet

audible
Synonyms—perceptible, discernible, distinct (able to be heard)
Antonyms—silent, indistinct (quiet or not able to be heard)

authentic
Synonyms—original, trustworthy, credible
Antonyms—corrupt, untrustworthy, fake

autonomous
Synonyms—independent, self-governing
Antonyms—dependent, helpless, subjugated (controlled by others)

B

baffle
Synonyms—confuse, stump, puzzle
Antonyms—clarify, elucidate (to make clear)

banal
Synonyms—usual, common, ordinary
Antonyms—unusual, different, special

barren
Synonyms—lifeless, empty, unfruitful (not able to support life)
Antonyms—productive, fruitful (able to support life)

belated
Synonyms—late, overdue
Antonyms—prompt, punctual (on time)

benevolent
Synonyms—kind, good-hearted
Antonyms—cruel, evil, malevolent (willing to cause harm)

benign
Synonyms—mild, peaceable, harmless
Antonyms—deadly, dangerous, harmful

berate
Synonyms—scold, criticize, reprimand (to scold or blame)
Antonyms—praise, encourage, uplift

bleak
Synonyms—grim, hopeless, desolate (deserted and empty)
Antonyms—hopeful, cheerful, encouraging

boisterous
Synonyms—noisy, loud, rambunctious (uncontrolled)
Antonyms—quiet, orderly, subdued (calm and under control)

bombastic
Synonyms—boastful, ostentatious (showy), pompous (full of oneself)
Antonyms—restrained, quiet, humble, reserved (private)

buttress
Synonyms—bolster, reinforce, support
Antonyms—weaken

C

cajole
Synonyms—coax, persuade, wheedle (to convince by asking nicely)
Antonyms—order, force, compel

camaraderie
Synonyms—friendship, companionship, togetherness
Antonyms—animosity, isolation

candid
Synonyms—truthful, straightforward, unrehearsed
Antonyms—dishonest, staged, set up

candor
Synonyms—honesty, directness, veracity (truthfulness)
Antonyms—insincerity, deceit, lying

capricious
Synonyms—willful, arbitrary, impulsive (acting without thought)
Antonyms—predictable, steady, sensible

captivate
Synonyms—dazzle, enchant, fascinate
Antonyms—bore, offend, repulse

caustic
Synonyms—burning, hurtful, sarcastic (cutting or mocking)
Antonyms—soothing, mild, innocuous (harmless)

chaos
Synonyms—disorder, confusion, pandemonium (an uproar or hubbub)
Antonyms—harmony, order, tranquility (peace)

circumvent
Synonyms—go around, avoid, elude (to get away from)
Antonyms—take on, confront, face

clandestine
Synonyms—secret, undercover, covert, surreptitious (hidden)
Antonyms—public, open, aboveboard, overt (open)

cloying
Synonyms—sticky, sentimental, clingy
Antonyms—independent, detached, cool

coerce
Synonyms—force, bully, pressure
Antonyms—coax, cajole, encourage

cogent
Synonyms—powerful, logical, persuasive
Antonyms—unconvincing, ineffective, illogical

cognizant
Synonyms—aware, informed, sentient (conscious)
Antonyms—ignorant, oblivious (not attentive)

coherent
Synonyms—understandable, clear
Antonyms—confused, meaningless

cohesive
Synonyms—close-knit, unified, interconnected
Antonyms—scattered, disorganized, fragmented

collaborate
Synonyms—work together, cooperate, join forces
Antonyms—separate, part ways, conflict

commend
Synonyms—praise, applaud, honor
Antonyms—criticize, put down, disapprove

compatible
Synonyms—harmonious, well-suited, congenial (friendly)
Antonyms—mismatched, clashing, incompatible

compel
Synonyms—force, require, pressure
Antonyms—discourage, prevent, dissuade (to advise against)

competent
Synonyms—skilled, qualified, proficient (good at)
Antonyms—inept, useless, bungling (prone to making mistakes)

complacent
Synonyms—self-satisfied, comfortable, smug (self-satisfied)
Antonyms—restless, dissatisfied, discontent

comply
Synonyms—obey, conform, follow
Antonyms—rebel, resist, defy

comprehensive
Synonyms—thorough, inclusive, complete
Antonyms—limited, partial, restricted

concise
Synonyms—short, to the point, succinct (brief)
Antonyms—rambling, long-winded, wordy

condescending
Synonyms—rude, snobbish
Antonyms—down-to-earth, friendly, kind

confident
Synonyms—sure, convinced, positive
Antonyms—insecure, shy, fearful

conform
Synonyms—comply, submit, follow
Antonyms—defy, disobey, flout (to go against or disregard)

conformity
Synonyms—compliance, submission
Antonyms—defiance, disobedience

congested
Synonyms—packed, jammed, blocked
Antonyms—empty, free, wide-open

congruent
Synonyms—alike, matching, harmonious (goes well together)
Antonyms—incompatible, mismatched, dissimilar

consensus
Synonyms—agreement, compromise, harmony
Antonyms—difference, disparity, confrontation

consequential
Synonyms—important, major, meaningful
Antonyms—trivial, insignificant

conservative
Synonyms—traditional, old-fashioned, conventional
Antonyms—progressive, adventurous, avant-garde (extremely modern)

constant
Synonyms—steady, persistent, incessant (unceasing)
Antonyms—irregular, occasional

constrain
Synonyms—hold back, restrict, inhibit (to slow down or prevent)
Antonyms—expand, develop, increase

consummate
Synonyms—ideal, perfect, superlative (the best)
Antonyms—inferior, awful, abysmal (very bad)

contaminate
Synonyms—pollute, spoil, taint (to spoil or damage)
Antonyms—purify, cleanse

contemporary
Synonyms—modern, up to date, new
Antonyms—old-fashioned, antique

contradict
Synonyms—disagree, oppose, challenge
Antonyms—support, concur (to agree)

conventional
Synonyms—usual, established, typical
Antonyms—uncommon, odd, original

converge
Synonyms—meet, come together, join
Antonyms—diverge, separate

convey
Synonyms—tell, express, communicate
Antonyms—hold back, contain

convoluted
Synonyms—complex, difficult
Antonyms—simple, uncomplicated, straightforward

corroborate
Synonyms—confirm, support, substantiate (to back up with evidence)
Antonyms—contradict, deny, challenge, refute

corrupt
Synonyms—dishonest, shady, crooked
Antonyms—truthful, honest, moral, upstanding

covert
Synonyms—secret, hidden, underground
Antonyms—open, public, exposed

criticize
Synonyms—disparage (to cut down), denigrate (to put down)
Antonyms—praise, commend

culpable
Synonyms—responsible, guilty, at fault
Antonyms—innocent, blameless

curtail
Synonyms—cut back, limit, shorten, restrict
Antonyms—increase, expand, lengthen

D

debased
Synonyms—corrupted, depraved (wicked)
Antonyms—upright, noble, dignified

decisive
Synonyms—determined, conclusive, sure
Antonyms—undetermined, indecisive, irresolute (unsure)

decorous
Synonyms—polite, proper, suitable
Antonyms—indecent, wrong, unsuitable

decry
Synonyms—devalue, disparage (to criticize), demean (to put down)
Antonyms—respect, approve, praise

deficient
Synonyms—lacking, insufficient, not enough
Antonyms—ample, adequate, enough

deficit
Synonyms—deficiency, loss, shortage
Antonyms—excess, surplus, extra

definite
Synonyms—certain, explicit, indubitable (not questionable)
Antonyms—uncertain, questionable, refutable

defy
Synonyms—disregard, flout (to go against)
Antonyms—obey, respect, follow

delete
Synonyms—remove, take away, expunge (to get rid of)
Antonyms—add, build up, create

deleterious
Synonyms—damaging, hurtful, injurious (harmful)
Antonyms—helpful, good for the health, beneficial, harmless

denigrate
Synonyms—malign, impugn, slander (to put down)
Antonyms—encourage, boost, celebrate

deplete
Synonyms—diminish, reduce, use up
Antonyms—fill, increase, enhance

deplore
Synonyms—despise, hate, undervalue
Antonyms—appreciate, accept, value

deprecate
Synonyms—ridicule, disparage (to criticize), denigrate (to put down)
Antonyms—commend, approve, bolster, support

deprive
Synonyms—take away, rob, remove
Antonyms—give, confer, bestow (to give)

desire
Synonyms—want, longing, craving
Antonyms—disinterest, apathy (lack of interest), repulsion (extreme dislike)

desolate
Synonyms—barren, lifeless, devoid (empty)
Antonyms—inhabited, lively, fruitful (productive)

destitute
Synonyms—poor, indigent (without money)
Antonyms—wealthy, secure, prosperous

destroy
Synonyms—eliminate, obliterate (to wipe out), raze (to completely destroy)
Antonyms—build, fix, improve

detach
Synonyms—remove, segregate, separate
Antonyms—join, put together, assemble

deter
Synonyms—stop, halt, hinder
Antonyms—aid, inspire, incite (to promote)

detractor
Synonyms—critic, enemy
Antonyms—supporter, benefactor, friend

detrimental
Synonyms—bad, harmful, unfavorable
Antonyms—positive, helpful, useful

devastate
Synonyms—destroy, wreck, annihilate (to demolish)
Antonyms—save, protect, expand, augment (to add to)

devious
Synonyms—dishonest, evil, duplicitous (scheming)
Antonyms—honest, forthright, righteous

diffuse
Synonyms—spread out, expanded, propagated
Antonyms—condensed, confined, succinct (brief)

digress
Synonyms—stray, ramble, deviate (to go off in another direction)
Antonyms—focus, be direct, stay on course

diligent
Synonyms—hard-working, earnest, persistent
Antonyms—thoughtless, careless, lazy

diminish
Synonyms—decrease, dwindle, reduce
Antonyms—prolong, increase, enhance, extend

diminutive
Synonyms—petite, small, short
Antonyms—big, enormous, huge

dire
Synonyms—critical, very important, desperate, grave (serious)
Antonyms—trivial, unimportant, silly

disagree
Synonyms—conflict, go against, dissent (to differ in opinion)
Antonyms—agree, concur (to have the same opinion), acquiesce (to accept without protesting)

discern
Synonyms—recognize, distinguish, perceive
Antonyms—confuse, misunderstand, discombobulate

disclose
Synonyms—tell, expose, reveal, make known
Antonyms—suppress, hide, disavow (to deny)

discomfort
Synonyms—unpleasantness, irritation, pain, anguish (great pain)
Antonyms—comfort, peacefulness, ease

disconcerting
Synonyms—disturbing, unbalancing, upsetting
Antonyms—quieting, calming, comforting

discord
Synonyms—disharmony, conflict
Antonyms—harmony, peacefulness

discrepancy
Synonyms—variation, difference, incongruity
Antonyms—consistency, sameness, reliability

dismal
Synonyms—bleak, sad, horrible
Antonyms—bright, hopeful, encouraging

dismay
Synonyms—disappointment, discouragement, trepidation (anxiety or fear)
Antonyms—encouragement, security, confidence

dismiss
Synonyms—send away, discard, push aside
Antonyms—permit, allow, keep, maintain

disparage
Synonyms—mock, criticize, belittle (to put down)
Antonyms—lift up, support, encourage, sanction (to support)

disparate
Synonyms—at variance, contrasting, different
Antonyms—similar, invariable, like

disparity
Synonyms—imbalance, gap, inequity
Antonyms—equity, likeness, sameness

dispute
Synonyms—bicker, argue, contend
Antonyms—harmonize, agree, go along with

disruptive
Synonyms—disorderly, disturbing
Antonyms—unifying, peaceful, calming

disseminate
Synonyms—publicize, scatter, radiate, disperse
Antonyms—condense, conceal, hide

dissipate
Synonyms—deplete, use up, squander (to waste)
Antonyms—save, preserve, conserve (to save)

distinct
Synonyms—separate, clearly defined, explicit (obvious)
Antonyms—vague, unsure, ambiguous (poorly defined)

distorted
Synonyms—warped, bent out of shape, perverted
Antonyms—straight, pure, invariable

diverge
Synonyms—separate, deviate (to go off course)
Antonyms—converge, join

diverse
Synonyms—dissimilar, different, varied
Antonyms—conforming, uniform, similar

divide
Synonyms—split up, disjoin, partition (to cut up)
Antonyms—join, add, combine

divulge
Synonyms—bring to light, confess, tell
Antonyms—protect, suppress, hide, conceal

dominant
Synonyms—superior, controlling, main
Antonyms—subordinate, inferior, auxiliary (additional)

dominate
Synonyms—rule over, influence, overshadow
Antonyms—follow, submit, acquiesce (to go along with)

dubious
Synonyms—suspicious, doubtful, disputable
Antonyms—reliable, true, unambiguous

duplicitous
Synonyms—two-faced, shady, dishonest
Antonyms—trustworthy, reliable, truthful, honest

durable
Synonyms—rugged, tough, tenacious (persistent)
Antonyms—flimsy, fragile, weak

duress
Synonyms—hardship, suffering, threat
Antonyms—ease, support, peace

E

endure
Synonyms—bear, withstand, suffer, tolerate, cope with
Antonyms—give up, surrender, cave in

effusive
Synonyms—expressive, gushing, unrestrained
Antonyms—reserved, restrained, aloof

egotism
Synonyms—narcissism, self-absorption (focusing only on one's self and one's own desires)
Antonyms—selflessness, compassion, thoughtfulness

elaborate
Synonyms—ornate, refined, complicated
Antonyms—plain, simple, uncomplicated

elated
Synonyms—thrilled, joyful, euphoric (extremely happy)
Antonyms—deflated, melancholy, disappointed

elusive
Synonyms—mysterious, puzzling, baffling (difficult to understand)
Antonyms—clear, understandable, concise (brief and clear)

eminent
Synonyms—prestigious, well-known, illustrious (well-known in a positive manner)
Antonyms—unimportant, ordinary, unknown

emulate
Synonyms—copy, mimic, act like
Antonyms—act independently

encompass
Synonyms—include, circumscribe, encircle
Antonyms—exclude, leave out, remove

enervate
Synonyms—weaken, incapacitate, drain
Antonyms—animate, empower, strengthen

engage
Synonyms—deal with, undertake, employ
Antonyms—avoid, repulse, ignore, fire

engender
Synonyms—incite, provoke, rouse (to move to action)
Antonyms—calm, discourage, hinder (to block or stop), dissuade (to advise against)

enhance
Synonyms—heighten, improve, increase
Antonyms—devalue, weaken, reduce, lessen, undermine (to weaken)

enrich
Synonyms—improve, enhance, aggrandize (to make bigger)
Antonyms—decrease, impoverish (to make poorer)

enthrall
Synonyms—charm, captivate, mesmerize (to capture the attention of)
Antonyms—bore, disgust, repel

eradicate
Synonyms—eliminate, destroy, get rid of
Antonyms—maintain, protect

erratic
Synonyms—irregular, unpredictable, volatile (explosive)
Antonyms—steadfast, predictable, regular

espouse
Synonyms—advocate, defend, support
Antonyms—disallow, reject, forsake (to abandon)

essential

Synonyms—necessary, requisite (required), indispensable (very much needed)

Antonyms—trivial, unnecessary, extra

euphoric

Synonyms—excited, thrilled, very happy

Antonyms—depressed, grieving, sorrowful

exacerbate

Synonyms—embitter, intensify, irritate

Antonyms—calm down, alleviate (to lessen), placate (to please)

exasperate

Synonyms—provoke, rile up, infuriate (to make angry)

Antonyms—mollify (to soothe), tranquilize (to calm down)

exclude

Synonyms—keep out, omit, ostracize (to ban someone from a group)

Antonyms—include, welcome, allow in

exculpate

Synonyms—forgive, excuse, acquit (to free from guilt)

Antonyms—punish, accuse, incriminate (to make appear responsible for a crime)

exempt

Synonyms—not required to, immune

Antonyms—responsible, required to

exonerate

Synonyms—hold blameless, vindicate (to free from guilt), exculpate (to free from guilt)

Antonyms—condemn, convict, hold accountable

expand

Synonyms—enlarge, increase, swell

Antonyms—decrease, minimize, reduce

expansive

Synonyms—all-inclusive, broad, widespread

Antonyms—exclusive, narrow, limited

expedite

Synonyms—quicken, hurry, hasten

Antonyms—delay, slow down, hinder

expert

Synonyms—skilled, knowledgeable, experienced

Antonyms—amateur, inept (unskilled), novice (new at something)

extenuate

Synonyms—diminish, lessen

Antonyms—increase, worsen, exacerbate (to make worse)

extol

Synonyms—praise, exalt, acclaim (to rave about)

Antonyms—disapprove, condemn, disparage (to complain about)

extraneous

Synonyms—extra, not needed, unnecessary, irrelevant

Antonyms—vital, relevant

extricate

Synonyms—liberate, free

Antonyms—restrain, involve, constrain (to limit)

extrinsic

Synonyms—foreign, alien, external (outside)

Antonyms—native, natural, inherent (originating from within)

exuberant

Synonyms—cheerful, buoyant (high-spirited), ebullient (full of positive energy)

Antonyms—unenthusiastic, dull, lethargic (slow)

F

fabricate

Synonyms—manufacture, make up, formulate

Antonyms—disassemble, break apart

fallacy

Synonyms—falsehood, lie, deception

Antonyms—truth, fact, reality

fanatic

Synonyms—zealot, radical (extremist)

Antonyms—conservative, disinterested party, unbeliever, infidel (non-believer)

fecund

Synonyms—propagating, fertile, fruitful (able to reproduce)

Antonyms—infertile, sterile, barren (unable to reproduce)

felicitous

Synonyms—appropriate, suitable, apropos (appropriate)

Antonyms—inopportune, poorly-timed, irrelevant

feral

Synonyms—wild, savage, untamed

Antonyms—tamed, mild-mannered, civilized

fervent

Synonyms—sincere, impassioned

Antonyms—unenthusiastic, unfeeling, dispassionate (unmoved)

flagrant

Synonyms—shameless, undisguised, brazen (brash)

Antonyms—obscure, contained, camouflaged (hidden)

flamboyant

Synonyms—glamorous, over-the-top, pretentious (showy)

Antonyms—refined, dull, common

forbid

Synonyms—prohibit, disallow, ban

Antonyms—facilitate, advance, admit (to allow)

formal

Synonyms—official, established, conventional

Antonyms—casual, informal, unofficial

forthright

Synonyms—sincere, honest, candid (open and direct)

Antonyms—dishonest, sneaky, lying

fortitude

Synonyms—courage, endurance, tenacity (persistence)

Antonyms—cowardice, laziness

foster

Synonyms—champion, support, nurture

Antonyms—neglect, halt, starve, deprive (to withhold support)

fragile

Synonyms—breakable, weak, frail

Antonyms—strong, durable, sturdy, rugged

frenetic

Synonyms—obsessive, overwrought (very upset), maniacal (frenzied, like a madman)

Antonyms—normal, balanced, calm

frivolity

Synonyms—whimsicality, silliness, childishness, playfulness

Antonyms—seriousness, sternness

frugal

Synonyms—economical, penny-pinching, thrifty

Antonyms—wasteful, spendthrift, lavish

furtive

Synonyms—secretive, clandestine (hidden), stealthy (done in a sneaky way)

Antonyms—candid, straightforward, overt (done in an obvious way)

futile

Synonyms—pointless, purposeless, trifling (having no value)

Antonyms—useful, worthwhile, efficacious (effective)

G

gargantuan

Synonyms—huge, gigantic, enormous

Antonyms—tiny, infinitesimal (infinitely small), minute (really small or insignificant)

generate

Synonyms—make, create, produce

Antonyms—end, terminate, destroy

genial

Synonyms—cordial, amiable, kindly (likeable)

Antonyms—disagreeable, unfriendly, surly (gruff)

grandiose

Synonyms—exaggerating, pompous (full of oneself), ostentatious (acting like a "show-off")

Antonyms—humble, lowly, unimposing (humble)

gratuitous

Synonyms—excessive, uncalled for, unnecessary

Antonyms—warranted, necessary, vital

greedy

Synonyms—gluttonous, insatiable (strong desire for selfish gain)

Antonyms—generous, giving, satisfied, metered (controlled)

gregarious

Synonyms—sociable, outgoing, good-natured

Antonyms—shy, introverted (turning inward to oneself), antisocial (unfriendly or aloof)

guileless

Synonyms—truthful, honest, straightforward

Antonyms—cunning, deceitful, tricky

gullible

Synonyms—simple, credulous (easily fooled)

Antonyms—sophisticated, skeptical, incredulous (unbelieving)

H

hackneyed

Synonyms—stale, common, trite (something overdone or constantly repeated)

Antonyms—original, fresh, authentic

haughty

Synonyms—snotty, narcissistic (focused on the self), arrogant (feeling superior to others)

Antonyms—humble, polite, self-effacing (humble)

heinous

Synonyms—wicked, repugnant (very bad), atrocious (awful)

Antonyms—honorable, wonderful, pleasing

heretic

Synonyms—pagan, unbeliever, iconoclast (one who goes against a belief system)

Antonyms—believer, loyalist, adherent (one who follows a belief system)

hesitate
Synonyms—pause, defer (to put off), balk (to refuse to move forward)
Antonyms—charge into, perform, hasten (to speed up)

honorable
Synonyms—well-regarded, law-abiding, esteemed (well-respected)
Antonyms—unethical, unjust, corrupt, dishonorable, base (lowly)

I

imitate
Synonyms—copy, mimic, impersonate (to act like someone), emulate (to strive to be like)
Antonyms—differ from, diverge from

immature
Synonyms—childish, infantile (like an infant)
Antonyms—experienced, mature, adult, seasoned

impede
Synonyms—block, hinder, stymie (thwart)
Antonyms—facilitate, accelerate, bolster (to support), expedite (to speed up)

impersonate
Synonyms—mimic, copy, imitate (to act like)
Antonyms—differ from

impetuous
Synonyms—hasty, rash (acting with little thought)
Antonyms—cautious, thoughtful, planned

impulsive
Synonyms—unpredictable, erratic (irregular), hasty (acting quickly, without thought)
Antonyms—deliberate, planned, designed (well-thought-out)

inarticulate
Synonyms—stammering, incomprehensible, tongue-tied (not well-spoken)
Antonyms—intelligible, clear, understandable, eloquent (well-spoken)

incisive
Synonyms—clever, acute, sharp (quick-witted)
Antonyms—dull, half-witted, incompetent (not capable)

incompatible
Synonyms—opposite, clashing (conflicting), disparate (different)
Antonyms—suitable, harmonious, simpatico (compatible)

incongruent
Synonyms—unlike, conflicting, inconsistent
Antonyms—alike, equal, analogous (similar)

incontrovertible
Synonyms—irrefutable, unquestionable, sure
Antonyms—questionable, inconclusive, unconvincing

hypocrisy
Synonyms—phoniness, fraudulence (fakeness), duplicity (lying)
Antonyms—honesty, sincerity, genuineness

hypothetical
Synonyms—supposed, presumed, guessed
Antonyms—factual, actual, real

incorporate
Synonyms—include, join, merge, mix
Antonyms—exclude, divide, separate

incriminate
Synonyms—accuse, involve, blame
Antonyms—free, exonerate (to remove from guilt)

indecision
Synonyms—ambivalence, hesitancy, tentativeness
Antonyms—certainty, assurance, decisiveness

independent
Synonyms—self-determining, free, self-sufficient, liberated
Antonyms—dependent

indeterminate
Synonyms—inexact, inconclusive, imprecise (not accurate)
Antonyms—conclusive, definite, irrefutable (certain)

indict
Synonyms—accuse, condemn, blame
Antonyms—hold blameless, exonerate (to excuse), acquit (to find not guilty)

indifference
Synonyms—disinterest, apathy (lack of interest)
Antonyms—concern, involvement, interest

indistinct
Synonyms—poorly defined, murky (unclear), ambiguous (not clearly marked or understood)
Antonyms—obvious, well-defined, discernible (distinct)

induce
Synonyms—motivate, cause, instigate (to set in motion)
Antonyms—hinder, block, impede (to slow or stop), dissuade (to advise against)

inept
Synonyms—unskillful, clumsy, incompetent (not capable), bungling (prone to making mistakes)
Antonyms—skillful, masterful, competent (capable), dexterous (demonstrating skill)

inevitable
Synonyms—unavoidable, impending (happening soon), destined (bound by destiny to happen)
Antonyms—avoidable, unlikely, uncertain

infamous
Synonyms—disreputable (having a bad reputation), notorious (well-known in a negative way)
Antonyms—righteous, noble, reputable

informal
Synonyms—casual, unofficial, unfussy
Antonyms—fussy, formal, stiff (acting in a strict manner)

ingenious
Synonyms—gifted, intelligent, resourceful (clever)
Antonyms—foolish, unimaginative, unskillful

inherent
Synonyms—built-in, natural, innate (found naturally within)
Antonyms—acquired, unnatural, learned

inhibit
Synonyms—constrain, suppress, restrain, prevent
Antonyms—assist, encourage, support

inhibited
Synonyms—shy, subdued, reserved (quiet or timid in manner)
Antonyms—outrageous, loud, boisterous (noisy)

initiate
Synonyms—start, begin, inaugurate (to implement)
Antonyms—end, finish, cease (to stop)

initiative
Synonyms—drive, motivation, gumption
Antonyms—idleness, laziness

innocuous
Synonyms—inoffensive, mild, harmless
Antonyms—offensive, shocking, wild

insipid
Synonyms—dull, tedious, boring
Antonyms—exciting, interesting, fun

insolence
Synonyms—crudeness, disrespect, impertinence (lack of respect)
Antonyms—respect, obedience, humility

instigate
Synonyms—start, initiate (to begin), foment (to stimulate to action)
Antonyms—suppress, not allow, dissuade (to advise against)

integrate
Synonyms—put together, merge, harmonize
Antonyms—separate, leave out, cast aside

intimidating
Synonyms—coercive, threatening, compelling
Antonyms—easy-going, non-threatening

intrepid
Synonyms—fearless, courageous, undaunted (unafraid)
Antonyms—cautious, fearful, afraid

inundate
Synonyms—overload, flood, overwhelm
Antonyms—relieve, lessen

invariable
Synonyms—unchanging, consistent, constant, steady
Antonyms—variable, changing, inconsistent, wavering

invigorate
Synonyms—energize, stimulate, enliven
Antonyms—drain, discourage, deflate

invincible
Synonyms—strong, unbeatable, indomitable (unable to be conquered)
Antonyms—weak, downtrodden, vulnerable

irate
Synonyms—angry, furious, enraged
Antonyms—calm, peaceful, pacified (soothed)

irrational
Synonyms—illogical, nonsensical
Antonyms—rational, logical, sensible

irregular
Synonyms—variable, unsteady, inconsistent, unusual, variegated (full of variety)
Antonyms—regular, steady, predictable, consistent, normal, uniform

irresolute
Synonyms—uncertain, undecided, indecisive
Antonyms—resolute, certain, decisive

irritate
Synonyms—annoy, upset, aggravate
Antonyms—please, soothe, placate (to make happy)

J

jeopardize
Synonyms—endanger, threaten
Antonyms—protect, support, empower

jovial
Synonyms—happy, upbeat, good-natured
Antonyms—cranky, grumpy, glum (sullen)

judicious
Synonyms—thoughtful, cautious, prudent (wise)
Antonyms—reckless, ill-considered, imprudent (unwise)

K

keen
Synonyms—sharp, quick, astute (smart)
Antonyms—dull, unintelligent, obtuse

L

laborious
Synonyms—difficult, hard, demanding
Antonyms—easy, relaxed, undemanding

lackluster
Synonyms—dull, boring, uninteresting
Antonyms—brilliant, captivating, interesting

lament
Synonyms—mourn, regret, grieve
Antonyms—celebrate

languid
Synonyms—slow, sluggish, weak
Antonyms—energetic, vital, strong

languish
Synonyms—droop, decline, suffer
Antonyms—thrive, grow, flourish

latent
Synonyms—unexpressed, inactive, hidden, undeveloped
Antonyms—expressed, active, actualized, developed

lavish
Synonyms—extravagant, posh, opulent (abundant)
Antonyms—poor, bare, understated, low-key

lax
Synonyms—relaxed, loose, permissive, lenient (not strict)
Antonyms—strict, tight, rigid

lazy
Synonyms—unmotivated, unenergetic, indolent (avoiding work)
Antonyms—driven, energetic, hardworking, industrious

legitimate
Synonyms—actual, real, verified (shown to be true)
Antonyms—illegitimate, false, fake, unreal

lenient
Synonyms—allowing, permissive, forgiving, lax (not strict)
Antonyms—strict, rigid, restrictive, punishing

lethargic
Synonyms—slow, lazy, sluggish, inactive
Antonyms—quick, energetic, vital, active

liability
Synonyms—obligation, debt, weakness, disadvantage
Antonyms—asset, strength, advantage

linger
Synonyms—stay, loiter, delay
Antonyms—leave, flee, rush, expedite (to hurry)

livid
Synonyms—angry, irate, furious
Antonyms—calm, pleased, contented

lofty
Synonyms—high, ambitious, pretentious (showy)
Antonyms—low, lowly, meager (very poor or not enough)

loquacious
Synonyms—talkative, chatty, wordy, garrulous (talkative)
Antonyms—silent, unresponsive, concise (brief), taciturn (unexpressive), terse (short)

lucid
Synonyms—clear, understandable, rational
Antonyms—unclear, muddled, confusing

M

malevolence
Synonyms—hatred, ill will, malice (intent to harm)
Antonyms—goodness, kindness, benevolence (good will)

malingering
Synonyms—lazy, shirking (avoiding duties)
Antonyms—hardworking, industrious

malignant
Synonyms—harmful, dangerous
Antonyms—beneficial, harmless, benign (not harmful)

malleable
Synonyms—changeable, bendable, pliable (easy to bend)
Antonyms—unchangeable, inflexible, rigid

mature
Synonyms—full-grown, developed, ripe
Antonyms—immature, undeveloped, underdeveloped

mediocre
Synonyms—unimpressive, ordinary, average, so-so
Antonyms—impressive, extraordinary, excellent, stellar (outstanding)

mercurial
Synonyms—ever-changing, unpredictable, fickle (not loyal), capricious (quick to change)
Antonyms—steady, constant, predictable

meticulous
Synonyms—neat, careful, detailed, precise (accurate)
Antonyms—messy, sloppy, imprecise (lacking accuracy)

misconception
Synonyms—misunderstanding, misperception, false belief
Antonyms—fact, truth

mitigate
Synonyms—reduce, lessen, relieve
Antonyms—worsen, exacerbate (to make more severe)

moderate
Synonyms—mild, medium, average
Antonyms—extreme, excessive, intense

modicum
Synonyms—bit, tidbit, morsel (a tiny amount)
Antonyms—load, large amount

mollify
Synonyms—soothe, calm, pacify (to calm)
Antonyms—enrage, aggravate, irritate, anger

moribund
Synonyms—dying, ending, declining, terminal (at the end)
Antonyms—vital, thriving, alive, living

morose
Synonyms—negative, dark, sullen (gloomy)
Antonyms—positive, happy, cheerful

mundane
Synonyms—ordinary, commonplace, everyday
Antonyms—extraordinary, unique, original

munificent
Synonyms—generous, lavish, liberal (giving freely)
Antonyms—stingy, miserly, withholding

mutable
Synonyms—changeable, flexible, malleable (able to be changed)
Antonyms—inflexible, rigid, steadfast

N

naive
Synonyms—innocent, trusting, newcomer
Antonyms—experienced, sophisticated

narcissistic
Synonyms—self-absorbed, conceited, selfish
Antonyms—generous, altruistic (helping others)

nebulous
Synonyms—vague, unclear
Antonyms—precise, specific, well-defined

neglect
Synonyms—forget, abandon, overlook
Antonyms—nurture, care for, foster

nemesis
Synonyms—arch enemy, opponent, adversary
Antonyms—best friend, collaborator, ally (friend)

nocturnal
Synonyms—nighttime, vampirish
Antonyms—daytime, diurnal (during the day)

nonchalant
Synonyms—casual, relaxed, laid-back
Antonyms—formal, stiff, uptight

notorious
Synonyms—disreputable (having a bad reputation), infamous (well-known for a bad reason)
Antonyms—unknown, unfamiliar, unheard of

novel
Synonyms—new, unique, imaginative
Antonyms—ordinary, everyday, unoriginal

novice
Synonyms—beginner, trainee, neophyte (new learner)
Antonyms—expert, authority, professional

nurture
Synonyms—care for, foster, protect
Antonyms—neglect, abandon, ignore, harm

O

objective
Synonyms—fair, unbiased, open-minded
Antonyms—prejudiced, partial, subjective (biased)

obliterate
Synonyms—demolish, eliminate, eradicate (wipe out)
Antonyms—assemble, build, create

oblivious
Synonyms—unresponsive, unaware, forgetting
Antonyms—mindful, conscious, alert

obscure
Synonyms—unknown, minor, unseen
Antonyms—famous, prominent, recognized

obsolete
Synonyms—outdated, irrelevant, archaic (old)
Antonyms—contemporary, current, trendy, modern

obstinate
Synonyms—stubborn, headstrong, obdurate, tenacious
    (determined)
Antonyms—obedient, yielding (giving in), accommodating (eager
    to please others)

obtrusive
Synonyms—obvious, prominent, blatant (highly noticeable)
Antonyms—ordinary, unremarkable, inconspicuous
    (unnoticeable)

occlude
Synonyms—block, obstruct, impede (to hold back)
Antonyms—assist, facilitate, ease

omnipotent
Synonyms—supreme, invincible (unstoppable)
Antonyms—powerless, weak, helpless

onerous
Synonyms—burdensome, tedious (repetitive and boring), arduous
    (difficult and demanding)
Antonyms—easy, effortless, trouble-free

opinionated
Synonyms—inflexible, unbending, dogmatic (having rigid
    opinions)
Antonyms—mellow, easygoing, laid-back

opponent
Synonyms—rival, foe, challenger
Antonyms—friend, colleague, teammate, ally (friend)

opportune
Synonyms—well-timed, advantageous (helpful)
Antonyms—inconvenient, unfortunate

optimistic
Synonyms—hopeful, positive, sanguine (confident)
Antonyms—pessimistic, gloomy

opulent
Synonyms—lavish, luxurious, sumptuous (expensive)
Antonyms—inadequate, meager (very poor or not enough),
    impoverished (poor)

ordinary
Synonyms—common, usual, regular, normal
Antonyms—extraordinary, exceptional, unique

ornate
Synonyms—lavish, bejeweled, adorned (decorated)
Antonyms—plain, simple, basic

orthodox
Synonyms—conventional, mainstream, usual
Antonyms—innovative, pioneering, ground-breaking

ostentatious
Synonyms—flashy, flamboyant, pretentious (showy)
Antonyms—modest, down-to-earth, humble

ostracize
Synonyms—banish, ignore, cast out
Antonyms—welcome, include, embrace

overt
Synonyms—open, unconcealed, blatant (obvious)
Antonyms—hidden, covert (concealed), clandestine (secret)

P

parched
Synonyms—dry, dehydrated, waterless
Antonyms—wet, saturated, drenched

pariah
Synonyms—outcast, untouchable, exile
Antonyms—insider, hero, idol

passion
Synonyms—enthusiasm, zeal, delight
Antonyms—indifference, apathy (lack of interest)

passive
Synonyms—sluggish, lifeless, inert (inactive)
Antonyms—active, lively, energetic

pathetic
Synonyms—pitiful, wretched, lame
Antonyms—admirable, excellent, worthy

penitent
Synonyms—sorry, apologetic, contrite (sorry)
Antonyms—unrepentant, shameless, unremorseful

perceptive
Synonyms—insightful, observant
Antonyms—insensitive, oblivious (unaware)

perish
Synonyms—die, pass away, expire
Antonyms—live, survive, endure

perplexing
Synonyms—puzzling, bewildering, mystifying
Antonyms—simple, effortless, trouble-free, clear, understandable

persevere
Synonyms—persist, continue, keep on
Antonyms—quit, surrender, give up

perturb
Synonyms—annoy, disturb, bother
Antonyms—please, delight, gratify (make happy)

pervasive
Synonyms—omnipresent, all-encompassing (found everywhere)
Antonyms—contained, limited

pessimistic
Synonyms—gloomy, negative
Antonyms—optimistic, hopeful

pious
Synonyms—religious, reverent
Antonyms—disrespectful, heretical (going against established beliefs)

placate
Synonyms—soothe, pacify, appease (to calm down)
Antonyms—enrage, anger, infuriate (to anger)

placid
Synonyms—calm, peaceful, easygoing
Antonyms—anxious, stressed, agitated (upset)

plausible
Synonyms—believable, possible, likely
Antonyms—improbable, far-fetched, questionable

popular
Synonyms—appealing, well-liked, admired
Antonyms—disliked, ill-favored, unpopular

potent
Synonyms—powerful, strong, effective
Antonyms—weak, unsuccessful, incapable

practical
Synonyms—useful, sensible, no-nonsense
Antonyms—unrealistic, unreasonable, impractical

precede
Synonyms—lead, go before
Antonyms—follow, trail

predatory
Synonyms—aggressive, rapacious (out to kill)
Antonyms—harmless, passive (inactive)

predominant
Synonyms—major, principal, most common
Antonyms—secondary, insignificant

pretentious
Synonyms—showy, conceited, self-important
Antonyms—practical, down-to-earth, humble

privilege
Synonyms—advantage, benefit
Antonyms—disadvantage, drawback, shortcoming

procrastinate
Synonyms—postpone, delay
Antonyms—advance, proceed, progress, hurry

proficient
Synonyms—skilled, talented, capable
Antonyms—incompetent, clumsy, inept (unskilled)

proliferate
Synonyms—increase, flourish, spread, thrive (to do well)
Antonyms—reduce, diminish, dwindle

propagate
Synonyms—spread, transmit, publicize
Antonyms—suppress, hold back

propensity
Synonyms—tendency, inclination, penchant
Antonyms—reluctance, aversion (dislike)

proponent
Synonyms—supporter, advocate, fan
Antonyms—opponent, foe, antagonist (enemy)

propriety
Synonyms—respectability, politeness
Antonyms—rudeness, discourtesy

prosaic
Synonyms—dull, ordinary, commonplace
Antonyms—inspiring, stirring, exciting

prosperous
Synonyms—wealthy, affluent, abundant
Antonyms—unsuccessful, disadvantaged

proximity
Synonyms—closeness, convenience, nearness
Antonyms—distance, remoteness

prudent
Synonyms—wise, cautious, practical
Antonyms—foolish, risky, reckless

punitive
Synonyms—penalizing, disciplinary, retaliatory (punishing)
Antonyms—rewarding, incentivizing, inducing (encouraging), enticing (tempting)

purify
Synonyms—cleanse, distill, filter, sanitize
Antonyms—soil, pollute, muddy

Q

quell
Synonyms—crush, defeat, conquer, suppress
Antonyms—incite, provoke, inflame, encourage

querulous
Synonyms—difficult, irritable, argumentative, cantankerous
Antonyms—amiable, friendly, good-natured, genial (likable)

quarrelsome
Synonyms—querulous, cranky, grouchy, bad-tempered
Antonyms—affable, likable, good-humored, kind

quiescent
Synonyms—quiet, sluggish, passive (inactive), dormant (inactive)
Antonyms—active, lively, energetic, vigorous

R

random
Synonyms—accidental, haphazard, chance, casual
Antonyms—predictable, intentional, planned, on purpose

rational
Synonyms—logical, reasonable, coherent (makes sense)
Antonyms—unreasonable, absurd, illogical

rebut
Synonyms—deny, disprove, invalidate
Antonyms—accept, believe, recognize, support

recede
Synonyms—ebb, diminish, draw back
Antonyms—advance, press forward, progress

reclusive
Synonyms—isolated, solitary, withdrawn
Antonyms—outgoing, friendly, sociable

reconcile
Synonyms—reunite, resolve, bring together
Antonyms—separate, split, break up

recuperate
Synonyms—recover, get well, improve
Antonyms—decline, weaken, deteriorate (to get worse)

refined
Synonyms—polished, developed, cultivated
Antonyms—coarse, crude, rough

remedy
Synonyms—cure, restore, fix
Antonyms—worsen, aggravate, exacerbate (make worse)

remorse
Synonyms—guilt, sorrow, regret, shame
Antonyms—indifference, hard-heartedness, pride

remote
Synonyms—distant, isolated, far
Antonyms—close, nearby

renovate
Synonyms—renew, refresh, repair
Antonyms—demolish, destroy

renounce
Synonyms—reject, abandon, deny
Antonyms—accept, embrace

replete
Synonyms—full, stuffed, plentiful
Antonyms—hungry, empty, bare

reprehensible
Synonyms—criminal, wicked, disgraceful
Antonyms—honorable, noble, praiseworthy

repress
Synonyms—restrain, control, suppress, stifle (to hold back)
Antonyms—express, release, free (to let go)

reputable
Synonyms—trustworthy, dependable, respectable, legitimate
Antonyms—questionable, shady, dishonest

resilient
Synonyms—flexible, elastic, rebounding
Antonyms—rigid, unyielding, stiff

resplendent
Synonyms—dazzling, magnificent, glorious, stunning
Antonyms—unimpressive, ordinary, forgettable

restrain
Synonyms—control, confine, hold back
Antonyms—free, release, liberate

retain
Synonyms—keep, save, preserve
Antonyms—discard, throw away, let go

revere
Synonyms—admire, respect, esteem (to regard highly)
Antonyms—disapprove, dislike, object to

robust
Synonyms—healthy, strong, vigorous
Antonyms—weak, feeble, frail

routine
Synonyms—usual, ordinary, normal
Antonyms—exceptional, uncommon

S

sagacious
Synonyms—wise, shrewd, learned, perceptive
Antonyms—foolish, thoughtless, irrational

saturate
Synonyms—soak, flood, inundate (to overwhelm)
Antonyms—dehydrate, desiccate (to dry)

scrutinize
Synonyms—examine, inspect, analyze
Antonyms—ignore, disregard, overlook

secrete
Synonyms—conceal, hide, stash
Antonyms—reveal, disclose, divulge (to reveal)

sedentary
Synonyms—inactive, immobile, lethargic (slow)
Antonyms—active, lively, energetic

sequential
Synonyms—in order, chronological (sorted by time)
Antonyms—disordered, chaotic, random

serene
Synonyms—calm, peaceful, tranquil
Antonyms—busy, lively, hectic

skeptical
Synonyms—doubtful, unconvinced, disbelieving
Antonyms—persuaded, converted, won over

solace
Synonyms—comfort, support, relief
Antonyms—irritation, annoyance, hurt

soporific
Synonyms—dull, sleep-inducing, monotonous (boring)
Antonyms—stimulating, exciting, lively, energizing

sparse
Synonyms—limited, scarce, inadequate, scant (a small amount)
Antonyms—abundant, plentiful, profuse (in good supply)

spontaneous
Synonyms—unplanned, spur-of-the-moment, impromptu
Antonyms—structured, deliberate, premeditated (planned)

squander
Synonyms—waste, spend, misuse
Antonyms—save, keep, conserve

rupture
Synonyms—break, burst, rip open
Antonyms—heal, mend, repair

stagnant
Synonyms—still, inactive, inert (not active)
Antonyms—moving, mobile, dynamic

sterile
Synonyms—antiseptic, disinfected, sanitary
Antonyms—contaminated, dirty, soiled

stimulate
Synonyms—encourage, motivate, inspire
Antonyms—discourage, dampen, stifle (to hold back)

strenuous
Synonyms—taxing, straining, demanding, arduous (difficult)
Antonyms—easy, effortless, painless

strict
Synonyms—firm, exacting, rigorous
Antonyms—lenient, relaxed, easygoing

submissive
Synonyms—obedient, passive (inactive), compliant (willing to obey)
Antonyms—assertive, pushy, aggressive

substantial
Synonyms—considerable, extensive, sizeable, significant
Antonyms—minor, insignificant, limited

substantiate
Synonyms—verify, prove, corroborate
Antonyms—disprove, refute, invalidate

subtle
Synonyms—slight, understated, delicate
Antonyms—obvious, noticeable, apparent

sullen
Synonyms—brooding, grim, gloomy
Antonyms—cheerful, smiling, joyful

summon
Synonyms—call, beckon, gather
Antonyms—dismiss, release

superficial
Synonyms—shallow, surface
Antonyms—deep, profound, meaningful

superfluous
Synonyms—extra, surplus (more than is needed)
Antonyms—indispensable, necessary, vital, essential

supply
Synonyms—provide, give, contribute
Antonyms—remove, take away, deprive (to withhold from)

support
Synonyms—maintain, encourage, sustain (to keep going)
Antonyms—abandon, ignore, forsake

suppress
Synonyms—prevent, repress (to hold down), stifle (to hold back), constrain (to limit)
Antonyms—spread, express, distribute

surge
Synonyms—rush, flow, pour, gush
Antonyms—stagnate, stand still, pool (to gather in one place)

surplus
Synonyms—extra, spare, leftover
Antonyms—basic, essential

surreptitious
Synonyms—secret, sneaky, stealthy, covert (hidden)
Antonyms—open, honest, direct

surrogate
Synonyms—substitute, replacement, stand-in
Antonyms—real, permanent, genuine

sustain
Synonyms—support, maintain, keep going
Antonyms—quit, stop, give up, abandon

T

tame
Synonyms—domestic, friendly, docile (obedient)
Antonyms—wild, untamed, feral (not domesticated)

tardy
Synonyms—late, slow, delayed
Antonyms—prompt, punctual, timely

tedious
Synonyms—boring, dull, dreary, monotonous
Antonyms—interesting, motivating, fascinating

temperate
Synonyms—moderate, pleasant, mild
Antonyms—extreme, severe, intense

temperamental
Synonyms—unpredictable, moody, volatile (explosive)
Antonyms—reliable, dependable, even-tempered

tenacious
Synonyms—stubborn, persistent, determined
Antonyms—unsure, hesitant, irresolute (undecided)

tentative
Synonyms—cautious, hesitant, uncertain
Antonyms—sure, definite, secure

tenuous
Synonyms—weak, flimsy, fragile
Antonyms—strong, sound, robust

tense
Synonyms—worried, anxious, stressed, uptight
Antonyms—relaxed, calm, tranquil, peaceful

terminate
Synonyms—end, finish, conclude, cease
Antonyms—begin, commence, originate

terse
Synonyms—abrupt, brief, concise (to the point), brusque (abrupt)
Antonyms—rambling, long-winded, wordy

therapeutic
Synonyms—healing, beneficial, helpful
Antonyms—harmful, destructive, unsafe, detrimental

tolerant
Synonyms—broadminded, understanding, forbearing (patient)
Antonyms—intolerant, unforgiving, rigid, impatient

toxic
Synonyms—poisonous, deadly, lethal
Antonyms—harmless, safe

tranquil
Synonyms—peaceful, calm, relaxing, serene
Antonyms—noisy, chaotic, frenzied

transgression
Synonyms—wrongdoing, disobedience, offense
Antonyms—good deed, kindness, favor

transient
Synonyms—temporary, brief, fleeting, short-lived
Antonyms—permanent, lasting, eternal, enduring

translucent
Synonyms—clear, transparent, see-through
Antonyms—opaque, dense, thick

treacherous
Synonyms—unsafe, dangerous, hazardous, perilous
Antonyms—harmless, safe, risk-free

trepidation
Synonyms—fear, anxiety, apprehension
Antonyms—composure, level-headedness, equanimity (calmness)

trivial
Synonyms—minor, insignificant, petty, negligible (not important)
Antonyms—crucial, essential, important, necessary, vital

truncate
Synonyms—shorten, abbreviate, trim
Antonyms—lengthen, extend, elongate (to make longer)

turbulent
Synonyms—chaotic, confused, tumultuous (in turmoil)
Antonyms—orderly, calm

U

unheralded
Synonyms—unannounced, unpredicted, unexpected
Antonyms—forecasted, foretold, expected

uniform
Synonyms—unchanging, unvarying, standardized, homogeneous (the same)
Antonyms—different, dissimilar, unlike, diverse

unpalatable
Synonyms—unpleasant, distasteful, disagreeable
Antonyms—enjoyable, pleasing, satisfying

unparalleled
Synonyms—matchless, unequaled, incomparable, supreme
Antonyms—common, ordinary, everyday, regular

unstinting
Synonyms—generous, giving
Antonyms—stingy, tightfisted

untenable
Synonyms—indefensible, unreasonable
Antonyms—justifiable, understandable

utilitarian
Synonyms—useful, practical, functional
Antonyms—ineffective, nonfunctional

utopian
Synonyms—perfect, ideal
Antonyms—problematic, flawed

V

vague
Synonyms—unclear, hazy, indistinct (not clear)
Antonyms—definite, distinct, evident (clear)

valid
Synonyms—legitimate, reasonable, sensible
Antonyms—invalid, illegitimate, unsound, fallacious (not true)

validate
Synonyms—confirm, approve, certify, authorize
Antonyms—invalidate, cancel, disapprove, deny

valid
Synonyms—authentic, legal, legitimate, official
Antonyms—invalid, counterfeit, void (not valid)

verdant
Synonyms—green, lush, luxuriant
Antonyms—bare, stripped, withered

versatile
Synonyms—adaptable, resourceful, multitalented
Antonyms—limited, narrow, restricted

vex
Synonyms—annoy, pester, irritate, exasperate (frustrate)
Antonyms—please, satisfy, calm

virtuoso
Synonyms—expert, master, ace, whiz
Antonyms—amateur, beginner, dabbler, hobbyist

viscous
Synonyms—thick, sticky, gluey
Antonyms—thin, runny

vitality
Synonyms—energy, liveliness, durability
Antonyms—weariness, sluggishness, lethargy (lack of energy)

vital
Synonyms—essential, fundamental, crucial
Antonyms—unimportant, insignificant, trivial

vivacious
Synonyms—lively, cheerful, spirited
Antonyms—slow, languid (lacking energy), lethargic (slow)

vivid
Synonyms—bright, vibrant, colorful
Antonyms—dull, dreary, faded, lackluster

volatile
Synonyms—explosive, unpredictable, unstable
Antonyms—calm, placid, inert (inactive)

W

wane
Synonyms—diminish, decline, fade
Antonyms—increase, develop, wax (to fade or decline)

waver
Synonyms—hesitate, fluctuate, vacillate (to be indecisive)
Antonyms—decide, resolve, choose

Y

youthful
Synonyms—young, vigorous, vital
Antonyms—aged, decrepit (old), mature, languid

Z

zealous
Synonyms—eager, passionate, fervent (full of passion)
Antonyms—bored, lethargic (slow), listless (lacking energy)

voluntary
Synonyms—unpaid, honorary, pro bono (done without pay)
Antonyms—paid, compensated, remunerated

vulnerable
Synonyms—unprotected, in danger, at risk
Antonyms—secure, protected

whimsical
Synonyms—fanciful, quirky, eccentric (unusual)
Antonyms—normal, regular, ordinary

wordy
Synonyms—rambling, long-winded, verbose (full of words)
Antonyms—concise (brief), taciturn (quiet), reticent (quiet)

zeal
Synonyms—enthusiasm, passion, eagerness
Antonyms—disinterest, indifference, apathy (lack of interest)

APPENDIX C: MATH FORMULAS

MATH FORMULAS AND TERMS

The following formulas and terms are common in middle school and high school math. Committing them to memory will serve you well on your tests.

Perimeter

Add the lengths of the sides.

Square

$P = 4s$

Rectangle

$P = 2l + 2w$

Triangle

$P = s_1 + s_2 + s_3$

Circle (circumference)

$C = \pi d$ or $2\pi r$

Area

Always express area in square units. Multiply the dimensions of the shape (length and width).

Square

$A = s^2$

Rectangle

$A = lw$

Triangle

Multiply thebase by the height, and divide by 2.

$A = \frac{1}{2}bh$

Circle

$A = \pi r^2$

Volume

Always express volume in cubic units.

Cube

$V = s^3$

Rectangular Solid

$V = lwh$

Cylinder

$V = \pi r^2 h$

Angle Measures

Straight line = 180°

Triangle = 180°

Rectangle = 360°

Square = 360°

Circle = 360°

Polygon = $(n - 2)180°$ where n = # of sides

Percent Change

$$\frac{\% \text{ change}}{100} = \frac{\text{difference}}{\text{original \#}}$$

Percent to Decimal

$25\% = \frac{25}{100} = 0.25$

Reverse for Decimal to Percent

Percent to Fraction

$25\% = \frac{25}{100} = \frac{1}{4}$

Reverse for Fraction to Percent

Distance/Rate/Time

To find distance, use $D = RT$ (Distance = Rate × Time)

To find rate, use $R = \frac{D}{T}$ (Rate = Distance ÷ Time)

To find time, use $T = \frac{D}{R}$ (Time = Distance ÷ Rate)